Upgrading and Repairing PCs, Second Edition

SCOTT MUELLER

Upgrading and Repairing PCs, 2nd Edition

©1992 by Que Corporation

Library of Congress Catalog No.: 91-67632
ISBN: 0-88022-856-3

95 94 93 92   7 6 5 4 3 2 1

Interpretation of the printing code: the rightmost double-digit number is the year of the book's printing; the rightmost single- digit number, the number of the book's printing. For example, a printing code of 92-1 shows that the first printing of the book occurred in 1992.

Publisher: Lloyd J. Short

Acquisitions Manager: Rick Ranucci

Product Development Manager: Thomas H. Bennett

Managing Editor: Paul Boger

Book Designer: Scott Cook

Production Analyst: Mary Beth Wakefield

Production Team: Claudia Bell, Scott Boucher, Jeanne Clark, Keith Davenport, Phil Kitchel, Juli Pavey, Cindy L. Phipps, Joe Ramon, Louise Shinault

CREDITS

Product Director
Brenda Carmichael
Timothy S. Stanley

Production Editor
Rebecca Whitney

Editors
Anne C. Clarke
Don Eamons
Beth Hoger
Frances R. Huber
Louise M. Lambert
Lori A. Lyons
Susan Pink, TechRight
MS Editorial Services
Susan M. Shaw
Colleen Totz

Technical Editor
Jerry L. Cox

Composed in Cheltenham and MCPdigital by Que Corporation

DEDICATION

To my family: Lynn, Amanda, and Emerson. "We're not hitchhiking anymore...we're riding!"

Scott Mueller is president of Mueller Technical Research, an international personal computer research and corporate training firm. Since 1982, Mueller Technical Research has specialized in the industry's most accurate and effective corporate technical seminars and documentation.

For more than ten years, Mr. Mueller has developed, refined, and presented successful personal computer training courses and seminars. As an internationally recognized seminar trainer and a renowned authority on data-recovery techniques and strategies, he has designed, written, and taught comprehensive seminars in all areas of PC hardware and software. He specializes in systems hardware, systems software, data-recovery techniques, local area networks, hardware upgrade, troubleshooting, repair, and major business applications software packages. He directs seminars on topics that cover industry-standard hardware, data recovery, hardware service, maintenance, and troubleshooting for both classic and PS/2 systems. These seminars include advanced operating-systems courses featuring DOS, OS/2, and Windows.

Mr. Mueller's seminars are practical, intensive, hands-on learning experiences. He has logged literally millions of miles presenting his seminars throughout North and South America, Canada, Europe, and Australia. Mueller Technical Research maintains a variety of clients that include Fortune 500 companies, the U.S. and foreign governments, major software and hardware corporations, as well as PC enthusiasts and entrepreneurs. His seminars are offered both publicly and in custom on-site versions.

Mr. Mueller has many popular books and course materials to his credit, among them the best-selling *Que's Guide to Data Recovery*. He already has begun research for his next book, about upgrading and repairing Apple Macintosh computers.

For more information about seminars available through Mueller Technical Research, please contact marketing director Philip Skoblikoff at Mueller Technical Research, 21718 N. Mayfield, Barrington, IL 60010-9733. Phone: 708-726-0709; Fax: 708-726-0710; CompuServe ID: 73145,1566.

TRADEMARK ACKNOWLEDGMENTS

Que Corporation has made every attempt to supply trademark information about company names, products, and services mentioned in this book. Trademarks indicated below were derived from various sources. Que Corporation cannot attest to the accuracy of this information. Trademarks of other products mentioned in this book are held by the companies producing them.

EtherNet is a trademark, and 3Com is a registered trademark of 3Com Corporation.

AT&T is a registered trademark of American Telephone & Telegraph Company.

Apple and Macintosh are registered trademarks of Apple Computer, Inc.

SideKick is a registered trademark of Borland International, Inc.

PCTools is a trademark of Central Point Software.

Kickstart is a trademark of Commodore-Amiga, Inc.

COMPAQ, COMPAQ Deskpro 286, COMPAQ Deskpro Model 1, and COMPAQ Deskpro Model 2 are registered trademarks of COMPAQ Computer Corporation.

FASTBACK is a registered trademark of Fifth Generation Systems, Inc.

SpinRite is a trademark of Gibson Research Corporation.

Vopt is a trademark, and Vfeature Deluxe is a registered trademark of Golden Bow Systems.

Above Board is a trademark of Intel Corporation.

IBM PC*jr*, IBM PC XT, IBM PC XT 286, PS/1, PS/2, and Personal Computer XT are trademarks; IBM, IBM PC, IBM PC AT, Micro Channel, OS/2, PS/2 Model 25, PS/2 Model 30, PS/2 Model 50, Personal Computer AT, PS/2, PS/2 Model 50 Z, PAL, Personal Computer AT, PS/2 Model 60, PS/2 Model 70, PS/2 Model 80, and Selectric are registered trademarks of International Business Machines Corporation.

Kaypro is a registered trademark of Kaypro Corporation.

1-2-3 is a registered trademark of Lotus Development Corporation.

ACKNOWLEDGMENTS

This second edition of *Upgrading and Repairing PCs* is the culmination of more than three years of additional research and development. Several people have helped me with both the research and production of this book. I would like to thank the following individuals:

Lynn Mueller and Phil Skoblikoff, of Mueller Technical Research, for helping with the product research and last-minute editor queries; Chris Huffman, at Micro 2000, for providing technical information about various PC operations and diagnostics products; Mike Siewruk, at Landmark, for providing information about and assistance with diagnostics products; Jim Buell, of Accurite Technologies, and Philip Potasiak, of Toshiba, for technical information on floppy disks and drives; Terri Guerin, at IBM, for providing access to IBM technical information; John Rourke, Geoff Lohff, Tom Kellar, and David Means, who have helped teach my seminars over the years, and who also have supplied information and made valuable suggestions for improving both the seminars and this book. Shiv Goyle of Abcom Computer Rental for providing access to a variety of systems.

Thanks to all the people who have attended the seminars I have given. You may not realize how much I learn from each of you! Also, thanks to those of you who have written to me with questions and suggestions concerning this book; I welcome all of your comments.

Thanks to all the people at Que Corporation who have worked on this project, especially to Rick Ranucci, for being tough when it was necessary. A special thanks to Brenda Carmichael, for being understanding and compassionate, providing moral support when it was needed, and for putting up with my methods of operation.

CONTENTS AT A GLANCE

TABLE OF CONTENTS

5 IBM-Compatible (and Not-So-Compatible) Computers 303

III   Hardware Considerations

6   System Teardown and Inspection

IV   System Maintenance, Backups, Upgrades, and Diagnostics

11   Maintaining Your System: Preventive Maintenance, Backups, and Warranties 731

Introduction

Welcome to *Upgrading and Repairing PCs*, 2nd Edition. This book is geared for people who want to upgrade, repair, maintain, and troubleshoot their own or their companies' computers. Designed to cover the range of hardware that is compatible with IBM's Personal Computer and Personal System/2 series of systems, it covers also actual IBM systems as well as all available IBM-compatibles or clones.

What Are the Main Objectives of This Book?

Upgrading and Repairing PCs focuses on several objectives. One is to help you understand the family of computers that stems from the original IBM PC. The book examines each system in depth, and outlines the differences among the models and presents options for configuring each system at the time you purchase it, including not only systems from IBM but also all the IBM-compatible systems. Much information about available clone and compatible systems is presented. Sections of the book provide detailed information about each internal component that makes up a personal computer system, from the processor to the keyboard and video display.

Another objective is to help you understand the PS/2 systems from IBM. The book examines, from an upgrade-and-repair point of view, how these systems differ from earlier systems.

Upgrading and Repairing PCs helps you gain an understanding of the peripheral and add-on market for IBM-compatible systems. The IBM-compatible microcomputer family is moving forward rapidly in power and capabilities. Processor performance increases with every new chip design. Available storage, with directly addressable memory and peripheral storage such as hard disks, is increasing quickly. The book examines the options available in modern, high-performance PC configurations and how to use them to your advantage; it focuses on much of the hardware and software available today and specifies the optimum configurations for achieving maximum benefit for the time and money you spend. And, *Upgrading and Repairing PCs* discusses all areas of system improvement such as floppy disks, hard disks, central processor units, math coprocessors, and power-supply improvement.

The primary objective of this book is to help you learn how to maintain, upgrade, and repair your PC system. The book discusses proper system and component care; it specifies the most failure-prone items in different PC systems and tells you how to locate and identify a failing component. You will learn about powerful diagnostics hardware and software that enables a system to help you determine what is causing a problem and about proper repair procedures. When you finish reading this book, you should have the knowledge to perform repairs on nearly all systems and components.

Who Should Use This Book?

Upgrading and Repairing PCs is designed for people who want a good understanding of how their PC systems work. Each section gives full explanations of and reasons for each problem or situation you might encounter so that you can better handle tough problems. You will gain an understanding of disk configuration and interfacing, for example, that can improve your diagnostics and troubleshooting skills. You will develop a "feel" for what goes on in a system so that you can rely on your own judgment and observations and not some table of canned troubleshooting "steps." The book is geared for people who are truly interested in their systems and how they operate.

This book is written for people who will select, install, configure, maintain, and repair systems that they or their companies use. To accomplish these tasks, you need a level of knowledge much higher than average system users. You must know exactly which tool to use for a task and how to use the tool correctly. This book can help you achieve this level of knowledge.

What Is in This Book?

Chapter 1 is an introduction to the development of the IBM PC and compatibles. Chapter 2 provides detailed information about the different types of systems you encounter and what separates one type of system from another. Chapter 2 explains also the memory architecture of the different system types, including conventional, extended, and expanded memory. This information helps you build a foundation of knowledge essential for the remainder of the book.

Chapters 3 and 4 describe each IBM PC and PS/2 model and list differences among individual versions of each system. Technical specifications for each system are highlighted in these chapters also. This information is useful not only for supporting actual IBM equipment but also for people whose IBM-compatible systems are not supplied with extensive documentation. You learn how to compare and contrast systems with the IBM standard.

Chapter 5 discusses compatible systems. It provides detailed information about differences in compatible systems and standard IBM systems, and also lists important features of different compatible systems. The chapter is useful especially if you make purchasing decisions. You can use Chapter 5 as a general guideline for features that make a certain compatible a good or bad choice.

The proper teardown, disassembly, and inspection procedures for a system are examined in Chapter 6, and each component that makes up a typical system, from the power supply to the microprocessor, is discussed in Chapter 7.

Chapters 8 and 9 describe in detail floppy disk drives and hard disk drives. This information is invaluable when you install drives either as replacements or upgrades in a system, as well as if you troubleshoot and repair malfunctioning drives. You will find especially interesting information about newer IDE and SCSI interface drives, used in most of the latest IBM and compatible systems.

Chapter 10 covers standard peripherals such as video boards and monitors, and communications boards such as serial and parallel ports. Differences between serial-port designs that can affect performance are discussed, as well as newer high-speed modems.

Chapter 11 focuses on preventive maintenance and backup procedures. The chapter emphasizes proper system care and cleaning and examines how to maintain a system so that a minimum number of problems occur. Data backup is discussed also.

Chapter 12 lists specific system upgrades and examines how they may be accomplished. It discusses how to add to a system different floppy drives (such as 3 1/2-inch drives) and more or larger hard disk drives. Other topics include speeding up a system by upgrading its processor, adding memory, and converting from one type of system to another—from an XT to an AT, or from a 286 AT to a 386, for example.

Chapter 13 focuses on system diagnostics and the required tools needed to perform such diagnostics. It describes manufacturer-provided diagnostics as well as different aftermarket diagnostics utilities. A new section in this edition discusses some of the hardware diagnostic boards.

Chapters 14 and 15 examine hardware and software troubleshooting. These chapters explain the most common problems and procedures you use to successfully discover the source of a problem. Chapter 16 concludes the book.

The appendix lists many tables and data with valuable reference information. You probably will refer to this section of the book repeatedly when you're troubleshooting system problems. The tables and charts in the appendix are one of my most valuable reference sources. Any information I have found useful in upgrading and repairing IBM systems is included in the appendix. Most of the information never has appeared all in one book.

I believe that *Upgrading and Repairing PCs* will prove to be the best book of its kind on the market. It offers not only the breadth of IBM and compatible equipment but also much in-depth coverage of each topic. This book is valuable as a reference tool for understanding how various components in a system interact and operate, and as a guide to repairing and servicing problems you encounter. *Upgrading and Repairing PCs* is far more than just a "repair" manual. I sincerely hope that you enjoy it.

The Background and Features of Personal Computers

PART

I

Personal Computer Background

System Features

Personal Computer Background

M any discoveries and inventions contributed to the development of the machine known today as the personal computer. Examining a few important developmental landmarks can bring the whole picture into focus.

Personal Computing History

The invention of the transistor, or semiconductor, was one of the most important developments leading to the personal computer revolution. The transistor was invented in 1948 by John Bardeen, Walter Brattain, and William Shockley (engineers at Bell Laboratories). The transistor, essentially a solid-state electronic switch, replaced the vacuum tube. Because the transistor consumed significantly less power, a computer system built with transistors was much smaller and more efficient than a computer system built with a vacuum tube.

The tube was inefficient as a switch. It consumed a great deal of electrical power and gave off enormous heat—a significant problem in the earlier systems. Tubes were notoriously unreliable also; one failed every two hours or so in the larger systems.

The conversion to transistors began a trend toward miniaturization. Today's small laptop PC systems, which run on batteries, have more computing power than many earlier systems that filled rooms and consumed huge amounts of electrical power.

In 1959, Texas Instruments invented the integrated circuit (IC), a semiconductor circuit that contains more than one transistor on the same base (or substrate material) and connects the transistors without wires. The first IC contained only 6 transistors; the Intel 486 microprocessor used in many of today's systems has 1.2 million transistors. Today ICs can be built with several million transistors on-board.

In 1969, Intel introduced a 1K-bit memory chip much larger than anything else available at the time. (One K-bit equals 1,024 bits, and a byte equals 8 bits; this chip therefore stored 128 bytes—not much by today's standards.) Because of Intel's success in chip manufacturing and design, Busicomp, a Japanese calculator-manufacturing company, asked Intel to produce 12 different logic chips for one of its calculator designs. Rather than produce the 12 separate chips, Intel engineers included all the functions of the chips in a single chip. In addition to just incorporating all the functions and capabilities of the 12-chip design into one multipurpose chip, they designed the chip to be controlled by a program that could alter the function of the chip. The chip then was "generic" in nature: it could function in designs other than just a calculator. Previous designs were hard-wired for one purpose with built-in instructions; this chip would read from memory a variable set of instructions, which Intel already was producing. The idea was to design almost an entire computing device on one chip. The first microprocessor, the Intel 4004, a 4-bit processor, was introduced in 1971. The chip operated on 4 bits of data at a time. The 4004 chip's successor was the 8008 8-bit microprocessor in 1972.

In 1973, some of the first microcomputer kits based on the 8008 chip were developed. These kits were little more than demonstration tools and did little except blink lights. In late 1973, Intel introduced the 8080 microprocessor, which was ten times faster than the earlier 8008 chip and addressed 64 kilobytes of memory. This breakthrough was the one the personal computer industry was waiting for.

MITS introduced the Altair kit in a cover story in the January 1975 issue of *Popular Electronics* magazine. The Altair kit, considered to be the first personal computer, included an 8080 processor, a power supply, a front panel with a large number of lights, and 256 bytes (not kilobytes) of memory. The kit sold for $395 and had to be assembled. The computer included open architecture (slots) that prompted various add-ons and peripherals from aftermarket companies. The new processor inspired other companies to write programs, including the CP/M (Control Program for Microprocessors) operating system and the first version of Microsoft BASIC.

IBM introduced what can be called its first *personal computer* in 1975. The Model 5100 had 16K of memory, a built-in 16-line-by-64-character display, a built-in BASIC language interpreter, and a built-in DC-300 cartridge tape drive for storage. The system's $9,000 price placed it out of the mainstream personal computer marketplace, dominated by experimenters (hackers) who built low-cost kits ($500 or so) as a hobby. The IBM system obviously was not in competition for this low-cost market and did not sell well. The Model 5100 was succeeded by the 5110 and 5120 before IBM introduced the IBM Personal Computer (Model 5150). This series of systems precedes the IBM PC and uses the same model numbering scheme, but the systems share nothing in common with the IBM PC. The PC is more closely related to the IBM System/23 DataMaster, introduced in 1980.

In 1976, a new company, Apple Computer, introduced the Apple I (for $695). This system consisted of a main circuit board screwed to a piece of plywood. A case and power supply were not included. Only a handful of these computers were made, and they reportedly have sold to collectors for more than $20,000. The Apple II, introduced in 1977, helped set the standard for nearly all the important microcomputers to follow, including the IBM PC.

The microcomputer world was dominated in 1980 by two types of computer systems. One type, the Apple II, claimed a large following of loyal users and a gigantic software base that was growing at a fantastic rate. The other type consisted not of a single system but included all the many systems that evolved from the original MITS Altair. These systems were compatible with each other and were distinguished by their use of the CP/M operating system and expansion slots that followed the S-100 (for slot with 100 pins) standard. All these systems were built by a variety of companies and sold under various names but for the most part used the same software and plug-in hardware.

The IBM Personal Computer

At the end of 1980, IBM had decided to compete in the rapidly growing low-cost personal computer market. The company established an Entry Systems Division, in Boca Raton, Florida, to develop the system. This small group consisted of 12 engineers and designers under the direction of Don Estridge. The team's chief designer was Lewis Eggebrecht. The division developed IBM's first real PC. (IBM considered the 5100 system, developed in 1975, to be an intelligent programmable terminal rather than a genuine computer, even though it truly was a computer.) Nearly all these engineers moved from working on the System/23 DataMaster project, a small, office computer system introduced in 1980 (and the direct predecessor of the IBM PC).

Much of the PC's design was influenced by the DataMaster's design. On the DataMaster's single-piece design, the display and keyboard were integrated into the unit. Because these features were limiting, they became external units on the PC although the PC keyboard layout and electrical designs were copied from the DataMaster. Several other parts of the IBM PC system also were copied from the DataMaster, including the expansion bus, or input-output slots, which included not only the same physical 62-pin connector, but also the almost identical pin specifications. This copying was possible because the PC used the same interrupt controller and a similar direct memory access (DMA) controller as the DataMaster. Expansion cards already designed for the DataMaster could then be easily "ported" to the PC. Because the DataMaster used an Intel 8085 CPU, which had a 64K address limit, the design team was prompted to use the 8088, which offered a 1-megabyte address limit, but was similar in instruction set and electrical design.

Estridge and the design team rapidly developed the design and specifications for the new system. In addition to borrowing from the System/23 DataMaster's design, the team studied the marketplace, which had enormous influence on the IBM PC's design. The designers looked at the prevailing standards, learned from the success of those systems, and incorporated into the new PC all the features of the popular systems— and more. With the parameters for design made obvious by the market, IBM produced a system that filled perfectly its niche in the market.

IBM brought its system from idea to delivery in one year by using existing designs and purchasing as many components as possible from outside vendors. IBM contracted out the PC's languages and operating system, for example, to a small company named Microsoft. (IBM originally had contacted Digital Research, which invented CP/M, but that company apparently was not interested in the proposal. Microsoft was interested, however, and since has become one of the largest software companies in the world.) The use of outside vendors was also an open invitation for the aftermarket to jump in and support the system. And it did.

On Wednesday, August 12, 1981, a new standard took its place in the microcomputer industry with the debut of the IBM PC. Since then, IBM has sold more than 10 million PCs, and the PC has grown into a large family of computers and peripherals. More software has been written for this family than for any other system on the market.

The IBM-Compatible Marketplace "Ten Years Later"

In the more than ten years since the original IBM PC was introduced, many changes have occurred. In ten years, the computer industry has advanced from 4.77 MHz 8088-based systems to 50 MHz 486-based systems more than *50 times faster* than the original IBM PC. (I am referring to processing speed, not just clock rates.) The original PC had only (as much as) two 160K floppy drives for storage, whereas modern systems easily can have several gigabytes of hard disk storage. A rule of thumb is that available processor performance and disk storage capacity at least doubles every two years. This pattern from the past ten years shows no signs of changing.

In addition to performance and storage capacity, another major change since the original IBM PC was introduced is that IBM is not the only manufacturer of "IBM-compatible" systems. IBM invented the IBM-compatible standard, of course, and continues to set standards that compatible systems follow, but it does not dominate the market as before. Hundreds of system manufacturers produce computers compatible with IBM's systems, not to mention the thousands of peripheral manufacturers with components that expand and enhance IBM and IBM-compatible systems.

The IBM-compatible market should thrive and prosper. New technology will be integrated into these systems and enable them to grow with the times. Because of both the high value these types of systems can offer for the money and the large amount of software available to run on them, IBM and IBM-compatible systems likely will dominate the personal computer marketplace for perhaps the next ten years as well.

Chapter Summary

This chapter traced the development of personal computing from the transistor to the introduction of the IBM PC. Intel's continuing development of the integrated circuit (IC) led to a succession of microprocessors and reached a milestone with the 1973 introduction of the 8080 chip. In 1975, MITS introduced the Altair computer kit, based on the 8080 microprocessor. IBM jumped into the personal computer market with the Model 5100 in 1975.

In 1976, Apple sold its first computers, followed in 1977 by the enormously successful Apple II. Because of its success, the Apple II played a major role in setting standards for all later microcomputers.

Finally, in 1981, IBM introduced its Personal Computer to a microcomputer world dominated by the Apple II and the somewhat Apple-compatible computers that evolved from the Altair, both of which used the CP/M operating system. The IBM PC, designed with the needs of the market in mind and with many of its components produced by outside vendors, immediately set the new standard for the microcomputer industry. This standard has evolved to meet the needs of today's users, with more powerful systems that offer performance levels not even imagined in 1981.

Chapter 2, "System Features," describes the technical fundamentals of IBM personal computers and their compatibles, differences between PC and AT systems, the structure and use of memory, and how to obtain and use maintenance manuals.

System Features

This chapter discusses the differences in system architecture of IBM and compatible systems, and explains memory structure and use. It discusses also how to obtain the service manuals necessary for maintaining and upgrading your computer.

Types of Systems

Many types of IBM and compatible systems are on the market today. Most systems are similar to one another, but a few important differences in system architecture have become more apparent as operating environments such as Windows and OS/2 become more and more popular. Operating systems such as OS/2 1.x require at least a 286 CPU platform on which to run, and OS/2 2.x requires at least a 386 CPU. Environments such as Windows offer different capabilities and operating modes based on the capabilities of the hardware platform you run it on. Knowing and understanding the differences in these hardware platforms will allow you to plan for, install, and utilize modern operating systems and applications to optimally use the hardware.

All IBM and compatible systems can be broken down into two basic system types, or classes, of hardware, with a few subcategories:

1. PC and XT types of systems:

    8-bit Industry Standard Architecture (ISA) bus

2. AT types of systems:

   16-bit Industry Standard Architecture (ISA) bus

   16-bit PS/2 Micro Channel Architecture (MCA) bus

   32-bit PS/2 Micro Channel Architecture (MCA) bus

   32-bit Enhanced ISA (EISA) bus

AT systems can be broken down further into subcategories: systems with the standard ISA slots, systems with Micro Channel Architecture slots, and systems with Enhanced ISA slots. Many AT-type systems have 80386 or higher processors. The 386 and higher systems have distinct capabilities regarding memory addressing, memory management, and possible 32-bit-wide access to data. Most systems with 80386DX or higher chips have 32-bit slots to take full advantage of the 32-bit data-transfer capabilities. Note that the 386SX or SL chips have the full instruction-set capabilities of the full 32-bit 386DX processor; they have only a 16-bit hardware data path, however, and are not found in systems with 32-bit MCA or EISA slots.

The standard ISA and MCA architectures were developed by IBM and copied by other manufacturers for use in compatible systems. In September 1988 a consortium of compatible manufacturers, led by COMPAQ, introduced a new slot system: Extended Industry Standard Architecture (EISA). The system is a 32-bit slot for use with 386DX or higher systems. Conventional (but false) speculation says that IBM-compatible manufacturers developed EISA to circumvent the small royalties IBM charges competitors who use the ISA or MCA slot design in their systems. This is not true, however, because manufacturers of EISA systems must pay IBM the same licensing fees as do manufacturers of ISA or MCA systems. EISA was developed not to circumvent licensing fees, but to show technological leadership and enable COMPAQ and other companies to have some design freedom and control over their systems. Whether EISA, *an alternative* to the IBM-designed MCA, becomes a useful standard depends on the popularity of systems that use the slot. Four years after EISA's introduction, only a few hundred thousand EISA systems have been sold, and several million MCA systems have been sold.

Table 2.1 summarizes the primary differences between a standard PC (or XT) system and an AT system. This information distinguishes between these systems and includes all IBM and compatible models.

This list should help you understand the material in table 2.1:

ISA	Industry Standard Architecture
EISA	Extended Industry Standard Architecture
MCA	Micro Channel Architecture
NMI	Non-maskable interrupt
DMA	Direct Memory Access
RAM	Random-access memory
ROM	Read-only memory
UART	Universal Asynchronous Receiver/Transmitter
ESDI	Enhanced Small Device Interface
BIOS	Basic input-output system
CMOS	Complementary Metal-Oxide Semiconductor
EISA	Enhanced Industry Standard Architecture

Table 2.1 Differences between PC (or XT) and AT Systems

System attributes	PC or XT type	AT type
Supported processors	All Intel 80xx	286 or higher
Processor modes	Real	Real/protected/virtual real
Expansion-slot width	8-bit	16-bit/32-bit
Slot type	ISA	ISA/EISA/MCA
Interrupts	8 + NMI	16 + NMI
DMA channels	4	8
Maximum RAM	1 megabyte	16 or 4096 megabytes
Motherboard ROM space	F0000-FFFFF	0E0000-0FFFFF/FE0000-FFFFFF
Floppy controller	250 KHz rate	250/300/500/1000 KHz rates
Boot drive	360K or 720K	1.2M/1.44M/2.88M
Hard disk BIOS	Adapter	Motherboard or adapter
Keyboard interface	Unidirectional	Bidirectional
CMOS setup/clock	No	Yes
Serial port UART	8250B	16450/16550

This table highlights the primary differences between the PC and AT architecture. Using the information in this table, you can properly categorize virtually any system as a PC type or AT type. A COMPAQ Deskpro, for example, is a PC system, and the Deskpro 286 and Deskpro 386 are AT-type systems. IBM's XT Model 286 is actually an AT-type system. The AT&T 6300 qualifies as a PC-type system, and the 6310 is an AT-type system.

You usually can identify PC and XT types of systems by their Intel-design 8088 or 8086 processors; many possibilities are available, however. Some systems have the NEC V-20 or V-30 processors, but these processors are functionally identical to the Intel chips. A few PC or XT systems have an 80286 or 80386 processor for increased performance. These systems usually have one or more 8-bit slots of the same system-bus design featured in the original IBM PC. The design of these slots includes only half the total DMA and interrupts of a true AT design, which limits severely the use of expansion slots by different adapter boards that require the use of these resources. This type of system can run most software that runs under MS-DOS but is limited in more advanced operating systems such as OS/2. This type of system cannot run OS/2 or any software designed to run under OS/2, nor can it run Windows in standard or enhanced mode. These systems also cannot have more than 1 megabyte of processor-addressable memory, of which only 640K is available for user programs and data.

You usually can identify AT systems by their Intel-design 80286, 80386, or higher processors. Some AT systems differ in the types of slots included on the main system board. The earlier standard called for 8- and 16-bit slots compatible with the original IBM PC and AT. The newer standard, IBM's Micro Channel Architecture (MCA), consists of 16- and 32-bit slots, with the 32-bit slots present in only 80386DX or higher systems.

Some manufacturers have integrated proprietary 32-bit slots in their non-Micro Channel AT systems, but usually no expansion boards are available except memory boards produced by the system manufacturer. Because of these nonstandard implementations, several manufacturers have announced a standard 32-bit AT-type slot to compete with the IBM Micro Channel Architecture. Compared to the 8-bit ISA design, the basic AT system (16-bit ISA) provides twice the number of interrupts and DMA channels for adapter boards to use, and EISA has even greater capabilities than the basic AT ISA design. This capability enables greater system expansion with fewer conflicts among adapters.

PC systems decode 64K of memory for the motherboard ROM, using the last segment in the 1 megabyte of total space. The actual addresses for this memory are F0000-FFFFF in hexadecimal. An AT system decodes

128K at the end of the first megabyte and at the end of the last (16th) megabyte of memory. The addresses are 0E0000-0FFFFF and FE0000-FFFFFF in hexadecimal. In the AT system, each set of 128K bytes of ROM space is the same code: double mapped—only 128K total is available as the amount of actual memory, but the system has it positioned in two different places so that the total memory consumed is 256K. Double mapping is required in the AT systems because of the microprocessor design.

PC systems usually have double-density (DD) floppy controllers, but AT systems must have a controller capable of high-density (HD) and double-density operation. Some newer systems, such as the PS/2 Model 57, also have a controller capable of extra-high density (ED). These systems can run the 2.88M floppy drive. Because of the different controller types, the boot drive on a PC system must be the DD, 5 1/4-inch 360K or 3 1/2-inch 720K drives, but the AT needs the 5 1/4-inch 1.2M or the 3 1/2-inch 1.44M or 2.88M drives for proper operation. You can use a double-density disk drive as the boot drive in an AT system; the problem is that your boot drive is *supposed* to be a high-density drive. Many applications that run on only AT-type systems are packaged on high-density disks. The OS/2 operating system, for example, is packaged on high-density disks and cannot be loaded from double-density disks. The capability to boot and run OS/2 is a basic AT-compatibility test.

The PC-type systems use a hard disk controller with an on-board hard disk, ROM BIOS. The controller ROM contains a set of built-in tables for supported drives or has an *autoconfigure* option that can configure a drive dynamically by building a table entry on the spot and storing it directly on the drive. On AT-type systems, the controller BIOS and the supported drive table usually are embedded in the motherboard ROM. This motherboard-resident hard disk BIOS is designed for a particular type of controller, and other controllers used must "look like" or emulate the one expected by the motherboard code. This situation is especially true for ST-412 and ESDI interface drives. SCSI (Small Computer System Interface) adapters, however, normally have their own on-board BIOS because they normally do not emulate the ST-412 or ESDI controllers, and most compatible manufacturers have not yet cloned the SCSI support found in the motherboard BIOS on some IBM PS/2 systems.

A subtle difference between PC/XT and AT systems is in the keyboard interface. AT systems use a bidirectional keyboard interface with an Intel 8042 processor "running the show." This processor has ROM built-in and can be considered a part of the total system ROM package. The PC/XT systems used an 8255 Programmable Peripheral Interface (PPI) chip, which supports only a unidirectional interface. A keyboard can be configured to work with only one of the interface designs. With many keyboards, you can alter the way the keyboard interfaces by flipping a switch on the bottom of the keyboard. Others, like IBM's Enhanced 101-key keyboard, detect which type of system they are plugged into and switch automatically. The older XT and AT keyboards work with only the type of system for which they were designed.

The AT architecture uses CMOS memory and a real-time clock, and the PC-type systems usually don't. (An exception is the PS/2 Model 30, which has a real-time clock even though it is an XT-class system.) A *real-time clock* is the built-in clock implemented by a special CMOS memory chip on the motherboard in an AT system. You can have a clock added on some expansion adapters in a PC system, but DOS does not recognize the clock unless a special program is run first. The CMOS memory in the AT system also stores the system's basic configuration. On a PC or XT type of system, all these basic configuration options (such as the amount of installed memory, the number and types of floppy drives and hard disks, and the type of video adapter) are set by using switches and jumpers on the motherboard, and various adapters.

The serial-port control chip (UART) is a National Semiconductor 8250B for the PC-type systems; AT systems use the newer NS 16450 or 16550 chips. Because these chips differ in subtle ways, the BIOS software must be designed for a specific chip. In the AT BIOS, designed for the 16450 and 16550 chips, using the older 8250B chip can result in strange problems such as lost characters at higher transmission speeds.

Some differences (such as the expansion slots, the system interrupts, and the DMA channel availability) are absolute. Other differences, such as which processors are supported, are less absolute. The AT systems, however, must use the 80286 or higher; the PC systems can use the entire Intel family of chips, from the 8086 to the 80386 and even the NEC V-20 and V-30. Other parameters are less absolute. Your own system might not follow the true standard properly. If your system does not follow all the criteria listed for it, especially if it is an AT-type system, you can expect compatibility and operational problems.

All the items listed in table 2.1 are meaningful and required in order for a system to follow the true industry-standard definition of an AT- or PC/XT-class system.

The System Memory Map

The *memory map* is one of the most important areas of the system. It shows all the memory possible for the system to address and how the memory is used in a particular type of system.

A PC- or XT-compatible system has 1 megabyte of memory workspace, sometimes called RAM (random-access memory), that is addressable by the processor. The 1M of RAM is divided into several sections, some of which have special uses. Conventional programs and data can reside in the portion of RAM space called *user memory*, conventionally limited to the first 640K of the total RAM. The next 128K, called *video RAM*, is reserved for use by video adapters. When text and graphics are displayed on-screen, they reside in this space.

The following 128K is reserved for ROM (read-only memory) control programs and other special memory uses for all the adapter boards plugged into the system slots. ROM is a subset of RAM, which stores programs that cannot be changed. The programs are stored on special chips that have fused circuits so that the PC cannot alter them. ROM is useful for permanent programs that always must be present while the system is running. Graphics boards, hard disk controllers, communications boards, and expanded memory boards, for example, are adapter boards that might use some of this memory.

The last 128K of memory is reserved for ROM on the motherboard. The basic input-output system (BIOS) as well as the POST (Power-On Self Test) and bootstrap loader reside in this space. These programs are the master test and control programs for the system and enable the system to load an operating system from a floppy or hard disk.

Figure 2.1 represents all the memory in an XT system and shows how the memory can be allocated. Each symbol on a line is equal to 1 kilobyte of memory. Each line or segment is 64K, and the entire map is 1,024K, or 1 megabyte.

These symbols are used in figure 2.1:

.	Program-accessible memory (user-installed RAM)
v	Video RAM
a	Adapter-board ROM and special-purpose RAM
r	Motherboard ROM BIOS
b	IBM Cassette BASIC (*r* on compatibles)

```
Conventional (base) memory

         : 0---1---2---3---4---5--6---7--8---9---A---B---C---D---E---F---
   00000: ................................................................
   10000: ................................................................
   20000: ................................................................
   30000: ................................................................
   40000: ................................................................
   50000: ................................................................
   60000: ................................................................
   70000: ................................................................
   80000: ................................................................
   90000: ................................................................

Upper memory area (UMA)
   A0000: vvvvvvvvvvvvvvvvvvvvvvvvvvvvvvvvvvvvvvvvvvvvvvvvvvvvvvvvvvvvvvvvvv
   B0000: vvvvvvvvvvvvvvvvvvvvvvvvvvvvvvvvvvvvvvvvvvvvvvvvvvvvvvvvvvvvvvvvvv
   C0000: aaaaaaaaaaaaaaaaaaaaaaaaaaaaaaaaaaaaaaaaaaaaaaaaaaaaaaaaaaaaaaaa
   D0000: aaaaaaaaaaaaaaaaaaaaaaaaaaaaaaaaaaaaaaaaaaaaaaaaaaaaaaaaaaaaaaaa
   E0000: rrrrrrrrrrrrrrrrrrrrrrrrrrrrrrrrrrrrrrrrrrrrrrrrrrrrrrrrrrrrrrrr
   F0000: rrrrrrrrrrrrrrrrrrrrrrrrrbbbbbbbbbbbbbbbbbbbbbbbbbbbbbbbrrrrrrrrr
```

Fig. 2.1

1-megabyte memory map (for PC- and XT- class systems).

Note that addresses A0000 to F0000 are reserved for various purposes. At least ten segments, each with 64K, are not reserved, which provides a total of 640K of memory for DOS and programs. The rest of the reserved space can be used completely in some systems and sparsely in others. Not all video adapters, for example, use all 128K of the space allocated to them. Adapters that use less enable DOS to use the additional memory for programs and data.

In an AT system, the memory map extends beyond the 1-megabyte boundary and continues to 16 megabytes. For this reason, in the computer industry, any memory greater than 1 megabyte is called *extended memory*. Because a small portion (128K) of the last megabyte is reserved for a duplicate of the AT ROM BIOS, not all of the last megabyte can be used for programs and data. This additional (128K) ROM located at the end of the last megabyte of addressable memory makes the total reserved space in an AT 512K greater than the 384K reserved in an XT system.

For an AT system to "see" (or be able to address) any memory beyond the standard 1 megabyte of address space, the 80286 or 80386 processor must be in its protected mode of operation. *Protected mode*, the native mode of these processors, has access to more memory, a modified instruction set, and other operational differences.

Unfortunately, because of these operational differences, the system cannot be compatible with the original IBM PC systems. Intel designed within the 80286 and 80386 an 8086/8088 mode called *real mode*, which enables full compatibility with the earlier processors. It is unfortunate that this compatibility is necessarily complete. An AT running in this mode is not really an AT; it is more like a "turbo" PC!

The 80286 can emulate the 8086 or 8088, but it cannot provide its own native features at the same time. You cannot extend DOS to take advantage of an AT's protected-mode features; you need an entirely new operating system written from the ground up. This operating system, known as OS/2, switches rapidly between real and protected mode, and the AT seems to run DOS software and new OS/2-specific programs. Even under OS/2, however, the DOS mode can run only within the first megabyte of the 16 total possible on an AT.

Figure 2.2 shows the total 16M map for an AT-type system in protected mode. This figure has been condensed to fit here by sectioning out most of the extended memory area. A full-length version of this figure is in the Appendix of this book. You can see where the real-mode addressable memory ends and extended memory picks up. An 80286 or 80386 system running in protected mode is required in order to address memory beyond the 1M boundary. The following symbols are used in figure 2.2:

.	Program-accessible memory (user-installed RAM)
v	Video RAM
a	Adapter-board ROM and special-purpose RAM
r	Motherboard ROM BIOS
b	IBM Cassette BASIC (r on compatibles)
h	High-Memory Area (HMA, allocated by HIMEM.SYS)

Notice the duplicate of the ROM BIOS that appears at the end of the 16th megabyte. The memory in these last two segments is a mirror image of the contents of the last two segments in the first megabyte, which is required so that the 286 and higher CPU designs can switch between the real and protected modes of operation. Don't confuse this type of memory with shadow ROM—high-speed RAM that contains a copy of the ROM BIOS and is relocated to occupy the 0E0000-0FFFFF area. Shadow ROM is possible only on 386 or higher systems and cannot easily be shown on these maps.

```
Conventional (base) memory
            : 0---1---2---3---4---5---6---7---8---9---A---B---C---D---E---F---
    000000: ................................................................
    010000: ................................................................
    020000: ................................................................
    030000: ................................................................
    040000: ................................................................
    050000: ................................................................
    060000: ................................................................
    070000: ................................................................
    080000: ................................................................
    090000: ................................................................

Upper memory area (UMA)
    0A0000: vvvvvvvvvvvvvvvvvvvvvvvvvvvvvvvvvvvvvvvvvvvvvvvvvvvvvvvvvvvvvvvvvv
    0B0000: vvvvvvvvvvvvvvvvvvvvvvvvvvvvvvvvvvvvvvvvvvvvvvvvvvvvvvvvvvvvvvvvvv
    0C0000: aaaaaaaaaaaaaaaaaaaaaaaaaaaaaaaaaaaaaaaaaaaaaaaaaaaaaaaaaaaaaaaaa
    0D0000: aaaaaaaaaaaaaaaaaaaaaaaaaaaaaaaaaaaaaaaaaaaaaaaaaaaaaaaaaaaaaaaaa
    0E0000: rrrrrrrrrrrrrrrrrrrrrrrrrrrrrrrrrrrrrrrrrrrrrrrrrrrrrrrrrrrrrrrrr
    0F0000: rrrrrrrrrrrrrrrrrrrrrrrrbbbbbbbbbbbbbbbbbbbbbbbbbbbbbbrrrrrrrrr

Extended memory
            : 0---1---2---3---4---5---6---7---8---9---A---B---C---D---E---F---
    100000: hhhhhhhhhhhhhhhhhhhhhhhhhhhhhhhhhhhhhhhhhhhhhhhhhhhhhhhhhhhhhhhhhh

XMS (Extended memory specification) memory
    110000: ................................................................
    120000: ................................................................
    130000: ................................................................
    140000: ................................................................
    150000: ................................................................
    160000: ................................................................
    170000: ................................................................
    180000: ................................................................
    190000: ................................................................
    1A0000: ................................................................
    1B0000: ................................................................
    1C0000: ................................................................
    1D0000: ................................................................
    1E0000: ................................................................
    1F0000: ................................................................
            : 0---1---2---3---4---5---6---7---8---9---A---B---C---D---E---F---
    200000: ................................................................
    210000: ................................................................
    220000: ................................................................
    230000: ................................................................
    240000: ................................................................
    250000: ................................................................
    260000: ................................................................

                            .
                            .
                            .

The map continues following the same segment pattern.

                            .
                            .
                            .

    E70000: ................................................................
    E80000: ................................................................
    E90000: ................................................................
    EA0000: ................................................................
    EB0000: ................................................................
    EC0000: ................................................................
    ED0000: ................................................................
    EE0000: ................................................................
    EF0000: ................................................................
            : 0---1---2---3---4---5---6---7---8---9---A---B---C---D---E---F---
    F00000: ................................................................
    F10000: ................................................................
    F20000: ................................................................
    F30000: ................................................................
```

```
F40000:  .............................................................
F50000:  .............................................................
F60000:  .............................................................
F70000:  .............................................................
F80000:  .............................................................
F90000:  .............................................................
FA0000:  .............................................................
FB0000:  .............................................................
FC0000:  .............................................................
FD0000:  .............................................................
FE0000:  rrrrrrrrrrrrrrrrrrrrrrrrrrrrrrrrrrrrrrrrrrrrrrrrrrrrrrrrrrrrrrr
FF0000:

         rrrrrrrrrrrrrrrrrrrrrrrrbbbbbbbbbbbbbbbbbbbbbbbbbbbbbbbbbbrrrrrrrrr
```

Fig. 2.2

16-megabyte memory map (for AT-class systems).

Some systems incorporate *expanded memory*. Unlike conventional (the first megabyte) or extended (the second through 16th megabytes) memory, expanded memory is *not* directly addressable by the processor except through a small 64K window. Expanded memory is a segment-switching scheme in which a memory adapter has on-board a large number of 64K segments. The system uses one available segment to map into the board. After this 64K is filled with data, the board "rotates" the filled segment out and a new, empty one in to take its place.

Segment E000 in the first megabyte usually is used for mapping. Lotus, Intel, and Microsoft—founders of the LIM specification for expanded memory (LIM EMS)—decided to use this segment because it is largely unused by most adapters. Programs must be written specially to take advantage of this segment-swapping scheme, and then only data normally can be placed in this segment because it is above the area of contiguous memory (640K) that DOS can use. For example, a program cannot run while it is "swapped out" and therefore not visible by the processor. This type of memory generally is useful only in systems that do not have extended (processor-addressable) memory available to them. Chapter 10, "Peripherals," describes expanded and extended memory use in much more detail.

DOS Program Memory

Many people have trouble understanding how the reserved memory affects the map as a whole. You need to know what goes where in this reserved area to understand how your hardware and software interact together, and to prevent conflicts.

Much is written about the "DOS 640K barrier." In reality, no actual barrier is at this location. DOS works with the entire RAM address space on a PC, which is 1 megabyte. Your programs cannot use all this space because some of it is reserved for the system's own use. DOS can read and write to the entire megabyte but can manage the loading of programs in only the contiguous-memory portion of the megabyte (640K).

DOS can use all the memory available until it runs into an obstruction. The first obstruction in the system is the video RAM, the topic of the following section. This obstruction is in different locations, depending on which video adapter is installed in the system. The different video adapters also use varying amounts of RAM for their operations. The higher-resolution adapters usually use more memory than those offering lower resolution because of the larger number of pixels (picture elements) and colors on the screen.

According to IBM's definition of the PC standard, the reserved video RAM begins at address A0000, which is right at the 640K boundary. The remaining memory after 640K is reserved for use by the graphics boards, other adapters, and the motherboard ROM BIOS.

Video Memory

A video adapter installed in your system uses some of your system's memory to hold graphics or character information for display. Some of the more advanced adapters, such as the EGA, VGA, or XGA adapters, also have an on-board ROM mapped into the system's space reserved for such types of adapters. Generally, the higher the resolution and color capabilities of the video adapter, the more memory the video adapter uses.

In the standard system-memory map, a total of 128K is reserved for video RAM, which is where the adapter stores currently displayed information. If the adapter has additional on-board memory that is hidden or swapped out, the total memory on the card might be more than 128K. The reserved video memory is located in segments A000 and B000, and space for any ROM on the video board is reserved in segment C000.

This section examines how standard video adapters use the system's memory. Figures 2.3 through 2.7 show where in a system each type of standard video adapter uses memory. Each symbol in these figures is equal to 1K of memory.

Figure 2.3 shows where the Monochrome Display Adapter (MDA) uses the system's memory. This adapter uses only a 4K portion of the reserved video RAM from B0000-B0FFF. Because the ROM code that is used to operate this adapter is actually a portion of the motherboard ROM, no additional ROM space is used in segment C000.

These symbols are used in figure 2.3:

.   Empty memory addresses

M   Monochrome Display Adapter (MDA) video RAM

```
        : 0---1---2---3---4---5---6---7---8---9---A---B---C---D---E---F---
A0000: ................................................................
B0000: MMMM............................................................
        : 0---1---2---3---4---5---6---7---8---9---A---B---C---D---E---F---
C0000: ................................................................
D0000: ................................................................
```

Fig. 2.3

The Monochrome Display Adapter's (MDA's) memory map.

Figure 2.4 shows where the Color Graphics Adapter (CGA) uses the system's memory. The CGA uses a 16K portion of the reserved video RAM from B8000-BBFFF. Because the ROM code that is used to operate this adapter is a portion of the motherboard ROM, no additional ROM space is used in segment C000.

These symbols are used in figure 2.4:

.   Empty memory addresses

C   Color Graphics Adapter (CGA) video RAM

```
        : 0---1---2---3---4---5---6---7---8---9---A---B---C---D---E---F---
A0000: ................................................................
B0000: ...........................................CCCCCCCCCCCCCCCCCC.....................
        : 0---1---2---3---4---5---6---7---8---9---A---B---C---D---E---F---
C0000: ................................................................
D0000: ................................................................
```

Fig. 2.4

The Color Graphics Adapter's (CGA) memory map.

Figure 2.5 shows where the Enhanced Graphics Adapter (EGA) uses the system's memory. This adapter uses all 128K of the video RAM from A0000-BFFFF. The ROM code that is used to operate this adapter is on the adapter itself and consumes 16K of memory from C0000-C3FFF.

These symbols are used in figure 2.5:

.   Empty memory addresses

E   Enhanced Graphics Adapter (EGA) video RAM

R   Video adapter ROM BIOS addresses

```
        : 0---1---2---3---4---5---6---7---8---9---A---B---C---D---E---F---
A0000: EEEEEEEEEEEEEEEEEEEEEEEEEEEEEEEEEEEEEEEEEEEEEEEEEEEEEEEEEEEEEEEEEE
B0000: EEEEEEEEEEEEEEEEEEEEEEEEEEEEEEEEEEEEEEEEEEEEEEEEEEEEEEEEEEEEEEEEEE
        : 0---1---2---3---4---5---6---7---8---9---A---B---C---D---E---F---
C0000: RRRRRRRRRRRRRRRRRR..............................................
D0000: ................................................................
```

Fig. 2.5

The Enhanced Graphics Adapter's (EGA) memory map.

Figure 2.6 shows where the IBM PS/2 Display Adapter uses the system's memory. The IBM PS/2 Display Adapter, essentially a Video Graphics Array (VGA) on a board for the standard PC and AT types of systems, uses all 128K of the video RAM from A0000-BFFFF. The ROM code that operates this adapter is on the adapter itself and consumes 24K of memory from C0000-C5FFF.

These symbols are used in figure 2.6:

.   Empty memory addresses

V   Video Graphics Array (VGA) or MultiColor Graphics Array (MCGA) video RAM

R   Video adapter ROM BIOS addresses

S   Scratch-pad memory

Fig. 2.6

The IBM PS/2 Display Adapter's (IBM VGA card) memory map.

```
       : 0---1---2---3---4---5---6---7---8---9---A---B---C---D---E---F---
 A0000: VVVVVVVVVVVVVVVVVVVVVVVVVVVVVVVVVVVVVVVVVVVVVVVVVVVVVVVVVVVVVVVVVV
 B0000: VVVVVVVVVVVVVVVVVVVVVVVVVVVVVVVVVVVVVVVVVVVVVVVVVVVVVVVVVVVVVVVVVV
       : 0---1---2---3---4---5---6---7---8---9---A---B---C---D---E---F---
 C0000: RRRRRRRRRRRRRRRRRRRRRRRRR..SSSSSS........SS......................
 D0000: ................................................................
```

Note that the IBM PS/2 Display Adapter uses the strange "scratch pad" memory. This memory use was not documented clearly in the technical-reference information for the adapter. In particular, the 2K of memory used at CA000 can cause problems with other cards if they are addressed in this area. If you try to install a hard disk controller with a 16K BIOS at C8000, for example, the system locks up during boot-up because of the conflict with the video-card memory. You can solve the problem by altering to D8000 the start address of the disk controller BIOS. Most "normal" VGA cards restrict their memory use to the 32K range, from C0000-C7FFF. This arrangement should prevent conflicts with most other adapters. A standard, compatible VGA adapter memory map should look like figure 2.7.

These symbols are used in figure 2.7:

.   Empty memory addresses

V   Video Graphics Array (VGA) or MultiColor Graphics Array (MCGA) video RAM

R   Video adapter ROM BIOS addresses

```
       : 0---1---2---3---4---5---6---7---8---9---A---B---C---D---E---F---
A0000: VVVVVVVVVVVVVVVVVVVVVVVVVVVVVVVVVVVVVVVVVVVVVVVVVVVVVVVVVVVVVVVVV
B0000: VVVVVVVVVVVVVVVVVVVVVVVVVVVVVVVVVVVVVVVVVVVVVVVVVVVVVVVVVVVVVVVVV
       : 0---1---2---3---4---5---6---7---8---9---A---B---C---D---E---F---
C0000: RRRRRRRRRRRRRRRRRRRRRRRRRRRRRRRRRRRR.............................
D0000:
```

Fig. 2.7

A "normal" VGA adapter's memory map.

On PS/2 systems with the Video Graphics Array (VGA) or MultiColor Graphics Array (MCGA), the built-in display systems also use all 128K of the reserved video RAM space; because these display systems are built into the motherboard, however, the control BIOS code is built into the motherboard ROM BIOS and needs no space in segment C000. Figure 2.8 shows where such PS/2 systems use the system memory.

These symbols are used in figure 2.8:

.   Empty memory addresses

V   Video Graphics Array (VGA) or MultiColor Graphics Array (MCGA) video RAM

```
A0000: VVVVVVVVVVVVVVVVVVVVVVVVVVVVVVVVVVVVVVVVVVVVVVVVVVVVVVVVVVVVVVVVV
B0000: VVVVVVVVVVVVVVVVVVVVVVVVVVVVVVVVVVVVVVVVVVVVVVVVVVVVVVVVVVVVVVVVV
       : 0---1---2---3---4---5---6---7---8---9---A---B---C---D---E---F---
C0000: ...............................................................
D0000: ...............................................................
```

Fig. 2.8

The PS/2 motherboard VGA and MCGA memory use.

Each type of video adapter on the market uses two types of memory: video RAM stores the display information, and ROM code, which controls the adapter, must exist somewhere in the system's memory. The ROM code built into the motherboard ROM on standard PC and AT systems controls adapters such as the MDA and CGA. All the EGA and VGA adapters for the PC and AT systems use the full 128K of video RAM and some ROM space at the beginning of segment C000. IBM's technical-reference manuals say that the memory between C0000 and C7FFF is reserved specifically for ROM on video adapter boards. Note that the VGA and MCGA built into the motherboards of the PS/2 systems have the ROM-control software built into the motherboard ROM in segments E000 and F000 and require no other code space in segment C000.

The low-end adapters such as the MDA and CGA allow DOS access to more than 640K of system memory. DOS can use all available contiguous memory in the first megabyte—which means all—memory until the video adapter RAM is encountered. The video memory *wall* begins at

A0000 for the EGA, MCGA, and VGA systems; the MDA and CGA do not use as much video RAM, however, which leaves some space that can be used by DOS and programs. The figures show that the MDA enables an additional 64K of memory for DOS (all of segment A000), bringing the total for DOS program space to 704K. Similarly, the CGA enables a total of 736K of possible contiguous memory. The EGA, VGA, or MCGA is limited to the normal maximum of 640K of contiguous memory because of the larger amount used by video RAM. The maximum DOS-program memory workspace therefore depends on which video adapter is installed (see table 2.2).

Table 2.2 DOS Memory Limitations from Video Adapter	
Video adapter	**Maximum memory**
Monochrome Display Adapter (MDA)	704K
Color Graphics Adapter (CGA)	736K
Enhanced Graphics Adapter (EGA)	640K
Video Graphics Array (VGA)	640K
MultiColor Graphics Array (MCGA)	640K

Using this memory to 736K might be possible depending on the video adapter, the types of memory boards installed, ROM programs on the motherboard, and the type of system. You can use some of this memory if your system has an 80386 or higher processor. With special software, such as Quarterdeck's QEMM, that can operate these chips' unique memory-management capabilities, you can remap extended memory to use this space. Systems that lack this memory-management capability cannot remap and use this memory.

Adapter ROM and RAM Memory

Segments C000 and D000 are reserved for use by adapter-board ROM and RAM. These boards use space as shown in table 2.3.

Table 2.3 Default Memory Use of Various Adapter Boards

Adapter	Memory use
IBM EGA ROM	16K at C0000
IBM PS/2 (VGA) display adapter ROM	24K at C0000
IBM PS/2 (VGA) display adapter scratch RAM	2K at CA000
Most other EGA/VGA adapter ROMs	32K at C0000
IBM XT 10M hard disk controller ROM	8K at C8000
IBM XT 20M hard disk controller ROM	4K at C8000
IBM ESDI fixed disk adapter/A	16K at C8000
Most other hard disk controller ROMs	16K at C8000
Token Ring network adapter ROM	8K at CC000
Token Ring network adapter RAM	16K at D8000
LIM expanded memory adapter RAM	64K at D0000

This list is a small sample of some of the boards that use space in these segments. Note that some of the apparent uses overlap, which is not allowed in a single system. If two adapters have overlapping ROM or RAM addresses, usually neither board operates properly. Each board functions if you remove or disable the other one, but they do not work together. With many adapter boards you can change the actual memory locations to be used with jumpers, switches, or driver software, which might be necessary to allow two boards to coexist in one system.

Note that the LIM EMS specification normally uses the entire range of segment D000 for expanded memory. The use of segment D000 by the LIM EMS cuts in half the amount of available ROM and RAM space for other adapters, forcing many adapters, such as the Token Ring network adapter, to be reconfigured so that their memory use excludes this segment.

This type of conflict can cause problems for troubleshooters. If you install a Token Ring network card and an Intel Above Board (an EMS board) and then follow the factory-set default configuration with each one, neither adapter card works in the same system. You must read the documentation for each adapter to find out what memory addresses the adapter uses and how to change the addresses to allow coexistence with another adapter. Most of the time, you can work around these problems by reconfiguring the board or changing jumpers, switch settings, or software-driver parameters. For the Token Ring card, you can change the software-driver parameters in the CONFIG.SYS file to move the memory the card uses from D8000 to something closer to C4000. This change enables the two boards to coexist and "stay out of each other's way."

You can use a chart or template to "mock up" the memory configuration of an adapter before you install it in a system by penciling, on the template, where each adapter will use memory. You end up with a "picture" of the system's memory layout and the relationship of each adapter that uses memory addresses. This procedure helps you anticipate conflicts with memory addressing and ensures that you configure each board correctly the first time. After you configure a system, the template you created showing how each board in the system uses memory is important documentation when you consider new adapter purchases. New adapters incorporating a ROM that the system must recognize must fit in the available workspace.

Motherboard ROM Memory

The ROM memory is part of the RAM in each system. Manufacturers permanently store this memory by fusing circuits in special chips called programmable read-only memory (PROM) chips. The chips store programs that must be invoked every time the system is turned on. Because these programs must be available immediately, they cannot be loaded from a device such as a disk drive. In fact, ROM programs instruct the system during the boot-up procedure.

Segments E000 and F000 in the memory map are reserved for the motherboard ROM software. Both segments are considered reserved for the motherboard ROM, but only the AT systems actually reserve this entire area. PC systems reserve only segment F000 and enable ROM or RAM to use segment E000 on other adapter cards. This information might be important when you attempt to "cram" an expanded memory adapter into a system that already has a full complement of other boards using memory in segments C000 and D000.

One thing that can be confusing is the difference between a segment address and a full address. For example, in my PS/2 system, my SCSI host adapter has 16K ROM on the card addressed from D4000 to D7FFF—the actual address range used. These numbers expressed in segment:offset form are D400:0000 to D700:0FFF. The segment portion is composed of the most significant four digits, and the offset portion is composed of the least significant four digits. Because each portion overlaps by one digit, the ending address of this ROM can be expressed in four different ways:

D000:7FFF = D0000+07FFF = D7FFF

D700:0FFF = D7000+00FFF = D7FFF

D7F0:00FF = D7F00+000FF = D7FFF

D7FF:000F = D7FF0+0000F = D7FFF

Adding together the segment and offset numbers makes possible even more combinations:

D500:2FFF = D5000+02FFF = D7FFF

D6EE:111F = D6EE0+0111F = D7FFF

As you can see, several combinations are possible. The correct and generally accepted way to write this address is either D7FFF or D700:0FFF.

Each system has on the motherboard a set of chips that stores the ROM BIOS. The ROM contains several routines, or modules, designed to operate the system. The main functions are listed:

- *Power-On Self Test*, the POST, is a set of routines that tests the motherboard, memory, disk controllers, video adapters, keyboard, and other primary system components. This routine is useful when you troubleshoot system failures or problems.

- The *basic input-output system* (BIOS) is the software interface, or "master control program," to all the hardware in the system. With the ROM BIOS, a program easily can access features in the system by calling a ROM BIOS program module instead of talking directly to the device.

- The *bootstrap loader* routine initiates a search for an operating system on a floppy disk or hard disk. If an operating system is found, it is loaded into memory and given control of the system.

Systems produced by IBM and other companies have different ROM BIOS software installed. How close in function this software is to what IBM has is a critical issue with any compatible. Compatible software must duplicate the functionality of an IBM ROM in order for software to run on the systems as it would on an equivalent IBM system. Fortunately, this software has been relatively easy to duplicate functionally. Modern compatibles are at no real disadvantage.

Many different ROM-interface programs are in the IBM motherboards, but the location of these programs is mostly consistent. Figures 2.9 through 2.12 show the memory use in segments E000 and F000.

Figure 2.9 shows the memory use in an IBM PC and XT with a 256K motherboard. These symbols are used in figure 2.9:

.   Empty memory addresses

b   IBM ROM Cassette BASIC

R   Motherboard ROM BIOS (CBIOS, for Compatibility BIOS)

x   Decoded by motherboard (unavailable)

Fig. 2.9

Motherboard ROM memory use in IBM PC and XT with 256K motherboard.

```
        : 0---1---2---3---4---5---6---7---8---9---A---B---C---D---E---F---
 E0000: ................................................................
 F0000: xxxxxxxxxxxxxxxxxxxxxxxxxxbbbbbbbbbbbbbbbbbbbbbbbbbbbbbbbbRRRRRRRR
```

Figure 2.10 shows the memory use in most PC- or XT-compatible systems. These systems lack the Cassette BASIC found in IBM's BIOS.

These symbols are used in figure 2.10:

.   Empty memory addresses (unavailable)

x   Empty memory decoded by motherboard (unavailable)

R   Video adapter ROM BIOS addresses

Fig. 2.10

Motherboard ROM memory use in most PC- or XT-compatibles.

```
        : 0---1---2---3---4---5---6---7---8---9---A---B---C---D---E---F---
 E0000: ................................................................
 F0000: xxxxxxxxxxxxxxxxxxxxxxxxxxxxxxxxRRRRRRRRRRRRRRRRRRRRRRRRRRRRRRRRRR
```

Figure 2.11 shows the memory use in an XT with a 640K motherboard and in the PS/2 Model 25 and Model 30. These systems have additional BIOS code compared to the original PC and XT. Note that the Cassette BASIC remains in the same addresses. These symbols are used in figure 2.11:

.   Empty memory (available for other uses)

R   Video adapter ROM BIOS addresses

b   IBM ROM Cassette BASIC

Fig. 2.11

Motherboard ROM memory use in an IBM XT with a 640K motherboard and in the PS/2 Model 25 and Model 30.

```
        : 0---1---2---3---4---5---6---7---8---9---A---B---C---D---E---F---
 E0000: ................................................................
 F0000: RRRRRRRRRRRRRRRRRRRRRRRRRRbbbbbbbbbbbbbbbbbbbbbbbbbbbbbbbbRRRRRRRR
```

Figure 2.12 shows the memory use in an XT-286 and AT. Note that the system board decodes segment E000 even though no code is there, because this area was planned for future ROM expansion; the expansion was implemented later, in the PS/2 systems, for a protected-mode BIOS called ABIOS (for Advanced BIOS). These symbols are used in figure 2.12:

x   Empty memory decoded by motherboard (unavailable)

R   Motherboard ROM BIOS (CBIOS: Compatibility BIOS)

b   IBM ROM Cassette BASIC

```
            : 0---1---2---3---4---5---6---7---8---9---A---B---C---D---E---F---
    E0000: xxxxxxxxxxxxxxxxxxxxxxxxxxxxxxxxxxxxxxxxxxxxxxxxxxxxxxxxxxxxxxxxxx
    F0000: RRRRRRRRRRRRRRRRRRRRRRRRRRRRbbbbbbbbbbbbbbbbbbbbbbbbbbbbbRRRRRRRRR
```

Fig. 2.12

Motherboard ROM memory use in an IBM XT-286 and IBM AT.

Figure 2.13 shows memory use in the PS/2 models with a 286 or higher processor, including ISA and MCA systems. Segment E000 contains the Advanced BIOS (ABIOS), used in protected mode. These symbols are used in figure 2.13:

x   Empty memory decoded by motherboard (unavailable)

R   Motherboard ROM BIOS (CBIOS-Compatibility BIOS)

```
            : 0---1---2---3---4---5---6---7---8---9---A---B---C---D---E---F---
    E0000: xxxxxxxxxxxxxxxxxxxxxxxxxxxxxxxxxxxxxxxxxxxxxxxxxxxxxxxxxxxxxxxxxx
    F0000: RRRRRRRRRRRRRRRRRRRRRRRRRRRRRRRRRRRRRRRRRRRRRRRRRRRRRRRRRRRRRRRRRR
```

Fig. 2.13

Motherboard ROM memory use in most AT-compatible systems.

Figure 2.14 shows that PS/2 systems use more of the allocated ROM space for their motherboard ROM BIOS. These symbols are used in figure 2.14:

A   Advanced ROM BIOS (ABIOS: for protected-mode operation)

R   Motherboard ROM BIOS (CBIOS: Compatibility BIOS)

b   IBM ROM Cassette BASIC

```
            : 0---1---2---3---4---5---6---7---8---9---A---B---C---D---E---F---
    E0000: AAAAAAAAAAAAAAAAAAAAAAAAAAAAAAAAAAAAAAAAAAAAAAAAAAAAAAAAAAAAAAAAA
    F0000: RRRRRRRRRRRRRRRRRRRRRRRRRRRRbbbbbbbbbbbbbbbbbbbbbbbbbbbbbRRRRRRRRR
```

Fig. 2.14

Motherboard ROM memory use in PS/2 models with a 286 or higher processor, including both ISA bus and MCA bus systems.

The PS/2 Models with 286 and higher processors each have an additional 64K of Advanced BIOS code, to be used when the systems are running protected-mode software, used by powerful operating systems such as OS/2.

Earlier AT systems, which don't have the Advanced BIOS code, can run OS/2 but must load the equivalent of the Advanced BIOS software from disk rather than have it already loaded in ROM. The code in segment E000 in these systems is not purely Advanced BIOS (protected mode only) code, but contains routines used in real mode as well. IBM has not just placed all of the real mode BIOS code in segment F000, and the protected-mode BIOS in segment E000, as you might imagine. Rather, all the code is distributed throughout segments E000 and F000.

This situation can affect other things also, such as SCSI adapters. Most systems that have a SCSI adapter and hard disk will have to load a special protected-mode driver in order for the adapter to work under OS/2, because the on-board BIOS runs in only real mode and not in protected mode. The IBM SCSI adapters, however, include both real- and protected-mode BIOS software on-board, and operate hard disks under any operating system with no funny drivers. For this reason, I highly recommend IBM SCSI adapters; also, I have not had the SCSI interfacing problems that many other people have had. When other manufacturers of SCSI adapters clone the BIOS from IBM's adapter, then I can recommend them as well.

The ROM maps of most compatibles equal the IBM system with which they are compatible. The only exception is the Cassette BASIC portion, a special Microsoft version designed for the original IBM PC, with built-in ROM to enable diskless operation. Users of these systems can save and load programs and data to or from a cassette tape recorder plugged into the cassette port on the back of an original IBM PC. Because no other IBM system (and virtually no compatible) has a cassette port (all have the Cassette BASIC interpreter in ROM), this type of BASIC language interpreter by itself is useless.

The disk version of BASIC from IBM uses Cassette BASIC as an overlay to save the duplication of the software code on the disk; IBM's BASICA.COM expects to find Cassette BASIC in ROM and does not work without it. Because no compatible system has Cassette BASIC in ROM, none will run IBM's BASICA.COM program from the PC DOS disk.

If you have a non-IBM system, you must get from your system's manufacturer an equivalent version of Microsoft BASIC called GW-BASIC (Graphics Workstation BASIC). The GWBASIC.EXE file has the equivalent program code of the IBM BASICA.COM file and enables interpreted BASIC programs to run exactly as they would on an IBM system.

DOS 5 and later versions from IBM still include the BASICA interpreter; however, non-IBM versions with the "generic" Microsoft MS-DOS no longer include the GW-BASIC interpreter. All DOS 5 and higher versions (IBM and others) have a crippled version of the Microsoft QuickBASIC Compiler. The compiler is crippled so that you can compile programs in memory but not create .EXE files on disk. To do so, you must purchase a copy of QuickBASIC.

Reviewing System-Memory Maps

You have learned how memory is used in systems compatible with the IBM standard. The reserved memory is deducted from what is available for programs and data because the reserved memory usually cannot be used by an operating system.

Table 2.4 lists the maximum available memory for the different systems.

Table 2.4 Maximum Addressable and Usable Memory	
System type	**Maximum addressable memory (RAM)**
PC/XT (or AT real mode)	1,024K (1 megabyte)
AT (protected mode)	16,384K (16 megabytes)
AT 386 or greater	4,194,304K (4,096 megabytes)
System type	Maximum usable memory
PC/XT (or AT real mode)	640K (0.625 megabytes)
AT (protected mode)	15,872K (15.5 megabytes)
Most AT 386 or greater	15,872K (15.5 megabytes)
Some AT 386 or greater	4,193,792K (4,095.5 megabytes)

By reviewing the table, you can see that the next "barrier" to cross is the 15.5M barrier.

Even though the 386 and higher processors can address four gigabytes of memory, most systems still are limited to 16 total megabytes of useful addressable memory, because no direct memory access (DMA) operations can occur beyond the 16-megabyte area. This limitation is primarily in the DMA controllers and not the processor. The memory beyond 16 megabytes usually can be used for *non-operating system memory*, used for adapters, caches, or other items not controlled by the operating system running on the machine. Because limitations in memory beyond 16 megabytes vary among computers, you should consult the manufacturer if you intend to use it.

Documentation

One of the biggest problems in troubleshooting, servicing, or upgrading a system is being able to find proper documentation. As with the system units, IBM has set the standard for the type of documentation a manufacturer makes available. Some compatible manufacturers duplicate the size and content of IBM's manuals, and other manufacturers provide no documentation at all. Generally, the type of documentation provided for a system is proportionate to the size of the manufacturing company. (Large companies can afford to produce good documentation.) Some of this documentation unfortunately is essential for even the most basic troubleshooting and upgrading tasks. Other documentation is necessary only for software and hardware developers with special requirements.

Types of Documentation

Four types of documents are available for each system. Some manuals cover an entire range of systems, which can save money and shelf space. You can get these types of manuals:

- Guide-to-operations (GTO) manuals (called quick-reference manuals for the PS/2)

- Technical-reference (TR) manuals

- Hardware-maintenance service (HMS) manuals

- Hardware-maintenance reference (HMR) manuals

A guide-to-operations manual is included in the purchase of a system. For PS/2 systems, these manuals have been changed to quick-reference manuals. They contain basic instructions for system setup, operation, testing, relocation, and option installation. A *customer-level* basic diagnostics disk (usually called a Diagnostics and Setup Disk) normally is included also in a system. For PS/2 machines, a special disk—the Reference Disk—contains the setup and configuration programs as well as both customer-level and technician-level diagnostics.

For PC and XT types of systems, you can find listings of all the jumper and switch settings for the motherboard. These settings specify the number of floppy disk drives, math-chip use, memory use, type of video adapter, and other items. For AT systems, the basic diagnostics disk has also the SETUP routine (used to set the date and time), installed memory, installed disk drives, and installed video adapters. This information is saved by the SETUP program into CMOS battery backed-up memory. For PS/2 systems, the included disk (called the Reference Disk) contains the special programmable option-select (POS) configuration routine and a hidden version of the advanced diagnostics.

Technical-Reference Manuals

The technical-reference manuals provide system-specific hardware and software interface information for the system. The manuals are intended for people who design hardware and software products to operate with these systems or people who must integrate other hardware and software into a system. Three types of technical-reference manuals are available: One is a technical-reference manual for a particular system; another covers all the options and adapters; and a third covers the ROM BIOS interface. For PS/2 systems, one hardware interface technical-reference manual covers all the PS/2 systems with updates for newer systems as they become available.

Each system has a separate technical-reference manual or an update to the hardware interface technical-reference manual. These publications provide basic interface and design information for the system units. They include information about the system board, math coprocessor, power supply, video subsystem, keyboard, instruction sets, and other features of the system. You need this information for integrating and installing aftermarket floppy and hard disk drives, memory boards, keyboards, network adapters, or virtually anything you want to plug into your system. This manual often contains schematic diagrams showing the circuit layout of the motherboard and pinouts for the various connectors and jumpers. It also includes listings of the floppy and hard disk drive tables, which show the range of drives that can be installed on a particular system. Power specifications for the power supply also are in this manual. You need these figures in order to determine whether the system has adequate current to power a particular add-on device.

The options and adapters technical-reference manual begins with a starter manual augmented with supplements. The basic manual covers a few IBM adapter cards, and supplements for new adapters and options are issued continually. These publications provide interface and design information about the options and adapters available for the various systems. This information includes a hardware description, programming considerations, interface specifications, and BIOS information.

The third manual is the BIOS interface technical-reference manual. This publication provides basic input-output system (BIOS) interface information. This compendium covers every BIOS that has been available in IBM's systems. The manual is designed for developers of hardware or software products that operate with the IBM PC and PS/2 products.

Hardware-Maintenance Manuals

Each hardware maintenance library consists of two manuals: a hardware-maintenance service manual and a hardware-maintenance reference manual. These real-service manuals are written for service technicians. IBM and local computer-retail outlets use these manuals to diagnose and service your system.

For IBM systems, two sets of manuals are available. One set covers the PC, XT, Portable PC, AT, and PS/2 Model 25 and Model 30. The other manual set covers the PS/2 systems except Model 25 and Model 30: these systems are considered as old PC or XT systems rather than as true PS/2 systems.

Manuals are purchased in starter form and then updated with supplements covering new systems and options. The PS/2 Model 25 and Model 30, for example, are covered by supplements that update the PC maintenance library; the PS/2 Model 80 is covered by a supplement to the PS/2 maintenance library.

The basic hardware-maintenance service manual for the PC or PS/2 contains all the information you need to troubleshoot and diagnose a failing system. This book contains special flowcharts that IBM calls maintenance-analysis procedures (MAPs), which can help you find a correct diagnosis in a step-by-step manner. It contains information about jumper positions and switch settings, a detailed parts catalog, and disks containing the advanced diagnostics. The hardware-maintenance service manual is an essential part of a troubleshooter's toolkit.

Many technicians with troubleshooting experience never need to use the maintenance-analysis procedures (MAPs), but when they have a tough problem, the MAPs help them organize a troubleshooting session. The MAPs tell you to check the switch and jumper settings before the cables, to check the cables before replacing the drive or controller, and so on. This type of information is extremely valuable and can work over a range of systems without getting too specific.

The basic hardware-maintenance reference manual for the PC or PS/2 contains general information about the systems. It describes the diagnostic procedures and field-replaceable unit (FRU) locations, system adjustments, and component removal and installation. The information in it is useful primarily to users with no experience in disassembling and reassembling a system or who have difficulty identifying components within the system. Most people do not need this manual after the first time they take down a system for service.

Obtaining Documentation

You cannot accurately troubleshoot or upgrade a system without the technical-reference manual. Because of the specific nature of the information in the manual, the information must be obtained from the manufacturer of the system. The IBM AT Technical Reference Manual, for example, is useless to a person with a COMPAQ Deskpro 286. A person with a Deskpro 286 must get the manual from COMPAQ.

The hardware-maintenance service manual also is a necessary item, but it is not available from most manufacturers. The manual is not nearly as system-specific as the technical-reference manual; the one from IBM works well for most compatibles. Some information, such as the parts catalog, is specific to IBM systems and does not apply to compatibles, but most of the book has general information.

Many knowledgeable reviewers use the IBM advanced diagnostics, included with the hardware-maintenance service manual, as an acid test for compatibility. If the system truly is compatible, it should pass the tests with flying colors. (Most systems pass.) Many manufacturers do not have or sell a book or disk equivalent to the hardware-maintenance service manual. COMPAQ, for example, has a service manual, but does not sell it or any parts to anyone who is not a COMPAQ-authorized dealer. Servicing or upgrading these systems therefore is more costly, and limited by how much your dealer helps you. Buyers are fortunate that sufficient third-party diagnostics work with most compatible systems such as the COMPAQ systems.

To get hardware-service documentation, contact the dealer who sold you the system and then, if necessary, contact the manufacturer. (Contacting the manufacturer is often more efficient because dealers rarely stock these items.) You can get the items easily from IBM. To order the IBM manuals, call this toll-free number:

1-800-IBM-PCTB (1-800-426-7282)

TB is the abbreviation for technical books. The service is active Monday through Friday, from 8 a.m. to 8 p.m. Eastern time. When you call, you can request copies of the *Technical Directory*—a catalog listing all the part numbers and prices of available documentation. You can inquire also about the availability of technical-reference or service documentation covering newly announced products that might not be listed yet in this directory.

For other manufacturers' manuals, the process of obtaining these types of manuals might (or might not) be so easy. Most larger-name companies run responsible service and support operations that include providing technical documentation. Others either do not have or are unwilling to part with such documentation, to protect their service departments or their dealers' service departments from competition. Contact the manufacturer directly, and the manufacturer can direct you to the correct department so that you can inquire about this information.

Chapter Summary

Apart from the overall similarity between IBM computers and their compatibles, important differences in system architecture exist. The two basic types of IBM and compatible computers can be broken down into PC, XT, and AT categories. This chapter has discussed the differences between them.

The system-memory map was examined in detail to show how computers organize and use RAM and ROM. The differences between conventional, extended, and expanded memory were explained. The chapter has described DOS program memory and video memory and their operation. The chapter ended with a discussion about how to obtain the service manuals necessary for maintaining and upgrading your computer.

PART II

IBM PC, PS/2, and Compatible Systems

IBM Personal Computer Family Hardware

This chapter explains and interprets IBM's original family of personal computer system units and accessories. It separates and identifies each personal computer system offered by IBM, including the complete original line of PC systems that have been discontinued. Because the entire original line has been discontinued, much of this chapter can be considered a history lesson. The information still is valuable, however, because many people still own and manage these older systems, which are more likely to break down than newer ones. The original line of systems often are called Industry Standard Architecture (ISA) systems, or *Classic* PCs. IBM calls them *Family/1* systems. The PS/2 (or *Family/2*) systems are examined in Chapter 4, "IBM Personal System/2 Family Hardware."

This chapter is a reference specific to the original line of true IBM PC, XT, and AT systems. IBM-compatible systems are examined separately in Chapter 5, "IBM-Compatible (and Not-So-Compatible) Computers," but even people that do not own IBM systems will find Chapter 5 filled with interesting and useful information. After all, the idea behind most "IBM-compatible" systems is to clone, copy, or emulate the features of a particular IBM system or combination of systems. For upgrade and repair purposes, most PC compatible systems are treated in the same manner as IBM systems. Most compatible systems can exchange parts easily with IBM systems and vice versa. In fact, most of the parts that make up IBM systems are made by third-party companies, and you can purchase these same parts outside of IBM to save money.

In Chapter 2, "System Features," you learned that all systems can be broken down into two basic *types*: PC/XT or AT. AT types of systems often are broken down into several subtypes. These subtypes can be classified as systems that use 286 or 386/486 processors and systems with Industry Standard Architecture (ISA), Extended Industry Standard Architecture (EISA), or Micro Channel Architecture (MCA) slots. You can use this chapter to compare a compatible system with a specific IBM system in a feature-by-feature comparison. This kind of comparison is often interesting because compatibles usually offer many more features and options at a lower price.

System-Unit Features By Model

In the following sections, you learn the makeup of all the various versions or models of the specific systems and also technical details and specifications of each system. Every system unit has a few standard parts. The primary component is the motherboard, which has the CPU (central processing unit, or microprocessor) and other primary computer circuitry. Each unit also includes a case with an internal power supply, a keyboard, certain standard adapters or plug-in cards, and usually some form of disk drive.

You receive an explanation of each system's various submodels and details about the differences between and features of each model. You learn about the changes from model to model and version to version of each system.

Included for your reference is part-number information for each system and option. This information is *for comparison and reference purposes only* because all these systems have been discontinued and generally are no longer available. IBM still stocks and sells component parts and assemblies, however, for even these discontinued units. You can (and usually should) replace failed components in these older systems with non-IBM replacement parts because you invariably can obtain upgraded or improved components compared to what IBM offers, and at a greatly reduced price.

An Introduction to the PC

IBM introduced the IBM Personal Computer August 12, 1981, and officially withdrew the machine from marketing April 2, 1987. During the nearly 6-year life of the PC, IBM made only a few basic changes to the system. The basic motherboard circuit design was changed in April 1983 to accommodate 64K RAM chips. Three different ROM BIOS versions were used during the life of the system; most other specifications, however, remained unchanged. Because IBM no longer markets the PC system, and because of the PC's relatively limited expansion capability and power, the standard PC is obsolete by most standards.

The system unit supports only floppy disk drives unless the power supply is upgraded or an expansion chassis is used to house the hard disk externally. IBM never offered an internal hard disk for the PC but many third-party companies stepped in to fill this void with upgrades. The system unit included many configurations with single or dual floppy disk drives. Early on, one version even was available with no disk drives, and others used single-sided floppy drives. The PC motherboard was based on the 16-bit Intel 8088 microprocessor and included the Microsoft Cassette BASIC language built into ROM. For standard memory, the PC offered configurations with as little as 16K of RAM (when the system was first announced) and as much as 256K on the motherboard. Two motherboard designs were used. Systems sold before March 1983 had a motherboard that supported a maximum of only 64K of RAM, and later systems supported a maximum of 256K on the motherboard. In either case, you added more memory (as much as 640K) by installing memory cards in the expansion slots.

The first bank of memory chips in every PC is soldered to the motherboard. Soldered memory is reliable but not conducive to easy servicing because the solder prevents you from easily exchanging failing memory chips located in the first bank. The chips must be unsoldered and the defective chip replaced with a socket so that a replacement can be plugged in. When IBM services the defective memory, IBM advises you to exchange the entire motherboard. Considering today's value of these systems, replacing the motherboard with one of the many compatible motherboards on the market may be a better idea. Repairing the same defective memory chip in the XT system is much easier because all memory in an XT is socketed.

The only disk drive available from IBM for the PC is a double-sided (320 or 360K) floppy disk drive. You can install a maximum of two drives in the system unit by using IBM-supplied drives, or four using half-height third-party drives and mounting brackets.

The system unit has five slots that support expansion cards for additional devices, features, or memory. All these slots support full-length adapter cards. In most configurations, the PC included at least a floppy disk controller card. You need a second slot for a monitor adapter, which leaves three slots for adapter cards.

All models of the PC have a fan-cooled, 63.5-watt power supply. This low-output power supply doesn't support much in the way of system expansion, especially power-hungry items, such as hard disks. Usually, this low-output supply must be replaced by a higher-output unit, such as the one used in the XT. Figure 3.1 shows an interior view of a PC system unit.

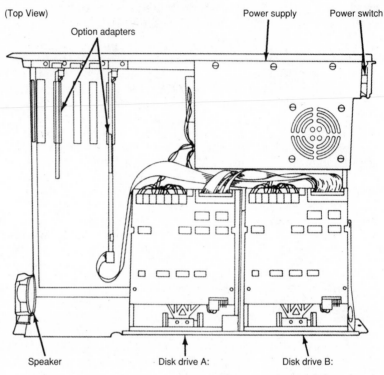

(Top View)   Power supply   Power switch

Option adapters

Speaker   Disk drive A: Disk drive B:

Fig. 3.1

The IBM PC system-unit interior view.

Courtesy of International Business Machines Corporation.

An 83-key keyboard with an adjustable typing angle is standard equipment on the PC. The keyboard is attached to the rear of the system unit by a 6-foot coiled cable. Figure 3.2 shows the back panel of the PC.

Most model configurations of the PC system unit included these major functional components:

    Intel 8088 microprocessor
    ROM-based diagnostics (POST)
    BASIC language interpreter in ROM
    256 kilobytes of dynamic RAM
    Floppy disk controller

One or two 360K floppy drives
A 63 1/2-watt power supply
Five I/O expansion slots
Socket for the 8087 math co-processor

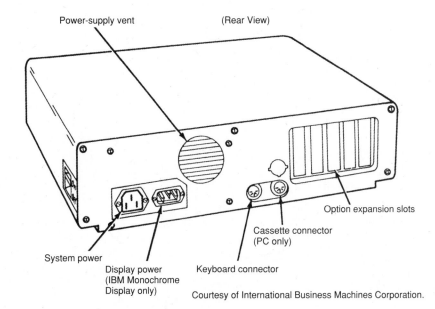

Power-supply vent   (Rear View)

Option expansion slots

System power

Cassette connector
(PC only)

Display power
(IBM Monochrome
Display only)

Keyboard connector

Courtesy of International Business Machines Corporation.

Fig. 3.2

The IBM PC system-unit
rear view.

PC Models and Features

Although several early-model configurations of the IBM PC were avail-
able before March 1983, only two models were available after that time.
The later models differ only in the number of floppy drives: one or two.
IBM designated these models as follows:

IBM PC 5150 Model 166: 256K RAM, one 360K drive

IBM PC 5150 Model 176: 256K RAM, two 360K drives

The PC never was available with a factory-installed hard disk, primarily
because the system unit has a limited base for expansion and offered few
resources with which to work. After IBM started selling XTs with only
floppy disk drives (on April 2, 1985), the PC became obsolete. The XT
offered much more for virtually the same price. Investing in a PC after
the XT introduction was questionable.

IBM finally withdrew the PC from the market April 2, 1987. IBM's plans for the system became obvious when the company didn't announce a new model with the Enhanced Keyboard, as it did with other IBM systems.

With some creative purchasing, you can make a usable system of a base PC by adding the requisite components, such as a full 640K of memory and hard and floppy drives. You still may have a slot or two to spare. Unfortunately, expanding this system requires replacing many of the boards in the system unit with boards that combine the same functions in less space. Only you can decide when your money is better invested in a new system.

Before you can think of expanding a PC beyond even a simple configuration, and to allow for compatibility and reliability, you must address two major areas:

> ROM BIOS level (version)
> Power supply

In most cases, the power supply is the most critical issue because all PCs sold after March 1983 already have the latest ROM BIOS. If you have an earlier PC system, you also must upgrade the ROM because the early versions lack some required capabilities. Both problems, and also other expansion issues related to all systems in the PC family, are addressed in Chapter 7, "Primary System Components," and Chapter 12, "System Upgrades and Improvements." Table 3.1 shows the part numbers for the IBM PC system unit.

Table 3.1 IBM PC Part Numbers

Description	Number
PC system unit, 256K, one double-sided drive	5150166
PC system unit, 256K, two double-sided drives	5150176
Options	
PC expansion-unit Model 001 with 10M fixed disk	5161001
Double-sided disk drive	1503810
8087 math coprocessor option	1501002
BIOS update kit	1501005

PC Technical Specifications

Technical information for the Personal Computer system and keyboard is described in this section. Here, you find information about the system architecture, memory configurations and capacities, standard system features, disk storage, expansion slots, keyboard specifications, and physical and environmental specifications. This kind of information may be useful in determining what parts you need when you are upgrading or repairing these systems. Figure 3.3 shows the layout and components on the PC motherboard.

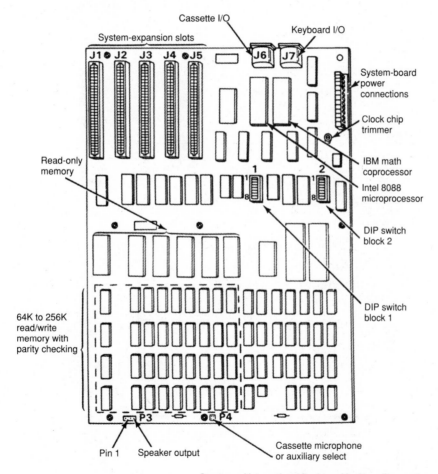

Courtesy of International Business Machines Corporation.

Fig. 3.3

The IBM PC system board.

System architecture

Microprocessor	8088
Clock speed	4.77 MHz
Bus type	ISA (Industry Standard Architecture)
Bus width	8-bit
Interrupt levels	8
Type	Edge-triggered
Shareable	No
DMA channels	3
DMA burst mode supported	No
Bus masters supported	No
Upgradeable processor complex	No

Memory

Standard on system board	16K, 64K or 256K
Maximum on system board	256K
Maximum total memory	640K
Memory speed (ns) and type	200ns dynamic RAM
System board memory-socket type	16-pin DIP
Number of memory-module sockets	27 (3 banks of 9)
Memory used on system board	27 16K-by-1-bit or 64K-by-1-bit DRAM chips in 3 banks of 9, one soldered bank of 9 16K-by-1-bit or 64K-by-1-bit chips
Memory cache controller	No
Wait states:	
System board	1
Adapter	1

Standard features

ROM size	40K
ROM shadowing	No
Optional math coprocessor	8087
Coprocessor speed	4.77 MHz
Standard graphics	None standard
RS232C serial ports	None standard
UART chip used	NS8250B
Maximum speed (bits per second)	9,600 bps
Maximum number of ports supported	2
Pointing device (mouse) ports	None standard
Parallel printer ports	None standard
Bidirectional	No
Maximum number of ports supported	3
CMOS real-time clock (RTC)	No
CMOS RAM	None

Disk storage

Internal disk and tape drive bays	2 full-height
Number of 3 1/2-/5 1/4-inch bays	0/2
Standard floppy drives	1×360K
Optional floppy drives:	
5 1/4-inch 360K	Optional
5 1/4-inch 1.2M	No
3 1/2-inch 720K	Optional
3 1/2-inch 1.44M	No
3 1/2-inch 2.88M	No
Hard disk controller included	None

continues

Expansion slots	
Total adapter slots	5
Number of long and short slots	5/0
Number of 8-/16-/32-bit slots	5/0/0
Available slots (with video)	3

Keyboard specification	
101-key Enhanced Keyboard	No, 83-key
Fast keyboard speed setting	No
Keyboard cable length	6 feet

Physical specifications	
Footprint type	Desktop
Dimensions:	
Height	5.5 inches
Width	19.5 inches
Depth	16.0 inches
Weight	25 pounds

Environmental specifications	
Power-supply output	63.5 watts
Worldwide (110/60,220/50)	No
Auto-sensing/switching	No
Maximum current:	
104-127 VAC	2.5 amps
Operating range:	
Temperature	60-90 degrees F
Relative humidity	8-80 percent
Maximum operating altitude	7,000 feet
Heat (BTUs/hour)	505
Noise (Average dB, operating, 1m)	43
FCC classification	Class B

An Introduction to the PC Convertible

IBM marked its entry into the laptop computer market on April 2, 1986 by introducing the IBM 5140 PC Convertible. The system superseded the 5155 Portable PC (IBM's transportable system), which no longer was available. The IBM 5140 system wasn't a very successful laptop system. Other laptops offered more disk storage, higher processor speeds, more readable screens, lower cost, and more compact cases, which pressured IBM to improve the Convertible. Because the improvements were limited to the display, however, this system never gained respect in the marketplace.

The PC Convertible was available in two models. The Model 2 had a CMOS 80C88 microprocessor, 64 kilobytes of ROM, 256 kilobytes of RAM, an 80-column-by-25-line detachable liquid crystal display, two 3 1/2-inch floppy disk drives, a 78-key keyboard, an AC adapter, and a battery pack. Also included were software programs called Application Selector, SystemApps, Tools, Exploring the IBM PC Convertible, and Diagnostics. The Model 22 is the same basic computer as the Model 2 but with the diagnostics software only. You can expand either system to 512K of RAM by using 128K RAM memory-card features, and you can include an asynchronous modem in the system unit. With aftermarket memory expansion, the computers can reach 640K.

At the back of each system unit is an extendable bus interface. This 72-pin connector enables you to attach the following options to the base unit: a printer, a serial or parallel adapter, and a CRT display adapter. Each feature is powered from the system unit. The CRT display adapter operates only when the system is powered from a standard AC adapter. A separate CRT display or a television set attached through the CRT display adapter requires a separate AC power source.

Each system unit includes a detachable liquid crystal display (LCD). When the computer is not mobile, the LCD screen can be replaced by an external monitor. When the LCD is latched in the closed position, it forms the cover for the keyboard and floppy disk drives. Because the LCD is attached with a quick-disconnect connector, you can remove it easily to place the 5140 system unit below an optional IBM 5144 PC Convertible monochrome or IBM 5145 PC Convertible color display.

The PC Convertible system unit has these standard features:

> Complementary Metal-Oxide Semiconductor (CMOS) 80C88 microprocessor

Two 32K CMOS ROMs containing these items:

POST (Power-On Self Test) of system components
BIOS (basic input-output system) support
BASIC language interpreter

256K CMOS RAM (expandable to 512K)

Two 3 1/2-inch 720K (formatted) floppy drives

An 80-column-by-25-line detachable LCD panel (graphics modes: 640-by-200 resolution and 320-by-200 resolution)

LCD controller

16K RAM display buffer

8K LCD font RAM

Adapter for optional printer (#4010)

Professional keyboard (78 keys)

AC adapter

Battery pack

The system-unit options for the 5140 are shown in this list:

128K memory card (#4005)
Printer (#4010)
Serial/parallel adapter (#4015)
CRT display adapter (#4020)
Internal modem (#4025)
Printer cable (#4055)
Battery charger (#4060)
Automobile power adapter (#4065)

Two optional displays are available for the PC Convertible:

IBM 5144 PC Convertible Monochrome Display Model 1
IBM 5145 PC Convertible Color Display Model 1

PC Convertible Specifications and Highlights

This section lists some technical specifications for the IBM 5140 PC Convertible system. The weights of the unit and options are listed because weight is an important consideration when you carry a laptop system. Figure 3.4 shows the PC Convertible motherboard components and layout.

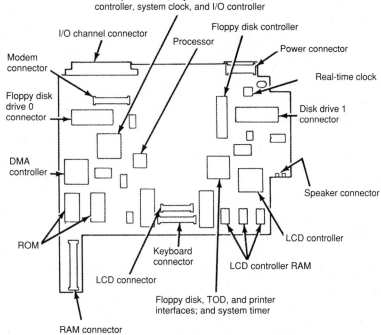

Interrupt controller, keyboard controller, audio
controller, system clock, and I/O controller

I/O channel connector

Floppy disk controller

Processor

Power connector

Modem
connector

Real-time clock

Floppy disk
drive 0
connector

Disk drive 1
connector

DMA
controller

Speaker connector

ROM

LCD controller

Keyboard
connector

LCD controller RAM

LCD connector

RAM connector

Floppy disk, TOD, and printer
interfaces; and system timer

Courtesy of International Business Machines Corporation.

Fig. 3.4

The PC Convertible
system board.

Dimensions	
Depth:	360 mm (14.17 inches) 374 mm (14.72 inches) including handle
Width:	309.6 mm (12.19 inches) 312 mm (12.28 inches) including handle
Height:	67 mm (2.64 inches) 68 mm (2.68 inches) including footpads

Weight	
Models 2 and 22 (including battery)	5.5 kg (12.17 pounds)
128K/256K memory card	40 g (1.41 ounces)
Printer	1.6 kg (3.50 pounds)
Serial/parallel adapter	470 g (1.04 pounds)
CRT display adapter	630 g (1.40 pounds)
Internal modem	170 g (6 ounces)
Printer cable	227 g (8 ounces)
Battery charger	340 g (12 ounces)
Automobile power adapter	113 g (4 ounces)
5144 PC Convertible monochrome display	7.3 kg (16 pounds)
5145 PC Convertible color display	16.9 kg (37.04 pounds)

To operate the IBM 5140 PC Convertible properly, you must have PC DOS Version 3.2 or later. Previous DOS versions aren't supported because they don't support the 720K floppy drive. Using the CRT display adapter and an external monitor requires that the system unit be operated by power from the AC adapter rather from the battery.

PC Convertible Models and Features

This section covers the options and special features available for the PC Convertible. Several kinds of options are available, from additional memory to external display adapters, serial/parallel ports, modems, and even printers.

Memory Cards

A 128K or 256K memory card expands the base memory in the system unit. You can add two of these cards, for a system-unit total of 640K with one 256K card and one 128K card.

Optional Printers

An optional printer attaches to the back of the system unit or to an optional printer-attachment cable for adjacent printer operation. The printer's intelligent, microprocessor-based, 40 cps, non-impact dot-matrix design makes it capable of low-power operation. The optional printer draws power from and is controlled by the system unit. Standard ASCII 96-character, upper- and lowercase character sets are printed with a high-resolution, 24-element print head. A mode for graphics capability is provided also. You can achieve near-letter-quality printing by using either a thermal transfer ribbon on smooth paper or no ribbon on heat-sensitive thermal paper.

Serial/Parallel Adapters

A serial/parallel adapter attaches to the back of the system unit, a printer, or other feature module attached to the back of the system unit. The adapter provides an RS-232C asynchronous communications interface and a parallel printer interface, both compatible with the IBM personal computer asynchronous communications adapter and the IBM personal computer parallel printer adapter.

CRT Display Adapters

A CRT display adapter attaches to the back of the system unit, printer, or other feature module attached to the back of the system unit. This adapter enables you to connect to the system a separate CRT display, such as the PC Convertible monochrome display or PC Convertible color display. By using optional connectors or cables, you can use the CRT display adapter also to attach a standard CGA type of monitor. Because composite video output is available, you can use a standard television set also.

Internal Modems

With an internal modem, you can communicate with compatible computers over telephone lines. It runs Bell 212A (1200 bps) or Bell 103A (300 bps) protocols. The modem comes as a complete assembly, consisting of two cards connected by a cable. The entire assembly is installed inside the system unit. This modem, made for IBM by Novation, doesn't follow the Hayes standard for commands and protocols and therefore is incompatible with most communications software. Fortunately, you still can operate a regular modem through the serial port, although you lose the convenience and portability.

Printer Cables

The printer cable is 22 inches (0.6 meter) long with a custom 72- pin connector attached to each end. With this cable, you can operate the Convertible printer when it is detached from the system unit and place the unit for ease of use and visibility.

Battery Chargers

The battery charger is a 110-volt input device that charges the system's internal batteries. It does not provide sufficient power output for the system to operate while the batteries are being charged.

Automobile Power Adapters

An automobile power adapter plugs into the cigarette-lighter outlet in a vehicle with a 12-volt, negative-ground electrical system. You can use the unit while the adapter charges the Convertible's battery.

The IBM 5144 PC Convertible Monochrome Display

The 5144 PC Convertible monochrome display is a 9-inch (measured diagonally) composite video display attached to the system unit through the CRT display adapter. It comes with a display stand, an AC power cord, and a signal cable that connects the 5144 to the CRT display adapter. This display does not resemble—and is not compatible with— the IBM monochrome display for larger PC systems. The CRT adapter emits the same signal as the one supplied by the Color Graphics Adapter for a regular PC. This display is functionally equivalent to the display on the IBM Portable PC.

The IBM 5145 PC Convertible Color Display

The 5145 PC Convertible color display is a 13-inch color display attached to the system unit through the CRT display adapter. It comes with a display stand, an AC power cord, a signal cable that connects the 5145 to the CRT display adapter, and a speaker for external audio output. The monitor is a low-cost unit compatible with the standard IBM CGA type of display.

Special software available for the Convertible includes these programs:

- The *Application Selector* program, installed as an extension to DOS, provides a menu-driven interface to select and run applications software, the SystemApps, and Tools.

- The *SystemApps* program provides basic functions similar to many memory-resident programs on the market. This application, which includes Notewriter, Schedule, Phone List, and Calculator, is equivalent in function to the popular SideKick program.

- You can use the menu-driven *Tools* program as a front end for DOS to control and maintain the system (copying and erasing files, copying disks, and so on). With DOS, additional functions are available, including printing, formatting, and configuring the Application Selector function keys. This program presents many DOS functions in an easy-to-use menu format.

This additional software, except system diagnostics, is not included with the Model 22. Table 3.2 shows the part numbers of the IBM Convertible system units.

Table 3.2 IBM Convertible Part Numbers	
5140 PC Convertible system units	**Number**
Two drives, 256K with system applications	5140002
Two drives, 256K without system applications	5140022

An Introduction to the XT

Introduced March 8, 1983, the PC XT with a built-in 10M hard disk (originally standard, later optional) caused a revolution in personal computer configurations. At the time, having even a 10M hard disk was something very special. XT stands for XTended (extended). IBM chose this name because the IBM PC XT system includes many features not available in the standard PC. The XT has eight slots, allowing increased expansion capabilities; greater power-supply capacity; completely socketed memory; motherboards that support expansion to 640K without using an expansion slot; and optional hard disk drives. To obtain these advantages, the XT uses a completely different motherboard circuit design than the PC.

The system unit was available in several models, with a variety of disk drive configurations: one 256K floppy disk drive, two 256K floppy disk drives, one floppy disk and one hard disk drive, or two floppy disk drives and one hard disk drive. The floppy disk drives are full-height drives in the earlier models, and half-height drives in more recent models. You therefore can have two floppy drives and a hard disk in a standard IBM configuration.

IBM also offered 10M and 20M, full-height hard disks. A double-sided (320/360K) floppy disk drive in a full- or half-height configuration is available also. A 3 1/2-inch 720K floppy disk drive is available in more recent models. The 3 1/2-inch drives are available in a normal internal configuration or as an external device. You can install a maximum of two floppy disk drives and one hard disk drive in the system unit, using IBM-supplied drives. With half-height hard disks, you can install two hard drives in the system unit.

The XT is based on the same 8- and 16-bit Intel 8088 microprocessor as the PC and runs at the same clock speed. Operationally, the systems are identical except for the hard disk. All models have at least one 360K floppy disk drive and a keyboard. For standard memory, the XT offers 256K or 640K on the main board. The hard disk models also include a serial adapter.

The system unit has eight slots that support cards for additional devices, features, or memory. Two of the slots support only short option cards because of physical interference from the disk drives. The XT has at least a disk drive adapter card in the floppy-disk-only models, and a hard disk controller card and serial adapter in the hard disk models. Either five or seven expansion slots (depending on the model) therefore are available. Figure 3.5 shows the interior of an XT.

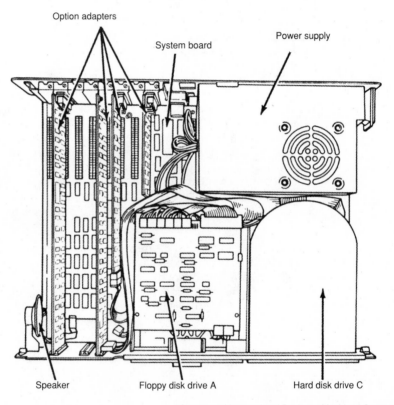

Option adapters

System board

Power supply

Speaker

Floppy disk drive A

Hard disk drive C

Fig. 3.5

The IBM PC XT interior.

Courtesy of International Business Machines Corporation.

All XT models include a heavy-duty, fan-cooled, 135-watt power supply to support the greater expansion capabilities and disk drive options. The power supply has more than double the capacity of the PC's supply.

An 83-key keyboard was standard equipment with the early XT models, but was changed to an enhanced 101-key unit in the more recent models. The keyboard is attached to the system unit by a 6-foot coiled cable.

All models of the PC XT system unit contain these major functional components:

> Intel 8088 microprocessor
> ROM-based diagnostics (POST)
> BASIC language interpreter in ROM
> 256K or 640K of dynamic RAM
> Floppy disk controller
> One 360K floppy drive (full- or half-height)
> 10M or 20M hard disk drive with interface (enhanced models)
> Serial interface (enhanced models)
> Heavy-duty, 135-watt power supply
> Eight I/O expansion slots
> Socket for 8087 math coprocessor

XT Models and Features

The XT was available in many different model configurations, but originally only one model was available. This model included a 10M hard disk, marking the first time that a hard disk was standard equipment in a personal computer and was properly supported by the operating system and peripherals. This computer helped change the industry standard for personal computers from one or two floppy disk drives to one or more hard disks.

Today, most people wouldn't consider a PC to be even usable without a hard disk. The original XT was expensive, however, and buyers couldn't *unbundle*, or delete, the hard disk from the system at purchase time for credit and add it later. This fact distinguished the XT from the PC and misled many people to believe that the only difference between the two computers was the hard disk. People who recognized and wanted the greater capabilities of the XT without the standard IBM hard disk had to wait.

The original Model 087 of the XT included a 10M hard disk, 128K of RAM, and a standard serial interface. IBM later increased the standard memory in all PC systems to 256K. The XT reflected the change in Model 086, which was the same as the preceding 087 except for a standard 256K of RAM.

On April 2, 1985, IBM introduced new models of the XT without the standard hard disk. Designed for expansion and configuration flexibility, the new models enabled you to expand a floppy disk system to a hard disk system. The XT therefore could be considered in configurations that previously only the original PC could fill. The primary difference between the PC and the XT is the XT's expansion capability, provided by the larger power supply, eight slots, and better memory layout. These models cost only $300 more than equivalent PCs, rendering the original PC no longer a viable option.

The extra expense of the XT can be justified with the first power-supply replacement you make with an overworked PC. The IBM PC XT is available in two floppy disk models:

5160068 XT with one full-height 360K disk drive

5160078 XT with two full-height 360K disk drives

Both these models have 256K of memory and use the IBM PC XT motherboard, power supply, frame, and cover. The asynchronous communications adapter isn't included as a standard feature with these models.

IBM introduced several more models of the PC XT on April 2, 1986. These recent models are significantly different from previous models. The most obvious difference, the Enhanced Keyboard, is standard with these newer computers. A 20M (rather than 10M) hard disk and high-quality, half-height floppy disk drives are included. The new half-height floppy disk drives allow for two drives in the space that previously held only one floppy drive. With two drives, backing up floppy disks became easy. A new 3 1/2-inch floppy disk drive, storing 720K for compatibility with the PC Convertible laptop computer, was released also. These more recent XT system units are configured with a new memory layout allowing for 640K of RAM on the motherboard without an expansion slot. This feature conserves power, improves reliability, and lowers the cost of the system.

One 5 1/4-inch, half-height, 360K floppy disk drive and 256K of system-board memory are standard with the XT Models 267 and 268. Models 277 and 278 have a second 5 1/4-inch floppy disk drive. Models 088 and 089 are expanded PC XTs with all the standard features of the Models 267 and 268, a 20M hard disk, a 20M fixed disk drive adapter, an asynchronous communications adapter, and an additional 256K of system-board memory—a total of 512K.

The following list shows the highlights of these new models:

Enhanced Keyboard standard on Models 268, 278, and 089

101 keys
Recappable
Selectric typing section
Dedicated numeric pad
Dedicated cursor and screen controls
Two additional function keys
9-foot cable

Standard PC XT keyboard on Models 267, 277, and 088

More disk capacity (20M)

New features

20M fixed disk
20M fixed disk adapter
5 1/4-inch, half-height, 360K floppy drive
3 1/2-inch, half-height, 720K floppy drive

New 3 1/2-inch 720K floppy drive, for added flexibility

Capacity for three storage devices within the system unit

Capacity to expand to 640K bytes memory on system board without using expansion slots

These newest XT models have an extensively changed ROM BIOS. The new BIOS is 64K and internally similar to the BIOS found in ATs. The ROM includes support for the new keyboard and 3 1/2-inch floppy disk drives. The POST also was enhanced.

The new XTs are incompatible in some respects with some software programs. These problems so far have centered on the new keyboard and the way the new ROM addresses the keys. These problems aren't major and were solved quickly by the software companies.

Seeing how much IBM changed the computer without changing the basic motherboard design is interesting. The ROM is different, and the board now can hold 640K of memory without a card in a slot. The memory trick is a simple one. IBM designed this feature into the board originally and chose to unleash it with these models of the XT.

During the past several years, I have modified many XTs to have 640K on the motherboard, using a simple technique designed into the system by IBM. A jumper and chip added to the motherboard can alter the memory addressing in the board to enable the system to recognize 640K. The new addressing is set up for 256K chips, installed in two of the four banks. The other two banks of memory contain 64K chips—a total of 640K. Chapter 12 has a set of detailed instructions for modifying an IBM XT in this way.

XT Technical Specifications

Technical information for the XT system, described in this section, gives information about the system architecture, memory configurations and capacities, standard system features, disk storage, expansion slots, keyboard specifications, and also physical and environmental specifications. This information can be useful in determining what parts you need when you are upgrading or repairing these systems. Figure 3.6 shows the layout and components on the XT motherboard.

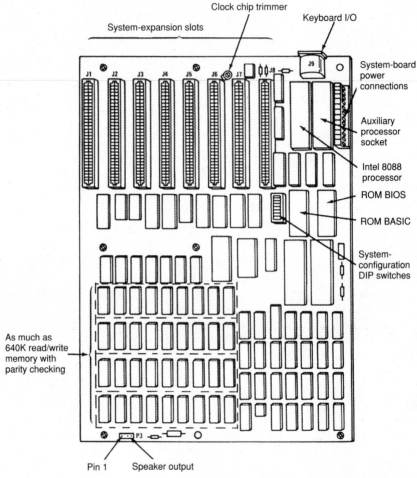

Fig. 3.6

The XT system board.

Courtesy of International Business Machines Corporation.

System architecture

Microprocessor	8088
Clock speed	4.77 MHz
Bus type	ISA (Industry Standard Architecture)
Bus width	8-bit
Interrupt levels	8
Type	Edge-triggered
Shareable	No
DMA channels	3
DMA burst mode supported	No
Bus masters supported	No
Upgradeable processor complex	No

Memory

Standard on system board	256K or 640K
Maximum on system board	256K or 640K
Maximum total memory	640K
Memory speed (ns) and type	200ns dynamic RAM
System board memory-socket type	16-pin DIP
Number of memory-module sockets	36 (4 banks of 9)
Memory used on system board	36 64K×1-bit DRAM chips in 4 banks of 9, or 2 banks of 9 256K×1-bit and 2 banks of 9 64K×1-bit chips
Memory cache controller	No
Wait states:	
System board	1
Adapter	1

Standard features

ROM size	40K or 64K
ROM shadowing	No
Optional math coprocessor	8087

continues

Standard features

Coprocessor speed	4.77 MHz
Standard graphics	None standard
RS232C serial ports	1 (some models)
UART chip used	NS8250B
Maximum speed (bits per second)	9,600 bps
Maximum number of ports supported	2
Pointing device (mouse) ports	None standard
Parallel printer ports	1 (some models)
Bidirectional	No
Maximum number of ports supported	3
CMOS real-time clock (RTC)	No
CMOS RAM	None

Disk storage

Internal disk and tape drive bays	2 full-height or 4 half-height	
Number of 3 1/2 or 5 1/4-inch bays	0/2 or 0/4	
Standard floppy drives	1×360K	
Optional floppy drives:		
5 1/4-inch 360K	Optional	
5 1/4-inch 1.2M	No	
3 1/2-inch 720K	Optional	
3 1/2-inch 1.44M	No	
3 1/2-inch 2.88M	No	
Hard disk controller included:	ST-506/412 (Xebec Model 1210)	
ST-506/412 hard disks available	10/20M	
Drive form factor	5 1/4-inch	
Drive interface	ST-506/412	
Drive capacity	10M	20M
Average access rate (ms)	85	65
Encoding scheme	MFM	MFM
BIOS drive type number	1	2
Cylinders	306	615

Disk storage		
Heads	4	4
Sectors per track	17	17
Rotational speed (RPMs)	3600	3600
Interleave factor	6:1	6:1
Data transfer rate (kilobytes/second)	85	85
Automatic head parking	No	No

Expansion slots	
Total adapter slots	8
Number of long and short slots	6/2
Number of 8-/16-/32-bit slots	8/0/0
Available slots (with video)	4

Keyboard specifications	
101-key Enhanced Keyboard	Yes
Fast keyboard speed setting	No
Keyboard cable length	6 feet

Physical specifications	
Footprint type	Desktop
Dimensions:	
Height	5.5 inches
Width	19.5 inches
Depth	16.0 inches
Weight	32 pounds

Environmental specifications	
Power-supply output	130 watts
Worldwide (110/60,220/50) Auto-sensing/switching	No No

continues

Environmental specifications	
Maximum current:	
90-137 VAC	4.2 amps
Operating range:	
Temperature	60-90 degrees F
Relative humidity	8-80 percent
Maximum operating altitude	7,000 feet
Heat (BTUs/hour)	717
Noise (Average dB, operating, 1m)	56
FCC classification	Class B

Table 3.3 shows the part numbers of the XT system units.

Table 3.3 IBM XT Model Part Numbers

Description	Number
XT system unit/83-key keyboard, 256K:	
one full-height 360K drive	5160068
one half-height 360K drive	5160267
two full-height 360K drives	5160078
two half-height 360K drives	5160277
XT system unit/101-key keyboard, 256K:	
one half-height 360K drive	5160268
two half-height 360K drives	5160278
XT system unit/83-key keyboard, 256K, one serial, one full-height 360K drive, 10M hard disk	5160086
XT system unit/83-key keyboard, 640K, one serial, one half-height 360K drive, 20M fixed disk	5160088
XT system unit/101-key keyboard, 640K, one serial, one half-height 360K drive, 20M fixed disk	5160089
Option numbers	
PC expansion-unit Model 002, 20M fixed disk	5161002
20M fixed disk drive	6450326

Description	Number
20M fixed disk adapter	6450327
10M fixed disk drive	1602500
10M fixed disk adapter	1602501
5 1/4-inch, half-height, 360K drive	6450325
5 1/4-inch, full-height, 360K drive	1503810
3 1/2-inch, half-height, 720K internal drive	6450258
3 1/2-inch, half-height, 720K external drive	2683190
8087 math coprocessor option	1501002
Asynchronous serial adapter	1502074
Enhanced Keyboard accessories	
Clear keycaps (60) with paper inserts	6341707
Blank light keycaps	1351710
Blank dark keycaps	1351728
Paper inserts (300)	6341704
Keycap-removal tools (6)	1351717

An Introduction to the 3270 PC

On October 18, 1983, IBM announced a special version of the XT, the 3270 PC. The 3270 PC combines the functions of IBM's 3270 display system with those of the XT. This system is basically a standard XT system unit with three to six custom adapter cards added to the slots. The keyboard and display for this system also are special and attach to some of the special adapter cards. The 3270 PC Control Program runs all this hardware. This combination can support as many as seven concurrent activities: one local PC DOS session, four remote mainframe sessions, and two local electronic notepads. With the help of the 3270 PC Control Program, information can be copied between windows, but a PC DOS window cannot receive information.

The 3270 PC included a new keyboard that addresses some complaints about the Personal Computer keyboard. The keyboard has more keys and an improved layout. The Enter and Shift keys are enlarged. The cursor keys are separate from the numeric keypad and form a small group between the main alphanumeric keys and the numeric keypad. At the top of the keyboard, 20 function keys are arranged in two rows of 10. To help clarify keystroke operations, the new keyboard is annotated. Blue legends designate PC-specific functions; black legends indicate 3270 functions. The keyboard is greatly improved, but most new keys and features don't work in PC mode. Often, you must obtain special versions of programs or disregard most of the new keys.

3270 PC Models and Features

The 3270 PC includes several specialized expansion boards that can be added to an XT. This section examines those expansion boards.

The 3270 System Adapter

The 3270 system adapter supports communication between the 3270 PC and the remote 3274 controller through a coaxial cable. One physical 3274 connection can support four logical connections.

The Display Adapter

A display adapter is used in place of the PC's monochrome or Color/ Graphics Display Adapter and provides text-only displays in eight colors. The PC's extended-character graphics are available, but bit-mapped graphics capabilities are not supported unless you add the accessory extended graphics card.

The Extended Graphics Adapter

The Extended Graphics Adapter provides storage and controls necessary for displaying local graphics in high- or medium-resolution mode. High-resolution mode is available in two colors at 720-by-350 or 640-by-200 pixels. Note that this isn't the same as the newer XGA (eXtended Graphics Array), which is either available for, or included with, certain PS/2 systems.

Medium-resolution mode is available with a choice of two sets of four colors at 360-by-350 or 320-by-200 pixels. To run in medium-resolution mode, your system must have an available system-expansion slot adjacent to the display adapter card. If you install a Programmed Symbols feature (discussed in the following section) next to the display adapter, you must use the slot adjacent to the PS feature. Because the aspect ratio differs for each display monitor, applications programs must control the aspect ratio parameter; a circle on the 5150/5160 PC with the Color Graphics Adapter looks slightly elliptical on the 3270 PC with the XGA unless you change this parameter.

Programmed Symbols

The Programmed Symbols (PS) adapter provides graphics capabilities available on IBM 3278/3279 display stations. This card provides storage for as many as six 190-symbol sets whose shapes and codes are definable. Symbol sets are loaded (and accessed for display) under program control. To accept this board, your system must have an available system-expansion slot adjacent to the display adapter card. If an XGA feature is installed, you must use the slot adjacent to the XGA. The PS card is available in distributed-function terminal (DFT) mode only and can be used in only one of the four host sessions.

The Keyboard Adapter

You use the keyboard adapter to adapt the 3270-style keyboard to the system unit. The keyboard connects to this board rather than to the motherboard, as it does for the PC. The board is short and must be installed in the special eighth slot in the XT system unit.

The standard XT system unit provides eight expansion slots; at least five of the slots normally are filled on delivery with the 3270 system adapter, the display adapter, the keyboard adapter, the disk drive adapter, and the hard disk controller. If you add options such as the graphics adapter and a memory multifunction card, you can see that even with the XT as a base, slots are at a premium in this system.

Software

The 3270 PC runs under control of the 3270 PC Control Program in conjunction with PC DOS and supports concurrent operation of as many as four remote-host interactive sessions, two local notepad sessions, and one PC DOS session. The Control Program enables users to associate sessions with display screen windows and to manage the windows by a set of functions that IBM named *advanced screen management*.

Windows

You can define windows that permit viewing of all (as many as 2,000 characters) or part of a presentation space. In IBM's vocabulary, a *presentation space* is a logical display area presented by a single host. PC DOS presentation spaces are 2,000 characters (25 lines by 80 characters), remote host spaces are as many as 3,440 characters, and notepad presentation spaces are 1,920 characters.

As many as seven windows can appear on-screen at one time. Every window is associated with a distinct presentation space. Windows can be as large as the screen or as small as 1 character, and can be positioned at any point within their presentation space. A window 20 characters wide and four lines long, for example, shows the first 20 characters of the last four lines of a host session display. You can change window size and position in the presentation space at any time without affecting the content of the presentation space.

At any time, only one window on the 3270 PC screen can be the active window. When you enter information from the keyboard, the information is directed to the session associated with the active window. You can switch between active windows by using keystroke commands.

You can define the foreground and background colors of host session windows not using extended data-stream attributes. You can define the background color for the 5272 screen also (the color to be displayed in areas not occupied by windows).

Special Facilities

In addition to advanced screen-management functions, the Control Program offers a number of related special facilities that help you take further advantage of the 3270 environment.

Data can be copied within or between any presentation spaces except into the PC DOS screen. You copy by marking a block of data in one window and marking a destination in some other window, much the same as a block copy in a word processor.

You can think of the notepads as local electronic scratch pads you can use at your convenience. You can save and restore the contents of a notepad at any time by using PC DOS files as the storage medium.

You can define as many as ten screen configurations, each of which describes a set of windows configured in any way, and they can display on command any one configuration. Use PC DOS files to store the configuration information.

You can print a full copy of the display screen on a local printer. Similarly, you can print a full copy of a PC DOS presentation space on a local printer. You also can print a full copy of any host presentation space on a local printer, a 3274 attached printer, or a 43xx display/printer.

The Control Program maintains at the bottom of the screen a status line that displays current configuration information, including the name of the active window. The program includes a help function and displays active workstation functions and sessions and an on-line tutorial that explains and simulates system functions. The tutorial is a standard PC DOS program that can be run on any IBM PC.

The Control Program, assisted by a host-based IBM 3270 PC file-transfer program, can initiate transfers of ASCII, binary, and EBCDIC files to and from remote hosts.

A drawback to this software is that it is memory resident and consumes an enormous amount of space. The result is that in the PC DOS session, not many applications can run in the leftover workspace. Your only option—reboot the computer without loading the Control Program—is a clumsy and time-consuming procedure. Even with this tactic, the drastic differences in the display hardware and the keyboard still render this computer much less than "PC compatible." The AT version of this system offers a solution to the memory problem by enabling much of the Control Program to reside in the AT's extended memory, above the 1M memory limit of the PC and XT.

The Significance of the 3270

The 3270 PC is a great system to use if you are a corporate worker who deals every day with many information sources (most of which are available through an IBM mainframe SNA network). Corporate information managers greatly appreciate the concurrent access to several SNA-based databases. The 3270 PC provides essential tools for viewing, extracting, combining, and manipulating information: multiple concurrent-terminal sessions, cut-and-paste capability between sessions, PC productivity tools, and up- and downloading host files from PC DOS files.

For simple 3270 terminal-emulation capability, however, this system is more than you need. In addition, the display and keyboard make this system partially incompatible with the rest of the PC world. Many PC applications do not run properly on this system. If you depend more on PC DOS applications than on the mainframe, or if you consider the multiple mainframe sessions unimportant, using one of the simpler 3270 emulation adapters is more cost-effective.

An Introduction to the XT 370

On October 18, 1983, IBM introduced another special version of the XT, the XT 370, consisting of a standard PC XT chassis with three special cards added. These adapters are special S/370-emulation cards that enable the computer to execute the mainframe system 370 instruction set. The boards enable you to run VM/CMS and emulate 4M of virtual memory. You can download programs and compilers from the mainframe and execute them directly on the XT. You switch between 370 mode and the standard XT by using a *hot key*, or special keystroke, sequence.

XT/370 Models and Features

The three cards that make up the XT 370—the PC 370-P card, the PC 370-M card, and the PC 3277-EM card—are examined in this section.

The P card implements an emulation of the 370 instruction set. The card has three microprocessors. One processor is a heavily modified Motorola 68000 produced under license to IBM. This chip implements the general-purpose registers, the PSW, instruction fetch and decode logic, and 72 commonly used S/370 instructions. Because Motorola manufactures the chip under license to IBM, the chip probably will not appear as a Motorola product.

A second processor is a slightly modified Motorola 68000, which is listed in Motorola's catalog. The chip emulates the remaining nonfloating-point instructions, manipulates the page table, handles exception conditions, and performs hardware housekeeping.

The third microprocessor, a modified Intel 8087 that executes S/370 floating-point instructions, is interfaced as a peripheral rather than the normal 8087 coprocessor linkage.

The M card has 512K of parity-checked RAM. You can access this memory from the P card or from the XT's native 8088 processor. Concurrent requests are arbitrated in favor of the 8088. The M card resides in an XT expansion slot but is connected to the P card by a special edge connector. Sixteen-bit-wide transfers between M card memory and the P card are carried out through this connector (normal XT memory transfers operate in 8-bit-wide chunks).

Operating in native PC mode, the M card's memory is addressed as contiguous memory beginning at the end of the 256K memory of the system's motherboard. In native PC mode, the XT 370 has 640K of usable RAM; some of the M card's memory is not used.

Operating in 370 mode, only the 512K RAM of the M card is usable (the memory on the motherboard is not available). The first 480K of this memory implements 480K of real S/370 space. The remaining 32K on the M card functions as a microcode control-storage area for the second P card microprocessor.

The first 64K (of 480K) of S/370 memory are consumed by VM/PC; 416K of real memory remains for user programs. User programs larger than 416K are handled through paging.

The PC 3277-EM card attaches the XT 370 to an S/370 mainframe by a local or remote 3274 control unit (connection through coaxial cable). When VM/PC is running, the EM card uses the IBM monochrome or color display. Under VM/PC, the EM card is used also to up- and download data between a host VM system and the XT 370.

The XT 370 can run in native PC XT mode or in S/370 mode under the VM/PC Control Program. Under VM/PC, the user can use a "hot key" to alternate between a local CMS session and a remote 3277 session (or, optionally, a 3101-emulation session). VM/PC does not offer a true VM-like environment. Rather, VM/PC provides an environment in which CMS applications can run. Non-CMS VM applications do not run on the XT 370.

The VM/PC system, which must be licensed, is provided on six floppy disks and includes the VM/PC Control Program, CMS, XEDIT, EXEC2, local and remote file-transfer utilities, and the 370 Processor Control package.

Estimations of the XT 370 CPU's performance indicate that it is about half of a 4331 when the XT 370 is running a commercial instruction mix. When the XT 370 is running scientific codes, you can expect twice the performance as from the 4331. The CPU generally is categorized as a 0.1 MIPS (million instructions per second) processor. This size does not sound impressive when you're used to multi-MIPS, single-chip microprocessors, but remember that 0.1-million S/370 instructions likely will produce substantially more computing than 0.1-million instructions of your standard microprocessor chip.

The XT 370 running in S/370 mode can access the 512K on the M card. Of this 512K, 32K is reserved for microcode control storage, and 65K is used by the VM/PC Control Program; 416K remains for user programs. If a user program requires more memory than 416K, VM/PC uses a paging area on the XT 370's hard disk and swaps pieces of the program in and out of memory according to use.

Swapping on the small 10M or 20M hard disks is considerably slower than on the large disks used with mainframes. Programs larger than 416K, therefore, probably will run very slowly. Field test users report long delays in loading large programs into memory, even when the programs are well under the maximum for nonpaging operation. Delays are due to the relatively slow operation of the XT 370 hard disks. Because of size and speed problems, many users of these systems should consider larger and faster hard disks.

An Introduction to the Portable PC

IBM introduced the Portable PC February 16, 1984. The IBM Portable PC, a "transportable" personal computer, has a built-in, 9-inch, amber composite video monitor; one 5 1/4-inch, half-height floppy disk drive (with space for an optional second drive); an 83-key keyboard; two adapter cards; a floppy disk controller; and a Color/Graphics Monitor Adapter (CGA). The unit has also a universal-voltage power supply capable of overseas operation on 220-volt power. Figure 3.7 shows the Portable PC exterior.

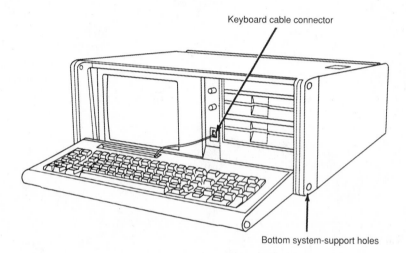

Keyboard cable connector

Bottom system-support holes

Fig. 3.7

The IBM Portable PC.

Courtesy of International Business Machines Corporation.

The system board used in the IBM Portable PC is the same board used in the original IBM XT's, with 256K of memory. Because the XT motherboard was used, eight expansion slots are available for the connection of adapter boards, although only two slots can accept a full-length adapter card. The power supply is basically the same as an XT's, with physical changes for portability and a small amount of power drawn to run the built-in monitor. In function and performance, the Portable PC system unit has identical characteristics to an equivalently configured IBM PC XT system unit. Figure 3.8 shows the Portable PC interior view.

IBM withdrew the Portable PC from the market April 2, 1986, a date that coincides with the introduction of the IBM Convertible laptop PC. The Portable PC is rare because not many were sold. The system was misunderstood by the trade press and user community. Most people did not understand that the system was an XT and not really a PC. Maybe if IBM had called the system the Portable XT, it would have sold better.

Color/Graphics Monitor Adapter

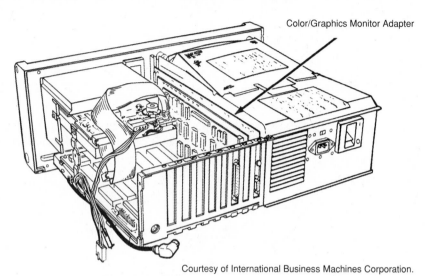

Courtesy of International Business Machines Corporation.

Fig. 3.8

The IBM Portable PC's interior.

The Portable PC system unit has these major functional components:

Intel 8088 microprocessor

ROM-based diagnostics (POST)

BASIC language interpreter in ROM

256K of dynamic RAM

Eight expansion slots (two long slots, one 3/4-length slot, and five short slots)

Socket for 8087 math coprocessor

Color/Graphics Monitor Adapter

9-inch, amber, composite video monitor

Floppy disk interface

One or two half-height 360K floppy drives

114-watt universal power supply (115 V to 230 V, 50 Hz to 60 Hz)

Lightweight 83-key keyboard

Enclosure with carrying handle

Carrying bag for the system unit

Portable PC Technical Specifications

The technical data for the Portable PC system is described in this section, which includes information about the system architecture, memory configurations and capacities, standard system features, disk storage, expansion slots, keyboard specifications, and also physical and environmental specifications. This information can be useful in determining what kinds of parts you need when you are upgrading or repairing these systems. Figure 3.6 previously showed the XT motherboard, also used in the Portable PC.

System architecture	
Microprocessor	8088
Clock speed	4.77 MHz
Bus type	ISA (Industry Standard Architecture)
Bus width	8-bit
Interrupt levels	8
Type	Edge-triggered
Shareable	No
DMA channels	3
DMA burst mode supported	No
Bus masters supported	No
Upgradeable processor complex	No

Memory	
Standard on system board	256K
Maximum on system board	256K
Maximum total memory	640K
Memory speed (ns) and type	200ns dynamic RAM
System board memory-socket type	16-pin DIP
Number of memory-module sockets	36 (4 banks of 9)
Memory used on system board	36 64K×1-bit DRAM chips in 4 banks of 9 chips
Memory cache controller	No

Memory	
Wait states:	
System board	1
Adapter	1

Standard features	
ROM size	40K
ROM shadowing	No
Optional math coprocessor	8087
Coprocessor speed	4.77 MHz
Standard graphics	None standard
RS232C serial ports	None standard
UART chip used	NS8250B
Maximum speed (bits per second)	9,600 bps
Maximum number of ports supported	2
Pointing device (mouse) ports	None standard
Parallel printer ports	None standard
Bidirectional	No
Maximum number of ports supported	3
CMOS real-time clock (RTC)	No
CMOS RAM	None

Disk storage	
Internal disk and tape drive bays	2 half-height
Number of 3 1/2-/5 1/4-inch bays	0/2
Standard floppy drives	1×360K
Optional floppy drives:	
5 1/4-inch 360K	Optional
5 1/4-inch 1.2M	No
3 1/2-inch 720K	Optional
3 1/2-inch 1.44M	No
3 1/2-inch 2.88M	No
Hard disk controller included	None

continues

Expansion slots

Total adapter slots	8
Number of long and short slots	5/3
Number of 8-/16-/32-bit slots	8/0/0
Available slots (with video)	6

Keyboard specifications

101-key Enhanced Keyboard	No
Fast keyboard speed setting	No
Keyboard cable length	6 feet

Physical specifications

Footprint type	Desktop
Dimensions:	
Height	8.0 inches
Width	20.0 inches
Depth	17.0 inches
Weight	31 pounds

Environmental specifications

Power-supply output	114 watts
Worldwide (110/60,220/50)	Yes
Auto-sensing/switching	No
Maximum current:	
90-137 VAC	4.0 amps
Operating range:	
Temperature	60-90 degrees F
Relative humidity	8-80 percent
Maximum operating altitude	7,000 feet
Heat (BTUs/hour)	650
Noise (Average dB, operating, 1m)	42
FCC classification	Class B

Table 3.4 shows the part numbers for the Portable PC:

Table 3.4 IBM Portable PC Model Part Numbers	
Description	Number
256K, one 360K half-height drive	5155068
256K, two 360K half-height drives	5155076
Half-height 360K floppy disk drive	6450300

The disk drive used in the Portable PC was a half-height drive, the same unit specified for use in the PC*jr*. When the Portable PC was introduced, PC*jr* was the only one IBM sold with the half-height drive.

An Introduction to the AT

IBM introduced the Personal Computer AT (for Advanced Technologies) August 14, 1984. The IBM AT system included many features previously unavailable in IBM's PC systems such as increased performance, an advanced microprocessor, high-capacity floppy disk and hard disk drives, larger memory space, and an advanced coprocessor. Despite its new design, the IBM AT retains compatibility with most existing hardware and software products for the earlier systems.

In most cases, IBM AT system performance is expected to be three to five times faster than the IBM XT for single applications running DOS on both computers. The performance increase is due to the combination of the 80286 processor, the 16-bit memory, and the hard disk capabilities.

The system unit has been available in several models: a floppy-disk-equipped base model (068) and several hard-disk-enhanced models. Based on a high-performance, 16-bit, Intel 80286 microprocessor, each computer includes Cassette BASIC language in ROM and a clock and calendar with battery backup. All models are equipped with a high-capacity (1.2M) floppy disk drive, a keyboard, and a lock. For standard memory, the base model offers 256K, and the enhanced models offer 512K. In addition, the enhanced models have a 20M or a 30M hard disk drive and a serial or parallel adapter. Each system can be expanded through customer-installable options. You can add memory (to 512K) for the base model by adding chips to the system board. You can expand all models to 16M by installing memory cards.

IBM offers these disk drives: a 30M hard disk drive; a 20M hard disk drive; a second, high-capacity (1.2M) floppy disk drive; a double-density (320/360K) floppy disk drive; and a new 3 1/2-inch 720K drive. You can install as many as two floppy disk drives and one hard disk drive or one floppy disk drive and two hard disk drives in the system unit. To use the high-capacity floppy disk drives properly, you must have special floppy disks—5 1/4-inch, high-coercivity, double-sided, soft-sectored disks, available from many sources. The double-sided floppy disk drive (320/360K) is available for floppy disk compatibility with the standard PC or XT systems; the 3 1/2-inch drive, for compatibility with the PC Convertible laptop and the PS/2 series. You can exchange disks reliably between the 1.2M and the standard 360K drives if you use the proper method and understand the recording process. This information is covered elsewhere in this book. For complete reliability, however, you should purchase the 360K drive.

The system unit has eight slots that support cards for additional devices, features, or memory. Six slots support the advanced 16-bit or 8-bit option cards. Two slots support only 8-bit option cards. All system-unit models, however, use one 16-bit slot for the fixed disk and floppy disk drive adapter. The enhanced models use an additional 8-bit slot for the serial or parallel adapter. The result is seven available expansion slots for the base model and six available expansion slots for enhanced models. Figure 3.9 shows the interior of an AT system unit.

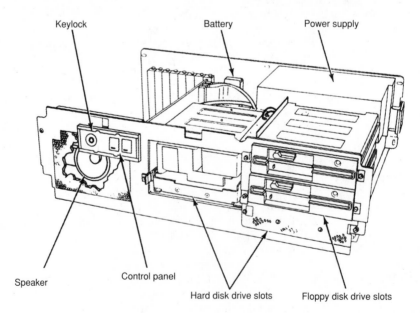

Keylock   Battery   Power supply

Speaker   Control panel   Hard disk drive slots   Floppy disk drive slots

Fig. 3.9

The IBM AT system-unit interior.

Courtesy of International Business Machines Corporation.

All models include a universal power supply; a temperature-controlled, variable-speed cooling fan; and a security lock with key. The user selects the power supply for a country's voltage range. The cooling fan significantly reduces the noise in most environments; the fan runs slower when the system unit is cool and faster when the system unit is hot. When the system is locked, no one can remove the system-unit cover, boot the system, or enter commands or data from the keyboard, thereby enhancing the system's security.

The keyboard is attached to the system unit by a 9-foot, coiled cable that enables the AT to adapt to a variety of workspace configurations. The keyboard includes key-location enhancements and mode indicators for improved keyboard usability. Figure 3.10 shows the rear panel of an AT.

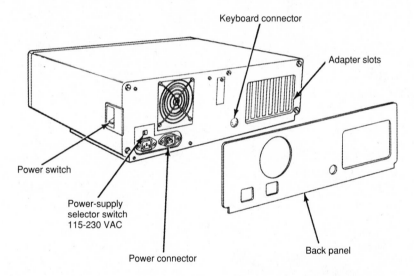

Courtesy of International Business Machines Corporation.

Fig. 3.10

The IBM AT rear view.

Every system unit for the AT models has these major functional components:

        Intel 80286 microprocessor
        ROM-based diagnostics (POST)
        BASIC language interpreter in ROM
        8086-compatible real address mode
        Protected virtual address mode
        256K of dynamic RAM (base model)
        512K of dynamic RAM (enhanced models)
        1.2M double-sided floppy drive
        20M or 30M hard disk drive (enhanced models)

Hard disk and floppy disk interface
Serial or parallel interface (enhanced models)
Clock-calendar and configuration with battery backup
Keylock
84-key keyboard
Enhanced, 101-key 3270-style keyboard
Switchable worldwide power supply
Eight I/O expansion slots (six 16-bit, two 8-bit)
Socket for 80287 math coprocessor

AT Models and Features

Since the introduction of the AT, several models have become available. First, IBM announced two systems: a base model (068) and an enhanced model (099). The primary difference between the two systems was the standard hard disk that came with the enhanced model. IBM has introduced two new AT systems since the first systems, each offering new features.

The first generation of AT systems have a 6 MHz system clock that dictates the processor cycle time. The *cycle time*, the system's smallest interval of time, represents the speed at which operations occur. Every operation in a computer takes at least one or (usually) several cycles to complete. Therefore, if two computers are the same in every way except for the clock speed, the system with the faster clock rate executes the same operations in a shorter time proportional to the difference in clock speed. Cycle time and clock speed are two different ways of describing the same thing. Discussions of clock speed are significant when you consider buying the AT because not all models have the same clock speed.

The first two AT models were the 068 (base) model, which had 256K on the motherboard and a single 1.2M floppy disk drive, and the model 099 (enhanced), which had a 20M hard disk drive, a serial/parallel adapter, and 512K on the motherboard. IBM designated the motherboard on these computers as Type 1, which is larger than the later Type 2 board and uses an unusual memory layout. The memory is configured as four banks of 128K chips—a total of 512K on the board. This configuration sounds reasonable until you realize that a 128K chip does not exist. IBM created this type of memory device by stacking a 64K chip on top of another one and soldering the two together. My guess is that IBM had many 64K chips to use, and the AT was available to take them.

On October 2, 1985, IBM announced a new model of the AT, the Personal Computer AT Model 239. The system has all the standard features of the AT Model 099, but has also a 30M hard disk rather than a 20M hard disk. A second, optional 30M hard disk drive expands the Model 239's hard disk storage to 60M. This unit's motherboard, a second-generation design IBM calls Type 2, is about 25 percent smaller than the Type 1 but uses the same mounting locations, for physical compatibility. All important items, such as the slots and connectors, remain in the same locations. Other major improvements in this board are in the memory. The 128K memory chips have been replaced by 256K devices. Now only two banks of chips are needed to get the same 512K on the board.

The AT Model 239 includes these items:

> 512K of RAM (standard)
>
> Type 2 motherboard with 256K memory chips
>
> Serial/parallel adapter (standard)
>
> 30M hard disk (standard)
>
> New ROM BIOS (dated June 10, 1985)
>
>> ROM supports 3 1/2-inch 720K floppy drives without using external driver programs
>>
>> ROM supports 22 hard disk types, including the supplied 30M disk
>>
>> POST fixes clock rate to 6 MHz

The Type 2 motherboard's design is much improved over Type 1's; the Type 2 motherboard has improved internal-circuit timing and layout. Improvements in the motherboard indicated that the system would be pushed to higher speeds—exactly what happened with the next round of introductions.

In addition to obvious physical differences, the Model 239 includes significantly different ROM software from the previous models. The new ROM supports more types of disks, and its new POST prevents alteration of the clock rate from the standard 6 MHz models. Because support for the 30M hard disk is built into the new ROM, IBM sells also a 30M hard disk upgrade kit that includes the new ROM for the original AT systems. This $1,795 kit represents unfortunately the only legal way to obtain the newer ROM.

The 30M hard disk drive upgrade kit for the Personal Computer AT Models 068 and 099 includes all the features in the 30M hard disk drive announced for the AT Model 239. The upgrade kit also has a new basic input-output subsystem (BIOS), essential to AT operation. The new ROM BIOS supports 22 drive types (compared to the original 15 in earlier ATs), including the new 30M drive. To support the 30M hard disk drive, a new diagnostics floppy disk and an updated guide-to-operations manual are shipped with this kit.

The 30M update kit includes these items:

> 30M hard disk drive
> Two ROM BIOS modules
> Channel keeper bar (a bracket for the fixed disk)
> Data cable for the hard disk
> Diagnostics disk
> An insert to the AT guide-to-operations manual

Some people were upset initially that IBM had "fixed the microprocessor clock" to 6 MHz in the new model, thereby disallowing any possible "hot rod" modifications. Many other people realized that the clock crystal on all the AT models was socketed so that the crystal could be replaced easily by a faster one. More important, because the AT circuit design is modular, changing the clock crystal does not have repercussions throughout the rest of the system, as is the case in the PC and PC XT. For the price of a new crystal (from $1 to $30) and the time needed to plug it in, someone easily could increase an AT's speed by 30 percent, and sometimes more. Because IBM now retrofits the ROM into earlier models or the 30M hard disk upgrade, you no longer can implement a simple speedup alteration.

Many people believed that this change was made to prevent the AT from being "too fast" and therefore competing with IBM's minicomputers. In reality, the earlier motherboard was run intentionally at 6 MHz because IBM did not believe that the ROM BIOS software and critical system timing was fully operational at a higher speed. Users who increased the speed of their early computers often received DOS error messages from timing problems. Many companies selling speedup kits sold software to help smooth over these problems, but IBM's official solution was to improve the ROM BIOS software and motherboard circuitry and to introduce a system running at a faster speed. If you want increased speed no matter what model you have, several companies sell clock-crystal replacements that are frequency synthesizers rather than a fixed type of crystal. The units can wait until the POST is finished and change midstream to an increased operating speed.

On April 2, 1986, IBM introduced the Personal Computer AT Models 319 and 339. These two similar systems are an enhancement of the earlier Model 239. The primary difference from the Model 239 is a faster clock crystal that provides 8 MHz operation. The Model 339 has a new keyboard, the Enhanced Keyboard, with 101 keys rather than the usual 84. Model 319 is the same as Model 339, but includes the original keyboard.

Highlights of the Models 319 and 339 are shown in this list:

> Faster processor speed (8 MHz)
>
> Type 2 motherboard, with 256K chips

512K of RAM (standard)

Serial/parallel adapter

30M hard disk (standard)

New ROM BIOS (dated 11/15/85)

Support for 23 types of hard disks, including the supplied 30M disk

Support for 3 1/2-inch drives, at both 720K and 1.44M capacities

POST fixes clock rate to 8 MHz

Support for 101-key Personal Computer Enhanced Keyboard (keyboard standard on Model 339)

Recappable keys

Selectric typing section

Dedicated numeric pad

Dedicated cursor and screen controls

12 function keys

Indicator lights

9-foot cable

The most significant physical difference in these new systems is the Enhanced Keyboard on the Model 339. The keyboard, similar to a 3270 keyboard, has 101 keys. It could be called the IBM "corporate" keyboard because it is standard on all new desktop systems. The 84-key PC keyboard still is available, with a new 8 MHz model, as the Model 319.

These new 8 MHz systems are available only in an enhanced configuration with a standard 30M hard drive. This configuration affects the aftermarket because IBM essentially is taking away sales of peripherals. Customers benefit, however, because IBM has decided to become a competitor in the peripheral market; drives and other peripherals are priced more competitively. If you want hard disk drives larger than IBM's 30M, you must tolerate two drives or sell the standard 30M unit. The days of the diskless PC seem to be over!

ROM support for 3 1/2-inch disk drives at both 720K and 1.44M exists only in Models 339 and 319. This configuration is important if you want to add these types of floppy disk drives as internal units, to accommodate media interchange with the PS/2 series. Earlier AT systems still can use the 720K and 1.44M drives, but they might need software drivers loaded from disk in order to have complete support.

AT Technical Specifications

Technical information for the AT system is described in this section. You will find information about the system architecture, memory configurations and capacities, standard system features, disk storage, expansion slots, keyboard specifications, as well as physical and environmental specifications. This type of information can be useful in determining what types of parts are needed when you are upgrading or repairing these systems. Figures 3.11 and 3.12 show the layout and components on the two different AT motherboards.

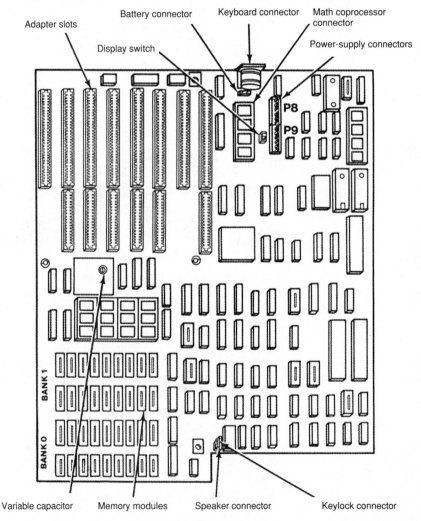

Fig. 3.11

The IBM AT Type 1 system board.

Courtesy of International Business Machines Corporation.

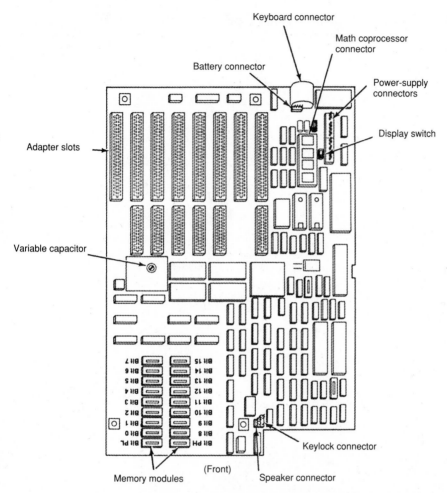

Keyboard connector

Math coprocessor
connector

Battery connector

Power-supply
connectors

Display switch

Adapter slots

Variable capacitor

Bit 7   Bit 15
Bit 6   Bit 14
Bit 5   Bit 13
Bit 4   Bit 12
Bit 3   Bit 11
Bit 2   Bit 10
Bit 1   Bit 9
Bit 0   Bit 8
Bit PL   Bit PH

Keylock connector

(Front)

Memory modules   Speaker connector

Courtesy of International Business Machines Corporation.

Fig. 3.12

The IBM AT Type 2
system board.

System architecture	
Microprocessor	80286
Clock speed	6 or 8 MHz
Bus type	ISA (Industry Standard Architecture)
Bus width	16-bit
Interrupt levels	16
Type	Edge-triggered

continues

System architecture

Shareable	No
DMA channels	7
DMA burst mode supported	No
Bus masters supported	No
Upgradeable processor complex	No

Memory

Standard on system board	512K
Maximum on system board	512K
Maximum total memory	16M
Memory speed (ns) and type	150ns dynamic RAM
System board memory-socket type	16-pin DIP
Number of memory-module sockets	18 or 36 (2 or 4 banks of 18)
Memory used on system board	36 128K-by-1-bit DRAM chips in 2 banks of 18, or 18 256K-by-1-bit chips in one bank
Memory cache controller	No

Wait states:

System board	1
Adapter	1

Standard features

ROM size	64K
ROM shadowing	No
Optional math coprocessor	80287
Coprocessor speed	4 or 5.33 MHz
Standard graphics	None standard
RS232C serial ports	1 (some models)
UART chip used	NS16450
Maximum speed (bits per second)	9,600 bps

Standard features

Maximum number of ports supported	2
Pointing device (mouse) ports	None standard
Parallel printer ports	1 (some models)
Bidirectional	Yes
Maximum number of ports supported	3
CMOS real-time clock (RTC)	Yes
CMOS RAM	64 bytes
Battery life	5 years

Disk storage

Internal disk and tape drive bays	1 full-height and 2 half-height	
Number of 3 1/2-, 5 1/4-inch bays	0/3	
Standarderfloppy drives	1×1.2M	
Optional floppy drives:		
5 1/4-inch 360K	Optional	
5 1/4-inch 1.2M	Standard	
3 1/2-inch 720K	Optional	
3 1/2-inch 1.44M	Optional (8 MHz models)	
3 1/2-inch 2.88M	No	
Hard disk controller included:	ST-506/412 (Western Digital WD1002-WA2 or WD1003-WA2)	
ST-506/412 hard disks available	20/30M	
Drive form factor	5 1/4-inch	
Drive interface	ST-506/412	
Drive capacity	20M	30M
Average access rate (ms)	40	40
Encoding scheme	MFM	MFM
BIOS drive type number	2	20
Cylinders	615	733
Heads	4	5
Sectors per track	17	17
Rotational speed (RPMs)	3600	3600

continues

Disk storage

Interleave factor	3:1	3:1
Data transfer rate (kilobytes/second)	170	170
Automatic head parking	Yes	Yes

Expansion slots

Total adapter slots	8
Number of long and short slots	8/0
Number of 8-/16-/32-bit slots	2/6/0
Available slots (with video)	5

Keyboard specifications

101-key Enhanced Keyboard	Yes (8 MHz models)
Fast keyboard speed setting	Yes
Keyboard cable length	6 feet

Physical specifications

Footprint type	Desktop
Dimensions:	
Height	6.4 inches
Width	21.3 inches
Depth	17.3 inches
Weight	43 pounds

Environmental specifications

Power-supply output	192 watts
Worldwide (110/60,220/50)	Yes
Auto-sensing/switching	No
Maximum current:	
90-137 VAC	5.0 amps

Environmental specifications	
Operating range:	
Temperature 60-90 degrees F	
Relative humidity	8-80 percent
Maximum operating altitude	7,000 feet
Heat (BTUs/hour)	1229
Noise (Average dB, operating, 1m)	42
FCC classification	Class B

Table 3.5 shows the AT system-unit part-number information.

Table 3.5 IBM AT Model Part Numbers

Description	Number
AT 6 MHz/84-key keyboard, 256K:	
one 1.2M floppy drive	5170068
AT 6 MHz/84-key keyboard, 512K, serial/parallel:	
one 1.2M floppy drive, 20M hard disk	5170099
one 1.2M floppy drive, 30M hard disk	5170239
AT 8 MHz/84-key keyboard, 512K, serial/parallel:	
one 1.2M floppy drive, 30M hard disk	5170319
AT 8 MHz/101-key, 512K, serial/parallel:	
one 1.2M floppy drive, 30M hard disk	5170339
System options	
20M fixed disk drive	6450205
30M fixed disk	6450210
30M fixed disk drive upgrade kit	6450468
360K half-height floppy disk drive (AT)	6450207
1.2M high-capacity drive	6450206
3 1/2-inch, half-height, 720K external drive (AT)	2683191
Serial/parallel adapter	6450215
80287 math coprocessor option	6450211
Floor-standing enclosure	6450218
Enhanced Keyboard accessories	
Clear keycaps (60) with paper inserts	6341707
Blank light keycaps	1351710
Blank dark keycaps	1351728
Paper inserts (300)	6341704
Keycap-removal tools (6)	1351717

3270-AT

IBM announced the AT 3270 on June 18, 1985. This computer, basically the same as the original 3270 PC, is configured with an AT, rather than an XT, as the base. New software enhancements and adapter cards use the DOS memory space better and can place much of the Control Program in the extended-memory area, beyond the 1M boundary. Much of this capability comes from the *XMA card*, from IBM. Because much of the Control Program can reside in the area above 1M, DOS can find more room for applications software. Although this configuration doesn't eliminate the incompatibilities in the display hardware or keyboard, it at least makes available the memory needed to run an application.

The AT 3270 system has the same basic adapters as the standard 3270 PC. This system differs, however, in the capability of enabling the Control Program to reside in the memory space above 1M (*extended memory*), which doesn't exist on a standard PC or XT. IBM made several changes in the Control Program for this system and in special memory adapters, such as the XMA card. These changes enhanced the compatibility of the AT 3270 system over the original 3270 PC.

For more information about the AT 3270 system, refer to the section on the 3270 PC in this chapter.

The AT-370

The AT-370 is basically the same system as the XT 370 except for its use of an AT as the base unit. The same three custom processor boards that convert an XT into an XT-370 also plug into an AT. This system is at least two to three times faster than the XT version. The custom processor boards also are available as an upgrade for existing ATs. For a more complete description of this system, refer to the section "3270 PC Models and Features" earlier in this chapter.

An Introduction to the XT Model 286

On September 9, 1986, IBM introduced a new AT-type system disguised inside the chassis and case of an XT. This XT Model 286 system features increased memory, an Intel 80286 microprocessor, and as many as three internal drives. The computer combined an XT's cost-effectiveness, flexibility, and appearance with the high-speed, high-performance technology of the Intel 80286 microprocessor. This model may look like an XT, but underneath, it's all AT.

The IBM XT Model 286 can operate as much as three times faster than earlier models of the XT in most applications. It has a standard 640K of memory. Various memory-expansion options enable users to increase its memory to 16M.

Standard features in this system include a half-height, 1.2M, 5 1/4-inch, double-sided floppy disk drive; a 20M hard disk drive; a serial/parallel adapter card; and the IBM Enhanced Keyboard. You can select an optional, internal, second floppy disk drive from the following list:

Half-height, 3 1/2-inch, 720K floppy drive
Half-height, 3 1/2-inch, 1.44M floppy drive
Half-height, 5 1/4-inch, 1.2M floppy drive
Half-height, 5 1/4-inch, 360K floppy drive

The IBM XT Model 286's performance stems primarily from the AT motherboard design, with 16-bit I/O slots and an Intel 80286 processor running at 6 MHz. In addition to the type of processor used, clock speed and memory architecture are the primary factors in determining system performance. Depending on the model, the IBM AT's clock speed is 6 or 8 MHz, with 1 wait state, and the XT Model 286 processes data at 6 MHz, with 0 wait states. The elimination of a wait state improves performance by increasing processing speed for system memory access. The 0-wait-state design makes the XT Model 286 definitely faster than the original AT models that ran at 6 MHz and about equal in speed to the 8 MHz AT systems. Based on tests, the XT Model 286 also is about three times faster than an actual XT.

Because the XT Model 286 is an AT-class system, the processor supports both real and protected modes. Operating in real address mode, the 80286 is 8088 compatible; therefore, you can use most software that runs on the standard PC systems. In real address mode, the system can address as much as 1M of RAM. Protected mode provides a number of advanced features to facilitate multitasking operations. Protected mode provides separation and protection of programs and data in multitasking environments. In protected mode, the 80286 can address as much as 16M of real memory and 1 gigabyte of virtual memory per user. In this mode, the XT Model 286 can run advanced operating systems such as OS/2 and UNIX. When the XT Model 286 was introduced, it was the least-expensive IBM system capable of running a true multitasking operating system.

The IBM XT Model 286 has a standard 640K of RAM. Memory options enable the system to grow to 15 1/2M, much higher than the 640K limit in other PC XTs. If you add an operating system such as OS/2 or Windows, you can take advantage of the larger memory capacities that the XT Model 286 provides.

A 20M hard disk drive is a standard feature in the XT Model 286, as is a 5 1/4-inch, 1.2M, high-capacity floppy disk drive. A similar floppy disk drive is standard on all models of the Personal Computer AT. Floppy disks formatted on a 1.2M floppy disk drive therefore can be read by an AT or an XT Model 286. The 1.2M floppy disk drive also can read floppy disks formatted with PC-family members that use a 320/360K floppy disk drive. Figure 3.13 shows the interior of an XT 286 system unit.

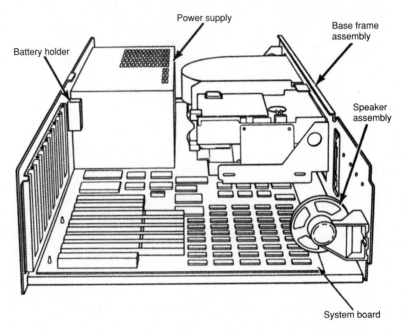

Fig. 3.13

The IBM XT-286 system unit interior.

Courtesy of International Business Machines Corporation.

The XT Model 286 features the IBM Enhanced Keyboard with indicator lights. Many IBM personal computers use the Enhanced Keyboard, but the XT Model 286 was the first PC XT to feature keyboard indicator lights. The Caps Lock, Num Lock, and Scroll Lock lights remind users of keyboard status, which helps to prevent keyboard-entry errors.

The IBM XT Model 286 has eight I/O slots, to accommodate peripheral-device adapter cards and memory-expansion options. Five slots support the advanced 16-bit cards or 8-bit cards; three support only 8-bit cards. Two of the three 8-bit slots support only short cards.

A hard disk and floppy drive adapter card are standard features in the XT Model 286. This multifunction card takes only one 16-bit slot and supports as many as four disk drives (two floppy disk drives and two hard disk drives).

The serial/parallel adapter, another standard feature, is a combination card that requires only one slot (either type) and provides a serial and a parallel port. The parallel portion of the adapter has the capacity to attach devices, such as a parallel printer, that accept eight bits of parallel data. The fully programmable serial portion supports asynchronous communications from 50 bps to 9600 bps. The serial portion requires an optional serial-adapter cable or a serial-adapter connector. When one of these options is connected to the adapter, all the signals in a standard EIA RS-232C interface are available. You can use the serial port for interfacing a modem, a remote display terminal, a mouse, or other serial device. The XT Model 286 supports as many as two serial/parallel adapters.

A standard IBM XT Model 286 offers these features:

80286 processor at 6 MHz with 0 wait states

640K of motherboard memory

1.2M floppy drive

20M hard disk

Five 16-bit and three 8-bit expansion slots

Fixed disk/floppy disk drive adapter (occupies one 16-bit expansion slot)

Serial/parallel adapter (occupies one 16-bit expansion slot)

Enhanced Keyboard with indicator lights

Time-and-date clock with battery backup

BASIC language in ROM

XT Model 286 Models and Features

The XT Model 286 processor is as much as 2 1/2 times faster internally than the preceding XT family and as much as 25 percent faster than the AT Model 239, depending on specific applications. The XT Model 286 is compatible with most hardware and software supported by the IBM personal computer family.

A 20M fixed disk and a 1.2M, 5 1/4-inch floppy disk drive are standard on the XT Model 286. One additional floppy disk drive can be installed internally as drive B.

You can add as a second half-height floppy drive any type of floppy drive, including both the high- and double-density versions of the 5 1/4- and 3 1/2-inch drives.

If you want to be able to read standard 5 1/4-inch data or program floppy disks created by the XT Model 286 on other PC systems, you might want to add a 5 1/4-inch 360K floppy disk drive, which provides full read/write compatibility with those systems. If read/write compatibility is not important, you can add a second, 1.2M, high-capacity floppy disk drive.

You can add any 3 1/2-inch drive, including the 720K and 1.44M versions. Because the 1.44M does not have any read/write compatibility problems with the 720K drives, however, and the 1.44M drives always can operate in 720K mode, I suggest adding only the 1.44M, 3 1/2-inch drives rather than the 720K versions. The higher-density drive is only a small extra expense compared to the double-density version. Most people do not know that full ROM BIOS support for these 1.44M drives is provided in the XT Model 286.

All internal floppy disk drives use the fixed disk and floppy disk drive adapter, standard on the XT Model 286.

For flexibility, you can choose an external floppy disk drive. The external 3 1/2-inch floppy disk drive provides compatibility with systems that have these drives.

XT Model 286 Technical Specifications

The technical information for the AT system described in this section covers the system architecture, memory configurations and capacities, standard system features, disk storage, expansion slots, keyboard specifications, and also physical and environmental specifications. You can use this information to determine the parts you need when you are upgrading or repairing these systems. Figure 3.14 shows the layout and components on the XT 286 motherboard.

System architecture	
Microprocessor	80286
Clock speed	6 MHz
Bus type	ISA (Industry Standard Architecture)
Bus width	16-bit
Interrupt levels	16
Type	Edge-triggered
Shareable	No
DMA channels	7
DMA burst mode supported	No
Bus masters supported	No
Upgradeable processor complex	No

continues

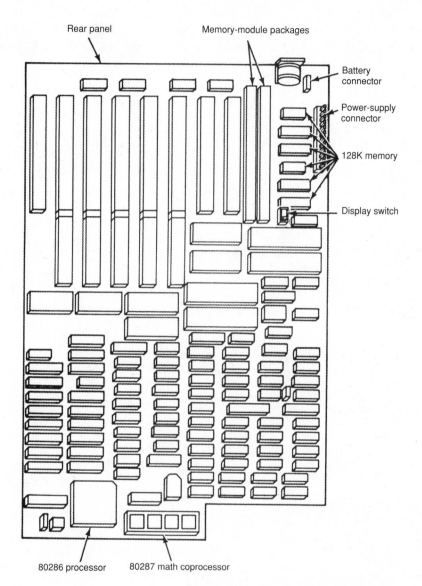

Rear panel

Memory-module packages

Battery connector

Power-supply connector

128K memory

Display switch

80286 processor

80287 math coprocessor

Courtesy of International Business Machines Corporation.

Fig. 3.14

The IBM XT-286 system board.

Memory

Standard on system board	640K
Maximum on system board	640K
Maximum total memory	16M
Memory speed (ns) and type	150ns dynamic RAM
System board memory-socket type	9-bit SIMM
Number of memory-module sockets	2
Memory used on system board	One bank of 4 64K×4-bit and 2 64K×1-bit DRAM parity chips, and one bank of 2 9-bit SIMMs
Memory cache controller	No
Wait states:	
System board	0
Adapter	1

Standard features

ROM size	64K
ROM shadowing	No
Optional math coprocessor	80287
Coprocessor speed	4.77 MHz
Standard graphics	None standard
RS232C serial ports	1
UART chip used	NS16450
Maximum speed (bits per second)	9,600 bps
Maximum number of ports supported	2
Pointing device (mouse) ports	None standard
Parallel printer ports	1
Bidirectional	Yes
Maximum number of ports supported	3
CMOS real-time clock (RTC)	Yes
CMOS RAM	64 bytes
Battery life	5 years

Disk storage

Internal disk and tape drive bays	1 full-height and 2 half-height
Number of 3 1/2-/5 1/4-inch bays	0/3
Standard floppy drives	1×1.2M
Optional floppy drives:	
5 1/4-inch 360K	Optional
5 1/4-inch 1.2M	Standard
3 1/2-inch 720K	Optional
3 1/2-inch 1.44M	Optional
3 1/2-inch 2.88M	No

Disk storage

Hard disk controller included:	ST-506/412 (Western Digital WD1003-WA2)
ST-506/412 hard disks available	20M
Drive form factor	5 1/4-inch
Drive interface	ST-506/412
Drive capacity	20M
Average access rate (ms)	65
Encoding scheme	MFM
BIOS drive type number	2
Cylinders	615
Heads	4
Sectors per track	17
Rotational speed (RPMs)	3600
Interleave factor	3:1
Data transfer rate (kilobytes/second)	170
Automatic head parking	No

Expansion slots

Total adapter slots	8
Number of long and short slots	6/2
Number of 8-/16-/32-bit slots	3/5/0
Available slots (with video)	5

Keyboard specifications

101-key Enhanced Keyboard	Yes
Fast keyboard speed setting	Yes
Keyboard cable length	6 feet

Physical specifications

Footprint type	*Desktop*
Dimensions:	
Height	5.5 inches
Width	19.5 inches
Depth	16.0 inches
Weight	28 pounds

continues

Environmental specifications	
Power-supply output	157 watts
Worldwide (110/60,220/50)	Yes
Auto-sensing/switching	Yes
Maximum current:	
90-137 VAC	4.5 amps
Operating range:	
Temperature	60-90 degrees F
Relative humidity	8-80 percent
Maximum operating altitude	7,000 feet
Heat (BTUs/hour)	824
Noise (Average dB, operating, 1m)	42
FCC classification	Class B

Table 3.6 lists the XT Model 286 system-unit part numbers.

Table 3.6 IBM XT-286 Model Part Numbers

Description	Number
XT Model 286 system unit, 6 MHz 0 wait state, 640K, serial/parallel:	
1.2M floppy drive, one 20M hard disk	5162286
Optional accessories	
5 1/4-inch, half-height 360K drive	6450325
3 1/4-inch, half-height 720K internal drive	6450258
3 1/2-inch, half-height 720K external drive	2683190
80287 math coprocessor option	6450211
Enhanced Keyboard accessories	
Clear keycaps (60) with paper inserts	6341707
Blank light keycaps	1351710
Blank dark keycaps	1351728
Paper inserts (300)	6341704
Keycap removal tools (6)	1351717

Chapter Summary

This chapter has examined all the systems that make up the original line of IBM personal computers. Because these systems still are used, and probably will be for years, the information in this chapter is useful as a reference tool.

The chapter has described the makeup of all the versions or models of each system, as well as their technical details and specifications. Each system unit's main components were listed also.

Each system's submodels were discussed, which should help you better understand the differences among systems that might look the same on the outside but differ internally.

Pricing information was listed too, for historical and reference purposes, because IBM no longer manufactures these systems.

Chapter 4 provides the same type of analysis for IBM's PS/2 system family.

IBM PS/2 and PS/1 System Hardware

This chapter identifies and describes each of the IBM Personal System/1 (PS/1) and Personal System/2 (PS/2) system units and standard features. The chapter begins by explaining the major differences between the IBM PC and the PS/1 and PS/2 systems—why the PS/2 is so similar to, yet so different from, the classic PC line.

The chapter continues with a discussion of the primary PS/2 models, which are based closely on the original PC line. These original systems sometimes are called Industry Standard Architecture (ISA) systems, and they include the standard ISA type of 8-bit and 16-bit I/O expansion slots.

The chapter also examines the PS/2 models and their respective submodels with the Micro Channel Architecture (MCA) slot design, which is dramatically different from the original ISA design.

Differences between PS/2 and PC Systems

Except for the obvious differences in appearance between PS/2 systems and the earlier "classic" (ISA) line of systems, the two types are quite similar. For troubleshooting and repair, you can consider the PS/2 as simply another type of PC-compatible system. All the troubleshooting techniques used on the other systems apply to the PS/2, although some repairs are conducted differently. For example, because each PS/2 motherboard includes a built-in floppy disk controller, if you determine that this controller is defective (using the same troubleshooting techniques as for the earlier systems), you must replace the entire motherboard. In contrast, on a PC system with the same problem, you replace only the floppy controller card, a much less costly operation.

After working on a PS/2 system for some time, you will discover several positive features of these systems:

■ The PS/2 is much more reliable than the earlier types of systems, for several reasons:

Robotic assembly of most of the system eliminates most human error during assembly.

The presence of fewer cables than other systems—or no cables at all—eliminates one of the biggest problem areas for repairs.

Better shielding than in other systems prevents reception and transmission of stray signals.

■ The PS/2 systems have no switches or jumpers to set, a feature that eliminates many service calls due to operator installation or configuration errors.

■ The systems can be taken apart and reassembled with no tools or only a few tools for special operations. Stripping down a PS/2 system to the motherboard usually takes less than one minute.

You will also discover several negative features as well:

■ Because the motherboard includes so many features, it is likely to be replaced more often than in other systems.

■ Parts are more expensive than for other systems, and items such as the motherboards, power supplies, and floppy drives can be much more expensive. Because of greatly reduced frequency of repair and the decreased labor required for each repair, however, maintaining a PS/2 system costs about half as much as maintaining other systems.

The primary areas of difference between PS/2 and PC systems are design and construction, video, and I/O adapter board slots.

Design and Construction

The design and construction of typical PS/2 systems is fascinating—they weren't designed in a day. The systems were designed with automated assembly in mind. Because parts and components are modular, technicians and users can remove and reinstall most of them without using any tools.

The no-tool disassembly concept carries over to the floppy and hard disk drives. To remove the floppy disk drive, you hold the front of the drive while bending a plastic tab and pull the drive from the system unit. To replace the drive, you slide the drive back into the case until it snaps into place. As a technician, you can amaze people who are unfamiliar with these systems when you open the system, remove a drive, replace it with a new unit, and close the system, all within 30 seconds. People who usually work on other types of systems, or who have never seen the inside of a PS/2, are usually quite impressed.

Parts and Availability

The small amount of labor required to service PS/2 systems is helping to change the repair and service industry. The modular construction should make labor less expensive than parts on the repair bill. Parts pricing and availability are much more important when you service a PS/2.

The availability and price of parts, however, can be a problem. A PS/2 system doesn't have many parts; the PS/2 motherboard contains many components that other systems house on expansion adapter cards. Furthermore, most PS/2 disk drives have integrated or built-in controllers, and items such as logic boards, which attach to the drives, are not available separately. Having so much integration makes PS/2s much easier to repair but may require replacing the motherboard more often than in earlier systems, in which many times simply replacing an inexpensive adapter could solve a problem.

Because many of the custom chips used in the PS/2 boards are unavailable separately, PS/2 motherboards are very difficult to repair. Unlike motherboards in other systems, PS/2 motherboards usually must be replaced (or exchanged) rather than repaired. Although very little motherboard repair occurs even with non-PS/2 systems—because repairing a motherboard is usually more costly than replacing it—the repair or replacement issue is more important with PS/2s because the PS/2 motherboard contains so many more components (and therefore more potential places for things to go wrong) than other motherboards. IBM is the primary source of new or exchange motherboards for the PS/2.

Cables

Another design feature of the PS/2 is that several models contain no cables, which is amazing when you think of the earlier systems with their mazes of cables for carrying power and data. Eliminating cables makes components easier to install and also removes perhaps the largest single source of errors and problems. PS/2 systems are also much better shielded against stray signals because of their circuit and case design.

Video

The PS/2 video subsystem differs greatly from a PC subsystem. The original PC systems had a Monochrome Display Adapter (MDA), Color Graphics Adapter (CGA), or Enhanced Graphics Adapter (EGA) available as a plug-in board. The PS/2 Models 25 and 30 have on the motherboard a built-in video adapter: the MultiColor Graphics Array (MCGA). PS/2 Models 50 and up (as well as the 25-286 and 30-286) contain a built-in video subsystem: the Video Graphics Array (VGA), which is a higher-end system. The MCGA is a subset of the VGA and lacks color capability in the highest-resolution mode. Some newer systems, such as Models P75, 90, and 95, include eXtended Graphics Array (XGA) on either the motherboard or a card. The newer XGA standard is a super-VGA type of adapter that includes more resolution and colors than the standard VGA and retains backward compatibility.

The VGA and XGA support all video modes available in the earlier MDA, CGA, and EGA, as well as some newer VGA- and XGA-specific modes. Because this downward compatibility is almost 100 percent, few programs are unable to run on a VGA- or an XGA-equipped system, although programs not written specifically for VGA or XGA cannot take advantage of their extra resolution and color capability.

Because VGA and XGA supersede EGA and all other previous standards, IBM has stopped producing all other video adapters, including EGA. For a while, IBM sold a VGA card for upgrading PC systems to VGA; this 8-bit board, called the IBM PS/2 Display Adapter, plugged into any IBM PC or PC-compatible system. IBM discontinued the board, leaving only aftermarket boards available for upgrading older systems. Most video-card vendors have followed IBM's lead and have also discontinued EGA boards. These vendors have successfully cloned the VGA and XGA technology, providing many video-card choices for upgrading PC and PC-compatible systems. In fact, IBM has been assisting video board manufacturers in developing clones of the XGA.

In contrast to other graphics adapters, VGA and XGA have analog output and require displays that can accept this signal. Other graphics adapters use a digital signal and work with monitors designed to accept the signal. Therefore, if you are upgrading a system to VGA or XGA, you probably also need to add a new monitor to your shopping list. Some monitors, such as the NEC MultiSync and the Sony Multiscan, accept both digital and analog signals. These monitors offer a flexibility for working with older digital systems not found in IBM's monitors, but they can be more expensive. If you have such a monitor and are upgrading your system's video adapter to VGA or XGA, you do not need a new monitor.

The change to analog displays comes for two primary reasons: color and money. With an analog display, many colors become available without a big jump in cost. VGA is designed to display as many as 262,144 colors, which would require a digital interface design with at least 18 lines to transmit all this color information to the monitor. Using an interface with 18 digital driver circuits on the video card, running through a thick cable containing at least 18 shielded wires, to a monitor with 18 digital receiver circuits, would cost thousands of dollars. A much simpler and less costly approach is to convert the digital color information to analog information for transmission and use by the display. This approach reduces the amount of circuitry required and allows for a much smaller cable. Analog transmission can send the same color information through fewer wires and circuits.

Micro Channel Architecture (MCA) Slots

Perhaps the most important difference between PS/2 systems and other systems is the I/O adapter board interface bus, or slots. PS/2 Models 50 and higher incorporate a new bus interface called Micro Channel Architecture (MCA). MCA is a new slot design that is incompatible with the ISA slot system but offers improvements in many areas. The first consequence of this bus is that a design adapter that plugs into the ISA 8-bit or 8/16-bit slots cannot plug into MCA slots. MCA is both physically and electrically different from ISA.

MCA Advantages

MCA was designed to meet strict FCC regulations for Class B certification. These requirements are much stricter than for Class A, which covers allowable emissions in a location zoned as commercial or industrial.

Class B requirements are for systems sold in residential environments and are designed to eliminate electrical interference with devices such as TV and radios. Meeting Class B requirements should give these systems a distinct advantage as clock rates (speeds) go ever higher. People in the communications and radio industry know that as the frequency of an oscillator increases, so does the problem of noise emissions. MCA has many ground connections for shielding, including a ground pin no further than one-tenth of an inch from any signal line in the slot. The Appendix of this book includes a pinout diagram of ISA and MCA bus slots.

MCA is designed to eliminate the bane of adapter board installers: setting jumpers and switches to configure the adapters. In surveys, IBM found that as many as 60 percent of all technician service calls were "no problem" calls; they were switch- and jumper-setting sessions. No wonder switches and jumpers are a problem, considering the number of switches and jumpers on some memory and multifunction boards. Setting them correctly can be very difficult, and nearly impossible without the board's original manual because each manufacturer's board is different. If you buy new boards, you might save money if you buy whatever board is on sale; you probably will end up with many different adapter boards, however, most with hard-to-read manuals and a bunch of jumpers and switches to set.

IBM's answer to this problem is called Programmable Option Selection (POS), a built-in feature on all MCA-equipped systems. The POS uses a special file called an Adapter Description File (with the file extension ADF) that comes with each adapter. The ADF file contains all possible setting attributes for the board and is read in by the system start-up disk or reference disk. The reference disk contains a special configuration routine that reads all the files and decides on nonconflicting settings for each board. The operator might need to select particular settings when two boards conflict. When the settings are set, they are stored in CMOS (battery-saved memory) and are available every time the system is started. The settings can be stored on disk also for backup, in case of a battery failure, or to quickly restore a configuration to several systems. The POS feature saves much labor and time, and is affecting the upgrade and repair industry: Many manufacturers have established switchless setups for their adapters to make them more "PS/2-like."

Finally, MCA-equipped systems are much more reliable than ISA-equipped systems, for several reasons. The rest of this section discusses the reliability of the MCA system, particularly timing considerations.

MCA Reliability

One reason that MCA-equipped systems are more reliable than those with ISA bus interfaces is that the MCA is well shielded. MCA-equipped systems therefore are more immune to noise from radio transmissions or any electrical noise.

This reason might be minor compared with the timing of the MCA bus. The MCA is asynchronous, which means that communication between adapters and the system board doesn't depend on timing. This feature solves a relatively common problem with bus systems. Have you ever had problems getting a system to work, only to find that moving a board to a different slot or switching two boards allows the system to operate normally? (By the way, I don't think that any IBM service manual officially suggests this solution.) The problem that moving or switching boards solves is one of timing. Each slot is supposed to carry the same signals as all the other slots, but that doesn't exactly happen. Effects on the bus, such as capacitance and signal propagation delays, can cause timing windows to "appear" differently in different slots, which can affect a board's functioning in that slot. MCA eliminates this type of problem; it is designed so that a board can tell it to "wait"—in effect, slowing the system by adding wait states until the board is ready.

Another timing-related problem is known to people who use some of the "turbo" IBM-compatible systems. In these "hypersystems," some boards cannot keep up with the system speed and do not work at all. On some systems, some of these boards can work if the system is slowed by adding wait states to operations or by reducing the speed of the system clock—but then the system doesn't really operate at its full performance capacity. Many communications, networking, and memory adapters can be speed-limiting in this way. With MCA, the bus cycles at a fixed, constant speed among all the systems, no matter what the microprocessor clock speed; the MCA always waits for a board, inserting wait states until the board is ready to proceed. Although this process might slow the system somewhat, the board and system work. Therefore, the same adapter functions in the 10 MHz Model 50 or the 50 MHz Model 90, regardless of their different clock speeds.

Other MCA design parameters for performance improvements exist, but they are more difficult to see. Most benchmarks have not proven any performance advantage in MCA systems over those with the standard ISA slots. IBM has demonstrated MCA coprocessing capabilities, however, which showed excellent performance. Taking full advantage of

MCA's performance capabilities requires new bus master adapter designs. These new designs are adapters with processors that can function independently of the system or even take control of it. For now, MCA provides increased reliability and easy setup and use. The improvements incorporated into this bus make it the standard bus for the future; for now, however, many more systems in use still have the earlier ISA bus design.

Fortunately, most troubleshooting techniques and methods apply equally to the MCA and the ISA bus systems. The MCA systems suffer fewer failures overall, and are much easier to set up and install. The real question is, how much are customers willing to pay for these features?

PS/2 System-Unit Features By Model

This section provides a reference to all the PS/2 systems that IBM has produced. The standard parts included with each system unit include the items in this list:

- Motherboard with the CPU (central processing unit, or microprocessor) and other primary computer circuitry
- Case with internal power supply
- Keyboard
- Standard adapters or plug-in cards
- Some form of disk drive (usually)

This section includes also various kinds of information about each system unit:

- A listing of specific components
- Technical data and specifications
- An explanation of each submodel, with details about differences and features of each model, including changes from model to model and version to version
- Price of each system and option

Note Prices shown are the IBM list prices and usually will not reflect true purchase prices. Normally, a standard discount of 30 percent is subtracted from the retail price. Retail prices are provided for comparison and reference only. If a model has been discontinued, the price given represents the retail list price at the time the system was withdrawn.

Decoding PS/2 Model Numbers

With the large variety of PS/2 systems now available, you might have difficulty telling from the model number how one differs from another. IBM's model-designation scheme started out with some reasoning behind it, but the increasingly large number of models made the original scheme difficult to adhere to and resulted in many inconsistencies in model designations. To restore consistency and enable greater understanding of the product line, IBM recently created a new model-designation scheme. This section provides an explanation of the older, inconsistent scheme, as well as the new method.

This list shows examples of the use of the old system:

Model	Meaning
Model 70-121	120M HD, one floppy disk drive
Model 30-E41	10 MHz 286, 45M HD, one floppy disk drive
Model 70-B61	25 MHz 486, 60M HD, one floppy disk drive

Table 4.1 describes the original PS/2 model designation meanings used by IBM for the PS/2 Models 25, 25-286, 30, 30-286, 50, 55, 60, 65, 70, P70, P75, and 80.

Table 4.1 PS/2 Model Designation Codes (for Original Models)

Model	Meaning
2	20M hard disk drive
3	30M hard disk drive (except A3*)
4	45M hard disk drive
6	60M hard disk drive
8	80M hard disk drive
**0	Medialess (no hard disk, no floppy disk drives)
**1	1 floppy disk drive
**1	Monochrome display (25 only)
**2	2 floppy disk drives
**4	Color display (25, 25-286 only)
**6	10 MHz 286; 1 floppy disk (25-286 only)
0**	Space-saving keyboard (25-286 only)
12*	120M hard disk drive
A2*	25 MHz 386; 120M hard disk drive
B2*	25 MHz 486; 120M hard disk drive
16*	160M hard disk drive
A16	160M hard disk drive
32*	320M hard disk drive
40*	400M hard disk drive
A**	25 MHz 386 processor
A3*	25 MHz 386 processor; 320M hard disk drive
B**	25 MHz 486 processor
C**	Color display
E**	10 MHz 286 (30-286 only)
E6*	16 MHz 386; 60M hard disk drive (70 only)
G**	Enhanced keyboard
L0*	Token-ring LAN adapter (25 only)
LE*	EtherNet LAN adapter (55 only)
LT*	16/4 token-ring LAN adapter (55 only)
M**	Monochrome display

Represents any number or letter

Table 4.2 describes the new model-designation meanings used by IBM for the PS/2 Models 35, 40, L40, 56, 57, 90, and 95.

Table 4.2 PS/2 Model Designation Codes (for Newer Models)

Model	Meaning
0**	Standard processor complex design
1**	Advanced processor complex design
2**	16/4 token-ring LAN adapter
4	20 MHz 386SX
G	20 MHz 486SX
J	25 MHz 486
K	33 MHz 486
M	50 MHz 486
**0	No hard disk, one floppy disk drive
**3	40M hard disk drive
**4	60M hard disk drive
**5	80M hard disk drive
**9	160M hard disk drive
**D	320M hard disk drive
**F	400M hard disk drive
**X	Medialess (no hard disk, no floppy disk drives)

This list shows examples of the use of the new system:

Model	Meaning
Model 35-24X	Token ring, 20 MHz 386SX, no media
Model 40-040	20 MHz 386SX, 1 floppy disk drive, no hard disk
Model 95-0KF	33 MHz 486, 400M hard disk drive

Table 4.3 provides a reference list of all IBM PS/2 models that use the Industry Standard Architecture (ISA) bus and shows their standard.

Table 4.3 IBM PS/2 System Models with ISA Bus

Part number	CPU	MHz	PLANAR MEMORY Std.	Max.	STANDARD Floppy drive	Hard disk	Bus type
25							
8525-001	8086	8	512K	640K	1×720K	—	ISA/8
8525-G01	8086	8	512K	640K	1×720K	—	ISA/8
8525-004	8086	8	512K	640K	1×720K	—	ISA/8
8525-G04	8086	8	512K	640K	1×720K	—	ISA/8
25 LS							
8525-L01	8086	8	640K	640K	1×720K	—	ISA/8
8525-L04	8086	8	640K	640K	1×720K	—	ISA/8
30							
8530-001	8086	8	640K	640K	1×720K	—	ISA/8
8530-002	8086	8	640K	640K	2×720K	—	ISA/8
8530-021	8086	8	640K	640K	1×720K	30M	ISA/8
PS/1 286							
2011-M01	286	10	512K	2.5M	1×1.44M	—	ISA/16
2011-C01	286	10	512K	2.5M	1×1.44M	—	ISA/16
2011-M34	286	10	1M	2.5M	1×1.44M	30M	ISA/16
2011-C34	286	10	1M	2.5M	1×1.44M	30M	ISA/16
PS/1 SX							
2121-C42	386SX	16	2M	6M	1×1.44M	40M	ISA/16
2121-B82	386SX	16	2M	6M	1×1.44M	80M	ISA/16
2121-C92	386SX	16	2M	6M	1×1.44M	129M	ISA/16
25 286							
8525-006	286	10	1M	4M	1×1.44M	—	ISA/16
8525-G06	286	10	1M	4M	1×1.44M	—	ISA/16
8525-036	286	10	1M	4M	1×1.44M	30M	ISA/16
8525-G36	286	10	1M	4M	1×1.44M	30M	ISA/16
25 SX							
8525-K00	386SX	16	1M	16M	1×1.44M	—	ISA/16
8525-K01	386SX	16	4M	16M	1×1.44M	—	ISA/16
8525-L01	386SX	16	4M	16M	1×1.44M	—	ISA/16
30 286							
8530-E01	286	10	1M	4M	1×1.44M	—	ISA/16
8530-E21	286	10	1M	4M	1×1.44M	20M	ISA/16
8530-E31	286	10	1M	4M	1×1.44M	30M	ISA/16
8530-E41	286	10	1M	4M	1×1.44M	45M	ISA/16

Total/ available slots	STANDARD Video	KB	Date introduced	Date withdrawn	List price
2/2	MCGA	SS	08/04/87	—	$1,350
2/2	MCGA	Enh	08/04/87	—	$1,395
2/2	MCGA	SS	08/04/87	—	$1,695
2/2	MCGA	Enh	08/04/87	—	$1,740
2/1	MCGA	Enh	06/02/88	—	$2,139
2/1	MCGA	Enh	06/02/88	—	$2,484
3/3	MCGA	Enh	04/04/89	12/27/90	$1,695
3/3	MCGA	Enh	04/02/87	07/05/89	$1,695
3/3	MCGA	Enh	04/02/87	12/27/90	$2,255
0	VGA	Enh	06/26/90	—	$995
0	VGA	Enh	06/26/90	—	$1,449
0	VGA	Enh	06/26/90	—	$1,649
0	VGA	Enh	06/26/90	—	$1,999
0	VGA	Enh	10/07/91	—	$1,699
2/2	VGA	Enh	10/07/91	—	$2,199
2/2	VGA	Enh	10/07/91	—	$2,499
2/2	VGA	SS	05/10/90	—	$2,135
2/2	VGA	Enh	05/10/90	—	$2,135
2/2	VGA	SS	05/10/90	—	$2,705
2/2	VGA	Enh	05/10/90	—	$2,705
2/2	VGA	Enh	01/21/92	—	$ *
2/1	VGA	Enh	01/21/92	—	$ *
2/1	VGA	Enh	01/21/92	—	$ *
3/3	VGA	Enh	09/13/87	05/04/92	$1,625
3/3	VGA	Enh	09/13/88	09/11/91	$1,795
3/3	VGA	Enh	09/26/89	01/17/92	$1,795
3/3	VGA	Enh	04/23/91	05/04/92	$1,995

continues

Table 4.3 Continued

Part number	CPU	MHz	PLANAR MEMORY Std.	Max.	STANDARD Floppy drive	Hard disk	Bus type
35 SX							
8535-040	386SX	20	2M	16M	1×1.44M	—	ISA/16
8535-043	386SX	20	2M	16M	1×1.44M	40M	ISA/16
35 LS							
8535-14X	386SX	20	2M	16M	—	—	ISA/16
8535-24X	386SX	20	2M	16M	—	—	ISA/16
40 SX							
8540-040	386SX	20	2M	16M	1×1.44M	—	ISA/16
8540-043	386SX	20	2M	16M	1×1.44M	40M	ISA/16
8540-045	386SX	20	2M	16M	1×1.44M	80M	ISA/16
L40 SX							
8543-044	386SX	20	2M	18M	1×1.44M	60M	ISA/16

* Sales of this system unit are limited to the educational market. Suggested pricing was not available before press time.

Table 4.4 provides a reference list of all IBM PS/2 models that use the Micro Channel Architecture (MCA) bus and shows their standard features

Table 4.4 IBM PS/2 System Models with MCA Bus

Part number	CPU	MHz	PLANAR MEMORY Std.	Max.	STANDARD Floppy drive	Hard disk	Bus type
50							
8550-021	286	10	1M	1M	1×1.44M	20M	MCA/16
50Z							
8550-031	286	10	1M	2M	1×1.44M	30M	MCA/16
8550-061	286	10	1M	2M	1×1.44M	60M	MCA/16
55 SX							
8555-031	386SX	16	2M	8M	1×1.44M	30M	MCA/16
8555-041	386SX	16	4M	8M	1×1.44M	40M	MCA/16
8555-061	386SX	16	2M	8M	1×1.44M	60M	MCA/16
8555-081	386SX	16	4M	8M	1×1.44M	80M	MCA/16

Total/ available slots	STANDARD Video	KB	Date introduced	Date withdrawn	List price
3/3	VGA	Any	06/11/91	—	$1,745
3/3	VGA	Any	06/11/91	—	$2,255
3/2	VGA	Any	10/17/91	—	$1,820
3/2	VGA	Any	06/11/91	—	$2,425
5/5	VGA	Any	06/11/91	—	$2,000
5/5	VGA	Any	06/11/91	—	$2,545
5/5	VGA	Any	06/11/91	—	$2,845
0	VGA	SS	03/26/91	—	$2,495

Keyboards available include the Enhanced (101-key), Space-Saving (84-key), and Host-Connected (122-key). If "Any" is indicated, purchaser can choose any of the three.

Total available slots	STANDARD Video	KB	Date introduced	Date withdrawn	List price
4/3	VGA	Enh	04/02/87	05/03/89	$3,595
4/3	VGA	Enh	06/07/88	07/23/91	$1,695
4/3	VGA	Enh	06/07/88	07/23/91	$1,975
3/3	VGA	Enh	05/09/89	09/11/91	$2,745
3/3	VGA	Enh	06/11/91	05/25/92	$2,745
3/3	VGA	Enh	05/09/89	09/11/91	$2,945
3/3	VGA	Enh	06/11/91	05/25/92	$2,945

continues

Table 4.4 Continued

Part number	CPU	MHz	PLANAR MEMORY Std.	Max.	STANDARD Floppy drive	Hard disk	Bus type
55 LS							
8555-LT0	386SX	16	4M	8M	—	—	MCA/16
8555-LE0	386SX	16	4M	8M	—	—	MCA/16
56 SX							
8556-043	386SX	20	4M	16M	1×2.88M	40M	MCA/16
8556-045	386SX	20	4M	16M	1×2.88M	80M	MCA/16
56 SLC							
8556-055	386SLC	20	4M	16M	1×2.88M	80M	MCA/16
8556-059	386SLC	20	4M	16M	1×2.88M	160M	MCA/16
56 LS							
8556-14x	386SX	20	4M	16M	—	—	MCA/16
8556-24x	386SX	20	4M	16M	—	—	MCA/16
56 SLC LS							
8556-15x	386SLC	20	4M	16M	—	—	MCA/16
8556-25x	386SLC	20	4M	16M	—	—	MCA/16
57 SX							
8557-045	386SX	20	4M	16M	1×2.88M	80M	MCA/16
8557-049	386SX	20	4M	16M	1×2.88M	160M	MCA/16
57 SLC							
8557-055	386SLC	20	4M	16M	1×2.88M	80M	MCA/16
8557-059	386SLC	20	4M	16M	1×2.88M	160M	MCA/16
M57 SLC							
8557-255	386SLC	20	4M	16M	1×2.88M	80M	MCA/16
8557-259	386SLC	20	4M	16M	1×2.88M	160M	MCA/16
60							
8560-041	286	10	1M	1M	1×1.44M	44M	MCA/16
8560-071	286	10	1M	1M	1×1.44M	70M	MCA/16
65 SX							
8565-061	386SX	16	2M	8M	1×1.44M	60M	MCA/16
8565-121	386SX	16	2M	8M	1×1.44M	120M	MCA/16
8565-321	386SX	16	2M	8M	1×1.44M	320M	MCA/16

Total available slots	STANDARD Video	KB	Date introduced	Date withdrawn	List price
3/2	VGA	Enh	10/09/90	05/25/92	$2,745
3/2	VGA	Enh	10/09/90	05/25/92	$2,395
3/3	VGA	Any	02/25/92	—	$2,745
3/3	VGA	Any	02/25/92	—	$3,030
3/3	VGA	Any	02/25/92	—	$3,560
3/3	VGA	Any	02/25/92	—	$4,030
3/2	VGA	Any	02/25/92	—	$2,445
3/2	VGA	Any	02/25/92	—	$2,890
3/2	VGA	Any	02/25/92	—	$2,980
3/2	VGA	Any	02/25/92	—	$3,420
5/5	VGA	Any	06/11/91	—	$3,465
5/5	VGA	Any	06/11/91	—	$3,935
5/5	VGA	Any	02/25/92	—	$3,995
5/5	VGA	Any	02/25/92	—	$4,465
5/3	XGA	Any	10/17/91	02/25/92	$5,995
5/3	XGA	Any	02/25/92	—	$5,995
8/7	VGA	Enh	04/02/87	10/31/90	$2,750
8/7	VGA	Enh	04/02/87	10/31/90	$3,085
8/7	VGA	Enh	03/20/90	07/23/91	$3,145
8/7	VGA	Enh	03/20/90	07/23/91	$3,715
8/7	VGA	Enh	10/30/90	07/23/91	$5,465

continues

Table 4.4 Continued

Part number	CPU	MHz	PLANAR MEMORY Std.	Max.	STANDARD Floppy drive	Hard disk	Bus type
70 386							
8570-E61	386DX	16	2M	6M	1×1.44M	60M	MCA/32
8570-061	386DX	20	2M	6M	1×1.44M	60M	MCA/32
8570-081	386DX	20	4M	6M	1×1.44M	80M	MCA/32
8570-121	386DX	20	2M	6M	1×1.44M	120M	MCA/32
8570-161	386DX	20	4M	6M	1×1.44M	160M	MCA/32
8570-A61	386DX	25	2M	8M	1×1.44M	60M	MCA/32
8570-A81	386DX	25	4M	8M	1×1.44M	80M	MCA/32
8570-A21	386DX	25	2M	8M	1×1.44M	120M	MCA/32
8570-A16	386DX	25	4M	8M	1×1.44M	160M	MCA/32
70 486							
8570-B61	486DX	25	2M	8M	1×1.44M	60M	MCA/32
8570-B21	486DX	25	2M	8M	1×1.44M	120M	MCA/32
P70 386							
8573-031	386DX	16	2M	8M	1×1.44M	30M	MCA/32
8573-061	386DX	20	4M	8M	1×1.44M	60M	MCA/32
8573-121	386DX	20	4M	8M	1×1.44M	120M	MCA/32
P75 486							
8573-161	486DX	33	8M	16M	1×1.44M	160M	MCA/32
8573-401	486DX	33	8M	16M	1×1.44M	400M	MCA/32
80 386							
8580-041	386DX	16	1M	4M	1×1.44M	44M	MCA/32
8580-071	386DX	16	2M	4M	1×1.44M	70M	MCA/32
8580-081	386DX	20	4M	4M	1×1.44M	80M	MCA/32
8580-111	386DX	20	2M	4M	1×1.44M	115M	MCA/32
8580-121	386DX	20	2M	4M	1×1.44M	120M	MCA/32
8580-161	386DX	20	4M	4M	1×1.44M	160M	MCA/32
8580-311	386DX	20	2M	4M	1×1.44M	314M	MCA/32
8580-321	386DX	20	4M	4M	1×1.44M	320M	MCA/32
8580-A21	386DX	25	4M	8M	1×1.44M	120M	MCA/32
8580-A16	386DX	25	4M	8M	1×1.44M	160M	MCA/32
8580-A31	386DX	25	4M	8M	1×1.44M	320M	MCA/32
90 XP 486							
8590-0G5	486SX	20	4M	64M	1×1.44M	80M	MCA/32
8590-0G9	486SX	20	4M	64M	1×1.44M	160M	MCA/32
8590-0H5	486SX	25	4M	64M	1×1.44M	80M	MCA/32
8590-0H9	486SX	25	4M	64M	1×1.44M	160M	MCA/32
8590-0J5	486DX	25	8M	64M	1×1.44M	80M	MCA/32

Total/ available slots	STANDARD Video	KB	Date introduced	Date withdrawn	List price
3/3	VGA	Enh	06/07/88	07/23/91	$3,945
3/3	VGA	Enh	09/26/89	09/11/91	$4,095
3/3	VGA	Enh	06/11/91	—	$3,675
3/3	VGA	Enh	09/26/89	09/11/91	$4,745
3/3	VGA	Enh	06/11/91	—	$4,295
3/3	VGA	Enh	09/26/89	09/11/91	$5,845
3/3	VGA	Enh	06/11/91	01/17/92	$4,875
3/3	VGA	Enh	09/26/89	09/11/91	$6,445
3/3	VGA	Enh	06/11/91	—	$5,475
3/3	VGA	Enh	09/26/89	09/11/91	$7,745
3/3	VGA	Enh	06/20/89	09/11/91	$8,345
2/2	VGA	Enh	03/20/90	07/23/91	$5,995
2/2	VGA	Enh	05/09/89	07/23/91	$7,695
2/2	VGA	Enh	05/09/89	—	$6,695
4/4	XGA	Enh	11/12/90	—	$10,645
4/4	XGA	Enh	11/12/90	—	$13,295
8/7	VGA	Enh	04/02/87	10/31/90	$4,000
8/7	VGA	Enh	04/02/87	10/31/90	$4,500
8/7	VGA	Enh	10/30/90	—	$4,595
8/7	VGA	Enh	04/02/87	12/27/90	$6,995
8/7	VGA	Enh	03/20/90	01/29/91	$6,945
8/7	VGA	Enh	10/30/90	—	$5,095
8/7	VGA	Enh	08/04/87	12/27/90	$9,395
8/7	VGA	Enh	03/20/90	—	$7,145
8/7	VGA	Enh	03/20/90	01/29/91	$9,645
8/7	VGA	Enh	10/30/90	—	$7,095
8/7	VGA	Enh	03/20/90	—	$8,695
4/3	XGA	Enh	04/23/91	01/17/92	$4,945
4/3	XGA	Enh	04/23/91	01/17/92	$5,545
4/3	XGA	Enh	10/17/91	—	$5,945
4/3	XGA	Enh	10/17/91	—	$6,545
4/3	XGA	Enh	10/30/90	01/17/92	$7,295

continues

Table 4.4 Continued

Part number	CPU	MHz	PLANAR MEMORY Std.	Max.	STANDARD Floppy drive	Hard disk	Bus type
8590-0J9	486DX	25	8M	64M	1×1.44M	160M	MCA/32
8590-0K9	486DX	33	8M	64M	1×1.44M	320M	MCA/32
8590-0KD	486DX	33	8M	64M	1×1.44M	320M	MCA/32
8590-0KF	486DX	33	8M	64M	1×1.44M	400M	MCA/32
95 XP 486							
8595-0G9	486SX	20	4M	64M	1×1.44M	160M	MCA/32
8595-0GF	486SX	20	4M	64M	1×1.44M	400M	MCA/32
8595-0H9	486SX	25	8M	64M	1×1.44M	160M	MCA/32
8595-0HF	486SX	25	8M	64M	1×1.44M	400M	MCA/32
8595-0J9	486DX	25	8M	64M	1×1.44M	160M	MCA/32
8595-0JD	486DX	25	8M	64M	1×1.44M	320M	MCA/32
8595-0JF	486DX	25	8M	64M	1×1.44M	400M	MCA/32
8595-0KD	486DX	33	8M	64M	1×1.44M	320M	MCA/32
8595-0KF	486DX	33	8M	64M	1×1.44M	400M	MCA/32

Keyboards available include the Enhanced (101-key), Space-Saving (84-key), and Host-Connected (122-key). If "Any" is indicated, the purchaser can choose any of the three.

PS/1

Announced June 26, 1990, the IBM PS/1 Computer was designed for consumers who have little or no knowledge about computers and who intend to use their computers at home. The PS/1 system is based on a 10 MHz 80286 processor with 512K or 1M of memory standard (depending on model). On October 7, 1991, IBM expanded its PS/1 product line by introducing several new PS/1 systems with 386SX processors. These newer systems address a broader market, including small businesses and the advanced computing requirements of second-time buyers. An upgrade is available from IBM. You can exchange the original systems for the new 386SX versions.

Each PS/1 system comes with an IBM Enhanced Keyboard, VGA display, IBM mouse, 2400 bps internal modem, IBM DOS, Microsoft Works, and tutorials that enable the purchaser to run a variety of applications immediately after setting up the system. Included with U.S. models is software to access the IBM PS/1 on-line Users' Club, through the Prodigy on-line communications service. Several models are available so that you can select the type of display (black and white, or color) and the system-unit configuration (a single floppy drive with 512K of memory or a single floppy drive and 30M hard disk with 1M of memory).

Total/ available slots	STANDARD Video	KB	Date introduced	Date withdrawn	List price
4/3	XGA	Enh	10/30/90	01/17/92	$7,895
4/3	XGA	Enh	10/17/91	—	$9,795
4/3	XGA	Enh	10/30/90	—	$11,745
4/3	XGA	Enh	10/17/91	—	$12,495
8/6	XGA	Enh	04/23/91	01/17/92	$7,745
8/6	XGA	Enh	04/23/91	01/17/92	$10,395
8/6	XGA	Enh	10/17/91	—	$9,245
8/6	XGA	Enh	10/17/91	—	$11,895
8/6	XGA	Enh	10/30/90	01/17/92	$10,045
8/6	XGA	Enh	10/30/90	01/17/92	$11,995
8/6	XGA	Enh	04/23/91	01/17/92	$12,745
8/6	XGA	Enh	10/30/90	—	$13,895
8/6	XGA	Enh	04/23/91	—	$14,645

Highlights of the PS/1 include the items in this list:

- 10 MHz 286 processor
- 12-inch Video Graphics Array (VGA) display (color or black-and-white)
- IBM mouse
- 101-key IBM keyboard
- Built-in 2400 bits-per-second (bps) modem
- Free three-month subscription to Prodigy
- PS/1 Club, an on-line customer support service
- Microsoft Works integrated application software
- Ease of set-up and use
- Preloaded DOS and menu interface (on hard disk models)
- Possibility of future expansion with PS/1 options
- Special IBM warranty

The 386SX models also offer the following additional features:

- 16 MHz 386SX processor
- 2M RAM, expandable to 6M on the system board
- 12-inch Color Video Graphics Array (VGA) display

IBM has announced a special model (B84) of the PS/1 that will be similar to the B82 but will come preloaded with OS/2 version 2.0. With OS/2 version 2.0, PS/1 users will be able to run DOS, Windows, and OS/2 applications, exploiting virtually all software available, regardless of the environment for which the software was designed.

System Features

IBM designed the PS/1 to enable home consumers to buy everything in one convenient place. Most consumers can set up and use the PS/1 in 15 minutes. The setup is simple: Take the components out of the box, attach cables, plug in the system, and push one button. Because the user interface (in ROM) and DOS already are installed on the system, users select what they want to do from the first screen and (on the floppy-drive system) are prompted to insert the proper floppy disk or (on the hard-drive system) are presented with the program they select after the machine goes to the hard disk, on which all the software included with the PS/1 was preloaded.

One special feature of the PS/1 is its warranty. Although most repair service is available easily through IBM authorized dealers, you have also another option. IBM's Express Maintenance service provides parts directly to customers, normally within 48 hours. Because the PS/1 is a totally modular, snap-together unit, replacing any part of the system is a relatively easy task. You therefore have an alternate route for service if the dealer is too far away or does not have needed parts in stock.

The IBM PS/1 computer comes in several models. The following list includes the major features of each model.

286 models:

> 2011-M01: Black-and-white display, 512K memory
> 2011-C01: Color display, 512K memory
> 2011-M34: Black-and-white display, 30M hard disk, 1M memory
> 2011-C34: Color display, 30M hard disk, 1M memory

386SX models:

> 2121-C42: Color display, 40M hard disk, 2M memory
> 2121-B82: Color display, 80M hard disk, 2M memory
> 2121-C92: Color display, 129M hard disk, 2M memory

All PS/1 models also include a 2400 bps modem, software, and service— all in one box. On hard disk models, all the software and DOS are preloaded, and everything is configured for an immediate start after you plug in the system.

The more powerful PS/1models—the B82 and C92—also feature an 80 MB or 129MB hard drive, two 11-inch AT-compatible expansion slots, and come preloaded with Microsoft Windows 3.0 and Productivity Pack for Windows customized for the PS/1. These systems deliver enough power to run the latest DOS, Windows, and OS/2 software applications. They are ideal for small businesses or home offices. With Microsoft Productivity Pack, customers easily can learn more about Windows 3.0. The design of these systems enables two hard drives to be stacked one on top of the other. By adding the new 129 MB hard drive, you can expand the C92's storage capacity to 260 MB. *Note:* After its introduction, the C92, which has the 129MB hard disk standard, was available only through Sears Brand Central outlets. All other dealers or retail outlets can sell only the B82 as the top model. IBM did not make clear how long this exclusive distribution of the highest-end PS/1 would last, so you should check whether other outlets will carry it when you are ready to purchase. The only difference between the B82 and C92 models is the 80MB versus 129MB standard hard disk.

IBM is offering a comprehensive 386SX upgrade package for owners of the 286-based PS/1 systems. This upgrade will be available from December 1991 through December 1992. The PS/1 upgrade package will enable current PS/1 owners to exchange their 286 system unit for the PS/1 386SX B82 system unit.

The standard service and support provided with the PS/1 system is excellent. Although, if necessary, most repair service can be obtained easily through IBM authorized dealers, another route is available. IBM has a special toll-free service called Express Maintenance, which provides parts directly to the customer, normally within 48 hours.

Support is available from the PS/1 Club, an on-line support service, exclusively available to PS/1 owners through Prodigy seven days a week, 18 hours a day, 365 days a year. PS/1 owners receive product support in four ways:

- "Answer Bank," a database with answers to hundreds of commonly asked questions about computers

- "Info Exchange," an electronic bulletin board where users can write to other PS/1 Club members or to an IBM expert who will reply within 24 hours

- "Write to Us," where users can send comments and suggestions directly to IBM

- "News to Use," an on-line posting of PS/1-related announcements and usability tips

The PS/1 is compatible with the PS/2 Model 30-286 at the BIOS level (although the BIOS is not identical) and at most hardware interfaces. The PS/1 also is compatible with the original IBM AT system. The 286 PS/1 is about 50 percent faster than the IBM AT, whereas the 386SX versions are more than twice as fast as an AT. All PS/1 systems incorporate many features that would have been extra-cost options on the original IBM AT system. Because the PS/1, like the PS/2, has many features integrated on its motherboard, many standard types of adapter cards—such as graphics adapters, some disk controllers, and many memory upgrades—do not work with it.

System Expansion and Restrictions

The PS/1 has some significant limitations and restrictions to expansion. The biggest limitation is that the system has no standard expansion slots! Several 386SX models have a larger chassis that includes 2 slots standard, but these slots accept only 3/4-length (11 inch) boards. For systems that do not have any standard slots, an optional extra-cost expansion chassis provides three slots, but none of them accepts full-length expansion cards. Two of the slots in the expansion unit accept 3/4-length cards and the third accepts only a 1/2-length board (8 inches). This setup effectively prevents the use of many types of expansion cards such as network adapters, memory boards, and many others, because many of those boards are the full 13.1 inches long. The expansion chassis cannot be used for additional slots on units that include two standard slots. These units will be limited to having only two slots.

The PS/1 has 512K or 2MB of memory installed permanently on the motherboard, depending on the system. An additional connector especially for memory is available, which can be used to bring the installed memory up to as much as 16MB; however, IBM offers a board with a maximum of only 4M for this connector. This connector is nonstandard, so industry standard memory devices such as 9-bit or 36-bit SIMMs cannot be used. Third-party companies now offer memory-expansion cards with larger amounts of memory for the PS/1.

The limited number and kinds of possible expansion slots is a serious limitation, but less of a problem than it might seem at first, because of the special connectors the PS/1 provides for various options. The modem that comes with the system plugs into a special motherboard connector and does not require a slot. An additional music and game adapter is optionally available that plugs into another special mother-board connector. Finally, a single hard disk and a second floppy disk drive can be added also without requiring an expansion slot.

Although the PS/1 offers many options for expansion that do not require the expansion chassis, the fact that the expansion chassis is an extra-cost item and supports only 1/2- and 3/4-length boards is nevertheless a significant limitation to the system.

A final limitation of the PS/1 is that the system's memory is not parity-checked as has been the standard in all other IBM systems since the original IBM PC. Parity-checked memory is memory that uses an extra bit for every eight bits of memory to allow a cross-check of memory accuracy. The status of parity is monitored continuously in most systems so that if a memory value contains an error, it is found immediately and does not go undetected.

On the PS/1, memory errors can go undetected more easily than in other IBM or IBM-compatible systems that do offer standard parity-checking. This statement might sound shocking and seem to reflect a seriously crippling feature of the system, but, in comparison, Apple Macintosh systems also do not have parity-checked memory as a standard feature. A computer does not require parity-checking to function, but the more "mission critical" that information accuracy is, the more parity-checking becomes an issue. The lack of parity-checking makes the PS/1 less suited for business applications use.

Table 4.5 describes the technical specifications for the 286 PS/1.

Table 4.5 PS/1 286 Technical Specifications

System architecture

Microprocessor	80286
Clock speed	10 MHz
Bus type	ISA (Industry Standard Architecture)
Bus width	16-bit
Interrupt levels	16
Type	Edge-triggered
Shareable	No
DMA channels	7
DMA burst mode supported	No
Bus masters supported	No
Upgradeable processor complex	No
Standard on system board	512K (x01) 1M (x34)
Maximum on system board	2.5M
Maximum total memory	8.5M
Memory speed and type	120ns dynamic RAM

continues

Table 4.5 Continued

Memory

System-board memory socket type	Proprietary card
Number of memory-module sockets	1
Number available in standard	0 (x34)
configuration	1 (x01)
Memory used on system board	Soldered 512K bank, 512K/2M cards
Parity-checked memory	No
Memory cache controller	No
Wait states:	
System board	1
Adapter	1

Standard

ROM size	256K
ROM shadowing	No
User interface menu in ROM	Yes
Optional math coprocessor	No
Standard graphics	VGA (Video Graphics Array)
Standard display	Included
Monochrome	(M01,M34)
Color	(C01,C34)
Audio earphone jack	Yes
2400 bps modem	U.S./Canada only
Hayes-compatible	Yes
Phone cord and splitter included	Yes
RS232C serial ports	Optional, (requires expansion chassis)
UART chip used	NS16450
Maximum speed (bits/second)	19,200 bps
DMA data transfer support	No
Maximum number of ports	1
Pointing device (mouse) ports	1
IBM mouse included	Yes
Parallel printer ports	1
Bidirectional	Yes
CMOS real-time clock (RTC)	Yes
CMOS RAM	64 bytes
Battery life	10 years
Replaceable	Yes (Dallas module)

Disk storage

Internal disk and tape drive bays	2
Number of 3 1/2- and 5 1/4-inch bays	2/0
Standard floppy disk drives	1×1.44M
Optional floppy disk drives:	

Disk storage

5 1/4-inch 360K	Optional
5 1/4-inch 1.2M	Optional
3 1/2-inch 720K	No
3 1/2-inch 1.44M	Standard
3 1/2-inch 2.88M	No
Hard disk controller included	IDE connector on system board
IDE hard disks available	30M
Drive form factor	3 1/2-inch
Drive interface	IDE
Average access rate (ms)	19
Encoding scheme	RLL
BIOS drive type number	35
Cylinders	921
Heads	2
Sectors per track	33
Rotational speed (RPM)	3600
Interleave factor	4:1
Data transfer rate (K/second)	248
Automatic head parking	Yes

Expansion slots

Total adapter slots	0
Number of long and short slots	0/0
Number of 8-/16-/32-bit slots	0/0/0
Available slots	0
With optional expansion unit:	
Total adapter slots	3
Number of long and short slots	2/1
Number of 8-/16-/32-bit slots	0/3/0
Available slots	3

Keyboard specifications

101-key Enhanced Keyboard	Yes
Fast keyboard speed setting	Yes
Keyboard cable length	6 feet

Security features

Keylock:	
Locks cover	No
Locks keyboard	No
Keyboard password	No
Power-on password	No
Network server mode	No

continues

Table 4.5 Continued

Physical specifications

Footprint type	Desktop
Dimensions:	
Height	14.25 inches
Width footprint	10.75 inches
Width display	12.0 inches
Depth	17.0 inches
Weight:	
Color display	38.0 pounds
Mono display	31.0 pounds

Environmental specifications

Power supply:	
Worldwide (110/60, 220/50)	Yes
Auto-sensing and switching	Yes
Maximum current:	
90-137 VAC; color	2.5 amps
80-259 VAC; color	2.0 amps
90-137 VAC; mono	2.0 amps
80-259 VAC; mono	1.25 amps
Operating range:	
Temperature	50-95 degrees F
Relative humidity	8 to 80 percent
Heat (BTUs/hour)	358
FCC classification	Class B

Table 4.6 describes the technical specifications for the 386SX PS/1.

Table 4.6 PS/1 386SX Technical Specifications

System architecture

Microprocessor	80386SX
Clock speed	16 MHz
Bus type	ISA (Industry Standard Architecture)
Bus width	16-bit
Interrupt levels	16
Type	Edge-triggered
Shareable	No
DMA channels	7
DMA burst mode supported	No
Bus masters supported	No
Upgradeable processor complex	No

Memory

Standard on system board	2M
Maximum on system board	6M
Maximum total memory	16M
Memory speed and type	100ns dynamic RAM
System-board memory socket type	Proprietary card
Number of memory-module sockets	1
Number available in standard configuration	1
Memory used on system board	Soldered 2M bank, 2M/4M cards
Parity-checked memory	No
Memory cache controller	No
Wait states:	
System board	0-2
Adapter	0-2

Standard features

ROM size	256K
ROM shadowing	Yes
User interface menu in ROM	Yes
Optional math coprocessor	387SX
Coprocessor speed	16 MHz
Standard graphics	VGA (Video Graphics Array)
Standard display	Color, included
Audio earphone jack	Yes
2400 bps modem	U.S./Canada only
Hayes-compatible	Yes
Phone cord and splitter included	Yes
RS232C serial ports	Optional
UART chip used	NS16450
Maximum speed (bits/second)	19,200 bps
DMA data transfer support	No
Maximum number of ports	1
Pointing device (mouse) ports	1
IBM mouse included	Yes
Parallel printer ports	1
Bidirectional	Yes
CMOS real-time clock (RTC)	Yes
CMOS RAM	64 bytes
Battery life	10 years
Replaceable	Yes (Dallas module)

Disk storage

Internal disk and tape drive bays	2 (C42)
	3 (B82, C92)
Number of 3 1/2- and 5 1/4-inch bays	2/0 (C42)
	3/0 (B82, C92)
Standard floppy disk drives	1×1.44M

continues

Table 4.6 PS/1 386SX Technical Specifications

Disk storage

Optional floppy disk drives:	
5 1/4-inch 360K	Optional
5 1/4-inch 1.2M	Optional
3 1/2-inch 720K	No
3 1/2-inch 1.44M	Standard
3 1/2-inch 2.88M	No
Hard disk controller included	IDE connector on system board
IDE hard disks available	40M (C42)
	80M (B82)
	129M (C92)
Drive form factor	3 1/2-inch
Drive interface	IDE
Average access rate (ms)	21
Encoding scheme	RLL
Automatic head parking	Yes

Expansion slots

Total adapter slots	0 (C42)
	2 (B82, C92)
Number of long and short slots	0/0 (C42)
	0/2 (B82, C92)
Number of 8-/16-/32-bit slots	0/0/0 (C42)
	0/2/0 (B82, C92)
Available slots	0 (C42)
	2 (B82, C92)
With optional expansion unit:	
Total adapter slots	3 (C42)
Number of long and short slots	2/1 (C42)
Number of 8-/16-/32-bit slots	0/3/0 (C42)
Available slots	3 (C42)

Keyboard specifications

101-key Enhanced Keyboard	Yes
Fast keyboard speed setting	Yes
Keyboard cable length	6 feet

Security features

Keylock:	
Locks cover	No
Locks keyboard	No
Keyboard password	No
Power-on password	No
Network server mode	No

Physical specifications	
Footprint type	Desktop
Dimensions:	
Height	14.25 inches (C42)
	15.75 inches (B82, C92)
Width footprint	10.75 inches
Width display	12.0 inches
Depth	17.0 inches
Weight:	
Color display	39.0 pounds
Environmental specifications	
Power supply:	
Worldwide (110/60, 220/50)	Yes
Auto-sensing and switching	Yes
Maximum current:	
90-137 VAC; color	2.5 amps
80-259 VAC; color	2.0 amps
Operating range:	
Temperature	50-95 degrees F
Relative humidity	8 to 80 percent
Heat (BTUs/hour)	358
FCC classification	Class B

Table 4.7 shows the primary specifications and costs of the various PS/1 models, and table 4.8 shows the accessories available from IBM for the PS/1.

PS/2 Model 25

The PS/2 Model 25, the lowest-priced PS/2 family member, was introduced August 11, 1987 (see fig. 4.1). The Model 25 (8525) is a general-purpose system that incorporates the PC-style 8-bit slot architecture, enabling this system to accept most current adapters. The Model 25 uses the Intel 8086 processor and operates at 8 MHz with 0 wait states to read-only memory (ROM). This system is 40 percent smaller and more than twice as fast as the original IBM PC.

The Model 25's display is integrated into the system unit, which makes it look similar to the Apple Macintosh. With the Model 25, you can choose one of two keyboards: the IBM Space-Saving Keyboard or the IBM Enhanced Keyboard, which has a numeric keypad. You also can choose one of two displays: monochrome or color. A second 3 1/2-inch floppy disk drive, a 20M hard disk, and an additional 128K of RAM memory are available.

Table 4.7 PS/1 Model Summary

Part number	CPU	MHz	PLANAR MEMORY Std.	PLANAR MEMORY Max.	STANDARD Floppy drive	STANDARD Hard disk	Bus type
PS/1 286							
2011-M01	286	10	512K	2.5M	1×1.44M	—	ISA/16
2011-C01	286	10	512K	2.5M	1×1.44M	—	ISA/16
2011-M34	286	10	1M	2.5M	1×1.44M	30M	ISA/16
2011-C34	286	10	1M	2.5M	1×1.44M	30M	ISA/16
PS/1 SX							
2121-C42	386SX	16	2M	6M	1×1.44M	40M	ISA/16
2121-B82	386SX	16	2M	6M	1×1.44M	80M	ISA/16
2121-C92	386SX	16	2M	6M	1×1.44M	129M	ISA/16

Keyboards available include the Enhanced (101-key), Space-Saving (84-key), and Host-Connected (122-key). If "Any" is indicated, purchaser could choose any of the three. PS/1

Table 4.8 PS/1 Special Accessories

Description	Part number	Price	Notes
PS/1 286 to 386SX upgrade	93F2059	$1,045	Trade in x01 Model for B82 Model
PS/1 286 to 386SX upgrade	93F2059	845	Trade in x34 Model for B82 Model
PS/1 color display upgrade	1057108	699	Upgrade for mono systems
PS/1 512K memory card	1057035	109	Upgrades to 1M on motherboard
PS/12M memory card	1057660	279	Upgrades to 2.5M on motherboard
PS/12M memory card	92F9935	279	Upgrades to 4M on 386SX motherboard
PS/14M memory card	92F9694	549	Upgrades to 6M on 386SX motherboard
5 1/4-inch 360K PS/1 286 drive	1057139	299	Attaches to PS/1
5 1/4-inch 360K PS/1 SX drive	92F9333	299	Attaches to PS/1
5 1/4-inch 1.2M PS/1 286 drive	1057191	299	Attaches to PS/1
5 1/4-inch 1.2M PS/1 SX drive	92F9334	299	Attaches to PS/1
3 1/2-inch 1.44M PS/1 drive	1057039	249	PS/1 internal drive

Total/ available slots	STANDARD		Date introduced	Date withdrawn	List price
	Video	KB			
0	VGA	Enh	06/26/90	—	$995
0	VGA	Enh	06/26/90	—	$1,449
0	VGA	Enh	06/26/90	—	$1,649
0	VGA	Enh	06/26/90	—	$1,999
0	VGA	Enh	10/07/91	—	$1,699
2/2	VGA	Enh	10/07/91	—	$2,199
2/2	VGA	Enh	10/07/91	—	$2,499

Models Mxx have a built-in monochrome analog display, and Models Cxx have the Color Analog Display.

Description	Part number	Price	Notes
30M 3 1/2-inch IDE drive	1057036	$ 599	For PS/1-M01/C01
80M 3 1/2-inch IDE drive	92F9937	1,060	For PS/1 386SX
129M 3 1/2-inch IDE drive	92F9938	1,500	For PS/1 386SX
PS/1 adapter expansion unit	1057028	169	Three slots: two 11-inch, one 9.5-inch
AT serial/parallel adapter	6450215	161	Requires expansion unit
Audio card/joystick connector	1057735	129	Attaches to 286 motherboard
Audio card/joystick connector	92F9932	129	Attaches to 386SX motherboard
Audio card/joystick for 286	1057064	249	Includes joystick, MIDI connector
Second joystick	1057109	39	Includes Y-cable for 1057064
PS/1 two-piece dust cover set	95F1136	20	Water-repellent, antistatic

The PS/1 286 to 386 upgrade is not sold through dealers and must be ordered by calling IBM Direct at 1-800-421-5448. This upgrade will be available through 12/92.

The Model 25 offers the same text and graphics capabilities as the IBM PS/2 Model 30. The built-in MultiColor Graphics Array (MCGA) can display as many as 256 colors on the system's color monitor (from a palette of more than 256,000 colors) or 64 shades of gray on the monochrome monitor.

Two 8-bit expansion slots enable you to attach many existing personal computer cards. A 12-inch analog display (color or monochrome), a display adapter, an RS-232C serial adapter, a parallel adapter, and a floppy disk drive adapter are standard, increasing the function of the standard unit. Figure 4.2 shows the rear panel of the Model 25.

Each model of the PS/2 Model 25 includes these features:

- Approximately twice the speed of the IBM PC or IBM XT

- Two 8-bit expansion slots (one full-size and one 8-inch), which allows attachment of many existing PC cards

- Integrated MultiColor Graphics Array (MCGA) graphics

    Displays 256 colors from 262,144 possible colors

    Displays 64 shades of gray

- 512K of RAM standard, expandable to 640K on the motherboard

- Integrated floppy disk controller for as many as two 3 1/2-inch 720K drives

- One 3 1/2-inch (720K) floppy disk drive

- 12-inch analog display (color or monochrome)

- IBM Space-Saving Keyboard or Enhanced Keyboard

- Integrated serial port, parallel port, mouse port, and keyboard port

- Audio earphone connector

- Math coprocessor socket

- Advanced technology that eliminates jumpers and switches

Some PC adapters do not work in the Model 25 for various reasons. Because of the integrated functions on the Model 25 motherboard, certain options (such as PC types of memory upgrades, floppy controllers, and graphics adapters) might conflict with what is already present on the motherboard. Moreover, because of physical constraints, adapter cards thicker than 0.8 inch might not work, and one of the two slots is a half-length slot. The integrated MCGA does not support modes that support the 5151 Monochrome Display. The Model 25 has analog graphics output and does not support digital display devices. Figures 4.3 and 4.4 illustrate the locations of internal components of the PS/2 Model 25.

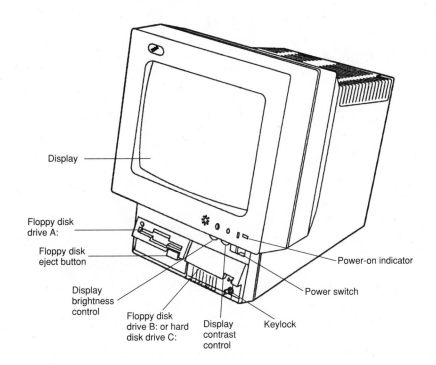

Display

Floppy disk
drive A:

Floppy disk
eject button

Display
brightness
control

Floppy disk
drive B: or hard
disk drive C:

Display
contrast
control

Keylock

Power-on indicator

Power switch

Fig. 4.1

PS/2 Model 25
(front view).

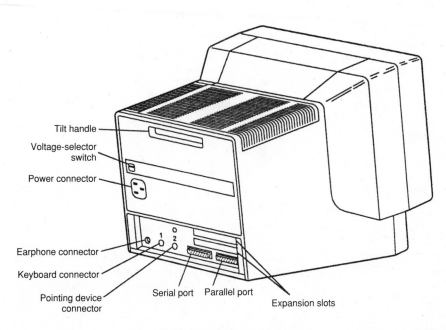

Tilt handle

Voltage-selector
switch

Power connector

Earphone connector

Keyboard connector

Pointing device
connector

Serial port

Parallel port

Expansion slots

Fig. 4.2

PS/2 Model 25
(rear view).

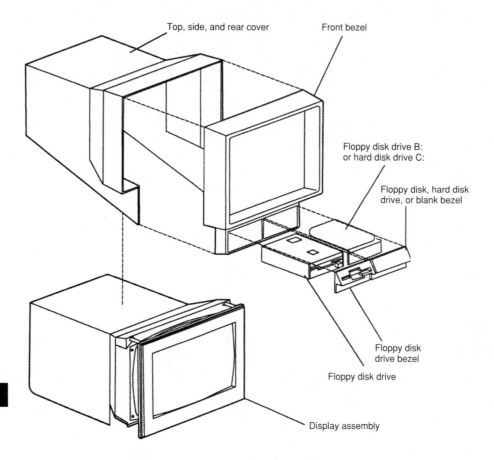

Top, side, and rear cover

Front bezel

Floppy disk drive B:
or hard disk drive C:

Floppy disk, hard disk
drive, or blank bezel

Floppy disk
drive bezel

Floppy disk drive

Display assembly

Fig. 4.3

PS/2 Model 25
interior (part 1).

IBM has expanded the usefulness of the Model 25 in two main ways: by offering a version for use on a local area network (LAN) and by providing hard disks for data and program storage.

LAN Support

On June 2, 1988, IBM introduced a specially configured version of the Model 25, called the Model 25 LAN Station, or LS. This system is basically a standard Model 25 preconfigured with the IBM Token Ring Network PC Adapter for use in a LAN. The Model 25 LS is available in both monochrome (8525-L01) and color (8525-L04) versions. The Models L01 and L04 include the Enhanced Keyboard and 640K of RAM. Because the Token Ring Adapter II card uses the half-length expansion slot, the LS models have only a single full-length expansion slot remaining in the system unit for other adapter boards. Both models come with one 3 1/2-inch (720K) floppy disk drive. A second 720K floppy or a 20M hard drive is available.

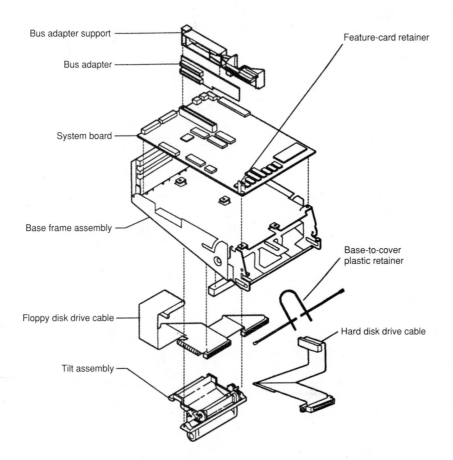

Bus adapter support

Bus adapter

System board

Base frame assembly

Floppy disk drive cable

Tilt assembly

Feature-card retainer

Base-to-cover
plastic retainer

Hard disk drive cable

Fig. 4.4

PS/2 Model 25
interior (part 2).

LAN software for operating on a network is not supplied with this system and must be purchased separately. Because many people buy LAN software from a third party such as Novell, the fact that the software support is "unbundled" is beneficial. You then can choose which software to use.

Hard Disk Drives

For increased storage, IBM made a 20M hard disk drive for the Model 25. Each system has the capacity to use one hard disk drive. On models with two floppy disk drives, the 20M hard disk replaces the second floppy disk drive.

The IBM PS/2 Model 25 20M hard disk drive (78X8958) features 20M of storage, 3 1/2-inch hard disk technology, a stepper motor head-actuator mechanism, and a keylocked bezel, which disables the keyboard. It has also a built-in controller that plugs into a special port on the motherboard and does not occupy an expansion slot. (Because the controller is integrated on the drive, the term IDE—Integrated Drive Electronics—is used to describe this type of drive.) The hard disk drive is essentially the same one used in the Model 30. The built-in controller on this drive unit conserves a precious slot in the Model 25. Because the Model 25 has only two slots, conserving one of them is an important consideration.

IBM produced another hard disk for the Model 25—the 20M hard disk drive with adapter (27F4130). The controller uses RLL encoding and achieves higher data-transmission speeds than the built-in controller on the other hard drive. Like the currently available hard drive for the Model 25, the older drive uses 3 1/2-inch hard disk technology, a stepper motor head-actuator mechanism, and a keylocked bezel, which disables the keyboard. The older drive uses a higher-speed stepper motor and also has a special actuator that parks the heads automatically when the power is turned off. This drive, however, required a separate controller, which occupies one of only two slots available in the Model 25; probably because of this limitation, IBM has discontinued production of this hard disk drive.

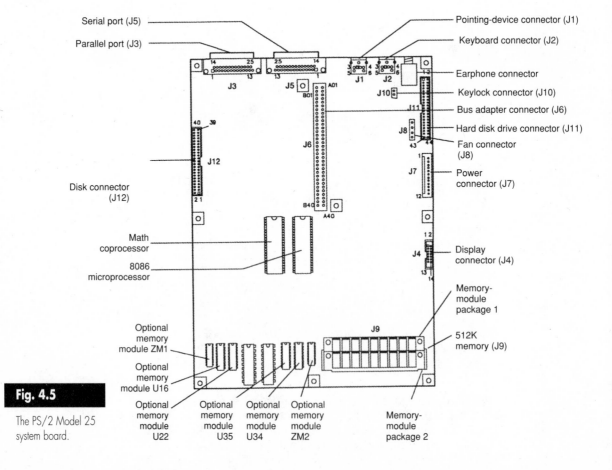

Fig. 4.5

The PS/2 Model 25 system board.

Table 4.9 lists the PS/2 Model 25 technical specifications; figure 4.5 shows the PS/2 Model 25 system board.

Table 4.9 PS/2 Model 25 Technical Specifications

System architecture

Microprocessor	8086
Clock speed	8 MHz
Bus type	ISA (Industry Standard Architecture)
Bus width	8-bit
Interrupt levels	8
Type	Edge-triggered
Shareable	No
DMA channels	3
DMA burst-mode supported	No
Bus masters supported	No
Upgradeable processor complex	No

Memory

Standard on system board	512K
Maximum on system board	640K
Maximum total memory	640K
Memory speed and type	150ns dynamic RAM
System board memory-socket type	9-bit SIMM (single in-line memory module)
Number of memory-module sockets	2
Number available in standard configuration	0
Memory used on system board	Two 256K 9-bit SIMMs, one socketed bank of four 64Kx4-bit and two 64Kx1-bit chips
Memory cache controller	No
Wait states:	
System board	0
Adapter	4

Standard features

ROM size	64K
ROM shadowing	No
Optional math coprocessor	8087
Coprocessor speed	8 MHz
Standard graphics	MCGA (MultiColor Graphics Array)
Built-in display	Yes
Monochrome	Model 8525-xx1
Color	Model 82525-xx4
Dot pitch (mm)	0.38
Audio earphone jack	Yes

continues

Table 4.9 Continued

Standard features

Color Model 8525-xx4	
Dot pitch (mm)	0.38
Audio earphone jack	Yes
RS232C serial ports	1
UART chip used	NS8250B
Maximum speed	9,600 bps
Maximum number ports	2
Pointing device (mouse) ports	1
Parallel printer ports	1
Bidirectional	Yes
Maximum number ports	2
CMOS real-time clock (RTC)	No
CMOS RAM	None

Disk storage

Internal disk and tape drive bays	2	
Number of 3 1/2- and 5 1/4-inch bays	2/0	
Standard floppy disk drives	1×720K	
Optional floppy disk drives:		
5 1/4-inch 360K	Optional	
5 1/4-inch 1.2M	No	
3 1/2-inch 720K	Standard	
3 1/2-inch 1.44M	No	
3 1/2-inch 2.88M	No	
Hard disk controller included:	(IDE connector on system board and/or an ST-506/412 RLL controller in the short slot)	
IDE/ST-506 hard disks available	20M	
Drive form factor	3 1/2-inch	
Drive interface	IDE	ST-506
Average access rate (ms)	80	38
Encoding scheme	MFM	RLL
BIOS drive type number	26	36
Cylinders	612	402
Heads	4	4
Sectors per track	17	26
Rotational speed (RPM)	3600	3600
Interleave factor	3:1	3:1
Data transfer rate (K/second)	170	260
Automatic head parking	No	Yes

Expansion slots

Total adapter slots	2
Number of long and short slots	1/1
Number of 8-/16-/32-bit slots	2/0/0
Available slots	2

Keyboard specifications

101-key Enhanced Keyboard	Yes (Gxx,Lxx)
84-key Space-Saving Keyboard	Yes (0xx)
Fast keyboard speed setting	No
Keyboard cable length:	
Space-Saving Keyboard	5 feet
Enhanced Keyboard	6 feet

Security features

Keylock:	
Locks cover	Yes (with optional hard disk)
Locks keyboard	Yes
Keyboard password	No
Power-on password	No
Network server mode	No

Physical specifications

Footprint type	Desktop
Dimensions:	
Height	15.0 inches
Width footprint	9.5 inches
Width display	12.6 inches
Depth	14.7 inches
Weight:	
001/G01	31.0 pounds
L01	32.0 pounds
004/G04	36.0 pounds
L04	37.0 pounds
Carrying case	Optional

Environmental specifications

Power-supply output	90 watts (001/G01) 115 watts (004/G04)
Worldwide (110/60,220/50)	Yes
Auto-sensing/switching	Manual switch
Maximum current:	
90-137 VAC	2.8 amps
80-259 VAC	1.7 amps
Operating range:	
Temperature	60-90 degrees F
Relative humidity	8-80 percent
Maximum operating altitude	7,000 feet
Heat (BTUs/hour)	683
Noise (Avg dB, operating, 1m)	44 dB
FCC classification	Class B

Table 4.10 shows the primary specifications and costs of the different versions of PS/2 Model 25.

Table 4.10 IBM PS/2 Model 25 Model Summary

Part number	CPU	MHz	PLANAR MEMORY Std.	PLANAR MEMORY Max.	STANDARD Floppy drive	STANDARD Hard disk	Bus type
25							
8525-001	8086	8	512K	640K	1×720K	—	ISA/8
8525-G01	8086	8	512K	640K	1×720K	—	ISA/8
8525-004	8086	8	512K	640K	1×720K	—	ISA/8
8525-G04	8086	8	512K	640K	1×720K	—	ISA/8
25 LS							
8525-L01	8086	8	640K	640K	1×720K	—	ISA/8
8525-L04	8086	8	640K	640K	1×720K	—	ISA/8

Models that end in xx1 have the monochrome analog display as a built-in feature; models that end in xx4 have the color display. The 25 LS models include also an IBM Token Ring Adapter II card in the half-length slot.

PS/2 Model 30

The IBM PS/2 Model 30 (IBM 8530), announced April 2, 1987, is a general-purpose system designed to offer more features and performance than the IBM PC and XT—especially in display graphics—and at a lower price. This system includes as standard many features built into the system board, including a graphics adapter, a parallel port, a serial port, a clock calendar, 640K of RAM, and a mouse port. The Model 30 also uses many existing PC adapter cards for further expansion due to its ISA 8-bit slots. Figure 4.6 shows a front view and figure 4.7 shows a rear-panel view of the Model 30. As of December 27, 1990, all versions of the PS/2 Model 30 have been discontinued and no longer are available.

The Model 30 is based on an 8086 microprocessor, running at 8 MHz with 0 wait states. Performance is enhanced by the use of a 16-bit-wide data path to the motherboard memory, which results in internal processing speed nearly comparable to a 6 MHz AT and more than twice as fast as the 8088-based PC or XT.

Total/ available slots	STANDARD		Date introduced	Date withdrawn	List price
	Video	KB			
2/2	MCGA	SS	08/04/87	—	$1,350
2/2	MCGA	Enh	08/04/87	—	$1,395
2/2	MCGA	SS	08/04/87	—	$1,695
2/2	MCGA	Enh	08/04/87	—	$1,740
2/1	MCGA	Enh	06/02/88	—	$2,139
2/1	MCGA	Enh	06/02/88	—	$2,484

Keyboards available include the Enhanced (101-key), Space-Saving (84-key), and Host-Connected (122-key). If "Any" is indicated, purchaser can choose any of the three.

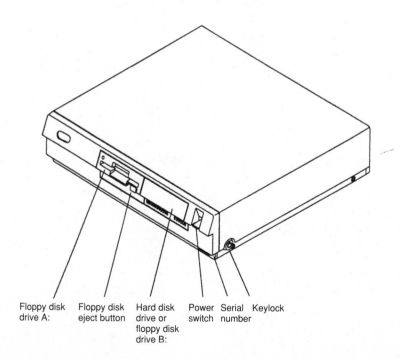

Floppy disk drive A: Floppy disk eject button Hard disk drive or floppy disk drive B: Power switch Serial number Keylock

Fig. 4.6

PS/2 Model 30.

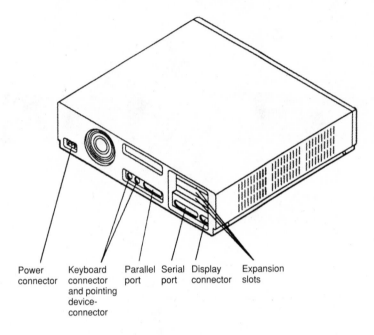

Fig. 4.7

PS/2 Model 30
(rear view).

Power
connector

Keyboard
connector
and pointing
device-
connector

Parallel
port

Serial
port

Display
connector

Expansion
slots

Major features of the Model 30 include the items in this list:

- Many functions are integrated on the motherboard, including disk controllers, graphics, and ports

- Integrated MCGA graphics displays as many as 256 colors or 64 shades of gray

- Approximately twice the performance speed of 8088-based IBM PC and IBM XT systems

- Smaller design, with reduced power requirements

- Worldwide power supply

- Switchless installation and configuration

- 640K random-access memory (RAM)

- 16-bit access to motherboard memory

- Integrated floppy disk controller for two 720K drives

- Integrated serial port, parallel port, mouse port, and keyboard port

- IBM Enhanced Keyboard

- Time-of-day clock with extended-life battery

■ Socket for a math coprocessor

■ Three expansion slots to accommodate PC or XT 8-bit adapter cards

Figure 4.8 shows an interior view of the Model 30.

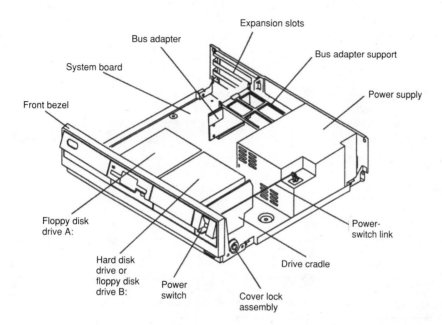

Fig. 4.8

PS/2 Model 30 interior.

The Model 30 was available in three versions: the 30-001, with one 3 1/2-inch (720K) floppy drive; the 30-002, with two 3 1/2-inch (720K) floppy drives; and the 30-021, with a 20M hard disk drive and a single 3 1/2-inch (720K) floppy drive. All models included 640K RAM.

Graphics Adapter

MultiColor Graphics Array (MCGA), the graphics adapter function integrated into the Model 30 motherboard, supports all Color Graphics Adapter (CGA) modes when an analog PS/2 display is attached. Other digital displays are incompatible. In addition to providing existing CGA mode support, MCGA supports four expanded modes, a subset of the VGA processor on Models 50 and higher:

640×480 by 2 colors—all points addressable

320×200 by 256 colors—all points addressable

40×25 by 16 colors for text (8-by-16-character box)

80×25 by 16 colors for text (8-by-16-character box)

The integrated graphics adapter automatically switches from color to 64 shades of gray when connected to a monochrome analog display. This feature allows users who prefer a monochrome display to execute color-based applications without compatibility problems or troublesome software reconfiguration.

Table 4.11 lists the PS/2 Model 30 technical specifications.

Table 4.11 PS/2 Model 30 Technical Specifications

System architecture	
Microprocessor	8086
Clock speed	8 MHz
Bus type	ISA (Industry Standard Architecture)
Bus width	8-bit
Interrupt levels	8
Type	Edge-triggered
Shareable	No
DMA channels	3
DMA burst mode supported	No
Bus masters supported	No
Upgradeable processor complex	No

Memory	
Standard on system board	640K
Maximum on system board	640K
Maximum total memory	640K
Memory speed and type	150ns dynamic RAM
System board memory-socket type	9-bit SIMM (single in-line memory module)
Number of memory-module sockets	2
Number available in standard configuration	0
Memory used on system board	Two 256K 9-bit SIMMs, one soldered bank of four 64K×4-bit and two 64K×1-bit chips.
Memory cache controller	No
Wait states:	
System board	0
Adapter	4

Standard features

ROM size	64K
ROM shadowing	No
Optional math coprocessor	8087
Coprocessor speed	8 MHz
Standard graphics	MCGA (MultiColor Graphics Array)
RS232C serial ports	1
UART chip used	NS8250B
Maximum speed (bits per second)	9,600 bps
Maximum number of ports supported	2
Pointing device (mouse) ports	1
Parallel printer port	1
Bidirectional	Yes
Maximum number of ports supported	2
CMOS real-time clock (RTC)	Yes
CMOS RAM	None
Battery life	5 years
Replaceable	Yes (replace bus adapter)

Disk storage

Internal disk and tape drive bays	2
Number of 3 1/2- and 5 1/4-inch bays	2/0
Standard floppy drives	1×720K
2×720K (002)	
Optional floppy drives:	
5 1/4-inch 360K	Optional
5 1/4-inch 1.2M	No
3 1/2-inch 720K	Standard
3 1/2-inch 1.44M	No
3 1/2-inch 2.88M	No
Hard disk controller included	IDE connector on system board
IDE hard disks available	20M
Drive form factor	3 1/2-inch
Controller type	IDE
Average access rate (ms)	80
Encoding scheme	MFM
BIOS drive type number	26
Cylinders	612
Heads	4
Sectors per track	17

continues

Table 4.11 Continued

Disk storage

Rotational speed (RPM)	3600
Interleave factor	3:1
Data transfer rate (K/second)	170
Automatic head parking	No

Expansion slots

Total adapter slots	3
Number of long and short slots	3/0
Number of 8-/16-/32-bit slots	3/0/0
Available slots	3

Keyboard specifications

101-key Enhanced Keyboard	Yes
Fast keyboard speed setting	No
Keyboard cable length	3 feet

Security features

Keylock:	
Locks cover	Yes
Locks keyboard	Yes
Keyboard password	No

Table 4.12 shows the primary specifications and costs of the different versions of PS/2 Model 30.

Table 4.12 IBM PS/2 Model 30 Model Summary

Part number	CPU	MHz	PLANAR MEMORY Std.	Max.	STANDARD Floppy drive	Hard disk	Bus type
30							
8530-001	8086	8	640K	640K	1×720K	—	ISA/8
8530-002	8086	8	640K	640K	2×720K	—	ISA/8
8530-021	8086	8	640K	640K	1×720K	30M	ISA/8

All models of the 8530 have been discontinued and are no longer available from IBM.

Security features	
Power-on password	No
Network server mode	No

Physical specifications	
Footprint type	Desktop
Dimensions:	
Height	4.0 inches
Width	15.6 inches
Depth	16.0 inches
Weight:	
00x	17.5 pounds
021	21.0 pounds

Environmental specifications	
Power-supply output	70 watts
Worldwide (110/60,220/50)	Yes
Auto-sensing/switching	Yes
Maximum current:	
90-137 VAC	1.5 amps
180-265 VAC	0.75 amps
Operating range:	
Temperature	60-90 degrees F
Relative humidity	8-80 percent
Maximum operating altitude	7,000 feet
Heat (BTUs/hour)	341
Noise (Average dB, operating, 1m)	37.5 dB
FCC classification	Class B

Total/ available slots	STANDARD Video	KB	Date introduced	Date withdrawn	List price
3/3	MCGA	Enh	04/04/89	12/27/90	$1,695
3/3	MCGA	Enh	04/02/87	07/05/89	$1,695
3/3	MCGA	Enh	04/02/87	12/27/90	$2,255

Figures 4.9 and 4.10 show the system boards for the PS/2 Model 30 (8530-001) and the PS/2 Model 30.

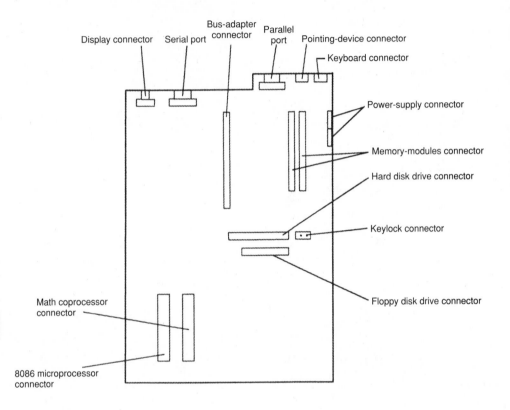

Fig. 4.9

PS/2 Model 30 (8530-001) system board.

PS/2 Model 25 286

Introduced on May 10, 1990 the PS/2 Model 25 286 (8525) unit is an enhanced version of the PS/2 Model 25. It is a standard Model 25 with an upgraded motherboard that makes it an AT-type system. This system features an 80286 microprocessor, expanded system-board memory (1M to 4M), high-density 3 1/2-inch (1.44M) floppy disk drives, and an integrated 12-inch VGA color monitor. The Model 25 286 utilizes the 80286 processor operating at 10 MHz with 1 wait state to system memory and has the following integrated functions: parallel port, serial port, pointing device port, keyboard port, an audio earphone connector, 1.44M floppy disk drive support, and VGA graphics. The Model 25 286 is offered in floppy drive only and 30M hard disk models with the IBM

Enhanced (101-key) or Space-Saving (84-key) Keyboard. It features 1M standard memory, with a maximum of 4M on the system board. The Model 25 286 is physically very similar to the Model 25 (see figs. 4.1 through 4.4 earlier in this chapter, which show exterior and interior views of the Model 25).

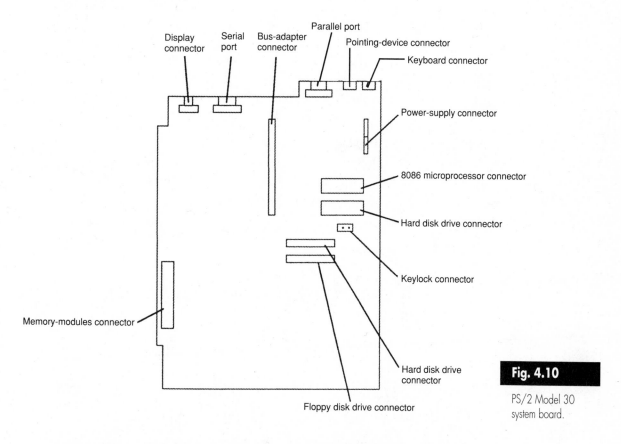

Fig. 4.10

PS/2 Model 30 system board.

The Model 25 286 differs significantly from the Model 25: It is a full AT-class system, and the original Model 25 is a PC-class system. They differ in virtually every way except appearance. (Refer to figures 4.1 through 4.4.) The Model 25 286 has a high-density floppy disk controller and a full VGA adapter integrated on the system board. An integrated color display is the only one offered. System memory can be increased to 4M on the system board and can address a maximum of 16M, providing functionality with DOS and Windows. As an AT-class system, the Model 25 286 is capable of running OS/2; the Model 25 is not. The Model 25 286 makes a perfect LAN workstation, although it is not sold preconfigured as one.

Like the Model 25, the Model 25 286 is compatible with the IBM AT at the BIOS interface level (although the BIOS is not identical) and at most hardware interfaces. Because many features are integrated on the motherboard in this system, many cards—graphics adapters, some disk controllers, and others—do not work with this system, and memory adapters that are not flexible in setting the starting memory address might not work either.

The motherboard in this system is identical to that of the Model 30 286. The BIOS is the same as the Model 30 286 as well, at least for the later versions.

The versions of this PS/2 model differ in type of keyboard (Enhanced or Space-Saving) and whether a 30M hard disk is included. Hard disks are available from IBM that will fit this system in sizes from 20M through 45M, but only the 30M is installed as standard. Hard disks are available from other manufacturers as well.

Figure 4.11 shows the Model 25 286 (and also 30 286) motherboard.

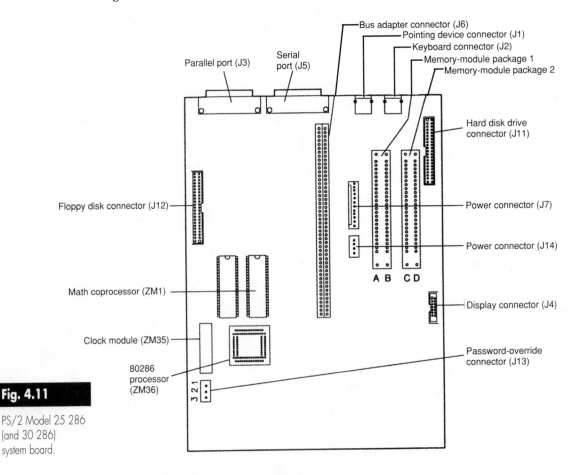

Fig. 4.11

PS/2 Model 25 286 (and 30 286) system board.

Table 4.13 lists the technical specifications for the PS/2 Model 25 286.

Table 4.13 PS/2 Model 25 286 Technical Specifications

System architecture

Microprocessor	80286
Clock speed	10 MHz
Bus type	ISA (Industry Standard Architecture)
Bus width	16-bit
Interrupt levels	16
Type	Edge-triggered
Shareable	No
DMA channels	7
DMA burst mode supported	No
Bus masters supported	No
Upgradeable processor complex	No

Memory

Standard on system board	1M
Maximum on system board	4M
Maximum total memory	16M
Memory speed and type	120ns dynamic RAM
System board memory-socket type	9-bit SIMM (single in-line memory module)
Number of memory-module sockets	4
Number available in standard configuration	2
Memory used on system board	256K/1M 9-bit SIMMs
Memory cache controller	No
Wait states:	
System board	1
Adapter	1

Standard features

ROM size	128K
ROM shadowing	No
Optional math coprocessor	80287
Coprocessor speed	6.67 MHz
Standard graphics	VGA (Video Graphics Array)
Built-in display	Yes
Monochrome	No
Color	(006,G06)
Dot pitch (mm)	.28
Audio earphone jack	Yes
RS232C serial ports	1
UART chip used	NS16450

continues

Table 4.13 Continued

Standard features

Maximum speed	19,200 bps
Maximum number of ports supported	2
Pointing device (mouse) ports	1
Parallel printer ports	1
Bidirectional	Yes
Maximum number of ports supported	2
CMOS real-time clock (RTC)	Yes
CMOS RAM	64 bytes
Battery life	10 years
Replaceable	Yes (Dallas module)

Disk storage

Internal disk and tape drive bays	2
Number of 3 1/2- and 5 1/4-inch bays	2/0
Standard floppy drives	1×1.44M

Optional floppy drives

5 1/4-inch 360K	Optional
5 1/4-inch 1.2M	No
3 1/2-inch 720K	No
3 1/2-inch 1.44M	Standard
3 1/2-inch 2.88M	No

Hard disk controller included:		IDE connector on system board			
IDE hard disks available		20/30/45M			
Drive form factor		3 1/2-inch			
Drive interface		IDE			
Drive capacity	20M	20M	30M	30M	45M
Average access rate (ms)	80	27	27	19	32
Encoding scheme	MFM	RLL	RLL	RLL	RLL
BIOS drive type number	26	34	33	35	37
Cylinders	612	775	614	921	580
Heads	4	2	4	2	6
Sectors per track	17	27	25	33	26
Rotational speed (RPM)	3600	3600	3600	3600	3600
Interleave factor	2:1	3:1	3:1	4:1	3:1
Data transfer rate (K/second)	255	270	250	248	260
Automatic head parking	No	No	No	Yes	Yes

Expansion slots

Total adapter slots	2
Number of long and short slots	1/1

Expansion slots	
Number of 8-/16-/32-bit slots	0/2/0
Available slots	2

Keyboard specifications	
101-key Enhanced Keyboard	Yes (Gxx)
84-key Space-Saving Keyboard	Yes (0xx)
Fast keyboard speed setting	Yes
Keyboard cable length:	
Space-Saving Keyboard	5 feet
Enhanced Keyboard	6 feet

Security features	
Keylock:	
Locks cover	Yes (x36)
Locks keyboard	No
Keyboard password	Yes
Power-on password	Yes
Network server mode	Yes

Physical specifications	
Footprint type	Desktop
Dimensions:	
Height	15.0 inches
Footprint width	9.5 inches
Display width	12.6 inches
Depth	14.7 inches
Weight:	
x06	35.3 lbs
x36	37.0 lbs
Carrying case	Optional

Environmental specifications	
Power-supply output	124.5 watts
Worldwide (110/60,220/50)	Yes
Auto-sensing/switching	Manual switch
Maximum current:	
90-137 VAC	3.0 amps
80-259 VAC	1.7 amps
Operating range:	
Temperature	60-90 degrees F
Relative humidity	8-80 percent
Maximum operating altitude	7,000 feet
Heat (BTUs/hour)	654
Noise (Average dB, operating, 1m)	51 dB
FCC classification	Class B

Table 4.14 shows the primary specifications and costs of the different versions of PS/2 Model 25 286.

Table 4.14 IBM PS/2 Model 25 286 Model Summary

Part number	CPU	MHz	PLANAR MEMORY Std.	Max.	STANDARD Floppy drive	Hard disk	Bus type
25 286							
8525-006	286	10	1M	4M	1×1.44M	—	ISA/16
8525-G06	286	10	1M	4M	1×1.44M	—	ISA/16
8525-036	286	10	1M	4M	1×1.44M	30M	ISA/16
8525-G36	286	10	1M	4M	1×1.44M	30M	ISA/16

Keyboards available include the Enhanced (101-key), Space-Saving (84-key), and Host-Connected (122-key). If "Any" is indicated, purchaser could choose any of the three.

PS/2 Model 30 286

The IBM PS/2 Model 30 286 (8530), introduced September 13, 1988, was the first PS/2 system with the full 16-bit ISA slot design in the original IBM AT and IBM XT 286 systems. Some people considered the Model 30 286 a reintroduction of the IBM AT; in slot design, it was. IBM supports both original Industry Standard Architecture (ISA) and Micro Channel Architecture (MCA). MCA-equipped PS/2 systems, however, are still (and will be for some time) IBM's primary platform. Figure 4.12 shows a front view and figure 4.13 shows a rear view of the Model 30 286.

The PS/2 Model 30 286 is a 80286 version of the Model 30. Although it shares the shape and form of the Model 30, its motherboard and circuitry are very different. The Model 30 is a PC-type system, and the Model 30 286 is an AT-type system. The Model 30 286 has processor performance equal to the Model 50 and includes a 1.44M floppy disk drive and VGA graphics. The Model 30 286 uses the Intel 80286 processor and operates at 10 MHz with 1 wait state to ROM. In addition to accepting most IBM PC and XT adapter cards, the Model 30 286 accepts most AT adapter cards. Figure 4.14 shows an interior view if the Model 30 286.

You can think of the Model 30 286 as equal to the Model 50, except that it uses ISA slots rather than MCA slots. The Model 30 286 is very similar to the Model 25 286. In fact, the motherboards in the two systems are identical. The Models 25 286 and 30 286 could be considered identical systems in hardware and BIOS; they differ only in physical shape and form.

| Total/ available slots | STANDARD | | Date introduced | Date withdrawn | List price |
	Video	KB			
2/2	VGA	SS	05/10/90	—	$2,135
2/2	VGA	Enh	05/10/90	—	$2,135
2/2	VGA	SS	05/10/90	—	$2,705
2/2	VGA	Enh	05/10/90	—	$2,705

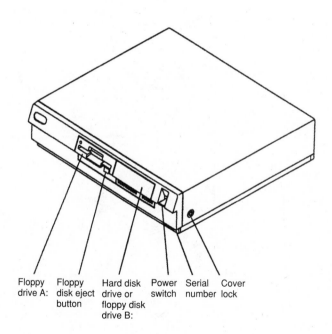

Floppy drive A: Floppy disk eject button Hard disk drive or floppy disk drive B: Power switch Serial number Cover lock

Fig. 4.12

PS/2 Model 30 286.

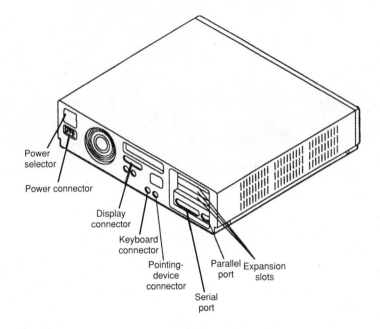

Fig. 4.13

PS/2 Model 30 286
(rear view).

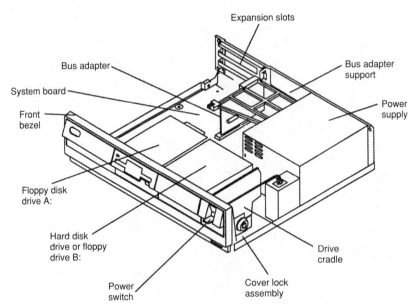

Fig. 4.14

PS/2 Model 30 286
(interior view).

The PS/2 Model 30 286 includes these standard features:

- Greatly improved performance over the XT, the AT, and 8086-based versions of the Model 25 and Model 30
- 10 MHz 80286 16-bit microprocessor, 1 wait state
- Optional 80287 coprocessor
- 16-bit ISA bus for adapters
- Three full-sized slots
- 1M random-access memory (RAM) standard
- Memory expansion to 4M on the system board
- 1.44M, 3 1/2-inch floppy disk drive
- Universal, automatic voltage-sensing power supply
- Keyboard port, serial/asynchronous port, parallel port, mouse port, and Video Graphics Array (VGA) port
- IBM Enhanced Keyboard
- Switchless installation and configuration

Several versions of the Model 30 286 have been available. The Model E01 (8530-E01) was a single floppy disk drive version of the Model 30 286 (without a hard disk drive). An optional 3 1/2-inch 20M hard disk drive (27F4969) was available for this model. The second model (8530-E21) included the 20M drive as a standard feature. Otherwise, these models were identical. The 30 286 was then available with 30M and 45M IDE (Integrated Drive Electronics) hard disk drives that plug into a modified slot connector on the motherboard. As of May 4, 1992, even these newer models will have been discontinued. Currently, all 8530 systems have been withdrawn from marketing by IBM.

The PS/2 Model 30 286 is compatible with the PC, XT, and AT at the BIOS level and at most hardware interfaces. Because many components are included on the motherboard, however, many boards that could be used in the standard PC, XT, or AT systems do not work in the Model 30 286, even though it has the ISA-style slots. Boards not likely to work include graphics adapters, some memory adapters (especially those that are not flexible in setting the starting memory address), and some other cards. Because of the built-in VGA, an analog display is required.

Available versions of this model differ only in the standard hard disk supplied with the unit. Available models offer no hard drive, a 30M hard drive, or a 45M hard drive. Hard disks for installation after you purchase the system are available from other manufacturers.

Table 4.15 lists the technical specifications for the PS/2 Model 30 286.

Table 4.15 PS/2 Model 30 286 Technical Specifications

System architecture

Microprocessor	80286
Clock speed	10 MHz
Bus type	ISA (Industry Standard Architecture)
Bus width	16-bit
Interrupt levels	16
Type	Edge-triggered
Shareable	No
DMA channels	7
DMA burst mode supported	No
Bus masters supported	No
Upgradeable processor complex	No

Memory

Standard on system board	1M
Maximum on system board	4M
Maximum total memory	16M
Memory speed (ns) and type	120ns dynamic RAM
System board memory-socket type	9-bit SIMM (single in-line memory module)
Number of memory module sockets	4
Number available in standard configuration	2
Memory used on system board	256K/1M 9-bit SIMMs
Memory cache controller	No
Wait states:	
System board	1
Adapter	1

Standard features

ROM size	128K
ROM shadowing	No
Optional math coprocessor	80287
Coprocessor speed	6.67 MHz
Standard graphics	VGA (Video Graphics Array)
RS232C serial ports	1
UART chip used	NS16450
Maximum speed (bits/second)	19,200 bps
Maximum number of ports	2
Pointing device (mouse) ports	1

Standard features

Parallel printer ports	1
Bidirectional	Yes
Maximum number of ports	2
CMOS real-time clock (RTC)	Yes
CMOS RAM	64 bytes
Battery life	10 years
Replaceable	Yes (Dallas module)

Disk storage

Internal disk and tape drive bays	2				
Number of 3 1/2- and 5 1/4-inch bays	2/0				
Standard floppy drives	1×1.44M				
Optional floppy drives:					
5 1/4-inch 360K	Optional				
5 1/4-inch 1.2M	No				
3 1/2-inch 720K	No				
3 1/2-inch 1.44M	Standard				
3 1/2-inch 2.88M	No				
Hard disk controller included:	IDE connector on system board				
IDE hard disks available	20/30/45M				
Drive form factor	3 1/2-inch				
Drive interface	IDE				
Drive capacity	20M	20M	30M	30M	45M
Average access rate (ms)	80	27	27	19	32
Encoding scheme	MFM	RLL	RLL	RLL	RLL
BIOS drive type number	26	34	33	35	37
Cylinders	612	775	614	921	580
Heads	4	2	4	2	6
Sectors per track	17	27	25	33	26
Rotational speed (RPM)	3600	3600	3600	3600	3600
Interleave factor	2:1	3:1	3:1	4:1	3:1
Data transfer rate (K/second)	255	270	250	248	260
Automatic head parking	No	No	No	Yes	Yes

Expansion slots

Total adapter slots	3
Number of long and short slots	3/0
Number of 8-/16-/32-bit slots	0/3/0
Available slots	3

Keyboard specifications

101-key Enhanced Keyboard	Yes
Fast keyboard speed setting	Yes
Keyboard cable length	6 feet

continues

Table 4.15 Continued

Security features

Keylock:
    Locks cover   Yes
    Locks keyboard   No
Keyboard password   Yes
Power-on password   Yes
    Network server mode   Yes

Physical specifications

Footprint type   Desktop
Dimensions:
    Height   4.0 inches
    Width   16.0 inches
    Depth   15.6 inches

Table 4.16 shows the primary specifications and costs of the various versions of PS/2 Model 30 286.

Table 4.16 IBM PS/2 Model 30 286 Model Summary

Part number	CPU	MHz	PLANAR MEMORY Std.	Max.	STANDARD Floppy drive	Hard disk	Bus type
30 286							
8530-E01	286	10	1M	4M	1×1.44M	—	ISA/16
8530-E21	286	10	1M	4M	1×1.44M	20M	ISA/16
8530-E31	286	10	1M	4M	1×1.44M	30M	ISA/16
8530-E41	286	10	1M	4M	1×1.44M	45M	ISA/16

Note: *All the 30 286 models have been withdrawn and no longer are available from IBM.*

Physical specifications	
Weight	17.0 lbs (E01)
	19.0 lbs

Environmental specifications	
Power-supply output	90 watts
Worldwide (110/60,220/50)	Yes
Auto-sensing/switching	Manual switch
Maximum current:	
90-137 VAC	2.5 amps
180-265 VAC	1.3 amps
Operating range:	
Temperature	60-90 degrees F
Relative humidity	8-80 percent
Maximum operating altitude	7,000 feet
Heat (BTUs/hour)	438
Noise (Average dB, operating, 1m)	46 dB
FCC classification	Class B

Total/ available slots	STANDARD Video	KB	Date introduced	Date withdrawn	List price
3/3	VGA	Enh	09/13/87	05/04/92	$1,625
3/3	VGA	Enh	09/13/88	09/11/91	$1,795
3/3	VGA	Enh	09/26/89	01/17/92	$1,795
3/3	VGA	Enh	04/23/91	05/04/92	$1,995

PS/2 Model 35 SX

The PS/2 Model 35 SX (8535), introduced June 11, 1991, uses the 80386SX microprocessor operating at 20 MHz with 0 to 2 wait states and has the following integrated functions: parallel port, serial port, pointing device port, video graphics array (VGA 16-bit) port, keyboard port, 1.44M (million bytes) floppy disk drive support, math coprocessor socket, and three single in-line memory module (SIMM) sockets (two available for memory expansion). The PS/2 Model 35 SX is a three-slot, two-bay system; it is offered in floppy disk drive only (040) and a 40M hard disk model (043). All models come with 2M memory (expandable to 16M) standard on the system board. This system uses the 16-bit ISA for expansion, and its slots are full length. IBM's first 386 system using the ISA bus shows that, although the company's emphasis is on the MCA bus, it continues to support and enhance its offerings in the ISA realm.

All versions of the PS/2 Model 35 are compatible with the IBM AT at the BIOS interface level (although the BIOS is not identical) and at most hardware interfaces. This system also uses the same motherboard as the PS/2 Model 40 SX. The only difference is that the bus adapter in the Model 40 supports five slots rather than three, as in the Model 35. Because many features are already integrated in these systems, many standard ISA adapters such as graphics, memory, disk controller, and other cards might not operate.

The PS/2 Floor Stand option is available if you want to install the system unit vertically.

LAN Version

A special version of the Model 35, the Model 35 LS, provides a local area network (LAN) workstation solution and is available with all the standard features of the Model 35 SX, with this exception: No disk devices of any kind are installed in this medialess system; rather, a 16/4 token ring adapter or IBM EtherNet adapter with Remote Initial Program Load (RIPL) occupies one of the three adapter slots. The 35 LS-24X includes an IBM 16/4 token ring adapter as a standard feature; the 35 LS-14X model includes an IBM EtherNet adapter as a standard feature.

With the RIPL ROM, the system can "boot" DOS or OS/2 from the LAN server machine. The diskless Model 35 LS is fully upgradeable to the Model 35 SX configurations.

The Models 35 SX and LS both have a universal power supply with an autosense circuit. No manual switching is required. The Models 35 SX and LS, therefore, can easily be used worldwide.

Standard versions of Model 35 SX differ only in the choice of whether to have a hard disk; the LS version is completely diskless. In other respects, the models are similar.

Keyboard Options

Both the PS/2 Model 35 SX and 35 LS support the IBM Enhanced Keyboard (101/102 keys), Space-Saving Keyboard (84/85 keys), and the IBM Host-Connected Keyboard (122 keys). The Host-Connected Keyboard is similar to the 3270 keyboard offered with 3270 IBM PC and IBM AT systems. This keyboard is similar in design to that of a 3270 terminal keyboard and offers keys dedicated to 3270 functions. The Host-Connected Keyboard is supported by the BIOS in this system and cannot be retrofitted to PS/2 systems that do not have the proper BIOS support. When you purchase a Model 35 SX or LS, you must choose any one of these three keyboards.

Floppy Drive Support

The Model 35 SX has BIOS support for the new 2.88M floppy drive. Although this drive does not come standard in this system, one is available from IBM. The Model 35 SX is one of the first systems to support this drive.

One very interesting feature of the Model 35 SX is its selectable-boot feature. As part of the system CMOS setup program, the user can specify which drive should be booted from and in which order the boot process should try each drive selected. The system supports an internally mounted 5 1/4-inch 1.2M drive in addition to the standard 3 1/2-inch 1.44M drive, and you can specify either drive as the primary boot device. You also can specify booting only from the hard disk, or even from a network file server (RIPL). This setup offers flexibility not found on many other systems.

The Model 35 SX system unit has two drive bays that can accommodate 5 1/4-inch or 3 1/2-inch devices, unlike many other PS/2 systems. Most older PS/2 systems cannot fit 5 1/4-inch devices internally.

Table 4.17 gives the specifications for the PS/2 model 35 SX.

Table 4.17 PS/2 Model 35 SX Technical Specifications

System architecture

Microprocessor	80386SX
Clock speed	20 MHz
Bus type	ISA (Industry Standard Architecture)
Bus width	16-bit
Interrupt levels	16
Type	Edge-triggered
Shareable	No
DMA channels	7
DMA burst mode supported	No
Bus masters supported	No
Upgradeable processor complex	No

Memory

Standard on system board	2M
Maximum on system board	16M
Maximum total memory	16M
Memory speed and type	85ns dynamic RAM
System-board memory socket type	36-bit SIMM (single in-line memory module)
Number of memory-module sockets	3
Number available in standard configuration	2
Memory used on system board	1M/2M/4M/8M 36-bit SIMMs
Memory cache controller	No
Wait states:	
System board	0-2
Adapter	1

Standard features

ROM size	128K
ROM shadowing	Yes
Optional math coprocessor	80387SX
Coprocessor speed	20 MHz
Standard graphics	VGA (Video Graphics Array)
8-/16-/32-bit controller	16-bit
Bus master	No
Video RAM (VRAM)	256K
RS232C serial ports	1
UART chip used	NS16450
Maximum speed (bits/second)	19,200 bps
Maximum number of ports	2

Standard features

Pointing device (mouse) ports	1
Parallel printer ports	1
Bidirectional	Yes
Maximum number of ports	2
CMOS real-time clock (RTC)	Yes
CMOS RAM	64 bytes
CMOS battery life	10 years
Replaceable battery	Yes (Dallas module)

Disk storage

Internal disk and tape drive bays	2	
Number of 3 1/2-/5 1/4-inch bays	0/2	
Selectable boot drive	Yes	
Bootable drives	All physical drives	
Standard floppy drives	1×1.44M	
None (24X)		
Optional floppy drives:		
5 1/4-inch 360K	Optional	
5 1/4-inch 1.2M	Optional	
3 1/2-inch 720K	No	
3 1/2-inch 1.44M	Standard	
3 1/2-inch 2.88M	Optional	
Hard disk controller included:	IDE connector on system board	
IDE hard drives available	40/80M	
Drive form factor	3 1/2-inch	
Drive interface	IDE	
Drive capacity	40M	80M
Average access rate (ms)	17	17
Read-ahead cache	32K	32K
Encoding scheme	RLL	RLL
Cylinders	1038	1021
Heads	2	4
Sectors per track	39	39
Rotational speed (RPM)	3600	3600
Interleave factor	1:1	1:1
Data transfer rate (K/second)	1170	1170
Automatic head parking	Yes	Yes

Expansion slots

Total adapter slots	3
Number of long and short slots	3/0
Number of 8-/16-/32-bit slots	0/3/0
Available slots	3

continues

Table 4.17 Continued

Keyboard specifications

Keyboard choices	122-key Host-Connected Keyboard
	101-key Enhanced Keyboard
	84-key Space-Saving Keyboard
Fast keyboard speed setting	Yes
Keyboard cable length	10 feet

Security features

Keylock:	
Locks cover	Yes
Locks keyboard	No
Keyboard password	Yes
Power-on password	Yes
Network server mode	Yes

Physical specifications

Footprint type	Desktop
Orientation	Horizontal (vertical with optional stand)

Table 4.18 shows the primary specifications and costs of the various versions of PS/2 Model 35 SX and LS.

Table 4.18 IBM PS/2 Model 35 SX/LS Model Summary

Part number	CPU	MHz	PLANAR MEMORY Std.	Max.	STANDARD Floppy drive	Hard disk	Bus type
35 SX							
8535-040	386SX	20	2M	16M	1×1.44M	—	ISA/16
8535-043	386SX	20	2M	16M	1×1.44M	40M	ISA/16
35 LS							
8535-14X	386SX	20	2M	16M	—	—	ISA/16
8535-24X	386SX	20	2M	16M	—	—	ISA/16

Keyboards available include the Enhanced (101-key), Space-Saving (84-key), and Host-Connected (122-key). If "Any" is indicated, purchaser could choose any of the three.

Physical specifications

Dimensions:	
Height	4.5 inches
Width	14.2 inches
Depth	15.6 inches
Weight:	
24X	22.4 lbs
040	23.8 lbs
043	20.9 lbs

Environmental specifications

Power-supply output	118 watts
Worldwide (110/60,220/50)	Yes
Auto-sensing/switching	Yes
Maximum current:	
90-137 VAC	3.5 amps
180-265 VAC	1.75 amps
Operating range:	
Temperature	50-95 degrees F
Relative humidity	8-80 percent
Maximum operating altitude	7,000 feet
Heat (BTUs/hour):	
24X	123
040	130
043	144
FCC classification	Class B

Total/ available slots	STANDARD Video	KB	Date introduced	Date withdrawn	List price
3/3	VGA	Any	06/11/91	—	$1,745
3/3	VGA	Any	06/11/91	—	$2,255
3/2	VGA	Any	10/17/91	—	$1,820
3/2	VGA	Any	06/11/91	—	$2,425

The 35 LS-24X includes an IBM 16/4 Token Ring Adapter as a standard feature, whereas the 35 LS-4X model includes an IBM EtherNet Adapter as a standard feature.

PS/2 Model 40 SX

The PS/2 Model 40 SX (8540), introduced June 11, 1991, uses the 80386SX microprocessor operating at 20 MHz with 0 to 2 wait states to system memory. The Model 40 SX ships with 2M system board memory (expandable to 16M on planar), 3 1/2-inch drive options, and 16-bit VGA. The system also provides five full-size, customer-accessible, 8-/16-bit expansion card slots. The 80386SX microprocessor PS/2 Model 40 SX has the following integrated functions: parallel port, serial port, pointing device port, VGA port, keyboard port, 1.44M floppy disk drive support, math coprocessor socket, and three single in-line memory module (SIMM) sockets (two available for memory expansion).

The Model 40 SX has a universal power supply with an autosense circuit. No manual switching is required. Therefore, the Model 40 SX can easily be used worldwide.

The PS/2 Model 40 SX is compatible with the IBM AT at the BIOS interface level (although the BIOS is not identical) and at most hardware interfaces. This system also uses the same motherboard as the PS/2 Model 35 SX. The only difference is that the bus adapter in the Model 40 supports five slots rather than three, as in the Model 35. Because many features are already integrated in these systems, many standard ISA adapters such as graphics, memory, disk controller, and other cards might not operate.

The standard versions of the Model 40 SX differ only by whether and what kind of hard disk drive they provide: a floppy-drive-only model (8540-040), a 40M hard disk model (8540-043), or an 80M hard disk model (8540-045). In other respects the versions are similar.

The PS/2 Floor Stand option is available if you want to install the system unit vertically.

Keyboard Options

The PS/2 Model 40 SX supports the IBM Enhanced Keyboard (101/102 keys), Space-Saving Keyboard (84/85 keys), and the IBM Host-Connected Keyboard (122 keys). The Host-Connected Keyboard is similar to the 3270 keyboard offered with 3270 IBM PC and IBM AT systems. This keyboard is similar in design to a 3270 terminal keyboard and offers keys dedicated to 3270 functions. The Host-Connected Keyboard is supported by the BIOS in this system and cannot be retrofitted to PS/2 systems that do not have the proper BIOS support.

When you purchase a Model 40 SX, you can choose any of these three keyboards. The keyboard can be specified only in new equipment orders and cannot be ordered separately for on-order or installed equipment.

Floppy Drive Support

The Model 40 SX has BIOS support for the new 2.88M floppy drive. Although this drive does not come standard in this system, one is available from IBM. The Model 40 SX is one of the first systems to support this drive.

One very interesting feature of the Model 40 SX is its selectable-boot feature. As part of the system CMOS setup program, you can specify from which drive it should be booted and in which order the boot process should try each drive selected. The system supports an internally mounted 5 1/4-inch 1.2M drive in addition to the standard 3 1/2-inch 1.44M drive; you can specify either drive as the primary boot device. You also can specify booting only from the hard disk, or even from a network file server (RIPL). This setup offers flexibility not found on many other systems.

The Model 40 SX has two or three available drive bays (depending on whether the model has a hard disk) and supports up to two hard disks and a variety of optional floppy disk devices, including a 5 1/4-inch internally mounted 1.2M floppy drive or a 2.88M 3 1/2-inch floppy drive. Because of a selectable boot feature, you can boot the system from any installed drive.

Table 4.19 lists the technical specifications for the PS/2 model 40 SX.

Table 4.19 PS/2 Model 40 SX Technical Specifications

System architecture

Microprocessor	80386SX
Clock speed	20 MHz
Bus type	ISA (Industry Standard Architecture)
Bus width	16-bit
Interrupt levels	16
Type	Edge-triggered
Shareable	No
DMA channels	7
DMA burst mode supported	No
Bus masters supported	No
Upgradeable processor complex	No

Memory

Standard on system board	2M
Maximum on system board	16M
Maximum total memory	16M

continues

Table 4.19 Continued

Memory

Memory speed and type	85ns dynamic RAM
System board memory-socket type	36-bit SIMM (single in-line memory module)
Number of memory-module sockets	3
Number available in standard configuration	2
Memory used on system board	1M/2M/4M/8M 36-bit SIMMs
Memory cache controller	No
Wait states:	
System board	0-2
Adapter	1

Standard features

ROM size	128K
ROM shadowing	Yes
Optional math coprocessor	80387SX
Coprocessor speed	20 MHz
Standard graphics	VGA (Video Graphics Array)
8-/16-/32-bit controller	16-bit
Bus master	No
Video RAM (VRAM)	256K
RS232C serial ports	1
UART chip used	NS16450
Maximum speed (bits per second)	19,200 bps
Maximum number of ports	2
Pointing device (mouse) ports	1
Parallel printer ports	1
Bidirectional	Yes
Maximum number of ports	2
CMOS real-time clock (RTC)	Yes
CMOS RAM	64 bytes
CMOS battery life	10 years
Replaceable	Yes (Dallas module)

Disk storage

Internal disk and tape drive bays	4
Number of 3 1/2- and 5 1/4-inch bays	1/3
Selectable boot drive	Yes
Bootable drives	All physical drives
Standard floppy drives	1x1.44M
Optional floppy drives:	
5 1/4-inch 360K	Optional

Disk storage

5 1/4-inch 1.2M	Optional
3 1/2-inch 720K	No
3 1/2-inch 1.44M	Standard
3 1/2-inch 2.88M	Optional
Hard disk controller included:	IDE connector on system board
IDE hard drives available	40/80M
Drive form factor	3 1/2-inch
Drive interface	IDE

Drive capacity	40M	80M
Average access rate (ms)	17	17
Read-ahead cache	32K	32K
Encoding scheme	RLL	RLL
Cylinders	1038	1021
Heads	2	4
Sectors per track	39	39
Rotational speed (RPM)	3600	3600
Interleave factor	1:1	1:1
Data transfer rate (K/second)	1170	1170
Automatic head parking	Yes	Yes

Expansion slots

Total adapter slots	5
Number of long and short slots	5/0
Number of 8-/16-/32-bit slots	0/5/0
Available slots	5

Keyboard specifications

Keyboard choices:	
122-key Host-Connected Keyboard	
101-key Enhanced Keyboard	
84-key Space-Saving Keyboard	
Fast keyboard speed setting	Yes
Keyboard cable length	10 feet

Security features

Keylock:	
Locks cover	Yes
Locks keyboard	No
Keyboard password	Yes
Power-on password	Yes
Network server mode	Yes

continues

Table 4.19 Continued

Physical specifications

Footprint type	Desktop
Orientation	Horizontal/vertical (stand included)
Dimensions:	
Height	6.7 inches
Width	17.3 inches
Depth	15.5 inches
Weight:	
	26.3 lbs (040)
	27.8 lbs

Table 4.20 shows the primary specifications and costs of the various versions of PS/2 Model 40 SX.

Table 4.20 IBM PS/2 Model 40 SX Model Summary

Part number	CPU	MHz	PLANAR MEMORY Std.	Max.	STANDARD Floppy drive	Hard disk	Bus type
40 SX							
8540-040	386SX	20	2M	16M	1×1.44M	—	ISA/16
8540-043	386SX	20	2M	16M	1×1.44M	40M	ISA/16
8540-045	386SX	20	2M	16M	1×1.44M	80M	ISA/16

Keyboards available include the Enhanced (101-key), Space-Saving (84-key), and Host-Connected (122-key). If "Any" is indicated, the purchaser could choose any of the three.

Environmental specifications

Power-supply output	197 watts
Worldwide (110/60,220/50)	Yes
Auto-sensing/switching	Manual switch
Maximum current:	
90-137 VAC	6.0 amps
180-265 VAC	3.0 amps
Operating range:	
Temperature	50-95 degrees F
Relative humidity	8-80 percent
Maximum operating altitude	7,000 feet
Heat (BTUs/hour)	190
FCC classification	Class B

Total/ available slots	STANDARD Video	KB	Date introduced	Date withdrawn	List price
5/5	VGA	Any	06/11/91	—	$2,000
5/5	VGA	Any	06/11/91	—	$2,545
5/5	VGA	Any	06/11/91	—	$2,845

PS/2 Model L40 SX

The PS/2 Model L40 SX, announced March 26, 1991, is a small, light-weight, battery-operated (AC/DC) portable laptop system. The PS/2 Model L40 SX is designed for people who want a high-function portable that is easy to carry and has the speed and capacity to support advanced applications. Standard features include a 20 MHz 80386SX processor; 2M of 80ns memory (expandable to 18M); 60M 2 1/2-inch hard disk; 3 1/2-inch 1.44M floppy disk drive; 10mm-thick, cold fluorescent, black-and-white LCD with VGA resolution; 84/85 key keyboard; and serial, parallel, keypad/mouse, VGA, and external expansion I/O ports for attaching external devices. In addition, each system includes an external 17-key numeric keypad, an AC adapter, a rechargeable battery pack, and a carrying case. Options for the PS/2 Model L40 SX include a one-slot expansion chassis, a data/fax modem (for the U.S. and Canada); a second serial adapter; a Trackpoint pointing device; 2M, 4M, or 8M memory upgrades; a quick charger; and a car-battery adapter.

The PS/2 Model L40 SX physical package is based on a clamshell design. It fits in most attache cases and weighs 7.7 pounds, including the rechargeable battery pack. The PS/2 Model L40 SX features the familiar IBM keyboard size and layout; 80386SX architecture; large, easy-to-read display; high-capacity hard disk; and efficient battery-power management, while maintaining the light weight of a notebook portable. Compared to the IBM PS/2 Model P70, the PS/2 Model L40 SX adds battery operation, clamshell design, black-on-white LCD, and a smaller, lighter package.

System Expansion and Restrictions

The Model L40 SX is designed to be compatible with the IBM AT at the BIOS interface level and at most hardware interfaces, and the system is very expandable. Many I/O connections are provided as standard. An external numeric keypad, included with the unit, plugs into the standard mouse port. The numeric keypad has a mouse port to enable numeric keypad and mouse connections to operate concurrently. The L40 has a standard serial port, parallel port, VGA display port, and a special external expansion port reserved for an expansion chassis or base station called the Communications Cartridge I.

The PS/2 Communications Cartridge I is a one-slot expansion unit that you use with the Model L40 SX. The unit contains one half-size card slot that was especially designed to support Token-Ring, 3270 or 5250 communications adapter cards. Although the Communications Cartridge I was designed primarily for these communications adapters, other types of adapters should also work, but are technically not supported by IBM.

The expansion of the system has some limitations. Unless you purchase the Communications Cartridge I expansion chassis, for example, there are slots available for attaching adapters and cards other than the specific IBM PS/2 Model L40 SX options. Also, when the VGA port is operational, the integrated LCD is not operational—a drawback when you use the system for presentations with a large-screen projector. Additionally, because the IBM PS/2 internal data/fax modem for Model L40 SX and the IBM PS/2 serial adapter for Model L40 SX use the same internal connector, only one of these options can be installed per system. Finally, external keyboards are not supported.

Power Management

The L40 boasts very efficient power management. A suspend-resume function is provided. You suspend an application by closing the clamshell and leaving the power switch on. When the clamshell is opened, the application resumes at the point at which it was suspended. During suspension, system components are automatically powered off, except for the real-time clock and application memory. The system can be set to resume at a specific time. An internal backup battery is provided to prevent disruption of the application or system when the rechargeable battery pack is being changed.

To reduce the frequency of recharging the batteries, trickle recharging occurs during AC operation. To conserve and prolong battery life between recharges, a switch is provided for user selection of system speed under manual or automatic control. In automatic mode, the hardware initiates low clock-speed operation during idle periods. In manual mode, the processor runs at the default clock speed set by the user when the system is configured. The clock-speed settings are 20 MHz, 10 MHz, and 5 MHz.

In an effort to conserve even more battery power, the hardware supports sleep mode. Sleep mode conserves battery power during idle times between clock cycles and keystrokes by putting system components in an idle state that results in low power usage. (Sleep mode is not operational when an external display is attached.) This function is exploited by DOS and OS/2. The L40 SX has an informative LCD display that uses international symbols that indicate operational and environmental status. These status indicators include: a battery gauge, humidity, temperature-limit indicator, modem carrier detect, Numeric Lock, Scroll Lock, speaker enabled, suspend mode, floppy disk drive in use, and hard drive in use indicators.

Environment Protection

The system's temperature and humidity sensors do not allow the unit to operate under incorrect environmental conditions. This feature is essential considering that a laptop system may spend time in a parked car, garage, or some other environment unsuitable for computer use. Few other systems offer this kind of protection.

Imagine leaving your system in your car for a few hours in the winter. After bringing the system inside, condensation forms on the circuitry and even on the hard disk platters. If you power up the system, the circuits or the hard drive might be destroyed. The L40 intervenes and does not allow the system to operate until safe temperature and humidity exist in the system's environment.

Table 4.21 lists the technical specifications for the PS/2 model L40 SX.

Table 4.21 PS/2 Model L40 SX Technical Specifications

System architecture

Microprocessor	80386SX
Clock speed	20/10/5 MHz
Bus type	ISA (Industry Standard Architecture)
Bus width	16-bit
Interrupt levels	16
Type	Edge-triggered
Shareable	No
DMA channels	7
DMA burst mode supported	No
Bus masters supported	No
Upgradeable processor complex	No

Memory

Standard on system board	2M
Maximum on system board	18M (16M + 2M EMS)
Maximum total memory	18M
Memory speed and type	80ns CMOS RAM
System board memory-socket type	36-bit CMOS SIMMs, specially keyed
Number system-board memory modules	2
Number available in standard configuration	2
Memory used on system board	2M soldered, and 2M/4M/ 8M 36-bit CMOS SIMMs
Memory cache controller	No
Wait states:	
System board	0-2

Standard features

ROM size	128K
ROM shadowing	Yes
Optional math coprocessor	80387SX
Coprocessor speed	20 MHz
Standard graphics	VGA (Video Graphics Array)
8-/16-/32-bit controller	8-bit
Bus master	No
Video RAM (VRAM)	256K
Built-in display	Yes
Type LCD	
Dimensions (Diag/H×W)	10 inches/6 × 8 inches
Number of grayshades	32
Backlit/sidelit	Sidelit
Supertwisted	Yes
Contrast ratio	12:1
Detachable	No
External monitor port	Yes
External display disables LCD	Yes
LCD indicators	Yes
RS232C serial ports	1
UART chip used	NS16450
Maximum speed (bits/second)	19,200 bps
Maximum number of ports supported	2
Internal modem	Optional
Hayes-compatible	Yes
Asynchronous/synchronous	Yes/Yes
FAX capable	Yes
Group III compatible	Yes
FAX software included	Yes
Send/receive FAX	Yes/Yes
Maximum speed (bps):	
Data 2400 bps	
FAX 9600 bps	
Pointing device (mouse) ports	1
Parallel printer ports	1
Bidirectional	Yes
Maximum number of ports supported	1
CMOS real-time clock (RTC)	Yes
CMOS RAM	64 bytes
CMOS battery life	5 years
Replaceable	Yes

Disk storage

Internal disk and tape drive bays	2
Number of 3 1/2-/5 1/4-inch bays	1/0
Standard floppy drives	1×1.44M

continues

Table 4.21 Continued

Disk storage

Hard disk controller included:	IDE connector on system board
IDE hard disks available	60M
Drive form factor	2 inches
Drive interface	IDE
Average access rate (ms)	19
Encoding scheme	RLL
Cylinders	822
Heads	4
Sectors per track	38
Rotational speed (RPM)	3600
Interleave factor	1:1
Data transfer rate (K/second)	1140
Automatic head parking	Yes

Expansion slots

Total adapter slots	0
Available slots	0

Keyboard specifications

101-key Enhanced Keyboard	Yes (with external keypad)
84-key keyboard	Yes
Fast keyboard speed setting	Yes
Keyboard detachable	No

Security features

Keylock:	
Locks cover	No
Locks keyboard	No
Keyboard password	Yes
Power-on password	Yes
Network server mode	Yes

Physical specifications	
Footprint type	Laptop
Dimensions:	
Height	2.1 inches
Width	12.8 inches
Depth	10.7 inches
Weight: with battery	7.7 lbs
Carrying case	Leather, included

Environmental specifications	
Power supply:	
Worldwide (110/60,220/50)	Yes
Auto-sensing/switching	Yes
Maximum current:	
90-265 VAC	2.7 amps
Operating range:	
Temperature	41-95 degrees F
Relative humidity	5-95 percent
Maximum operating altitude	8000 feet
Heat (BTUs/hour)	136
Noise (Average dB, operating, 1m)	32 dB
FCC classification	Class B

Miscellaneous	
A/C adapter included	Yes
Quick charger	Optional
Car cigarette lighter adapter	Optional
Battery pack included	Yes
Battery charge duration	3 hours
Setup and power-management software	Yes
Speed-setting switch and software	Yes

Table 4.22 shows the primary specifications and costs of the different versions of PS/2 Model L40 SX. Table 4.23 shows accessories available from IBM for the PS/2 Model L40 SX.

Table 4.22 IBM PS/2 Model L40 SX Model Summary

| Part number | CPU | MHz | PLANAR MEMORY | | STANDARD | | Bus type |
			Std.	Max.	Floppy drive	Hard disk	
L40 SX							
8543-044	386SX	20	2M	18M	151.44M	60M	ISA/16

Table 4.23 IBM PS/2 Model L40 SX Special Accessories

Description	Part number	Price	Notes
Communications Cartridge I	3541001	$595	One slot expansion chassis
Rechargeable battery pack	79F0197	130	3 hours use/up to 500 charges
Quick charger	79F0192	132	Charges in 2 1/2 hours rather than 8 hours
Car battery adapter	79F1012	165	Lighter socket runs and recharges L40
Leather carrying case	79F3981	71	Included with L40SX, black leather
Deluxe carrying case	79F0981	115	Cloth case, pockets and compartments
Airline travel hard case	79F3844	247	Plastic, padded, wheels, storage
Serial adapter for L40 SX	79F0979	119	Second serial, N/A with internal FAX or modem

PS/2 Model 50

The IBM PS/2 Model 50, which uses MCA, was introduced April 2, 1987, as an entry-level desktop system in the PS/2 family. Figure 4.15 shows a front view of the Model 50. As of July 23, 1991, all models of the 50 and 50 Z were discontinued and no longer are available from IBM.

The Model 50 features a 10 MHz 286 processor running with 0 or 1 wait state, depending on the model version, and 1M of memory on the system board. System-board memory can be expanded to 2M on Model 50 Z

Total/ available slots	STANDARD Video	KB	Date introduced	Date withdrawn	List price
0	VGA	SS	03/26/91	—	$2,495

systems but is limited to 1M on the standard model (8550-021). As much as 16M of additional memory can be added with memory adapter cards. The IBM Model 50 comes standard with a 1.44M, 3 1/2-inch floppy disk drive; a 20M, 30M, or 60M hard disk drive (depending on the model); a serial port; a parallel port; a mouse port; and a Video Graphics Array (VGA) port. Figure 4.16 shows the rear panel of the Model 50.

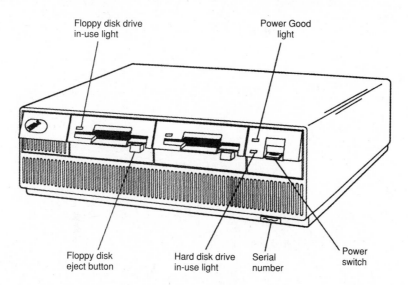

Floppy disk drive in-use light

Power Good light

Floppy disk eject button

Hard disk drive in-use light

Serial number

Power switch

Fig. 4.15

PS/2 Model 50.

The 80286 10 MHz 16-bit microprocessor running with 1 wait state enables the 50-021 to perform approximately 20 percent faster than the IBM XT 286 or the IBM AT Model 339. The Model 50 Z systems (8550-031 and 8550-061) run with 0 wait states to motherboard memory access, which translates into an additional 20 percent performance increase for most computational tasks.

The Model 50 has two levels of BIOS, which total 128K: a Compatibility BIOS (CBIOS) with memory addressability of up to 1M provides support for real-mode-based application programs. An additional version of BIOS, Advanced BIOS (ABIOS), provides support for protected-mode-based multitasking operating systems and has extended memory addressability of up to 16M.

Note   Real mode is a mode in which the 80286 processor can emulate 8086 or 8088 processors for compatibility purposes. DOS runs under this mode. Protected mode, not found in the 8086 or 8088 processors, allows for specialized support of multitasking. Advanced multitasking operating systems such as OS/2 run under this mode.

Additional features of the system unit include four 16-bit I/O slots (with one slot occupied by the disk controller adapter); a 94-watt, automatic voltage-sensing, universal power supply; a time-and-date clock with battery backup; a socket for an 80287; an additional position for a second 3 1/2-inch floppy disk drive; and the IBM Enhanced Keyboard. Figure 4.17 shows an interior view of the Model 50.

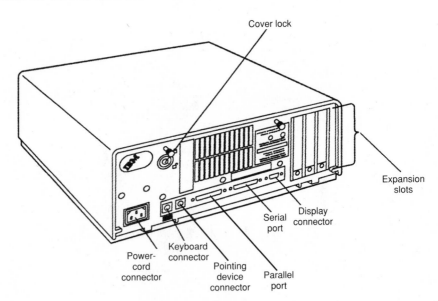

Fig. 4.16

PS/2 Model 50 rear panel view.

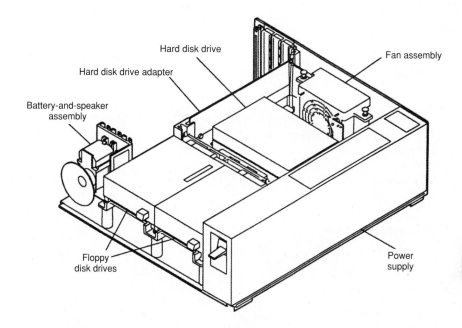

Hard disk drive

Fan assembly

Hard disk drive adapter

Battery-and-speaker
assembly

Floppy
disk drives

Power
supply

Fig. 4.17

PS/2 Model 50
interior view.

Model 50 Z

On June 2, 1988, IBM introduced the PS/2 Model 50 Z (actually the 8550-031 and the 8550-061). These models offer improved performance and greater hard disk capacity. Higher-speed (85ns) memory provides 0-wait-state processor performance and can be upgraded to 2M on the system board. The 50 Z comes with a 30M or 60M hard disk drive, which provides greater capacity and improved average access time over the standard 20M hard disk in Model 50-021.

Floppy Drive Support

The standard 1.44M drive in all the Model 50 systems can format, read, and write to either 720K (double density) or 1.44M (high density) floppy disks. In double-density mode, this drive is fully compatible with the 720K (3 1/2-inch) floppy disk drive. In high-density mode, the standard drive doubles the data capability to 1.44M and the data rate to 500K bits per second.

Note Because of the capabilities and design of the disk media, you should not use the 1.44M drive to format a 720K (1M unformatted) disk as 1.44M, or to format a 1.44M (2M unformatted) disk as 720K.

A 5 1/4-inch external disk drive (360K) is available that enables you to convert or operate existing 5 1/4-inch applications. To operate, this drive requires the External Diskette Drive Adapter/A. The adapter card plugs into the connector for the 3 1/2-inch drive B. When the external drive is installed, it becomes drive B. Unfortunately, the external disk drive consumes one slot and the drive B position.

System Expansion

In response to user complaints about the storage capacity of the original 20M Model 50, IBM offers the PS/2 60M hard disk drive as an upgrade option. You can install this drive by replacing the existing 20M hard disk in the PS/2 Model 50 (8550-021) or 30M in the Model 50 Z (8550-031). No trade-in is available for the earlier drive. This drive provides 60M of storage and a faster access time of 27ms. The replacement adapter card required for the 50-021 is included.

For additional memory, IBM offers the PS/2 1-8M Memory Expansion Adapter/A and the PS/2 2-8M Memory Expansion Adapter/A—16-bit, full-length circuit cards. You can expand either card to a maximum of 8M by using optional memory kits. You can configure the adapter memory from 1M to 8M by using either the 0.5M memory module kit or the 2M memory module kit. These cards can be installed in any open expansion slot on the Model 50. The adapter is easy to set up because it contains no jumpers or hardware switches. An additional feature is an on-board ROM that contains a POST and microcode to initialize the card.

These memory cards also provide support for two different operating modes: expanded memory and extended memory. Used as expanded memory, the adapter card's memory is compatible with applications written to the LIM EMS V4.0 standard. In addition, you can use the adapter card's memory as extended memory for DOS or OS/2. By installing two adapters, each filled to 8M, a user can reach the system address limit of 16M for the Model 50.

Because of the 0 wait states on the 50 Z systems, IBM offers a special motherboard memory upgrade for only these systems. This upgrade consists of one 2M, 85ns memory kit, which you install on the system board of the 50-031 or 50-061, replacing the standard 1M of memory. This upgrade brings the system board to its maximum capacity of 2M for these models.

Table 4.24 lists the technical specifications for the PS/2 Model 50.

Table 4.24 PS/2 Model 50 Technical Specifications

System architecture

Microprocessor	80286
Clock speed	10 MHz
Bus typeMCA	(Micro Channel Architecture)
Bus width	16-bit
Interrupt levels	16
Type	Level-sensitive
Shareable	Yes
DMA channels	15
DMA burst mode supported	Yes
Bus masters supported	15
Upgradeable processor complex	No

Memory

Standard on system board	1M
Maximum on system board	2M 1M (021)
Maximum total memory	16M
Memory speed and type	85ns dynamic RAM 150ns dynamic RAM (021)
System board memory-socket type	36-bit SIMM (single in-line memory module) 9-bit SIMM (021)
Number of memory-module sockets	1 2 (021)
Number available in standard configuration	0
Memory used on system board	1M/2M 36-bit SIMM 512K 9-bit SIMMs (021)
Memory cache controller	No
Wait states:	
System board	0 1 (021)
Adapter	0-1

Standard features

ROM size	128K
ROM shadowing	No
Optional math coprocessor	80287
Coprocessor speed	10 MHz
Standard graphics	VGA (Video Graphics Array)

continues

Table 4.24 Continued

Standard features

8-/16-/32-bit controller	8-bit
Bus master	No
Video RAM (VRAM)	256K
RS232C serial ports	1
UART chip used	NS16550
Maximum speed (bits per second)	19,200 bps
FIFO mode enabled	No
Maximum number of ports	8
Pointing device (mouse) ports	1
Parallel printer ports	1
Bidirectional	Yes
Maximum number of ports	8
CMOS real-time clock (RTC)	Yes
CMOS RAM	64 bytes
Battery life	5 years
Replaceable	Yes

Disk storage

Internal disk and tape drive bays	3		
Number of 3 1/2- and 5 1/4-inch bays	3/0		
Standard floppy drives	1×1.44M		
Optional floppy drives:			
5 1/4-inch 360K	Optional		
5 1/4-inch 1.2M	Optional		
3 1/2-inch 720K	No		
3 1/2-inch 1.44M	Standard		
3 1/2-inch 2.88M	No		
Hard disk controller included:	IDE connector on Interposer Card ST-506 Controller (021)		
ST-506/IDE hard disks available	20/30/60M		
Drive form factor	3 1/2-inch		
Drive capacity	20M	30M	60M
Drive interface	ST-506	IDE	IDE
Average access rate (ms)	80	39	27
Encoding scheme	MFM	RLL	RLL
BIOS drive type number	30	33	None
Cylinders	611	614	762
Heads	4	4	6
Sectors per track	17	25	26
Rotational speed (RPM)	3600	3600	3600
Interleave factor	1:1	1:1	1:1
Data transfer rate (K/second)	510	750	780
Automatic head parking	No	No	Yes

Expansion slots	
Total adapter slots	3
Number of long and short slots	3/0
Number of 8-/16-/32-bit slots	0/3/0
Number of slots with video ext.	1
Available slots	3

Keyboard specifications	
101-key Enhanced Keyboard	Yes
Fast keyboard speed setting	Yes
Keyboard cable length	6 feet

Security features	
Keylock:	
Locks cover	Yes
Locks keyboard	No
Keyboard password	Yes
Power-on password	Yes
Network server mode	Yes

Physical specifications	
Footprint type	Desktop
Dimensions:	
Height	5.5 inches
Width	14.2 inches
Depth	16.5 inches
Weight	23.0 lbs
	21.0 lbs (021)

Environmental specifications	
Power-supply output	94 watts
Worldwide (110/60,220/50)	Yes
Auto-sensing/switching	Yes
Maximum current:	
90-137 VAC	2.7 amps
180-265 VAC	1.4 amps
Operating range:	
Temperature	60-90 degrees F
Relative humidity	8-80 percent
Maximum operating altitude	7,000 feet
Heat (BTUs/hour)	494
Noise (Average dB, operating, 1m)	46 dB
FCC classification	Class B

Figures 4.18 and 4.19 show the layout and components on Model 50 and 50 Z motherboards, respectively.

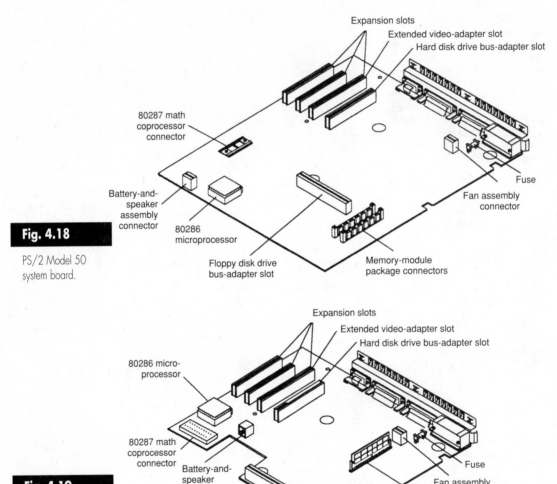

Fig. 4.18

PS/2 Model 50 system board.

Fig. 4.19

PS/2 Model 50Z system board.

Table 4.25 shows the primary specifications and costs of the different versions of PS/2 Model 50.

PS/2 Model 55 SX

The PS/2 Model 55 SX, introduced May 9, 1989, has been one of IBM's top-selling systems because of the system's reasonable performance, modular construction, low price, and compact, efficient design. Model 55 SX systems use the 386 SX processor running at 16 MHz. They have 2M as standard memory in the 30M and 60M hard drive configurations, and 4M as standard memory in the 40M and 80M hard drive configurations. These Model 55 SX systems have the capability of supporting up to 16M of memory and have offered hard disks from 30M to 80M. Additional features include 1.44M, 3 1/2-inch floppy disk drive; ports (keyboard, pointing device, serial/asynchronous, parallel, VGA); three MCA I/O slots, and an Enhanced Keyboard. Figure 4.20 shows a front view and figure 4.21 shows a rear panel view of a Model 55 SX.

Also available are special diskless versions of the Model 55 SX with preinstalled IBM Token Ring or EtherNet Adapters. These "Lxx" versions are designed as LAN workstations and have the capability to boot directly from the LAN server system. The -LEx models include an IBM Ethernet Adapter, and the -LTx models include an IBM Token Ring Network Adapter. Although these models come without any drives, they can be upgraded later with both floppy and hard disk drives.

The PS/2 Model 55 SX is designed to maintain compatibility with many software products currently operating under DOS and OS/2 on the IBM AT and the rest of the PS/2 family. These systems have full 80386 memory management capability, which means that they can operate in 32-bit software mode. Figure 4.22 shows an interior view of the Model 55 SX.

The various models of the 55 SX differ only in the size of the preinstalled hard disk. Models have been available with 30M, 40M, 60M, and 80M drives. The 30M and 60M drive models have been discontinued by IBM, and the 40M and 80M models have taken their place.

Table 4.25 IBM PS/2 Model 50 Model Summary

Part number	CPU	MHz	PLANAR MEMORY Std.	Max.	STANDARD Floppy drive	Hard disk	Bus type
50							
8550-021	286	10	1M	1M	1×1.44M	20M	MCA/16
50 Z							
8550-031	286	10	1M	2M	1×1.44M	30M	MCA/16
8550-061	286	10	1M	2M	1×1.44M	60M	MCA/16

Note: *All 50 and 50 Z models have been withdrawn from marketing by IBM.*

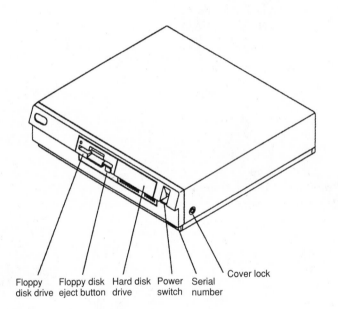

Floppy disk drive Floppy disk eject button Hard disk drive Power switch Serial number Cover lock

Fig. 4.20

PS/2 Model 55 SX.

Total/ available slots	STANDARD Video	KB	Date introduced	Date withdrawn	List price
4/3	VGA	Enh	04/02/87	05/03/89	$3,595
4/3	VGA	Enh	06/07/88	07/23/91	$1,695
4/3	VGA	Enh	06/07/88	07/23/91	$1,975

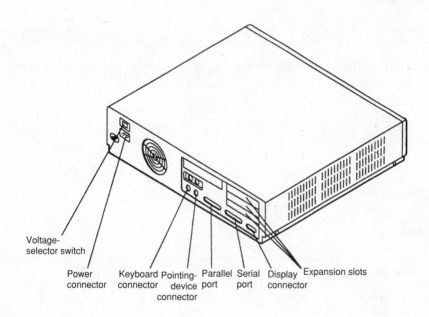

Voltage-
selector switch

Power
connector

Keyboard
connector

Pointing-
device
connector

Parallel
port

Serial
port

Display
connector

Expansion slots

Fig. 4.21

PS/2 Model 55 SX
rear panel view.

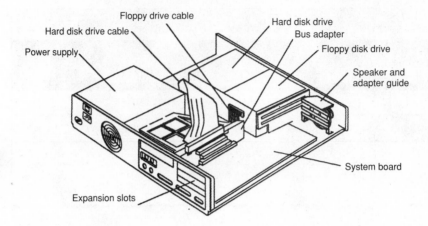

Table 4.26 lists the technical specifications for the PS/2 model 55SX.

Table 4.26 PS/2 Model 55 SX Technical Specifications

System architecture

Microprocessor	80386SX
Clock speed	16 MHz
Bus type	MCA (Micro Channel Architecture)
Bus width	16-bit
Interrupt levels	16
Type	Level-sensitive
Shareable	Yes
DMA channels	15
DMA burst mode supported	Yes
Bus masters supported	15
Upgradeable processor complex	No

Memory

Standard on system board	4M
Maximum on system board	8M
Maximum total memory	16M
Memory speed and type	100ns dynamic RAM
System board memory socket type	36-bit SIMM (single in-line memory module)
Number of memory module sockets	2
Number available in standard configuration	1
Memory used on system board	1M/2M/4M 36-bit SIMMs

Memory

Memory cache controller	No
Wait states:	
System board	0-2
Adapter	0-4
Standard features	
ROM size	128K
ROM shadowing	Yes
Optional math coprocessor	80387SX
Coprocessor speed	16 MHz
Standard graphics	VGA (Video Graphics Array)
8-/16-/32-bit controller	8-bit
Bus master	No
Video RAM (VRAM)	256K
RS232C serial ports	1
UART chip used	NS16550A
Maximum speed (bits/second)	19,200 bps
FIFO mode enabled	Yes
Maximum number of ports	8
Pointing device (mouse) ports	1
Parallel printer ports	1
Bidirectional	Yes
Maximum number of ports supported	8
CMOS real-time clock (RTC)	Yes
CMOS RAM	64 bytes
Battery life	10 years
Replaceable	Yes (Dallas module)

Disk storage

Internal disk and tape drive bays	2
Number of 3 1/2- and 5 1/4-inch bays	2/0
Standard floppy drives	1×1.44M
	None (LT0,LE0)
Optional floppy drives:	
5 1/4-inch 360K	Optional
5 1/4-inch 1.2M	Optional
3 1/2-inch 720K	No
3 1/2-inch 1.44M	Standard
3 1/2-inch 2.88M	No
Hard disk controller included:	IDE connector on bus adapter
IDE hard disks available	30M/40M/60M/80M
Drive form factor	3 1/2-inch
Drive interface	IDE

continues

Table 4.26 Continued

System architecture

Drive capacity	30M	40M	60M	80M
Average access rate (ms)	27	17	27	17
Read-ahead cache	No	32K	No	32K
Encoding scheme	RLL	RLL	RLL	RLL
BIOS drive type number	33	None	None	None
Cylinders	614	1038	762	1021
Heads	4	2	6	4
Sectors per track	25	39	26	39
Rotational speed (RPM)	3600	3600	3600	3600
Interleave factor	1:1	1:1	1:1	1:1
Actual transfer rate (K/second)	750	1170	780	1170
Automatic head parking	No	Yes	Yes	Yes

Expansion slots

Total adapter slots	3
Number of long and short slots	3/0
Number of 8-/16-/32-bit slots	0/3/0
Number of slots with video ext.	1
Available slots	3
Keyboard specifications:	
101-key Enhanced Keyboard	Yes
Fast keyboard speed setting	Yes
Keyboard cable length	6 feet

Security features

Keylock:	
Locks cover	Yes
Locks keyboard	No
Keyboard password	Yes
Power-on password	Yes
Network server mode	Yes

Physical specifications

Footprint type	Desktop
Dimensions:	
Height	4.0 inches
Width	16.0 inches
Depth	15.6 inches
Weight	15.5 lbs (LT0,LE0)
	19.0 lbs

Environmental specifications

Power-supply output	90 watts
Worldwide (110/60,220/50)	Yes

Environmental specifications	
Auto-sensing/switching	Manual switch
Maximum current:	
90-137 VAC	2.5 amps
180-265 VAC	1.3 amps
Operating range	
Temperature	60-90 degrees F
Relative humidity	8-80 percent
Maximum operating altitude	7,000 feet
Heat (BTUs/hour)	438
Noise (Average dB, operating, 1m)	40 dB
FCC classification	Class B

Figure 4.23 shows the Model 55 SX motherboard components and layout.

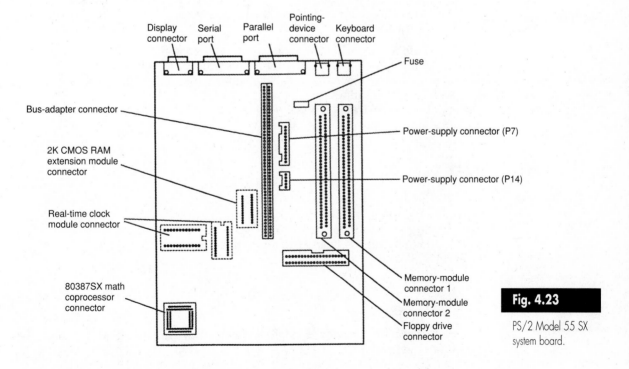

Fig. 4.23

PS/2 Model 55 SX
system board.

Table 4.27 shows the primary specifications and costs of the various versions of PS/2 Model 55 SX.

PS/2 Model 56 SX, SLC, LS, and LS SLC

The PS/2 Model 56, introduced February 25, 1992, is an MCA system designed to replace the PS/2 Model 55 SX. The system has a 386SX or 386SLC 20 MHz processor, and offers improvements such as increased speed, configuration flexibility, and a Small Computer System Interface (SCSI) input/output interface. For improved graphics performance, video is provided through an enhanced 16-bit VGA controller integrated on the system board. Several models are offered including models with SCSI hard disk capacities of 80M and 160M, with or without the 386SLC processor option, and LAN versions with built-in token ring or EtherNet adapters.

The SLC models use a new custom, high-speed processor. The new IBM 386SLC processor is designed and manufactured in IBM's Burlington, Vermont, semiconductor facility. The 386SLC chip powers the PS/2 cached processor option. This processor includes a built-in cache controller and 8K cache similar to 486 processors. The 386SLC is up to 88 percent faster than the standard 386SX processor. The standard Model 56 SX systems can be upgraded to the SLC processor by adding the PS/2 cached processor option.

The PS/2 Model 56 is designed for desktop operation but ships with a vertical stand, allowing the customer the flexibility of horizontal or vertical orientation. The mechanical package allows for expansion with three 16-bit slots for MCA adapters and two bays for I/O devices. One of the bays contains an extra-high-density 3 1/2-inch 2.88M (million bytes) media sense floppy disk drive. Another bay contains an SCSI hard disk.

SCSI Standard

The SCSI controller is integrated in the system board, so a slot is not required, and the controller can support up to seven SCSI devices (including the standard SCSI hard disk). Two of the additional SCSI devices can be attached internally and the remaining devices externally with the external SCSI connector.

System Memory

The system ships with one 4M single in-line memory module (SIMM) located in the first SIMM socket on the motherboard. The PS/2 Model 56 supports up to 16M of 70ns memory on the system board in three SIMM sockets, all of which are addressable by direct memory address (DMA). Because the system board supports the full 16M, memory should not be installed via adapter cards in the bus. The Model 56 supports 2M, 4M, and 8M memory SIMMs (70ns only). To take advantage of enhanced performance via interleaved memory, SIMMs should be installed using all 2M or all 4M SIMMs. One, two, or three 2M SIMMs provide memory interleaving. Two or three 4M SIMMs also provide memory interleaving. The 8M SIMMs do not provide interleaving, but do allow the maximum capacity of 16M to be reached.

Keyboard Options

The PS/2 Model 56 supports the IBM Enhanced Keyboard (101/102 keys), Space-Saving Keyboard (84/85 keys), and the IBM Host-Connected Keyboard (122 keys). The Host-Connected Keyboard is similar to the 3270 keyboard offered with 3270 IBM PC and IBM AT systems. This keyboard is similar in design to that of a 3270 terminal keyboard and offers keys dedicated to 3270 functions. The Host-Connected Keyboard is supported by the BIOS in this system and cannot be retrofitted to PS/2 systems that do not have the proper BIOS support.

When you purchase a Model 56, you can choose any of these three keyboards. The keyboard can be specified only in new equipment orders and cannot be ordered separately for on-order or installed equipment.

Floppy Drive Support

The Model 56 includes a standard 2.88M floppy disk drive. This drive is fully compatible with 1.44M and 720K floppy disk drives. The drive includes a media sensor, which prevents accidentally formatting floppy disks to the wrong capacity (which can result in data loss).

DOS 5.0 is the minimum DOS version supported on this system. Because of the 2.88M floppy disk drive, versions of DOS prior to 5.0 (or other operating systems or applications) might not format floppy disk media correctly. Use of the proper level of operating system along with the new 2.88M floppy disk drive provides media sensing of 720K, 1.44M, and 2.88M floppy disks, giving greater ease in formatting, reading, and writing floppy disks.

Table 4.27 IBM PS/2 Model 55 SX Model Summary

Part number	CPU	MHz	PLANAR MEMORY Std.	Max.	STANDARD Floppy drive	Hard disk	Bus type
55 SX							
8555-031	386SX	16	2M	8M	1×1.44M	30M	MCA/16
8555-041	386SX	16	4M	8M	1×1.44M	40M	MCA/16
8555-061	386SX	16	2M	8M	1×1.44M	60M	MCA/16
8555-081	386SX	16	4M	8M	1×1.44M	80M	MCA/16
55 LS							
8555-LT0	386SX	16	4M	8M	—	—	MCA/16
8555-LE0	386SX	16	4M	8M	—	—	MCA/16

The LT0 model includes an IBM 16/4 Token Ring Adapter, and the LE0 model includes an IBM

Initial Microcode Load

One very special feature of the Model 56 is called Initial Microcode Load (IML). The ROM BIOS is stored on the hard disk in a protected 3M partition and loaded from the disk during a "pre-boot" process. The formatted capacity of the hard disk is reduced by 3M, and the total user-accessible capacity might vary slightly, based on operating environments. This partition is protected from normal access and does not appear to the system when it is running FDISK or FORMAT. In fact, the partition is so well protected that the system BIOS cannot even access this system partition with standard Int 13h commands. For all intents and purposes the hard disk is simply 3M smaller than it would normally be. The 3M system partition also contains a copy of the Reference disk, which means that the Setup program is effectively in ROM as well! The setup program is accessed by pressing Ctrl-Alt-Ins when the cursor shifts to the right-hand portion of the screen during a boot operation.

Having a disk-based ROM offers an unprecedented level of control over the system compared to other models. For example, updating the ROM BIOS to a new version simply requires booting from a newer Reference disk and selecting the option that updates the system partition. This feature enables IBM to keep in step with ROM upgrades for new features and fix bugs in the BIOS without the expense and hassle of replacing ROM chips.

Total/ available slots	STANDARD Video	KB	Date introduced	Date withdrawn	List price
3/3	VGA	Enh	05/09/89	09/11/91	$2,745
3/3	VGA	Enh	06/11/91	05/25/92	$2,745
3/3	VGA	Enh	05/09/89	09/11/91	$2,945
3/3	VGA	Enh	06/11/91	05/25/92	$2,945
3/2	VGA	Enh	10/09/90	05/25/92	$2,745

EtherNet adapter. Both of these models are also diskless.

The optional 386SLC processor was designed, developed, and manufactured by IBM under a long-standing agreement with Intel. This chip has the same 32-bit internal, 16-bit external design as the Intel 386SX and is fully compatible with Intel 386 architecture. Intel participated in testing the 386SLC and determined the processor to be compatible with the Intel 386 architecture. IBM designed the 386SLC with 8K of internal cache and an internal cache controller, which improves performance by accessing data from high-speed cache memory rather than system memory, whenever possible. This is very similar to the 486 and is the primary reason for the increased performance. Performance has been further enhanced by optimizing commonly used instructions.

LS models are designed as LAN stations and include no disk drives. These diskless models are available in several versions, with or without the 386SLC processor. The -1xx models include an IBM EtherNet adapter in one of the three slots, and the -2xx models include an IBM Token Ring network adapter in one of the three slots.

Table 4.28 lists the technical specifications for the PS/2 Model 56.

Table 4.28 PS/2 Model 56 Technical Specifications

System architecture

Microprocessor	80386SX (04x)
	80386SLC (05x)
Optional microprocessor	80386SLC (04x)
Clock speed	20MHz
Bus type	MCA (Micro Channel Architecture)
Bus width	16-bit
Interrupt levels	16
Type	Level-sensitive
Shareable	Yes
DMA channels	15
DMA burst mode supported	Yes
Bus masters supported	15
Upgradeable processor complex	No

Memory

Standard on system board	4M
Maximum on system board	16M
Maximum total memory	16M
Memory speed and type	70ns dynamic RAM
System board memory socket type	36-bit SIMM (single in-line memory module)
Number of memory module sockets	3
Number available in standard configuration	2
Memory used on system board	2M/4M/8M 36-bit SIMMs
Memory interleaving	Yes (2MB/4MB SIMMs only)
Memory cache controller	No
Wait states:	
System board	0-2
Adapter	0-4

Standard features

ROM size	128K
ROM shadowing	Yes
BIOS extensions stored on disk	Yes
Setup and Diagnostics stored on disk	Yes
Optional math coprocessor	80387SX
Coprocessor speed	20 MHz

continues

Standard features

Standard graphics	VGA
8-/16-/32-bit controller	16-bit
Bus master	No
Video RAM (VRAM)	256K
RS232C serial ports	1
UART chip used	Custom (compatible with NS16550A)
Maximum speed (bits/second)	345,600
FIFO mode enabled	Yes
Supports DMA data transfer	Yes
Maximum number of ports	8
Pointing device (mouse) ports	1
Parallel printer ports	1
Bidirectional	Yes
Supports DMA data transfer	Yes
Maximum number of ports	8
CMOS real-time clock (RTC)	Yes
CMOS RAM	64 bytes + 2K extension
Battery life	10 years
Replaceable	Yes (Dallas module)

Disk storage

Internal disk and tape drive bays	4
Number of 3 1/2-inch and 5 1/4-inch bays	1/3

System architecture

Selectable boot drive	Yes
Bootable drives	All physical drives
Standard floppy drives	1×2.88M
Optional floppy drives:	
5 1/4-inch 360K	Optional
5 1/4-inch 1.2M	Optional
3 1/2-inch 720K	No
3 1/2-inch 1.44M	Optional
3 1/2-inch 2.88M	Standard
Hard disk controller included:	SCSI integrated on system board
Bus master	Yes
Devices supported per adapter	7
Adapters supported per system	4
SCSI hard disks available	60M/80M/120M/160M/320M/400M
Drive form factor	3 1/2-inch
Drive interface	SCSI

	60M	80M	120M	160M	320M	400M
Drive capacity	60M	80M	120M	160M	320M	400M
Average access rate (ms)	23	17	23	16	12.5	11.5
Read-ahead cache	32K	32K	32K	32K	64K	128K
SCSI transfer mode	Async	Async	Async	Async	Sync	Sync

continues

Table 4.28 Continued

System architecture

Encoding scheme	RLL	RLL	RLL	RLL	RLL	RLL
Cylinders	920	1021	920	1021	949	1201
Heads	4	4	8	8	14	14
Sectors per track	32	39	32	39	48	48
Rotational speed (RPM)	3600	3600	3600	3600	4318	4318
Interleave factor	1:1	1:1	1:1	1:1	1:1	1:1
Data transfer rate (K/second)	960	1170	960	1170	1727	1727
Automatic head parking	Yes	Yes	Yes	Yes	Yes	Yes

Expansion slots

Total adapter slots	3
Number of long and short slots	3/0
Number of 8-/16-/32-bit slots	0/3/0
Number of slots with video ext.	1
Available slots	3
	2 (1xx, 2xx)

Keyboard specifications

Keyboard choices:	
	122-key Host-Connected Keyboard
	101-key Enhanced Keyboard
	84-key Space-Saving Keyboard
Fast keyboard speed setting	Yes
Keyboard cable length	10 feet

Security features

Keylock:	
Locks cover	Yes
Locks keyboard	No
Keyboard password	Yes
Power-on password	Yes
Network server mode	Yes

Physical specifications

Footprint type	Desktop
Orientation	Horizontal/vertical
Dimensions:	
Height	4.5 inches
Width	14.2 inches
Depth	15.6 inches
Weight	24 lbs

continues

Environmental specifications	
Power-supply output	118 watts
Worldwide (110/60,220/50)	Yes
Auto-sensing/switching	Yes
Maximum current:	
90-137 VAC	3.5 amps
180-265 VAC	1.75 amps
Operating range:	
Temperature	50-95 degrees F
Relative humidity	8-80 percent
Maximum operating altitude	7,000 feet
Heat (BTUs/hour)	154
FCC classification	Class B

PS/2 Model 57 SX

The PS/2 Model 57 SX, introduced June 11, 1991, is an MCA system designed to complement and enhance the PS/2 Model 55 SX, the PS/2 Model 65 SX, and the low end of the PS/2 Model 70 386 family. The system has a 386SX 20 MHz processor and offers improvements such as increased speed, configuration flexibility, and a Small Computer System Interface (SCSI) input/output interface. For improved graphics performance, video is provided through an enhanced 16-bit VGA controller integrated on the system board. Several models are offered with SCSI hard disk capacities of 80M and 160M.

On October 17, 1991, IBM introduced a new custom, high-speed processor upgrade for the Model 57. The new upgrade option utilizes the powerful IBM 386SLC processor, designed and manufactured in IBM's Burlington, Vermont, semiconductor facility. The 386SLC chip powers the PS/2 cached processor option. This processor includes a built-in cache controller and 8K cache similar to 486 processors. The 386SLC is up to 88 percent faster than the standard 386SX processor.

The PS/2 Model 57 SX is designed for desktop operation but ships with a vertical stand, allowing the customer the flexibility of horizontal or vertical orientation. The mechanical package allows for expansion with five 16-bit slots for MCA adapters and four bays for I/O devices. One of the four bays contains an extra-high-density 3 1/2-inch 2.88M (million bytes) media sense floppy disk drive. Another bay contains a SCSI hard disk. Additional 5 1/4-inch and/or 3 1/2-inch devices, floppy disk drives, hard disks, tape and CD-ROM drives, and similar devices might be installed in the two remaining bays.

SCSI Standard

The SCSI controller is integrated in the system board, so a slot is not required, and the controller can support as many as seven SCSI devices (including the standard SCSI hard disk). Two of the additional SCSI devices can be attached internally and the remaining devices externally with the external SCSI connector.

System Memory

The system ships with one 4M single in-line memory module (SIMM) located in the first SIMM socket on the motherboard. The PS/2 Model 57 SX supports up to 16M of 70ns memory on the system board in three SIMM sockets, all of which are addressable by direct memory address (DMA). Because the system board supports the full 16M, memory should not be installed with adapter cards in the bus. The Model 57 SX supports 2M, 4M, and 8M memory SIMMs (70ns only). To take advantage of enhanced performance with interleaved memory, SIMMs should be installed using all 2M or all 4M SIMMs. One, two, or three 2M SIMMs provide memory interleaving. Two or three 4M SIMMs also provide memory interleaving. The 8M SIMMs do not provide interleaving, but do allow the maximum capacity of 16M to be reached.

Keyboard Options

The PS/2 Model 57 supports the IBM Enhanced Keyboard (101/102 keys), Space-Saving Keyboard (84/85 keys), and the IBM Host-Connected Keyboard (122 keys). The Host-Connected Keyboard is similar to the 3270 keyboard offered with 3270 IBM PC and IBM AT systems. This keyboard is similar in design to that of a 3270 terminal keyboard and offers keys dedicated to 3270 functions. The Host-Connected Keyboard is supported by the BIOS in this system and cannot be retrofitted to PS/2 systems that do not have the proper BIOS support.

When you purchase a Model 57, you can choose any of these three keyboards. The keyboard can be specified only in new equipment orders and cannot be ordered separately for on-order or installed equipment.

Floppy Drive Support

The Model 57 is the first system in the PC world to be shipped with a standard 2.88M floppy disk drive (although the drive is supported as an option in several other PS/2 systems). This drive is fully compatible with

1.44M and 720K floppy disk drives. The drive includes a media sensor, which prevents accidentally formatting floppy disks to the wrong capacity (which can result in data loss).

DOS 5.0 is the minimum DOS version supported on this system. Because of the 2.88M floppy disk drive, versions of DOS prior to 5.0 (or other operating systems or applications) might not format floppy disk media correctly. Use of the proper level of operating system along with the new 2.88M floppy disk drive provides media sensing of 720K, 1.44M, and 2.88M floppy disks, making it easier to format, read, and write floppy disks.

Initial Microcode Load

One special feature of the Model 57 is called Initial Microcode Load (IML). The ROM BIOS is stored on the hard disk in a protected 3M partition and loaded from the disk during a "pre-boot" process. The formatted capacity of the hard disk is reduced by 3M, and the total user-accessible capacity might vary slightly, based on operating environments. This partition is protected from normal access and does not appear to the system when running FDISK or FORMAT. In fact, the partition is so well protected that the system BIOS cannot even access this system partition with standard Int 13h commands. For all intents and purposes the hard disk is 3M smaller than it would normally be. The 3M system partition also contains a copy of the Reference disk, which means that the Setup program is effectively in ROM as well. The setup program is accessed by pressing Ctrl-Alt-Ins when the cursor shifts to the right-hand portion of the screen during a boot operation.

Having a disk-based ROM offers an unprecedented level of control over the system compared to other models. Updating the ROM BIOS to a new version, for example, simply requires booting from a newer Reference disk and selecting the option that updates the system partition. This feature enables IBM to keep in step with ROM upgrades for new features and fix bugs in the BIOS without the expense and hassle of replacing ROM chips.

The optional 386SLC processor was designed, developed, and manufactured by IBM under a long-standing agreement with Intel. This chip has the same 32-bit internal, 16-bit external design as the Intel 386SX and is fully compatible with Intel 386 architecture. Intel participated in testing the 386SLC and has determined the processor to be compatible with the Intel 386 architecture. IBM designed the 386SLC with 8K of internal cache and an internal cache controller that improves performance by accessing data from high-speed cache memory rather than system memory, whenever possible. This is very similar to the 486, and is the primary reason for the increased performance. Performance has been further enhanced by optimizing commonly used instructions.

Table 4.29 shows the primary specifications and costs of the various versions of PS/2 Model 56.

Table 4.29 IBM PS/2 Model 56 Model Summary

Part number	CPU	MHz	PLANAR MEMORY Std.	Max.	STANDARD Floppy drive	Hard disk	Bus type
56 SX							
8556-043	386SX	20	4M	16M	1×2.88M	40M	MCA/16
8556-045	386SX	20	4M	16M	1×2.88M	80M	MCA/16
56 SLC							
8556-055	386SLC	20	4M	16M	1×2.88M	80M	MCA/16
8556-059	386SLC	20	4M	16M	1×2.88M	160M	MCA/16
56 LS							
8556-14x	386SX	20	4M	16M	—	—	MCA/16
8556-24x	386SX	20	4M	16M	—	—	MCA/16
56 SLC LS							
8556-15x	386SLC	20	4M	16M	—	—	MCA/16
8556-25x	386SLC	20	4M	16M	—	—	MCA/16

Keyboards available include the Enhanced (101-key), Space-Saving (84-key), and Host-Connected

Because of IBM's deal with Intel, you may see other compatible systems using the 386SLC processor. Until then, only IBM systems will contain the new chip. Because of the enhanced 486-like design, installation of this chip will allow the Model 57 to perform faster than nearly all 25 MHz 386DX-based systems from IBM and other manufacturers. The 386SLC processor option card installs easily in the math coprocessor socket on the Model 57 SX system board. There is a socket on the 386SLC module for installation of a math coprocessor if you want one, or one has already been installed in the system.

Total/ available slots	STANDARD Video	KB	Date introduced	Date withdrawn	List price
3/3	VGA	Any	02/25/92	—	$2,745
3/3	VGA	Any	02/25/92	—	$3,030
3/3	VGA	Any	02/25/92	—	$3,560
3/3	VGA	Any	02/25/92	—	$4,030
3/3	VGA	Any	02/25/92	—	$2,445
3/2	VGA	Any	02/25/92	—	$2,890
3/2	VGA	Any	02/25/92	—	$2,980
3/2	VGA	Any	02/25/92	—	$3,420

(122-key). If "Any" is indicated, purchaser could choose any of the three.

On October 17, 1991, IBM pre-announced the PS/2 Ultimedia Model M57 SLC (8557-255). This enhanced version of the 57 includes the 386SLC processor module, for performance nearly double that of the standard Model 57. It also includes OS/2 2.0, whose availability coincides with the availability of this system in March 1992. This system also has complete multimedia capability. It adds the following standard product improvements to the model standard Model 57:

■ Multimedia front panel with stereo headphone jack, mono microphone jack, volume control, and enhanced loudspeaker.

■ 16-bit eXtended Graphics Array (XGA) adapter card with 1M VRAM supports 640×480 with 65,000 colors or 1024×768 with 256 colors.

- 16-bit audio adapter card with I/O to the front panel supports FM-quality stereo.

- IBM PS/2 mouse.

- 160M SCSI fixed disk.

- A new CD-ROM/XA drive (PS/2 CD-ROM II) with connection to the multimedia front panel, supporting existing CD-ROM formats and enabled to support new CD-ROM/XA formats.

- A CD containing three operating systems or environments, a variety of multimedia application samplers, and an "Introducing Ultimedia" demonstration.

- Operating systems supplied on CD-ROM include IBM OS/2 Version 2.0, IBM DOS 5.0, and Microsoft Windows 3.0 with Microsoft Multimedia Windows Extensions 1.0.

The PS/2 Ultimedia Model M57 SLC (8557-255) includes the IBM 386 SLC microprocessor as a standard item. This system is designed for desktop and floor standing operation (a floor stand is included). The mechanical package has five Micro Channel slots and four bays for I/O devices. The Audio Capture and Playback Adapter and the XGA Adapter are installed in two of the slots, leaving three slots for future expansion. A 3 1/2-inch 2.88M media sense disk drive, an SCSI fixed disk, and a CD-ROM/XA drive are installed in three of the bays. An additional 5 1/4-inch or 3 1/2-inch device, optical disk drive, fixed disk drive, tape drive, CD-ROM drive, or a similar device can be installed in the one remaining bay.

The primary video in the Ultimedia is provided by the 16-bit IBM PS/2 XGA Display Adapter/A. Additionally, an enhanced VGA port is provided, for direct video display/monitor connections or indirect connections via the video feature bus connections to Micro Channel slot #2.

With OS/2 Version 2.0 as a standard feature, users can run OS/2, DOS, and Windows applications. Multimedia applications supported in any of the operating systems can be used effectively by the PS/2 Ultimedia Model M57 SLC user. XGA graphics and CD-ROM/XA are leading-edge technologies. They offer capabilities yet to be exploited, making this one of the most advanced multimedia systems available. IBM intends to make IBM multimedia extensions to OS/2 generally available in 1992. These extensions will exploit the CD-ROM Extended Architecture (CD-ROM/XA) capabilities for interleaved data and compressed audio enabled by the PS/2 CD-ROM II drive. IBM also intends to provide the new PS/2 CD-ROM II drive as an optional feature on all IBM SCSI-supported PS/2 systems in the future.

Table 4.30 lists the technical specifications for the PS/2 model 57 SX.

Table 4.30 PS/2 Model 57 SX Technical Specifications

System architecture

Microprocessor	80386SX (04x)
	80386SLC (05x)
Optional microprocessor	80386SLC (04x)
Clock speed	20MHz
Bus type	MCA (Micro Channel Architecture)
Bus width	16-bit
Interrupt levels	16
Type	Level-sensitive
Shareable	Yes
DMA channels	15
DMA burst mode supported	Yes
Bus masters supported	15
Upgradeable processor complex	No

Memory

Standard on system board	4M
Maximum on system board	16M
Maximum total memory	16M
Memory speed and type	70ns dynamic RAM
System board memory socket type	36-bit SIMM (single in-line memory module)
Number of memory module sockets	3
Number available in standard configuration	2
Memory used on system board	2M/4M/8M 36-bit SIMMs
Memory Interleaving	Yes (2MB/4MB SIMMs only)
Memory cache controller	No
Wait states:	
System board	0-2
Adapter	0-4

Standard features

ROM size	128K
ROM shadowing	Yes
BIOS extensions stored on disk	Yes
Setup and Diagnostics stored on disk	Yes
Optional math coprocessor	80387SX
Coprocessor speed	20 MHz
Standard graphics	VGA
	XGA (255, 259)
8-/16-/32-bit controller	16-bit
Bus master	No
	Yes (XGA)

continues

Table 4.30 Continued

Standard features

Video RAM (VRAM)	256K (1M on XGA)
RS232C serial ports	1
UART chip used	Custom (compatible with NS16550A)
Maximum speed (bits/second)	345,600
FIFO mode enabled	Yes
Supports DMA data transfer	Yes
Maximum number of ports	8
Pointing device (mouse) ports	1
Parallel printer ports	1
Bidirectional	Yes
Supports DMA data transfer	Yes
Maximum number of ports	8
CMOS real-time clock (RTC)	Yes
CMOS RAM	64 bytes + 2K extension
Battery life	5 years
Replaceable	Yes

Disk storage

Internal disk and tape drive bays	4
Number of 3 1/2-inch and 5 1/4-inch bays	1/3
Selectable boot drive	Yes
Bootable drives	All physical drives
Standard floppy drives	1×2.88M
Optional floppy drives:	
5 1/4-inch 360K	Optional
5 1/4-inch 1.2M	Optional
3 1/2-inch 720K	No
3 1/2-inch 1.44M	Optional
3 1/2-inch 2.88M	Standard
Hard disk controller included: board	SCSI integrated on system
Bus master	Yes
Devices supported per adapter	7
Adapters supported per system	4
SCSI hard disks available	60M/80M/120M/160M/320M/400M

Disk storage

Drive interface   SCSI

	60M	80M	120M	160M	320M	400M
Drive capacity	60M	80M	120M	160M	320M	400M
Average access rate (ms)	23	17	23	16	12.5	11.5
Read-ahead cache	32K	32K	32K	32K	64K	128K
SCSI transfer mode	Async	Async	Async	Async	Sync	Sync
Encoding scheme	RLL	RLL	RLL	RLL	RLL	RLL
Cylinders	920	1021	920	1021	949	1201
Heads	4	4	8	8	14	14
Sectors per track	32	39	32	39	48	48
Rotational speed (RPM)	3600	3600	3600	3600	4318	4318
Interleave factor	1:1	1:1	1:1	1:1	1:1	1:1
Data transfer rate (K/second)	960	1170	960	1170	1727	1727
Automatic head parking	Yes	Yes	Yes	Yes	Yes	Yes

PS/2 Ultimedia Model M57 SLC (8557-255)

CD-ROM/XA drive characteristics:

Formats	CD-DA, CD-ROM, CD-ROM/XA
Capacity	Typically 600M, media-dependent
Access time	380ms
Burst (64K) transfer rate	1.5M/sec
Sustained transfer rate	150K/second
Latency	56ms to 150ms

Expansion slots

Total adapter slots	5
Number of long and short slots	5/0
Number of 8-/16-/32-bit slots	0/5/0
Number of slots with video ext.	1
Available slots	5

Keyboard specifications

Keyboard choices:

         122-key Host-Connected Keyboard
         101-key Enhanced Keyboard
         84-key Space-Saving Keyboard

Fast keyboard speed setting	Yes
Keyboard cable length	10 feet

Security features

Keylock:	
Locks cover	Yes
Locks keyboard	No
Keyboard password	Yes
Power-on password	Yes
Network server mode	Yes

continues

Table 4.30 Continued

Physical specifications	
Footprint type	Desktop
Orientation	Horizontal/vertical (stand included)
Dimensions:	
Height	6.7 inches
Width	17.3 inches
Depth	15.5 inches
Weight	32.0 lbs

Environmental specifications	
Power-supply output	197 watts
Worldwide (110/60,220/50)	Yes
Auto-sensing/switching	Manual switch
Maximum current:	
90-137 VAC	6.0 amps
180-265 VAC	3.0 amps
Operating range:	
Temperature	50-95 degrees F
Relative humidity	8-80 percent
Maximum operating altitude	7,000 feet
Heat (BTUs/hour)	120
FCC classification	Class B

PS/2 Model 60

The IBM PS/2 Model 60, introduced April 2, 1987, is a midrange, desk-side system in the PS/2 family using 16-bit MCA I/O slots. As of October 31, 1990, IBM has withdrawn all versions of the Model 60, and the system is no longer available. Figure 4.24 shows a front view of the Model 60.

The system unit features a 10 MHz microprocessor running with 1 wait state, enabling the Model 60 to perform approximately 20 percent faster than the IBM XT 286 or the IBM AT Model 339. The system-board limit of 1M memory is provided. The Model 60 comes standard with a 1.44M, 3 1/2-inch floppy disk drive; a 44M or a 70M hard disk drive; a disk controller; a serial port; a parallel port; a mouse port; a VGA port; and an 80287 coprocessor socket.

The system has two levels of BIOS, which total 128K: a Compatibility BIOS (CBIOS) with memory addressability of up to 1M provides support for real-mode-based application programs, and Advanced BIOS (ABIOS) provides support for protected-mode-based multitasking operating systems and has extended memory addressability up to 16M.

Additional features of the system unit include eight 16-bit MCA I/O slots (with one slot occupied by the disk controller adapter); an automatic voltage-sensing, universal power supply; a time-and-date clock with battery backup; an additional slot for a second 3 1/2-inch floppy disk drive; and the IBM Enhanced Keyboard. Figure 4.25 shows the rear panel and figure 4.26 shows the interior view of a Model 60.

IBM produced two versions of the Model 60, differing only in the hard disk and controller board supplied. The 70M drive is included with the 60-071 and also can be added as a second drive in that system. The 70M drive attaches using the high-performance Enhanced Small Device Interface (ESDI) disk adapter provided with the system unit and does not require an additional expansion slot. The ESDI adapter (standard in the 60-071) can connect up to two drives and allows for an extremely high data-transfer rate of 10 mbps (megabits per second) as well as increased reliability.

The standard Model 60-041 includes an ST-506/412 hard disk controller, which can connect up to two drives. The maximum transfer rate for this controller is 5 mbps (half that possible with the ESDI controller).

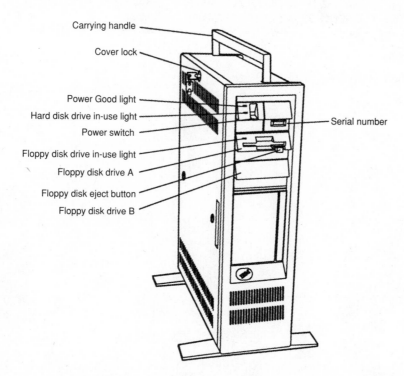

Carrying handle

Cover lock

Power Good light

Hard disk drive in-use light

Power switch

Floppy disk drive in-use light

Floppy disk drive A

Floppy disk eject button

Floppy disk drive B

Serial number

Fig. 4.24

PS/2 Model 60.

Table 4.31 shows the primary specifications and costs of the various versions of PS/2 Model 57 SX.

Table 4.31 IBM PS/2 Model 57 SX Model Summary

Part number	CPU	MHz	PLANAR MEMORY Std.	Max.	STANDARD Floppy drive	Hard disk	Bus type
57 SX							
8557-045	386SX	20	4M	16M	1×2.88M	80M	MCA/16
8557-049	386SX	20	4M	16M	1×2.88M	160M	MCA/16
57 SLC							
8557-055	386SLC	20	4M	16M	1×2.88M	80M	MCA/16
8557-059	386SLC	20	4M	16M	1×2.88M	160M	MCA/16
M57 SLC							
8557-255	386SLC	20	4M	16M	1×2.88M	80M	MCA/16
8557-259	386SLC	20	4M	16M	1×2.88M	160M	MCA/16

Keyboards available include the Enhanced (101-key), Space-Saving (84-key), and Host-Connected

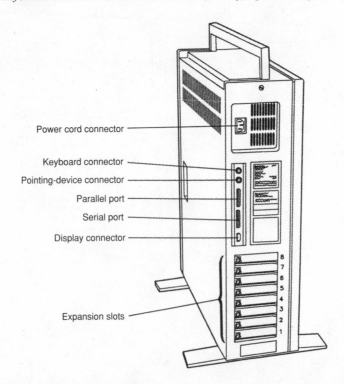

Power cord connector

Keyboard connector
Pointing-device connector
Parallel port
Serial port
Display connector

Expansion slots

Fig. 4.25

PS/2 Model 60 rear panel view.

Total/ available slots	STANDARD Video	KB	Date introduced	Date withdrawn	List price
5/5	VGA	Any	06/11/91	—	$3,465
5/5	VGA	Any	06/11/91	—	$3,935
5/5	VGA	Any	02/25/92	—	$3,995
5/5	VGA	Any	02/25/92	—	$4,465
5/3	XGA	Any	10/17/91	02/25/92	$5,995
5/3	XGA	Any	02/25/92	—	$5,995

(122-key). If "Any" is indicated, purchaser could choose any of the three.

Table 4.32 lists the technical specifications for the PS/2 Model 60.

Table 4.32 PS/2 Model 60 Technical Specifications

System architecture

Microprocessor	80286
Clock speed	10 MHz
Bus type	MCA (Micro Channel Architecture)
Bus width	16-bit
Interrupt levels	16
Type	Level-sensitive
Shareable	Yes
DMA channels	15
DMA burst mode supported	Yes
Bus masters supported	15
Upgradeable processor complex	No

continues

Table 4.32 Continued

Memory

Standard on system board	1M
Maximum on system board	1M
Maximum total memory	16M
Memory speed and type	150ns dynamic RAM
System board memory socket type	9-bit SIMM (single in-line memory module)
Number of memory module sockets	4
Number available in standard configuration	0
Memory used on system board	256K 9-bit SIMMs
Memory cache controller	No
Wait states:	
System board	1
Adapter	0-1
Standard features	
ROM size	128K
ROM shadowing	No
Optional math coprocessor	80287
Coprocessor speed	10 MHz
Standard graphics	VGA (Video Graphics Array)
8-/16-/32-bit controller	8-bit
Bus master	No
Video RAM (VRAM)	256K
RS232C serial ports	1
UART chip used	NS16550
Maximum speed (bits/second)	19,200 bps
FIFO mode enabled	No
Maximum number of ports	8
Pointing device (mouse) ports	1
Parallel printer ports	1
Bidirectional	Yes
Maximum number of ports	8
CMOS real-time clock (RTC)	Yes
CMOS RAM	64 bytes + 2K extension
Battery life	5 years
Replaceable	Yes

Disk storage

Internal disk and tape drive bays	4
Number of 3 1/2-/5 1/4-inch bays	2/2
Standard floppy drives	1×1.44M
Optional floppy drives:	
5 1/4-inch 360K	Optional
5 1/4-inch 1.2M	Optional
3 1/2-inch 720K	No

Disk storage

3 1/2-inch 1.44M	Standard				
3 1/2-inch 2.88M	No				

Hard disk controller included: ESDI controller
ST-506 controller (041)

ST-506/ESDI hard disks available: 44M/70M/115M/314M
Drive form factor 5 1/4-inch

	44M	44M	70M	115M	314M
Drive capacity	44M	44M	70M	115M	314M
Drive interface	ST-506	ST-506	ESDI	ESDI	ESDI
Average access rate (ms)	40	40	30	28	23
Encoding scheme	MFM	MFM	RLL	RLL	RLL
BIOS drive type	31	32	None	None	None
Cylinders	733	1024	583	915	1225
Heads	7	5	7	7	15
Sectors per track	17	17	36	36	34
Rotational speed (RPM)	3600	3600	3600	3600	3600
Interleave factor	1:1	1:1	1:1	1:1	1:1
Data transfer rate (K/second)	510	510	1080	1080	1020
Automatic head parking	Yes	Yes	Yes	Yes	Yes

Expansion slots

Total adapter slots	8
Number of long and short slots	8/0
Number of 8-/16-/32-bit slots	0/8/0
Number of slots with video ext.	1
Available slots	7

Keyboard specifications

101-key Enhanced Keyboard	Yes
Fast keyboard speed setting	Yes
Keyboard cable length	10 feet

Security features

Keylock:	
Locks cover	Yes
Locks keyboard	No
Keyboard password	Yes
Power-on password	Yes
Network server mode	Yes

Physical specifications

Footprint type	Floor-standing
Dimensions:	
Height	23.5 inches
Width	6.5 inches
Depth	19.0 inches
Weight	47.0 lbs

continues

Table 4.32 Continued

Environmental specifications

Power-supply output	207 watts (041)
	225 watts (071)
Worldwide (110/60,220/50)	Yes
Auto-sensing/switching	Yes
Maximum current:	
90-137 VAC	5.3 amps
180-265 VAC	2.7 amps
Operating range:	
Temperature	60-90 degrees F
Relative humidity	8-80 percent
Maximum operating altitude	7,000 feet
Heat (BTUs/hour)	1240
Noise (Average dB, operating, 1m)	46 dB
FCC classification	Class B

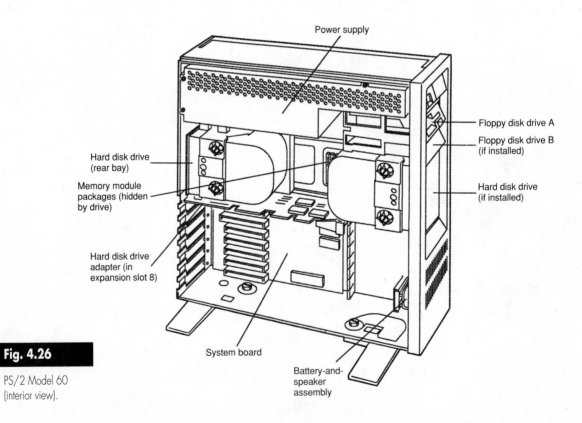

Fig. 4.26

PS/2 Model 60
(interior view).

Figure 4.27 shows the motherboard components and layout of a Model 60.

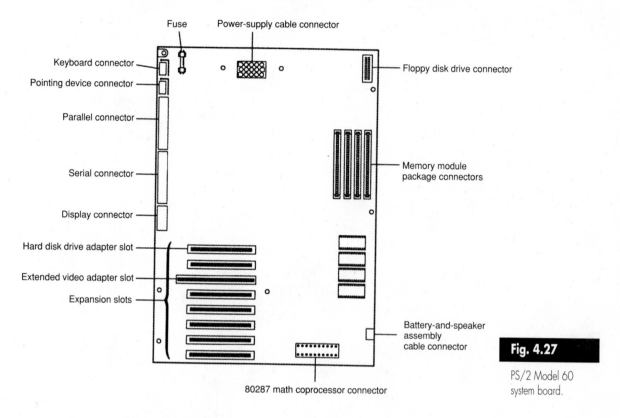

Fuse Power-supply cable connector

Keyboard connector

Pointing device connector

Parallel connector

Serial connector

Display connector

Hard disk drive adapter slot

Extended video adapter slot

Expansion slots

Floppy disk drive connector

Memory module
package connectors

Battery-and-speaker
assembly
cable connector

80287 math coprocessor connector

Fig. 4.27

PS/2 Model 60
system board.

PS/2 Model 65 SX

The PS/2 Model 65 SX, introduced March 20, 1990, is based on the Intel 80386SX processor running at 16 MHz and uses 16-bit MCA I/O slots. All models of the Model 65 SX were discontinued on July 23, 1991, and are no longer available from IBM. Figure 4.28 and figure 4.29 show front and rear panel views of the Model 65, respectively.

Standard features of the Model 65 SX include a 1.44M, 3 1/2-inch, half-height floppy disk drive; VGA graphics adapter; 2M of memory; a 250-watt power supply; a time-and-date clock with battery backup; and the IBM Enhanced PC Keyboard. Two memory SIMM sockets are provided on the system board; one contains 2M of 100ns memory. Both versions of the Model 65 SX can be expanded to 8M of memory on the system board and support up to 16M total system memory. This can be done by removing the standard 2M SIMM and using 4M SIMMs instead. Figure 4.30 shows an interior view of the Model 65.

The hard disk drive controller is the PS/2 Micro Channel SCSI (Small Computer System Interface) Adapter. This bus master adapter provides additional expansion capability and an interface for the 3 1/2-inch, half-height SCSI hard disk drives of either 60M (8565-061) or 120M (8565-121).

The Model 65 SX has two levels of BIOS, which total 128K: a Compatibility BIOS (CBIOS) with memory addressability of up to 1M provides support for real-mode-based application programs, and Advanced BIOS (ABIOS) provides support for protected-mode-based multitasking operating systems and has extended memory addressability up to 16M.

Design enhancements to these systems offer significant advantages in configuration flexibility and expansion. In addition to providing seven available adapter slots, the standard configuration supports as many as five or six internal drives.

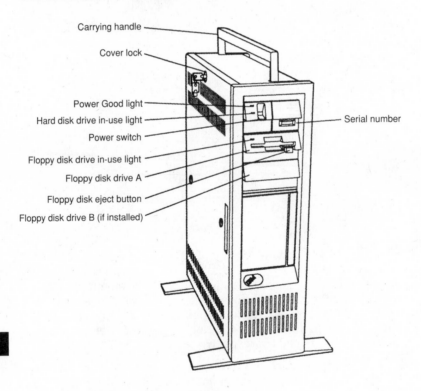

Fig. 4.28

PS/2 Model 65 SX.

Drive Support

The PS/2 65 SX design provides five drive bays. The three bays in the front of the system are user-accessible; they can contain devices that require insertion and removal of media. The remaining two bays are designed for nonaccessible devices such as hard disks. The accessible bays consist of two 3 1/2-inch, half-height bays and one 5 1/4-inch, full-height bay. The top 3 1/2-inch, half-height bay contains a standard 1.44M floppy disk drive; the second 3 1/2-inch, half-height bay and the 5 1/4-inch, full-high bay are open for expansion purposes.

The standard hard disk drive configuration of the PS/2 Model 65 SX contains one SCSI hard disk drive located in one of the two nonaccessible bays. The other nonaccessible bay contains the necessary hardware to install a second IBM SCSI hard disk drive. The accessible 5 1/4-inch, full-height bay can be converted into two 3 1/2-inch, half-height bays through the use of the optional Fixed Disk Drive Kit A (1053) (6451053). This conversion allows the installation of third and fourth IBM SCSI hard disk drives.

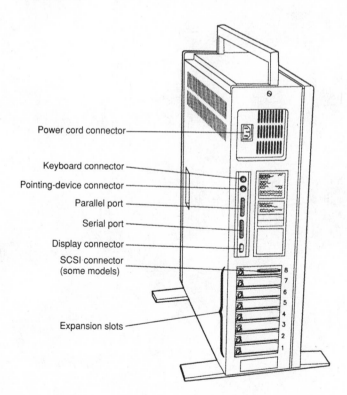

Power cord connector

Keyboard connector

Pointing-device connector

Parallel port

Serial port

Display connector

SCSI connector
(some models)

Expansion slots

Fig. 4.29

PS/2 Model 65 SX
rear panel view.

Table 4.33 shows the primary specifications and costs of the various versions of PS/2 Model 60.

Table 4.33 IBM PS/2 Model 60 Model Summary

Part CPU	MHz	Std.	PLANAR MEMORY Max.	drive	STANDARD Floppy disk	Hard type	Bus number
60							
8560-041	286	10	1M	1M	1×1.44M	44M	MCA/16
8560-071	286	10	1M	1M	1×1.44M	70M	MCA/16

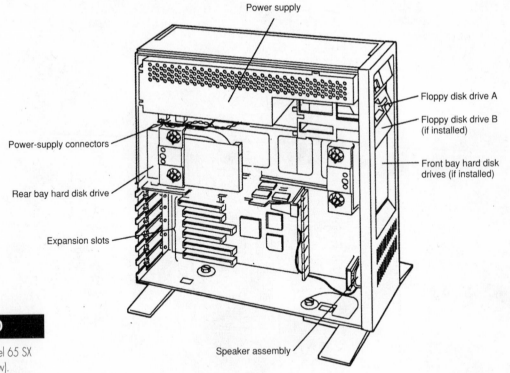

Fig. 4.30

PS/2 Model 65 SX (interior view).

Total/available slots	STANDARD Video	KB	Date introduced	Date withdrawn	List price
8/7	VGA	Enh	04/02/87	10/31/90	$2,750
8/7	VGA	Enh	04/02/87	10/31/90	$3,085

The drive controller is the IBM PS/2 Micro Channel SCSI Adapter—a 16-bit MCA master adapter. Internal cabling is provided to support the standard hard disk drive and two additional internal SCSI devices. External SCSI devices attach directly to the IBM PS/2 Micro Channel SCSI Adapter external port, using the PS/2 card to option cable.

The specifications for the IBM PS/2 Micro Channel SCSI Adapter are as follows:

- Industry-standard interface (ANSI standard X3.131-1986)
- PS/2 16-bit intelligent bus master adapter
- Support for as many as seven physical SCSI devices
- Support for internal and external SCSI devices (single-ended)
- Micro Channel data transfer rate of up to 8.3M per second
- Support for asynchronous or synchronous SCSI devices

Table 4.34 lists the technical specifications for the PS/2 Model 65 SX.

Table 4.34 PS/2 Model 65 SX Technical Specifications

System architecture

Microprocessor	80386SX
Clock speed	16 MHz
Bus type	MCA (Micro Channel Architecture)
Bus width	16-bit
Interrupt levels	16

continues

Table 4.34 Continued

System architecture

Type	Level-sensitive
Shareable	Yes
DMA channels	15
DMA burst mode supported	Yes
Bus masters supported	15
Upgradeable processor complex	No

Memory

Standard on system board	2M
Maximum on system board	8M
Maximum total memory	16M
Memory speed and type	100ns dynamic RAM
System board memory socket type	36-bit SIMM (single in-line memory module)
Number of memory module sockets	2
Number available in standard configuration	1
Memory used on system board	1M/2M/4M 36-bit SIMMs
Memory cache controller	No
Wait states:	
System board	0-2
Adapters	0-4

Standard features

ROM size	128K
ROM shadowing	Yes
Optional math coprocessor	80387SX
Coprocessor speed	16 MHz
Standard graphics	VGA
8-/16-/32-bit controller	8-bit
Bus master	No
Video RAM (VRAM)	256K
RS232C serial ports	1
UART chip used	NS16550A
Maximum speed (bits/second)	19,200 bps
FIFO mode enabled	Yes
Maximum number of ports	8
Pointing device (mouse) ports	1
Parallel printer ports	1
Bidirectional	Yes
Maximum number of ports	8
CMOS real-time clock (RTC)	Yes
CMOS RAM	64 bytes + 2K extension
Battery life	10 years
Replaceable	Yes (Dallas module)

Disk storage

Internal disk and tape drive bays	5 or 6 (reconfigurable)					
Number of 3 1/2 and /5 1/4-inch bays	4/1 or 6/0 (reconfigurable)					
Standard floppy drives	1×1.44M					
Optional floppy drives:						
5 1/4-inch 360K	Optional					
5 1/4-inch 1.2M	Optional					
3 1/2-inch 720K	No					
3 1/2-inch 1.44M	Standard					
3 1/2-inch 2.88M	No					
Hard disk controller included:	16-bit SCSI adapter					
Bus master	Yes					
Devices supported per adapter	7					
Adapters supported per system	4					
SCSI hard disks available:	60M/80M/120M/160M/320M/400M					
Drive form factor	3 1/2-inch					
Drive interface	SCSI					
Drive capacity	60M	80M	120M	160M	320M	400M
Average access rate (ms)	23	17	23	16	12.5	11.5
Read-ahead cache	32K	32K	32K	32K	64K	128K
SCSI transfer mode	Async	Async	Async	Async	Sync	Sync
Encoding scheme	RLL	RLL	RLL	RLL	RLL	RLL
Cylinders	920	1021	920	1021	949	1201
Heads	4	4	8	8	14	14
Sectors per track	32	39	32	39	48	48
Rotational speed (RPM)	3600	3600	3600	3600	4318	4318
Interleave factor	1:1	1:1	1:1	1:1	1:1	1:1
Data transfer rate (K/sec)	960	1170	960	1170	1727	1727
Automatic head parking	Yes	Yes	Yes	Yes	Yes	Yes

Expansion slots

Total adapter slots	8
Number of long and short slots	8/0
Number of 8-/16-/32-bit slots	0/8/0
Number of slots with video ext.	1
Available slots	7

Keyboard specifications

101-key Enhanced Keyboard	Yes
Fast keyboard speed setting	Yes
Keyboard cable length	10 feet
Keylock:	
Locks cover	Yes
Locks keyboard	No
Keyboard password	Yes

continues

Table 4.34 Continued	
Keyboard specifications	
Power-on password	Yes
Network server mode	Yes
Physical specifications	
Footprint type:	Floor-standing
Dimensions:	
Height	23.5 inches
Width	6.5 inches
Depth	19.0 inches
Weight	52.0 lbs
Environmental specifications	
Power-supply output	250 watts
Worldwide (110/60,220/50)	Yes
Auto-sensing/switching	Yes
Maximum current:	
90-137 VAC	5.3 amps
180-265 VAC	2.7 amps
Operating range:	
Temperature	60-90 degrees F
Relative humidity	8-80 percent
Maximum operating altitude	7,000 feet
Heat (BTUs/hour)	1218
Noise (Average dB, operating, 1m)	54 dB
FCC classification	Class B

Figure 4.31 shows the motherboard components and layout for the Model 65.

PS/2 Model 70 386

The PS/2 Model 70 386, introduced June 2, 1988, is a desktop, high-end system in the PS/2 family. The Model 70 386 includes Micro Channel Architecture (MCA). Figure 4.32 shows a front view of the Model 70.

The basic system features a 16 MHz, 20 MHz, or 25 MHz 80386 microprocessor and 2M or 4M of high-speed memory on the motherboard. Motherboard memory is expandable to 6M or 8M depending on the model; you can expand total memory to 16M with memory adapters. The Model 70 386 comes with a 1.44M, 3 1/2-inch floppy disk drive and either a 60M or 120M hard disk drive with integrated controller (IDE) as standard. A serial port, parallel port, mouse port, and VGA port also are standard. Figure 4.33 shows a rear panel view of the Model 70.

The top-of-the-line 70 386-Axx models feature a 25 MHz 80386 32-bit microprocessor and an Intel 82385 memory cache controller with a high-speed 64K static memory cache. This memory cache lets the Model 70 386 perform approximately 150 percent faster than the 20 MHz versions of the Model 80. The Model 70 386 is about 250 percent faster than the Model 50.

The Model 70 386 has two levels of BIOS, which total 128K: a Compatibility BIOS (CBIOS) with memory addressability of up to 1M provides support for real-mode-based application programs; and Advanced BIOS (ABIOS) provides support for protected-mode-based multitasking operating systems and has extended memory addressability up to 16M.

Additional features of the Model 70 386 include one 16-bit and two 32-bit I/O slots. Because all the hard disks available with the Model 70 386 have integrated (embedded) controllers, no slot is lost to a disk controller

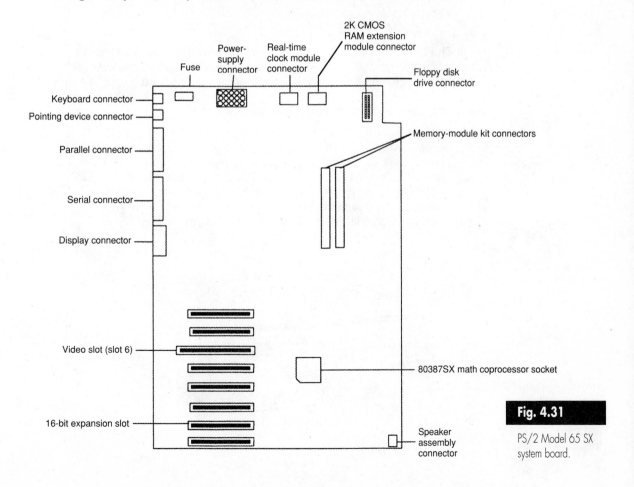

Fig. 4.31

PS/2 Model 65 SX system board.

Table 4.35 shows the primary specifications and costs of the various versions of PS/2 Model 65 SX.

Table 4.35 IBM PS/2 Model 65 SX Model Summary

Part number	CPU	MHz	PLANAR MEMORY Std.	Max.	STANDARD Floppy drive	Hard disk	Bus type
65 SX							
8565-061	386SX	16	2M	8M	1×1.44M	60M	MCA/16
8565-121	386SX	16	2M	8M	1×1.44M	120M	MCA/16
8565-321	386SX	16	2M	8M	1×1.44M	320M	MCA/16

Note: *All Model 65 units are discontinued.*

card. The Model 70 386 also has a 132-watt, automatic voltage-sensing, universal power supply; a time-and-date clock with battery backup; an additional slot for a second 3 1/2-inch floppy disk drive; an optional 16 MHz, 20 MHz, or 25 MHz 80387 coprocessor; and the IBM Enhanced Keyboard. Figure 4.34 shows the interior view of the Model 70.

Several versions of the Model 70 386 are available. They differ mainly in clock speed, installed hard disk storage, and memory capabilities. Available system clock speeds are 16 MHz, 20 MHz, and 25 MHz, AND hard disks are available with 60M, 80M, 120M, and 160M of capacity. The 25 MHz models offer memory expansion to 8M on the system board and feature an upgradeable processor on a daughterboard (currently, only a single upgrade is available to a 25 MHz 80486DX processor).

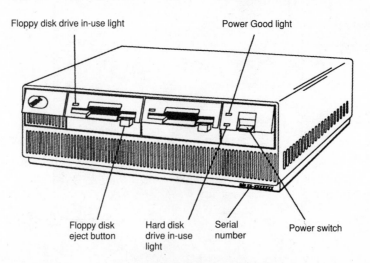

Floppy disk drive in-use light · Power Good light

Floppy disk eject button · Hard disk drive in-use light · Serial number · Power switch

Fig. 4.32

PS/2 Model 70.

Total/ available slots	STANDARD Video	KB	Date introduced	Date withdrawn	List price
8/7	VGA	Enh	03/20/90	07/23/91	$3,145
8/7	VGA	Enh	03/20/90	07/23/91	$3,715
8/7	VGA	Enh	10/30/90	07/23/91	$5,465

The 25 MHz models have a few outstanding differences from the other models that give this system a higher than expected performance level. The 70 386-Axx models use an Intel 82385 cache controller chip, which manages 64K of extremely high-speed static memory. This memory is accessed at 0 wait states and uses a special algorithm to ensure an exceptionally high bit ratio for cache memory access. Because of this system's speed, this version of the Model 70 386 requires extremely fast (80ns) memory, which the other models do not need. Remember this requirement when you purchase additional memory for this system and when you make repairs.

The 80387 math coprocessor chip selected for each system unit must match the main processor in speed, and the 80387 chips (especially the 25 MHz chip) are expensive. These chips are no longer being sold by IBM and must be obtained from other sources.

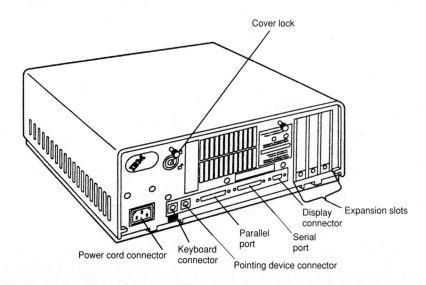

Cover lock

Display connector
Expansion slots
Serial port
Parallel port
Pointing device connector
Keyboard connector
Power cord connector

Fig. 4.33

PS/2 Model 70 rear panel.

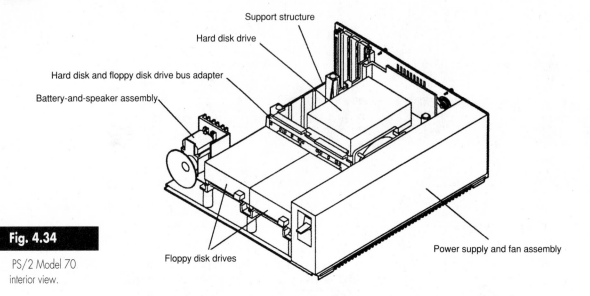

Support structure

Hard disk drive

Hard disk and floppy disk drive bus adapter

Battery-and-speaker assembly

Floppy disk drives

Power supply and fan assembly

Fig. 4.34

PS/2 Model 70
interior view.

Table 4.36 lists the technical specifications for the PS/2 Model 70 386.

Table 4.36 PS/2 Model 70 386 Technical Specifications

System architecture

Microprocessor	80386DX
Clock speed	16 MHz (Exx)
	20 MHz (0xx,1xx)
	25 MHz (Axx)
Bus type	MCA (Micro Channel Architecture)
Bus width	32-bit
Interrupt levels	16
Type	Level-sensitive
Shareable	Yes
DMA channels	15
DMA burst mode supported	Yes
Bus masters supported	15
Upgradeable processor complex	No
	Yes (Axx)

Memory

Standard on system board	4M
Maximum on system board	6M
	8M (Axx)
Maximum total memory	16M

Memory

Memory speed and type	85ns dynamic RAM
	80ns dynamic RAM (Axx)
System board memory socket type	36-bit SIMM (single in-line memory module)
Number of memory module sockets	3
	4 (Axx)
Number available in standard configuration	1
	2 (Axx)
Memory used on system board	1M/2M 36-bit SIMMs
Paged memory logic	Yes
Memory cache controller	No
	Yes (Axx)
Internal/external cache	External
Standard memory cache size	64K
Cache memory speed and type	25ns static RAM
Wait states:	
System board	0-5 (Axx, 95 percent 0 wait states)
	0-2
Adapter	0-7 (Axx, 95 percent 0 wait states)
	0-4

Standard features

ROM size	128K
ROM shadowing	Yes
Optional math coprocessor	80387DX
Coprocessor speed	16 MHz (Exx)
	20 MHz (0xx,1xx)
	25 MHz (Axx)
Standard graphics	VGA (Video Graphics Array)
8-/16-/32-bit controller	8-bit
Bus master	No
Video RAM (VRAM)	256K
RS232C serial ports	1
UART chip used	NS16550A
Maximum speed (bits/second)	19,200 bps
FIFO mode enabled	Yes
Maximum number of ports	8
Pointing device (mouse) ports	1
Parallel printer ports	1
Bidirectional	Yes
Maximum number of ports	8

continued

Table 4.36 PS/2 Model 70 386 Technical Specifications

System architecture

CMOS real-time clock (RTC)	Yes
CMOS RAM	64 bytes + 2K extension
Battery life	5 years
Replaceable	Yes

Disk storage

Internal disk and tape drive bays	3
Number 3 1/2-inch and 5 1/4-inch bays	3/0
Standard floppy drives	1×1.44M
Optional floppy drives:	
5 1/4-inch 360K	Optional
5 1/4-inch 1.2M	Optional
3 1/2-inch 720K	No
3 1/2-inch 1.44M	Standard
3 1/2-inch 2.88M	No
Hard disk controller included:	IDE connector on Interposer Card
IDE hard disks available:	60M/80M/120M/160M
Drive form factor	3 1/2-inch
Drive interface	IDE

Drive capacity	60M	80M	120M	160M
Average access rate (ms)	27	17	23	16
Read-ahead cache	No	32K	No	32K
Encoding scheme	RLL	RLL	RLL	RLL
Cylinders	762	1021	920	1021
Heads	6	4	8	8
Sectors per track	26	39	32	39
Rotational speed (RPM)	3600	3600	3600	3600
Interleave factor	1:1	1:1	1:1	1:1
Data transfer rate (K/second)	780	1170	960	1170
Automatic head parking	Yes	Yes	Yes	Yes

Expansion slots

Total adapter slots	3
Number of long and short slots	3/0
Number of 8-/16-/32-bit slots	0/1/2
Number of slots with video ext.	1
Available slots	3

Keyboard specifications

101-key Enhanced Keyboard	Yes
Fast keyboard speed setting	Yes
Keyboard cable length	6 feet

Security features	
Keylock:	
Locks cover	Yes
Locks keyboard	No
Keyboard password	Yes
Power-on password	Yes
Network server mode	Yes
Physical specifications	
Footprint type	Desktop
Dimensions:	
Height	5.5 inches
Width	14.2 inches
Depth	16.5 inches
Weight	21.0 lbs
Environmental specifications	
Power-supply output	132 watts
Worldwide (110/60,220/50)	Yes
Auto-sensing/switching	Yes
Maximum current:	
90-137 VAC	2.7 amps
180-265 VAC	1.4 amps
Operating range:	
Temperature	60-90 degrees F
Relative humidity	8-80 percent
Maximum operating altitude	7,000 feet
Heat (BTUs/hour)	751
Noise (average dB, operating, 1m)	40 dB
FCC classification	Class B

Figures 4.35, 4.36, and 4.37 show the components and layouts of the three different types of Model 70 motherboards.

Table 4.37 shows the primary specifications and costs of the various versions of PS/2 Model 70 386.

Table 4.37 IBM PS/2 Model 70 386 Model Summary

Part number	CPU	MHz	PLANAR MEMORY Std.	Max.	STANDARD Floppy drive	Hard disk	Bus type
70 386							
8570-E61	386DX	16	2M	6M	1×1.44M	60M	MCA/32
8570-061	386DX	20	2M	6M	1×1.44M	60M	MCA/32
8570-081	386DX	20	4M	6M	1×1.44M	80M	MCA/32
8570-121	386DX	20	2M	6M	1×1.44M	120M	MCA/32
8570-161	386DX	20	4M	6M	1×1.44M	160M	MCA/32
8570-A61	386DX	25	2M	8M	1×1.44M	60M	MCA/32
8570-A81	386DX	25	4M	8M	1×1.44M	80M	MCA/32
8570-A21	386DX	25	2M	8M	1×1.44M	120M	MCA/32
8570-A16	386DX	25	4M	8M	1×1.44M	160M	MCA/32

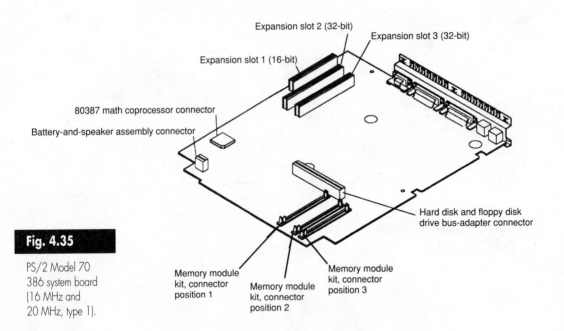

Fig. 4.35

PS/2 Model 70 386 system board (16 MHz and 20 MHz, type 1).

Total/ available slots	STANDARD		Date introduced	Date withdrawn	List price
	Video	KB			
3/3	VGA	Enh	06/07/88	07/23/91	$3,945
3/3	VGA	Enh	09/26/89	09/11/91	$4,095
3/3	VGA	Enh	06/11/91	—	$3,675
3/3	VGA	Enh	09/26/89	09/11/91	$4,745
3/3	VGA	Enh	06/11/91	—	$4,295
3/3	VGA	Enh	09/26/89	09/11/91	$5,845
3/3	VGA	Enh	06/11/91	01/17/92	$4,875
3/3	VGA	Enh	09/26/89	09/11/91	$6,445
3/3	VGA	Enh	06/11/91	—	$5,475

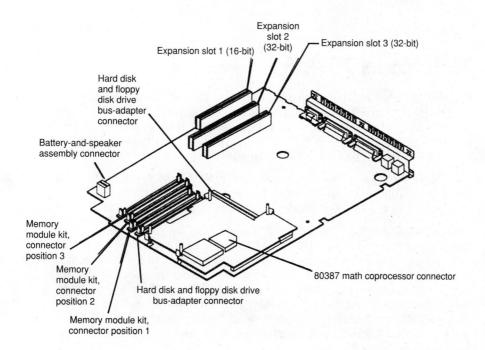

Fig. 4.36

PS/2 Model 70 386 system board (16 MHz and 20 MHz, type 2).

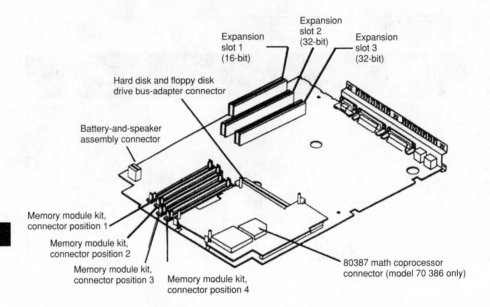

Expansion
slot 2
(32-bit)

Expansion
slot 1
(16-bit)

Expansion
slot 3
(32-bit)

Hard disk and floppy disk
drive bus-adapter connector

Battery-and-speaker
assembly connector

Memory module kit,
connector position 1

Memory module kit,
connector position 2

Memory module kit,
connector position 3

Memory module kit,
connector position 4

80387 math coprocessor
connector (model 70 386 only)

Fig. 4.37

PS/2 Model 70
386 system board
(25 MHz, type 3).

PS/2 Model 70 486

The IBM PS/2 Model 70 486, introduced June 20, 1989, is essentially a
Model 70 386-Axx with the 486 25 MHz Power Platform upgrade. The 25
MHz 80486 32-bit microprocessor replaces the 386 processor module
standard in the Model 70 386. The Model 70 496 is no different from a
Model 70 386 with the Power Platform added later.

The Model 70 486 has been discontinued by IBM as of 09/11/91 and is no
longer available. The 486 Power Platform, however, is still available for
upgrading existing 25 MHz Model 70 386 systems.

The basic system features a 25 MHz 80486 32-bit microprocessor with a
built-in 8K memory cache. With this processor and memory cache, this
unit can perform approximately 100 percent faster than the 386 version.
Also included is 4M of high-speed memory on the motherboard, expandable to 8M, with total memory expandable to 16M (with memory adapters). This system comes with a 1.44M, 3 1/2-inch floppy disk drive and
either a 60M or 120M hard disk drive with integrated controller (IDE) as
standard. Also standard are a serial port, a parallel port, a mouse port,
and a VGA port.

The Model 70 486 has two levels of BIOS, which total 128K: A Compatibility BIOS (CBIOS) with memory addressability of up to 1M provides
support for real-mode-based application programs; and an additional
version of BIOS, Advanced BIOS (ABIOS), provides support for

protected-mode-based multitasking operating systems and has extended memory addressability of up to 16M.

Additional features of the Model 70 486 include one 16-bit and two 32-bit I/O slots. Because all the hard disks available with the Model 70 have integrated (embedded) controllers, no slot is lost to a disk controller card. The Model 70 486 also has a 25 MHz 80387 math coprocessor; a 132-watt, automatic voltage-sensing, universal power supply; a time-and-date clock with battery backup; an additional slot for a second 3 1/2-inch floppy disk drive; and the IBM Enhanced Keyboard.

Table 4.38 lists the technical specifications for the PS/2 Model 70 486.

Table 4.38 PS/2 Model 70 486 Technical Specifications	
System architecture	
Microprocessor	80486
Clock speed	25 MHz
Bus type	MCA (Micro Channel Architecture)
Bus width	32-bit
Interrupt levels	16
Type	Level-sensitive
Shareable	Yes
DMA channels	15
DMA burst mode supported	Yes
Bus masters supported	15
486 burst mode enabled	No
Upgradeable processor complex	Included
Memory	
Standard on system board	2M
Maximum on system board	8M
Maximum total memory	16M
Memory speed and type	80ns dynamic RAM
System board memory socket type	36-bit SIMM (single in-line memory module)
Number of memory module sockets	4
Number available in standard configuration	3
Memory used on system board	2M 36-bit SIMMs
Paged memory logic	Yes
Memory cache controller	Yes
Internal/external cache	Internal
Standard memory cache size	8K
Optional external memory cache	No
Wait states:	
System board	0-5 (95 percent 0 wait states)
Adapter	0-7

continues

Table 4.38 Continued

Memory

Standard features

ROM size	128K
ROM shadowing	Yes
Math coprocessor	Built-in
Coprocessor speed	25 MHz
Standard graphics	VGA
8-/16-/32-bit controller	8-bit
Bus master	No
Video RAM (VRAM)	256K
RS232C serial ports	1
UART chip used	NS16550A
Maximum speed (bits/second)	19,200 bps
FIFO mode enabled	Yes
Maximum number of ports	8
Pointing device (mouse) ports	1
Parallel printer ports	1
Bidirectional	Yes
Maximum number of ports	8
CMOS real-time clock (RTC)	Yes
CMOS RAM	64 bytes + 2K extension
Battery life	5 years
Replaceable	Yes

Disk storage

Internal disk and tape drive bays	3			
Number of 3 1/2- and 5 1/4-inch bays	3/0			
Standard floppy drives	1×1.44M			
Optional floppy drives:				
5 1/4-inch 360K	Optional			
5 1/4-inch 1.2M	Optional			
3 1/2-inch 720K	No			
3 1/2-inch 1.44M	Standard			
3 1/2-inch 2.88M	No			
Hard disk controller included:	IDE connector on Interposer Card			
IDE hard disks available:	60M/80M/120M/160M			
Drive form factor	3 1/2-inch			
Drive interface	IDE			
Drive capacity	60M	80M	120M	160M
Average access rate (ms)	27	17	23	16
Read-ahead Cache	No	32K	No	32K
Encoding scheme	RLL	RLL	RLL	RLL
Cylinders	762	1021	920	1021
Heads	6	4	8	8
Sectors per track	26	39	32	39

Disk storage

Rotational speed (RPM)	3600	3600	3600	3600
Interleave factor	1:1	1:1	1:1	1:1
Data transfer rate (K/second)	780	1170	960	1170
Automatic head parking	Yes	Yes	Yes	Yes

Expansion slots

Total adapter slots	3
Number of long and short slots	3/0
Number of 8-/16-/32-bit slots	0/1/2
Number of slots with video ext.	1
Available slots	3

Keyboard specifications

101-key Enhanced Keyboard	Yes
Fast keyboard speed setting	Yes
Keyboard cable length	6 feet

Security features

Keylock:	
Locks cover	Yes
Locks keyboard	No
Keyboard password	Yes
Power-on password	Yes
Network server mode	Yes

Physical specifications

Footprint type	Desktop
Dimensions:	
Height	5.5 inches
Width	14.2 inches
Depth	16.5 inches
Weight	21.0 lbs

Environmental specifications

Power-supply output	132 watts
Worldwide (110/60,220/50)	Yes
Auto-sensing/switching	Yes
Maximum current:	
90-137 VAC	2.7 amps
180-265 VAC	1.4 amps
Operating range:	
Temperature	60-90 degrees F
Relative humidity	8-80 percent
Maximum operating altitude	7,000 feet
Heat (BTUs/hour)	751
Noise (Average dB, operating, 1m)	40 dB
FCC classification	Class B

Table 4.39 shows the primary specifications and costs of the various versions of PS/2 Model 70 486.

Table 4.39 IBM PS/2 Model 70 486 Model Summary

Part number	CPU	MHz	PLANAR MEMORY Std.	Max.	STANDARD Floppy drive	Hard disk	Bus type
70 486							
8570-B61	486DX	25	2M	8M	1×1.44M	60M	MCA/32
8570-B21	486DX	25	2M	8M	1×1.44M	120M	MCA/32

PS/2 Model P70 386

The PS/2 Model P70 386 (8573), introduced May 9, 1989, is a high-function, high-performance portable system designed to complement the PS/2 Model 70 386 desktop family of products. IBM has made the PS/2 Model P70 386 in 16 MHz and 20 MHz versions with 30M, 60M, and 120M hard disks. Effective July 23, 1991, IBM discontinued two versions of the Model P70 386: the 16 MHz model (031) and the 20 MHz, 60M disk model (061). The Model P70 386-121 (120M disk) continues to be sold. Figure 4.38 shows a front view of the Model P70.

The Model P70 386 includes MCA I/O slots, a VGA 16-grayscale plasma display, and a fully compatible PS/2 Enhanced Keyboard, all neatly integrated into a single package. It features an 80386DX processor, high-density memory technology, and a wide range of integrated features, supporting up to 16M of high-speed memory (4M standard, expandable up to 8M on system board), 120M or more disk storage, and an optional 80387 math coprocessor. Like most PS/2 systems, all models come standard with a 1.44M, 3 1/2-inch floppy disk drive, a pointing device port, a serial/asynchronous port, a parallel port, a VGA port, and an external storage device port. Figure 4.39 shows the rear panel view of the Model P70.

Exceptional features for a portable computer include the Model 70's two MCA expansion slots (one full and one half-length) and its ergonomic briefcase portable design. The expansion slots can be used for products such as the IBM PS/2 300/1200/2400 Internal Modem/A or P70 386 Token Ring Adapter. Figure 4.40 shows the interior view of the P70.

Total/ available slots	STANDARD Video	KB	Date introduced	Date withdrawn	List price
3/3	VGA	Enh	09/26/89	09/11/91	$7,745
3/3	VGA	Enh	06/20/89	09/11/91	$8,345

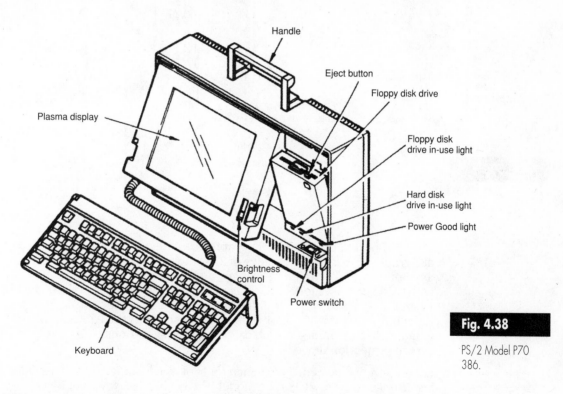

Fig. 4.38

PS/2 Model P70
386.

One exception to the norm is the external storage device port. The equivalent of the drive B internal floppy disk port, as found in the desktop Model 70, it permits attachment of externally powered devices, such as the IBM 360K external disk drive and some other manufacturers' backup devices. A cable (part number 23F2716) 35.5 centimeters or

14 inches long is available for attaching external drives. The cable features a Hoshiden Connector to attach to the P70 386 with an industry standard 37-pin D-shell connector that connects to the externally powered devices.

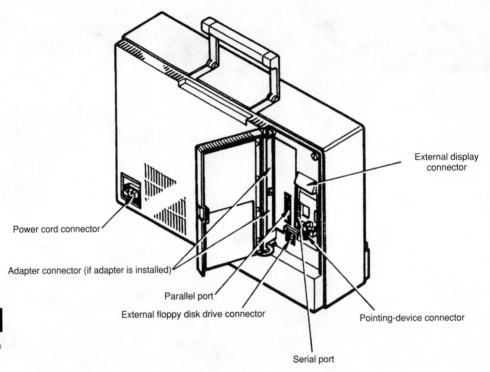

External display connector

Power cord connector

Adapter connector (if adapter is installed)

Parallel port

External floppy disk drive connector

Pointing-device connector

Serial port

Fig. 4.39

PS/2 Model P70 386
rear panel view.

The VGA port supports all VGA graphics and text modes including 640×480 graphics, 320×200 graphics in 256 colors, and 720×400 text using any optional PS/2 VGA color display; and yet maintains compatibility with CGA and EGA modes. The gas plasma display normally shuts down when an external display is connected. You can override this feature and force both displays to operate simultaneously, with the external display in monochrome mode—which is ideal for presentations using large-screen projection devices.

In addition, the system is designed for tool-free installation and includes security features in BIOS. The Model P70 386 has two levels of BIOS, which total 128K: A Compatibility BIOS (CBIOS) with memory addressability of up to 1M provides support for real-mode-based application programs; and an additional version of BIOS, Advanced BIOS (ABIOS), provides support for protected-mode-based multitasking operating systems and has extended memory addressability of up to 16M.

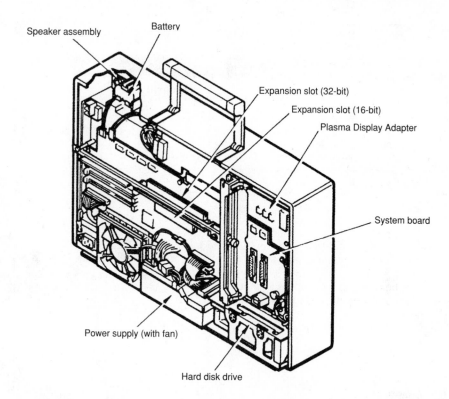

Speaker assembly
Battery
Expansion slot (32-bit)
Expansion slot (16-bit)
Plasma Display Adapter
System board
Power supply (with fan)
Hard disk drive

Fig. 4.40

PS/2 Model P70 386
interior view.

The P70 386 uses hard drives with integrated controllers (IDE). These drives plug directly into a special MCA IDE connector on the mother-board. All models use high-speed (85ns) memory, and have memory paging and ROM shadowing to improve performance. Several accessories are available for the system, including three different carrying cases, the external storage device cable, and a keyboard extension cable.

Table 4.40 lists the technical specifications for the PS/2 Model P70 386.

Table 4.40 PS/2 Model P70 386 Technical Specifications	
System architecture	
Microprocessor	80386DX
Clock speed	20 MHz
	16 MHz (031)
Bus type	MCA (Micro Channel Architecture)
Bus width	32-bit
Interrupt levels	16

continues

Table 4.40 Continued

System architecture

Type	Level-sensitive
Shareable	Yes
DMA channels	15
DMA burst mode supported	Yes
Bus masters supported	15
Upgradeable processor complex	No

Memory

Standard on system board	4M
Maximum on system board	8M
Maximum total memory	16M
Memory speed and type	85ns dynamic RAM
System board memory socket type	36-bit SIMM (single in-line memory module)
Number of memory module sockets	4
Number available in standard configuration	2
Memory used on system board	1M/2M 36-bit SIMMs
Page memory logic	Yes
Memory cache controller	No
Wait states:	
System board	0-2
Adapter	0-4

Standard features

ROM size	128K
ROM shadowing	Yes
Optional math coprocessor	80387DX
Coprocessor speed	20 MHz
	16 MHz (031)
Standard graphics	VGA
8-/16-/32-bit controller	8-bit
Bus master	No
Video RAM (VRAM)	256K
Integrated display	Yes
Type	Gas plasma, orange
Size (diagonal measure)	10 inches
Gray-shades	16
RS232C serial ports	1
UART chip used	NS16550A
Maximum speed (bits/second)	19,200 bps
FIFO mode enabled	Yes
Maximum number of ports	8

Standard features

Pointing device (mouse) ports	1
Parallel printer ports	1
Bidirectional	Yes
Maximum number of ports	8
CMOS real-time clock (RTC)	Yes
CMOS RAM	64 bytes + 2K extension
Battery life	5 years
Replaceable	Yes

Disk storage

Internal disk and tape drive bays	2		
Number of 3 1/2-/5 1/4-inch bays	2/0		
Standard floppy drives	1×1.44M		
Optional floppy drives:			
5 1/4-inch 360K	Optional		
5 1/4-inch 1.2M	Optional		
3 1/2-inch 720K	No		
3 1/2-inch 1.44M	Standard		
3 1/2-inch 2.88M	No		
Auxiliary storage connector	Yes		
Drives supported	5 1/4-inch 360K		
Cable adapter	Optional		
Hard disk controller included:	MCA IDE connector on system board		
IDE hard disks available	30M/60M/120M		
Drive form factor	3 1/2-inch		
Drive interface	MCA IDE		
Drive capacity	30M	60M	120M
Average access rate (ms)	19	27	23
Encoding scheme	RLL	RLL	RLL
Cylinders	920	762	920
Heads	2	6	8
Sectors per track	32	26	32
Rotational speed (RPM)	3600	3600	3600
Interleave factor	1:1	1:1	1:1
Data transfer rate (K/second)	960	780	960
Automatic head parking	Yes	Yes	Yes

Expansion slots

Total adapter slots	2
Number of long and short slots	1/1
Number of 8-/16-/32-bit slots	0/1/1
Number of slots with video ext.	0
Available slots	2

continues

Table 4.40 Continued

Keyboard specifications

101-key Enhanced Keyboard	Yes
Fast keyboard speed setting	Yes
Keyboard cable length	1.2 feet (14 inches)
Keyboard extension cable	Optional, 6 feet

Security features

Keylock:	
Locks cover	No
Locks keyboard	No
Keyboard password	Yes
Power-on password	Yes
Network server mode	Yes

Physical specifications

Footprint type	Portable
Dimensions:	
Height	12.0 inches
Width	18.3 inches
Depth	16.5 inches
Weight	20.8 lbs
Carrying handle	Yes
Carrying case	Optional, three styles available

Environmental specifications

Power-supply output	85 watts
Worldwide (110/60,220/50)	Yes
Auto-sensing/switching	Yes
Maximum current:	
90-137 VAC	2.4 amps
180-264 VAC	1.2 amps
Operating range:	
Temperature	50-95 degrees F
Relative humidity	8-80 percent
Maximum operating altitude	7,000 feet
Heat (BTUs/hour)	480
Noise (Average dB, operating, 1m)	39 dB
FCC classification	Class B

Figure 4.41 shows the components and layout of the Model P70 motherboard.

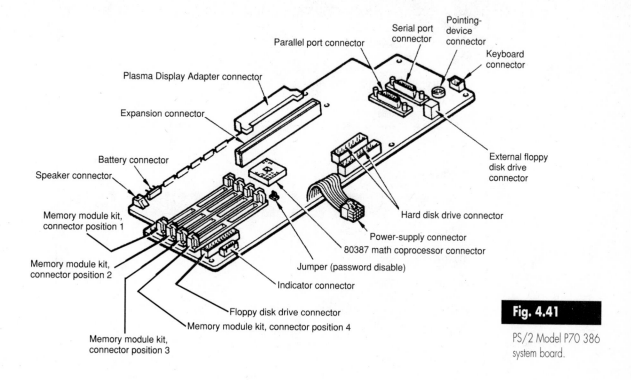

Fig. 4.41

PS/2 Model P70 386 system board.

Table 4.41 shows the primary specifications and costs of the various versions of PS/2 Model P70 386. Table 4.42 shows accessories available from IBM for the PS/2 Model P70 386.

Table 4.41 IBM PS/2 Model P70 386 Model Summary

Part number	CPU	MHz	PLANAR MEMORY Std.	Max.	STANDARD Floppy drive	Hard disk	Bus type
P70 386							
8573-031	386DX	16	2M	8M	1×1.44M	30M	MCA/32
8573-061	386DX	20	4M	8M	1×1.44M	60M	MCA/32
8573-121	386DX	20	4M	8M	1×1.44M	120M	MCA/32

Table 4.42 IBM PS/2 Model P70 386 Special Accessories

Description	Part number	Price	Notes
Hartmann leather case	23F3192	$360	For P70 (not P75), pockets
Hartmann nylon case	23F3193	185	For P70 (not P75), pockets
Airline travel hard case	79F3205	299	Plastic, padded, wheels, storage
External storage device cable	23F2716	101	P70 360K, P75 360K/1.2M
Keyboard extension cable	79F3210	82	For P70/75, six-foot cable

PS/2 Model P75 486

The PS/2 Model P75 486, introduced November 12, 1990, is a high-end addition to IBM's portable computer family. The Model P75 486 features the powerful 486DX processor, operating at 33 MHz, and MCA slots. For several months after the introduction of this system, no other company had a portable that was as fast or as powerful. In fact, nearly every company that has tried to introduce a 33 MHz 486 portable has run into problems with the FCC in obtaining the proper Class B certification. This highlights one of the distinct advantages that IBM has with the Micro Channel Architecture: IBM will be able to make systems faster and faster, while keeping them within noise-emission guidelines set by the FCC, because of the superior electrical characteristics of the MCA bus over the ISA or EISA bus.

The PS/2 Model P75 486 enables applications that require portability to run on a system which rivals many desktop or even floor-standing tower systems in capacity. This system allows a portable application to use the

Total/ available slots	STANDARD Video	KB	Date introduced	Date withdrawn	List price
2/2	VGA	Enh	03/20/90	07/23/91	$5,995
2/2	VGA	Enh	05/09/89	07/23/91	$7,695
2/2	VGA	Enh	05/09/89	—	$6,695

processing power of the 486DX processor operating at 33 MHz, up to 16M of main storage, hard disk capacity to 400M, an external SCSI port, and four MCA adapter slots. Because of the built-in SCSI interface, internal hard disk drives can be easily upgraded to well over 1 gigabyte in capacity. This system has one of the largest disk storage capabilities for a portable system.

The PS/2 Model P75 486 has the following features:

- 33 MHz 486DX processor on removable card
- 8M memory expandable to 16M
- Four slots (two full-length 32-bit, two half-length 16-bit)
- High-resolution eXtended Graphics Array (XGA) video port
- VGA 16-gray scale plasma display
- Choice of 160M or 400M disk drives
- Full-size PS/2 Enhanced Keyboard
- 3 1/2-inch 1.44M floppy disk drive
- External SCSI port
- AC operation (only)
- Maximum expansion

The PS/2 P75 486 offers power not previously available in a portable machine. It can be used as a network server or workstation for temporary offices at conventions, sporting events, and other temporary work locations. This system is ideal where a maximum system configuration must be carried along.

The PS/2 P75 486 does not run on batteries and has no "low-power" devices that would limit performance and expandability. Due to the extreme power and integration of this unit, it currently ranks as IBM's most expensive PC, at more than $18,000.

In addition to the powerful processor, the PS/2 P75 486 features a SCSI hard disk drive up to 400M as standard. With 3 1/2-inch SCSI drives becoming available in the gigabyte-capacity range and higher, it will be easy to upgrade this system to even larger-capacity storage.

The XGA graphics adapter built-in on the unit offers graphics resolution of 1,024 × 768. Because this device also is configured as a bus master, the performance is far beyond a standard VGA, even at VGA resolution. A device driver package is included with drivers for many popular applications and environments, such as OS/2 and Windows.

Several accessories are available, including the IBM PS/2 travel case (part number 79F3205). This hard case is constructed of molded plastic with easy-rolling wheels and an integrated, telescopic handle for pulling. The interior is padded and provides space for the P75 (or P70 386), cables, and a mouse. The case is designed to provide an easy, safe way to transport the system. It conforms to FAA luggage regulations, so it can be carried on board aircraft and stored under the seat.

Also available is a keyboard extension cable. The keyboard extension cable (part number 79F3210) gives users the flexibility of placing the keyboard and the system unit farther apart for more comfort and convenience.

Table 4.43 lists the technical specifications for the PS/2 Model P75 486.

Table 4.43 PS/2 Model P75 486 Technical Specifications

System architecture

Microprocessor	80486DX
Clock speed	33 MHz
Bus type	MCA (Micro Channel Architecture)
Bus width	32-bit
Interrupt levels	16
Type	Level-sensitive
Shareable	Yes
DMA channels	15
DMA burst mode supported	Yes
Bus masters supported	15
486 burst mode enabled	No
Upgradeable processor complex	Yes

Memory

Standard on system board	8M
Maximum on system board	16M
Maximum total memory	16M

Memory

Memory speed and type	70ns dynamic RAM
System board memory socket type	36-bit SIMM (single in-line memory module)
Number of memory-module sockets	4
Number available in standard configuration	2
Memory used on system board	2M/4M 36-bit SIMMs
Paged memory logic	Yes
Memory cache controller	Yes
Internal/external cache	Internal
Standard memory cache size	8K
Optional external memory cache	No
Wait states:	
System board	0-5 (95 percent 0 wait states)
Adapter	0-7

Standard features

ROM size	128K
ROM shadowing	Yes
Math coprocessor	Built-in to 486
Coprocessor speed	33 MHz
Standard graphics	XGA (eXtended Graphics Array)
8-/16-/32-bit controller	16/32-bit
Bus master	Yes
Video RAM (VRAM)	1M
Integrated display	Yes, VGA mode only
Type	Gas plasma, orange
Size (diagonal measure)	10 inches
Grayshades	16
RS232C serial ports	1
UART chip used	NS16550A
Maximum speed (bits/second)	19,200 bps
FIFO mode enabled	Yes
Maximum number of ports	8
Pointing device (mouse) ports	1
Parallel printer ports	1
Bidirectional	Yes
Maximum number of ports	8
CMOS real-time clock (RTC)	Yes
CMOS RAM	64 bytes + 2K extension
Battery life	5 years
Replaceable	Yes

Disk storage

Internal disk and tape drive bays	2
Number of 3 1/2- and 5 1/4-inch bays	2/0

continues

Table 4.43 Continued

Disk storage

Standard floppy drives	1×1.44M					
Optional floppy drives:						
5 1/4-inch 360K	Optional					
5 1/4-inch 1.2M	Optional					
3 1/2-inch 720K	No					
3 1/2-inch 1.44M	Standard					
3 1/2-inch 2.88M	No					
Auxiliary storage connector	Yes					
Drives supported	5 1/4-inch 360K, 1.2M					
Cable adapter	Optional					
Hard disk controller included:	SCSI integrated on system board					
Bus master	Yes					
Devices supported per adapter	7					
Adapters supported per system						
SCSI hard disks available:	60M/80M/120M/160M/320M/400M					
Drive form factor	3 1/2-inch					
Drive interface	SCSI					
Drive capacity	60M	80M	120M	160M	320M	400M
Average access rate (ms)	23	17	23	16	12.5	11.5
Read-ahead cache	32K	32K	32K	32K	64K	128K
SCSI transfer mode	Async	Async	Async	Async	Sync	Sync
Encoding scheme	RLL	RLL	RLL	RLL	RLL	RLL
Cylinders	920	1021	920	1021	949	1201
Heads	4	4	8	8	14	14
Sectors per track	32	39	32	39	48	48
Rotational speed (RPM)	3600	3600	3600	3600	4318	4318
Interleave factor	1:1	1:1	1:1	1:1	1:1	1:1
Data transfer rate (K/second)	960	1170	960	1170	1727	1727
Automatic head parking	Yes	Yes	Yes	Yes	Yes	Yes

Expansion slots

Total adapter slots	4
Number of long and short slots	2/2
Number of 8-/16-/32-bit slots	0/2/2
Number of slots with video ext.	1
Available slots	4

Keyboard specifications

101-key Enhanced Keyboard	Yes
Fast keyboard speed setting	Yes
Keyboard cable length	1.2 feet (14 inches)
Keyboard extension cable	Optional, 6 feet

Security features

Keylock:	
Locks cover	No
Locks keyboard	No
Keyboard password	Yes
Power-on password	Yes
Network server mode	Yes

Physical specifications

Footprint type	Portable
Dimensions:	
Height	12.0 inches
Width	18.3 inches
Depth	6.1 inches
Weight	22.1 lbs
Carrying handle	Yes
Carrying case	Optional hard-shell case

Environmental specifications

Power-supply output	120 watts
Worldwide (110/60,220/50)	Yes
Auto-sensing/switching	Yes
Maximum current:	
90-137 VAC	3.0 amps
180-264 VAC	1.5 amps
Operating range:	
Temperature	50-104 degrees F
Relative humidity	8-80 percent
Maximum operating altitude	7000 feet
Heat (BTUs/hour)	751
Noise (average dB, operating, 1m)	39 dB
FCC classification	Class B

Table 4.44 shows the primary specifications and costs of the various versions of PS/2 Model P75 486. Table 4.45 shows accessories available from IBM for the PS/2 Model P75 486.

Table 4.44 IBM PS/2 Model P75 486 Model Summary

Part number	CPU	MHz	PLANAR MEMORY Std.	Max.	STANDARD Floppy drive	Hard disk	Bus type
P70 386							
8573-161	486DX	33	8M	16M	1×1.44M	160M	MCA/32
8573-401	486DX	33	8M	16M	1×1.44M	400M	MCA/32

Table 4.45 IBM PS/2 Model P75 486 Special Accessories

Description	Part number	Price	Notes
Airline-travel hard case	79F3205	299	Plastic, padded, wheels, storage
Keyboard extension cable	79F3210	82	For P70/75, 6-foot cable
External storage device cable	23F2716	101	P70 360K, P75 360K/1.2M

PS/2 Model 80 386

IBM originally introduced the PS/2 Model 80 on April 2, 1987. Since then, many new models in the 80 family have been introduced and some have been discontinued. The Model 80 is a floor-standing, high-end system in the PS/2 family and includes MCA. Figure 4.42 shows a front view of the Model 80.

The basic Model 80 386 features a 16 MHz, 20 MHz, or 25 MHz 80386 microprocessor and 4M of high-speed (80ns) memory on the motherboard. Motherboard memory is expandable to 8M, depending on the model, and the total RAM can be expanded to 16M with memory adapters. This system comes standard with a 1.44M, 3 1/2-inch floppy disk drive and a wide variety of ST-506, ESDI, or SCSI hard disk drives ranging from 44M through 400M. Also standard are a serial port, a parallel port, a mouse port, and a VGA port. Figure 4.43 shows the rear panel view of the Model 80.

Total/ available slots	STANDARD Video	KB	Date introduced	Date withdrawn	List price
4/4	XGA	Enh	11/12/90	—	$10,645
4/4	XGA	Enh	11/12/90	—	$13,295

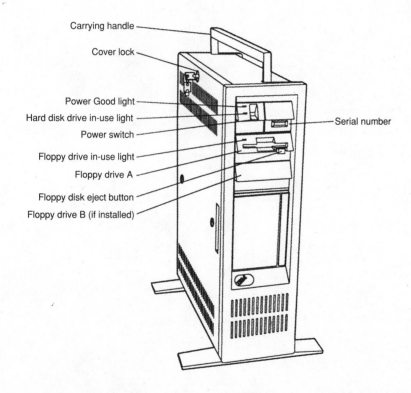

Carrying handle

Cover lock

Power Good light

Hard disk drive in-use light

Power switch

Floppy drive in-use light

Floppy drive A

Floppy disk eject button

Floppy drive B (if installed)

Serial number

Fig. 4.42

PS/2 Model 80 386.

The 80386 32-bit microprocessor running at 16 MHz, 20 MHz, or 25 MHz coupled with the MCA and high-speed memory allows the Model 80 to perform three to four times faster than the IBM AT Model 339. The 80387 math coprocessor running at the system clock rate allows the Model 80 to perform math calculations four to five times faster than an IBM AT Model 339 with an 80287 math coprocessor.

The Model 80 386 has two levels of BIOS, which total 128K: A Compatibility BIOS (CBIOS) with memory addressability of up to 1M provides support for real-mode-based application programs; and an additional version of BIOS, Advanced BIOS (ABIOS), provides support for protected-mode-based multitasking operating systems and has extended memory addressability of up to 16M.

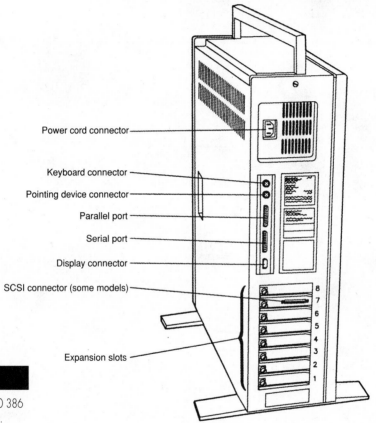

Power cord connector

Keyboard connector

Pointing device connector

Parallel port

Serial port

Display connector

SCSI connector (some models)

Expansion slots

Fig. 4.43

PS/2 Model 80 386
rear panel view.

Additional features of the system unit include eight I/O bus slots, of which five are 16-bit slots and three are 16/32-bit slots. Each system includes a hard disk controller that occupies one 16-bit slot. This controller is either an ST-506/412, ESDI or SCSI controller. The Model 80 also has a 225-watt or 242-watt, automatic voltage-sensing, universal power supply with auto-restart; a time-and-date clock with battery backup; an additional position for a second 3 1/2-inch floppy disk drive; an additional position for a second full-height 5 1/4-inch hard disk; and the

IBM Enhanced Keyboard. Figure 4.44 shows the interior view of the Model 80.

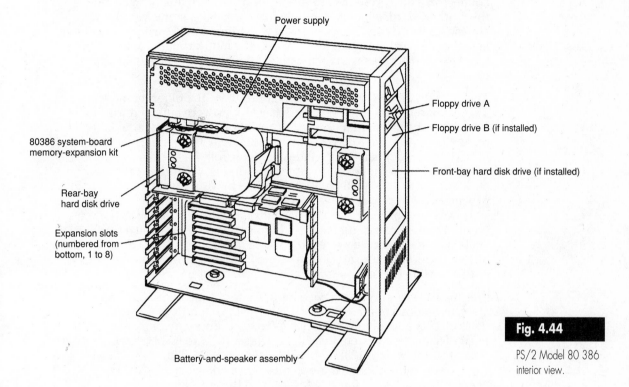

Power supply

Floppy drive A

Floppy drive B (if installed)

80386 system-board memory-expansion kit

Front-bay hard disk drive (if installed)

Rear-bay hard disk drive

Expansion slots (numbered from bottom, 1 to 8)

Battery-and-speaker assembly

Fig. 4.44

PS/2 Model 80 386 interior view.

The auto-restart feature on the power supply enables the computer to restart automatically when AC power returns after a power decrease or outage. This feature enables the system to be programmed for unattended restart after power outages—a useful feature on a computer in a network file-server application.

Model 80 has a variety of configurations; three different Model 80 system boards are available. The motherboards differ primarily in the clock rate of the processor and the arrangement of the MCA slots. The 16 MHz and 20 MHz models have three 32-bit slots and five 16-bit MCA slots. One of the 16-bit slots includes a video extension connector. These motherboards also allow a maximum of 4M to be installed using two nonstandard memory connectors. None of the Model 80 systems used standard SIMM connectors; they use a custom-designed card, making the memory upgrades available only from IBM.

The 25 MHz model differs from the others in that it has four 32-bit slots and four 16-bit slots, with two of the 16-bit slots having the video extension connector. These systems also incorporate a 64K static RAM cache on the motherboard, which essentially makes these systems run at 0 wait states. These motherboards support a maximum of 8M using two custom 4M memory cards plugged directly into the motherboard. Any additional memory beyond these maximums must be installed using an adapter card.

The hard disk drive interfaces also differentiate the different models. Three different disk interfaces and drive types were supplied with the Model 80. The 041 model used an ST-506 type controller that would handle up to two hard drives. The 071, 111, and 311 systems used an ESDI (Enhanced Small Device Interface) controller and drive. The ESDI controller would support up to two hard drives. The other (newer) models all include the IBM 16-bit MCA SCSI bus master adapter. This card provides an internal as well as external SCSI port for connecting devices. This card supports up to seven hard disks, and the system supports up to four of these cards. IBM has SCSI drives available from 60M through 400M to install in these systems. Also, because these drives are all in the 3 1/2-inch form factor (at least the ones from IBM), you can fit up to six of them inside the unit.

The 16 MHz systems also have a motherboard that always runs at 1 wait state, and does not offer ROM shadowing, in which the slower (150ns) ROM BIOS is copied into faster (80ns) motherboard memory chips. The ROM BIOS on this system board performs a ROM to RAM copy operation on start-up that uses 128K of the total 16M of RAM. This copy then is used for all subsequent ROM operations, and because the ROM now effectively resides in 80ns RAM, access to these routines is improved significantly. The chips then are re-addressed into the original BIOS locations and write protected. This means that you essentially have write-protected RAM acting as ROM, which can then run with fewer wait states. The 20 MHz systems incorporate a memory-paging scheme that reduces the number of wait states to 0 most of the time. All system board memory is accessed by a special paging scheme that allows for 0 wait state access to all 512 bytes within a single page. When access occurs outside the available page, you must perform a page swap requiring 2 wait states. Overall, this scheme allows for faster access to memory than a nonpaging, 1 wait state system. The 25 MHz systems incorporate a full-blown memory cache system that performs most operations in 25ns Static RAM. These systems are nearly always running at an apparent 0 wait states due to the efficiency of the cache.

Table 4.46 lists the technical specifications for the PS/2 Model 80 386.

Table 4.46 PS/2 Model 80 386 Technical Specifications

System architecture

Microprocessor	80386DX
Clock speed	16 MHz (041,071)
	20 MHz (081,111,121,161,311,321)
	25 MHz (Axx)
Bus type	MCA (Micro Channel Architecture)
Bus width	32-bit
Interrupt levels	16
Type	Level-sensitive
Shareable	Yes
DMA channels	15
DMA burst mode supported	Yes
Bus masters supported	15
Upgradeable processor complex	No

Memory

Standard on system board	4M
Maximum on system board	4M
	8M (Axx)
Maximum total memory	16M
Memory speed and type	80ns dynamic RAM
System board memory socket type	Nonstandard memory card
Number of memory module sockets	2
Number available in standard configuration	1
Memory used on system board	1M/2M/4M card
Paged memory logic	Yes
	No (041,071)
Memory cache controller	No
	Yes (Axx)
Internal/external cache	External
Standard memory cache size	64K
Cache memory speed and type	25ns static RAM
Wait states:	
System board	0-5 (Axx, 95 percent 0 wait states)
	0-2 (081,111,121,161,311,321)
	1 (041,071)
Adapter	0-7 (Axx)
	0-4

Standard features

ROM size	128K
ROM shadowing	Yes
	No (041,071)

continues

Table 4.46 Continued

Standard features

Optional math coprocessor	80387DX
Coprocessor speed	16 MHz (041,071)
	20 MHz (081,111,121,161,311,321)
	25 MHz (Axx)
Standard graphics	VGA (Video Graphics Array)
8-/16-/32-bit controller	8-bit
Bus master	No
Video RAM (VRAM)	256K
RS232C serial ports	1
UART chip used	NS16550A
	NS16550 (041,071)
Maximum speed (bits/second)	19,200 bps
FIFO mode enabled	Yes
	No (041,071)
Maximum number of ports	8
Pointing device (mouse) ports	1
Parallel printer ports	1
Bidirectional	Yes
Maximum number of ports	8
CMOS real-time clock (RTC)	Yes
CMOS RAM	64 bytes + 2K extension
Battery life	5 years
Replaceable	Yes

Disk storage

Internal disk and tape drive bays	5 or 6 (reconfigurable)
	4 (041,071,111,311)
Number of 3 1/2-/5 1/4-inch bays	4/1 or 6/0 (reconfigurable)
	2/2 (041,071,111,311)
Floppy drives standard	1×1.44M
Optional floppy drives	
5 1/4-inch 360K	Optional
5 1/4-inch 1.2M	Optional
3 1/2-inch 720K	No
3 1/2-inch 1.44M	Standard
3 1/2-inch 2.88M	No
Hard disk controller included:	SCSI adapter
	(081,121,161,321,Axx)
	ESDI controller (071,111,311)
	ST-506 controller (041)
SCSI host adapter type	16-bit SCSI adapter
Bus master	Yes
Devices supported per adapter	7

Disk storage

Adapters supported per system	4				
ST-506/ESDI hard disks available:	44M/70/115M/314M				
Drive form factor	5 1/4-inch				
Drive capacity	44M	44M	70M	115M	314M
Drive interface	ST-506	ST-506	ESDI	ESDI	ESDI
Average access rate (ms)	40	40	30	28	23
Encoding scheme	MFM	MFM	RLL	RLL	RLL
BIOS drive type	31	32	None	None	None
Cylinders	733	1023	583	915	1225
Heads	7	5	7	7	15
Sectors per track	17	17	36	36	34
Rotational speed (RPM)	3600	3600	3600	3600	3283
Interleave factor	1:1	1:1	1:1	1:1	1:1
Data transfer rate (K/second)	510	510	1080	1080	930
Automatic head parking	Yes	Yes	Yes	Yes	Yes

SCSI hard disks available:	60M/80M/120M/160M/320M/400M					
Drive form factor	3 1/2-inch					
Drive interface	SCSI					
Drive capacity	60M	80M	120M	160M	320M	400M
Average access rate (ms)	23	17	23	16	12.5	11.5
Read-ahead cache	32K	32K	32K	32K	64K	128K
SCSI transfer mode	Async	Async	Async	Async	Sync	Sync
Encoding scheme	RLL	RLL	RLL	RLL	RLL	RLL
Cylinders	920	1021	920	1021	949	1201
Heads	4	4	8	8	14	14
Sectors per track	32	39	32	39	48	48
Rotational speed (RPM)	3600	3600	3600	3600	4318	4318
Interleave factor	1:1	1:1	1:1	1:1	1:1	1:1
Data transfer rate (K/sec.)	960	1170	960	1170	1727	1727
Automatic head parking	Yes	Yes	Yes	Yes	Yes	Yes

Expansion slots

Total adapter slots	8
Number of long and short slots	8/0
Number of 8-/16-/32-bit slots	0/5/3
	0/4/4 (Axx)
Number of slots with video ext.	1
	2 (Axx)
Available slots	7
Keyboard specifications	
101-key Enhanced Keyboard	Yes
Fast keyboard speed setting	Yes
Keyboard cable length	10 feet
Security features	

continues

Table 4.46 Continued

Expansion slots

Keylock:	
Locks cover	Yes
Locks keyboard	No
Keyboard password	Yes
Power-on password	Yes
Network server mode	Yes

Physical specifications

Footprint type	Floor-standing
Dimensions:	
Height	23.5 inches
Width	6.5 inches
Depth	19.0 inches
Weight	45.3 lbs
	52.0 lbs (041,071,111,311)

Environmental specifications

Power-supply output	242 watts
	225 watts (041,071,111,311)
Worldwide (110/60,220/50)	Yes
Auto-sensing/switching	Yes
Maximum current:	
90-137 volts AC	5.3 amps
180-265 volts AC	2.7 amps
Operating range:	
Temperature	60-90 degrees F
Relative humidity	8-80 percent
Maximum operating altitude	7,000 feet
Heat (BTUs/hour)	1390
	1245 (041,071,111,311)
Noise (average dB, operating, 1m)	40 dB
	46 dB (041,071,111,311)
FCC classification	Class B

Figures 4.45 and 4.46 show the components and layout of the Model 80 type 1 and type 2 motherboards.

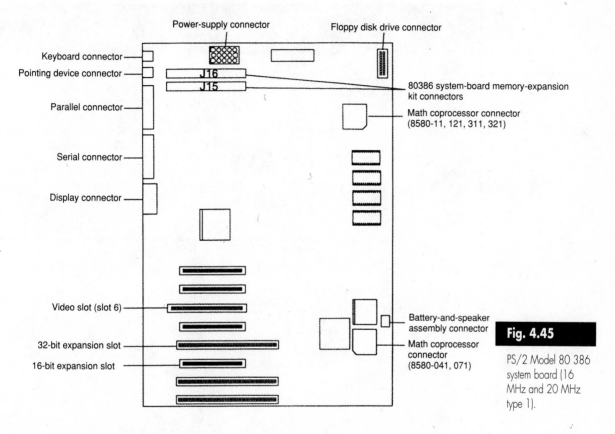

Power-supply connector

Floppy disk drive connector

Keyboard connector

Pointing device connector

J16

J15

80386 system-board memory-expansion kit connectors

Parallel connector

Math coprocessor connector (8580-11, 121, 311, 321)

Serial connector

Display connector

Video slot (slot 6)

Battery-and-speaker assembly connector

32-bit expansion slot

Math coprocessor connector (8580-041, 071)

16-bit expansion slot

Fig. 4.45

PS/2 Model 80 386 system board (16 MHz and 20 MHz type 1).

Table 4.47 shows the primary specifications and costs of the various versions of PS/2 Model 80 386.

Table 4.47 IBM PS/2 Model 80 386 Model Summary

Part number	CPU	MHz	PLANAR MEMORY Std.	Max.	STANDARD Floppy drive	Hard disk	Bus type
80 386							
8580-041	386DX	16	1M	4M	1×1.44M	44M	MCA/32
8580-071	386DX	16	2M	4M	1×1.44M	70M	MCA/32
8580-081	386DX	20	4M	4M	1×1.44M	80M	MCA/32
8580-111	386DX	20	2M	4M	1×1.44M	115M	MCA/32
8580-121	386DX	20	2M	4M	1×1.44M	120M	MCA/32
8580-161	386DX	20	4M	4M	1×1.44M	160M	MCA/32
8580-311	386DX	20	2M	4M	1×1.44M	314M	MCA/32
8580-321	386DX	20	4M	4M	1×1.44M	320M	MCA/32
8580-A21	386DX	25	4M	8M	1×1.44M	120M	MCA/32
8580-A16	386DX	25	4M	8M	1×1.44M	160M	MCA/32
8580-A31	386DX	25	4M	8M	1×1.44M	320M	MCA/32

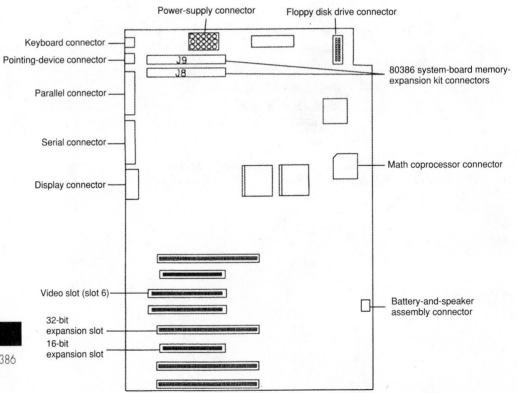

Fig. 4.46

PS/2 Model 80 386 system board (25 MHz type 2).

Total/ available slots	STANDARD Video	KB	Date introduced	Date withdrawn	List price
8/7	VGA	Enh	04/02/87	10/31/90	$4,000
8/7	VGA	Enh	04/02/87	10/31/90	$4,500
8/7	VGA	Enh	10/30/90	—	$4,595
8/7	VGA	Enh	04/02/87	12/27/90	$6,995
8/7	VGA	Enh	03/20/90	01/29/91	$6,945
8/7	VGA	Enh	10/30/90	—	$5,095
8/7	VGA	Enh	08/04/87	12/27/90	$9,395
8/7	VGA	Enh	03/20/90	—	$7,145
8/7	VGA	Enh	03/20/90	01/29/91	$9,645
8/7	VGA	Enh	10/30/90	—	$7,095
8/7	VGA	Enh	03/20/90	—	$8,695

PS/2 Model 90 XP 486

The PS/2 Model 90 XP 486, introduced October 30, 1990, is a powerful and expandable MCA-based desktop system. Through an unusual design, the system's 32-bit 80486 processor is on a removable processor complex, allowing processor upgrade from the 25 MHz to the more powerful 33 MHz or 50 MHz system. This capability to upgrade can extend the life of the system as customer requirements for enhanced processor performance grow.

Highlights of the Model 90 include:

■ Processor complex with 80486 20, 25, 33, or 50MHz processor

■ 8M standard memory, expandable to 64M on the system board

■ XGA graphics integrated on system board

■ PS/2 SCSI 32-bit bus master adapter with cache

■ Four internal storage device bays

■ Four 32-bit Micro Channel expansion slots

■ Two DMA serial ports and one DMA parallel port

■ Selectable boot and disk loaded ROM BIOS

The PS/2 Model 90 XP 486 features the 20 MHz, 25 MHz, 33 MHz, or 50 MHz 80486 microprocessor. The processor includes an internal memory cache controller, an internal 8K memory cache, and an internal floating point processor unit. The PS/2 256K cache option provides additional memory cache capability beyond the 8K internal memory cache. The PS/2 256K cache option is supported on 486DX models of Model 90 and Model 95. This capability provides investment protection and flexibility for the user.

The Model 90 system provides four internal drive bays and four 32-bit MCA I/O slots (one slot is used for the IBM PS/2 Micro Channel SCSI Adapter with cache, leaving three available for expansion). The PS/2 Micro Channel SCSI adapter with cache allows up to seven SCSI devices to be attached to the Model 90. The Model 90 also supports an internal 5 1/4-inch floppy disk device. The 5 1/4-inch Slim High Disk Drive (part number 6451066) is an internal 5 1/4-inch, 1.2M floppy disk drive with electrical button eject. This drive does not require an attachment card or expansion slot for installation and is supported in Models 90 and 95.

The Model 90 memory subsystem has been designed for optimum performance with interleaved memory; it features parity memory checking for added reliability and data integrity. All system memory (up to 64M) is supported on the system board, eliminating the need for memory adapters in any of the expansion slots. Although the Model 90 supports a maximum of 64M of memory, only 16M of that is addressable by DMA. This effectively limits the use of memory past 16M to nonsystem operations such as caching, virtual memory, or other functions. The system board has a total of eight memory sockets, two of which are used by a pair of 2M SIMMs (single in-line memory modules) to provide the standard 4M of memory. Optional 1M, 2M, and 4M memory SIMMs (70ns, 80ns, and 85ns only) are supported in matched pairs to provide various memory configurations up to 64M. Although 80ns and 85ns memory SIMMs are supported, 70ns memory SIMMs provide optimum memory subsystem performance.

The eXtended Graphics Array (XGA), high-performance, 32-bit bus master video subsystem is a standard feature of the PS/2 Model 90 XP 486 system. The integrated XGA provides $1024 \times 768 \times 16$ colors or $640 \times 480 \times 256$ colors as standard and can be optionally expanded to $1024 \times 768 \times 256$ colors with the addition of one PS/2 video memory expansion option. XGA supports all VGA modes and is optimized for use with window managers and other graphical user interfaces, allowing for highly interactive pop-up icons and pull-down menus. XGA also provides hardware support for 132-character text mode (using 8515 or 8514 display) and 16-bit direct color mode (64K colors at 640×480 resolution). MCA slot 3 of the PS/2 Model 90 XP 486 system contains a video feature bus connector that can be used to install a video adapter.

Other features of the Model 90 include the dual direct memory address (DMA) serial ports and a DMA parallel port included as standard. One of the serial port connectors is standard 25-pin D-shell, and the other connector is 9-pin D-shell. The 9-pin D-shell connector requires an adapter for attaching devices with 25-pin D-shell connectors. The DMA serial port provides support for speeds from 300 bits per second to 345.6K bits per second. It reduces processor loading and overhead when used in high-speed communications and supports speeds up to 345.6K bits per second.

The Model 90 offers the selectable-boot feature. As part of the system CMOS setup program, the user can specify which drive should be booted from and in which order the boot process should try each drive (for example, boot first from drive A, then drive C, and load BASIC). This step enables the user to boot or load a program from the optional 5 1/4-inch internal floppy disk drive as if it were drive A.

Initial Microcode Load

One special feature that the Model 90 has is called Initial Microcode Load (IML). The Model 90 stores the BIOS, configuration programs, and diagnostics on the hard disk in a protected 3M system partition and loaded from the disk during a "pre-boot" process. (The system programs also are provided on the PS/2 Model 90 XP 486 Reference Disk.) The formatted capacity of the hard disk is reduced by 3M, and the total user-accessible capacity might vary slightly, based on operating environments. This partition is not affected when the drive is formatted using the DOS or OS/2 FORMAT command.

The Initial Microcode Load (IML) loads the BIOS program from the hard disk drive into system memory. This process makes updating the BIOS an easy task when the time comes. Rather than pulling and replacing ROM chips on the motherboard, all you have to do is obtain a newer copy of the reference floppy disk and restore the system programs using that disk. Updates are available from your dealer or directly from IBM.

For example, a problem has been noted with Model 90 systems that have more than 8M of memory. To fix the problem, you need the Model 90 Reference Disk Version 1.02 or higher. To obtain the latest version, call 1-800-426-7282, weekdays between 8 a.m. and 8 p.m., Eastern Standard time. Specify the floppy disk for IBM PS/2 Model 90 XP 486. In Canada, call 1-800-465-1234 weekdays between 8 a.m. and 4:30 p.m. Eastern Standard time. In Alaska, call (414) 633-8108. The update will be sent to you and is installed in a menu-driven fashion. Because IBM sets the standards in this industry, you probably will see other compatible vendors adopting this disk-based BIOS approach as well. The flexibility and ease of upgrading are welcome.

On October 17, 1991, IBM enhanced the PS/2 Model 90 XP family with new Intel 486SX 25MHz (0Hx) models. The new systems come equipped with a new 486SX 25MHz processor complex, which provides improved performance over the previous 25MHz 486DX processor—and at a lower price. The new processor complex provides improved Micro Channel performance, better bus arbitration, and enhancements to the memory controller, making it ideal for multitasking or operating in heavily loaded networked environments. An improved physical design with fewer parts provides for greater reliability. The new processor complex also incorporates a conventional math coprocessor socket. Because of the improved price and performance of the new 25 MHz systems, earlier models using the 486SX 20MHz (0Gx) and 486 25MHz (0Jx) processor complex are being withdrawn. Because the 486SX lacks the integrated math coprocessor unit, a socket for the addition of the optional 487SX Math coprocessor is provided. In addition, these entry-level models can be upgraded to the more powerful 486/33MHz or the 486/50MHz processors with the IBM PS/2 486/33 and 486/50 processor upgrade options.

Table 4.48 lists the technical specifications for the PS/2 Model 90 XP 486.

Table 4.48 PS/2 Model 90 XP 486 Technical Specifications

System architecture

Microprocessor and clock speed	80486SX 20 MHz (0Gx)
	80487SX 20 MHz
	80486SX 25 MHz (0Hx)
	80487SX 25 MHz
	80486DX 25 MHz (0Jx)
	80486DX 33 MHz (0Kx)
	80486DX 50 MHz
Bus type	MCA (Micro Channel Architecture)
Bus width	32-bit
Interrupt levels	16
Type	Level-sensitive
Shareable	Yes
DMA channels	15
DMA burst mode supported	Yes
Bus masters supported	15
486 burst mode enabled	Yes
Upgradeable processor complex	Yes
Processor upgrades available	20 MHz 487SX
	25 MHz 486SX
	25 MHz 486DX
	33 MHz 486DX
	50 MHz 486DX

Memory

Standard on system board	4M (0Gx)
	8M (for all others)
Maximum on system board	64M
Maximum total memory	64M
Memory speed and type	70ns dynamic RAM
System board memory socket type	36-bit SIMM (single in-line memory module)
Number of memory module sockets	8
Number available in standard configuration	6 (0Gx)
	4 (for all others)
Memory used on system board	2M/4M/8M SIMMs
Memory interleaving	Yes
Paged memory logic	Yes
Memory cache controller	Yes
Internal/external cache	Internal
Standard memory cache size	8K
Optional external memory cache	No (0Gx, 0Hx)
	Yes
External cache size	256K
Cache memory speed and type	17ns static RAM
Wait states:	
System board	0-5 (95 percent 0 wait states)
Adapter	0-7
ROM size	128K
ROM shadowing	Yes
BIOS extensions stored on disk	Yes
Setup and Diagnostics stored on disk	Yes
Optional math coprocessor	80487SX (0Gx)
	Built-in to 486DX
Coprocessor speed	20 MHz (0Gx)
	25 MHz (0Jx)
	33 MHz (0Kx)
	50 MHz
Standard graphics	XGA (eXtended Graphics Array)
8-/16-/32-bit controller	32-bit
Bus master	Yes
Video RAM (VRAM)	512K
RS232C serial ports	2
UART chip used	Custom (compatible with NS16550A)
Maximum speed (bits/second)	345,600 bps
FIFO mode enabled	Yes
Supports DMA data transfer	Yes
Maximum number of ports	8
Pointing device (mouse) ports	1
Parallel printer ports	1
Bidirectional	Yes

continues

Table 4.48 Continued

Memory

Supports DMA data transfer	Yes
Maximum number of ports	8
CMOS real-time clock (RTC)	Yes
CMOS RAM	64 bytes + 2K extension
Battery life	5 years
Replaceable	Yes

Disk storage

Internal disk and tape drive bays	4
Number of 3 1/2-/5 1/4-inch bays	3/1
Selectable boot drive	Yes
Bootable drives	All physical drives
Standard floppy drives	1×1.44M
Optional floppy drives:	
5 1/4-inch 360K	Optional
5 1/4-inch 1.2M	Optional
3 1/2-inch 720K	No
3 1/2-inch 1.44M	Standard
3 1/2-inch 2.88M	No
Hard disk controller included:	32-bit SCSI adapter with 512K cache
Bus master	Yes
Devices supported per adapter	7
Adapters supported per system	4
SCSI hard disks available:	60M/80M/120M/160M/320M/400M
Drive form factor	3 1/2-inch
Drive interface	SCSI

Drive capacity	60M	80M	120M	160M	320M	400M
Average access rate (ms)	23	17	23	16	12.5	11.5
Read-ahead cache	32K	32K	32K	32K	64K	128K
SCSI transfer mode	Async	Async	Async	Async	Sync	Sync
Encoding scheme	RLL	RLL	RLL	RLL	RLL	RLL
Cylinders	920	1021	920	1021	949	1201
Heads	4	4	8	8	14	14
Sectors per track	32	39	32	39	48	48
Rotational speed (RPM)	3600	3600	3600	3600	4318	4318
Interleave factor	1:1	1:1	1:1	1:1	1:1	1:1
Data transfer rate (K/second)	960	1170	960	1170	1727	1727
Automatic head parking	Yes	Yes	Yes	Yes	Yes	Yes

Expansion slots

Total adapter slots	4
Number of long and short slots	4/0
Number of 8-/16-/32-bit slots	0/0/4
Number of slots with video ext.	1
Available slots	3

Keyboard specifications

101-key Enhanced Keyboard	Yes
Fast keyboard speed setting	Yes
Keyboard cable length	6 feet

Security features

Keylock:	
Locks cover	Yes
Locks keyboard	No
Keyboard password	Yes
Power-on password	Yes
Network server mode	Yes

Physical specifications

Footprint type	Desktop
Dimensions:	
Height	5.5 inches
Width	17.3 inches
Depth	16.9 inches
Weight	25.0 lbs

Environmental specifications

Power-supply output	194 watts
Worldwide (110/60,220/50)	Yes
Auto-sensing/switching	Yes
Maximum current:	
90-137 VAC	4.8 amps
180-264 VAC	2.4 amps

Operating range

Temperature	50-95 degrees F
Relative humidity	8-80 percent
Maximum operating altitude	7,000 feet
Heat (BTUs/hour)	662
FCC classification	Class B

Table 4.49 shows the primary specifications and costs of the various versions of PS/2 Model 90 XP 486.

Table 4.49 PS/2 Model 90 XP 486 Model Summary

Part number	CPU	MHz	PLANAR MEMORY Std.	Max.	STANDARD Floppy drive	Hard disk	Bus type
90 XP 486							
8590-0G5	486SX	20	4M	64M	1×1.44M	80M	MCA/32
8590-0G9	486SX	20	4M	64M	1×1.44M	160M	MCA/32
8590-0H5	486SX	25	4M	64M	1×1.44M	80M	MCA/32
8590-0H9	486SX	25	4M	64M	1×1.44M	160M	MCA/32
8590-0J5	486DX	25	8M	64M	1×1.44M	80M	MCA/32
8590-0J9	486DX	25	8M	64M	1×1.44M	160M	MCA/32
8590-0K9	486DX	33	8M	64M	1×1.44M	320M	MCA/32
8590-0KD	486DX	33	8M	64M	1×1.44M	320M	MCA/32
8590-0KF	486DX	33	8M	64M	1×1.44M	400M	MCA/32

PS/2 Model 95 XP 486

The PS/2 Model 95 XP 486, introduced October 30, 1990, is a high-performance, highly expandable floor-standing system based on MCA. Like the Model 90, through an unusual design, this system's 32-bit 80486 processor is on a removable processor complex, allowing a processor upgrade from the 25 MHz to the more powerful 33 MHz or 50 MHz system. This capability to upgrade can extend the life of the system as customer requirements for enhanced processor performance grow.

Highlights of the Model 95 include:

- Processor complex with 80486 20, 25, 33, or 50MHz processor
- 8M standard memory, expandable to 64M on the system board
- Enhanced Performance XGA Display Adapter/A standard
- PS/2 SCSI 32-bit bus master adapter with cache
- Seven internal storage device bays
- Eight 32-bit Micro Channel expansion slots
- One DMA serial port and one DMA parallel port
- Selectable boot and disk loaded ROM BIOS

Total/ available slots	STANDARD Video	KB	Date introduced	Date withdrawn	List price
4/3	XGA	Enh	04/23/91	01/17/92	$4,945
4/3	XGA	Enh	04/23/91	01/17/92	$5,545
4/3	XGA	Enh	10/17/91	—	$5,945
4/3	XGA	Enh	10/17/91	—	$6,545
4/3	XGA	Enh	10/30/90	01/17/92	$7,295
4/3	XGA	Enh	10/30/90	01/17/92	$7,895
4/3	XGA	Enh	10/17/91	—	$9,795
4/3	XGA	Enh	10/30/90	—	$11,745
4/3	XGA	Enh	10/17/91	—	$12,495

The PS/2 Model 95 XP 486 features the 20, 25, 33, or 50 MHz 80486 micro-processor. The processor includes an internal memory cache controller, an internal 8K memory cache, and an internal floating point processor unit. The PS/2 256K cache option provides additional memory cache capability beyond the 8K internal memory cache. The PS/2 256K cache option is supported on 486DX models of Model 90 and Model 95. This capability provides investment protection and flexibility for the user.

The system provides a total of seven storage device bays: Two can ac-commodate 5 1/4-inch half-high drives and the other five support 3 1/2-inch devices. Up to five high-speed SCSI hard disk drives can be installed internally, and a variety of other storage devices can be installed, such as CD-ROM drives, 5 1/4-inch floppy disk drives, and tape backup de-vices. The PS/2 Micro Channel SCSI adapter with cache allows as many as seven SCSI devices to be attached to the PS/2 Model 95. The PS/2 Model 95 also supports an internal 5 1/4-inch floppy disk device. The 5 1/4-inch Slim High Disk Drive (part number 6451066) is an internal 5 1/4-inch, 1.2M floppy disk drive with electrical button eject. This drive does not require an attachment card or expansion slot for installation and is supported in the Models 90 and 95.

The system provides eight 32-bit MCA slots: Two are used by the SCSI and XGA adapters, leaving six for other expansion adapters. A direct memory access (DMA) serial port and DMA parallel port are provided as standard. The Model 95 also features the capability of booting from any drive and an easy way to upgrade BIOS capability.

The Model 95 memory subsystem has been designed for optimum performance with interleaved memory; it features parity memory checking for added reliability and data integrity. All system memory (up to 64M) is supported on the system board, eliminating the need for memory adapters in any of the expansion slots. Although the Model 95 supports a maximum of 64M of memory, only 16M of that is addressable by DMA. This amount effectively limits the use of memory past 16M to nonsystem operations such as caching, virtual memory, or other functions. The system board has a total of eight memory sockets, two of which are used by a pair of 2M SIMMs (single in-line memory modules) to provide the basic standard 4M of memory. (Note that the amount of standard memory can vary according to the model from 4M to 8M.) Optional 1M, 2M, and 4M memory SIMMs (70ns, 80ns, and 85ns only) are supported in matched pairs to provide various memory configurations up to 64M. Although 80ns and 85ns memory SIMMs are supported, 70ns memory SIMMs provide optimum memory subsystem performance.

The Extended Graphics Array (XGA) Display Adapter/A with its high-performance 32-bit bus master video subsystem is a standard feature of the PS/2 Model 95 XP 486. The XGA adapter provides $1024 \times 768 \times 16$ colors or $640 \times 480 \times 256$ colors as standard and can be optionally expanded to $1024 \times 768 \times 256$ colors with the addition of one PS/2 video memory expansion option. XGA supports all VGA modes and is optimized for use with window managers and other graphical user interfaces, allowing for highly interactive pop-up icons and pull-down menus. XGA also provides hardware support for 132-character text mode (using 8515 or 8514 display) and 16-bit direct color mode (64K colors at 640×480 resolution).

Other specific features of the Model 95 include a direct memory address (DMA) serial port and a DMA parallel port as standard. The DMA serial port provides support for speeds from 300 bits per second to 345.6K bits per second, which reduces processor loading and overhead when used in high-speed communications.

The Model 95 offers the selectable-boot feature. As part of the system CMOS setup program, the user can specify which drive should be booted from and in which order the boot process should try each drive (for example, boot first from A drive, then C drive, and load BASIC). This allows the user to boot or load a program from the optional 5 1/4-inch internal floppy disk drive as if it were drive A.

Initial Microcode Load

One special Model 95 feature is Initial Microcode Load (IML). The Model 95 stores the BIOS, configuration programs, and diagnostics on the hard disk in a protected 3M partition and loaded from the disk during a "pre-boot" process. (The system programs also are provided on the PS/2 Model 95 Reference Disk.) The formatted capacity of the hard disk is reduced by 3M, and the total user-accessible capacity might vary slightly, based on operating environments. This partition is not affected when the drive is formatted using the DOS or OS/2 FORMAT command.

The Initial Microcode Load (IML) loads the BIOS program from the hard disk drive into system memory. This step makes updating the BIOS an easy task when the time comes. Rather than pulling and replacing ROM chips on the motherboard, all you have to do is obtain a newer copy of the reference floppy disk and restore the system programs using that disk. Updates are available from your dealer or directly from IBM.

For example, a problem has been noted with Model 95 systems that have more than 8M of memory. To fix the problem, you need the Model 95 Reference Disk Version 1.02 or higher. To obtain the latest version, call 1-800-426-7282, weekdays between 8 a.m. and 8 p.m., Eastern Standard time. Specify the floppy disk for IBM PS/2 Model 90 XP 486. In Canada, call 1-800-465-1234 weekdays between 8 a.m. and 4:30 p.m. Eastern Standard time. In Alaska, call (414) 633-8108. The update will be sent to you and is installed in a menu-driven fashion. Because IBM sets the standards in the computer industry, other IBM-compatible vendors probably will adopt this disk-based BIOS approach. The flexibility and ease of upgrading are welcome.

On October 17, 1991, IBM enhanced the PS/2 Model 95 XP family with new Intel 486SX 25 MHz (0Hx) models. The new systems come equipped with a new 486SX 25 MHz processor complex, which provides improved performance over the previous 25 MHz 486DX processor at a lower price. The new processor complex provides improved Micro Channel performance, better bus arbitration, and enhancements to the memory controller, making it ideal for multitasking or operating in heavily loaded networked environments. An improved physical design with fewer parts provides greater reliability. The new processor complex also incorporates a conventional math coprocessor socket. Because of the improved price and performance of the new 25 MHz systems, earlier models using the 486SX 20MHz (0Gx) and 486 25 MHz (0Jx) processor complex are being withdrawn. Because the 486SX lacks the integrated math coprocessor unit, a socket for the addition of the optional 487SX math coprocessor is provided. In addition, these entry-level models may be upgraded to the more powerful 486/33MHz or the 486/50MHz processors with the IBM PS/2 486/33 and 486/50 processor-upgrade options.

Table 4.50 lists the technical specifications for the PS/2 model 95XP 486.

Table 4.50 PS/2 Model 95 XP 486 Technical Specifications

System architecture

Microprocessor and clock speed	80486SX 20 MHz (0Gx)
	80487SX 20 MHz
	80486SX 25 MHz (0Hx)
	80487SX 25 MHz
	80486DX 25 MHz (0Jx)
	80486DX 33 MHz (0Kx)
	80486DX 50 MHz
Bus type	MCA (Micro Channel Architecture)
Bus width	32-bit
Interrupt levels	16
Type	Level-sensitive
Shareable	Yes
DMA channels	15
DMA burst mode supported	Yes
Bus masters supported	15
486 burst mode enabled	Yes
Upgradeable processor complex	Yes
Processor upgrades available	20 MHz 487SX
	25 MHz 486DX
	33 MHz 486DX
	50 MHz 486DX

Memory

Standard on system board	4M (0Gx)
	8M (for all others)
Maximum on system board	64M
Maximum total memory	64M
Memory speed and type	70ns dynamic RAM
System-board memory socket type	36-bit SIMM (single in-line memory module)
Number of memory module sockets	8
Number available in standard configuration	6 (0Gx)
	4 (for all others)
Memory used on system board	2M/4M/8M SIMMs
Memory interleaving	Yes
Paged memory logic	Yes
Memory cache controller	Yes
Internal/external cache	Internal
Standard memory cache size	8K

Memory

Optional external memory cache	No (0Gx, 0Hx)
	Yes (for all others)
External cache size	256K
Cache memory speed and type	17ns static RAM
Wait states:	
System board	0-5 (95 percent 0 wait states)
Adapter	0-7
Standard features	
ROM size	128K
ROM shadowing	Yes
BIOS extensions stored on disk	Yes
Setup and Diagnostics stored on disk	Yes
Optional math coprocessor	80487SX (0Gx)
	Built-in to 486DX
Coprocessor speed	20 MHz (0Gx)
	25 MHz (0Jx)
	33 MHz (0Kx)
	50 MHz
Standard graphics	XGA (eXtended Graphics Array)
8-/16-/32-bit controller	32-bit
Bus master	Yes
Video RAM (VRAM)	512K
RS232C serial ports	2
UART chip used	Custom (compatible with NS16550A)
Maximum speed (bits/second)	345,600 bps
FIFO mode enabled	Yes
Supports DMA data transfer	Yes
Maximum number of ports	8
Pointing device (mouse) ports	1
Parallel printer ports	1
Bidirectional	Yes
Supports DMA data transfer	Yes
Maximum number of ports	8
CMOS real-time clock (RTC)	Yes
CMOS RAM	64 bytes + 2K extension
Battery life	5 years
Replaceable	Yes

Disk storage

Internal disk and tape drive bays	7
Number of 3 1/2 and 5 1/4-inch bays	5/2
Selectable boot drive	Yes
Bootable drives	All physical drives
Standard floppy drives	1×1.44M

continues

Table 4.50 Continued

System architecture

Optional floppy drives:	
5 1/4-inch 360K	Optional
5 1/4-inch 1.2M	Optional
3 1/2-inch 720K	No
3 1/2-inch 1.44M	Standard
3 1/2-inch 2.88M	No

Hard disk controller included:	32-bit SCSI adapter with 512K cache
Bus master	Yes
Devices supported per adapter	7
Adapters supported per system	4

SCSI hard disks available:	60M/80M/120M/160M/320M/400M					
Drive form factor	3 1/2-inch					
Drive interface	SCSI					
Drive capacity	60M	80M	120M	160M	320M	400M
Average access rate (ms)	23	17	23	16	12.5	11.5
Read-ahead cache	32K	32K	32K	32K	64K	128K
SCSI transfer mode	Async	Async	Async	Async	Sync	Sync
Encoding scheme	RLL	RLL	RLL	RLL	RLL	RLL
Cylinders	920	1021	920	1021	949	1201
Heads	4	4	8	8	14	14
Sectors per track	32	39	32	39	48	48
Rotational speed (RPM)	3600	3600	3600	3600	4318	4318
Interleave factor	1:1	1:1	1:1	1:1	1:1	1:1
Data transfer rate (K/second)	960	1170	960	1170	1727	1727
Automatic head parking	Yes	Yes	Yes	Yes	Yes	Yes

Expansion slots

Total adapter slots	8
Number of long and short slots	8/0
Number of 8-/16-/32-bit slots	0/0/8
Number of slots with video ext.	2
Adapter form factor	IBM RISC system/6000
Available slots	6

Keyboard specifications	
101-key Enhanced Keyboard	Yes
Fast keyboard speed setting	Yes
Keyboard cable length	6 feet
Keylock:	
Locks cover	Yes
Locks keyboard	No
Keyboard password	Yes
Power-on password	Yes
Network server mode	Yes

Physical specifications	
Footprint type	Floor-standing
Dimensions:	
Height	19.8 inches
Width	8.0 inches
Depth	20.0 inches
Weight	51.0 lbs

Environmental specifications	
Power-supply output	329 watts
Worldwide (110/60,220/50)	Yes
Auto-sensing/switching	Yes
Maximum current:	
90-137 VAC	8.3 amps
180-264 VAC	4.7 amps
Operating range:	
Temperature	50-95 degrees F
Relative humidity	8-80 percent
Maximum operating altitude	7,000 feet
Heat (BTUs/hour)	1123
FCC classification	Class B

Table 4.51 shows the primary specifications and costs of the various versions of PS/2 Model 95 XP 486.

Table 4.51 IBM PS/2 Model 95 XP 486 Model Summary

Part number	CPU	MHz	PLANAR MEMORY Std.	Max.	STANDARD Floppy drive	Hard disk	Bus type
95 XP 486							
8595-0G9	486SX	20	4M	64M	1×1.44M	160M	MCA/32
8595-0GF	486SX	20	4M	64M	1×1.44M	400M	MCA/32
8595-0H9	486SX	25	8M	64M	1×1.44M	160M	MCA/32
8595-0HF	486SX	25	8M	64M	1×1.44M	400M	MCA/32
8595-0J9	486DX	25	8M	64M	1×1.44M	160M	MCA/32
8595-0JD	486DX	25	8M	64M	1×1.44M	320M	MCA/32
8595-0JF	486DX	25	8M	64M	1×1.44M	400M	MCA/32
8595-0KD	486DX	33	8M	64M	1×1.44M	320M	MCA/32
8595-0KF	486DX	33	8M	64M	1×1.44M	400M	MCA/32

PS/2 BIOS Information

To uniquely identify each PS/2 system model through software, IBM encodes each system with a unique set of identifying information. By using this information and comparing it to a chart showing what versions have been available, you might be able to determine whether a system has an out-of-date ROM release that might be causing problems. A review of this information shows just how many different systems IBM has released.

To identify one system from another, one item that many technicians use is the ROM BIOS date of creation. The date is stored in the ROM at absolute address FFFF:5. To see this date, you can use the DOS DEBUG program as follows:

1. Run the DEBUG program by typing the DEBUG command at the C: prompt:

   C:\>DEBUG

2. When the debug prompt (-) appears, type the following command and press Enter:

   -D FFFF:5 L 8

   This command instructs debug to dump the memory in segment FFFF and offset 5, for a length of 8 bytes.

3. Read the screen display, which looks something like the following line, showing the BIOS date, unless the compatible BIOS is non-standard and does not store the date there:

   FFFF:0000   30 31 2F-31 38 2F 38 39   01/18/89

Total/ available slots	STANDARD Video	KB	Date introduced	Date withdrawn	List price
8/6	XGA	Enh	04/23/91	01/17/92	$7,745
8/6	XGA	Enh	04/23/91	01/17/92	$10,395
8/6	XGA	Enh	10/17/91	—	$9,245
8/6	XGA	Enh	10/17/91	—	$11,895
8/6	XGA	Enh	10/30/90	01/17/92	$10,045
8/6	XGA	Enh	10/30/90	01/17/92	$11,995
8/6	XGA	Enh	04/23/91	01/17/92	$12,745
8/6	XGA	Enh	10/30/90	—	$13,895
8/6	XGA	Enh	04/23/91	—	$14,645

4. To exit DEBUG, press Q.

The screen will look something like this when you are done:

```
C:\>DEBUG
-D FFFF:5 L 8
FFFF:0000          30 31 2F-31 38 2F 38 39    01/18/89
-Q
```

Although many people use the BIOS date of creation to identify a system, IBM uses other information in addition to the version of BIOS to uniquely identify the system. IBM has given each PS/2 system a model ID byte (or model byte), a submodel byte, and a revision byte. With these three pieces of information, you can clearly identify any PS/2 system by booting the Reference Disk and executing the "Display Revision Levels" option at the main menu. The display that results looks something like this:

```
     Model Byte: F8
 Sub-Model Byte: 0B
       Revision: 00
```

The values are in hexadecimal because they represent raw byte values. Many diagnostics programs can locate this information for a given system because a standard way to retrieve the information involves executing an Int 15h instruction with the AH register set to C0, which returns a pointer to the location of the desired information.

You also can find out this information by using DEBUG. The first step in the procedure involves (A)ssembling at memory offset 100h a short program that will (MOV)e the value C0 into the AH register. Then execute (Int)errupt 15h, and (Int)errupt 3h. The Int 15 function C0 causes the ES and BX registers to contain the address of the System Configuration Parameters table. This table is in memory and contains information about how the system is configured and the model ID information you are looking for. The Int 3 is a breakpoint instruction that will cause the program to stop and display the register contents.

After the program is assembled in memory, the (G)o instruction tells DEBUG to run the program, which occurs until the Int 3 instruction is reached and causes the program to stop, gives DEBUG control of the system, and displays the current contents of the registers. The correct location of the System Configuration Table then is in the ES:BX registers. For my P70 system that would be E000:7CED, but the address will vary for other systems. When you run these steps, be sure to substitute whatever is reported on your system in the ES and BX registers for the address in the (D)ump command. The "L A" part of the (D)ump command says that the (L)ength of data to dump is Ah (10) bytes. This includes the first two bytes of the table, which is a word indicating the length of the remaining portion of the table. Normally this word has a value of 0008h, which means that the remainder of the table is 8 bytes long.

To find out the model byte, submodel byte, and revision number of your system you can execute these steps using DOS DEBUG. You should notice that the address given in the (D)ump instruction will differ between systems. You must substitute whatever values are reported by the ES and BX registers:

```
C:\>DEBUG
-A 100
xxxx:0100 MOV AH,C0
xxxx:0102 INT 15
xxxx:0104 INT 3
xxxx:0105
-G

AX=00FF  BX=7CED  CX=0000  DX=0000  SP=FFEE  BP=0000
SI=0000  DI=0000
DS=269A  ES=E000  SS=269A  CS=269A  IP=0104    NV UP EI PL
ZR NA PE NC
269A:0104 CC              INT    3
-D E000:7CED L A
E000:7CE0                                          08 00
F8                      ...
E000:7CF0  0B 00 F6 40 00 00 00
...@...
-Q
```

Starting with the address reported in the ES:BX registers, the third, fourth and fifth bytes listed after the (D)ump command are the model byte, sub-model byte, and revision number, respectively. In this case they are F8, 0B, and 00.

Table 4.52 is a relatively complete compilation of IBM BIOS ID information. Some systems have had BIOS changes during their life span. One piece of information this table provides is the total number of ST-506 drive types each BIOS supports. These types often are used when installing ST-506 or IDE hard disk drives. If the BIOS of your system is included in table 4.53, you can look up the IBM BIOS Hard Drive Table in this appendix and establish the exact drive types supported by your system.

Table 4.52 IBM ROM BIOS Model/Submodel/Revisions

System description	CPU	Clock speed	Bus type/ width	ROM BIOS date	ID byte	Sub-model byte	Rev	ST506 drive types
PC	8088	4.77 MHz	ISA/8	04/24/81	FF	—	—	—
PC	8088	4.77 MHz	ISA/8	10/19/81	FF	—	—	—
PC	8088	4.77 MHz	ISA/8	10/27/82	FF	—	—	—
PC-XT	8088	4.77 MHz	ISA/8	11/08/82	FE	—	—	—
PC-XT	8088	4.77 MHz	ISA/8	01/10/86	FB	00	01	—
PC-XT	8088	4.77 MHz	ISA/8	05/09/86	FB	00	02	—
PC*jr*	8088	4.77 MHz	ISA/8	06/01/83	FD	—	—	—
PC Convertible	80C88	4.77 MHz	ISA/8	09/13/85	F9	00	00	—
PS/2 25	8086	8 MHz	ISA/8	06/26/87	FA	01	00	26
PS/2 30	8086	8 MHz	ISA/8	09/02/86	FA	00	00	26
PS/2 30	8086	8 MHz	ISA/8	12/12/86	FA	00	01	26
PS/2 30	8086	8 MHz	ISA/8	02/05/87	FA	00	02	26
PC-AT	286	6 MHz	ISA/16	01/10/84	FC	—	—	15
PC-AT	286	6 MHz	ISA/16	06/10/85	FC	00	01	23
PC-AT	286	8 MHz	ISA/16	11/15/85	FC	01	00	23
PC-XT 286	286	6 MHz	ISA/16	04/21/86	FC	02	00	24
PS/1	286	10 MHz	ISA/16	12/01/89	FC	0B	00	44
PS/2 25 286	286	10 MHz	ISA/16	06/28/89	FC	09	02	37
PS/2 30 286	286	10 MHz	ISA/16	08/25/88	FC	09	00	37
PS/2 30 286	286	10 MHz	ISA/16	06/28/89	FC	09	02	37
PS/2 35 SX	386SX	20 MHz	ISA/16	03/15/91	F8	19	05	37
PS/2 35 SX	386SX	20 MHz	ISA/16	04/04/91	F8	19	06	37
PS/2 40 SX	386SX	20 MHz	ISA/16	03/15/91	F8	19	05	37
PS/2 40 SX	386SX	20 MHz	ISA/16	04/04/91	F8	19	06	37
PS/2 L40 SX	386SX	20 MHz	ISA/16	02/27/91	F8	23	02	37
PS/2 50	286	10 MHz	MCA/16	02/13/87	FC	04	00	32
PS/2 50	286	10 MHz	MCA/16	05/09/87	FC	04	01	32

continues

Table 4.52 Continued

System description	CPU	Clock speed	Bus type/ width	ROM BIOS date	ID byte	Sub-model byte	Rev	ST506 drive types
PS/2 50Z	286	10 MHz	MCA/16	01/28/88	FC	04	02	33
PS/2 50Z	286	10 MHz	MCA/16	04/18/88	FC	04	03	33
PS/2 55 SX	386SX	16 MHz	MCA/16	11/02/88	F8	0C	00	33
PS/2 57 SX	386SX	20 MHz	MCA/16	07/03/91	F8	26	02	None
PS/2 60	286	10 MHz	MCA/16	02/13/87	FC	05	00	32
PS/2 65 SX	386SX	16 MHz	MCA/16	02/08/90	F8	1C	00	33
PS/2 70 386	386DX	16 MHz	MCA/32	01/29/88	F8	09	00	33
PS/2 70 386	386DX	16 MHz	MCA/32	04/11/88	F8	09	02	33
PS/2 70 386	386DX	16 MHz	MCA/32	12/15/89	F8	09	04	33
PS/2 70 386	386DX	20 MHz	MCA/32	01/29/88	F8	04	00	33
PS/2 70 386	386DX	20 MHz	MCA/32	04/11/88	F8	04	02	33
PS/2 70 386	386DX	20 MHz	MCA/32	12/15/89	F8	04	04	33
PS/2 70 386	386DX	25 MHz	MCA/32	06/08/88	F8	0D	00	33
PS/2 70 386	386DX	25 MHz	MCA/32	02/20/89	F8	0D	01	33
PS/2 70 486	486DX	25 MHz	MCA/32	12/01/89	F8	0D	?	?
PS/2 70 486	486DX	25 MHz	MCA/32	09/29/89	F8	1B	00	?
PS/2 P70 386	386DX	16 MHz	MCA/32	?	F8	50	00	?
PS/2 P70 386	386DX	20 MHz	MCA/32	01/18/89	F8	0B	00	33
PS/2 P75 486	486DX	33 MHz	MCA/32	?	F8	52	00	?
PS/2 80 386	386DX	16 MHz	MCA/32	03/30/87	F8	00	00	32
PS/2 80 386	386DX	20 MHz	MCA/32	10/07/87	F8	01	00	32
PS/2 80 386	386DX	25 MHz	MCA/32	11/21/89	F8	80	01	?
PS/2 90 XP 486	486SX	20 MHz	MCA/32	?	F8	2D	00	?
PS/2 90 XP 486	487SX	20 MHz	MCA/32	?	F8	2F	00	?
PS/2 90 XP 486	486DX	25 MHz	MCA/32	?	F8	11	00	?
PS/2 90 XP 486	486DX	33 MHz	MCA/32	?	F8	13	00	?
PS/2 90 XP 486	486DX	50 MHz	MCA/32	?	F8	2B	00	?
PS/2 95 XP 486	486SX	20 MHz	MCA/32	?	F8	2C	00	?
PS/2 95 XP 486	487SX	20 MHz	MCA/32	?	F8	2E	00	?
PS/2 95 XP 486	486DX	25 MHz	MCA/32	?	F8	14	00	?
PS/2 95 XP 486	486DX	33 MHz	MCA/32	?	F8	16	00	?
PS/2 95 XP 486	486DX	50 MHz	MCA/32	?	F8	2A	00	?

The ID byte, submodel byte, and revision numbers are in hexadecimal.
— = This feature is not supported.
None = Only SCSI drives are supported.
?=No information available

Summary of IBM Hard Disk Drives

The tables in this section are a complete reference to all of the hard disk drives supplied by IBM in any XT, AT, or PS/2 system. This reference can be useful in determining which types of drives came with each system, and upgrades are possible.

You usually can easily install an upgraded drive of the same interface type in a given system. If I have a PS/2 Model 50Z that came with a 30M MCA IDE hard drive, for example, I easily can upgrade that system to any of the other MCA IDE drives that were available, such as the 120MB or 160MB units. Because the drives use the exact same interface, it would be a simple plug-in upgrade. Using this information, you can more easily "recycle" hard drives from systems that have since received upgrades.

Here are the standard and optional hard drives installed by IBM in its systems, grouped by interface

Table 4.53 IBM-Installed ST-506/412 Hard Drives Used in the XT, AT, and PS/2 Model 25

Drive form factor	5 1/4	5 1/4	5 1/4	5 1/4	3 1/2
Capacity	10MB	20MB	20MB	30MB	20MB
Physical/logical interface	ST506	ST506	ST506	ST506	ST506
Average access rate (ms)	85	65	40	40	38
Read-ahead cache (K)	—	—	—	—	—
Encoding scheme	MFM	MFM	MFM	MFM	RLL
BIOS drive type number	1	2	2	2	36
Cylinders	306	615	615	733	402
Heads	4	4	4	5	4
Sectors/track	17	17	17	17	26
Rotational speed (RPM)	3600	3600	3600	3600	3600
Standard interleave factor	6:1	3:1	3:1	3:1	3:1
Data transfer rate (K/second)	85	170	170	170	260
Automatic head parking	No	No	Yes	Yes	Yes

Table 4.54 IBM-Installed ST-506/412 Hard Drives Used in the XT, AT, and PS/2 Models 50, 60, and 80

Drive form factor	3 1/2	5 1/4	5 1/4
Capacity	20MB	44MB	44MB
Physical/logical interface	ST506	ST506	ST506
Average access rate (ms)	80	40	40
Read-ahead cache (K)	—	—	—
Encoding scheme	MFM	MFM	MFM
BIOS drive type number	30	31	32
Cylinders	611	732	1023
Heads	4	7	5
Sectors/track	17	17	17
Rotational speed (RPM)	3600	3600	3600
Standard interleave factor	1:1	1:1	1:1
Data transfer rate (K/second)	510	510	510
Automatic head parking	No	Yes	Yes

Table 4.55 IBM-Installed XT IDE Drives Used in the PS/2 Models 25, 30, 25 286 and 30 286

Drive form factor	3 1/2	3 1/2	3 1/2	3 1/2	3 1/2
Capacity	20MB	20MB	30MB	30MB	45MB
Physical interface	IDE	IDE	IDE	IDE	IDE
Logical interface	XT	XT	XT	XT	XT
Average access rate (ms)	80	27	27	19	32
Read-ahead cache (K)	—	—	—	—	—
Encoding scheme	MFM	RLL	RLL	RLL	RLL
BIOS drive type number	26	34	33	35	37
Cylinders	612	775	614	921	580
Heads	4	2	4	2	6
Sectors/track	17	27	25	33	26
Rotational speed (RPM)	3600	3600	3600	3600	3600
Standard interleave factor	2:1	3:1	3:1	4:1	3:1
Data transfer rate (K/second)	255	270	250	248	260
Automatic head parking	No	No	No	Yes	Yes

Table 4.56 IBM-Installed ATA IDE Drives Used in the PS/2 Models 35, 40, and L40

Drive form factor	2 1/2	3 1/2	3 1/2
Capacity	60MB	40MB	80MB
Physical interface	IDE	IDE	IDE
Logical interface	ATA	ATA	ATA
Average access rate (ms)	19	17	17
Read-ahead cache (K)	—	32K	32K

Encoding scheme	RLL	RLL	RLL
BIOS drive type number	—	—	—
Cylinders	822	1038	1021
Heads	4	2	4
Sectors/track	38	39	39
Rotational speed (RPM)	3600	3600	3600
Standard interleave factor	1:1	1:1	1:1
Data transfer rate (K/second)	1140	1170	1170
Automatic head parking	Yes	Yes	Yes

Table 4.57 IBM-Installed MCA IDE Drives Used in the PS/2 Models 50Z, 55, 70 386, and P70 386

Drive form factor	3 1/2	3 1/2	3 1/2	3 1/2	3 1/2	3 1/2	3 1/2	3 1/2
Capacity	30MB	30MB	30MB	40MB	60MB	80MB	120MB	160MB
Physical interface	IDE	IDE	IDE	IDE	IDE	IDE	IDE	IDE
Logical interface	ST506	ST506	ESDI	ESDI	ESDI	ESDI	ESDI	ESDI
Average access rate (ms)	39	27	19	17	27	17	23	16
Read-ahead cache (K)	—	—	—	32K	—	32K	—	32K
Encoding scheme	RLL	RLL	RLL	RLL	RLL	RLL	RLL	RLL
BIOS drive type number	33	33	—	—	—	—	—	—
Cylinders	614	614	920	1038	762	1021	920	1021
Heads	4	4	2	2	6	4	8	8
Sectors/track	25	25	32	39	26	39	32	39
Rotational speed (RPM)	3600	3600	3600	3600	3600	3600	3600	3600
Standard interleave factor	1:1	1:1	1:1	1:1	1:1	1:1	1:1	1:1
Data transfer rate (K/second)	750	750	960	1170	780	1170	960	1170
Automatic head parking	No	No	Yes	Yes	Yes	Yes	Yes	Yes

Table 4.58 IBM-Installed ESDI Drives Used in the PS/2 Models 60 and 80

Drive form factor	5 1/4	5 1/4	5 1/4
Capacity	70MB	115MB	314MB
Physical/logical interface	ESDI	ESDI	ESDI
Average access rate (ms)	30	28	23
Read-ahead cache (K)	—	—	—
Encoding scheme	RLL	RLL	RLL
BIOS drive type number	—	—	—
Cylinders	583	915	1225
Heads	7	7	15
Sectors/track	36	36	34
Rotational speed (RPM)	3600	3600	3283
Standard interleave factor	1:1	1:1	1:1
Data transfer rate (K/second)	1080	1080	930
Automatic head parking	Yes	Yes	Yes

Table 4.59 IBM-Installed SCSI Drives Used in the PS/2 Models 56, 57, 65, P75, 80, 90, and 95

Drive form factor	3 1/2	3 1/2	3 1/2	3 1/2	3 1/2	3 1/2
Capacity	60MB	80MB	120MB	160MB	320MB	400MB
Physical/logical interface	SCSI	SCSI	SCSI	SCSI	SCSI	SCSI
Average access rate (ms)	23	17	23	16	12.5	11.5
Read-ahead cache (K)	32K	32K	32K	32K	64K	128K
SCSI transfer mode	Async	Async	Async	Async	Sync	Sync
Encoding scheme	RLL	RLL	RLL	RLL	RLL	RLL
BIOS drive type number	—	—	—	—	—	—
Cylinders	920	1021	920	1021	949	1201
Heads	4	4	8	8	14	14
Sectors/track	32	39	32	39	48	48
Rotational speed (RPM)	3600	3600	3600	3600	4318	4318
Standard interleave factor	1:1	1:1	1:1	1:1	1:1	1:1
Data transfer rate (K/second)	960	1170	960	1170	1727	1727
Automatic head parking	Yes	Yes	Yes	Yes	Yes	Yes

Table 4.60 Standard PS/2 Accessories

Description	Part number	Price	Notes
PS/2 mouse driver	6450350	$101	2-button mouse, DOS
Trackpoint	1397040	106	Mouse/trackball
Dual serial adapter/A	6451013	231	For 50-95, NS16550, 9-pin plug
Serial/parallel adapter	6450215	161	25-40(not L40), NS16450, 9-pin
Floor stand	95F5606	45	Vertical mount for 35 LS/SX

Table 4.61 PS/2 Processor/Coprocessor Upgrades

Description	Part	Price	Notes
16 MHz 387SX math coprocessor	27F4676	$ 387	For Models 55 and 65
25 MHz 486DX power platform	6450876	1,900	70-Axx, trade-in 25 MHz 386DX
20 MHz 487SX chip upgrade	6451230	840	90/95-0Gx, trade-in 20 MHz 486SX
25 MHz 486DX processor complex	6450755	1,845	90/95-0Gx, trade-in 20 MHz 486SX
33 MHz 486DX processor complex	6451094	3,595	90/95-0Gx, trade-in 20 MHz 486SX
33 MHz 486DX processor complex	6451094	2,500	90/95-0Jx, trade-in 25 MHz 486DX
50 MHz 486DX processor complex	6450757	6,445	90/95-0Gx, trade-in 20 MHz 486SX
50 MHz 486DX processor complex	6450757	5,345	90/95-0Jx, trade-in 25 MHz 486DX
50 MHz 486DX processor complex	6450757	3,695	90/95-0Kx, trade-in 33 MHz 486DX
Processor complex 256K cache	6451095	1,995	External cache for 486DX complex

IBM no longer sells Intel math coprocessors other than the 80487SX. Math coprocessors other than the 80487SX must be purchased directly from Intel or from Intel distributors or dealers.

Table 4.62 PS/2 Memory Modules and Adapters

Description	Part number	Price	Notes
ISA 8-bit memory adapters			
Expanded memory adapter (XMA)	2685193	$1,395	2M RAM, LPT port, XT/AT/30
ISA bus 16-bit memory adapters			
0-12M multifunction adapter	30F5364	495	COM/LPT port, 30 286
All ChargeCard	34F2863	495	Memory manager for 25/30 286
3M expanded memory adapter	34F2864	1,830	ChargeCard, 0-12M card, 3M RAM
4M expanded memory kit	34F2866	1,285	ChargeCard, 4M system-board RAM
MCA bus 16-bit memory adapters			
1-8M 80286 memory optional/85ns	6450685	510	1M, EMS 4.0 for 50/55/60/65
2-8M 80286 memory optional/85ns	6450609	630	2M, EMS 4.0 for 50/55/60/65
MCA bus 32-bit adapters			
2-14M enhanced adapter/85ns	87F9856	745	2M, for 70/P70/80
4-14M enhanced adapter/85ns	87F9860	995	4M, for 70/P70/80
Memory module kits (SIMMs)			
25 system board memory/120ns	78X8955	51	128K kit (6 chips) for 25
512K memory module kit/120ns	30F5348	140	2-256K SIMMs for 30F5364/ 1497259, 25/30 286 system board
2M memory module kit/120ns	30F5360	250	2-1M SIMMs for 30F5364/ 1497259, 34F2866 25/30 286 system board
1M memory module kit/85ns	6450603	125	1M SIMM for 6450605/ 6450609, 6450685/34F3077/ 34F3011, 50Z/55/65/70 386 (Not Axx/Bxx)/P70 386
2M memory module kit/85ns	6450604	250	2M SIMM for 6450605/ 6450609, 6450685/34F3077/ 34F3011, 50Z/55/65/ 70 (Not Axx/Bxx)/P70 386
34M memory module kit/85ns	87F9977	495	4M SIMM for 35/40/55/65 34F3011/34F3077

continues

Table 4.62 PS/2 Memory Modules and Adapters

Description	Part number	Price	Notes
2M memory module kit/80ns	6450608	250	2M SIMM for 35/40/70 -Axx/Bxx
8M memory module kit/80ns	6450129	1,000	8M SIMM for 35/40
2M memory module kit/70ns	6450902	285	2M SIMM for 57/90/95
4M memory module kit/70ns	6450128	565	4M SIMM for 57/P75/90/95
8M memory module kit/70ns	6450130	1,135	8M SIMM for 35/40/57/P75 /90/95
2M memory module kit/80ns	79F0999	415	2M CMOS SIMM for L40 (keyed)
4M memory module kit/80ns	79F1000	825	4M CMOS SIMM for L40 (keyed)
8M memory module kit/80ns	79F1001	1,645	8M CMOS SIMM for L40 (keyed)
1M system board kit/80ns	6450375	528	1M card for 80-041
2M system board kit/80ns	6450379	250	2M card for 80 (except Axx)
4M system board kit/80ns	6451060	500	4M card for 80-A21/A31

Table 4.63 PS/2 Floppy Drives, Adapters, and Cables

Description	Part number	Price	Notes
5 1/4-inch floppy drives			
5 1/4-inch external 360K drive	4869001	$489	For all PS/2s
5 1/4-inch external 1.2M drive	4869002	509	For 50-95, requires 6451007
5 1/4-inch internal 1.2M drive	6451006	365	For 60/65/80
5 1/4-inch internal 1.2M slim drive	6451066	310	For 35/40/57/90/95
3 1/2-inch floppy drives			
3 1/2-inch internal 720K drive	78X8956	180	For 25 S/N < 100,000
3 1/2-inch internal 720K 1/3-height drive	6451056	159	For 25 S/N > 100,000
3 1/2-inch internal 720K 1/3-height drive	6451027	159	For 30-001
3 1/2-inch internal 1.44M 1/3-height drive	6451063	263	For 25-006/G06
3 1/2-inch internal 1.44M drive	6450353	263	For 30-E01/50-80, not 55/P70 386
3 1/2-inch internal 1.44M slim drive	6451130	263	35/40/57, not L40, media-sense

Description	Part number	Price	Notes
3 1/2-inch internal 1.44M 1/3-height drive	6451072	263	50-95, not 55/P70/30-E01
3 1/2-inch internal 2.88M slim drive	6451106	325	35/40/57, not L40, media-sense

Floppy disk drive adapters

Description	Part number	Price	Notes
5 1/4-inch external drive adapter	6450244	72	360K for 25-40, not L40
5 1/4-inch external drive adapter/A	6450245	72	360K for 50-80, not 55/P70 386
5 1/4-inch floppy disk drive adapter/A	6451007	216	For 1.2M/360K in 50-95

Cables and miscellaneous

Description	Part number	Price	Notes
5 1/4-inch external 360K cable	6451033	21	For 30-001/021 external drive
5 1/4-inch external 360K cable	27F4245	18	For 30-Exx external drive
5 1/4-inch external drive adapter cable	6451124	40	For 35/40 and 4869001
External storage device cable	23F2716	101	P70 360K,P75 360K/1.2M
3 1/2-inch internal drive kit	6451037	30	Cable/Bezel for 6451353
3 1/2-inch internal 1/3-height drive kit	6451034	25	Cable/Bezel for 6451072
3 1/2-inch internal 1/3-height drive kit B	6451035	30	For 6451026 in 55 LS
Drive upgrade kit for 35 LS	6451127	45	For 6451130/6451106/6451066

IBM preformatted floppy disks

Description	Part number	Price	Notes
5 1/4-inch 10 360K disks	6023450	44	Cardboard slipcase
5 1/4-inch 10 360K disks with case	6069769	45	Plastic library case/stand
5 1/4-inch 10 1.2M disks	6109660	54	Cardboard slipcase
5 1/4-inch 10 1.2M disks with case	6109661	55	Plastic library case/stand
3 1/2-inch 10 720K disks with case	6404088	33	Plastic library case/stand
3 1/2-inch 10 1.44M disks with case	6404083	49.50	Plastic library case/stand
3 1/2-inch 10 2.88M disks with case	72X6111	99	Plastic library case/stand

Table 4.64 PS/2 Hard Disks, Adapters and Cables

Description	Part number	Price	Notes
IDE hard disk drives			
20M 3 1/2-inch 80ms IDE drive	78X8958	$ 787	For 25
20M 3 1/2-inch 27ms IDE drive	6451075	787	For 25-xx6, Req 6451071
30M 3 1/2-inch 19ms IDE drive	6451076	695	For 25-xx6, Req 6451071
40M 3 1/2-inch 17ms IDE drive	6451047	500	For 55 LS

continues

Table 4.64 Continued

Description	Part number	Price	Notes
40M 3 1/2-inch 17ms IDE drive	6451073	500	For 35/40
80M 3 1/2-inch 17ms IDE drive	6451043	750	For 55 LS
80M 3 1/2-inch 17ms IDE drive	6451074	750	For 35/40
SCSI hard disk drives			
60M 3 1/2-inch 23ms, 32K cache	6451049	1,000	Async, 1.25M/sec Xfer rate
80M 3 1/2-inch 17ms, 32K cache	6451045	750	Async, 1.25M/sec Xfer rate
120M 3 1/2-inch 23ms, 32K cache	6451050	1,670	Async, 1.5M/sec Xfer rate
160M 3 1/2-inch 16ms, 32K cache	6451046	1,250	Async, 1.5M/sec Xfer rate
320M 3 1/2-inch 12.5ms, 64K cache	6451234	2,585	Sync, 2.0M/sec Xfer rate
400M 3 1/2-inch 11.5ms, 128K cache	6451235	3,125	Sync, 2.0M/sec Xfer rate
SCSI host adapter			
SCSI Adapter/A	6451109	495	16-bit Bus Master
SCSI Adapter/A with 512K cache	6451110	995	32/16-bit Bus Master
SCSI external terminator	6451039	110	For Adapter with Cache
Cables and miscellaneous			
Fixed Disk Drive Kit A	6451071	65	Installation kit for 25-xx6
Fixed Disk Upgrade Kit/35	6451128	15	For 6451073/6451074 in 35 LS
SCSI Installation Kit A	6451053	90	For 3 1/2-inch drive in 60/65/80
Fixed Disk Drive Kit D	6451120	20	For 60/120M drives in 90/95
SCSI card to option cable	6451139	220	Includes terminator, replaces 6451041
SCSI option to option cable	6451042	90	Connect external options
CD-ROM drives			
Internal 600M CD-ROM drive	6451113	1,250	Requires SCSI adapter
External 600M CD-ROM drive	3510001	1,550	Requires SCSI adapter
CD-ROM installation kit/A	6450847	35	Install in 5 1/4-inch bay
3 1/2-inch 128M rewritable drive	6450162	1,795	Requires SCSI adapter
Optical drive kit A	6451126	29	For 6450162 in 60/80 (non-SCSI)
3 1/2-inch rewritable cartridge	38F8645	70	128M cartridge for 6450162
3 1/2-inch rewritable cartridge	38F8646	315	5-128M cartridges for 6450162

Description	Part number	Price	Notes
8mm tape backup drives and accessories			
2.3G internal SCSI drive	6451121	6,500	For 95/3511, requires SYTOS
2.3G external SCSI drive	6451121	6,915	Requires SCSI adapter and SYTOS
SCSI cable for external drive	31F4187	315	Connects tape drive to system
SCSI device-to-device cable	31F4186	78	Chains tape to other devices
8mm data cartridge	21F8595	29.25	Stores 2.3 gigabytes
8mm cleaning cartridge	21F8593	40	For cleaning heads
SYTOS plus V1.3 for DOS	04G3375	150	Data compression
SYTOS plus V1.3 for OS/2 PM	04G3374	195	Data compression, FAT/HPFS
SCSI expansion units			
3510 external SCSI storage unit	35100V0	360	1 half-height, 3 1/2-inch, 5 1/4-inch bay
3511 external SCSI storage unit	3511003	3,845	7 bays, 3 1/2/5 1/4-inch, 320M drive

Table 4.65 PS/2 Video Displays and Adapters

Description	Part number	Price	Notes
Analog displays			
8504 12-inch VGA Mono Display	8504001	$ 342	640×480
8507 19-inch XGA Mono Display	8507001	600	1024×768
8604 16-inch XGA Mono Display	8604001	850	1024×768
PS/1 Color Display Upgrade	1057108	699	Upgrade for mono systems
8512 14-inch Color Display	8512001	599	640×480, .41mm stripe
8513 12-inch VGA Color Display	8513001	665	640×480, .28mm dot, stand
8514 16-inch XGA Color Display	8514001	1,645	1024×768, .31mm dot, stand
8515 14-inch XGA Color Display	8515021	866	1024×768, .28mm dot, stand
8518 14-inch VGA Color Display	8518001	749	640×480, .28mm dot, stand
8516 14-inch XGA Touch Screen	8516001	1,695	1024×768, .28mm dot, stand

continues

Table 4.65 Continued

Description	Part number	Price	Notes
Analog display adapters			
XGA Adapter/A	75X5887	795	1024×768, For 55-95 (Not 60/P70)
Video Memory Expansion Option	75X5889	280	512K Video RAM for XGA
8514/A Display Adapter	1887972	980	1024×768×16, for 50-80 (Not P70)
8514/A Memory Expansion Kit	1887989	283	1024×768×256 colors
Miscellaneous display accessories			
Display Stand for 8512	1501215	36	Tilt-swivel stand
TouchSelect for 12-inch displays	91F7951	670	Adds Touch screen to 8513
Privacy Filter for 8512	1053405	154	Prevents side view of display
Privacy Filter for 8513	1053401	154	Prevents side view of display
Privacy Filter for 8514	1053402	154	Prevents side view of display
Privacy Filter for 8515	1053403	154	Prevents side view of display

Table 4.66 PS/2 Network Adapters and Accessories

Description	Part number	Price	Notes
ISA bus Token Ring Network (TRN) adapters			
TRN Adapter II	25F9858	395	4Mbps for 25-40 (not L40)
TRN 16/4 Adapter	25F7367	895	16/4Mbps for 25-40 (not L40)
TRN 16/4 Trace & Performance	74F5121	1,220	16/4Mbps for 25-40 (not L40)
MCA bus Token Ring Network (TRN) adapters			
TRN Adapter/A (full-length)	69X8138	395	4Mbps, for 50-95
TRN Adapter/A (half-length)	39F9598	448	4Mbps for P70/75 (and 50-95)
TRN 16/4 Adapter/A	16F1133	895	16/4Mbps for 50-95
TRN 16/4 Adapter/A (half)	74F9410	895	16/4Mbps, 50-95, 80 percent faster
TRN 16/4 Trace & Perf./A	74F5130	1,220	16/4Mbps for 50-95
TRN 16/4 Busmaster Server/A	74F4140	1,030	16/4Mbps for 50-95 servers only

Description	Part number	Price	Notes
MCA bus EtherNet network adapters			
PS/2 EtherNet Adapter/A	6451091	575	10Mbps for 50-95, including boot ROM
Miscellaneous network adapter accessories			
TRN adapter cable	6339098	36	Connect card to LAN
TRN L-shaped connector cable	79F3229	50	For 74F9410 and P70/75
TRN 8230 4Mbps media filter	53F5551	55	For unshielded twisted pair
TRN Adapter II boot ROM	83X7839	99	EPROM for 25F9858
TRN Adapter/A boot ROM	83X8881	96	EPROM for 69X8138/39F9598
TRN 16/4 Adapter/A boot ROM	25X8887	99	EPROM for 25F7367/16F1133

Chapter Summary

This chapter has presented information about the PS/2 line of systems from IBM, including information about all the various PS/2 models and submodels, from low-end to high-end systems. The low-end PS/2 systems—the PS/2 Models 25, 30, PS/1, 25 286, 30 286, 35 SX, 40 SX, and L40 SX—are based closely on the original PC line and include the standard ISA-type of expansion slots. The higher-end PS/2 Models 50, 50Z, 55 SX, 57 SX, 60, 65 SX, 70 386, P70 386, P75, 80, 90, 95, and their respective submodels use the newer MCA slot design, which is dramatically different from the original ISA bus.

Chapter 5 examines IBM-compatible systems, including details on the available types of compatible systems and some of the criteria you might use to justify purchasing a particular IBM-compatible system over another IBM-compatible or an IBM system.

IBM-Compatible (and Not-So-Compatible) Computers

The open architecture of IBM systems has allowed a variety of non-IBM companies to introduce systems that are functionally identical to IBM's own. These systems often do more than just run the same software; many are hardware copies of IBM systems and are virtually identical in almost every respect. For this reason, many of these types of systems are called *clones*. Every time IBM makes a change in a system, compatibles or clones follow with the same kind of change.

Recent developments at IBM have made it difficult for clone-makers to keep up. IBM has introduced into the PC arena several new standards that are technological hurdles for other manufacturers to leap. The first major difficulty was the Micro Channel Architecture (MCA). These systems are much more difficult to copy than were the original ISA bus systems. Also, IBM is being stricter about what it allows as "cloning." Protecting massive amounts of development work and money poured into a new system is good business; IBM is more rigidly enforcing its patents and license agreements with respect to MCA clones. Although every manufacturer that develops even an IDA or EISA system owes IBM licensing fees and royalties, IBM has been lax in enforcing payments. IBM seems to have become more bold with its enforcement of these licenses. Most people believe that anybody can make ISA or EISA systems free of charge, as though the designs are in the public domain, but such is not the case. IBM holds in its portfolio many patents that ensure that anyone who develops an IBM-compatible PC, no matter which bus it uses, must license from IBM some of the technology for the system. The patents IBM holds for newer systems virtually guarantee that no compatible will be developed without such licensing. Several MCA-based compatibles exist, though not many, compared to ISA or EISA systems. Tandy sells a PS/2 compatible, the Model 5000MC, and several other companies sell Micro Channel systems.

IBM has introduced other standards that compatibles will have to follow. Perhaps the most prominent standard is the newer XGA video standard. IBM has licensed the XGA chipset technology to INMOS, a company that now can sell the chips to anyone who wants to make an XGA clone adapter. In essence, IBM is helping cloners develop their own XGA boards: IBM will benefit if the new standard is widely supported. Other standards include the IBM SCSI host adapters, which have complete real mode and protected mode BIOS support, and the 2.88M floppy drives that IBM introduced in the PS/2 Model 57. IBM even has introduced a custom version of the Intel 386SX processor, the 386SLC, which has features from the 486 design, including a built-in cache. This version has been licensed back to Intel, perhaps for others to purchase.

This chapter examines compatibles from several points of view. The primary view is that of the system installer and repair person. Such a person has strict criteria for what makes a "good" compatible system. For a system even to be in the running, for example, it must come with proper and adequate documentation. A lack of documentation is the nemesis of any installer or repair person, and a system without documentation simply is not acceptable. From this same point of view, several other items are presented for your consideration when you shop for a compatible system. What you learn here can and should be applied to the selection of any IBM or compatible system. These guidelines will direct you to a system that will be compatible, serviceable, and upgradeable for many years.

Examining Types of Compatibles

Although many brands, makes, and models of IBM and IBM-compatible systems exist, all the systems can be broken down into several types or categories. Any IBM or compatible system can be classified as one of two primary system types:

PC XT compatible
AT compatible

Any system that runs IBM software can be put in one of these categories. A COMPAQ Deskpro 486/50, for example, is really just another AT compatible—although, compared to the original IBM AT, the COMPAQ Deskpro 486/50 offers a great deal more performance. Even IBM's own systems can be classified as compatibles; the PS/2 Model 30, for example, is really a PC XT compatible that, again, offers much more performance than the original PC or XT.

The distinction between the two types of systems comes primarily from the architectural differences in the microprocessors making up the systems. Intel processors have two basic modes of operation: real and protected modes. Systems that can run only in real mode are considered PC XT-compatible systems, and they never will make the jump to the next level of systems software, called OS/2. Systems that can run also in protected mode will run OS/2 and can be classified as AT-compatible systems.

AT compatibles that run the Micro Channel interface have different types of expansion adapters available, and are different from the viewpoint of the system installer, upgrader, or repair person. These systems are much easier to work on, have fewer components, are more reliable, and offer greater potential for performance. AT compatibles with 386 or greater processors have access to an additional mode, called virtual 8086 mode, which allows multiple real-mode simulations not only to coexist in memory but also to process simultaneously in a true multitasking environment. These systems offer also an improved method for switching from real to protected mode, which OS/2 does frequently when it runs older DOS programs. The 386- (or higher) based AT compatibles also offer improved memory-switching capabilities.

Another, and totally different, method of categorizing systems is to separate clones from compatibles. A clone usually is defined as a system that is a virtual duplicate of one of IBM's systems: The system is the same physically and electronically, as well as being capable of running the same software as a given IBM system. For example, a clone of the IBM AT would use a motherboard that's not only electronically but also physically compatible with the AT. The board therefore has the same mounting-screw hole, standoff, slot connector, and keyboard connector locations as the IBM board. Such a board could be physically interchanged in a system with the IBM board, or vice versa. This capability would apply also to the power supply, disk drives, and perhaps even the chassis. Because of the wealth of physical replacement parts available to fit IBM systems, a clone of one of these systems will have access to the same wealth of parts. Clones therefore not only are very easy to upgrade or repair, but also the cost of upgrading and repairing them is extremely low.

A system that isn't a clone physically, but that will run the same software and even take the same plug-in cards as an IBM system, is defined as compatible. COMPAQ makes compatible systems that are not clones, for example. These systems use motherboards with completely different mounting hardware and connector locations than IBM, so physical interchangeability is impossible. This incompatibility isn't only in the power supply; even the floppy disk drives in a COMPAQ system are incompatible physically with those in an IBM system.

Some manufacturers go out of their way, in fact, to make their systems as physically incompatible as possible with any other system. Then replacement parts, repairs, and upgrades are virtually impossible to find—except, of course, from the original system manufacturer, at a significantly higher price than the equivalent part would cost to fit an IBM or clone system. For example, if the motherboard in my IBM AT dies, I can find any number of replacement boards to bolt to the AT chassis, with my choice of processors and clock speeds and at ridiculously low prices. If the motherboard dies in your COMPAQ Deskpro, you'll pay for a replacement available only from COMPAQ, and you have virtually no opportunity to select a board with a faster or better processor than the one that failed. In other words, upgrading one of these systems is almost out of the question.

No matter what the differences, there are certainly cases in which each system type is suitable for a particular need.

Learning the Levels of Compatibility

In developing a compatible computer, you can achieve a few basic levels of similarity to IBM systems. In order of increasing desirability, these are the levels of similarity:

> Operating-system level
> ROM BIOS level
> Hardware (register) level
>   A. Motherboard and CPU
>   B. Peripherals and I/O controllers
> Physical (dimensional) level

Compatibility at the Operating-System Level

For the most part, compatibles at only the first (operating system) level are the least desirable and generally are shunned by the industry. The reason is that operating-system compatibles use licensed, customized versions of Microsoft's MS-DOS, or perhaps OS/2. These systems don't run the IBM version of MS-DOS or OS/2; they also have a ROM basic input-output system (BIOS) not quite like any from IBM. Compatibility is not possible when the ROM isn't identical to IBM's and when DOS makes calls to the ROM BIOS for specific functions.

Any software will run on a version of MS-DOS or OS/2 that has been customized for a nonstandard ROM—as long as the software runs on top of DOS and makes no calls, either to the ROM BIOS or directly to the hardware. This type of software sometimes is called "well behaved" software. Most popular software does make calls to ROM, however; such hardware and software are "ill behaved." Most popular software programs therefore either cannot run on operating-system-level compatibles or require special versions for the systems in question.

Many systems have been developed for compatibility at only the operating-system level. A few examples are the DEC Rainbow 100, the Texas Instruments Professional, and the Tandy 2000. Compatibility at only the operating-system (OS) level definitely is not fashionable now, and most people would be well advised to stay away from any system with this limitation.

An interesting tidbit of information is that the development of OS/2 might encourage the emergence of new systems compatible at only the OS level, largely because software running under OS/2 is isolated from the hardware. Because no software accesses the hardware, OS/2 itself can mask any differences between various manufacturers' hardware systems. ROM-level compatibility also might become unimportant because OS/2 can (and does, on most systems) load the ROM from disk; what used to be called the ROM BIOS code is effectively now part of the OS/2 system. For all of this activity to take place, you will have to get a special custom version of OS/2 from the same company that manufactured your hardware.

Compatibility at the ROM BIOS Level

A large number of systems, however, are compatible at the ROM level. The ROM BIOS interface in these systems appears, to software, to be exactly like the ROM BIOS of a particular IBM system. Generally, the same software that runs on a particular IBM system can run on this kind of system. The actual BIOS code differs from IBM's, but only in the area of the actual interface to the hardware.

This difference is necessary because compatibles operating at this level have hardware that differs from any particular IBM system. This feature generally doesn't cause problems unless you attempt to run actual BIOS code from an IBM system in this type of compatible. This situation rarely happens, though: Making a copy of IBM's ROM BIOS chips and placing them in the motherboard of a compatible system is not legal. The procedure wouldn't work anyway, unless that system truly was hardware compatible with the specific IBM system from which the ROM was copied. Systems that are compatible at this level usually run IBM DOS, unless the hardware is very different from the IBM standard. Software that runs on top of DOS remains unaffected unless, again, a special dependence on a different hardware feature exists.

With OS/2, compatibility at only this level is a problem. As indicated, when OS/2 is loaded it loads a copy of a ROM BIOS from disk. This copy is the *protected mode ROM BIOS*, or *Advanced BIOS (ABIOS)*. A system compatible only at this level won't run IBM OS/2, which may or may not be a problem. If your particular system manufacturer does not offer a customized version of OS/2 containing new ABIOS code designed specifically for your system, a real problem occurs: You might never be able to run OS/2 because the IBM version will run on only true hardware-compatible systems. Unlike DOS, no "generic" versions of OS/2 are available because of the amount of customization necessary for certain hardware systems. Usually, compatibility at the BIOS level becomes a real problem only to owners of AT-class compatibles, because PC XT-class compatibles never will run OS/2 anyway. An important development is that IBM now supports its versions of DOS and OS/2 on compatible systems. The company does not guarantee that its versions will run on everything, but it is making significant efforts to eliminate areas of incompatibility.

In some instances, system owners with compatibility at only the ROM level are locked out of certain upgrades. For example, specialized upgrades, such as processor accelerator boards, run only on systems that are truly hardware compatible with IBM's PC XT or AT. Most of these boards don't run on systems that are BIOS compatible but have not reached the third level of compatibility—the hardware level.

Compatibility at the Hardware Level

To be a true hardware-level compatible, a system must match a particular IBM system at the basic motherboard hardware level. In other words, the system must use the same hardware interrupt request (IRQ) channels, direct memory access (DMA) channels, and I/O port addresses for the same purposes that IBM does, and the system must offer the same slot or bus interface—at the same clock rate—that IBM does. The majority of today's systems offer this level of compatibility, which means that an adapter board that works in a particular IBM system unit will work also in a comparable unit of the compatible. ROM code should be much the same as IBM's; in some cases, you might be able to run IBM's own ROMs in a system such as this one. For AT-type systems, actual IBM OS/2 should boot and run. A customized version from the system's original equipment manufacturer (OEM) might exist, but that does not necessarily preclude the use of the IBM OS/2.

Some differences in the hardware might make the system marginally compatible. The system and bus clock rate and the number of wait states inserted by the system during bus cycles, for example, can have a big effect on which peripherals do or don't work. The AST Premium 286 offers a jumper-selectable wait-state setting of 0 or 1. Running with 0 wait states, the system picks up about 20 to 30 percent in speed over running with 1 wait state. Many plug-in boards aren't affected, but some are. Certain memory boards, network boards, and other communications adapters won't work at the 0 wait state setting; the board in question acts as though it were defective. Resetting the motherboard to insert 1 wait state slows down the system but allows the boards in question to run without problems.

COMPAQ takes a good approach with its systems. The COMPAQ Deskpro systems run at clock rates between 8 MHz and 50 MHz or more. Few conventional AT adapter boards run at these higher speeds, but the COMPAQ uses a dual bus and clock system that runs the standard AT bus at 8 MHz with 1 wait state. All the adapter cards act the same as though they were in actual IBM AT slots. To improve memory-access performance, you must purchase—from COMPAQ—a separate board for memory that will work at the full system clock rate and reduced number of wait states. These boards usually are proprietary in design and plug into special slots designed by the OEM just for this purpose.

Peripherals and I/O controllers are hardware-compatibility issues that usually are glossed over. Differences in these devices exist between the PC XT and AT types of systems. For example, in PC XT systems, IBM used a serial port (RS-232C) that incorporates a National Semiconductor 8250B Universal Asynchronous Receiver Transmitter (UART) device. In the AT, IBM used a newer chip by National Semiconductor: the 16450 UART. In many PS/2 systems, an NS 16550AN chip is used. Mixing serial ports with these respective UARTs was never a problem under DOS, but under OS/2 you must have the 16450 or 16550 version in your AT. If you have instead the PC XT type of serial port with the 8250, serial communications of any kind either won't operate or will work unreliably under OS/2.

Similar problems exist with the hard disk controllers in AT systems. For the AT, IBM used a version of Western Digital 1002-WA2 or the later model 1003-WA2. These controllers have no on-board ROM BIOS and, instead, run from the BIOS interface built into the motherboard ROM. To successfully run OS/2 on your AT-compatible system, you must follow that standard. In other words, a hard disk controller with an on-board ROM BIOS that doesn't work in protected mode, or that isn't hardware-register-compatible with the Western Digital controllers, won't work for protected-mode environments such as OS/2 or Novell NetWare.

Finally, the graphics adapter can be a sensitive issue in a protected-mode environment. The reason is that every graphics adapter beyond the standard Color Graphics Adapter (CGA) has an on-board ROM BIOS interface. Because this on-board BIOS might not operate in protected mode, any protected-mode operating system then would load the correct drivers from disk to run the graphics board. Many users of some of the first EGA- and VGA-compatible cards found that their particular early-model EGA or—especially—early-model VGA adapters did not operate under OS/2. For standard types of adapters, such as serial ports, disk controllers, and graphics boards, the solution to this problem is to get boards that are truly hardware-register-compatible with the ones IBM has used. For other nonstandard types of peripherals that must work under OS/2, such as tape drives or CD-ROM drives, you must get special OS/2 drivers from the OEM of the particular unit.

Compatibility at the Physical (Dimensional) Level

The final level of compatibility is that of the clone system. These systems have all the previous levels of compatibility, (operating system, ROM BIOS, and hardware) as well as the capability to interchange parts physically from IBM systems. As stated, this capability makes a system incredibly easy, as well as inexpensive, to maintain and upgrade. This level of compatibility ensures that the widest selection of upgrade components will be available.

The bottom line is that most users will want a compatible or clone that is at least truly hardware compatible with one of IBM's systems. Sometimes it isn't easy to tell. Remember that this level of compatibility is much more important for AT-type systems than for PC- or XT-type systems because of OS/2 and its dependence on the hardware. The best way around this problem is to purchase AT-type systems from an OEM who has the proper customized version of OS/2 to go along with the system. PC or XT system owners don't have to worry about this problem, but do note that most of the best "accelerator" products for these systems on the market are very hardware dependent.

Knowing What To Look For (Selection Criteria)

As a consultant, I often am asked to make a recommendation for a system purchase. Making these types of recommendations is one of the most frequent tasks a consultant performs. Many consultants charge a large fee for this advice. Unfortunately, most "consultants" don't have any rhyme or reason to their selections and instead base their choices solely on magazine reviews or, even worse, on some personal bias. To help eliminate this haphazard selection process, I have developed a simple checklist that will help you select a system. This list takes into consideration several important system aspects overlooked by most such checklists. The goal is to ensure that the selected system truly is compatible and has a long life of service and upgrades ahead.

Compatible-Selection Checklist

It helps to think like an engineer when you make your selection. Consider every aspect and detail of the systems in question. For instance, you will want to consider all future uses and upgrades. Technical support at a professional (as opposed to a user) level is extremely important; what support will be provided? Is there documentation, and does it cover everything else?

You will want also to evaluate nonstandard parts and make sure that the OEM provides a spare-parts program that lets you purchase these parts when the system needs service. In addition, you should identify standard parts and their sources so that you can substitute parts where you want or need them, and establish avenues for purchase other than the OEM. It helps to identify the interfaces present at all connectors so that you can locate products which can plug into these connectors.

In short, a checklist is a good idea. Here is one for you to use in evaluating any IBM-compatible system. You might not have to meet every one of these criteria to consider a particular system, but if you miss more than a few of these checks, consider staying away from that system. The items at the top of the list are the most important, and the items at the bottom are perhaps of lesser importance than some (although I think each item is important!). The rest of this chapter discusses in detail the criteria in this checklist.

1. Is technical documentation available?

   ❏ Technical-reference manual?
   ❏ Service or maintenance manual?
   ❏ Manufacturer-supplied diagnostics?

2. Is there an OEM version of

   ❏ MS-DOS?
   ❏ OS/2?

3. Is the ROM BIOS a current version developed by a known BIOS manufacturer with documentation and support? Examples include:

   ❏ Most "name" systems such as IBM and COMPAQ
   ❏ American Megatrends Inc. (AMI)
   ❏ Award Software
   ❏ Phoenix Software

4. Is the system design conservative? In particular:

   ❏ Is the motherboard memory (RAM and ROM) socketed?
   ❏ Is the CPU socketed?
   ❏ Are parts rated for full operating speed?
   ❏ Do the slots run at 8 MHz with wait state 1?
   ❏ Is the power supply adequate for upgrades?
   ❏ Does the system run cool?

5. Does the system adhere to established hardware standards? In particular:

   ❏ Does the IRQ and DMA use match IBM's?
   ❏ Does the I/O port use match IBM's?
   ❏ Does the CMOS memory and clock work like IBM's?

6. Is technical and service support available? In particular:

   ❏ Are spare parts available (especially unique components)?
   ❏ Is technical support available directly from the OEM?

If you can answer Yes to all these questions, the system definitely is worth purchasing! Some systems, because of unique constraints, might not pass every check in the list. COMPAQ, for example, although perhaps the premier compatible manufacturer, does not make a system service manual available to the purchaser; only dealers get this information. Also, you must obtain technical support or spare parts through the dealer because COMPAQ does not deal directly with the purchaser of the system. You must weigh these drawbacks in your consideration of such a system.

Items 1 and 2, as well as parts of item 4, definitely eliminate from consideration the typical no-name systems built in some garage. Systems such as "Joe's Computer Shack Super-Turbo-American-Generic-Limited-Plus AT" won't meet these criteria. When you call Joe and ask him whether you can buy the technical-reference manual, he usually doesn't have one. Then you are at Joe's mercy whenever you have a technical question that needs an answer. More than likely, Joe doesn't have answers to any but the simplest questions—not a workable alternative to the manual! Remember that you received a "generic" version of MS-DOS with your system. That version is fine for DOS, but are you aware that no plans exist for a generic version of OS/2? The OS/2 operating system is more hardware-specific than DOS, and a generic version will be difficult to support. IBM has decided to support its version of OS/2 on compatible systems, and therefore it may not be a problem, but IBM cannot make any guarantees. What do you think Joe will say when his Turbo AT customers call and ask why the IBM OS/2 package doesn't run properly on his system?

Note that these selection criteria will fully qualify many systems on the market. Most of the time you must purchase these systems from bigger-name companies, and the systems might cost a little more than the "generic" systems referred to earlier. Often, however, the extra expense is justified down the road when service and support are necessary.

Documentation

As mentioned, extensive documentation is an important factor to consider when you're planning to buy a system. This section examines four forms of documentation: system documentation, technical-reference manuals, hardware-maintenance and service manuals, and advanced diagnostics software.

System Documentation

One of the most important things your system can have is good system documentation. Without it, repairing, upgrading, or troubleshooting a system is nearly impossible. Many people are intimidated by the volume, technical nature, and cost of some of the documentation available for a system, but consider the purchase a necessary evil. This area separates the true manufacturers from the guy who slaps together motherboards and cases in a garage. Good documentation also keeps you from trying the two worst approaches when you have a question or problem: trial and error, or a dealer.

Of these approaches, many consider trial and error to be much more productive than calling your computer dealer. Some dealers, of course,

are fully capable and can support properly a typical end user. Few dealers, however, want to become closely involved in your upgrade project,
especially with a system purchased more than a year earlier, and no dealer
will repair your system for free. Unless you want to waste innumerable
hours with sometimes unresponsive technical-support departments
or simply play a guessing game when you troubleshoot or upgrade your
system, demand that certain technical-reference documents for your
system be made available to you. Expect in most cases to have to locate
these documents as well as pay for them when you find them. Free reference documents rarely are included with the system, and in some cases
can be difficult to obtain.

Technical-Reference Manuals

The technical-reference manual is the most important of all the manuals
available for a system. I refuse to purchase any system that does not
have an appropriate technical-reference manual. Remember that many
manufacturers include such information with the system as part of the
standard documentation. I sometimes buy the manual long before I buy
the system because the information in the manual is necessary for me to
conduct a proper review of the system.

Chapter 2, "System Features," provided information about the contents
of the manuals produced by IBM. IBM (as well as most name-brand system
vendors) excels in this area. IBM system documentation sets a standard
that is difficult for other manufacturers to follow. Having documentation
as good as IBM's is not really necessary, but a basic technical-reference
manual with detailed information is essential. You'll need this information
in order to install certain floppy drives, hard drives, memory adapters
and chips, communications adapters, and practically anything else. Expect to pay between $25 and $200 for a good technical-reference manual,
unless of course it was provided for free as part of the standard package.
Contact the original equipment manufacturer (OEM) to obtain the manual
for your system. Chapter 2 has more information about obtaining this
documentation for IBM systems.

Hardware-Maintenance and Service Manuals

Service manuals are desirable for anyone who has to troubleshoot a
system. This type of manual isn't an absolute necessity and, in fact, several manufacturers have none. Other manufacturers (such as COMPAQ)
have service manuals but refuse to make them available to users, which
might be OK because of the wealth of third-party diagnostics and repair
utilities. In many cases, the actual IBM documentation is satisfactory—
especially for a clone, but might work well even for a compatible.

Hardware-maintenance and service manuals from IBM contain several items:

- Jumper and switch settings for IBM systems
- A parts catalog for IBM systems
- Detailed diagnostic flowcharts
- Advanced diagnostics disks

The first two items don't do a compatible owner any good, but the last two items are valuable in almost all cases for IBM systems or compatibles. The diagnostic flowcharts, called *maintenance-analysis procedures* (MAPs) by IBM, are quite useful. These flowcharts are a list of step-by-step instructions for troubleshooting a failure down to the smallest plug-in part in a system. "Down to the smallest plug-in part" generally means down to the board level, but items such as memory are "troubleshot" down to the failed component.

MAPs are written in a manner that enables you to follow a logical progression. You check and test a cable before scrapping a controller card, for example, or test a controller card before tossing a disk drive, or check switch and jumper settings before even touching any hardware. Although someone with experience in troubleshooting and diagnosis may not use MAPs often, these flowcharts can be handy when all your own tried-and-true procedures have failed. MAPs are especially handy when the pressure is on and you're not thinking clearly.

Advanced diagnostics are included in hardware-maintenance and service manuals. The manual for the PC, XT, Portable, and AT comes with two diagnostics disks: one for PC-type systems and the other for AT-type systems. Supplements (updates) are available for newer systems not covered by the original diagnostics, such as the PS/2 Models 25 and 30. The updates include the proper diagnostics for these systems. Other updates are available for the XT-286, which comes with a new disk that replaces and supersedes the original AT disk supplied with the starter manual.

The hardware-maintenance and service manual for PS/2 Micro Channel systems comes with the same Reference Disk you received when you bought the system. You might not have realized that you already had the advanced diagnostics for these systems (only PS/2 Models 50 and higher, which have the MCA bus) without having to purchase the hardware-maintenance and service manual, as with the PC, XT, and AT. The Advanced Diagnostics for these systems are hidden on the Reference Disk and can be activated by a special "back door" command. This command becomes known to anyone who pays for the hardware-maintenance and service manual, in which the activation command is fully documented.

The idea is to prevent an average user from knowing about and subsequently "wandering around in" the advanced diagnostics, because many of the disk tests can destroy data and should not be run by inexperienced personnel.

What is the command to activate the Advanced Diagnostics for the PS/2? Simply boot the Reference Disk, go to the main menu, and press Ctrl-A (for Advanced). The standard menu then is replaced by a new one: the Advanced Diagnostics menu. That's it. Even though you already have the diagnostics, you still might want to consider getting a copy of the manual; it contains valuable information.

Advanced Diagnostics Software

Advanced diagnostics software is a powerful set of routines that can inspect and test all major areas of the system and several minor ones. Additionally, any peripherals that are fully compatible with IBM's own can be tested by these diagnostics. The advanced diagnostics run on any system compatible at the hardware level with any IBM system. In fact, the Advanced Diagnostics software can be used as a sort of acid test for compatibility. (Remember how people used such products as Microsoft's Flight Simulator or Lotus 1-2-3 for testing compatibility? I always used instead the IBM advanced diagnostics, which gave me a much better evaluation of a system's performance and compatibility.)

The diagnostics software can test also most add-on devices similar to those from IBM. For example, you can test the hard disk and controller as long as the interface is compatible with what IBM used. Graphics boards can be tested as though they were the specific IBM board that they replaced; examples of the IBM boards are the Color Graphics Adapter (CGA), Enhanced Graphics Adapter (EGA), and so on. I usually find that any hardware-compatible system passes at least the motherboard tests (they work even without an actual IBM ROM), memory tests, floppy controller and disk tests, and hard disk controller and drive tests. Non-IBM graphics boards usually fail the IBM tests, and most non-IBM communications boards such as terminal emulators and network adapters are not even recognized. This is the case even if they are in an IBM system unit.

In a later chapter, you can read about some aftermarket (non-OEM) replacements for the advanced diagnostics that might or might not be available from your system's manufacturer. Several replacements have been adjusted to work with compatible systems, perhaps better than the diagnostics from IBM. In many cases, the replacements have also more powerful test and diagnostic routines than those in the IBM version.

System Software

The operating-system software for your computer is extremely important. The software is an essential part of the system because nothing can be done without it. The operating-system software should be considered equal in importance to the ROM BIOS code that runs the system because the operating system is in fact an extension of or replacement for the ROM BIOS. You might ask, "Why didn't they just put the entire DOS in ROM? And then, when I turn on the system, it will be ready to go." The answer is that an operating system is complicated and often changed. Would you want to take your system in for service every time a new DOS was introduced? Also, would you want to be restricted to using only one type of DOS? Of course not. Therefore, the system designers put in the system as little of an operating system as possible in the form of ROM chips or firmware. *Firmware* indicates a program burned into a ROM chip; software that is "hard" is called "firmware."

The importance of system software is easy to understand. Now, where do you get this software? Hopefully, you can get it from the company that makes your system. The original equipment manufacturer (OEM) of the system must supply this software because it is highly customized to the particular hardware design. Unfortunately, many lower-cost compatibles do not have OEM versions of any operating systems. And, a system with no real operating system can cause problems. Where do you get one? Where do you get upgrades to new versions? Will new versions be produced for other systems but not for yours? These tough questions are examined in this section.

OEM-Licensed DOS (from Microsoft)

Asked which operating system they use, many people respond, "MS-DOS." Others might say that they use IBM DOS or COMPAQ DOS. Those who say that they use MS-DOS, however, might not be entirely correct. What is MS-DOS? And what, for instance, is the difference between MS-DOS and IBM DOS?

MS-DOS stands for *Microsoft Disk Operating System*, a collection of programs designed and produced by Microsoft and IBM in a special joint-development agreement. The programs are designed specifically to run on IBM (and IBM-compatible) systems. Microsoft owns the source code and sells licenses to various system OEMs, who then adapt the code to run on their systems. The OEMs then produce the documentation and provide all support for their specific version of DOS. Microsoft has not yet officially sold MS-DOS as a stand-alone retail product. It has offered a DOS 5.0 *upgrade* as a retail product, but only for systems that already have a version of DOS on them. Microsoft still officially does not sell a bootable stand-alone version of DOS at the retail level. Therefore, technically no such thing as "pure" retail MS-DOS exists—usually only specific MS-DOS "flavors," or implementations, given names (such as IBM DOS, COMPAQ DOS, AT&T DOS, AST DOS, and so on) by the OEMs that produce them.

This analogy is from the automotive world: General Motors often produces a variety of different makes and models of automobiles based on exactly the same chassis. Suppose that I drive a 1989 Pontiac Firebird. If you ask me what type of car I drive, I could answer, "I drive a GM F-body automobile." The answer is correct, but not sufficiently detailed. True, the Firebird is an F-body (a GM Corporate designation), but so is the Chevrolet Camaro. You don't buy a pure or otherwise generic F-body car from General Motors; you buy either a Firebird or a Camaro. GM does not sell raw F-bodies to the public.

Rather, GM Corporate "sells" the bodies to the Pontiac and Chevrolet Motor Divisions, and they customize the autos to produce the final result. In 1989, at the F-body assembly plant in Van Nuys, California, Firebirds and Camaros were manufactured simultaneously by the same workers, on the same assembly line. The frames, engines, transmissions, brakes, axles, suspensions, and virtually all mechanical items are exactly the same between the two cars. The cars differ only in interior and exterior appearance items and trim. The same can be said for the Mitsubishi 3000 GT and the Dodge Stealth, both manufactured in a Mitsubishi factory in Japan. These two cars are identical also, except for exterior sheet metal and ornamentation.

DOS and OS/2 are sold in much the same way: licensed by Microsoft and IBM to a particular computer-system manufacturer who then adapts the raw DOS source code to run properly on its own system. Because each manufacturer customizes DOS for its specific systems, you benefit the most by using the DOS from your system's manufacturer. Microsoft produces a generic version licensed to no-name clone makers, available as a retail product in the form of an upgrade, but you are better off to stick (if possible) with the DOS from your system's OEM.

The auto analogy helps to answer the second question, "What is the difference between MS-DOS and IBM DOS?" You can see that, as stated, the question can't be answered in definite terms. IBM DOS is a retail product that can be dissected and analyzed. MS-DOS, however, is a general term that applies to all the different DOS products produced from the same "assembly line" beginnings. The computer question is the same as the automotive question: "What is the difference between a GM F-body automobile and a Pontiac Firebird?" How do you answer? The

Firebird is an F-body automobile, but not all F-bodies are Firebirds. Some end up as Camaros. Likewise, IBM DOS is an MS-DOS "flavor," but so are COMPAQ DOS, AT&T DOS, Zenith DOS, AST DOS, Toshiba DOS, NEC DOS, and so on.

Now a problem occurs. Remember Joe, from Joe's Computer Shack? Suppose that he wanted to sell an implementation of MS-DOS for his systems, and called Microsoft. Microsoft spoke to Joe about licensing MS-DOS and told him that he could get a binary adaptation kit (BAK) including source code to DOS that would have to be customized for his systems. Joe found out also that he would have to write and print all the documentation and produce all the packaging for his product, which he could call "Joe's DOS." Then he was told about licensing fees, which run into tens and even hundreds of thousands of dollars. Because Joe sells only five or six systems a week and runs a small store, he can hardly justify the costs and does not have the programming staff required to do the adaptation. So, Joe told his customers to buy IBM DOS; after all, his systems are 100 percent compatible with IBM's, right?

Wrong. Joe's customers began calling. "Why can't I run BASIC programs?" "Why don't some of the systems recognize the date and time during boot-up?" "Why am I having so many problems with overwriting floppy data in drive A: when I switch disks?" "On some systems, why does the hard disk have constant errors?" Joe then told his customers to buy COMPAQ DOS because, in that version, the entire BASIC interpreter is provided on disk and does not rely on Cassette BASIC, found only in the ROM of true IBM systems. This solution might not have solved the other problems. In fact, new calls came in. "Why does the MODE command no longer operate properly?"

Today, many "Joes" still sell low-cost, generic compatibles and clones, and Microsoft has recognized this situation. As of DOS V3.2, Microsoft has made a special version of MS-DOS just for generic compatibles: the Microsoft MS-DOS Packaged Product. A dealer such as Joe can get this version from Microsoft on a small-quantity basis but must agree in writing to perform all the testing to verify that the version works correctly on his systems, provide all support to end users who purchase the product, and then sell it only with one of his tested computers. You supposedly cannot buy this generic MS-DOS without a computer system. Upgrades and bug fixes are handled by Joe or, possibly, directly by Microsoft. This generic version is not "tweaked" to run better on any certain system but rather is designed to run on IBM or 100 percent compatible systems. Any system not fully compatible with IBM still must use a specially customized version of DOS licensed from Microsoft and produced by the OEM. If the generic version does not work on a particular system for some reason, Microsoft probably will not fix the problem.

With the introduction of DOS V5.0, Microsoft began selling DOS upgrades as a retail product directly to the public. It is interesting to note, however, that this product isn't bootable and works only on systems on which DOS already is running. Another interesting bit of information is that, technically, you still cannot purchase the generic version of DOS in a standard bootable form without a computer. The license agreements between compatible vendors who want to sell the MS-DOS Packaged Product remains the same.

Although Microsoft still does not have dealers selling standard DOS bootable copies as a stand-alone item through the retail channel, you rarely will encounter resistance in purchasing a generic copy of MS-DOS. It seems that many dealers are willing to sell DOS on the "gray market," perhaps without Microsoft's direct approval. I have purchased several copies of generic MS-DOS (full product, not just the upgrade) with no problems. Therefore it seems that virtually anyone can easily buy the generic version of MS-DOS.

With various manufacturer versions of DOS, the bottom line is this: To ensure that your system really is fully compatible with current and later releases of DOS, you should buy your system from an OEM that has a direct license from Microsoft for DOS and that produces its own DOS product. You could buy an AST Premium 386, for example, because AST has a license from Microsoft and produces its own DOS product (AST DOS) specifically for its systems. In all honesty, you rarely will have problems with various compatibles not running the prepackaged "generic" Microsoft DOS. In fact, most compatibles will run IBM DOS, if not the BASIC interpreter, quite well. The criteria of having an OEM-produced DOS for all systems is not mandatory, but having an OEM DOS is valuable insurance against future problems. I recommend running IBM DOS on compatibles because IBM offers the most support for bug fixes and updates. It is second to none in this respect; for example, it already has released at least four versions of DOS 5, to fix a variety of small bugs and problems not yet fixed in other OEM versions, including Microsoft's. IBM also now supports its version on compatibles, and anyone can purchase it or an upgrade through normal retail channels.

OEM-Licensed OS/2 (from Microsoft)

In examining OS/2 in the same manner as DOS, you will find that the issues are more straightforward: No generic version of OS/2 is available from Microsoft. OS/2 is available only as a licensed product to OEMs, who must adapt it to their systems. If you have purchased an AT-class system whose manufacturer does not produce an implementation of OS/2, you might be in trouble. (Joe's customers will be in trouble when they find out that Joe has no specific version of OS/2 for them and that they must take their chances with the IBM version.) As a professional consultant, I cannot have my clients left out in the cold like this. For me to recommend a system for purchase, either an OEM version of OS/2 specifically for that system must be available, or the system must run IBM OS/2. Any system that is 100 percent hardware compatible with IBM obviously runs the IBM versions of OS/2. Most compatibles so far run the IBM version with no problems, and IBM is dedicated to supporting OS/2 on compatibles as well. For now, however, I would not purchase a system in a "hope" that might turn out to be just a "dream."

You should understand that even if your motherboard is fully compatible with IBM's AT systems and would run OS/2, it must be compatible also at the adapter-card hardware level. By adding nonstandard adapter cards to an IBM AT, you can render it incapable of running OS/2. For example, IBM OS/2 comes with drivers for Western Digital register-compatible hard disk controllers. Because IBM used the 1002-WA2 and 1003-WA2, these controllers work well, as do any others that are register compatible with them, including most AT-style ST-506/412 MFM or RLL controllers and most ESDI controllers.

SCSI controllers are more problematic. Generally, you need special OS/2 drivers for your particular SCSI adapter. If your AT system, however, has a hard disk controller with a built-in nonstandard ROM used to run the card or uses an 8-bit interface to the system board or a proprietary compression system, you might need a special OS/2 driver program in order for the controller to work. The driver must be supplied by the OEM of the board you use. Be prepared to wait. For example, I am using in one of my systems a SCSI host adapter that provides an incredibly fast and powerful interface to hard disks and other devices. For quite some time, however, I could not boot OS/2 because the company that produces the adapter did not have OS/2 drivers readily available, and the adapter's on-board BIOS did not run in protected mode. Be prepared for similar experiences in obtaining drivers for other adapter cards that deviate from established standards. On my PS/2 system, however, using IBM's SCSI adapter, which has a real and protected mode BIOS, I can run any operating system, with no special drivers needed to support the hard disks.

All these problems will be solved with time and effort. Most (if not all) the early Video Graphics Array (VGA) adapters, for example, did not work with OS/2, but nearly all the current versions do. People who purchased the earlier boards should upgrade or exchange their board for one that really works.

If OS/2 compatibility is important to you, *make sure that you have an up-front guarantee that the operating system will be supported,* either by a specific version for the system, or by being compatible enough to run IBM's version.

ROM BIOS

The issue of ROM BIOS compatibility is important. If the BIOS is not compatible, any number of problems can result. Several reputable companies that produce compatibles have developed their own proprietary ROM BIOS that works just like IBM's. These companies also frequently update their ROM code, to keep in step with the latest changes IBM has incorporated into its ROMs. Because IBM generally does not sell ROM upgrades or provide them for its systems unless the upgrade is absolutely necessary (IBM decides what is necessary), keeping current with an actual IBM system is more difficult than with most of the compatible systems on the market. Also, many of the compatibles' OEMs have designed ROMs that work specifically with additional features in their systems while effectively masking the effects of these improvements from any software that would "balk" at the differences.

OEMs

Many OEMs independently have developed their own compatible ROMs. Companies such as COMPAQ, Zenith, and AT&T have developed their own BIOS product, which has proven compatible with IBM's. These companies also offer upgrades to newer versions that often can offer more features and improvements or fix problems with the older versions. If you use a system with a proprietary ROM, make sure that it is from a larger company with a track record and one that will provide updates and fixes as necessary.

Several companies have specialized in the development of a compatible ROM BIOS product. The three major companies that come to mind in discussing ROM BIOS software are American Megatrends Inc. (AMI), Award Software, and Phoenix Software. Each company licenses its ROM BIOS to a motherboard manufacturer so that the manufacturer can worry about the hardware rather than the software. To obtain one of these ROMs for a motherboard, the OEM must answer many questions about the design of the system so that the proper BIOS can be either developed or selected from those already designed. Combining a ROM BIOS and a motherboard is not a haphazard task. No single, generic, compatible ROM exists, either. AMI, Award, and Phoenix ship to different manufacturers many variations of their BIOS code, each one custom-tailored to that specific system, much like DOS can be.

AMI

Although AMI customizes the ROM code for a particular system, it does not sell the ROM's source code to the OEM. An OEM must obtain each new release as it becomes available. Because many OEMs don't need or want every new version developed, they might skip several version changes before licensing a new one. The AMI BIOS is very popular and now is in a large number of systems. One special AMI feature is that it is the only third-party BIOS manufacturer to make its own motherboard as well. Knowing that both the motherboard and the BIOS originate from the same source gives me peace of mind.

The AMI BIOS has had a few problems with different keyboards and keyboard controller chips, and earlier versions also had some difficulty with certain IDE hard disk drives. To eliminate these types of problems, make sure that your BIOS is dated 4/9/90 or later, and has keyboard controller F or later. To locate this information, power-on the system and observe the character string on the lower left of the screen:

    xxxx-yyyy-ddmmyy-Kr

xxxx-yyyy is the motherboard manufacturer and model code. For example, xxxx represents DAMI if the motherboard is an AMI motherboard. ddmmyy is the date code, which should be 040990 or later to prevent problems. The r in Kr is the keyboard controller revision, which should be F or later. You sometimes can have keyboard lockups and problems running Windows or OS/2 if you do not have the latest keyboard controller chip.

The AMI BIOS has the standard features, including a built-in setup program activated by pressing the Del key in the first few seconds of booting up your computer. AMI offers user-definable hard disk types, essential for optimal use of many IDE or ESDI drives. A unique AMI BIOS feature is that, in addition to the setup, it has a built-in, menu-driven, diagnostics package, essentially the same as its stand-alone AMIDIAG product. Unfortunately, the diagnostics fall far short of ideal, and the Power-On Self Test seems to have suffered from the inclusion of the menu-driven diagnostics. Neither the POST nor the menu-driven diagnostics is capable of properly handling memory errors, for example, and the hard disk low-level formatter works only at the BIOS level rather than at the controller register level. These limitations often have prevented it from being capable of formatting severely damaged disks. I would rather have a "beefed-up" Power-On Self Test than menu-driven diagnostics.

You can be sure that because of the highly refined AMI diagnostics' popularity, nearly all problems have been worked out. Another AMI feature is that it offers BBS support, at this number:

    (404) 246-5825

Award

Award is unique among BIOS manufacturers because it sells its BIOS code to the OEM and allows the OEM to customize the BIOS. Of course, then the BIOS no longer is Award BIOS, but rather a highly customized version. AST uses this approach on its systems, as do other manufacturers, for total control over the BIOS code, without having to write it from scratch. Although AMI or Phoenix customize the ROM code for a particular system, they do not sell the ROM's source code to the OEM. Some OEMs that seem to have developed their own ROM code started with a base of source code licensed to them by Award or some other company.

The Award BIOS has all the normal features you expect, including a built-in setup program activated by pressing Ctrl-Alt-Esc. This setup offers user-definable drive types, required in order to fully utilize IDE or ESDI hard disks. The Power-On Self Test is good, and Award runs a BBS for support, at this number:

(408) 370-3139

In all, the Award BIOS is high quality, has minimal compatibility problems, and offers a high level of support.

Phoenix

The Phoenix BIOS for many years has been a standard of compatibility by which others are judged. It was one of the first third-party companies to legally reverse-engineer the IBM BIOS using a "clean room" approach. In this approach, a group of engineers studied the IBM BIOS and wrote a specification for how that BIOS should work and what features should be incorporated. This information then was passed to a second group of engineers who had never seen the IBM BIOS. They could then legally write a new BIOS to the specifications set forth by the first group. This work would then be unique and not a copy of IBM's BIOS; however, it would function the same way. This code has been refined over the years and has very few compatibility problems compared to some of the other BIOS vendors.

The Phoenix BIOS excels in two areas that make it high on my list of recommendations. One is that the Power-On Self Test is the best in the industry. The BIOS outputs an extensive set of beep codes that can be used to diagnose severe motherboard problems which would prevent normal operation of the system. In fact, this POST can isolate memory failures in Bank 0 right down to the individual chip with beep codes alone. The Phoenix BIOS also has an excellent setup program free from unecessary frills, but that offers all of the features one would expect, such as user-definable drive types, and so on. The built-in setup is activated by typing either Ctrl-Alt-S or Ctrl-Alt-Esc, depending on the version of BIOS you have.

The second area in which Phoenix excels is in the documentation. Not only are the manuals that you get with the system detailed, but also Phoenix has written a set of BIOS technical-reference manuals that are a standard in the industry. The set consists of three books, titled *System BIOS for IBM PC/XT/AT Computers and Compatibles*, *CBIOS for IBM PS/2 Computers and Compatibles*, and *ABIOS for IBM PS/2 Computers and Compatibles*. Phoenix is one of few vendors who have done extensive research on the PS/2 BIOS and produce virtually all of the ROMs in PS/2 Micro Channel clones on the market. In addition to being an excellent reference for the Phoenix BIOS, these books serve as an outstanding overall reference to anybody's IBM-compatible BIOS. Even if you never have a system with a Phoenix BIOS, I highly recommend these books, published by Addison-Wesley and available through most bookstores.

Phoenix is also one of the largest OEMs of Microsoft MS-DOS. Many of you that have MS-DOS probably have also the Phoenix OEM version. Phoenix licenses its DOS to other computer manufacturers so long as they use the Phoenix BIOS. Because of its close relationship with Microsoft, it has access to the DOS source code, which helps in eliminating compatiblity problems.

Although Phoenix does not operate a support BBS by itself, its largest nationwide distributor does—Micro Firmware Inc. It can be reached at

Micro Firmware Inc. (Phoenix Distributors) BBS = (405)321-3553

Unless the ROM BIOS is a truly compatible, custom OEM version such as COMPAQ's, you might want to install in the system the ROM BIOS from one of the known quantities, such as AMI, Award, or Phoenix. These companies' products are established as ROM BIOS standards in the industry, and frequent updates and improvements ensure that a system containing these ROMs will have a long life of upgrades and service.

Conservative Design

For systems I recommend for business use, a principle of conservative design is important. Stay away from systems advertised to perform "impossible" feats of speed and performance or with features and prices simply too good to be true. Many of these systems use substandard components and often run at higher speeds than the components were designed to handle. These systems will have had limited testing and debugging and can have frustrating lockups, incompatibilities, and servicing problems.

If the expansion bus is running too fast or with inaccurate timing, many adapter cards don't run properly or at all in the system. If a system improperly runs a form of RLL encoding, with drives and cabling never designed for the additional band width, serious problems with data integrity will result. If a cheap power supply is used and runs at (or past) its limit, a system will experience a number of problems and failures. All these issues deal with the original design of the system. I believe in conservatism and a little overkill with these matters, which is part of the reason that my own systems, and those I recommend for others, run so well for so long.

Using Correct Speed-Rated Parts

Many substandard parts are used in some systems. A system is sold as a 25 MHz system, for example, but when you look "under the hood," you find a CPU rated for only 20 MHz. You call the dealer, who says that the systems are "burned in" to ensure that the parts run at the specified speed. If the company that manufactures the chip installed in this system had tested the chip to run reliably at 25 MHz, it would have labeled the part accordingly. After all, the company could sell the chip for more money if it worked at the higher clock speed. Unfortunately, the chip usually does not work, at least not reliably. Don't purchase a system if the systems-operation speed exceeds the design of the respective parts.

You usually find this sort of design in some compatibles that are running very fast and that also have unusually good prices. Ask before you buy: "Are the parts really manufacturer-rated for the system speed?"

Table 5.1 provides a speed decoding chart for the CPU chips you see in IBM-compatible systems.

Table 5.2 shows the different available Intel and Intel-compatible processors and the maximum speeds at which they run. As you can see, for a given processor, a variety of different speed versions are available.

Slot Speed

For true compatibility and board exchangeability, you must know how fast a certain system runs the slots. Most high-speed compatibles using Industry Standard Architecture (ISA), otherwise known as the AT bus, employ a dual clock which ensures that the system slots for both PC XT or AT systems do not run the bus at a rate faster than 8 MHz or with less than 1 wait state. If the system can allow faster operation, you are free to try it. If the system bus cannot be slowed to this level, however, you will see that many adapter cards do not work in that system. Many memory cards are speed-sensitive, especially the expanded-memory types of boards. Also, most of the network adapters or other highly specialized communications adapters are speed sensitive as well.

Note that because Micro Channel Architecture (MCA) or Extended Industry Standard Architecture (EISA) systems have strict timing definitions that must be adhered to as part of their respective standards, slot speed isn't an issue with these systems. Because of the standard definitions laid out for MCA and EISA, they also are free of some of the problems that have plagued various ISA systems in these areas.

Table 5.1 Speed Decoding Chart

CPU or NDP chip	Suffix	Maximum speed
8088/8086/8087	No marks	5 MHz
	-3	6 MHz
	-2	8 MHz
	-1	10 MHz
80286 or higher	-6	6 MHz
	-8	8 MHz
	-10	10 MHz
	-12	12 MHz
	-16	16 MHz
	-20	20 MHz
	-25	25 MHz
	-33	33 MHz
	-50	50 MHz

Table 5.2 Intel and Intel-Compatible Microprocessor Clock Rates

Processor	Type	5	6	8	10	12	16	20	25	33	40	50	66
8086	CPU	✓	✓	✓	✓								
8088	CPU	✓	✓	✓	✓								
8087	NDP	✓	✓	✓	✓								
80286	CPU		✓	✓	✓	✓	✓	✓					
80287	NDP		✓	✓	✓	✓							
80287 XL	NDP					✓							
80287 XLT	NDP					✓							
80386 DX	CPU						✓	✓	✓	✓			
80387 DX	NDP						✓	✓	✓	✓			
80386 SX	CPU						✓	✓	✓				
80387 SX	NDP						✓	✓	✓				
80386 SL	CPU						✓	✓	✓				
80386 SLC	CPU							✓					
80486 SX	CPU						✓	✓	✓				
80487	CPU+NDP						✓	✓	✓	✓	✓		
80486 SL	CPU						✓	✓	✓				
80486 DX	CPU+NDP								✓	✓	✓	✓	✓
80586	CPU+NDP												✓

CPU = Central processing unit
NDP = Numeric data processor (math coprocessor)

Power-Supply Output

I always try to make sure that adequate power output is available from the power supply to run expansion devices added to the system. The power supply should supply sufficient airflow also to cool the system adequately. The system chassis lid or case might feel warm but should never feel hot to the touch. Most of the time, the power-output specification is stamped on the system's power supply or is listed in its technical-reference manual. Consult the technical manual for each disk drive you purchase, as well as for each adapter you intend to plug in, to see whether sufficient power is available to reliably run all these devices. Chapter 7 examines the consequences of overstressing the power supply.

Adhering to Standards

Check to see that certain standards are followed. IBM has declared specific uses for certain interrupt request (IRQ) lines, direct memory access (DMA) channels, and I/O ports. Be certain that the CMOS memory and real-time clock are set up the same way they are set up in the IBM units (that is, make sure that data is organized the same way and that the port locations are the same. Make sure that your system follows IBM standards. (An example of a system that did not follow these standards is the AT&T 6300 system. This machine had severe compatibility problems with standard plug-in boards because of nonstandard use of interrupts and DMA channels. Locating items, therefore, such as disk controllers or other boards that worked properly in the system, was very difficult.) You usually can find this information in a system's technical-reference manual. Several charts in the Appendix describe these items and how they are allocated in an IBM system unit.

Support

Support from the system manufacturer is important. Some manufacturers rely solely on their vendors (dealers) to provide support, which isn't always a good idea because dealers rarely can provide true technical support. In addition to simply being able to ask technical questions, the source of support should include a spare-parts program and be able to exchange major components for rebuilt replacements. Most larger companies, such as IBM, Tandy, AT&T, Toshiba, NEC, and Dell, support their own products directly as well as through the dealer. Others, such as COMPAQ, don't support their products directly; any support you seek must be handled through your dealer.

Spare-Parts Programs

In any system, look for the availability of a spare-parts program. In other words, can you obtain any unique parts that make up a system? The parts can include motherboards, power supplies, proprietary adapter cards, special memory boards and chips, unique hardware, and cosmetic parts such as cases, front panels, and so on. In this regard, I like the way that *Popular Mechanics* magazine reviews an automobile. The end of the review is a list with the cost of most of the commonly replaced items on a car, such as brakes, front and rear body parts, alternators, and so on. The list provides much insight into comparing a low-cost foreign model (which has exorbitant parts and maintenance prices) with a domestic model (which has cheaper, more commonly available parts).

Because of the number of systems sold, many suppliers are available for these types of items for any of IBM's systems. You can buy a power supply or any type of drive or adapter at a low cost because of the competition. Other vendors prefer to lock you into high-cost custom parts, which you cannot find at a discount. For example, every COMPAQ item that can be physically different from an IBM item is different. You must get your power supplies, your motherboards, and often your disk drives from COMPAQ. And COMPAQ does not sell any parts directly; you must go through dealers.

In the end, purchasing a system with an ample supply of parts available and supported by the aftermarket pays off. The IBM PS/2 systems are difficult to find parts for, and most of the parts must be purchased from IBM. Few aftermarket power supplies are available, but many companies supply third-party disk drives and adapter cards that fit the unique interiors of these systems. Little concern exists over any lack of aftermarket support for the PS/2; plenty of support is available due to the sheer number of these systems sold. Some people have held off on a PS/2 purchase until repair and service parts for these systems are more readily available from the aftermarket.

Exchanging Major Components

Most larger manufacturers offer a board-exchange policy. For expensive components such as the motherboard, you can trade in a defective component for a good one for much less money than in an outright purchase. You might want to consider this information when you look at other vendors' systems.

Chapter Summary

This chapter showed that there are several ways to break down the compatible marketplace. You saw that a system can be classified as an XT- or AT-class system, and as either a clone or a compatible system. The chapter examined the compatible marketplace from the point of view of a system installer or troubleshooter, keeping in mind that you can plan to upgrade a system later. The chapter provided a quick guide and checklist for what to look for in a compatible system that meets the needs of a business user, is serviceable for years to come, and has plenty of upgrade options.

Chapter 6 uses detailed information to describe how to tear down and inspect your system.

PART

III

Hardware
Considerations

System Teardown and Inspection

This chapter examines procedures for tearing down and inspecting a system. It describes the types of tools required, the procedure for disassembling the system, and the various components that make up the system. A special section discusses some of the test equipment you can use, and another section covers some problems you might encounter with the hardware (screws, nuts, bolts, and so on).

Using the Proper Tools

To troubleshoot and repair PC systems properly, you need a few basic tools:

- Simple hand tools for basic disassembly and reassembly procedures

- Diagnostics software and hardware for testing components in a system

- Wrap plugs for diagnosing port problems

- Test and measurement devices, such as volt-ohm meters, that allow accurate measurement of voltage and resistance, and logic probes and pulsers, that allow analysis and testing of digital circuits

■ Chemicals, such as contact cleaners, component freeze sprays, and compressed air for cleaning

In addition, you might need also soldering and unsoldering tools for problems that require these operations. These basic tools are discussed in more detail in the following section. Diagnostics software and hardware is discussed in Chapter 13.

Hand Tools

It becomes apparent immediately when you work with PC systems that the tools required for nearly all service operations are simple and inexpensive. You can carry most of the required tools in a small pouch. Even a top-of-the-line "master mechanic's" set fits inside a briefcase. The cost of these toolkits ranges from about $20 for a small-service kit to $500 for a briefcase-size deluxe kit. Compare these costs to what might be necessary for an automotive technician. Most spend between $5,000 to $10,000 or more for the tools they use!

In this section you learn about the tools required to make up a set capable of basic, board-level service on PC systems. One of the best ways to start such a set of tools is with a small kit sold especially for servicing PCs.

This list shows the basic tools you can find in one of the small "PC toolkits" sold for about $30:

3/16-inch nut driver
1/4-inch nut driver
Small Phillips screwdriver
Small flat-blade screwdriver
Medium Phillips screwdriver
Medium flat-blade screwdriver
Chip extractor
Chip inserter
Tweezers
Claw-type parts grabber
T10 and T15 TORX drivers

You use nut drivers to remove the hexagonal-headed screws that secure the system-unit covers, adapter boards, disk drives, power supplies, and speakers in most systems. The nut drivers work much better than a conventional screwdriver.

Because some manufacturers have substituted slotted-head (Phillips) screws for the more standard hexagonal head screws, the standard screwdrivers can be used for these systems.

You use the chip-extraction and -insertion tools to install or remove memory chips (or other, smaller chips) without bending any pins on the chip. Usually, you pry out larger chips, such as microprocessors or ROMs, with the small screwdriver.

The tweezers and parts grabber can be used to hold any small screws or jumper blocks that are difficult to hold in your hand. The parts grabber is especially useful when you drop a small part into the interior of a system; usually, you can remove the part without completely disassembling the system.

Finally, the TORX driver is a special, star-shaped driver that matches the special screws found in most COMPAQ systems and in many other systems as well.

Although this basic set is useful, you should supplement it with some other small hand tools, such as:

> Needlenose pliers
> Wire cutter or wire stripper
> Metric nut drivers
> Tamper-proof TORX drivers
> Vise or clamp
> File

Pliers are useful for straightening pins on chips, applying or removing jumpers, crimping cables, or grabbing small parts.

The wire cutter or stripper obviously is useful in making or repairing cables or wiring.

The metric nut drivers can be used in many clone or compatible systems, as well as in the IBM PS/2 systems, which all use metric hardware.

The tamper-proof TORX drivers can be used to remove TORX screws with the tamper-resistant pin in the center of the screw. A tamper-proof TORX driver has a hole drilled in it to allow clearance for the pin.

You can use a vise for installing connectors on cables and for crimping cables to the shape you want, as well as for holding parts during delicate operations.

Finally, you can use the file for smoothing rough metal edges on cases and chassis, as well as for trimming the faceplates on disk drives for a perfect fit.

With this simple set of hand tools, you are equipped for nearly every PC repair or installation situation. The total cost for these tools should be less than $150, making your tool set economical as well.

Soldering and Unsoldering Tools

For certain situations, such as repairing a broken wire, reattaching a component to a circuit board, removing and installing chips that are not in a socket, or adding jumper wires or pins to a board, you must use a soldering iron to make the repair. Even if you do only board-level service, you will need a soldering iron in some situations.

You need a low-wattage iron, usually about 25 watts. More than 30 watts generates too much heat and can damage the components on the board. Even with a low-wattage unit, you must limit the amount of heat to which you subject the board and its components. You can do this with quick and efficient use of the soldering iron, as well as with the use of heat-sinking devices clipped to the leads of the device being soldered. A *heat sink* is a small, metal, clip-on device designed to absorb excessive heat before it reaches the component that the heat sink is protecting.

To remove components originally soldered into place from a printed circuit board, you can use a soldering iron with a *solder sucker*. This device normally is constructed as a small tube with an air chamber and a plunger-and-spring arrangement. (I do not recommend the "squeeze bulb" type of solder sucker.) The unit is "cocked" when you press the spring-loaded plunger into the air chamber. When you want to remove a device from a board, you heat with the soldering iron the point at which one of the component leads joins the circuit board, from the underside of the board, until the solder melts. As soon as melting occurs, move the solder-sucker nozzle into position and press the actuator. This procedure allows the plunger to retract, and create a momentary suction that inhales the liquid solder from the connection and leaves the component lead dry in the hole.

Always do the heating and suctioning from the underside of a board, not from the component side. Repeat this action for every component lead joined to the circuit board. When you master this technique, you can remove a small chip, such as a 16-pin memory chip, in a minute or two with only a small likelihood of damage to the board or other components. Larger chips with many pins can be more difficult to remove and resolder without damaging other components or the circuit board.

If you intend to add soldering and unsoldering skills to your arsenal of abilities, you should practice. Take a useless circuit board and practice removing various components from the board; then reinstall the components. Try to remove the components from the board by using the least amount of heat possible. Also, perform the solder-melting operations as quickly as possible, and limit the time the iron is applied to the joint. Before you install any components, clean out the holes through which the leads must project, and mount the component into place. Then apply the solder from the underside of the board, using as little heat and solder as possible. Attempt to produce joints as clean as the joints that the board manufacturer performed by machine. Soldered joints that do not look "clean" may keep the component from making a good connection with the rest of the circuit. This "cold-solder joint" normally is created by not using enough heat. *Remember that you should not practice your new soldering skills on the motherboard of a system you are attempting to repair.* Don't attempt to work on real boards until you are sure of your skills.

Using Proper Test Equipment

In some cases you must use specialized devices to test a system board or component. This test equipment is not expensive or difficult to use, but can add much to your troubleshooting abilities. I consider wrap plugs and a voltmeter required gear for proper system testing. The wrap plugs allow testing of serial and parallel ports and their attached cables. A volt-ohm meter (VOM) can serve many purposes, including checking for voltage signals at different points in a system, testing the output of the power supply, and checking for continuity in a circuit or cable.

Logic probes and pulsers are not considered mandatory equipment, but they can add to your troubleshooting proficiency. You use the logic probe to check for the existence and status of digital signals at various points in a circuit. You use the logic pulser to inject signals into a circuit to evaluate the circuit's operation. Using these devices effectively requires more understanding of how the circuit operates. Chapter 14, "Hardware Troubleshooting Guide," explains where some of these devices can be useful.

Wrap Plugs

For diagnosing serial- and parallel-port problems, you need wrap plugs, used to circulate, or "wrap," signals. The plugs enable the serial or parallel port to send data to itself for diagnostic purposes. Several types of wrap plugs are available. You need one for the 25-pin serial port, one for the 9-pin serial port, and one for the 25-pin parallel port (see table 6.1). IBM sells the plugs separately, as well as a special version that includes all three types in one plug.

Table 6.1 Wrap Plug Types

Description	IBM part number
Parallel-port wrap plug	8529228
Serial-port wrap plug, 25-pin	8529280
Serial-port wrap plug, 9-pin (AT)	8286126
Tri-connector wrap plug	72X8546

The handy tri-connector unit contains in one, compact unit all commonly needed plugs. The unit costs approximately $30 from IBM. Be aware that most professional diagnostics packages (especially the ones I recommend) include the three types of wrap plugs as part of the package. If you're handy, you can even make your own wrap plugs for testing. Wiring diagrams for the three types of wrap plugs are in the Appendix of this book.

Meters

Many troubleshooting procedures require that you measure voltage and resistance. You take these measurements by using a hand-held volt-ohm meter (VOM). The meters can be analog devices (using an actual meter) or digital-readout devices. The VOM has a pair of wires, called *test leads*, or *probes*. The test leads make the connections so that you can take readings. Depending on the meter's setting, the probes will measure electrical resistance, direct-current voltage (DCV), or alternating-current voltage (ACV).

Usually, each system-unit measurement setting has several ranges of operation. DC voltage, for example, usually can be read in several scales to a maximum of 200 millivolts, 2 volts, 20 volts, 200 volts, and 1,000 volts. Because computers use both +5 and +12 volts for various operations, you should use the 20-volt-maximum scale for making your measurements. Making these measurements on the 200-millivolt or 2-volt scales could "peg the meter" and possibly damage it because the voltage would be much higher than expected. Using the 200-volt or 1,000-volt scales works, but the readings at 5 volts and 12 volts are so small in proportion to the maximum that accuracy is low.

If you are taking a measurement and are unsure of the actual voltage, start at the highest scale and work your way down. Some better system-unit meters have an autoranging capability: The meter automatically selects the best range for any measurement. This type of meter is much easier to operate. You just set the meter to the type of reading you want, such as DC volts, and attach the probes to the signal source. The meter selects the correct voltage range and displays the value. Because of their design, these types of meters always have a digital display rather than a meter needle.

I prefer the small, digital meters. You can buy them for only slightly more than the analog style, and they're extremely accurate. Some are not much bigger than a cassette tape; they fit in a shirt pocket. Radio Shack sells a good unit (made for Radio Shack by Beckman) in the $30 price range, which is only a half-inch thick, weighs 3 1/2 ounces, and is digital and autoranging as well. This type of meter works well for most if not all PC troubleshooting and test uses.

You should be aware that many analog meters can be dangerous to digital circuits. These meters use a 9-volt battery to power the meter for resistance measurements. If you use this type of meter to measure resistance on some digital circuits, you can damage the electronics because you are essentially injecting 9 volts into the circuit. The digital meters universally run on 3 to 5 volts or less.

Logic Probes and Logic Pulsers

A logic probe can be useful in diagnosing problems with digital circuits. In a digital circuit, a signal is represented as either high (+5 volts) or low (0 volts). Because these signals might be present for only a short time (measured in millionths of a second), or might be oscillating or switching on and off rapidly, a simple voltmeter is useless. A logic probe is designed to display these signal conditions easily.

Logic probes are especially useful in troubleshooting a dead system. Using the probe, you can determine whether the basic clock circuitry is operating and whether other signals necessary to system operation are present. In some cases, a probe can help you also cross-check the signals at each pin on an IC chip. You can compare the signals present at each pin to what a known, good chip of the same type would show—a comparison helpful in isolating a failed component. Logic probes can be useful also in troubleshooting some disk drive problems by letting you test the signals present on the interface cable or drive-logic board.

A companion tool to the probe is the *logic pulser*. A pulser is designed to test circuit reaction by delivering into a circuit a logical high (+5 volt) pulse, usually lasting 1 1/2 to 10 millionths of a second. Compare the reaction to that of a known functional circuit. This type of device normally is used much less frequently than a logic probe, but in some cases can be helpful in testing a circuit.

Now that you've examined the tools needed to tear down and inspect your system, let's examine procedures for disassembling it.

Chemicals

Chemicals can be used to help clean, troubleshoot, and even repair a system. For the most basic function, cleaning components and electrical connectors and contacts, one of the most useful chemicals is 1,1,1 trichloroethelyne. This substance, sometimes sold as "carbo-chlor," is a very effective cleaner. It can be used to clean electrical contacts and components, and will not damage most plastics and board materials. In fact, carbo-chlor can be very useful for cleaning stains on the system case and keyboard.

Compressed air often is used as an aid in system cleaning. Normally composed of Freon or carbon dioxide, compressed gas is used as a blower to remove dust and debris from a system or component. Be careful when you use these devices: Some of them can generate a tremendous static charge as the compressed gas leaves the nozzle of the can. Be sure that you are using the kind approved for cleaning or dusting off computer equipment, and consider wearing a static grounding strap as a precaution. Freon TF is known to generate these large static charges; Freon R12 is less severe. Of course, because both chemicals are damaging to the ozone layer, they are being phased out by most suppliers. Expect to see new versions of these compressed-air devices with carbon dioxide or some other less-harmful propellant.

CAUTION: If you use the propellant Freon R12 (dichlorodifluoromethane), *do not expose the gas to an open flame or other heat source.* If you burn this substance, a highly toxic gas called *phosgene* is generated. Phosgene, used as a nerve gas in WWII, can be deadly.

Freon R12 is the substance in your automobile air conditioner and your kitchen refrigerator. Automobile service technicians are instructed *never* to smoke near air-conditioner systems.

Related to compressed-air products are chemical-freeze sprays. These sprays are used to quickly cool down a suspected failing component to restore it to operation. These substances are not used to repair a device, but rather to confirm that you have found the failed device. Often, a component's failure is heat-related; cooling it temporarily restores it to normal operation. If the circuit begins operating normally, the device you are cooling is the suspect device.

A Word about Hardware

This section discusses some problems you might encounter with the hardware (screws, nuts, bolts, and so on) used in assembling a system.

Types of Hardware

One of the biggest aggravations you encounter in dealing with various systems on the market is the different hardware types and designs that hold the units together.

For example, most system hardware types use screws that can be driven with 1/4-inch or 3/16-inch hexagonal drivers. IBM uses these screws in all original PC, XT, and AT systems. Other manufacturers might use different hardware. COMPAQ, for example, uses TORX screws in most of its systems. A TORX screw has a star-shaped hole driven by the correct-size TORX driver. These drivers carry size designations, such as T-8, T-9, T-10, T-15, T-20, T-25, T-30, T-40, and so on. A variation on the TORX screw is the tamper-proof TORX screw, found in IBM's power supplies and in other manufacturers' power supplies and other assemblies. These screws are identical to the regular TORX screws except that a pin sticks up exactly in the middle of the star-shaped hole in the screw. This pin prevents the standard TORX driver from entering the hole to grip the screw; a special tamper-proof driver with a corresponding hole for the pin is required. An alternative is to use a small chisel to knock out the pin in the screw. Usually, a device sealed with these types of screws is considered a complete, replaceable unit and rarely, if ever, needs to be opened.

The more standard slotted-head and Phillips-head screws are used by many manufacturers as well. Using tools on these screws is relatively easy, but tools do not grip these fasteners as well as hexagonal head or TORX screws, and the heads can be rounded off more easily than other types. Extremely cheap versions tend to lose bits of metal as they're turned with a driver, and the metal bits can fall onto the motherboard. Stay away from cheap fasteners whenever possible; the headaches from dealing with stripped screws aren't worth it.

English versus Metric

Another area of aggravation with hardware is that two types of thread systems are available: English and metric. IBM used mostly

English-threaded fasteners in its original line of systems, but many other manufacturers used metric-threaded fasteners in their systems.

The difference becomes apparent especially with disk drives. American-manufactured drives use English fasteners; drives made in Japan or Taiwan use metric fasteners. Whenever you replace a floppy drive in an early-model IBM unit, you encounter this problem. All American floppy drive manufacturers have either gone out of business or ceased making floppy drives. IBM used Tandon and Control Data Corporation (CDC) as suppliers for the original line of systems, but these companies no longer make floppy drives. Their drives used English fasteners. Companies that make floppy drives, such as Mitsubishi, Sony, Teac, Panasonic, and others, all use metric fasteners. Try to buy the correct screws and any other hardware, such as brackets, with the drive because they might be difficult to find at a local hardware store. The OEM's drive manual has the correct data about a specific drive's hole locations and thread size.

Most hard disks still are made by American manufacturers, so most hard disks use English fasteners also. Japanese drives use metric fasteners, of course.

> **CAUTION:** Some screws in a system might be length-critical, especially screws used to retain disk drives. You can destroy some hard disks by using a screw that's too long. You can puncture or dent the sealed disk chamber by tightening the screw. When you install a new type of drive in a system, always make a trial fit of the hardware and see how far the screws can be inserted in the drive before they interfere with components on the drive.

Disassembly Procedures

The process of physically disassembling and reassembling systems isn't difficult. Because of marketplace standardization, only a couple of different types and sizes of screws (with a few exceptions) are used to hold the systems together, and the physical arrangement of the major components is similar even among systems from different manufacturers. Also, not many individual components are in each system. This section breaks down the disassembly and reassembly procedure into these sections:

- Case or cover assembly
- Adapter boards
- Disk drives

- Power supply
- Motherboard

This section discusses how to remove and install these components for each system-unit primary system type: PC, XT, AT, and various PS/2 systems.

PC- and XT-Type Systems

The procedure for disassembling the PC- or XT-type systems offered by IBM and other manufacturers is simple. Only two tools are required: a 1/4-inch nut driver for the external screws holding the cover in place and a 3/16-inch nut driver for all other screws.

Removing the Cover

To remove the system-unit cover:

1. Turn off the system and unplug the power cord from the system unit.

2. Turn the system unit around so that the rear of the unit is facing you, and locate the screws that hold the system-unit cover in place (see fig. 6.1).

3. Use the 1/4-inch nut driver to remove the cover screws.

4. Slide the cover toward the front of the system unit until it stops. Lift up the front of the cover and remove it from the chassis.

To remove all adapter boards from the system unit, first remove the system-unit cover, as described earlier. Then proceed as follows for each adapter:

1. Note which slots all the adapters are in. If possible, make a diagram or drawing.

2. Use the 3/16-inch nut driver to remove the screw holding the adapter in place (see fig. 6.2).

3. Note the position of any cables plugged into the adapter before removing them. In a correctly wired system, the colored stripe on one side of the ribbon cable always denotes pin number 1. The power connector is shaped so that it can be inserted only the correct way.

4. Remove the adapter by lifting with even force at both ends.

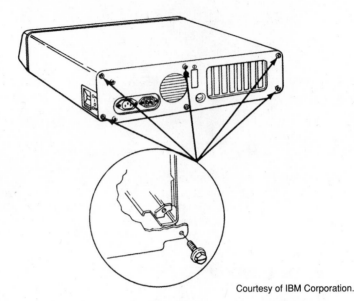

Courtesy of IBM Corporation.

Fig. 6.1

The screws holding the PC and XT system-unit cover in place.

5. Note the positions of any jumpers or switches on the adapter, especially when documentation for the adapter isn't available. Even when documentation is available, undocumented jumpers and switches often are used by manufacturers for special purposes, such as testing or unique configurations.

Jumpers and switches normally are named on the circuit board. SW1 and SW2 are used for switch 1 and switch 2, for example, and J1 and J2 are used for jumper 1 and jumper 2. If these jumpers or switches later are disturbed, you can return to the original configuration—as long as you noted it when the adapter was first removed. The best procedure usually is to make a diagram showing these features for a particular card.

Removing Disk Drives

Removing drives for PC- and XT-type systems is fairly easy. The procedures are similar for both floppy and hard disk drives.

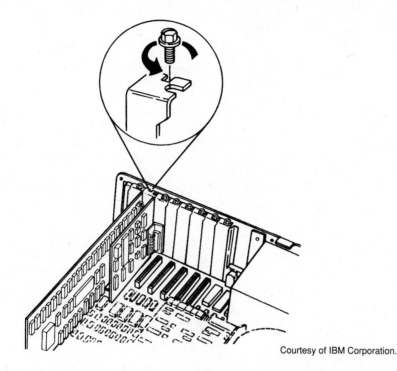

Courtesy of IBM Corporation.

Fig. 6.2

Removing the screw
that holds the adapter
in place.

Before you remove your hard disks from the system, back them up and park the heads. The possibility always exists that data will be lost or the drive damaged from rough handling. Hard disks are discussed in more detail in Chapter 9.

When you remove the drives from a PC- or XT-type system, first remove the cover and all adapters, as previously described. Then proceed as follows:

1. Lift up the front of the chassis so that the unit is standing with the rear of the chassis down and the disk drive facing straight up. Locate any drive-retaining screws in the bottom of the chassis and remove them. On IBM equipment, you find these screws in XT systems with hard disks or half-height floppy drives (see fig. 6.3). These screws might be shorter than others used in the system. You must reinstall a screw of the same length in this location later; using a screw that's too long can damage the drive.

2. Set the chassis flat on the table and locate the drive-retaining screws on the outboard sides of the drive. Remove them (see fig. 6.4 and fig. 6.5).

3. Slide the disk drive forward about two inches and disconnect the power and signal cables from the drive (see fig. 6.6 and fig. 6.7). In a correctly wired system, the odd-colored stripe on one side of the ribbon cable always denotes pin number 1. The power connector is shaped so that it can be inserted only the correct way.

4. Slide the drive completely out of the unit.

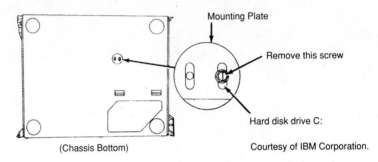

Fig. 6.3

Removing the retaining screws from the bottom of the chassis.

(Chassis Bottom)

Mounting Plate

Remove this screw

Hard disk drive C:

Courtesy of IBM Corporation.

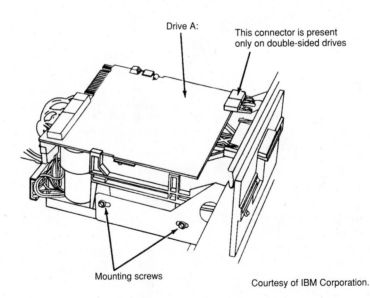

Drive A:

This connector is present only on double-sided drives

Fig. 6.4

Removing the retaining screws from the outboard sides of a floppy disk drive.

Mounting screws

Courtesy of IBM Corporation.

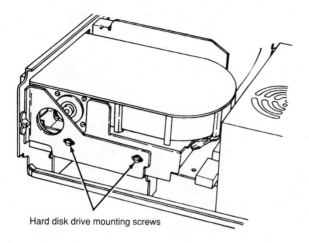

Hard disk drive mounting screws

Courtesy of IBM Corporation.

Fig. 6.5

Removing the retaining screws from the outboard sides of the hard disk drive.

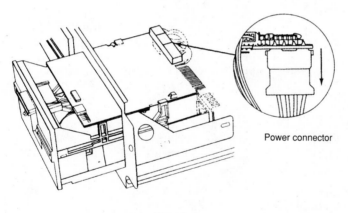

Power connector

(Side View)

Courtesy of IBM Corporation.

Fig. 6.6

The power connector on a floppy disk drive.

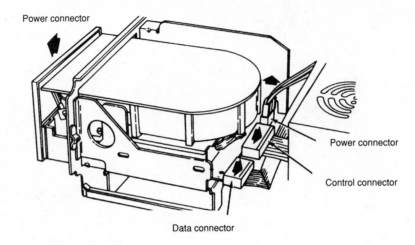

Power connector

Power connector

Control connector

Data connector

Courtesy of IBM Corporation.

Fig. 6.7

Disconnecting the power and signal cables from the hard disk drive.

Removing the Power Supply

In PC- and XT-type systems, the power supply is mounted in the system unit with four screws in the rear and two interlocking tabs on the bottom. Removing the power supply usually requires that you remove the disk drives before getting the power supply out. You will have to at least loosen the drives to slide them forward for clearance when you remove the supply.

To remove the power supply, first remove the cover, all adapter boards, and the disk drives, as described earlier. If sufficient clearance exists, you might not have to remove the adapter boards and disk drives. Then proceed as follows:

1. Remove the four power-supply retaining screws from the rear of the system-unit chassis (see fig. 6.8).

2. Disconnect the cables from the power supply to the motherboard (see fig. 6.9). Disconnect the power cables from the power supply to the disk drives. Always grasp the connectors themselves; never pull on the wires.

3. Slide the power supply forward about a half-inch to disengage the interlocking tabs on the bottom of the unit. Lift the power supply out of the unit (see fig. 6.10).

Power supply mounting screws

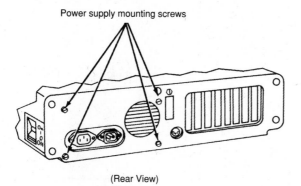

(Rear View)

Courtesy of IBM Corporation.

Fig. 6.8

Removing the power-supply retaining screws from the rear of the chassis.

System/expansion board power connectors

Power supply

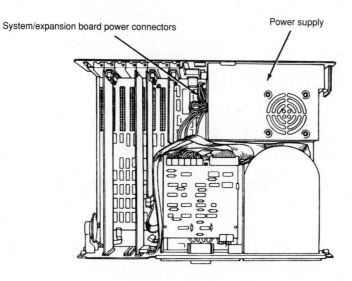

System unit

(Top View)   Courtesy of IBM Corporation.

Fig. 6.9

Disconnecting the cables from the power supply to the motherboard.

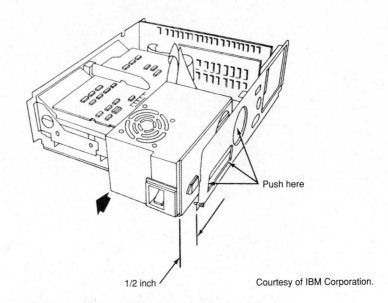

Push here

1/2 inch

Courtesy of IBM Corporation.

Fig. 6.10

Sliding the power
supply forward to
disengage the
interlocking tabs on the
unit's bottom.

Removing the Motherboard

After all the adapter cards are removed from the unit, you can remove
the system board, or *motherboard*. The motherboard in PC- and XT-type
systems is held in place by only two screws and several plastic standoffs
that elevate the board from the metal chassis so that it does not touch
the chassis and cause a short. The standoffs slide into slots in the chassis. *These standoffs should remain with the motherboard.* You do not have
to extract these standoffs from the motherboard to remove it; you just
remove the motherboard with the standoffs still attached. When you
reinstall the motherboard, make sure that the standoffs slide properly in
their slots. If one or more standoffs have not properly engaged the chassis, you might crack the motherboard when you tighten the screws or
install adapter cards.

To remove the motherboard, first remove all adapter boards from the
system unit, as described earlier. Then proceed as follows:

1. Disconnect from the motherboard all electrical connectors, including those for the keyboard, power supply, and speaker.

2. Locate and remove the motherboard retaining screws.

3. Slide the motherboard away from the power supply about a half-
   inch until the standoffs have disengaged from their mounting slots
   (see fig. 6.11).

4. Lift the motherboard up and out of the chassis.

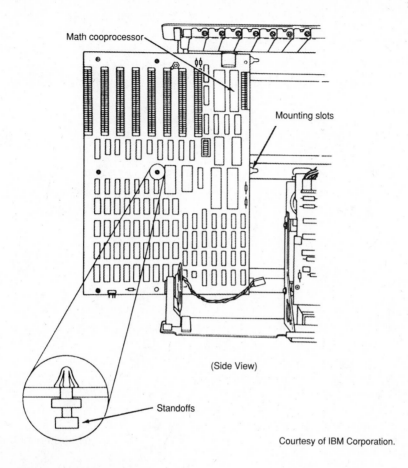

Math cooprocessor

Mounting slots

(Side View)

Standoffs

Courtesy of IBM Corporation.

Fig. 6.11

Sliding the
motherboard away
from the power supply
until standoffs
disengage from
mounting slots.

AT-Type Systems

Disassembling an AT-type system offered by IBM or another manufacturer requires only two tools: a 1/4-inch nut driver for the external
screws holding the cover in place and a 3/16-inch nut driver for all the
other screws.

Most of the procedures are exactly like those for the PC- and XT-type
systems. One difference, however, is that IBM used a different method
for mounting the disk drives in the AT. Plastic or fiberglass rails are attached to the drives, and the drives slide into the system-unit chassis on
these rails. The chassis has guide tracks for the rails, which enables you
to remove the drive from the front of the unit without having to access
the side to remove any mounting screws.

Removing the Cover

To remove the system-unit cover:

1. Turn off the system and unplug the power cord from the system unit.

2. Turn the system unit around so that you're facing the rear of the unit. Locate the five screws that hold the system-unit cover in place (see fig. 6.12).

3. Use the 1/4-inch nut driver to remove the cover screws.

4. Slide the cover toward the front of the system unit until it stops. Lift up the front of the cover and remove it from the chassis.

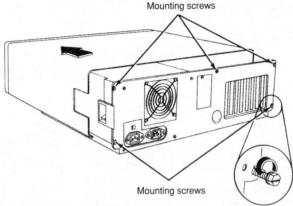

Mounting screws

Mounting screws

Courtesy of IBM Corporation.

Fig. 6.12

Removing the screws holding the AT system-unit cover in place.

Removing Adapter Boards

To remove all the adapter boards from the system unit, first remove the system-unit cover, as described earlier. Then proceed as follows for each adapter:

1. Note which slot each adapter is in. If possible, make a diagram or drawing.

2. Use the 3/16-inch nut driver to remove the screw holding the adapter in place (refer to fig. 6.2.).

3. Note the positions of any cables plugged into the adapter before you remove them. In a correctly wired system, the colored stripe on one side of the ribbon cable always denotes pin number 1. Some connectors have keys that enable them to be inserted only the correct way.

4. Remove the adapter by lifting with even force at both ends.

5. Note the positions of any jumpers or switches on the adapter, especially when documentation for the adapter is not available. Even when documentation is available, undocumented jumpers and switches often are used by manufacturers for special purposes, such as testing or unique configurations. It's a good idea to know the existing settings in case they are disturbed.

Removing Disk Drives

Removing drives from AT systems is very easy. The procedures are similar for both floppy and hard disk drives.

Always back up hard disks completely and park the heads before removing disks from the system. The possibility always exists that data will be lost or the drive damaged from rough handling.

To remove the drives from an AT-type system, first remove the cover, as described earlier. Then proceed as follows:

1. Depending on whether the drive is a hard disk or floppy disk drive, it is retained by either a metal keeper bar with two screws or two small, L-shaped metal tabs each held in place by a single screw. Locate these screws and remove them, along with the tabs or keeper bar (see fig. 6.13 and fig. 6.14).

2. Slide the disk drive forward about two inches and disconnect from the drives the power cables, signal and data cables, and the ground wire (see fig. 6.15 and fig. 6.16). In a correctly wired system, the colored stripe on one side of the ribbon cable always denotes pin number 1. The power connector is shaped so that it can be inserted only the correct way.

3. Slide the drive completely out of the unit.

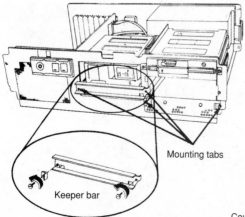

Mounting tabs

Keeper bar

Courtesy of IBM Corporation.

Fig. 6.13

Removing mounting tabs and the keeper bar on a hard disk drive.

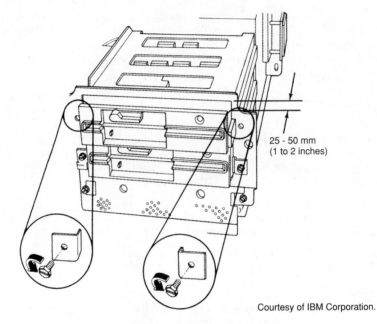

25 - 50 mm
(1 to 2 inches)

Fig. 6.14

Removing the mounting tabs on a floppy disk drive.

Courtesy of IBM Corporation.

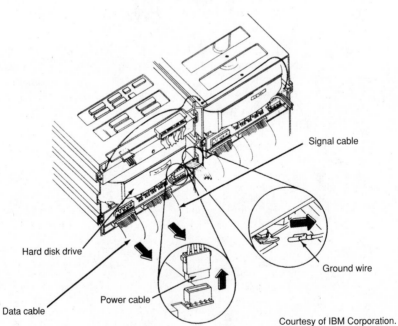

Signal cable

Fig. 6.15

Disconnecting the hard disk drive power cable, signal and data cables, and ground wire.

Hard disk drive

Ground wire

Data cable

Power cable

Courtesy of IBM Corporation.

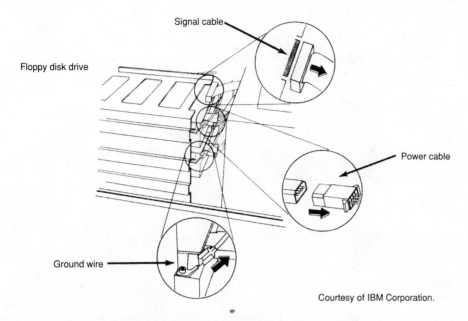

Signal cable

Floppy disk drive

Power cable

Ground wire

Courtesy of IBM Corporation.

Fig. 6.16

Disconnecting the floppy disk drive power cable, signal cable, and ground wire.

Removing the Power Supply

In AT systems, the power supply is mounted in the system unit with four screws in the rear and two interlocking tabs on the bottom. Removing the power supply usually requires that you slide the disk drives forward for clearance when you remove the supply.

To remove the power supply, first remove the cover, loosen the disk drive mounting screws, and move the disk drive forward about two inches, as described earlier. Then proceed as follows:

1. Remove the four power-supply retaining screws from the rear of the system-unit chassis (see fig. 6.17).

2. Disconnect the cables from the power supply to the motherboard (see fig. 6.18). Disconnect the power cables from the power supply to the disk drive. Always grasp the connectors themselves; never pull on the wires.

3. Slide the power supply forward about a half-inch to disengage the interlocking tabs on the bottom of the unit. Lift the power supply out of the unit.

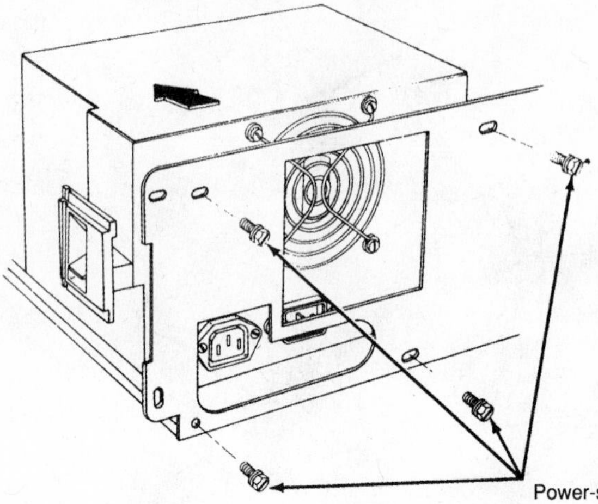

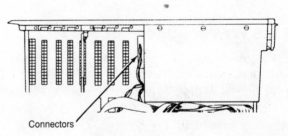

Power-supply mounting screws

Courtesy of IBM Corporation.

Fig. 6.17

Removing the power-supply retaining screws from the rear of the chassis.

Connectors

Courtesy of IBM Corporation.

Fig. 6.18

Disconnecting the cables from the power supply to the motherboard.

Removing the Motherboard

After all the adapter cards are removed from the unit, you can remove the motherboard. The motherboard in AT-type systems is held in place by only two screws and several plastic standoffs that elevate the board from the metal chassis so that it does not touch the chassis and cause a short. You should not separate the standoffs from the motherboard; remove the board and the standoffs as a unit. The standoffs slide into slots in the chassis. When you reinstall the motherboard, make sure that the standoffs are located properly in their slots. If one or more standoffs have not engaged the chassis properly, you might crack the motherboard when you tighten the screws or install adapter cards.

To remove the motherboard, first remove all adapter boards from the system unit, as described earlier. Then proceed as follows:

1. Disconnect from the motherboard all electrical connectors, including those for the keyboard, power supply, speaker, battery, and keylock.

2. Locate and remove the motherboard retaining screws.

3. Slide the motherboard away from the power supply about a half-inch until the standoffs have disengaged from their mounting slots (see fig. 6.19).

4. Lift the motherboard up and out of the chassis.

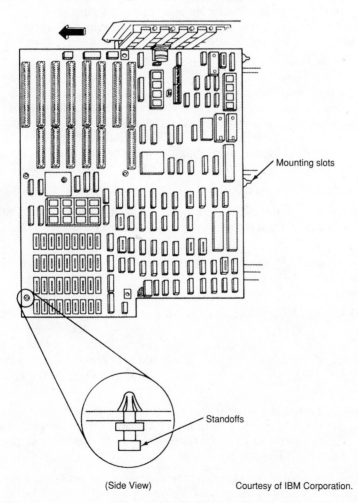

Mounting slots

Standoffs

(Side View)   Courtesy of IBM Corporation.

Fig. 6.19

Disengaging standoffs from their mounting slots.

PS/2 Systems

The disassembly of IBM's PS/2 systems is incredibly easy. In fact, ease of disassembly and reassembly is one of the greatest features of these systems. In addition to being easy to service and repair, they were designed to be assembled primarily by robots and automated machinery. This type of machinery does not handle conventional fasteners such as screws, nuts, and bolts very well. Most PS/2 systems therefore are assembled with a great deal of "snap together" technology. The screws that are used have a special self-centering design, in which the screw end is tapered so that it is self-guiding, to mate with the threads in the hole. Automated robotic machinery then can insert and tighten the screws more easily and accurately, and without stripping the threads. This approach to construction makes these systems not only easier to assemble by machine but also much easier for people to disassemble and reassemble.

If you can disassemble one PS/2 system, you see how easily the others come apart as well, especially systems that are similar or identical physically. Although a variety of PS/2 designs exist, they're all similar in many respects. The three primary original types of PS/2 chassis design are the 30/30-286/55 SC, the 50/70, and the 60/65/80. Other designs, including the 90, 95, and 35/40/57, are similar in many ways to the three primary types. Models 25 and 25-286 are unique in that they have a built-in display.

- Models 25 and 25-286 have a unique design with a built-in monitor.

- Models 30, 30-286, and 55 SC share a common chassis and mechanical design, although their circuit boards are different.

- The newer 35, 40, and 57 systems physically are nearly identical to each other, especially the 40 and 57 units. The 35 differs from the 40 and 57 only slightly in construction (and has the same motherboard as the 40).

- Models 50, 50 Z, and 70 represent the "ultimate" in ease of disassembly and reassembly. These units have not a single cable in their default configuration and are snapped together almost entirely without conventional fasteners. Models 50 Z and 70 especially share many physical components and are difficult to tell apart from the outside.

- Models 60, 65 SC, and 80 are full-size, floor-standing systems. These systems are virtually identical to each other from a physical standpoint and share most of their physical components, even though the motherboards are different.

- The newer Model 90 is similar to the 50/70 systems in construction, but is unique in some ways. The newer Model 95 is similar to the 60/65/80 systems, but also differs in some ways.

The following section discusses, step-by-step, disassembly and reassembly procedures for the PS/2 systems. A section covers each of the three main system types. The disassembly procedures for the three primary designs can be applied to the other, similar PS/2 system designs as well.

Models 30, 30-286, and 55 SC

This section describes the disassembly procedures for the PS/2 Model 30, Model 30-286, and Model 55 SC. The systems are modular in nature, and most of the procedures are simple.

Removing the Cover

To remove the system-unit cover:

1. Park the hard disk.

2. Turn off the system and unplug the power cord from the wall socket.

3. Disconnect all external options.

4. If the keylock option is installed, make sure that the lock is in the unlocked position and the key removed.

5. Loosen all four screws located at the bottom corners on the sides of the system. Slide the cover back and lift it up and away.

6. Remove the rear cover that covers the system's back panel. You remove this cover by loosening the screw on each corner of the rear cover on the back of the system. Then pull the rear cover back and away from the system unit (see fig. 6.20).

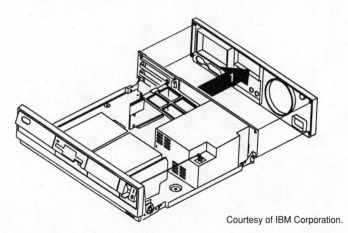

Courtesy of IBM Corporation.

Fig. 6.20

Removing the rear cover (Models 30, 30-286, and 55 SC).

Removing the 3 1/2-inch Floppy Disk Drive

The procedure for removing the floppy drive is very simple. Proceed as follows:

1. Remove the front cover (the bezel) from the drive by pushing down on the two plastic tabs on top of the bezel.

2. Pull the bezel off and away from the front of the system.

3. Disconnect the disk cabling by gently pulling the cable away from the drive.

4. Remove the plastic nails from each side of the drive bracket.

5. Press up on the plastic tab under the front of the drive.

6. Pull the drive forward out of the system (see fig. 6.21).

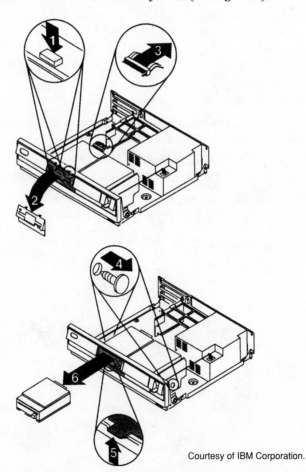

Fig. 6.21

Removing a 3 1/2-inch floppy disk drive (Models 30, 30-286, and 55 SC).

Courtesy of IBM Corporation.

Removing the Fixed Disk Drive

Before removing the fixed disk, make sure that the heads have been parked. You can use the Reference Disk to perform this task. Simply boot the disk, and select the Move the computer option from the main menu. If this option is not present, IBM supplied your system with only self-parking drives; you park them by simply turning off the power. Even if the option is present, you still might have a self-parking drive (refer to Chapter 4 for more information). You can remove the drive by following these steps (which are similar to the steps for removing a floppy drive):

1. Remove the front cover (the bezel) from the drive by pushing down on the two plastic tabs on top of the bezel and pulling it off and away from the front of the system.

2. Disconnect the disk cabling by gently pulling the cable away from the drive.

3. Remove the plastic nails from each side of the drive bracket.

4. Press upward on the plastic tab under the front of the drive, and pull the drive forward out of the system.

Removing Adapters

To remove all adapter cards from the system unit, first remove the system-unit cover, as described earlier. Then proceed as follows for each adapter:

1. Remove the screw from the bracket retaining the card.

2. Slide the adapter sideways out of the system unit (see fig. 6.22).

If you add new options, their installation might require that you remove the plastic insert on the rear panel. Also, if you add a 3/4-length adapter, you must adjust the sliding support bracket to support the adapter properly.

Removing the Bus Adapter

These systems have a bus adapter card that contains the slots. This adapter plugs into the motherboard. To remove the device, proceed as follows:

1. Push in on the two tabs on top of the bus adapter support.

2. Gently rotate the end of the support upward and disengage the tabs in the power supply.

3. Lift up and remove the bus adapter (see fig. 6.23).

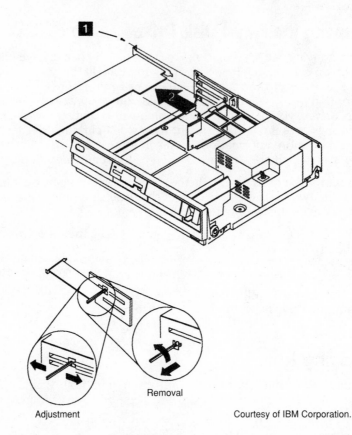

Fig. 6.22

Removing adapter
cards (Models 30,
30-286, and 55 SC).

Adjustment

Removal

Courtesy of IBM Corporation.

Removing the Power Supply

When you remove the power supply, first remove the rear cover and the
bus adapter support, as described earlier. Then proceed as follows:

1. Disconnect the power connector from the power supply to the
   motherboard by pulling the connector straight up.

2. Disengage the power-switch link from the power supply.

3. Remove the three screws that secure the power supply to the system frame. The screws are at the back of the power supply.

4. Gently slide the power supply toward the front of the system to
   disengage the power supply from the base of the frame.

5. Lift the power supply up and away from the unit (see fig. 6.24).

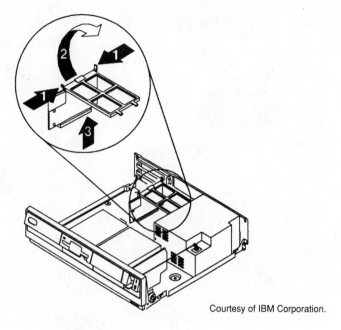

Courtesy of IBM Corporation.

Fig. 6.23

Removing the bus adapter (Models 30, 30-286, and 55 SC).

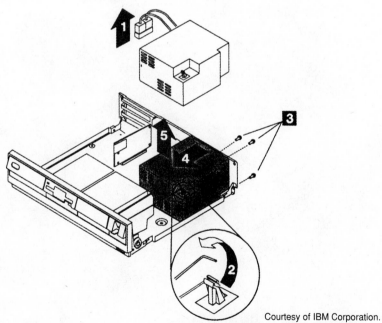

Courtesy of IBM Corporation.

Fig. 6.24

Removing the power supply (Models 30, 30-286, and 55 SC).

Removing Single In-line Memory Modules (SIMMs)

One benefit of using single in-line memory modules (SIMMs) is that they're easy to remove or install. When you remove memory modules, remember that because of physical interference you must remove the memory-module package closest to the disk drive bus-adapter slot before you remove the package closest to the edge of the motherboard. To remove a SIMM properly, follow this procedure:

1. Gently pull the tabs on each side of the SIMM socket outward.

2. Rotate or pull the SIMM up and out of the socket (see fig. 6.25).

Be careful not to damage the connector. If you damage the motherboard-SIMM connector, you could be looking at an expensive repair. Never force the SIMM; it should come out easily. If it doesn't, you are doing something wrong.

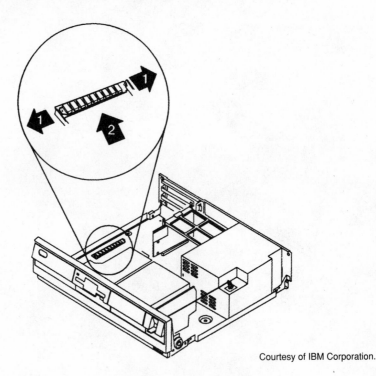

Fig. 6.25

Removing a SIMM (Models 30, 30-286, and 55 SC).

Courtesy of IBM Corporation.

Removing the Motherboard

The motherboard is held in place by several screws, all of which must be taken out. Proceed as follows:

1. Remove all screws.

2. Carefully slide the motherboard to the left.

3. Lift the motherboard out of the system unit (see fig. 6.26).

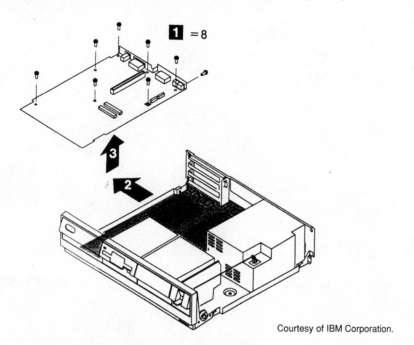

Courtesy of IBM Corporation.

Fig. 6.26

Removing the motherboard (Models 30, 30-286, and 55 SC).

Models 50, 50 Z, and 70

This section describes the disassembly procedures for the PS/2 Models 50, 50 Z, and 70. These systems are modular in nature, and most of the procedures are simple.

Removing the Cover

To remove the system-unit cover:

1. Park the hard disk. Nearly all these systems come with self-parking hard disks; only the 20M drive used in the Model 50 does not. Self-parking drives require no manual parking operation. Because no parking program is necessary, the reference disks for the Model 70 do not have a head-parking program or menu selection.

2. Turn off the system and unplug the power cord from the wall socket.

3. Unlock the cover.

4. Loosen the two cover thumbscrews on the back of the system.

5. Slide the cover toward you and lift it off (see fig. 6.27).

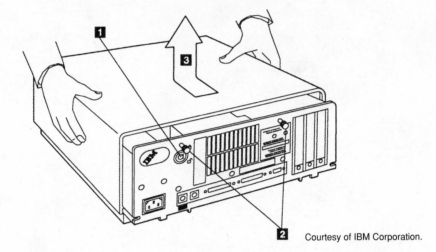

Fig. 6.27

Removing the cover
(Models 50 and 70).

Courtesy of IBM Corporation.

Removing the Battery-and-Speaker Assembly

The battery and speaker are contained in a single assembly. To remove this assembly, follow these steps:

1. To avoid accidentally discharging the battery, remove the battery from its holder before removing the battery-and-speaker assembly: bend the tabs on the holder toward the rear and pull the battery straight up. Remember to install this assembly before replacing the battery.

2. Push the tab on the bottom of the speaker unit to disengage the speaker assembly from the support structure.

3. Lift the entire battery-and-speaker assembly up and out of the system (see fig. 6.28).

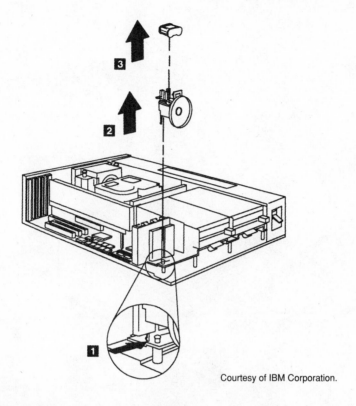

Courtesy of IBM Corporation.

Fig. 6.28

Removing the battery-
and-speaker assembly
(Models 50 and 70).

Removing the Fan Assembly

The fan assembly in Model 70 systems is an integral part of the power supply. In these systems, the fan is screwed directly to the power supply. You remove the fan by removing the power supply.

In Model 50 systems, remove the fan assembly as follows:

1. Disengage the two plastic pushbutton tabs on either side of the fan assembly by prying them upward. If necessary, use the small pry tool located at the front, right corner of the system.

2. Pull the entire assembly up and out of the system (see fig. 6.29).

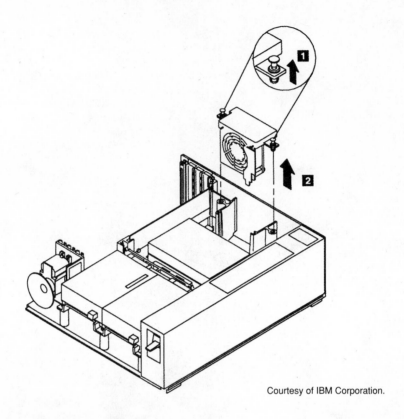

Fig. 6.29

Removing the fan
assembly (Models 50
and 70).

Removing Adapters

An important part of removing adapter boards in these systems is to
make a diagram of the adapter and cable locations.

T I P   You should put all adapters back in the same slot from which they
were removed. Otherwise, the CMOS memory configuration must
be run.

To remove the adapters, follow these steps:

1. Make sure that all cables are disconnected.

2. Loosen the retaining thumb screw at the base of the card bracket.

3. Grasp the option adapter and gently pull it up and out of the system unit (see fig. 6.30).

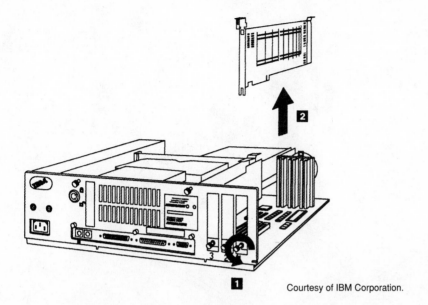

Courtesy of IBM Corporation.

Fig. 6.30

Removing an adapter
(Models 50 and 70).

Removing the 3 1/2-Inch Floppy Disk Drive

Removing floppy drives from 3 1/2-inch floppy disk drive systems is a simple task. Just push up on the tab underneath the floppy drive, and slide the drive out toward you.

Removing Fixed Disk Drives

Removing the hard disk from a fixed disk drive is almost as easy as removing a floppy drive. Before removing the hard disk, make sure that you've backed up all the information on the fixed disk and parked the heads. Then follow these steps:

1. Press down the two plastic tabs on the side where the power supply is located.

2. Slide the fixed disk drive toward the power supply and up.

3. Grasp the adapter at each end, and gently pull the adapter up (see fig. 6.31).

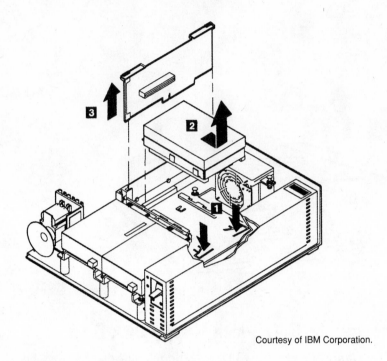

Courtesy of IBM Corporation.

Fig. 6.31

Removing the fixed
disk drive (Models 50
and 70).

Removing the Drive-Support Structure

To remove the support structure from the system unit, you first must
remove these components:

> Cover
> Battery-and-speaker assembly
> Fan assembly
> Adapters
> Floppy disk drives
> Fixed disk drives

When these items have been removed, pull up all six white, plastic,
pushbutton lock tabs, and lift the assembly up (see fig. 6.32). If necessary, you can use the small pry tool on the front, right side of the system
to pry up the lock tabs.

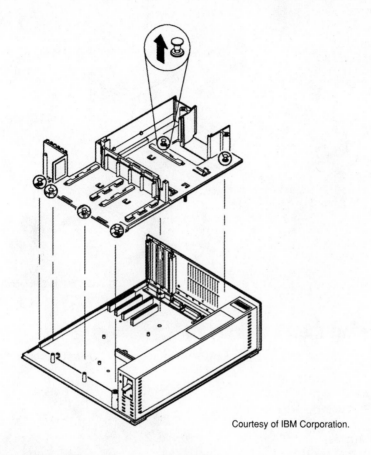

Courtesy of IBM Corporation.

Fig. 6.32

Removing the drive-support structure (Models 50 and 70).

Removing the Power Supply

To remove the power supply, follow these steps:

1. Remove the screw on the front, left side of the system.

2. Remove the two screws on the back of the power supply.

3. Slide the power supply to the right, and remove from the system unit (see fig. 6.33).

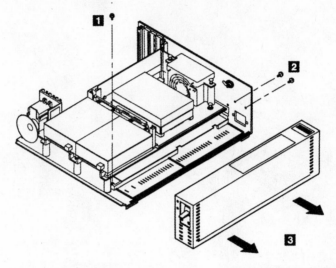

Courtesy of IBM Corporation.

Fig. 6.33

Removing the power
supply (Models 50
and 70).

Removing the Motherboard

To remove the motherboard from the system unit, you first must remove
these components:

> Cover
> Battery-and-speaker assembly
> Fan assembly
> Adapters
> Floppy disk drives
> Fixed disk drives
> Disk-support structure
> Power supply

After you remove all these components from the system unit, removing
the motherboard requires only these two steps:

1. Remove all six retaining screws (three on the back of the system
   unit and three on the motherboard).

2. Gently lift the motherboard up and out of the system (see fig. 6.34).

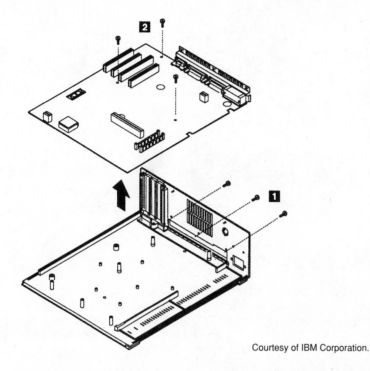

Courtesy of IBM Corporation.

Fig. 6.34

Removing the
motherboard (Models
50 and 70).

Removing Single In-line Memory Modules (SIMMs)

A benefit of using single in-line memory modules (SIMMs) is that they are
easy to remove or install. When you remove memory modules, remember that, because of physical interference, you must remove the
memory-module package closest to the disk drive bus-adapter slot before removing the package closest to the edge of the motherboard. To
remove a SIMM properly, follow the steps shown for the 30, 30-286, and
55 SC (see fig. 6.35).

CAUTION: Be careful not to damage the connector. If you damage
the motherboard-SIMM connector, you could have an expensive
repair. Never force the SIMM; it should come out easily. If it
doesn't, you are doing something wrong.

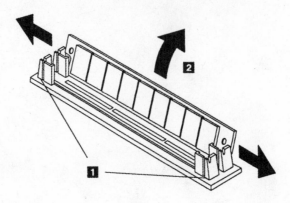

Courtesy of IBM Corporation.

Fig. 6.35

Removing a SIMM
(Models 50 and 70).

Models 60, 65 SC, and 80

This section describes the disassembly procedures for the PS/2 models
60, 65 SC, and 80, These floor-standing PS/2 systems are not as easy to
work on or as modular as the desktop systems, but they're still easy to
service compared with the earlier PC- and AT-type systems. Most repair
procedures do not even involve using any tools.

Removing the Cover

To remove the system-unit cover, follow these steps:

1. Park the hard disk. Because all Model 60, 65 SC, and 80 systems
   delivered from IBM include self-parking hard disks, no manual parking operation is necessary. The reference disks for these systems
   do not include a head-parking program or menu selection because
   they are unnecessary with self-parking drives.

2. Turn off the system, and unplug the power cord from the wall
   socket.

3. Disconnect all external options.

4. Unlock the cover lock.

5. Loosen the two cover screws on the side of the system.

6. Tilt the cover toward you.

7. Lift the cover up (see fig. 6.36).

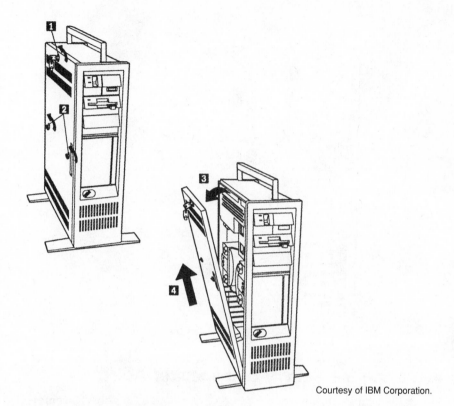

Courtesy of IBM Corporation.

Fig. 6.36

Removing the cover
(Models 60, 65 SC,
and 80).

Removing Adapters

An important part of removing adapter boards in these systems is to make a diagram of the adapter and cable locations.

> Put all adapters back in the same slot from which they were removed. Otherwise, the CMOS memory configuration must be run.   **T I P**

To remove the adapters, follow these steps:

1. Make sure that all cables are disconnected.

2. Loosen the retaining thumb screw at the base of the card bracket.

3. Grasp the option adapter, and gently pull it up and out of the system unit (see fig. 6.37).

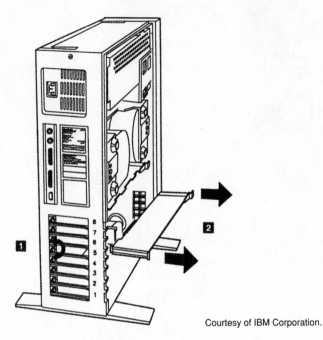

Courtesy of IBM Corporation.

Fig. 6.37

Removing an adapter
(Models 60, 65 SC,
and 80).

Removing the Battery-and-Speaker Assembly

The battery and speaker are contained in a single assembly. To remove this assembly, follow these steps:

1. To avoid accidentally discharging the battery, remove the battery from its holder before removing the battery-and-speaker assembly: bend the tabs on the holder toward the rear, and pull the battery straight up. Remember to install this assembly before replacing the battery.

2. Disconnect the battery-and-speaker assembly cable.

3. Push the tab on the bottom of the speaker unit to disengage the speaker assembly from the support structure (see fig. 6.38).

4. Lift the entire battery-and-speaker assembly up and out of the system.

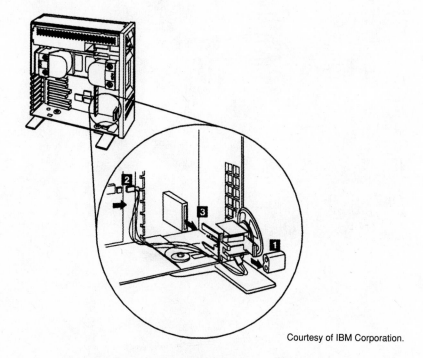

Courtesy of IBM Corporation.

Fig. 6.38

Removing the battery-and-speaker assembly (Models 60, 65 SC, and 80).

Removing the Front Bezel

These models have a large front panel, or bezel, that you must remove to gain access to the floppy disk drives. The panel snaps off easily if you follow this procedure:

1. Grasp the bottom near the feet of the unit.

2. Pull out (see fig. 6.39). The bezel should snap off freely.

Removing the Power Supply

To remove the power supply, you first must remove the cover and front bezel. Then follow these steps:

1. Disconnect all cables from the power supply.

2. Remove the three screws that retain the power supply. One screw is near the power switch, and the other two are near the back of the supply.

3. Lift the power supply out the side of the unit (see fig. 6.40).

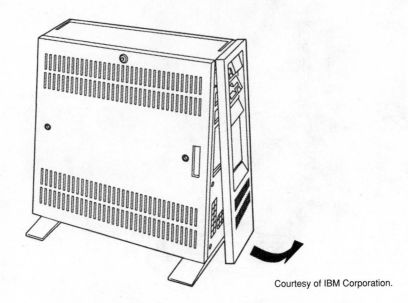

Fig. 6.39

Removing the bezel
(Models 60, 65 SC,
and 80).

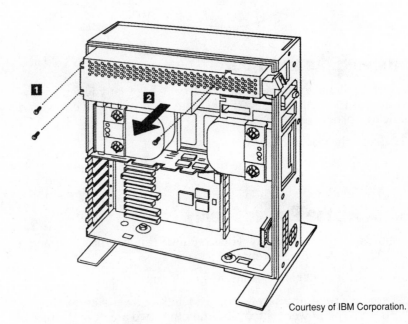

Fig. 6.40

Removing the power
supply (Models 60,
65 SC, and 80).

Removing Floppy Disk Drives

The floppy drives are located next to the power supply. Removing floppy drives from these systems requires only these two steps:

1. Push the tab underneath the floppy drive up while you simultaneously press a tab on the rear of the drive sideways.

2. Slide the drive out the front of the unit (see fig. 6.41).

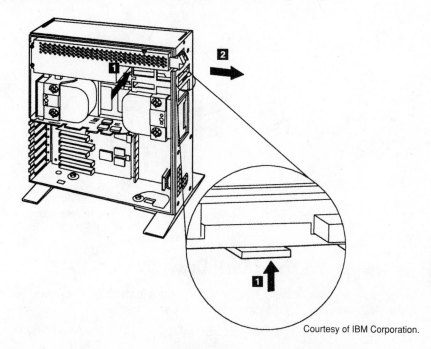

Courtesy of IBM Corporation.

Fig. 6.41

Removing a disk drive (Models 60, 65 SC, and 80).

Removing the Floppy Disk Drive Cable Retainer

Floppy disk drive systems use a retainer to hold cables in place when the floppy drives are plugged in. To remove this cable retainer, follow these steps:

1. Press the tabs located on the side of the cable retainer.

2. Rotate the retainer out toward the back of the system unit.

3. Pull off the retainer (see fig. 6.42).

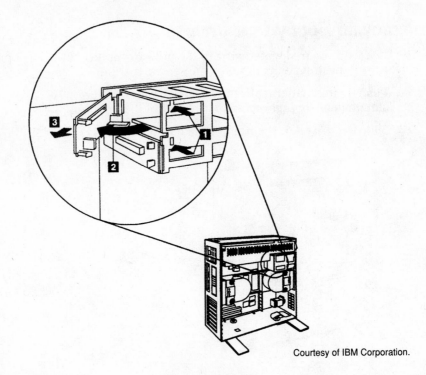

Fig. 6.42

Removing the disk drive cable retainer (Models 60, 65, SC and 80).

Courtesy of IBM Corporation.

Removing the Fixed Disk Drive D

Make sure that you have a backup of the information on the drive before removing the disk. Then follow these steps:

1. Disconnect the ground wire and all cables from the fixed disk drive.

2. Turn both thumb screws counterclockwise.

3. Remove the front bezel.

4. Slide the fixed disk drive out the front of the system unit (see fig. 6.43). Note that drive D must be removed before drive C because of physical interference.

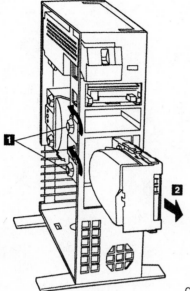

Courtesy of IBM Corporation.

Fig. 6.43

Removing fixed disk
drive D (Models 60,
65 SC, and 80).

Removing the Fixed Disk Drive C

Make sure that you have a backup of the information on the drive before
removing the drive. Then proceed as follows:

1. Disconnect the ground wire and all cables from the fixed disk drive.

2. Turn both thumb screws counterclockwise.

3. Remove the front bezel.

4. Slide the drive a little toward the front and lift the fixed disk drive
   sideways out of the system (see fig. 6.44). Note that drive D must be
   removed before drive C because of physical interference.

Removing the Fixed Disk Drive-Support Structure

A large, metal hard disk drive support structure is used to clamp the
hard disks in place. You must remove this structure in order to remove
the motherboard. Follow these steps:

1. Remove the four screws located on the front portion of the
   structure.

2. Slide the structure forward, and lift it up and sideways out of the
   system (see fig. 6.45).

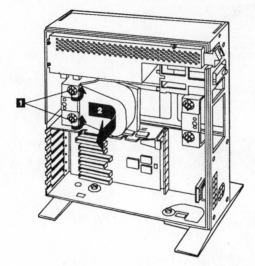

Fig. 6.44

Removing fixed disk drive C (Models 60, 65 SC, and 80).

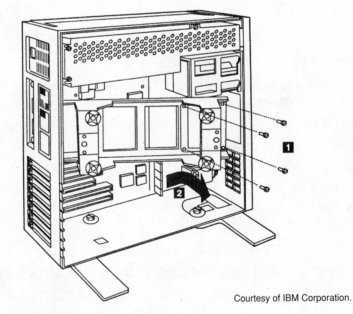

Fig. 6.45

Removing the fixed disk drive support structure (Models 60, 65 SC, and 80).

Removing the Motherboard

To remove the motherboard from the system unit, you first must remove the cover, any adapters, the fixed disk drives, and the fixed disk support structure. With these components removed from the system unit, removal of the motherboard requires these three steps:

1. Disconnect all cables from the motherboard.

2. Remove all eight retaining screws.

3. Gently lift the motherboard up and out of the system (see fig. 6.46).

Now that you've examined the procedures for disassembling a system, let's examine the different components that make up a system.

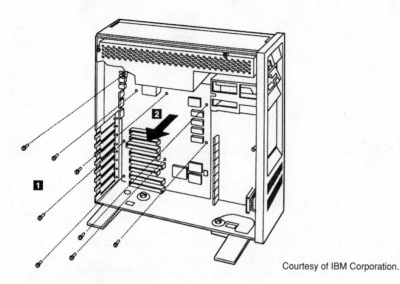

Courtesy of IBM Corporation.

Fig. 6.46

Removing the motherboard (Models 60, 65 SC, and 80).

Motherboard Layouts

The most important single part of every system is the system board, or motherboard. The boards differ for each type of system available. Sometimes a manufacturer even changes the motherboard for a system to add features or improve the design. IBM has made such changes for several of its systems. In some cases, the changes from one type to another are subtle—higher-density memory chips, for example, are used in the PC Type 2 motherboard. This change is difficult to detect just by looking. At other times, changes are more complete, as in the AT Type 2 motherboard. This board is completely different from the Type 1 design in both layout and size. The only unchanged items are the mounting and connector positions.

This list shows the changes in the different motherboards used in standard PC systems.

PC motherboards

Type 1	Used 16K RAM chips in four banks—a 64K total; had Version 1 or 2 of the ROM BIOS, which now is obsolete
Type 2	Used 64K RAM chips in four banks—a 256K total; had ROM BIOS Version dated 10/27/82, the last version offered

XT motherboards

Type 1	Used 64K RAM chips—a 256K total; used ROM BIOS Version dated 11/8/82
Type 2	Used 256K RAM chips in two banks and 64K RAM chips in two banks—a 640K total. Used ROM BIOS Versions dated 01/10/86 or 05/09/86

AT motherboards

Type 1	Used 128K, stacked RAM chips; ran 6 MHz and used BIOS Version dated 01/10/84 or 06/10/85
Type 2	Physically smaller than Type 1 and used 256K RAM chips; supplied with ROM BIOS Versions dated 06/10/85 (6 MHz) or 11/15/85 (8 MHz)

Non-IBM systems also have different system-board designs. Some manufacturers have even used a backplane type of design, in which the only components on the "motherboard" are the slot connectors. All circuitry, including the main CPU, is contained on adapter boards. When a system is designed in this way, the motherboard is called a *backplane*. Zenith, for example, favors this design in many of its desktop systems. Upgrading a system built like this can be easy. To change from an 80286-based system to a 80386-based system, for example, you just change one card. See Chapter 7 for more information about motherboards and their design.

IBM PS/2 systems have gone the opposite route from backplane design. These systems incorporate as much circuitry as possible on the motherboard. For example, disk controllers, video circuits, serial and parallel ports, and mice ports are included on the motherboard. With this design, these systems have fewer total system parts, a more standard base configuration on which to build, and easy diagnosis and servicing. Unfortunately, when an on-board component fails, the entire motherboard must be replaced, which is much more expensive than if the component were on a plug-in board.

To be upgraded more easily, many newer PS/2 systems have a processor-complex architecture, a design evolved from the backplane type in some compatible systems. The primary difference in this design is that the motherboard still contains the majority of the system circuitry, and only the main central processing unit (CPU) chip and any necessary support and control circuits are placed on a small circuit board. The circuit board then plugs into the main motherboard.

This smaller processor complex (or *daughterboard*, as it often is called) is plugged into a special connector designed specifically for the processor complex. Replacement processor complexes are available with higher-speed processors or larger memory caches that enable a system to be upgraded in performance and capability. As a fringe benefit, serviceability is improved because in case of failure a portion of the motherboard can be replaced easily.

Table 6.2 shows all the PS/2 systems that use a processor-complex design, and the upgrades available for these systems:

Table 6.2 Boards Using Processor-Complex Design

System	Standard speed	Standard CPU	Available upgrades
Model 70-Axx	25 MHz	386DX	25 MHz 486DX
Model 70-Bxx	25 MHz	486DX	None introduced yet
Model P75-xxx	33 MHz	486DX	None introduced yet
Model 90-0Gx	20 MHz	486SX	25, 33, or 50 MHz 486
Model 90-0Hx	25 MHz	486SX	33 or 50 MHz 486
Model 90-0Jx	25 MHz	486DX	33 or 50 MHz 486
Model 90-0Kx	33 MHz	486DX	50 MHz 486
Model 95-0Gx	20 MHz	486SX	25, 33, or 50 MHz 486
Model 95-0Hx	25 MHz	486SX	33 or 50 MHz 486
Model 95-0Jx	25 MHz	486DX	33 or 50 MHz 486
Model 95-0Kx	33 MHz	486DX	50 MHz 486

The 486SX systems can be upgraded also by just swapping the 486SX chip for a 487SX. The 487SX chip is equivalent to a 486DX chip of the same speed. Also, the processor complexes used in the Model 90 systems can be upgraded further by adding to the processor-complex optional 256K external cache memory.

The upgradeable CPU concept was not pioneered by IBM. Many other compatible manufacturers in fact have employed this type of design for several years. Now that IBM has jumped on the upgradeable CPU bandwagon, however, other compatible vendors will follow suit. COMPAQ already has responded by introducing such systems. Many others surely will follow.

The upgradeable CPU design sounds good, but the available upgrades are expensive, especially from name-brand companies such as IBM and COMPAQ. For the cost of an upgrade from IBM, you can purchase an entire equivalent compatible system, including display. Because upgrades such as these usually are available only from the system OEM, not only are the costs high, but also your choices can be limited.

Chapter Summary

This chapter has discussed the initial teardown and inspection of a system and looked at the types of tools required, from simple hand tools to meters for measuring voltage and resistance. It mentioned some of the problems you might encounter with the actual hardware (screws, nuts, bolts, and so on) in a system.

The chapter also has discussed the physical-disassembly procedure and how to recognize the different components that make up a system. A variety of designs are used in system motherboards. The traditional motherboard design has been enhanced by placing directly on the motherboard some devices that formerly were external, including disk controllers, video adapters, and large amounts of memory. Some companies have shifted to a backplane design, in which the majority of the motherboard circuitry is on a card that can be replaced or upgraded easily. Even more companies are shifting to the processor-complex design, in which the main CPU and support chips are separated from the rest of the motherboard on a small daughtercard that also is easy to replace or upgrade.

Primary System Components

This chapter studies the primary components that make up a typical system's base configuration. These components include:

- Motherboards
- Microprocessors
- Memory
- Slots
- Standard adapters
- Power supply
- Keyboards

Most systems are supplied with a system unit and a keyboard. The system unit includes a motherboard, which contains a microprocessor, usually some memory, and slots for expansion of the system. Many systems include one or more standard adapter boards in these slots, such as adapters for disk controllers or serial and parallel ports. At least one floppy disk drive typically is included as well. (For more on floppy disk drives, see Chapter 8.) A system unit houses a power supply, which provides the correct voltage and current to run the system. The keyboard is an external device attached to the system unit by a cable. Knowing how all these components operate can help when you're trying to track down problems or repair systems.

These components comprise only the base configuration. You need additional devices to complete a typical system. Many systems, for example, don't include a display adapter, the display itself, or ports for the connection of printers or modems. Systems often include only a minimum of memory, which you must expand before you can perform any serious computing. Also, the base configuration of some systems doesn't include a hard disk. Many new systems, however, do include a hard disk, serial and parallel ports, a display adapter, and even the display. For more information about the peripherals used in a typical system, see Chapter 10.

Motherboards

Easily the most important component in a PC system is the main or *motherboard*. Sometimes the terminology can be confusing because IBM refers to the motherboard as a system board or *planar*. The terms "motherboard," "system board," and "planar" are interchangeable. Each motherboard in the PS/2 family contains functionally the same components as the motherboards in the original PC family, and more.

Not all systems have a motherboard in the true sense of the word. Some systems' components, normally found on a motherboard, are located instead on an expansion adapter card plugged into a slot. In these systems, the board with the slots is called not a motherboard, but a *backplane*. Systems using this type of construction are called *backplane systems*.

Each system design, the motherboard and the backplane, has advantages and disadvantages. Most original personal computers were designed as backplanes in the late 1970s. Apple and IBM shifted the market to the now-traditional motherboard with a slot-type design because this type of system generally is cheaper to mass-produce than one with the backplane design. The advantage of a backplane system, however, is that you easily can upgrade it to a new processor and new level of performance by changing a single card. For example, you can upgrade a system with an 80286-based processor card to an 80386-based card just by changing the card. In a motherboard-design system, you must change the motherboard itself, a more formidable task.

Slightly different from a true backplane design is the processor-complex design, first used in some compatibles such as those from AST and ALR, and now in the newer IBM PS/2 systems and in systems from COMPAQ. In this design, the main processor and support chips reside on a replaceable card, and the majority of system circuits are still on the motherboard.

In effect, you have a modular motherboard design. You can replace the processor complex with a more powerful one for less money than a complete motherboard upgrade, and usually for less than if the entire motherboard circuitry were mounted on a replaceable card. Of course, companies such as IBM and COMPAQ charge a high price for their upgrades. Consider this factor when you purchase one of these systems. The processor-complex design seems to be gaining popularity in systems with the 486 processor. These systems offer a single machine that can accept processor-complex modules with either a 20 MHz 486SX, or 25 MHz, 33 MHz, and 50 MHz 486DX processors, enabling a very long upgrade path by changing only the processor module.

Market realities have confused the distinction between upgrades for these two system designs. Intel, for example, sells for the AT the Inboard 386/AT board, which contains an 80386 processor and memory. You can justifiably call this board a "mothercard" because it replaces many functions of the motherboard into which it is plugged. The original motherboard now acts much like a backplane. Zenith and Kaypro are known for producing systems in the backplane design, but most other manufacturers have followed IBM in producing typical motherboard-based systems.

Any given system usually has a motherboard designed specifically for that system. The motherboard in IBM's original AT system, for example, was a new design produced especially for that system. After a motherboard is produced, however, it sometimes is revised during the life of a system. Beginning with systems sold during October 1985, for example, the AT motherboard design was changed to increase reliability and reduce manufacturing costs. The new design, called Type 2, was found also on the AT versions -319 and -339, where it increased the clock speed of the system to 8 MHz. For more information about speed, see the section "Microprocessor Speed Ratings," later in this chapter.

Be aware, then, that two apparently identical systems may in fact have different physical motherboard designs or revisions, often depending on when the system was manufactured. Sometimes the revisions are minor, as in the IBM XT, but they can be major, as in the AT example cited in the preceding paragraph. Chapter 2 discusses the changes IBM made in motherboards between the different model systems.

IBM sometimes uses a motherboard first designed for one system in another system. The Portable PC is an example. The IBM Portable PC contains an XT Type 1 motherboard. The PS/2 Models 25-286 and 30-286 use the same motherboards. Usually, however, all the various models in a system use the same motherboard design. The differences among the models are primarily in configuration and optional accessories.

Newer systems seem to go through more motherboard revisions and redesigns than the older systems did, largely the result of increased automation in the design and assembly of these systems. Implementing a design change for new motherboards is now an easy task, considering the powerful CAD-CAM (computer-aided design and computer-aided manufacturing) systems designers use today.

Microprocessors

The microprocessor, or central processing unit (CPU), is the "brain" of the PC and performs all the system's calculating and processing. All the IBM PC and PS/2 units and compatibles use microprocessors compatible with the Intel family of chips.

Data Bus and Address Bus

One of the most common ways to describe a microprocessor is the size of the processor's data bus and address bus. A *bus* is simply a series of connections designed to carry common signals. Imagine running a pair of wires from one end of a building to another. If you connect a 110-volt AC power generator to the two wires at any point and place outlets at convenient locations along the wires, you have constructed a "power bus." No matter which outlet you plug in to, you have access to the same "signal," which in this example is 110-volt AC power.

Any transmission medium with more than one outlet at each end can be called a bus. A typical computer system has several buses, and a typical microprocessor has two important buses for carrying data and memory-addressing information: the data bus and the address bus.

The microprocessor bus discussed most often is the *data bus*, the bundle of wires (or pins) used to send and receive data. The greater number of signals that can be sent at one time, the more data can be transmitted in a specified interval and, therefore, the faster the bus.

Data in a computer is sent as digital information, consisting of a time interval in which a single wire carries 5 volts to signal a "1" data bit, or 0 volts to signal a "0" data bit. Therefore, the greater number of wires you have, the greater number of individual bits you can send in the same time interval. A chip such as the 80286, which has 16 wires for transmitting and receiving such data, is said to have a 16-bit data bus. A 32-bit chip such as the 80386 has twice as many wires dedicated to simultaneous data transmission and can send twice as much information in the same time interval as a 16-bit chip.

A good way to understand this flow of information is to consider an automobile highway and the traffic it carries. If a highway has only one lane in each direction of travel, only one car at a time can pass in a certain direction. If you want to have more traffic flow, you can add another lane and then have twice as many cars pass in a specified time. You can think of an 8-bit chip as the single-lane highway because with this chip one byte flows at a time. (One byte equals eight individual bits.) The 16-bit chip, with two bytes flowing at a time, resembles a two-lane highway. To move a large amount of automobiles, as in larger cities, you might have four lanes (in each direction), which corresponds to a 32-bit data bus and the capability to move four bytes of information at a time.

Just as you can describe a highway by its width, you can describe a chip by the "width" of its data bus. When you read an advertisement describing a computer system as a 16-bit or 32-bit system, the ad usually is referring to the data bus of the CPU. This number provides a rough idea of the chip's (and therefore the system's) performance potential.

Table 7.1 shows specifications, including the data-bus sizes, for the Intel family of microprocessors used in IBM and compatible PCs.

Table 7.1 INTEL CPU Specifications

Processor	Register size	Data bus	Address bus	Integral cache	Math Co-processor	Number of transistors	Date introduced
8088	16-bit	8-bit	20-bit	No	No	29,000	June '79
8086	16-bit	16-bit	20-bit	No	No	29,000	June '78
286	16-bit	16-bit	24-bit	No	No	130,000	February '82
386SX	32-bit	16-bit	24-bit	No	No	275,000	June '88
386SL	32-bit	16-bit	24-bit	No	No	855,000	October '90
386SLC	32-bit	16-bit	24-bit	8K	No	N/A	October '91
386DX	32-bit	32-bit	32-bit	No	No	275,000	October '85
486SX	32-bit	32-bit	32-bit	8K	No	1,185,000	April '91
487SX	32-bit	32-bit	32-bit	8K	Yes	1,200,000	April '91
486DX	32-bit	32-bit	32-bit	8K	Yes	1,200,000	April '89
586	32-bit	32-bit	32-bit	N/A	Yes	3,000,000	1992

The fact that not all the chips are "pure" sometimes confuses the data-bus issue. Some processors have an internal data bus (made up of data paths, and of storage units called *registers*) that is different from the external data bus. The 8088 and 80386SX are examples of this structure. Each chip has an internal data bus twice the width of the external bus. These designs sometimes are called *hybrid designs* and usually are low-cost versions of a "pure" chip. The 80386SX, for example, can pass data around internally with a full 32-bit register size; for communications with the outside world, however, the chip is restricted to a 16-bit-wide data path. This design enables a systems designer to build a lower-cost motherboard with only a 16-bit bus design and still maintain full compatibility with the full 32-bit 80386.

Completely different from the data bus, the *address bus* is the set of wires carrying the addressing information used to describe the memory location to which the data is being sent or from which the data is being retrieved. As with the data bus, each wire in an address bus carries a single bit of information. This single bit is a single digit in the address. The more wires (digits) used in calculating these addresses, the greater the total number of address locations. The size (or width) of the address bus indicates the maximum amount of random-access memory (RAM) a chip can address.

The highway analogy can be used to show how the address bus fits in. If the data bus is the highway, and the size of the data bus is equivalent to the highway's width, then the address bus relates to the house number or street address number. The size of the address bus is equivalent to the number of digits in the house address. If you live on a street where the address is limited to a two-digit number, then no more than 100 (00 to 99) distinct addresses can exist for that street. Add another digit, and the total number of available addresses increases to 1,000 (000 to 999).

Remember that because a computer works in the binary numbering system, a two-digit number gives only four unique addresses (00, 01, 10, and 11), and a three-digit number provides only eight addresses (000 to 111). Examples are the 8086 and 8088 processors, each of which use a 20-bit address bus with a maximum of 1,048,576 bytes (one megabyte) of address locations.

Table 7.2 describes the memory-addressing capabilities of Intel microprocessors.

Table 7.2 Intel Microprocessor Memory-Addressing Capabilities			
Processors	8088/8086	286, 386SX 386SL, 386SLC	386DX, 486SX/487SX, 486DX, 586
Address bus width (in bits)	20	24	32
Bytes	1,048,576	16,777,216	4,294,967,296
Kilobytes (1024 bytes)	1,024	16,384	4,194,304
Megabytes (1024 kilobytes)	1	16	4,096
Gigabytes (1024 megabytes)	—	—	4

The data bus and address bus are independent of one another, and chip designers can use whatever size they want for each bus. Usually, however, chips with larger data buses have larger address buses. The sizes of the buses can provide important information about a chip's relative power, measured in two important ways. The size of the data bus is an indication of the chip's information-moving capability, and the size of the address bus tells you how much memory a certain chip can handle.

Using a Math Coprocessor Chip

Each central processor can use a math coprocessor chip as an option. Some CPU chips have a math coprocessor built-in. The coprocessors provide hardware for arithmetic functions that would place excessive drain on the main CPU. Table 7.3 summarizes the coprocessors available for the Intel family of microprocessors.

Math chips (as coprocessors sometimes are called) can perform certain mathematical operations at 10 to 100 times the speed of the corresponding main processor. Math chips also are much more accurate in these calculations than the primary CPU.

A drawback to using a coprocessor, however, is that the instruction set is different from that in the primary CPU. A program must detect the existence of the coprocessor and then execute instructions written explicitly for that coprocessor. Otherwise, the math coprocessor chip simply draws power and does nothing else. Fortunately, most modern programs that can benefit from the use of the coprocessor can correctly detect and use the coprocessor if it is present in a system. These programs are usually math-intensive programs such as spreadsheets, statistical programs, and some graphics programs such as computer-aided design (CAD) software. A word processor doesn't benefit from a math chip and, for this reason, doesn't use it.

Table 7.3 Coprocessor Summary for Intel Microprocessors

Processor	Coprocessor
8086	8087
8088	8087
286	287
386SX	387SX
386SL	387SX
386SLC	387SX
386DX	387DX
486SX	487SX
487SX	Built-in
486DX	Built-in

In programs that utilize the chip, the increase in performance in an application can be dramatic—usually a multifold increase in speed. If the primary applications you run take advantage of a math coprocessor, you should upgrade your system to include one.

Most PCs are socketed for the coprocessor as an option, but almost no systems include it as standard equipment. Exceptions are, of course, any system with a 486DX or 487SX processor. These processors have the math unit built-in. A few systems on the market don't even have a socket for the coprocessor because of cost and size considerations. Usually, these systems are the low-cost or portable systems such as the IBM PS/1 or the older laptop PC Convertible or PC*jr*. For more specific information about math coprocessors, see the discussions of the specific chips— 8087, 287, 387, and 487SX—in the following section. Table 7.4 shows some of the specifications of the various math coprocessors.

Table 7.4 Intel Math Coprocessor Specifications

Name	Power consumption	TEMPERATURE RATINGS Case min.	Case max.	Number of transistors	Date introduced
8087	3 watts	0°C	85°C	45,000	1980
287	3 watts	0°C	85°C	45,000	1982
287XL	1.5 watts	−65°C	110°C	40,000	May '90
387SX	1.5 watts	0°C	85°C	120,000	June '88
387DX	1.5 watts	−65°C	110°C	120,000	Feb. '87

Examining Microprocessors

IBM and compatible vendors have used all the Intel chips in different PC systems over the years. To understand fully the capabilities of a certain system, as well as to perform any type of servicing, you must at least know what type of processor runs under the hood. Table 7.5 summarizes which microprocessors operate with most IBM systems.

Table 7.5 Microprocessors Operating with IBM Systems	
Processor	**System units**
8086	PS/2 25, 30
8088	PC, XT, Convertible, Portable, PC*jr*
286	AT, XT-286, PS/1, PS/2 25-286, 30-286, 50, 50 Z, 60
386SX	PS/1 SX, PS/2 25SX, 35, 40, L40, 55, 57, 65
386SLC	PS/2 57M
386DX	PS/2 70, P70, 80
486SX	PS/2 90, 95
487SX	PS/2 90, 95
486DX	PS/2 70, P75, 90, 95

The following sections examine these microprocessors in more detail.

8086 and 8088

Intel first introduced the 8086 microprocessor in 1976. This microprocessor was one of the first 16-bit chips on the market and, at the time, had one of the largest memory-address spaces (20 bits, or 1M) available. The design's only problem was that it was costly. Both the chip and a motherboard designed for the chip were expensive. The cost was high because the system included the 16-bit data bus, which is more expensive to design than a system using an 8-bit bus. The generally price-sensitive marketplace was slow to accept the 8086. Although having 16 bits was desirable, mainstream systems then were all 8-bit systems. Users apparently weren't willing to pay for the extra performance in the full 16-bit design. This situation led Intel to introduce the 8088 chip in 1978.

The 8088 is just a lower-cost version of the 8086. The 8088 is identical to the 8086 with the exception of the external communications circuits, which are modified—restricted—to conform to an 8-bit design. With this hybrid chip, a systems designer could offer a system that could run 16-bit software (using the 16-bit internal registers) and have access to 1M of memory (because of the 20-bit address bus), and still keep the cost in line with the then-current 8-bit designs. The 8088 is referred to as a 16-bit processor because of the internal 16-bit-wide registers and data paths, even though the external data bus is only eight bits wide.

The 8088 is the microprocessor at the heart of all of IBM's PC- and XT-based computers. IBM originally selected this chip because of the cost issue. The 8088 enabled the original design team to put together the original IBM PC 5150-001 and sell it for $1,355. (This price was for a 16K system unit with no drives! A similarly configured Apple II system at that time cost around $1,600.)

The IBM PC and XT motherboards run the 8088 processor chip at a clock speed of 4.77 MHz. Contrast this speed to that of many clones on the market, which run their chips at sometimes more than double this rate by using faster versions of the 8086/88. The speed at which the processor operates has a direct effect on the speed of program execution. For more information about speed, see this chapter's section "Microprocessor Speed Ratings."

The PS/2 Models 25 and 30 use the 8086, which IBM previously had ignored. Many compatible systems, such as the COMPAQ Deskpro and the AT&T 6300, had been using the 8086 for some time. The 8086's improved communications capability gives it about a 20 percent improvement in throughput over an identical-speed (in MHz) 8088. This improvement is one reason that IBM can claim that the 8 MHz 8086-based Model 30 is 2 1/2 times faster than the 4.77 MHz 8088-based PC or XT, even though 8 MHz is not more than twice the clock speed.

80186 and 80188

The 80186 and 80188 have the same relationship to each other that the 8086 and 8088 have. The 80186 is a full 16-bit design; the 80188 is the hybrid chip that compromises the 16-bit design with an 8-bit external communications interface.

This pair of microprocessors is similar to the earlier 8086 and 8088 in other ways. The 80186 is just a slightly modified version of the 8086, with a few improvements and many built-in support functions that normally would require external chips. Compared CPU to CPU, the 80186 is almost exactly the same as the 8086, but the 8018X chips have many CPU support functions built in. The chips in the 8018X series effectively combine in a single chip 15 to 20 of the most common 808X series system components. This design can greatly reduce the total number of components in a computer design and offer the same levels of performance.

Although the 8018X chips help the systems designer who wants to reduce the component count in a system design, the chips place design restrictions on the final product. Using one of these chips to construct a system that is very compatible with the IBM PC seems to be difficult. The 186 and 188 incorporate some new instructions and capabilities—but not many when compared with the 286 and 386 chips. These slight differences seem to cause problems with the 186 and 188 when they're supposed to emulate the 86 and 88 chips. A few systems—and even a "turbo" board or two for the IBM PC and XT systems—have been built using these chips. Overall, however, systems designers in the IBM-compatible realm have overlooked the 80186 and 80188.

In addition to the compatibility problem, the chips didn't offer much performance improvement over the earlier 8086 and 8088, and the 80286 was a much better component to use. Also, the individual components the 8018X series was designed to replace had become inexpensive, which made the 8018X chips less attractive. In spite of these limitations, the 8018X chips have found a following among board designers for highly intelligent peripheral adapter cards, such as local area network adapters, because of the decrease in chips needed: The processors can fit easily on an adapter that plugs in to one of the slots of the motherboard.

8087

The 8087 chip, often called the NDP (numeric data processor), math coprocessor, or simply the math chip, is a coprocessor designed to perform math operations at many times the speed and accuracy of the main processor. The primary advantage of using this chip is the increased execution speed of a number-crunching program, such as a spreadsheet. Using the 8087 has several minor disadvantages, however, including software support, cost, power consumption, and heat production.

The primary disadvantage in installing the 8087 chip in a PC is that you notice speedup only with programs written to use this coprocessor, and then not for all operations. Only math-intensive programs—spreadsheets, statistical programs, CAD software, and engineering software—support the chip. Even then the effects vary from application to application, and support is limited to specific areas. Lotus 1-2-3, for example, which supports the coprocessor, does not actually use the coprocessor for more common operations such as addition, subtraction, multiplication, and division. Applications that do not usually use the 8087 at all include word processing programs, communications software, database programs, presentation-type graphics programs, and many more.

As a test, I developed two spreadsheets, each with 8,000 cells. The first spreadsheet had addition, subtraction, multiplication, and division tasks split evenly among the 8,000 cells. The second spreadsheet had 8,000 cells with formulas using SQRT, SIN, COS, and TAN calculations split among the cells. The results are surprising. This table shows the recalculation times:

	XT without 8087	XT with 8087
Sheet #1 (standard math)	21 seconds	21 seconds
Sheet #2 (high-level math)	195 seconds	21 seconds

This table shows that the addition of an 8087 to a standard IBM XT did nothing for the first spreadsheet but calculated the second sheet in almost 1/10 the time. Therefore, if your spreadsheets consist of nothing but addition, subtraction, multiplication, and division calculations, save your money. You will derive no benefit from the math chip. For a spreadsheet consisting of engineering types of calculations or business math in which high-level functions are used, however, the addition of the math chip might speed up your recalculations by as much as ten times. The instruction set and chip design were intended specifically for math calculations. The uneven effect of coprocessors is customary for most applications. You must decide whether the total performance benefits are worthwhile.

The 8087 chip can be fairly expensive, ranging from under $100 to about $150, depending on the maximum speed rating. Although $100 might sound like a lot of money for a single chip, the benefits can be valuable. Just remember to purchase the chip with the correct maximum-speed rating: greater than or equal to the actual speed at which your system will run the chip.

To find the actual speed at which your system will run the chip, look for the information in your technical-reference manual. I cannot stress enough the importance of good documentation.

The 8087 must always run at the same rate of speed as the main processor, whatever the speed. The reason is that the main CPU and the coprocessor must run in synchronization with each other. In an IBM XT, for example, the 8088 runs at 4.77 MHz, and so does the 8087. You must purchase an 8087 designed to run at this speed (4.77 MHz) or faster, or the chip will fail. To add a math chip to a system that uses an 8087 coprocessor, therefore, just purchase one that runs equal to or better than the speed of your system's CPU. To find the speed of the system's CPU, you can look at the technical specifications listed in Chapters 3 and 4, or you can look up the information in the system's technical-reference manual.

Systems that use the 80286 or 80386 do not run the CPU and math chip in synchronization. They are asynchronous, which means that the chips can run at different speeds. The 80287 math chip usually runs at two-thirds of that speed (as it does in the IBM AT), but that might not always be the case. Some systems might run them at the same speed. The PS/2 50 and 60, for example, run the 80287 at 10 MHz, the same speed as the 80286 CPU. Note that even though the 387 chips run asynchronously, most systems are designed such that they normally run at the same clock speed as the main CPU, unlike most 286/287 system designs.

Math chips are quite power-hungry because of the number of transistors included. A typical 8088 has only about 29,000 transistors on-board, but the 8087 has about 45,000. (Nearly all the 45,000 transistors are dedicated to math functions, which is the reason that the 8087 can perform math so well.) This figure translates to nearly double the calculating horsepower, as well as double the electrical power drain. In a heavily loaded PC, the 8087 could be the straw that breaks the camel's back: the power supply might be insufficient to operate under the increased load. The chip draws nearly one-half amp of current.

Another problem is the amount of heat generated—a healthy 3 watts of energy. This heat level can raise the chip temperature to more than 150 degrees Fahrenheit (158 degrees is the approved maximum temperature for most 8087s). For this reason, the chips are made of ceramic. The power and heat are not a problem in the XT or Portable because these systems are built to handle it. The PC, however, usually requires a higher-watt power supply to handle the load.

In spite of some of the drawbacks, most newer programs are being written to support the 8087 chip, and the prices are coming down. For different design reasons, the 8087 chip has much more effect on the speed of the PC and XT than the 80287 has on the AT. Installing an 8087 can extend the useful life of the PC or XT because the chip closes some of the performance gap between the PC- or XT-based computers and the AT-based computers. In short, the chip is an asset whenever the software supports it.

80286

The 80286 microprocessor is the CPU behind the IBM AT. This chip, manufactured by Intel and introduced in 1981, is in the same family as the 8088 used by the PC and the XT. When IBM developed the AT, it naturally selected the 80286 as the basis for the new system because the chip provided much compatibility with earlier systems. The 80286 is upwardly compatible with the 8086 and 8088, which means that software written for those chips should run on the 80286.

The 80286 has two modes of operation: real address mode and protected virtual address mode. The two modes are distinct enough from one another to make the 80286 resemble two different chips in one. In real mode, an 80286 acts essentially the way an 8086 chip would and is fully object-code-compatible with the 8086 (or 8088). A processor with *object-code compatibility* can run already compiled programs just as they are and execute every system instruction in the same manner as the 8086/88.

An 80286 chip in real mode is limited; it cannot perform any additional operations or use any extra features designed into the chip. The AT is run in real mode most of the time. PC DOS is limited to support for real mode only. Unfortunately, the power of the system therefore is greatly restricted. In real mode, the processor can address only 1M, the same amount of memory as the 8088. Because of this restriction, an AT running PC DOS is little more than an extremely fast PC. This capability might sound sufficient, but that is not the AT's destiny. Real mode was created so that much of the 8086- and 8088-based software could run with little or no modification until new software could be written to use the chip in protected mode.

In the protected mode of operation, the 80286 truly is something new. In this mode, the processor automatically maps 1 gigabyte (1,024M) of memory into a 16M physical address space. The 80286 also supports multitasking operation in the form of memory protection to isolate the operating system and ensure the safety of every task's programs and data. Programs run in protected areas of memory so that if one of the programs on a multiple-program system locks up or fails, the entire system doesn't need a reset or cold boot. What happens in one area of memory cannot affect the programs running in other areas.

In protected mode, a program "believes" that it has access to 1 gigabyte of memory. The 286 chip, however, can address only 16 megabytes of physical hardware memory. When a program calls for more memory than physically exists, the CPU swaps to disk some of the currently running code and enables the program to use the newly freed space. The program does not know about this swapping, and instead acts as though 1 gigabyte of actual memory exists. This *virtual memory* is controlled completely by the operating system and built-in hardware on the chip. Because of virtual memory, the size of programs under OS/2 or UNIX can grow to be extremely large, even though you never actually have more than 16M available. Programs that require a lot of swapping and virtual memory management run slowly, however, so most software manufacturers will still indicate that a certain amount of memory is needed to run their programs effectively. Because of swapping overhead, the more physical memory you can install, the faster systems running OS/2 or UNIX will run.

All the features of the 80286 in protected mode are attractive, but they generally are unavailable because PC DOS runs only in real mode. You might ask, "Why doesn't IBM and Microsoft rewrite DOS so that it runs in both real and protected modes?" They have! The result is called OS/2.

OS/2 1.X can run most old DOS programs just as they ran before, in real mode, and also can run a new breed of software in protected mode. In protected mode, OS/2 allows true software multitasking and access to the entire 1 gigabyte of virtual or 16M physical address space provided by the 286. Other operating systems, such as UNIX or XENIX, also support the AT in protected mode. OS/2 is not yet as popular as DOS has been, and not as many applications have been developed for protected mode OS/2.

80287

The 80287 numeric data processor works with the 80286 in the AT. This chip is much the same as the 8087 chip in a PC or XT, but you should notice some different considerations and circumstances. Because the AT has a healthy power supply and generous, thermostatically controlled fan cooling, for example, the heat and power problems mentioned when discussing the 8087 generally don't apply when discussing the 287.

The 80287 has basically the same internal-processing capabilities as the 8087, but its interface is modified to work with the 80286. The interface between the 80286 and 80287 is different from the one for the 8086 and 8087. The 80286 and 80287 don't run in synchronization as do the 8086 and 8087. Because of the use of an asynchronous interface, the 286 and 287 chips can run at different speeds, and the interface between them is not as efficient as with the 8086 and 8087. In most AT-class systems using an 80286 CPU, the 80286 internally divides the system clock by 2 to derive the processor clock, and the 80287 internally divides the system clock frequency by 3. For this reason, most AT-type computers run the 80287 at one-third the system clock rate, which is also two-thirds the clock speed of the 80286.

The 80287 math coprocessor has two clock input modes, controlled by the status of pin 39 on the 80287. If pin 39 is low (grounded), then the 80287 will run at the input clock frequency. If pin 39 is high, then the 80287 will divide the input clock frequency by 3. If a higher-performance 80287 is desired, the motherboard designer can use a separate oscillator to drive the 80287 at virtually any speed desired.

In an 8 MHz IBM AT Model 339, for example, a 16 MHz crystal-controlled system clock feeds the 80286 processor chip that internally divides the signal's frequency by 2 (8 MHz), which then is used as the processor clock. The 80287 math coprocessor internally divides the system clock's frequency by 3 (5.33 MHz), which then becomes the 80287 clock signal. Therefore, the 80286 runs at 8 MHz, and the 80287 runs at 5.33 MHz. Most AT-compatibles use this design, although the primary system clock (from which all of these frequencies are derived) in most compatibles is usually higher in speed than 16 MHz.

Note that other systems might be different. In an IBM XT Model 286 (an AT-type system), for example, the system clock runs at 12 MHz, divided by 2 inside the 80286, which runs at 6 MHz. To run the 80287, IBM takes a different route from the standard AT. The video-oscillator crystal, which is 14.31818 MHz, is used in combination with a separate 8284 clock generator that divides the frequency by 3 to get a 4.77 MHz signal, which is sent to the 80287. The 80287 in this case is set to run off the input frequency with no internal division. For the XT Model 286, therefore, the system clock is 12 MHz, the 286 clock is 6 MHz, and the 287 clock is 4.77 MHz. In a "normal" AT system with a 12 MHz system clock, the 287 clock would have been only 4.00 MHz, which is one of the reasons that the XT Model 286 is slightly faster than a "normal" AT.

PS/2 Models 50, 50 Z, and 60 use different circuitry. The result is that the 286 and 287 both run at the same 10 MHz frequency in these systems. The PS/2 Model 25-286 and 30-286, however, follow the standard AT-type design in which the 286 runs at 10 MHz and the 287 runs at 6.67 MHz. As you can see, the motherboard designer determines all these specifications; if you want to know specific information about your system, look in the technical-reference manual for the system. Table 7.6 shows 80286 and 80287 clock speeds (in MHz) for most AT-type systems.

Table 7.6 80286 and 80287 Clock Speeds for Standard AT-Type Systems

System clock	80286 clock	80287 clock
12.00	6.00	4.00
16.00	8.00	5.33
20.00	10.00	6.67
24.00	12.00	8.00
32.00	16.00	10.67

Imagine this scenario: Two competitive users from a company have computers. One user has an IBM XT, and another has an AT (6 MHz). Both use 1-2-3 as their primary application. The AT user delights in being able to out-calculate the XT user by a factor of three times. The XT user wants to get the faster AT system but instead purchases an 8087 math chip for $100 and installs it. The XT user then finds that the XT calculates many spreadsheets ten times faster than before, or more than three times faster than the AT. This feat frustrates the AT user, who thought that the AT was a faster system. The AT user therefore purchases an 80287 for $100 and discovers that the AT is equal in speed to the XT for many sheet recalculations. In a few situations, however, the XT still outruns the AT.

The AT user then wants to know why the 80287 chip, which costs twice as much as the equivalent chip for the XT, did not make the AT "superior" to the XT by any significant margin for spreadsheet recalculations. (For any other "normal" processing—processing that does not involve or use the math functions—the AT still holds its superiority in speed.)

The answer is in the 80287 chip. Because it has the same math unit internally as the 8087 chip, at equal clock rates they should perform the same. The original 80287 is not "better" than the 8087 in any real way, unlike the superiority of the 80286 to the 8086 or 8088. The 80287 in the 6 MHz AT runs at only 4 MHz, and the interface between the 80286 and 80287 is asynchronous, not synchronous as is the 8088- or 8086-to-8087 interface. Because of these elements, the performance gain in most AT systems from adding the coprocessor is overall much less substantial than the same type of upgrade for the PC- or XT-type systems.

How can you improve this differential in performance gain? Because the 80286 and the 80287 run asynchronously, the clock signal that drives the 287 might come from another source, which might run the chip at any speed. PS/2 systems have circuitry that enables both processors in the Models 50, 50 Z, and 60 to run at 10 MHz.

Some companies that sell coprocessor chips have designed a simple speedup circuit that includes a crystal and an 8284 clock generator chip, all mounted on a special socket. This special socket is plugged into your 287 socket, and then the 287 is plugged in on top of the special socket. These small circuit boards (which might not be much bigger than a single socket) sometimes are called *daughterboards*. Because the crystal and clock generator then are separate from the motherboard circuitry, the daughterboard can run the 80287 at any speed you want, up to the maximum rating of the chip.

You could, for example, add an 80287-10 to your old 6 MHz AT and run the 287 at 10 MHz with one of these daughterboards; without the daughterboard, the chip would run at only 4 MHz. The boards are available from any of the math coprocessor chip vendors, such as MicroWay or Hauppauge. I highly recommend their use if you run math-intensive programs because the chip vendors usually bundle the board in "free" if you buy a higher-speed (more expensive) 80287 chip. Remember that this type of speedup cannot apply to systems that use 8087 or 80387 chips because these systems run those chips at the same speed as the main processor. In those systems, the math coprocessor always must run at exactly the same speed as the main CPU.

The only way to know for sure at what speeds your 287 processor will run is to consult your system's technical-reference manual. To take advantage of the asynchronous clocking between the 286 and 287, many math-chip vendors have designed small daughterboards that fit between the 287 chip and socket and supply a new clock signal for the chip to use. With this sort of mechanism, you can run the math chip at speeds as much as 8, 10, or 12 MHz or more. You can decide at what speed the math chip should run without affecting the rest of the system in any way.

A newer variation on the 80287 has been introduced by Intel, called the 287 XL and XLT. In fact, the original 287 has been discontinued and only the 287 XL and XLT are available today. The XL version is designed as a replacement for the standard 287 math coprocessor. The XLT version is functionally identical to the XL but has a PLCC (plastic leadless chip carrier) case, which is required by some laptop systems. These XL chips are completely redesigned and are patterned after the 387 instead of the 8087. The XL chips consume much less power than the original 287 chips because they are constructed with CMOS (Complimentary Metal-Oxide Semiconductor) technology. The XL chips perform about 20 percent faster than the original 287 at any given clock rate due to their improved design. The design improvements also extend to the instruction set, which includes 387 trigonometric functions not found in the regular 287 coprocessors. The XL chips are offered in one speed rating only, which is 12.5 MHz. They also can be run at lower speeds.

Because the XL chips are designed after the 387 math chips, you should note that many older diagnostics programs will incorrectly identify the XL chips. Some diagnostics will simply indicate that the 287 XL is a 387, and other diagnostics may incorrectly fail the math coprocessor tests if a 287 XL is installed. Intel provides a special diagnostics program called CHKCOP (which stands for CHecK COProcessor) that can test all of its math coprocessors. This program can be obtained on disk from Intel's customer support department or can be downloaded directly from the Intel BBS (503-645-6275).

If you decide, after considering all these issues, to invest in a 287 chip, note that only the XL or XLT versions are available now, and they are rated for up to 12.5 MHz operation. Adding the 287 to an AT is a good idea if the software you use supports the chip. You also should consider using one of the math coprocessor speedup daughterboards, which will run the newer XL chips at the maximum 12 MHz rating regardless of your system's clock speed. Otherwise, the benefits may not be enough to justify the cost.

80386DX, SX, SL, and SLC

The Intel 80386 is a full 32-bit processor optimized for high-speed operation and multitasking operating systems. The 80386 originally caused quite a stir in the PC industry because of the performance levels it brought to a desktop system. Introduced by Intel in 1985, the chip didn't appear in commercial PC-type systems until late 1986 and 1987. The chip debuted in the COMPAQ Deskpro 386 and several other IBM AT clones, and finally in an IBM system: the PS/2 Model 80. Since then, IBM has introduced several other systems that also use the 386 chip. Compared with 8088 and 80286 systems, the 386 chip offers staggering performance in almost all areas of operation. But performance isn't the only issue here. This chip has other capabilities that should get your attention.

The 386 can execute the same instructions as a 286 and an 8086/8088 in fewer clock cycles. The 386 also can switch to and from protected mode under software control without resetting the system, which saves an enormous amount of time. (The 286 cannot switch from protected mode.) The 386 can address 4 gigabytes of physical memory and make software act as though 64 terabytes of memory exists through the built-in virtual memory manager. The 386 has a new mode, called virtual real mode, that can enable several real-mode sessions to run simultaneously under a manager.

Probably the most exciting feature of this chip (other than speed) is its available modes of operation:

- Real mode
- Protected mode
- Virtual real (sometimes called Virtual 86) mode

Real mode is an "8086-compatible" mode just like that of the 286 chip. The 386 running in real mode can run unmodified 8086-type software. A 386 system running in this mode is acting as a "turbo PC." PC DOS and any software written to run under DOS need this mode to run. OS/2 enables DOS programs to run in this mode, but only one program at a time. A program running in this mode has access to a maximum of 1M of memory.

Protected mode is fully compatible with the 286 chip's protected mode. Many people call this mode of operation the chip's "native mode" because an advanced operating system, such as OS/2, runs in protected mode. In 386 protected mode, Intel extended the memory-addressing capabilities with a new memory-management unit (MMU) that allows highly sophisticated memory paging and program switching. Because these features are added as true extensions of the 286 type of MMU, the 386 remains fully compatible with the 286 at a system-code level.

Virtual real mode is entirely new. In this mode, the processor can run with hardware memory protection while simulating an 8086's real-mode operation. Multiple copies of PC DOS and other operating systems therefore can run simultaneously on this processor, each in a protected area of memory and oblivious to the others. If the programs in one segment crash, the rest of the system is protected. Software commands can "reboot" the blown partition. A PC with a 386 has the capability therefore to "become" multiple PCs under software control.

These capabilities have become realities under the control of specialized operating systems such as Windows and OS/2 2.X. Under Windows, a 386-based system can run a copy of PC DOS with an application in each window. Each window allows access to 1M of memory and acts as though it were a window on a stand-alone PC. Because each window's applications also run simultaneously or even truly multitask, all the programs run simultaneously and no task switching is done with software: All the multitasking capability is in the hardware instead. OS/2 can exploit these features even further than Windows. OS/2 2.X can manage the operation of 386 protected mode and virtual real modes simultaneously. This means that you can run native OS/2 programs as well as multitask several DOS real mode applications. In fact, OS/2 also can run any Windows software. These capabilities aren't possible with lesser processors such as the 286.

Because the 386 is a full 32-bit processor, the chip has 32-bit internal registers, a 32-bit internal data bus, and a 32-bit external data bus. The chip has an on-board memory-management unit (MMU) that enables a

(32-bit) 4-gigabyte physical address space and a (46-bit) 64-terabyte virtual memory space. The 386 sports 275,000 transistors in a very-large-scale-integrated (VLSI) circuit. The chip, which comes in a 132-pin package, draws approximately 400 milliamperes (ma)—less power than even the 8086. This characteristic is caused by the chip's construction in Complementary Metal-Oxide Semiconductor (CMOS) materials. CMOS design enables devices to consume extremely low levels of power.

Some special versions of the 386 are available. One is the 386SX. This chip was code-named the "P9" chip during its development and received much press. The chip's SX version bears the same relationship to the standard 386 as the 8088 does to the 8086. In other words, the 386SX is restricted in communications to using only a 16-bit external interface, even though all the internals are the same as in the standard 386. The 386SX was designed as a low-cost alternative for systems designers looking for 386 capabilities with 286-system pricing.

In addition to the 16-bit external interface, another area of restriction is that the 386SX uses only a 24-bit memory-addressing scheme rather than the full 32-bit scheme implemented in the standard 386. The SX therefore can address only a maximum of 16M of physical memory rather than the 4 gigabytes of physical memory the 386 normally can address. This limit isn't a problem for most current systems because they really cannot utilize memory beyond 16M. Most system architecture doesn't allow direct memory access (DMA) transfers to or from memory beyond the 16M boundary even if the system could accept the memory.

One often-heard fallacy about the 386SX is that you can plug one into a 286 system and give the system 386 capabilities—not completely true. The new SX chip is not pin-compatible with the 286 and does not plug into the same socket. Although several upgrade products have been designed to adapt the chip to a 286 system, much of the performance gain from changing from 286 to 386 architecture would be lost because of the restricted 16-bit interface to memory and peripherals. The bottom line is that a 16 MHz 386SX is not faster than a 16 MHz 286, but does offer improved memory-management capabilities. The capability to run 386-specific software is another important advantage that the 386SX has over any 286 or older designs. The 386SX chip has made its mark in new systems designs, signaling the end of the 286 because of the superior memory-management unit and the extra virtual 8086 mode that the 286 does not have.

A variation on the 386SX chip is the 386SL. This low-power CPU is designed for laptop systems where low power consumption is needed. The SL chips offer special power-management features which are important to systems that run on batteries. The SL chip offers several "sleep" modes that conserve power. These chips also include an extended architecture that includes a System Management Interrupt (SMI), which allows access to the power-management features. Also included in the SL chips is special support for LIM expanded memory functions and a cache controller. The cache controller is designed to control a 16K to 64K processor cache, which must be provided externally to the processor. These extra functions account for the higher transistor count (855,000 transistors) in the SL chips compared to even the 386DX processor (275,000 transistors).

Intel also has introduced a special companion to the 386SL chip, called the 82360SL I/O subsystem. The 82360SL provides many common peripheral functions, such as serial and parallel ports, a direct memory access (DMA) controller, interrupt controller, and power-management logic for the 386SL processor. This one chip subsystem works with the processor to provide an ideal solution for portable or laptop systems in which small size and low power consumption are important.

Another variation on the original 386SX is the IBM 386SLC. This IBM enhanced chip adds some of the features of the 486, such as the 8K cache, to result in a chip that performs nearly as well as a 486SX for much lower cost. In fact, IBM states that the SLC chip is as much as 80 percent faster than the standard SX chip, which allows a 20 MHz 386SLC to outperform even 33 MHz 386DX systems. This chip was first available in the PS/2 Model 57 and now can be found in several other PS/2 systems. The design and manufacturing of this chip are possible because IBM has fully licensed Intel's processor designs, giving it the capability to legally produce (and modify) 386 chips. Currently, no other manufacturer has this type of relationship with Intel. The 386 clone processors produced by other manufacturers have had to be reverse-engineered without Intel's blessing, usually resulting in a lawsuit from Intel.

Manufacturers such as AMD and Chips and Technologies have developed clones of the Intel 386DX and SX processors, despite the expected legal problems with Intel. These 386-compatible chips are available in speeds up to 40 MHz, while Intel produces 386 chips only up to 33 MHz. Intel will not offer the 386 faster than 33 MHz because that speed begins to tread on the performance domain of the lower-speed 486 processors. In fact, Intel has been cutting the prices on the 486 line to entice the industry to shift over to the 486 as the mainstream system. Because of the high performance and built-in upgradeability offered by the 486 line, this is probably where the industry will rapidly go. Unfortunately for Intel, other companies, such as AMD and Chips and Technologies, also are working on 486 clones.

80387DX and 80387SX

The 80387 coprocessor is a high-performance math chip designed specifically to work with the 386. Because Intel lagged behind in originally developing the 387 coprocessors, some early 386 systems were designed with a socket for a 287 coprocessor. Performance levels associated with that union, however, leave much to be desired. Although the 387 chip runs asynchronously with the 386, it normally runs at the same clock speed as the 386. The 387 coprocessor has two basic designs: The 387DX coprocessor is designed to work with the 386DX processor, and the 387SX coprocessor is designed to work with the 386SX, SL, or SLC processors. All 387 chips are constructed using a low-power-consumption CMOS design.

Originally, Intel offered several different speed versions of the 387DX coprocessor. When Intel designed the 33 MHz version, it decided that a whole new mask was required. The *mask* is the photographic blueprint of the processor and is used to etch the intricate signal pathways into a silicon chip. To reliably achieve the higher speed, a smaller mask was required to reduce the lengths of the signal pathways in the chip. Intel reduced the feature size from 1.5 microns to 1 micron. This action reduced the size of the actual silicon chip by 50 percent. In addition to reducing the size, other design improvements were engineered into the new mask, resulting in an improvement in processing efficiency of 20 percent. The 33 MHz version therefore would outperform other versions even at slower clock rates.

At the time, I was recommending that my clients purchase the 33 MHz version of the 387DX, even if it was for a 20 MHz application, because this chip would run 20 percent faster than a 20 MHz-rated 387. As of October 1990, however, Intel upgraded the entire 387DX line to the improved mask, resulting in a 20 percent performance boost across the board. You can easily identify these improved 387DX coprocessors by looking at the 10-digit code under the "387" part number. The older (slower) chips begin this line with the letter S, and the improved (faster) chips do not begin this line with an S. More recently, Intel has discontinued all 387DX processors, except the 33 MHz version, which of course always used the new design. Remember that even though the chip is rated for 33 MHz, it runs at any lower speeds.

The 387SX coprocessors are designed to work specifically with the 386SX, SL, or SLC processors. All versions of the 387SX use the improved mask design. When you are selecting a 387SX for your system, be sure that you purchase one rated at a speed equal to or higher than your system will run. Currently, 387SX chips are available from Intel at speeds up to 25 MHz.

Installing a 387DX is easy, but you must be careful to orient the chip in its socket properly, or the chip will be destroyed. The most common cause for burned pins on the 387DX is incorrect installation. In many systems, the 387DX is oriented differently from other large chips. Carefully follow the manufacturer's installation instructions to avoid damaging the 387DX. Intel's warranty doesn't cover chips that are installed incorrectly.

Several manufacturers have developed clones of the Intel 387 coprocessors. Some of these were touted as being faster than the original Intel chips, but they may not be faster than the newer Intel 387DX or 387SX coprocessors with the improved mask design. Intel also has significantly reduced the prices on its own coprocessors, which means that the clones are usually the same price as the Intel version. Unless the compatible chips can offer far greater performance at a lower price than Intel, be wary of compatibility problems. Note that the general compatibility record for these clone chips has been very good.

When the 387s were first introduced, the 33 MHz 387DX chips listed for more than $2,000! Today, the list price for that chip is just under $200, with street prices even lower. This cost is so low that this upgrade should be considered by many individuals. If the software you run supports the chip, the performance gains can be very impressive.

Weitek Coprocessors

In 1981, several Intel engineers formed Weitek Corporation. Weitek has developed math coprocessors for a number of systems, including those based on Motorola processor designs. Intel originally contacted Weitek to develop a math coprocessor for the Intel 386 CPU because Intel was behind in its own development of a 387 math coprocessor. The result was the Weitek 1167, which was a custom math coprocessor that uses a proprietary Weitek instruction set, and which is not compatible with the Intel 387. The Weitek 1167 was not a single chip, but instead was a daughterboard consisting of several chip elements that would plug into a special 112-pin Weitek socket. This daughterboard included a socket for an Intel 387 coprocessor so that a system could have both coprocessors installed, allowing software that ran either Weitek or Intel math instructions to work. The 1167 was replaced in April 1988 by a single chip version, called the 3167. Weitek also introduced the 4167 for 486 systems in November 1989.

To use the Weitek processors, your system needs to have the required socket, which is incompatible with the 387 math coprocessor or 486SX processor enhancement sockets. Many computers contain a square socket for a Weitek math coprocessor. This socket has three rows of holes on all four sides. In many computers, such as the COMPAQ 386, the inner two rows of pins are compatible with the Intel 387. This gives you the option of using a 387DX or the Weitek math coprocessor. If you want to install a 387DX in the Weitek socket, however, you must use *extreme caution* to orient the chip correctly; otherwise, you could damage both the computer and the 387DX. Read your technical-reference documentation to determine the correct procedure for installing the

387DX in your computer. Some computers use the Weitek socket but *do not* support the 387DX, such as the Tandy 4000. Contact your computer manufacturer or dealer for more specific information.

Unfortunately, even if you have the socket for the Weitek processor, your software probably does not support it. One problem is that the Weitek coprocessors require the 386 to run in protected mode. Because DOS programs run in real mode, you cannot use the Weitek without a special program called a DOS extender. Only a handful of applications support these coprocessors, and they are mostly high-end scientific or CAD programs.

Even if a program does support the Weitek processors specifically, it will almost always support the Intel coprocessors as well. With the performance improvements Intel has been making with respect to mask redesign and efficiency upgrades, the Weitek processors do not really offer much of a performance advantage. The Intel 387 supports basic math (addition, subtraction, multiplication, and division), exponential, logarithmic, and trigonometric functions, and can perform these operations much more quickly than the 386. Because all math functions can be processed by the 387, this leaves the 386 free to perform other system operations until the math coprocessor returns its result. This coprocessing gives the Intel 387 its overall advantage. The Weitek coprocessors perform basic math functions faster than the 387, but basic math is all they can do. They cannot process higher math functions like the 387, which means that the 386 must perform the higher math functions. Because the 386 is much slower than the 387 in performing higher math functions, the calculations will take longer and other system operations must either wait or interrupt the calculation in progress.

Before purchasing one of the Weitek coprocessors, you first should determine whether your software will support them, and then contact the software company to determine whether the Weitek really has a performance advantage over the more standard Intel coprocessors.

80486 and Beyond

The Intel 80486 microprocessor was introduced in late 1989, and systems using this chip appeared during 1990. The original chip has grown into a family of itself, with several different versions available. This chip has two main features over the earlier processors: integration and upgradeability. The 486 integrates functions such as the math coprocessor, cache controller, and cache memory right into the chip. The 486 also has been designed with upgradeability in mind, with double-speed "overdrive" upgrades as well as math coprocessor and external cache upgrades.

The 486 processor is fabricated using low-power CMOS technology. It has the same register and data-bus dimensions as the 386DX processor: a 32-bit internal-register size, a 32-bit external data bus, and a 32-bit address bus. The standard chip contains 1.2 million transistors on a piece of silicon no larger than your thumbnail—more than four times the number of components on the 386 processors and a good indication of the chip's power.

The standard 486DX contains a processing unit, a built-in math coprocessor, a memory-management unit, and an 8K internal RAM cache system. This cache is one of the reasons that the 486 offers approximately double the performance of the older 386 systems at the same clock rate. This means that a 20 MHz 486 will perform about as well as a 40 MHz 386 system, and the faster 486s are way beyond any 386 in performance. The 486 is fully compatible with previous Intel processors such as the 386.

Since the introduction of the chip, the 486 family has grown, and several versions are available. Four primary versions of the 486 are shown in the following list:

486SX	486DX without math coprocessor
487SX	486SX plus math coprocessor
486DX	CPU with built-in math coprocessor
486 OverDrive	Double-speed CPU and math coprocessor

All these chips have the full 32-bit architecture and 8K built-in memory cache discussed earlier, but they differ in a few areas. The 486SX is designed to be a lower-cost version of the 486, and therefore does not incorporate the math coprocessor portion. What is hard to understand at first is that Intel does not have a provision for adding a math coprocessor to 486SX systems. In fact, there is no math coprocessor socket in any 486 system. If this sounds confusing, read on, because this brings us to the most important aspect of 486 design—upgradeability!

Perhaps you have seen Intel advertisements featuring a 486SX system with a neon "vacancy" sign pointing to an empty socket next to the CPU chip. Unfortunately, I don't think that these ads have transmitted the message properly, because few people I talk to really understand the implications presented by these ads. That socket next to the CPU in a 486SX system is not a math coprocessor socket, but instead is called a *processor enhancement socket*. In fact, most people do not understand that Intel does not offer a math coprocessor for 486SX systems—it offers a 487SX processor and math coprocessor chip for this socket. The 487SX is not really a math coprocessor, but instead is a complete 486SX processor with the built-in math coprocessor enabled. In other words, the 486SX is a regular 486DX with the math unit disabled, and the 487SX is a complete 486SX with the math unit enabled. So if you are thinking that the 487SX with math unit sounds exactly like the 486DX, then you are right! The only difference between a 487SX and a 486DX is the pinout, which renders them physically incompatible by design.

Therefore, if you add a 487SX to the processor enhancement socket of a 486SX system, the 487 completely shuts down the original 486SX, and the new processor takes over both CPU and math coprocessor functions. That is one of the reasons why the 487SX is so expensive; you are really buying more than you think.

So, just what is this processor enhancement socket really all about? Intel has finally announced a line of 486 OverDrive processors that will plug into this socket and double the system clock rate! This true one-chip upgrade doubles the CPU performance as well as adds the math coprocessor capability. These OverDrive processors essentially make the 487SX chip obsolete because they include the math coprocessor function as well as the double clock feature. These OverDrive processors will be available for 486SX systems in 16/33 MHz, 20/40 MHz, and 25/50 MHz versions and will enable anyone who purchases a low-cost 486SX system today to purchase a single chip that will double the system's performance at a later date. With the cost of the 486SX systems about equal to 386 systems that lack this upgrade feature, the 486SX will soon become the standard entry-level system.

486DX systems do not have this processor enhancement socket, but they are not out of the upgrade game. Intel has announced OverDrive DX processors that will replace the 486DX CPU directly. Although this sounds like a cleaner upgrade to me, something still bothers me about the SX systems, in which the original CPU has nothing to do after the upgrade is installed. Because the original CPU must be removed when you are installing the OverDrive upgrade in place of the original 486DX processor, the CPU probably will have to be returned for a "core charge." This also should help to keep down the price of the OverDrive upgrade. The 486DX OverDrive processors will be available in several speeds, including 25/50 MHz and 33/66 MHz versions. Imagine upgrading from 33 MHz to 66 MHz by simply changing one chip in the system! This will allow what was originally a 33 MHz system to outperform a 50 MHz system, unless Intel offers an OverDrive processor for the 50 MHz systems as well. Imagine a 50/100 MHz processor!

Another member of the 486 family, the 486SL chip, is basically an SX constructed in a low-power design. The SL chip is designed to be installed in laptop or notebook systems that run on batteries. The SL chips feature special power-management techniques such as sleep mode and clock throttling, to reduce power consumption when necessary.

Note All the chips in the 486 family include the internal 8K memory cache and cache controller—one reason that the chips are so much faster than the 386 processors. In general, a 486 chip is twice as fast as the equivalently rated 386 processor. Therefore, a 20 MHz 486SX is equal in speed to a 386 running at 40 MHz, and a 66 MHz OverDrive 486DX is approximately equal to a 132 MHz 386 chip! The next level of performance from Intel will be 586 chips running at 50 or 66 MHz, with four times the power of the 486.

The 486 processor family is designed for high performance because of the integration of formerly external devices such as cache controllers, cache memory, and math coprocessors. 486 systems also are designed for upgradeability. These systems can be upgraded by simple processor additions or swaps that can effectively double the speed of the system. Because of these features, I recommend the 486SX as the ideal entry-level system, especially in a business environment. Your investment will be protected in the future by a universally available, low-cost processor upgrade.

Microprocessor Speed Ratings

A common area of misunderstanding about microprocessors is their speed ratings. This section covers speed in general and then moves on to some specifics about different Intel-family processors.

A computer system's clock speed is measured as a frequency, usually expressed as a number of cycles per second. A crystal oscillator controls clock speeds using a small sliver of quartz in a small, tin container. As voltage is applied to the quartz, it begins to vibrate (oscillate) at a harmonic rate dictated by the shape and size of the crystal (sliver). The oscillations emanate from the crystal in the form of a current that alternates at the harmonic rate of the crystal. This alternating current is the clock signal. Because a typical computer system runs millions of these cycles per second, the abbreviation of megahertz, MHz, is used to measure speed. One hertz is equal to one cycle per second. One megahertz is 1,000,000 hertz.

Note The hertz was named for the German physicist Heinrich Rudolph Hertz, who in 1885 confirmed through experimentation the electromagnetic theory, which stated that light is a form of electromagnetic radiation and is propagated as waves.

A single cycle is the smallest element of time for the microprocessor, but not much can occur within a single cycle. Every action requires at least one cycle and usually multiple cycles. To transfer data to and from memory, for example, an 8086 chip needs four cycles plus wait states. (A wait state is a clock tick in which nothing happens to make sure that the microprocessor isn't getting ahead of the rest of the computer.) A 286 needs only two cycles plus wait states for the same transfer. As for executing instructions, most processor instructions take anywhere from 2 to 100 or more cycles to execute. One reason the 80386 is so fast is that it has an average instruction-execution time of 4.4 clock cycles. If two processors have the same cycling time, the processor that can execute instructions in fewer cycles is faster. For example, a 6 MHz 8086-based system is about half as fast as a 6 MHz 80286-based system, even though the clock rates are the same.

How can two different processors that run at exactly the same clock rate perform differently, with one running "faster" than the other? The answer is simple: efficiency. Here's an analogy: Suppose that you are comparing two engines. An engine has a crankshaft revolution, called a cycle. This cycling time is measured in revolutions per minute (RPM). If you have two engines that run the same maximum RPM, the engines should run the car at the same speed, right?

Wrong! Suppose that you're shopping for a fast sports car, and you decide to compare the Mazda Miata and the Chevrolet Corvette. You stop first at the Mazda dealership and look at the Miata. You ask the dealer, "What's the redline on the engine?" The dealer tells you that the Miata has a 4-cylinder engine that redlines at 6,500 RPM. You are impressed with the high RPM rating, so you record the information and go on to see the Chevrolet dealer, who steers you toward a new Corvette model. You ask the same question about engine redline, and the dealer tells you that the Corvette has a V-8 engine that redlines at 5,700 RPM. You now figure that because the Mazda engine turns 6,500 RPM, it will propel that car much faster than the Corvette, whose engine can turn only 5,700 RPM. Although a simplistic comparison of engine maximum RPM ratings shows the Miata to be faster, road tests show exactly the opposite. In fact, road tests show that the Corvette is a faster vehicle by a wide margin. You can see that comparing two vehicles' performance based solely on engine redline is inaccurate. You would never make such a comparison because you know that many more factors than just engine redline are involved in determining vehicle speed and acceleration capability.

Unfortunately, we often make the same type of poor comparison in evaluating computers. Using engine RPM to compare how fast two cars can run is similar to using MHz to compare how "fast" two computers can run. A better specification to use when you are comparing the two vehicles would be engine horsepower, a measurement of the amount of "work" that each engine can perform. Of course, this would then have to be adjusted for the weight of the vehicle, the coefficient of drag, drive-line gearing, parasitic losses, and so on. In effect, too many other variables are involved for any sort of simplistic paper comparison to be made, even if you first picked a more meaningful specification to compare than engine redline. The best way to evaluate which of the two vehicles is faster is through road testing. In a computer, this would be equivalent to taking some of your software and running benchmarks or comparative performance tests.

The big V-8 engine in the Corvette does more "work" in each crankshaft revolution (or cycle) than the 4-cylinder engine in the Mazda. In the same manner, an 80286 can perform much more "work" in a single CPU cycle than an 8088: it's simply more efficient. The 386 is even better; it is about four times more efficient than the 8088 in instruction execution. Although an 8088 requires nearly 20 cycles for the average processor instruction to execute, the same average instruction takes only four cycles on a 386 chip. Combine that with a higher clock rate and you know why a 16 MHz 386 system is about ten times faster than a 4.77 MHz 8088-based system. The 486 is about twice as efficient as the 386 due primarily to an on-chip memory cache. In essence, a 50 MHz 486 would perform approximately equal to a 100 MHz 386. So as you can see, you must be careful in comparing MHz to MHz when two different systems are involved, because much more is involved in total system performance.

Clock speed is a function of a system's design and usually is controlled by an oscillator, in turn controlled by a quartz crystal. Typically, you divide the crystal-oscillation frequency by some amount to obtain the processor frequency. The divisor amount is determined by the original design of the processor (Intel), by related support chips, and also by how the motherboard was designed to use these chips together as a system. For example, in IBM's PC and XT systems, the main crystal frequency is 14.31818 MHz, divided by 3 by an 8284 clock generator chip to obtain a 4.77 MHz processor clock speed. In an IBM AT system, the crystal speeds are either 12.00 or 16.00 MHz, divided by 2 internally inside the 80286 in a 6.00 or 8.00 MHz processor clock speed, respectively.

If all other variables, such as the type of processor, number of wait states (empty cycles) added to memory accesses, width of the data bus, and so on are equal, you can compare two systems by their respective clock rates. Be careful with this type of comparison, however, because unknown variables, such as the number of wait states, often can influence the speed of a particular system and cause the unit with the lower clock rate to run faster than you expect, or likewise cause a system with a numerically higher clock rate to run slower than it "should." In particular, the construction and design of the memory subsystem can have an enormous impact on a system's final execution speed.

In building a processor, a manufacturer tests it for operation at different speeds, temperatures, and pressures. After the processor is tested, it receives a stamp indicating the maximum safe speed at which the unit will operate under the wide variation of temperatures and pressures encountered in normal operation. The rating system usually is simple. For example, if you remove the lid of an IBM PS/2 Model 50, you can see markings on the processor that look like this:

```
80286-10
```

This number indicates that the chip is an 80286 that runs at a maximum operating speed of 10 MHz. The chip is acceptable for any application in which the chip runs at 10 MHz or less. If you have a system such as the AT Model 339 or Model 319, which uses an 80286-8, and the processor fails, you can replace the processor with an 80286 rated at 8 MHz or higher. The 80286-6, rated at only 6 MHz, is not suitable as a replacement because its maximum speed rating is less than the 8 MHz at which the AT runs the chip.

Sometimes the markings don't indicate the actual speed. In the 8086, for example, a "-3" translates to 6 MHz operation. Table 7.7 lists the available microprocessors and coprocessors and the manufacturers' markings and corresponding clock rates.

A disturbing practice you may occasionally find is the sale of systems with substandard speed-rated components, especially microprocessors. The microprocessor is probably the single most expensive part in a system, and the lower-speed components often cost much less than their higher-speed counterparts. The price can even sometimes double when you move from one speed designation to another. Some manufacturers use the lower-rated part to save a substantial amount of money in the system manufacturing process.

You may wonder how a chip can even run at a greater speed without failing. Most chips, in fact, can run at a higher speed than they're rated. For example, 386-16 chips probably can run at 20 MHz in a normal environment. In checking that part, Intel tested at many temperature and pressure extremes as well as for an amount of time that enabled it to know that the component always will perform to the rated specification; the part is guaranteed to run at the rated speed. To offer such a guarantee means that the manufacturer must have some "cushion" in the design, a cushion that's lost when the part is run beyond the rated speed.

Table 7.7 Intel-Compatible Microprocessor Clock Rates

Processor	Type	Available maximum speed ratings (in MHz)											
		5	6	8	10	12	16	20	25	33	40	50	66
8086	CPU	✓	✓	✓	✓								
8088	CPU	✓	✓	✓	✓								
8087	NDP	✓	✓	✓	✓								
80286	CPU		✓	✓	✓	✓	✓	✓					
80287	NDP		✓	✓	✓	✓							
80287 XL	NDP				✓								
80287 XLT	NDP				✓								
80386 DX	CPU						✓	✓	✓	✓	✓		
80387 DX	NDP						✓	✓	✓	✓	✓		
80386 SX	CPU						✓	✓	✓				
80387 SX	NDP						✓	✓	✓				
80386 SL	CPU						✓	✓	✓				
80486 SX	CPU						✓	✓	✓				
80487 SX	CPU+NDP						✓	✓	✓				
80486 SL	CPU						✓	✓	✓				
80486 DX	CPU+NDP								✓	✓		✓	✓
486 OverDrive							✓	✓	✓	✓	✓	✓	✓
80586	CPU+NDP											✓	

CPU = Central processing unit
NDP = Numeric data processor (math coprocessor)
The OverDrive 486 processors will operate at double the clock rate of the system they are installed in. OverDrive 486 processors are available at 16/33MHz, 20/40MHz, 25/50MHz, and 33/66MHz.

Sometimes a manufacturer will hide the CPU under a heat sink, which prevents you from reading the rating printed on the chip. A *heat sink* is a metal device that draws heat away from an electronic device. Although having a heat sink is generally a good idea, Intel designs its chips to run at rated speed without heat sinking.

Testing Microprocessors

Microprocessor manufacturers have specialized equipment designed to test their own processors, but you have to settle for a little less. The best microprocessor testing device to which you have access is a known, functional system. You then can use the diagnostics available from IBM and other systems manufacturers to test the motherboard and processor functions. Most all systems now have processors mounted in a socket for easy replacement, because the processor is easily the single most expensive chip in the system.

Landmark offers specialized diagnostics software, called Service Diagnostics, written to test various microprocessors. Special versions are available for each processor in the Intel family. If you don't want to purchase this kind of software, you can perform a "quick and dirty" evaluation of your microprocessor by using the normal diagnostics program supplied with your system. Because the microprocessor is the brain in a system, most systems don't function with a defective one. If a system seems to have a dead motherboard, try replacing the microprocessor with one from another motherboard known to function properly. You might find that the processor in the original board is the culprit. If the system continues to "play dead," however, the problem obviously lies elsewhere.

Known Defective Chips

Your system occasionally can have problems—sometimes built-in at the factory—with bugs or design defects. These types of defects are rare, but some examples exist. Learning to recognize when you have one of these defects can be beneficial. Otherwise, strange problems can occur that might cause you to repair or replace other areas of the system unnecessarily. This section describes several known defects in system processors.

Early 8088s

A bug in some early 8088 microprocessors allowed interrupts to occur after a program changed the stack segment register. An interrupt usually is not allowed until the instruction after the one that changes the stack segment register. This subtle bug might cause problems in older systems. Most programmers have adopted coding procedures that work around the bug, but you have no guarantee that these procedures are in all software. Another problem is that the bug might affect chip operation with an 8087 math coprocessor. Approximately 200,000 IBM PC units (early units sold during 1981 and 1982) were manufactured with the defective chip.

Originally, in the 8087 math-coprocessor chip package, IBM always included an 8088 to be installed with the math chip, a practice which led to rumors that the parts were somehow "matched." The rumors were unfounded; IBM had just found an easy way to prevent machines using its 8087 chips from using the defective 8088. Because the cost of the chip was negligible, IBM included a bug-free 8088 and eliminated many potential service problems.

If you're unsure about the 8088 chip in a system, you can use diagnostics software to diagnose the problem, or you can identify a good or bad chip from its appearance. If you can open the unit to look at the 8088 chip, the manufacturer and copyright date printed on the chip provide clues to which version you have. An 8088 chip made by a manufacturer other than Intel is bug-free because Intel licensed the chip mask to other manufacturers so that they could produce the chips. The company began this licensing program after the bug already had been fixed. If a chip was manufactured by Intel, older (defective) parts have only a 1978 copyright date; newer (good) parts have 1978 and 1981 copyright dates, or some later year.

This marking on Intel 8088 chips indicates a chip with the interrupt bug:

```
8088
(c) INTEL 1978
```

The following markings on Intel 8088 chips indicate chips on which the bug is corrected:

```
8088
(c) INTEL '78 '81
```

```
8088

(c) INTEL '78 '83
```

Many diagnostics programs can identify the chip, but you can do it yourself with DEBUG, in DOS versions 2.0 and later. Just load DEBUG at the " - " prompt, and enter the commands shown in the following example. Note that XXXX indicates a segment address, which varies from system to system:

```
    -A 100
XXXX:0100]   MOV ES,AX
[XXXX:0102]   INC AX
[XXXX:0103]   NOP
[XXXX:0104
    -T
AX=0001 BX=0000 CX=0000 DX=0000 SP=FFEE BP=0000 SI=0000 DI=0000
DS=XXXX ES=0000 SS=XXXX CS=XXXX IP=0103 NV UP EI PL NZ NA PO NC
XXXX:0103 90          NOP
    -Q
```

The A 100 command tells DEBUG to assemble some instructions, of which three were then entered. The T command then executes a Trace, which should normally execute a single instruction, display the contents of the 8088's registers, and then stop. The Trace command usually executes only one instruction. However, when the instruction is an MOV to a segment register, as in this case, then the Trace command should execute the second instruction before interrupting the program. The third instruction is a dummy no-operation instruction.

Look at the value shown by DEBUG for the register AX. If AX is equal to 0000, then you have found a bugged microprocessor. If AX is 0001, then the second instruction in the test was executed properly and the chip is good. If the second instruction is executed, it increments the value of the AX register by 1.

In this example, after executing the Trace, AX equals 0001, which indicates a good chip. Note that if you try this on 286 or higher systems, the test will fail! This test is valid only for 8088s.

If you have an 8087 and a 4.77 MHz 8088 dated '78, or that fails this test, you can get a free replacement 8088. Contact Intel Customer Support for the replacement. Only 4.77-MHz 8088 chips may need to be upgraded. The 8088-2 and 8088-1 do not require replacement. You also can purchase a replacement 8088 for less than $10 from most chip houses. If your chip is bad or you suspect that it is, a replacement is cheap insurance.

Early 80386s

Some early 16 MHz Intel 386DX processors had a small bug you might encounter in troubleshooting what seems to be a software problem. The bug, apparently in the chip's 32-bit multiply routine, manifests itself only when you're running true 32-bit code, in a program such as OS/2 2.X, UNIX/386, or Windows in Enhanced mode. Some specialized 386 memory-management software systems also might invoke this subtle bug, but 16-bit operating systems, such as DOS and OS/2 1.X, probably will not.

The bug usually causes a system to lock up. Diagnosing this problem therefore can be difficult because the problem generally is intermittent and software-related. Running tests to find the bug is difficult; only Intel, with proper test equipment, can determine whether your chip is bugged. Some programs can diagnose the problem and identify a defective chip, but they cannot identify all defective chips. If a program indicates a bad chip, you certainly have a defective one; if the program passes the chip, you still might have a defective one.

Intel requested that its 386 customers return possibly defective chips for screening, but many vendors did not return them. Intel tested returned chips and replaced defective ones. The known defective chips later were sold to bargain liquidators or systems houses that wanted chips which would not run 32-bit code. The "known defective" chips were stamped with a *16-bit SW Only* logo, indicating that they were authorized to run only 16-bit software.

Chips that passed the test, and all subsequent chips produced as bug-free, were marked with a double sigma ($\Sigma\Sigma$) code, which indicates a good chip. 386DX chips not marked with either *16-bit SW Only* or the $\Sigma\Sigma$ designation have not been tested by Intel and might be defective. They look like this:

80386-16

Return these chips to the system manufacturer, who then will return the chip for a free replacement.

The following marking indicates that a chip has not yet been screened for the defect; it might be either good or bad:

80386-16
16-bit SW Only

This marking indicates that the chip has been tested and has the 32-bit multiply bug. The chip works with 16-bit software, such as DOS, but not with 32-bit, "386-specific" software such as Windows/386.

The following mark on a chip indicates that it has been tested as defect-free. This chip fulfills all the capabilities promised for the 80386.

```
80386-16
  ΣΣ
```

Because this problem was discovered and corrected before Intel officially added the DX to the part number, if you have a chip labeled as 80386DX or 386DX, it does not have this problem.

Another problem with the 386DX can be more specifically stated. When 386-based versions of XENIX or other UNIX implementations are run on a computer containing a 387DX math coprocessor, the computer will lock up under certain conditions. The problem won't occur in the DOS environment. For the lockup to occur, all of the following must happen simultaneously:

- Demand page virtual memory must be active

- A 387DX must be installed and in use

- DMA (direct memory access) must occur

- The 386 must be in a wait state

When all these conditions are true at the same instant, the 386DX ends up waiting for the 387DX and vice versa. Both processors will continue waiting for each other indefinitely. The problem lies within certain versions the 386DX, not with the 387DX math coprocessor.

Intel published this problem (Errata 21) immediately after it was discovered, to inform its OEM customers. At that point, it became the responsibility of each manufacturer to implement a fix in its hardware or software product. Some manufacturers, like COMPAQ and IBM, responded accordingly by modifying their motherboards to prevent these lockups from occurring.

The Errata 21 problem is present only in the B Stepping version of the 386DX and not the later D Stepping version. You can easily identify the D Stepping version of the 386DX by the letters DX in the part number— for example, 386DX-20. If the chip is labeled with DX as part of the part number, the chip does not have this problem.

Other Processor Problems

Some other problems with processors and math coprocessors are worth noting.

After removing a math coprocessor from an AT-type system, you must rerun your computer's SETUP program. Some AT-compatible SETUP programs do not properly unset the math coprocessor bit. If you receive a Power-On Self Test (POST) error message because the computer cannot find the math chip, you may have to temporarily unplug the battery from the system board. All SETUP information will be lost, so be sure to write down the hard drive type, floppy drive type, and memory and video configurations before unplugging the battery. This information is critical in correctly reconfiguring your computer.

Another strange problem occurs with some of the IBM PS/2 Model 80 systems when a 387DX is installed. Some of the 8580 Model 111 and 311 systems with math coprocessors installed may experience trouble with noise coming from the speaker. You may hear crackling or beeping noises while the computer is running. The following computers may have this problem:

- 8580 Model 111, with serial numbers below 6019000
- 8850 Model 311, with serial numbers below 6502022

If you are experiencing this problem and your system conforms to these models and serial numbers, you should contact IBM service for a motherboard replacement.

Memory

The CPU's (microprocessor's) architecture dictates a computer's memory capacity. The 8088 and 8086, with 20 address lines, can keep track of and reference as much as 1,024K (1M) of memory. Because the PC's hardware design reserves the top 384K of that memory for special purposes, you have access to 640K for your programs and data. The 286 and 386SX CPUs have 24 address lines; they can keep track of as much as 16M of memory. The 386DX, 486, and 586 CPUs, used in many newer systems, have a full set of 32 address lines; they can keep track of a staggering four gigabytes of memory.

Both the 80286 and 80386 emulate the 8086 by implementing a hardware operating mode called *real mode*. In real mode, all Intel processors—even the mighty 80386—are restricted to using only 1M, and the motherboard design still reserves 384K of that amount. Only in protected mode can the 80286 and 80386 use their maximum potential for memory addressing.

A limitation specific to 80386- or higher-based systems is that the motherboard designs don't fully use the memory beyond 16M. Some motherboards don't address even that memory. You can identify these systems by their lack of some type of special 32-bit slot. Even systems with a 32-bit slot don't enable direct memory access (DMA) transfers between devices and any memory greater than 16M; this situation limits severely the usefulness of memory in that region. This means that most of the time, the memory past 16M can be used for video memory extensions, ROM extensions, or as a scratchpad area for a program or adapter card.

Today you must deal with two primary types of memory architecture: the PC type and the AT type. The PC-type system has a 1M boundary, with 384K reserved by the hardware; the AT-type system has a 16M (16,384K) boundary, with 0.5M (512K) reserved by the hardware. The 1M and 16M figures serve as "walls" in memory capacity; the current motherboard and operating-system structure prevent your using greater amounts of memory, even if the system is capable (as with the 80386, for example).

The computer market offers several types of "fixes" for this problem, but most are limited solutions. Some involve software such as a new or different operating system. Other solutions involve specialized hardware, such as expanded memory adapters, or special memory-control and -management programs that take advantage of unique 80386 capabilities. For PCs and XTs, hardware design activity has produced a couple of techniques for "tricking" a system into using vast amounts of memory without affecting the microprocessor. These expanded memory boards are examined in more detail in Chapter 10.

The following sections discuss different types of motherboard memory, how memory is organized in a system, the system ROM, memory speed ratings, and ways to test memory.

Motherboard Memory

A system usually has some type of primary circuit board. As mentioned, most systems use a motherboard, which contains slots for expansion adapters. Other systems have adopted the backplane design, in which the primary circuit board is a card plugged into a slot. In each case, the primary circuit contains the system's processor and an amount of installed memory.

Accessing memory installed directly on a motherboard is faster on many systems than accessing memory through an expansion slot. Even without a speed advantage, you have an advantage in saving slots. The more memory you can get on the motherboard, the fewer memory-expansion adapters you need.

Most faster, 80386- and higher-based systems have a special 32-bit slot for adding memory to the system. Systems that do not have this slot, however, face a large speed reduction for memory addressed through a standard 16-bit slot. On some systems, such as the IBM Model 70, a special caching system on the motherboard controls memory access at an extremely high rate of speed. The caching systems contain high-speed memory that serves as a buffer between the microprocessor and memory. The cache acts as an intelligent buffer, which often can ensure that nearly all memory locations accessed by the processor are found in the cache and presented to the processor at high speed and with no wait states. Memory addresses read by the processor that are not in the cache must be accessed at a slower rate, with added wait states. Some processors, such as the 386SLC, 486, and 586, have a high-performance cache built right in to the processor itself. These systems may also have additional cache memory on the motherboard for even higher performance.

Physical Storage and Organization

Motherboard memory can be physically installed in several forms. Older systems conventionally used Dual In-line Pin (DIP) memory chips individually plugged into sockets or even soldered directly to a board. Most modern systems now use a memory package called a single in-line memory module (SIMM). These modules combine several chips on a small circuit board that is plugged into a retaining socket. This section will describe these devices and show how they are physically and logically organized in a system.

Memory Chips

Several types of memory chips have been used in PC system motherboards. Most of these chips are the single-bit-wide chips, available in several capacities:

16K by 1 Bit

These devices, used in the original IBM PC with a Type 1 motherboard, are quite small in capacity compared with the current standard. You won't find much demand for these chips except for owners of original IBM PC systems.

64K by 1 Bit

These chips were used in the standard IBM PC Type 2 motherboard and in the XT Type 1 and 2 motherboards. Many memory adapters, such as the popular vintage-AST 6-pack boards, use these chips also.

128K by 1 Bit

These chips, used in the IBM AT Type 1 motherboard, often were a strange physical combination of two 64K chips stacked on top of one another and soldered together. True single-chip versions were used also for storing the parity bits in the IBM XT 286.

256K by 1 Bit

These chips are popular in the majority of current motherboards and memory cards. The IBM XT Type 2 and IBM AT Type 2 motherboards, as well as most compatible systems, use these chips.

1,024K by 1 Bit

These 1-megabit chips are very popular in systems today because of the low cost of these chips. These chips are often used in single in-line memory modules (SIMMs) found in systems today. (See the following section for more information on SIMMs.)

4,096K by 1 Bit

Four-megabit chips have gained popularity recently and now are used in many compatible motherboards and memory cards. They are used primarily in the 4M and 8M SIMMs, and generally are not sold as individual chips.

16,384K by 1 Bit

Sixteen-megabit chips are new on the market. They are not yet popular but will probably find use in new, high-capacity SIMM modules. The use of these chips in SIMMs will allow unbelievable memory capacities in very little physical space.

Banks of Memory

DIP memory chips, as well as SIMMs, are allocated on the motherboard (and on memory cards) in banks. The banks usually correspond to the data-bus capacity of the system's microprocessor. In 8088-based systems, for example, memory banks are 8 data bits plus 1 parity bit or 9 bits (usually 9 chips) wide; in 8086, 286-, and 386SX-based systems, memory banks are 16 bits plus 2 parity bits or 18 bits (usually 18 chips) wide. 386DX and higher systems have memory banks that are 32 bits plus 4 parity bits or 36 bits wide. Most of these systems will use four 9-bit SIMMs or one 36-bit SIMM per bank.

You should know the bank layout and position on your motherboard and memory cards. This is important when you are adding memory to the system, as well as for troubleshooting and repair. Memory diagnostics report error locations by bank and bit addresses. You will need to locate the physical chip (or SIMM) location based on the numbers reported by a memory diagnostics program.

The IBM PC Type 2 and XT Type 1 motherboard contains 4 banks of memory labeled as Bank 0, 1, 2, and 3. Each bank uses nine 64K-by-1-bit chips. The total number of chips present is 4 times 9, or 36 chips, organized as shown in figure 7.1.

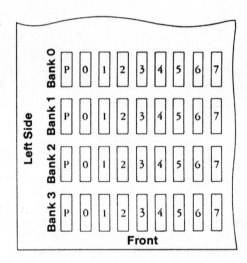

Fig. 7.1

Organization of memory on an IBM XT Type 1 motherboard showing four 9-bit Banks.

Courtesy of IBM Corporation.

This layout is used in several motherboards, including the Type 1 and 2 PC motherboards and the Type 1 and 2 XT motherboards. Most PC or XT clones also follow this same scheme. Note that the parity chip is the leftmost chip in each of the banks on the XT motherboard.

In an AT-type system with a 286 or 386SX processor, the memory is organized into larger banks of 18 chips, or in some cases two 9-bit SIMMs. The organization of the single bank of memory (Bank 0) on an IBM AT Type 2 motherboard is shown in figure 7.2.

In this application, the chips in a single bank are organized in two vertical columns rather than in rows. The IBM AT Type 1 motherboard is different, with two banks of 18 chips laid out horizontally and two rows per bank. The first bank (Bank 0) is toward the front of the system, which is opposite the orientation in the PC and XT. The physical orientation used on a particular motherboard or memory card is arbitrary and determined by the board's designers. Documentation covering your specific system or card will come in very handy. You can determine the layout of a given motherboard or adapter card through some simple testing. This testing takes time, however, and may not be convenient to perform—especially after you are having a problem with a system.

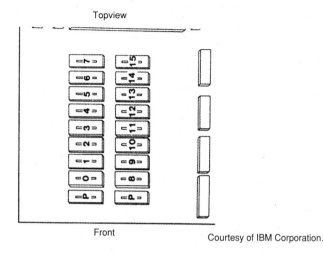

Topview

Front

Courtesy of IBM Corporation.

Fig. 7.2

Organization of memory on an IBM AT Type 2 motherboard showing a single 18-bit bank.

One-bit-wide chips used to be almost a universal standard among PC systems, but today many systems use 2-bit- or 4-bit-wide chips. Because the "wider" chips are more dense, you can assemble banks of memory with fewer chips. To construct a 16-bit bank (with parity) of 128K bytes with 128K-by-1-bit chips, for example, you need 18 chips. You could construct a similar 16-bit bank of 128K bytes, however, using eight 128K-by-2-bit chips and two additional 128K-by-1-bit chips for the parity bits.

As an alternative to individual memory chips, most modern systems have adopted the single in-line memory module (SIMM) for memory storage. For more information about SIMMs, see the section "Single In-line Memory Modules (SIMMs)."

Parity Checking

One standard IBM has set for the industry is that each 8-bit byte of memory storage is accompanied by an additional parity bit. The parity bit enables a system to have a built-in cross-check for the integrity of each byte in the system. IBM uses odd parity as a standard for its systems; as the eight individual bits in a byte are being stored, a special chip called a 74LS280 parity generator/checker on the motherboard (or memory card) evaluates the data bits by counting the total number of 1s. If an even number is counted, then a 1 is created by the parity generator/checker chip and stored as the ninth bit (parity bit) in the parity memory chip. This gives a total sum for all 9 bits, which is now an odd number. If the original sum of the 8 data bits was an odd number, then the parity bit created would be 0, keeping the 9-bit total sum as odd. You can see that the parity bit is always created such that the sum of all 9 bits (8 data bits plus 1 parity bit) is always an odd number. Here are some examples:

```
Bit:            Parity      0 1 2 3 4 5 6 7
Value:            0         1 0 1 1 0 0 1 1
```

In this example, because the total number of data bits with a value of 1 is an odd number (5), the parity bit must have a value of 0 to ensure an odd sum for all nine bits.

```
Bit:            Parity      0 1 2 3 4 5 6 7
Value:            1         0 0 1 1 0 0 1 1
```

In this example, because the total number of data bits with a value of 1 is an even number (4), the parity bit must have a value of 1 to force an odd sum for all nine bits.

When the system reads memory back from storage, the system checks the parity information. If a (9-bit) byte has an even number of bits with a value of 1, that byte must have an error. The system cannot tell which bit has changed, or if only a single bit has changed. If three bits changed, for example, the byte still flags a parity-check error; if two bits have changed, however, the bad byte passes unnoticed. When a parity-check error is detected, the motherboard parity-checking circuits generate a Non-Maskable Interrupt (NMI), which halts processing and diverts the system's attention to the error. The NMI causes a routine in the ROM to be executed. The routine clears the screen and then displays a message in the upper left corner of the screen. The exact message differs depending on the type of computer system. These examples show parity-check messages for three types of systems:

For the IBM PC: PARITY CHECK X

For the IBM XT: PARITY CHECK X
                                   YYYYY (Z)

For the IBM AT and late-model XT: PARITY CHECK X
                                   YYYYY

where X is 1 or 2:
    1 = Error occurred on the motherboard
    2 = Error occurred in an expansion slot

YYYYY represents a number from 00000 through FFFFF, which indicates, in hexadecimal notation, the byte in which the error has occurred

(Z) is (S) or (E):
    (S) = Parity error occurred in the system unit
    (E) = Parity error occurred in the expansion chassis

Note

An expansion chassis was a rare option IBM sold for the original PC and XT systems. This unit consisted of a backplane motherboard with eight slots, one of which contained a special extender/receiver card that was cabled to a similar extender/receiver card placed in the main system. Due to the extender/receiver cards in the main system and the expansion chassis, the net gain was six slots.

The third (and final) step is that the ROM parity-check routine halts the CPU. The system locks up and you must perform a hardware reset or power-off/on cycle to restart the system. Unfortunately, all unsaved work is lost in the process.

Most IBM-compatible systems do not halt the CPU and instead offer you a choice of either rebooting the system or continuing as though nothing happened. Additionally, these systems may display the parity error message in a different format from IBM, although the information presented is basically the same. For example, systems with the Phoenix BIOS display these messages:

```
Memory parity interrupt at YYYY:YYYY
Type (S)hut off NMI, Type (R)eboot, other keys to continue
```

or

```
I/O card parity interrupt at YYYY:YYYY
Type (S)hut off NMI, Type (R)eboot, other keys to continue
```

The first of these two messages indicates a motherboard parity error (Parity Check 1), and the second indicates an expansion-slot parity error (Parity Check 2). Notice that the address given for the memory error is in a segment:offset form rather than a straight linear address such as with IBM's message. The segment:offset address form still gives you the precise location of the error to a resolution of a single byte. Finally, you can see that you have three ways to proceed after viewing this error message. You can press S, which will shut off parity checking altogether and resume system operation at the point where the parity check first occurred. Pressing R would force the system to reboot, losing any unsaved work. Pressing any other key will cause the system to resume operation with further parity checking still enabled. If the problem reoccurs, it will likely cause another parity check interruption.

Although many compatibles allow you to continue processing after a parity check, and even allow for the disabling of further parity checking, this feature can be dangerous if misused. The idea is that you can save any unsaved work, but be careful how you do this. Remember, the parity check is telling you that memory has been corrupted. Do you want to save a potentially corrupt file over your last good one? Definitely not! Be sure that you save your work to a different file for safety. In fact, you should save only to floppy disks and avoid writing to the hard disk at all. After saving the work, you should determine the cause of the parity errors and repair the system. Unfortunately, you may be tempted to use the S option to shut off further parity checking and simply continue using the system as if nothing were wrong. Doing so resembles unscrewing the oil pressure warning indicator bulb in your car so that it does not bother you anymore! If a problem were to occur, you would no longer be notified. You can use the S option so long as your next actions are to save your work and then troubleshoot and repair the system.

IBM PS/2 systems have a slightly different way of communicating parity check errors than the older IBM systems. To indicate motherboard parity errors, the message would look like this:

```
110
YYYYY
```

To indicate parity errors from an expansion slot, the message would look like this:

```
111
YYYYY
```

In these messages, the YYYYY is the address of the parity error, as before. As with the older IBM systems, the system will be halted after these messages are displayed.

Chapter 14 explains how to use the memory error address numbers to help locate the defective component so that the system can be repaired.

Single In-line Memory Modules (SIMMs)

A SIMM is a tiny board with memory chips soldered to it. These small boards plug into special connectors on motherboards or memory cards. Because the individual memory chips are soldered to the SIMM, removing and replacing individual memory chips becomes unfeasible. Instead, you must remove and replace the entire SIMM if any part of it fails. In essence, the SIMM is treated as though it were one large "memory chip."

IBM-compatibles have basically two main types of SIMMs, with several subcategories. The two main types are 9-bit and 36-bit SIMMs. The 9-bit SIMMs are physically smaller than the 36-bit versions. Depending on just how much memory is contained on the SIMM, you will find chips on one or both sides. SIMMs for other types of computer systems that are not IBM-compatible may be slightly different. For example, Apple computers use either 8-bit or 32-bit SIMMs because Apple systems do not have parity-checked memory. Interestingly, you can use the IBM compatible 9-bit or 36-bit SIMMs to replace the 8-bit or 32-bit SIMMs in Apple systems, but you absolutely cannot use 8- or 32-bit SIMMs in IBM-compatible systems. If you must service both IBM and Apple systems, simply stock only the IBM-compatible SIMMs because you can use them in either type of system.

The following figures show both SIMM types. Figure 7.3 shows a typical 9-bit SIMM, and figure 7.4 shows a typical 36-bit SIMM. Note that the 9-bit SIMMs have 30 pins, and the 36-bit SIMMs have 72 pins. The pins are numbered from left to right and are connected through to both sides of the module. Note that all dimensions are in inches and millimeters (mm).

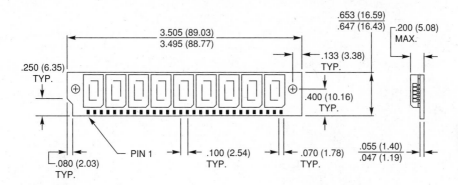

Fig. 7.3

A typical 9-bit (30-pin) SIMM.

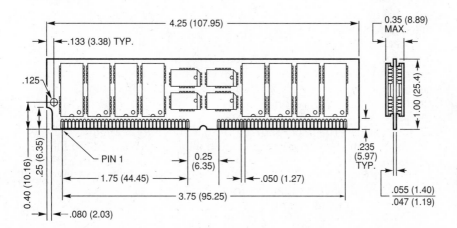

Fig. 7.4

A typical 36-bit (72-pin) SIMM.

A SIMM is extremely compact, considering the amount of memory it holds. SIMMs are available in several capacities, including the following:

9-bit SIMM capacities:

256K
1,024K (1M)
4,096K (4M)

36-bit SIMM capacities:

1,024K (1M)
2,048K (2M)
4,096K (4M)
8,192K (8M)
16,384K (16M)

Two main types of 9-bit SIMMs are available. Most compatibles use what many refer to as the "generic" type of SIMM, which has a standard pin configuration. IBM systems that use 9-bit SIMMs, starting with the XT-286 introduced in 1986, require a SIMM with a slightly modified pinout from what many other systems use. These are known as "IBM style" 9-bit SIMMs, and they differ from the generic ones by having different signals on five of the pins. You can modify a generic SIMM to work in the IBM systems, and vice versa, but purchasing the SIMM with the correct pinout to begin with is much easier. Be sure that you identify to the SIMM vendor which type you want when you are purchasing the 9-bit SIMMs. The 36-bit SIMMs do not have different pinouts to contend with, and are differentiated only by capacity and speed.

The 36-bit SIMMs are ideal for 386 and higher systems because they represent an entire bank of memory (32 data bits plus 4 parity bits) in these systems. This means that you can usually add or remove memory in single SIMM modules when you are configuring systems that use the 36-bit versions. The 9-bit SIMMs are very clumsy used in a system with a 32-bit memory architecture because these SIMMs must be added or removed in quantities of four to make up a complete bank. Even a 286 system would require two 9-bit SIMMs for a single bank of memory. Remember that a bank is the smallest amount of memory that can be addressed by the processor at one time, and usually corresponds to the data bus width of the processor. Note that some of the higher-end 486 systems use interleaved memory, which may require two 36-bit SIMMs to make up a single "bank" because memory accesses are alternated between the SIMMs to improve performance. The PS/2 Models 90 and 95 are examples of systems that use interleaved memory and require two 36-bit SIMMs for a single bank.

In addition to being available in different capacities, SIMMs also are found with different access time ratings just like stand-alone memory chips. The ratings vary from about 120ns (nanoseconds) on the slow side for SIMMs used in older 286-based systems, to 60 or 70ns SIMMs used in the fastest 486 systems. You cannot always replace a SIMM with a larger-capacity unit and expect it to work. For example, the IBM PS/2 Model 70-Axx or Bxx systems will accept 36-bit SIMMs of 1M or 2M capacity, which are 80ns or faster. Although an 80ns 4M SIMM is available, it will not work in these systems. The PS/2 Model 55 SX and 65 SX, however, will accept 1M, 2M, or 4M 36-bit SIMMs. A larger-capacity SIMM will work only if the motherboard has been designed to accept it in the first place. You should consult the technical-reference manual for your system to determine the correct capacity and speed to use.

SIMMs were designed to eliminate *chip creep*, which plagues systems with memory chips installed in sockets. Chip creep occurs when a chip works its way out of its socket, caused by the normal thermal cycling from powering a system on and off. Eventually, chip creep leads to poor contact between the chip leads and the socket, and memory errors and problems begin.

The original solution for chip creep was to solder all the memory chips to the printed circuit board. This approach, however, made chips difficult to replace. Also, because memory chips fail more frequently than most other types of chips, soldering chips to the board made the units hard to service.

The SIMM incorporates the best features of both socketed and soldered devices. The chips are soldered to the SIMM, but you can replace the socketed SIMM if necessary. This solution is a good one, but it can greatly increase the cost of repairing parts; rather than replace just one defective chip, you must replace what amounts to an entire bank. The PS/2 Model P75, for example, comes with two 4M SIMMs for a total of 8M of standard memory. If a single bit fails in this system, you must replace one of the two SIMMs, which currently list for $565 from IBM. Note that you can get these same 4M SIMMs for nearly half that price from third parties. The point is that this is certainly more expensive than replacing a single 256K chip. Of course, this system has about 10 times the memory and processing power of any system that might contain individual 256K chips. It would take 288 256K chips to equal what those two SIMMs contain. Troubleshooting a problem with two devices compared to 288 of them is certainly much easier, not to mention the reliability of the two SIMMs compared to 288 individual chips in sockets.

SIMMs are in nearly all systems on the market, including nearly all of IBM's PS/2 systems, the XT-286, many compatibles, and even the Apple Macintosh systems. Because a SIMM is not a proprietary memory system but an industry-standard device, you should be able to purchase one at most of the same places you purchase a normal memory chip. You will find some differences in pinouts and specifications other than speed and capacity between some SIMMs, so be sure that you obtain the correct SIMMs for your applications. In general, a SIMM is a much better alternative than fully soldered memory and definitely better than a board loaded with socketed chips.

Knowing the organization of memory in your systems, whether it is supplied via chips or SIMMs, is necessary when you need to diagnose defective memory. You should consult your technical-reference manual to determine the physical organization of memory for your system. Chapter 14 presents some helpful tips in determining this organization for any system.

Memory Organization

Systems designers have reserved for internal uses a certain portion of the maximum amount of memory in each system. The reserved memory is used for such things as graphics and ROM programs. The remaining memory, *user memory*, is the portion of memory in which an operating system loads itself and any applications programs. Table 7.8 lists the amount of memory available on different systems.

Table 7.8 Memory Allocation

System type	PC	AT
Maximum addressable memory (RAM)	1,024K	16,384K
Reserved memory		
Video memory	128K	128K
Adapter board ROM and RAM	192K	128K
Motherboard ROM	64K	128K
Duplicate of motherboard ROM	n/a	128K
Remaining RAM	640K	15,872K

Figure 7.5 shows how the real- and protected-mode memory space is allocated. The beginning of this memory-allocation graph shows memory

used by real mode, which is also the first megabyte of protected mode. The last part of the memory-allocation graph shows the last megabyte of protected-mode memory.

Use these guidelines when you refer to figure 7.5:

. = Program-accessible memory (user-installed RAM)
v = Video RAM
a = Adapter board ROM and special-purpose RAM
r = Motherboard ROM BIOS
b = IBM Cassette BASIC (would be "r" on Compatibles)
h = High Memory Area (HMA, allocated by HIMEM.SYS)

Video memory is a 128K portion of memory reserved for storing graphics and text material for display. The memory is located from memory address A0000 to BFFFF. Lower-resolution adapters might use only a portion of this video memory, but the higher-resolution EGA and VGA adapters use it all.

Adapter-board ROM and RAM space is allocated for different adapter cards that need a place for their on-board control software. Some network boards use the space for RAM to transfer data to and from the system. Expanded memory adapters that conform to the Lotus-Intel-Microsoft Expanded Memory Standard (LIM EMS) use 64K of this space for a bank-switching scheme to access the rest of the memory on the EMS adapter board.

Motherboard ROM space is just that: space for the motherboard-control program, sometimes called the basic input-output system (BIOS). On IBM systems only, the requisite Cassette BASIC interpreter also is located in this space. Note that this memory is duplicated at the end of the protected-mode space, because of the way in which switching from real to protected modes happens and the idiosyncrasies of the 80286 and 80386 processors.

The High Memory Area (HMA) is allocated by the DOS driver HIMEM.SYS. This driver allows real-mode programs running under DOS, or even DOS itself, to use the first 64K of extended memory to store programs or data. DOS 5.0 and higher versions use this area to store a portion of COMMAND.COM and the DOS buffers allocated in CONFIG.SYS.

The remaining extended memory is governed and controlled by HIMEM.SYS as Extended Memory Specification (XMS) memory. Protected mode programs that require access to this memory can have access in a controlled fashion and several protected mode programs can share use of this memory.

```
        Conventional (Base) Memory:
            :0---1---2---3---4---5---6---7---8---9---A---B---C---D---E---F---]
        000000:................................................................
        010000:................................................................
        020000:................................................................
        030000:................................................................
        040000:................................................................
        050000:................................................................
        060000:................................................................
        070000:................................................................
        080000:................................................................
        090000:................................................................
        Upper Memory Area (UMA):
        0A0000:vvvvvvvvvvvvvvvvvvvvvvvvvvvvvvvvvvvvvvvvvvvvvvvvvvvvvvvvvvvvvvvvv
        0B0000:vvvvvvvvvvvvvvvvvvvvvvvvvvvvvvvvvvvvvvvvvvvvvvvvvvvvvvvvvvvvvvvvvv
        0C0000:aaaaaaaaaaaaaaaaaaaaaaaaaaaaaaaaaaaaaaaaaaaaaaaaaaaaaaaaaaaaaaaaa
        0D0000:aaaaaaaaaaaaaaaaaaaaaaaaaaaaaaaaaaaaaaaaaaaaaaaaaaaaaaaaaaaaaaaaa
        0E0000:rrrrrrrrrrrrrrrrrrrrrrrrrrrrrrrrrrrrrrrrrrrrrrrrrrrrrrrrrrrrrrrrr
        0F0000:rrrrrrrrrrrrrrrrrrrrrrrrbbbbbbbbbbbbbbbbbbbbbbbbbbbbbbbbrrrrrrrr
        Extended Memory:
            :0---1---2---3---4---5---6---7---8---9---A---B---C---D---E---F---
        100000:hhhhhhhhhhhhhhhhhhhhhhhhhhhhhhhhhhhhhhhhhhhhhhhhhhhhhhhhhhhhhhhhh
        Extended Memory Specification (XMS) Memory:
        110000:................................................................
        120000:................................................................
        130000:................................................................
        140000:................................................................
        150000:................................................................
        160000:................................................................
        170000:................................................................
        180000:................................................................
        190000:................................................................
        1A0000:................................................................
        1B0000:................................................................
        1C0000:................................................................
        1D0000:................................................................
        1E0000:................................................................
        1F0000:................................................................
            :0---1---2---3---4---5---6---7---8---9---A---B---C---D---E---F---
        200000:................................................................
        210000:................................................................
        220000:................................................................
        230000:................................................................
        240000:................................................................
        250000:................................................................
        260000:................................................................
        E70000:................................................................
        E80000:................................................................
        E90000:................................................................
        EA0000:................................................................
        EB0000:................................................................
        EC0000:................................................................
        ED0000:................................................................
        EE0000:................................................................
        EF0000:................................................................
            :0---1---2---3---4---5---6---7---8---9---A---B---C---D---E---F---
        F00000:................................................................
        F10000:................................................................
        F20000:................................................................
        F30000:................................................................
        F40000:................................................................
        F50000:................................................................
        F60000:................................................................
        F70000:................................................................
        F80000:................................................................
        F90000:................................................................
        FA0000:................................................................
        FB0000:................................................................
        FC0000:................................................................
        FD0000:................................................................
        FE0000:rrrrrrrrrrrrrrrrrrrrrrrrrrrrrrrrrrrrrrrrrrrrrrrrrrrrrrrrrrrrrrrrr
        FF0000:rrrrrrrrrrrrrrrrrrrrrrrrbbbbbbbbbbbbbbbbbbbbbbbbbbbbbbbbrrrrrrrr
```

Fig. 7.5

16 megabyte memory map.

System ROM

The system ROM for each IBM computer contains three primary programs: the POST (Power-On Self Test), the basic input-output system (BIOS), and Cassette BASIC. Compatibles have the first two but lack Cassette BASIC. Placing a small essential set of software in ROM enables the computer to bootstrap itself automatically and to retain flexibility for easy future changes.

Over the years, the ROM in various PC models has undergone changes almost always associated with either a completely new system or a new motherboard design for an existing system. There are several reasons for these changes. The introduction of the XT, for example, gave IBM a good opportunity to fix a few things in the ROM and also add necessary new features, such as automatic support for a hard disk. IBM retrofitted many of the same changes into the PC's ROM at the same time.

Because an in-depth knowledge of the kinds of ROM is something a programmer might find useful, IBM makes the necessary information available in the technical-reference manuals sold for each system. A new ROM BIOS technical-reference manual covers all IBM systems in one book. Complete ROM listings (with comments) accompanied the earlier technical-reference manuals, but that specific information is not supplied in the later ones.

Certain things about ROM, however, are important to know. IBM has had more than 20 specifically different ROM BIOS programs for the PC and PS/2 families. Each one is different in some respects from all the others. Sometimes a single system has had different versions of ROM over the course of the system's availability. For example, at least three versions of the ROM existed for the PC, XT, and AT systems. Because a couple of important changes have been made in the ROM software (sometimes called firmware), knowing which ROM is in your system can be useful.

The ROM version you have is indicated by the date encoded in the chip. The ROM also contains an identification byte (the second-to-last byte) indicating the system type and a part number for reference. The value of the byte at location FFFFE (hexadecimal) corresponds to the system type (see table 7.9).

To determine which BIOS module is installed in your system, you can display the date the BIOS module design was completed. Just key in this four-statement BASIC program:

```
10 DEF SEG=&HF000
20 For X=&HFFF5 to &HFFFF
30 Print Chr$(Peek(X));
40 Next
```

Table 7.9 IBM ROM Versions

ID byte	Submodel byte	System	Date	Revision number
FF	00	PC	04/24/81	—
FF	00	PC	10/19/81	—
FF	00	PC	10/27/82	—
FE	00	PC XT	11/08/82	—
FD	00	PC*jr*	06/01/83	—
FC	00	PC AT	01/10/84	—
FC	00	PC AT	06/10/85	1
FC	01	PC AT	11/15/85	0
FC	02	PC XT 286	04/21/86	0
FC	04	PS/2 Model 50	02/13/87	0
FC	04	PS/2 Model 50 Z	04/18/88	3
FC	05	PS/2 Model 60	02/13/87	0
FB	00	PC XT	01/10/86	1
FB	00	PC XT	05/09/86	2
FA	00	PS/2 Model 30	09/02/86	0
FA	00	PS/2 Model 30	12/12/86	1
F9	00	PC Convertible	09/13/85	1
F8	00	PS/2 Model 80/16	03/30/87	0
F8	01	PS/2 Model 80/20	10/07/87	0

You can identify your ROM version by running this small program, which displays only the date. If you also want to see the model ID byte, submodel byte, and revision number of the ROM, a short DEBUG routine in the "PS/2 BIOS Information" section of Chapter 4 can show you this information.

After determining your BIOS date, you can look in table 7.9 for an exact match. If your system is not listed there, a more lengthy and complete table is in the Appendix of this book. For example, I have an XT with the date 11/08/82. The date clearly indicates the first XT ROM version, as shown in the chart; I can see that two versions are later than mine. In addition, I have an XT 286 with a ROM date of 04/21/86. According to the chart, this ROM is the only one IBM ever installed in the system, so

I know that I have the latest (and only) version of the ROM in my system. Note that this ROM has the same ID byte as the AT but differs in the submodel byte. This difference means that IBM considers the XT 286 to be an AT; software that looks at the ID byte to determine the type of system it is running on (such as DOS and OS/2) conclude that it's running on an AT. To the software and hardware, therefore, the XT Model 286 is an AT.

The date is important: It has the same relative meaning as does a version number for software. IBM later began to code an official revision number, which is what the last column represents. Versions now can be identified by this number as well. The ID is the most significant piece of information, followed by the submodel byte and, within a submodel, the revision numbers.

For example, the PS/2 50Z has a revision number of 3, which means that it's the fourth version developed for this submodel (the Model 50 and 50 Z are the same submodel). The original Model 50 has the first ROM (revision 0); the revision 1 and 2 ROMs never surfaced in a system (although IBM must have used these revisions only in-house). This situation is analogous to having a program go from Version 1.0 to Version 1.3. What happened to Versions 1.1 and 1.2? Only IBM knows for sure.

If you have a PC, a date later than or equal to 10/27/82 indicates that you don't need a BIOS update. A date of 10/19/81 or earlier in a PC indicates that you probably should install a BIOS update. The update enables the system to recognize the full 640K memory space and to use an adapter with an extended BIOS, such as a fixed disk controller, Enhanced Graphics Adapter, PC network adapter, expansion unit, or IBM Personal Computer cluster adapter.

Only IBM Personal Computer Models 1, 13, 14, 64, and 74 require an update of the BIOS. All these units were sold before March 1983. Computers sold after March 1983 had the 10/27/82 ROM. Models with an expansion unit Model 1 attached don't need further updating because the new BIOS was included with this option. Later models (including 104, 114, 164, 166, 174, and 176) were built with the new functions included in their respective BIOS. PCs originally manufactured with the early BIOS modules have a serial number of 0300960 or lower. PCs with the newest ROM also have the letter *B* stamped in white ink inside a circle on the back of the system chassis.

If you are interested in a PC ROM upgrade, IBM introduced a BIOS Update Kit (part number 1501005) on April 6, 1984. (The part number represents the number for the upgrade kit, not the part number of the chip.) This $35 replacement-parts kit updates with a new BIOS module earlier models of the Personal Computer system board (which uses 16K memory modules). Buying this newer chip is a good idea, but IBM has discontinued it and it is no longer in stock. If no alternative is found, you might as well place a glass dome over the PC and donate it to the Smithsonian: The PC would have more value as a museum piece than as a computer.

Several liquidators have purchased large quantities of the original 10/27/82 ROM chips from IBM. The chips are exact NOS (New Old Stock) originals and not copies or illegal duplicates. You can purchase them for about $25 from Mentor Electronics, Inc. Their address and phone number are listed in the vendor list in the back of this book.

You also can contact Phoenix, Award, or AMI, who all manufacture IBM-compatible ROM BIOS chips for compatible motherboard manufacturers. Phoenix sells, for example, a chip specifically customized for the IBM PC motherboard. These companies are all listed in the vendor list in the back of the book.

The XT has had three ROMs. The first ROM is in the majority of XT systems and in the Portable PC. The two newer ROMs are different from the preceding one and even have a different ID byte. The two newer XT ROMs, structured much like an AT's, are 64K in total size rather than 40K, like the older ROM.

Much of the newest ROM deals with a greatly revised and enhanced POST, as well as interfacing to the new Enhanced Keyboard. The new ROM supports such things as the AT 1.2M drive and the 3 1/2-inch 720K drives in PS/2 systems. Note that although the ROM appears to support the high-density 1.2M drive, the existing disk controller will not. The changes were significant for the newer XTs—enough for IBM to assign the system an entirely new ID byte. This change means that the term "IBM compatible" again is redefined. Of all these new features, the only real apparent difference is support for the new keyboard and floppy disk drives.

Some interesting things are happening to the AT ROM. Newer ATs with the IBM 30M hard disk have been supplied with a controversial new ROM significantly different from previous versions. One change is an alteration of the drive tables encoded in the chip to support more hard disk parameter tables, including the new 30M drive. The ROM dated 6/10/85 supports 23 different types of hard disks and the 3 1/2-inch floppy disk drives at the 720K capacity.

Another (somewhat controversial) change has been an alteration in the POST to cause the system to fail POST diagnostics if you have altered the system's clock rate to be faster than the normal 6 MHz. This feature effectively prevents you from using some of the commonly available "speedup kits," which run the system at a faster clock rate through the installation of a faster clock crystal. You probably have this version of ROM if you have an IBM 30M drive or an AT that uses 256K RAM chips on the motherboard. Find the date in the ROM and refer to table 7.9 to be sure.

This "speed fixing" might sound like a bad move by IBM, but it was intended to eliminate some potential problems with floppy disk timing that many users experience with a speedup. The aftermarket at one time offered variable-speed clock crystal kits that would take care of the speed problem for the newer chips by keeping the system at normal speed during bootup operations, thus fooling the Power-On Self Test (POST). These devices no longer are being marketed, but you can easily upgrade to a compatible ROM BIOS from Phoenix, Award, or AMI, which does not include the speed test. Of course, what IBM put in, you can take out—with an EPROM burner. I modified my own XT-286 ROM to eliminate the speed check during the POST; instructions for doing this to any system are in Chapter 12.

The newest ROM for the AT is in the units running at 8 MHz in stock form. The ROM appears much like the preceding one, with additional timing and POST changes to handle properly the increased speed, but also includes a couple of significant changes. The hard disk tables have one new entry, for a total of 24 drives supported by the ROM. The floppy drive tables have been updated to support the 3 1/2-inch floppy disk drives at the full 1.44M capacity of the PS/2 systems. In addition, this ROM fully supports the newer Enhanced Keyboard.

This type of ROM information should be particularly useful if you have a mixture of PC equipment in your company, with perhaps some of it dating back several years. Knowing the exact configuration of all your equipment can help when you're dealing with different systems. Subtle, hidden differences in your systems often cause some strange problems.

Speed Ratings

Memory-chip speed is reported in elements of time called nanoseconds. One *nanosecond* is the time that light takes to travel 11.72 inches. PC system memory speeds vary from about 200 to about 20 nanoseconds.

Different systems require memory chips that perform at different levels of performance. The memory speed required depends on many things, but probably the most important factor is the system-clock speed. To calculate the cycle time for a system, divide the system-clock frequency into 1 second. *Cycle time* is the amount of time for one cycle. If your system runs at 8 MHz, it performs 8 million cycles per second. You just divide 1 second by 8 million to calculate the time it takes for one cycle—in this case, 125 nanoseconds, or 0.000000125 seconds. For example, table 7.10 shows the cycle times for ATs and XTs.

Table 7.10 AT and XT Cycle Times

XT clock rate (MHz)	System timing cycle time (ns)
4.77	210
5	200
6	167
7	143
8	125
9	111
10	100

AT system clock rate (MHz)	Timing cycle time (ns)
6	167
8	125
10	100
12	83
16	63
20	50
25	40
33	30
40	25
50	20
66	15

The cycle times in the table don't show the required speed for memory chips, which the system designer determines. Usually, at least two cycles are required for memory access because of the way the microprocessors work. A system designer also can add wait states, which are "do-nothing" cycles, to memory access; wait states slow down the system enough to work with slower-speed memory chips. As you can see, the 25 MHz and faster systems can really use some fast memory. These systems therefore typically employ some sort of caching or memory interleaving scheme. Because having a great deal of very fast memory is far too costly, a smaller cache or "intelligent buffer" of ultrahigh-speed memory can be used to supply the processor's demands. The cache is supplied by the rest of the RAM system, which consists of chips with much slower rates. By interleaving the memory in the system, one bank can be working while another is being accessed. By alternating accesses between two banks, the effective speed of memory can be doubled.

When you replace a failed memory module, you must pay attention to the speed requirements for the module. Otherwise, the replacement won't work. You can substitute a different speed chip only if the speed of the replacement chip is equal to or faster than that of the failed chip. Substituting faster memory usually doesn't provide improved performance, because the system still operates the memory at the same speed. In some cases, however, in systems not engineered with a great deal of "forgiveness" in the timing between the memory and the system, substituting faster memory chips might improve reliability.

Whether your memory has failed or is simply not fast enough, you will notice the same common symptoms. The usual effect is that the system is frequently reporting parity check errors, or does not operate at all. The POST also might report errors.

Some people believe that you must have all the chips in a single bank rated at the exact same speed. Other users, who carry this "memory superstition" to even greater lengths, believe that all the chips must be from the same manufacturer or even from the same lot. These suppositions are not true.

As long as your chip is the correct type and meets all the specifications (pinouts, width, depth, and refresh timing), the access time always can be less (faster) than the application requires. The faster chips always can replace a slower chip of the same "type." Some people have had problems when "mixing" chips because they were using a chip that either did not meet the minimum required specifications, or was incompatible in pinout or design. Within chips of the same design, when the minimum speed is met, faster ones may be substituted. When stocking spare chips for service, I usually purchase chips much faster than necessary because I can use these to replace slower chips, but not vice versa.

A discussion of how memory chips work is beyond the scope of this book, but knowledge in this area tells you that faster-access chips always can replace slower ones, even in the same bank. If you use chips that are slower than required or with incorrect pinouts, width, depth, or RAS-versus-CAS sequencing, you will have many parity check errors and general memory problems.

If you're unsure about what chips you should buy for your system, contact the system manufacturer or a reputable chip supplier.

To check a chip's rating, examine the chip. For example, here's what a typical 256K-by-1-bit 100-nanosecond chip looks like:

```
41256-10
8804
```

The number 41256 is the manufacturer's part number. Some sort of pictorial logo usually is included on the chip to indicate the manufacturer. The 256 portion of the part number identifies the chip as a 256K chip. After the part number is a suffix. In this case, the –10 figure indicates 100 nanoseconds. Other speeds *usually* are indicated in the same manner, but some differences can occur. The following list shows suffixes you might see, and the speeds they represent:

Suffix	Speed (in nanoseconds)
–20	200
–15	150
–3	150
–12	120
–10	100
–85	85
–80	80
–70	70

Note that I have thrown in some inconsistencies, such as the "–3" indicating 150ns. This is true for some Hitachi and NEC chips. Also, it is difficult to determine (except by common sense) when the indication is the actual speed, as in "–70", or when you are to multiply by 10, as in "–15". If you are unsure about a chip, the one true source of accurate information is the chip manufacturer's data book or catalog. Simply determine who made the chip by observing the manufacturer's logo, and contact them for their documentation. A chart showing many of these logos is included in the Appendix, which can be helpful if you are trying to ID a chip.

The number 8804 on the lower part of this chip indicates that the chip was manufactured during the fourth week of 1988. Sometimes the date code appears in Julian format. The normal form of a Julian-format date code is the number of days after 1/1/1900. For example, the date 1/1/1992 equals 33,604 days after the first day of the century.

Testing Memory

The best way to test memory is to install and use it, with your PC system acting as the testing tool. Dedicated systems designed to test chips are available, but the systems usually are expensive or limited in capability. For example, one commercially available unit for testing chips sells for $200 but can test only 64K or 256K chips, and the unit cannot even tell you whether the chip's speed meets specifications.

You need, in addition to your otherwise functioning system, a memory-test program. Many programs are available, usually included in a diagnostics program. The POST, which is in the ROM, can be an effective test for problem memory, but usually a larger and more sophisticated disk-based program does a better job. The diagnostics program that accompanies a system usually is adequate, but even better programs are available. Chapter 13 discusses these programs in detail.

Types of Slots

As discussed earlier in this chapter, several different motherboard designs have been included in the various IBM computers. A major criterion that sets one motherboard apart from another is the number and type of slots available for expansion. Knowing the major differences and similarities in these slots is important because they serve as the foundation for all future expansion of the system. The following sections examine the type and slot design in the various system models.

Differences between Slots

IBM and compatible systems today have several types of slot designs in two main families: those based on Industry Standard Architecture (ISA) slots, including the Extended Industry Standard Architecture (EISA) extensions, and those based on Micro Channel Architecture (MCA) slots. Each main slot or bus design has a primary connector and one or more extension connectors, which adds capabilities for certain systems. MCA also adds a special video-extension connector on one of the slots. This list shows the types of slots:

- Industry Standard Architecture (ISA)

    8 - bit connector

    16 - bit extension connector

    32 - bit Extended Industry Standard Architecture (EISA) extension connector

■ Micro Channel Architecture (MCA)

16-bit connector

16-bit connector with video-extension connector

32-bit extension connector

Figure 7.6 shows the physical layout of the different MCA connector types. For the ISA and EISA systems, the physical layout is such that the 16-bit extension connector is in line with the 8-bit primary connector portion. If the slot is an EISA 32-bit type, then the 32-bit EISA extension connector is actually underneath the 8- and 16-bit connectors. This is why an EISA card has two levels of contacts on the edge connector. The lowest level sinks into the slot connector all the way to make contact with the EISA 32-bit extension connector, and the upper portion makes contact with the 8- and 16-bit connectors. If you are inserting an 8- or 16-bit card into an EISA slot, special stops in the slot prevent the card from sinking any further into the connector than it should.

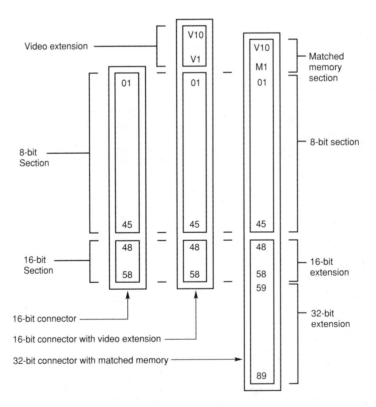

Fig. 7.6

Micro Channel Architecture (MCA) slot layout.

Some motherboards have proprietary expansion slots that were designed for special-purpose adapter boards. These slots are usually unique to the particular system, and unfortunately the only place you will find cards to plug into these slots is from the motherboard manufacturer. Companies such as AST and COMPAQ have included these types of slots in their systems for specialized expansion cards such as memory and processor upgrade cards. I usually try to avoid systems that have proprietary slot designs because it usually means only very limited and expensive upgrades will be offered, and offered only by the motherboard manufacturer. Standard slots offer a multitude of upgrade options and virtually unlimited potential.

Examining Expansion-Slot Design Differences

The basic IBM PC established the original slot design, known now as the PC-family 8-bit slot. This type of slot is designed to transfer data 8 bits at a time and has 20 addressing lines to allow the handling of 1M of memory. All PC-motherboard configurations have had five expansion slots. The XT introduced later had eight slots. Because of the larger number, the slots had to be positioned closer together; they are approximately an inch apart in the PC and only about 3/4-inch apart in the XT. Because of this design, some of the extremely thick, or double-stacked, expansion cards that fit well in a PC require two adjacent slots in an XT.

Because most board manufacturers realize that many of their boards will be installed in XTs, boards usually are designed to fit the XT systems. The only modern cards that seem to cause problems in XT systems are some of the "hard disks on a card." (The Hardcard from Plus Development Corporation, however, is an example of a hard card that doesn't occupy two slot spaces.)

In the XT or Portable PC, the eighth slot—the one closest to the power supply—is a special slot; only certain cards can be installed there. A card installed in the eighth slot must supply to the motherboard on pin B8 a special "card-selected" signal, which few cards have been designed to do. (The IBM asynchronous adapter card and the keyboard/timer card from a 3270 PC are two examples of cards that fit in the eighth slot.) Additionally, the timing requirements for the eighth slot are stricter.

The reason this strange slot is in the XT is that IBM developed the system to support a special configuration called the 3270-PC, which is really an XT with from three to six special adapter boards installed. The eighth slot was designed specifically to accept the keyboard/timer adapter from the 3270 PC. This board needed special access to the motherboard because it replaced the motherboard keyboard circuitry. Special timing and the card-selected signal made this access possible. (Contrary to what many users believe, the eighth slot has nothing to do with the IBM expansion chassis.) The IBM expansion chassis, by the way, is a box developed by IBM that looked like another system unit. Because the IBM XT had eight slots, one full-height floppy drive, and one full-height hard drive, the expansion gave room for more expansion slots and additional floppy and hard drives.

Like the XT, the AT has eight slots. Because of the greater addressing capability of the 80286 microprocessor, however, some slots are equipped to handle many more signals than the PC or XT, to tap the power and speed the processor is capable of providing. IBM took the safe route for the most part and kept the slot design the same, but it added extension connectors to six of the slots to carry the extra wires. Therefore, you can plug any standard PC or XT expansion card into the AT with no changes.

The slot-extension connector physically interferes with cards that have a *skirt*, which is an extended area of the card that drops down toward the motherboard just after the connector. To handle these cards, IBM omitted the extension connector from two of the slots so that they could physically handle any skirted PC or XT expansion card. Some XT cards, however, don't work properly in the AT even though you can physically plug them in.) Rather than use earlier PC or XT boards, most often you will purchase expansion cards designed specifically for the AT. Boards designed specifically for the AT take advantage of the full 16-bit slot; they can perform a 16-bit transfer rather than an 8-bit transfer and achieve greater speed. Some dedicated AT cards also take advantage of the fact that the AT is a larger box that supports cards a half-inch taller, thereby allowing more circuitry on the board.

Two heights are available for cards commonly found in AT systems: those that use the full 4.8 inches of available space and those that are only 4.2 inches tall. The shorter cards became an issue when IBM introduced the XT Model 286. Because this model has an AT motherboard in an XT case, it needs AT-type boards with the 4.2-inch maximum height. Most board makers trimmed down their boards a little; now many of them make only 4.2-inch-tall boards, used in either the standard AT or the XT Model 286. The precise dimensional limits for XT and AT expansion boards are shown in this list:

XT ISA card
4.2 inches (106.68 mm) high
13.13 inches (333.5 mm) long
0.5 inches (12.7 mm) wide

AT ISA card
4.8 inches (121.92 mm) high
13.13 inches (333.5 mm) long
0.5 inches (12.7 mm) wide

EISA card
5.0 inches (127.0 mm) high
13.13 inches (333.5 mm) long
0.5 inches (12.7 mm) wide

Figure 7.7 shows the physical specifications of a standard 8-bit ISA (XT-type) expansion card. Figure 7.8 shows the specifications for a 16-bit ISA (AT-type) expansion card. Figure 7.9 shows the physical specifications for a 32-bit EISA expansion card.

Some XT-type cards do not work in ISA or EISA slots, even though you can physically plug them in, because of problems with interrupts, DMA channels, ROM address conflicts, and so on.

Micro Channel Architecture is the all-new bus design in all IBM PS/2 50 and higher models. This slot design is superior in every way to the older ISA bus. Because the new design is different, no boards that plug into an ISA bus system plug into an MCA system, or vice versa. The number of pins, their signals, and even the physical dimensions of the new bus connectors are different from the old ISA bus design.

Three types of slots are involved in MCA design (refer to fig. 7.6). Every slot has a 16-bit connector; it is the basis of MCA. This connector is the primary one, found in all MCA systems.

MCA systems based on the 386DX or higher processor chips have several slots with a 32-bit extension connector, designed to enable higher transfer rates and performance by taking advantage of the processors' increased communications and memory-addressing capabilities. Even though the 32-bit extension is an extension to the original connector, as the 16-bit extension connector was in the ISA design, the 32-bit extension was designed at the same time as the rest of MCA. Because the extension connector was designed directly into MCA and not added later, the design is more integrated than something that was added later. Figures 7.10 and 7.11 show the physical specifications of 16-bit and 32-bit Micro Channel Architecture adapter boards.

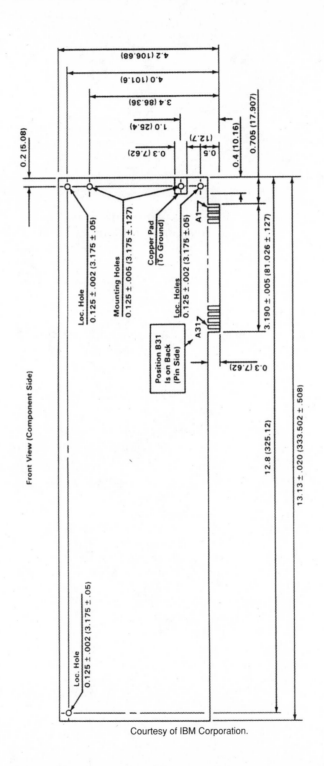

Fig. 7.7

8-bit ISA (XT-type) card specifications.

Courtesy of IBM Corporation.

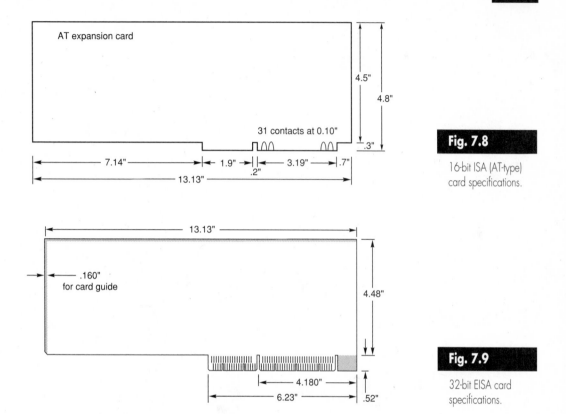

Fig. 7.8

16-bit ISA (AT-type)
card specifications.

Fig. 7.9

32-bit EISA card
specifications.

The third type of MCA slot, a standard 16-bit MCA connector, has an added special video-extension connector. This special slot is in almost every MCA system, and normally only one slot in each system would have this design. The slot is designed to allow a high-resolution video card special access to the motherboard VGA circuitry so that the new card does not need to duplicate this circuitry. No matter what new type of video board you add to an MCA system, all your programs will run because you never lose the built-in VGA circuits. The built-in VGA circuits do not have to be disabled. Instead, your new card coexists with the VGA circuits and can even "borrow" some things, such as the digital-to-analog converter, which can make the add-on video boards less expensive because they can use circuitry on the motherboard rather than build in duplicates of that circuitry.

MCA systems achieve a new level of "ease of use," as anyone who has set up one of these systems can tell you. An MCA system has no jumpers and switches—neither on the motherboard nor on any expansion adapter. You don't need an electrical engineering degree to be able to plug a card into a PC.

The new MCA bus has many other advantages. These advantages and the general implementation of the bus are listed in Chapter 4.

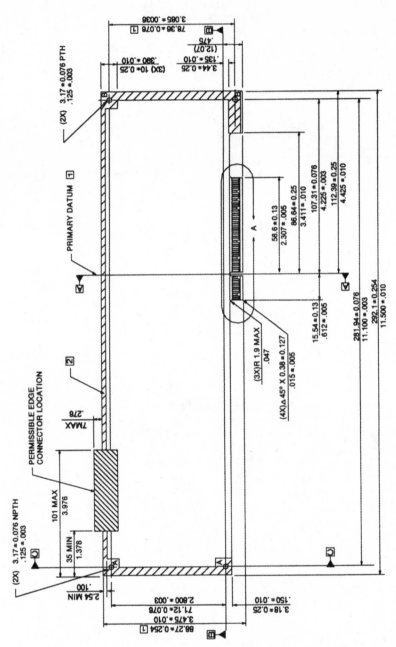

Fig. 7.10

Micro Channel
Architecture 16-bit
adapter specifications.

Courtesy of IBM Corporation.

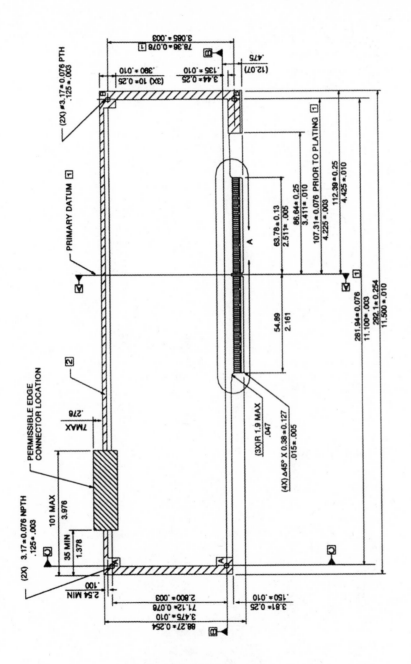

Courtesy of IBM Corporation.

Fig. 7.11

Micro Channel
Architecture 32-bit
adapter specifications.

Diagnosing Problems

Have you ever "fixed" a problem with two boards or a system unit by shuffling boards from one slot to another? All the slots in a system are supposed to be identical to each other. The only exceptions are the strange eighth slot in the XT and the 8-bit slots in the AT, which are the same as the other slots minus the extension connector. Although each slot is supposed to be "generic" in determining which board goes where, a timing problem sometimes can crop up.

MCA runs asynchronously with the main processor. Because IBM has published strict timing requirements for boards that plug into an MCA slot, these "slot swapping" sessions to resolve timing problems should become a thing of the past. MCA is much more reliable as far as these types of problems are concerned than the standard ISA or even EISA designs.

Recommended Board Placement

This section provides some simple recommendations for placing boards in slots in a system. Electrically, there's no reason a board must be placed in a certain slot. (The XT's eighth slot is the only exception.) The timing and signals in the AT's slots are all the same, for example; the only difference is that two of the slots are missing the 16-bit extension connectors. Because the signals for the absent connectors still are present on the motherboard, an enterprising person with a soldering iron could put the missing extension connectors back in place. So, what's a good rule for board placement?

Think about air circulation as you add boards and cables to a system. If you place the longest boards in the outboard slots and the shorter boards in the inboard slots, you promote the cross-ventilation airflow essential for system cooling. Remember also to route cables so that they don't restrict airflow, or try to limit the airflow restriction as much as possible.

T I P If you have a board that expands your system memory, place it in a slot as near to the power supply as possible; because the board is closer to the motherboard circuitry, it might help avoid parity-check errors. Being closer to the motherboard circuitry cuts down on memory-access times. Parity-check errors often are created because of timing problems.

Standard System Adapters

With all the different configurations available for each system, you might have difficulty knowing what you're supposed to do—and what you need to add—to end up with a system that does what you want it to do. This section describes adapters included with each system: cards or circuit boards that plug into an expansion connector or bus slot.

The IBM PC almost always was supplied with at least a floppy controller. ("Diskless" versions of the PC were available, but they were few and far between, and not many dealers wanted to order one of these PCs.) The standard floppy controller can address a total of four drives. The drives must be double-density drives because the PC and XT floppy controllers support only the low data rate of 250K Hz; the AT floppy controllers, however, support higher data rates (300 KHz and 500 KHz). Part of what defines an AT system is that it has a floppy controller that can support the 300K Hz and 500K Hz data rates.

The PC/XT controller has both an internal and an external connector, each of which supports a daisy chain of two drives. A *daisy chain* is a single cable that runs from the controller and "stops" at each of the two (maximum) drives. IBM and compatibles use a daisy-chain arrangement, which differs from a radial connection. A *radial* connection is equivalent to a star arrangement: Each disk drive has a separate cable that radiates from the centrally located controller. IBM-compatible systems do not use a radial connection.

The XT base models were configured exactly the same way as the PC—that is, with the floppy disk controller. The XT and the PC used the same controller. The enhanced XT models that featured a hard disk also had a separate hard disk controller. As a bonus, IBM added a serial port card in the "funny" eighth slot in these systems.

The hard disk controller IBM used for the XT was the Xebec Model 1210, made by Xebec Corporation. Although IBM wrote a custom ROM for the controller, Xebec shipped a compatible version of ROM with orders for the 1210 controller from Xebec. IBM supplied two different versions of ROM for the hard disk controller: one version for the 10M hard disk systems and a newer ROM with the 20M hard disk systems. The controller had also at least two different revisions, identical in performance and operation, even though the newer units had fewer components.

The AT comes with a single disk controller card at minimum. In the AT, this card is a dual-function controller because it handles the floppy and hard disk interface.

The disk controllers used in the AT systems were made for IBM by Western Digital. IBM used two different versions of the Western Digital family of controllers in the AT and XT 286. The original unit was the Western

Digital WD 1002-WA2. The later AT systems and the XT 286 came with the WD 1003A-WA2. The latter controller was reduced in height to fit inside the shorter XT 286 chassis. The AT enhanced model includes the IBM serial/parallel adapter card, which enables you to attach printers, modems, or both.

None of these systems in their default configuration, without additional options, is a functional system. All of them need at least some sort of video board in order to operate. Additional memory is virtually a requirement for most of the systems. PC and XT systems need a printer port and a clock calendar to be configured "normally" by today's standards. Also, units that don't include a standard hard disk must add the disk alone (as in the AT) or both a disk and controller (as in the PC or XT).

Compare this situation to the PS/2 systems, which include these items on the motherboard:

- A video interface in the form of a Multi-Color Graphics Array (MCGA), Video Graphics Array (VGA), or Extended Graphics Array (XGA) subsystem

- At least 640K of memory (some include as much as 8M or more)

- A serial, parallel, and mouse port

- A built-in floppy controller

All but the lower-end Models 25 and 30 include at least a 20M hard disk. Literally, all you have to add to a standard PS/2 configuration is a monitor, and some systems include that. This system is a far cry from the original PC, which was like buying a car and having to remember that you needed wheels, seats, headlights, and so on.

This new trend of "bundling" everything with the system, however, has drawbacks. For one thing, the initial price seems higher. You cannot save money by shopping around and getting the best prices for each individual component, as you could with earlier systems. Also, when a component in the PS/2 system fails, the part usually is built into the motherboard, which you then must replace. Replacing the motherboard is expensive when the system is out of warranty. And, finally, you cannot be as creative with "individualizing" the configuration to your own specific needs, as was possible with the earlier piecemeal systems.

The Power Supply

One of the most failure-prone components in PC systems is the power supply. You therefore should investigate this subject in some depth. You need to know both the function and limitations of a power supply, and its potential problems and their solutions.

Here's an overview of what the supply is supposed to do in PC systems. The power supply in a PC is designed to convert the 120-volt, 60Hz, AC current into something the computer can use—specifically, both 5- and 12-volt DC current. Usually, the digital electronic components and circuits in the system (motherboard, adapter cards, and disk drive logic boards) use the 5-volt power, and the motors (disk drive motors and the fan) use the 12-volt power. You must ensure a good, steady supply of both types of current so that the system can operate properly.

The power supply also ensures that the system doesn't run without proper power levels. The power supply will actually prevent the computer from starting up until all the correct power levels are present. Each power supply completes internal checks and tests before allowing the PC to start up. The power supply sends to the motherboard a special signal, called Power Good. If this signal is not present, the computer does not run. The effect of this setup is that when the AC voltage dips and the power supply becomes overstressed or overheated, the Power Good signal goes down and forces a system reset or complete shutdown. If your system has ever seemed dead when the power switch is on and the fan and hard disks are running, you know the effects of losing the Power Good signal.

IBM used this conservative design with the view that if the power goes low or the supply is overheated or overstressed, causing output power to falter, the computer shouldn't be allowed to operate. You even can use the Power Good feature as a method of designing and implementing a reset switch for the PC. The Power Good line is wired to the 8284 or 82284 clock generator chip, which controls the clock and reset lines to the microprocessor. When you ground the Power Good line with a switch, the chip and related circuitry stop the processor by killing the clock signal and then reset the processor when the Power Good signal appears after you release the switch. The result is a full hardware reset of the system.

On the other hand, the AT shines in the power department. It has a 192-watt capacity supply with a variable-speed, thermostatically controlled cooling fan to take care of any high-heat situations. Other than normal failures, supply difficulties don't exist for the AT. A normal failure is one caused not specifically by overloading, power surges, or any other torture, but rather just a failure of the power supply from normal defects or thermal expansion or contraction.

PS/2 systems have been built with proper power supplies as well. In fact, most modern systems have an adequate power supply from inception. Most manufacturers have learned the hard way that a little overengineering in this area pays off.

Troubleshooting Power-Supply Problems

A weak or inadequate power supply can put a damper on your ideas for system expansion. Some systems were designed with beefy power supplies, as if to anticipate a great deal of system add-on or expansion components. XT and AT systems were built in this manner. Some systems have inadequate power supplies from the start, however, and cannot accept the number and types of power-hungry options you might want to add.

In particular, the PC's 63 1/2-watt supply is inadequate for all but the most basic system. Add a graphics board, a hard disk, an 8087 chip, and 640K of memory, and you will kill the system in no time. The total power draw of all the items in the system determines the adequacy of the power supply.

Another problem with underengineered power supplies is that they run hot and force the system to do so as well. The repeated heating and cooling of solid-state components eventually causes a computer system to fail, and engineering principles dictate that the hotter a PC's temperature, the shorter its life. Many people recommend replacing the PC supply with the 130-watt supply from an XT, which solves the problem. You can bolt in the XT supply, and use the same mounting and physical configuration of the original PC supply. The only problem with this recommendation is the price: IBM's XT power supply, part number 8529247, sells for $290. (An interesting note: The PC supply costs $344.)

An alternative to the XT and PC power supplies is a 200-watt unit from PC Power and Cooling, which sells for $169. With almost four times the output capabilities of the PC supply and nearly twice that of the XT, this unit is built like a tank. To help reduce the temperature of the system further, the supply has two cooling fans. The PC Cooling Systems unit also has four disk drive power connectors and is a bolt-in swap that uses the same mounting screws and connectors as the originals.

T I P   If you seal the ventilation holes on the bottom of the PC chassis, starting from where the disk drive bays begin and all the way to the right side of the PC, you drop the interior temperature some 10 to 20 degrees Fahrenheit—not bad for two cents worth of electrical tape. IBM "factory-applied" this tape on every XT and XT-286 it sold. The result is greatly improved interior aerodynamics and airflow over the heat-generating components.

T I P

A frequent question that relates to the discussion of temperature concerns whether you should turn off a system when you're not using it. The answer is No—you should not repeatedly turn a system on and off. The reason is simple but not obvious to most. Many people believe that flipping system power on and off frequently is harmful because it electrically "shocks" the system. The real culprit, however, is temperature. In other words, it's not so much electrical "shock" as thermal shock that destroys a system.

Regardless of whether you turn a system on or off ten times or a thousand times a day, if you allow it to heat and cool frequently, you're asking for problems. When you heat and cool metal, it hardens and—along with the solder in your system—becomes brittle. The constant expansion and contraction then eventually cause the work-hardened metal to crack, which causes the failure. Also, socketed devices tend to work their way out of their sockets, and the movement enables corrosion to work into sockets and connector joints. Many "blown" power supplies are nothing more than a cracked or broken solder joint or a failed transistor that died when it separated from its heat sink. (The heat-sink glue fails after repeated heating and cooling.)

Repairing these problems is simple, but the process is cumulative, and recurring thermal stress will cause the problem to return. Keeping the unit at a constant temperature seems to be the most important contribution to system longevity.

Power-Supply Ratings

IBM provides charts with the technical specifications of each of its system-unit power supplies. The charts are in each system's technical-reference manual and often are on stickers on the power supply.

Tables 7.11 and 7.12 list power-supply specifications for each of IBM's units. The input specifications are listed as voltages; the output specifications as amps, at several voltage levels. IBM reports output wattage level as "specified output wattage." You can convert amperage figures to output wattage by using this simple formula:

Wattage = voltage * amperage

Table 7.11 Power-Supply Specifications for PC Systems

	PC	PPC	XT	XT-286	AT
Input voltage range					
Minimum voltage	104	90	90	90	90
Maximum voltage	127	137	137	137	137
Universal (220v)?	No	Yes	No	Yes	Yes
Switch/Automatic	—	Switch	—	Auto	Switch
Output amperage					
+5	7.00	11.20	15.00	20.00	19.80
−5	0.30	0.30	0.30	0.30	0.30
+12	2.00	4.40	4.20	4.20	7.30
−12	0.25	0.25	0.25	0.25	0.30
Calculated output wattage	63.5	113.3	129.9	154.9	191.7
Specified output wattage	63.5	114.0	130.0	157.0	192.0

Most power supplies are considered to be *universal*, or *worldwide*: they run on the 220-volt, 50-cycle current used in Europe and many other parts of the world. Most power supplies that can switch to 220-volt input are automatic, but a few require you to set a switch on the back of the power supply to indicate which type of power you will access. (The automatic units sense the current and then switch automatically.)

My PS/2 P70, for example, runs on both 110- and 220-volt power; all I have to do is plug it in and the system automatically recognizes the incoming voltage and switches circuits accordingly. This is different from my older AT, which runs on both levels of power but requires me to flip a switch manually to select the proper circuits within the power supply.

Power-Use Calculations

One way to see whether your system is capable of expansion is to calculate the levels of power drain in the different system components and then deduct the total from the maximum power supplied. This calculation might help you decide when to upgrade the power supply to a more capable unit.

Table 7.12 Power-Supply Specifications for PS/2 Systems				
Model	**Part number**	**Worldwide power**	**Manual/Auto**	**Output wattage**
25	8525-xx1	Yes	Manual	90
	8525-xx4	Yes	Manual	115
30	8530-0xx	Yes	Auto	70
25 286	8525-xxx	Yes	Manual	124.5
30 286	8530-Exx	Yes	Manual	90
35 SX	8535-xxx	Yes	Auto	118
40 SX	8540-0xx	Yes	Manual	197
50	8550-0xx	Yes	Auto	94
55 SX	8555-xxx	Yes	Manual	90
57 SX	8557-0xx	Yes	Manual	197
60	8560-041	Yes	Auto	207
	8560-071	Yes	Auto	225
65 SX	8565-xxx	Yes	Auto	250
70 386	8570-xxx	Yes	Auto	132
70 486	8570-Bxx	Yes	Auto	132
P70 386	8573-xxx	Yes	Auto	85
P75 486	8573-xxx	Yes	Auto	120
80 386	8580-xxx	Yes	Auto	225
	8580-Axx	Yes	Auto	242
90 XP 486	8590-0xx	Yes	Auto	194
95 XP 486	8595-0xx	Yes	Auto	329

Suppose, for example, that you examine some typical power-consumption figures for components in an IBM PC system unit. The PC comes with a 63 1/2-watt power supply. The levels of power to be concerned about are the 5- and 12-volt levels. The PC power supply can provide 7.0 amps of 5-volt power and 2.0 amps of 12-volt power. The following calculation shows what happens when you subtract the amount of power necessary to run the different system components:

5-volt power		7.0 amps
Less:	Motherboard (full memory, 8087)	–4.0
	Video adapter	–1.0
	Two full-height floppy drives	–1.2 (0.6 each)
	Multifunction (6-pack type) board	–1.0
		———
Remaining power		–0.2
12-volt power		2.0 amps
Less:	Two full-height floppy drives	–0.9 (0.9 each)
	Cooling fan	–0.25
		———
Remaining power		0.85

As you can see, with this system you're in trouble. The 5-volt portion of the supply in this configuration is already overloaded, and you have only three slots full and no hard disk. A typical full-height hard disk consumes 1.5 amps of 5-volt power, and a half-height drive draws 0.8 amps. Needless to say, you don't have enough power left for anything.

With 12-volt power, at least the basic configuration isn't overloaded. Suppose that you want to add a hard disk, however. The full-height drives draw about 4.0 amps of power for the first 5 to 10 seconds and then drop to a continuous draw of about 2.0 amps. A typical half-height drive draws about 2.2 amps of power during the first 5 to 10 seconds and then tapers off to about 0.9 amps of continuous draw. In this example, you might have enough 12-volt power for a small, half-height hard disk. Some of the newer 3 1/2-inch hard disks don't draw very much power because a disk drive's power draw is almost directly related to the drive's physical size. Some of the hard disks on a card operate on very low power also. For a typical PC system, however, even these units are too much to handle unless you're willing to replace the power supply with one that has more capacity.

In this example, you need an upgraded power supply, which you can purchase from many sources, including IBM and the aftermarket. Most users choose at least a 130-watt supply, or better. The PC Power and Cooling unit described earlier has 20.0 amps of 5-volt output and 8.0 amps of 12-volt output, nearly four times what's available in a standard IBM PC. Using this supply in a PC ensures that the system has enough power to drive nearly anything you can add to the unit.

Many people wait until an existing unit fails before they replace it with an upgraded version. If you're on a tight budget, this "if it ain't broke, don't fix it" attitude works. Power supplies, however, often do not just fail; they can fail in an intermittent fashion or allow fluctuating power levels to reach the system, which results in unstable operation. You might be blaming system lockups on software bugs when the culprit is an overloaded power supply. If you've been running with your original power supply for a long time, you should expect some problems.

One thing to consider is that the figures most manufacturers report for maximum power output are full-duty-cycle figures, which means that these levels of power can be supplied continuously. You usually can expect a unit that continuously supplies some level of power to supply more power for some noncontinuous amount of time. A supply usually can offer 50 percent greater output than the continuous figure indicates for as long as one minute. This cushion often is used to supply the necessary power to start spinning a hard disk. After the drive has spun to full speed, the power draw drops to some value within the system's continuous supply capabilities. Drawing anything over the rated continuous figure for any long length of time causes the power supply to run hot and fail early, and can prompt several nasty symptoms in the system.

You should make these types of calculations for your system:

- The first figures you need are the output-level specifications for your power supply. These specifications are in your system's technical-reference manual. (The figures for IBM's systems are in table 7.11.)

- Then you need power-consumption figures for each type of component in the system. Most boards draw less than 1 amp; some boards, however, such as network adapters or internal modems, can draw even more. Disk drives are power hungry, and draw both 5- and 12-volt power. Get the consumption figures for these types of products from the manufacturers of the products. IBM has a technical-reference manual for options and adapters for IBM boards and disk drives. The original equipment manufacturers (OEM) manuals for your disk drives and adapter boards usually contain this type of information.

In Chapter 14, you learn about the symptoms you can expect from a blown or failing power supply and the steps necessary to correct the problem. The chapter also tells you how to test the supply for correct operation.

Replacement Units

As mentioned earlier, replacement power supplies are available from many manufacturers. Consider the power supply's shape, or *form factor*. For example, the power supply used in the IBM AT differs physically from the one used in the PC or XT. Therefore, AT and PC supplies are not interchangeable.

The differences are in the size, shape, screw-hole positions, connector type, number of connectors, and switch position. The XT power supply has the same form factor as the PC supply, however, and would bolt in with no modifications required to the system or the supply. The two power supplies differ only in power-output capabilities.

IBM has used only two different form-factor supplies for the original line of systems:

1. The PC type, used in the PC, XT, and XT-286. The most (electrically) powerful version of this supply was the one used in the XT-286. All are physically interchangeable.

2. The AT type, used in all models of the IBM AT systems.

In PS/2 systems, only the power supplies from the Models 60, 65, and 80 use the same form factor and are interchangeable. Several different output level power supplies have been available for these systems, including 207-, 225-, 242-, and 250-watt versions. The most powerful 250-watt unit was supplied originally for the Model 65 SX, although it will fit perfectly in the other Model 60 or 80 systems. Most of the other PS/2 systems have power supplies unique to the system. I have not found any company manufacturing aftermarket supplies for the PS/2 systems, probably because the IBM factory-supplied units are more than adequate for their intended application. A great number of third-party companies are repairing and reselling IBM PS/2 power supplies at prices greatly below what IBM charges for the same thing. Be sure to scan the vendor list in the back of this book for some recommended vendors of these parts.

One risk with some of the compatibles is that they might not use one of the two original PC family form-factor supplies. If a system uses the PC-type or AT-type form-factor power supply, replacement units are available from hundreds of vendors. You often have a smorgasbord of supplies from which to choose—everything from heavy-duty units at different levels of capability to units available at different noise levels.

An unfortunate user of a system with a nonstandard form-factor supply doesn't have this kind of choice and must get a replacement from the original manufacturer of the system—and usually pay through the nose for the unit. Although you can find PC and AT form-factor units for as little as $50, the proprietary units from some manufacturers run as much as $400. When *Popular Mechanics* magazine reviews an automobile, it always lists the replacement costs of the most failure-prone and replacement-prone components, from front bumpers to alternators to taillights. PC buyers often overlook this type of information, and discover too late the consequences of having nonstandard components in a system.

An example of compatible systems with proprietary power-supply designs are those from COMPAQ. None of its systems use the same form-factor supply as the IBM systems, which means that COMPAQ usually is the only place you can get a replacement. If the power supply in your COMPAQ Deskpro system "goes south," you can expect to pay $395 for a replacement, and the replacement unit will be no better or quieter than the one you're replacing. You have little choice in the matter because almost no one offers COMPAQ form-factor power supplies except COMPAQ. An exception is that PC Power and Cooling offers excellent replacement power supplies for the earlier COMPAQ Portable systems and for the Deskpro series. These replacement power supplies have higher-output power levels than the original supplies from COMPAQ and cost much less.

Keyboards

This section examines the keyboards available for IBM and compatible systems. IBM has had three different keyboard designs during the last few years:

- 83-key PC and XT keyboard
- 84-key AT keyboard
- 101-key Enhanced Keyboard

The Enhanced Keyboard has appeared in three different versions, but all three are the same electrically and can be interchanged. The three different versions are:

- Enhanced Keyboard without LED panel (lock indicators)
- Enhanced Keyboard with LED panel (lock indicators)
- Enhanced Keyboard (PS/2 logo)

The first two keyboards are the same cosmetically, but the second unit was designed for systems that support the full bidirectional capability needed to operate the LED panel that shows the status of the Caps Lock, Num Lock, and Scroll Lock keys. The third version is the same as the second, except for a logo on top that matches the PS/2 system logo. Electrically, these keyboards are the same, but the first one is missing a small add-on circuit board to control the lights. PC- or XT-type systems cannot operate these lights because they do not have the bidirectional interface necessary for light operation. If you use an XT and the IBM Enhanced Keyboard with the LED panel, the lights remain dark.

Any IBM keyboard can be ordered separately as a spare part. The newer Enhanced Keyboards come with an externally detachable keyboard that plugs into the keyboard port with a special connector, much like a telephone connector. The other end of the cable is one of two types:

- Earlier systems use a 5-pin DIN connector.

- PS/2 systems use a new, miniature, 6-pin DIN connector.

Because of the interchangeability of the newer Enhanced Keyboards, I can plug a 101-key unit from an XT into a PS/2 system simply by switching the cables. I also can plug the PS/2-style 101-key unit into any XT or AT system by switching cables. The PS/2-style cable is available in two different lengths. Because of the vastly superior "feel" of the IBM keyboards, I often equip compatible systems with these keyboards. In fact, IBM has spun off its keyboard and printer division (Lexmark), which is now selling keyboards on the open market to the compatible industry. Purchased from either Lexmark or from other third-parties, new IBM keyboards have sold for as low as $80 or less. Table 7.13 shows the part numbers of all the IBM keyboards and cables. These numbers can serve as a reference when you are seeking an IBM keyboard from IBM direct or from third-party companies.

The original 83/84-key keyboards are sold with a cable that has the larger, 5-pin DIN connector already attached. Enhanced Keyboards are always sold without a cable. You must order the proper cable as a separate item. Cables are available to connect the keyboards to either the older system units that use the larger DIN connector or to PS/2 systems (and many compatibles) that use the smaller mini-DIN connector.

PC and AT keyboards are different from each other. In addition to having different key layouts, the internal electronics are different. The 83-key keyboard uses an 8048 processor, and the other keyboards use a 6805 processor internally and an 8042 processor on the motherboard.

Table 7.13 IBM Keyboard and Cable Part Numbers

Description	Part number
83-key U.S. keyboard assembly with cable	8529297
Cable assembly for 83-key unit	8529168
84-key U.S. keyboard assembly with cable	8286165
Cable assembly for 84-key unit	8286146
101-key U.S. keyboard without LED panel	1390290
101-key U.S. keyboard with LED panel	6447033
101-key U.S. keyboard (PS/2 logo)	1392090
6-foot Enhanced Keyboard cable (DIN plug)	6447051
6-foot Enhanced Keyboard cable (mini-DIN plug)	61X8898
6-foot Enhanced Keyboard cable (mini-DIN plug with additional shielding)	27F4984
10-foot Enhanced Keyboard cable (mini-DIN plug)	72X8537

The 101-key keyboard was designed to replace both the 83-key and 84-key units, and theoretically replaces the earlier keyboards for any system. One problem, however, is that the individual system ROM BIOS might not be capable of operating the 101-key keyboard correctly. If this is the case, the 101-key keyboard does not work (as with all three ROM versions of the IBM PC), or only the new added keys (F11 and F12 function keys) do not work.

You usually can tell whether your system has complete ROM BIOS support for the 101-key unit: when you plug in the keyboard and turn on the system unit, the Num Lock light automatically comes on and the numeric keypad portion of the keyboard is enabled. This method of detection isn't 100 percent accurate, but if the light goes on, your BIOS generally supports the keyboard. A notable exception is the IBM AT BIOS dated 06/10/85; it turns on the Num Lock light but still does not properly support the Enhanced Keyboard. Many users are irritated because the numeric keypad is automatically enabled when their system reboots. Some think that this is a function of the Enhanced Keyboard because they know that none of the earlier keyboards seemed to operate this way. Remember that this function isn't really a keyboard function— instead it's a function of the motherboard ROM BIOS, which identifies an enhanced 101-key unit and turns on the Num Lock as a "favor." Some

472

compatible BIOS versions enable you to specify in the Setup routine whether the numeric keypad (Num Lock) should be activated when you boot your computer. The Phoenix BIOS has this convenient function. In systems that cannot disable the automatic numeric keypad enable feature, I simply use one of the many public domain programs available for turning off the Num Lock function. Placing the program command to disable Num Lock in the AUTOEXEC.BAT file turns off the numeric keypad each time the system reboots.

Because of the processor in each keyboard, the keyboards are intelligent devices; they are computers in their own right, with their own built-in processor capable of running a self-test when they're turned on.

83-Key PC and XT Keyboard

One of the most criticized components of the original PC and XT systems was the IBM keyboard; the 83-key keyboard has an awkward layout. The Shift keys are small and in the wrong place on the left side. The Enter key also is too small. These oversights were disturbing because IBM had produced the Selectric typewriter, perceived as a standard for keyboard layout. Figure 7.12 shows the layout of the original 83-key PC and XT keyboard.

Fig. 7.12

PC and XT 83-key keyboard layout.

84-Key AT Keyboard

When the AT was introduced, it included a new keyboard—the 84-key unit (see fig. 7.13). This keyboard corrected many of the problems of the original PC and XT keyboards. The position and arrangement of the numeric keypad was modified. The Enter key was made much larger, like that of a Selectric typewriter. The Shift key positions and sizes were corrected. IBM also finally added LED indicators for the status of the Caps Lock, Scroll Lock, and Num Lock toggles.

Fig. 7.13

AT 84-key keyboard layout.

Enhanced 101-Key

IBM then introduced the "corporate" Enhanced 101-key Keyboard for the newer XT and AT models (see fig. 7.14). I use the word "corporate" because this unit now is supplied with every type of system and terminal IBM sells. This universal keyboard has a further improved layout over that of the 84-key unit, with perhaps the exception of the Enter key, which reverted to a smaller size. The 101-key Enhanced Keyboard was designed to conform to international regulations and specifications for keyboards. In fact, other companies such as DEC and TI had already been using designs similar to the IBM 101-key unit even earlier than IBM. These 101-key units came in versions with and without the status indicator LEDs, depending on whether the unit was sold with an XT or AT system.

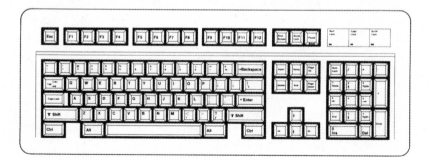

Fig. 7.14

101-key keyboard layout for the XT, AT, and PS/2.

The 101-key keyboard layout can be divided into four sections:

- Typing area
- Numeric keypad
- Cursor and screen controls
- Function keys

The 101-key arrangement is similar to the Selectric keyboard layout. The Tab, Caps Lock, Shift, Enter, and Backspace keys have a larger striking area and are located in the familiar Selectric locations. Ctrl and Alt keys are on each side of the space bar. The typing area and numeric keypad have home-row identifiers for touch typing.

The cursor and screen-control keys have been separated from the numeric keypad, which is reserved for numeric input. (As with other PC keyboards, you can use the numeric keypad for cursor and screen control when the keyboard is not in Num Lock mode.) A division-sign key and an additional Enter key have been added to the numeric keypad.

The cursor-control keys are arranged in the inverted T format. The Insert, Delete, Home, End, Page Up, and Page Down keys, located above the dedicated cursor-control keys, are separated from the numeric keypad. The function keys, spaced in groups of four, are located across the top of the keyboard. The keyboard has two additional function keys (F11 and F12). The Esc key is isolated in the upper left corner of the keyboard. Dedicated Print Screen/Sys Req, Scroll Lock, and Pause/Break keys are provided for commonly used functions.

One of the Enhanced Keyboard's many useful features is removable keycaps. With clear keycaps and paper inserts, you can customize the keyboard. Keyboard templates are available to provide specific operator instructions. IBM also provides a 9-foot cable for attaching the keyboard to the system unit.

The new keyboard probably will be on any desktop system IBM introduces for quite some time. If you want to change older systems to use the new keyboard, however, you may have problems with ROM BIOS support. IBM changed the ROM on the systems to support the new keyboard properly, and most compatible vendors have followed suit for newer systems. Older machines may require a ROM upgrade to properly use some of the features on the 101-key enhanced keyboards, such as the F11 and F12 keys.

In a somewhat informal test, I plugged the new keyboard into an earlier XT. The keyboard seemed to work well. None of the keys that didn't exist previously, such as F11 and F12, were operable, but the new arrow keys and the numeric keypad did work. The Enhanced Keyboard seems to work on XT or AT systems but will not function on the original PC systems. Many compatible versions of the 101-key Enhanced Keyboards have a manual XT-AT switch on the bottom, which may allow the keyboard to work in an original PC system. IBM sells its 101-key Enhanced Keyboard as a separate item for $275, but you can get this board for as little as $80 or less from third-party companies, or maybe slightly more from Lexmark. Other manufacturers also offer enhanced keyboards that work on XTs and AT-type systems.

Cleaning a Keyboard

One of the best ways to maintain a keyboard in top condition is periodic cleaning. As preventive maintenance, you should vacuum the keyboard weekly. Or, you can use the canned compressed air available at electronics-supply houses. Before you dust a keyboard with the compressed air, turn the keyboard upside down so that particles of dirt and dust collected inside fall out.

On all the keyboards, each keycap is removable, which can be handy if a key sticks or acts erratically. For example, a common problem is a key that doesn't work every time you press it. This problem usually results from dirt collecting under the key. An excellent tool for removing keycaps on most any keyboard is the "U"-shaped chip-puller tool. You simply slip the hooked ends of the tool under the keycap, squeeze the ends together to grip the underside of the keycap, and lift up. IBM sells a tool specifically for removing keycaps from its keyboards, but the chip puller works better. After removing the cap, spray some compressed air into the space under the cap to dislodge the dirt. Then replace the cap and check the action of the key.

When you remove the keycaps, be careful not to remove the space bar on the original 83-key PC and 84-key AT-type keyboards. This bar is very difficult to reinstall. The newer 101-key units use a different wire support that is removed and replaced much more easily.

Spills also can be a problem. If you tip a soft drink or cup of coffee into a keyboard, you don't necessarily have a disaster. You should immediately (or as soon as possible) flush out the keyboard with distilled water. Partially disassemble the keyboard and use the water to wash the components. (See the following section for disassembly instructions.) If the spilled liquid has dried, let the keyboard soak in some of the water for a while. Then, when you're sure that the keyboard is clean, pour another gallon or so of distilled water over it and through the key switches to wash away any residual dirt. After the unit dries completely, it should be perfectly functional. You may be surprised to know that you can drench your keyboard with water, and it will not harm the components. Just make sure that you use distilled water, which is free from residue or mineral content. Also make sure that the keyboard is fully dry before you attempt to use it, or some of the components might short out: Water is a conductor of electricity.

Disassembly Procedures and Cautions

Repairing and cleaning a keyboard often requires that you take it apart. When you perform this task, you should know when to stop. An IBM keyboard generally has these four major parts:

- Cable

- Case

- Keypad assembly

- Keycaps

You easily can break down a keyboard to these major components and replace any of them, but don't disassemble the keypad assembly or you'll be showered with tiny springs, clips, and keycaps. Finding all these parts (several hundred of them) and piecing the unit back together is not a fun way to spend time. You also may not be able to assemble the keyboard as well as it was. Figure 7.15 shows a typical keyboard with the case opened.

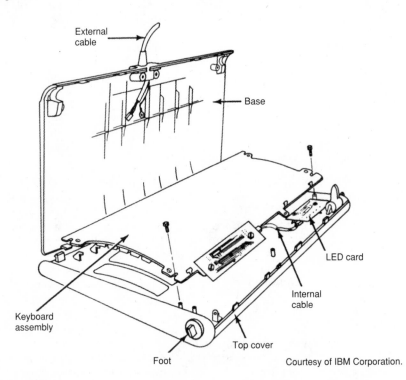

Courtesy of IBM Corporation.

Fig. 7.15

Typical keyboard components.

Another problem is that you cannot purchase the smaller parts separately, such as contact clips and springs. The only way to obtain these parts is from another keyboard. If you ever have a keyboard that's beyond repair, keep it around for these parts. They might come in handy some day.

Most repair operations are limited to changing the cable or cleaning some component of the keyboard, from the cable contact ends to the key contact points. The keyboard cable takes quite a bit of abuse, and therefore can fail easily. The ends are stretched, tugged, pulled, and generally handled roughly. The cable uses strain reliefs, but you still might have problems with the connectors making proper contact at each end or even with wires that have broken inside the cable. You might want to carry a spare cable for every type of keyboard you have. Extra cables provide inexpensive insurance.

All keyboard cables plug into the keyboard and PC with connectors, and you can change the cables easily without having to splice wires or solder connections. With the earlier 83-key PC and 84-key AT keyboards, you must open the case to access the connector where the cable attaches. On the newer 101-key Enhanced Keyboards, the cable plugs into the keyboard from the outside of the case, using a modular jack and plug similar to a telephone jack. This design, one of the best features of this keyboard, also makes the keyboard universally usable on nearly any system except the original PC.

The only difference, for example, between the Enhanced Keyboards for an AT and a PS/2 system is the attached cable. PS/2 systems use a tan cable with a smaller plug on the computer side. The AT cable is black and has the larger DIN-type plug on the computer side. You can interchange the Enhanced Keyboards as long as you use the correct cable for the system.

If you plug an Enhanced Keyboard into a system that didn't originally support the LEDs for indicating Caps Lock, Scroll Lock, or Num Lock, these lights remain inactive while the keyboard is plugged in. If the system originally supported the lights but doesn't have ROM support for the Enhanced Keyboard, the Num Lock light does not come on during a system boot. If the system fully supports the Enhanced Keyboard in ROM, the Num Lock light comes on during a boot so that the numeric keypad functions in numeric mode. You have to use the separate arrow keys on the keyboard or manually turn off the numeric lock. If you don't like this "improvement," you can include in your AUTOEXEC.BAT file a program that turns off the numeric lock. The Public Software Library is a good source for this type of program; its address and phone number are in the vendor list at the back of this book.

The only feasible ways to repair a keyboard are to replace the cable and clean the individual keyswitch assemblies, the entire keypad, or the cable contact ends. The individual spring and keyswitch assemblies are not available as a separate part, and disassembling the unit to that level is not advisable because of the difficulty in reassembling it. Other than cleaning a keyboard, the only thing you can do is replace the entire keypad assembly (virtually the entire keyboard) or the cable.

Chapter 14 describes the steps in troubleshooting keyboard problems and discusses the sequence in which you should proceed.

Chapter Summary

This chapter has thoroughly described the various system units in the IBM personal computers and their assorted components: the motherboard, microprocessor, memory, slots, standard adapters, power supply, and keyboards. The information you've received in this chapter can help you understand why many items in PC and PS/2 systems operate as they do. Understanding the way the system operates gives you valuable insight into many of the problems that can occur with these systems. This understanding can turn you into an expert trouble-shooter—you can use creativity to solve problems rather than just recite a problem solution from memory. In-depth troubleshooting of these system components is discussed in Chapter 14.

Floppy Disk Drives

This chapter examines, in detail, floppy disk drives and disks. It explores how floppy disk drives and disks function, how DOS uses a disk, what types of disk drives and disks are available, and how to properly install and service drives and disks. You learn about all the types of drives available for today's personal computer systems; these drives include both the 5 1/4-inch and 3 1/2-inch drives in both high- and double-density versions. The chapter discusses also the newer, extra-high-density 3 1/2-inch disks. You might find especially interesting the discussion about the addition of the 3 1/2-inch drives to the early PC-family systems, which enables them to be compatible with many newer systems.

Drive Components

This section describes the components that make up a typical drive and examines how these components operate together to read and write data—the physical operation of the drive. All floppy drives, regardless of type, consist of several basic common components. To properly install and service a disk drive, you must be able to identify these components and understand their function (see fig. 8.1).

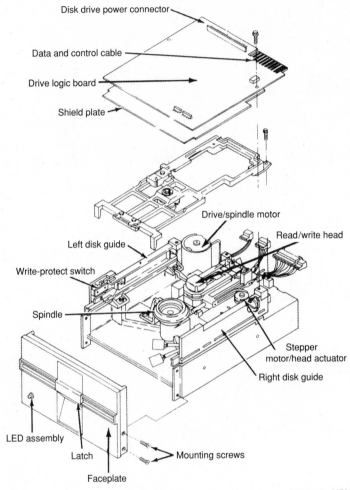

Disk drive power connector

Data and control cable

Drive logic board

Shield plate

Drive/spindle motor

Read/write head

Left disk guide

Write-protect switch

Spindle

Stepper motor/head actuator

Right disk guide

LED assembly

Latch

Mounting screws

Faceplate

Fig. 8.1

A typical full-height disk drive.

Courtesy of IBM Corporation.

Read/Write Heads

A disk drive has two read/write heads, making the modern floppy disk drive a double-sided drive (see fig. 8.2). A head exists for each side of the disk, and both heads are used for recording and reading on their respective disk sides. At one time, single-sided drives were available for PC systems (the original PC had such drives), but today single-sided drives are a fading memory.

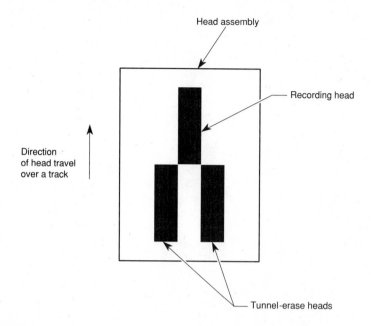

Head assembly

Recording head

Direction
of head travel
over a track

Tunnel-erase heads

Fig. 8.2

Composite construction
of a typical floppy
drive head.

Note Many people do not realize that the first head is the bottom
one. Single-sided drives, in fact, use only the bottom head;
the top head is replaced by a felt pressure pad. Another bit of
disk trivia is that the top head (Head 1) is not directly over
the bottom head—the top head is located either 4 or 8 tracks
inward from the bottom head, depending on the drive type.
Therefore, what we conventionally call "cylinders" should
more accurately be called "cones."

The head mechanism is moved by a motor called a *head actuator*. The
heads can move in and out over the surface of the disk in a straight line
to position themselves over various tracks. The heads move in and out
tangentially to the tracks that they record on the disk. Because the
heads are mounted on the same rack, or mechanism, they move in unison and cannot move independently of each other. The heads are made
of soft ferrous (iron) compounds with electromagnetic coils. Each head
is a composite design, with a record head centered within two tunnel-
erase heads in the same physical assembly (refer to fig. 8.2).

The recording method is called *tunnel erasure*; as the track is laid down,
the trailing tunnel erase heads erase the outer bands of the track, trimming it cleanly on the disk. The heads force the data to be present only
within a specified narrow "tunnel" on each track. This process prevents

the signal from one track from being confused with the signals from adjacent tracks. If the signal were allowed to "taper off" to each side, problems would occur. The forcibly trimmed track prevents this problem.

Alignment is the placement of the heads with respect to the tracks they must read and write. Head alignment can be checked only against some sort of reference-standard disk recorded by a perfectly aligned machine. These types of disks are available, and you can use one to check your drive's alignment.

The two heads are spring-loaded and physically grip the disk with a small amount of pressure. Because PC Compatible floppy disk drives spin at only 300 or 360 RPM, this pressure doesn't present an excessive friction problem. Some newer disks are specially coated with Teflon or other compounds to further reduce friction and enable the disk to slide more easily under the heads. Because of the contact between the heads and the disk, a buildup of the oxide material from the disk eventually forms on the heads. The buildup periodically can be cleaned off the heads as part of a preventive-maintenance or normal service program.

The Head Actuator

The *head actuator* is a mechanical motor device that causes the heads to move in and out over the surface of a disk. These mechanisms for floppy disk drives universally use a special kind of motor, a *stepper motor*, that moves in both directions an amount equal to or less than a single revolution. This type of motor does not spin around; rather, the motor can complete only a partial revolution in each direction. Stepper motors move in fixed increments, or *detents*, and must stop at a particular detent position. Stepper motors are not infinitely variable in their positioning. Each increment of motion, or a multiple thereof, defines each track on the disk. The motor can be commanded by the disk controller to position itself according to any relative increment within the range of its travel. To position the heads at track 25, for example, the motor is commanded to go to the 25th detent position.

The stepper motor usually is linked to the head rack by a coiled, split steel band. The band winds and unwinds around the spindle of the stepper motor, translating the rotary motion into linear motion. Some drives use a worm gear arrangement rather than a band. With this type, the head assembly rests on a worm gear driven directly off the stepper motor shaft. Because this arrangement is more compact, you normally find worm gear actuators on the smaller 3 1/2-inch drives. A stepper motor usually has a full travel time of about 1/5 of a second—about 200 milliseconds. On average, a half-stroke is 100 milliseconds, and a one-third stroke is 66 milliseconds. The timing of a one-half or one-third stroke of the head-actuator mechanism often is used to determine the reported average-access time for a disk drive. *Average-access time* is the normal amount of time the heads spend moving at random from one track to another.

The Spindle Motor

The *spindle motor* spins the disk. The normal speed of rotation is either 300 or 360 RPM, depending on the type of drive. The 5 1/4-inch HD drive is the only drive that spins at 360 RPM; all others, including the 5 1/4-inch DD, 3 1/2-inch DD, 3 1/2-inch HD, and 3 1/2-inch ED drives, spin at 300 RPM. Most earlier drives used a mechanism on which the spindle motor physically turned the disk spindle with a belt, but all modern drives use a direct-drive system with no belts. The direct-drive systems are more reliable and less expensive to manufacture, as well as smaller in size. The earlier belt-driven systems have more rotational torque available to turn a sticky disk, because of the torque multiplication factor of the belt system. Most newer direct-drive systems use an automatic torque-compensation capability that automatically sets the disk-rotation speed to a fixed 300 or 360 RPM and compensates with additional torque for sticky disks or less torque for slippery ones. This type of drive eliminates the need to adjust the rotational speed of the drive.

Most newer direct-drive systems use this automatic-speed feature, but many earlier systems require that you periodically adjust the speed. Looking at the spindle provides you with one clue to the type of drive you have. If the spindle contains strobe marks for 50 Hz and 60 Hz strobe lights (fluorescent lights), the drive probably has an adjustment for speed somewhere on the drive. Drives without the strobe marks almost always include an automatic tachometer-control circuit that eliminates the need for adjustment. The technique for setting the speed involves operating the drive under fluorescent lighting and adjusting the rotational speed until the strobe marks appear motionless, much like the "wagon wheel effect" you see in old Western movies. The procedure is described later in this chapter, in the "Setting the Floppy Drive Speed Adjustment" section.

To locate the spindle-speed adjustment, you must consult the original equipment manufacturer's (OEM) manual for the drive. IBM provides the information for its drives in the *Technical Reference Options and Adapters* manual as well as in the hardware-maintenance reference manuals. Even if IBM had sold the drives, they most likely are manufactured by another company, such as Control Data Corporation (CDC), Tandon, YE-Data (C. Itoh), Alps Electric, or Mitsubishi. I recommend contacting these manufacturers about the original manuals for your drives.

Circuit Boards

A disk drive always incorporates one or more *logic* boards, circuit boards that contain the circuitry used to control the head actuator, read/write heads, spindle motor, disk sensors, and any other components on the drive. The logic board represents the drive's interface to the controller board in the system unit.

The standard interface used by all PC types of floppy disk drives is the Shugart Associates SA-400 interface. The interface, invented by Shugart in the 1970s, has been the basis of most floppy disk interfacing. The selection of this industry-standard interface is the reason that you can purchase "off the shelf" drives (raw, or bare, drives) that can plug directly into your controller. (Thanks, IBM, for sticking with industry-standard interfacing; it has been the foundation of the entire PC upgrade and repair industry!)

Some other computer companies making non-IBM-compatible systems (especially Apple, for example) have stayed away from industry standards in this and other areas, which can make tasks such as drive repair or upgrades a nightmare—unless, of course, you buy all your parts from them. For example, in both the Apple II series as well as the Mac, Apple has used nonstandard proprietary interfaces for the floppy drives.

The Mac uses an interface based on a proprietary chip called either the IWM (Integrated Woz Machine) or the SWIM (Super Woz Integrated Machine) chip, depending on which Mac you have. These interfaces are incompatible with the industry standard SA-400 interface used in IBM-compatible systems, which is based on the nonproprietary NEC PD765 chip. In fact, the Apple drives use an encoding scheme called GCR (group-coded recording), which is very different from the standard MFM (modified frequency modulation) used in most other systems. The GCR encoding scheme, in fact, cannot be performed by the NEC-type controller chips, which is why it is impossible for IBM-compatible systems to read Mac floppy disks. To Apple's credit, the Mac systems with the SWIM chip include drives that can read and write both GCR and MFM schemes, enabling these systems to read and write IBM floppy disks.

Unfortunately, because the electrical interface to the drive is proprietary, you still cannot easily (or cheaply) purchase these drives as bare units from a variety of manufacturers, as you can for IBM-compatible systems. IBM uses true industry standards in these and other areas, which is why the PC, XT, AT, and PS/2 systems, as well as most IBM-compatible vendors' systems are so open to upgrade and repair.

Logic boards for a drive can fail and usually are difficult to obtain as a spare part. One board often costs more than replacing the entire drive. I recommend keeping failed or misaligned drives that might otherwise be discarded so that they can be used for their remaining good parts—such as logic boards. The parts can be used to restore a failing drive in a very cost-effective manner.

The Faceplate

The *faceplate*, or bezel, is the plastic piece that comprises the front of the drive. These pieces, usually removable, come in different colors and configurations.

Most drives use a bezel slightly wider than the drive. These types of drives must be installed from the front of a system because the faceplate is slightly wider than the hole in the system-unit case. Other drive faceplates are the same width as the drive's chassis; these drives can be installed from the rear—an advantage in some cases. In the later-version XT systems, for example, IBM uses this design in its drives so that two half-height drives can be bolted together as a unit and then slid in from the rear, to clear the mounting-bracket and screw hardware. On occasion, I have filed the edges of a drive faceplate to install the drive from the rear of a system—which made the installation much easier in some cases.

Connectors

All disk drives have at least two connectors—one for power to run the drive and the other to carry the control and data signals to and from the drive (see fig. 8.3). These connectors are fairly standardized in the computer industry; a 4-pin in-line connector (called Mate-N-Lock, by AMP) is used for power, and a 34-pin edge connector is used for the data and control signals. Some smaller 3 1/2-inch drives use a tiny version of the power connector, and some drives can have the other connector modified as well. The manufacturers make these drives, however, for special applications in which the different style of connectors might be required.

Fig. 8.3

A disk drive power-supply cable connector.

The following chart shows the definition of the pins on the drive power-cable connector:

Pin number	Signal	Wire color
Pin 1	+12 Vdc	Yellow
Pin 2	Ground	Black
Pin 3	Ground	Black
Pin 4	+5 Vdc	Red

In the PS/2 systems, for example, IBM uses a special version of a Mitsubishi 3 1/2-inch drive called the MF-355W-99; for a standard PC- or AT-type system, however, you want the MF-355B-82 (black faceplate) or MF-355B-88 (beige faceplate). These latter drives include an adapter that enables the standard power connector and disk drive control and data connector to be used. These types of drives are ideal for upgrading earlier systems. Most drive-upgrade kits sold today include the drive, appropriate adapters for the power and control and data cables, 5 1/4-inch frame adapter and faceplate, and rails for AT installations. The frame adapter and faceplate enable the drive to be installed where a 5 1/4-inch half-height drive normally would go.

Drive-Configuration Devices

You must locate several items on a drive that you install in a system. These items control the configuration and operation of the drive and must be set correctly depending on which type of system the drive is installed in and exactly where in the system the drive is installed.

You must set or check these items during installation:

> Drive select jumper
> Terminating resistor
> Diskette Changeline or Ready jumper
> Media sensor jumper

You learn how to configure these items later in this chapter. In this section, you learn what function these devices perform.

Drive Select Jumpers

Each drive in a controller and drive subsystem must have a unique drive number. The *drive select jumper* is set to indicate to the controller the number of a particular drive. The jumper indicates whether the specific drive should respond as drive 0 or 1 (A: or B:). Some idiosyncrasies can be found when you're setting this jumper in various systems, because of strange cable configurations or other differences. Most drives allow four different settings, labeled DS1, DS2, DS3, and DS4. Some drives start with 0, and thus the four settings are labeled DS0, DS1, DS2, and DS3. On some drives, these jumpers are not labeled! If they are not labeled, you have several resources available for information about how to set the drive: the OEM manual, your experience with other similar drives, or simply an educated guess. I recommend first checking the manual if it is available; if not, then perhaps you can rely on your past experiences and make an educated guess.

You might think that the first drive select position corresponds to A: and that the second position corresponds to B:, but in most cases you would be wrong. The configuration that seems correct is wrong because of some creative rewiring of the cable. IBM, for example, crosses the seven wires numbered 10 through 16 (the drive select, motor enable, and some ground lines) in the floppy interface cable between drives B: and A: to allow both drives to be jumpered the same way, as though they both were drive B:. This type of cable is shown later in this chapter.

If you had set the DS jumper on the drives using this type of cable with the twisted lines, you would have set both drives to the second drive select position. This setup enabled dealers and installers to buy the drives by IBM and to install them with a minimum of hassle. Sometimes this setup confuses people who attempt to install drives properly without knowing about the twisted-cabling system.

If the cable has a straight-through design, in which lines 10 through 16 are not twisted between the B: and A: connectors, you would in fact jumper the drives as you might have thought originally—that is, drive A: would be set to the first drive select position, and drive B: would be set to the second drive select position.

If you install a drive and it either does not respond or responds in unison with the other drive in the system in calling for drive A:, you probably have the drive select jumper set incorrectly for your application. If two drives respond in unison, the drive intended to be B: has been set as A:. If neither drive responds, the one intended as A: has been set as B:.

Terminating Resistors

The terminating resistor must be set, or enabled, on the drive at the end of the cable furthest from the controller. In most systems, this drive should also be the lowest-lettered drive (A:) of the pair. The drive plugged into the connector in the center of the cable must have the terminating resistor (or terminator) removed or disabled for proper operation.

The terminating resistor is designed to absorb any signals that reach the end of a cabling system so that no reflection of the signals echoes, or bounces, back down the line in the opposite direction. Engineers sometimes call this effect *signal ringing*. Simply put, noise and distortion can disrupt the original signal and prevent proper communications between the drive and controller. Another function of proper termination is to place the proper resistive load on the output drivers in the controller and drive.

A terminating resistor already is installed in the controller to terminate the cable at that end; you must be concerned only about properly terminating the drive end. Sometimes a system operates even with incorrect terminator installation, but the system might experience sporadic disk errors. Additionally, with the wrong signal load on the controller and drives, you run the risk of damaging them by causing excessive power output because of a low resistance load.

The terminating resistor usually looks like a memory chip—a 16-pin dual in-line package (DIP) device. The device is actually a group of eight resistors physically wired in parallel with each other to terminate separately each of the eight data lines in the interface subsystem. Normally, this "chip" is a different color from other black chips on the drive. Orange, blue, or white are common colors for a terminating resistor. Be aware that not all drives use the same type of terminating resistor, however, and it might be physically located in different places on different manufacturer's drive models. The OEM manual for the drive comes in handy in this situation because it shows the location, physical appearance, enabling and disabling instructions, and even the precise value required for the resistors. Do not lose the terminator if you remove it from a drive; you might need to reinstall it later if you relocate the drive to a different position in a system or even to a different system. Some drives use a resistor network in a single in-line pin (SIP) package, which looks like a slender device with eight or more pins in a line.

Some drives, especially those made by Toshiba, have a permanently installed terminating resistor enabled or disabled by a simple jumper. This type of terminating resistor is preferable to one you can remove and then lose. Most 3 1/2-inch drives use *distributed termination*, a technique for termination in which each drive has a lower-value terminating resistor and therefore carries a part of the termination load. These terminating resistors are fixed permanently to the drive and never have to be removed. This feature makes configuring these drives one step simpler.

The Diskette Changeline and Ready Jumper

In an XT-type system, pin 34 of the disk drive interface is not used, but in an AT system this pin is used to carry a signal called *Diskette Changeline*, or DC. Although the XT does not use pin 34, most drives that don't support the DC signal can optionally use the pin to carry a signal called *ready*, or RDY.

The AT uses the Diskette Changeline signal to determine whether the disk has been changed, or more accurately, whether the same disk loaded during the previous disk access still is loaded in the floppy drive. *Disk Change* is a pulsed signal that changes a status register in the controller to let the system know that a disk has been either inserted or ejected. This register is set to indicate that a disk has been inserted or removed (changed) by default. The register is cleared when the controller sends a step pulse to the drive and the drive responds, acknowledging that the heads have moved. At this point, the system knows that a specific disk is in the drive. If the disk change signal is not received before the next access, the system can assume that the same disk is still in the drive. Any information read into memory during the previous access therefore can be reused without rereading the disk.

Because of this process, some systems can buffer or cache the contents of the file allocation table or directory structure of a disk in the system's memory. By eliminating unnecessary rereads of these areas of the disk, the apparent speed of the drive is increased. If you move the door lever or eject button on a drive that supports the disk change signal, the DC pulse is sent to the controller, thus resetting the register indicating that the disk has been changed. This procedure causes the system to purge buffered or cached data that had been read from the disk because the system then cannot be sure that the same disk is still in the drive.

AT-class systems use the DC signal to increase significantly the speed of the floppy interface. Because the AT can detect whether you have changed the disk, the AT can keep a copy of the disk's directory and file allocation table information in RAM buffers. On every subsequent disk access, the operations are much faster because the information does not have to be reread from the disk in every individual access. If the DC signal has been reset (has a value of 1), the AT knows that the disk has been changed and appropriately rereads the information from the disk.

You can observe the effects of the DC signal by trying a simple experiment. Boot DOS on an AT-class system and place in drive A: a formatted floppy disk with data on it. Drive A: can be any type of drive except 5 1/4-inch double-density, although the disk you use can be anything the drive will read, including a double-density 360K disk, if you want. Then type this command:

    DIR A:

The disk drive lights up, and the directory is displayed. Note the amount of time spent reading the disk before the directory is displayed on-screen. Without touching the drive, enter the dir a: command again, and watch the drive-access light and screen. Note again the amount of time that passes before the directory is displayed. The drive A: directory should appear almost instantly the second time because virtually no time is spent reading the disk. The directory information was simply read back from RAM buffers rather than read again from the disk. Now open and close the drive door, and keep the disk in the drive. Type dir a: again. The disk again takes some time reading the directory before displaying anything, because the AT "thinks" that you have changed the disk.

The PC and XT controllers (and systems) are not affected by the status of the DC signal. These systems "don't care" about signals on pin 34. The PC and XT systems always operate under the assumption that the disk is perpetually changed, and they reread the disk directory and file allocation table during every access—one reason that these systems are slower in using the floppy disk drives.

A problem can occur when certain drives are installed in an AT system. As mentioned, some drives use pin 34 for a ready signal. The RDY signal is sent when a disk is installed and rotating in the drive. If you install a drive that has pin 34 set to send RDY, the AT "thinks" that it is continuously receiving a disk change signal, which will cause problems: Usually the drive fails with a Drive not ready error and renders the drive inoperable. If the drive is not sending a signal on pin 34 and if the system thinks that the drive is not a 360K drive, the system never recognizes that a disk is changed. Therefore, even if you change the disk, the AT still acts as though the first disk is in the drive, and holds the first disk's directory and file allocation table information in RAM. The information is written automatically to any subsequent disks written to in the drive.

If you ever have seen an AT-class system with a floppy drive that shows "phantom directories" of the previously installed disk, even after you have changed or removed it, you have experienced this problem first-hand. The negative side effect is that all disks after the first one you place in this system are in extreme danger. You likely will overwrite the directories and file allocation tables of many disks with information from other disks. Data recovery from such a catastrophe can require quite a bit of work with utility programs such as the Norton Utilities. These problems with disk change most often are traced to an incorrectly configured drive. Another possibility is that the disk-eject sensor mechanism no longer operates correctly. A temporary solution to the problem is to press the Ctrl-Break or Ctrl-C key combination every time you change a floppy disk in the drive. These commands cause DOS to flush the RAM buffers manually and reread the directory and file allocation table during the next disk access.

All drives except 5 1/4-inch double-density (360K) drives support the Disk Change signal. Therefore, if your system thinks that one of these drives is installed, the drive is expected to provide the signal. If the system thinks that the installed drive is a 360K drive, no signal is expected on pin 34.

To summarize, PC and XT systems are not affected by pin 34, but on AT systems, non-360K drives must have pin 34 set to send Disk Change. If the drive is a 360K drive and you want to install it in an AT, pin 34 must be disabled (usually preconfigured as such, or set by removing a jumper). Never set a 360K drive (or any other drive for that matter) to send a signal called Ready (RDY) on pin 34, because no IBM-compatible system can use this signal. The only reason it exists on some drives is that it happens to be a part of the standard Shugart SA-400 disk interface that was not adopted by IBM.

The Media Sensor Jumper

This configuration item exists only on the 3 1/2-inch 1.44M drives. The jumper selection, called the *media sensor (MS) jumper*, must be set to enable a special media sensor in the disk drive, which senses a media sensor hole found only in the 1.44M high-density (HD) and the 2.88M extra-high density (ED) floppy disks.

This setup enables the drive to determine the level of recording strength to use, and is required for most installations of these drives because of a bug in the design of the Western Digital hard disk and floppy controllers used by IBM in the AT systems. This bug prevents the controller from properly instructing the drive to switch to double-density mode when you write or format double-density disks. With the media sensor enabled, the drive no longer depends on the controller for density mode switching, and relies only on the drive's media sensor. Unless you are sure that your disk controller does not have this flaw, you must be sure that your HD drive includes the media sensor, and that it is properly enabled. The 2.88M drives universally rely on media sensors to determine the proper mode of operation. The 2.88M drives, in fact, have two separate media sensors because the ED disks include a media sensor hole in a different position than the HD disks.

With only a few exceptions, high-density 3 1/2-inch drives installed in most IBM-compatible systems do not operate properly in double-density mode unless the drive has control over the write current (recording level) via an installed and enabled media sensor. Exceptions are found primarily in systems with floppy controllers integrated on the motherboard, including most IBM PS/2 systems as well as most laptop or notebook systems from other manufacturers. These systems have floppy controllers without the bug referred to earlier, and can correctly switch the mode of the drive without the aid of the media sensor. In these systems, it technically does not matter whether you enable the media sensor. If the media sensor is enabled, the drive mode is controlled by the disk you insert, as is the case with most IBM-compatible systems. If the media sensor is not enabled, the drive mode is controlled by the floppy controller, which in turn is controlled by DOS.

If a disk is already formatted (correctly), DOS reads the volume boot sector to determine the current disk format, and the controller then switches the drive to the appropriate mode. If the disk has not been formatted yet, DOS has no idea what type of disk it is, and the drive remains in its native HD or ED mode.

When you format a disk in systems without an enabled media sensor (such as most PS/2s), the mode of the drive depends entirely on the FORMAT command issued by the user, regardless of the type of disk inserted. For example, if you insert a DD disk into an HD drive in an IBM PS/2 Model 70 and format the disk by entering FORMAT A:, the disk is formatted as though it is an HD disk because you did not issue the correct parameters to cause the FORMAT command to specify a DD format. On a system with the media sensor enabled, this type of incorrect format would fail and you would see the `Invalid media or Track 0 bad` error message from FORMAT. In this case, the media sensor prevents an incorrect format from occurring on the disk, a safety feature most IBM PS/2 systems lack. Some newer PS/2 systems, such as the 35, 40, 56, 57, 90, and 95, include drives with an enabled media sensor. These PS/2s work more like a standard IBM-compatible system during disk formatting.

The Floppy Disk Controller

The floppy disk controller consists of the circuitry either on a separate adapter card or integrated on the motherboard, which acts as the interface between the floppy drives and the system. Most PC- and XT- class systems used a separate controller card that occupied a slot in the system. The AT systems normally had the floppy controller and hard disk controller built into the same adapter card and also plugged into a slot. In most of the more modern systems built since then, the controller is integrated on the motherboard. In any case, the electrical interface to the drives has remained largely static, with only a few exceptions.

The original IBM PC and XT system floppy controller was a 3/4-length card that could drive as many as four floppy disk drives. Two drives could be connected to a cable plugged into a 34-pin edge connector on the card, and two more drives could be plugged into a cable connected to the 37-pin connector on the bracket of this card. These connectors and the pinouts for the controller are shown in figures 8.4 and 8.5.

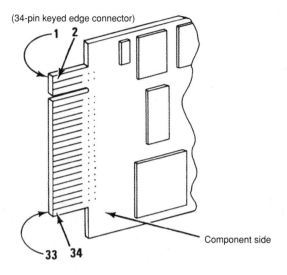

(34-pin keyed edge connector)

Component side

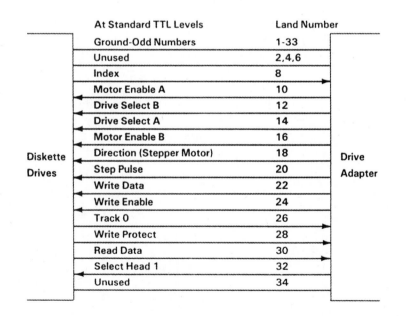

	At Standard TTL Levels	Land Number	
	Ground-Odd Numbers	1-33	
	Unused	2,4,6	
	Index	8	
	Motor Enable A	10	
	Drive Select B	12	
	Drive Select A	14	
	Motor Enable B	16	
Diskette	Direction (Stepper Motor)	18	Drive
Drives	Step Pulse	20	Adapter
	Write Data	22	
	Write Enable	24	
	Track 0	26	
	Write Protect	28	
	Read Data	30	
	Select Head 1	32	
	Unused	34	

Fig. 8.4

A PC and XT floppy controller internal connector.

Courtesy of IBM Corporation.

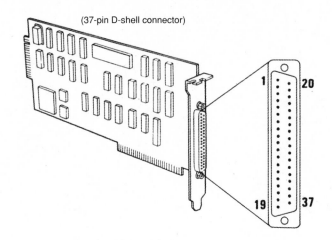

(37-pin D-shell connector)

At Standard TTL Levels	Pin Number
Unused	1-5
Index	6
Motor Enable C	7
Drive Select D	8
Drive Select C	9
Motor Enable D	10
Direction (Stepper Motor)	11
Step Pulse	12
Write Data	13
Write Enable	14
Track 0	15
Write Protect	16
Read Data	17
Select Head 1	18
Ground	20-37

External Drives

Drive Adapter

Courtesy of IBM Corporation.

Fig. 8.5

A PC and XT floppy controller external connector.

The AT used a board made by Western Digital, which included both the floppy and hard disk controllers in a single adapter. The connector location and pinout for the floppy controller portion of this card is shown in figure 8.6. IBM used two variations of this controller during the life of the AT system. The first one was a full 4.8 inches high, which used all the vertical height possible in the AT case. This board was a variation of the Western Digital WD1002-WA2 controller, sold through distributors and dealers. The second-generation card was only 4.2 inches high, which enabled it to fit into the shorter case of the XT-286 as well as the taller AT cases. This card was equivalent to the Western Digital WD1003-WA2, also sold on the open market.

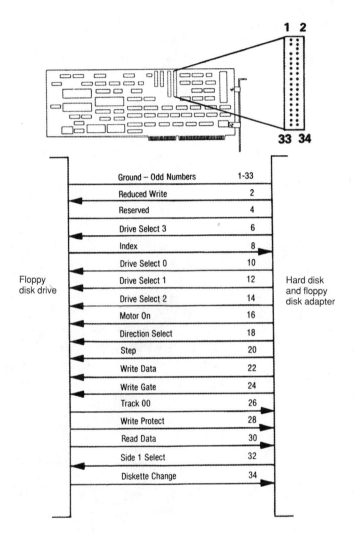

Ground – Odd Numbers	1-33
Reduced Write	2
Reserved	4
Drive Select 3	6
Index	8
Drive Select 0	10
Drive Select 1	12
Drive Select 2	14
Motor On	16
Direction Select	18
Step	20
Write Data	22
Write Gate	24
Track 00	26
Write Protect	28
Read Data	30
Side 1 Select	32
Diskette Change	34

Floppy disk drive

Hard disk and floppy disk adapter

Fig. 8.6

An AT floppy controller connector.

Courtesy of IBM Corporation.

Disk Physical Specifications and Operation

PC Compatible systems now use one of as many as five standard types of floppy drives. Also, there are five types of disks that can be used in the drives. This section examines the physical specifications and operations of these drives and disks.

Drives and disks are in two classes: 5 1/4-inch and 3 1/2-inch. The physical dimensions and components of a typical 5 1/4-inch disk and a 3 1/2-inch disk are shown later in this chapter.

The physical operation of a disk drive is fairly simple to describe. The disk rotates at either 300 or 360 RPM; the faster mode is reserved for high-density controllers and drives. With the disk spinning, the heads can move in and out approximately one inch, and write either 40 or 80 tracks. The tracks are written on both sides of the disk and therefore sometimes are called *cylinders*. A single cylinder comprises the tracks on the top and bottom of the disk. The heads record by using a tunnel-erase procedure in which a track is written to a specified width, and then the edges of the track are erased to prevent interference with any adjacent tracks.

The tracks are recorded at different widths for different drives. Table 8.1 shows the track widths in both millimeters and inches for the five types of floppy drives supported in PC systems.

Table 8.1 Floppy Disk Track-Width Specifications

Drive type	Number of tracks	Track width
5 1/4-inch 360K	40 per side	0.300 mm; 0.0118 inches
5 1/4-inch 1.2M	80 per side	0.155 mm; 0.0061 inches
3 1/2-inch 720K	80 per side	0.115 mm; 0.0045 inches
3 1/2-inch 1.44M	80 per side	0.115 mm; 0.0045 inches
3 1/2-inch 2.88M	80 per side	0.115 mm; 0.0045 inches

The differences in recorded track width can result in data-exchange problems between drives. The 5 1/4-inch drives are affected because the double-density drives record a track width nearly twice that of the high-density drives. A problem occurs, therefore, if a high-density drive is used to update a double-density disk with previously recorded data on it.

Even in 360K mode, the high-density drive cannot completely overwrite the track left by the 40-track drive. A problem occurs when the disk is returned to the person with the 360K drive: that drive read the new data as embedded within the remains of the previously written track. The drive cannot distinguish either signal, and an Abort, Retry, Ignore error message appears on-screen. The problem does not occur if a new disk (one that never has had data recorded on it) is first formatted in a 1.2M drive with the /4 option, which formats the disk as a 360K disk.

Note You can also format a 360K disk in a 1.2M drive with the /N:9 /T:40 or /F:360 options, depending on the DOS version. The 1.2M drive then can be used to fill the brand-new and newly formatted 360K disk to its capacity, and every file will be readable on the 40-track, 360K drive.

I use this technique all the time to exchange data disks between AT systems that have only the 1.2M drive and between XT or PC systems that have only the 360K drive. The key is to start with either a new disk or one wiped clean magnetically by a bulk eraser or degaussing tool. Just reformatting the disk does not work by itself because formatting does not actually erase a disk; instead it records data across the entire disk.

In addition to a track-width specification, there are specifications for the precise placement of tracks on a disk. A 5 1/4-inch DD disk has tracks placed precisely 1/48-inch apart. The outermost track on side 0 (the bottom of the disk) is the starting point for measurements, and this track (cylinder 0, head 0) has a radius of exactly 2.25 inches. Because Head 1 (the top of the disk) is offset by four tracks inward from Head 0, the radius of cylinder 0, Head 1 is 2.2500 inches – (1/48 inch * 4) = 2.1667 inches. Therefore, to calculate the exact track radius R in inches for any specified cylinder C and head position on a 360K disk, use these formulas:

For Head 0 (bottom): R = 2.2500 inches – C/48 inches
For Head 1 (top): R = 2.1667 inches – C/48 inches

That the tracks on top of the disk (Head 1) are offset toward the center of the disk from the tracks on the bottom of the disk (Head 0) might be surprising: in effect, the cylinders are cone shaped. Figure 8.7 shows the physical relationship between the top and bottom heads on a floppy drive. In this figure, both heads are positioned at the same cylinder. You can see that the top track of the cylinder is closer to the center of the disk than is the bottom track.

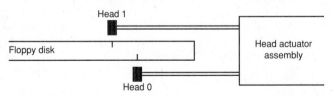

Fig. 8.7

Floppy disk drive head offset.

Courtesy of IBM Corporation.

I first saw this positioning in one of my data-recovery seminars. One of the experiments I perform is to stick a pin through a disk with data on it. The objective is to recover as much data as possible from the disk. Normally, I can resolve the damage down to only a few unreadable sectors on either side of the disk and then easily recover all but these damaged sectors. As I was trying to determine the exact location of the hole by its cylinder, head, and sector coordinates, I noticed that the damaged sectors were always located several cylinders apart on the top and bottom of the disk. Because I had stuck the pin straight through the disk, I realized that any offset had to be in the tracks themselves. I then removed the disk from its jacket to look more closely at the holes.

When I want to "see" the tracks on a disk, I use a special type of solution called Magnetic Developer, a fine-powdered iron suspended in a trichloroethelyne solution. When this developer, which dries quickly, is sprayed on the disk, the iron particles align themselves directly over magnetized areas of the disk and show very graphically the exact physical appearance and location of the tracks and sectors on the disk. You can see every individual track and sector on the disk "develop." With a microscope, I can locate the exact sectors and tracks damaged by the hole on either side of the disk. That the tracks on top of the disk start and end further toward the center of the disk became obvious with this method. If you want to do similar experiments or simply "see" the magnetic image of your disks, you can obtain the Magnetic Developer solution from Sprague Magnetics (its address and phone number are in the vendor list in the Appendix of this book). By the way, after viewing this magnetic image, the disk "cookie" can be washed off with distilled water, placed back into a new jacket, and reused!

The high-density 5 1/4-inch disk track dimensions are similar to the double-density disk, except that the tracks are spaced precisely 1/96-inch apart, and the top head (Head 1) is offset eight tracks inward from the bottom head (Head 0). The physical head offset between Head 0 and Head 1 is the same as DD disks because there are twice as many tracks in the same space as on a DD disk. The calculations for a given track radius R in inches for any cylinder C and head are as follows:

> For Head 0 (bottom): R = 2.2500-inch–C/96-inch
> For Head 1 (top): R = 2.1667-inch–C/96-inch

All the different 3 1/2-inch disks (DD, HD, ED) are dimensionally the same in track and cylinder spacing. The track and cylinder dimensions of these disks start with the radius of Cylinder 0, Head 0 (the bottom head outer track) defined as 39.5 millimeters. Tracks inward from this track are spaced precisely 0.1875 millimeters apart, and the top head (Head 1) is offset inward by eight tracks from Head 0. The radius, in millimeters, of the outer track on top of the disk (Cylinder 0, Head 1) therefore can be calculated as

> 39.5 mm–(0.1875 * 8) = 38.0 mm

Now you can calculate the radius R in millimeters of any specified cylinder C and head using these formulas:

> For Head 0 (bottom): R = 39.5mm–(0.1875mm * C)
> For Head 1 (top): R = 38.0mm–(0.1875mm * C)

An interesting note about the dimensions of the 3 1/2-inch disks is that the dimensional standards all are based in the metric system, unlike the 5 1/4-inch disks. I could have converted these numbers to their English equivalents for comparison with the 5 1/4-inch disk figures, but rounding would have sacrificed some accuracy in the numeric conversion. For example, many texts often give the track spacing for 3 1/2-inch disks as 135 TPI (tracks per inch). This figure is an imprecise result of metric-to-English conversion and rounding. The true spacing of 0.1875 mm between tracks converts to a more precise figure of 135.4667 TPI. The figures presented here are the specifications as governed by the ANSI standards X3.125 and X3.126 for 360K and 1.2M disks, and by Sony, Toshiba, and Accurite, which all are involved in specifying 3 1/2-inch disk standards.

Disk Magnetic Properties

A subtle problem with the way a disk drive works magnetically is that the recording volume varies depending on the type of format you are trying to apply to a disk. The high-density formats use special disks that require a much higher volume level for the recording than do the double-density disks. My classes nearly always are either stumped or incorrect (unless they have read ahead in the book) when they answer this question: "Which type of disk is magnetically more sensitive: a 1.2M disk or a 360K disk?" If you answer that the 1.2M disk is more sensitive, you are wrong! The high-density disks are approximately half as sensitive magnetically as the double-density disks.

The high-density disks are called *high-coercivity disks* also because they require a magnetic field strength much higher than do the double-density disks. Magnetic field strength is measured in *oersteds*. The 360K floppy disks require only a 300-oersted field strength in order to record, and the high-density 1.2M disks require a 600-oersted field strength. Because the high-density disks need double the magnetic field strength for recording, you should not attempt to format a 1.2M high-density disk as though it were a 360K disk, or a 360K disk as though it were a 1.2M high-density disk.

The latter case in particular seems to appeal to people looking for an easy way to save money. They buy inexpensive 360K disks and format them in a 1.2M drive, to the full 1.2M capacity. Most of the time, this format seems to work, with perhaps a large amount of bad sectors; otherwise, most of the disk might seem usable. You should not store important data on this incorrectly formatted disk, however, because the data is recorded at twice the recommended strength and density. Eventually, the adjacent magnetic domains on the disk begin to affect each other and can cause each other to change polarity or weaken because of the proximity of these domains, and because the double-density disk is more sensitive to magnetic fields. This process is illustrated later in this chapter, in the "Media Coercivity and Thickness" section. Eventually, the disk begins to erase itself and deteriorates. The process might take weeks, months, or even longer, but the result is inevitable—a loss of the information stored on the disk.

Another problem results from this type of improper formatting: You can imprint the 360K disk magnetically with an image that is difficult to remove. The high-density format will have placed on the disk a recording at twice the strength it should have been. How do you remove this recording and correct the problem? If you attempt to reformat the disk in a 360K drive, the drive writes in a reduced write-current mode and in some cases cannot overwrite the higher-volume recorded image you mistakenly placed on the disk. If you attempt to reformat the disk in the high-density drive with the /4 (or equivalent) parameter, which indicates 360K mode, the high-density drive uses a reduced write-current setting and again cannot overwrite the recording.

You can correct the problem in several ways. You can throw away the disk and write it off as a learning experience, or you can use a bulk eraser or degaussing tool to demagnetize the disk. These devices can randomize all the magnetic domains on a disk and return it to an essentially factory-new condition. You can purchase a bulk-erasing device at electronic-supply stores for about $25.

The opposite problem with disk formatting is not as common, but some have tried it anyway: formatting a high-density disk with a double-density format. You should not (and normally cannot) format a 1.2M high-density disk to a 360K capacity. If you attempt to use one, the drive changes to reduced write-current mode and does not create a magnetic field strong enough to record on the "insensitive" 1.2M disk. The result in this case is normally an immediate error message from the FORMAT command: Invalid media or Track 0 bad - disk unusable. Fortunately, the system usually does not allow this particular mistake to be made.

The 3 1/2-inch drives don't have the same problems as the 5 1/4-inch drives—at least for data interchange. Because both the high-density and double-density drives write the same number of tracks and these tracks are always the same width, no problem occurs when one type of drive is used to overwrite data written by another type of drive. A system manufacturer therefore doesn't need to offer a double-density version of the 3 1/2-inch drive for systems equipped with the high-density or extra high-density drive. The HD and ED drives can perfectly emulate the operations of the 720K DD drive, and the ED drive can perfectly emulate the 1.44M HD drive.

The HD and ED drives can be trouble, however, for inexperienced users who try to format disks to incorrect capacities. Although an ED drive can read, write, and format DD, HD, and ED disks, a disk should be formatted and written at only its specified capacity. An ED disk therefore should be formatted only to 2.88M, and never to 1.44M or 720K. *You must always use a disk at its designated format capacity.* You are asking for serious problems if you place a 720K disk in the A: drive of a PS/2 Model 50, 60, 70, or 80 and enter FORMAT A:. This step causes a 1.44M format to be written on the 720K disk, which renders it unreliable at best and requires a bulk eraser to reformat it correctly. If you decide to use the resulting incorrectly formatted disk, you will have an eventual massive data loss.

This particular problem could have been averted if IBM had used media sensor drives in all PS/2 systems. Drives that use the disk media-sensor hole to control the drive mode are prevented from incorrectly formatting a disk. The hardware causes the FORMAT command to fail with an appropriate error message if you attempt to format the disk to an incorrect capacity.

By knowing how a drive works physically, you can eliminate most of these user "pilot error" problems and distinguish this kind of easily solved problem from a more serious hardware problem. You will be a much better user as well as a troubleshooter of a system if you truly understand how a drive works.

Logical Operation

Each type of drive can create disks with different numbers of sectors and tracks. This section examines how DOS sees a drive. It gives definitions of the drives according to DOS and the definitions of cylinders and clusters.

How DOS Uses a Disk

A technical understanding of the way DOS maintains information on your disks is not necessary to use a PC, but you will be a more informed user if you understand the general principles.

To DOS, data on your PC disks is organized in tracks and sectors. Tracks are narrow, concentric circles on a disk. Sectors are pie-shaped slices of the disk. DOS versions 1.0 and 1.1 read and write 5 1/4-inch double-density disks with 40 tracks (numbered 0 through 39) per side and 8 sectors (numbered 1 through 8) per track. DOS versions 2.0 and higher automatically increase the track density from 8 to 9 sectors, for greater capacity on the same disk. On an AT with a 1.2M disk drive, DOS V3.0

supports high-density 5 1/4-inch drives that format 15 sectors per track and 80 tracks per side; DOS V3.2 supports 3 1/2-inch drives that format 9 sectors per track and 80 tracks per side; DOS V3.3 supports 3 1/2-inch drives that format 18 sectors per track and 80 tracks per side. The distance between tracks and, therefore, the number of tracks on a disk is a built-in mechanical and electronic function of the drive. Tables 8.2 and 8.3 summarize the standard disk formats supported by DOS version 5.0 and higher.

Table 8.2 5 1/4-inch Floppy Disk Drive Formats

	Double-density (DD)	High-density (HD)
Bytes per sector	512	512
Sectors per track	9	15
Tracks per side	40	80
Sides	2	2
Capacity (kilobytes)	360	1,200

Table 8.3 3 1/2-inch Floppy Disk Drive Formats

	Double-density (DD)	High-density (HD)	Extra-high density (ED)
Bytes per sector	512	512	512
Sectors per track	9	18	36
Tracks per side	80	80	80
Sides	2	2	2
Capacity (kilobytes)	720	1,440	2,880

You can calculate the capacity differences between different formats by multiplying the sectors per track by the number of tracks per side together with the constants of two sides and 512 bytes per sector.

Like blank sheets of paper, new disks contain no information. Formatting a disk is similar to adding lines to the paper so that you can write straight across. Formatting places on the disk the information DOS needs in order to maintain a directory and file table of contents. Using the

/S (system) option in the FORMAT command resembles making the paper a title page. FORMAT places on the disk the portions of DOS required to boot the system.

DOS reserves the track nearest to the outside edge of a disk (track 0) almost entirely for its purposes. Track 0, Sector 1 contains the "boot record," or "boot sector," the system needs in order to begin operation. The next few sectors contain the file allocation table, the disk "room reservation clerk" that keeps records of which clusters (rooms) on the disk have information and which are empty. Finally, the next few sectors contain the root directory, in which DOS stores information about the files on the disk; you see this information when you use the DIR command.

In computer-industry jargon, this process is "transparent to the user," which means that you don't have to (and generally cannot) decide where information is stored on disks. That this process is "transparent," however, doesn't necessarily mean that you shouldn't be aware of the decisions DOS makes for you.

When DOS writes data, it always begins by attempting to use the earliest available data sectors on the disk. Because the file might be larger than the particular block of available sectors that were selected, DOS then writes the remainder of the file in the next available block of free sectors. In this manner, files can become fragmented as they are written to fill a hole on the disk created by the deletion of some smaller file. The larger file completely fills the hole; then DOS continues to look for more free space across the disk, from the outermost tracks to the innermost tracks. The rest of the file is deposited in the next available free space.

This procedure continues until eventually all the files on your disk are intertwined. This situation is not really a problem for DOS because it was designed to manage files in this way. The problem is a physical one: Retrieving a fragmented file that occupies 50 or 100 separate places across the disk takes much longer than if the file were in one piece. Also, if the files were in one piece, recovering data in the case of a disaster would be much easier. You should consider unfragmenting a disk periodically simply because it can make recovery from a disk disaster much easier; many people, however, unfragment disks for the performance benefit in loading and saving files that are in one piece.

How do you unfragment a disk? DOS does not provide an easy method. To unfragment a floppy disk, you can copy all the files one by one to an empty disk, delete the original files from the first disk, and then recopy the files. With a hard disk, you can back up all the files, reformat the disk, and restore the files. This procedure is time consuming, to say the least.

Because DOS does not provide a good way to unfragment a disk, many software companies have produced utility programs that can easily unfragment disks in a clean and efficient manner. These programs can restore file contiguity without reformat and restore operations. My favorite for an extremely safe, easy, and *fast* unfragmenting program is the Vopt utility, by Golden Bow. In my opinion, no other unfragmenting utility even comes close to this amazing $50 package. Golden Bow's address and phone number are in the vendor list in the Appendix in this book.

> **WARNING:** These unfragmenting programs, inherently dangerous by nature, do not eliminate the need for a good backup program. Before using an unfragmenting program, make sure that you have a good backup. What shape do you think your disk would be in if the power failed during an unfragmenting session. Also, some programs have had bugs or have been incompatible with new releases of DOS.

Cylinders

The term *cylinder* usually is used in place of *track*. A cylinder is all the tracks that are under read/write heads on a drive at one time. For floppy drives, because a disk cannot have more than two sides and the drive has two heads, normally there are two tracks per cylinder. As you learn in Chapter 9, hard disks can have many disk platters, each with two heads, for many more tracks per single cylinder.

Clusters

A cluster is called an *allocation unit* also in DOS version 4.0 and higher. The term is appropriate because a single cluster is the smallest unit of the disk that DOS can allocate when it writes a file. A cluster is one or more sectors—usually two or more. Having more than one sector per cluster reduces the file-allocation table size and enables DOS to run faster because it has fewer individual allocation units of the disk with which to work. The tradeoff is in some wasted disk space. Because DOS can manage space only in the cluster size unit, every file consumes space on the disk in increments of one cluster. Table 8.4 lists the default cluster sizes used by DOS for different disk formats.

Table 8.4 DOS Default Cluster and Allocation Unit Sizes

Disk or volume size	Cluster and allocation unit size	FAT type
5 1/4-inch, 360K	2 sectors, or 1,024 bytes	12-bit
5 1/4-inch, 1.2M	1 sector, or 512 bytes	12-bit
3 1/2-inch, 720K	2 sectors, or 1,024 bytes	12-bit
3 1/2-inch, 1.44M	1 sector, or 512 bytes	12-bit
3 1/2-inch, 2.88M	2 sectors, or 1,024 bytes	12-bit

K = 1,024 bytes
M = 1,048,576 bytes

The high-density disks have smaller cluster sizes, which seems strange because these disks have many more individual sectors than do double-density disks. The probable reason is that because these high-density disks are faster than their double-density counterparts, IBM and Microsoft thought that the decrease in wasted disk space cluster size and speed would be welcome. You learn later that the cluster size on hard disks can vary much more between different versions of DOS and different disk sizes. Table 8.5 shows the floppy disk logical parameters.

Table 8.5 Floppy Disk Logical DOS-Format Parameters

	Current formats					Obsolete formats		
Disk size (inches)	3 1/2	3 1/2	3 1/2	5 1/4	5 1/4	5 1/4	5 1/4	5 1/4
Disk capacity (kilobytes)	2880	1440	720	1200	360	320	180	160
Media descriptor byte	F0h	F0h	F9h	F9h	FDh	FFh	FCh	FEh
Sides (heads)	2	2	2	2	2	2	1	1
Tracks per side	80	80	80	80	40	40	40	40
Sectors per track	36	18	9	15	9	8	9	8
Bytes per sector	512	512	512	512	512	512	512	512
Sectors per cluster	2	1	2	1	2	2	1	1
FAT length (sectors)	9	9	3	7	2	1	2	1
Number of FATs	2	2	2	2	2	2	2	2
Root directory length (sectors)	15	14	7	14	7	7	4	4

continues

Table 8.5 Continued								
	Current formats					**Obsolete formats**		
Maximum root entries	240	224	112	224	112	112	64	64
Total sectors per disk	5760	2880	1440	2400	720	640	360	320
Total available sectors	5726	2847	1426	2371	708	630	351	313
Total available clusters	2863	2847	713	2371	354	315	351	313

Types of Floppy Drives

Five types of standard floppy drives are available for an IBM-compatible system. The drives can be summarized most easily by their formatting specifications (refer to tables 8.2 and 8.3).

Most drive types can format multiple types of disks. For example, the 3 1/2-inch ED drive can format and write on any 3 1/2-inch disk. The 5 1/4-inch HD drive also can format and write on any 5 1/4-inch disk (although, as mentioned, sometimes track-width problems occur). This drive can even create some older obsolete formats, including single-sided disks and disks with eight sectors per track.

As you can see from table 8.5, the different disk capacities are determined by several parameters, some of which seem to remain constant on all drives, while others change from drive to drive. For example, all drives use 512-byte physical sectors, which remains true for hard disks as well. Note, however, that DOS treats the sector size as though it could be a changeable parameter, although the BIOS does not.

Note also that now all standard floppy drives are double sided. IBM has not shipped PC systems with single-sided drives since 1982; these drives are definitely considered obsolete. Also, IBM never has utilized any form of single-sided 3 1/2-inch drives, although that type of drive appeared in the first Apple Macintosh systems in 1984. IBM officially began selling and supporting 3 1/2-inch drives in 1986, and has used only double-sided versions of these drives.

The 360K 5 1/4-inch Drive

The 5 1/4-inch low-density drive is designed to create a standard-format disk with 360K capacity. Although I persistently call these low-density drives, the industry term is "double-density." I use "low-density" because I find the term "double-density" to be somewhat misleading, especially when I am trying to define these drives in juxtaposition to the high-density drives.

The term *double density* arose from the use of the term *single density* to indicate a type of drive that used frequency modulation (FM) encoding to store approximately 90 kilobytes on a disk. This type of obsolete drive never was used in any IBM-compatible systems, but was used in some older systems such as the original Osborne-1 portable computer. When drive manufacturers changed the drives to use Modified Frequency Modulation (MFM) encoding, they began using the term "double density" to indicate it, as well as the (approximately doubled) increase in recording capacity realized from this encoding method. All modern floppy disk drives use MFM encoding, including all types listed in this section. Encoding methods such as FM, MFM, and RLL are discussed in Chapter 9, "Hard Disk Drives."

The 360K 5 1/4-inch drive normally records 40 cylinders of two tracks each, with each cylinder numbered starting with 0 closest to the outside diameter of the floppy disk. Head position (or side) 0 is recorded on the underside of the floppy disk, and Head 1 records on the top of the disk surface. This drive normally divides each track into nine sectors, but it can optionally format only eight sectors per track to create a floppy disk compatible with DOS versions 1.1 or earlier. This type of format rarely (if ever) is used today.

The 360K 5 1/4-inch drives as supplied in the first IBM systems all were full-height units, which means that they were 3.25 inches tall. Full-height drives are obsolete now and have not been manufactured since 1986. Later units used by IBM and most compatible vendors have been the half-height units, which are only 1.6 inches tall. You can install two half-height drives in place of a single full-height unit. These drives, made by different manufacturers, are similar except for some cosmetic differences.

The 360K 5 1/4-inch drives spin at 300 RPM, which equals exactly 5 revolutions per second, or 200 milliseconds per revolution. All standard floppy controllers support a 1:1 interleave, in which each sector on a specific track is numbered (and read) consecutively. To read and write to a disk at full speed, a controller sends data at a rate of 250,000 bits per second. Because all low-density controllers can support this data rate, virtually any controller supports this type of drive, depending on ROM BIOS code that supports these drives.

All standard IBM-compatible systems include ROM BIOS support for these drives; therefore, you usually do not need special software or driver programs in order to use them. This statement might exclude some aftermarket (non-IBM) 360K drives for PS/2 systems that might require some type of driver in order to work. The IBM-offered units use the built-in ROM support to enable these drives to work. The only requirement usually is to run the Setup program for the machine to enable it to properly recognize these drives.

The 1.2M 5 1/4-inch Drive

The 1.2M high-density floppy drive first appeared in the IBM AT system introduced in August 1984. The drive required the use of a new type of disk to achieve the 1.2M format capacity, but it still could read and write (although not always reliably) the lower-density 360K disks.

The 1.2M 5 1/4-inch drive normally recorded 80 cylinders of two tracks each, starting with cylinder 0, at the outside of the disk. This situation differs from the low-density 5 1/4-inch drive in its capability to record twice as many cylinders in approximately the same space on the disk. This capability alone suggests that the recording capacity for a disk would double, but that is not all. Each track normally is recorded with 15 sectors of 512 bytes each, increasing the storage capacity even further. In fact, these drives store nearly four times the data of the 360K disks. The density increase for each track required the use of special disks with a modified media designed to handle this type of recording. Because these disks initially were expensive and difficult to obtain, many users attempted incorrectly to use the low-density disks in the 1.2M 5 1/4-inch drives and format them to the higher 1.2M-density format. This attempt results in data loss and unnecessary data-recovery operations.

A compatibility problem with the 360K drives stems from the 1.2M drive's capability to write twice as many cylinders in the same space as the 360K drives. The 1.2M drives easily can position their heads over the same 40 cylinder positions used by the 360K drives through "double stepping," a procedure in which the heads are moved every two cylinders to arrive at the correct positions for reading and writing the 40 cylinders on the 360K disks. The problem is that because the 1.2M drive normally has to write 80 cylinders in the same space in which the 360K drive writes 40, the heads of the 1.2M units had to be made dimensionally smaller. These narrow heads can have problems overwriting tracks produced by a 360K drive that has a wider head, because the narrower heads on the 1.2M drive cannot "cover" the entire track area written by the 360K drive. This problem and possible solutions to it are discussed later in this chapter.

The 1.2M 5 1/4-inch drives spin at 360 RPM, or 6 revolutions per second, or 166.67 milliseconds per revolution. The drives spin at this rate no matter what type of disk is inserted—either low- or high-density. To send or receive 15 sectors (plus required overhead) six times per second, a controller must use a data-transmission rate of 500,000 bits per second (500 kilohertz, or KHz). All standard high- and low-density controllers support this data rate and, therefore, these drives. This support of course would depend also on proper ROM BIOS support of the controller in this mode of operation. When a standard 360K disk is running in a high-density drive, it also is spinning at 360 RPM; a data rate of 300,000 bits per second (300 KHz) therefore is required in order to work properly. All standard AT-style low- and high-density controllers support the 250 KHz, 300 KHz, and 500 KHz data rates. The 300 KHz rate is used only for high-density 5 1/4-inch drives reading or writing to low-density 5 1/4-inch disks.

Virtually all standard AT-style systems have a ROM BIOS that supports the controller's operation of the 1.2M drive, including the 300 KHz data rate.

The 720K 3 1/2-inch Drive

The 720K, 3 1/2-inch, double-density drives first appeared in an IBM system with the IBM Convertible laptop system introduced in 1986. In fact, all IBM systems introduced since that time have 3 1/2-inch drives as the standard supplied drives. This type of drive has been offered also by IBM as an internal or external drive for the AT or XT systems. Note that outside the IBM-compatible world, other computer-system vendors (Apple, Hewlett-Packard, and so on) offered 3 1/2-inch drives for their systems well before the IBM-compatible world "caught on."

The 720K, 3 1/2-inch, double-density drive normally records 80 cylinders of two tracks each, with 9 sectors per track, resulting in the formatted capacity of 720 kilobytes. It is interesting to note that many disk manufacturers label these disks as 1.0-megabyte disks, which is true. The difference between the actual 1.0 megabyte of capacity and the usable 720K after formatting is that some space on each track is occupied by the header and trailer of each sector, the inter-sector gaps, and the index gap at the start of each track before the first sector. These spaces are not usable for data storage and account for the differences between the unformatted and formatted capacities. Most manufacturers report the unformatted capacities because they do not know on which type of system you will format the disk. Apple Macintosh systems, for example, can store 800K of data on the same disk because of a different formatting technique. Note also that the 720K of usable space does not account for the disk areas DOS reserves for managing the disk (boot sectors, FATs, directories, and so on) and that because of these areas, only 713K remains for file data storage.

IBM-compatible systems have used 720K, 3 1/2-inch, double-density drives primarily in XT-class systems because the drives operate from any low-density controller. The drives spin at 300 RPM, and therefore require only a 250 KHz data rate from the controller to operate properly. This data rate is the same as for the 360K disk drives, which means that any controller that would support a 360K drive would support also one of the 720K drives.

The only issue to consider in installing a 720K, 3 1/2-inch drive is whether the ROM BIOS offers the necessary support. An IBM system with a ROM BIOS date of 06/10/85 or later has built-in support for 720K drives and requires no driver in order to use them. If your system has an earlier ROM BIOS date, the DRIVER.SYS program from DOS V3.2 or higher—as well as the DRIVPARM config.sys command in some OEM DOS versions—is all you need in order to provide the necessary software support to operate these drives. Of course, a ROM BIOS upgrade to a later version negates the need for "funny" driver software, and is usually the preferred option when you add one of these drives to an older system.

The 1.44M 3 1/2-inch Drive

The 3 1/2-inch, 1.44M, high-density drives first appeared from IBM in the PS/2 product line introduced in 1987. Although IBM has not officially offered this type of drive for any of its older systems, most compatible vendors started offering the drives as options in systems immediately after IBM introduced the PS/2 system.

The drives record 80 cylinders consisting of two tracks each with 18 sectors per track, resulting in the formatted capacity of 1.44 megabytes. Most disk manufacturers label these disks as 2.0-megabyte disks, and the difference between this unformatted capacity and the formatted usable result is lost during the format. Note that the 1,440K of total formatted capacity does not account for the areas DOS reserves for file management, leaving only 1423.5K of actual file-storage area.

These drives spin at 300 RPM, and in fact must spin at that speed to operate properly with your existing high- and low-density controllers. To utilize the 500 KHz data rate, the maximum from most standard high- and low-density floppy controllers, these drives could spin at only 300 RPM. If the drives spun at the faster 360 RPM rate of the 5 1/4-inch drives, they would have to reduce the total number of sectors per track to 15 or else the controller could not keep up. In short, the 1.44M 3 1/2-inch drives store 1.2 times the data of the 5 1/4-inch 1.2M drives, and the 1.2M drives spin exactly 1.2 times faster than the 1.44M drives. The data rates used by both high-density drives are identical and compatible with the same controllers. In fact, because these 3 1/2-inch high-density drives can run at the 500 KHz data rate, a controller that can support a 1.2M 5 1/4-inch drive can support the 1.44M drives also. If you are using a low-density disk in the 3 1/2-inch high-density drive, the data rate is reduced to 250 KHz, and the disk capacity is 720K.

The primary issue in a particular system utilizing a 1.44M 3 1/2-inch drive is one of ROM BIOS support. An IBM system with a ROM BIOS date of 11/15/85 or later has built-in support for these drives, and no external driver support program is needed. You might need a generic AT setup program because IBM's setup program hasn't offered the 1.44M drive as an option. Another problem relates to the controller and the way it signals the high-density drive to write to a low-density disk. The problem is discussed in detail in the following section.

The 2.88M 3 1/2-inch Drive

The new 2.88M drive was developed by Toshiba Corporation in the 1980s, and officially announced in 1987. Toshiba began production manufacturing of the drives and disks in 1989, and then several vendors began selling the drives as upgrades for systems. DOS version 5.0 and higher officially supports the new drives, and most newer compatible ROM BIOS and disk controllers include support as well. Toshiba has indicated that it is developing a mass-market upgrade package to allow the installation and support of these drives in older compatible systems. The package will include a new disk controller, the 2.88M drive, cables, and either a new BIOS or software driver.

Handling Recording Problems with 1.44M 3 1/2-inch Drives

A serious problem awaits many users who use the 1.44M 3 1/2-inch drives: If the drive is installed improperly, any write or format operations performed incorrectly on 720K disks can end up trashing data on low-density disks. The problem is caused by the controller's inability to signal the high-density drive that a low-density recording will take place.

High-density disks require a higher write-current or signal strength when they record than do the low-density disks. A low-density drive can record at only the lower write-current, which is correct for the low-density disks; the high-density drive, however, needs to record at both high and low write-currents depending on which type of disk is inserted in the drive. If a signal is not sent to the high-density drive telling it to lower or reduce the write-current level, the drive stays in its normal high write-current default mode, even when it records on a low-density disk. The signal normally should be sent to the drive by the controller, but many controllers do not provide this signal properly for the 1.44M drives.

It seems that the Western Digital controller used by IBM would enable the reduced write-current (RWC) signal only if the controller also were sending data at the 300 KHz data rate, indicating the special case of a low-density disk in a high-density drive. The RWC signal is required to tell the high-density drive to lower the head-writing signal strength to be proper for the low-density disks. If the signal is not sent, the drive defaults to the higher write-current, which should be used for only high-density disks. If the controller were transmitting the 250 KHz data rate, the controller knows that the drive must be a low-density drive and therefore no RWC signal was necessary because the low-density drives can write only with reduced current.

This situation presented a serious problem for owners of 1.44M drives using 720K disks because the drives spin the disks at 300 RPM, and, in writing to a low-density disk, use the 250 KHz data rate—not the 300 KHz rate. This setup "fools" the controller into "thinking" that it is sending data to a low-density drive, which causes the controller to fail to send the required RWC signal. Without the RWC signal, the drive then records improperly on the disk, possibly trashing any data being written or any data already present. Because virtually all compatibles use controllers based on the design of the IBM AT floppy disk controller, most share the same problem as the IBM AT.

Drive and disk manufacturers devised the perfect solution for this problem, short of using a redesigned controller. They built into the drives a *media sensor*, which, when it is enabled, can override the controller's RWC signal (or lack of it) and properly change the head-current levels within the drive. Essentially, the drive chooses the write-current level independently from the controller when the media sensor is operational.

The sensor is a small, physical or optical sensor designed to feel, or "see," the small hole on the high-density 3 1/2-inch disks located opposite the write-enable hole. The extra hole on these high-density or extra-high density disks is the media sensor's cue that the full write-current should be used in recording. If an ED disk is detected, the ED drive enables the vertical recording heads. Low-density disks do not have these extra holes; therefore, when the sensor cannot see a media-sensor hole, it causes the drive to record in the proper reduced write-current mode for a double-density disk.

Some people, of course, foolishly attempt to override the function of these sensors by needlessly punching an extra hole in a low-density disk, to fool the drive's sensor into acting as though an actual high-density disk has been inserted. Several "con artist" companies have made a fast buck by selling media sensor hole-punchers to unwary or misinformed people. These "shyster" disk-punch vendors try to mislead you into believing that there is no difference between the low- and high-density disks except for the hole, and that punching the extra hole makes the low-density disk a legitimate high-density disk. This, of course, is absolutely untrue: The high-density disks are very different from low-density disks. The differences between the disks are explained in more detail later in this chapter.

Another reason that this hole-punching is needless is that if you want to record a high-density format on a low-density disk, you only have to remove the jumper from the drive that enables the media sensor. Removing the media sensor jumper still allows the drive to work properly for high-density disks writing at the full write-current level, but unfortunately also allows the higher write-current to be used on low-density disks as well because then the drive has no way of knowing the difference. If you really want to risk your data to low-density disks formatted as high-density disks, you can save yourself the cost of the $40 hole-punchers. Note that even if you attempt to format or record properly on a 720K disk, you still will be working at the higher write-current, and will risk trashing the disk.

Many newer systems, including the IBM PS/2 series, Toshiba laptops, and most others with floppy controllers built in to the motherboard, do not need 1.44M drives with media sensors. Their controllers have been fixed to allow the RWC signal to be sent to the drive even when the controller is sending the 250 KHz data rate. This setup allows for proper operation no matter what type of disk or drive is used, as long as the user formats properly. Because these systems do not have a media sensor policing users, they easily can format low-density disks as though they were high-density disks regardless of what holes are on the disk. In summary, if you use a PS/2, for example, you can trash all the data you want by using low-density disks as though they were high-density disks without punching any holes. I hope that you don't do this, of course— I am just stating that you can.

Handling Recording Problems with 1.2M and 360K Drives

The 5 1/4-inch drives have their own special problems. One major problem resulting in needless data destruction is that the tracks sometimes are recorded at different widths for different drives. These differences in recorded track width can result in problems with data exchange between different 5 1/4-inch drives.

As shown in table 8.1, the recorded track-width difference affects only the 5 1/4-inch drives because the 5 1/4-inch low-density drives record a track width more than twice that of the 5 1/4-inch high-density drives. This difference presents a problem if a high-density drive is used to update a low-density disk with previously recorded data on it. The high-density drive, even in 360K mode, cannot completely overwrite the track left by the 40-track drive. A problem occurs when the disk is returned to the person with the 360K drive, because that drive sees the new data as "embedded" within the remains of the previously written track. The 360K drive cannot distinguish either signal, and an Abort, Retry, Ignore error message results.

The way around this problem is to start with a brand-new disk that has never been formatted, and to format it in the 1.2M drive with the /4 (or equivalent) option. This procedure causes the 1.2M drive to place the proper 360K format on the disk. The 1.2M drive then can be used to fill the disk to its 360K capacity, and every file will be readable on the 40-track 360K drive because there were no previous wider data tracks to confuse the 360K drive. I use this trick all the time to exchange data disks between AT systems that have only a 1.2M drive and XT or PC systems that have only a 360K drive. The key is to start with a brand-new disk or a disk wiped clean magnetically by a bulk eraser. Simply reformatting the disk does not work because formatting actually writes data to the disk.

Note that because all the 3 1/2-inch drives write tracks of the same width, these drives have no disk-interchange problems related to track width.

Analyzing Floppy Disk Construction

The 5 1/4-inch and 3 1/2-inch disks each have unique construction and physical properties.

The flexible (or floppy) disk is contained within a plastic jacket. The 3 1/2-inch disks are covered by a more rigid jacket than are the 5 1/4-inch disks; the disks within the jackets, however, are virtually identical except, of course, for the size.

There are differences and similarities between these two different-size disks. Let's look at the physical properties and construction of each disk type.

When you look at a typical 5 1/4-inch floppy disk, you see several things (see fig. 8.8). Most prominent is the large, round hole in the center. When you close the disk drive's "door," a cone-shaped clamp grabs and centers the disk through the center hole. Many disks come with hub-ring reinforcements—thin, plastic rings like those used to reinforce three-ring notebook paper—intended to help the disk withstand the mechanical forces of the clamping mechanism. The high-density disks usually lack these reinforcements because the difficulty in accurately placing them on the disk means that they will cause alignment problems.

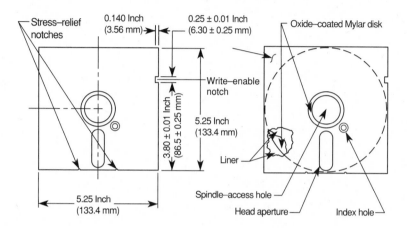

Fig. 8.8

Construction of a 5 1/4-inch floppy disk.

On the right side, just below the center of the hub hole, is a smaller, round hole called the *index hole*. If you carefully turn the disk within its protective jacket, you see a small hole in the disk. The drive uses the index hole as the starting point for all the sectors on the disk—sort of the "prime meridian" for the disk sectors. A disk with a single index hole is a *soft-sectored* disk; the software (operating system) decides the actual number of sectors on the disk. Some older equipment, such as Wang word processors, used hard-sectored disks, which had an index hole to demarcate individual sectors. Do not use hard-sectored disks in a PC.

Below the hub hole is a slot shaped somewhat like a long racetrack, through which you can see the disk surface. Through this *media-access hole*, the disk drive heads read and write information to the disk surface.

At the right side, about one inch from the top, is a rectangular punch from the side of the disk cover. If this *write-enable notch* is present, writing to the disk has been enabled. Disks without this notch (or with the notch taped over) are *write-protected* disks. The notch might not be on all disks, particularly those you have purchased with programs on them.

On the rear of the disk jacket, at the bottom, two very small, oval notches flank the head slot. The notches relieve stress on the disk and help prevent it from warping. The drive might use these notches also to assist in keeping the disk in the proper position in the drive.

Because the 3 1/2-inch disks use a much more rigid plastic case, which helps stabilize the disk, the disks can record at track and data densities greater than the 5 1/4-inch disks (see fig. 8.9). A metal shutter protects the media-access hole. The shutter is manipulated by the drive, and remains closed whenever the disk is not in a drive. The media then is insulated from the environment and from your fingers. The shutter also obviates the need for a disk jacket.

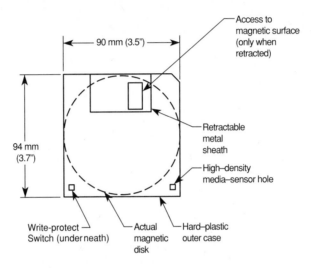

Fig. 8.9

Construction of a 3 1/2-inch floppy disk.

Rather than an index hole in the disk, the 3 1/2-inch disks use a metal center hub with an alignment hole. The drive "grasps" the metal hub, and the hole in the hub enables the drive to position the disk properly.

On the lower-left part of the disk is a hole with a plastic slider—the write-protect/-enable hole (refer to fig. 8.9). When the slider is positioned so that the hole is visible, the disk is write protected; the drive is prevented from recording on the disk. When the slider is positioned to cover the hole, writing is enabled and you can record on the disk. For more permanent write-protection, some commercial software programs are supplied on disks with the slider removed so that you cannot easily enable recording on the disk.

On the other (right) side of the disk from the write-protect hole, there might be in the disk jacket another hole called the *media-density-selector hole*. If this hole is present, the disk is constructed of a special media and is therefore a high-density or extra-high-density disk. If the media-sensor hole is exactly opposite the write-protect hole, it indicates a 1.44M HD disk. If the media-sensor hole is located more toward the top of the disk (the metal shutter is at the top of the disk), it indicates an ED disk. No hole on the right side means that the disk is a low-density disk. Most 3 1/2-inch drives have a media sensor that controls recording capability based on the existence or absence of these holes.

Both the 3 1/2-inch and 5 1/4-inch disks are constructed of the same basic materials. They use a plastic base (usually Mylar) coated with a magnetic compound. The compound is usually a ferric- (iron-) oxide-based compound for the standard density versions; a cobalt ferric compound usually is used in the higher-coercivity (higher-density) disks. A newly announced disk type, called *extended density*, uses a barium ferric compound. The rigid jacket material on the 3 1/2-inch disks often causes people to believe incorrectly that these disks are some sort of "hard disk" and not really a floppy disk. The disk "cookie" inside the 3 1/2-inch case is just as floppy as the 5 1/4-inch variety.

Floppy Disk Types and Specifications

This section examines all the types of disks you can purchase for your system. Especially interesting are the technical specifications that can separate one type of disk from another. This section defines all the specifications used to describe a typical disk.

Single- and Double-Sided Disks

Whether a disk is single- or double-sided is really an issue only for the lower-density disks. Because no single-sided high-density drives are manufactured, no need exists for disks to match the drives. The original IBM PC had single-sided drives, but they were discontinued in 1982.

A single-sided disk is constructed of the same material as a double-sided disk. The only difference seems to be that only the single-sided disks are "certified" (whatever that means) on only one side, and the double-sided disks are certified on both sides. Because the single-sided disks are cheaper than the double-sided versions, many PC users quickly determined that they could save some money if they used the single-sided disks even in double-sided drives.

The reason that this reasoning can work is that it is economically impractical for disk manufacturers to make some disks with recording surfaces on one side and other disks with recording surfaces on both sides. Today's single-sided disks look, and usually behave, exactly the same as double-sided disks. The result of this—depending on the brand of disks you buy—is that you can generally format and use "single-sided" disks successfully in double-sided drives, at a savings in disk costs. Unfortunately, the savings now are so small that this practice is obsolete, if not risky.

The danger in this practice is that some manufacturers do not burnish, or polish, the unused (top) side to the same level of smoothness as the used (bottom) side. This practice can cause accelerated wear on the top head. In single-sided drives, because the top head was replaced by a soft, felt pad, the rougher top side caused no problems. For the cost, it is not worth using with the wrong disks. I recommend the conservative route: Spend the small amount of extra money for double-sided disks of the correct density and you will rarely have to recover damaged data.

Density

Density, in simplest terms, is a measure of the amount of information that can be packed reliably into a specific area of a recording surface. The keyword here is *reliably*.

Disks have two types of densities: longitudinal density and linear density. *Longitudinal density* is indicated by how many tracks can be recorded on the disk, often expressed as a number of tracks per inch (TPI). *Linear density* is the capability of an individual track to store data, often indicated as a number of bits per inch (BPI). Unfortunately, both types of densities often are interchanged incorrectly in discussing different disks and drives. Table 8.6 provides a rundown of each available type of disk.

Table 8.6 Floppy Disk Media Specifications

	5 1/4-inch			3 1/2-inch		
	Double density	Quad density	High density	Double density	High density	Extra-high density
Media parameters	(DD)	(QD)	(HD)	(DD)	(HD)	(ED)
Tracks per inch (TPI)	48	96	96	135	135	135
Bits per inch (BPI)	5,876	5,876	9,646	8,717	17,434	34,868
Media doping agent	Ferrite	Ferrite	Cobalt	Cobalt	Cobalt	Barium
Coercivity (Oersteds)	300	300	600	600	720	750
Thickness (micro inches)	100	100	50	70	40	100
Recording polarity	Horiz.	Horiz.	Horiz.	Horiz.	Horiz.	Vertical

It is notable that IBM skipped the quad-density disk type—that is, no IBM system has used a quad-density drive, or required quad-density disks. Don't purchase a quad-density disk unless you just want a better-quality double-density disk.

Both the quad- and double-density disks store the same linear data on each track. They use the same formula for the magnetic coating on the disk, but the quad-density versions represent a more rigorously tested, higher-quality disk. The high-density disks are entirely different, however. To store the increased linear density, an entirely different magnetic coating was required. In both the 5 1/4-inch and 3 1/2-inch high-density disks, a high-coercivity coating is used to allow the tremendous bit density for each track. A high-density disk never can be substituted for a double- or quad-density disk because the write-current must be different for these very different media formulations and thicknesses.

The extra-high density 3 1/2-inch disk in the chart is newly available in some systems. This type of disk, invented by Toshiba, is available from several other vendors as well. The extra-high density disks use a barium-ferric compound to cover the disk with a thicker coating, which enables a vertical recording technique to be used. In vertical recording, the magnetic domains are recorded vertically rather than flat. The higher density results from their capability to be stacked much more closely together. These types of drives can read and write the other 3 1/2-inch disks because of their similar track dimensions on all formats.

Media Coercivity and Thickness

The *coercivity specification* of a disk refers to the magnetic-field strength required to make a proper recording on a disk. Coercivity, measured in oersteds, is a value indicating magnetic strength. A disk with a higher coercivity rating requires a stronger magnetic field to make a recording on that disk. With lower ratings, the disk can be recorded with a weaker magnetic field. In other words, *the lower the coercivity rating, the more sensitive the disk*.

Another factor is the thickness of the disk. The thinner the disk, the less influence a region of the disk has on another adjacent region. The thinner disks therefore can accept many more bits per inch without eventually degrading the recording.

When I ask someone whether the high-density disks are more sensitive or less sensitive than the double-density disks, the answer is almost always "more sensitive." But you can see that this is not true. The high-density disks are in fact as much as half as sensitive as the double-density disks. A high-density drive can record with a much higher volume level at the heads than can the standard double-density drive. For these high-density drives to record properly on a double-density disk, the drive must be capable of using a reduced write-current mode and enable it whenever the lower-density disks are installed. A big problem with users and floppy disks then can occur.

Most AT-system users cringe when they see the price of the high-density disks their drives require, as do PS/2-system users with high-density 3 1/2-inch disks. These users, in an attempt to save money, are tempted to use the lower-density disks as a substitute. Some users attempt to format the "regular" disk at the high-density capacity. This formatting is facilitated by DOS, which always attempts to format a disk to the maximum capacity of the drive's capabilities, unless specifically ordered otherwise through the use of proper parameters in the FORMAT command. If you use no parameters and simply enter FORMAT A:, however, the disk is formatted as though it were a high-density disk. Many users think that this procedure somehow is equivalent to using the single-sided disks in place of double-sided ones. I can assure you that this is not true—it is much worse. *Do not use double-density disks in place of high-density disks*, or you will experience severe problems and data loss from improper coercivity, media thickness, and write-current specifications.

The reasons for using the high-coercivity thin disks are simple. In designing the high-density drives, engineers found that the density of magnetic flux reversals caused adjacent flux reversals to begin to affect each other. The effect was that they started to cancel each other out, or cause shifts in the polarity of the domain. Data written at the high densities eventually began to erase itself. As an analogy, imagine a wooden track on which you place magnetic marbles, evenly spaced four inches apart in a specific pattern of magnetic polarity. At this distance, the magnetic forces from each marble are too weak to affect the adjacent marbles. Now imagine that the marbles must be placed only two inches apart. The magnetic attraction and repulsion forces now might start to work on the adjacent marbles so that they begin to rotate on their axis and thus change the direction of polarity and the data they represent.

You could eliminate the interaction of the magnetic domains by either spacing them further apart or making the domains "weaker," therefore reducing their sphere of influence. If the marbles were made half as strong magnetically as they were before, you could get them twice as close together without any interaction between them. This principle was behind the high-coercivity, thin media disks. Because they are weaker magnetically, they need a higher recording strength in order to store an image properly.

Try a simple experiment to verify this principle. Attempt to format a high-density disk in a low-density format. DOS responds with a Track 0 bad, Disk unusable message. The disk did not seem to accept a recording in low-density mode because the low-density recording is also low volume. The disk cannot make a recording on the disk, and therefore the Track 0 bad message is displayed.

It is unfortunate for users that the opposite attempt appears to work: that you can format a standard double-density disk as though it were a high-density disk and the FORMAT command or DOS does not seem to be affected. You might notice a large number of "bad sectors," but DOS allows the format to be completed anyway.

This situation is unfortunate for two reasons. First, you are recording on the (low-density) disk with a density that requires weak magnetic domains to eliminate interaction between the adjacent domains. A low-density disk unfortunately stores magnetic domains twice as strong as they should be, and eventually they interact. You will experience mysterious data losses on this disk over the next few days, weeks, or months.

Second, you have just placed a recording on this disk at twice the signal strength it should be. This "industrial strength" recording might not be removable by a normal disk drive, and the disk might be magnetically saturated. You might not ever be able to reformat it correctly as a double-density disk because a double-density reformat uses reduced write-current. The reduced write-current might not be capable of overwriting the high write-current signal that had been recorded incorrectly. The best way to remove this "burned in" recording then is to use a bulk eraser to renew the disk by removing all magnetic information. In most cases, however, a fresh format can overcome the magnetic image of the previous one, even if the write-current had been incorrect.

Do not use the wrong media for the format you are attempting to perform. You must use the correct type of disk. Note that the 3 1/2-inch disks have a perfect mechanism—the media sensor for deterring users. If you are sure that all your high-density 3 1/2-inch drives contain this sensor, set to function (by way of a jumper or switch), you are saved from your own ignorance. A drive with a media sensor sets the write-current and operating mode by the actual disk inserted. You are prevented from taking a 720K disk and attempting to cram 1.44 megabytes on it. Remember that IBM did not make using this sensor a requirement because it fixed the controller problem that necessitated it; therefore, incorrectly formatting a disk is easy on the PS/2 system. Also, if you want to format a low-density 3 1/2-inch disk incorrectly with a high-density format using an IBM PS/2 system, you don't need one of the "disk converters" or hole punchers.

Soft and Hard Sectors

Disks are either *soft sectored* or *hard sectored*; for the PC, soft-sectored disks have only one index hole on the disk surface. Once every revolution, the hole is visible through the hole in the protective jacket, and the drive, controller, and DOS use the hole to establish the location of the first sector on a track. Hard-sectored disks have a hole for each sector; therefore, each hole marks the beginning of a new sector. If you try to use a hard-sectored disk in a PC, the machine gets confused. Sometimes hard-sectored disks are not labeled specifically as hard-sectored, but rather specify "10 sectors" or "16 sectors." Don't buy them. (I have not even seen these disks for sale in quite some time.)

Formatting and Using High- and Low-Density Disks

This section describes how the different density capabilities of the high- and low-density drives sometimes can cause problems in formatting disks. You must always ensure that a disk initially is formatted to the density in which it was supposed to be run. In some cases, you should have a high-density drive format a low-density disk. You can perform this formatting with the correct format commands. The following section describes how to use DOS correctly so that your disks are formatted properly.

Reading and Writing 360K Disks in 1.2M Drives

Having 1.2M drives *read* or *write* to a 360K disk is a simple task. Just place a previously formatted 360K disk in the drive and use it normally. In other words, pretend that the drive is a 360K drive. Nothing special must be done. You can either read or write on the disk with absolutely no problems...yet.

You will have a problem if you decide to return the disk to a 360K drive and attempt to read it. Remember that the recorded track width of the 1.2M drive is half the track width of the 360K drive; therefore, if are any tracks have been *previously recorded by an actual 360K drive*, the tracks are twice as wide as the tracks recorded by the 1.2M drive. If you write to the disk with the 1.2M drive, you cannot overwrite the entire track width—only the center portion of it. When you return this disk to a 360K drive, the wider head system in the 360K drive then sees two signals on any overwritten tracks, and the new data is nestled within the image of the old data that could not be completely covered by the 1.2M drive. An immediate Abort, Retry, Ignore error from DOS usually is displayed for any updated portions of the disk.

To solve this problem easily, if you want to record data in an AT 1.2M drive and later read it properly in a 360K drive, make sure that you use *brand-new* disks for recording in the 1.2M drive. Because a new disk has no magnetic information on it, the smaller recorded track width can be written on the 1.2M drive and read properly in the 360K drive: The more narrow track is written in "clean space." The 360K drive, therefore, no longer is confused by any "ghost images" of previously recorded wider tracks. Other than starting with a brand-new disk, your only other option is to use a disk erased by a bulk eraser. You cannot erase a disk by reformatting it if has been in use. Formatting records actual data on the disk, and causes the track-width problem. The new or bulk-erased disk in fact must be formatted by the 1.2M drive for this procedure to work again. Remember the simple rule: Any track recorded by a 360K drive *cannot be overwritten* by a 1.2M drive, even in the 360K format.

How do you format a 360K disk in a 1.2M drive? If you just execute the FORMAT command without parameters, DOS attempts to format the disk to its maximum capacity. Because the 1.2M drives have no media-sensing capability, DOS assumes that the disk capability is equal to the maximum capability of the drive, and attempts to create a 1.2M format on the disk. The write-current is increased also during a recording in this format, which is incompatible with the 360K media. To format the 360K disk correctly, therefore, look at the alternative command examples in table 8.7.

Table 8.7 Proper Formatting of 5 1/4-inch 360K Disks in a 1.2M Drive

Command	DOS version					
	5.0	4.0	3.3	3.2	3.1	3.0
FORMAT d: /4	Yes	Yes	Yes	Yes	Yes	Yes
FORMAT d: /N:9 /T:40	Yes	Yes	Yes	Yes	No	No
FORMAT d: /F:360	Yes	Yes	No	No	No	No

d: = The drive to format
N = Number of sectors per track
T = Tracks per side
F = Format capacity

Each example command accomplishes the same function, which is to place on a 360K disk a 40-track, 9-sector format using reduced write-current mode.

Reading and Writing 720K Disks in 1.44M Drives

The 3 1/2-inch drives do not have the same problems as the 5 1/4-inch disks—that is, at least not with data interchange. Because both the high- and low-density drives write the same number of tracks and are the same width, one type of drive can be used to overwrite data written by another type of drive. Because of this capability, IBM does not need to offer a low-density version of the 3 1/2-inch drives for the PS/2 systems. These systems (except Models 25 and 30) include only the HD or ED drives, which are capable of imitating perfectly the 720K drives in the Model 25 and Model 30. The high-density drives can be trouble, however, in the hands of an inexperienced (or cheapskate) user. You *must* be sure to use only the 1.44M high-density disks in the 1.44M format, and only the 720K disks in the 720K format. You will encounter serious problems if you stick a 720K disk in a drive in a PS/2 without a media sensor drive and enter the command FORMAT A:. If you decide to use the formatted disk anyway, massive data loss eventually will occur.

Problems with incorrect formatting could have been averted if IBM had universally used disk drives that included the media sensor. This special switch senses the unique hole found only on the right side of high-density disks. Drives that use this hole to control the status of reduced write-current never can format a disk incorrectly. The hardware saves you by causing the FORMAT command to end in failure with an appropriate error message if you attempt to format the disk incorrectly.

If you purchase a 1.44M drive for upgrading an older system, the drive must have this sensor to control operation of the drive. IBM introduced the PS/2 system before the media sensor had been agreed on by the drive and disk manufacturers, and already had fixed the controller problem that required it; therefore, IBM did not use drives with media sensors in the PS/2 system. Newer PS/2 systems, such as Models 35, 40, 56, 57, 90, and 95 have been shipped with media sensor drives.

The 1.44M drives and 720K drives do not have all the same problems as the 5 1/4-inch drives, primarily because all the 3 1/2-inch drives have the same recorded track width. The 1.44M or 2.88M drive has no problem recording 720K disks. For these reasons (and more), I applaud the industry move to the 3 1/2-inch drives. The sooner we stop using 5 1/4-inch disk drives, the better.

The only other problem with formatting, other than incorrectly selecting a drive without a media sensor or failing to enable it during the drive-installation procedure, is naive users attempting to format disks at a capacity for which they were not designed. *You must have a 720K (double-density) disk in order to write a 720K format; a 1.44M (high-density) disk in order to write a 1.44M format; and a 2.88M (extra-high-density) disk in order to write an extra-high-density format.* No ifs, ands, or buts. This chapter has explained already that this requirement stems from differences in the coercivity of the media and the levels of recording current used in writing the disks.

When you enter a standard format command with no parameters, DOS always attempts to format the disk to the drive's maximum capacity. If you insert a 720K disk in a 1.44M drive, therefore, and enter the FORMAT command with no parameters, DOS attempts to create a 1.44M format on the disk. If the drive has a media sensor, the FORMAT command aborts with an error message. The media sensor does not communicate to DOS the correct information to format the disk—it just *prevents* incorrect formatting. You still must know the correct commands. Table 8.8 shows the correct FORMAT command and parameters to use in formatting a 720K disk in a 1.44M drive.

Table 8.8 Proper Formatting of 3 1/2-inch 720K Disks in a 1.44M Drive

| Command | DOS version | | |
	5.0	4.0	3.3
FORMAT d: /N:9 /T:80	Yes	Yes	Yes
FORMAT d: /F:720	Yes	Yes	No

d: = The drive to format
N = Number of sectors per track
T = Tracks per side
F = Format capacity
DOS versions earlier than 3.3 do not support the 1.44M drive.

Reading and Writing 1.44M Disks in 2.88M Drives

The 2.88M extra-high-density (ED) drive used in some newer systems, such as the PS/2 Model 57, is a welcome addition to any system. This drive offers a capacity twice as great as the standard 1.44M HD drive, and also offers full backward compatibility with the 1.44M HD drive and the 720K DD drive.

The 2.88M ED drive uses a technique called *vertical recording* to achieve its great linear density of 36 sectors per track. This technique increases density by magnetizing the domains perpendicular to the recording surface. By essentially placing the magnetic domains on their ends and stacking them side by side, density increases enormously.

The technology for producing heads that can perform a vertical or perpendicular recording has been around awhile. It is not the heads or even the drives that represent the major breakthrough in technology; rather, it is the media that is special. Standard disks have magnetic particles shaped like tiny needles, which lie on the surface of the disk. Orienting these acicular particles in a perpendicular manner to enable vertical recording is very difficult. The particles on a barium ferrite floppy disk are shaped like tiny, flat, hexagonal platelets that easily can be arranged to have their axis of magnetization perpendicular to the plane of recording. Although barium ferrite has been used as a material in the construction of permanent magnets, no one has been able to reduce the grain size of the platelets enough for high-density recordings.

Toshiba has perfected a glass-crystallization process for manufacturing the ultrafine platelets used in coating the barium ferrite disks. This technology, patented by Toshiba, is being licensed to a number of disk manufacturers, all of whom are producing barium ferrite disks using Toshiba's process. Toshiba also made certain modifications to the design of standard disk drive heads to enable them to read and write the new barium ferrite disks as well as standard cobalt or ferrite disks. This technology is being used not only in floppy drives but also is appearing in a variety of tape drive formats.

The disks are called 4MB disks in reference to their unformatted capacity. Actual formatted capacity is 2,880K, or 2.88M. Because of space lost in the formatting process, as well as space occupied by the volume boot sector, file-allocation tables, and root directory, the total usable storage space is 2,863K.

A number of manufacturers are making these drives, including Toshiba, Mitsubishi, Sony, and Panasonic. During the next few years, they should become more popular in higher-end systems.

Table 8.9 Proper Formatting of 3 1/2-inch 1.44M Disks in a 2.88M Drive

Command	DOS version 5.0
FORMAT d: /N:18 /T:80	Yes
FORMAT d: /F:1.44	Yes

d: = The drive to format
N = Number of sectors per track
T = Tracks per side
F = Format capacity
DOS V5.0 or higher is required in order to support the 2.88M drive.

Format Summary

This section is a short guide to the DOS FORMAT command. With newer DOS versions supporting more and different types of disk hardware, the once-simple FORMAT command has become more complex. Especially with the advent of DOS V5.0, the number of parameters and options available for the FORMAT command has increased dramatically. This section discusses the FORMAT command and these optional parameters. You will see a simple guide to proper formatting of disks, as well as a thorough description of the FORMAT command parameters and options.

This chapter has emphasized that a specific disk must always be formatted to its designated capacity. Formatting a disk to a capacity different from what it was designed for results only in an eventual loss of data from the disk. Because all the higher-density drives can format all the lower-density disks of the same form factor, knowing when a particular command option is required can be pretty complicated.

The basic rule is that a drive always formats in its native mode unless specifically instructed otherwise through the FORMAT command parameters. Therefore, if you insert a 2.88M ED disk in a 2.88M ED A: drive, you then can format that disk by simply entering FORMAT A:—no optional parameters are necessary in that case. If you insert any other type of disk (DD or HD), however, you absolutely *must* enter the appropriate parameters in the FORMAT command to change the format mode from the default 2.88M mode to the mode appropriate for the inserted disk. Even though the drive might have a media sensor that can detect which type of disk is inserted in the drive, the sensor does not communicate to the controller or DOS, which does not know which disk it is. In effect, all the sensor does is forcibly control the drive write mode, and also forces the FORMAT command to fail if you do not enter the correct parameters for the inserted disk type.

Table 8.10 shows the proper format command for all possible variations in drive and disk types. It shows also which DOS versions support the various combinations of drives, disks, and FORMAT parameters.

To use this table, just look up the drive type and disk type you have. You then can see the proper FORMAT command parameters to use as well as the DOS versions that support the combination you want.

With the advent of DOS V5.0, the FORMAT command has received a number of new functions and capabilities, all expressed through two new parameters: /Q (Quickformat) and /U (Unconditional). Precisely describing the effect of these parameters on the FORMAT command is difficult, especially considering that they have different effects on hard disks and floppy disks. Table 8.11 summarizes the functions of these new parameters, and relates the new functions to the older versions of DOS.

Table 8.10 Proper Disk Formatting

DOS version	Drive type	Disk type	Proper format command
DOS 2.0+	5 1/4-inch 360K	DD 360K	FORMAT d:
DOS 3.0+	5 1/4-inch 1.2M	HD 1.2M	FORMAT d:
DOS 3.0+	5 1/4-inch 1.2M	DD 360K	FORMAT d: /4
DOS 3.2+	5 1/4-inch 1.2M	DD 360K	FORMAT d: /N:9 /T:40
DOS 4.0+	5 1/4-inch 1.2M	DD 360K	FORMAT d: /F:360
DOS 3.2+	3 1/2-inch 720K	DD 720K	FORMAT d:
DOS 3.3+	3 1/2-inch 1.44M	HD 1.44M	FORMAT d:
DOS 3.3+	3 1/2-inch 1.44M	DD 720K	FORMAT d: /N:9 /T:80
DOS 4.0+	3 1/2-inch 1.44M	DD 720K	FORMAT d: /F:720
DOS 5.0+	3 1/2-inch 2.88M	ED 2.88M	FORMAT d:
DOS 5.0+	3 1/2-inch 2.88M	HD 1.44M	FORMAT d: /F:1.44

+ = *Includes all higher versions*
d: = *Specifies drive to format*
DD = *Double-density*
HD = *High-density*
ED = *Extra-high-density*

Table 8.11 DOS FORMAT Command Internal Operations

	DOS version					
	2-4	5	5	5	5	5
Hard disk FORMAT operations						
FORMAT parameters	Any	None	Any	/Q	/U	/Q/U
Disk previously formatted?	—	Yes	No	Yes	Yes	Yes
Check DOS volume boot sector	No	Yes	Yes	Yes	No	Yes
Save UNFORMAT information	No	Yes	No	Yes	No	No

	DOS version					
	2-4	5	5	5	5	5
Read verify (scan) disk	Yes	Yes	Yes	No	Yes	No
Overwrite DVB, FATs, and root directory	Yes	Yes	Yes	Yes	Yes	Yes
Overwrite data area	No	No	No	No	No	No
Floppy disk FORMAT operations						
FORMAT parameters	Any	None	Any	/Q	/U	/Q/U
Disk previously formatted?	—	Yes	No	Yes	Yes	Yes
Check DOS volume boot sector	No	Yes	Yes	Yes	No	Yes
Save UNFORMAT information	No	Yes	No	Yes	No	No
Read verify (scan) disk	Yes	Yes	Yes	No	Yes	No
Overwrite data area	Yes	No	Yes	No	Yes	No

/Q = Quick format
/U = Unconditional format
— = Does not matter
DVB = DOS volume boot sector
FAT = File allocation table

From this table you should be able to discern the function of a specific FORMAT command relative to the use of the /Q and /U parameters. For example, suppose that you are using DOS V5.0 and you insert a brand-new 1.44M disk in a 1.44M drive A: on your system. If you enter the command FORMAT A: with no other parameters, what will happen? By looking at table 8.11, you can see that the default operation of the FORMAT command in this case would be

1. Check the DOS volume boot sector.

2. Perform a read verify (or scan) of the entire disk.

3. Overwrite the DVB, FATs, and the root directory.

4. Overwrite the entire data area of the disk.

These functions do not necessarily happen in this order; in fact, the last three items listed occur simultaneously as the format progresses. Now suppose that you write some files on this disk and reenter the same FORMAT A: command. As you can see from table 8.11, the functions of the FORMAT command are very different this time. The steps occur something like this:

1. Check the DOS volume boot sector.

2. Save UNFORMAT information.

3. Perform a read verify (or scan) of the entire disk.

4. Overwrite the DVB, FATs, and the root directory.

The default operation of FORMAT on a disk that is already formatted has changed dramatically with DOS V5.0. The biggest differences between this and older versions of DOS is that DOS 5 and higher versions will (by default) save a backup copy of the disk's DOS volume boot sector, file-allocation tables, and root directory. This information, which is placed in a special format in sectors near the end of the disk, is designed to be utilized by the UNFORMAT command to restore these areas of the disk and therefore undo the work of the FORMAT command. In addition to saving this critical UNFORMAT information, the FORMAT command also defaults to *not* overwriting the data area of the disk; therefore, the UNFORMAT command can "restore" the disk data. The UNFORMAT does not actually restore the data—only the saved UNFORMAT information. The disk data is never lost. Older DOS versions do not check the disk to see whether it is formatted, and always overwrite the entire floppy disk.

The /Q parameter stands for Quickformat. The basic function of /Q, to eliminate the (sometimes lengthy) read verify scan for disk defects that otherwise would occur, can be performed only on a disk that already has been formatted. Any existing defect marks on the disk are preserved by using /Q. The net effect of /Q is to greatly speed up the formatting procedure for disks that were already formatted. It's a quick way to delete all the files from a disk quickly and efficiently.

The /U parameter stands for Unconditional. This parameter has two distinctly different effects depending on whether you are formatting a floppy disk or a hard disk. On a floppy disk, the /U parameter instructs the FORMAT command to overwrite the entire disk and skip saving UNFORMAT information because it would be useless anyway if the data were overwritten. On a hard disk, the purpose of /U is only to suppress saving UNFORMAT information. FORMAT on a hard disk *never* overwrites the data area of the disk, even with the /U parameter! If you have experience with the FORMAT command, you know that FORMAT never has overwritten data on a hard disk, no matter what version of IBM or MS-DOS you are using. (On some older OEM versions, such as COMPAQ and AT&T, DOS did overwrite the entire hard disk.)

When you combine the /Q and /U parameters, you get the fastest reformat possible. /Q prevents the scan for defects, which is the longest operation during formatting, and /U eliminates saving UNFORMAT information. The FORMAT command is restricted to simply erasing the DOS volume boot sector, FATs, and root directory, which it can do very quickly. In fact, a format using the /Q and /U parameters takes only a few seconds to complete no matter how large the disk.

For more information on the DOS FORMAT command, a master FORMAT command reference chart is in the Appendix of this book. This explicit chart explains what all the format parameters do, and even describes some useful undocumented parameters I discovered.

Caring for and Handling Floppy Disks and Drives

Most computer users know the basics of disk care. Disks can be damaged or destroyed easily by:

Touching the recording surface with your fingers or anything else

Writing on a disk label with a ballpoint pen or pencil

Bending the disk

Spilling coffee or other substances on the disk

Overheating a disk (leaving it in the hot sun or near a radiator, for example)

Exposing a disk to stray magnetic fields

Despite all these cautions, disks are rather hardy storage devices; I can't say that I have ever destroyed one by just writing on it with a pen, because I do so all the time. I am careful, however, not to press too hard, which can put a crease in the disk. Also, simply touching a disk does not necessarily ruin it but rather gets the disk and your drive head dirty with oil and dust. The danger to your disks comes from magnetic fields that, because they are unseen, can sometimes be found in places you never dreamed of.

For example, all color monitors (and color TV sets) have, around the face of the tube, a degaussing coil used to demagnetize the shadow mask inside when the monitor is turned on. The coil is connected to the AC line and controlled by a thermistor that passes a gigantic surge of power to the coil when the tube is powered on, which then tapers off as the tube warms up. The degaussing coil is designed to remove any stray magnetism from the shadow mask at the front area of the tube. Residual magnetism in this mask can bend the electron beams so that the picture appears to have strange colors or be out of focus.

If you keep your disks anywhere near (within one foot) of the front of the color monitor, you expose them to a strong magnetic field every time you turn on the monitor. Keeping disks in this area is not a good idea because the field is designed to demagnetize objects, and indeed works well for demagnetizing disks. The effect is cumulative and irreversible.

Another major disk destructor is the telephone. The mechanical ringer in a typical phone uses a powerful electromagnet to move the striker into the bell. The ringer circuit uses some 90 volts, and the electromagnetic fields have sufficient power to degauss a disk lying on the desk next to or partially underneath the phone. *Keep disks away from the telephone*. A telephone with an electronic ringer might not cause this type of damage to a disk, but be careful anyway.

Another source of powerful magnetic fields is an electric motor, found in vacuum cleaners, heaters or air conditioners, fans, electric pencil sharpeners, and so on. Do not place these devices near areas where you store disks.

Airport X-Ray Machines and Metal Detectors

People associate myths with things they cannot see, and we certainly cannot see data as it is stored on a disk, nor the magnetic fields that can alter the data.

One of my favorite myths to dispel is that the airport X-ray machine somehow damages disks. I have a great deal of experience in this area from having traveled around the country for the past 10 years or so with disks and portable computers in hand. I fly about 150,000 miles per year, and my portable computer equipment and disks have been through X-ray machines more than 100 times each year.

Most people commit a fatal mistake when they approach the airport X-ray machines with disks or computers: they don't pass the stuff through. Seriously, X-rays are in essence just a form of light, and disks and computers are just not affected by it. What can damage your magnetic media is the *metal detector*. Time and time again, someone with magnetic media or a portable computer approaches the security check. He freezes and says, "Oh no, I have disks and a computer—they have to be hand inspected." The person then refuses to place the disk and computer on the X-ray belt, and either walks through the metal detector with disks and computer in hand or passes the items over to the security guard, in very close proximity to the metal detector. Metal detectors work by monitoring disruptions in a weak magnetic field. A metal object inserted in the field area causes the field's shape to change, which the detector observes. This principle, which is the reason that the detectors are sensitive to metal objects, can be dangerous to your disks; the X-ray machine, however, is the safest area through which to pass either your disk or computer.

The X-ray machine is not dangerous to magnetic media because it merely exposes the media to electromagnetic radiation at a particular (very high) frequency. Blue light is an example of electromagnetic radiation of a different frequency. The only difference between X-rays and blue light is in the frequency, or wavelength, of the emission.

Electromagnetic radiation is technically a form of wave energy characterized by oscillating electric and magnetic fields perpendicular to one another. An electromagnetic wave is produced by an oscillating electric charge. This wave is not the same thing as a magnetic field. When matter intercepts electromagnetic energy, the energy is converted to thermal, electrical, mechanical, or chemical energy, but not to a magnetic field. Simply put, an electromagnetic wave generates either heat or an electrical alternating current in an object through which the wave passes.

I have been electrically shocked, for example, by touching metal objects in the vicinity of a high-powered amateur-radio transmitter. Your microwave oven induces thermal (kinetic) or even electrical energy in objects because of the same principle. Although a microwave oven is designed to induce kinetic energy in an irradiated substance's molecules, most of you know that when you place conductive (metal) objects in the microwave, an alternating electrical current also is generated, and you might even see sparks. This activity is a generation of electrical or mechanical energy, not of a magnetic field. Because a disk is not a good conductor, the only noticeable effect a high-powered electromagnetic field has on a floppy disk is the generation of kinetic (or thermal) energy. In other words, the only way that X-rays, visible light, or other radiation in these areas of the electromagnetic spectrum can damage a disk is by heating it.

Consider also that if electromagnetic radiation could truly magnetize a disk as a magnetic field can, all magnetic media (disks and tapes) in the world would be in danger. Much electromagnetic radiation is passing through you at this moment, and through all your disks and tapes as well. There is no danger of magnetic damage because the radiation's effect on an object is to impart electrical, thermal, mechanical, or chemical energy—*not to magnetize the object*. I am *not* saying that you cannot harm a disk with electromagnetic radiation, because you certainly can; the damage, however, is from the heating effects of the radiation.

You probably know what the sun's extremely powerful electromagnetic radiation can do to a disk. Just leave a disk lying in direct sunlight awhile and you can see the thermal effects of this radiation. A microwave oven would have basically the same cooking effect on a disk, only more intense! Seriously, at the levels of electromagnetic radiation to which we normally are exposed, or which are present in an airport X-ray machine, there is certainly no danger to your disks. The field strength is far too low to raise the temperature of the disk in any perceptible manner, and this radiation has no magnetic effect on a disk.

Some people worry about the effect of X-ray radiation on their system's EPROM (erasable programmable read-only memory) chips. This concern might actually be more valid than worrying about disk damage because EPROMs are erased by certain forms of electromagnetic radiation. In reality, however, you do not need to worry about this effect either. EPROMs are erased by direct exposure to very intense ultraviolet light. Specifically, to be erased, an EPROM must be exposed to a 12,000 uw/cm2 UV light source with a wavelength of 2537 angstroms for 15 to 20 minutes, and at a distance of one inch. Increasing the power of the light source or decreasing the distance from the source can shorten the erasure time to a few minutes. The airport X-ray machine is different by a factor of 10,000 in wavelength, and the field strength, duration, and distance from the emitter source are nowhere near what is necessary for EPROM erasure. Be aware that many circuit-board manufacturers use X-ray inspection on circuit boards (with components including EPROMs installed) to test and check quality control during manufacture.

I have conducted my own tests: I passed one disk through different airport X-ray machines for two years, averaging two or three passes a week. The same disk still remains intact with all the original files and data, and never has been reformatted. I have also several portable computers with hard disks installed; one of them has been through the X-ray machines safely every week for more than four years. I prefer to pass computers and disks through the X-ray machine because it offers the best shielding from the magnetic fields produced by the metal detector standing next to it. Doing so also significantly lowers the "hassle factor" with the security guards, because if I have it X-rayed, they usually do not require that I plug it in and turn it on.

Drive-Installation Procedures

The procedure for installing floppy drives is simple. You install the drive in two phases. The first phase is to configure the drive for the installation, and the second is to perform the physical installation. Of these two steps, the first one usually is the most difficult to perform, depending on your knowledge of disk interfacing and whether you have access to the correct OEM drive manuals.

Drive Configuration

Configuring a floppy drive consists of setting the jumpers and switches mounted on the drive to match the system in which the drive will be installed, as well as tailoring the function of the drive to the installer's requirements. Every drive has a stable of jumpers and switches, and many drives are different from each other. You will find no standards for what these jumpers and switches are called, where they should be located, or how they should be implemented. There are some general guidelines to follow, but to set up a specific drive correctly and know all the options available, you must have information from the drive's manufacturer, normally found in the original equipment manufacturer's (OEM) manual. The manual is a "must have" item when you purchase a disk drive.

Although additional options might be available, most drives have several configuration features that must be set properly for an installation. These standard options typically need attention during an installation procedure:

> Drive select jumper
> Terminating resistor
> Diskette Changeline or Ready jumper
> Media sensor jumper

Each configuration item was discussed in more detail earlier in this chapter. The following section describes how these items are to be set for various installations.

Floppy drives are connected by a cabling arrangement called a *daisy chain*. The name is descriptive because the cable is strung from controller to drive to drive in a single chain. All drives have a drive select (sometimes called DS) jumper that must be set to indicate a certain drive's physical drive number. The point at which the drive is connected on the cable does not matter; the DS jumper indicates how the drive should respond. Most drives allow four settings, but the controllers used in all PC systems support only two on a single daisy-chain cable. The PC and XT floppy controllers, for example, will support four drives but only on two separate cables—each one a daisy chain with a maximum of two drives.

Every drive on a particular cable must be set to have unique drive select settings. In a normal configuration, the drive you want to respond as the first drive (A:) is set to the first drive select position, and the drive you want to respond as the second drive (B:) is set to the second drive-select position. On some drives, the DS jumper positions are labeled 0, 1, 2, and 3; other drives use the numbers 1, 2, 3, and 4 to indicate the same positions. For some drives then, a setting of DS0 is drive A:. For others, however, DS1 indicates drive A:. Likewise, some drives use a setting of DS1 for drive B:, and others use a DS2 setting to indicate drive B:. On some drives, the jumpers on the drive circuit board are unlabeled! In this case, consult the drive's manual to find out the descriptions of each jumper setting on the drive. A typical daisy-chain drive cable with this included "twist" is connected as shown in figure 8.10.

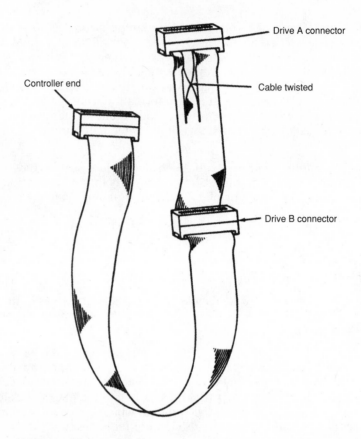

Controller end

Drive A connector

Cable twisted

Drive B connector

Fig. 8.10

A floppy controller cable showing the location of "the twist."

You should make sure that the DS settings for every drive on a single daisy-chain cable are different, or both drives will respond to the same signals. If you have incorrect DS settings, both drives respond simultaneously or neither drive responds at all.

The type of cable you use can confuse the drive select configuration. IBM puts in its cables a special twist that electrically changes the DS configuration of the drive plugged in after the twist. This twist causes a drive physically set to the first DS position (A:) to appear to the controller to be set to the second DS position (B:). If the first drive on the cable was before the twist in the cable and was set to the second DS position (B:), the controller would see a conflict. To the controller, both drives would appear to be set to the second DS position (B:), although physically they looked as though they were set differently. In essence, the system would think that two B: drives were installed. The adjustment for this problem is simple: When this type of cable is used, both drives should be set to the second DS position. The drive plugged in to the connector furthest from the controller, which is after the twist in the cable, then would have the physical second-DS-position setting appear to be changed to a first-DS-position setting. Then the system would see this drive as A:, and the drive plugged into the middle cable connector still would appear as B:.

An IBM-style floppy cable is a 34-pin cable with lines 10 through 16 sliced out and cross-wired (twisted) between the drive connectors (refer to fig. 8.10). This twisting "cross-wires" the first and second drive-select and motor-enable signals, and therefore inverts the DS setting of the drive following the twist. All the drives in a system using this type of cable, therefore—whether you want them to be A: or B:—are physically jumpered the same way; installation and configuration are simplified because both floppies can be preset to the second DS position. Some drives used by IBM, in fact, have had the DS "jumper" setting permanently soldered into the drive logic board.

Most bare drives you purchase will have the DS jumper already set to the second position, which is correct for the majority of systems that use a cable with the twisted lines. Although this setting is correct for the majority of systems, if you are using a cable with no twist, you will have to alter this setting on at least one of the two drives. Some systems come with only a single floppy drive and no provisions for adding a second one. These types of systems often use a floppy cable with only one drive connector attached. This type of cable would not have any twisted lines, so how would you set up a drive plugged into this cable? Because there is no twist, the DS setting you make on the drive is exactly what the controller would see. You can attach only one drive, and it should appear to the system as A:—therefore, you would set the drive to the first DS position.

Most IBM-compatibles use a floppy cable with the twisted lines between the drive connectors. Drives plugged into this type of cable have their DS jumpers set to the second position. Drives on a single floppy cable or a cable with no twisted lines are set to the first DS position.

A terminating resistor should be placed (or enabled) in any drive plugged into the physical end of a cable. The function of this resistor is to prevent reflections or echoes of signals from reaching the end of the cable. All new drives will have this resistor installed by default. The terminating resistor should be removed or disabled for drives that are not the farthest away from the controller. Most 3 1/2-inch floppy drives use the distributed-termination technique, in which the installed terminating resistors are permanently installed, and are nonremovable and cannot be disabled. The resistor value in these drives is adjusted appropriately so that, in effect, the termination is distributed among both drives. When you mix 5 1/4-inch and 3 1/2-inch drives, you should enable or disable the terminators on the 5 1/4-inch drives appropriately, according to their position on the cable, and ignore the nonchangeable settings on the 3 1/2-inch drives.

In a typical cabling arrangement for two 5 1/4-inch floppies, for example, the terminating resistor is installed in drive A: (at the end of the cable), and this resistor is removed from the other floppy drive on the same cable (B:). The letter to which the drive responds is not important in relation to terminator settings; the important issue is that the drive at the end of the cable has the resistor installed and functioning and that other drives on the same cable have the resistor disabled or removed.

The terminating resistor usually looks like a memory chip; it might be white, blue, black, gray, or some other color, and memory chips usually are just black. IBM always labels the resistor with a T-RES sticker for easy identification. On some systems, the resistor is a built-in device enabled or disabled by a jumper or series of switches. If you have the removable type, be sure to store the resistor in a safe place because you might need it later. Figure 8.11 shows the location and appearance of the terminating resistor or switches on a typical floppy drive. Because most 3 1/2-inch drives have a form of automatic termination, there is no termination to configure; also, some 5 1/4-inch drives, such as Toshiba drives, have a permanently installed terminating resistor enabled or disabled by a jumper labeled TM.

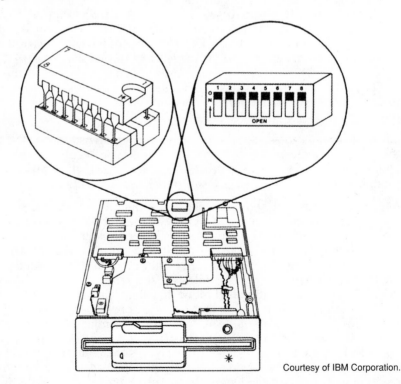

Fig. 8.11

A typical floppy drive terminating resistor, or termination switch.

Courtesy of IBM Corporation.

Table 8.12 explains how a drive should be configured relative to the drive-select jumper and terminating resistor. You can use the table as a universal drive-select and terminating-resistor configuration chart that applies to all types of drives, including floppy disk drives and hard disks.

Table 8.12 Configuring Drive-Select Jumpers and Terminating Resistors

	Twisted cable	Straight cable
First (A:) drive (end connector)	DS = second TR installed	DS = first TR installed
Second (B:) drive (center connector)	DS = second TR removed	DS = second TR removed

DS = Drive select position
TR = Terminating resistor

The assumption in table 8.12 is that you always plug drive B: into the center connector on the cable and drive A: into the end connector. This arrangement might seem strange at first, but it is virtually required if you ever assemble a single-drive system. The logical first (A:) drive should be the end, or last, drive on the cable, and should be terminated. The twist in the cable is almost always between the two drive connectors on a cable and not between the controller and a drive.

Two other options might be available for you to set: the status of pin 34 on the drive's connector, and the function of a media-sensor feature. The guidelines for setting these options follow.

If the drive is a 5 1/4-inch 360K drive, set the status of pin 34 to Open (disconnected) regardless of the type of system in which you are installing the drive. The only other option normally found for pin 34 on 360K drives is Ready (RDY), which is incorrect. If you are using only a low-density controller, as in a PC or XT, pin 34 is ignored no matter what is sent on it. If the drive you are installing is a 5 1/4-inch 1.2M or 3 1/2-inch 720K, 1.44M, or 2.88M drive, be sure to set pin 34 to send the Disk Change (DC) signal. The basic rule is simple:

> For 360K drives only, pin 34 = Open (disconnected)
> For any other drive, pin 34 = Disk Change

The media-sensor setting is the easiest to describe. Only 1.44M and 2.88M drives have a media sensor. The best rule to follow is to set these drives so that the sensor is enabled; this step enables the sensor to control the drive's recording mode and, therefore, the drive's write-current level.

Physical Installation

When you physically install a drive, you plug in the drive (refer to Chapter 6). Here, your concerns are using the correct brackets and screws for the system and the correct drive you are installing.

A special bracket usually is required whenever you install a half-height drive in place of an earlier full-height unit (see fig. 8.12). The brackets enable you to connect the two half-height drives together as a single full-height unit for installation. Remember also that nearly all floppy drives now use metric hardware; only the early, American-manufactured drives use the standard English threads.

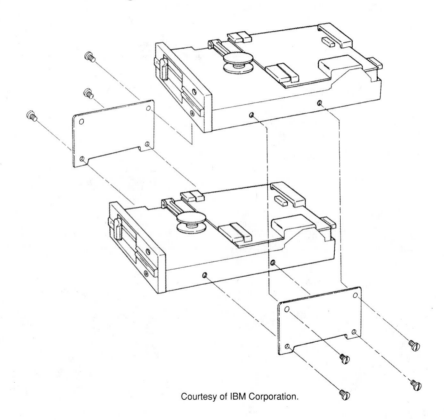

Fig. 8.12

Installing half-height drives with adapter plates.

Courtesy of IBM Corporation.

You can get these adapter plates from most vendors who sell drives, but sometimes they charge as much as $10 for basically a piece of sheet metal with four holes drilled in it! Several companies in the Appendix of this book specialize in cables, brackets, screw hardware, and other items useful in assembling systems or installing drives. I have also made up the template shown in figure 8.13, which will guide you if you want to make your own. I usually use a piece of galvanized sheet metal like that used in ventilation ductwork for the stock, which can be easily obtained at most hardware stores.

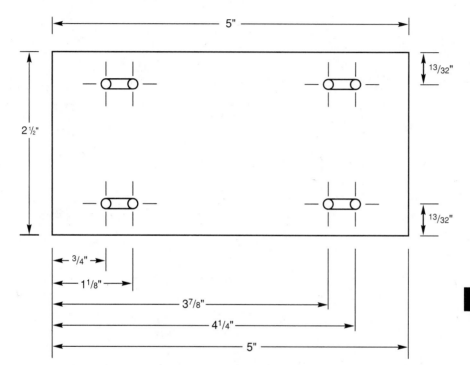

Another piece of drive-installation paraphernalia you need are the rails used in installing disk drives in AT systems. Most IBM-compatible systems follow the IBM standard for rail design. Again, you can purchase these from some of the vendors listed in the Appendix in this book. If you want to construct your own, figure 8.14 shows the construction of a typical IBM-style drive rail. These rails can be made from metal, but usually are made from plastic. They probably can even be made from wood. Drives installed in an AT are grounded to the system chassis through a separate ground wire and tab, which is why the rails do not need to be made from a conductive material. I find it more cost effective to purchase the rails rather than make them.

As you might expect, COMPAQ uses a slightly different rail construction. The vendors mentioned in the Appendix who sell cables, brackets, and other installation accessories also carry the COMPAQ-style rails.

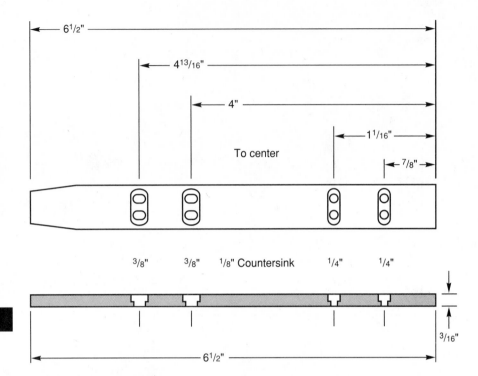

Fig. 8.14

A typical AT-drive
mounting rail.

When you connect a drive, make sure that the power cable is installed
properly. The cable normally is keyed so that it cannot be plugged in
backward. Also, install the data and control cable. If no key is in this
cable, which allows only a correct orientation, use the colored wire
in the cable as a guide to the position of pin 1. This cable is oriented
correctly when you plug it in so that the colored wire is plugged into
the disk drive connector toward the cut-out notch in the drive edge
connector.

Floppy Drive Installation Summary

To install and set up a floppy drive properly, you must understand and
set up primarily four different configuration items on the drive:

> Drive select jumper setting
> Terminating resistor enabled or disabled
> Send disk change/No signal on pin 34
> Enable media sensor

This section has explained the proper settings for these items in virtually any installation situation you might encounter.

For more information about configuring and installing a specific drive, you can use several resources. Obviously, this book contains much information about configuring and installing floppy disk drives—be sure that you have read it all! The best source of information about certain drives or controllers is the original equipment manufacturer's (OEM) documentation. These manuals tell you where all configuration item are located on the drive, what they look like, and how to set them. Unfortunately, most of the time you do not receive this detailed documentation when you purchase a drive or controller; instead, you must contact the OEM to obtain it.

Correcting Problems from Improper Drive Installation or Use

The majority of floppy drive problems I see are caused primarily by improper drive configuration, installation, or operation. Unfortunately, floppy drive configuration and installation is much more complicated than the average technician seems to realize. Even if you have had your drive "professionally" installed, it still might have been done incorrectly.

This section describes some of the most common problems that stem from improperly installing or configuring a drive. Also discussed are several problems that can occur from improperly using drives and disks. Solutions to these problems are presented also.

Handling the "Phantom Directory" (Disk Change)

One of the most common mistakes I have seen people make in installing a disk drive is incorrectly setting the signals sent by the drive on pin 34 of the cable to the controller. All drives *except* the 360K drive must be configured so that a Disk Change (DC) signal is sent along pin 34 to the controller.

If you have not enabled the DC signal when the system expects that it should have been, you might end up with trashed disks as a result. For example, a PC user with disk in hand might say to you, "Moments ago, this disk contained my document files, and now it seems as though my entire word processing program disk has mysteriously transferred to it. When I attempt to run the programs that now seem to be on this disk, they crash or lock up my system." Of course, in this case the disk has been damaged, and you will have to perform some data-recovery magic to recover the information for the user. My book *Que's Guide to Data Recovery* contains more information about data-recovery techniques. A good thing about this particular kind of problem is that recovering most—if not all—the information on the disk is entirely possible.

You also can observe this installation defect manifested in the "phantom directory" problem. For example, you place a disk with files on it in the A: drive of your AT-compatible system and enter the DIR A: command. The drive starts spinning, the access light on the drive comes on, and after a few seconds of activity, the disk directory scrolls up the screen. Everything seems to be running well. Then you remove the disk and insert in drive A: a different disk with different files on it and repeat the DIR A: command. This time, however, the drive barely (if at all) spins before the disk directory scrolls up the screen. When you look at the directory listing that has appeared, you discover in amazement that it is the same listing as on the first disk you removed from the drive.

You should understand that the disk you have inserted in the drive is in danger. If you write on this disk in any way, you will cause the file-allocation tables and root-directory sectors from the first disk (which are stored in your system's memory) to be copied over to the second disk, thereby "blowing away" the information on the second disk. Most AT-compatible systems with high- or low-density controllers utilize a floppy disk caching system that buffers the FATs and directories from the floppy disk that was last read in system RAM. Because this data is kept in memory, these areas of the disk do not have to be reread as frequently. This system greatly speeds access to the disk.

Opening the door lever or pressing the eject button on a drive normally sends the Disk Change signal to the controller, which in turn causes DOS to flush out the floppy cache. This action causes the next read of the disk drive to reread the FAT and directory areas. If this signal is not sent, the cache is not flushed when you change a disk, and the system acts as though the first disk still is present in the drive. Writing to this newly inserted disk writes not only the new data but also either a full or partial copy of the first disk's FAT and directory areas. Also, the data is written to what was considered free space on the first disk, which might not be free on the subsequent disk and results in damaged files and data.

There are several simple solutions to this problem. One is temporary; the other is permanent. For a quick, temporary solution, press Ctrl-Break or Ctrl-C immediately after changing any disk, to force DOS to flush manually the floppy I/O buffers. This method is exactly how the old CP/M operating system used to work. After pressing Ctrl-Break or Ctrl-C, the next disk access rereads the FAT and directory areas of the disk and places fresh copies in memory. In other words, you must be sure that every time you change a disk, the buffer gets flushed. Because these commands work only from the DOS prompt, you must not change a disk while working in an application.

A more permanent and correct solution to the problem is simple—just correct the drive installation. In my experience, incorrect installation is the root cause of this problem nine out of ten times. Remember this simple rule: *If a jumper block is on the disk drive labeled DC, you should install a jumper there.* If you are absolutely certain that the installation was correct—for instance, the drive has worked perfectly for some time, but then suddenly develops this problem—check the following list of items, all of which can prevent the Disk Change signal from being sent:

- Drive configuration (pilot error!). Make sure that the DC jumper is enabled.

- Bad cable. Check for continuity on pin 34.

- Bad Disk Change sensor. Clean sensor or replace drive and retest.

- Bad drive logic board. Replace drive and retest.

- Bad controller. Replace controller and retest.

- Wrong DOS OEM version. (Pilot error again!)

The last of these checklist items can stump you because the hardware seems to be functioning correctly. As a rule, you should use only the DOS supplied by the same OEM as the computer system on the system. For example, use IBM DOS on IBM systems, COMPAQ DOS on COMPAQ systems, Zenith DOS on Zenith systems, Toshiba DOS on Toshiba systems, Tandy DOS on Tandy systems, and so on. This problem is most noticeable with some laptop systems that apparently have a modified floppy controller design, such as some Toshiba laptops. On many of these systems, you *must* use the correct (Toshiba, for example) OEM version of DOS.

Handling Incorrect Media-Sensor Operation

Incorrect media-sensor operation occurs on only 1.44M or 2.88M, 3 1/2-inch, high-density drives, the only drives that have a media sensor. Again, this is largely a drive-configuration problem because the installer did not enable the sensor when it should have been enabled. You would think that the sensor would be set correctly when you purchase a drive, but that is not always the case. Never assume that a drive is pre-configured properly for your system. Remember that drive manufacturers sell drives for systems other than IBM-compatibles. Sometimes it is hard to remember that many other types of computers exist other than just IBMs or IBM clones.

If the media sensor is not operational, the controller likely will leave the drive in a state in which high write-current always is applied to the heads during write operations. This state is OK for high-density disks, but when low-density disks are used, random and sporadic read and write failures occur, usually ending with the DOS message `Abort, Retry, Ignore, Fail?`.

Another symptom of incorrect media-sensor operation would be generating double-density disks that seem eventually to lose data—maybe over a few weeks or months. This loss often can be traced back to an improperly configured media sensor on the drive. In some systems, the problem might be more obvious, such as not being capable of formatting or writing successfully on 720K disks. If your system can format a 720K disk to 1.44M without punching any extra holes in the disk, it is an immediate alert that the media sensor is not enabled.

Handling Problems Caused By Using Double-Density Disks at High Density

If you attempt to format a 5 1/4-inch, double-density disk at high-density format, you usually will hear several retries from the drive as DOS finds a large amount of bad sectors on the disk. When the format is completed, hundreds of kilobytes in bad sectors usually are reported. Most people would never use this disk. Because the 5 1/4-inch disks are so radically different from one another in terms of magnetic coercivity and media formulation, the double-density disks do not work well carrying a high-density format.

Problems are seen more often with the 3 1/2-inch disks because the double-density disks are not nearly as different from the high-density disks compared to the 5 1/4-inch versions, although they indeed are different. Because the 3 1/2-inch DD and HD disks differ less, however, a double-density, 3 1/2-inch disk usually accepts a high-density format with no bad sectors reported. This acceptance is unfortunate because it causes most users to feel that they are safe in using the disk for data storage.

A 3 1/2-inch, double-density disk with a 1.44M, high-density format initially seems to work with no problem. If you fill this type of double-density disk with 1.44M of data and store it on a shelf, you will notice that eventually the recording degrades and the data becomes unreadable. Several months might pass before you can detect the degradation, but then it is too late. From talking to hundreds of my clients, I have found that the average "half life" of such a recording is approximately six months from the time the data is written to the time that one or more files suddenly have unreadable sectors. In six months to a year, much of the rest of the disk rapidly degrades until all the data and files have extensive damage. The recording simply destroys itself during this time.

I have substantiated this situation with my own testing and my clients' experiences. If the data is reread and rewritten periodically before any degradation is noticeable, then the recording can be "maintained" for longer periods of time before data is lost.

The technical reasons for this degradation were explained earlier in this chapter. In a sense, the disk eventually performs a self-erasure operation. Again, the time frame for damage seems to be approximately six months to a year from the time the data is written. I certainly expect my disks to hold data for more than six months; in fact, data written properly to your disks should be readable many, many years from now.

If you have been using double-density, 3 1/2-inch disks with high-density formats, you are asking for problems. Using these types of disks for backup, for instance, is highly inappropriate! Many people use double-density disks as high-density disks to save money. You should realize that high-density disks are not very expensive anymore; *data-recovery services, however, are very expensive.* I do not condone incorrectly formatting disks, and I certainly would not want anyone to use one of those ridiculous disk "hole punchers." There are good reasons that I rarely am in data-recovery situations with my own data; yet I have seen people seem to wipe out data and crash systems by just *breathing* near a PC!

If you have a disk that has been formatted improperly and is developing read problems, the first thing to do is DISKCOPY the disk immediately to another proper-density disk. Then you can survey the damage and make repairs to the new copy. Chapter 15 describes how to repair some simple problems with the FAT, directory, and other management areas of the disk. For a more detailed investigation into the subject of data recovery, see *Que's Guide to Data Recovery*.

Handling Track-Width Problems from Writing on 360K Disks with a 1.2M Drive

As discussed earlier in this chapter, the 5 1/4-inch, high-density drives usually write a narrower track than the 5 1/4-inch, double-density drives. Therefore, when you use a high-density drive to update a double-density disk originally formatted or written in a double-density drive, the wider tracks written by the double-density drive are not completely overwritten by the high-density drive. Of course, if the double-density disk is newly formatted and subsequently written in only a high-density drive (although at the proper 360K format), there is no problem with overwrites—that is, until you update the disk with a double-density (wide-track) drive and then update it again with a high-density (narrow-track) drive. In that case, you again have a wider track with a narrow-track update embedded within—but not completely covering—it.

You must remember *never* to use a high-density drive to write on a double-density disk that was previously written by a double-density drive. This procedure would make the disk unreadable by the double-density drive, but usually still readable by the high-density drive. In fact, the best way to recover information from a disk that has been incorrectly overwritten in this manner is to use a high-density disk drive to perform a DISKCOPY operation of the disk to a new, blank, never-formatted, low-density disk.

Handling Off-Center Disk Clamping

Clamping the disk off-center in the drive has to be absolutely the most frequently encountered cause of problems with floppy drives. In my worldwide troubleshooting seminars, we run the PC systems with the lid off for most of the course. Whenever someone has a problem reading or booting from a floppy disk, I look down at the top of the exposed disk drive on the system while it is spinning to see whether the disk has been clamped by the drive hub in an off-center position. *More often than not, that is the problem.* I know that the disk is clamped off-center because the disk wobbles while it rotates. Ejecting and reinserting the disk so that it is clamped properly usually makes the disk reading or booting problem disappear immediately. This step might solve the problem in most cases, but it is not much help if you have formatted or written a disk in an off-center position. In that case, all you can do is try to DISKCOPY the improperly written disk to another disk and attempt various data-recovery operations on both disks.

I have used a technique for inserting floppy disks that has eliminated this problem for me. After inserting a disk into a drive, I always take an extra half-second to wiggle the drive lever or door, first down, and then up, and then down again to clamp the disk rather than simply push the door or lever down once to clamp it. The reason is that the first partial closing of the lever serves to center the disk in its jacket so that the second motion allows the drive hub to clamp the disk properly in a centered position. If I were in charge of training for a large organization, I would make sure that all the basic PC starter classes taught proper disk handling, including insertion and on-center clamping in the drive.

Note that the 3 1/2-inch drives are virtually immune to this type of problem because of the different type of clamping and centering mechanisms they use. Some 5 1/4-inch drives have adopted a more reliable clamping mechanism similar to the 3 1/2-inch drives. Canon makes some of these new 5 1/4-inch drives, used by IBM and COMPAQ. The newest version used by IBM in some of its PS/2 systems is totally motorized. You merely slide the disk into the drive slot, and the drive grabs the disk and electrically pulls it in and centers it. These drives also include a motorized eject button.

Realigning Misaligned Drives

If your disk drives are misaligned, you will notice that other drives cannot read disks created in your drive, and you might not be able to read disks created in other drives. This situation can be dangerous if you allow it to progress unchecked. If the alignment is bad enough, you probably will notice it first in the inability to read original application-program disks, while still being able to read your own created disks. Chapter 13 discusses the Drive Probe program from Accurite for checking the alignment and operation of floppy drives.

To solve this problem, you can have the drive realigned. I don't always recommend realigning drives because of the low cost of simply replacing the drive compared to aligning one. Also, an unforeseen circumstance catches many people off guard: You might find that your newly aligned drive might not be able to read all your backup or data disks created while the drive was out of alignment. If you replace the misaligned drive with a new one and keep the misaligned drive, you can use it for DISKCOPY purposes to transfer the data to newly formatted disks in the new drive.

Repairing Floppy Drives

Attitudes about repairing floppy drives have changed over the years primarily because of the decreasing cost of drives. When drives were more expensive, people often considered repairing the drive rather than replacing it. With the cost of drives decreasing every year, however, certain labor- or parts-intensive repair procedures have become almost as expensive as replacing the drive with a new one.

Because of the cost considerations, repairing floppy drives usually is limited to cleaning the drive and heads and lubricating the mechanical mechanisms. On drives that have a speed adjustment, adjusting the speed to within the proper operating range is common also. Note that most newer half-height drives and virtually all 3 1/2-inch drives do not have an adjustment for speed. These drives use a circuit that automatically sets the speed at the required level and compensates for variations with a feedback loop. If such an auto-taching drive is off in speed, the reason usually is that the circuit failed. Replacement of the drive usually is necessary.

Cleaning Floppy Drives

Sometimes read and write problems are caused by dirty drive heads. Cleaning a drive is easy. You can proceed in two ways. In one method, you use one of the simple head-cleaning kits available from computer- or office-supply stores. These devices are easy to operate and don't require the system unit to be open for access to the drive. The other method is the manual method: You use a cleaning swab with a liquid such as pure alcohol, Freon, or trichloroethelyne. With this method, you must open the system unit to expose the drive and, in many cases (especially in earlier full-height drives), also remove and partially disassemble the drive. The manual method can result in a better overall job, but usually the work required is not worth the difference.

The cleaning kits come in two styles: The wet type uses a liquid squirted on a cleaning disk to wash off the heads; the dry kit relies on abrasive material on the cleaning disk to remove head deposits. I recommend that you never use the dry drive-cleaning kits. Always use a wet system in which a liquid solution is applied to the cleaning disk. The dry disks can prematurely wear the heads if used improperly or too often; wet systems are very safe to use.

The manual drive-cleaning method requires that you have physical access to the heads, in order to swab them manually with a lint-free foam swab soaked in a cleaning solution. This method requires some level of expertise: Simply jabbing at the heads incorrectly with a cleaning swab might knock the drive heads out of alignment. You must use a careful in-and-out motion, and lightly swab the heads. No side-to-side motion (relative to the way the heads travel) should be used; this motion can snag a head and knock it out of alignment. Because of the difficulty and danger of this manual cleaning, for most applications I recommend a simple wet-disk cleaning kit because it is the easiest and safest method.

One question that comes up repeatedly in my seminars is "How often should you clean a disk drive?" Only you can answer that question. What type of environment is the system in? Do you smoke cigarettes near the system? If so, cleaning would be required more often. Usually, a safe rule of thumb is to clean drives about once a year if the system is in a clean office environment, in which no smoke or other particulate matter is in the air. In a heavy-smoking environment, you might have to clean every six months or perhaps even more often. In dirty industrial environments, you might have to clean every month or so. Your own experience is your guide in this matter. If DOS reports drive errors in the system by displaying the familiar DOS `Abort`, `Retry`, `Ignore` prompt, you should clean your drive to try to solve the problem. If cleaning does solve the problem, you probably should step up the interval between preventive-maintenance cleanings.

In some cases, you might want to place a (very small) amount of lubricant on the door mechanism or other mechanical contact points inside the drive. *Do not use oil.* I use a pure silicone lubricant. Oil collects dust rapidly after you apply it and usually causes the oiled mechanism to gum up later. Silicone does not attract dust in the same manner and can be used safely. Use very small amounts of silicone; do not drip or spray silicone inside the drive. You must ensure that the lubricant is applied only to the part that needs it. If the lubricant gets all over the inside of the drive, it may cause unnecessary problems.

Setting the Floppy Drive Speed Adjustment

Most older 5 1/4-inch floppy disk drives, especially full-height drives, have a small variable resistor used to adjust the drive's rotational speed. In particular, the Tandon and CDC full-height drives used by IBM in the PC and XT systems have this adjustment. The location of this variable resistor is described in the hardware-maintenance reference manuals IBM sells for these systems.

If you have a Tandon drive, you make the adjustment through a small, brass screw on a variable resistor mounted on the motor control board, attached to the rear of the drive (see fig. 8.15). The resistor is usually blue, and the screw is brass. To gauge the speed, you can use a program such as Drive Probe, by Accurite; IBM's Advanced Diagnostics, supplied with the hardware-maintenance and service manual; or even a purely mechanical method that relies on a fluorescent light to act as a strobe.

The software methods use a disk to evaluate the running speed of the drive. Usually, you turn the screw until the speed reads correctly (300 RPM) according to the program you use. The mechanical method requires you to remove the drive from the system and place it upside down on a bench. Sometimes the drive is set sideways on the power supply so that the drive's case is grounded. Then the underside of the drive is illuminated by a standard fluorescent light. The lights acts as a strobe that flashes 60 times per second because of the cycling speed of the AC line current. On the bottom of the drive spindle are strobe marks for 50 Hz and 60 Hz (see fig. 8.16). Because 60 Hz power is used in the United States, you should use the 60 Hz marks. The 50 Hz marks are used for (50 cycle) European power. While the drive is running, turn the small screw until the strobe marks appear to be stationary, much like the "wagon wheel effect" you see in old western movies. When the marks are completely stationary as viewed under the light, the drive's rotation speed is correct.

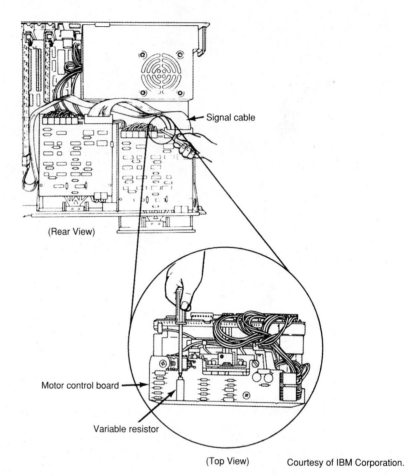

Signal cable

(Rear View)

Motor control board

Variable resistor

(Top View)   Courtesy of IBM Corporation.

Fig. 8.15

The drive-speed adjustment for the Tandon TM-100 series drive.

With CDC drives, the adjustment resistor is mounted on the logic board, which is on top of the drive. The small, brass screw to the left of the board is the one you want. Other drives also might have an adjustment. The best way to tell whether a drive has a speed adjustment is to look for the telltale strobe marks on the spindle of the drive. If the marks are there, the drive probably has an adjustment; if the marks are not there, the drive probably has an automatic speed circuit and requires no adjustment. The OEM manual for the drive has information about all these adjustments (if any) and where you make them.

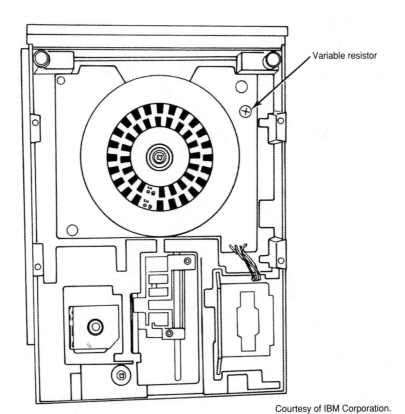

Variable resistor

Courtesy of IBM Corporation.

Fig. 8.16

Strobe marks and speed adjustment on a typical half-height drive.

Aligning Floppy Disk Drives

Aligning disk drives is usually no longer done because of the high relative cost. To align a drive properly requires access to an oscilloscope (for about $500), a special analog-alignment disk ($75), and the OEM service manual for the drive; also, you must spend half an hour to an hour aligning the drive.

A new program, Drive Probe, by Accurite, uses special test disks called High-Resolution Diagnostic (HRD) disks. These disks are as accurate as the analog alignment disks (AAD), and eliminate the need for an oscilloscope to align a drive. You cannot use any program that relies on the older Digital Diagnostic Disk (DDD) or Spiral format test disks because they are not accurate enough to use to align a drive. The Drive Probe and HRD system can make an alignment more cost-effective than before, but it is still a labor-intensive operation. Figure 8.17 shows the main menu of the Accurite Drive Probe program, which offers various functions, including fully automatic or manual drive testing.

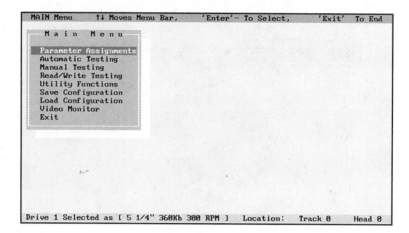

Fig. 8.17

The main menu screen from Accurite Drive Probe.

With the price of most types of floppy drives hovering at or below the $75 mark, aligning drives usually is not a cost-justified alternative to replacement. One exception exists. In a high-volume situation, drive alignment might pay off. Another alternative is to investigate local organizations that perform drive alignments, usually for $25 to $50. Weigh this cost against the replacement cost and age of the drive. I have purchased new 360K floppy drives for *as low as $30*. At these prices, alignment is no longer a viable option.

Chapter Summary

This chapter has examined floppy drives and floppy media (disks) in great detail. One of the most important things to do when you're installing a drive in a system is to ensure that the drive is configured correctly. This chapter has discussed drive configuration also. With this information, installing drives correctly should be an easy task.

Many problems that confound floppy drive users, such as reading and writing double-density disks with high-density drives, were discussed in this chapter. It has discussed thoroughly the differences between high- and double-density drives and disks, and mentioned the consequences of using the wrong type of disk in the wrong drive. Simple drive servicing, such as cleaning and speed adjustment, were explained so that these operations can be performed in-house. After reading this chapter, you should know much about floppy drives. Chapter 9 discusses hard disk drives.

Hard Disk Drives

To most users, the hard disk drive is the most important yet most mysterious part of a computer system. A *hard disk drive* is a sealed unit that holds the data in a system. When the hard disk fails, the consequences are usually very serious. To maintain, service, and expand a PC system properly, you must fully understand the hard disk unit.

Most computer users want to know how hard disk drives work, and what to do when a problem occurs. Few books about hard disks, however, are written for the PC manager or user. This chapter corrects the situation.

This chapter thoroughly describes the hard disk, from the drives to the cables and controllers that run them. In particular, it examines the construction and operation of a hard disk drive. You learn about the various disk interfaces you can select, the shortcomings and strengths of working with each one, and the procedures for configuring, setting up, and installing various drives. The chapter introduces the basic procedures necessary to integrate a hard disk drive into a PC system.

Definition of a Hard Disk

A hard disk drive contains rigid, disc-shaped platters usually constructed of aluminum or glass. Unlike floppy disks, the platters cannot bend or flex, hence the term *hard disk*. In most hard disk drives, the platters cannot be removed; for that reason, IBM calls them *fixed disk drives*. Although there are removable-platter hard disk drives, their nonstandard nature, higher cost, and reliability problems make them unpopular.

Hard disk drives often are called *Winchester drives*. This term dates to the 1960s, when IBM developed a high-speed hard disk drive that had 30 megabytes of fixed-platter storage and 30 megabytes of removable-platter storage. The drive had platters that spun at high speeds and heads that floated over the platters while they spun in a sealed environment. That drive, the *30-30 drive*, soon received the nickname "Winchester," after the famous Winchester 30-30 rifle. After that time, drives that used a high-speed spinning platter with a floating head also became known as Winchester drives. The term has no technical or scientific meaning; it is a slang term synonymous with *hard disk*.

Hard Disk Drive Operation

The basic physical operation of a hard disk drive is similar to that of a floppy disk drive: A hard drive uses spinning disks with heads that move over the disks and store data in tracks and sectors. In many other ways, however, hard disk drives are different from floppy disk drives.

Hard disks usually have multiple platters, each with two sides on which to store data. Most drives have at least two or three platters, which results in four or six sides. The identically positioned tracks on each side of every platter together make up a *cylinder*. A hard disk drive has one head per platter side, and all the heads are mounted on a common carrier device, or *rack*. The heads are moved in and out across the disk in unison; they cannot move independently because they all are mounted on the same rack.

Hard disks operate much faster than floppy drives. Most hard disks spin at 3600 RPM, approximately ten times faster than a floppy drive. Until recently, 3600 RPM was a constant among drive manufacturers. Now, however, a few hard drives spin faster. The drive I use, for example, spins at 4317 RPM, and others spin as fast as 5600 RPM. High rotational speed combined with a fast head-positioning mechanism and more sectors per track make one hard disk faster than another—the same thing that makes hard drives so much faster than floppy drives at storing and retrieving data.

The heads in a hard disk do not (should not!) touch the platters during normal operation. When the heads are powered off, however, they land on the platters as they stop spinning. While the drive is on, a cushion of air keeps each head suspended a short distance above or below the platter. If the cushion is disturbed by a particle of dust or a shock, the head may come in contact with the platter spinning at full speed. When contact with the spinning platters is hard enough to do damage, it is called a *head crash*, and the results may be a few lost bytes of data to a totally trashed disk. Most drives have special lubricants on the platters and hardened surfaces that can withstand the daily "takeoffs and landings" as well as more severe abuse.

Because the platter assemblies are sealed from the environment and are nonremovable, they can have high track densities. Many have 1,000 or more tracks per inch of media. Head Disk Assemblies (HDAs), which contain the platters, are assembled and sealed in clean rooms under absolutely sanitary conditions. Because few companies repair HDAs, the repair or replacement of items inside the sealed HDA can be expensive. Every hard disk ever made eventually fails; the only question is when the disk will fail.

Many PC users think that hard disks are fragile. In my troubleshooting seminars, however, I have run hard disks for days with the lids off, and have even removed and installed the covers while the drives were operating. Those drives worked perfectly and continue to work to this day with the lids either on or off. Of course, I do not recommend that you try this with your own drives, nor would I do it to my larger, more expensive drives.

Magnetic Data Storage

Learning how magnetic data storage works will help you develop a feel for how your disk drives operate and can improve how you work with disk drives and disks.

Nearly all disk drives in personal computer systems operate on magnetic principles. Optical disk drives are used only as secondary peripheral devices—the computer to which they are connected still has a magnetic storage medium as its primary disk system. Optical disk drives and media have a long way to go before they will replace magnetic storage in PC systems.

Magnetic drives such as floppy disk drives and hard disk drives operate using *electromagnetism*. This basic principle of physics states that as an electric current flows through a conductor a magnetic field is generated around the conductor. This magnetic field then can influence magnetic material in the field. By reversing the direction of the flow of electric current, the magnetic field's polarity also is reversed. An electric motor operates using electromagnetism to exert pushing and pulling forces on magnets attached to a rotating shaft.

Another effect of electromagnetism is that if a conductor is passed through a magnetic field, an electrical current is generated. As the polarity of the magnetic field changes, so does the direction of the electric current flow. An electrical generator, or *alternator*, operates by rotating electromagnets past coils of wire conductors in which large amounts of electrical current can be induced. This two-way operation of electromagnetism is how data can be recorded on a disk and read back later.

The read/write heads in your disk drives (both floppy and hard disks) are constructed basically as U-shaped pieces of magnetic material, much like a horseshoe magnet. Because of the shape, the generated magnetic fields are concentrated in the gap between the ends of the U. The drive head material is not a magnet; it consists of material, such as iron, in which a magnetic field can be generated. This U-shaped piece of iron is wrapped with coils of wire, through which an electric current can flow. When the disk drive logic passes a current through these coils, it generates a magnetic field in the drive head. This magnetic field is concentrated in the head gap area resting on or just above the surface of the disk. The field's polarity is based on the direction of the flow of electric current through the coils.

A computer disk consists of some form of substrate material (such as mylar for floppy disks or aluminum for hard disks) on which a layer of magnetizable material has been deposited. This material is usually a form of iron oxide with various other elements added. The polarities of the magnetic fields of the individual magnetic particles on a disk are normally in a state of disarray. Because the fields of the individual particles point in different directions, each individual, tiny, magnetic field is cancelled by one that points in the opposite direction, for a total effect of no observable or cumulative field polarity.

The magnetic field generated by the drive head is focused in the head gap area, and the head gap is either touching or in close proximity to the surface of the disk. This strong magnetic field causes the particles in the disk surface near the head to become polarized in whatever direction the field in the head gap is pointing. Particles in the area near the head gap are aligned in the same direction. When the individual magnetic domains no longer cancel one another (but instead are aligned in the same direction), an observable magnetic field exists in that region of the disk. This local field is generated by the many magnetic particles that are now operating as a team to produce a detectable cumulative field of a unified direction. The term *flux* is applied to describe a magnetic field with a given direction.

As the disk surface rotates under the drive head, the head can lay a magnetic flux over a region of the disk. When the electrical current flow through the coils in the head is reversed, so is the magnetic field polarity in the head gap. This also causes the flux being placed on the disk to reverse. The *flux reversal* is a change in polarity of the alignment of magnetic particles in the disk surface.

A drive head places flux reversals on a disk to record data. For each data bit (or bits) written, a pattern of flux reversals is placed on the disk in specific areas known as bit cells. A *bit cell* is an area of the disk controlled by the time and rotational speed in which flux reversals are placed by a drive head. The particular pattern of flux reversals used to store a given data bit or bits is referred to as the *encoding method*. The drive logic or controller takes the data to be stored and encodes it as a series of flux reversals over a period of time according to the encoding method used. Popular encoding methods are Modified Frequency Modulation (MFM) or Run Length Limited (RLL) encoding. All floppy disk drives use the MFM scheme. Hard disks use MFM, RLL, or modifications to those methods. These encoding methods are described in more detail later in this chapter.

When a drive head is passed over a disk surface in which a magnetic flux has been previously placed, a current of a specific direction is generated in the head coils. The direction of this current flow depends on the direction of the flux. When the head passes over an area where the flux direction reverses, the current flow being generated in the head coils reverses also. The currents generated in the head while it is passing over a disk in read mode are virtually identical (although much weaker) to the currents passed through the heads during the recording of the disk. Sensitive electronics in the drive and controller assembly then can amplify and decode these weak electrical currents back into data that is (theoretically) identical to the data originally recorded.

Disks are both recorded and read using this basic method: Data is recorded on a disk by passing electrical currents through an electromagnet (the drive head) that generates a magnetic field stored on the disk. Data on a disk is read by passing the head back over the surface of the disk; as the head encounters a stored magnetic field, it generates an electrical current that is the same as the current originally used to record the disk.

Sectors

A disk track is too large an area to manage effectively as a single storage unit. Most disk tracks can store 8,000 or more bytes of data, which would be very inefficient for storing small files. For that reason, a disk track is divided into several numbered divisions known as *sectors*. These sectors represent slices of a track.

Different types of disk drives and disks split tracks into different numbers of sectors, depending on the density of the tracks. For example, floppy disk formats use from 8 to 36 sectors per track; hard disks usually store data at a higher density and can use from 17 to 64 sectors per track. Sectors created by standard formatting procedures on PC systems have a capacity of 512 bytes, but this capacity may change in the future.

Track sectors are numbered starting with 1, unlike the tracks or cylinders (which are numbered from 0). For example, a 1.2-megabyte floppy disk contains 80 cylinders numbered from 0 to 79, and each track on each cylinder has 15 sectors numbered from 1 to 15.

When a disk is formatted, additional areas are created on the disk for the disk controller to use for sector numbering and the identification of the start and end of each sector. These areas precede and trail each sector's data area, which accounts for the difference between a disk's unformatted and formatted capacities. For example, a 2.0-megabyte floppy disk (3 1/2-inch) has a capacity of 1.44 megabytes when it is formatted, and a 38-megabyte hard disk has a capacity of only 32 megabytes when it is formatted. All disks have the same sort of reserved and available areas.

It is usually stated that each disk sector is 512 bytes in size. This statement is technically false. Each sector does allow for the storage of 512 bytes of data, but the data area is only a portion of the sector. Each sector on a disk typically occupies 571 bytes of the disk, of which only 512 bytes are usable for user data.

You may find it helpful to think of each sector as a page in a book. In a book, each page contains text, but the entire page is not filled with text. Rather, each page has top, bottom, left, and right margins. Information such as chapter titles (track and cylinder numbers) and page numbers (sector numbers) is placed in the margins. The "margin" areas of a sector are created and written to during the format process for the disk. Formatting also fills the data area of each sector with dummy values. After the disk is formatted, the data area can be altered by normal writing to the disk. The sector header and trailer information cannot be altered, unless you reformat the disk.

Each sector on a disk has a *prefix portion* or header that identifies the start of the sector and a sector number, and a *suffix portion* or trailer that contains a *checksum* (which helps ensure the integrity of the data contents). Each sector also contains 512 bytes of data. The data bytes normally are set to the value of hexadecimal F6 when the disk is physically, or low-level, formatted. (Low-level formatting is explained in the following section.) In addition to the gaps within sectors, there are gaps between sectors on each track, and gaps between tracks, none of which contains usable data space. The prefix, suffix, and gaps account for the lost space between the unformatted capacity of a disk and the formatted capacity.

Table 9.1 shows the format for each track and sector on a typical hard disk with 17 sectors per track.

Table 9.1 Typical 17-Sector/-Track Disk Sector Format

Bytes	Name	Description
16	Post index gap	All 4Eh, at the track that begins after the Index mark
13	ID VFO lock	All 00h; synchronizes the VFO for the ID
1	Sync byte	A1h; notifies the controller that data follows
1	Address mark	FEh; defines that ID field data follows
2	Cylinder number	A value that defines the actuator position
1	Head number	A value that defines the head selected
1	Sector number	A value that defines the sector
2	CRC	Cyclic redundancy check to verify ID data
3	Write turn-on gap	00h written by format to isolate the ID from DATA
13	Data sync VFO lock	All 00h; synchronizes the VFO for the DATA
1	Sync byte	A1h; notifies the controller that data follows
1	Address mark	F8h; defines that user DATA field follows
512	User DATA	The area for user DATA
2	CRC	Cyclic redundancy check to verify DATA
3	Write turn-off gap	00h; written by DATA update to isolate DATA
15	Inter-record gap	All 00h; a buffer for speed variation
693	Pre-index gap	All 4Eh, at track end before Index mark

571 total bytes per sector
512 usable bytes per sector
10416 total bytes per track
8704 usable bytes per track

The usable space on each track is about 20 percent less than the unformatted capacity. This example is true for most disks, although some may vary slightly. The sector prefix is extremely important because it contains the numbering information that defines the cylinder, head, and sector. This information is written only during the original (low-level) format of the disk. On a typical inexpensive hard disk on which thermal gradients cause dimensional changes in the media, the data updates rewrite the 512-byte data area and the CRC that follows it may not be placed exactly in line with the sector header information.

This situation eventually causes read or write failures of the `Abort`, `Retry`, `Fail`, `Ignore` variety. You can correct this problem by reformatting the disk, which rewrites the header and data information. Then when you restore the data to the disk, the data areas are rewritten and align with the newly written sector headers.

Table 9.1 refers to a hard disk track with 17 sectors. Although this capacity is typical, more advanced hard disks place as many as 64 or more sectors per track, and the specific formats of those sectors may vary slightly from the example.

Disk Formatting

You usually have two types of formats to consider:

> The physical, or *low-level*, format

> The logical, or *high-level*, format

When you format a floppy disk, the DOS FORMAT command performs both kinds of formats simultaneously. To format a hard disk, however, the operations must be done separately. Moreover, a hard disk requires a third step, between the two formats, in which the partitioning information is written to the disk. *Partitioning* is required because a hard disk is designed to be used with more than one operating system. Separating the physical format in a way that is always the same regardless of the operating system being used and regardless of the high-level format (which would be different for each operating system) makes possible the use of multiple operating systems on one hard drive. The partitioning step allows more than one type of DOS to use a single hard disk or a single DOS to use the disk as several volumes or logical drives. A volume or logical drive is anything that DOS assigns a drive letter.

Consequently, formatting a hard disk involves three steps:

1. Low-level format

2. Partitioning

3. High-level format

During a low-level format, the disk's tracks are divided into a specific number of sectors. The sector header and trailer information is recorded, as are inter-sector and inter-track gaps. Each sector's data area is filled with a dummy value (usually 512 bytes F6h bytes, but other values or even patterns of bytes can be used). For floppy disks, the number of sectors recorded on each track depends on the type of disk and drive; for hard disks, the number of sectors per track depends on the drive interface and controller. Here are some examples of hard disk sectoring for different types of interfaces:

Interface	Sectors per track
ST-506/412 MFM or IDE	17
ST-506/412 RLL or IDE	25 or 26
ESDI, SCSI, or IDE	32 and greater

During the high-level format, DOS puts on the disk its structure for managing files and data. DOS places a volume boot sector, a file allocation table (FAT), and a root directory on each formatted logical drive. These data structures (discussed in detail in Chapter 15) enable DOS to manage the space on the disk, keep track of files, and even manage defective areas so that they do not cause problems.

High-level formatting is not really formatting: it is creating a table of contents for the disk. The low-level format is the real format, in which tracks and sectors are written on the disk. As mentioned, the single DOS FORMAT command performs both low-level and high-level format operations on a floppy disk but performs only the high-level format for a hard disk. Hard disk low-level formats require a special utility usually supplied by the system or controller manufacturer.

Basic Hard Disk Drive Components

Many types of hard disks are on the market, but nearly all drives share the same basic physical components. Some differences may exist in the implementation of these components (and in the quality of materials used to make them), but the operational characteristics of most drives are similar. The components found in a typical hard disk drive follow (see fig. 9.1).

- Disk platters
- Read/write heads
- Head actuator mechanism
- Spindle motor
- Spindle motor ground strap
- Logic board
- Cables and connectors
- Configuration items (such as jumpers or switches)
- Bezel

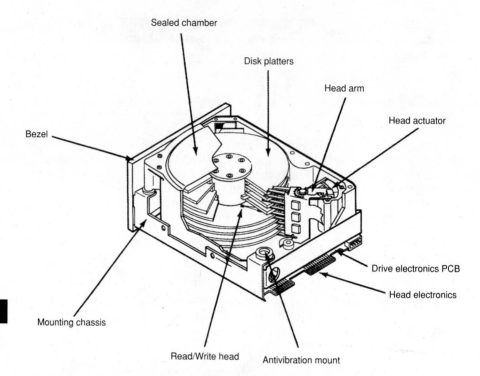

Sealed chamber

Disk platters

Head arm

Head actuator

Bezel

Head actuator

Drive electronics PCB

Head electronics

Mounting chassis

Read/Write head   Antivibration mount

Fig. 9.1

Hard disk drive
components.

The platters, spindle motor, heads, and head actuator mechanisms usually are contained in a sealed chamber called the *Head Disk Assembly* (HDA). The HDA usually is treated as a single component; it is rarely ever opened. Other parts external to the drive's HDA, such as the logic boards, bezel, and other configuration or mounting hardware, can be disassembled from the drive.

Platters and Media (Disks)

A typical hard disk has one or more platters, or disks. The most common types of disks in use are those with 5 1/4-inch or 3 1/2-inch diameter platters. There are larger drives with 8-inch or even 14-inch platters, but these expensive, high-capacity drives typically have not been associated with PC systems. Quite a few drives have 2 1/2-inch platters, primarily for use in laptop systems.

Most hard drives have several platters, although some of the smaller, half-height drives have only 1. The number of platters a drive can have is limited by the drive's physical size. So far, the maximum number of platters for the 5 1/4-inch full-height drives is 11; the half-height 5 1/4-inch and 3 1/2-inch drives have as many as 8 platters.

Each platter usually is made of an aluminum metal alloy, for strength and light weight. Some drives use platters made of glass. The glass substrate results in a smoother disk and higher densities. Glass platter drives usually are manufactured in only the 2 1/2-inch form factor. The 5 1/4-inch and 3 1/2-inch platters are usually 1/8-inch thick. The platters are covered with a thin layer of a magnetically retentive substance or media in which information is stored. Two popular types of media are used on hard disk platters:

Oxide media
Thin film media

Most older drives and many low-end drives have oxide media on the drive platters. Oxide media has been used since 1955, and has remained popular because of its relatively low cost and ease of application.

Oxide media is made of various compounds containing iron oxide as the active ingredient. A magnetic layer is created by coating the aluminum platter with a syrup containing iron-oxide particles. This media is spread evenly across the disk by spinning the platters at high speed—the material flows from the center of the platter to the outside because of centrifugal force. This force creates an even coating of material on the drive, with few imperfections. The surface then is cured and polished. Finally, a protective lubricating layer of material is added and burnished smooth. Normally, this media is about 30 millionths of an inch thick. If you could peer into a drive with oxide-media-coated platters, you would see that they are brownish or amber.

As drive densities increase, the media needs to be thinner and more perfectly formed. The capabilities of oxide coatings have been exceeded by most higher-capacity drives. Because oxide media is very soft, disks are prone to head crash damage if the drive is jolted during operation.

Thin film media is thinner, harder, and more perfectly formed. It was developed as a high-performance media to enable a new generation of drives to have lower head-recording heights, which in turn made possible increases in drive density. Most higher-capacity or higher-quality drive systems have thin film media rather than an oxide coating.

Thin film media is aptly named. The thickness of the media is much less than can be achieved by the oxide coating method. Thin film media is also known as *plated*, or *sputtered*, media because of the various processes used to get the thin film of media on the platters.

Plated media is manufactured by placing the media material on the disk with an electroplating mechanism, much like chrome plating on the bumper of a car. The aluminum platter is immersed in a series of chemical baths that coat the platter with layers of metallic film. The final layer is about three-millionths of an inch of a cobalt alloy that is the actual media.

Thin-film sputtered disks are created by first coating the aluminum platters with a layer of nickel phosphorus and then applying the cobalt alloy magnetic material with a continuous vacuum deposition process called *sputtering*. During this process, magnetic layers as thin as two-millionths of an inch are deposited on the disk, similar to the way that silicon chip wafers are coated with metallic film in the semiconductor industry. The sputtering technique then is used again to lay down an extremely hard, one-microinch protective carbon coating. The platters are usually electrically charged so that they attract the media particles as they are vaporized. The requirements of a near-perfect vacuum make sputtering the most expensive of the processes described here.

The surfaces of sputtered platters contain magnetic layers as thin as two-millionths of an inch. Because this surface is also very smooth, the head can float close to the disk surface. The head can float six to eight millionths of an inch over the surface. With the head closer, the density of the magnetic field can be increased to provide greater storage capacity. Additionally, the increased intensity of the magnetic field provides the higher signal amplitudes needed for good signal-to-noise performance.

Both the sputtering and plating processes result in a very thin, hard film of media on the platters. Because the thin film media is so hard, it has a better chance of surviving contact with the heads at high speed. Oxide coatings are scratched more easily. Because the thin film media can accurately handle much greater densities, it is on most larger-capacity drives and many of the newer 3 1/2-inch platter drives. If you could open a drive to peek at the platters, the thin film platters would look like the silver surface of a mirror.

The sputtering process results in the most perfect, thinnest, and hardest disk surface that can be commercially obtained. It is now used in the majority of drives equipped with thin film media. Having a thin film media surface on a drive translates into increased storage capacity in a smaller area with fewer head crashes, and a drive that will provide many years of trouble-free use.

Read/Write Heads

A hard disk drive usually has one read/write head for each platter side, which makes the usual range of heads from 2 to 22. Many controller and drive systems translate the number of heads to a different value. For example, in a PS/2 Model 70-121 with a 120-megabyte hard disk, the drive has 8 heads and 920 cylinders; the controller translates this number to appear as 64 heads and 115 cylinders. The multiple heads are connected, or "ganged," on a single movement mechanism. The heads therefore move in unison across the platters.

Mechanically, read/write heads are simple. Each head is on an arm that is spring-loaded to force the head into a platter. Each platter is "squeezed" by the heads above and below it. If you could open a drive safely and lift the top head with your finger, it would snap back into the platter when you released it. If you could pull down on one of the heads underneath a platter, spring tension would cause it to snap back up into the platter when you released it. Figure 9.2 shows a typical hard disk head-actuator assembly from a voice coil drive.

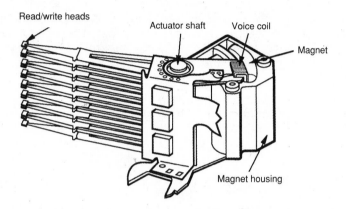

Read/write heads   Actuator shaft   Voice coil

Magnet

Magnet housing

Fig. 9.2

Read/write heads and actuator assembly.

When the drive is at rest, the heads are forced into the platters by spring tension, but when the drive is spinning at full speed, air pressure develops underneath the heads and lifts them off the surface of the platter. On a fully spinning drive, the gap between the heads and the platter is usually between 5 and 20 millionths of an inch. The small size of this gap is why the disk drive's Head Disk Assembly (HDA) is never opened: Any particle of dust or dirt that gets into this mechanism could cause the heads to read improperly, or possibly to oscillate and strike the platters while at full speed. The latter event, a head crash, may damage (scratch) the platter, or—worse—the head.

To ensure the cleanliness of the interior of the drive, the HDA is assembled in a class 100 or better clean room; a cubic foot of air cannot contain more than one hundred 0.5 micron particles. A single person breathing while standing motionless spews out 500 such particles in a single minute. These rooms contain special air-filtration systems that continuously evacuate and refresh the air. A drive's HDA should not be opened unless it is inside such a room. Because the clean environment is very expensive to produce, few companies except those that manufacture the drives are prepared to service hard disk drives.

Three basic types of heads are used in the modern hard disk drive:

- Ferrite heads
- Thin film heads
- Magneto-resistive (MR) heads

Ferrite heads are the traditional type of magnetic head design. They have an iron-oxide core wrapped with electromagnetic coils. A magnetic field is produced by energizing the coils; a field can be induced also by passing a magnetic field near the coils. This process gives the heads full read and write capability. Ferrite heads are larger and heavier than thin film heads and therefore require a larger flying height to record on the disk. Ferrite heads are relatively cheap to produce and are plentiful.

Many refinements have been made to the original (monolithic) ferrite head design. A type of ferrite head called a *composite ferrite head* has a smaller ferrite core bonded with glass in a ceramic housing. This design permits a smaller head gap, which allows higher track densities. These heads are less susceptible to stray magnetic fields than the older, monolithic design.

To further extend the performance of ferrite heads, an enhancement called *metal-in-gap* (MIG) technology has been developed. In MIG ferrite heads, a metal substance is sputtered into the recording gap on the tailing edge of the head. This material offers increased resistance to magnetic saturation, allowing a higher-density recording. MIG ferrite heads also produce a sharper gradient in the magnetic field for a more well-defined magnetic pulse. These heads enable the use of higher-coercivity thin film disks and can lower flying heights.

Thin film heads are produced in the same manner as a semiconductor chip. These heads are really a complex circuit. They offer an extremely narrow and controlled head gap created by sputtering a hard aluminum material. Because this material completely encloses the gap, this area is very hard and well protected, minimizing the chance of damage from contact with the media. The core is a combination of iron and nickel alloy two to four times more magnetic than a ferrite head core.

Thin film heads produce a sharply defined magnetic pulse that allows extremely high densities to be written. Because they do not have a conventional coil, thin film heads are more immune to variations in coil impedance due to temperature variations. Thin film heads are small and lightweight, and can fly at a much lower height than the ferrite heads. Flying height has been reduced to as little as two-millionths of an inch in some designs. Because the reduced height enables a much stronger signal to be picked up and transmitted between the head and platters, the signal-to-noise ratio increases, which improves accuracy. At the high track and linear densities in some drives, a standard ferrite head would not be able to pick out the data signal from the background noise. When thin film heads are used, their small size enables more platters to be stacked in a drive. Most of the highest-capacity drives use thin film heads to achieve their tremendous densities.

Magneto-resistive heads (MR heads) are a new technology, pioneered by IBM. Using this technology, several 1-gigabyte 3 1/2-inch drives are on the market, and 2-gigabyte and larger drives also have been developed. MR heads are two heads in one, a standard inductive thin film head for writing and a special magneto-resistive head for reading. Because two separate heads are built into one assembly, each head can be optimized to its task. Accordingly, the write head (thin film) writes a wider track than the read head (magneto-resistive) reads. The read head then is less susceptible to picking up stray magnetic information from adjacent tracks.

MR heads rely on the fact that the resistance of a current-carrying magnetic conductor changes slightly when an external magnetic field is present. Rather than put out a voltage by converting a magnetic field flux reversal, as a normal head would, the MR head senses the flux reversal and changes resistance. A small current flows through the heads, and the change in resistance is measured by this sense current. This type of design enables the output to be three or more times more powerful than a thin film head during a read. In effect, MR heads are "power read" heads, somewhat like power steering in a car.

MR head construction involves additional cost and complexity beyond that required for other types of heads, because a number of special features or steps must be added:

- Additional wires must be run to and from the head to carry the sense current.

- Four to six more masking steps are required.

- Because MR heads are so sensitive, they are very susceptible to stray magnetic fields and must be shielded.

These factors contribute to the additional cost of the MR head. This type of technology generally is used only in the absolutely highest-capacity applications, in which the increased density offered by the magneto-resistive head design is required. Most 3 1/2-inch hard disks with capacities of 1-gigabyte and higher use this technology.

Head Actuator Mechanism

Possibly more important than the heads themselves is the mechanical system that moves them, the *head actuator*. This mechanism moves the heads across the disk and positions them accurately over the desired cylinder. Many variations on head actuator mechanisms are in use, and they are one of two different basic types:

- Stepper motor actuators
- Voice coil actuators

The use of one or the other type of positioner has profound effects on a drive's performance and reliability. The effect is not limited to speed, but includes accuracy, sensitivity to temperature, position, vibration, and overall reliability. To put it bluntly, a drive equipped with a stepper motor actuator is much less reliable (by a factor of five to ten or more) than a drive equipped with a voice coil actuator.

The head actuator is the most important single specification in the drive. The type of head actuator mechanism in a drive tells you a great deal about the drive's performance and reliability characteristics. Table 9.2 shows the two types of hard disk drive head actuators and the affected performance parameters.

Table 9.2 Characteristics of Stepper Motor versus Voice Coil Drives		
Characteristic	**Stepper motor**	**Voice coil**
Relative access speed	Slow	Fast
Temperature sensitive	Yes (very)	No
Positionally sensitive	Yes	No
Automatic head parking	Not usually	Yes
Preventive maintenance	Periodic format	None required
Relative reliability	Poor	Excellent

Generally, a stepper motor drive has a slow average access rating, is temperature-sensitive during read and write operations, is sensitive to the physical orientation during read and write operations, does not automatically park its heads over a save zone during power-down, and usually requires annual or biannual reformats to realign the sector data with the sector header information due to mistracking. Overall, stepper motor drives are inferior to drives with voice coil actuators.

Some stepper motor drives feature automatic head parking at power-down. If you have a newer stepper motor drive, refer to the drive's technical-reference manual to determine whether your drive has this feature. (Other than removing the lid and watching as you power-off—which is definitely *not* recommended—the documentation is the only reliable way to tell.) Sometimes you can hear a noise after power-down, but that can be deceptive because some drives use a solenoid-activated spindle break, which makes a noise as the drive is powered off and does not involve head parking.

Floppy disk drives position their heads using a stepper motor actuator. The accuracy of the stepper mechanism is suited to a floppy drive because the track densities are usually nowhere near those of a hard disk. Many of the less expensive, low-capacity hard disks also use a stepper motor system. Most hard disks with capacities of more than 40 megabytes have voice coil actuators, as do all drives with capacities of more than 100 megabytes. In IBM's product line, a drive of 40 or more megabytes is a voice coil drive. On IBM systems with drives of less than 40 megabytes (usually 20 or 30 megabytes), both voice coil and stepper motor drives have been used.

This breakdown does not necessarily apply to other system manufacturers, but it is safe to say that hard disk drives with less than 80-megabyte capacity may have either type of actuator, and virtually all drives with greater than 80-megabyte capacities have voice coil actuators. The cost differential between voice coil drives and stepper motor drives of equal capacity is only 30 to 50 percent: If you can purchase a 40-megabyte stepper motor hard disk for $300, you can buy a 40-megabyte voice coil unit for $400 to $500. Although this 30 to 50 percent rule usually holds true, you can find 80-megabyte voice coil drives for the same price as 40-megabyte steppers, so it pays to shop carefully.

Stepper Motor

A *stepper motor* is an electrical motor that can "step," or move from position to position, with mechanical detents. If you were to grip the spindle of one of these motors and spin it by hand, you would notice a clicking or buzzing. The sensation is much like that of the volume control on some stereo systems. Stepper motors cannot position themselves between step positions; they can stop at only the predetermined detent positions. The motors are small (between 1 and 3 inches) and can be square, cylindrical, or a flat pancake design. They are outside the sealed HDA, although the spindle of the motor penetrates the HDA through a sealed hole. The stepper motor is located in one of the four corners of the hard disk drive and is usually easily visible.

Mechanical Links

The stepper motor is mechanically linked to the head rack by either a split-steel band coiled around the motor spindle or a rack-and-pinion gear mechanism. As the motor steps, each detent, or click-stop position, represents the movement of one track through the mechanical linkage. Some systems use several motor steps for each track. In positioning the heads, if the drive is told to move to track 400, the motor begins the stepping motion, proceeds to the 400th detent position, and stops, leaving the heads over the desired cylinder.

The most widely used stepper motor actuator systems use a *split metal band mechanism* to transmit the rotary stepping motion to the in-and-out motion of the head rack. The band is made of special alloys to limit thermal expansion and contraction as well as stretch. One end of the band is coiled around the spindle of the stepper motor, and the other is connected directly to the head rack. The band is inside the sealed HDA and is not visible from the outside of the drive.

Some companies (notably Miniscribe) use a *rack-and-pinion gear mechanism* to link the stepper motor to the head rack. This procedure involves a small pinion gear on the spindle of the stepper motor that moves a rack gear in and out. The rack gear is connected to the head rack, causing it to move. The rack-and-pinion mechanism is more durable than the split metal band mechanism and provides slightly greater physical and thermal stability. One problem, however, is *backlash*, the amount of play in the gears. Backlash increases as the gears wear, and eventually renders the mechanism useless.

Temperature Fluctuation Problems

Stepper motor mechanisms are affected by a variety of problems. The biggest problem is temperature. As the drive platters heat and cool, they expand and contract, respectively; the tracks then move in relation to a predetermined track position. The stepper mechanism does not allow the mechanism to move in increments of less than a single track to correct for these temperature-induced errors. The drive positions the heads to a particular cylinder according to a predetermined number of steps from the stepper motor, with no room for nuance.

The low-level formatting of the drive places the initial track and sector marks on the platters at the positions where the heads are currently located, as commanded by the stepper motor. If all subsequent reading and writing occur at the same temperature as the initial format, the heads always record precisely within the track and sector boundaries.

At different temperatures, however, the head position does not match the track position. When the platters are cold, the heads miss the track location because the platters have shrunk and the tracks have moved toward the center of the disk. When the platters are warmer than the formatted temperature, the platters will have grown larger, and the track positions are located outward. Gradually, as the drive is used, the data is written inside, on top of, and outside the track and sector marks. Eventually the drive fails to read one of these locations, and usually a DOS `Abort, Retry, Ignore` error message appears.

The temperature sensitivity of stepper motor drives may also cause the "Monday morning blues." When the system is powered up cold (on Monday, for example), a 1701, 1790, or 10490 Power-On Self Test (POST) error occurs. If you leave the system on for about 15 minutes, the drive can come up to operating temperature and the system then may boot normally. This problem sometimes occurs in reverse too, when the drive gets particularly warm, such as when a system is in direct sunlight, or in the afternoon when room temperature is highest. In that case, the symptom is a DOS error message with the familiar `Abort, Retry, Ignore` prompt.

Temperature-induced mistracking problems can be solved by reformatting the drive and restoring the data. Then the information is placed on the drive at the current head positions for each cylinder. Over time the mistracking recurs, necessitating another reformat-and-restore operation, which is a form of periodic preventive maintenance for stepper motor drives. An acceptable interval for this maintenance is once a year or perhaps twice a year if the drive is extremely temperature-sensitive.

Reformatting a hard drive, because it requires a complete backup-and-restore operation, is inconvenient and time consuming. To help with these periodic reformats, most low-level format programs offer a special reformat option that copies the data for a specific track to a spare location, reformats the track, and then copies the data back to the original track. When this type of format operation is finished, there is no need to restore your data because it already has been done for you.

CAUTION: *Never* use a so-called nondestructive format program without first making a complete backup. This type of program does wipe out the data as it operates. "Destructive-reconstructive" more accurately describes its operation. If there is a problem with the power, the system, or the program (maybe a bug that stops the program from finishing), all of the data will not be restored properly, and some tracks may be wiped clean. Although such programs save you from having to do the manual restore operation when the format is complete, they do not remove your obligation to perform a backup first.

Beware of programs whose advertising is filled with marketing hype and miracle claims for making a hard disk "better than new." One company even boasted in its advertisements that by using its program you will "Never have any problems" with your hard disk—an outrageous claim.

What the ads don't say is that a low-level format program performs these same feats of "magic" without the misleading or exaggerated claims and unnecessary hype. Also, annual or biannual formatting is not necessary with voice coil actuator drives because they do not exhibit these types of mistracking errors.

Voice Coil

A *voice coil actuator* is found on higher-quality hard disk drives, including most drives with capacities greater than 40 megabytes and all drives with capacities exceeding 80 megabytes. A voice coil actuator is significantly better than the standard stepper motor actuator in performance and reliability.

A voice coil actuator works by pure electromagnetic force. The construction of this mechanism is similar to a typical audio speaker, which uses a stationary magnet surrounded by a voice coil connected to the speaker's paper cone. Energizing the coil causes the coil to move, which produces sound from the speaker cone. In a typical hard disk voice-coil system, an electromagnetic coil moves on a track through a stationary magnet, with no contact—other than magnetic interaction—between the coil and the magnet. The coil mechanism is connected directly to the head rack. As the electromagnetic coils are energized, they attract or repulse the magnet and move the head rack. Such systems are extremely quick and efficient, and most are much quieter than a system driven with a stepper motor.

Unlike a stepper motor, a voice coil actuator has no click stops, or detent positions. Rather, a different system stops the head rack over a particular cylinder as the actuator slides the heads in and out smoothly (like a trombone slide). When the drive is manufactured, one side of one platter is deducted from normal read/write usage; on this platter are recorded a special set of index marks that indicate proper track positions. Because the head sitting above this platter has no recording capability, the marks never can be erased. When the drive is commanded to move the heads to a specific track (track 400, for example), the internal drive electronics use the signals received by this special head to indicate the position of the heads. As the heads are moved, the track counters are read from the index surface. When the requested track is detected under the head rack, the heads are commanded to stop moving. The electronics then fine-tune the position so that, before writing is allowed, the heads are positioned precisely over the track, where the strongest signals are received by the index head.

The complete name for this system sometimes is called a *dedicated surface, closed loop, servo-controlled mechanism. Dedicated surface* refers to the platter surface that is lost in order to store the special index tracks.

Because the dedicated platter surface cannot be used to store normal data, most voice coil drives have an odd number of heads. In fact, that is usually a clue indicating a voice coil actuator. *Closed loop* indicates that the index (or servo) head is wired to the positioning electronics in a closed-loop system. This loop is called a *feedback loop* also. The feedback from this index head is used to accurately position the other heads. It acts as a guide head to the rest of the rack. *Servo-controlled* refers to this index or the servo head, which is used to dictate or control head-positioning accuracy.

Not all voice coil drives have an odd number of heads, because many drives bury the servo or guidance information in the sector gaps or headers on each track, eliminating the need for an entire surface dedicated to this information. Such mechanisms are called *embedded servo, closed loop actuators*. A few drives begin with an odd number of heads; after deducting the one for servo purposes, an even number of heads remains.

A voice coil actuator with servo control is not affected by temperature changes as a stepper motor is. When the temperature is cold and the platters have shrunk (or when the temperature is hot and the platters have expanded), the voice coil system compensates because it never positions to predetermined track positions. Rather, it searches for the specific track and uses the servo head to position the head rack precisely over that track at the track's current position, regardless of the temperature.

Automatic Head Parking

When a hard disk drive is powered off, the spring tension in each head arm pulls the heads back into the platters. The drive is designed to sustain thousands of takeoffs and landings, but it is wise to ensure that the landing occurs at a spot on the platter where there is no data. Some amount of abrasion occurs during the landing and takeoff process, which removes just a "micropuff" of the media; if the drive is jarred during the landing or takeoff process, real damage can occur.

One benefit of using a voice coil actuator is *automatic head parking*. In a drive with a voice coil actuator, the heads are positioned and held by magnetic force. When power is removed from the drive, the magnetic field holding the heads stationary over a particular cylinder dissipates, enabling the head rack to skitter across the drive surface and potentially cause damage. In the voice coil design, therefore, the head rack is attached to a weak spring at one end and a head stop at the other end. When the system is powered on, the spring normally is overcome by the magnetic force of the positioner. When the drive is powered off, however, the spring gently drags the head rack to a park-and-lock position before the drive slows down and the heads land.

On a drive with a voice coil actuator, the parking mechanism is activated by simply turning off the system. There is no need to run a program to park or retract the heads. In case of a power outage, the heads even park themselves automatically. (The drives automatically unpark when the system is powered on.)

Types of Voice Coil Actuators

There are two main types of voice-coil positioner mechanisms:

- Linear voice-coil actuators
- Rotary voice-coil actuators

The types differ only in the physical arrangement of the magnets and coils.

Linear actuators move the heads in and out over the platters in a straight line, much like a "tangential tracking" turntable. The coil moves in and out on a track surrounded by the stationary magnets.

Rotary actuators use the same magnets and coil, but the coil is spun around a spindle and is surrounded by the stationary magnets. The rotary motion is transmitted directly to the heads because the head arms are mounted to the coils. The physical movement of this type of system is exactly like a conventional turntable: The head arms swing in and out over the surface of the platters like the record tonearm, and the voice coil mechanism is at the arm-pivot location. Most higher-end drives are rotary actuator systems, and rotary actuators far outnumber linear actuators.

Air Filters

Hard disk drives have air filters that are not changeable (because they never really get dirty). A hard disk for a PC system is a permanently sealed unit, not comparable to many mainframe hard disk drives. Many mainframe drives circulate air from outside the drive through a filter that must be changed periodically.

A hard disk on a PC system does not circulate air. The filter inside the unit filters only the small particles of media scraped off the platters during head takeoff and landing, and the metal flakes or small particles dislodged inside the drive. Because hard disk drives are permanently sealed and do not circulate outside air, they can run in extremely dirty environments.

> **CAUTION:** Airborne particulates such as cigarette smoke normally do not affect a PC system hard disk drive because outside air is filtered before entering the drive. Many other components in the system (such as floppy drives, keyboards, connectors, and sockets), however, will sustain damage from cigarette smoke.

The only way air gets into or out of a hard disk is from a change in atmospheric pressure. All drives have a pressure-equalization system with a filtered port to bleed air into or out of the HDA as necessary (see fig. 9.3). Little air moves across this barrier, and the filter is a submicron type of permanent filter that cannot be changed.

Recirculating filter

Rotary voice coil

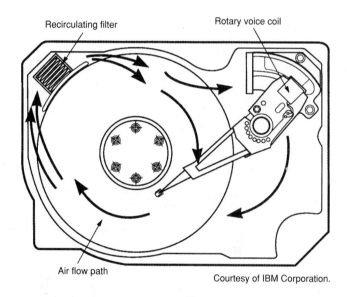

Air flow path

Courtesy of IBM Corporation.

Fig. 9.3

Air circulation in a hard disk.

Spindle Motors

The motor that spins the platters is called the *spindle motor* because it is connected to the spindle around which the platters revolve. Spindle motors are always connected directly; no belts or gears are used. The motors must be noise-free; otherwise they transmit "rumble" to the platters and disrupt reading and writing operations. The motors must be precisely controlled for speed. The platters on nearly all hard disks revolve at exactly 3600 RPM, and the motor has a control circuit with a feedback loop to monitor and control this speed precisely. Because this speed control must be automatic, the drives do not have a speed adjustment, and nothing can be done if the speed is off. Some diagnostics programs, such as the Norton Utilities, can measure hard drive rotational speed.

On most drives, the spindle motor is on the bottom of the drive, just outside the sealed HDA. Some companies, such as Maxtor, build the motor directly into the HDA, and mount the motor in the center of the platters. Maxtor can place eight platters in a normal 5 1/4-inch, full-height, form-factor drive. Having that many platters would be impossible if the motor were outside the platters: the drive would be too tall.

 **Note**   Spindle motors, particularly on the larger form-factor drives, can consume a great deal of 12-volt power. Most drives require two to three times the normal operating power when the motor is first spinning the platters. This heavy draw lasts about 15 seconds, until the drive platters have reached a stable 3600 RPM.

Spindle Ground Strap

Most drives have a special grounding strap attached to a ground on the drive and resting on the center spindle of the platter spindle motor. This device is the single most likely cause of excessive drive noise.

The *grounding strap* usually is made of copper and often has a carbon or graphite button that contacts the motor spindle. The grounding strap dissipates static generated by the spindle motor. If the platters and motor generate static due to friction, and no place exists for this electrical potential to bleed off, static may discharge through the heads or the internal bearings in the motor. When static discharges through the internal bearings in the motor, it burns the lubricants inside the sealed bearings. The grounding strap bleeds off this static buildup so that no damage is done to the rest of the drive.

Where the spindle of the motor contacts the carbon contact button (at the end of the ground strap) spinning at 3600 RPM, the button often wears, creating a flat spot. The flat spot causes the strap to vibrate and produce a high-pitched squealing or whining noise. The noise may come and go, depending on temperature and humidity. Sometimes, banging the side of the machine can jar the strap so that the noise changes or goes away. *I am not suggesting that you bang on your system.* (Most people mistake this noise for something much more serious, such as a total drive-motor failure or bearing failure, which rarely occurs.)

If the spindle grounding strap has become loose, you can remedy the situation in several ways:

■ Dampen the vibration of the strap by attaching some foam tape or rubber to it.

- Lubricate the contact point.
- Tear off the strap.

On some drives, the spindle motor strap is in an easily accessible position. On other drives, you have to partially disassemble the drive and remove the drive logic board or other external items to get to the strap.

Of these suggested solutions, the first one is the best. The best way to correct this problem is to glue or otherwise affix some rubber to the strap. This procedure changes the harmonics of the strap and usually dampens vibrations. Most manufacturers now use this technique on newly manufactured drives. An easy way to do this on older drives is with double-stick foam tape (place it on the back side of the ground strap).

Another technique is to place a small piece of foam tape on the back of the strap. You also can use a dab of silicone RTV (room-temperature vulcanizing) rubber or caulk on the back of the strap. (Use the low-volatile noncorrosive silicone RTV sealer commonly sold at auto-parts stores. The noncorrosive silicone will be listed on the label as being safe for automotive oxygen sensors. This low-volatile silicone is free from corrosive acids that can damage the copper strap. It is described also as low odor because it does not have the familiar vinegar odor of corrosive silicone.) Dab a small amount on the copper strap (do not interfere with the contact location), and the problem should be solved permanently.

Lubrication of the strap is also an acceptable solution. You will want some sort of conducting lube, such as a graphite compound (the kind used on frozen car locks). Any lubricant will work, as long as it is conductive, but do not use standard oil or grease. Simply dab a small amount of lubricant on the end of a toothpick and place a small drop directly on the point of contact.

The last solution is not an acceptable one. Tearing off the strap eliminates the noise, but it has a number of other possible ramifications. Although the drive will work (silently) without it, an engineer placed the ground strap there for a reason. Imagine those ungrounded static charges leaving the platters through the heads, perhaps in the form of a spark—possibly even damaging the thin film heads. You should choose one of the other solutions.

The only reason I even mention this last solution is that several people have told me that tech-support staff members at some of the hard drive vendors, and even manufacturers, told them to remove the strap, which—of course—I do not recommend.

Logic Boards

A disk drive, including a hard disk drive, has one or more logic boards mounted on it. The logic boards contain the electronics that control the drive's spindle and head actuator systems and present data to the controller in some agreed-on form. With some drives, the controller is located on the drive, which can save on a system's total chip count.

Many disk drive failures occur in the logic board and not in the mechanical assembly. (This statement does not seem logical, but it is accurate.) You can repair many failed drives therefore by replacing the logic board and not the entire drive. Replacing the logic board, moreover, lets you regain access to the data on the failed drive—something that replacing the entire drive precludes.

Logic boards can be removed or replaced because they simply plug into the drive. They usually are mounted with standard screw hardware. If a drive is failing and you have a spare, you may be able to verify a logic-board failure by taking the board off the known good drive and mounting it on the bad one. If your suspicions are confirmed, you can order a new logic board from the drive manufacturer. You may be able also to purchase a refurbished unit, or even trade in your old drive or logic board. The drive manufacturer will have details on what services it can offer. To reduce costs further, many third-party vendors also can supply replacement logic-board assemblies. These companies often charge much less than the drive manufacturers for the same components. (See the vendor list in the Appendix for vendors of drive components, including logic boards.)

Cables and Connectors

This section describes the different types of cables and connectors you encounter in working with different types of hard disks. Note that the pinout specifications for these cables and connectors are in the Appendix of this book.

ST-506/412 and ESDI

Standard drives that interface through ST-506/412 (Seagate Technologies Model 506/412) or ESDI (Enhanced Small Device Interface) nearly always have four connectors (see fig. 9.4):

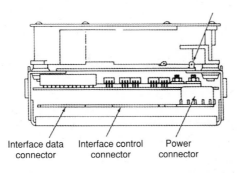

Interface data connector   Interface control connector   Power connector

(Rear View)   Courtesy of IBM Corporation.

Fig. 9.4

ST-506/412 or ESDI hard disk connectors.

- Interface control connector
- Interface data connector
- Power connector
- Ground connector (tab)

Of these, the interface connectors are the most important because they carry the drive's instructions and the data to and from the drive. The *interface control connector* is a 34-pin connector that can be daisy-chained between two drives and a single controller. This cable-and-connector system passes instructions from the controller to the drive or drives to cause head movements and other operations. The drive acknowledges these actions to the controller through the interface control connector cable.

The daisy-chain arrangement is much like that used for floppy drives. It has two usable channels—out of a maximum of four—to which the drive will respond. The channels are labeled drive selects 1, 2, 3, and 4. Although it may appear as though you could string four drives on a single daisy-chain cable, the design of the system and the controllers makes only the first two usable on PC controllers.

The *interface data connector*, or *data cable*, is a 20-pin cable that runs from the controller to one drive. This cable is not daisy-chained. A two-drive system has one control cable from the controller to each of two drives, plus two separate data cables, one for each drive. The controller has three connectors, to support the two-drive maximum limit. As its name suggests, the data cable carries data to and from the drive.

The *power connector* is usually the same as one for a floppy, and the same power-supply connector plugs into it. The drives use both 5- and 12-volt power; the 12-volt power runs the drive's motors and head actuator. Make sure that your power supply can adequately supply power for the hard disk drives installed in your PC system. Many hard drives draw quite a bit more power than a floppy drive.

Ensuring an adequate power supply is particularly important with IBM AT systems. These systems have a power supply with three disk drive power connectors, labeled P10, P11, and P12. The three power connectors may seem equal, but the technical-reference manual for these systems indicates that 2.8 amps of 12-volt current is available on P10 and P11, and that only 1.0 amp of 12-volt current is available on P12. Because most full-height hard drives draw much more power than 1.0 amp, especially at start-up, the P12 connector can be used only by floppy drives or half-height hard drives. Some 5 1/4-inch drives draw as much as 4 amps of current during the first few seconds of start-up. These drives also can draw as much as 2.5 amps during normal operation.

Sometimes you can solve random boot-up failures by simply plugging the hard drive into a suitable power connector (P10 or P11 on the IBM AT). Most IBM-compatible PC systems have a power supply with four or more disk drive power connectors that provide equal power, but some use power supplies designed like the IBM AT.

A *grounding tab* provides a positive ground connection between the drive and the system's chassis. In a typical IBM PC or IBM XT system, because the hard disk drive is mounted directly to the chassis of the PC using screws, the ground wire is unnecessary. On AT-type systems from IBM and others, the drives are installed on plastic or fiberglass rails, which do not provide a proper ground. These systems must provide a grounding wire, plugged into the drive at this grounding tab. Failure to ground the drive may result in improper operation, intermittent failure, or general read and write errors.

SCSI and IDE Interfaces

Small Computer System Interface (SCSI) and Integrated Drive Electronics (IDE) drives usually have a single data and control connector. With these two interface standards, the disk controller normally is built into the drive.

SCSI drives plug into a SCSI bus. The computer also plugs into the SCSI bus through a host adapter plugged into a slot. Some newer PC systems, such as the PS/2 Model 57, include a SCSI host adapter built directly into the motherboard. The host adapter connects to the SCSI drive with a single 50-pin cable. Power and grounding cables normally are separate from this 50-pin cable. Because the SCSI system is a daisy-chain arrangement, more than one drive can be attached using the same cable. A PC system normally is limited to seven SCSI devices in addition to the SCSI host adapter (which counts as the eighth device).

Some ESDI and ST-506/412 implementations include the disk controller as part of the drive assembly. ESDI or ST-506/412 drives that combine the entire disk controller with the drive usually are called *embedded controller,* or Integrated Drive Electronics (IDE), *drives.* With these devices, the drive and controller are in a single unit that plugs directly into a bus slot. For example, PS/2 Model 70 systems use Micro Channel IDE drives, which plug directly into a Micro Channel bus slot (usually through an angle adapter or Interposer card). Other companies, such as COMPAQ, use AT-bus (16-bit) IDE drives or XT-bus (8-bit) IDE drives in their systems. The first IDE drives were called Hardcards.

Because an IDE drive plugs into a standard slot on the motherboard, it is the simplest drive interface. Systems with IDE drives normally have a special 40-pin connector on the motherboard for the IDE drives. This connector might look like a built-in hard disk controller connector, but it is not. A standard ST-506/412 or ESDI controller plugged into the 98-pin AT-bus uses only about 40 of the pins. An AT hard disk controller normally uses only Interrupt 14 (a single pin on the bus); the special IDE connector therefore does not need any other interrupt pins. This is where the IDE interface came from: To save a "real" slot from being used, the motherboard manufacturers provided a specially modified 16-bit (AT) bus slot that had only the pins needed by a typical hard disk controller. That connector is basically the same as one of the regular slot connectors minus any unneeded signals. This connector has been standardized and is called the AT Attachment, or ATA, connector. A pinout chart showing the signals on this connector is in the Appendix.

If your motherboard does not have one of these connectors, you can purchase an adapter card that changes your 98-pin slot connector into a 40-pin IDE connector. These adapter cards are nothing more than buffered cables; they are not really controllers. The controller is built into the drive.

The primary advantage of IDE drives is cost. By eliminating the separate controller or host adapter and simplifying the cable connections, IDE drives cost much less than a standard controller-and-drive combination. They also have increased reliability because the controller is built into the drive. Therefore, the *data separator* (the divisor between the digital and analog signals on the drive) keeps close to the media. Because the drive has a short analog signal path, it is less susceptible to external noise and interference.

The biggest drawback to the IDE interface is expandability. IDE drives are not suited to bigger, high-performance systems requiring large-capacity, high-performance drives. Incompatibilities among different manufacturers' standards make it difficult to install more than one IDE drive on a system. Because the controller is mounted on the drive, to add a second drive you must disable its controller and have it use the controller on the first drive. This process can be difficult because of the many different kinds of controllers on the drives. In many cases, to add an IDE second drive you must use one from the same manufacturer as the first, for compatibility.

An additional drawback to IDE drives is that they are forever locked into a specific type of bus. IDE drives are available for these buses:

- AT bus (16-bit ISA)
- XT bus (8-bit ISA)
- Micro Channel bus

These different IDE drives are normally not interchangeable, although some adapters change some signals to enable the AT-bus drives to work in an 8-bit slot. No such adapters exist for converting the AT bus to Micro Channel, however. An AT-bus IDE drive therefore can never be used with a Micro Channel system, and a Micro Channel IDE drive can never be used in an Industry Standard Architecture (ISA) system.

Another problem with these three different IDE standards is that only the AT-bus version has become a true industry standard. The ANSI committee has approved an implementation of IDE, the ATA interface, that works on the AT bus. Although ATA interface drives theoretically are compatible, many options are in the interface specification, and each drive vendor has implemented custom ATA commands unique to its drives.

Configuration Items

To configure a hard disk drive for installation in a system, a couple of items must be set. These configuration items usually are mounted on the disk drive logic board, which usually is located on the bottom of the drive.

The items that must be set or configured on a hard disk are similar to those on a floppy drive:

- Drive select jumper
- Terminating resistor

These items perform the same functions as on a floppy drive.

Drive Select Jumpers

The *drive select jumper* selects the channel to which the drive should respond. The drive controller sends control signals on two channels— one for each drive. Each drive in a system must be set to respond to a different drive select channel, which limits the number of drives per controller to two. If a system has only one drive, the drive must be set to channel 1. Systems with two drives must have the lowest-letter drive (usually C) set to channel 1 and the other drive (usually D) set to channel 2.

With hard drives (as with floppy drives), IBM systems use a cable that twists around the drive select and motor-enable lines (pins 25 through 29 are crossed) to invert the channels for the last drive on the cable. This procedure ensures that all drives in the system have the same drive select settings, which makes the installation of a hard disk easier because IBM preconfigures all its drives to use the second channel or drive select position. Both drives connected to such a cable seem to have the same drive select setting (the second one). Both drives therefore look as though they are set to be drive D. The drive at the end of the cable is plugged into a connector that has the lines twisted so that the drive's setting is inverted; what appears to be a "D:" setting is changed automatically to "C:". See Chapter 8, "Floppy Disk Drives," for a more detailed discussion of the intricacies of twisted cables.

If you are using a cable with the IBM-type of twist, both hard disks on a single controller must be set to the second drive select position. If you are using a straight-through cable, both drives must carry different drive select settings; the drive set to the first drive select position must respond as C, and the other must respond as D. The typical hard disk cabling system uses three cables for two drives. One cable is a single 34-pin control cable, daisy-chained to both drives. This cable has the optional twist. The cable looks much like the 34-pin cable for floppy drives, but if it is twisted the cables are not interchangeable because different lines are twisted. Pins 25 through 29 would be inverted on the hard disk control cable, and pins 10 through 16 would be inverted on the floppy cable. The other two cables are 20-pin data cables; one is available for each drive and is plugged into a single connector for each one on the controller. These data cables are never twisted and are not daisy-chained.

Terminating Resistors

A hard disk always is shipped from the factory with a terminating resistor. When you install a drive, remove the terminator from any drive that is not at the end of the control cable. The drive at the end of the control cable (drive C) must have the terminator installed.

The functions of the terminating resistor are the same for hard disk drives and floppy drives. The idea is to provide electrical signal termination so that the control signals to and from the drive and controller are not reflected and echo along the cable. The terminating resistor provides the proper signal-to-noise ratio and the proper electrical load for the controller. Improper drive termination results in drives that do not read or write, or do so only with excessive problems. Improper termination also can damage the controller because of excessive electrical loads.

The Bezel

Most hard disk drives offer as an option a front faceplate, or *bezel* (see fig. 9.5). A bezel usually is supplied as an option for the drive rather than as a standard item.

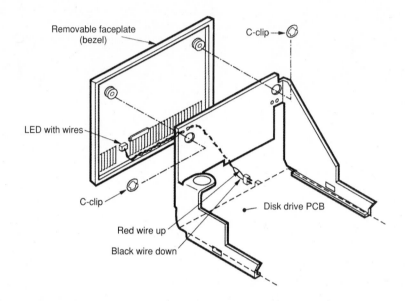

Fig. 9.5

A typical hard drive faceplate.

Bezels come in several sizes and colors to match various PC systems. For standard full-height, 5 1/4-inch, form-factor drives, you have only one choice of bezel. For half-height drives, bezels come in half-height and full-height forms. Using a full-height bezel on a half-height drive enables a single drive to be installed in the bay of a PC or XT without leaving a hole in the front of the system. To add a second half-height drive, you may want to order the half-height bezels so that you can stack the old and new drives. There are many faceplate configurations for 3 1/2-inch drives, including bezels to fit 3 1/2-inch drive bays as well as 5 1/4-inch drive bays. You can even have a choice of colors (usually black, cream, or white).

Some bezels have a light-emitting diode (LED) that flickers when your hard disk is in use. The LED is mounted in the bezel; the wire hanging off the back of the LED plugs into the drive. In some drives, the LED is mounted on the drive; the bezel has a clear or colored see-through window so that you can see the light flicker on the drive.

In IBM AT systems, becuase the hard disk is hidden by the unit's cover, a bezel is not needed. Using a bezel may prevent the cover from sitting properly on the chassis. One type of problem occurs with AT hard disk installations: if the drive has an LED, the LED may remain on as though it were a "power-on" light rather than an access light. This happens because the controller in the AT has a direct connection for the LED, thus altering the drive LED function. Some controllers have a jumper that enables the controller to run the drive in *latched* or *unlatched* mode. Latched mode means that the drive is selected continuously, and the drive LED will remain lit; in unlatched mode (which we are more accustomed to), the LED lights only when the drive is accessed. Check to see whether your controller has this jumper.

Hard Disk Features

To make the best decision in purchasing a hard disk for your system or to understand what differentiates one brand of hard disk from another, you must consider many features. This section examines issues you should consider when you evaluate drives:

- Actuator mechanism
- Media
- Head parking
- Reliability
- Speed
- Shock mounting
- Cost

Actuator Mechanism

A drive with high performance and reliability has two basic physical properties:

- Voice coil actuator mechanism
- Thin film media

Drives with stepper motor actuators should be used only when cost far outweighs other considerations. You should not use them in portable systems or systems that must operate under extremes of temperature, noise, or vibration. Don't use them where preventive maintenance cannot be provided, because they require periodic reformats to maintain data integrity. Finally, you should not use these drives in demanding situations, such as in a network file server. Drives with stepper motor actuators perform adequately in low-volume-usage systems, as long as you provide preventive maintenance at least annually or semiannually and the environment can be controlled.

Voice coil actuator drives should be used in all other situations, especially where extreme demands are put on the drive. These drives are ideal for portable systems or systems that suffer extremes of temperature, noise, or vibration. They are ideal when a fast drive must be used, such as for a network file server. A voice coil drive requires little or no preventive maintenance, so the first low-level format is usually the only low-level format ever done. Less maintenance (reformatting) enables this type of drive to be used for high-volume situations in which a single support person maintains many PC systems. They are more expensive but the payoffs they provide in reliability, performance, and maintenance in the long run more than offset their initial cost.

Head Parking

Head parking is a big and often misunderstood issue with hard disks. When a hard disk comes to a stop, the heads land on the media. The process happens as the drive slows down; therefore, when the head does land, the drive is not turning very fast. On some drives, the story ends here: The heads land on the cylinder they were last positioned over—usually over an area of the disk that contains data.

A drive with a voice coil actuator offers an *automatic head parking* feature. These drives have a spring attached to the head. While the drive is running, an electric coil overcomes the spring tension and moves the head around the disk. When power is lost, the spring automatically pulls the head rack away from data areas of the disk to a special landing zone.

Voice coil drives park drive heads automatically, but most stepper motor drives do not. To find out whether your drive autoparks, find out what kind of actuator it has.

Some newer stepper drives do incorporate a parking mechanism. One example is the Seagate ST-251. This popular stepper drive autoparks the heads using an ingenious system in which the drive spindle motor is used as a generator powering the stepper motor to park the heads. When the drive is powered off, you hear the stepper motor drive the heads to the landing zone. Seagate seems to be using this type of mechanism in more of its stepper motor drives.

Software is available to let you park the heads of drives that lack the automatic parking feature. The software is not quite as reliable as automatic parking because it does not park the heads if the power goes off unexpectedly.

The head-parking program is on the diagnostics disk supplied in the guide-to-operations manual. The parking program is supplied also on the Advanced Diagnostics disk supplied with the hardware-maintenance service manual. Simply boot these disks and select menu item number 3, Prepare system for moving. The heads of all attached disks will be parked. Then shut down the system. This procedure invokes a program on the disk called SHIPDISK.COM. There are different SHIPDISK.COM files for XT and AT systems.

Several years ago, IBM issued a warning to its dealers recommending that they not run SHIPDISK.COM from the DOS prompt. IBM said a slight chance exists that you can lose data because the program can wipe out track 0 of the disk. The memo indicated that SHIPDISK.COM should be run only from the menu.

SHIPDISK.COM parks the disks and then executes a software interrupt to return to the diagnostics disk menu. The interrupt is set only by the special diagnostics DOS found on the diagnostics disk; it is not set by standard DOS. If you run this program at the DOS prompt, random code is run in the system when the SHIPDISK.COM program attempts to return to the diagnostics DOS menu through the untamed interrupt. In an *untamed interrupt*, the interrupt pointer has not been set to indicate the location of the program routine to run when the interrupt is invoked. The system goes to a random location and executes whatever is there, which usually locks up the system immediately. This lockup is assumed mistakenly to be intentional, but it is not. Sometimes the random code not only locks up the system but also causes random data to be written to the drive. If this happens at track 0, the partition table is wiped out and access to the drive is made impossible. *Do not run SHIPDISK.COM from the DOS prompt.* Run it from the diagnostics menu.

For AT systems, IBM supplies a separate program, SHUTDOWN.EXE, that can be run from the DOS prompt. This program is on the AT diagnostics and advanced diagnostics disks. You can copy this program to the hard disk and enter the SHUTDOWN command at the DOS prompt. You will see a picture of a switch, which turns off as the heads are parked. The program then halts the system, requiring a complete power-down. This program does not work on a non-AT type of system.

 Note Do not run a hard disk parking program not designed for your system. If a parking program is written to park a disk of a specific number of cylinders, it may not function properly on other drives.

If your hard drive is a stepper motor actuator drive without automatic parking, it should come with a parking program. If your system is from IBM, these programs come on the diagnostics and setup disks that came with the system. If you have a compatible, you also probably received such a program on your setup disk. Additionally, some public-domain programs will park a stepper motor hard disk.

Should you park the heads every time you shut down the drive? Some people think so, but IBM says that you do not have to park the heads on a drive unless you are moving the drive. My experiences are in line with IBM's recommendations, although a more fail-safe approach is to park the heads at every shutdown. Remember that voice coil drives park their heads automatically every time and require no manual parking operations. For stepper motor drives, I recommend that users park the heads at every shutdown. The procedure is simple and cannot hurt.

Reliability

When you shop for a drive, you may notice a feature called *the mean time between failures*, or MTBF, described in the brochures. MTBF figures usually range from 20,000 hours to 50,000 hours or more. I recommend that you ignore these figures because there is no measurable difference in reliability between drives based on these figures. These figures are just theoretical—not actual—statistical values. Most drives that boast these figures have not even been manufactured for that length of time. One year of 5-day workweeks with 8-hour days equals 2,080 hours of operation. If you never turn off your system for 365 days and run the full 24 hours per day, you operate your system 8,760 hours each year.

Statistically, for the MTBF figures to have real weight, you must take a sample of drives and measure the failure rate for at least twice the rated figure, which means that you should watch the test drives for 40,000 to 100,000 hours to measure how many fail in that time. To be accurate, you must wait until all the drives fail, and record the operating hours at each failure. Then after they fail, you average the running time for all the test samples, which gives you the average life expectancy of the drive. For a reported MTBF of 30,000 hours (most common), the test sample should be run for 30,000 to 60,000 hours (3.4 to 6.8 years) to be accurate, yet the drive carries this specification on the day it is introduced.

I also have seen vendors "play" with these numbers. For example, CDC rated its Wren II half-height drive at 20,000 hours MTBF (this drive is one of the most reliable in the world), but I saw a reseller rate the same unit at 50,000 hours. Some of the worst drives I have used boast high MTBF figures, and some of the best drives have lower ones. These figures do not necessarily translate to reliability in the field.

Speed

When you select a hard disk, an important feature to consider is the speed of the drive. Hard disks come in a wide range of speeds. The best indicator of the drive's speed is usually its price. An old saying from the automotive world is appropriate here: "Speed is money. How fast do you want to go?"

You can measure the speed of a disk drive in two ways:

- Average seek time
- Transfer rate

Average seek time, normally measured in milliseconds, is the average amount of time takes to move the heads from one cylinder to another a random distance away. One way to measure this specification is to run many random track-seek operations and divide the timed results by the number of seeks performed. This method provides an average time for a single seek. The standard way to measure average seek time used by many drive manufacturers involves measuring the time it takes the heads to move across one third of the cylinders. Average seek time depends only on the drive; the interface or controllers have little effect on this specification. (In some instances, the setup of the controller to the drive can affect seek times; this subject is discussed later.) This rating is a gauge of the capabilities of the head actuator.

A different measurement, called average access time, involves another element, called latency. *Latency* is the average time (in milliseconds) it takes for a sector to be available after the heads have reached a track. On average, this figure is one-half the time it takes for a single rotation of the disk, which is 8.33 ms at 3600 RPM. A measurement of average access time is the sum of the average seek time and latency. This number provides the average amount of time required before a randomly requested sector can be accessed.

Latency is a factor in disk read and write performance. Decreasing the latency increases the speed of access to data or files, accomplished only by spinning the drive platters faster. The drive I am using spins at 4318 RPM, for a latency of 6.95 ms. Some drives spin at 5600 RPM or faster, which results in an even faster latency time. In addition to increasing performance where real-world access to data is concerned, spinning the platters faster also increases the data-transfer rate after the heads have arrived at the desired sectors.

The transfer rate is more important to overall system performance than any other specifications. *Transfer rate* is the rate at which the drive and controller can send data to the motherboard. The transfer rate depends not only on the drive, but more so on the interface used as well as the disk controller and even system throughput. The drive is rarely the limiting factor controlling this figure. The drive interface limits the maximum transfer rate possible. The theoretical maximum throughput of the ST-506/412 interface, for example, is 5 megabits per second, and the ESDI is limited to 24 megabits per second. These rates are the absolute limits; the actual transfer rate depends on the controller and the drive.

You can sometimes double or triple the transfer rate on a PC system by changing the controller, without changing the drive. The setup and installation of a drive and controller system can have a big effect on the observed throughput. An improper system setup cannot take full advantage of a component's performance capabilities. Proper drive and controller setup are described later in this chapter, in the section "Disk Installation Procedures."

The speed at which the heads can move usually is rated in average access time, measured in milliseconds. The average access time is about 85 ms to 115 ms for the drives in the original IBM XT, and 35 ms to 40 ms for the drives in the AT. That difference is as large as it looks. Anything less than 40 ms is considered reasonable, and some of the fastest drives clock in at around 10 ms. These drives cost $1000 or more. A drive with a time greater than 40 ms is considered really slow (or antique), but these drives are cheap. There is a high correlation between price and performance in hard disk drives.

Shock Mounting

Most hard disks manufactured today have a *shock-mounted* HDA, which means that a rubber cushion is between the disk drive body and the mounting chassis. Some drives use more rubber than others, but for the most part, a shock mount is a shock mount. Most hard disks have shock mounts—the exceptions are usually among very inexpensive drives. These inexpensive units (such as the Seagate ST-225) lack rubber-isolation mounts for the HDA. Do not use a drive that lacks shock mounting in a portable PC system or in a system in which environmental conditions are less favorable than in a comfortable office. I never recommend a drive that lacks some form of shock mounting.

Cost

The cost of a hard disk drive varies from the $200 Seagate ST-225 20M drive at the low end to the $5,000 Maxtor XT 8760 650M drive at the high end. The largest influences on cost are disk capacity and type of head actuator mechanism. As capacities increase, so does the cost. A drive

with a voice coil actuator costs about 30 to 50 percent more than a drive
of equal capacity but with a stepper motor actuator.

Drive Parameter Tables

When you are selecting a drive for a PC system, consider how the drive
will be supported. How will the system know what type of drive is connected? IBM systems typically store the drive setup or type information
in ROM. The IBM XT uses a controller with a ROM that contains the hard
disk controller BIOS (basic input-output system) and a table of four drive
types indicating the supported drives. You set jumpers or switches on
that controller to indicate which of the four drives you are installing. IBM
AT systems have a 15-, 22-, or 23-entry drive table in the motherboard
ROM. The Setup program supplied with the system selects and stores
the drive type in the CMOS memory.

Perhaps the easiest way to deal with the drive-table problem is to use
only drives supported by the system's existing ROM table. Because IBM
places the drive table for the XT on the hard disk controller, many aftermarket controllers will have different drive tables, and most aftermarket
XT controllers store the drive parameters on the drive itself.

IBM XT Drive Selection

IBM XT hard disk controllers have used two different ROMs over the
years, but they each have only four entry tables, which means that only
four different drives can be supported by a single ROM. Thus, virtually
every time you want to add a different type of hard disk to an IBM XT,
you must reburn the ROM with the correct values for the new drive. You
can try to anticipate future upgrades and burn in the values for those
drives as well.

A new generation of controllers for the IBM PC and IBM XT alleviates the
problem with the IBM XT disk controller. These new controllers request
the type of drive being connected and store the information in a specially reserved track on the drive. Every time the system is booted, the
information is read from that location and the system has the correct
drive type. Thus, a drive table with an infinite number of entries is possible. Regardless of the parameters for your drive, the system can support it because this "autoconfigure ROM" is built into the controller. No
matter what type of disk drive you select, make sure that your controller
is an *autoconfigure type*; it eliminates problems with table entries that do
not match your drives. (Specific recommendations for these controllers
are discussed in this chapter, in the section "Recommended Aftermarket
Controllers.")

Table 9.3 lists the drive parameters in IBM XT (Xebec 1210) hard disk controllers.

Table 9.3 IBM XT Hard Disk Controller Drive Parameter Tables

IBM 10M Hard Disk Controller (Xebec 1210)

Entry	Type	Cyls	Heads	WPC	Ctrl	LZ	S/T	Meg	MB
0	—	306	2	0	00h	00h	00h	5.08	5.33
1	—	375	8	0	05h	00h	00h	24.90	26.11
2	—	306	6	256	05h	00h	00h	15.24	15.98
3	—	306	4	0	05h	00h	00h	10.16	10.65

IBM 20M Hard Disk Controller (Xebec 1210)

Entry	Type	Cyls	Heads	WPC	Ctrl	LZ	S/T	Meg	MB
0	1	306	4	0	05h	305	17	10.16	10.65
1	16	612	4	0	05h	663	17	20.32	21.31
2	2	615	4	300	05h	615	17	20.42	21.41
3	13	306	8	128	05h	319	17	20.32	21.31

Entry = Controller table position
Type = Drive type number
Cyls = Total number of cylinders
Heads = Total number of heads
WPC = Write precompensation starting cylinder
Ctrl = Control byte, values as follows:

> *Bit 0   01h, drive step rate (see table)*
> *Bit 1   02h, drive step rate (see table)*
> *Bit 2   04h, drive step rate (see table)*
> *Bit 3   08h, more than eight heads*
> *Bit 4   10h, embedded servo drive*
> *Bit 5   20h, OEM defect map at (Cyls + 1)*
> *Bit 6   40h, disable ECC retries*
> *Bit 7   80h, disable disk access retries*

Xebec 1210 Drive Step Rate Coding (Control Byte)

> *00h, 3-millisecond step rate*
> *04h, 200-microsecond buffered step*
> *05h, 70-microsecond buffered step*
> *06h, 30-microsecond buffered step*
> *07h, 15-microsecond buffered step*

LZ = Landing zone cylinder for head parking
S/T = Number of sectors per track
Meg = Drive capacity in megabytes
MB = Drive capacity in millions of bytes

The Landing Zone field and Sectors per Track fields are not used in the 10M (original) controller and contain 00h values for each entry.

Note *MB* and *Meg* sometimes are used interchangeably, but this is not exactly correct. MB is one million bytes, or 1,000,000 bytes. Meg (or M) is one megabyte, which is equal to 1,048,576 bytes. (1 megabyte = 1 kilobyte times 1 kilobyte, and 1 kilobyte = 1024 bytes. Thus, 1 megabyte = 1024 times 1024 = 1,048,576.)

To select one of the drive table entries in the IBM XT controllers (Xebec 1210), you would set the drive table selection jumper (Jumper W5) (see fig. 9.6). Jumper pins 1 and 2 define drive 0 (C), 3 and 4 define drive 1 (D). For example, to select table entry 2 for the first drive (C), you would set the jumper Off at position 1 and On at position 2.

		Controller table entry			
Jumper pins		#0	#1	#2	#3
Drive 0	1	O≡O	O≡O	O O	O O
"	2	O≡O	O O	O≡O	O O
Drive 1	3	O≡O	O≡O	O O	O O
"	4	O≡O	O O	O≡O	O O

IBM AT, PS/1, and PS/2 Drive Selection

IBM AT systems are different. Rather than use a ROM on the controller card to support the card and drive tables, IBM incorporated the hard disk ROM BIOS as part of the main system ROM that resides on the motherboard. This ROM contains a hard disk table with at least 15 entries. Later AT ROMs have tables with 23 entries. The XT 286 (really a late-model AT) has a table with 24 entries. And some PS/1 and PS/2 systems have as many as 44 entries. In each of these tables, entry 15 is reserved and not usable. The tables are downward compatible in the newer systems. For example, the PS/2 Model 80-111 has 32 table entries in its ROM, and the entries in the earlier systems match exactly on the specifications. Drive type 9, for example, is the same in all these systems, from the earliest AT to the newest PS/2 systems. Note that compatible systems are not consistent in regard to drive tables. The Appendix lists a number of hard disk drive tables for different compatible systems.

Table 9.4 lists the entries in the IBM motherboard ROM BIOS hard disk parameter table for AT or PS/2 systems using ST-506/412 (standard or IDE) controllers.

Table 9.4 IBM AT and PS/2 Hard Disk Drive Types

Type	Cyls	Heads	WPC	Ctrl	LZ	S/T	Meg	MB
1	306	4	128	00h	305	17	10.16	10.65
2	615	4	300	00h	615	17	20.42	21.41
3	615	6	300	00h	615	17	30.63	32.12
4	940	8	512	00h	940	17	62.42	65.45
5	940	6	512	00h	940	17	46.82	49.09
6	615	4	65535	00h	615	17	20.42	21.41
7	462	8	256	00h	511	17	30.68	32.17
8	733	5	65535	00h	733	17	30.42	31.90
9	900	15	65535	08h	901	17	12.06	117.50
10	820	3	65535	00h	820	17	20.42	21.41
11	855	5	65535	00h	855	17	35.49	37.21
12	855	7	65535	00h	855	17	49.68	52.09
13	306	8	128	00h	319	17	20.32	21.31
14	733	7	65535	00h	733	17	42.59	44.66
15	0	0	0	00h	0	0	0	0
16	612	4	0	00h	663	17	20.32	21.31
17	977	5	300	00h	977	17	40.55	42.52
18	977	7	65535	00h	977	17	56.77	59.53
19	1024	7	512	00h	1023	17	59.50	62.39
20	733	5	300	00h	732	17	30.42	31.90
21	733	7	300	00h	732	17	42.59	44.66
22	733	5	300	00h	733	17	30.42	31.90
23	306	4	0	00h	336	17	10.16	10.65
24	612	4	305	00h	663	17	20.32	21.31
25	306	4	65535	00h	340	17	10.16	10.65
26	612	4	65535	00h	670	17	20.32	21.31
27	698	7	300	20h	732	17	40.56	42.53
28	976	5	488	20h	977	17	40.51	42.48
29	306	4	0	00h	340	17	10.16	10.65

Type	Cyls	Heads	WPC	Ctrl	LZ	S/T	Meg	MB
30	611	4	306	20h	663	17	20.29	21.27
31	732	7	300	20h	732	17	42.53	44.60
32	1023	5	65535	20h	1023	17	42.46	44.52
33	614	4	65535	20h	663	25	29.98	31.44
34	775	2	65535	20h	900	27	20.43	21.43
35	921	2	65535	20h	1000	33	29.68	31.12
36	402	4	65535	20h	460	26	20.41	21.41
37	580	6	65535	20h	640	26	44.18	46.33
38	845	2	65535	20h	1023	36	29.71	31.15
39	769	3	65535	20h	1023	36	40.55	42.52
40	531	4	65535	20h	532	39	40.45	42.41
41	577	2	65535	20h	1023	36	20.29	21.27
42	654	2	65535	20h	674	32	20.44	21.43
43	923	5	65535	20h	1023	36	81.12	85.06
44	531	8	65535	20h	532	39	80.89	84.82
45	0	0	0	00h	0	0	0.00	0.00
46	0	0	0	00h	0	0	0.00	0.00
47	0	0	0	00h	0	0	0.00	0.00

Type = Drive type number
Cyls = Total number of cylinders
Heads = Total number of heads
WPC = Write precompensation starting cylinder
Ctrl = Control byte, values as follows:

Bit 0	*01h, not used (XT=drive step rate)*
Bit 1	*02h, not used (XT=drive step rate)*
Bit 2	*04h, not used (XT=drive step rate)*
Bit 3	*08h, more than 8 heads*
Bit 4	*10h, not used (XT=embedded servo)*
Bit 5	*20h, OEM defect map at (Cyls + 1)*
Bit 6	*40h, disable disk retries*
Bit 7	*80h, disable disk retries*

LZ = Landing zone cylinder for head parking
S/T = Number of sectors per track
Meg = Drive capacity in megabytes
MB = Drive capacity in millions of bytes
Table entry 15 is reserved as a CMOS pointer to indicate that the actual type is greater than 15.

Most IBM systems do not have every entry in table 9.4. The maximum usable type number varies for each specific ROM version. The maximum usable type for each IBM ROM is indicated in table 9.5. If you have a compatible, table 9.5 may be inaccurate for many of the entries past type 15. (Most compatibles follow the IBM table for at least the first 15 entries.) A number of compatible-system drive tables are in the Appendix in the back of this book, including tables for a number of different compatible systems from COMPAQ to Zenith.

Most IBM PS/2 systems now are supplied with hard disk drives that have the defect map written as data on the cylinder that is one cylinder beyond the highest reported cylinder. This special data is read by the IBM PS/2 Advanced Diagnostics low-level format program, which automates the entry of the defect list and eliminates the chance for human error (as long as you use only the IBM PS/2 Advanced Diagnostics program for hard disk low-level formatting).

Table 9.5 does not apply to IBM ESDI or SCSI hard disk controllers, host adapters, and drives. Because ESDI and SCSI controllers and host adapters query the drive directly for the required parameters, no table entry selection is necessary. The table for ST-506/412 drives, however, is still in the ROM BIOS of most PS/2 systems, even if the model came standard with the ESDI or SCSI disk subsystem.

Table 9.5 Number of Drive Types in Various IBM BIOS Versions

System description	ROM BIOS date	ID byte	Submodel byte	Revision	ST506 drive types
PS/2 25	06/26/87	FA	01	00	26
PS/2 30	09/02/86	FA	00	00	26
PS/2 30	12/12/86	FA	00	01	26
PS/2 30	02/05/87	FA	00	02	26
PC-AT	01/10/84	FC	Not supported		15
PC-AT	06/10/85	FC	00	01	23
PC-AT	11/15/85	FC	01	00	23
PC-XT 286	04/21/86	FC	02	00	24
PS/1	12/01/89	FC	0B	00	44
PS/2 25-286	06/28/89	FC	09	02	37
PS/2 30-286	08/25/88	FC	09	00	37
PS/2 30-286	06/28/89	FC	09	02	37

System description	ROM BIOS date	ID byte	Submodel byte	Revision	ST506 drive types
PS/2 35 SX	03/15/91	F8	19	05	37
PS/2 35 SX	04/04/91	F8	19	06	37
PS/2 40 SX	03/15/91	F8	19	05	37
PS/2 40 SX	04/04/91	F8	19	06	37
PS/2 L40 SX	02/27/91	F8	23	02	37
PS/2 50	02/13/87	FC	04	00	32
PS/2 50	05/09/87	FC	04	01	32
PS/2 50 Z	01/28/88	FC	04	02	33
PS/2 50 Z	04/18/88	FC	04	03	33
PS/2 55 SX	11/02/88	F8	0C	00	33
PS/2 60	02/13/87	FC	05	00	32
PS/2 65 SX	02/08/90	F8	1C	00	33
PS/2 70 386	01/29/88	F8	09	00	33
PS/2 70 386	04/11/88	F8	09	02	33
PS/2 70 386	12/15/89	F8	09	04	33
PS/2 70 386	01/29/88	F8	04	00	33
PS/2 70 386	04/11/88	F8	04	02	33
PS/2 70 386	12/15/89	F8	04	04	33
PS/2 70 386	06/08/88	F8	0D	00	33
PS/2 70 386	02/20/89	F8	0D	01	33
PS/2 P70 386	01/18/89	F8	0B	00	33
PS/2 80 386	03/30/87	F8	00	00	32
PS/2 80 386	10/07/87	F8	01	00	32

Numbers in ID byte, Submodel byte, and Revision columns are in hexadecimal.

Because the hard disk ROM BIOS of the IBM AT is built into the motherboard ROM, you cannot easily change the type of hard disk controller on an IBM AT. A new controller must be exactly like the original controller, or else the ROM BIOS on the motherboard will not operate the new controller correctly. If the new controller has ROM on board, it will conflict with the system board ROM. Therefore, to install a hard disk controller other than one exactly like the original on an IBM AT, you must use an alternative installation method like one of the following:

- Disable motherboard ROM support of the hard disk controller and use a controller that has a built-in ROM. To disable motherboard ROM support of the hard disk controller, run the Setup program and tell the system that no hard disk drives are installed. This process disables the hard disk BIOS on the motherboard and enables the controller's own BIOS to be recognized and used. Then you can use an autoconfigure type controller with dynamically variable drive tables on an IBM AT. The replacement hard drive controller must have on-board ROM BIOS.

A drive not directly supported by the CMOS memory setup routine normally is not recognized by an operating system that runs in protected mode, including OS/2, XENIX (UNIX), and Novell Advanced NetWare. Therefore, if you are purchasing a hard disk controller that has on-board ROM for an IBM AT, you may need special drivers for OS/2, XENIX, or NetWare. Because most ROMs do not function in protected mode, the drivers must be loaded from disk instead.

- Modify the drive-table entries so that the drive is supported. You can accomplish this task by downloading, patching, and reburning the original motherboard ROM chips. This method is considered impractical at best.

- Replace the motherboard ROM with a compatible ROM, such as one from Phoenix or Award. Each company sells a set of AT ROMs for about $50. These ROMs usually have a full 47 entries in their drive tables, and some contain as many as 255 entries. One of these entries probably will match the new drive.

- Use ROM dubbing. Golden Bow and Washburn & Company have released ROM dubbing boards that patch themselves into the motherboard ROM, which enables you to replace one of the existing drive types with a different drive type. You can keep the standard controller, run under protected mode, and support virtually any type of drive. These dubbing kits sell for about $100.

Capacity

Four figures commonly are used in advertising drive capacity:

- Unformatted capacity in millions of bytes (MB)
- Unformatted capacity in megabytes (Meg)
- Formatted capacity in millions of bytes (MB)
- Formatted capacity in megabytes (Meg)

Table 9.5 shows the formatted capacities of drives in millions of bytes (MB) and megabytes (Meg). Both figures are included because advertisements for drives or discussions of drives sometimes include either figure.

For example, the formatted capacity of a Control Data Corporation (Imprimis) Wren III half-height SCSI drive is as follows:

Bytes per sector: 512
Sectors per track: 35
Tracks per head: 1022
Heads: 5
Total bytes: 91,571,200

The 91.5 million bytes (MB) is equal to only 87.33 megabytes (Meg) of capacity. Most marketing departments for drive vendors choose to use the larger one, referring to a drive as a 91.5 MB drive rather than as an 87.33 Meg drive. Both numbers are correct. They could choose instead to refer to the drive's unformatted capacity, which in this case is 106 MB, or 101 Meg. The figures that can be used for a CDC Wren III half-height SCSI drive follow:

Unformatted capacity: 106 M (101 Meg)
Formatted capacity: 91.5 M (87.33 Meg)

Any of these four figures—formatted or unformatted capacity in Meg or MB—is technically correct and accurate in describing the capacity of the drive.

Specific Brands and Recommendations

I recommend only voice coil drives because they are much more reliable and durable than stepper motor drives and the benefits far outweigh the small additional cost. Generally, the use of thin film (sputtered or plated) media is a bonus also, although many high-quality drives still use oxide-coated media. For high-performance, consider drives and controllers with SCSI, ESDI, or IDE. These interfaces offer much greater reliability and performance than the ST-506/412 interface.

I recommend the manufacturers listed in this section. The list does not cover all manufacturers because new companies and drives are introduced all the time.

When reliability and performance are paramount, consider the following companies, which make some of the highest-quality drives in the industry:

Seagate (high-end Imprimis models)
Maxtor/Miniscribe
Micropolis
IBM/Western Digital

For some, cost is the more important consideration. Many manufacturers of midrange drives that use voice coil actuators make them available at a lower cost. The Seagate ST-4000 series, for example, is sold in such high volumes (Seagate is the largest disk drive company) that it is priced very competitively. Many other companies also offer reasonably priced voice coil drives. Some of the best bargains are from these companies:

Seagate (lower cost models)
Conner Peripherals
Microscience (voice coil only)

Hard Disk Controllers

You must consider many options when you evaluate and select a hard disk interface and controller for your system. Compatibility and the speed of the controller are probably the most important initial considerations.

In many PC systems, the hard disks and controllers are installed already. Using devices that are interface-compatible with existing controllers and drives is much simpler and less expensive than forcing a change to some new standard. Many times, you can change the brand of controller, keep the interface specification the same, and gain as much as a threefold increase in speed with the same drives. If you are willing to begin from scratch and select a controller and disk together without requiring that they work with your other drives or controllers, you have much more leeway in choosing a subsystem.

This section examines the standard controllers and describes how you can work with these controllers, as well as replace them with much faster units. Also discussed are the different types of drive interfaces: ST-506/412, ESDI, IDE and SCSI. Choosing among these interfaces is important because the choice also affects your disk drive purchases and the ultimate speed of the controllers.

The primary job of the hard disk controller is to transmit and receive data and control signals to and from the drive. Hard disks can transmit and receive data as fast as they spin; while the drive is turning, raw data pulses are transmitted to the controller, which sends the signals to the system's motherboard.

The information stored on a floppy or hard disk is arranged in a series of concentric circular rings called *tracks*. Each track on a disk is divided into *sectors*, which are shaped much like slices of a pie. The number of sectors on a disk varies, depending on the density of the disk and the encoding scheme. Disks have 17, 25, 26, 32, 34, 35, 36, or more sectors per track. (Other numbers of sectors per track are possible, but these are the ones I have seen on drives for PC systems.) Two things usually do not change among different drives: the rotational speed of the drive (usually 3600 RPM) and the number of bytes in each sector (512 bytes).

In discussing disk drives, especially hard disk drives, a popular specification to note is the drive's reported average access time—the (average) time it takes for the heads to be positioned from one track to another. Because it takes longer to move across all the tracks on the disk than to move to only one track, average access time often is calculated by making hundreds or thousands of individual random seeks across the disk, observing the total time taken, and dividing that time by the number of random seeks completed. This process gives the average amount of time for each seek. Unfortunately, the importance of this specification often is overstated, especially in relation to a specification known as the *data-transfer rate*.

The transfer rate of data between the drive and the motherboard is more important than access time because most drives spend more time reading and writing information than simply moving the heads around on the disk. The speed with which a program or data file is loaded or read is affected most by the data-transfer rate. Sorting large files, which involves a lot of random access to individual records of the file (and therefore many seek operations), is helped greatly by a faster-seeking disk drive. Other file-load and -save operations are affected most by the rate at which data can be read and written to and from the drive. The data-transfer rate depends more on the disk controller than on the drive.

The *disk controller* is the device that controls the transfer of data to and from the drive. A specific disk's maximum transfer rate is dictated primarily by the number of sectors per track; other factors, such as rotational speed and the amount of data in each sector, tend to remain constant among different drives. (Drives are made that spin faster than 3600 RPM, but I do not know of any using a sector size other than 512 bytes.) A drive with 17 sectors per track has the same transfer rate as other drives with 17 sectors per track. Variations in data-transfer rates among drives with the same number of sectors per track operating at the same rotational speed result from the capabilities of different disk controllers. Not all controllers accept and transfer data at the maximum rate possible for the drive. Moreover, not all motherboards are fast enough to accept data at the drive's full rate even if the controller could manage it.

Interleave Selection

When a disk is formatted by a low-level format program, the sectors are numbered according to an interleave ratio. Interleave specification or alteration is always done by a low-level format routine because it is the only type of program that can write to the sector header area. In most cases you need to know the best interleave value for your controller and system combination. The following section describes the interleave ratio and how you can determine the best value for your system.

As an example, suppose that a disk has 17 sectors on each track and you want to number the sectors on each track consecutively.

Now suppose that the controller is commanded to position the heads to a specific track and read all 17 sectors from that track. The heads move and arrive at the desired track. After an average of one-half of a disk revolution, the sector numbered 1 arrives under the heads. While the disk is spinning at 3600 RPM (60 revolutions per second), the data is read from sector 1, and as the data is being transferred to the system board, the disk continues to spin. Finally the data is moved to the motherboard, and the controller is ready for sector 2 (see fig. 9.7).

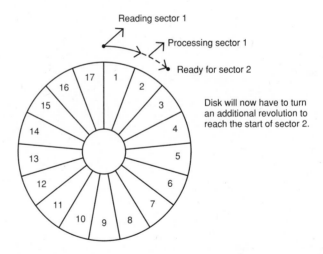

Reading sector 1

Processing sector 1

Ready for sector 2

Disk will now have to turn an additional revolution to reach the start of sector 2.

Fig. 9.7

A hard disk interleave ratio too low for the controller.

There is a problem here. Because the disk continues to spin at such a high rate of speed, the next sector passes under the head as the controller does its work, and the heads now are coming to sector 3. Because you now want to read sector 2, the controller must wait (as the disk spins around again) until the start of sector 2 comes under the heads. After an additional disk revolution, sector 2 arrives under the heads and is read. While the controller is transferring the data to the motherboard, sector 3 passes under the heads. When the controller finally is ready to read sector 3, the heads are coming to the start of sector 4.

As you can see, the timing of this procedure is not working out. The controller must wait while the disk spins another revolution, until the start of sector 3 comes underneath the heads, before it can be read. At this pace, 17 full revolutions of the disk are required in order to read all 17 sectors. Because each revolution takes 1/60 of 1 second, it will take 17/60 of 1 second to read this track, almost one-third of a second—a long time by computer standards.

Can this performance be improved? You notice that after reading a specific sector from the disk, the controller takes some time to transfer the sector data to the motherboard. The next sector that the controller can catch in this example is the second sector away from the first one. In other words, the controller seems to be capable of catching every second sector.

I hope that now you can imagine the perfect solution to this problem: simply *number* the sectors out of order. The new numbering scheme takes into account how fast the controller works; the sectors are numbered so that each time the controller is ready for the next sector, the sector coming under the heads is numbered as the next sector the controller will want to read. Figure 9.8 shows this new sector-numbering scheme.

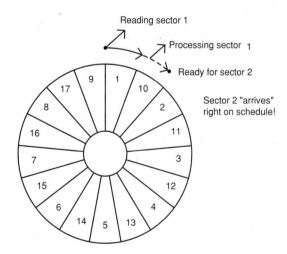

Reading sector 1

Processing sector 1

Ready for sector 2

Sector 2 "arrives" right on schedule!

Fig. 9.8

A hard disk interleave ratio matching the controller's capabilities.

The new numbering system eliminates the extra disk revolution previously required to pick up each sector. With the new scheme, the controller will read all 17 sectors on the disk in only two complete revolutions. Renumbering the sectors on the disk in this manner is called *interleaving*, normally expressed as a ratio. The interleave ratio in the preceding example is 2 to 1 (also written as 2:1), which means that the next numbered sector is 2 sectors away from the preceding one, and only 2 complete revolutions are needed to read an entire track. Reading the track takes only 2/60 of one second at the 2 to 1 interleave, rather than 17/60 of one second required to read the disk at the 1 to 1 interleave—an improvement of *800 percent* in data-transfer rate.

This example depicts a system in which the ideal interleave is 2:1. I used this example because most controllers that came in older AT systems worked in exactly this manner. If you set one for a 1:1 interleave, you make the drive eight times slower than it should be. Most disk controllers sold in the last couple of years should be able to support a 1:1 interleave on AT-class systems. In today's systems, a 1:1 interleave controller should be considered standard issue, and I would not accept anything less in a new system.

The correct interleave for a system depends primarily on the controller, and secondarily on the speed of the system that the controller is plugged into. A controller and system that can handle a *consecutive sector interleave* (a 1 to 1 interleave) must transfer data as fast as the disk drive can present it; this used to be quite a feat, but is now commonplace. Table 9.6 presents theoretical maximum data-transfer rates at various interleaves, disk spindle speeds, and track densities.

Advances in controller technology have made a 1 to 1 interleave both possible and affordable. AT and PS/2 systems can easily handle this transfer rate. The only system units that cannot effectively use a 1 to 1 interleave are the original 4.77 MHz PC- and XT-type systems. Those systems have a maximum throughput to the slots of just under 400K per second, not fast enough to support a 1:1 interleave controller. The IBM PS/2 systems with Micro Channel Architecture slots (including the Model 50 and higher) all include controllers that support a 1 to 1 interleave as a standard feature. IBM was among the first personal computer manufacturers to sell systems with disk data-transfer rates this fast.

A 1-to-1 interleave with a 17-sector disk is one thing, but with ESDI or SCSI drives spinning at 5400 RPM and having 75 or more sectors per track, this results in *more than three megabytes of data transfer each second.*

The interleave used in standard-issue IBM XT systems with hard drives is 6 to 1; in IBM AT systems, it is 3 to 1. The best interleave for these systems is one lower than standard in each case: The best interleave for the Xebec 1210 controller in a 4.77 MHz IBM PC or IBM XT is 5 to 1, and the best interleave for the Western Digital 1002 and 1003 controllers in a 6 MHz or 8 MHz IBM AT system is 2 to 1. IBM selected the higher values, resulting in lower performance; but IBM is known for conservatism. If you redo the low-level format on these systems to the lower interleave number, you gain about 20 to 30 percent in data-transfer performance, at no cost except for some of your time.

Table 9.6 Maximum Data-Transfer Rates in Kilobytes per Second

Speed (RPM)	Sectors/track	Interleaves					
		1:1	2:1	3:1	4:1	5:1	6:1
3600	17	510	255	170	128	102	85
3600	25	750	375	250	188	150	125
3600	26	780	390	260	195	156	130
3600	27	810	405	270	203	162	135
3600	32	960	480	320	240	192	160
3600	33	990	495	330	248	198	165
3600	34	1020	510	340	255	204	170
3600	35	1050	525	350	263	210	175
3600	36	1080	540	360	270	216	180
3600	37	1110	555	370	278	222	185
3600	38	1140	570	380	285	228	190
3600	39	1170	585	390	293	234	195
4318	48	1727	864	576	432	345	288
3600	87	2610	1305	870	653	522	435
5400	75	3375	1688	1125	844	675	563

I usually recommend the Norton Utilities for performing hard disk drive interleave testing. The Calibrate program included with the Norton Utilities can test and change the interleave on most hard disks through a nondestructive low-level format.

Standard Controllers

IBM supplies standard disk controllers in its systems, but most of the controllers are made for IBM by an outside vendor. If you know the original manufacturer, you might be able to purchase the same part directly and save the markup.

Note The interleave factor can be too loose or too tight (a high number is loose; a low number is tight). Operating with an interleave factor that is too loose results in lower performance. Operating with an interleave factor that is too tight is more serious: The controller misses the next sector every time, which drastically slows the disk speed. Regardless of the interleave factor—whether it is too loose, just right, or too tight—the disk functions with no errors. This is the reason that so many systems remain interleaved incorrectly; the only way to know that your system is interleaved incorrectly is to run performance tests at different interleaves. One of the tested interleave values will result in the best transfer rate. If your system is not set to that value, you will want to perform a low-level format to reset it (remember to make a complete backup of the disk before you start the reformatting procedure).

If you purchase from IBM either the XT Fixed Disk Controller or the AT Fixed Disk Controller, for example, the price is about $300 each. On the other hand, you can buy the same controllers for about $100 from a distributor. This pricing disparity applies to virtually every component in the early IBM systems and to many components in the IBM PS/2 systems. The closer to the source of manufacture you can get to buy a part, the less you have to pay. You can save a lot and be assured of the same or better quality—and full compatibility with the original IBM parts.

IBM PC and IBM XT Controllers

The hard disk controller used in the original 10MB IBM XT is the Xebec 1210 controller, manufactured by Xebec Corporation. The Xebec 1210 is an ST-506/412 controller that uses Modified Frequency Modulation (MFM) encoding to record data on a drive. (MFM is discussed later in this chapter, under "Data-Encoding Schemes.") This controller's ROM is produced by IBM and contains the hard disk BIOS. If you purchase the controller from Xebec, you get a slightly different but completely compatible ROM. Xebec allows system integrators to copy its ROM in order to modify the built-in drive tables for a specific drive.

The later version of the IBM controller is supplied on IBM XT systems with a 20MB hard disk. This controller is the Xebec 1210 with a new ROM that contains different drive tables. Xebec never sold an autoconfigure version of this controller, which would have made integrating different drives easier.

The Xebec 1210 is one of the slowest controllers, supporting at best a 5 to 1 interleave on a stock IBM PC or IBM XT system. If you use the IBM Advanced Diagnostics program for the IBM PC or IBM XT, the low-level formatter produces a standard 6 to 1 interleave, which results in a paltry 85K-per-second data-transfer rate. By changing the interleave to 5 to 1, you can wring 102K per second from this controller.

One benefit of using the Xebec 1210 controller is that Xebec makes a Model 1220 that combines the function of the floppy controller for two floppy drives, is hardware compatible with the 1210, and works with the IBM or standard Xebec ROM. The floppy controller then is removed from the system, and the 1220 ends up saving a slot.

I recommend replacing this controller with an autoconfigure controller whenever you get the chance. Most other controllers also are significantly faster than the Xebec.

IBM AT Controllers

For the AT, IBM uses two controllers made by Western Digital: the WD 1002-WA2 and the WD 1003A-WA2. The WD 1003 is an upgraded WD 1002 with a much lower chip count. The WD 1003 is shorter than the WD 1002, to fit into the IBM XT 286.

The WD 1002 is used in the IBM AT as a combination hard disk and floppy disk controller. The WD 1002 and the WD 1003 are standard ST-506/412 controllers that supply MFM encoding to the drive. Neither contains a ROM BIOS; instead, support is built in to the motherboard ROM. Both support a 2 to 1 interleave, even on a standard 6 MHz IBM AT system. The IBM Advanced Diagnostics low-level formatter can put down a 2 to 1 interleave, but the default is 3 to 1. Most users can realize a performance gain if they simply reformat to the lower interleave.

IBM PS/2 Systems with ISA Bus

The IBM PS/2 Models with ISA bus slots use IDE hard drives. The IDE interface in these systems is built into the motherboard. The Model 25, 25-286, 30, and 30-286 systems use an 8-bit XT IDE interface. These 8-bit XT IDE drives are difficult to find because few manufacturers other than IBM and Western Digital make them; the upgradeability of these systems therefore is significantly limited.

The Model 35 and 40 systems use the industry-standard AT Attachment (ATA) IDE interface, the standard IDE interface. Because nearly all hard disk manufacturers make a multitude of drives with the ATA IDE interface, these systems are easy to upgrade. Just purchase the new drive, plug it in, and run Setup. ATA IDE drives are available in capacities up to and beyond 1 gigabyte.

IBM PS/2 Systems with MCA Bus

The IBM PS/2 Models come with MicroChannel Architecture (MCA) bus slots ST-506/412, ESDI and SCSI drives. Most ST-506/412 and ESDI drives have the controller on the drive. This is a form of IDE interface, but is designed for the MCA bus and is not compatible with the more industry-standard ATA IDE interface. Few companies other than IBM and Western Digital make replacement MCA IDE drives for these systems. Even though the connection to the system is through a MCA IDE interface, the controller built into the drive can be either ST-506/412 or ESDI.

Systems that do not use the IBM MCA IDE interface drives use ST-506/412, ESDI, or SCSI drives. In all but the SCSI systems, a separate controller card is plugged into one of the MCA slots, and up to two drives are cabled to the controller. If the system uses a SCSI interface to hard disks, a SCSI host adapter card is in one of the slots, or the system has a SCSI host adapter built into the motherboard. This seems to be similar in appearance to the IDE interface because a single cable runs from the motherboard to the SCSI drive, but SCSI supports as many as seven different devices (some of which may not be hard disks); IDE supports only two devices, which must be either a hard disk or a tape drive.

PS/2 systems with SCSI drives are easily the most upgradeable because virtually any third-party SCSI drive will plug in and function. The ESDI drives require that you purchase a drive compatible with IBM's ESDI controller. The IBM ESDI controller expects the defect information to be in a special format that many third-party drives do not have. The ST-506/412 models are relatively easy to upgrade, but when you use that interface you return to being limited by the ROM BIOS hard disk drive support table. Unlike most compatible systems, IBM systems do not support a user-definable drive type.

Recommended Aftermarket Controllers

Many companies manufacture disk controllers for IBM and IBM-compatible systems. Many newer systems include IDE drives, which have the controller built in and offer a high level of performance at a low cost. Other systems are using SCSI drives because of the inherent flexibility of the SCSI bus to support many drives and other peripherals.

I recommend IDE drives for most standard installations because the connections are so simple and the drives are inexpensive for the power. SCSI drive systems are recommended for higher-end systems, or when upgradeability and flexibility are most important.

Silicon Valley makes a line of IDE adapters that are excellent for systems without the special IDE connector on the motherboard. It also has a special adapter that enables you to put AT IDE drives in 8-bit XT systems, which few other cards do.

For SCSI host adapters, I recommend IBM for MCA cards, and Adaptec or Future Domain for ISA or EISA bus cards. All these adapters work well and come complete with the necessary formatting and operating software. OS/2 has built-in support for IBM and Adaptec SCSI adapters. This support is a consideration in many cases because it eliminates having to deal with external drivers.

Data Technology Corporation has an excellent line of standard controllers for the ST-506/412 drives. Its controllers support a 1:1 interleave on AT systems, and it is one of the few remaining vendors that still makes XT controllers. One of the most popular controller manufacturers, Western Digital, has discontinued all of its disk controller products, leaving a hole in the industry because many have relied on these controllers for years. Fortunately, DTC makes excellent alternatives to the WD products. In fact, it has a complete line of controllers that offers everything WD offered and, in some cases, even more. DTC's address and phone information is in the vendor list in the back of this book.

Interface Specifications

You can use several types of hard disk drive interfaces in PC systems:

- ST-506/412
- ESDI
- SCSI
- IDE

Of these interfaces, only ST-506/412 and ESDI are true disk interfaces. SCSI and IDE are system-level interfaces that usually incorporate one of the other two disk interfaces internally. For example, most SCSI and IDE drives incorporate ESDI into the disk drive electronics and use the higher-level SCSI or IDE to talk to the drive controller.

In data recovery, it helps to know the disk interface you are working with because many data-recovery problems involve drive setup and installation problems. Each interface requires a slightly different method of installation and drive configuration. If the installation or configuration is incorrect or accidently altered by the system user, it may prevent access to data on a drive. Accordingly, anyone who wants to become proficient in data recovery must be an expert in installing and configuring various types of hard disks and controllers.

One advantage of working with IBM personal computer systems and compatibles is that IBM relies on industry-standard devices for its PC and PS/2 peripherals. Vendors of IBM-compatible systems have followed this wise plan. Therefore, you can take virtually any disk drive off the shelf, plug it in, and be ready to go. This "plug and play" capability results in affordable hard disk storage and a variety of options in capacities and speed.

ST-506/412 Interface

The ST-506/412 interface was developed by Seagate Technologies around 1980. The interface, designed for the Seagate ST-506 drive, was a 6-megabyte unformatted or 5-megabyte formatted drive in a full-height, 5 1/4-inch form factor. By today's standards, it is a tank! In 1981 Seagate introduced the ST-412 drive, which added a *buffered seek* feature to the interface. This drive was a 10-megabyte formatted or 12-megabyte unformatted drive and also qualifies today as a tank. The ST-412 is one of the drives IBM originally selected for the XT.

Most drive manufacturers who made hard disks for PC systems adopted the Seagate standard, which helped to make this interface popular. One important feature is the interface's "plug and play" design. No custom cables or special modifications are needed for the drives. The only item to customize is the drive table support in the system.

The ST-506/412 interface does not quite make the grade in today's high-performance PC systems. It was designed for a 5-megabyte drive; no manufacturers use this interface on drives larger than 152 megabytes with MFM encoding or 233 megabytes with RLL encoding. Drives larger than those use ESDI or SCSI.

Data-Encoding Schemes

Encoding schemes are used in telecommunications for converting digital data bits into various tones for transmission over a telephone line. For disk drives, the digital bits are converted, or *encoded*, into a pattern of magnetic impulses, or *flux reversals*, stored on the disk. They are decoded later when the data is read from the disk while a *modem (modulator/demodulator)* does the conversion to and from the encoded data in telecommunications. An endec (*encoder/decoder*) device accomplishes the conversion to flux reversals and the reconversion back to digital data for a disk drive.

Several encoding schemes are used for disk drives, but two are the most popular in PC applications:

Modified Frequency Modulation (MFM)
Run Length Limited (RLL 2,7 or 1,7)

The primary difference between these two encoding schemes is the bit density they can achieve. The ST-506/412 interface specification requires that the endec be located on the controller. However, because the endec is on the controller, some controller manufacturers were able to change the endec to enable the drive to store data using RLL encoding.

The standard ST-506/412 MFM format specifies that the drive will contain 17 sectors per track, with each sector containing 512 bytes of data. The encoding scheme determines the efficiency of the recording on the disk. With an RLL encoding scheme, the number of sectors per track is raised to 25 or 26, which results in about 50 percent more data on each track, and a 50 percent greater data-transfer rate at the same interleave value.

MFM Encoding

MFM stands for *Modified Frequency Modulation,* a type of encoding scheme for converting digital information into magnetic flux changes stored on a disk drive. MFM is a fixed-length scheme, in which a set pattern of bits always uses the same amount of linear space on the disk. The MFM encoding scheme was devised as a way to build in clocking information with data pulses. This method always spaces the flux reversals on the disk evenly in time, to separate the beginnings of one bit from another. MFM encoding enables even single-bit errors to be detected easily and corrected by the controller electronics.

Under the ST-506/412 interface, if the data is encoded with MFM, the number of sectors per track is 17. Floppy disk drives also use MFM encoding for data storage.

RLL Encoding

RLL stands for *Run-Length Limited.* The abbreviation usually is followed by two numbers (RLL 2,7, for example). The first number indicates the minimum run of 0 bits between two 1s (or the *length*), and the second number indicates the maximum number of 0s between two 1s (or the *limit*).

In RLL encoding, the intervals between flux changes are less regular and more prone to error than in MFM encoding. Essentially, every MFM bit cell is divided into three RLL bit cells, each of which may have a flux reversal. RLL encoding places more stringent demands on the timing of the controller and drive electronics because it allows flux reversals to occur at highly irregular intervals. With RLL encoding, virtually no clocking information exists; therefore, accurately reading the timing of the flux changes is paramount. Additionally, because the length of the code is not fixed, a single-bit error cannot be detected and may corrupt as many as five bits. For both of these reasons, an RLL controller must have a more sophisticated error-detection and error-correction routine than an MFM controller.

The great benefit of RLL encoding is the increased density of data storage on the disk and the resulting increased transfer rate—a nominal increase of 50 percent over MFM encoding. A drive that stores 20 megabytes under MFM encoding can store 30 megabytes under RLL. The density of the flux reversals per inch of track does not change. What does change is the timing between the flux reversals and the bit or byte meanings of various groups of these flux reversals. The data density changes, not the magnetic density.

You may find it helpful to compare data encoding to secret codes like the ones children use. Imagine a code in which each letter of the alphabet is converted to the letter at the opposite end of the alphabet: The letter *A* is converted to *Z*, *B* to *Y*, and so on. This encoding scheme can be used to encode a message in writing. Note that a message encoded using this scheme is no more "dense" than the original message; if the original message was 500 letters long, the encoded message is also 500 letters long.

Suppose that you develop a new code in which words are represented by a unique letter or symbol. Using this new code, a 500-letter message might be coded as a 50-symbol message. The advantage of the new encoding scheme is that it is ten times more efficient than the previous one. The disadvantages are that the new scheme is more difficult to interpret quickly, an error in the new scheme results in the loss of an entire word, rather than a single letter (which could be corrected easily in context), and many symbols must be memorized.

This denser encoding scheme is how RLL works; with approximately the same "flux density," the drive can store 50 percent more information than it could with MFM encoding. The problems are primarily ones of reliability and data integrity.

Because of the design of the ST-506/412 interface, the MFM endec or RLL endec resides on the controller card in a slot in the PC, which is where the encoding and decoding takes place. As a result, unfortunately, the endec is placed a long way from the data transmitting and receiving source. Changing a system that has a controller with an MFM endec to a controller with an RLL endec is like changing a modem from a 2400 bps unit to a 14,400 bps unit to "increase the density" of the signal transmitted over the phone line. If the procedure is done with local calling (or a high-quality phone line) in mind, few problems should result; a bad phone line, however, can render the higher-speed connection unusable.

The endec's physical placement in the controller under the ST-506/412 interface is not optimum and not recommended for most PC systems. Unfortunately, computer magazines often include ads that say, "Try the new Super Turbo Kontroller that will increase your disk capacity and speed by 50 or even 100 percent!" What the ads do not tell you is that you may be in for a hassle with continuous read/write errors, constant reformatting, and constant data loss.

This endec placement does provide acceptable results if you are using an IDE ST-506/412 drive (such as a Hardcard), in which the controller is part of the drive unit. Because the endec is attached to the drive without cables and with an extremely short electrical distance, the propensity for timing- and noise-induced errors is greatly reduced or eliminated. For example, IBM and COMPAQ use IDE-based ST-506/412 RLL-encoded drives in their systems with no decrease in reliability—in fact, reliability is increased.

Accurate RLL encoding and decoding places many demands on the drive and controller. The sensitivity to timing means that the drive must be a high-quality unit, with a voice coil actuator and thin film media. (A stepper motor drive has too many tracking- and temperature-induced errors.) Thin film media has a much greater signal-to-noise ratio and bandwidth than conventional oxide media, thereby reducing the possibility for errors using RLL encoding. Most drive manufacturers "RLL certify" only ST-506/412 drives that use a voice coil head actuator and have thin film media.

The reason that I usually mention the ST-506/412 interface in discussing RLL encoding is that, with the ESDI, IDE, and SCSI and with IDE versions of the ST-506/412 interface, the data separator or endec is part of the drive and cannot be changed by the controller. Only pure digital information is sent to the drive (or drive/controller combination), which does the encoding and decoding internally, which amounts to a local telephone call between the endec and the disk platters. This local communication makes the ESDI, IDE, and SCSI interfaces much more reliable than the older non ST-506/412 interface; they share none of the problems associated with RLL encoding over the ST-506/412 interface. Nearly all ESDI, IDE, and SCSI drives use RLL encoding. With these interfaces, RLL encoding is much less of an issue for discussion; the endec is built into the drive and has nothing to do with the type of controller card or interface in your system.

ESDI

ESDI, or *Enhanced Small Device Interface*, is a specialized hard disk and tape drive interface established as a standard in 1983 by Maxtor Corporation. Maxtor led a consortium of drive manufacturers to adopt its proposed interface as a new high-performance standard. Provisions for increased reliability were made, such as building the encoder/decoder or endec into the drive. ESDI is a very-high-speed interface, capable of a maximum 24-megabits-per-second transfer rate. Most drives running ESDI, however, still are limited to a maximum of 10 or 15 megabits per second.

One of ESDI's most important features is that it has been adopted throughout the industry without each manufacturer making changes; thus, ESDI is a "plug and play" type of interface. Enhanced commands enable the controller to read a drive's capacity parameters directly from the drive and control defect mapping, making it even more of a "plug and play" interface than the ST-506/412 interface. When you install an ESDI drive, you do not have to use a setup program to tell the system what "type" of hard disk you have installed, because ESDI enables the controller or motherboard ROM BIOS to read drive parameters directly from the hard disk. This enhanced communication protocol lets IBM avoid the drive table problem in its high-end ESDI systems.

The ESDI's enhanced defect mapping commands provide a standard way for the PC system to read a defect map from a drive, which means that the manufacturer's defect list can be written to the drive as a file. The defect list file then can be read by the controller and low-level format software, eliminating the need for the installer to type these entries from the keyboard and enabling the format program to update the defect list with new entries if it finds new defects during the low-level format or the surface analysis.

Most ESDI implementations have drives formatted to 32 sectors per track or higher (80 or more sectors per track are possible), many more sectors per track than the standard ST-506/412 MFM implementation of 17 sectors per track or the ST-506/412 RLL implementation of 26 sectors per track. The greater density results in two or more times the data-transfer rate, with a 1 to 1 interleave. Almost without exception, ESDI controllers support a 1 to 1 interleave, which allows for more than one megabyte-per-second or greater transfer rate.

Because ESDI is much like the ST-506/412 interface, it can replace that interface without affecting software in the system. Most ESDI controllers are register-compatible with the older ST-506/412 controllers, which enables OS/2 and other non-DOS operating systems to run with few or no problems. The ROM BIOS interface to ESDI is similar to the ST-506/412 standard, and many low-level disk utilities that run on one will run on the other. To take advantage of the ESDI defect mapping and other special features, however, use a low-level format and surface-analysis utility designed for ESDI (such as the ones usually built into the controller ROM BIOS and called by DEBUG).

Until the last year or so, most high-end systems from major manufacturers were equipped with ESDI controllers and drives. More recently, manufacturers have been dropping their ESDI systems for SCSI. The SCSI interface allows for much greater expandability, supports more types of devices than ESDI, and offers equal or greater performance. I no longer recommend that ESDI drives be installed in systems, unless you are upgrading a system that already has an ESDI controller.

IDE Interface

The *Integrated Drive Electronics* (IDE) interface is a new name for something that has been available for some time: a Hardcard. In a drive with IDE, the disk controller is built into the drive, and the drive/controller assembly plugs into a slot on the motherboard. This type of drive/controller combination greatly simplifies drive installation because there are no separate power or signal cables from the system or controller to the drive. Also, with the controller and the drive assembled as a unit, the number of total components is reduced, signal paths are shorter, and the electrical connections are more noise-resistant, resulting in a more reliable design than is possible using a separate controller connected to the drive by cables.

With a Hardcard, the entire drive/controller unit is mounted directly into a slot; by contrast, an IDE drive is usually mounted in the more secure, standard position that would be occupied by a standard hard disk. A cable then connects the drive/controller unit directly to a slot on the motherboard. A hard disk controller does not require every single interface pin in the Industry Standard Architecture (ISA) XT or AT bus. Therefore, most manufacturers that build systems with IDE drives design a special connector on the motherboard for the IDE drive. This connector looks the same as a normal 8-bit or 16-bit slot but contains only the signal pins required by a standard type XT or AT hard disk controller. For example, because an AT style disk controller uses only interrupt line 14, the motherboard AT IDE connector supplies only that interrupt line; no other interrupt lines are needed. The XT IDE motherboard connector supplies interrupt line 5 because that is what an XT controller would use.

The XT or AT IDE connectors on motherboards in many systems are nothing more than a "stripped down" slot, designed only for the matching XT or AT type controller/drive. Many people who use IDE drives believe that a hard disk controller is built into their system's motherboard. They get this impression because the hard disk seems to plug directly into the motherboard, but the controller is really in the drive. I do not know of any PC systems with hard disk controllers built into the motherboard.

There are three main types of IDE interfaces, with differences based on three different bus standards:

- XT IDE (8-bit)
- AT Attachment (ATA) IDE (16-bit)
- MCA IDE (Micro Channel 16-bit)

The XT and AT versions have standardized on a 40-pin single connector at the drive and motherboard, and the MCA version uses a 72-pin connector. To install an IDE drive in a system in which the motherboard does not have a dedicated IDE connector for an IDE drive, you can plug an adapter card into a standard slot; these adapters adjust the physical configuration of the slot to the standard IDE 40-pin or 72-pin connector. Some of these card adapters have buffer circuitry to improve the bus connection to the drive, but they are nothing more than bus adapters.

In PS/2 systems, IBM sometimes uses an *interposer card*, an adapter that changes the physical Micro Channel slot to the 72-pin MCA IDE edge connector. XT IDE drives work only in XT-class 8-bit ISA slot systems, AT IDE drives work only in AT-class 16-bit ISA slot systems, and MCA IDE drives work only in Micro Channel systems (such as the IBM PS/2 Model 50 or higher). At least one company (Silicon Valley) offers adapter cards for XT systems that will run ATA IDE drives. This is great because very few XT IDE drives are being manufactured because of low market demand.

SCSI

SCSI (pronounced "scuzzy") stands for *Small Computer System Interface*. This interface has its roots in SASI, the *Shugart Associates System Interface*. SCSI is not a disk interface but a systems-level interface. It is not a type of controller; instead, you can plug as many as eight controllers into a single SCSI system, and they can talk to one another. One of these controllers is a *host adapter* and functions as the gateway between the SCSI bus and the system. The SCSI does not work directly with a hard disk, and the disk drive still needs a controller to talk to the SCSI.

You could, for example, use ST-506/412 and ESDI drives and their respective controllers, which would plug into the SCSI. The system would have a SCSI host adapter, which would enable it to talk to the attached devices, much like a small local area network (LAN). A single SCSI bus can support as many as eight *logical units*, or ports; because one of these is the adapter card in your PC, the other seven can be other peripherals. You could have a graphics scanner, a tape backup unit, an optical CD-ROM drive, an ST-506/412 hard disk controller with up to two drives, and an ESDI controller with two drives, and still have two ports free.

Most disk drive/controller/SCSI port combinations are all-in-one units, rather than a standard controller with one or two drives plugged into a SCSI adapter. When you purchase a SCSI hard disk, you usually are purchasing the drive, controller, and SCSI adapter in one circuit. This type of drive usually is called an *embedded SCSI drive*; the SCSI is built into the drive and precludes attaching another drive to the controller portion of the unit. The controller internal to the embedded SCSI drive is not directly accessible. Embedded SCSI drives are in standard use, limiting you to seven hard disk drives attached to one SCSI host adapter (because each of the seven SCSI bus addresses can support only one drive rather than two). You could, however, add a second, third, and fourth SCSI adapter to your system and support a total of 28 hard disks (except that DOS would recognize only the first 24 of those drives).

You do not need to know what type of controller (ESDI or ST-506/412, for example) is inside the SCSI drive, because your system cannot talk directly to the controller as though it were plugged into the system bus, like a standard controller. Instead, communications go through the SCSI host adapter installed in the system bus. You can access the drive only with the SCSI protocols. Because of the increasing availability of devices with embedded controllers and SCSI ports, many SCSI-based peripherals (such as tape drives and scanners) are likely to be available for PC systems in the future.

Apple originally rallied around the SCSI as an inexpensive way out of the bind it put itself in with the Macintosh. When the engineers at Apple realized the problem in making the Macintosh a closed system (with no slots), they decided that the easiest way to gain expandability was to build a SCSI port into the system, which is how external peripherals now can be added to the slotless Macs. Because PC systems always have been expandable, the push toward SCSI has not been necessary. With eight bus slots supporting different devices and controllers in IBM and IBM-compatible systems, SCSI was not needed.

SCSI is now becoming popular in the IBM-based computer world because of the great expandability it offers and the number of devices available with built-in SCSIs. One thing that stalled acceptance of SCSI in the PC marketplace was the lack of a real standard—the SCSI standard has been designed primarily by a committee. No single manufacturer has led the way, at least in the IBM arena; each has its own interpretation of how SCSI should be implemented.

SCSI is a standard, in much the same way that RS-232 is a standard. However, the SCSI standard (like the RS-232 standard) defines only the hardware connections, not the driver specifications required to communicate with the devices. Software ties the SCSI subsystem into your PC, but unfortunately most of the driver programs work only for a specific device and a specific host adapter. For example, a graphics scanner comes with its own SCSI host adapter to connect to the system, and a CD-ROM drive comes with another (different) SCSI host adapter and driver software that works only with that SCSI adapter. On a system with those two SCSI adapters, you would need a third SCSI host adapter to run SCSI hard disk drives, because the host adapters supplied by the scanner and CD-ROM companies do not include a built-in, self-booting BIOS that supports hard disk drives. SCSI has become somewhat of a mess in the IBM world because of the lack of a host adapter standard, a software interface standard, and standard ROM BIOS support for hard disk drives attached to the SCSI bus.

The lack of capability to run hard disks off the SCSI bus and to boot from these drives and use a variety of operating systems is a problem that results from the lack of an interface standard. The standard IBM XT and AT ROM BIOS software was designed to talk to ST-506/412 hard disk controllers. The software easily was modified to work with ESDI because ESDI controllers are similar to ST-506/412 controllers at the register level. (This similarity at the register level enabled manufacturers to easily design self-booting, ROM-BIOS-supported ESDI drives.) IBM adopted the ESDI interface in its PS/2 systems and incorporated an ESDI BIOS into either the disk controller or the motherboard on the PS/2 systems. SCSI is so different from standard disk interfaces that a new set of ROM BIOS routines would be necessary to support the system so that it could self-boot. The newer IBM PS/2 systems that come with SCSI drives include this support built-in to the motherboard BIOS or as an extension BIOS on the SCSI host adapter.

Companies such as Adaptec and Future Domain have produced SCSI cards with built-in ROM BIOS support for the SCSI for several years, but these BIOS routines were limited to running the drives under DOS only. The BIOS would not run in the AT-protected mode, and other operating systems included drivers for only the standard ST-506/412 and ESDI controllers. Thus, running SCSI was impossible under many non-DOS operating systems. IBM is supporting many third-party SCSI host adapters in OS/2 2.X, which means that you do not need to worry about a protected mode BIOS on the SCSI adapter.

Because of the lead taken by Apple in developing systems software (operating systems and ROM) support for SCSI, peripherals connect to Apple systems in fairly standard ways. Until recently, this kind of standard-setting leadership was lacking for SCSI in the IBM world. This changed on March 20, 1990, however, because IBM introduced several "standard" SCSI adapters and peripherals for the IBM PS/2 systems, with complete ROM BIOS and full operating system support.

My portable system uses an IBM SCSI host adapter with 2 megabytes of cache and a 1 gigabyte 3 1/2-inch SCSI drive. The adapter has a 16/32K ROM BIOS that gives the system full support of SCSI hard disks under

DOS, OS/2, and other operating systems. The system is self-booting and has a complete ROM BIOS-based Power-On Self Test (POST) and advanced diagnostics support. The ROM even operates in the protected mode of 80286 and higher processors, which means different drivers are not required for protected-mode-based operating systems such as OS/2 and UNIX.

Several manufacturers now ship SCSI products with drivers that support the IBM SCSI host adapters. Hard disks were never a problem; support for them is built into the card. The example set by IBM will become the SCSI standard for others to emulate in the IBM-compatible world; companies that have been making SCSI host adapters will have to update their adapters to emulate the IBM adapters. With IBM's support, the SCSI bus will probably become the de facto standard peripheral interface for the IBM-compatible world, as it has for the Apple Macintosh.

Disk Installation Procedures

This section describes the installation of a typical hard disk and its integration in a particular PC system. To install a hard drive in an IBM-compatible system, you must perform several procedures: configure the drive correctly, physically install it, low-level format it, configure it to receive an operating system, high-level format it, and install the system software.

The following sections describe each step. The steps are simple to execute and, if done properly, result in the successful installation of a bootable hard disk. Special attention is given to issues of reliability and data integrity, to ensure that the installation is long lasting and trouble-free.

Drive Configuration

Configuring a hard disk drive is similar to configuring a floppy drive, but it is much less complicated. You need to set only two things: the drive select jumper and a terminating resistor.

The example shows the installation of a standard ST-506/412 drive into an IBM XT or IBM AT system. An ESDI installation is similar in most respects, but SCSI installations can be different because of the lack of standards for IBM and IBM-compatible PC systems. If you are installing a SCSI drive, follow the installation instructions that come with the drive and host adapter, and for best results, purchase all the components from one company.

Drive Select Jumpers

Before you can install a hard disk, you must configure it. The first item to configure is the drive select jumper setting. You must set the drive select jumper so that the drive and controller can communicate on the same channel. Separate channels are available for as many as four drives in the ST-506/412 and ESDI controller specifications; SCSI systems allow as many as seven controllers with as many as four drives on each controller. The more standard, embedded SCSI systems have a single controller built into, or embedded in, the drive, which reduces the total to seven possible drive addresses, called *logical units*.

Setting the drive select jumpers for a hard disk is almost the same as setting these jumpers for floppy disk drives. Both drives must have the drive select jumpers set depending on the type of cable being used. The following section discusses the cables and how they affect drive select jumper settings.

Data and Control Cables

Two cables—a 34-pin control cable and a 20-pin data cable—run from the controller to a hard disk drive. The control cable is run in a daisy-chain arrangement to one or two hard disks. The cable is wired either in a straight-through design or with a twist in some of the wires before the last physical connector on the cable (the drive C connector).

The data cable is wired straight through. Two data-cable connector positions are on the controller—one for each of two drives. These cables are not daisy-chained but run from the controller to each drive separately.

IBM always uses a twist in the fixed disk control cable to fool the first drive (C:). In this case, wires 25 through 29 are twisted. You must not use a floppy drive cable as a hard disk control cable if the floppy cable also is twisted. IBM twists different wires on the floppy drive cable (wires 10 through 16) than on the fixed disk control cable. I prefer to use a straight cable because it eliminates this confusion and makes the cable usable for either floppy drives or hard disks.

The drive select setting is simple if you have the twisted cable. The drive at the last physical connector on the end of the cable after the twist is drive C. It is set as the second drive select position. The second position is labeled DS1 if the first setting is labeled DS0, or DS2 if the first position is DS1. The drive plugged into the connector between the controller card and the other drive on the control cable is drive D. It also is set to the second drive select position regardless of whether the cable is twisted.

If the cable is not twisted, set drive C to the first drive select position (labeled DS0 or DS1) and drive D to the second drive select position (labeled DS1 or DS2).

To make sure that the cables are connected properly, check that the odd-colored wire in the cable is aligned toward the notches in the drive circuit boards. This ensures that pin 1 on the cable aligns with pin 1 on the drive.

Power Cables

To complete the required cable connections to the hard drive, you need a spare power connector. IBM PC and XT power supplies have only two-drive power connectors. IBM and other companies sell a *power splitter cable*, or Y cable, that can adapt one cable from the power supply so that it powers two drives. If you add a power splitter to a system, make sure that the power supply can handle the load of the additional drive or drives. If the original power supply is not adequate, purchase an after-market unit that can supply adequate power. Most better aftermarket supplies have four drive power connectors, eliminating the need for the splitter cables.

Terminating Resistors

You must install a terminating resistor on the drive farthest from the controller—the last one on the daisy chain. In an IBM-compatible system, the terminating resistor is installed on drive C:. The other drive plugged into the middle of the cable (drive D:) must not have a terminating resistor. (See the OEM drive manual to locate the terminating resistor.) After the drive is removed, you should store it in a safe place because you will need it if the drive is moved to an end cable connector in the future.

Physical Installation

The physical installation of a hard disk is much the same as for a floppy drive. You must have the correct screws, brackets, and faceplates for the specific drive and system before you can install the drive (see fig. 9.9).

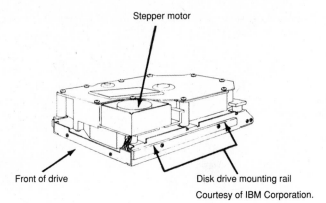

Stepper motor

Front of drive

Disk drive mounting rail

Courtesy of IBM Corporation.

IBM AT systems require plastic rails that are secured to the sides of the drives so that they can slide into the proper place in the system. COMPAQ uses a different type of rail. When you purchase a drive, the vendor usually includes the IBM-type rails, so be sure to specify whether you need the special COMPAQ type. IBM PC-type and XT-type systems do not need rails but may need a bracket to enable double-stacking of half-height drives. Several companies in the vendor list specialize in drive-mounting brackets, cables, and other hardware accessories.

There are different faceplate, or bezel, options; make sure that you have the correct bezel for your application. The IBM AT, for example, does not need a faceplate; if a faceplate is on the drive, remove it. If you are installing a half-height drive in a full-height bay, you may need a blank half-height bezel to fill the hole, or you may want to order a half-height drive with a full-height bezel so that no hole is created.

System-to-Disk Configuration

With the drive physically installed, you can begin configuring the system to the drive. You have to tell the system about the drive so that the system can boot from it when it is powered on. How you set and store this information depends on the type of drive and system. Standard setup procedures are used for most hard disks except SCSI drives. SCSI drives normally follow a custom setup procedure that varies depending on which host adapter you are using. If you have SCSI drives, follow the instructions included with the host adapter to configure the drives.

To begin the setup procedure for non-SCSI drives, you need to know several details about the hard disk drive, controllers, and system ROM BIOS. To continue properly, you must have the OEM manuals for these devices; when you purchase disk or controller products, make sure that the vendor includes these manuals. (Many vendors do not include the manuals unless you specifically ask for them.) For IBM-supplied disks and controllers, you can get the original manufacturer's documentation if the drive was made by a third party, or use the IBM documentation if the drives are IBM drives. The IBM controller cards and drives are fully documented in the *IBM Technical Reference Options and Adapters* manual. You may also need to purchase updates to these manuals to get the details for some drives announced later than the original manuals. The technical-reference manuals for the system also may be useful.

You need to know the following facts about the drive you are installing:

> Number of cylinders
> Number of heads
> Starting cylinder for write precompensation
> Range of acceptable head step pulse timing
> Locations of defects by cylinder and head

All this information, except the defect list, is in the drive manual. IDE drives may have two sets of these parameters: the physical drive parameters, and a different set recommended by the drive manufacturer. The recommended values are the ones to use because the built-in controllers used in many IDE drives automatically translate these parameters internally within the drive. The defect list is usually on a sticker on the top or front of the drive—or possibly on a piece of paper attached to the drive. IDE drives normally do not have a defect sticker because they are preformatted and the defects are already marked. Copy and record the defect information because you will need it later for a proper low-level format.

You need to know also various facts about the controller you are installing. If the controller is one of the recommended autoconfigure XT-type controllers, you need to know the following:

> Interrupt Request Channel (IRQ) used
> DMA channel (DRQ) used
> ROM memory locations used
> Start location for the autoconfigure routine
> I/O ports used
> Possible head step pulse rates
> Best interleave

If the controller is not an autoconfigure type, you need to know the following:

> Built-in drive-table values
> Method for selecting drive types

If the controller is an AT type, the list is much simpler:

> Interrupt request channel used
> I/O ports used
> Possible head step pulse rates
> Best interleave

An AT-type controller does not have (or should not have) an on-board ROM or autoconfigure routine. (If you have one that does, you are on your own with OS/2, XENIX, and network software.) AT controllers also do not use DMA channels for data transfer; instead, they use the high-speed I/O ports in the AT. For most of these controllers, like those used by IBM, the head step pulse rate is fixed by the motherboard ROM BIOS at 35μsec. The motherboard ROM also contains the drive types, and you use the Setup program to select the desired type.

If the system is an AT-type, you need the following information about the ROM BIOS:

> Supported drive-type values
> Selected head step pulse rate

For IBM systems, this documentation is provided in the technical-reference manuals. The Appendix includes a list of the supported drive types, and the head step rate selected is 35μsec. For other non-IBM systems, you can find this information in the system technical-reference manual.

When you have collected the necessary information, the next step is to tell the system the kind of drive that is attached so that the system can boot from the drive (eventually). This chapter discusses the installation of a drive in both an XT-type and an AT-type of system. The same drive is installed on both systems. With knowledge of drive interfacing, you can install just about any drive in any system.

The example drive is a Maxtor XT-1140, which is an ST-506/412 drive designed for MFM encoding. This drive is a full-height 5 1/4-inch platter drive that fits easily into an IBM XT or IBM AT system. The drive capacity is 140M unformatted, 119M formatted. You can use the drive in a system with an ST-506/412 interface controller. It is a fairly high-performance drive with an advertised 27ms seek time (across 119M), and it has 8 platters with 15 read/write heads plus 1 servo head.

First, you need to read the drive manual and locate the required information. In this case, you need the following information:

> 918 cylinders
> 15 heads
> No write precompensation required
> 2 to 3100μs head step pulse timing acceptable
> 2 to 13μs head step pulse timing optimum
> 7 defects total:
>
> > Cyl 188 Head 7
> > Cyl 217 Head 5
> > Cyl 218 Head 5
> > Cyl 219 Head 5
> > Cyl 601 Head 13

Cyl 798 Head 10
Cyl 835 Head 5

The next step is to physically install the drive. Set the drive select jumper depending on the type of cable being used, and ensure that the last physical drive on the control cable has the terminating resistor in place (and that any other drive has the terminating resistor removed).

Autoconfigure Controllers for IBM PC and IBM XT

To install the example drive in an IBM XT, I could use the original IBM XT controller (Xebec 1210), but the built-in tables in that controller do not match my drive. I would have to download the ROM to disk and patch it to contain the correct drive-table values. If you can wield the DOS DE-BUG program and have access to an EPROM burner, you can patch the correct table into one of the existing four table positions on the controller, and the controller will operate correctly with the drive. (I used this procedure on my vintage 1983 XT controller. The system works fine, but its best interleave is 5 to 1.)

Faster autoconfigure ROM controllers are available at such low prices that a better alternative is to purchase one. This example describes the installation of a Scientific Micro Systems Omti 5520A-10 controller, which has complete autoconfigure capability and supports a 2 to 1 interleave in the IBM PC and XT. Although this controller is no longer available, Data Technology Corporation (DTC) makes a DTC5150XL controller that offers even more features. The installation and configuration of all autoconfigure controllers are very similar. DTC also makes a DTC5160XL controller that is an RLL version of the previous controller. These controllers support co-residency, which means that they can be added to a system which already has an existing controller. These controllers can be installed with no hassle, run three times faster than the old Xebec controller, and cost less than $100. (Times have changed—an original Xebec 1210 cost me $795 in 1983.)

The next set of required information for the example installation follows:

Interrupt Request Channel (IRQ) = 5
DMA channel (DRQ) = 3
ROM locations used = C8000 to C9FFF
I/O ports = 320 to 32F
Autoconfigure start location = C8006
Step pulse rates = 10, 25, 50, 70, 200, and 3000µs
Best interleave = 2 to 1 (4.77 MHz XT)

You need some of this information to ensure that the card is uniquely configured compared with other cards in the system. The system cannot have another card using the same IRQ, DMA, ROM, or I/O ports as this card. Keep this information for future reference, and cross-check for conflicts when you add other cards to the system. The autoconfigure start location, step pulse rates, and interleave information is necessary for completing the drive setup.

The next step is to activate the controller's built-in autoconfigure routine. When you do so, an autoconfigure controller prompts you for information about the drive (otherwise found in ROM tables), and then records the information directly on the drive in an area reserved by the controller on the first track. The advantage of the autoconfigure controller is that when you change drives, the controller can adapt. You never have to patch ROM-based tables with an EPROM burner because this drive stores them dynamically on the drive. After the routine is completed, the controller reads this information every time the system is powered up, and "knows" how to boot from the drive.

One potential problem with storing the parameters on the drive is that if they are accidentally overwritten, the drive is inaccessible. For this reason, you must be careful with any program that performs a low-level format on the drive. Most nondestructive formatters, such as the Norton Utilities Calibrate program, refuse to reformat the first track of any drive, to avoid overwriting any of this special autoconfigure data.

To run the autoconfigure routine, follow these steps:

1. Boot DOS 3.3 or higher.

2. Run the DOS DEBUG program.

3. At the DEBUG prompt, enter the information to tell DEBUG to move the system instruction pointer to the autoconfigure ROM start location. For this specific controller, you enter:

   G=C800:6

Because autoconfigure controllers from different manufacturers have different starting locations for the ROM BIOS format routine built-in to the controller, look in the manual to find the starting location for the specific controller you are installing. Table 9.7 provides the controller BIOS low-level format addresses used with DEBUG for several popular controller brands.

After you enter the last DEBUG instruction, the autoconfigure routine asks several questions about the drive and controller: how many heads and cylinders the drive has, what the starting write precompensation cylinder is, and how fast the step pulses should be sent. Use the information you gathered about the drive and controller to answer these questions.

Table 9.7 Controller BIOS Low-level Format Addresses

Controller brand	Low-level format address
Western Digital	g=C800:5
DTC	g=C800:5
Adaptec	g=C800:CCC
Seagate	g=C800:5
SMS-OMTI	g=C800:6

The C800 value may be different on these controllers because of jumper settings modified from the defaults, which can alter the segment address of the BIOS. Although C800 is the default segment address for ROM BIOS on most controllers, these addresses may be changed by altering jumper settings on the controller. Other ROM BIOS segment addresses used may include CC00, D800, or others.

In the example, you would indicate that the controller should pulse the drive with step pulses spaced 10µs apart. To establish this figure, look at the range of spacing the drive will accept, compare it to what the controller can send, and select the fastest rate that both can agree on. This procedure is similar to configuring a serial printer and serial port for 9600 bps transmission. Why not go as fast as the hardware will allow? The Maxtor XT-1140 manual states that drive seek performance on this particular drive degrades if step pulses are sent at intervals greater than 13µs. Setting this specification to a setting that is optimum for your drive can really "tweak" a drive's seek performance.

The autoconfigure program also asks you to specify the desired interleave. An interleave of 2 to 1 is the best value for the example controller in a 4.77 MHz IBM PC or IBM XT system. This interleave value was determined by a simple trial-and-error testing session in which the disk was formatted at various interleaves, from 6 to 1 (the IBM XT default) down to 1 to 1. The transfer rate improved with each lower interleave until 1 to 1, at which point the transfer rate slowed by more than 800 percent. At 1 to 1, this controller cannot keep up with the rate at which the next sector comes under the heads; it requires 17 full revolutions of the disk to read a track, compared with 2 revolutions to read a track at a 2 to 1 interleave.

Finally, the autoconfigure program asks whether the drive has defects and gives you the opportunity to enter them. The example drive has seven defects (printed on a sticker on top of the drive as well as included on a printed sheet). Entering this information causes the low-level format program to specially mark these tracks with invalid checksum figures, ensuring that these locations are never read or written to. Later, when DOS is used to high-level format the disk, the DOS format program will be unable to read these locations and will mark the file allocation table with information so that the locations will never be utilized. If you do not enter these locations properly, data or program files could use these defective tracks and become corrupted. Always mark these locations.

With the controller used for this example, the low-level format is part of the autoconfigure routine. After you answer the questions, the drive is low-level formatted, the defects are marked, and a scan is made for defects that were marked improperly or became bad after the manufacturer's original tests. Finally, the autoconfigure information is written to a specially reserved track on the disk. When this process is completed, the drive is ready for DOS installation.

IBM AT Setup Program and Drive Types

To install the Maxtor XT-1140 in an IBM AT, I could simply use the original IBM AT controller (Western Digital WD1003A-WA2); however, I would have to live with the slow 2:1 interleave this controller provides. A better choice would be to upgrade the controller with a Data Technology Corporation DTC7280 controller. This controller does not have on-board ROM to worry about and is not an autoconfigure type. For IBM AT-type systems, you set the drive type by looking up the drive information in the table of types located in the system ROM. You match the drive parameters to one of the table entries in the system ROM. If you want to run an ST-506/412 drive with RLL encoding, I recommend the DTC7287, which also includes an autoconfigure feature that works perfectly on AT systems.

The required information for installing the DTC7280 controller is as follows:

> Interrupt Request Channel (IRQ) = 14
> I/O ports = 1F0 to 1F7
> Step pulse rate = 35μs (selected by BIOS)
> Best interleave = 1 to 1

Because this controller also contains a floppy controller, some additional information specific to the floppy controller portion of the card is required:

> Interrupt Request Channel (IRQ) = 6
> DMA channel (DRQ) = 2
> I/O ports = 3F0 to 3F7

Considerations before Low-Level Formatting

In a low-level format (LLF), which is a real format, the tracks and sectors of the disk are outlined and written. During the LLF, data is written across the entire disk. An improper low-level format results in lost data and many read and write failures. You need to consider several things before initiating a low-level format.

Data Backup

Low-level formatting is the primary standard repair procedure for hard disk drives that are having problems. Because data values are copied to the drive at every possible location during an LLF, necessary data-recovery operations must be performed *before* an LLF operation.

> **CAUTION:** After an LLF has been performed, you cannot recover any information previously written to the drive.

System Temperature

Sector header and trailer information is written or updated only during the LLF operation. During normal read and write activity, only the 512 bytes plus a checksum value in the trailer are written in a sector. Temperature-induced drive instability, particularly sensitivity to temperature changes, during read and write operations can become a problem.

When a 5 1/4-inch platter drive is low-level formatted five minutes after power-up at a relatively cold platter temperature of 70 degrees F, the sector headers and trailers and the 512-byte dummy data values are written to each track on each platter at specific locations. Suppose that you save a file on a drive that has been running for several hours and at a platter temperature of 140 degrees F. The data areas of only several sectors are updated. But with the drive platters as much as 70 degrees warmer than when the drive was formatted, each aluminum drive platter has expanded in size, by 2.5-thousandths of an inch (taking into account the coefficient of linear thermal expansion of aluminum). Each track could have moved outward a distance of approximately 1.3-thousandths of an inch. Most 5 1/4-inch hard disks have track densities between 500 and 1000 tracks per inch, with distances of only 1 to 2 thousandths of an inch between adjacent tracks. As a result, the thermal expansion of a typical hard disk platter could cause the tracks to migrate from one-half to more than one full track of distance underneath the heads. If the drive head movement mechanism does not compensate for these thermally induced dimensional changes in the platters, severe mistracking results.

When this happens, the data areas in each sector that have been updated at the higher temperature fail to line up with the sector header and trailer information. If the sector header and trailer information cannot be read properly, DOS usually issues an error message like this one:

```
Sector not found reading drive A
Abort, Retry, Ignore, Fail?
```

The data is misaligned with the sector boundaries on those tracks. This thermal effect can work in reverse also: If the drive is formatted and written to while it is extremely hot, it may not read properly while cold because of dimensional changes in the platters. This problem occurs with drives that have the "Monday morning blues," in which they do not boot up and run properly when they are first powered on after being off for an extended period of time (over a weekend, for example). If you leave the power to the system on for some time so that the drive can warm up, the system then may boot and run normally. If this happens, the next step is to back up the drive completely and initiate a new low-level format at the proper operating temperature (described next). This procedure enables the drive to work normally again until temperature-induced mistracking becomes great enough to cause the problem again.

Knowing that temperature fluctuations can cause mistracking, you should understand the reason for the following basic rules for disk use:

- Leave the system's power on for at least 30 minutes before performing a low-level format on its hard disk. This step ensures that the platters are at a normal operating temperature and have dimensionally stabilized.

- Allow a system to warm up for 5 to 30 minutes after power-on before storing any data on the hard disk.

You may want to consider running the drive constantly. Doing so would extend its trouble-free lifespan significantly because the temperature and dimensions of the platters would stay relatively constant.

These kinds of temperature-fluctuation problems are more of a problem with drives that have open-loop stepper motor actuators (which offer no thermal compensation) than with the closed-loop voice coil actuators (which follow temperature-induced track migration and compensate completely, resulting in no tracking errors even with large changes in platter dimensions).

Drive Operating Position

Another consideration before formatting a drive is ensuring that the drive is formatted in the operating position it will have when it is installed in the system. Gravity can place on the head actuator different loads that can cause mistracking if the drive changes between a vertical and a horizontal position.

Additionally, drives that are not properly shock mounted (such as the Seagate ST 2xx series) should be formatted only when they are installed in the system because the installation screws exert twisting forces on the drive's Head Disk Assembly (HDA), which can cause mistracking. If you format the drive with the mounting screws installed tightly, it may not read with the screws out, and vice versa. Be careful not to over-tighten the mounting screws because doing so can stress the HDA. This is usually not a problem if the drive's HDA is isolated from the frame by rubber bushings.

In summary, for a proper low-level format, the drive should be

- At a normal operating temperature
- In a normal operating position
- Mounted in the host system (if the drive HDA is not shock-mounted or isolated from the drive frame by rubber bushings)

Because many different makes and models of controllers differ in how they write data to a drive, it is best to format the drive using the same make and model of controller as the controller that will be used in the host system. Some brands of controllers work exactly alike, however, so this is not an absolute requirement. Usually, if the controller establishes the drive type using its own on-board ROM rather than the system Setup program, it will be incompatible with other controllers.

Defect Mapping

Before formatting the disk, you need to know whether the drive has defects that have to be mapped out. Most drives come with a list of defects discovered by the manufacturer during the drive's final quality-control testing. These defects must be marked so that they are not used later to store programs or data.

Defect mapping is one of the most critical aspects of low-level formatting. To understand the defect-mapping procedures, you first must understand what happens when a defect is mapped on a drive.

The manufacturer's defect list usually indicates defects by cylinder and track. When this information is entered, the low-level format program marks these tracks with invalid checksum figures in the header of each of the sectors, which ensures that nothing can read or write to these locations. When DOS does a high-level format of the disk, the DOS FORMAT program cannot read these locations and marks the involved clusters in the file allocation table (FAT) so that they will never be used.

The list of defects the manufacturer gives you is probably more extensive than what a program could determine from your system because the manufacturer's test equipment is far more sensitive than a regular disk controller. Do not expect a format program to automatically find the defects; you will probably have to enter them manually. An exception to this is the new IBM PS/2 systems, in which the defect list is encoded in a special area of the drive not accessible by normal software. The IBM PS/2 low-level format program (included on the Reference disk that comes with IBM PS/2 systems) reads this special map, thereby eliminating the need to enter these locations manually.

Most new drives are not low-level formatted by the manufacturer. Even if you bought a drive that had been low-level formatted, you would not know the temperature and the operating position of the drive when it was formatted. For best results, perform your own low-level format on a drive after you receive it. If you bought a system with a drive already installed by the manufacturer or dealer, they probably did a low-level format for you. To be safe, however, you might want to do a new low-level format in the system's new environment.

Although an *actual defect* is technically different from a *marked defect*, they should correspond to one another if the drive is formatted properly. For example, I can enter the location of a good track into the low-level format program as a defective track. The low-level format program then corrupts the checksum values for each of the sectors on that track, rendering them unreadable and unwriteable. When the DOS FORMAT program encounters that track, it finds it unreadable and marks the clusters occupying that track as bad in the FAT. After that, as the drive is used, DOS ensures that no data ever is written to that track. The drive stays in that condition until I redo the low-level format of that track, indicate that the track is not to be marked defective, and redo the high-level format that no longer will find the track unreadable and therefore allow those clusters to be used. In general, unless an area is marked as defective in the low-level format, it will not be found by the high-level format and DOS will use it for data storage.

Defect mapping becomes a problem when someone formats a hard disk and fails to enter the manufacturer's defect list, which contains actual defect locations, so that the low-level format can establish these tracks or sectors as marked defects. Letting a defect go unmarked will cost you data when the area is used to store a file that subsequently cannot be retrieved. Unfortunately, the low-level format program does not automatically find and mark any areas that are defective on a disk. The manufacturer defect list is produced by very sensitive test equipment that tests the drive at an analog level. Most manufacturers indicate areas as defective even if they are just marginal. The problem is that a marginal area today may be totally unreadable in the future. You should avoid any area suspected as being defective by entering the location during the low-level format so that the area is marked; then DOS is forced to avoid the area.

Currently Marked Defects Scan

Most low-level format programs have the capability to perform a scan for previously marked defects on a drive. Some programs call this operation a defect scan; IBM calls it Read Verify in the IBM Advanced Diagnostics. This type of operation is nondestructive and reports by cylinder and head position all track locations marked bad. Do not mistake this for a true scan for defective tracks on a disk, which is a destructive operation normally called a surface analysis (discussed later, in the "Surface Analysis" section).

If a drive was previously low-level formatted, you should scan the disk for previously marked defects before running a fresh low-level format for several reasons:

- *Ensure that the previous low-level format correctly marked all manufacturer-listed defects.* Compare the report of the defect scan to the manufacturer's list, and note discrepancies. Any defects on the manufacturer's list but not found by the defect scan were not marked properly.

- *Look for tracks that are marked as defective but are not on the manufacturer's list.* These tracks may have been added by a previously run surface-analysis program, in which case they should be retained, or they may result from typographical errors in marking the manufacturer's defect on the part of the previous formatter. One of my drive's manufacturer's list showed Cylinder 514 Head 14 as defective. A defect scan, however, showed that track as good but Cylinder 814 Head 14 marked as bad. Because the latter location was not on the manufacturer's list and the transcription of a 5 to an 8 would be an easy mistake to make, I concluded that a typographical error was the cause and reformatted the drive, marking Cylinder 514 Head 14 as bad, and enabling Cylinder 814 Head 14 to be formatted as a good track, thus "unmarking" it.

If you run a surface analysis and encounter defects in addition to those on the manufacturer's list, you can do one of two things. If the drive is under warranty, consider returning it. If the drive is out of warranty, grab a pen and write on the defect list sticker, adding the bad tracks discovered by the surface-analysis program. (The IBM PS/2 low-level formatter built into the Reference disk automatically performs a surface analysis immediately after the low-level format; if it discovers additional defects, it adds them automatically to the defect list recorded on the drive.) Adding new defects to the sticker in this manner means that these areas are not forgotten when the drive is subsequently reformatted.

Manufacturer's Defect List

The manufacturer tests a new hard disk using sophisticated analog test instruments that perform an extensive analysis of the surface of the platters. This kind of testing can indicate the functionality of an area of the disk with great accuracy, precisely measuring information such as the signal-to-noise ratio and recording accuracy.

Some manufacturers have more demanding standards than others about what they consider defects. Many people are bothered by the fact that when they purchase a new drive, it comes with a list of defective locations. Some even demand that the seller install a defect-free drive. The seller can satisfy this request by substituting a drive made by a company with less-stringent quality control, but the drive will be of poorer quality. The manufacturer who produces drives with more listed defects usually has a higher-quality product because the number of listed defects depends on the level of quality control. What constitutes a defect depends on who is interpreting the test results.

To mark the manufacturer defects listed on the drive, consult the documentation that goes with your low-level format program. For most drives, the manufacturer's defect list shows the defects by cylinder and head; other lists locate the defect down to the bit that is bad on the track, starting with the index location.

> **WARNING:** Make sure that all manufacturer's defects have been entered before proceeding with the low-level format.

Some systems automatically mark the manufacturer's defects, using a special defect file recorded on the drive by the manufacturer. For such a system, you need a special low-level format program that knows how to find and read this file. Automatic defect-map entry is standard for IBM PS/2 systems and for most ESDI and all SCSI systems. Consult the drive or controller vendor for the proper low-level format program and defect-handling procedures for your drive.

Note Do not mark defective clusters on the disk with a data-recovery utility such as Norton, Mace, or PC Tools because they cannot mark the sectors or tracks at the low-level format level. The bad cluster marks they make are stored only in the FAT, and are erased during the next high-level format operation.

Surface Analysis

A defect scan is a scan for marked defects; a surface analysis is a scan for actual defects. A surface analysis ignores tracks already marked defective by a low-level format and tests the unmarked tracks. The surface-analysis program writes 512 bytes to each sector on the good tracks, reads the sectors back, and compares the data read to what was written. If the data does not verify, the program (like a low-level format) marks the track bad by corrupting the checksum values for each of the sectors on that track.

Surface-analysis programs are destructive: they write over every sector, except those already marked bad. A surface-analysis program should be run immediately after a low-level format, to determine whether defects have appeared in addition to the manufacturer's defects entered during the low-level format. A defect scan after the low-level format and the surface analysis shows the cumulative tracks marked bad by both programs.

> **CAUTION:** Some surface-analysis programs perform a track backup-and-restore operation before and after corrupting a track. To keep your data safe, however, perform a complete backup of the disk before using a surface-analysis program.

If the manufacturer's defect list has been lost, you can use the surface-analysis program to indicate which tracks are bad, but this program can never duplicate the accuracy or sensitivity of manufacturer testing.

For example, if a spot in the sector were performing to 51 percent of capacity, it would be good enough to pass in a PC surface analysis. The next day, due to variances in the drive and electronics, that same spot might perform at only 49 percent of capacity, failing a surface analysis. If you must use a surface analysis as your only source of defect information for a drive, be sure to use the option of increasing the number of times each track will be tested, and run the program over an evening or weekend for a higher probability of catching an elusive or intermittent bad track.

Some low-level format and surface-analysis programs have hype-filled advertisements that make misleading and even false claims of performance and capability. Some programs even "unmark" defects that have been purposely marked by the initial, properly done low-level format according to the manufacturer's supplied list of defects, because the program determines that the area in question is not defective. (This is unbelievable!) If the drive is a good one, no surface-analysis program can possibly find all the defects on the manufacturer's list. Only testing at the analog level could indicate these defects because most manufacturers include slightly marginal areas on their list.

For example, I have a 40-megabyte drive that has 27 manufacturer defects on the bad-track list; this drive is probably the highest-quality 40-megabyte unit sold. Most cheaper 40-megabyte drives would have 5 or fewer defects on the bad-track list. I have run virtually every surface-analysis program on this drive, and none could find more than 5 of the 27 defects.

I do not normally run a surface analysis after low-level formatting, for several reasons:

- Compared to formatting, surface analysis takes a long time. Most surface-analysis programs take two to five times longer than a low-level format to complete. A low-level format of a 120M drive takes about 15 minutes, and a surface analysis of the same drive takes an hour or more. Moreover, if you increase the accuracy of the surface analysis by allowing multiple passes, the surface analysis takes even longer.

- With high-quality drives, I never find defects beyond what the manufacturer specified. In fact, the surface-analysis programs do not even find all the manufacturer's defects if I do not enter them manually. Because the high-quality (voice coil) drives that I use have been tested by the manufacturer to a greater degree than a program can perform on my system, I simply mark all the defects from the manufacturer's list in the low-level format and am done with it. If I were using low-quality (stepper motor) drives or installing a used and out-of-warranty drive, I would consider performing the surface analysis after the low-level format.

Defect-Free Drives

Although some manufacturers claim that the drives they sell or install are defect-free, this is not really true. The defects are mapped out and replaced by spare sectors and tracks. This type of defect mapping, usually called *sector sparing*, insulates the operating system from having to handle the defects. IDE and SCSI drives universally use sector sparing to hide defects, so they all seem defect free.

When you finish the low-level format and surface analysis of a hard disk in non-IDE or non-SCSI installations, several areas on the disk have been marked defective by corrupting the checksum values in the sector headers on the indicated tracks. When the high-level format scans the disk, it locates the defective sectors by failing to read them during the defect scan portion of the high-level format operation. The clusters or allocation units that contain these unreadable sectors are then marked bad in the FAT. When the CHKDSK command is executed, you get a report of how many of these bad clusters are on the disk. The CHKDSK report looks like this (although yours will have different numbers):

```
Volume DRIVE C     created 06-02-1990 9:14p
Volume Serial Number is 3311-1CD3
 117116928 bytes total disk space
     73728 bytes in 3 hidden files
    593920 bytes in 268 directories
 106430464 bytes in 4068 user files
    143360 bytes in bad sectors
   9875456 bytes available on disk
      2048 bytes in each allocation unit
     57186 total allocation units on disk
      4822 available allocation units on disk
    655360 total bytes memory
    561216 bytes free
```

The `143360 bytes in bad sectors` are really only 70 clusters, or allocation units, because each allocation unit contains 2048 bytes.

When I did the low-level format of this disk, I entered 14 defects, which caused 14 tracks to be corrupted. This disk has 17 sectors per track; therefore, 238 total sectors (17 sectors times 14 tracks) have been corrupted by the low-level format program. Therefore, 121856 total bytes have been marked bad (238 sectors times 512 bytes per sector).

This number does not agree with the total reported by CHKDSK because DOS must mark entire allocation units, not individual sectors. Each allocation unit is made up of 4 sectors (2,048 bytes) on this disk. Therefore:

1 track = 17 sectors = 4 allocation units plus 1 extra sector

DOS must mark a whole allocation unit as bad in the file allocation tables even if only one sector in the unit is bad; therefore, DOS marks five allocation units as bad for each marked track. In bytes, this becomes:

5 allocation units = 20 sectors = 10,240 bytes (20 sectors times 512 bytes)

Therefore, 10,240 bytes are marked as bad in the FAT for each track marked in the low-level format. And 10,240 bytes per track marked bad times 14 total marked tracks equals 143,360 total bytes marked bad.

From these calculations, you can see that all of the correct defect mapping is in place. The bytes in bad sectors will never be used by files, so they will never bother you. This number should not change over the life of the drive, unless new defects are entered in a subsequent low-level format or surface-analysis program.

The relationship between CHKDSK results and disk defects is not as clear with all drives and controllers. For example, I have an IBM PS/2 Model 70-121 that has a 120M IBM drive with an MCA IDE drive with an embedded ESDI controller. (The controller is built into the drive.) I formatted this drive using IBM Advanced Diagnostics for the IBM PS/2 (included free with the system). After finishing the high-level format, I ran CHKDSK and it reported no bad sectors. Could this be true? Not really. In fact, this drive has more than 140 defects, and all have been correctly marked. How could that be? If the defects were marked, the high-level format should have been unable to read those locations, and CHKDSK would have reported the xxxxxx bytes in bad sectors message. The answer lies in how the drive and controller operate together.

IBM advertises this drive as having 32 sectors per track and 920 cylinders with 8 heads, but it actually has 33 sectors per track—or a spare sector on every track. When a defect location is given to the low-level format program, it removes the defective sector from use by not numbering it as one of the 32 sectors on that track. Then the program gives the spare sector the number that the defective one would have been given—the defective sector becomes the spare. Through this technique, the disk can have up to one defect for every track on the drive (7,360 total) without losing capacity. Moreover, entire spare tracks are available on several spare cylinders past 920; if more than one sector on a track is defective, those extra tracks can be used. The disk has enough spare sectors and tracks to accommodate all possible defects. This kind of defect mapping is standard on many newer drives, including the drives on new IBM PS/2 systems.

Interleave Selection

When the disk is formatted by a low-level format program, the program numbers the sectors according to a specific interleave ratio. Interleave specification or alteration is always done by a low-level format routine, which is the only type of program that can write to the sector header area. In most cases, you need to know the best interleave value for your specific controller and system combination in order to run the low-level format.

Software for Low-Level Formatting

You often can choose from several types of low-level format programs, but no single low-level format program works on all drives or all systems. Because low-level format programs must operate very closely with the controller, they are often specific to a controller or controller type. Therefore, ask the controller manufacturer for the formatting software it recommends.

If the controller manufacturer supplies a low-level format program (usually in the controller's ROM), use its program because it is the one most specifically designed for your system and controller. The manufacturer's program can take advantage of special defect-mapping features, for example. A different format program might not only fail to use a manufacturer-written defect map but also overwrite and destroy it.

IBM supplies a low-level format program for its PS/2 systems. With Models 50 and higher, the program is included in the Advanced Diagnostics portion of the Reference disk that comes with the system. With system models lower than 50, users can purchase the Advanced Diagnostics program separately.

For a general-purpose ST-506/412 or ESDI low-level format program, I recommend the hTEST/hFORMAT program by Kolod Research. For the ST-506/412 interface only, I recommend the IBM Advanced Diagnostics or the HDtest program by Jim Bracking, a user-supported product found on many electronic bulletin boards, including CompuServe. For low-level formatting of IDE drives, I recommend the MicroScope program from Micro 2000. (These companies are listed in the vendor list at the back of this book.) For SCSI systems and systems on which the other recommended programs do not work, contact the controller or interface manufacturer and find out what it can supply or recommend.

Controller ROM-Based Format Software

An autoconfigure ROM can alter or specify the drive type information (such as the number of cylinders and heads). If the controller has an autoconfigure ROM, you are probably limited to using the format routine built into the controller's autoconfigure system because only the built-in formatter can write to disk the special information for the controller.

IBM Advanced Diagnostics

The standard low-level format program for IBM systems is the Advanced Diagnostics program. For the IBM PS/2 Models 50 and above, this formatting software is provided on the Reference disk included with the system. To get this software for other IBM PS/2 systems (lower than the 50), you must purchase the hardware-maintenance service manuals, which cost several hundred dollars.

To access the Advanced Diagnostics portion of the Reference disk, you press Ctrl-A (for Advanced) at the Reference disk main menu. The "secret" advanced diagnostics will appear. IBM does not document this feature in the regular system documentation, because it does not want the average user "wandering around" in this software. The Ctrl-A procedure is documented in the service manuals.

The IBM PS/2 low-level format programs are excellent, and are the only low-level format programs you should use on these systems. Only the IBM format tools know to find, use, and update the IBM-written defect map.

For standard IBM AT or IBM XT systems, the Advanced Diagnostics low-level format program is fine at formatting and testing hard disks and has the standard features associated with this type of program. However, the AT version does not allow an interleave selection of 1 to 1; this may not be a problem for most, but it renders the program useless if you upgrade to a controller that can handle a 1 to 1 interleave.

The IBM PC/XT version allows only a 6 to 1 interleave selection, which renders it useless on most IBM PC and IBM XT systems because most controllers can handle between 2 to 1 and 5 to 1 interleaves. Using the IBM XT formatting program results in a very slow system. An additional problem with the IBM PC/XT version is that it does not allow the entry of the manufacturer's defect list, an unforgivable oversight that makes the IBM PC/XT low-level format program definitely *not* recommended. Fortunately, most PC- or XT-type system users use aftermarket autoconfigure-type controllers that come with a proper built-in ROM-based formatter.

hTEST/hFORMAT

For AT-type systems and other systems with controllers that do not have an autoconfigure routine, the hTEST/hFORMAT program from Kolod Research is excellent. It is probably the most sophisticated hard disk technician's tool, and has many capabilities that make it a desirable addition to your toolbox.

HTEST/hFORMAT includes an interleave testing program called Hoptimum, which tests a disk at different interleave values to determine which interleave offers the best performance. After making this determination, the program can redo the disk at the new interleave by performing a low-level format one cylinder at a time, backing up and restoring each cylinder as it goes. Thus, the program can calculate the best interleave, reset the disk to that interleave, and retain the data on the drive, all while you are eating lunch. Be sure to back up the disk before starting this process, because a power interruption might leave you with a corrupted disk. Never trust a disk formatting program with data that is not backed up.

hTEST/hFORMAT also performs an excellent surface analysis. The low-level format and surface-analysis tools are in full control of the disk controller and can detect errors that the controller normally masks with controller error-correction codes (ECC). You can set the analysis to run for a number of passes on each track, thus improving its capability to detect a marginal track. If you have lost the original defect list or you suspect that the disk has defects in addition to the ones on the manufacturer's defect list, hTEST/hFORMAT is the program to have.

Because hTEST/hFORMAT works independently of the operating system, it is compatible with DOS, OS/2, XENIX, Novell NetWare, and other software. The program has a host of additional functions, such as controller and drive test programs and a program that prints currently marked defects on the drive.

The only drawback of hTEST/hFORMAT is that its sophistication comes with some difficulty of use. The number of options and capabilities can be bewildering to people who are not well-versed in hard disk technology. Nevertheless, the program costs only about $100, and is an essential part of my toolkit.

HDtest

HDtest, by Jim Bracking, is an excellent user-supported software program. This program is distributed through electronic bulletin boards and public-domain software libraries. You can also obtain the program from the Public Software Library, in the vendor listing in the Appendix. It costs $35, but you can try it for free.

HDtest has an easy-to-use interface and pull-down menu system. The program offers all functions normally associated with a standard low-level format program and some extras:

- Normal formatting
- Defect mapping
- Surface analysis
- Interleave test
- Nondestructive low-level reformat
- Hard disk tests (duplicate of the IBM Advanced Diagnostics hard disk tests), including tests for drive seek, head selection, error detection and correction, and a read/write/verify of the diagnostics cylinder

This program can also run low-level ROM BIOS commands to the controller.

HDtest includes most of what you would want in a low-level format program and hard disk diagnostics utility. Its only limitation is the systems it supports: the system must be compatible with the IBM XT or IBM AT and use ST-506/412 drives supported by an installation in which the drive type has been properly defined. The program does not work with ESDI or SCSI drives and does not support the IBM PS/2 defect map written on the drive.

SCSI Low-Level Format Software

If you are using a SCSI drive, you probably have to use a low-level format program provided by the manufacturer of the host adapter (SCSI). The design of these devices varies enough that a register-level program can work only if it is tailored to the individual controller.

The interface to the SCSI drive is through the host adapter. SCSI is a standard, but there are no true standard host adapters, except for those from IBM. For IBM PS/2 systems with SCSI drives, IBM supplies formatting and defect-management software on the Reference disk. That software performs everything that needs to be done to a SCSI hard disk connected to an IBM host adapter. IBM has defined a standard interface to its adapter through an Int 13h and Int 4Bh BIOS interface in a ROM installed on the card. The IBM adapters also include a special ABIOS (Advanced BIOS) interface that runs in the processor's protected mode of operation (for use under protected-mode operating systems such as OS/2).

I do not know of any other SCSI host adapters with all this interface software built into ROM. For others, you have to load drivers to match each interface you need to support. This situation causes many problems for these other adapters, particularly when they run under OS/2. Without the proper driver, these other adapters cannot run under protected mode, even if they have an Int 13h BIOS interface in ROM. The IBM host adapter, by contrast, runs in all modes with no drivers.

Because of the lack of an IBM SCSI adapter for Industry Standard Architecture (ISA) bus systems, manufacturers of these types of SCSI adapters have had no IBM lead to follow. This has caused some disparity among different SCSI host adapters from different manufacturers. You must therefore obtain hard disk formatting and defect management software from the same manufacturer as your host adapter. The particular SCSI drive you use is not important in this case, because the software is keyed to the host adapter.

IDE Low-Level Format Software

IDE drives are in a situation similar to SCSI host adapters. Each manufacturer has defined extensions to the standard Western Digital 1002/1003 AT interface, which was further standardized for IDE drives as the CAM (Common Access Method) ATA (AT Adapter) interface. Unfortunately, the CAM ATA specification does not completely specify the IDE standard, and many manufacturers have proprietary extensions to the standard. To prevent improper low-level formatting, many of these IDE drives have special codes that must be sent to the drive to unlock the format routines. These codes vary among manufacturers.

Fortunately, one manufacturer has produced a low-level format program that knows all the manufacturer-specific IDE format commands and routines, and can automatically identify and format a drive properly. The program, called MicroScope, is a comprehensive diagnostics program that can format virtually all IDE drives on the market, including those by Seagate (Imprimis), Conner Peripherals, Western Digital, Maxtor, and Fujitsu. It also performs defect mapping and surface-analysis procedures. It is published by Micro 2000, Inc. Its address and phone information are in the vendor list at the back of this book.

If possible, however, you should obtain low-level format and defect-management software from the drive manufacturer. The custom nature of the ATA interface drives is the source of some myths about IDE. Many people say, for example, that you cannot perform a low-level format on an IDE drive. This statement is untrue! What is true is that most ATA drives have a custom command set that must be used in the format process; the standard format commands defined by the ATA specification usually do not work. Without the proper manufacturer-specific format commands, you cannot format the drive, or you will format it improperly, possibly damaging the servo information on the drive and rendering it inoperable. In that case, you have to send the drive back to the manufacturer for re-servoing. The servo information guides the head actuator and dictates the track and sector positioning for the drive. To low-level format IDE drives properly, you need the correct utility, normally one provided by the manufacturer.

Western Digital provides a utility called WDAT that formats Western Digital IDE drives perfectly. This utility is available for downloading from the Western Digital electronic bulletin board system (BBS). The phone numbers and parameters for the Western Digital BBS are as follows:

> (714) 753-1234 = 1200/2400bps, 8-bit, no parity, 1 stop bit
> (714) 753-1068 = 9600bps, 8-bit, no parity, 1 stop bit

The WDAT utility works for Western Digital ATA IDE drives, but it does not work for other vendor's drives.

Many other drive manufacturers have BBSs for downloading formatting and drive utility software. See the Appendix for a list of company BBS phone numbers and parameters.

Other drives present other problems. For example, the Conner Peripherals drives in the COMPAQ systems can be formatted by COMPAQ's advanced diagnostics software, which is normally provided only to dealers. The Conner drives installed in COMPAQ systems are slightly modified from standard Conner drives; the only real difference is in the manufacturer-specific commands, especially those related to formatting.

Surface Analysis

After the hard disk low-level format, you can perform a surface analysis to locate additional defects. A surface analysis normally writes a data pattern to each sector on the drive and attempts to read that pattern back. It then compares the read information to what was originally written; a failure to compare exactly results in that sector or the entire track being marked corrupt, as in the low-level format.

Because of variations in read and write accuracy, surface analysis normally should be performed only immediately after a fresh low-level format. This precaution ensures that the surface analysis finds real defects on the drive, rather than mistracking problems from sector data not matching the headers and trailer information on the track, as might be caused by temperature variations in the platters.

A surface analysis tests only the tracks not marked bad by the low-level format. It does not reformat marked-bad tracks as good ones, even if they are good. Normally, a surface analysis should not find defects beyond what the manufacturer has already marked, except in the case of problems or drive mishandling. If the drive is new or still under warranty, I recommend returning it if a surface analysis finds new defects.

Defect List Maintenance

Traditionally, a defect list is printed on a sticker on the hard disk cover. If additional defects are found during the life of the drive, you must enter these defects manually during the low-level format process.

Most IDE and SCSI drives used in the IBM PS/2 systems feature a defect map written in a specially hidden area of the drive. The drive's surface-analysis program or low-level format program updates this area if additional defects are encountered. Only programs that know about this defect area and its format can read and update it. (The only program I know of that does this is the IBM PS/2 Advanced Diagnostics formatter found on the Reference disks.) The defect area is not accessible through normal means because it is beyond the drive's reported last cylinder. Even programs that can access a drive in an absolute sector mode (such as Norton Utilities) cannot read past the last reported cylinder as understood by the hardware. This special area of the disk can be read only through special BIOS calls. The technical-reference manuals for the PS/2 systems contain more information about this defect map and its format.

If IDE or SCSI drives are installed in compatible systems, they will also have automatic defect management. In these cases the software you use is provided by the manufacturer of the SCSI host adapter or the IDE drive itself.

If you are using a drive combination with a printed (manual) defect list on the drive, you are responsible for maintaining that list. Because there is no defect map on the drive, you must make sure that all marginal areas are marked by the low-level format program. If a surface analysis turns up new areas, write the new defects on the sticker; then the next time you run a low-level format program, you will remember to enter and re-mark these areas.

To check the accuracy of the sticker on a disk before running a low-level format on a drive that has been previously formatted, run a nondestructive scan for tracks currently marked bad. A *nondestructive scan* searches each sector of the disk, looking for the corrupt sector header checksum bytes that indicate a sector has been intentionally marked bad by a low-level format program. Compare the results to the written list on the drive sticker to see if the previous formatter marked all the defects (or discovered and marked additional defects without adding them to the sticker). You may find that the person who performed the previous low-level format made an error in entering the defect locations from the sticker to the low-level format program, which means that a good area has been marked bad, and that the defective area is unmarked and currently in use. (Systems that incorporate the defect map in machine-readable form on the drive, such as the IBM PS/2 systems, never have this kind of operator-induced problem.)

Whatever type of defect management your drive and controller combination performs, make sure that all manufacturer defects, as well as additional defects found by the surface analysis, have been entered correctly and marked both in the low-level format and on the written manufacturer defect list (so that they will also be marked on subsequent low-level formats). If you trust subsequent surface-analysis scans with the marking of additional defect areas, you may be surprised to see that some marginal areas read as good one time and bad another. Make sure that an area discovered as bad once will be marked bad from that time forward by subsequent low-level format operations.

Surface-Analysis Software

A good low-level format program provides surface-analysis routines. The original IBM XT and AT Advanced Diagnostics low-level format programs include surface analysis as an option to perform after the format. On the IBM PS/2 Advanced Diagnostics program, the surface analysis is no longer optional and is performed automatically during the low-level format operation, which is one reason the IBM PS/2 low-level format routines take so long and make multiple passes through the disk. The first pass is the format, the second pass is a destructive write test, and the last pass is a read and verify of all sectors of the disk. This procedure extends the time for the operation to the equivalent of three or four consecutive low-level format operations.

Other commercial low-level format programs also include surface analysis routines. The hTEST/hFORMAT program includes comprehensive surface-analysis capability, as does the HDtest program. If you are using a controller-based format program and it includes a surface-analysis routine, use it.

Drive Partitioning

Partitioning a hard disk is the act of defining areas of the disk for an operating system to use as a volume. To DOS, a volume is an area of a disk denoted as a drive letter; for example, drive C: is volume C:, drive D: is volume D:, and so on. Some people think that you have to partition a disk only if you are going to divide it into more than one volume. This is a misunderstanding; a disk must be partitioned even if it will be the single volume C:.

When a disk is partitioned, a master partition boot sector is written at cylinder 0, head 0, sector 1—the first sector on the hard disk. This sector contains data describing the partitions by their starting and ending cylinder, head, and sector locations. The partition table also indicates to the ROM BIOS which of the partitions is bootable, and thus where to look for an operating system to load. A single hard disk can have from 1 to 24 partitions. This number includes all the hard drives installed in the system, which means that you can have as many as 24 separate hard disks with one partition each, a single hard disk with 24 partitions, or a combination of disks and partitions such that the total number of partitions is no more than 24. If you have more than 24 drives or partitions, DOS does not recognize them, although other operating systems may. What limits DOS is that a letter is used to name a volume, and the Roman alphabet ends with Z, the 24th volume when you begin with C.

FDISK

The DOS FDISK program is the accepted standard for partitioning hard disks. Partitioning prepares the boot sector of the disk such that the DOS FORMAT program can operate correctly, and enables different operating systems to coexist on a single hard disk.

If a disk is set up with two or more partitions, FDISK shows only two total DOS partitions, the *primary partition* and the *extended partition*. The extended partition is then divided into *logical DOS volumes*, which are partitions themselves. FDISK gives a false impression of how the partitioning is done. FDISK reports that a disk divided as C:, D:, E:, and F: is set up as two partitions, with a primary partition having a volume designator of C: and a single extended partition, with logical DOS volumes D:, E:, and F:. But in the real structure of the disk, each logical DOS volume is a separate partition with an extended partition boot sector describing it. Each drive volume constitutes a separate partition on the disk, and the partitions point to one another in a daisy-chain arrangement.

Different versions of DOS have different partitioning capabilities. DOS 2.x and later versions support hard disks and partitioning. The minimum size for a partition for any version of DOS is one cylinder. FDISK in DOS 4 or higher versions allocate partitions in megabytes, and the minimum size partition it will create is 1 megabyte. DOS 4 and higher allow partitions to be as large as 2 gigabytes. Versions of DOS earlier than 4.0 have a maximum partition size of 32 megabytes.

DOS 3.3 allows partitions of up to 32 megabytes. FDISK shows that a single extended partition can be as big as the rest of the disk past the primary partition, but that is not a true picture of the disk structure. This so-called single extended partition is not a partition but a pointer to the remainder of the disk where the DOS extended partitions reside. This extended partition must be split into logical DOS volumes, which are partitions themselves, of 32 megabytes or less. In the organization of the disk, the primary partition is assigned drive letter C and the extended partitions are assigned letters sequentially from D through Z. Each drive letter (which is a volume or partition) can be assigned only as much as 32 megabytes of disk space under DOS 3.3.

DOS 3.2 and earlier versions do not support an extended partitioning scheme and allow only a single partition for DOS (assigned the C: volume designator). The size limit of this partition is 32 megabytes due to the limit of 65,536 total sectors in a partition in DOS prior to version 4.0.

DOS versions 2.x support only 16-megabyte maximum partitions due to limitations of the 12-bit FAT system. A 12-bit FAT can manage a maximum of only 4,096 total clusters on a disk. The limit of 16 megabytes does not come from the FAT, but from the high-level DOS FORMAT command, which aborts with a `Track 0 bad—disk unusable` error message if the partition is larger than 16 megabytes. On a disk that has no marked bad tracks beyond the first 16 megabytes of the disk, you can ignore the error message and continue the setup of the disk with the SYS command. If the disk has defects beyond 16 megabytes, they are not properly marked in the FAT, which results in problems with data stored in these areas.

These problems were corrected by modified high-level format programs supplied with hard disks sold by most disk vendors. The modified high-level format programs enable partitions of up to 32 megabytes to be formatted properly. The only problem then is that each cluster or minimum allocation unit on the disk is 8,192 bytes (8K) because of the 12-bit FAT. A lot of disk space is wasted, especially with smaller files, because each file uses the disk in 8K increments.

With the current versions of DOS, problems of partition size and formatting are gone. FDISK allows partitions as large as the disk or as small as 1 megabyte. By combining the hard disks attached to a single system, you can have as many as 24 separate DOS-recognizable partitions among them.

Partitioning Software

Since DOS 3.3 and 4.0 first became available, there has been little need for disk partitioning utilities, except in special cases. If a system is having problems that cause you to consider using a partitioning utility, I recommend that you upgrade to a newer version of DOS instead. Using nonstandard partitioning programs to partition your disk places the data in these partitions in jeopardy and makes recovery of data lost in these partitions extremely difficult.

The reason that disk partitioning utilities other than FDISK exist is that the maximum partition size was 16 megabytes for DOS 2.x and 32 megabytes for DOS 3.x. These limits are bothersome for people with physical hard disks much larger than 32 megabytes, because they must divide the hard disk into many partitions to use all the disk. Versions of DOS prior to 3.3 cannot even create more than a single DOS-accessible partition on a hard disk. If you have a 120-megabyte hard disk and are using DOS 3.2 or earlier versions, you can access only 32 megabytes of that disk as a C: partition. To overcome this limitation, several software companies created enhanced partitioning programs you can use rather than FDISK. These programs create multiple partitions and partitions larger than 32 megabytes on a disk recognizable by DOS. These partitioning programs include a high-level format program because the FORMAT program in DOS 3.3 or earlier versions can format partitions only up to 32 megabytes.

Disk Manager by Ontrack, Speedstor by Storage Dimensions, and Vfeature Deluxe by Golden Bow are among the best-known of the partitioning utilities. They include low-level format capabilities, so they can be used as a single tool to set up a hard disk. They even include disk driver software that provides the capability to override the physical type selections in the system ROM BIOS, enabling a system to use all of a disk, even though the drive-type table in the system ROM BIOS does not have an entry that exactly matches the hard disk.

These nonstandard partitioning and formatting programs were given away by many drive vendors and integrators, which makes some purchasers of such products feel that they must use these drivers to operate the drive. In most cases, there are better alternatives; nonstandard disk partitioning and formatting can cause more problems that it solves.

For example, Seagate shipped Ontrack Disk Manager with its drives larger than 32M. One purpose of the program is to perform low-level formatting of the drive, which Disk Manager does well, and I recommend it highly for this function. If possible, however, you should avoid other program functions, including partitioning and high-level formatting.

When you use a program like Disk Manager to partition and high-level (DOS) format a drive, the drive is set up in a nonstandard way, different from pure DOS. This difference can cause trouble with utilities—including disk cache programs, disk test and interleave check programs, and data recovery or retrieval programs—written to function with a standard DOS disk structure. In many situations that a standard format would avoid, a nonstandard disk format can cause data loss and also make data recovery impossible.

If you do not use the device drivers provided by Disk Manager and programs like it, you retain more free RAM and a pure DOS (standard) disk structure, and you eliminate many potential problems, especially with disk-utility and data-recovery operations. With DOS 4.0 and later versions, very few systems require a program such as Disk Manager, and the penalties for having a nonstandard disk format far outweigh benefits.

In a few special cases, these types of disk driver programs are useful or even required. In general, disk device driver programs are *not* required for these systems:

- IBM XT system
- IBM AT systems with SCSI drives
- IBM AT systems with matching BIOS drive types
- IBM AT systems with IDE drives and similar-capacity BIOS drive types

- IBM AT systems with custom or user-definable BIOS drive types
- IBM AT systems with a controller featuring an on-board BIOS and either of the following:

    ST-506/412 RLL drives with 1024 or fewer cylinders
    ESDI drives with 1024 or fewer cylinders

- IBM AT systems with a controller featuring an on-board BIOS with translation mode and either of the following:

    ST-506/412 RLL drive
    ESDI drive

Disk device driver programs may be required for the following systems:

- IBM AT systems without a user-definable BIOS drive type and with an ST-506/412 MFM drive that is not supported well in the existing BIOS drive-type table
- IBM AT systems with an IDE drive and no BIOS drive-type table entry of a similar capacity
- IBM AT systems with a controller that does not support translation and ST-506/412 RLL or ESDI drives with more than 1024 cylinders

Situations in which the disk driver may be required are rare; in most cases, these disk drivers are definitely not recommended.

> **CAUTION:** If you are interested in future data recovery, you should *not* use Disk Manager, Speedstor, Vfeature Deluxe, or others like them to partition or high-level format your hard disks. Also do not use these programs to override a system's ROM BIOS drive-type settings. If you use these programs as anything but a low-level format, you are creating a nonstandard disk system. Software that does not run under DOS will not understand the disk, and if you execute programs that write to the disk without going through DOS, the program will write in the wrong place.

It is especially dangerous to use these partitioning programs to override your ROM BIOS disk-table settings. Consider the following disaster scenario.

Suppose that you have a Seagate ST-4096 hard disk, which has 1024 cylinders and 9 heads, and requires that your controller never perform a data write modification called *write precompensation* to cylinders of the disk. Some drives require this precompensation on the inner cylinders to compensate for "bit crowding" that takes place because of the higher density of data on the (smaller size) inner cylinders. The ST-4096 internally compensates for this effect and therefore needs no precompensation from the controller.

Now suppose that you install this drive in an IBM AT that does not have a ROM BIOS drive table that exactly matches the drive. The best matching type you can select is type 18, which enables you to use only 977 cylinders and 7 heads, or 56.77 megabytes of what should be a 76.5-megabyte hard disk. If your IBM AT is one of the older ones with a ROM BIOS dated 01/10/84, the situation is worse because its drive-table ends with type 14. In that case, you would have to select type 12 as the best match, giving you access to 855 cylinders and 7 heads, or only 49.68 megabytes of a 76.5-megabyte drive. ROM BIOS drive tables are listed in the Appendix of this book for reference. Most IBM-compatibles have a more complete drive-type table and would have an exact table match for this drive, allowing the full 76.5 megabytes to be used with no problems. For example, in most compatibles with a Phoenix ROM BIOS, you would select type 35, which would support the drive entirely.)

Now suppose that, not content with using only 57 or 50 megabytes of this 76.5-megabyte drive, you invoke the Disk Manager program that came with the drive and use it to low-level format the drive. Then you use the Disk Manager program to override the type 18 or type 12 settings in the drive table. The program instructs you to set up a very small C: partition (of only 1 megabyte), then partitions the remaining 75.5 mega-bytes of the disk as D:. This partitioning overrides the DOS 3.3 32-megabyte partition limitation. (If you had an IBM-compatible system that did not require the drive-type override, you would still need to use the Disk Manager partitioner to create partitions larger than the DOS 3.3 standard 32 megabytes.) Following that, you use Disk Manager to high-level format the C: and D: partitions, because the DOS high-level format in DOS 3.3 works only on volumes of 32 megabytes or less.

Disk Manager creates a special driver file called DMDRVR.BIN, which it installs in the CONFIG.SYS file through the DEVICE command. After the system boots from the C: partition and loads the DMDRVR.BIN device driver, the 75.5-megabyte D: partition is completely accessible.

Along comes an innocent user of the system who always boots from her own DOS floppy disk. After booting from the floppy, she tries to log into the D: partition. No matter what version of DOS this user boots from on the floppy disk, the D: partition seems to have vanished. An attempt to log into that partition results in an Invalid drive specification error message. No standard version of DOS can recognize that specially created D: partition if the DMDRVR.BIN device driver is not loaded.

An attempt by this user to recover data on this drive with a utility pro-gram such as Norton, Mace, or PC Tools results in failure because these programs interpret the drive as having 977 cylinders and 7 heads (type 18) or 855 cylinders and 7 heads (type 12). In fact, when these programs attempt to correct what seems to be partition-table damage, data will be corrupted in the vanished D: partition.

Thinking that there may be a physical problem with the disk, the innocent user boots and runs the Advanced Diagnostics software to test the hard disk. Because Advanced Diagnostics incorporates its own special boot code and does not use standard DOS, it does not examine partitioning but goes to the ROM BIOS drive-type table to determine the capacity of the hard disk. It sees the unit as having only 977 or 855 cylinders, indicated by the type 18 or 12 settings, as well as only 7 heads. The user then runs the Advanced Diagnostics hard disk tests, which use the last cylinder of the disk as a test cylinder for diagnostics read and write tests. This cylinder is subsequently overwritten by the diagnostics tests, which all pass because there is no physical problem with the drive.

This innocent user has just wiped out the D: drive data that happened to be on cylinder 976 in the type 18 setup or cylinder 854 in the type 12 setup. Had the drive been partitioned by FDISK, the last cylinder indicated by the ROM BIOS drive table would have been left out of any partitions, reserved so that diagnostics tests could be performed on the drive without damaging data.

Beyond the kind of disaster scenario just described, other potential problems can be caused by nonstandard disk partitioning and formatting, such as the following:

■ Data loss by using OS/2, UNIX, XENIX, Novell Advanced NetWare, or other non-DOS operating systems that do not recognize the disk or the nonstandard partitions. Using Windows 3.0 can also cause data loss because it looks to the ROM BIOS for the disk parameters. Writing to the drive under these operating systems destroys data.

■ Difficulty upgrading a system from one DOS version to another

■ Difficulty installing a different operating system, such as OS/2, on the hard disk

■ Data loss by using a low-level format utility to run an interleave test; the test area for the interleave test is the diagnostics cylinder, which contains data on disks formatted with Disk Manager

■ Data loss by accidentally deleting or overwriting the DMDRVR.BIN driver file and causing the D: partition to disappear after the next boot

■ Data-recovery difficulty or failure because nonstandard partitions do not follow the rules and guidelines set by Microsoft and IBM, and there is no documentation on their structure. The sizes and locations of the FATs and root directory are not standard, and the detailed reference charts in this book (which are valid for an FDISK-created partition) are inaccurate for nonstandard partitions.

I could continue, but I think you get the idea. I do not mean to pick on only Disk Manager; the Speedstor or Vfeature Deluxe programs present the same problems, as do other programs that provide the same features. If these utility programs are used only for low-level formatting, they do not cause problems. It is the drive-type override, partitioning, and high-level format operations that cause difficulty. If you consider data integrity important and want to be able to perform data recovery, follow these disk support and partitioning rules:

■ Every hard disk must be properly supported by system ROM BIOS, with no software overrides. If the system does not have a drive-table that supports the full capacity of the drive, either accept the table's limit or modify the table through hardware (by patching the ROM BIOS, upgrading to a new ROM BIOS, or using a disk controller with on-board ROM BIOS for drive support).

■ Use only FDISK to partition a hard disk. If you want partitions larger than 32M, use DOS 4.0 or later versions.

High-Level Format

The final step in the software preparation of a hard disk is the DOS high-level format. The primary function of the high-level format is to create a FAT and a directory system on the disk so that DOS can manage files.

Usually, you do the high-level format with the standard DOS FORMAT program, using the following syntax:

```
FORMAT C: /S /V
```

This step high-level formats drive C: (or volume C: in a multivolume drive), places the hidden operating system files on the first part of this partition, and prompts for the entry of a volume label to be stored on the disk at completion.

The high-level format program performs the following functions and procedures:

1. Scans the disk (read only) for tracks and sectors marked bad during the low-level format. Notes these tracks as unreadable.

2. Returns the drive heads to the first cylinder of the partition, and at that cylinder, head 1, sector 1, writes a DOS volume boot sector.

3. Writes a file allocation table (FAT) at head 1, sector 2. Immediately after this FAT, it writes a second copy of the FAT. These FATs are essentially blank except for bad cluster marks noting areas of the disk found unreadable during the marked defect scan.

4. Writes a blank root directory.

5. If the /S parameter is specified, copies the IBMBIO.COM, IBMDOS.COM, and COMMAND.COM files to the disk (in that order).

6. If the /V parameter is specified, prompts the user for a volume label, which is written as the fourth file entry in the root directory.

Now DOS can use the disk for storing and retrieving files, and the disk is a bootable disk.

During the first phase of the high-level format, a marked defect scan is performed. Defects marked by the low-level format operation show up during this scan as unreadable tracks or sectors. When the high-level format encounters one of these areas, it automatically performs up to five retries to read these tracks or sectors. If the unreadable area was marked by the low-level format, the read fails on all attempts.

After five retries, the DOS FORMAT program gives up on this track or sector and moves to the next. Areas unreadable after the initial read and the five retries are noted as bad clusters in the FAT. DOS 3.3 and earlier versions can mark only entire tracks bad in the FAT, even if only one sector was marked in the low-level format. DOS 4.0 and higher versions individually check each cluster on the track and recover those that do not involve the low-level marked-bad sectors. Because most low-level format programs mark all the sectors on a track as bad rather than the individual sector containing the defect, the result using either DOS 3.3 or 4.0 is the same: all clusters involving sectors on that track are marked bad in the FAT.

> **Note**
>
> Some low-level format programs mark only the individual sector that is bad on a track, rather than the entire track. This is true of the IBM PS/2 low-level formatters on the IBM PS/2 Advanced Diagnostics or Reference disk. In this case, high-level formatting with DOS 4.0 or higher versions results in fewer lost bytes in bad sectors because only the clusters containing the marked bad sectors are marked bad in the FAT. DOS 4.0 and higher display the Attempting to recover allocation unit x message, where x is the number of the cluster, in an attempt to determine whether a single cluster or all the clusters on the track should be marked bad in the FAT.
>
> If the controller and low-level format program together support sector and track sparing, the high-level format finds the entire disk defect-free, because all the defective sectors have been exchanged for spare good ones.

If a disk has been low-level formatted correctly, the number of bytes in bad sectors is the same before and after the high-level format. If the number does change after redoing a high-level format (reporting fewer bytes or none), the low-level format was not done correctly. Probably the manufacturer's defects were not marked, or Norton, Mace, PC Tools, or a similar utility was used to mark defective clusters on the disk. The utilities cannot mark the sectors or tracks at the low-level format level; the bad cluster marks they make are stored only in the FAT and erased during the next high-level format operation. Defect marks made in the low-level format consistently show as bad bytes in the high-level format, no matter how many times you run it.

Only a low-level format or a surface analysis tool can correctly mark defects on a disk; anything else makes only temporary bad cluster marks in the FAT. This kind of marking may be acceptable temporarily, but when additional bad areas are found on a disk, you should run a new low-level format of the disk and either mark the area manually or run a surface analysis to place a more permanent mark on the disk.

Here is a format tip for users of DOS 4.0. IBM has issued a number of Corrective Service Diskettes (CSDs) for DOS 4.0. The speed of the high-level FORMAT command for DOS 4.0 has been tremendously improved as of CSD UR29015, particularly in the handling of marked defects. Additionally, this CSD corrected a bug in the FORMAT command that caused the program to abort with an Invalid media or Track 0 bad — disk unusable error message. This situation happens if you are high-level formatting a partition larger than 32 megabytes and a marked defect is located in the area of the disk from 32 megabytes to 32 megabytes plus x, where x equals the size of the DOS volume boot sector, FATs, and root directory on that partition. Prior to receiving the patched FORMAT command in CSD UR29015 or higher, I had to boot OS/2 and high-level format the partition with the OS/2 1.1 high-level format program, then reboot DOS 4.0 and use the SYS command to make the disk bootable. The DOS 4.0 Corrective Service Diskettes corrects this problem. (See Chapter 15, "Software Troubleshooting Guide," for more information about Corrective Service Diskettes and how to get them.) DOS 5.0 and later versions do not exhibit this format problem.

Hard Disk Drive Repair

If a hard disk drive has a problem inside its sealed HDA (Head Disk Assembly), repairing the drive is usually not feasible. If the failure is in the logic board, that assembly can be replaced with a new or rebuilt assembly easily and for a much lower cost than replacing the entire drive.

Most hard disk problems are not really hardware problems; instead, they are "soft" problems, in which a new low-level format and defect mapping session can solve the problem. Soft problems are characterized by a drive that sounds normal but gives various read and write errors.

"Hard" problems are mechanical, such as when the drive sounds as if it contains loose marbles. Constant scraping and grinding noises from the drive, with no reading or writing capability, also qualifies as a hard error. In these cases, it is unlikely that a low-level format will put the drives back into service. If a hardware problem is indicated, first replace the logic board assembly. You can do this repair yourself and, if successful, you can recover the data from the drive.

If replacing the logic assembly does not solve the problem, contact the manufacturer or a specialized repair shop that has clean room facilities for hard disk repair. See the vendor list in the Appendix for a list of drive manufacturers and companies that specialize in hard disk drive repair.

The cost of HDA repair may be more than half the cost of a new drive, so you may want to consider replacing rather than repairing the drive. If the failed drive is an inexpensive 20-megabyte or 30-megabyte stepper motor drive, the better option is to purchase something better. If the drive is a larger, voice coil drive, however, it is usually more economical to repair rather than replace the drive because the replacement cost is much higher.

17xx, 104xx, 210xxxx Hardware Error Codes

When there is a failure in the hard disk subsystem at power-on, the Power-On Self Test (POST) finds the problem and reports it with an error message. The 17xx, 104xx, and 210xxxx errors during the POST or while running the Advanced Diagnostics indicate problems with hard disks, controllers, or cables. The 17xx codes apply to ST-506/412 interface drives and controllers; 104xx errors apply to ESDI drives and controllers; and 210xxxx errors apply to SCSI drives and host adapters.

A breakdown of these error messages and their meanings are shown in table 9.8.

Table 9.8 Hard Disk and Controller Diagnostic Error Codes

ST-506/412 fixed drive and controller error codes

Code	Description
1701	Fixed disk general POST error
1702	Drive/controller time-out error
1703	Drive seek error
1704	Controller failed
1705	Drive sector not found error
1706	Write fault error
1707	Drive track 0 error
1708	Head select error
1709	Error correction code (ECC) error
1710	Sector buffer overrun
1711	Bad address mark
1712	Internal controller diagnostics failure
1713	Data compare error
1714	Drive not ready
1715	Track 0 indicator failure
1716	Diagnostics cylinder errors
1717	Surface read errors
1718	Hard drive type error
1720	Bad diagnostics cylinder
1726	Data compare error
1730	Controller error
1731	Controller error
1732	Controller error
1733	BIOS undefined error return
1735	Bad command error
1736	Data corrected error
1737	Bad track error
1738	Bad sector error

continues

Table 9.8 Continued

ST-506/412 fixed drive and controller error codes

1739	Bad initialization error
1740	Bad sense error
1750	Drive verify failure
1751	Drive read failure
1752	Drive write failure
1753	Drive random read test failure
1754	Drive seek test failure
1755	Controller failure
1756	Controller error-correction code (ECC) test failure
1757	Controller head select failure
1780	Seek failure; drive 0
1781	Seek failure; drive 1
1782	Controller test failure
1790	Diagnostic cylinder read error; drive 0
1791	Diagnostic cylinder read error; drive 1

ESDI drive and adapter error codes

10450	Read/write test failed
10451	Read verify test failed
10452	Seek test failed
10453	Wrong device type indicated
10454	Controller test failed sector buffer test
10455	Controller failure
10456	Controller diagnostic command failure
10461	Drive format error
10462	Controller head select error
10463	Drive read/write sector error
10464	Drive primary defect map unreadable
10465	Controller; error-correction code (ECC) 8-bit error

ESDI drive and adapter error codes	
10466	Controller; error-correction code (ECC) 9-bit error
10467	Drive soft seek error
10468	Drive hard seek error
10469	Drive soft seek error count exceeded
10470	Controller attachment diagnostic error
10471	Controller wrap mode interface error
10472	Controller wrap mode drive select error
10473	Read verify test errors
10480	Seek failure; drive 0
10481	Seek failure; drive 1
10482	Controller transfer acknowledge error
10483	Controller reset failure
10484	Controller; head select 3 error
10485	Controller; head select 2 error
10486	Controller; head select 1 error
10487	Controller; head select 0 error
10488	Controller; read gate - command complete 2 error
10489	Controller; write gate - command complete 1 error
10490	Diagnostic area read error; drive 0
10491	Diagnostic area read error; drive 1
10499	Controller failure

SCSI drive and controller error codes	
096xxxx	SCSI adapter with cache (32-bit) errors
112xxxx	SCSI adapter (16-bit without cache) errors
113xxxx	System board SCSI adapter (16-bit) errors
210xxxx	SCSI fixed disk errors

First x in xxxx is SCSI ID number.
Second x in xxxx is logical unit number.
Third x in xxxx is host-adapter slot number.
Fourth x in xxxx is the drive capacity, in which A is 60MB, C is 120MB, E is 320MB, F is 400MB and U is undetermined.

Most of the time a seek failure indicates that the drive is not responding to the controller. This failure is usually caused by one of the following:

- Incorrect drive-select jumper setting
- Loose, damaged, or backward control cable
- Loose or bad power cable
- Stiction between drive heads and platters
- Bad power supply

If a diagnostics cylinder read error occurs, the most likely problems are these:

- Incorrect drive-type setting
- Loose, damaged, or backward data cable
- Temperature-induced mistracking

Correcting most of these problems is obvious. For example, if the drive-select jumper setting is incorrect, correct it. If a cable is loose, tighten it. If the power supply is bad, replace it. You get the idea.

If the problem is temperature related, the drive will usually read data acceptably at the same temperature at which it was written. Let the drive warm up for a while and then attempt to reboot it, or let the drive cool and reread the disk if the drive has overheated.

The stiction problem may not have an obvious solution; the next section addresses this problem.

Drive Spin Failure

Other than a faulty power-supply cable connection or a faulty power supply, stiction is the primary cause of a hard disk drive not spinning. *Stiction* (static friction) is a condition in which the drive heads are stuck to the platters in a way that the platter motor cannot overcome the sticking force and spin the drive up for operation. This situation happens more frequently than you might imagine.

The heads stick to the platters in the same way two very smooth pieces of glass might stick together. It is especially noticeable if the drive has been off for a week or more. It also seems more noticeable if the drive is operated under very hot conditions and then shut down. In the latter case, the excessive heat buildup in the drive softens the lubricant; after the drive is powered off, the platters cool rapidly and contract around the heads, which have settled in the lubricant coating. Drives with many platters and heads are more prone to this problem than drives with fewer ones.

To solve this problem, you must spin the platters with enough force to rip the heads loose from the platters. Usually this is accomplished by twisting the drive violently in the same plane as the platters, using the platter's inertia to overcome the sticking force. The heavy platters tend to remain stationary while you twist the drive and make the heads move around the platters.

Another technique is to spin the spindle motor, which rotates the platters inside the drive. To do this, you may have to remove the circuit board from the bottom of the drive to get to the spindle motor. In other cases, you can insert a stick into the gap between the bottom of the drive and the circuit board and push on the spindle motor with the stick. You will probably feel heavy resistance to rotation, then the platters will suddenly feel free as the heads are unstuck. Some drives use a spindle motor brake that is released by an electric solenoid, which may make turning the platters more difficult. If the brake has failed and is holding the platters from spinning, you must remove the brake from the spindle motor to allow it to spin. Because every drive is designed differently, consult the drive manual to see whether your drive has such a spindle braking system.

After you free the platters, reapply the power, and the drive should spin up normally. I have solved stiction problems many times using these methods, and have never lost data as a result. If you are nervous about handling your drive in this manner, consult a professional drive repair facility.

Logic Boards

A disk drive, including a hard disk drive, has one or more logic boards mounted on it. These boards contain the electronics that control the drive's spindle and head actuator systems and present data to the controller. Some drives have built-in controllers.

Logic boards on hard disks fail more often than the mechanical components. Most professional data-recovery companies stock a number of functional logic boards for popular drives. When a drive comes in for recovery, data-recovery professionals check the drive for problems such as installation or configuration errors, temperature mistracking, and stiction. If these are not the problem, they replace the logic board on the drive with a known good unit. Often the drive then works normally, and data can be read from it.

The logic boards on most hard disks can be removed and replaced easily; they simply plug into the drive. They are usually mounted with standard screw hardware. If a drive is failing, and you have a spare of the same type, you might be able to verify a logic board failure by removing the board from a known good drive and mounting it on the bad one. Then if your suspicions are confirmed, you can order a new logic board from the drive's manufacturer. Be prepared for sticker shock; parts like this may cost more than replacing the entire drive with a new or refurbished unit. A less-expensive option is buying a refurbished unit, or trading in the old board. (The drive manufacturer will have details on the savings.) Purchasing a new logic board may not always be cost effective, but borrowing one from a drive that works costs nothing, and it may let you recover all the data from the problem drive.

Chapter Summary

This chapter has examined hard disks and controllers, and explored the physical and logical operations of the disk. You learned about installing and configuring hard disks and controllers. Now you can use this information to select and configure a hard disk system correctly. A properly designed and installed hard disk system will give you fewer problems than a haphazardly installed system. Most problems are related to software, installation, or formatting, so you can use the information in this chapter to restore many failing drives to normal operation.

The next chapter continues your tour through the system and focuses on other peripherals such as video subsystems, memory boards, and communications adapters.

Peripherals

W hen you equip an IBM or compatible computer, you can choose from a wide variety of display options, memory adapters, and communications boards. In this chapter, you learn about the features and drawbacks of each of the available systems. All the standard video systems are discussed and examined, including the new MCGA and VGA standards that are part of the PS/2 systems from IBM. Memory adapters are discussed, including conventional, extended, and expanded memory boards. This chapter also covers communications adapters such as serial and parallel ports.

Video Display Hardware

During the early years of the IBM PC and compatibles, the video system choice was simply color or monochrome. Since then, many adapter and display options have hit the market. A video subsystem consists of two main components: an adapter that plugs into an expansion slot or is built into the motherboard, and a video display or monitor that is compatible with the video adapter. This chapter explores the range of available IBM-compatible video adapters and the displays that work with them.

With the PS/2 systems, IBM developed new video standards that have completely overtaken the older display standards in popularity and support. Abiding by industry standards for video displays and adapters is extremely important. Many video systems are not supported by every program and system peripheral. Therefore, I usually avoid discussing proprietary standards because they offer the typical mainstream system user little more than incompatibility problems. So far only IBM has been able to define true video standards for the IBM-compatible industry, although others have made attempts. Sometimes even IBM has failed to have its video standards adopted throughout the industry.

The following IBM display systems are standards in today's industry:

MDA	Monochrome Display Adapter
CGA	Color Graphics Adapter
EGA	Enhanced Graphics Adapter
VGA	Video Graphics Array
XGA	eXtended Graphics Array

These adapters and video standards are supported by virtually every program that runs on IBM or compatible equipment.

Adapters and Displays

Different display adapters can require different displays because of differences in horizontal and vertical scanning frequencies. (The preceding mini-table lists the horizontal and vertical scan rates produced by the adapters.)

The *vertical scan rate* indicates how often the screen flashes per second. High vertical scan rates reflect less flickering. Some monitors can even be damaged if an inappropriate adapter is used. The display must match the scan frequencies of the adapter, although some newer monitors, usually called *multiscan* or *multisync displays*, support multiple scanning frequencies. The various NEC, Mitsubishi, and Sony multisync or multiscan monitors are among the most popular.

When these newer monitors first became available, they had some problems interacting with the large variety of video adapters in use. When the user switched video modes with some of these multiscanning monitors, the monitor did not properly adjust for the changed signal, and the resultant image did not always occupy the full screen. Images sometimes appeared shrunken in the display's center or were off-center. Although these problems are less prevalent today, you should still check how a display operates with your adapter before making a purchase.

Note Some adapters, such as the XGA, run in an Interlaced mode at higher resolutions. *Interlacing* occurs when the adapter makes two passes to complete an image, drawing one half of the image during each scan. The vertical scanning frequency is therefore at a lower value than normal, and some users notice flickering. In the XGA, for example, the interlaced modes allow only 43.48 complete screen images to be drawn every second (compared to a rate of 60 on a normal television). System designers can greatly lessen this effect by using a display with a longer persistence phosphor, which blends the separate images and controls the flicker. If you are considering a video adapter that runs in an interlaced mode, be sure to use a display recommended by the adapter manufacturer. Try out the system before purchasing it just to be sure.

Monochrome Display and Adapter

The simplest display combination you can choose is the IBM Monochrome Display and Printer Adapter card. A character-only combination, the display has no inherent graphics capabilities. This combination was originally a top-selling option because the combination is fairly cost-effective. As a bonus, this combination also provides a printer interface that does not consume an extra slot. The display is known for clarity and high resolution, making this combination ideal for businesses—especially businesses that use word processing or spreadsheets. Figure 10.1 shows the Monochrome Display Adapter pinouts.

Because the monochrome display is a character-only display, you cannot run software that requires graphics. Originally, that drawback only kept the user from playing games on a monochrome display, but today even the most serious business software uses graphics and color to great advantage. With the 9-by-14 dots character box (matrix), the IBM monochrome monitor displays attractive characters. Table 10.1 summarizes features of the MDA's single mode or operation.

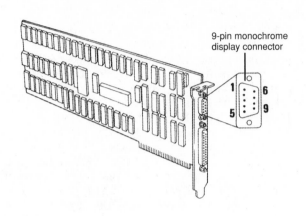

9-pin monochrome
display connector

At Standard TTL Levels

IBM Monochrome Display	Signal		Pin	IBM Monochrome Display and Printer Adapter
	Ground		1	
	Ground		2	
		Not Used	3	
		Not Used	4	
		Not Used	5	
	+ Intensity		6	
	+ Video		7	
	+ Horizontal		8	
	− Vertical		9	

Fig. 10.1

MDA connector specifications.

Table 10.1 IBM Monochrome Display Adapter (MDA) Specifications

Video standard	Resolution	Number of colors	Mode type	BIOS modes	Character format	Character box	Scan Frequency Vertical (Hz)	Horizontal (KHz)	Scan mode
DA (08/12/81)	720 × 350	4	Text	07h	80 × 25	9 × 14	50	18.432	Std

Colors *refers to different display attributes such as regular, highlight, reverse video, and underlined.*

Color Graphics Display and Adapter

For many years, the Color Graphics Adapter was the most common display adapter, although now its capabilities leave much to be desired. This adapter has two basic modes of operation: alphanumeric (A/N) or all points addressable (APA). In A/N mode, the card operates in a 40-column by 25-line mode or an 80-column by 25-line mode with 16 colors. In APA and A/N modes, the character set is formed with a resolution of 8 × 8 pixels. In APA mode, two resolutions are available: a medium-resolution color mode (320 × 200) with four colors available, and a two-color high-resolution mode (640 × 200). With the Color Graphics Adapter, you can choose from a number of monitors because the horizontal scanning rate of the CGA is the same as standard television (15.75 KHz). You can purchase a low-cost monochrome composite video monitor, and upgrade to a more expensive monitor later without reconfig-uring your software. Figure 10.2 and figure 10.3 show the pinouts for the Color Display Adapter.

Dot pitch indicates the distance between the dots making up the display. Smaller pitch values indicate sharper images. The IBM PC color monitor has a pitch of 0.43 mm, which is considered poor even by CGA standards, but because the monitor uses a black-matrix tube, it produces a good picture with vivid colors.

Most of the monitors sold for the CGA were RGBs, not composite monitors. The color signal of a composite monitor contains a mixture of colors that must be decoded or separated. RGB monitors receive red, green, and blue separately and combine the colors in different proportions to generate other colors. RGB monitors offer better resolution than composite monitors and do a much better job of displaying 80-column text.

Most companies that sold a CGA-type adapter have long since discontinued the product. With many VGA cards costing under $100, recommending a CGA makes little sense. For most applications, I recommend a VGA-compatible adapter and display because most software is being written for this standard. Table 10.2 gives the specifications for all CGA modes of operation.

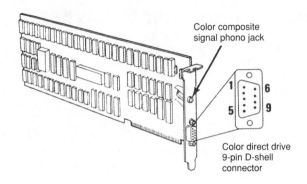

Color composite
signal phono jack

Color direct drive
9-pin D-shell
connector

At Standard TTL Levels

IBM Color Display or other Direct-Drive Monitor		Color/Graphics Direct-Drive Adapter
Ground	1	
Ground	2	
Red	3	
Green	4	
Blue	5	
Intensity	6	
Reserved	7	
Horizontal Drive	8	
Vertical Drive	9	

**Composite Phono Jack
Hookup to Monitor**

Fig. 10.2

CGA display
connector
specifications.

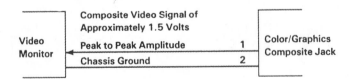

Video Monitor	Composite Video Signal of Approximately 1.5 Volts		Color/Graphics Composite Jack
	Peak to Peak Amplitude	1	
	Chassis Ground	2	

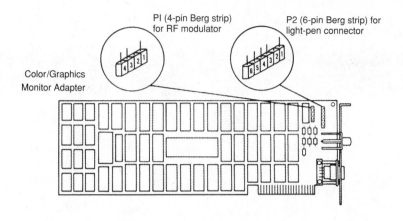

P1 (4-pin Berg strip) for RF modulator

P2 (6-pin Berg strip) for light-pen connector

Color/Graphics Monitor Adapter

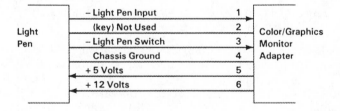

RF Modulator	+ 12 Volts	1	Color/Graphics Monitor Adapter
	(key) Not Used	2	
	Composite Video Output	3	
	Logic Ground	4	

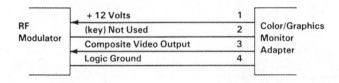

Light Pen	– Light Pen Input	1	Color/Graphics Monitor Adapter
	(key) Not Used	2	
	– Light Pen Switch	3	
	Chassis Ground	4	
	+ 5 Volts	5	
	+ 12 Volts	6	

Fig. 10.3

CGA RF modulator and light-pen connector specifications.

Enhanced Color Display and Adapter

The IBM Enhanced Graphics System, discontinued when the PS/2 systems were introduced, consisted of a graphics board, a graphics memory-expansion board, a graphics memory-module kit, and a high-resolution color monitor. The whole package originally cost about $1,800! The aftermarket gave IBM a great deal of competition in this area, and you could put together a similar system from non-IBM vendors for much less money.

Table 10.2 IBM Color Graphics Adapter (CGA) Specifications

Video standard	Resolution	Number of colors	Mode type	BIOS modes	Character format	Character box	Scan Frequency Vertical (Hz)	Horizontal (KHz)	Scan mode
CGA (08/12/81)	320 × 200	16	Text	00/01h	40 × 25	8 × 8	60	15.75	Std
	640 × 200	16	Text	02/03h	80 × 25	8 × 8	60	15.75	Std
	160 × 200	16	APA	—	—	—	60	15.75	Std
	320 × 200	4	APA	04/05h	40 × 25	8 × 8	60	15.75	Std
	640 × 200	2	APA	06h	80 × 25	8 × 8	60	15.75	Std

APA = All points addressable (graphics)
— = Not supported

One nice thing about the EGA was that you could build your system in modular steps. Because the card worked with any of the monitors IBM had at the time, you could use the card with the IBM Monochrome Display, the earlier IBM Color Display, or the new IBM Enhanced Color Display. With the EGA, the IBM color monitor displays 16 colors in 320 × 200 or 640 × 200 mode. With the EGA, the IBM monochrome monitor shows a resolution of 640 × 350 with a 9 × 14 character box (text mode). Figure 10.4 and figure 10.5 show you the pinouts and P-2 connector on the Enhanced Graphics Display Adapter.

With the EGA, the IBM Enhanced Color Display is capable of 640 × 350 with 16 colors. The character box for text is 8 × 14 compared to 8 × 8 for the earlier CGA board and monitor. The 8 × 8 character box can be used, however, to display 43 lines of text. Through software, the character box can be manipulated up to the size of 8 × 32. The 16 colors can be selected from a palette of 64.

You can enlarge a RAM-resident, 256-member character set to 512 characters by using the IBM memory expansion card. A 1,024 character set is added with the IBM graphics memory-module kit. These character sets are loaded from programs.

All this memory fits in the unused space between the end of RAM user memory and the current display adapter memory. The Enhanced Graphics Color Adapter has a maximum 128K of memory that maps into the RAM space just above the 640K boundary. If you install more than 640K, you probably will lose the extra memory after installing the EGA. The graphics memory-expansion card adds 64K to the standard 64K for a total of 128K. The IBM graphics memory-module kit adds another 128K, for a total of 256K. This second 128K of memory is only on the card and does not consume any of the PC's memory space. Note that because almost every aftermarket EGA card came configured with the full 256K of memory, expansion options were not necessary.

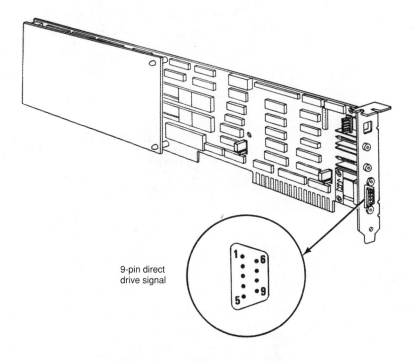

9-pin direct drive signal

	Signal Name - Description	Pin	
Direct Drive Display	Ground	1	**Enhanced Graphics Adapter**
	Secondary Red	2	
	Primary Red	3	
	Primary Green	4	
	Primary Blue	5	
	Secondary Green/Intensity	6	
	Secondary Blue/Mono Video	7	
	Horizontal Retrace	8	
	Vertical Retrace	9	

Fig. 10.4

EGA display connector specifications.

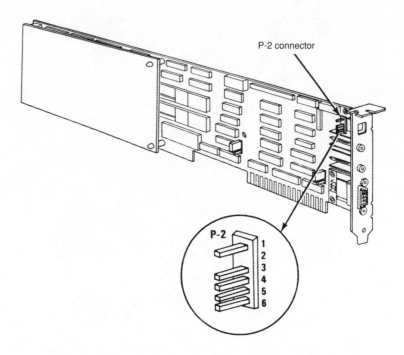

P-2 connector

P-2

	P-2 connector	Pin	
Light Pen Attachment	+Light Pen Input	1	Enhanced Graphics Adapter
	Not used	2	
	+Light Pen Switch	3	
	Ground	4	
	+5 Volts	5	
	12 Volts	6	

Fig. 10.5

EGA light-pen connector specifications.

The VGA system supersedes the EGA in many respects. The EGA had problems emulating the earlier CGA or MDA adapters, and some software that worked with the earlier cards would not run on the EGA until the programs were modified. Because the VGA system was installed in more than two million systems during its first year, a great deal of software support appeared in no time. It was more than two years after the EGA was introduced before a substantial amount of software support was available, however. Because the EGA graphics adapter is technically obsolete, I do not recommend further purchases of EGA display systems. Newer VGA systems have much more to offer and are even less expensive. Most manufacturers, including IBM, discontinued EGA products long ago. Table 10.3 shows the modes supported by the EGA adapter.

Table 10.3 IBM Enhanced Graphics Adapter (EGA) Specifications

Video standard	Resolution	Number of colors	Mode type	BIOS modes	Character format	Character box	Scan frequency Vertical (Hz)	Horizontal (KHz)	Scan mode
EGA (09/10/84)	320 × 350	16	Text	00/01h	40 × 25	8 × 14	60	21.85	Std
	640 × 350	16	Text	02/03h	80 × 25	8 × 14	60	21.85	Std
	720 × 350	4	Text	07h	80 × 25	9 × 14	50	18.432	Std
	320 × 200	16	APA	0Dh	40 × 25	8 × 8	60	15.75	Std
	640 × 200	16	APA	0Eh	80 × 25	8 × 8	60	15.75	Std
	640 × 350	4	APA	0Fh	80 × 25	8 × 14	50	18.432	Std
	640 × 350	16	APA	10h	80 × 25	8 × 14	60	21.85	Std

APA = All points addressable (graphics)

Professional Color Display and Adapter

The Professional Graphics Display System is a video display product that IBM introduced in 1984. At $4,290, the system was too expensive to become a mainstream product. The system is composed of a Professional Graphics Monitor and a Professional Graphics Card Set. When fully expanded, this card set uses three slots in an XT or AT system, which is a high price to pay, but the features are impressive. The PGA offers three-dimensional rotation and clipping as a built-in hardware function. The adapter can run 60 frames per second of animation because the Professional Graphics Adapter uses a built-in dedicated microcomputer. The PGA has an 8088 microprocessor, 320K of RAM, and 64K of ROM. The resolution of this system is 640 × 480 pixels. Note that the VGA system built into the PS/2 motherboards also has this resolution capability.

The expense and complexity of this system limit the system to supporting specialized applications only. The PGA system was designed for applications such as computer-aided design (CAD). The capabilities of an AT with this board and monitor set combined with software such as AutoCAD resulted in a system with the power and functionality of CAD systems that cost up to $50,000 or more at the time. The Professional Graphics card and monitor were targeted toward the engineering and scientific areas rather than financial or business applications. This system was discontinued when the PS/2 was introduced and has been replaced by the VGA and other higher-resolution graphics standards for these newer systems. Table 10.4 shows all supported PGA modes.

Table 10.4 IBM Professional Graphics Adapter (PGA) Specifications

Video standard	Resolution	Number of colors	Mode type	BIOS modes	Character format	Character box	Scan Frequency Vertical (Hz)	Scan Frequency Horizontal (KHz)	Scan mode
PGA (09/10/84)	320 × 200	16	Text	00/01	40 × 25	8 × 8	60	15.75	Std
	640 × 200	16	Text	02/03	80 × 25	8 × 8	60	15.75	Std
	320 × 200	4	APA	04/05	40 × 25	8 × 8	60	15.75	Std
	640 × 200	2	APA	06	80 × 25	8 × 8	60	15.75	Std
	640 × 480	256	APA	—	—	—	60	30.48	Std

APA = All points addressable (graphics)
— = Not supported

VGA Displays and Adapters

When IBM introduced the PS/2 systems on April 2, 1987, they also introduced the Video Graphics Array display standard. On that day, in fact, IBM also introduced the lower-resolution Multi-Color Graphics Array (MCGA) and higher-resolution 8514 adapters. The MCGA and 8514 adapters did not become de facto standards like the VGA, and both were discontinued. The VGA has become the mainstream video standard for PCs, and the newer XGA has become the higher-resolution standard.

Digital versus Analog

Unlike earlier video standards that were digital, the VGA video is an analog system. Why are the displays going from digital to analog, when most other electronic systems are going digital? Compact disc players (digital) have replaced many turntables (analog), while newer VCRs and camcorders have digital picture storage for smooth slow motion and freeze-frame capability. With digital televisions, you can watch several channels on a single screen by splitting the screen or placing a picture within another picture. The PBX systems in most companies are digital, and the entire telephone network is going digital. With everything else going digital, why did IBM decide to change the video to analog? The answer is color.

Most personal computer displays introduced before the PS/2 were digital. This type of display generates different colors by firing the red, green, and blue (RGB) electron beams in an on or off mode. You can display up to 8 colors (2 to the third power). In the IBM displays and adapters, another signal—intensity—doubles the number of color combinations from 8 to 16 by displaying each color at one of two intensity levels. This digital display is easy to manufacture and offers simplicity with consistent color combinations from system to system. The real drawback of the digital display system is the limited number of possible colors.

In the PS/2 systems, IBM went to an analog display circuit. Analog displays work like the digital displays that use the RGB electron beams to construct various colors, but each color in the analog display system can be displayed at varying levels of intensity, 64 levels in the case of the VGA. This versatility provides 262,144 possible colors (64 to the third power). To make realistic computer graphics, color is often more important than high resolution, because the human eye perceives a picture with more colors as more realistic. IBM moved graphics into an analog form to enhance the color capabilities.

Multi-Color Graphics Array

The Multi-Color Graphics Array (MCGA) is a graphics adapter that has been integrated into the motherboard of the Models 25 and 30. The MCGA supports all Color Graphics Adapter (CGA) modes when an IBM analog display is attached, but any previous IBM display is not compatible. In addition to providing existing CGA mode support, the MCGA includes four additional modes.

The MCGA uses as many as 64 shades of gray in converting color modes for display on monochrome displays so that those who prefer a monochrome display still can execute color-based applications.

The technical specifications of the MCGA are as follows:

- CGA compatible (31.5 KHz double-scanned)
- Not compatible with digital monitors
- 64K multiport RAM for displays
- Palette of 262,144 colors

■ Analog drive, subminiature 15-pin, D-shell connector

■ 70 Hz refresh rate in all but 640 × 480 mode

■ Loadable character font capability (512 characters)

■ Color summing to 64 gray shades in BIOS for monochrome display

Table 10.5 lists the MCGA display modes.

Table 10.5 IBM Multi-Color Graphics Array (MCGA) Specifications

Video standard	Resolution	Number of colors	Mode type	BIOS modes	Character format	Character box	Scan Frequency Vertical (Hz)	Scan Frequency Horizontal (KHz)	Scan mode
MCGA (04/02/87)	320 × 400	16	Text	00/01h	40 × 25	8 × 16	70	31.5	Std
	640 × 400	16	Text	02/03h	80 × 25	8 × 16	70	31.5	Std
	320 × 200	4	APA	04/05h	40 × 25	8 × 8	70	31.5	Dbl
	640 × 200	2	APA	06h	80 × 25	8 × 8	70	31.5	Dbl
	640 × 480	2	APA	11h	80 × 30	8 × 16	60	31.5	Std
	320 × 200	256	APA	13h	40 × 25	8 × 8	70	31.5	Dbl

APA = All points addressable (graphics)
DBL = Double scan

Systems with this display circuitry are all but discontinued by IBM, and no one ever developed an MCGA display adapter. VGA offers much more at little extra cost.

Video Graphics Array

PS/2 systems contain the primary display adapter circuits on the motherboard. The circuits are called the Video Graphics Array and are implemented by a single custom VLSI chip designed and manufactured by IBM. To adapt this new graphics standard to the earlier systems, IBM introduced the PS/2 Display Adapter. Also called a VGA card, this adapter contains the complete VGA circuit on a full-length adapter board with an 8-bit interface, giving earlier systems and compatibles the capability to have VGA graphics. IBM has since discontinued its VGA card, but many third-party units are available. Figures 10.6 and 10.7 show the video connectors and video pinouts.

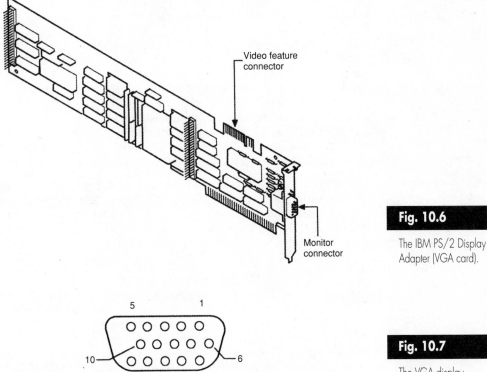

Video feature
connector

Monitor
connector

Fig. 10.6

The IBM PS/2 Display
Adapter (VGA card).

5   1

10   6

15   11

Fig. 10.7

The VGA display
connector.

The VGA BIOS (basic input-output system) is the control software
residing in the system ROM for controlling VGA circuits. With the BIOS,
software can initiate commands and functions without having to man-
ipulate the VGA directly. Programs become somewhat hardware-
independent and can call a consistent set of commands and functions
built into the system's ROM control software. Future implementations
of the VGA will be different in hardware but will respond to the same
BIOS calls and functions. New features will be added as a superset of the
existing functions. The VGA, therefore, will be compatible with the earlier graphics and text BIOS functions that were built into the PC systems
from the beginning. The VGA can run almost any software that was written originally for the MDA, CGA, or EGA.

In a perfect world, software programmers would write to the BIOS interface rather than directly to the hardware, and promote software inter-
changes between different types of hardware. More frequently, however,
the programmer wants the software to perform better and writes the
program to control the hardware directly. The programmer achieves a

higher-performance application dependent on the hardware to which it is first written. You have to make sure that your hardware is 100 percent compatible with the standard so that software written to a standard piece of hardware runs on your system. Note that just because a manufacturer claims this register level of compatibility does not mean that the product is 100 percent compatible or that all software runs as it would on a true IBM VGA. Most manufacturers have "cloned" the VGA system at the register level, which means that even applications which write directly to the video registers will function correctly. Also, the VGA circuits themselves emulate the older adapters even to the register level, and have an amazing level of compatibility with these earlier standards. This makes the VGA a truly universal standard.

The VGA displays up to 256 colors on-screen, from a palette of 262,144 (256K) colors. Because the VGA outputs an analog signal, you must have a monitor that accepts an analog input. The 200-line modes produced by the new MCGA and VGA are double-scanned; each of the lines is repeated twice before a new set is scanned. The 200-line modes, therefore, really consist of 400 lines, but the lines can be controlled only in pairs.

Color summing to 64 gray shades is done in the ROM BIOS for monochrome displays. The summing routine is initiated if the BIOS detects the monochrome display when the system is booted. This routine uses a formula that takes the desired color and rewrites the formula to involve all three color guns, producing varying intensities of gray. The color that would be displayed, for example, is converted into 30 percent red plus 59 percent green plus 11 percent blue to achieve the desired gray. Users who prefer a monochrome display, therefore, can execute color-based applications. Table 10.6 lists the VGA display modes.

8514 Display Adapter

The PS/2 Display Adapter 8514/A offered higher resolution and more colors than the standard VGA. This adapter is designed to use the PS/2 Color Display 8514 and plugs into a Micro Channel slot in any PS/2 model so equipped. All operation modes of the built-in VGA continue to be available. An IBM Personal System/2 8514 memory-expansion kit is available for the IBM Display Adapter 8514/A. This kit gives increased color and gray-scale support.

The IBM Display Adapter 8514/A has these advantages:

- Hardware assistance for advanced text, image, and graphics functions

- New high-content display modes

■ Increased color and monochrome capability

■ Support for the new family of IBM displays

■ MDA, CGA, EGA, and VGA modes available

■ 256/256K colors and 64/64 gray scales with memory-expansion kit

To take full advantage of this adapter, the 8514 display should be used because it is matched to the capabilities of the adapter. Note that IBM has discontinued the 8514/A adapter and specifies the XGA in its place. The 8514 display continues to be sold because it works well with the newer XGA. Table 10.7 shows all 8514 modes.

Table 10.6 IBM Video Graphics Array (VGA) Specifications

Video standard	Resolution	Number of colors	Mode type	BIOS modes	Character format	Character box	Scan Frequency Vertical (Hz)	Horizontal (KHz)	Scan mode
VGA (04/02/87)	360 × 400	16	Text	00/01h	40 × 25	9 × 16	70	31.5	Std
	720 × 400	16	Text	02/03h	80 × 25	9 × 16	70	31.5	Std
	320 × 200	4	APA	04/05h	40 × 25	8 × 8	70	31.5	Dbl
	640 × 200	2	APA	06h	80 × 25	8 × 8	70	31.5	Dbl
	720 × 400	16	Text	07h	80 × 25	9 × 16	70	31.5	Std
	320 × 200	16	APA	0Dh	40 × 25	8 × 8	70	31.5	Dbl
	640 × 200	16	APA	0Eh	80 × 25	8 × 8	70	31.5	Dbl
	640 × 350	4	APA	0Fh	80 × 25	8 × 14	70	31.5	Std
	640 × 350	16	APA	10h	80 × 25	8 × 14	70	31.5	Std
	640 × 480	2	APA	11h	80 × 30	8 × 16	60	31.5	Std
	640 × 480	16	APA	12h	80 × 30	8 × 16	60	31.5	Std
	320 × 200	256	APA	13h	40 × 25	8 × 8	70	31.5	Dbl

APA = All points addressable (graphics)
Del = Double scan

Note Although the 8514 does not support any VGA modes, it does have a VGA pass-through via the auxiliary video-extension connector (AVEC) slot in a PS/2 system. A system with the 8514 installed will still function in all VGA modes via the original VGA circuitry passing signals through the 8514 adapter. Compatibility with VGA software is ensured in this manner.

Table 10.7 IBM 8514 Specifications

Video standard	Resolution	Number of colors	Mode type	BIOS modes	Character format	Character box	Scan Frequency Vertical (Hz)	Scan Frequency Horizontal (KHz)	Scan mode
8514 (04/02/87)	1024 × 768	256	APA	H-0h	85 × 38	12 × 20	43.48	35.52	Il
	640 × 480	256	APA	H-1h	80 × 34	8 × 14	60	31.5	Std
	1024 × 768	256	APA	H-3h	146 × 51	7 × 15	43.48	35.52	Il

APA = All points addressable (graphics)
Il = Interlaced

XGA

IBM announced the PS/2 XGA Display Adapter/A on October 30, 1990, along with the Model 90 and Model 95. The PS/2 XGA Display Adapter/A is a high-performance 32-bit bus master adapter for Micro Channel-based systems. This video subsystem evolves from the VGA and provides greater resolution, more colors, and much better performance.

The original VGA combined all the functions of the earlier standard adapters (MDA, CGA, and EGA), along with new graphics resolutions ranging up to 640 × 480 pixels with 16 colors. At the same time, the 8514 Display Adapter/A was introduced to meet requirements for high-resolution 1024 × 768 (with 256 colors) graphics. The next logical step for video on PS/2 systems would be to combine the capabilities of both VGA and high-resolution graphics. The XGA was developed in the United Kingdom at IBM's Hursley Labs, as was the 8514/A adapter. Not surprisingly, the XGA maintains many of the 8514/A's features.

Combine a fast VGA, a graphics coprocessor, and bus mastering, and you have XGA. Being a bus master adapter means that the XGA can take control of the system as though it were the motherboard. In essence, a bus master is an adapter with its own processor that can execute operations independent of the motherboard. The XGA was introduced as the default graphics display platform with the Model 90 XP 486 and the Model 95 XP 486. In the desktop Model 90, the XGA is on the motherboard; in the Model 95 (a tower unit), it is located on a separate Micro Channel Architecture add-in board. This board, the XGA Display Adapter/A, is also available for other 386- and 486-based Micro Channel systems. Originally, I thought that IBM would make the 8514/A graphics system the next standard on PS/2 motherboards, but the XGA does everything the 8514/A could, and more.

The XGA adapter can be installed in any Micro Channel Architecture (MCA) systems that have 80386, 80386SX, or 80486 processors. These include systems such as the PS/2 models 55, 57, 65, 70, and 80.

The XGA comes standard with 512K of graphics memory, which can be upgraded to 1M with an optional video-memory expansion.

This list shows highlights of the XGA adapter features:

- 1024 × 768 with 256 colors (16 colors with standard memory)
- 40 × 480 with 256 colors
- DOS XGA adapter interface provides 8514/A compatibility
- Integrates a 16-bit compatible VGA
- Optimized for windowing operating systems
- Includes device drivers for DOS, OS/2, and Windows

The following software is delivered with the adapter:

- DOS XGA adapter interface with fonts
- Microsoft Windows/286 driver
- Microsoft Windows version 3 driver
- Fonts for Microsoft Windows
- IBM PS/2 mouse driver
- OS/2 driver
- Anti-aliased fonts for OS/2 Presentation Manager
- AutoCAD and AutoCAD/386 drivers

In addition to all VGA modes, the XGA offers several new modes of operation, shown in table 10.8.

Table 10.8 XGA Unique Modes of Operation

Maximum resolution	Maximum colors	Required VRAM
1024 × 768	256 colors	1M
1024 × 768	16 colors	512K
640 × 480	65536 colors	1M
1024 × 768	64 gray shades	1M
1024 × 768	16 gray shades	512K
640 × 480	64 gray shades	512K

The 65,536 color mode provides almost photographic output. The 16-bit pixel is laid out as 5 bits of red, 6 bits of green, and 5 bits of blue (5-6-5), or in other words, 32 shades of blue, 64 shades of green, and 32 shades of blue. (The eye notices more variations in green than in red or blue.) One major drawback of the current XGA implementation is the interlacing that occurs in the higher-resolution modes. With interlacing, you can use a less expensive monitor, but the display updates more slowly, resulting in a slight flicker.

Some added features, such as bus mastering, are designed to take advantage of the Micro Channel Architecture (MCA) bus, standard in the PS/2 Model 50 and higher. IBM has released full register specifications for the XGA, unlike the way it handled the 8514/A. In fact, at least one company is working with IBM to bring XGA chipsets to board and system manufacturers.

The XGA supports all existing VGA and 8514/A video modes. A large number of popular applications have been developed to support the 8514/A high-resolution 1024 × 768 mode. These applications are written to the 8514/A Adapter interface, a software interface between the application and the 8514/A hardware. The XGA's extended graphics function maintains compatibility at the same level. Because of the power on the XGA adapter, current VGA or 8514/A applications run much faster on the XGA.

The XGA has a much wider data path than the original 8-bit VGA systems. The new data path is a full 16 or 32 bits wide, depending on the system in which it is installed. Because of this, and because the XGA is a bus master (meaning that it has its own processor), it is as much as 90 percent faster than the VGA.

Much of the XGA's speed can be attributed also to its video RAM (VRAM), a type of dual-ported RAM designed for graphics-display systems. This memory can be accessed by both the processor on the XGA adapter as well as the system CPU simultaneously, allowing almost instant data transfer. The XGA VRAM is mapped into the system's address space. The VRAM normally is located in the top addresses of the 386's 4-gigabyte address space. Because no other cards normally use this area, conflicts should be rare. The XGA adapter also has an 8K ROM BIOS extension that must be mapped somewhere in segments C000 or D000. Note that the motherboard implementation of the XGA does not require its own ROM because the motherboard BIOS contains all the necessary code.

Until now, all PS/2 system units have had VGA video integrated on the system board. The system board VGA drives video data out to the Micro Channel auxiliary video extension connector (AVEC). This enables display adapters plugged into the AVEC slot to display this VGA data on the monitor connected to the adapter.

On the Model 90 XP 486, the XGA video subsystem is resident on the system board. The XGA maintains the same AVEC support as VGA did in the past. The PS/2 Model 95 XP 486 has no video adapter on the system board. Instead, video is generated by the XGA Display Adapter/A resident in a newly designed base video extension connector (BVEC) Micro Channel slot. This BVEC functions like the AVEC slot, although the signals are different. The new BVEC slot is wired to a standard AVEC slot, allowing other adapters to receive the VGA data as before.

The XGA is designed to fit into a 32-bit system, which means that it will work only in 386 or 486 systems. Many registers on the adapter are 32-bit, and the BIOS and other driver software were written using 386 instructions. Although a 386 or better is required, the adapter works in a 16-bit MCA slot, although somewhat slower. Therefore, the adapter can even be used in 386SX systems, such as the Models 55, 57, and 65.

IBM is providing full register-level documentation for the XGA. To ensure that XGA will become a de facto standard, IBM is licensing technology for other companies to produce XGA chipsets so that XGA-compatible adapters can be easily constructed by third-party companies. These companies will provide XGA adapters for standard ISA as well as EISA slot-based systems.

The XGA supports the 14-inch 8516 Color Display with its high-resolution 1024 × 768 capability, as well as the 16-inch IBM PS/2 Color Display 8514. In addition, other PS/2 monochrome and color displays including 8503, 8507, 8512, 8513, and 8604 can be used, depending on resolution and application requirements. Table 10.9 lists the supported displays.

Table 10.9 XGA-Supported Displays

Display	Description	Maximum resolution	Maximum colors
8503	12-inch mono	640 × 480	64 gray shades
8507	19-inch mono	1024 × 768	64 gray shades
8604	15-inch mono	1024 × 768	64 gray shades
8512	14-inch color	640 × 480	65536 colors
8513	12-inch color	640 × 480	65536 colors
8514	16-inch color	1024 × 768	256 colors
8515	14-inch color	1024 × 768	256 colors

Note Some of the lower-resolution displays limit the resolution and color capability of the XGA. The XGA adapter uses the monitor ID pins of the connector to determine which display is connected. The mode capabilities of the XGA card are determined by which of these pins are grounded to the Sync Return pin.

The following table shows how some IBM displays ID themselves to the graphics adapter.

Monitor type	Bit 2	Bit 1	Bit 0
IBM 8503	—	GND	—
IBM 8512	—	—	GND
IBM 8513	—	—	GND
IBM 8514	GND	—	GND

In the 15-pin VGA or XGA connector, ID Bits 0, 1, and 2 are found at pins 11, 12, and 4, respectively, and the Sync Return (Ground) is found at Pin 10. Before you purchase a third-party display for the XGA, be sure to determine whether the display IDs itself correctly. A display with an incorrect ID can yield improperly sized images, or an inability to activate particular modes, especially higher-resolution ones. Table 10.10 summarizes all the XGA modes.

IBM Analog Monitors

When IBM introduced the analog VGA, it had to introduce new monitors that were compatible with the new graphics standard. The following monitors have been introduced:

PS/2 Monochrome Display 8503

PS/2 Monochrome Display 8504

PS/2 Color Display 8512

PS/2 Color Display 8513

PS/2 Color Display 8514

PS/2 Color Display 8515

You can use the IBM PS/2 Monochrome Display 8503 with any of the newer IBM PS/2 system units or display adapters. The monochrome display, the least expensive IBM display for the Personal System/2, is the natural choice for users who don't need color. Different shades of gray are used for graphics. In text applications, the monochrome display produces sharper characters than color displays because of the high resolution. Monochrome displays are also ideal for a network file server system because of the occasional monitoring of server activity and performance. The 8503 display is the least expensive display available.

Table 10.10 IBM eXtended Graphics Array (XGA) Specifications

Video standard	Resolution	Number of colors	Mode type	BIOS modes	Character format	Character box	Scan Frequency Vertical (Hz)	Horizontal (KHz)	Scan mode
XGA (10/30/90)	360×400	16	Text	00/01h	40×25	9×16	70	31.5	Std
	720×400	16	Text	02/03h	80×25	9×16	70	31.5	Std
	320×200	4	APA	04/05h	40×25	8×8	70	31.5	Dbl
	640×200	2	APA	06h	80×25	8×8	70	31.5	Dbl
	720×400	16	Text	07h	80×25	9×16	70	31.5	Std
	320×200	16	APA	0Dh	40×25	8×8	70	31.5	Dbl
	640×200	16	APA	0Eh	80×25	8×8	70	31.5	Dbl
	640×350	4	APA	0Fh	80×25	8×14	70	31.5	Std
	640×350	16	APA	10h	80×25	8×14	70	31.5	Std
	640×480	2	APA	11h	80×30	8×16	60	31.5	Std
	640×480	16	APA	12h	80×30	8×16	60	31.5	Std
	320×200	256	APA	13h	40×25	8×8	70	31.5	Dbl
	1056×400	16	Text	14h	132×25	8×16	70	31.5	Std
	1056×400	16	Text	14h	132×43	8×9	70	31.5	Std
	1056×400	16	Text	14h	132×56	8×8	70	31.5	Std
	1056×400	16	Text	14h	132×60	8×6	70	31.5	Std
	1024×768	256	APA	H-0h	85×38	12×20	43.48	35.52	Il
	640×480	65536	APA	H-1h	80×34	8×14	60	31.5	Std
	1024×768	256	APA	H-2h	128×54	8×14	43.48	35.52	Il
	1024×768	256	APA	H-3h	146×51	7×15	43.48	35.52	Il

APA = All points addressable (graphics)
Dbl = Double scan
Il = Interlaced

Announced on June 11, 1991, the PS/2 8504 is a 12-inch analog display that replaces the 8503. It uses a Flatter Squarer Tube (FST) for reduced distortion as compared to earlier displays. The PS/2 8504 also incorporates a low-emissions circuit design, front controls, 300-degree swivel with tilt, and a smaller footprint than earlier displays. This monitor is suitable for systems in which cost matters and color is not required. Like many newer displays, the PS/2 8504 Monochrome Display is engineered to meet the recommendations for lower field emissions (VLMF).

The IBM Color Display 8512, a VGA-resolution 14-inch display, takes maximum advantage of the capabilities of the VGA or MCGA at a low cost. This display has a 0.41mm dot pitch, which is coarse compared to other displays, but it was designed to keep costs low.

The IBM Color Display 8513 is better for the VGA environment than the 8512 and is IBM's most widely sold display for VGA systems. The 8513 is a 12-inch color display and includes a tilt-swivel stand. Its visual characteristics surpass the 8512's in clarity and sharpness, primarily because of the 0.28mm dot pitch.

The IBM PS/2 Color Display 8514 is a 16-inch color display with a 1,024 × 768 pixel resolution capability. An XGA or 8514/A is required in order to exploit the 8514 display's full capabilities; however, it also works well with any standard VGA. The 8514 is intended for applications that require advanced functions, high resolution, and high performance. The larger screen size and the capability to display 146 columns and 51 rows offer additional advantages for applications such as spreadsheets and word processing.

The PS/2 Color Display 8515 was announced on March 20, 1990, and is an analog color display with a 14-inch screen that has a data area of 9.8 × 7.4 inches. It supports all XGA modes and has a maximum of 1024 × 768 pixel addressability. This display has a 0.28mm phosphor dot pitch and a display area 42 percent larger than the 8513. It is ideal for any VGA or XGA because it supports up to 1024 × 768 pixel resolution required for some XGA modes. The 8515 has a Very Low Magnetic Field (VLMF), meeting the extremely tough Scandinavian field-emission requirements. A tilt/swivel base is standard.

Troubleshooting and Servicing

Servicing most graphics adapters and monitors is fairly simple, although costly, because replacement of the adapter or display is the usual procedure. A defective or dysfunctional adapter or display is usually replaced as a single unit rather than repaired. Most of today's cards cost more to service than to replace, and the documentation required to service the adapters or displays properly is not always available. You cannot get schematic diagrams, parts lists, wiring diagrams, and so on, for most of the adapters or monitors. Many adapters now are constructed with surface-mount technology that requires a substantial investment in a rework station before you can remove and replace these components by hand. You cannot use a $25 pencil-type soldering iron on these boards!

Servicing displays is slightly different. Although a display often is replaced as a whole unit, many displays are too expensive to simply replace. Your best bet is to contact the company from whom the display was purchased. If your NEC Multisync display goes out, for example, a swap with another monitor can confirm that the display is the problem. After you narrow down the problem to the display, call NEC for the location of the nearest factory repair depot. Third-party service companies can repair most displays, and their prices are often much lower than "factory" service.

You usually cannot repair displays yourself. First, opening the case of a color display exposes you to as much as 35,000 volts of electricity. If you don't follow recommended safety precautions, you easily can electrocute yourself. Second, the required documentation is not always available. Without schematic diagrams, board layouts, parts lists, or other documentation, even an experienced service technician may not be able to properly diagnose and repair the display.

WARNING: You probably should not try to repair displays yourself. Touching the wrong item can be fatal. The display circuits can sometimes hold extremely high voltages for hours, days, or even weeks after the power is shut off. A qualified service person should discharge the tube and power capacitors before proceeding.

For most displays, you are limited to making simple adjustments, and for color displays, the adjustments can be quite formidable if you lack experience. Even factory service technicians often lack proper documentation and service information for newer models. They usually exchange your unit for another and repair the defective one later. Never buy a display that does not have a local factory repair depot.

If you have a problem with a display or adapter, it pays to call the manufacturer because it may have a known problem where a repair has been made available—as occurred with the IBM 8513 display. Large numbers of the IBM 8513 color displays were manufactured with components whose values change over time and may exhibit text or graphics out of focus. This problem haunted my IBM 8513. Opening up the monitor and adjusting the focus helped for a while, but the display became fuzzy again. I discovered that IBM replaces these displays at no cost when focusing is a problem. If you have a fuzzy 8513 display, you should contact IBM to see whether your display qualifies for a free replacement.

You can call IBM (800-IBM-SERV) or an IBM authorized dealer for assistance. This particular problem is covered under Engineering Change Announcement (ECA) 017.

Memory Boards

In discussing memory and memory adapter boards, you should consider the following three types of memory:

- Conventional memory
- Extended memory
- Expanded memory

Memory differs in several ways, from where the memory is located to what processors can address what types of memory. Figure 10.8 shows the relative "locations" of the different types of memory in relation to the system logical memory map.

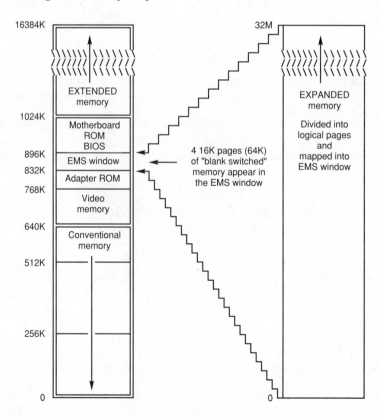

The relationship between conventional, extended, and expanded memory.

This map was constructed with an 80286-based system as a model. The 386 and 486 system map is basically the same, but the total amount of extended and conventional memory adds as much as 4 gigabytes. The 286 processor has a total of 16M of memory, including conventional and extended memories. These 16M provide all the memory addressable by the processor. Expanded memory lies completely out of the processor-addressable portion, except for the 64K window through which expanded memory is accessed. Expanded memory cannot be used for running applications programs, which explains why expanded memory is slower than conventional and extended memory.

Any system using an 8088 or 8086 processor, such as the original PC and XT or PS/2 Models 25 and 30, controls memory access through a 20-bit-wide address bus. An *address bus* is the numbering scheme used to uniquely identify all locations in random-access memory (RAM). The address bus width has an effect on how much RAM a system can address. With the 20-digit binary number used for addressing, these systems generate a total of 1M of memory locations. Any system using an 80286 processor, such as the XT-286, AT, and PS/2 Models 30-286, 50, and 60, uses a memory addressing system with 24 lines or digits. With this addressing system, a maximum of 16M of RAM is available. Any 386- or 486-based system, such as the PS/2 Models 35, 40, L40, 55, 57, 65, 70, P75, 80, 90, and 95, uses a 32-bit memory addressing system that allows for a total of 4 gigabytes of RAM. This amount of processor-addressable memory equals the IBM 3090 Model 600 Sierra mainframe system that costs $10 million—not bad for a system that sits on or beside a desk. The memory-addressing capabilities of the various processors in native (protected) modes are listed in table 10.11.

Table 10.11 Intel Processor Addressing			
		Processors	
	8088/8086	286/386SX 386SL, 386SLC	386DX 486/487SX 486DX, 586
Address bus size (bits)	20	24	32
Bytes	1,048,576	16,777,216	4,294,967,296
Kilobytes (1024 bytes)	1,024	16,384	4,194,304
Megabytes (1024 kilobytes)	1	16	4,096
Gigabytes (1024 megabytes)	—	—	4

These figures reflect only what is technically possible, not what is practical or immediately available. For example, because the Model 90 has eight 36-bit SIMM sockets, you could expand that system to 64M using 8M SIMMs. Any further memory would have to come from a card in a slot. Most systems are not nearly as gifted with memory-expansion capabilities as this, however, and the maximum you can fit in your system depends on many factors.

To put the memory-addressing capabilities of the 386 and 486 into perspective, 4 gigabytes of memory (4,096M) at a below market cost of $50 per megabyte for fast (70 nanoseconds or less) memory still would cost more than $200,000.

Microprocessor Operating Modes

When Intel designed the 80286 and 80386 microprocessors, the company wanted to add new features and retain compatibility with the large base of software that existed for the 8086 and 8088. Intel incorporated an 8086/8088 mode within the newer 286 and 386 processors. This combination is called *real mode*, or 8086/8088 compatibility mode. When the newer processors are in real mode, the emulation of the earlier 8086 is complete, including any limitations that apply to the earlier chip.

Protected mode is the native mode of the 286, 386, and 486. Protected mode enables these chips to perform as designed, with access to full memory-addressing capabilities, but is incompatible with software written for real mode. To run software written for real mode in protected mode entails rewriting the software. OS/2 can run DOS-based software by temporarily switching the processor to real mode. When this switch is in effect, all processing (multitasking) under OS/2 is suspended until protected mode is reactivated.

When Intel designed the 286, the company included a method of instructing the chip to go from real mode to protected mode. It did not, however, include a method for getting the chip back into real mode because the whole idea of protection is to prevent rampant software from crashing the system. Now Windows and OS/2 require the processor to switch often from protected to real mode. Switching rapidly between real and protected mode is how the compatibility box in OS/2 can run DOS and DOS applications software. Windows also runs the processor in protected mode. By switching the processor back into real mode, you can run a DOS application in an environment devoid of protection. The only documented way to switch from protected to real mode is to reset the chip by placing a high signal on the processor's reset pin.

When the chip is reset, the system reinitiates the boot process. Rebooting normally performs a power-on test of all memory and loads DOS from the first found disk drive. Rebooting wipes out anything running under OS/2 as if the operator used the Ctrl-Alt-Del combination. Before performing the reset, OS/2 places a special flag value in the CMOS battery backed-up memory present in every AT. This value is checked at boot time to see whether you are performing a real boot or a switch from protected mode. If a switch is indicated, normal booting procedures are skipped and the system is sent to a start-up code location.

While this reset operation is in progress, the system does not listen to hardware interrupts. Information coming in over a network adapter, communications port, keyboard, or other interrupt-driven device is lost. This operation resembles having to turn off the engine to shift your car from third to fourth gear. When the engine is off, you have no power steering or brakes, so you hope that no sudden curves are ahead.

The compatibility box enables DOS programs to run under OS/2. The compatibility box should not be used while communications programs are operating, including network software. You also should not use the compatibility box while the system is performing a real-time operation such as monitoring a laboratory instrument with a data acquisition adapter.

The 386 or greater processors have an instruction to switch modes. Using this instruction, these processors can switch modes much faster than the 286.

Virtual 8086 mode is unique to the 386 and higher chips and enables the user to run several protected real mode sessions as one or more subtasks. This mode emulates an entire 8086 system within the 80386 chip. Multiple DOS programs can run as though they were running on a single-processor DOS system. Each virtual machine requires 1M of space for the simulation. Only Windows and OS/2 support this kind of arrangement. Eventually, a 386 version of OS/2 that runs multiple DOS sessions in a multitasking environment may be developed.

Conventional Memory

Conventional memory exists between 0 kilobytes and 1M (with 384K reserved and 640K usable) on any IBM or compatible system. Conventional memory is used by 8088, 8086, 80286, or 80386 in real mode. An operating system cannot use the full megabyte of conventional memory because the hardware uses 384K (for video RAM, adapter ROM and RAM, and the motherboard ROM BIOS), leaving 640K of conventional memory for use.

The maximum addressable memory for the IBM PC is 1M, not 640K. Addressable memory is all the memory that the processor can address regardless of function. Usable memory is the subset of addressable memory that operating systems and user programs occupy. When IBM introduced the PC in 1981, the company indicated that the unit could have only 256K because that was all the memory you could access with IBM memory boards installed. By 1983, IBM indicated that the maximum amount of usable memory could be 640K.

Addressing any memory above 640K is a problem because 384K is reserved for system operations. How much memory DOS has access to depends on how your system uses that reserved space and how the memory adapters are installed. You face the following limitations with DOS:

- DOS cannot address memory beyond 1,024K because DOS runs in real mode with a maximum of only 1,024K of addressable memory.

- DOS manages its own code and program code in contiguous memory, starting with the first byte in the system at address 00000h. The first obstruction (such as the video RAM) is the cap that prevents further memory from being managed. A program running under DOS, however, can store data in any addressable memory, including memory beyond the DOS range.

Because of these limitations, DOS handles programs that fit in the 1M workspace, minus any reserved memory after the video RAM. Table 10.12 shows the maximum usable DOS memory available in systems equipped with different video adapters.

Table 10.12 Maximum Usable DOS Memory

DOS memory	Video adapter
736K	Color Graphics Adapter (CGA)
704K	Monochrome Display Adapter (MDA)
640K	Enhanced Graphics Adapter (EGA)
640K	Video Graphics Array (VGA)
640K	eXtended Graphics Array (XGA)

The 8086/8088 addresses 1M of memory. From this memory, BIOS, the adapter board, and video memory are subtracted, leaving from 640K to 736K free for DOS and DOS-based applications. If you have a CGA or MDA video board and want to use this extra memory, you have to find a card that supports 640K as a starting address. One card that comes to mind is the discontinued Hicard. Other cards may support 640K as a starting address, but you probably can get only 704K—not 736K— because most memory boards use designs that allow expansion in 64K increments. I do not know of any board (except Hicard) that allows the system to fill the remaining 32K without overlaying the CGA video memory.

Extended Memory

For even more memory expansion, you can install the more advanced 80286 and 80386 that support 16M and 4 gigabytes, respectively. The portion of memory beyond the first megabyte is called *extended memory*.

Extended memory is important for operating systems such as OS/2 that run in the protected mode of the 286, 386, and higher-level processors. This operating system takes full advantage of up to 16M of memory.

Real-mode operation, which is required for DOS, does not support access to extended memory. If users need to transfer data to and from extended memory, they must switch the system from real to protected mode. Hardships encountered in using extended memory led to the development of expanded memory.

Expanded Memory

Expanded memory is not in the processors' direct address space. You can access expanded memory by *bank switching* (memory paging), a technique that provides small windows of memory (physical pages) through which blocks of expanded memory are traded with your base memory. A program places data elements in expanded memory as a type of cold storage until the data is needed. One problem with this method is that the program must keep track of every piece of data placed in expanded memory. When the program requires data that has been placed in expanded memory, the program must consult its own internal database to recall the correct memory page.

The Expanded Memory Specification (EMS), created by Lotus, Intel, and Microsoft, describes a method in which four contiguous physical pages of 16K each (forming a block of 64K) can access up to 32M of expanded memory space through the Expanded Memory Manager (EMM). The page frame is located above 640K. Only video adapters, network cards, and similar devices are normally addressed between 640K and 1,024K.

When large programs seemed to be running out of memory in the 640K workspace, several manufacturers sought ways to make more memory available. Lotus Development Corporation first designed expanded memory because most 1-2-3 users eventually ran out of memory in developing huge spreadsheets. (The Lotus program keeps all active data in memory.) Lotus, Intel, and Microsoft collaborated to devise the LIM Expanded Memory Standard (EMS).

Problems with LIM EMS are caused by several things. First, because expanded memory is not actual memory to the processor, nothing important can be placed there. Second, the memory window sits above the video RAM area, where DOS cannot manage programs and where storing program code is forbidden. Third, Lotus could not place spreadsheet numeric values in expanded memory because every time the user pressed the Recalc button, every value had to be recalled from the EMS. This process slows down the program, harming Lotus's reputation for fast recalculation times. Data stored in EMS memory is limited to items such as labels.

Because of the program's need to keep a database of what was placed in expanded memory, you still can run out of conventional memory long before the expanded memory is even half gone. Using all of the expanded memory is impossible.

The AST Enhanced Expanded Memory Standard (EEMS) and the IBM Expanded Memory Adapter (XMA) are two subtypes of expanded memory on the market. These different implementations are not fully compatible with each other.

The new version of the LIM EMS, Version 4.0, combines the features of all three standards—EEMS, XMA, and the original LIM EMS—into a newer unified standard. Not all boards, however, fully support the EMS 4.0 specification. The newest boards from Intel, the AST boards, and the earlier AST boards support the new EMS 4.0 specification. The AST and subsequent LIM 4.0 improvements included increased page size and a capability to position page windows anywhere in the memory map.

Despite some of the drawbacks, investing in an EMS board may be worthwhile. With the new specification in LIM 4.X, a breed of memory-management programs has appeared with the capacity to manage multiple programs in the conventional memory workspace. Aided by the improved paging in the new specification, these programs can move programs and datasets in and out of expanded memory. DESQview is one of the more popular programs with this capability and has a strong following. All 16-bit expanded memory boards can function also as conventional or extended memory boards; however, 8-bit cards can never run as extended memory. When you convert a system to run OS/2 or Windows, for example, you can reconfigure expanded memory boards to operate as extended memory boards. Remember that expanded memory is obsolete with OS/2 and not needed in any protected-mode system.

Systems with a 386 processor never need an expanded memory board because the 386 chip has advanced memory-management capabilities that enable you to use the 4 gigabytes of possible extended memory space as simulated expanded memory. This simulation is fast because the memory-management capability is built into the processor. With a 386-based system, you need only conventional and extended memory because the drivers that simulate the change of extended to expanded memory usually are supplied with the 80386 systems. COMPAQ, for example, supplies users with a disk containing the COMPAQ Expanded Memory Manager (CEMM). This type of driver is now part of the IBM and Microsoft DOS 5.X package, under the name EMM386.EXE. (These emulators are for 80386-based systems only.)

Types of Memory Devices

You can break memory hardware down to its smallest removable component—the chip or the SIMM (single in-line memory module). In this section, you look at how to identify different memory chips and what effect the newer SIMMs have on the memory in your system. Most newer systems are installing memory in the SIMM format, which makes troubleshooting and diagnosing problems in memory much easier, and reduces labor in replacing these failed components. The real drawback to the SIMM is the cost.

Chips

At some point, you should be able to take a memory board out of a system, examine it, and identify the board's capacity by counting the installed chips. When you are repairing a memory board, you need this information to help locate the physical position of a defective memory chip, especially when you have an error's logical address location only.

Memory on a board usually is organized into banks of chips. A bank is the minimum amount of memory with which the processor communicates at one time. The size of a bank normally is determined by the width of the data bus on the system processor. Systems with an 8-bit processor data bus architecture will have banks that are 8 bits wide. Because most IBM-compatible systems use parity-checked memory, an additional bit is present for every 8 bits. A system with an 8-bit processor would have a memory bank that is 9 bits wide, systems with 16-bit processors would have banks 18 bits wide, and systems with 32-bit processors would have banks 36 bits wide. Because most chips are arranged as a memory column that is only 1 bit wide, a 9-bit bank would require 9 chips, an 18-bit bank would require 18 chips, and so on.

You should be able to identify how banks are placed on a given memory board or motherboard. Usually, some silk-screen writing on the board labels the banks as "Bank 0," "Bank 1," and so on. Each of the banks has 8 bits numbered 0 through 7, and an extra parity bit.

Examine a chip in one of the banks and look at the writing on the top. A typical memory chip resembles figure 10.9.

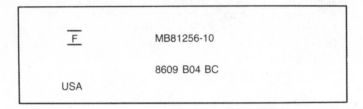

Fig. 10.9

Markings on a typical memory chip.

Each item on the chip means something. As mentioned in Chapter 7, the -10 corresponds to the speed of the chip in nanoseconds (a 100 nanosecond rating). MB81256 is the chip's part number, where you usually can find a clue about its capacity. The key digits are 1256, which indicate that this chip is 1 bit wide and has a depth of 256K. To make a full byte with parity, nine of these single-bit-wide chips are required. A chip with a part number KM4164B-10 indicates a 64K-by-1-bit chip at a speed of 100 nanoseconds. The following list of some common types of chips matches them with common part numbers:

4164	64K by 1 bit
4264	64K by 2 bits
4464	64K by 4 bits
41128	128K by 1 bit
42128	128K by 2 bits
44128	128K by 4 bits
41256	256K by 1 bit
42256	256K by 2 bits
44256	256K by 4 bits

Chips wider than 1 bit are used to construct banks of less than 9, 18, or 36 chips (depending on the system architecture). For example, in the IBM XT-286, which is an AT-type of 16-bit system, the last 128K bytes of memory on the motherboard consist of a bank with only 6 chips—4 that are 64K by 4 bits wide and 2 parity chips that are 1 bit wide, storing 18 bits.

In figure 10.9, the symbol centered between two lines is the manufacturer's logo, here for Fujitsu Microelectronics. A cross-reference showing manufacturer symbols is in the Appendix. The 8609 indicates the date of manufacture (ninth week of 1986), although some manufacturers use a

Julian date code that looks different. To decode the chip further, contact the manufacturer for a data book or catalog.

With the depth, width, and speed rating of the chip, you can order a replacement. Knowing the date of a chip can sometimes help you identify a bad batch of chips if the dates are consistent.

SIMMs

Single in-line memory modules (SIMMs) are more reliable and easier to replace than standard memory chips. Because each SIMM contains entire bytes of memory rather than individual bits, determination of the physical fault domain in troubleshooting problems is simpler. You no longer have to narrow the problem to a particular failed bit within a byte. With a SIMM, figuring out the failed byte is enough to determine the physical fault domain. The higher memory densities achieved by SIMMs contribute to their use in smaller systems. They can be used also to place more memory on a single adapter card. Smaller MCA boards make SIMMs necessary for any PS/2 MCA applications because of the limited space for more memory and features. PS/2 system boards are available with 8M or more on a single adapter board, a density that could be achieved only with SIMMs. The SIMM will replace the individual memory module within the next few years, at least for newer systems.

SIMMs usually are constructed with 256K-bit, 1-megabit or 4-megabit chips. SIMMs also are available in different widths and depths. Chapter 7 has more information on different types of SIMMs. Make sure that you can identify the parts in your system so that you can order proper replacements. Many of today's high-memory-content boards are packed with SIMMs. You can purchase a single memory board today with up to 16 full megabytes. This purchase is the only memory board you need for many systems and brings most systems up to full-expansion capacity. Of course, the 16M memory card for the faster systems may cost $8,000, which may be more expensive than the system.

Communications Ports

The basic communications ports in any PC system are the serial and parallel ports. The serial ports are used primarily for devices that must communicate bidirectionally with the system; such devices include modems, mice, scanners, digitizers, or any other device that "talks to" as well as receives information from the PC.

Parallel ports are used primarily for printers and operate normally as one-way ports, although sometimes they can be used bidirectionally. IBM sells a device and software called the Data Migration Facility, which is basically an adapter plug that enables two printer cables to be plugged into one another, and can be used to copy floppy disks from system to system. This device was designed to allow the transfer of data between systems that had different types of floppy drives.

Several companies also manufacture communications programs that perform high-speed transfers between PC systems using serial or parallel ports. I recommend the Fastlynx program from Rupp Corp. for this type of program. I also have an EPROM burner, from a company called Andratech, that plugs into a parallel port for communications with the system.

Serial Ports

The asynchronous serial interface is the primary system-to-system communications device. *Asynchronous* means that no synchronization or clocking signal is present, so characters may be sent with any arbitrary time spacing, as when a typist is providing the data.

Each character is framed by a standard start and stop signal. A single 0 bit, called the start bit, precedes each character to tell the receiving system that the next 8 bits constitute a byte of data. One or two stop bits follow the character to signal that the character has been sent. At the receiving end of the communication, characters are recognized by the start and stop signals instead of being recognized by the timing of their arrival. The asynchronous interface is character-oriented and has about 20 percent overhead for the extra information needed to identify each character.

Serial refers to data sent over one wire with each bit lining up in a series as they are sent. This type of communication is used over the phone system because this system provides one wire for data in each direction. Serial ports for the PC are available from many manufacturers. You usually can find them on one of the available multifunction boards or on a board with at least a parallel port. IBM made single cards with only a serial or a parallel port, but these were not very popular. All IBM AT models that included a hard disk also came with an IBM serial/parallel port board, and all XT models with IBM hard disks came with a single serial port card in slot 8. Figure 10.10 shows the standard 9-pin AT-style serial port, and figure 10.11 shows the more conventional 25-pin version.

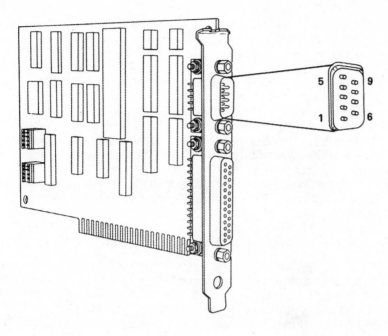

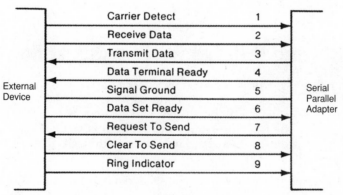

External Device	Carrier Detect	1	Serial Parallel Adapter
	Receive Data	2	
	Transmit Data	3	
	Data Terminal Ready	4	
	Signal Ground	5	
	Data Set Ready	6	
	Request To Send	7	
	Clear To Send	8	
	Ring Indicator	9	

Fig. 10.10

AT-style 9-pin serial-port connector specifications.

Fig. 10.11

Standard 25-pin serial-port connector specifications.

Many people incorrectly think that "a serial port is a serial port." Under DOS, for example, you can use the XT serial port card in an AT but cannot use the AT serial port card in an XT without some problems. Under OS/2, you cannot even use the XT serial port card in an AT. The differences are not caused by the interface, because all these cards use the 8-bit interface. The serial port UART (Universal Asynchronous Receiver Transmitter) chip and the control program for this chip are the problems. The control program is in the ROM BIOS on the system's motherboard. Under OS/2, the standard AT ROM BIOS does not function because the BIOS was not designed to run under protected mode. The serial port control programs must be loaded from disk when OS/2 is booted. This software does not run on ports with UART chips designed for PC or XT systems. Many users with less expensive AT clones are running PC or XT serial port cards because they are less expensive than the right card. These users are in for a surprise when they run OS/2 and discover that the serial ports do not work.

Serial ports may connect a variety of devices such as modems, plotters, printers, other computers, bar code readers, scales, and device control circuits. Basically, anything that needs a two-way connection to the PC uses the industry-standard Reference Standard number 232 revision c (RS-232c) serial port. This device enables data transfer between otherwise incompatible devices.

Serial- and Parallel-Port Configuration

Each time a character is received by a serial port, it has to get the attention of the computer by raising an Interrupt Request Line (IRQ). Eight-bit ISA bus systems have 8 of these lines, and systems with a 16-bit ISA bus have 16 lines. The 8259 interrupt controller chip usually handles these requests for attention. In a standard configuration, COM1 uses IRQ4, and COM2 uses IRQ3.

When a serial or parallel port is installed in a system, it must be configured to use specific I/O addresses (called ports), and interrupts (called IRQs for Interrupt ReQuest). The best plan is to follow the existing standards for how these devices should be set up. For configuring serial ports, you should use the addresses and interrupts as indicated in table 10.13.

Table 10.13 Standard Serial I/O Port Addresses and Interrupts

System	COMx	Port	IRQ
All	COM1	3F8h	IRQ4
All	COM2	2F8h	IRQ3
ISA bus	COM3	3E8h	IRQ4
ISA bus	COM4	2E8h	IRQ3
ISA bus	COM3	3E0h	IRQ4
ISA bus	COM4	2E0h	IRQ3
ISA bus	COM3	338h	IRQ4
ISA bus	COM4	238h	IRQ3
MCA bus	COM3	3220h	IRQ3
MCA bus	COM4	3228h	IRQ3
MCA bus	COM5	4220h	IRQ3
MCA bus	COM6	4228h	IRQ3
MCA bus	COM7	5220h	IRQ3
MCA bus	COM8	5228h	IRQ3

A problem can occur when the ROM BIOS logs in these ports. If the Power-On Self-Test (POST) does not find a 3F8 serial port but does find a 2F8, then the 2F8 serial port is mistakenly assigned to COM1. The reserved IRQ line for COM1 is IRQ4, but this serial port of 2F8 is using COM2's address, which means that it should be using IRQ3 instead of IRQ4. If you are trying to use BASIC or DOS for COM1 operations, therefore, the serial port or modem cannot work. Generally, never use COM1 without first using COM2.

Another problem is that IBM never built BIOS support in its original ISA bus systems for COM3 and COM4. Therefore, the DOS MODE command cannot work with serial ports above COM2 because DOS gets its I/O information from the BIOS, which finds out what's installed where in your system during the POST. The POST in these older systems checks only for the first two installed ports. PS/2 systems have an improved BIOS that checks for as many as eight serial ports, although DOS is limited to handling only four of them.

To get around this problem, most communications software and some serial peripherals (such as mice) support higher COM ports by addressing them directly, rather than making DOS function calls. For example, the communications program PROCOMM supports the additional ports even if your BIOS or DOS does not. Of course, if your system or software does not support these extra ports or you need to redirect data using the MODE command, trouble arises.

A couple of utilities enable you to append your COM port information to the BIOS, making the ports DOS-accessible. A program called Port Finder is one of the best, and is available in the "general hardware" data library of the IBMHW forum on CompuServe. Port Finder also can be obtained directly from the manufacturer at the following address:

> Port Finder
> mcTRONic Systems
> 7426 Cornwall Bridge Lane
> Houston, TX 77041-1709
> (713) 462-7687

Port Finder activates the extra ports by giving the BIOS the addresses and providing utilities for swapping the addresses among the different ports. Address-swapping allows programs that don't support COM3 and COM4 to access them. Software that already directly addresses these additional ports usually is unaffected.

Extra ports, however, must use separate interrupts. If you are going to use two COM ports at one time, they should be on opposite interrupts. Using the standard port and interrupt configurations, the possibilities for simultaneous operation are as follows:

> COM1 (IRQ4) and COM2 (IRQ3)
>
> COM1 (IRQ4) and COM4 (IRQ3)
>
> COM2 (IRQ3) and COM3 (IRQ4)
>
> COM3 (IRQ4) and COM4 (IRQ3)

Divide your COM port inputs into these groups of two, pairing serial devices that won't be used simultaneously on the same interrupt, and devices that will be used at the same time on different interrupts. Note again that PS/2 Micro Channel Architecture systems are entirely exempt from these types of problems because they have a BIOS that looks for the additional ports, and because the MCA bus can share interrupts without conflicts.

Parallel-port configuration is not so complicated. Even the original IBM PC has BIOS support for three LPT ports, and DOS has always had this support as well. Table 10.14 shows the standard I/O address and interrupt settings for parallel port use.

Table 10.14 Standard Parallel I/O Port Addresses and Interrupts				
System	**LPTx**	**Port**	**IRQ**
8-bit ISA	LPT1	3BCh	IRQ7
8-bit ISA	LPT2	378h	None
8-bit ISA	LPT3	278h	None
16-bit ISA	LPT1	3BCh	IRQ7
16-bit ISA	LPT2	378h	IRQ5
16-bit ISA	LPT3	278h	None
All MCA	LPT1	3BCh	IRQ7
All MCA	LPT2	378h	IRQ7
All MCA	LPT3	278h	IRQ7

Because the BIOS and DOS have always provided three definitions for parallel ports, problems with older systems are infrequent. However, problems can arise from the lack of available interrupt-driven ports for the ISA bus systems. Normally an interrupt-driven port is not absolutely required for printing operations; in fact, many programs do not use the interrupt-driven capability. However, the DOS print spooler does use the interrupt, as do network print programs and other types of background or spooler-type printer programs. Also, any high-speed laser-printer utility programs would often use the interrupt capabilities to allow for printing. If you use these types of applications on a port that is not interrupt driven, you see the printing slow to a crawl, if it works at all. The only solution is to use an interrupt-driven port. Note that because MCA bus PS/2 systems can share interrupts, they are completely exempt from this type of problem, and all parallel ports in these systems are interrupt driven on IRQ7.

To configure parallel and serial boards in ISA bus systems, you probably will have to set jumpers and switches. Because each board on the market is different, you always should consult the OEM manual for that particular card if you need to know how the card should or can be configured. IBM includes this information with each card's documentation. IBM also offers technical-reference options and adapters manuals as well as hardware-maintenance and service manuals, which also cover in detail all the jumper and switch settings for IBM adapter cards. Other manufacturers simply include with the card a manual that describes the card and includes the configuration information. The PS/2 MCA bus systems have an automatic or software-driven configuration that eliminates these configuration hassles.

Modem Standards

Bell Labs and the CCITT have set standards for modem protocols. Although the CCITT is actually a French term, it translates in English to the Consultative Committee on International Telephone and Telegraph. A protocol is a method by which two different entities agree to communicate. Bell Labs no longer sets new standards for modems, although several of its older standards are still used. Most modems built in the last few years conform to the CCITT standards. The CCITT is an international body of technical experts responsible for developing data communications standards for the world. The group falls under the organizational umbrella of the United Nations, and its members include representatives from major modem manufacturers, common carriers (such as AT&T), and governmental bodies.

The CCITT establishes communications standards and protocols in many areas, so one modem often adheres to several CCITT standards, depending on its various features and capabilities. Modem standards can be grouped into the following three areas:

■ Modulation standards

    Bell 103

    Bell 212A

    CCITT V.21

    CCITT V.22bis

    CCITT V.29

    CCITT V.32

    CCITT V.32bis

■ Error-correction standards

    CCITT V.42

■ Data-compression standards

    V.42bis

Other standards have been developed by different companies, and not Bell Labs or the CCITT. These are sometimes called *proprietary standards*, even though most of these companies publish full specifications on their protocols so that other manufacturers can develop modems to work with them. The following list shows some of the proprietary standards that have become fairly popular.

Proprietary standards

Modulation
HST
PEP
DIS

Error correction
MNP 1-4
Hayes V-series

Data compression
MNP 5
CSP

Almost all modems today claim to be "Hayes compatible," which does not refer to any communication protocol, but instead to the commands required to operate the modem. Because almost every modem uses the Hayes command set, this compatibility is a given and should not really affect your decisions about modems.

Modulation Standards

Modems start with *modulation*, which is the electronic signaling method used by the modem (from *mod*ulator to *dem*odulator). Modems must use the same modulation method to understand each other. Each data rate uses a different modulation method, and sometimes more than one method exists for a particular rate.

The three most popular modulation methods are frequency shift keying (FSK), phase shift keying (PSK), and quadrature amplitude modulation (QAM). FSK is a form of frequency modulation, otherwise known as FM. By causing and monitoring frequency changes in a signal sent over the phone line, two modems can send information. PSK is a form of phase modulation, in which the timing of the carrier signal wave is altered and the frequency stays the same. QAM is a modulation technique that combines phase changes with signal amplitude variations, resulting in a signal that can carry more information than the other methods.

Baud versus Bits Per Second (bps)

Baud rate and the bit rate are often confused in discussions about modems. Baud rate is the rate at which a signal between two devices changes in one second. If a signal between two modems can change frequency or phase at a rate of 300 times per second, for example, that device is said to communicate at 300 baud. Sometimes a single modulation change is used to carry a single bit. In that case, 300 baud would also equal 300 bits per second (bps). If the modem could signal two bit values for each signal change, the bit-per-second rate would be twice the baud rate, or 600 bps at 300 baud. Most modems transmit several bits per baud, so that the actual baud rate is much slower than the bit-per-second rate. In fact, people usually use the term *baud* incorrectly. We normally are not interested in the raw baud rate but in the bit-per-second rate, which is the true gauge of communications speed.

Bell 103

Bell 103 is a U.S. and Canadian 300 bps modulation standard. It uses frequency shift keying (FSK) modulation at 300 baud to transmit one bit per baud. Most higher-speed modems will communicate using this protocol even though it is largely obsolete.

Bell 212A

Bell 212A is the U.S. and Canadian 1200 bps modulation standard. It uses differential phase shift keying (DPSK) at 600 baud to transmit two bits per baud.

V.21

V.21 is an international data-transmission standard for 300 bps communications similar to Bell 103. Because of some differences in the frequencies used, Bell 103 modems are not compatible with V.21 modems. This standard is used primarily outside of the United States.

V.22

V.22 is an international 1200 bps data-transmission standard. This standard is similar to the Bell 212A standard, but is incompatible in some areas, especially in answering a call. This standard was used primarily outside of the United States.

V.22bis

V.22bis is a data-transmission standard for 2400 bps communications. *Bis* is Latin for *second*, indicating that this data transmission is an improvement to or follows V.22. This data transmission is an international standard for 2400 bps and is used inside and outside the United States.

V.22bis uses quadrature amplitude modulation (QAM) at 600 baud and transmits four bits per baud to achieve 2400 bps.

V.23

V.23 is a split data-transmission standard, operating at 1200 bps in one direction and 75 bps in the reverse direction. Therefore, the modem is only "pseudo-full-duplex," meaning that it can transmit data in both directions simultaneously, but not at the maximum data rate. This standard was developed to lower the cost of 1200 bps modem technology, which was expensive in the early 1980s. This standard was used primarily in Europe.

V.29

V.29 is a data-transmission standard at 9600 bps, which defines a half duplex (one-way) modulation technique. This standard is generally used in Group III facsimile (FAX) transmissions, and only rarely in modems. Because V.29 is a half-duplex method, it is substantially easier to implement this high-speed standard than to implement a high-speed full-duplex standard. As a modem standard, V.29 has not been fully defined, so V.29 modems of different brands seldom can communicate with each other. This does not affect FAX machines, which have a fully defined standard.

V.32

V.32 is a full-duplex (two-way) data transmission standard at 9600 bps. It is a full modem standard, and also includes forward error-correcting and negotiation standards. V.32 uses TCQAM (trellis coded quadrature amplitude modulation) at 2400 baud to transmit 4 bits per baud, resulting in the 9600 bps transmission speed. The trellis coding is a special forward error-correction technique that creates an additional bit for each packet of 4. This extra check bit is used to allow on-the-fly error correction to take place at the other end. It also greatly increases the resistance of V.32 to noise on the line. In the past, V.32 has been expensive to implement because the technology it requires is complex. Because a one-way 9600-bps stream uses almost the entire bandwidth of the phone line, V.32 modems implement *echo cancellation*, meaning that they cancel out the overlapping signal that their own modems transmit and just listen to the other modem's signal. This procedure is complicated and costly. Recent advances in lower-cost chipsets make these modems inexpensive, so they are becoming the de facto 9600 bps standard.

V.32bis

V.32bis is a relatively new 14,400 bps extension to V.32. This protocol uses TCQAM modulation at 2400 baud to transmit 6 bits per baud, for an effective rate of 14,400 bits per second. The trellis coding makes the connection more reliable. This protocol is also a full-duplex modulation protocol, with fallback to V.32 if the phone line is impaired. Although this high-speed standard is newly developed, it is rapidly becoming the communications standard for dial-up lines because of its excellent performance and resistance to noise. I recommend all modem purchases be V.32bis-type modems.

V.32fast

V.32fast is a new standard being proposed to the CCITT. V.32fast will be an extension to V.32 and V.32bis but will offer a transmission speed of 28,800 bits per second. This standard, when approved, probably will be as advanced as modem communications ever gets. Looming on the horizon is that the phone system eventually will be digital. All further development on analog transmission schemes will end, and new digital modems will be developed. V.32fast will be the best and last of the analog protocols when it debuts.

Error-Correction Protocols

Error correction refers to a capability that some modems have to identify errors during a transmission, and to automatically resend data that appears to have been damaged in transit. For error correction to work, both modems must adhere to the same correction standard. Fortunately, most modem manufacturers follow the same error-correction standards.

V.42

V.42 is an error-correction protocol, with fallback to MNP 4. MNP stands for Microcom Networking Protocol, and version 4 is an error-correction protocol as well. Because the V.42 standard includes MNP compatibility through Class 4, all MNP 4 compatible modems can establish error-controlled connections with V.42 modems. This standard uses a protocol called LAPM (Link Access Procedure for Modems). LAPM, like MNP, copes with phone-line impairments by automatically retransmitting data corrupted during transmission, assuring that only error-free data passes through the modems. V.42 is considered to be better than MNP 4 because it offers about a 20 percent higher transfer rate due to more intelligent algorithms.

Data-Compression Standards

Data compression refers to a built-in capability in some modems to compress the data they're sending, thus saving time and money for long-distance modem users. Depending on the type of files that are sent, data can be compressed to 50 percent of its original size, effectively doubling the speed of the modem.

V.42bis

V.42bis is a CCITT data-compression standard similar to MNP Class 5, but providing about 35 percent better compression. V.42bis is not actually compatible with MNP Class 5, but nearly all V.42bis modems include the MNP 5 data-compression capability as well.

This protocol can sometimes quadruple throughput, depending on the compression technique used. This fact has led to some mildly false advertising: for example, a 2400-bps V.42bis modem might advertise "9600 bps throughput" by including V.42bis as well, but this would be possible in only extremely optimistic cases, such as in sending text files that are very loosely packed. In the same manner, many 9600-bps V.42bis makers now advertise "up to 38.4K bps throughput" by virtue of the compression. Just make sure that you see the truth behind such claims.

V.42bis is superior to MNP 5 because it analyzes the data first, and then determines whether compression would be useful. V.42bis only compresses data that needs compression. Files found on bulletin board systems are often compressed already (using ARC, PKZIP, and similar programs). Further attempts at compressing already compressed data can increase the size of the data and slow things down. MNP 5 always attempts to compress the data, which slows down throughput on previously compressed files. V.42bis, however, will compress only what will benefit from the compression.

To negotiate a standard connection using V.42bis, V.42 also must be present. Therefore, a modem with V.42bis data compression is assumed to include V.42 error correction. These two protocols combined result in an error-free connection that has the maximum data compression possible.

Proprietary Standards

In addition to the industry standard protocols for modulation, error correction, and data compression that are generally set forth or approved by the CCITT, several protocols in these areas were invented by various companies and included in their products without any official endorsement by the CCITT. Some of these protocols are quite popular and have become pseudo-standards of their own.

The most successful proprietary protocols are the MNP (Microcom Networking Protocols) that were developed by Microcom. These error-correction and data-compression protocols are widely supported by other modem manufacturers as well. Another company successful in establishing proprietary protocols as limited standards is USRobotics, with its HST (high speed technology) modulation protocols. Because of an aggressive marketing campaign with bulletin board system operators, it captured a large portion of the market with its products.

This section will examine these and other proprietary modem protocols.

HST

The HST is a 14400 and 9600 bps modified half-duplex proprietary modulation protocol used by USRobotics. Though common in bulletin board systems, it is probably destined for extinction within the next few years as V.32 modems become more competitive in price. HST modems run at 9600 bps or 14400 bps in one direction, and 300 or 450 bps in the other direction. This is an ideal protocol for interactive sessions. Because echo-cancellation circuitry is not required, costs are lower.

USRobotics also makes modems that use standard protocols as well as *dual standards*, modems that incorporate both V.32bis and HST protocols. This gives you the best of the standard and proprietary worlds and allows you to connect to virtually any other system at that system's maximum communications rate. I use and recommend the dual-standard modems.

DIS

The DIS is a 9600-bps proprietary modulation protocol by CompuCom, which uses dynamic impedance stabilization (DIS), with claimed superiority in noise rejection over V.32. Implementation appears to be very inexpensive, but like HST, only one company makes modems with the DIS standard. Because of the lower costs of V.32 and V.32bis, this proprietary standard will likely disappear.

MNP

MNP (Microcom Networking Protocol) offers end-to-end error correction, meaning that the modems are capable of detecting transmission errors and requesting retransmission of corrupted data. Some levels of MNP also provide data compression.

As MNP evolved, different classes of the standard were defined, describing the extent to which a given MNP implementation supports the protocol. Most current implementations support Classes 1 through 5. Higher classes usually are unique to modems manufactured by Microcom, Inc. because they are proprietary.

MNP generally is used for its error-correction capabilities, but MNP Classes 4 and 5 also provide performance increases, with Class 5 offering real-time data compression. The lower classes of MNP usually are not important to you as a modem user, but they are included here for completeness.

- MNP Class 1 (block mode) uses asynchronous, byte-oriented, half-duplex (one-way) transmission. This method provides about 70 percent efficiency and error correction only, so it's rarely used today.

- MNP Class 2 (stream mode) uses asynchronous, byte-oriented, full-duplex (two-way) transmission. This class also provides error correction only. Because of protocol overhead (the time it takes to establish the protocol and operate it), throughput at Class 2 is only about 84 percent of that for a connection without MNP, delivering about 202 cps (characters per second) at 2400 bps (240 cps is the theoretical maximum). Class 2 is rarely used today.

- MNP Class 3 incorporates Class 2, and is more efficient. It uses a synchronous, bit-oriented, full-duplex method. The improved procedure yields throughput about 108 percent of that of a modem without MNP, delivering about 254 cps at 2400 bps.

- MNP Class 4 is a performance-enhancement class that uses Adaptive Packet Assembly and Optimized Data Phase techniques. Class 4 improves throughput and performance by about 5 percent, although actual increases depend on the type of call and connection, and can be as high as 25 to 50 percent.

- MNP Class 5 is a data-compression protocol that uses a real-time adaptive algorithm. It can increase throughput up to 50 percent, but the actual performance of Class 5 depends on the type of data being sent. Raw text files allow the highest increase, although program files cannot be compressed as much and the increase is smaller. On precompressed data (files already compressed with ARC, PKZIP, and so on), MNP 5 *decreases* performance, and therefore is often disabled on BBS systems.

V-Series

The Hayes V-series is a proprietary error-correction protocol by Hayes that was used in some of its modems. Since the advent of lower-cost V.32 and V.32bis modems (even from Hayes), the V-series has all but become extinct. These modems used a modified V.29 protocol, sometimes called a ping-pong protocol because it has one high-speed channel and one low-speed channel that alternate back and forth.

CSP

The CSP (CompuCom Speed Protocol) is an error-correction and data-compression protocol available on CompuCom DIS modems.

Modem Recommendations

V.32 high-speed transmission technology has decreased in cost, and therefore is displacing other high-speed proprietary protocols. Like 2400-bps modems, 9600-bps modems eventually will drop in cost to a couple hundred dollars or less.

Today, many 2400-bps modems come with MNP or V.42bis. They can connect to 9600-bps or faster modems with MNP or V.42bis, but the modulation speed will still be at 2400. Likewise, a V.42bis can connect to a V.32/42bis, but only at their highest common speed of 2400 bps. Of course, because they both have V.42bis data compression, throughput of up to 9600 bps is possible.

Probably the most universal modem is the USRobotics Courier HST Dual Standard, a high-speed modem that uses both the industry standard ultra-high speed V.32bis protocol and U.S. Robotics' own transmission standard as well. This modem also includes V.42bis, which enables throughput to hit 38.4K bps with the right data. The multiple protocols and standards in this modem make possible connections to almost any other modem at its full capability. You are limited only by the speed and protocols of the modem you are calling. This device's only drawback is its price, but its flexibility makes it cost effective.

Secrets of Modem Negotiation

If you are curious about the complex negotiations that occur when two modems connect, two detailed descriptions of *modem handshaking* follow. The two examples of connections use V.22bis and V.32. These sequences may differ slightly depending on your modem, and can get more complicated when you combine different modem types into one box.

This information is not particularly useful, but I find it fascinating and valuable to have a deeper understanding of how amazing some of the technology that we take for granted really is.

Making a V.22bis connection between two modems involves the following sequence of events:

1. The answering modem detects a ring, goes off-hook, and waits for at least two seconds of *billing delay* (required by phone company rules so that no data passes before the network recognizes that the call has been connected).

2. The answering modem transmits an *answer tone* (described in CCITT Recommendation V.25, occurs at 2100Hz, and lasts 3.3 ± 0.7 seconds). The answer tone tells manual-dial originators that they have reached a modem and can put their calling modem in data mode, and informs the network that data is going to be transferred so that echo suppressors in the network can be disabled. If the echo suppressors remain enabled, you cannot transmit in both directions at the same time. (The originating modem remains silent throughout this period.)

3. The answering modem goes silent for 75 ± 20 milliseconds (ms) to separate the answer tone from the following signals.

4. The answering modem transmits unscrambled binary 1s at 1200 bits per second (USB1), which cause the static, or hash sound, you hear after the answer tone. This sound is slightly higher in pitch than the answer tone because the signal's major components are at 2250 and 2550 Hz.

5. The originating modem detects the USB1 signal in 155 ± 10 ms, and remains silent for 456 ± 10 ms.

6. The originating modem transmits unscrambled double-digit 00s and 11s at 1200 bits (S1) for 100 ± 3 ms. A Bell 212 or V.22 modem does not transmit this S1 signal, and it is by the presence or absence of this single 100 ms signal that V.22bis knows whether to fall back to 1200 bps operation.

7. When the answering modem (which is still transmitting the USB1 signal) detects the S1 signal from the originator, it also sends 100 ms of S1 so that the originating modem knows that the answerer is capable of 2400 bps operation.

8. The originating modem then switches to sending scrambled binary 1s at 1200 bits (SB1). Scrambling has nothing to do with encryption or security, but is simply a method by which the signal is *whitened*, or randomized, to even out the power across the entire bandwidth. *White noise* is a term given by engineers to totally random noise patterns.

9. The answering modem switches to sending SB1 for 500 ms.

10. The answering modem switches to sending scrambled 1s at 2400 bps for 200 ms. After that, it is ready to pass data.

11. Six hundred ms after the originating modem hears SB1 from the answerer, it switches to sending scrambled 1s at 2400 bps. It does this for 200 ms, and then is ready to pass data.

The signals involved in a V.32 connection are more complicated than V.22bis because of the need to measure the total round-trip delay in the circuit so that the echo cancellers work. Making a V.32 connection involves the following sequence of events:

1. The answering modem detects a ring, goes off-hook, and waits two seconds (the billing delay).

2. The answering modem transmits a V.25 answer tone, but it is different from the previous example. The phase of signal is reversed every 450 ms, which sounds like little clicks in the signal. These phase reversals inform the network that the modems themselves are going to do echo cancellation, and that any echo cancellers in the network should be disabled so as not to interfere with the modems.

3. The originating V.32 modem does not wait for the end of the answer tone. After one second, it responds with an 1800 Hz tone, which in V.32 is known as signal AA. Sending this signal before the end of the answer tone allows the answering modem to know, very early, that it is talking to another V.32 modem.

4. When the answer tone ends (3.3 ± 0.7 seconds), if the answering modem heard signal AA, it proceeds to try to connect as V.32 immediately. If it did not hear AA, it first tries, for three seconds, to connect as a V.22bis modem (sends signal USB1 and waits for a response). If it does not get a response to USB1, it goes back to trying to connect as a V.32 modem because of the possibility that the calling V.32 modem didn't hear the answer tone, was manually dialed and switched to data mode late, or is an older V.32 model that does not respond to the answer tone.

5. To connect in V.32, the answering modem sends signal AC, which is 600 and 3000 Hz sent together, for at least 64 *symbol intervals* (1/2400 of a second). It then reverses the phase of the signal, making it into signal CA.

6. When the originating modem detects this phase reversal, in 64 ± 2 symbol intervals, it reverses the phase of its own signal, making AA into CC.

7. When the answer modem detects this phase reversal (in 64 ± 2 symbol intervals), it again reverses the phase of its signal, making CA back into AC. This exchange of phase reversals allows the modems to accurately time the total propagation (round trip) delay of the circuit so that the echo cancellers can be set to properly cancel signal echoes.

8. The modems go into a half-duplex exchange of training signals, to train the adaptive equalizers, test the quality of the phone line, and agree on the data rate to be used. The answering modem transmits first, from 650 to 3525 ms, and then goes silent.

9. The originating modem responds with a similar signal, but then leaves its signal on, while the answering modem responds one more time, establishing the final agreed-on data rate.

10. Both modems then switch to sending scrambled binary 1 (marks) for at least 128 symbol intervals, and then are ready to pass data.

As you can see, these procedures are quite complicated; considering the quality of a normal dial-up line these days, it is amazing that these devices actually work! Although you do not need to understand these communications protocols to use a modem, you can get an idea of what you're hearing when the connection is being established.

Parallel Ports

A parallel port has eight lines for sending all the bits for one byte of data simultaneously across eight wires. This interface is fast and usually is reserved for printers rather than computer-to-computer communications. The only problem with parallel ports is that cables cannot be extended for any great length without amplifying the signal, or else errors will occur in the signal.

The parallel port of the PC, XT, and AT is unidirectional. Data travels only one way from the computer to the port, to the parallel device. On the PS/2, the parallel port is bidirectional so that data can travel to or from the port.

Most applications do not use the bidirectional capability of the PS/2 parallel ports. The only application that uses the bidirectional capability is IBM's Data Migration Facility for exchanging data between systems with 5 1/4-inch disks and PS/2 systems with 3 1/2-inch disks. The printer port is used on earlier systems to send data to PS/2 systems that use the port as a receiving device. Data transfer with this method is faster than with the serial port because the parallel port sends data 8 bits at a time.

This bidirectional capability, however, may create a new use for the parallel port as a gateway for input from high-speed data-transfer devices that talk, such as scanners, bar code readers, and video cameras. Figure 10.12 shows the specifications for a standard 25-pin parallel-port connector.

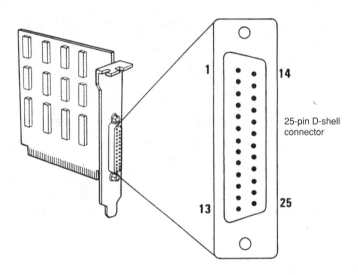

25-pin D-shell connector

At Standard TTL Levels

	Signal Name	Adapter Pin Number	
	− Strobe	1	
	+ Data Bit 0	2	
	+ Data Bit 1	3	
	+ Data Bit 2	4	
	+ Data Bit 3	5	
	+ Data Bit 4	6	
	+ Data Bit 5	7	
	+ Data Bit 6	8	
Printer	+ Data Bit 7	9	Printer
	− Acknowledge	10	Adapter
	+ Busy	11	
	+ P.End (out of paper)	12	
	+ Select	13	
	− Auto Feed	14	
	− Error	15	
	− Initialize Printer	16	
	− Select Input	17	
	Ground	18-25	

Fig. 10.12

Standard 25-pin parallel-port connector specifications.

Diagnosing Problems with Serial and Parallel Ports

To diagnose problems with serial and parallel ports, you need diagnostics software and a wrap plug for each type of port. The diagnostics software works with the wrap plugs to send signals through the port. The plug wraps around the port so that the same port receives the information it sent. This information is verified to ensure that the port works properly. For further information, see Chapter 14, "Hardware Troubleshooting Guide."

Many problems stem from using the wrong serial port card in a system. Most clone manufacturers are guilty of this practice in AT systems because the right card is more expensive. The big difference in serial ports is in the Universal Asynchronous Receiver Transmitter (UART) chip. UARTs are the primary port circuits. Several different versions exist, and they have different applications. Some of the UARTs should be used only in certain systems because the system ROM BIOS is designed specifically to support certain chips. OS/2, which replaces the ROM BIOS when it runs, also is designed for a specific UART. Using a port with the wrong UART results in problems such as the port hanging, incompatibilities with software, lost characters, or total functional failure.

Most UART chips used by IBM are made by National Semiconductor. Identify the chips by looking for the largest chip on the serial port card and reading the numbers on that chip. Usually the chips are socketed, and replacing only the chip may be possible. Table 10.15 lists UART chips in PC or AT systems.

Note The interrupt bug referred to in table 10.15 is a spurious interrupt generated by the 8250 at the end of an access. The ROM BIOS code in the PC and XT has been written to work around this bug. If a chip without the bug is installed, random lockups may occur. The 16450 or 16550(A) chips do not have the interrupt bug, and the AT ROM BIOS was written without any of the bug workarounds in PC or XT systems.

Table 10.15 UART Chips in PC or AT Systems

Chip	Description
8250	IBM used this original chip in the PC serial port card. The chip has several bugs, none of which is serious. The PC and XT ROM BIOS are written to anticipate at least one of the bugs. This chip was replaced by the 8250B.
8250A	Do not use the second version of the 8250 in any system. This upgraded chip fixes several bugs in the 8250, including one in the interrupt enable register, but because the PC and XT ROM BIOS expect the bug, this chip does not work properly with those systems. The 8250A should work in an AT system that does not expect the bug, but does not work adequately at 9600 bps.
8250B	The last version of the 8250 fixes bugs from the previous two versions. The interrupt enable bug in the original 8250, expected by the PC and XT ROM BIOS software, has been put back into this chip, making the 8250B the most desirable chip for any non-AT serial port application. The 8250B chip may work in an AT under DOS, but does not run properly at 9600 bps.
16450	IBM selected the higher-speed version of the 8250 for the AT. Because this chip has fixed the interrupt enable bug mentioned earlier, the 16450 does not operate properly in many PC or XT systems, because they expect this bug to be present. OS/2 requires this chip as a minimum, or the serial ports will not function properly. It also adds a scratch-pad register as the highest register. The 16450 is used primarily in AT systems because of its increase in throughput over the 8250B.
16550	This newer UART improves on the 16450. This chip cannot be used in a FIFO (first in, first out) buffering mode because of problems with the design, but it does enable a programmer to use multiple DMA channels and thus increase throughput on an AT or higher class computer system. I highly recommend replacing the 16550 UART with the 16550A.
16550A	This chip is a faster 16450 with a built-in 16-character Transmit and Receive FIFO (first in, first out) buffer that works. It also allows multiple DMA channel access. You should install this chip in your AT system serial port cards if you do any serious communications at 9600 bps or higher. If your communications program makes use of the FIFO, which most will today, it can greatly increase communications speed and eliminate lost characters and data at the higher speeds.

Various manufacturers make versions of the 16550A; National Semiconductor was the first. Its full part number for the 40-pin DIP is NS16550AN or NS16550AFN. Make sure that the part you get is the 16550A, and not the older 16550. You can contact any of the following distributors for the NS16550AN:

Fry's Electronics
Sunnyvale, CA 94088
(408) 733-1770

Jameco Electronics
1355 Shoreway Road
Belmont, CA 94002
(415) 592-8097

JDR Microdevices
2233 Branham Lane
San Jose, CA 95124
(800) 538-5000 and (408) 995-5430

MicroProcessors Unlimited
24000 S. Peoria Ave.
Beggs, OK 74421
(918) 267-4961

Some computers (particularly 4.77 MHz, 8088 machines) are not fast enough to support the higher communications speeds, especially 19200 or 38400 bps. Even if you have a faster system, if you are running a program that makes heavy use of extended memory, such as a RAM disk or a cache, you may lose characters. This problem occurs primarily on 286 machines. With some programs, like VDisk, it helps to reduce the sector size or the number of sectors transferred at a time (transfer block size) helps.

Some terminate-and-stay-resident (TSR) programs interfere with communications programs. If you are having trouble with a communications program, try to reboot with no CONFIG.SYS or AUTOEXEC.BAT file, to eliminate the TSR programs. Then you can retest the system.

Detecting Serial and Parallel Ports with DEBUG

If you cannot tell which ports (parallel and serial) the computer is using, check for the I/O ports by using DEBUG.

Follow these steps to use DEBUG:

1. Run DEBUG.

2. At the DEBUG prompt, type *D 40:0* and press Enter. This step displays the hexadecimal values of the active I/O port addresses, first serial and then parallel. Figure 10.13 shows a sample address.

Fig. 10.13

DEBUG used to display installed serial and parallel port I/O port addresses.

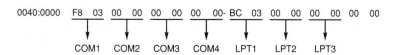

The address for each port is shown in the corresponding position. Because addresses are stored as words, the byte values are swapped and should be read backward. This example indicates one serial port installed at 03F8 and one parallel port installed at 03BC.

3. To exit DEBUG, press Q and press Enter.

Testing Serial Ports

You can perform several tests on serial and parallel ports. One of the most useful is a *loopback* test, which can be used to ensure the correct function of the serial or parallel port, as well as any attached cables. Loopback tests are basically internal (digital), or external (analog). Internal tests can be run by simply unplugging any cables from the port and executing the test via a diagnostics program.

The external loopback test is more effective. This test requires that a special loopback connector or wrap plug be attached to the port in question. When the test is run, the port is used to send data out to the loopback plug, which simply routes the data back into the port's receive pins so that the port is transmitting and receiving at the same time. A loopback or wrap plug is nothing more than a cable doubled back on itself. Most diagnostics programs that run this type of test include the loopback plug, and if not, these types of plugs can be easily purchased or even built. See the Appendix in this book for the necessary diagrams to construct your own wrap plugs.

If you want to purchase a wrap plug, I recommend the IBM tri-connector wrap plug. IBM sells this triple plug, as well as individual wrap plugs under the following part numbers:

Description	IBM part number
Parallel-port wrap plug	8529228
Serial-port wrap plug, 25-pin	8529280
Serial-port wrap plug, 9-pin (AT)	8286126
Tri-connector wrap plug	72X8546

As for the diagnostics software, IBM's own Advanced Diagnostics test both serial and parallel ports. If you have a PS/2 system with Micro Channel Architecture, IBM has already given you the Advanced Diagnostics on the Reference disk that came with the system. To activate this normally hidden Advanced Diagnostics, press Ctrl-A at the Reference Disk's main menu. For IBM systems that are not MCA, the Advanced Diagnostics must be purchased.

For any system, you can use the serial and parallel tests in the comprehensive diagnostics packages sold by several companies as a replacement for the IBM (or other manufacturer) -supplied Advanced Diagnostics. Programs such as Micro-Scope from Micro 2000, Service Diagnostics from Landmark, or QA-Plus FE from Diagsoft all have this type of test as part of their package. All include the necessary three wrap plugs as well. See the vendor list or Chapter 13, "System Diagnostics," for more information on these programs.

For testing serial ports exclusively, as well as any modems that are attached, I highly recommend an inexpensive ($19.95) program called the Modem Doctor. This comprehensive serial port and modem test program enables you to go beyond the simple loopback tests and test the complete communications system, including the cable and modem. The program is especially useful with the USRobotics modems or any other modem with a Hayes-compatible command structure. The program takes command of the modem and runs a variety of tests to determine whether it is functioning correctly. You can get the Modem Doctor from:

> The Modem Doctor
> Hank Volpe
> 108 Broadmoor Dr.
> Tonawanda, NY 14150
> 716-694-7484

This program works especially well in testing the new breed of 9600+ bps modems.

Chapter Summary

This chapter has discussed and examined several main peripherals that work with your systems. Descriptions were given of the various types of available video adapters and monitors, along with some recommendations. This chapter also has examined memory adapters and the available memory configurations. Finally, the chapter has looked at the serial and parallel communications ports on a system, with particular attention to modems.

System Maintenance, Backups, Upgrades, and Diagnostics

PART

IV

Maintaining Your System: Preventive Maintenance, Backups, and Warranties

Preventive maintenance can be the key to obtaining years of trouble-free service from your computer system. A properly administered preventive-maintenance program pays for itself many times over by reducing problem behavior, data loss, and component failure, and also by ensuring a long life for your system. In some cases, I have "repaired" an ailing system with nothing more than a preventive-maintenance session. Preventive maintenance also increases your system's resale value. This chapter describes preventive-maintenance procedures and how often you should perform them.

You will learn also the importance of creating backup files of your data and the various backup procedures available. A sad reality in the computer repair and servicing world is that hardware always can be fixed, but data cannot. Most hard disk troubleshooting and service procedures, for example, require that a low-level format be done. This low-level format overwrites any data still on the disk.

In Chapter 15, "Software Troubleshooting Guide," you learn some simple techniques for recovering data from a damaged disk or disk drive; these procedures are not fail-proof, however. For more information on Data Recovery procedures, see my book *Que's Guide to Data Recovery*.

Because data recovery depends a great deal on the type and severity of damage and the expertise of the recovery specialist, data-recovery services are very expensive. Most recovery services (including mine) charge a minimum of $100 or more per hour for these services and give no guarantees that the data will be completely recovered. Backing up your system as discussed in this chapter is the only guarantee you have that you will see your data again.

Most of the discussion of backing up systems in this chapter is limited to professional solutions—that is, solutions that require you to buy specially designed hardware and software. Backup solutions that employ floppy disk drives, such as the DOS BACKUP and RESTORE commands, are insufficient in many cases.

Finally, the last section in this chapter discusses the standard warranties and optional service contracts available for many systems. Although most of this book is written for people who want to perform their own maintenance and repair service, taking advantage of a good factory warranty that provides service for free definitely is prudent. Some larger computer companies, such as IBM, offer attractive service contracts that, in some cases, are cost-justified over self service. These types of options are examined in the final section.

Developing a Preventive-Maintenance Program

Developing a preventive-maintenance program is important to everyone who uses or manages personal computer systems. Two types of preventive maintenance procedures exist: active and passive.

Active preventive maintenance includes steps you can apply to a system that promote a longer, trouble-free life. This type of preventive maintenance primarily involves cleaning the system and its components. This section describes several active preventive-maintenance procedures, including cleaning and lubricating all major components, reseating chips and connectors, and reformatting hard disks.

Passive preventive maintenance includes steps you can take to protect a system from the environment, such as using power-protection devices; ensuring a clean, temperature-controlled environment; and preventing excessive vibration. In other words, passive preventive maintenance means treating your system well. This section also describes passive preventive-maintenance procedures.

Active Preventive-Maintenance Procedures

The frequency with which you should implement active preventive-maintenance procedures depends on the system's environment and the quality of the system's components. If your system is in an extremely dirty environment, such as a machine-shop floor or a gas-station service area, you might need to clean your system every three months.

For most clean office environments, however, you need to clean only every one to two years. Every system, though, is unique. If you open your system after one year and find tumbleweeds inside, you should shorten the cleaning interval.

Another active preventive-maintenance technique discussed in this section is reformatting hard disks. Low-level reformatting restores the track and sector marks to their proper locations and forces you to back up and restore all data on the drive. Not all drives require this procedure, but if you are using drives with a stepper-motor head actuator, periodic reformatting is highly recommended.

Again, you must use your own equipment and environment as your guide regarding how often you should reformat. If you have inexpensive, stepper-motor actuator, non-shock mounted hard disks that run in an environment in which the ambient temperature varies, you probably will have to reformat the drive about every six months. Higher-quality stepper-motor drives used in a good environment require reformatting only every year or two. Most drives with a voice-coil head actuator run indefinitely in a "nice" environment, such as a clean, temperature-controlled, non-smoking office, but may need occasional reformats if they are located on a machine-shop floor or other harsh industrial environment.

If your drives start returning DOS `Abort, Retry, Ignore` error messages within a year after the last reformatting session, you should reformat the drive at some interval shorter than a year—six months, for example. Only experience with your systems can tell you whether reformatting is necessary; this chapter provides only guidelines.

Cleaning a System

One of the most important operations in a good preventive-maintenance program is regular and thorough cleaning of the system. Dust buildup on the internal components can lead to several problems. One is that the dust acts as a thermal insulator which prevents proper system cooling.

Excessive heat shortens the life of system components and adds to the thermal stress problem caused by wider temperature changes between power-on and power-off states. Additionally, the dust may contain conductive elements that can cause partial short circuits in a system. Other elements in the dust and dirt accelerate corrosion of electrical contacts and cause improper connections. In all, the removal of any layer of dust and debris from within a computer system benefits that system in the long run.

All IBM and IBM-compatible systems use a forced-air cooling system that allows for even cooling inside the system. A fan is mounted in, on, or near the power supply and pushes air outside. This setup depressurizes the interior of the system relative to the outside air. The lower pressure inside the system causes outside air to be drawn into openings in the system chassis and cover. This draw-through, or depressurization, system is the most efficient cooling system that can be designed without an air filter. Air filters typically are not used with depressurization systems because there is no easy way to limit air intake to a single port that can be covered by a filter.

Some industrial computers from IBM and other companies use a forced-air system that uses the fan to pressurize, rather than depressurize, the case. This system forces air to exhaust from any holes in the chassis and case or cover. The key to the pressurization system is that all air intake for the system is at a single location—the fan. The air flowing into the system therefore can be filtered, by simply integrating a filter assembly into the fan housing. The filter must be cleaned or changed periodically. Because the interior of the case is pressurized relative to the outside air, airborne contaminants are not drawn into the system even though it may not be sealed. Any air entering the system must pass through the fan and filter housing, which removes the contaminants. Pressurization cooling systems are used primarily in industrial computer models designed for extremely harsh environments.

Most systems you have contact with are depressurization systems. Mounting any sort of air filter on these types of systems is impossible because air enters the system from too many sources. With any cooling system in which incoming air is not filtered, dust and other chemical matter in the environment is drawn in and builds up inside the computer. This buildup can cause severe problems if left unchecked.

One problem that can develop is overheating. The buildup of dust acts as a heat insulator, which prevents the system from cooling properly. The dust also might contain chemicals that conduct electricity. These chemicals can cause minor current shorts and create electrical signal paths where none should exist. The chemicals also cause rapid corrosion of cable connectors, socket-installed components, and areas where boards plug into slots.

Cigarette smoke contains chemicals that can conduct electricity and cause corrosion of computer parts. Therefore, you should avoid smoking near your computer equipment and encourage your company to develop and enforce a similar policy.

T I P

Floppy disk drives are particularly vulnerable to the effects of dirt and dust. Floppy drives are the source of a large "hole" within the system through which air is continuously drawn in. Therefore, they accumulate a large amount of dust and chemical buildup within a short time. Hard disk drives do not present quite the same problems with dust and dirt that floppy drives do. Because the head disk assembly (HDA) in a hard disk is a sealed unit, no dust or dirt can enter. Thus, cleaning a hard disk requires simply blowing the dust and dirt off from outside the drive. No internal cleaning is required, nor can it be performed.

Obtaining Required Tools and Accessories

To properly clean the system and all the boards inside requires certain supplies and tools. In addition to the tools required to disassemble the unit (see Chapter 6), you should have these items:

- Liquid cleaning solution
- Canned air
- A small brush
- Lint-free foam cleaning swabs

You might want to acquire these optional items also:

- Foam tape
- Low-volatile room-temperature vulcanizing (RTV) sealer
- Silicone lubricant
- Computer vacuum cleaner
- Antistatic wrist-grounding strap

Make sure that the liquid cleaning solution is designed to clean computers. The solution normally contains Freon, isopropyl alcohol, trichloro-ethelyne, or some mixture of these chemicals. Pure Freon is probably the best, but it is expensive. The material must be moisture-free and residue-free. I prefer the solution to be in liquid form—not a spray. Sprays are far too wasteful, and I almost never spray the solution directly on components. I prefer instead to wet a foam swab used for wiping the component. These electronic-component cleaning solutions are available at any good electronics-parts stores.

Canned air is just what its name suggests. You should be sure that you use "computer-grade" air, which (of course) costs more than regular air. Seriously, the type of compressed-air cans used for cleaning camera equipment can differ from the type used for cleaning static sensitive computer components. Canned air must be completely moisture- and residue-free and for computer use, and it should not contain Freon TF as the propellant. Freon TF is known for generating an extremely high static charge because of the friction created as it leaves the nozzle of the can.

Most older computer-grade canned air consisted of dichlorodifluoro-methane—Freon R12—the same chemical used in your car's air-conditioning system. Because of environmental concerns about destruction of the ozone layer, restrictions have been placed on the use of this chemical, and manufacturers are producing a variety of alternatives, one of which is pure carbon dioxide. These newer compressed-air products are safe for the ozone layer as well as for computer components.

T I P

The makeup of many of the chemicals used for cleaning electronic components has been changing because the chemicals originally used as propellants were environmentally unsafe and were contributing to the destruction of the Earth's ozone layer. Many of these older chemicals now are strictly regulated and no longer marketed. The companies that produce chemicals used for system cleaning and maintenance have introduced environmentally safe replacement chemicals. The only drawback is that many of these safer chemicals cost much more than those originally available.

Some people prefer to use a vacuum cleaner rather than canned air for cleaning a system, but canned air is better for cleaning in small areas. A vacuum cleaner is more useful in situations in which you do not want to remove the motherboard completely. You can use the vacuum cleaner to suck out dust and debris rather than blow them on other components, which sometimes happens when you use canned air. For outbound servicing (when you are going to the location of the equipment rather than the equipment coming to you), canned air is much easier to carry in a toolkit than even a small vacuum cleaner.

A small makeup, photographic (lens cleaning), or even paintbrush can be used to carefully loosen accumulated dirt and dust before spraying with the canned air or vacuuming with the vacuum cleaner. Just be careful about generating static electricity: doing so is easy to do when you are using one of these brushes, especially if the bristles are plastic. Wear a grounded wrist strap, and brush slowly and lightly to prevent static discharges from occurring.

Cleaning swabs are used for wiping off electrical contacts and connectors, as well as disk drive heads and other sensitive areas. The swabs should be made of foam, which does not leave lint or dust residue. Unfortunately, these foam cleaning swabs are more expensive than the typical cotton swabs. Do not use cotton swabs because they leave cotton fibers on everything they touch. Cotton fibers are conductive in some situations, and remain on drive heads, which can scratch disks. The foam swabs can be purchased at most electronics-supply stores.

Hard disks normally use a small copper strap to ground the spindle of the disk assembly to the logic board, thus bleeding off any static charge carried by the spinning disk platters. Unfortunately, this strap often can begin to harmonize, or vibrate, and result in an annoying squealing or whining noise. (Sometimes the noise is not unlike fingernails dragged across a chalkboard!)

To eliminate the source of irritation, you can stop the strap from vibrating by using one of two easy methods to weight it with a rubber dampener. One method is to use a piece of foam tape cut to match the size of the strap and stuck to the strap's back side. Another way to dampen the vibration is to use a low-volatile RTV sealer. You apply this silicone-type rubber to the back of the grounding strap. After it hardens to a rubber-like material, the sealer acts as a dampener to stop the vibrations that produce the annoying squeal. You can buy the RTV sealer from an automotive-supply house.

I prefer using the foam tape rather than the RTV because it is easier and neater to apply. If you use the RTV, be sure that it is the low-volatile type, which does not generate acid when it cures. This acid produces the vinegar smell common to the standard RTV sealer, and can be highly corrosive to the strap and anything else it contacts. The low-volatile RTV also eliminates the bad vinegar smell. You can purchase the foam tape at most electronics-supply houses, where it often is sold for attaching alarm switches to doors or windows. The low-volatile RTV is available from most auto-supply stores. To be sure that you buy low-volatile RTV, look for the packaging to state specifically that the product is either a low-volatile type or is compatible with automobile oxygen sensors.

Silicone lubricants are used to lubricate the door mechanisms on floppy disk drives, and any other part of the system that may require clean, non-oily lubrication. Other items you can lubricate are the disk drive head slider rails or even printer-head slider rails, which allow for smooth operation.

Using silicone rather than conventional oils is important because silicone does not gum up and collect dust and other debris. Always use the silicone sparingly, however; do not spray it anywhere near the equipment. Instead, apply a small amount to a toothpick or foam swab and dab the silicone on the components where needed. You can use a lint-free cleaning stick soaked in silicone lubricant to lubricate the metal print-head rails in a printer.

Remember that some of the cleaning operations described in this section might generate a static charge. You may want to use a static grounding strap in cases in which static levels are high to ensure that you do not damage any boards as you work with them.

With all these items on hand, you should be equipped for most preventive-maintenance operations.

Disassembling and Cleaning Procedures

To properly clean your system, you first must disassemble most of it. Some people go as far as removing the motherboard. Removing the motherboard results in the best possible job, but in the interest of saving time, you need to disassemble the system only to where the motherboard is completely visible.

All plug-in adapter cards must be removed, along with the disk drives. Although you can clean the heads of a floppy drive with a cleaning disk without opening the system unit's cover, you probably will want to do more thorough cleaning. In addition to the heads, you also should clean and lubricate the door mechanism and clean any logic boards and connectors on the drive. This procedure usually requires you to remove the floppy drive.

Next, do the same procedure with a hard disk: clean the logic boards and connectors, as well as lubricate the grounding strap. To do so, you must remove the hard disk.

Reseating Socketed Chips

A primary preventive-maintenance function is to undo the effects of chip creep. As your system heats and cools, it expands and contracts, and the physical expansion and contraction causes components plugged into sockets to gradually work their way out of those sockets. This process is called *chip creep*. To correct its effects, you must find all socketed components in the system and make sure that they are properly reseated.

In most systems, all the memory chips are socketed. Memory SIMM devices are retained securely in their sockets and cannot creep out. Memory SIPP devices (like SIMMs with pins rather than contacts) are not retained, and therefore can creep. Standard socketed memory chips are prime candidates for chip creep. Most other logic components are soldered in. You also can expect to find the ROM chips, the main processor or CPU, and the math coprocessor in sockets. In most systems, these items are the only components that are socketed; all others are soldered in.

Exceptions might exist, however. A socketed component in one system might not be socketed in another—even if both are from the same manufacturer. Sometimes this difference results from a parts-availability problem when the boards are manufactured. Rather than halt the assembly line when a part is not available, the manufacturer adds a socket instead of the component. When the component becomes available, it is plugged in and the board is finished.

To make sure that all these components are fully seated in their sockets, I place my hand on the underside of the board and then apply downward pressure with my thumb (from the top) on the chip to be seated. For larger chips, seat the chip carefully in two movements, and press separately on each end of the chip with your thumb to be sure that the chip is fully seated. (The processor and math coprocessor chips usually are seated in this manner.) In most cases, you hear a crunching sound as the chip makes its way back into the socket. Because of the great force sometimes required to reseat the chips, this operation is difficult if you do not remove the board.

For motherboards, forcibly seating chips can be dangerous if you do not directly support the board from the underside with your hand. Enough pressure on the board can cause it to bow or bend in the chassis, and the pressure can crack it before seating takes place. The plastic stand-offs that separate and hold the board up from the metal chassis are spaced too far apart to properly support the board under this kind of stress. Try this operation only if you can remove and support the board adequately from underneath.

You may be surprised to know that, even if you fully seat each chip, they might need reseating again within a year. The creep usually is noticeable within a year or less.

Cleaning Boards

After reseating any socketed devices that may have creeped out of their sockets, the next step is to clean the boards and all connectors in the system. For this step, the cleaning solution described and the lint-free swabs described earlier are needed.

First, clean the dust and debris off the board, and then clean any connectors on the board. To clean the boards, first gently wipe with a brush to loosen and remove any dust and debris. (Use the brush because spraying the board with compressed air does not remove all dirt and dust.) After you loosen the debris with the brush, you can spray it off or vacuum it up easily.

> **CAUTION:** Be careful with electrostatic discharge (ESD), which can damage components. Do not try this operation in the dead of winter in an extremely dry, high-static environment. Make sure that the humidity is high enough to prevent static.
>
> I recommend that you use an antistatic wrist-grounding strap, which should be connected to a ground on the card or board you are wiping. This strap ensures that no electrical discharge occurs between you and the board. An alternative method is to keep a finger or thumb on the ground of the motherboard or card as you wipe it off.

Cleaning Connectors and Contacts

Cleaning the connectors and contacts in a system promotes reliable connections between devices. On a motherboard, you will want to clean the slot connectors, power-supply connectors, keyboard connector, and speaker connector. For most plug-in cards, you will want to clean the edge connectors that plug into slots on the motherboard as well as any other connectors, such as external ones mounted on the card bracket.

Submerge the lint-free swabs in the liquid cleaning solution. If you are using the spray, hold the swab away from the system and spray a small amount on the foam end until the solution starts to drip. Then, use the soaked foam swab to wipe the connectors on the boards.

On the motherboard, pay special attention to the slot connectors. Be liberal with the liquid; resoak the foam swab repeatedly, and vigorously clean the connectors. Don't worry if some of the liquid drips on the surface of the motherboard. This solution is entirely safe for the whole board.

Use the solution to wash the dirt off the gold contacts in the slot connectors, and then douse any other connectors on the board. Clean the keyboard connector, the grounding positions where screws ground the board to the system chassis, power-supply connectors, speaker connectors, battery connectors, and so on.

If you are cleaning a plug-in board, pay special attention to the edge connector that mates with the slot connector on the motherboard. When people handle plug-in cards, they often touch the gold contacts on these connectors. Touching the gold contacts coats them with oils and debris, which prevents proper contact with the slot connector when the board is installed. Make sure that these gold contacts are free of all finger oils and residue.

> **CAUTION:** Many people use a common pink eraser to rub the edge connectors clean. I do not recommend this procedure, for two reasons. One, the eraser eventually removes some of the gold and leaves the tin solder or copper underneath exposed. Without the gold, the contact corrodes rapidly and requires frequent cleaning. The second reason to avoid cleaning with the eraser is that the rubbing action can generate a static charge. This charge can harm any component on the board. Rather than use an eraser, use the liquid solution and swab method described earlier.

You also will want to use the swab and solution to clean the ends of ribbon cables or other types of cables or connectors in a system. Clean the floppy drive cables and connectors, the hard disk cables and connectors, and any others you find. Don't forget to clean off the edge connectors that are on the disk drive logic boards as well as the power connectors to the drives.

Cleaning Drives

Because Chapter 8 explains the procedure for cleaning floppy drives, the information is not repeated here. The basic idea is to use the brush and canned air to dust off the interior of the drive, use the silicone lubricant on whatever items need lubrication, and follow up with a head cleaning, either manually with a foam swab or automatically with a cleaning disk.

For hard disks, take this opportunity to dampen or lubricate the grounding strap as described earlier. Dampening is the recommended solution because if you lubricate this point, the lubricant eventually dries up and the squeal can come back. Because the dampening is usually a more permanent fix for this sort of problem, I recommend it whenever possible.

Reformatting a Hard Disk

In addition to cleaning a system, periodically reformatting a hard disk is an operation often overlooked as part of a preventive-maintenance plan. Reformatting rewrites the sector header information in alignment with current head positions, which can drift in stepper motor head-actuator drives because of temperature- and stress-induced dimensional changes between the platters and heads. If these alignment variations continue unchecked, they eventually will cause read and write errors. Note that this reformatting operation applies to stepper motor head-actuator drives only and not to voice-coil drives, which maintain their positional accuracy. Note also that most IDE drives should never be reformatted, except with manufacturer-approved utilities. Most IDE drives use voice-coil head actuators anyway.

Reformatting a hard disk lays down new track and sector ID marks and boundaries, re-marks the manufacturer's defects, and performs a surface scan for new defects that might have developed since the last format. Temperature variations, case flexing, and physical positioning can add up to eventual read and write errors in a stepper-motor-actuated hard disk. This type of failure sometimes appears as a gradually increasing number of disk retries and other read and write problems. You also might notice difficulties when you boot the disk for the first time each day or if the system has been turned off for some time (over the weekend, for example). The cause of these problems is a mistracking between where the data has actually written on the drive and where the track and sector ID marks are located. If the drive is used in a variety of temperatures and environmental conditions, dimensional changes between the heads and platters can cause the data to be written at various improper offsets from the desired track locations.

The reformatting procedure for hard disks is the equivalent of aligning a floppy drive. For hard disks, however, the concern is not for the actual locations of each track, but that the drive heads are positioned accurately to the same track location each time. Because of the inherent problems in tracking with stepper motor drives and the lack of a track-following system, mistracking errors accumulate and eventually cause a failure to read or write a particular location. To correct this problem, you must lay down a new set of track and sector ID marks that correspond as closely as possible to the position from which the heads actually read and write data. To do this (with stepper motor drives), you must perform a low-level format.

To make the new format effective, you must do it at the drive's full operating temperature and with the drive in its final mounted position. If the drive runs on its side when it is installed, the format must be done in that position.

For inexpensive drives that lack a proper shock-mounting system (such as the Seagate ST-225, -238, -251, or any ST-2XX drive), make sure that the drive is completely installed before beginning low-level formatting. When you attach the mounting screws to these drives, you are placing screws almost directly into the Head Disk Assembly (HDA), which can cause the HDA to bend or warp slightly depending on how much you tighten the screws. Turn the screws just until they are a little more than finger-tight. Do not overtighten them, or your drive might fail if the screws ever loosen and the HDA stress is relaxed. Screws that are too tight can cause continuous read and write problems also, from stress in the HDA. Having this type of drive completely installed when you are formatting places the HDA under the same physical stress and distortion that it will be under when data is read and written, which makes the format much more accurate.

Refer to Chapter 9, which describes hard disk formatting procedures, for more information about the proper tools and procedures for reformatting a hard disk drive.

The frequency with which you should reformat a hard disk depends primarily on the types of drives you have. If the drives are inexpensive stepper motor types—the Seagate ST-2XX series, for example—and you have them formatted with a controller that uses RLL encoding, you probably should reformat the drives more than once a year. People who must support large numbers of these cheaper drives become known as "hard disk reformatting specialists." A joke in the industry is that some of these drives require winter and summer formats because of temperature sensitivity. This joke unfortunately can be the truth, in some cases.

High-quality voice coil drives normally are formatted only once, either at the factory, as in the case of most IDE drives, or by the installer, as is the case with most other types of hard disks. The best way to know how often to format a hard disk is to notice how often, on average, you must reformat a particular type of drive to repair read/write problems. You can avoid those problems by performing a format before any data loss occurs the next time.

As mentioned earlier, voice coil drives do not require reformatting the hard disk as do stepper motor drives. Voice coil drives do not develop difficulties with *hysteresis*, a measurement of how accurately a drive can repeatedly locate to a specified position. Hysteresis is measured by commanding a drive to position itself at a particular cylinder and, later (at a different temperature), commanding the drive to position itself at the same cylinder. The voice coil drive always positions itself at the same position relative to the disk platter because of the track-following servo guide head; the stepper motor drive, however, is fooled by temperature and other environmental or physical stress changes because it is essentially a *blind* positioning system.

IDE interface hard disks normally are formatted at the factory and should not be reformatted because many of them use proprietary bad-track marking schemes, and some place head guidance (servo) information between sectors on a track. An improper format program that does not recognize these "features" may overwrite them, possibly rendering the drive dysfunctional. Most IDE drives can be formatted by a manufacturer-supplied or -approved format program, if necessary. The Micro-Scope program mentioned in Chapter 9 can format most IDE drives.

Passive Preventive-Maintenance Procedures

Passive preventive-maintenance involves taking care of the system in an external manner: basically, providing the best possible environment— both physical as well as electrical—for the system to operate in. Physical concerns are conditions such as ambient temperature, thermal stress from power cycling, dust and smoke contamination, and disturbances such as shock and vibration. Electrical concerns are items such as electrostatic discharge (ESD), power-line noise and radio-frequency interference. Each of these environmental concerns is discussed in this section.

Examining the Operating Environment

Oddly enough, one of the most overlooked aspects of microcomputer preventive maintenance is protecting the hardware—and the sizable financial investment it represents—from environmental abuse. Computers are relatively forgiving, and they generally are safe in an environment that is comfortable for people. Computers, however, often are treated with no more respect than desktop calculators. The result of this type of abuse is many system failures.

Before you acquire a system, prepare a proper location for your new system, free of airborne contaminants such as smoke or other pollution. Do not place your system in front of a window: The system should not be exposed to direct sunlight or temperature variations. The environmental temperature should be as constant as possible. Power should be provided through properly grounded outlets, and should be stable and free from electrical noise and interference. Keep your system away from radio transmitters or other sources of radio frequency energy. This section examines these issues in more detail.

Heating and Cooling

Thermal expansion and contraction from temperature changes place stress on a computer system. Therefore, keeping the temperature in your office or room relatively constant is important to the successful operation of your computer system.

Temperature variations can lead to serious problems. You might encounter excessive chip creep, for example. If extreme variations occur over a short period, signal traces on circuit boards can crack and separate, solder joints can break, and contacts in the system undergo accelerated corrosion. Solid-state components such as chips can be damaged also, and a host of other problems can develop.

Temperature variations can play havoc with hard disk drives also. Writing to a disk at different ambient temperatures can, on some drives, cause data to be written at different locations relative to the track centers. Read and write problems then might accelerate later.

To ensure that your system operates in the correct ambient temperature, you first must determine your system's specified functional range. Most manufacturers provide data about the correct operating temperature range for their systems. Two temperature specifications might be available: one indicating allowable temperatures during operation and another indicating allowable temperatures under non-operating conditions. IBM, for example, indicates these temperature ranges as acceptable for the AT:

System on: 60 to 90 degrees Fahrenheit
System off: 50 to 110 degrees Fahrenheit

For the safety of the disk and the data it contains, avoid rapid changes in ambient temperatures. If rapid temperature changes occur—for example, when a new drive is shipped to a location during the winter and then brought indoors—let the drive acclimate to room temperature before turning it on. In extreme cases, condensation forms on the platters inside the drive Head Disk Assembly—disastrous for the drive if you turn it on before the condensation can evaporate. Most drive manufacturers specify a timetable to use as a guide in acclimating a drive to room temperature before operating it. You usually must wait several hours to a day before a drive is ready to use after it has been shipped or stored in a cold environment.

Most office environments provide a stable temperature in which to operate a computer system, but some do not. Be sure to give some consideration to the placement of your equipment.

Power Cycling (On/Off)

As you have just learned, the temperature variations a system encounters greatly stress the physical components in a system. The largest temperature variations a system encounters, however, are those that occur during system warmup when you initially turn it on. Turning on, also called powering on, a cold system subjects it to the greatest possible internal temperature variations. For these reasons, limiting the number of power-on cycles a system is exposed to greatly improves its life and reliability.

If you want a system to have the longest, most trouble-free life possible, you should limit the temperature variations in its environment. You can limit the extreme temperature cycling in two simple ways during a cold start-up: leave the system off all the time or leave it on all the time. Of these two possibilities, of course, you want to choose the latter option. Leaving the power on is the best way I know to promote system reliability. I recommend that you keep the system unit powered on continuously.

If you think about the way light bulbs typically fail, you can begin to understand that thermal cycling can be dangerous. Light bulbs burn out most often when you first turn them on, because the filament must endure incredible thermal stresses as it changes temperature—in less than one second—from ambient to several thousands of degrees. A bulb that remains on continuously lasts longer than one that is turned on and off repeatedly.

Some people argue that the reason you should leave a computer system on continuously is to prevent the electrical "shock" from the inrush of power when you start up a system. The cause of failure in a low-voltage solid-state circuit repeatedly powered on and off, however, is not inrushing electrons, but rather physical stresses caused by thermal expansion and contraction of the components. Component engineers agree, and tests prove, that a device left on continuously outlasts one that is powered on and off repeatedly.

Where problems can occur immediately at power-on is in the power supply. The start-up current draw for the system and for any motor during the first few seconds of operation is very high compared to the normal operating-current draw. Because the current must come from the power supply, the supply has an extremely demanding load to carry for the first few seconds of operation, especially if several disk drives will be started. Motors have an extremely high power-on current draw. This demand often overloads a marginal circuit or component in the supply and causes it to burn or break with a "snap." I have seen several power supplies die the instant a system was powered up. To enable your equipment to have the longest possible life, try to keep the temperature of solid-state components relatively constant, and limit the number of start-ups on the power supply. The only way I know to do so is to leave the system on.

Although it sounds as though I am recommending that you leave all of your computer equipment on 24 hours a day, seven days a week, I no longer recommend this type of operation. A couple of concerns have tempered my urge to leave everything running continuously. One is that an unattended operating system represents a fire hazard. I have seen monitors start themselves on fire after internally shorting, and systems whose cooling fans have frozen, enabling the power supply and entire system to overheat. I do not leave any system running in an unattended building. Another problem is wasted electrical power. Many companies have adopted austerity programs that involve turning lights and other items off when not in use. The power consumption of some of today's high-powered systems and accessories is not trivial. Also, an unattended operating system is more of a security risk than one that is powered off and locked.

Realities—such as the fire hazard of unattended systems running during night or weekend hours, security problems, and power-consumption issues—might prevent you from leaving your system on all the time. Therefore, you must compromise. Power on the system only one time daily. Don't power the system on and off several times every day. This good advice is often ignored, especially when several users share systems. Each user powers on the system to perform work on the PC and then powers off the system. These systems tend to have many more problems with component failures.

If you are concerned about running your hard disk continuously, let me dispel your fears. Running your hard disk continuously might be the best thing you can do for your drive. Leaving the drive powered on is the best method for reducing read and write failures caused by temperature changes. If you are using extremely inexpensive drives with stepper motor actuators, leaving the drive on greatly improves reliability and increases the time between low-level formats caused by mistracking. A drive's bearings and motors also function longer if you reduce the power-on temperature cycling. You might have had a disk that didn't boot after you turned the drive off for a prolonged period (over the weekend, for example) and you fixed the problem with a subsequent low-level format, but you most likely wouldn't have had the problem if you had left your drive on.

If you are in a building with a programmable thermostat, you have another reason to be concerned about temperatures and disk drives. Some buildings have thermostats programmed to turn off the heat overnight or over the weekend. These thermostats are programmed also to quickly raise the temperature just before business hours every day. In Chicago, for example, outside temperatures in the winter can dip to 20 degrees below 0 (not including a wind-chill factor). An office building's interior temperature can drop as low as 50 degrees during the weekend. When you arrive Monday morning, the heat has been on for only an hour or so, but the hard disk platters might have not yet reached even 60 degrees when you turn on the system unit. During the first 20 minutes of operation, the disk platters rapidly rise in temperature to 120 degrees or more. If you have an inexpensive stepper motor hard disk and begin writing to the disk at these low temperatures, you are setting yourself up for trouble. Again, many systems with these "cheap" drives don't even boot properly under these circumstances and must be warmed up before they even boot DOS.

T I P   If you do not leave a system on continuously, at least give it 15 minutes or more to warm up before writing to the hard disk. Power up the system and go get a cup of coffee, read the paper, or do some other task. This practice does wonders for the reliability of the data on your disk, especially cheaper units.

If you do leave your system on for long periods of time, make sure that the screen is blank if the system is not in use. The phosphor on the picture tube can burn if an image is left on-screen continuously. Higher-persistence phosphor monochrome screens are most susceptible, and the color displays with low-persistence phosphors are the least susceptible. If you ever have seen a monochrome display with the image of 1-2-3 permanently burned in—even with the display off—you know what I mean. Look at the monitors that display flight information at the airport—they usually show the effects of phosphor burn.

To eliminate information from the screen while leaving the monitor on, follow one of these methods:

- Turn the brightness and contrast levels all the way down. This technique is effective, but it is a manual method; you must remember to do it.

- To have the screen blank without operator intervention, you can buy one of the commonly available programs that accomplish this task. These programs usually run as terminate-and-stay-resident (TSR) programs. The program watches the clock and the keyboard simultaneously; if several minutes pass with nothing typed at the keyboard, the program shuts off all signals to the display and the screen blanks.

  TSR programs have their own quirks, such as incompatibilities with some software, but they generally are one of the best solutions in a large company.

- You can, of course, just turn off the display and leave on the system unit. This procedure saves the phosphor in the display and enables the system unit to benefit from reducing the temperature variation.

Static Electricity

Static electricity can cause numerous problems within a system. The problems usually appear during the winter months when humidity is low or in extremely dry climates where the humidity is low year-round. In these cases, you might need to take special precautions to ensure that the system functions properly.

Static discharges outside a system-unit chassis are rarely a source of permanent problems within the system. The usual effect of a static discharge to the case, keyboard, or even in close proximity to a system, is a parity check (memory) error or a locked-up system. In some cases, I have been able to cause parity checks or system lockups by simply walking past a system. Most static-sensitivity problems such as this one are caused by improper grounding of the system power. Be sure that you always use a three-prong, grounded power cord plugged into a properly grounded outlet. If you are unsure about the outlet, you can buy an outlet tester at most electronics-supply or hardware stores for only a few dollars.

Whenever you open a system unit or handle circuits removed from the system, you must be much more careful with static. You can damage permanently a component with a static discharge if the charge is not routed to a ground. I usually recommend handling boards and adapters first by a grounding point such as the bracket to minimize the potential for static damage.

An easy way to prevent static problems is with good power-line grounding, which is extremely important for computer equipment. A poorly designed power-line grounding system is one of the primary causes of poor computer design. The best way to prevent static damage is to prevent the static charge from getting into the computer in the first place. The chassis ground in a properly designed system serves as a static guard for the computer, which redirects the static charge safely to ground. For this ground to be complete, therefore, the system must be plugged into a properly grounded three-wire outlet.

If the static problem is extreme, you can resort to other measures. One is to use a grounded static mat underneath the computer. Touch the mat first before you touch the computer, to ensure that any static charges are routed to ground and away from the system unit's internal parts. If problems still persist, you might want to check out the electrical building ground. I have seen installations in which three-wire outlets exist but are not grounded properly. You can use an outlet tester to be sure that the outlet is wired properly.

Power-Line Noise

To run properly, a computer system requires a steady supply of clean noise-free power. In some installations, however, the power line serving the computer serves heavy equipment also, and the voltage variations resulting from the on-off cycling of this equipment can cause problems for the computer. Certain types of equipment on the same power line also can cause voltage *spikes*—short transient signals of sometimes 1,000 volts or more—that can physically damage a computer. Although these spikes are rare, they can be crippling. Even a dedicated electrical circuit used only by a single computer can experience spikes and transients, depending on the quality of the power supplied to the building or circuit.

During the site-preparation phase of a system installation, you should be aware of these factors to ensure a steady supply of clean power:

- If possible, the computer system should be on its own circuit with its own circuit breaker. This setup does not guarantee freedom from interference, but it helps.

- The circuit should be checked for a good, low-resistance ground, proper line voltage, freedom from interference, and freedom from brownouts (voltage dips).

- A three-wire circuit is a must, but some people substitute grounding-plug adapters to adapt a grounded plug to a two-wire socket. This setup is not recommended; the ground is there for a reason.

- Power-line noise problems increase with the resistance of the circuit, which is a function of wire size and length. To decrease resistance, therefore, avoid extension cords unless absolutely necessary, and then use only heavy-duty extension cords.

- Inevitably, you will want to plug in other equipment later. Plan ahead to avoid temptations to use too many items on a single outlet. If possible, provide a separate power circuit for noncomputer-related accessories.

Air conditioners, coffee makers, copy machines, laser printers, space heaters, vacuum cleaners, and power tools are some of the worst corrupters of a PC system's power. Any of these items can draw an excessive amount of current and play havoc with a PC system on the same electrical circuit. I've seen offices in which all the computers begin to crash at about 9:05 a.m. daily, which is when all the coffee makers are turned on!

Also, try to ensure that copy machines and laser printers do not share a circuit with other computer equipment. These devices draw a large amount of power.

Another major problem in some companies is partitioned offices. Many of these partitions are prewired with their own electrical outlets and are plugged into one another in a sort of power-line daisy chain, similar to chaining power strips together. I pity the person in the cubicle at the end of the electrical daisy chain, who will have very flaky power!

As a real-world example of too many devices sharing a single circuit, I can describe several instances in which a personal computer had a repeating parity check problem. All efforts to repair the system had been unsuccessful. The reported error locations from the parity check message also were inconsistent, which normally indicates a problem with power. The problem could have been the power supply in the system unit or the external power supplied from the wall outlet. This problem was solved one day as I stood watching the system. The parity check message was displayed at the same instant someone two cubicles away turned on a copy machine. Placing the computers on a separate line solved the problem.

By following the guidelines in this section, you can create the proper power environment for your systems and help to ensure trouble-free operation.

Radio-Frequency Interference

Radio-frequency interference (RFI) is easily overlooked as a problem factor. The interference is caused by any source of radio transmissions near a computer system. Living next door to a 50,000-watt commercial radio station is one sure way to get RFI problems, but less powerful transmitters cause problems too. I know of many instances in which portable radio-telephones have caused sporadic random keystrokes to appear, as though an invisible entity were typing on the keyboard. I also have seen RFI cause a system to lock up. Solutions to RFI problems are more difficult to state because every case must be handled differently. Sometimes, reorienting a system unit eliminates the problem because radio signals can be directional in nature. At other times, you must invest in specially shielded cables for cables outside the system unit, such as the keyboard cable.

One type of solution to an RFI noise problem with cables is to pass the cable through a *toroidal iron core*, a doughnut-shaped piece of iron placed around a cable to suppress both the reception and transmission of electromagnetic interference (EMI). If you can isolate an RFI noise problem in a particular cable, you often can solve the problem by passing the cable through a toroidal core. Because the cable must pass through the center hole of the core, it often is difficult, if not impossible, to add a toroid to a cable that already has end connectors installed.

Radio Shack sells a special snap-together toroid designed specifically to be added to cables already in use. This toroid looks like a thick-walled tube that has been sliced in half. You just lay the cable in the center of one of the halves, and snap the other half over the first. This type of construction makes it easy to add the noise-suppression features of a toroid to virtually any existing cable.

IBM also makes a special 6-foot long PS/2 keyboard cable with a built-in toroid core (part number 27F4984) that can greatly reduce interference problems. This cable has the smaller 6-pin DIN (PS/2 style) connector at the system end and the standard SDL (Shielded Data Link) connector at the keyboard end; it costs about $40.

The best, if not the easiest, way to eliminate the problem probably is to correct it at the source. You likely won't convince the 50,000-watt commercial radio station near your office to shut down, but if you are dealing with a small radio transmitter that is generating RFI, sometimes you can add to the transmitter a filter that suppresses spurious emissions. Unfortunately, problems sometimes persist until the transmitter is either switched off or moved some distance away from the affected computer.

Note that your own computer systems can be a source of RFI. Computer equipment must meet one of these two classifications to be certified and salable, according to the FCC (Federal Communications Commission): Class A or Class B. The Class A specification applies to computing devices sold for use in commercial, business, and industrial environments. Class B indicates that the equipment has passed more stringent tests and can be used in residential environments, in addition to any environments allowed under Class A.

The FCC does not really police users or purchasers of computer equipment so much as it polices the equipment manufacturers or vendors. Therefore, if you are using a Class A-rated system in your home, you don't need to worry about radio police showing up at your door. If, however, you are making or selling PCs that meet one of these conditions:

- Marketed through retail or direct-mail outlets

- Sold to the general public rather than commercial users only

- Operates on battery or 120-volt AC electrical power

you must obtain a Class B certification for these systems. Note that a system has to fit each of these three categories to be considered a personal computer and therefore be subject to the stricter Class B rules. Note also that the FCC considers all portable computer systems as meeting Class B standards because their portability makes them likely to be used in a residential setting.

The FCC standards for Class A and Class B certification governs two kinds of emissions: conductive emissions, radiated from the computer system into the power cord, and radio-frequency emissions, radiated from the computer system into space. Table 11.1 shows the conductive and radio-frequency emissions limitations to be eligible for both Class A and Class B ratings.

Table 11.1 FCC Class A and Class B Emission Limitations

CONDUCTIVE: Frequency (MHz)	Maximum signal level (mv) Class A	Class B
0.45 to 1.705	1000	250
1.705 to 30.0	3000	250

RADIATED: Frequency (MHz)	Maximum field strength (uv/M) Class A (10M)	Class B (3M)
30 to 88	90	100
88 to 216	150	150
217 to 960	210	200
960 and up	300	500

MHz = Megahertz
10M = Measured at 10 meters
3M = Measured at 3 meters
mv = Millivolts
uv/M = Microvolts per meter

Note that although some of the specific numbers listed for Class A seem lower than those required for Class B, you must consider that field-strength measurements normally decline under the inverse square law: The strength of the signal decreases as the square of the distance from the source. A rating of 100 microvolts per meter at 3 meters, therefore, would be approximately equal to a rating of about 9 microvolts per meter at 10 meters. This calculation just means that the limits to pass Class B certification are much tougher than they look, and certainly are much tougher than Class A limits. Additionally, Class A certification is tested and verified entirely by the manufacturer; Class B certification requires a sample of the equipment to be sent to the FCC for testing.

IBM and most other responsible manufacturers ensure that all systems they sell meet the stricter Class B designations. In fact, one of the primary reasons for the Micro Channel Architecture design was not only to meet but also to greatly exceed these FCC classifications. IBM knew that as computing clock speeds go up, so do the radio emissions. As clock rates of 66 MHz and higher become more common (and they will soon), IBM will have a distinct advantage over manufacturers still using the AT, or EYES, bus designs. Because vendors using ISA, or EYES, bus designs will have to invest in more expensive chassis and case shielding to combat the emission problem, IBM and other MicroChannel clones will gain a distinct manufacturing cost advantage.

Dust and Pollutants

Dirt, smoke, dust, and other pollutants are bad for your system. The power-supply fan carries airborne particles through your system, and they collect inside. If your system is used in an extremely harsh environment, you might want to investigate some of the industrial systems on the market designed for harsh conditions. IBM used to sell industrial-model XT and AT systems but discontinued them after introducing the PS/2. IBM has licensed several third-party companies to produce industrial versions of PS/2 systems.

Compatible vendors also have industrial systems; many companies make special *hardened* versions of their systems for harsh environments. Industrial systems usually use a different cooling system from the one used in a regular PC. A large cooling fan is used to pressurize the case rather than depressurize it, as most systems do. The air pumped into the case passes through a filter unit that must be cleaned and changed periodically. The system is pressurized so that no contaminated air can flow into it; air flows only outward. The only way air can enter is through the fan and filter system.

These systems also might have special keyboards impervious to liquids and dirt. Some flat-membrane keyboards are difficult to type on, but are extremely rugged; others resemble the standard types of keyboards, but have a thin, plastic membrane that covers all the keys. You can add this membrane to normal types of keyboards to seal them from the environment.

A new breed of humidifier can cause problems with computer equipment. This type of humidifier uses ultrasonics to generate a mist of water sprayed into the air. Although the extra humidity helps to cure problems with static electricity resulting from a dry climate, airborne water contaminants can cause many problems. If you use one of these systems, you might notice a white, ashlike deposit forming on components. The deposit is the result of abrasive and corrosive minerals suspended in the vaporized water. If these deposits collect on the disk drive heads, they will ruin the heads and scratch disks. The only safe way to run one of these ultrasonic humidifiers is with pure distilled water. If you use a humidifier, be sure that it does not generate these deposits.

If you do your best to keep the environment for your computer equipment clean, your system will run better and last longer. Also, you will not have to open your unit as often for complete preventive-maintenance cleaning.

Using Power-Protection Systems

Power-protection systems do just what the name implies: They protect your equipment from the effects of power surges and power failures. In particular, power surges and spikes can damage computer equipment, and a loss of power can result in lost data. In this section, you learn about the four primary types of power-protection devices available and under what circumstances you should use them.

Before considering any further levels of power protection, you should know that the power supply in your system (if your system is well-made) already affords you a substantial amount of protection. The power supplies in IBM equipment are designed to provide protection from higher-than-normal voltages and currents, and provide a limited amount of power-line noise filtering. Some of the inexpensive aftermarket power supplies probably do not have this sort of protection, so be careful if you have an inexpensive clone system. In those cases, further protecting your system might be wise.

To verify the levels of protection built in to the existing power supply in a computer system, an independent laboratory subjected several unprotected PC systems to various spikes and surges up to *6,000 volts*—considered the maximum level of surge that can be transmitted to a system by an electrical outlet. Any higher voltage would cause the power to arc to ground within the outlet itself. Note that none of the systems sustained permanent damage in these tests; the worst thing that happened was that some of the systems rebooted or shut down if the surge was more than 2,000 volts. Each system restarted when the power switch was toggled after a shutdown.

I do not use any real form of power protection on my systems, and they have survived near-direct lightning strikes and powerful surges. The most recent incident, only 50 feet from my office, was a direct lightning strike to a brick chimney that *blew the top of the chimney apart*. None of my systems (which were running at the time) was damaged in any way from this incident; they just shut themselves down. I was able to restart each system by toggling the power switches. An alarm system located in the same office, however, was destroyed by this strike. I am not saying that lightning strikes or even much milder spikes and surges cannot damage computer systems—another nearby lightning strike did destroy a modem and serial adapter installed in one of my systems. I was just lucky that the destruction did not include the motherboard.

This discussion points out an important oversight in some power-protection strategies: You may elect to protect your systems from electrical power disturbances, but do not forget to provide similar protection also from spikes and surges on the phone line.

The automatic shutdown of a computer during power disturbances is a built-in function of most high-quality power supplies. You can reset the power supply by flipping the power switch from on to off and back on again. Some power supplies, such as those in the in the PS/2 Model 80, have an *auto-restart function*. This type of power supply acts the same as others in a massive surge or spike situation: It shuts down the system. The difference is that, after normal power resumes, the power supply resets itself and powers the system back up. Because no manual switch resetting is required, this feature is desirable in systems functioning as a network file server or in a system in a remote location.

The first time I witnessed a large surge cause an immediate shutdown of all my systems, I was extremely surprised. All the systems were silent, but the monitor and modem lights were still on. My first thought was that everything was blown, but a simple toggle of each system-unit power switch caused the power supplies to reset, and the units powered up with no problem. Since that first time, this type of shutdown has happened to me several more times, always without further problems.

The following types of power-protection devices are explained in the sections that follow:

- Surge suppressors

- Line conditioners

- Standby power supplies (SPS)

- Uninterruptible power supplies (UPS)

Surge Protectors

The simplest form of power protection is any of the commercially available surge protectors; that is, devices inserted between the system and the power line. These devices, which cost between $20 and $200, can absorb the high-voltage transients produced by nearby lightning strikes and power equipment. Some surge protectors can be effective for certain types of power problems, but they offer only very limited protection.

Surge protectors use several devices, usually metal-oxide varistors (MOVs), that can clamp and shunt away all voltages above a certain level. MOVs are designed to accept voltages as high as 6,000 volts and divert any power above 200 volts to ground. MOVs can handle normal surges, but powerful surges such as a direct lightning strike can blow right through them. MOVs are not designed to handle a very high level of power, and self-destruct while shunting a large surge. These devices therefore cease to function after either a single large surge or a series of smaller ones. The real problem is that you cannot easily tell when they no longer are functional; the only way to test them is to subject the MOVs to a surge, which destroys them. Therefore, you never really know if your so-called surge protector is protecting your system.

Some surge protectors have status lights that let you know when a surge large enough to blow the MOVs has occurred. A surge suppressor without this status indicator light is useless because you never know when it has stopped protecting.

United Laboratories has produced an excellent standard that governs surge suppressors, called UL 1449. Any surge suppressor that meets this standard is a very good one, and definitely offers an additional line of protection beyond what the power supply in your PC already does. The only types of surge suppressors worth buying, therefore, should have two features: conformance to the UL 1449 standard and a status light indicating when the MOVs are blown. Units that meet the UL 1449 specification say so on the packaging or directly on the unit. If this standard is not mentioned, it does not conform, and you should avoid it.

Another good feature to have in a surge suppressor is a built-in circuit breaker that can be reset rather than a fuse. The breaker protects your system is the system or a peripheral develops a short. These better surge suppressors usually cost about $40.

Line Conditioners

In addition to high-voltage and current conditions, other problems can occur with incoming power. The voltage might dip below the level needed to run the system and result in a brownout. Other forms of electrical noise other than simple voltage surges or spikes might be on the power line, such as radio-frequency interference or electrical noise caused by motors or other inductive loads.

Remember two things when you wire together digital devices (such as computers and their peripherals). A wire is an antenna and has a voltage induced in it by nearby electromagnetic fields, which can come from other wires, telephones, CRTs, motors, fluorescent fixtures, static discharge, and, of course, radio transmitters. Digital circuitry also responds with surprising efficiency to noise of even a volt or two, making those induced voltages particularly troublesome. The wiring in your building can act as an antenna and pick up all kinds of noise and disturbances. A line conditioner can handle many of these types of problems.

A line conditioner is designed to remedy a variety of problems. It filters the power, bridges brownouts, suppresses high-voltage and current conditions, and generally acts as a buffer between the power line and the system. A line conditioner does the job of a surge suppressor, and much more. It is more of an active device functioning continuously rather than a passive device that activates only when a surge is present. A line conditioner provides true power conditioning and can handle myriad problems. It contains transformers, capacitors, and other circuitry that temporarily can bridge a brownout or low-voltage situation. These units usually cost several hundreds of dollars, depending on the power-handling capacity of the unit.

Backup Power

The next level of power protection includes backup power-protection devices. These units can provide power in case of a complete blackout, which provides the time needed for an orderly system shutdown. Two types are available: the standby power supply (SPS) and the uninterruptible power supply (UPS). The UPS is a special device because it does much more than just provide backup power: it is also the best kind of line conditioner you can buy.

Standby Power Supplies (SPS)

A standby power supply is known as an *off-line device*: It functions only when normal power is disrupted. An SPS system uses a special circuit that can sense the AC line current. If the sensor detects a loss of power on the line, the system quickly switches over to a standby battery and power inverter. The power inverter converts the battery power to 110-volt AC power, which then is supplied to the system.

SPS systems do work, but sometimes a problem occurs with the switch to battery power. If the switch is not fast enough, the computer system unit shuts down or reboots anyway, which defeats the purpose of having the backup power supply. A truly outstanding SPS adds to the circuit a *ferroresonant transformer*, a large transformer with the capability to store a small amount of power and deliver it during the switch time. Having this device is similar to having on the power line a buffer that you add to an SPS to give it almost truly uninterruptible capability.

SPS units also may or may not have internal line conditioning of their own; most cheaper units place your system directly on the regular power line under normal circumstances and offer no conditioning. The addition of a ferroresonant transformer to an SPS gives it additional regulation and protection capabilities due to the buffer effect of the transformer. SPS devices without the ferroresonant transformer still require the use of a line conditioner for full protection. SPS systems usually cost from $200 to several thousands of dollars, depending on the quality and power-output capacity.

Uninterruptible Power Supplies (UPS)

Perhaps the best overall solution to any power problem is to provide a power source that is both conditioned and that also cannot be interrupted—which describes an uninterruptible power supply. UPSs are known as on-line systems because they continuously function and supply power to your computer systems. Because some companies advertise ferroresonant SPS devices as though they were UPS devices, many now use the term *true UPS* to describe a truly on-line system. A true UPS system is constructed much the same as an SPS system; however, because you always are operating from the battery, there is no switching circuit.

In a true UPS, your system always operates from the battery, with a voltage inverter to convert from 12 volts DC to 110 volts AC. You essentially have your own private power system that generates power independently of the AC line. A battery charger connected to the line or wall current keeps the battery charged at a rate equal to or greater than the rate at which power is consumed.

When power is disconnected, the true UPS continues functioning undisturbed because the battery-charging function is all that is lost. Because you already were running off the battery, no switch takes place and no power disruption is possible. The battery then begins discharging at a rate dictated by the amount of load your system places on the unit, which (based on the size of the battery) gives you plenty of time to execute an orderly system shutdown. Based on an appropriately scaled storage battery, the UPS functions continuously, generating power and preventing unpleasant surprises. When the line power returns, the battery charger begins recharging the battery, again with no interruption.

UPS cost is a direct function of both the length of time it can continue to provide power after a line current failure, and how much power it can provide; therefore, purchasing a UPS that gives you enough power to run your system and peripherals as well as enough time to close files and provide an orderly shutdown would be sufficient. In most PC applications, this solution is the most cost-effective because the batteries and charger portion of the system must be much larger than the SPS type of device, and will be more costly.

Many SPS systems are advertised as though they were true UPS systems. The giveaway is the unit's "switch time." If a specification for switch time exists, the unit cannot be a true UPS because UPS units never switch. Understand, however, that a good SPS with a ferroresonant transformer can virtually equal the performance of a true UPS at a lower cost.

Because of a UPS's almost total isolation from the line current, it is unmatched as a line conditioner and surge suppressor. The best UPS systems add a ferroresonant transformer for even greater power conditioning and protection capability. This type of UPS is the best form of power protection available. The price, however, can be very high. A true UPS costs from $1 to $2 per watt of power supplied. To find out just how much power your system requires, look at the UL sticker on the back of the unit. This sticker lists the maximum power draw in watts, or sometimes in just volts and amperes. If only voltage and amperage are listed, multiply the two figures to calculate a wattage figure.

As an example, the back of an IBM PC AT Model 339 indicates that the system can require as much as 110 volts at a maximum current draw of 5 amps. The maximum power this AT can draw is about 550 watts. This wattage is for a system with every slot full, two hard disks and one floppy—in other words, the maximum possible level of expansion. The system should never draw any more power than that; if it does, a 5-ampere fuse in the power supply blows. This type of system normally draws an average 300 watts; to be safe when you make calculations for UPS capacity, however, be conservative and use the 550-watt figure. Adding a monitor that draws 100 watts brings the total to 650 watts or more. To run two fully loaded AT systems, you need an 1100-watt UPS. Don't forget two monitors, each drawing 100 watts; the total, therefore, is 1300 watts. Using the $1 to $2 per watt figure, a UPS of at least that capacity or greater will cost from $1300 to $2600 dollars—expensive, but unfortunately what the best level of protection costs. Most companies can justify this type of expense for only a critical-use PC, such as a network file server.

In addition to the total available output power (wattage), several other factors can differentiate one UPS from another. The addition of a ferroresonant transformer improves a unit's power conditioning and buffering capabilities. Good units have also an inverter that produces a true sine wave output; the cheaper ones may generate a square wave. A square wave is an approximation of a sine wave with abrupt up-and-down voltage transitions. The abrupt transitions of a square wave signal are not compatible with some computer equipment power supplies. Be sure that the UPS you purchase produces a signal compatible with your computer equipment. Every unit has a specification for how long it can sustain output at the rated level. If your systems draw less than the rated level, you have some additional time. Be careful, though: Most UPS systems are not designed for you to sit and compute for hours through an electrical blackout. They are designed to provide power to whatever is needed, to remain operating long enough to allow for an orderly shutdown. You pay a large amount for units that provide power for more than 15 minutes or so.

Using Data-Backup Systems

Making a backup of important data on a computer system is one thing that many users fail to do. A backup is similar to insurance: You need it only when you are in big trouble! Because of the cost in not only dollars, but also in time and effort, many users do not have adequate backup— which is not a problem until the day you have a catastrophe and suddenly find yourself without your important data or files. This section discusses several forms of backup hardware and software that can make the job both easier and faster, and—hopefully—cause more users to do it.

Backup is something a service technician should be aware of. After I repair a system that has suffered some kind of disk crash, I can guarantee that the disk subsystem will be completely functional. I cannot guarantee, however, that the original files are on the disks; in fact, the drive may have to be replaced. Without a backup, the system can be physically repaired, but the original data may be lost forever.

Nothing destroys someone's faith in computer technology faster than telling them that the last year or more of work (in the form of disk files) no longer exists. When I visit a customer site to do some troubleshooting or repair, I always tell my clients to back up the system before I arrive. They may be reluctant to do so at first, but it is better than paying a technician by the hour to do it. A backup must be done before I operate on a system, because I do not want to be liable if something goes wrong and data is damaged or lost. If the system is so dysfunctional that a backup cannot be performed, I make sure that the client knows that the service technician is not responsible for the data.

A good general rule is never to let a backup interval be longer than what you are willing to lose one day. You always can reload or even repurchase copies of software programs that might have been lost, but you cannot buy back your own data. Because of the extremely high value of data compared to the system itself, I have recommended for some time that service technicians become familiar with data-recovery principles and procedures. Being able to perform this valuable service gives you a fantastic edge over technicians who can only fix or replace the hardware.

Backup Policies

All users and managers of computer systems should develop a plan for regular disk backups. I recommend that one person in an office have the responsibility for performing these backups so that the job is not left undone.

A backup interval should be selected based on the amount of activity on the system. Some users find that daily backups are required, and others find that a weekly arrangement is more suitable. Backups rarely must be scheduled at more than weekly intervals. Some users settle on a mixed plan: perform weekly disk backups and daily backups of only the changed files.

The procedures for backing up and for dealing with copy protection are explained in the following sections.

Backup Procedures

You should back up to removable media such as cartridge or tape, which you remove from a system and store in a safe place. Backups performed on nonremovable media, such as another hard disk, are much more vulnerable to damage, theft, or fire; also, having multiple backups is much more expensive.

Because of the relatively low cost of hard disks, some users unfortunately install two hard disks and back up one to the other. Worse, some users split a single disk into two partitions and back up one partition to the other. These backups are false backups. If the system were subjected to a massive electrical surge or failure, the contents of both drives could be lost. If the system were stolen, again, both backups would be lost. Finally, if the system were physically damaged, such as in a fire or other mishap, both the data and the backup would be lost. These are good reasons that it is important to back up to removable media.

Perform your backups on a rotating schedule. I recommend using a tape-backup system with at least three tapes per drive, in which you back up data to the first tape the first week. The second week, you use a second tape. That way, if the second tape has been damaged, you can use the preceding week's backup tape to restore data. The third week, you should use still another, third, tape and place the first tape in a different physical location as protection against damage from fire, flood, theft, or another disaster.

The fourth week, you begin to rotate each tape so that the first (off-site) tape is used again for backup, and the second tape is moved off-site. This system always has two progressively older backups on-site, with the third backup off-site to provide for disaster insurance. Only removable media can provide this type of flexibility, and tape is one of the best forms of removable media for backup.

Dealing with Copy Protection

One thing standing in the way of proper backups of some of your software is copy protection, a system in which the original disk the software is on is modified so that it cannot be copied exactly by your system. When the programs on the disk are run, they look for this unique feature to determine whether the original disk is in the system. Some software makers force you to use master copies of their programs by using this technique to require that the original disks be placed in the floppy drive for validation even though the system might have the software loaded on the hard disk.

Some forms of copy protection load the software on a hard disk only from an original disk, and modify the hard disk loaded version so that it runs only if it remains on the system in a specified set of sectors. If the program ever is moved on the disk, it fails to operate. Because these requirements make the software highly prone to failure, copy protection has no place on software used in a business environment.

My personal response to copy protection is to refuse to use, buy, or recommend any software from a company engaged in this practice. With rare exceptions, I simply do not buy copy-protected software. Unprotected alternatives always are available for whatever type of program you want. You might even discover that the unprotected alternative is a better program. If you don't make the software-purchasing decisions in your organization, however, you may have little choice in this matter.

Experienced computer users know that you never should use original disks when you install or configure software. After I purchase a new program, I first make a copy and store the original disks. In fact, I use the original disks solely for making additional backup copies. Following this procedure protects me if I make a mistake in installing or using the software. Because of the need for backup and the fact that copy protection essentially prevents proper backup, a solution has been devised.

When you must use a piece of protected software, you can purchase special programs that enable you to back up and even remove the protection from most copy-protected programs on the market. Two such programs are CopyWrite, by Quaid Software Ltd., and Copy II PC, by Central Point Software. These programs cost about $50 and are absolutely necessary when you are forced to deal with copy-protected software.

Note that no matter what a software license agreement says, you have a legal right to back up your software; this right is guaranteed under U.S. copyright law. Do not let a software license agreement bamboozle you into believing otherwise.

The best way to fight copy protection is with your wallet. Most companies respond to this economic pressure; many of them have responded by removing the protection from their programs. Fortunately, because of this economic pressure by influential users, the scourge of copy protection has been almost eliminated from the business-software marketplace. Only a few remaining programs have this unfortunate defect; I hope that the protection will be eradicated from them as well.

Backup Software

In considering how to back up your system, you should be aware of both the hardware and software options available. This section first explores the software-only options; that is, using either what you get with DOS, or some more-powerful aftermarket software to back up using a floppy drive. You will learn that the aftermarket software usually offers many features and capabilities that the standard DOS BACKUP program does not have. After discussing software alternatives, this section looks at complete, dedicated hardware and software backup systems. Using specialized hardware is the best way to have an easy, effective, and safe way of backing up your system.

The BACKUP Command

The most basic backup software you can use are the DOS commands BACKUP and RESTORE. Since their introduction in Version 2.0 of DOS, and up to Version 3.3, these commands have frustrated users with their bugs and other problems. The versions supplied with DOS V4.0 and higher have been greatly improved, but they still do not offer what many aftermarket products offer. Because of the way BACKUP and RESTORE use the floppy drive as the hardware device, you can use this software only for backing up systems with low-capacity hard drives.

Aftermarket Software for Floppy Backups

Most aftermarket software offers convenience and performance features not found in the DOS BACKUP and RESTORE commands. If you are relegated to using the floppy disk drive as your backup hardware, you should do yourself a favor and investigate some of the aftermarket software designed for backup. I recommend FASTBACK, by Fifth Generation Systems, as well as the Norton (Symantec) and Central Point backup programs. The latter two are included in utility packages from these companies, including Norton Desktop for Windows and PC Tools.

Even with these programs, however, backing up a hard disk larger than 20 to 40 megabytes is not recommended because it requires using a large number of floppy disks. To explain, consider the system I use. My main portable system has a 1-gigabyte disk drive, which requires *728 1.44M floppy disks* for backup. Some backup programs perform data compression that can reduce that number by a third to a half; even optimistically, therefore, you still would need nearly 400 high-density disks. Because I always perform backups to a rotating set of media, with three backups in the rotation, I need somewhere from *1,200 to 2,184 HD disks for my backup.* That number handles only one of my systems; I have an aggregate of more than 1 gigabyte of disk space on several other systems as well. When you imagine trying to manage more than a thousand HD floppy disks, not to mention feeding 400 or more of them into a system for a day or so to perform each backup, you can see the problem associated with backing up large drives to floppy disks.

My solution is to back up the drive using either an 8mm videotape drive or a 4mm digital audiotape (DAT) drive. Either type of tape system easily backs up more than one gigabyte to a single tape, and can perform a complete backup of a full drive in just over three hours. Partial backups take only seconds or minutes.

Another feature of a tape drive is that, because it is an external unit, I can carry it around and use it to back up all my systems. Also, the media costs for tape are much less than for floppy disks: the 4mm 1.3 gigabyte tapes cost only $20 or less. Therefore, I can have three backups that cost less than $60—using floppy media would cost from $1,000 to $2,000 or more. You may not have a gigabyte of on-line storage to back up, but any amount over 40 megabytes starts to become unwieldy when you are using a floppy drive.

For a total of about $1,500 for some of the less-expensive DAT or 8mm units, I have a reliable, complete, high-speed, and simple backup of every system I own. If you have more than 40M to back up—or more than one system—a tape-backup device is the best way. Various tape-backup products are discussed in the following section.

Dedicated Backup Hardware

As explained earlier, you can choose from software and hardware options when you consider backup equipment. In this section, you learn about dedicated backup hardware, usually a tape or cartridge device designed for high-speed, high-capacity backup purposes.

Tape-Backup Systems

A good, reliable backup is important when you're using a large hard disk. With a disk of 40M or more, you should consider some form of hardware backup device other than only the floppy drive. Tape backup is available in configurations easily supporting hundreds of megabytes and more. Tape backup is fast and accurate.

Because your data is probably worth much more to you than the physical hardware on which it is stored, it is important to develop a backup system you will use. A tape system makes the backup convenient and, therefore, helps to ensure that you will complete it. If backing up your system is a difficult, time-consuming operation, you or the person responsible for doing it probably will not do it regularly (if ever). Tape units also can be set to perform unattended automatic backups during times when you are not using your computer, such as during the middle of the night.

These parameters describe the basic parameters of different tape-backup devices:

> Type of media used
> Hardware interface
> Backup software

These parameters are explained in the sections that follow.

QIC Standards

The Quarter-Inch Committee (QIC) issues standards for such things as tape-drive controller adapters, cartridge physical size, and commands that tape drives understand. You can write the committee at this address:

> Quarter-Inch Cartridge Drive Standards Group
> 311 East Cabrillo Street
> Santa Barbara, CA 93101

The QIC organization was formed to develop standard formats for DC-600 and DC-2000 data cartridge tape drives. Because quarter-inch tapes typically have been the market leaders, even suppliers of other systems generally follow QIC standards, such as the SCSI command set in QIC-104, and QIC-122 or QIC-123, which define data-compression methods. Data compression enables you to store more data on a certain length of tape. Vendors can change their backup software so that the codes are inserted at the beginning of the tape. Then, if the tape is read back by other tape drives, the readback drive can determine the method used.

Media

I like to use systems that employ industry-standard media. *Media* refers to the type of tape format used. The type of media you select dictates the capacity of the tape-unit storage. Many different types of systems use many different types of media, but I am concerned with only a handful of standard media types. Four primary standards are the 3M Data Cartridge 600 (or DC-600), DC-2000, 4mm digital audiotape (DAT), and 8mm (video) cartridge media. I recommend any of these types, depending on your requirements for capacity and performance. This list shows the different media types:

- *DC-600 cartridges*. Invented by 3M, the DC-600 cartridge is a relatively large tape, 4×6×0.665 in L×W×D, and has a heavy metal base plate. This long-running standard was introduced in 1971. Many variations of the DC-600 tapes exist; longer lengths have capacities anywhere from 60M, at the low end, to 525M or more at the high end.

- *DC-2000 cartridges*. Also invented by 3M, this cartridge is one of the most popular media for backup purposes. This tape is 2.415×3.188×0.570 inches in L×W×D, with a heavy metal base plate. Although early versions held only 20M, the most common ones now hold 80M or more. A variety of capacities result from the different tape formats available.

- *4mm DAT (digital audiotape) cartridges*. At first glance, this cartridge looks like a regular audiocassette but is slightly smaller. These cartridges come in several recording formats. The most widely used is digital data storage, or DDS, for short. Another format, DataDAT, is available as well. The recording technology is similar to digital audiotape decks and is done in a Helical-Scan format; it is licensed by Sony (the original DAT developer). DAT tapes can hold as much as 1.3 gigabytes (1 gigabyte = 1,024M).

- *8mm cartridges*. These cartridges, which use the 8mm videotape developed by Sony for camcorders, comprise one of the highest-capacity backup systems available. Most units store 2.3G, but even larger-capacity units are available. The recording is done physically as a Helical-Scan, the same method used in a video recorder.

The DC-600 drives now store from 60M to 525M or more, depending on the format and quality of tape used. The DC-2000 media stores only 40M to 80M or more per tape and might be suitable for low-end (such as home) use. Because the larger-capacity 4mm and 8mm units store more than 1 or 2 gigabytes on a tape, they are ideal for network server applications. These large-capacity units can cost from $1,500 to $6,000 or more, depending on the features included and—of course—where you buy it.

Make sure that the system is capable of handling your largest drive either directly or through the use of multiple tapes. With this unit, you can change tapes in the middle of a backup session to accommodate greater capacities; because this method is inconvenient and requires an operator, however, you eliminate unattended, overnight backups. For network applications or large storage requirements, or anything else for which you need top performance and the most reliable backup, you should select DC-600 or the 4mm or 8mm rather than the DC-2000 media.

I recommend only tape systems that use these media because they offer the greatest value per dollar, are the most reliable, and hold a large amount of data. Stay away from devices that use the 3M DC-1000 tapes, Phillips audiotapes, or VHS VCR tape systems. These systems often are slow, errorprone, and inconvenient to use; some do not handle larger capacities, and they are not standard.

Interface

Of the three primary hardware-interface standards, virtually all professional backup systems use the QIC-02 (for Quarter-Inch Committee 02) or SCSI (for *Small Computer Systems Interface*). The lower-end home-use systems use the Shugart Associates 400 (SA-400) interface, the standard floppy controller. The interface you select controls the backup speed, whether an adapter card and slot are required, and the reliability and capacity of the unit.

In the PC and XT systems with their 4-drive floppy controllers, you can use the extra connector on the back of the existing floppy controller for some tape-backup units. This connector saves the use of a slot in these systems. Unfortunately, the AT systems require some sort of multiplexer card to enable sharing one of the internal floppy ports or another complete floppy controller so that these systems can work.

I don't recommend these floppy interface systems in general because they are slow, and the floppy controller lacks any form of error-detection and -correction capability, which can make the backups unreliable. A system using the SA-400 interface has a maximum data rate of 2M per minute, less than half the QIC-02 or SCSI interfaces. These floppy interface systems are suitable for home computer users on a tight budget but should not be used in business or professional environments. Another problem is that the interface limits the capacity to 40M, and you might have to format the tapes before using them.

The QIC-02 interface, designed specifically for tape-backup products, represents an industry standard. Most companies offer products that use this interface. The QIC-02 can back up at a rate of 5M per minute. The interface usually is a short adapter card that requires a free slot in the system. You can buy these adapters separately and enable many systems to use the same externally mounted drive. A free slot is required, however, and might not be available with a regular PC.

Perhaps the best hardware interface is the Small Systems Computer Interface (SCSI), which enables your PC to back up at high data rates. The current norm is 5M per minute as limited by the tape drives. When faster media and drives are available, SCSI can take advantage of the greater speed.

The SCSI interface is supplied as a SCSI host adapter card that plugs into the system unit and can connect to the tape drive. The SCSI adapter requires a slot, but it can connect to other devices such as hard disk drives with embedded SCSI interfaces. The use of the lone host adapter for as many as six hard disk drives and one tape unit is a strong case in favor of SCSI as a general disk and tape interface. The use of SCSI in PCs, however, is still not as popular as the other dedicated interfaces. The reason: SCSI is not as standardized as most manufacturers want.

Stay with the "safe" QIC-02 for tape and ST-506/412 or ESDI for hard drives, or use SCSI for all the drives and tape units. The choice is yours. As long as you get all the necessary operating-systems drivers, you cannot go wrong with SCSI. I think that this interface definitely will become more popular, and it already is overtaking the other interfaces in system use.

Software

Now you need to consider the software that will run the tape system. Most manufacturers have written their own software, which is proprietary and used only by that manufacturer. In other words, even though you might be using a tape unit with the same media and interface, if the software is different you cannot interchange data between the units. One type of software does not recognize the data formats of another proprietary software system. An evolving standard for backup software, called SyTOS (Sytron tape operating system) is fast becoming an industry standard because it is endorsed (and sold) by IBM and many other vendors, as well as having versions that work on all major PC operating systems.

SyTOS has been selected by IBM as the standard software for its units. Because of market pressures to be compatible with IBM, COMPAQ and other system and tape-drive vendors are offering SyTOS with their tape systems. Because two systems that use the same media, interface, and software can read and write each other's tapes, you can have data interchangeability among different tape-unit manufacturers. You should consider using a system that runs SyTOS software for those reasons. Of course, the proprietary software is generally just as good, if not better, but you can exchange data tapes only with other users of the same systems.

All software should be capable of certain basic operations. Make sure that your software does what you want, and consider buying only software that has these features:

- Can back up an entire DOS partition (full volume backup)
- Can back up any or all files individually (file-by-file backup)
- Allows a selective file-by-file restore from a volume backup as well as a file-by-file backup
- Can combine several backups on a single tape
- Can run the software as commands from DOS BATCH files
- Works under a network

Also, make sure that the backup system has these features:

- Can span a large drive on multiple tapes
- Can be completely verified

If the software you are considering does not have any of these essential features, look for another system.

Physical Location: Internal or External

Physical location of the tape-backup units is a simple factor often not considered in detail. I almost never recommend any tape-backup unit mounted internally in a system unit. I recommend that you buy a tape unit externally mounted in its own chassis and one that connects to the system unit through a cable and connectors.

Tape units are relatively expensive, and I never want to tie up a backup unit for only one system. The amount of time that just one system spends using the unit makes this proposition wasteful. With an external unit, many systems can share the backup unit. I just equip every system unit with the required interface, if they aren't already equipped. Extra QIC-02 cards are available for about $100 each, and SCSI host adapters are about $200. Note that many systems now include a SCSI host adapter as part of the motherboard, or as a card already installed. I already share my system among more than five computers and will continue adding systems to the backup pool. In some companies, the backup unit is mounted on a wheeled cart so that workers easily can move it from computer to computer.

If you have only one system or if all your data is stored in a single file-server system, you might have a legitimate argument for using an internal tape drive. You might wish that you had an external system, however, on the day a new system arrives, or when the server is down and you have to get a new one up and running.

Recommendations

I recommend units from any manufacturer that meets these requirements:

Type of media:	DC-2000, DC-600, 4mm DAT, or 8mm
Hardware interface:	QIC-02 or SCSI
Software:	SyTOS

Many manufacturers have systems that meet these requirements.

Purchasing Warranty and Service Contracts

Extended warranties are a more recent trend in the computer industry. With the current fierce competition between hardware vendors, a good warranty is one way for a specific manufacturer to stand out from the crowd. Although most companies offer a one-year warranty on their systems, others offer longer warranty periods, such as two years or more.

In addition to extended-length warranties, some manufacturers offer free or nearly free on-site service during the warranty period. Many highly competitive mail-order outfits offer service such as this for little or no extra cost. Even IBM has succumbed to market pressure to lower service costs, and has an option for converting the standard 1-year warranty into a full blown, on-site service contract for only $40. This same option can be extended to cover monitors and printers for only a small additional cost.

T I P

IBM and other companies are beginning to offer extended-length warranties and free or low-cost on-site service. IBM has a somewhat unknown option to upgrade the standard 1-year warranties on its PS/2 systems into a full-blown, on-site service contract. Under this option, you can upgrade the standard Customer Carry-in Repair warranty to an IBM On-site Repair warranty for only $40 for the first year.

If you have only the carry-in warranty, as its name implies you must carry in your computer to a depot for service; with the on-site warranty, the service technician comes to you. One car trip to a service center costs me more than $40 in wasted gasoline and time. I gladly pay the fee to have the service technician come to see me. Be sure to ask for this option when you buy your system. If your dealer is unfamiliar with it, ask that your order include IBM feature code #9805.

In most normal cases, service contracts are not worth the price. In the retail computer environment, a service contract is often a way for a dealer or vendor to add income to a sale. Most annual service contracts add 10 to 15 percent of the cost of the system. A service contract for a $5,000 system, for example, *costs $500 to $750 per year.* Salespeople in most organizations are trained to vigorously sell service contracts. Much like in the automobile sales business, these contracts are largely unnecessary except in special situations.

The high prices of service contracts also might affect the quality of service you receive. Technicians could try to make their work seem more complex than it actually is to make you believe that the contract's price is justified. For example, a service technician might replace your hard disk or entire motherboard with a spare when all you need is low-level formatting for the hard disk or a simple fix for the motherboard such as a single memory chip. A "defective" drive, for example, probably is just returned to the shop for low-level formatting. Eventually, it ends up in somebody else's system. Replacing a part is faster and leaves the impression that your expensive service contract is worth the price because you get a "new" part. You might be much less impressed with your expensive service contract if the service people visit, do a simple troubleshooting procedure, and then replace a single $2 memory chip or spend 15 minutes reformatting the hard disk.

With some basic troubleshooting skills, some simple tools, and a few spare parts, you can eliminate the need for most of these expensive service contracts. Unfortunately, some companies practice deceptive servicing procedures to justify the expensive service contracts they offer. Users are made to believe that these types of component failures are the norm, and they have a mistaken impression about the overall reliability of today's systems.

T I P If you have many systems, you can justify carrying a spare-parts inventory, which can also eliminate the need for a service contract. For less than what a service contract costs for five to ten systems, you often can buy a complete spare system each year. Protecting yourself with extra equipment rather than service contracts is practical if you have more than ten computers of the same make or model. For extremely time-sensitive applications, you might be wise to buy a second system along with the primary unit—such as in a network file-server application. Only you can make the appropriate cost-justification analysis to decide whether you need a service contract or a spare system.

In some instances, buying a service contract can be justified and beneficial. If you have a system that must function at all times and is so expensive that you cannot buy a complete spare system, or for a system in a remote location far away from a centralized service operation, you might be wise to invest in a good service contract that provides timely repairs. Before contracting for service, you should consider your options carefully. These sources either supply or authorize service contracts:

- Manufacturers

- Dealers or vendors

- Third parties

Although most users take the manufacturer or dealer service, sometimes a third-party tries harder to close the deal; for example, it sometimes includes all the equipment installed, even aftermarket items the dealers or manufacturers don't offer. In other cases, a manufacturer might not have its own service organization; instead, it makes a deal with a major third-party nationwide service company to provide authorized service.

After you select an organization, several levels of service often are available. Starting with the most expensive, these levels of service typically include:

- Four-hour on-site response

- Next-day on-site response

- Courier service (a service company picks up and returns a unit)

- Carry-in, or "depot," service

The actual menu varies from manufacturer to manufacturer. For example, IBM offers only a full 24-hours-a-day, 7-days-a-week, on-site service contract. IBM claims that a technician is dispatched usually within four hours of your call. For older systems, but not the PS/2, IBM also offers a courier or carry-in service contract. Warranty work, normally a customer carry-in depot arrangement, can be upgraded to a full on-site contract for only $40. After the first-year $40 contract upgrade expires, you can continue the full on-site service contract for standard rates. Table 11.2 lists the rates for IBM service contracts after the warranty has expired.

Table 11.2 PS/2 Service-Contract Fees after Warranty for Annual IBM On-site Repair (IOR) Service

PS/2 model	Contract	PS/2 model	Contract
8525-x01/x02	$95	8570-0x1/1x1	$450
8525-x04/x05	$110	8570-Axx	$595
8525-x06/x36	$210	8570-Bx1	$645
8530-001	$190	8573-031/061	$385
8530-002	$140	8573-121	$385
8530-021	$190	8573-161	$750
8530-E01/E21	$190	8573-401	$850
8530-E31/E41	$190	8580-041	$360
8535-all	$260	8580-071	$425
8540-all	$400	8580-081	$550
8543-044	$430	8580-111/121	$500
8550-021	$220	8580-161	$600
8550-031/061	$220	8580-311	$575
8555-0x1	$260	8580-321	$605
8555-LT0/LE0	$260	8580-A21	$675
8557-045/049	$400	8580-A16/A31	$785
8560-041	$310	8590-0G5/0G9	$800
8560-071	$345	8590-0J5/0J9	$850
8565-061	$425	8590-0KD	$950
8565-121	$475	8595-0G9/0GF	$1,400
8565-321	$550	8595-0Jx	$1,450
8570-E61	$415	8595-0Kx	$1,550

If you have bought a service contract in the past, these prices might surprise you. With the PS/2 systems, IBM has rewritten the rules for PC servicing. The same type of on-site annual contract for an earlier 20M AT system, for example, costs nearly $600 annually, compared with $220 for the PS/2 Model 50. Smaller third-party service companies are having difficulty competing with these newer prices. IBM claims that the PS/2 systems are five times more reliable than the earlier systems, and the service-contract pricing is about one-third what the earlier systems cost. If the claims of additional reliability are true, IBM is doing well even with lower pricing. If the claims are not true (which is unlikely), IBM is losing money.

> **T I P**
>
> In summary, for most standard systems, a service contract beyond what is included with the original warranty is probably a waste of money. For other systems that have not yet achieved commodity status, or for systems that must be up and running at all times, you might want to investigate a service-contract option, even though you might be fully qualified and capable of servicing the system.
>
> The PS/2 systems are a somewhat special case; they have low-priced, on-site warranty upgrades and fairly inexpensive service contracts compared to the costs of the systems. Remember, however, that you can buy most, if not all, parts for these systems from non-IBM sources; also, third-party companies that specialize in difficult items such as motherboards and power supplies can repair these items. Only after carefully weighing every option and cost involved can you decide how your systems should be serviced.

Chapter Summary

This chapter has presented the steps you can take to ensure proper operation of your system. It has examined active and passive preventive maintenance—the key to a system that gives many years of trouble-free service. You have learned about the procedures involved in preventive maintenance and the frequency with which these procedures should be performed.

Backup was discussed as a way to be prepared when things go wrong. The only guarantee for being able to retrieve data is to back it up. In this chapter, you also have learned about backup options.

Finally, you have learned about the commonly available warranty and service contracts provided by computer manufacturers. Sometimes the contracts can save you from worrying about tough-to-service systems or systems whose parts are largely unavailable on short notice.

System Upgrades and Improvements

IBM and compatible systems are easy systems to upgrade and improve because of support from IBM and especially the aftermarket. Numerous options are available for extending a system in virtually any targeted area. You can extend the life of older systems by adding functions and features that match the newest systems on the market.

Upgrading a system can be a cost-effective way to keep up with advances in the computer industry and to extend the life of your system. In this chapter, you learn about these types of system upgrades:

- Expanding memory
- Upgrading a ROM BIOS
- Expanding a disk system
- Increasing system speed
- Improving a video subsystem
- Adding a reset switch
- Upgrading to a new version of DOS

> **CAUTION:** You must be careful not to overdo system upgrades. Most people throw far too much money and materials into a "junk" system. For example, upgrading a typical PC- or XT-class system into a 386 AT-class system is not practical cost-wise. Keep track of the cost of your upgrades. Changes to an existing system can become so expensive that purchasing a new system becomes the better choice. By making extensive changes in a system, you also risk creating a "Frankenstein" system with strange quirks and eccentric, if not flaky, operation. This type of system might be acceptable as a "toy" for your personal use but is not recommended for a system used in a business environment. In business, there's no room for a marginally functional or flaky system.

Upgrading by Expanding Memory

Adding memory to a system is one of the more useful upgrades you can perform, especially when you consider the increased capabilities of DOS, Windows, and OS/2 when given more memory with which to work. You can add three primary types of memory to a system: conventional, extended, and expanded. (These three types of memory are described in detail in Chapter 10.) *Conventional memory* is any memory in the first megabyte of a system's memory. Conventional memory is accessible in the processor's real mode of operation. *Extended memory* follows the first megabyte and normally extends to the 16th or 4,096th megabyte of memory. *Expanded memory* is off-line memory accessed by the processor in chunks that are "bank switched" in and out of the processor's view. Expanded memory is slow and clumsy for the system to use and generally is considered obsolete by today's standards. Consider adding only conventional or extended memory because conventional and extended memory are directly usable by DOS, Windows, and OS/2, and expanded memory is not.

This section discusses adding memory, including selecting and installing memory chips and testing the results of the installation.

Today, most systems are sold with the full 640K of usable conventional memory installed. You can add additional extended or expanded memory after filling the 640K conventional memory amount.

PC or XT systems cannot use extended memory because the processors in PC or XT systems cannot run in protected mode. Expanded memory, however, can enhance some of the capabilities—but generally not the speed—of these computer systems. IBM and Microsoft have added limited expanded-memory support to DOS starting with DOS 4.0. Expanded memory requires specialized hardware to implement the bank-switching techniques, so for PC and XT systems, you must purchase a special type of memory adapter with built-in switching capability. If you decide to add one or more of these expanded-memory adapters to a PC- or XT-type system, be sure that the adapter meets Expanded Memory Specification 4.0 (EMS 4.0) or higher standards in the hardware and the software. Many older expanded-memory adapters meet only the inferior EMS 3.x standards in hardware even though the software driver might comply with EMS 4.x. The major difference between the 3.x and 4.x EMS designs is that the newer 4.x versions provide a larger, variable-size paging area that can occupy a larger range of memory areas within the system memory map.

With AT-class systems, you can install both extended and expanded memory. Extended memory is more useful than expanded memory because you can use it fully under Windows and OS/2. Windows and OS/2 can take full advantage of the 16 megabytes of available conventional- and extended-memory space. The need or desire for expanded memory in AT systems is virtually nonexistent because it must be implemented in a slow and clumsy way. Fortunately, you easily can change almost any AT-type, 16-bit expanded memory board from expanded to extended memory by simply reconfiguring the adapter switches.

Because they use advanced AT chipsets, some 286 AT-class systems can use extended memory to emulate expanded memory. If your 286 systems have this capability, check your system documentation for more information. An enhanced Setup program usually controls this capability.

I do not recommend adding expanded memory to PC- or XT-type systems for several reasons. First, an expanded memory board with a couple of megabytes of expanded memory installed can cost more than the entire system is worth, especially when you consider that this memory will not function for Windows and that a PC- or XT-class system cannot run OS/2. I recommend purchasing instead a more powerful system with greater expansion capabilities, such as an inexpensive 386 or 486SX system.

If you decide to upgrade to a more powerful computer system, you cannot salvage the memory from a PC or XT system. The 8-bit memory boards are useless in AT or Micro Channel systems, and the speed of the memory chips usually is inadequate for newer systems. Many new systems use high-speed SIMM modules rather than chips. A pile of 150-nanosecond, 64K or 256K chips is useless if your next system is a PS/2 Model 90 or another high-speed system that uses SIMMs or memory devices faster than 150 nanoseconds. Be sure to weigh carefully your future needs for computing speed and a multitasking operating system (OS/2, for example) with the amount of money you will spend to upgrade current equipment.

Motherboard Memory

This section discusses *motherboard memory*—the memory installed on the motherboard—rather than the memory that resides on adapter boards. The first part of this section presents recommendations for selecting and installing chips. The last part has instructions for modifying an IBM XT Type 1 motherboard. This modification enables a full 640K of memory to be placed on the motherboard, to eliminate the need for memory-expansion boards. IBM's later XT Type 2 motherboards already include this modification.

Selecting and Installing Chips

If you are upgrading a motherboard with memory, follow the manufacturer's guidelines about which memory chips or SIMMs to purchase. The manufacturer of the motherboard indicates also the correct speed of the components. For example, IBM specifies different-speed memory for different systems. Table 12.1 lists the required installed memory speed for IBM motherboards.

Table 12.1 IBM Motherboard Memory Timing

System	CPU	Clock speed (MHz)	Wait states	Memory-access time (ns)	Notes
PC	8088	4.77	1	200	
XT	8088	4.77	1	200	
AT	286	6	1	150	
AT	286	8	1	150	
XT-286	286	6	0	150	Zero wait
PS/1	286	10	1	120	
25	8086	8	0	150	Zero wait
30	8086	8	0	150	Zero wait
25-286	286	10	1	120	
30-286	286	10	1	120	
35 SX	386SX	20	0-2	85	Paged memory
40 SX	386SX	20	0-2	85	Paged memory

System	CPU	Clock speed (MHz)	Wait states	Memory-access time (ns)	Notes
L40	386SX	20	0-2	80	Paged memory
50	286	10	1	150	
50Z	286	10	0	85	Zero wait
55 SX	386SX	16	0-2	100	Paged memory
57 SX	386SX	20	0-2	70	Paged memory
60	286	10	1	150	
65	386SX	16	0-2	100	Paged memory
70	386DX	16	0-2	85	Paged memory
70	386DX	20	0-2	85	Paged memory
70	386DX	25	0-5	80	External 64K cache
70	486DX	25	0-5	80	Internal 8K cache
P70	386DX	16	0-2	85	Paged memory
P70	386DX	20	0-2	85	Paged memory
P75	486DX	33	0-5	70	Internal 8K cache
80	386DX	16	0-2	80	Paged memory
80	386DX	20	0-2	80	Paged memory
80	386DX	25	0-5	80	External 64K cache
90	486SX	20	0-5	70	Interleaved memory, internal 8K cache
90	486SX	25	0-5	70	Interleaved memory, internal 8K cache
90	486DX	25	0-5	70	Interleaved memory, internal 8K cache, optional external 256K cache

continues

Table 12.1 Continued

System	CPU	Clock speed (MHz)	Wait states	Memory-access time (ns)	Notes
90	486DX	33	0-5	70	Interleaved memory, internal 8K cache, optional external 256K cache
90	486DX	50	0-5	70	Interleaved memory, internal 8K cache, optional external 256K cache
95	486SX	20	0-5	70	Interleaved memory, internal 8K cache
95	486SX	25	0-5	70	Interleaved memory, internal 8K cache
95	486DX	25	0-5	70	Interleaved memory, internal 8K cache, optional external 256K cache
95	486DX	33	0-5	70	Interleaved memory, internal 8K cache, optional external 256K cache
95	486DX	50	0-5	70	Interleaved memory, internal 8K cache, optional external 256K cache

In some cases, you can have slower-speed memory on an adapter than would be tolerated by the system on the motherboard. Many systems run the expansion slots at a fixed slower speed—8 MHz for most ISA bus systems—so that installed adapters will function properly. The PS/2 system memory adapters might be able to run more slowly than main memory because of the Micro Channel Architecture (MCA) interface's higher level of controls and capabilities. The MCA's asynchronous design enables adapters to remain independent of the processor's speed and request additional wait states as required to accommodate the slower adapters. (A wait state is an idle cycle in which the processor and system essentially wait for a component, such as memory, to "catch up.")

All the memory adapters that IBM offers for the PS/2 50 and 60, for example, use 120-nanosecond memory chips. These adapters also are specified for the Model 50Z, which normally runs with no wait states and requires 85-nanosecond memory on the motherboard. If these slower 120-nanosecond memory adapters are used in a Model 50Z, they cause the MCA in the 50Z to insert a wait state when the adapter memory is accessed by the system. Only the motherboard memory, therefore, runs with 0 wait states. Several third-party board manufacturers offer special 0-wait-state boards for the 50Z, which require faster access memory than 120ns.

In some systems, even the motherboard memory speed can be controlled. Systems with adjustable wait-state settings enable you to choose high performance by purchasing the proper high-speed memory or to choose lower performance by purchasing cheaper memory. Many compatibles offer a wait-state jumper, which controls whether the motherboard runs with zero wait states. To run with zero wait states may require faster access speed memory. Other systems can configure themselves dynamically to the memory installed. The PS/2 Model 90 and 95 system boards check the speeds of the SIMMs installed on the system board and adjust the number of wait states accordingly. Most other PS/2 systems simply check the speed of SIMMs installed on the system board and flag an error condition if the minimum speed requirements are not met.

The PS/2 systems that use 36-bit SIMMs can detect both the speed and capacity of the installed SIMMs through four special contacts called *presence detect pins*. The motherboard can use these pins to determine the installed SIMM's rated speed and capacity in much the same way that many modern cameras can tell what speed film you have loaded by "reading" a series of contacts on the film canister. In the Model 90 and Model 95, if the SIMM is slower than 70 nanoseconds, the system will add wait states so that the rest of the memory can keep up. In other systems, such as the Model 70, if memory slower than the required 80 or 85 nanoseconds is installed, a 225 POST error message (Wrong-speed memory on system board) is displayed, indicating that the installed memory is too slow.

The faster systems with 16 MHz or higher clock speeds require extremely fast memory to keep up with the processor. Because the speed requirements are so excessive, the cost of memory can be excessive as well. One alternative, adding several wait states to reduce the memory-speed requirements, greatly decreases performance—not what you want in a fast system. Several special memory-architecture schemes have been devised to reduce the number of wait states required, boost overall system performance, and keep costs down. The following list shows the most commonly used architecture schemes that increase memory performance:

- Paged memory
- Memory caching
- Interleaved memory

Paged memory is a simple scheme for improving memory performance that divides memory into pages from 512 bytes to a few kilobytes long. The paging circuitry then enables memory locations within a page to be accessed with zero wait states. If the desired memory location is outside the current page, one or more wait states are added to select the new page. Paged memory has become common in higher-end 286 systems as well as in many 386 systems. Many PS/2 systems, such as the Model 70 and Model 80 systems, use paged memory to increase performance and enable slower 80 or 85ns memory to be used.

Interleaved memory offers greater performance than paged memory. This higher-performance scheme combines two banks of memory into one, organized as even and odd bytes. With this combination, an access cycle can begin in the second bank while the first is already processing a previous access, and vice versa. By alternating access to even and odd banks, you can request data from one bank and, while the request is pending, move to the next bank and make another request. The first request becomes available while the second request is still pending, and so on. By interleaving access to memory in this manner, you can effectively double your memory-access performance without using faster memory chips. Many of the highest-performance systems use interleaved memory to achieve increased performance. Some systems that offer interleaved memory can use the interleaving function only if you install banks in matched capacity pairs, which usually means adding two 36-bit SIMMs of equal capacity at a time. If you add only a single bank or add two banks of different capacity, some systems still will function, but memory interleaving is disabled and a great deal of performance is lost. Consult your system's technical-reference manual for more information.

Memory caching is the most popular and usually the most effective scheme for improving memory performance. This technique relies on a small amount (8K to 256K) of raw, high-speed memory fast enough to keep up with the processor with zero wait states. This small bank of cache memory often is rated at *20 nanoseconds or less* in access speed. Because this rate is faster than normal Dynamic RAM components can handle, a special type of memory component, called Static RAM, is used. Static RAM devices do not need the constant refresh signals required by Dynamic RAM devices. This feature, combined with other design properties, results in incredibly fast access times and very high costs.

Although the static RAM is expensive, only a small amount is required in a caching scheme. It is used by a special cache controller circuit that stores frequently accessed RAM locations and also is preloaded with the RAM values that the cache controller expects to be accessed next. The cache acts as an intelligent buffer between the CPU and the slower Dynamic RAM.

A *cache hit* means that the particular value the CPU wanted was available in the cache RAM and that there will be no additional wait states to retrieve this value. A *cache miss* means that the value the CPU wanted had not been loaded into the cache RAM, and that wait states must be inserted while the value is retrieved. A good cache controller has a hit ratio of 95 percent or more: The system runs with zero wait states 95 percent of the time. The net effect is that the system acts as though nearly all of the memory is 20ns or less in speed, although most of the memory is actually much slower and therefore much less costly.

That the 486 SX and DX chips include a cache controller and 8K of internal cache RAM in the CPU is one of the reasons that systems which use these processors are so much faster than earlier systems. Systems with 386 SX or DX processors must use an external cache controller with externally provided cache RAM. The 386 SL provides a built-in cache controller, and the IBM-designed 386 SLC incorporates virtually the same cache controller and 8K of built-in cache RAM as the 486 processors. IBM therefore can claim an 80 percent performance increase over the regular 386 SX or DX chips for systems that use the 386 SLC processor.

Sometimes the amount of cache RAM a system has can be misleading in providing a performance increase. For example, adding the 256K external cache RAM option to a PS/2 Model 90 or 95 with a 486 DX processor offers only a small increase in performance relative to the 8K of cache memory already built in to the 486 CPU chip.

A cache integrated into a CPU can far outperform an external cache. Also, adding cache RAM does not result in a proportional increase in performance. One of my clone 386 SX systems was supplied with 16K of external cache on the motherboard, with sockets for an additional 16K. This system already outperforms by 20 percent my 386 DX system that runs at exactly the same clock rate but that has no cache. It was difficult to measure an additional 5 percent of performance by adding the second 16K of cache RAM to the clone system.

You cannot expect cache performance to be proportional to the amount of cache RAM you have, and you must be careful in comparing the amount of cache RAM in different systems. You may find that the system with the least cache RAM can outperform a system with a greater amount of cache RAM. It depends on the efficiency of the cache controller and the system design.

To get maximum system performance and reliability, the best recommendation when you add chips or SIMMs to a motherboard is to use memory rated at the speeds recommended by the manufacturer. Using faster memory may work, but it creates no performance benefit. The minimum access-time specification for motherboard memory in a specific system is in the technical-reference manual for the system. For IBM-compatible systems that lack proper documentation, you can use table 12.1 as a guide because most compatibles follow IBM's requirements. Because of the variety of system designs on the market, however, if possible you should acquire the proper information from the manufacturer.

For many systems (such as COMPAQ) with proprietary memory-expansion connectors, you must purchase all memory-expansion boards from that company. Even IBM used proprietary memory connectors in the PS/2 Model 80 systems. For other industry-standard systems that allow non-proprietary memory expansion, such as the IBM PC, XT, AT, most clone and compatible systems, as well as most PS/2 systems, you can purchase memory boards from hundreds of vendors. Be wary of purchasing systems with nonstandard memory connectors, such as COMPAQ and AST, because you may have additional problems and expense when you have to add or service memory.

Chip Installation

When you install or remove memory, these three problems are the ones you most likely will encounter:

- Electrostatic discharge
- Broken or bent pins
- Incorrect switch and jumper settings

This section discusses installing memory chips to avoid these problems, and mentions memory diagnostics programs used for testing memory after it is installed.

To prevent electrostatic discharge (ESD) when you install sensitive memory chips or boards, do not wear synthetic clothes or leather-soled shoes. Remove any static charge you may be carrying by touching the system chassis before you begin, or—better yet—wear on your wrist a good commercial grounding strap. These straps consist of a conductive wristband grounded at the other end by clipping a wire to the system chassis, usually with an alligator clip.

> **CAUTION:** Be sure to use a properly designed commercial wrist strap; *do not make one yourself.* Commercial units have a one-megohm resistor that acts as protection if you accidentally touch live power. The resistor ensures that you do not become "the path of least resistance" to ground and become electrocuted. An improperly designed wrist strap can cause the power to conduct through you to the ground and possibly kill you.

Broken or bent leads are another potential problem associated with installing memory. Sometimes the pins on new chips are bent in a V-shape, making them difficult to align with the socket holes. If you notice this problem, place the chip on its side and press gently to bend inward the pins on the table. Then, install the chips in the sockets one at a time. Chip-insertion and pin-straightening devices are available to make sure that the pins are straight and aligned with the socket holes; using one of these inexpensive tools can save you a great deal of time.

When you install a chip, you must place it in the socket with proper orientation. Each chip has a U-shaped notch that matches a similar mark on the socket. If the socket is not marked, you should use other chips as a guide. The orientation of the notch indicates the location of Pin 1 on the chip. Aligning this notch correctly with the others on the board ensures that you do not install the chip backward. Gently set each chip into a socket, and push the chip in firmly with both thumbs until the chip is fully seated.

Incorrect switch and jumper settings also can create problems when you install memory. After adding memory chips, you might have to alter motherboard switches or jumper settings. AT and PS/2 systems have no switches or jumpers for memory. Rather, you must run a setup program to inform the system of the total amount of memory installed. The PC includes two switch blocks with eight individual switches per block. Switch positions 1 through 4 of a PC's second switch block must be set to reflect the total installed memory. The XT has only one switch block, set to reflect the number of memory banks installed on the system board but not the expansion-card memory. The Appendix in this book provides more detailed information about the PC and XT motherboard switch settings.

Most memory-expansion cards also have switches or jumpers that must be set. You often must set two items when you configure a memory card. The first, a starting address for the memory on the card, usually enables the memory on the card to begin addressing in the system after any other previously installed memory. The second setting is for the total amount of memory installed on the card.

Because of the PS/2's influence in the market, many memory boards as well as other types of adapter cards are made without switches. These boards have instead a configuration program used to set up the card. The configuration is stored in a special nonvolatile memory device contained on the card; after the settings are set, the card can remember the settings permanently. The Intel Above Board 286 and Plus versions, for example, have this switchless setup and configuration capability. Following a menu-driven configuration program is much easier than flipping tiny switches or setting jumpers located on a card. Another benefit of the software configuration is that you don't even have to open up the system to reconfigure a card.

Before installing memory, be sure that the system power is off. Remove the PC cover and any installed cards. SIMMs snap easily into place, but chips can be more difficult to install. A chip-installation tool is not required, but it can make inserting the chips into sockets much easier. For removing chips, use a chip extractor or small screwdriver. Never try removing a RAM chip with your fingers because you can bend the chip's pins or poke a hole in your finger with one of the pins. You remove SIMMs by releasing the locking tabs and either pulling or rolling them out of their sockets.

After installing memory and putting the system back together, you probably will have to run a SETUP program to inform the system of the changes you have made. After running SETUP, you should run a memory-diagnostics program to test for failures.

At least two—and sometimes three—memory-diagnostic programs are available for all systems. In order of accuracy, these programs are

- POST (Power-On Self Test)
- User diagnostics disk
- Advanced diagnostics disk
- Aftermarket diagnostics software

PS/2 systems include the user diagnostics and advanced diagnostics programs on one reference disk. The disk ensures that PS/2 owners have all three memory-test programs. The POST is used every time you power up the system; you can press Ctrl-A at the opening menu to access the advanced diagnostics on the reference disk.

Owners of standard PC systems receive (in the guide-to-operations manual) a diagnostics disk that has a good memory test. PC owners should purchase the advanced diagnostics disk as part of the hardware-maintenance service manual package. If you have purchased this package, you should use the advanced diagnostics program.

Many additional diagnostics programs are available from aftermarket sources. I recommend the Landmark Service Diagnostics and Micro 2000 MicroScope programs as two very capable aftermarket diagnostics programs. Both companies are listed in the vendor list in the back of this book. Also, some good public-domain or user-supported shareware diagnostics programs are available for very low cost. The Public Software Library (see the vendor list) is a good source for public domain and user-supported programs.

Installing 640K on an XT Motherboard

This section describes how to install 640K of RAM on the system board in an IBM XT and an IBM Portable. The upgrade essentially changes what IBM calls an XT Type 1 motherboard into a Type 2 motherboard.

The upgrade consists of installing two banks of 256K chips and two banks of 64K chips on the motherboard, and then enabling the memory chips by adding a multiplexer/decoder chip to an empty socket provided for it, and a jumper wire. The jumper wire allows an existing memory decoder chip (U44) to enable the additional memory. These modifications are relatively easy to perform, and can be done with no soldering.

A memory chip address is selected by two signals called *row-address select* (RAS) and *column-address select* (CAS). These signals determine where a value in a chip is located. The signals are modified by installing the jumper as indicated in these instructions so that the first two banks can be addressed four times deeper than they were originally, thus using the additional address locations in the 256K chips rather than in the original 64K chips.

To install 640K on an IBM XT motherboard, you must obtain the following parts from a chip house or electronics-supply store (see the vendor list for sources):

- Eighteen 256K-by-1-bit 200-nanosecond (or faster) memory chips

- One 74LS158 (multiplexer/decoder) chip

- A small length of thin (30-gauge) jumper or wire-wrapping wire

After you have these parts, follow these steps:

1. Remove the motherboard (as explained in Chapter 6).

2. Plug the 74LS158 chip into the socket labeled U84.

   All motherboard components can be identified by an alphanumeric value. The letter usually indicates the type of component, and the number indicates a sequential component ID number for that type of component. The coding can differ among manufacturers, but most use this scheme for lettering:

U	Integrated circuit
Q	Transistor
C	Capacitor
R	Resistor
T	Transformer
L	Coil
Y	Crystal
D	Diode

   Usually, component numbering follows a pattern in which the numbers increase as you move from left to right along the first row of components. Then they begin again, at the left side and one row lower. You should be able to locate all the IC chips, starting with U1 in the upper left corner of the board and ending with U90 in the lower right corner.

3. Remove the IC installed in the socket labeled U44.

   In the next step, you insert a jumper wire that modifies the memory chip-select and -addressing signals.

4. Install a jumper wire connecting Pin 1 to Pin 8 on the chip removed from position U44. To avoid making changes you cannot undo later, it is easiest to wrap the ends of the jumper wire around the indicated IC pins. Be sure that the ends of the wire are wrapped securely around pins 1 and 8, and that the connection is good. Route the wire on the underside of the IC so that the wire is held in place when you install the chip. Reinstall the chip with the jumper in place. The IC might sit slightly higher in the socket because of the wire underneath it, so make sure that it is seated as far as it will go.

Be careful with the U44: It is a unique IBM programmable array logic (PAL) chip that you cannot purchase separately. A PAL chip is burned with a circuit pattern much like a ROM chip is burned with data values. The only way to obtain the chip is to purchase a new motherboard from IBM. Some chip houses, such as Microprocessors Unlimited (see the vendor list), sell a copy of this PAL chip with the jumper wire modification burned in. Using one of these modified PAL chips is an alternative to adding the jumper wire manually, but note that most companies charge $20 for the chip. Adding the wire yourself is much cheaper.

Another alternative to adding the jumper wire to the chip in U44 is to solder two jumper pins into the plated holes numbered 1 and 2 in the jumper pad labeled E2. Using a standard plug-in jumper, you install a jumper across the two added pins. I normally do not recommend this method unless you are experienced with a soldering iron. All IBM XT Type 2 motherboards already have this modification built in.

5. Remove the 18 existing 64K-by-1-bit chips from banks 0 and 1. Reinstall them in banks 2 and 3 if 64K chips are not already in these banks, or store them as spare chips.

6. Install the 18 new 256K-by-1-bit chips in banks 0 and 1.

7. Be sure that switches 3 and 4 of switch block SW1 are set to Off.

8. Replace the motherboard, and restore all other system components except memory cards.

Remember that the motherboard now has 640K on it and that no other boards must address that space. If other memory cards previously had been configured to supply memory in the first 640K area, these cards must be reconfigured or removed from the system.

9. Power up the system and test the installed memory for 640K without other memory adapter cards.

If all operations are successful, you have performed an inexpensive memory upgrade that matches the capabilities of the Type 2 XT motherboard from IBM.

Upgrading the ROM BIOS

In this section, you learn that ROM BIOS upgrades can improve a system in many ways. You learn also that the upgrades can be difficult and require much more than plugging in a generic set of ROM chips.

The ROM BIOS, or *read-only memory basic input-output system*, enables the operating system and software applications to interface with a system's hardware. The BIOS is the reason that DOS can operate on virtually any IBM-compatible system despite hardware differences. Because the BIOS communicates with the hardware, the BIOS must be specific to the hardware and match it completely. A hardware manufacturer who wants to license a BIOS must undergo a lengthy process with the BIOS company, to tailor the BIOS code to the hardware. This process is what makes upgrading a BIOS so difficult. BIOS almost always resides on ROM chips on the motherboard; however, some newer PS/2 systems from IBM have a disk-loaded BIOS that is much easier to upgrade.

In an older system, the BIOS often must be upgraded to take advantage of some other upgrade being installed. To install some of the newer IDE (Integrated Drive Electronics) hard drives and 1.44M floppy drives in older machines, for example, you might need a BIOS upgrade. Machines still are being sold with older revisions of BIOS that either do not support the user-definable drive-type feature required for easy installation of an IDE drive or that may have timing problems associated with IDE drives.

This list shows the primary functions of a ROM BIOS upgrade:

- Adding 720K, 1.44M, or 2.88M 3 1/2-inch floppy drive support to a system

- Eliminating controller- or device-driver-based hard disk parameter translation for MFM, RLL, IDE, or ESDI drives with 1,024 or fewer cylinders by using a user-definable hard drive type matched to the drive

- Adding 101-key Enhanced Keyboard support

- Correcting known bugs or compatibility problems with certain hardware and software

Because of the variety of motherboard designs on the market, ordering a BIOS upgrade often is more difficult than it sounds initially. If you have a name-brand system with a well-known design, the process can be simple. For many lesser-known compatible systems, however, you must provide the BIOS vendor with information about the system, such as the type of manufacturer's chipset the motherboard uses.

For most BIOS upgrades, you must obtain this information:

- The make and model of the system unit
- The type of CPU; for example, 286, 386, 386SX, 486, 486SX, and so on
- The make and version of the existing BIOS
- The part number of the existing ROM chips (you might have to peel back the label to read this information)
- The make, model, or part numbers of integrated motherboard chipsets, if used—for example, Chips & Technologies, SUNTAC, VLSI, OPTI, and others.

An *integrated chipset* is a group of chips on the original AT motherboard that perform the functions of up to hundreds of discrete chips. Many chipsets offer customizable features, available only if you have the correct BIOS. Most differences between systems today lie in the variety of integrated chipsets now used to manufacture PCs and the special initialization required to operate these chips. Even IBM uses third-party integrated chipsets from VLSI in PS/2 ISA-bus systems such as Models 30-286, 35 SX, and 40 SX.

The BIOS must support also variations in keyboard-controller programming and the way nonstandard features such as speed switching are handled. For example, a computer using the Chips & Technologies NEAT chipset must have a BIOS specifically made for it. The BIOS must properly initialize the NEAT chipset registers; otherwise, the machine will not even boot. The BIOS also must have support for this chipset's special features. Each one of the 20 or more popular chipsets for 286, 386, 486, and 586 machines requires specific BIOS support for proper operation. A generic BIOS might boot some systems, but certain features, such as shifting to and from protected mode or speed switching, might not be possible without the correct BIOS.

Keyboard Controller Chips

In addition to the main system ROM, AT-class computers have also a keyboard controller or keyboard ROM, which is actually a keyboard controller microprocessor with its own built-in ROM. The keyboard controller is usually an Intel 8042 microcontroller, which incorporates a microprocessor, RAM, ROM, and I/O ports. The keyboard controller usually is a 40-pin chip, often with a label that has a copyright notice identifying the BIOS code programmed into the chip.

The keyboard controller controls the reset and A20 lines and deciphers the keyboard scan codes. The A20 line is used in extended memory and other protected-mode operations. On many systems, one of the unused ports is used to select the CPU clock speed. Because of the tie-in with the keyboard controller and protected-mode operation, many problems with the keyboard controllers become evident when you use either Windows or OS/2. If you experience lockups or keyboard problems with either Windows or OS/2 software, or with any software that runs in protected mode, such as 1-2-3 Release 3.x, get a replacement from your BIOS vendor or system-board vendor.

No IBM system I know of has ever needed a replacement of the keyboard controller for upgrade purposes. (Replacement would be difficult because the chip normally is soldered in.) Most IBM-compatible vendors install the keyboard controller chip in a socket so that you easily can upgrade or replace it. If you upgrade the BIOS in your system, often the BIOS vendor includes a compatible keyboard controller as well. You usually do not have to buy the controller unless your old keyboard controller has a known problem with the new BIOS.

BIOS Manufacturers and Vendors

Several BIOS manufacturers have developed ROM BIOS software to use in upgrading IBM or IBM-compatible systems. These three companies are the largest manufacturers of ROM BIOS software:

- Phoenix
- American Megatrends International (AMI)
- Award

Phoenix pioneered the IBM-compatible BIOS and the legal means to develop a product fully compatible with IBM's BIOS without infringing on the corporation's copyright. Phoenix first made available many new features, such as user-defined hard drive types and 1.44M drive support. Phoenix also has by far the largest installed base of ROM BIOS chips worldwide. The Phoenix BIOS has also—in my opinion—the best Power-On Self Test available. This thorough POST presents a complete set of failure codes for diagnosing problems, especially the ones that occur when a system seems dead. The Appendix in the back of this book has a complete list of Phoenix BIOS POST error codes.

The Phoenix BIOS documentation, a complete three-volume reference package, is one of its most useful features. It includes *System BIOS for IBM PC/XT/AT Computers and Compatibles*, *CBIOS for IBM PS/2 Computers and Compatibles*, and *ABIOS for IBM PS/2 Computers and Compatibles*.

I recommend these excellent reference works, published by Addison-Wesley, even if you do not have the Phoenix BIOS (although some of its specific information does not apply to other systems).

The BIOS produced by AMI is very popular, and surpasses even Phoenix in new systems installations. The AMI BIOS offers a far less comprehensive Power-On Self Test than does Phoenix, but it has an extensive diagnostics program in ROM. You can even purchase the program separately, as AMIDIAG. The in-ROM version, however, lacks the capability to test memory—crucial if the failure is in the first bank. Because failures in the first bank of memory preclude the capability to run disk-based diagnostics, you must determine on your own which chip in the bank has failed. On the other hand, the BIOS is very compatible, available for a number of different chipsets and motherboards, and has been handled responsibly from a support level. When problems have occurred, AMI has fixed them, earning this program full compatibility with OS/2 and other difficult environments. The AMI BIOS is available through the distributors listed at the end of this section.

Because AMI manufactures its own motherboards, it has a distinct advantage over other companies. Knowing that the motherboard and BIOS are made by the same source means that any interaction problems between the BIOS and motherboard likely can be resolved quickly by the single vendor with no shifting of blame for the problem to another party. I recommend buying AMI's motherboards because you generally don't have to worry about compatibility problems between the AMI BIOS and AMI motherboard. Even if problems occur, AMI will correct them.

Award, the third-largest manufacturer of BIOS software, has made a name for itself with many system vendors because it licenses the BIOS code to them for further modification. AST, for example, purchased the rights to the Award BIOS for its own systems and now can modify the BIOS internally as though it had created the BIOS from scratch. In a sense, AST could develop its own custom BIOS using the Award code as a base, or starting point. Award also provides precustomized BIOS code for manufacturers. Although Award's BIOS is not yet as popular as the Phoenix and AMI BIOS, it is very popular, and compatibility even in tough environments such as OS/2 is ensured.

If you want to replace or upgrade your BIOS, you can obtain replacement chips from these recommended sources:

■ Micro Firmware, Inc., 1430 W. Lindsey Street, Norman, OK 73069-4314

(800) 767-5465 Order desk
(405) 321-8333 Technical support
(405) 321-8342 FAX
(405) 321-2616 Bulletin-board system (BBS)

Micro Firmware has an extensive line of Phoenix BIOS upgrades, with more than 50 common 8088, 286, 386, and 486 versions. This company develops BIOS upgrades for specific hardware platforms, even when the original motherboard manufacturer is no longer in business or provides its own support and upgrades. Many other BIOS vendors sell BIOS, developed by Micro Firmware, for specific platforms.

■ Washburn & Company Distributors, 3800 Monroe Avenue, Pittsford, NY 14534; (716) 248-3627

This licensed AMI distributor deals exclusively with AMI BIOS upgrades. Washburn has complete AMI motherboard and BIOS packages. A primary distributor for AMI, Washburn has great expertise in dealing with BIOS upgrade problems. It also sells Second Nature, a disk drive support product that might eliminate the need for a BIOS if all you want is additional hard disk or floppy drive support.

■ Upgrades Etc., Inc., 1521 N.E. 90th Street, Redmond, WA 98052; (800) 541-1943

Upgrades Etc., a source for Award BIOS upgrades, also offers a number of other BIOS types.

Alternatives to Upgrading the BIOS

Some companies, especially those who purchase only IBM systems, are timid about removing the BIOS and replacing it with a clone. If you, too, are leery of removing your system BIOS, another solution is available: You can purchase an accessory ROM to augment—rather than replace—your existing BIOS.

Second Nature is one of the best of these products. An accessory ROM for IBM and compatibles, it adds these important features to a system:

■ Greatly expanded BIOS hard disk parameter table

■ Support for 720K and 1.44M drives

No software drivers or other memory-resident programs are used when Second Nature is installed. The hard disk parameters supplied by Second Nature overlay existing drive parameters that are already in your system ROM BIOS. Second Nature, compatible with all popular operating systems—including DOS, Windows and OS/2—also has a built-in, low-level format-and-verify utility.

Most AT-type computers have four 28-pin ROM sockets, two of which normally are occupied already by the existing ROM BIOS chips. If there are no additional empty sockets (such as in the IBM XT-286 or some early IBM ATs) or if your computer cannot load accessory ROMS in the E000 memory segment (as with Sperry, Leading Edge, and some other AT clones), you can buy an optional card to install the Second Nature ROMs in any 8- or 16-bit slot. For more information about this product, contact Washburn & Company Distributors (see the vendor list at the back of this book).

Special ROM BIOS Related Problems

Some known problems exist in certain ROM BIOS versions as well as in some systems sold during the past few years. Several of these problems have the potential to affect a large number of individuals because either the problem is severe or a large number of systems have the problem. This section describes some of the more important known BIOS- and system-interaction problems, and provides solutions for the problems as well.

If you use an AT&T 6300 system, you will want to use BIOS Version 1.43, the most recent one. This version solves many problems with the 6300, and enables support of a 720K floppy disk drive. You can order BIOS Version 1.43 (for about $35) from AT&T National Parts; call (800) 222-PART, and order part number 105203780.

Some systems with the AMI BIOS have had problems with IDE hard disk drives. IDE (Integrated Drive Electronics) drives have been touted as being fully port-compatible with existing ST-506/412 (MFM or RLL) and ESDI drives. Some IDE drives, however, take somewhat longer than they should after certain commands to present valid data at their ports. In late 1989, AMI had received many reports of problems with IDE drives, especially Conner and Toshiba systems. Because of these timing problems, AMI BIOS versions dated earlier than April 9, 1990 (04/09/90) are not rated for use with IDE drives, and data loss can result if earlier versions are used. You might experience Drive C not ready errors with certain IDE drives, such as those from Conner Peripherals. If you have a computer with an IDE drive and an AMI BIOS dated earlier than April 9, 1990, you should get a newer BIOS from the system vendor.

To be sure that you have the correct AMI BIOS version, look in the lower left corner of the screen when you boot your computer, for this figure:

xxxx-zzzz-040990-Kr

The 040990 indicates a BIOS date of April 9, 1990, the minimum version to use. Older versions are OK only if you are *not* using IDE drives. The xxxx-zzzz indicates the BIOS type code and an OEM (original equipment manufacturer) ID number. For AMI-manufactured motherboards, for example, the BIOS type code is DAMI-(model code). The r indicates the keyboard controller chip revision level.

Modifying Your Existing BIOS

If you have access to the correct tools and knowledge, you can perform some interesting modifications or upgrades to your system by altering your existing ROM BIOS. This section discusses some things I have tried. These modifications have worked *for me*, but I am not necessarily recommending that anyone else perform them. If nothing else, the research and development of these modifications have taught me much about the way some things work in an IBM-compatible system, and I know that many of you will be interested in some of this information.

EPROM Programming Equipment

Some interesting modifications or upgrades and even repairs can be accomplished with a system by using an EPROM programmer, or "burner," as it is sometimes called. EPROM stands for Erasable Programmable Read-Only Memory, a type of chip that can have a program "burned," or fused, into it by way of an EPROM programmer device. These devices cost anywhere from about $150 to several thousands of dollars, depending on the capabilities of the device. Most cheaper ones are more than adequate for burning PC ROMs. Both JDR Microdevices and Jameco Electronics sell EPROM programmers; I use and recommend one from Andratech (see the vendor list). They either connect to a slot or use the standard serial or parallel ports for communications. The Andratech EPROM burner connects to a system parallel port, which gives it flexibility and performance not found in most other units. To erase an EPROM, you need also an EPROM eraser, an inexpensive device ($30 to $100) that exposes the EPROM chip to intense ultraviolet light for about three to five minutes. I use a simple one from DataRace (see the vendor list).

With an EPROM programmer, you can modify or customize your system ROM BIOS, as well as the ROM found on many expansion cards. You can do things such as add hard drives to the drive table, change sign-on or error messages, or make specific changes to increase performance or otherwise customize your system. The ability to alter ROMs gives you an extra level of capability in both upgrading and repairing systems. Note that you can use an EPROM programmer to work with ROMs from other types of computer systems as well; in fact, I have even altered the ROMs that operate several different General Motors automobiles, allowing me total control over such things as turbocharger boost settings, engine temperature calibrations, vehicle speed governors, torque converter clutch operation, and even fuel injector and spark advance curves.

Backing Up Your BIOS

One often-overlooked benefit of an EPROM programmer is that you can essentially "back up" your ROMs if they are damaged. Many hardware vendors, such as IBM, do not offer ROM upgrades for their systems, and the only way to repair a motherboard or card with a damaged ROM is to burn a new copy from a backup. The backup can be in the form of another EPROM chip with the original program burned in, or even in the form of a disk file. I keep files containing all of the ROMs in each of my motherboards and expansion cards in case I need to burn a new copy to fix one of my systems.

To create a disk file copy of your motherboard ROM BIOS, you can either place the ROM in an EPROM programmer and use the function provided by the device to read the EPROM into a disk file, or you can use the DOS DEBUG program to read your ROM BIOS from memory and transfer it to disk as a file. To use DEBUG in this manner, follow these instructions:

```
C:\>DEBUG               ;Run DEBUG
-N SEG-F.ROM            ;Name the file
-R BX                   ;Change BX register (high-order file size)
BX 0000                 ;  from 0
:1                      ;  to 1 (indicates 64K file)
-M F000:0 FFFF CS:0     ;Move BIOS data to current code segment
-W 0                    ;Write file from offset 0 in code segment
Writing 10000 bytes     ;  10000h = 64K
-Q                      ;Quit DEBUG
```

These instructions save the entire 64K segment range from F000:0000 to 000:FFFF as a file by first setting up the name and size of the file to be saved, and then moving (essentially copying) the ROM BIOS code to the current code segment when DEBUG was loaded. Then the data can be written to the disk. IBM AT systems and most compatibles have only 64K of BIOS, but PS/2 systems from IBM normally have a full 128K of BIOS code that resides in both segment E000 and F000. For these systems, repeat the procedure using E000:0 as the starting address in the Move command (rather than F000:0) and, of course, a different file name in the Name command. One important quirk of this procedure is that the commands should be entered in the order indicated here. In particular, the Name command must precede the Move command, or else some of the data at the beginning of the current code segment area will be trashed.

You also can use this routine to "back up" any adapter-board ROMs installed in your system. For example, to back up the ROM on the IBM SCSI adapter with cache, installed in my system, a similar DEBUG session will work. You must know the ROM's starting address and ending address or length to proceed. My SCSI adapter ROM is located at D400:0 and is 16K (4000h bytes) long, which means it ends at D400:3FFF. To save this ROM as a file, I can execute these instructions:

```
C:\>DEBUG                      ;Run DEBUG
-N SCSI.ROM                    ;Name the file
-R CX                          ;Change CX register (low-order file size)
CX 0000                        ;  from 0
:4000                          ;  to 4000 (indicates 16K file)
-M D400:0 3FFF CS:0            ;Move BIOS data to current code segment
-W 0                           ;Write file from offset 0 in code segment
Writing 04000 bytes            ;  4000h = 16K
-Q                             ;Quit DEBUG
```

Most EPROM programmers are supplied with software that runs in your PC and enables you to control the unit. Functions available include the capability to read a ROM and save it as a disk file or write a ROM from a disk file, and the capability to copy or test ROMs. The software also should be able to split a file into even and odd addresses for 16- or 32-bit systems, as well as combine two split files into one. Another requirement is the capability to calculate the proper checksum byte (usually the last byte) in the ROM so that diagnostics will pass it. All the programmers mentioned have these functions and more.

Removing the POST Speed Check

One problem in the IBM AT and XT-286 systems is that the clock speed is checked during the Power-On Self Test (POST). Checking the clock speed is probably a good idea, but it causes problems if you want to take advantage of the socketed clock crystal in these systems for a cheap and easy speedup. Most IBM-compatibles do not have such a speed check, and may run at different clock rates with usually no modifications to the BIOS required.

In IBM systems, the Verify Speed/Refresh Clock Rates test checks the system refresh rate (clock speed) to ensure that it is 6 or 8 MHz, depending on which IBM system you have. A marginally faster or slower rate causes the test to fail, and results in a POST error of one long and one short beep followed by a halt (HLT) instruction.

This test occurs at POST checkpoint 11h, which is sent to the manufacturer's test port 80h. A failure of this test as indicated by one of the POST-card products that read this port can be identified by reading 11h as the last value sent to the manufacturer's test port. To eliminate the test, and enable a higher than normal clock rate, you must patch the instruction at the proper location from a 73h (JAE - Jump if Above or Equal) to an EBh (JMP - Jump unconditionally); this patch causes the test for an abnormally high refresh rate (resulting in a low test value) to pass through the JAE instruction. When this instruction is changed to a JMP instruction, the test never passes through and falls into the error routine no matter how fast the rate.

Note that the test for a slow refresh rate is still intact, and fails if the clock is below 6 or 8 MHz, depending on the system. The JAE instruction occurs at F000:05BC in IBM AT systems with the 06/10/85 or 11/15/85 ROM BIOS versions, or at F000:05C0 in an XT-286 system. The original AT system with the 01/10/84 BIOS *does not have this test*. By creating a new set of chips with this value changed with an EPROM programmer, you can eliminate this speed check and enable faster clock rates to go unstopped.

Modifying ROM BIOS Hard Disk Drive Parameter Tables

Probably the most common change made to a BIOS is to add or change drives in existing hard drive tables. For example, I have added to one of my systems two new drive types, 25 and 26, which have these parameters:

Type	Cylinders	Heads	WPC	Ctrl	LZ	S/T	Meg	M
25	918	15	65535	08h	918	17	114.30	119.85
26	918	15	65535	08h	918	26	174.81	183.31

See Chapter 9 for more information about these parameters. In my old AT system, these table entries originally were unused (zeros), as are the remainder from 27 through 47. By burning a new set of ROMs with these two new completed entries, I can use my Maxtor XT-1140 drive to maximum capacity with either an MFM controller (as type 25) or an RLL controller (as type 26). This setup precludes the need for a controller BIOS to override the motherboard table values, and saves me some memory in the C000 or D000 segments, where an adapter ROM normally would reside. It also makes my system more standard. If you are interested in performing this modification, you should have the *IBM AT Technical Reference Manual*, which documents the position and format of the drive tables in the BIOS.

Changing the Hard Disk Controller Head Step Rate

Another, more complicated modification that can be performed is to increase the stepping rate of the hard disk controller. The first edition of this book briefly mentioned this modification, and someone wrote me expressing an interest in it. This edition explains the precise nature of this modification and what is being changed, to give you greater insight into how the BIOS and disk controller work together. The performance gain, in fact, is relatively slight; I see the change as a learning experience more than anything else.

The Western Digital AT Controllers (1002/1003/1006) used by IBM in the original AT system, as well as other compatible controllers, such as those from DTC (Data Technology Corporation) and Adaptec, have a default head-stepping rate of 35μsec. The fastest usable step rate is 16μsec—more than twice as fast. Most ST-506/412 hard disks have optimum stepping rates as low as 10μsec. By decreasing the rate to 16μsec, you can improve the seeking performance of the drive, resulting in an improvement of several milliseconds or more during an average seek. Because the standard rate is so slow compared to the optimum rate, many drives, especially fast-seeking drives, do not perform to their manufacturer-rated seek performance unless the step rate from the controller is optimized in this manner.

There are two ways to decrease the step rate to 16μsec. The easiest and best way is to simply set a jumper on the controller card; not all cards, however, support this option. In fact, only one of the many Western Digital ST-506/412 controllers—the WD1003-WAH (ST-506/412 MFM, no floppy support)—supports this option. None of the other WD cards for the AT enables changing the step rate by way of a jumper. Adaptec, on the other hand, has a jumper to select the step rate on all of its AT ST-506/412 controllers. Other than Adaptec's cards, most cards do not have a jumper and require instead other means of changing the step rate.

The second method of changing the step rate is universal, and works with virtually all AT bus ST-506/412 controllers, regardless of whether they are MFM or RLL or support floppy drives. This change is completed by changing two bytes in the ROM BIOS hard disk support code, which alters the way two specific commands are sent to the controller card.

First, let's discuss a little background on how the BIOS and controller operate. When DOS reads or writes data to or from a hard disk, it accesses the disk through the ROM BIOS. Specifically, DOS uses the Int 13h functions provided in the BIOS. Int 13h functions are commands incorporated into the BIOS of an AT system that enable DOS (or any other software) to perform specific commands in relation to the drive. These Int 13h commands then are translated into direct controller register level commands by the BIOS. The direct controller commands are called command control block (CCB) commands because each command must be presented to the controller in the form of a 7-byte command block with the command byte itself as the last (seventh) one. The other six bytes contain information such as the number of sectors on which to operate, as well as the cylinder and head positions where the command will operate.

Sixteen different Int 13h commands are available for hard disks in the IBM AT BIOS. Some of these commands perform functions that do not involve accessing the controller or drive, such as the Get Disk Type BIOS command. Most other commands, however, are translated by the BIOS into the required code to send one of eight total CCB commands to the controller. Table 12.2 shows the available Int 13h BIOS commands, and the specific CCB command the BIOS executes in the process.

Table 12.2 Int 13h AT Hard Disk BIOS and AT Controller Command Control Block (CCB) Commands

BIOS command	Description	CCB command	Description
00h	Reset Disk System	91h	Set Parameters
		10h	Recalibrate
01h	Get Status of Last Operation	—	—
02h	Read Sectors	20h	Read Sector
03h	Write Sectors	30h	Write Sector
04h	Verify Sectors	40h	Read Verify
05h	Format Track	50h	Format Track
08h	Read Drive Parameters	—	—
09h	Initialize Drive Characteristics	91h	Set Parameters
0Ah	Read Long	22h	Read Sector
0Bh	Write Long	32h	Write Sector
0Ch	Seek	70h	Seek
0Dh	Alternate Hard Disk Reset	10h	Recalibrate
10h	Test for Drive Ready	—	—
11h	Recalibrate Drive	10h	Recalibrate
14h	Controller Internal Diagnostic	80h	Diagnose
15h	Get Disk Type	—	—

Although only eight CCB commands are specific to the standard Western Digital (or compatible) AT hard disk controller, there are variations on some of the commands. Each CCB command consists of a single byte, with the most significant four bits (bits 4-7) of the byte indicating the actual command, and the least significant four bits (bits 0-3) indicating various command options. For two of the CCB commands, the option bits indicate and, in fact, set the step rate for the controller. By changing these bits, you also change the default step rate.

Table 12.3 shows the eight standard CCB commands:

Table 12.3 WD1002/WD1003/WD1006 AT Hard Disk Controller Command Control Block (CCB) Commands

CCB command	Description
10h-1Fh	Recalibrate
20h-23h	Read Sector
30h-33h	Write Sector
40h-41h	Read Verify
50h	Format Track
70h-7Fh	Seek
80h	Diagnose
91h	Set Parameters

In each of these commands, the CCB command byte is sent to the controller as the seventh byte of the total command block. The primary value is the first one listed in the chart. By setting the option bits, the command function can be altered. For example, the Read Sector command is 20h. By adding +1h to the command byte (making it 21h), automatic retries in case of errors are disabled. This step prevents the controller from automatically rereading the sector as many as 19 additional times in some cases; instead, the error is reported immediately. For error-correction code (ECC) errors, the controller simply attempts an immediate ECC correction, rather than rereading the sector as many as eight times in attempting to get a good read before making the ECC correction. You can disable retries only for the Read Sector, Write Sector, and Read Verify commands. This capability is useful especially during low-level formatting, surface analyzing, or even just Read Verify testing on the drive, because any errors are reported more accurately without automatic retrying taking place.

You can set another option for only the Read Sector and Write Sector commands. This option includes the ECC bytes, an additional four bytes of data past the data area of the sector; it would make the sector read or write include a total of 516 bytes rather than the normal 512. To set the "long" option, add +2h to the Read Sector or Write Sector CCB byte value. For example, to change the standard Read Sector command (20h) to include the ECC bytes, you add +2h, which results in a CCB command byte value of 22h. The option to include the ECC bytes during a read or write is especially useful in testing the ECC circuitry on the controller by specifically writing incorrect values and then reading them back to see the ECC in action.

For the Read Sector and Write Sector CCB commands, you can combine the disable-retries option with the long option by adding the two options together (+1h and +2h = +3h), resulting in a CCB command byte value of 23h (Read Sector) or 33h (Write Sector).

The last two commands, Recalibrate and Seek, have options that can be set through the option bits. For these two commands only, the option bits are used to set the stepping rate for subsequent seek commands to the drive. By adding a value from 1h through Fh to the CCB command byte for the Recalibrate or Seek commands, you can change the step rate from the default of 35μsec to something else. The following chart shows the different step rates possible by adding the step option to these commands:

Step option	Step rate (μsec)
0h	35
1h	500
2h	1000
3h	1500
4h	2000
5h	2500
6h	3000
7h	3500
8h	4000
9h	4500
Ah	5000
Bh	5500
Ch	6000
Dh	6500
Eh	3.2
Fh	16

In this case, you want to add Fh to change the step rate from the default of 35µsec to 16µsec. Notice that the other possible values are way too slow (from 500 to 6500µsec), and that the 3.2µsec rate is way too fast for most drives. To change the Recalibrate and Seek commands to use the 16µsec step rate, you must patch the BIOS, changing the 10h and 70h to 1Fh and 7Fh, respectively. You essentially are patching the code executed when an Int 13h, Function 11h (Recalibrate Drive) or Function 0Ch (Seek) BIOS command is executed. These BIOS routines contain the code that sends the 10h (Recalibrate) or 70h (Seek) CCB commands to the controllers. Because the other BIOS routines that also execute the CCB Recalibrate command do so by calling the same Int 13h Function 11h code, only one patch is required in order to change all instances of the CCB Recalibrate command.

Because these two commands can be in different positions in different BIOS, the following code shows you how to find them using the DOS DEBUG command:

```
C:\>DEBUG                     ;Run DEBUG
-S F000:0 L 0 C6 46 FE 10     ;Search ROM for Recalibrate
command
F000:30CF                     ; Found it!
-S F000:0 L 0 C6 46 FE 70     ;Search ROM for Seek command
F000:309A                     ; Found it!
-Q                            ;Quit
```

The first Search command locates the code sent to the controller for a CCB Recalibrate command, and the second Search locates the Seek command. The 10h (Recalibrate) command is at F000:30D2h in this example because the address returned by the Search command points to the beginning of the search string, not to the end. Remember to add 3 to each location returned for the actual location of the 10h or 70h command. For example, the 70h byte would be at F000:309Dh. These "found" locations vary from system to system; this example used an IBM AT Model 339 with an 11/15/85 BIOS. Therefore, you can change these bytes to 1Fh and 7Fh, respectively. You must have an EPROM programmer to record these changes in another set of chips.

This section has examined some simple changes you can make to a ROM BIOS with the help of an EPROM programmer. The steps involved in modifying or burning the ROMs were not described because these instructions normally are included with the programmer device you purchase.

Note Because I consider these types of modifications to be for "hacker" types, I do not necessarily recommend them for everyone, especially with systems whose reliability is critical. Some of this information should prove interesting to many of you who read this type of book.

Upgrading Disk Drives

The interfacing of a system to the different types of floppy and hard disk drives can be a problem sometimes because of the differences in controllers and support software. This section discusses adding floppy disk and hard disk drives to a system.

Upgrading a Floppy Disk Drive

To add floppy drives to an existing system, you must connect them to a controller board. Virtually every PC, XT, or AT comes equipped with at least one floppy disk controller. The controllers and system BIOS routines support different drives.

You should consider five types of drives when you add floppy disk drives to a system: 5 1/4-inch double (DD) or high-density (HD) drives, and 3 1/2-inch double- (DD), high- (HD), or extra-high-density (ED) drives. With 5 1/4-inch drives, you might be concerned about the track-width differences in 40- and 80-track drives. Because all 3 1/2-inch drives are 80-track drives, however, they do not share these compatibility problems. Because the ED or HD drives can read and write DD disks as well, a system with as few as two drives—one 5 1/4-inch HD drive and one 3 1/2-inch ED drive—can read and write any disk format. When you upgrade, therefore, you should add these higher-density drives whenever possible.

DOS version 3.3 or higher is required in order to support all disk formats except the newer ED 3 1/2-inch drive; DOS version 5.0 or later is required for ED drives. DOS versions earlier than 3.3 support fewer drives and probably should not be used anymore. Table 12.4 lists the floppy disk support provided in each DOS version.

Table 12.4 DOS Version Floppy Disk Format Support

Supported disk formats	DOS versions						
	1.0	1.1	2.0	3.0	3.2	3.3	5.0
5 1/4-inch DD (160K)	✓	✓	✓	✓	✓	✓	✓
5 1/4-inch DD (180K)			✓	✓	✓	✓	✓
5 1/4-inch DD (320K)		✓	✓	✓	✓	✓	✓
5 1/4-inch DD (360K)			✓	✓	✓	✓	✓
5 1/4-inch HD (1.2M)				✓	✓	✓	✓
3 1/2-inch DD (720K)					✓	✓	✓
3 1/2-inch HD (1.44M)						✓	✓
3 1/2-inch ED (2.88M)							✓

In addition to DOS support, the controller is another issue of concern. Standard controllers in PC and XT systems support only double-density drives. To save money, consider adding only the double-density versions of the 5 1/4-inch and 3 1/2-inch drives to PC- or XT-type systems because adding them requires no special controllers, cables, or software. DOS provides everything you need, in the DRIVER.SYS driver file, which can be used to support the 3 1/2-inch 720K drive in systems without built-in ROM support for that drive.

The HD drives use a higher data rate (500 KHz) than do the DD drives (250 KHz). To use these higher-density drives, you must have a controller and software capable of supporting the higher data rate. Because the newer extra-high-density drives require a 1 MHz data rate, faster than most current controllers are capable of, you probably need a controller upgrade to run those drives.

To use 1.2M or 1.44M drives in PC or XT systems, you must purchase a controller and software that can handle the high- or extra-high-density formats. Because the AT floppy controller already supports the 500 KHz data rate required by the 1.2M or 1.44M high-capacity drives, no additional controller is necessary. To upgrade your system with a newer 2.88M drive, however, you must have a new controller that supports the 1 MHz data rate.

The final issue to consider when you upgrade a floppy disk drive is BIOS support. Many older systems do not have BIOS support for the newer floppy disk drives. Therefore, even if you have the correct drive, controller, and DOS version, you still cannot use the drive correctly unless your BIOS supports it. Table 12.5 shows the IBM BIOS versions and the floppy disk drives they support.

Table 12.5 IBM BIOS Floppy Drive Support

System description	ROM BIOS date	ID byte	Submodel byte	Revision	Floppy BIOS support 5 1/4 DD	HD	3 1/2 DD	HD	ED
PC	04/24/81	FF	—	—	✓				
PC	10/19/81	FF	—	—	✓				
PC	10/27/82	FF	—	—	✓				
PC-XT	11/08/82	FE	—	—	✓				
PC-XT	01/10/86	FB	00	01	✓		✓		
PC-XT	05/09/86	FB	00	02	✓		✓		
PS/2 25	06/26/87	FA	01	00	✓		✓		
PS/2 30	09/02/86	FA	00	00	✓		✓		
PS/2 30	12/12/86	FA	00	01	✓		✓		
PS/2 30	02/05/87	FA	00	02	✓		✓		
PC-AT	01/10/84	FC	—	—	✓		✓		
PC-AT	06/10/85	FC	00	01	✓	✓	✓		
PC-AT	11/15/85	FC	01	00	✓	✓	✓	✓	
PC-XT 286	04/21/86	FC	02	00	✓	✓	✓	✓	
PS/1	12/01/89	FC	0B	00	✓	✓	✓	✓	
PS/2 25-286	06/28/89	FC	09	02	✓	✓	✓	✓	
PS/2 30-286	08/25/88	FC	09	00	✓	✓	✓	✓	
PS/2 30-286	06/28/89	FC	09	02	✓	✓	✓	✓	
PS/2 35 SX	03/15/91	F8	19	05	✓	✓	✓	✓	✓
PS/2 35 SX	04/04/91	F8	19	06	✓	✓	✓	✓	✓
PS/2 40 SX	03/15/91	F8	19	05	✓	✓	✓	✓	✓
PS/2 40 SX	04/04/91	F8	19	06	✓	✓	✓	✓	✓
PS/2 L40 SX	02/27/91	F8	23	02	✓	✓	✓	✓	
PS/2 50	02/13/87	FC	04	00	✓	✓	✓	✓	
PS/2 50	05/09/87	FC	04	01	✓	✓	✓	✓	
PS/2 50Z	01/28/88	FC	04	02	✓	✓	✓	✓	
PS/2 50Z	04/18/88	FC	04	03	✓	✓	✓	✓	

continues

Table 12.5 Continued

System description	ROM BIOS date	ID byte	Submodel byte	Revision	Floppy BIOS support 5 1/4		3 1/2		
					DD	HD	DD	HD	ED
PS/2 55 SX	11/02/88	F8	0C	00	✓	✓	✓	✓	
PS/2 57 SX	07/03/91	F8	26	02	✓	✓	✓	✓	✓
PS/2 60	02/13/87	FC	05	00	✓	✓	✓	✓	
PS/2 65 SX	02/08/90	F8	1C	00	✓	✓	✓	✓	
PS/2 70 386	01/29/88	F8	09	00	✓	✓	✓	✓	
PS/2 70 386	04/11/88	F8	09	02	✓	✓	✓	✓	
PS/2 70 386	12/15/89	F8	09	04	✓	✓	✓	✓	
PS/2 70 386	01/29/88	F8	04	00	✓	✓	✓	✓	
PS/2 70 386	04/11/88	F8	04	02	✓	✓	✓	✓	
PS/2 70 386	12/15/89	F8	04	04	✓	✓	✓	✓	
PS/2 70 386	06/08/88	F8	0D	00	✓	✓	✓	✓	
PS/2 70 386	02/20/89	F8	0D	01	✓	✓	✓	✓	
PS/2 70 486	12/01/89	F8	0D	?	✓	✓	✓	✓	
PS/2 70 486	09/29/89	F8	1B	00	✓	✓	✓	✓	
PS/2 P70 386	?	F8	50	00	✓	✓	✓	✓	
PS/2 P70 386	01/18/89	F8	0B	00	✓	✓	✓	✓	
PS/2 P75 486	?	F8	52	00	✓	✓	✓	✓	✓
PS/2 80 386	03/30/87	F8	00	00	✓	✓	✓	✓	
PS/2 80 386	10/07/87	F8	01	00	✓	✓	✓	✓	
PS/2 80 386	11/21/89	F8	80	01	✓	✓	✓	✓	
PS/2 90 XP 486	?	F8	2D	00	✓	✓	✓	✓	✓
PS/2 90 XP 486	?	F8	2F	00	✓	✓	✓	✓	✓
PS/2 90 XP 486	?	F8	11	00	✓	✓	✓	✓	✓
PS/2 90 XP 486	?	F8	13	00	✓	✓	✓	✓	✓
PS/2 90 XP 486	?	F8	2B	00	✓	✓	✓	✓	✓
PS/2 95 XP 486	?	F8	2C	00	✓	✓	✓	✓	✓
PS/2 95 XP 486	?	F8	2E	00	✓	✓	✓	✓	✓

System description	ROM BIOS date	ID byte	Submodel byte	Revision	Floppy BIOS support				
					5 1/4		3 1/2		
					DD	HD	DD	HD	ED
PS/2 95 XP 486	?	F8	14	00	✓	✓	✓	✓	✓
PS/2 95 XP 486	?	F8	16	00	✓	✓	✓	✓	✓
PS/2 95 XP 486	?	F8	2A	00	✓	✓	✓	✓	✓

The ID byte, submodel byte, and revision numbers are in hexadecimal form.

For example, table 12.5 shows that the original PC-AT (01/10/84) BIOS supports only the 5 1/4-inch drives, and that the second revision (06/10/85) adds the 720K drive support. The final AT BIOS (11/15/85) supports the 1.44M drive as well. Some of this information is undocumented by IBM; in fact, IBM states that the AT never supported the 1.44M drives. However, I have installed hundreds of them.

If your BIOS does not support a 720K drive, DOS can add support for a 720K drive by adding a DRIVPARM command in CONFIG.SYS. You also can load DRIVER.SYS by way of a command similar to DRIVPARM, for DOS versions that do not support the DRIVPARM command. For example, to support a 3 1/2-inch floppy disk drive on an older system without such support, you can use these commands:

> For a PC/XT-class system: DRIVPARM=/D:1 /F:2 /I

> For an AT-class system: DRIVPARM=/D:1 /F:2 /I /C

The /D parameter indicates which physical drive unit is being specified; in this case, 1 equals B:. The /F parameter indicates a 720K drive format. The /I parameter indicates that this drive is not supported in the BIOS. The /C parameter indicates that the drive has Disk Changeline support: The drive can alert the controller that the disk has been changed. Because the PC/XT controllers do not support a disk change, you cannot use /C with those systems. As an alternative, especially if you are using versions of DOS 4.0 or earlier (which lack the DRIVPARM command), you can use DRIVER.SYS instead:

> For a PC/XT-class system: DEVICE=\DOS\DRIVER.SYS /D:2 /F:2

> For an AT-class system: DEVICE=\DOS\DRIVER.SYS /D:2 /F:2 /C

The parameters have the same meaning for DRIVER.SYS as they do for DRIVPARM. The primary difference in using DRIVPARM or DRIVER.SYS comes after you boot your machine. Using DRIVPARM, the B: drive has the new, correct parameters, and functions as a normal 720K drive, as though your BIOS fully supported the drive. Using DRIVER.SYS, B: still acts as though it were a 360K drive; that is, if you execute a FORMAT B:

command, it formats the 3 1/2-inch disk to 360K. Your system recognizes a new drive letter one character higher than your last hard disk partition letter, which is the substitute letter for B: but with the correct parameters and operation. For example, if you have a hard disk with a single partition (volume) C:, DRIVER.SYS assigns the B: drive as D:. If you FORMAT D:, the B: drive operates in 720K mode. As B:, the drive is in 360K mode.

This situation is confusing, especially for novice users. I tell them, "If you stick a disk in B: and FORMAT B:, it works as a 360K drive; if you stick a disk in B: and FORMAT D:, it works as a 720K drive. But you can use an already formatted disk in B: as either B: or D:—get it?" Confusing! A much better alternative is to use DRIVPARM if your DOS version supports it. The first IBM DOS version to support DRIVPARM is 5.0; some MS-DOS versions supported the command as early as version 3.2.

You should know that DRIVPARM and DRIVER.SYS work only for adding 720K support to a system that does not have that support for the BIOS. The DRIVPARM and DRIVER.SYS commands do not work for adding 1.44M or 2.88M support to a system that lacks that support in the BIOS, even though the DOS manual seems to indicate that they will work. In these cases, you must either purchase a third-party driver program or upgrade your BIOS to support the new drive. I recommend only the BIOS-update method, which eliminates the need for special driver programs.

The PC and XT versions can connect to two drives internally, through the supplied cable, and to two drives externally, through a cable you can purchase. The AT controller supports two floppy drives and two hard disks. If you add large-capacity floppy drives to a PC or XT system, you must have a new controller card and driver programs that operate with the card to support the high-density drives. MicroSolutions sells these special controllers and software drivers, along with complete kits for installing 360K, 720K, 1.44M, and even 2.88M drives in any PC, XT, or AT system.

Adding a High-Density Floppy Drive to a PC/XT System

Adding high-density floppy drives (1.2M or 1.44M) to an XT-class (8088) machine can be a problem. Some people incorrectly believe that a new motherboard BIOS is necessary. It's not, because the XT hardware does not support high-density operation.

Special high-density floppy controllers for XTs are available. These controllers, however, include their own ROM BIOS extension that provides the BIOS-level support tailored for their specific controller. The main BIOS normally has nothing to do with supporting a high-density drive on an XT.

In some cases, the BIOS extension on an XT high-density controller might not work properly with some motherboard BIOS versions; ask the controller manufacturer for verification. You know that the controller BIOS is having problems when you see phantom-directory problems— that is, problems with the controller recognizing the Disk Change signal. If you have this problem, contact the manufacturer of the controller. The manufacturer should be able to recommend a solution, such as changing the BIOS on the controller card or installing a new motherboard BIOS. Of course, an incorrectly configured drive or bad cable also can cause these problems. Be sure to check your installation thoroughly.

Adding a Hard Disk to a System

When you add hard disks to a system, purchase the entire package from one company unless you are familiar with disk drive interfacing. Because IBM continues to use industry-standard interfaces, you can take a "plug and play" approach to hard disk interfacing: As long as your disk controller and drive interface match in type, they should work together. To learn more about the different hard disk installations, be sure to follow the information in Chapter 9. Especially if you want to install an ESDI or SCSI system, I recommend using a single supplier for the drive and adapter until you are familiar with these types of installations. Differences between these and the more common ST-506/412 interface can complicate the process.

Speeding Up a System

This section examines ways to increase a system's speed. For example, a common and easy way to increase a system's calculating performance is to add a math coprocessor. Products advertised to make your system run faster are discussed also in this section, along with indications of their relative performance gains.

Another type of performance improvement involves increasing the system clock rate, changing the processor for another type, or both. The idea of replacing the processor with a faster one can extend to replacing the entire motherboard. In this case, you do not really upgrade your system—you change it entirely. This "extreme" upgrade is not always recommended. This section examines also the cost benefit of these upgrades.

Math Coprocessors

Adding a math coprocessor is an easy way to upgrade a system's performance with minimum effort. Be sure that the software you use supports these chips; they lighten your wallet only when they are specifically recognized and supported by software. Depending on how your motherboard is designed and the type of main processor you have, you can add the appropriate math coprocessor chip.

These chips are rated for different speeds of operation. Be sure that the chip you purchase is designed to operate at the clock rate at which the system runs the math chip. Be careful with static discharges when you handle these chips; the chips are delicate and expensive. For more information about math coprocessors, refer to Chapter 7.

A math coprocessor upgrade does not speed up all system operations, or even all math operations. For example, I created a sample Lotus spreadsheet consisting of 10,000 cells of multiplication, division, addition, and subtraction. It showed no improvement in speed in a system with a math coprocessor compared to a system without one. The overhead to have these math operations transferred to the coprocessor, executed, and returned is not worth the additional speed gained; most software packages that support the coprocessor do not use it for addition, subtraction, multiplication, or division operations.

Because of the transfer overhead, the Lotus software does not use the math coprocessor for simple mathematical operations; rather, Lotus software calculates these kinds of instructions on the main processor. High-level math—such as exponentiation, trigonometry functions, and logarithms—are executed on the math coprocessor for an approximate tenfold increase in speed. As an upgrade, a math coprocessor is a very selective speed improvement. A math coprocessor works with software written specifically to recognize the coprocessor and only in limited areas within a program. A spreadsheet does not increase speed in all operations throughout a system.

To install a math coprocessor, follow these steps:

1. Turn off the system power.

2. Remove the system-unit cover assembly.

3. Touch the power supply to ensure that you are at the same electrical potential as the system unit.

4. Remove all plug-in adapter cards necessary to adequately access the coprocessor socket.

5. Locate the coprocessor socket on the motherboard. In almost all systems, the math coprocessor socket is next to the main processor.

6. Remove the math coprocessor from its protective holder, place the coprocessor on the socket, and align Pin 1 on the processor with Pin 1 in the socket. To align the pins, look for a notch in the chip, and make sure that the notch faces the same direction as the notches on other chips.

7. Carefully press the chip straight down, and make sure that all the pins are seated in the socket. Be careful not to bend pins.

8. If you are using a PC or XT, locate the DIP switch block of the PC on the system board, and flip switch position 2 to Off. On an AT or PS/2, run the Setup program so that the computer recognizes the addition of the coprocessor.

9. Reinstall all adapter boards that were removed.

10. Replace the system-unit cover.

11. Verify the operation of the math coprocessor by using either the diagnostics or advanced diagnostics disk.

Upgrading a PC-Type System Main Processor

Several methods are available for increasing the calculating speed of a PC, including replacing the processor with a more efficient unit, replacing the processor with an In-Circuit Emulator, and replacing the entire motherboard. This section describes how to increase the calculating speed of a PC-type system, including the IBM PC and XT and all PC or XT compatibles.

Replacing a Processor with an NEC V20 or V30 Chip

A simple way to increase the performance of an 8088- or 8086-based system is to use the more efficient alternative processors that NEC produces. These processors are plugged into the system as direct replacements for the original processors. The NEC unit selected varies according to the original processor type in the system. The processors are exchanged as follows:

Original processor	Replacement processor
Intel 8088	NEC V20
Intel 8086	NEC V30

The original processor in an IBM XT is a 4.77 MHz 8088. The replacement processor required is an NEC V20 rated for at least 4.77 MHz. The available V20 chips normally are rated to run at 8 MHz because the actual operating speed of 4.77 MHz is less than the rated 8 MHz. The chip's rating has nothing to do with the speed at which the chip runs; the running speed is controlled by the motherboard clock circuitry.

To install the NEC processor replacement, locate the 8088 or 8086 processor on the motherboard, remove the processor, and plug the NEC device into place. NEC chips are available for about $15 to $25, depending upon the chip, the speed rating, and the retailer.

This processor upgrade is very inexpensive and easy to install, but the speed increase is so small that it is difficult to detect. You should test-run applications and time different operations with a stopwatch to determine any time savings from using the new chip. The normal increase in performance is about 5 to 10 percent of the former speed. If an operation originally took 10 seconds to complete, the same operation takes 9 to 9 1/2 seconds with the new NEC chip. For only $15, however, a 5 percent average increase is not bad.

Another problem with this processor upgrade is that the NEC chips are not 100 percent compatible with Intel units. The IBM PS/2 Models 25 and 30 cannot use the NEC chips, for example, and some of the special disk-duplicating programs that back up copy-protected disks do not work when the NEC chips are installed.

There have been legal questions regarding the NEC V-series chips. Several years ago, when Intel could not meet the demand for the production of 8088 and 8086 systems, it licensed other manufacturers to make these chips. NEC, one of the manufacturers, was given the chip mask specifications for the Intel chips and complete access to the Intel processors' source code. NEC then created a new processor that mimics the Intel units but that is more efficient in several instructions. Intel has attempted to restrain NEC from manufacturing and importing these devices; they remain available, however.

Because of the very small performance gain and the potential for both incompatibility and legal problems, business users probably should avoid purchasing NEC chips. You might want to consider this upgrade for a home or experimental system, however, because of its low cost.

Increasing the Clock Rate

Another type of improvement to speed up your system is to increase the processor's clock rate. This type of upgrade is more difficult to implement for PC or XT systems because the clock crystal cannot be easily altered or replaced. The crystal is soldered, not socketed, in place, and the crystal is multiplexed—that is, it is used for other functions in addition to running the system clock.

The crystal in an IBM XT, for example, is a 14.31818 MHz unit whose frequency is divided by 3 by the timer circuits to generate the 4.77 MHz system clock. This 14.31818 MHz crystal frequency also is on the system bus (slot) connectors at Pin B30. (This signal is one of the PC bus specifications.) Many cards, such as video boards, depend on this oscillator signal to be present for their operation. The oscillator signal is divided by 4 to obtain a 3.58 MHz signal used to drive circuits in the Color Graphics Adapter. An upgrade that attempts to increase the clock rate of the main processor, therefore, probably would interfere with the original crystal and its subset function of generating a 14.31818 MHz oscillator signal for the system bus.

Several years ago, some devices sold for PC and XT systems could increase the clock rate for the main processor without interfering with other circuits on the motherboard. These devices have been mostly unavailable for some time. A much better alternative is to install a processor-enhancement card that has a 286 or 386 processor on board, or even to replace the entire motherboard.

In-Circuit Emulator Boards

You can upgrade your system with an In-Circuit Emulator (ICE) board also. This plug-in board emulates the 8088 or 8086 microprocessor chip by plugging an adapter cable into the processor chip socket. These boards are relatively economical for the enhancement they provide, and can offer a tremendous improvement in speed in most cases.

An ICE board is an adapter board that plugs into one of the system's expansion slots. The board also has a cable that plugs into the microprocessor socket and takes over the system as though it were a new processor. The boards I recommend have a 286 or 386 processor running at a high clock rate, and high-speed, 16- or 32-bit memory on board and wired to the included processor. Another feature of some of the better boards enables your processor to be installed on the ICE board. You can switch the original processor back into the circuit electrically for compatibility and reliability testing.

To install an ICE board, follow these steps:

1. Remove the main processor from the motherboard.

   In some units, you install the processor on the speedup board. Other units require that you store the original processor for safekeeping.

2. Plug the speedup board into an open slot, preferably next to the processor socket.

3. Run a cable from the board to the processor socket, and plug in the cable.

The installation is complete. These units have their own on-board memory, a full complement of 640K, or a small amount of cache memory. The high-speed memory is directly accessible by the 80286 or 80386 processor on the speedup board. Your system memory still is used on some of these units.

Some units run in synchronization with the motherboard clock circuits, and others do not. The units that run in synchronization handle input and output operations more efficiently, such as dealing with disk drive controllers and other expansion boards in the slots. The asynchronous units generally are somewhat slower because of their less-efficient design, although they can make up for it by running at much higher clock rates than a synchronous unit. For example, 12 MHz asynchronous boards speed up the system overall by the same amount as a 7.2 MHz synchronous board. Don't be fooled by a raw clock-rate figure; these figures often are misleading.

The asynchronous units have one distinct advantage: compatibility with more systems on the market. The synchronous units work only in systems with an 8088 processor running at 4.77 MHz. You cannot install synchronous units in any other systems, including those with an 8086 processor. This restriction rules out many "turbo" XT compatibles unless the turbo mode can be disabled and the system run at 4.77 MHz.

Typical speed increase in these units is about 350 to 450 percent for units based on the 286 processor, and 800 to 900 percent in 386-based units. Prices vary, but you should expect to pay $200 or so for 286-based units, and $400 or so for 386-based units. Table 12.6 lists recommended boards and their speed increases.

Table 12.6 Recommended ICE Boards

Board type and name	Approximate speed increase
Synchronous 80286 boards	
Orchid TinyTurbo 286	+350 percent
Orchid TwinTurbo 12	+450 percent
Asynchronous 80386 boards	
Sota Technology 386si	+800 percent

These devices also could monitor the system-reset line to detect a reboot operation, and automatically kicked the system into low gear until the POST was passed, thus working around the speed test. These devices unfortunately cost much more than a simple crystal change, and have for the most part been discontinued.

In-Circuit Emulator Boards for AT Systems

In-Circuit Emulator (ICE) boards for ATs are not as diverse or complicated as those for PC types of systems. They normally act as direct processor replacements: They plug into the processor socket and do not take up a slot as in the ICE boards used in PC or XT systems.

You install these processor upgrade boards by removing the 286 chip and installing the upgrade module in the 286 socket. Most processor-upgrade boards use the 386 SX chip, and run at 25 MHz. The small daughterboard also has a socket for a 387 SX math coprocessor. Because some of these upgrade boards have had compatibility problems with the original IBM ROM BIOS, most are supplied with a set of aftermarket BIOS chips as well. In many cases, this supply is itself an upgrade, because the new BIOS gives you enhancements discussed earlier in this chapter, including enhanced hard disk drive support and floppy drive support.

Several of these 386 SX processor-upgrade modules are on the market. I recommend those from Intel, Kingston, and Sota Technologies (addresses and phone numbers for these companies are in the vendor list in the back of this book).

These processor-upgrade modules are a relatively simple and effective way to double the performance of older AT computers. Because most of these devices sell for about $300, the cost is relatively low compared to the performance gain.

Replacing the AT Motherboard

You can choose from many motherboard replacements for AT systems, most of which use 386 or 486 processors. These motherboard upgrades do not share the same problems as in upgrading an XT in this manner because you do not have to worry about changing other system components to be compatible with the new motherboard. In general, because you are both starting and ending with an AT-class system, you do not have to worry about changing the existing disk controller, memory, serial ports, floppy controller, or floppy drives because they are already AT devices.

Be sure that the board you purchase has the correct screw holes for mounting in the existing chassis. Most AT replacement motherboards include both AT and XT form-factor mounting holes, to enable the boards to be mounted in a variety of system chassis. Some higher-performance upgrade motherboards work only in an AT chassis because they exploit the full AT motherboard form factor, and are designed specifically for only the larger AT case.

Adding a New Video Adapter Board

Adding a high-resolution video display adapter and monitor is a great way to breathe some life into an early system. This type of upgrade, however, can be expensive. High-resolution, color-graphics displays usually cost between $500 and several thousands of dollars, depending primarily on the size and resolution capability of the display. The video adapters cost much less than the displays, ranging anywhere from well under $100 to $500 or more.

Most video upgrades consist of adding either VGA- or XGA-level graphics capabilities to a system. Video-system upgrades to VGA- or XGA-level graphics ensure software compatibility with the majority of programs designed to support these industry-standard display adapters. Earlier display adapters, including the Enhanced Graphics Adapter (EGA), are obsolete and are not recommended for any system unless cost is the most important factor.

VGA and XGA graphics adapters support a variety of displays, including everything from inexpensive analog monochrome displays to high-resolution color without changing the video card. You can start with a monochrome VGA system for a very low cost, and upgrade to a full-color display when more money is available. The VGA and XGA senses the type of display (monochrome or color) and adjusts the display to a mode that uses shades of gray rather than color. No change in software configuration is necessary to make the adjustment.

VGA and XGA graphics adapters also support any software written for the older, obsolete display cards. With the emphasis on powerful graphics applications and graphical user interfaces such as OS/2 and Windows, I recommend video upgrades at the XGA level. Because XGA cards have built-in processors, these graphics cards are much faster than the previous VGA adapters and offer very high resolution and color capability. Chapter 10 has more information on video adapter and display capabilities.

Adding a Hardware Reset Switch

A switch that applies a full reset to your system keeps power moving to the system and rescues you from a system lockup. A reset switch saves much time and some of the wear and tear on your unit from using the power switch as a reset button. Because IBM and most compatible vendors have built full reset circuitry into the motherboard, the hardest part of adding a reset switch to your system is figuring out where to mount it.

Adding a reset button is possible on any system, including all IBM systems, because it has a power supply that provides a Power Good signal. On most IBM-compatible computers, the Power Good signal is on the connector that plugs into the rearmost power-supply connectors. In PC and XT systems, this signal traces through the motherboard to the 8284a chip at Pin 11. When the line is shorted to ground and returned to normal, the 8284a (82284 in an AT) clock-timer chip generates a reset signal on Pin 10. The reset signal is sent to the 8088 at Pin 21, and the boot process begins. In other systems with different processors and timer chips, such as AT or PS/2 systems, the Power Good signal also initiates a reset if the signal is grounded and returned to normal, although the wiring details vary.

In all IBM-compatible systems, when the CPU is reset, it begins to execute code at memory location F000:FFF0, known as the power-up reset vector. An immediate jump instruction at this location sends the CPU's instruction pointer to the start location for the particular system ROM. The system then begins the POST. The processor and DMA chips are tested first, but before initiating the full POST memory test, the memory location 0000:0472 is compared to the value 1234h. If they are equal, a *warm* start is indicated and the POST memory tests are skipped. If any other value is there, a *cold* start forces all memory to be tested.

This procedure is the basis of an effective reset switch. By setting the flag value at memory location 0000:0472, you can have the system perform either a cold or warm start when you press a reset button. The type of reset, a hardware reset, "unfreezes" a locked-up machine, unlike the Ctrl-Alt-Del software reset command.

To add a reset switch, you need these parts:

- Six inches of thin (about 20-gauge) insulated wire

- A single-pole, normally open, momentary-contact push-button switch

The idea behind installing a reset switch is to run a momentary-contact switch parallel with the Power Good line and ground. To do so, follow these steps:

1. Remove from the motherboard the power-supply connector containing the Power Good signal.

   Look in your technical-reference manual to make sure that you have the right connector and can identify the signal wire containing the Power Good signal. Sometimes this information also is on a sticker attached to the power supply.

2. Poke the stripped end of a wire into the hole in the power-supply connector in which the Power Good signal is carried.

3. Plug the connector, with the wire inserted, back in to the motherboard.

4. Run the other end of the wire under one of the screws that secures the motherboard. The screw serves as a ground.

5. Cut the wire in the middle, bare the ends, and attach the stripped wire ends to the normally open, single-pole, momentary-contact push-button switch.

6. Run the wire and the switch outside the case.

You should now have a functioning reset button. You can mount the switch to an available place in the unit, such as an empty card bracket, in which you can drill a small hole to accept the switch.

A simple button and wire are sufficient for adding a reset switch, but as a safety precaution you can place a 1/4-watt resistor with a value between 1K ohms and 2.7K ohms in-line with the wire from the Power Good line to the switch. The reason for adding the resistor is that the Power Good signal is provided by a PNP transistor inside the power supply with its emitter connected to the +5 volt signal. Without the resistor, shorting the Power Good signal to ground for a long period can burn out the transistor.

When you press the switch, you initiate the boot sequence. The boot process that occurs (warm or cold) depends on the status of memory location 0000:0472. The value at this location is 0000h when you first power up the system and until you press Ctrl-Alt-Del for the first time. If the last boot operation was a cold boot (an initial power-on), every subsequent time you press the reset button a cold boot occurs. After you press Ctrl-Alt-Del once to initiate a manual warm-boot sequence, every subsequent time you press the reset button you initiate a warm boot that skips the memory tests. To eliminate the need to press Ctrl-Alt-Del after you start the system every day to "set" the reset button for subsequent warm boot operations, you can enter a program using DEBUG that produces a WARMSET.COM program to run in your AUTOEXEC.BAT file. This simple program quickly sets the memory flag to indicate that a warm boot should be initiated when the reset switch is pressed.

To create WARMSET.COM, be sure that you have the DEBUG program available in the path, and enter these commands at the DOS prompt:

```
C:\>DEBUG
-N WARMSET.COM
-A 100
xxxx:0100 MOV AX,0040
xxxx:0103 MOV DS,AX
xxxx:0105 MOV WORD PTR [0072],1234
xxxx:010B INT 20
xxxx:010D
-R CX
CX 0000
:D
-W
Writing 0000D bytes
-Q
```

Unlike the Ctrl-Alt-Del combination, the hardware reset cannot be ignored by your system no matter how locked up the system is.

The Phoenix BIOS sets the warm-boot flag during every boot sequence, regardless of whether it's warm or cold. Immediately after power-up, therefore, the flag is zero, which causes the standard POST test to run. Immediately after the POST, the Phoenix BIOS sets the flag for a warm boot, because many compatibles that use the Phoenix BIOS have a reset button already integrated into the system. The reset button works in the same way as the button you can construct. Because of the warm boot flag's automatic setting, a warm boot occurs every time you press the reset button no matter what the previous boot was. If you want a cold boot to occur (including POST), you can create a COLDSET.COM program also using DEBUG.

To create COLDSET.COM, enter these commands:

```
C:\>DEBUG
-N COLDSET.COM
-A 100
xxxx:0100 MOV AX,0040
xxxx:0103 MOV DS,AX
xxxx:0105 MOV WORD PTR [0072],0000
xxxx:010B INT 20
xxxx:010D
```

```
-R CX
CX 0000
:D
-W
Writing 0000D bytes
-Q
```

This procedure causes a reset button to initiate a cold boot with POST tests no matter which BIOS you have. An interesting variation on these programs is to produce two additional companion programs called WARMBOOT.COM and COLDBOOT.COM. As their names indicate, they go one step farther than the WARMSET.COM and COLDSET.COM programs: They not only set the flag but also cause an immediate boot. You might wonder why you would need that operation when you can just press Ctrl-Alt-Del or turn the power off and on to reboot the system. The answer is that with these programs you can initiate the boot you want from a batch file with no operator intervention.

I use the WARMBOOT.COM program in batch files that copy new CONFIG.SYS files to my root directory, and then reboot the system automatically to initiate the new configuration. For example, one batch file copies a CONFIG.SYS file, which loads local area network (LAN) drivers as well as a new AUTOEXEC.BAT file to the root directory of the C: drive. The AUTOEXEC.BAT file has commands that automatically log on to the network. In seconds, my network is up and running, and I am automatically logged in, *with only one command*. You probably can come up with other uses for these programs.

To create WARMBOOT.COM, enter these commands:

```
C:\>DEBUG
-N WARMBOOT.COM
-A 100
xxxx:0100 MOV AX,0040
xxxx:0103 MOV DS,AX
xxxx:0105 MOV WORD PTR [0072],1234
xxxx:010B JMP FFFF:0
xxxx:0110
-R CX
CX 0000
:10
-W
Writing 00010 bytes
-Q
```

To create COLDBOOT.COM, enter these commands:

```
C:\>DEBUG
-N COLDBOOT.COM
-A 100
xxxx:0100 MOV AX,0040
xxxx:0103 MOV DS,AX
xxxx:0105 MOV WORD PTR [0072],0000
xxxx:010B JMP FFFF:0
xxxx:0110
-R CX
CX 0000
:10
-W
Writing 00010 bytes
-Q
```

Whether or not you have a reset button, the WARMBOOT.COM and COLDBOOT.COM programs can be useful.

Upgrading the DOS Version

An upgrade many users overlook is an upgrade to a new version of an operating system. You can complicate a DOS upgrade by using different OEM versions of DOS, but normally you should not have to reformat your hard disk when you upgrade from one version of DOS to another. If you are using nonstandard drivers or other non-DOS support programs, you might have to format the disk or use Norton Utilities or some other low-level utility to modify the disk's boot sector and root directory. This modification enables the SYS command in the new version to operate properly.

You can perform an operating-system upgrade in several ways. One is to use the automatic installation and upgrade facility built in to DOS. The automatic DOS upgrade and installation utility that comes with DOS 5.X versions works well. If you want to upgrade on your own, following the set of simple instructions in the following section will complete the upgrade in a relatively short amount of time.

To repartition your hard disk at the same time you are upgrading to a new DOS version, you must back up your entire hard disk, repartition and reformat it, and then restore all your original files. Then you can install the new version of DOS over your original (restored) version. Depending on the type of backup hardware you use, this procedure can be somewhat time-consuming.

Upgrading DOS the Easy Way

To perform a DOS-version upgrade the easy way, follow these steps:

1. Boot the new DOS version from drive A:.

2. Transfer the system files to C: with this command:

   SYS C:

3. Locate the DOS disk with the REPLACE program, insert it in drive A:, and execute this command:

   COPY REPLACE.* C:

4. Use this command to replace all DOS transient files on C: with new versions in all subdirectories and enable read-only files to be overwritten:

   C:REPLACE A:*.* C: /S /R

   Caution: This command replaces any file on the C: drive with a file of the same name on the DOS disks, no matter where on the C: drive the file is located. Any files on C: that have the same name as any of the DOS files on A: therefore are overwritten by this command.

5. Change the disk in drive A: to the second DOS floppy disk, and repeat the preceding step until you have inserted all of the DOS floppy disks.

6. Place the DOS boot disk back in drive A:.

7. Add any new DOS transient files to the C:\DOS directory with this command (assuming that you have a C:\DOS directory already in place on the hard disk):

   C:REPLACE A:*.* C:\DOS /A

8. Replace the boot disk with the second DOS floppy disk, and repeat the preceding step until you have inserted all DOS floppy disks.

When you are finished, the system will be capable of booting the new DOS version from the hard disk. This method ensures that all previous DOS files are overwritten by new versions, no matter in which subdirectories they are located.

If you use a directory other than C:\DOS to store your DOS program files, replace C:\DOS in the preceding steps with that directory. If you have problems with the SYS command, your original installation probably has a problem, which must be repaired before you can proceed. Note that the SYS commands in DOS 4.0 and higher versions are more tolerant of different configurations on the destination drive. If you have problems, I recommend *Que's Guide to Data Recovery* for additional reading on this subject.

Upgrading DOS the Hard Way

You must use the more difficult method of upgrading a DOS version to take advantage of newer DOS-version disk formatting capabilities. A common use for this method is upgrading from DOS 3.3 to 5.0, with a hard disk larger than 32 megabytes in capacity. Because DOS V3.3 could create disk partitions a maximum of only 32M in capacity, the disk must be currently partitioned into several volumes. Because DOS V5.0 allows partitions as large as 2 gigabytes, it's a good idea to use the upgrade as an opportunity to condense the multiple partitions into one partition that matches the total capacity of the drive.

This method requires first backing up the data on all the partitions because the existing partitions must be destroyed and re-created as a single partition.

To perform a DOS-version upgrade using the full backup, format, and restore method, follow these steps:

1. Boot the system from the original (older) version of DOS.

2. Execute a complete backup of all partitions using the backup method of your choice.

3. Boot the new version of DOS.

4. Use the new DOS FDISK command to remove the existing DOS partition or partitions.

5. Use the new DOS FDISK to create the new partition or partitions.

6. Perform a high-level format and install the new DOS system files with this command:

   FORMAT C: /S

7. Restore the previous partition backups to the new partition, but do not restore the original system files (IBMBIO.COM and IBMDOS.COM). Your restore program should have a way to enable you to selectively ignore certain files such as these. BACKUP and RESTORE in DOS V3.3 and higher always ignores the system files.

8. Locate the new DOS disk with the REPLACE program, insert it in drive A:, and execute this command:

   COPY REPLACE.EXE C:

9. Use this command to replace all DOS transient files on C: with new versions in all subdirectories and enable read-only files to be overwritten:

    REPLACE A:*.* C: /S /R

    Caution: This command replaces any file on the C: drive with a file of the same name on the DOS disks, no matter where on C: the file is located. Any files on C: that have the same name as any of the DOS files on A: therefore are overwritten by this command.

10. Place the second DOS floppy disk in drive A:, and repeat the preceding step until you have inserted all DOS floppy disks.

11. Place the boot disk back in drive A:.

12. Add new DOS transient files to the C:\DOS directory with this command:

    REPLACE A:*.* C:\DOS /A

13. Replace the boot disk with the second DOS floppy disk, and repeat the preceding step until you have inserted all DOS floppy disks.

When you are finished, the system will be capable of booting the new DOS version from the hard disk. If you store program files in a directory other than C:\DOS, replace C:\DOS with that directory. This method ensures that all previous DOS files are overwritten by new versions.

Backup procedures make this method very difficult unless you have a good backup system. You also must determine how to prevent your backup system from restoring the system files.

If you are using the DOS V3.3 or higher BACKUP and RESTORE commands, preventing the system files from being overwritten is much more simple. Because RESTORE never can restore the files IBMBIO.COM, IBMDOS.COM, and COMMAND.COM, the chances of overwriting them are eliminated.

You must use the new DOS version's FDISK command to remove and especially create the partitions in order for the newer DOS version's partitioning capabilities to become available. One variation on this method is to substitute a low-level format operation on the hard disk for step 4 of this procedure. One advantage of not repeating the low-level format is that any existing non-DOS partitions survive; with a low-level format, nothing is left on the disk. An advantage to the low-level format is that it rewrites the sectors and tracks, which might be a good idea for some older hard disks.

Chapter Summary

This chapter has examined many types of system upgrades, including memory expansion, disk system expansion, speeding up a system, improving the video subsystem, adding a reset switch, and upgrading to a new version of DOS. You should have some insight and useful recommendations to avoid pitfalls others have endured.

Upgrading a system can be a cost-effective way to keep up with the rest of the computing community and to extend the life of your system. By upgrading, however, you also can create a "Frankenstein" system with compatibility problems before realizing how much money you have poured into the system. You must learn when to say No to more upgrades and to recognize when it is time to buy a new system.

the hang. This step usually identifies the failed part. A complete list of these POST codes is in the Appendix in this book; the list covers several different BIOSes, including IBM, AMI, Award, and Phoenix.

Most BIOSes on the market in systems with an ISA or EISA bus output the POST codes to I/O port address 80h. Compaq is different: its systems send codes to port 84h. IBM PS/2 models with ISA bus slots, such as the Model 25 and 30, send codes to port 90h. Some EISA systems send codes to port 300h (most EISA systems also send the same codes to 80h). IBM MCA bus systems universally send codes to port 680h. With all these different addresses, you should be sure that the card you purchase will read the port addresses you need.

Several cards read only port address 80h. This port address is certainly the most commonly used, and works in most situations, but the cards do not work in Compaq systems, some EISA systems, and IBM PS/2 systems. A POST card designed specifically for the PS/2 MCA bus needs to read only port address 680h because the card cannot be used in ISA or EISA bus systems anyway.

To read a port address, a card needs to have only an 8-bit design; it does not have to have a 16-bit or 32-bit POST card. The two normal types of POST cards are those that plug into the 8-bit connector which is a part of the ISA or EISA bus, and those that plug into the MCA bus. Some companies, such as Ultra-X, offer both types of POST cards—one for MCA bus systems and one for ISA/EISA bus systems. Micro 2000 does not offer a separate card; rather, it includes with its POST Probe card a unique slot adapter that enables it to work in MCA bus systems as well as in ISA and EISA systems. Most other companies offer only ISA/EISA POST cards and have ignored the MCA bus.

Note that because the EISA bus includes the ISA bus as a subset, and only the 8-bit portion of the ISA bus is needed to even read the required port addresses, it is unnecessary to have a separate card specific to EISA bus systems. Beware, however, that at least one manufacturer sells a separate EISA card that it claims is designed specifically for the EISA bus. As long as an ISA card is properly designed to latch the correct port addresses, there is no reason for it not to function perfectly in both ISA and EISA bus systems. There is absolutely no need for a separate (and expensive) EISA card.

POST-code cards are invaluable in diagnosing what seem to be "dead" motherboards. Just pop the card into a slot, and observe the code on the card's display. Then look up the code in a list corresponding to the specific BIOS on the motherboard. These cards can be very helpful with tough problems such as a memory-bit failure in Bank 0, which does not allow error codes to be displayed on a CRT in most EGA or VGA systems.

POST-code cards can help also to troubleshoot other problems that occur so early in the POST tests that no error messages can be displayed. The only problem is that each manufacturer's BIOS runs different tests in a different order sequence, and even outputs different code numbers for the same tests. Therefore, without the proper documentation specific to the BIOS on the motherboard you are testing, the numbers shown on the POST card are meaningless! A "feature" that separates the many POST cards on the market is documentation.

The documentation supplied with the Micro 2000, Landmark, Data Depot and Ultra-X cards offers excellent information covering a wide variety of different BIOS vendor's codes. One company, MicroSystems Development (MSD) supplies its POST Card documentation both in printed form and on a disk with a built-in POST Code lookup program. This method is unique and desirable especially if you carry a laptop or portable system with you when you troubleshoot. The JDR Microdevices card offers less than most of the others in the way of documentation, but is also the least expensive card by a wide margin. The one other thing that distinguishes the JDR card is that it is designed to be left in a system permanently. The two-digit display can be moved to the back bracket of the card so that it can be read outside the system. There is also a connector for an external two-digit display. The other cards have the display on the card only, which is impossible to read if the system is closed up.

Some cards have additional features worth mentioning. The Micro 2000 card (called the POST Probe) includes a built-in logic probe for testing signals on the major motherboard components. The POST Probe includes a series of individually separate LED readouts for several important bus signals as well as power-supply voltage levels. The separate LEDs enable these bus signals to be monitored simultaneously. Sometimes you can help to determine the cause of a failure by noting which bus LED is lit at a certain time. The power-supply LEDs verify the output of the +5, -5, +12, and -12 volt signals from the supply. Another feature is meter-probe attachment points on which you can easily connect a voltmeter to the card for more accurate measurements.

The basic card functions in all ISA bus and EISA bus systems because of its capability to monitor any port addresses mentioned earlier in this section. As mentioned, this card includes a unique adapter that enables it to function in MCA bus systems as well. This card is the only one that functions in every system on the market. The extensive documentation not only covers the expected POST codes for different BIOS versions but also includes a detailed reference to the bus signals monitored by the card. A reference in the documentation enables even novices to use the included logic probe for some more-sophisticated motherboard tests. This card offers more features than others on the market.

The Data Depot Pocket POST is a unique card that includes an LED for monitoring bus signals. It can monitor a single signal at a time, which is selected by a jumper. The card includes LEDs for testing all the power-supply voltage levels, and includes attachment points for a voltmeter as well. The Pocket POST is designed for ISA and EISA bus systems, and can connect to any port addresses used in these systems for POST codes. As its name suggests, the card is small compared to most others, and therefore is easy to carry around. The entire package, including the comprehensive manual, fits in a standard (included) floppy disk case.

Ultra-X has two cards: the Quick-POST PC for ISA/EISA bus systems, and the Quick-POST PS/2 for MCA bus systems. Because the Quick-POST cards monitor only one port address each—80h for the PC card and 680h for the PS/2 card—the ISA/EISA version is less flexible than some others. The included documentation is excellent and covers a variety of BIOS versions. Both cards also include LEDs used to monitor the power-supply voltages.

The MicroSystems Development (MSD) card is unique because of its documentation on disk. A printed manual is supplied also. This POST Code Master is capable of monitoring either port address 80h or 84h. It also includes voltage-test LEDS for checking the power supply.

A second type of diagnostics card goes beyond the function of a basic POST-code card. In addition to monitoring POST codes, these cards include an on-board ROM that contains a more sophisticated diagnostics program than normally is in the motherboard ROM BIOS alone. Several cards that offer this function are the Kickstart II card, by Landmark, and the RACER II card, by Ultra-X. These cards not only monitor POST codes but also have a diagnostics program of their own in on-board ROM. Because of the extra expense of having these programs and other options on-board, the cards are more expensive than the standard POST-code cards.

The idea is valid, but I normally do not recommend this higher-level card because the standard POST-code cards provide 95 percent of the capabilities of these cards with no BIOS conflicts or other problems. Beyond the standard POST card functions, I usually rely on disk-based diagnostics for further tests that are more thorough than the tests on these cards. To eliminate conflicts with ROMs on other cards, in many cases other adapters must be removed from the system to execute the tests. Although these cards are quite capable, and function as a basic POST-code card if necessary, I find it more valuable to spend the extra money on a disk-based diagnostics program and stick to the basic POST-code cards. This way, I get the most functionality for my money.

System Diagnostics Disk

Every IBM computer comes with a guide-to-operations (GTO) or Quick Reference manual. The GTO manual is in a reddish purple binder; it includes a diagnostics disk to assist you in identifying problems your computer might have. PS/2 computers are supplied with a much smaller quick-reference guide that includes a reference disk. The disk contains both the regular and advanced diagnostics, as well as the normal SETUP program.

The diagnostics disk and corresponding manual provide step-by-step instructions for you to test the various parts of your computer system, including the system unit and many installed options, such as the expansion unit, keyboard, display, and printer. Unfortunately, these diagnostics are at "customer level" and are lacking in many respects. The tests cannot be run individually; you must always run them all together, and many of the better tests have been deleted. These diagnostics are a crippled version of the much more powerful advanced diagnostics IBM sells. Many compatible-system vendors do not segregate the diagnostics software like IBM does; many include an advanced-type diagnostics disk free with the system. For example, AST includes free with every system its diagnostics program, called ASTute. This program is similar to the IBM advanced diagnostics.

You must boot from the diagnostics disk to run the program because a special version of DOS resides on the diagnostics disk. The DOS version suppresses the system parity checking during the boot process. Disabling parity checking might enable a defective system to "limp" through the diagnostics, whereas normally the system continually locks up with the parity-check message. After the disk is loaded, the main diagnostics menu is displayed. The opening menu looks something like this:

```
The IBM Personal Computer
DIAGNOSTICS
Version 2.06
Copyright IBM Corp. 1981,1986
SELECT AN OPTION
    0 - SYSTEM CHECKOUT
    1 - FORMAT DISKETTE
    2 - COPY DISKETTE
    3 - PREPARE SYSTEM FOR MOVING
    4 - SETUP
    9 - END DIAGNOSTICS

SELECT THE ACTION DESIRED

?
```

Options 0, 1, and 2 are part of the diagnostics procedures. Option 3 is used to "park," or secure, the heads on a hard disk so that the system unit can be moved safely without damaging the disk or its contents. Option 4 is seen only on the AT version of the diagnostics and is used with the AT to identify installed options when you first set up your system.

Option 1 is used to format a disk. The format is different from a normal DOS format, however, and this routine should not be used for formatting disks for normal use under DOS. This option is designed to create a special "scratch disk" used by the diagnostics for testing purposes. Among other things, differences exist in the construction of the boot sector of this disk and a normal DOS disk.

Option 2 is used to copy a disk. This routine is exactly the same as the DISKCOPY command in normal DOS. Option 2 creates a mirror-image copy of a disk, the same in every way. This routine was designed to copy the diagnostics disk because the original disk should not be used for testing purposes, and the entire disk was designed to be a stand-alone usable system, without the presence of DOS. You use this option to make backups of your master diagnostics disk so that you can use the copies for actual testing purposes. The diagnostics disks can be copied by any other means as well because they are not copy protected. IBM never has protected the regular or advanced diagnostics, which enables you to make proper backups and keep the master disks safe.

For general testing, you select Option 0. When this option is selected, the diagnostics software loads from the disk various modules that perform a "presence test" to see whether the device to which the module corresponds is in the system. A list of installed devices is presented, and you are asked whether the list is correct.

For several reasons, this list does not always exactly match the system configuration. The only items listed are those that have diagnostic software modules on the disk. If you purchase a newer type of expansion item, such as a VGA graphics card, the diagnostics might instead identify this board as an EGA board, if the VGA module is not present on the disk. Because modules are not available for most expanded-memory boards, those boards almost never appear on the list, with the exception of IBM's XMA card. Nonstandard communications boards (boards containing other than normal serial or parallel ports) normally are not seen either.

If you have an IBM Token Ring network adapter in your system, for example, it never is incorporated in the list of installed devices because the diagnostics (or advanced diagnostics) disks do not incorporate the modules for these adapters. IBM instead provides a separate diagnostics program on its own disk for this adapter. Most standard devices should show up on the list, even if the particular device was not made by IBM.

Your hard disk controller should show up, for example, as should your video board (although it might incorrectly identify the type of video card), serial and parallel ports, conventional and extended (not expanded) memory, floppy drives, and the motherboard.

If an installed device shows up because it is installed in the system, and you know that the diagnostics software normally would find it but doesn't, then the device is configured incorrectly or has a serious problem. Signify that the list is incorrect by answering No when you are asked whether the installed device list is correct. Then add the item to the list. If an item appears that is not installed, use the same procedure to remove the item from the list. This list represents all the tests that can be run. The only way you can test an item is to have it appear on this list.

After going through the installed-devices list, you see another menu, similar to this one:

```
0 - RUN TESTS ONE TIME
1 - RUN TESTS MULTIPLE TIMES
2 - LOG UTILITIES
3 - END SYSTEM CHECKOUT
```

Option 0 normally is selected to test one or all of the items in the system. Option 1 enables you to test any (or all) of these items repetitively as many times as you want, or "forever." The forever option is handy because it enables you to run the diagnostics for an item continuously overnight or over a weekend to find particularly troublesome problems. This method can be an easy way to flesh out an intermittent problem. To record errors that occur while you're not present, you first select Option 2, which can be used to set up an error log. The log records the date, time, and error message to a floppy disk or printer so that you can review them at a later time.

If an error occurs while these tests are running, a numerical error message appears along with the date and time. These numbers, listed in this chapter and in the Appendix in this book, follow the same conventions as the numbers displayed by the POST, and are the same numbers in some cases. The diagnostic tests usually are much more powerful than the tests run in the POST.

Although the diagnostics do an excellent job of identifying specific problem areas or problem components, they provide limited assistance in telling you how to correct the source of the errors. Little documentation is provided with these diagnostics and, in fact, the information most often provided is "Have your system unit (or problem device) serviced." These diagnostics are a crippled version of the real diagnostics, which are part of the hardware-maintenance service manual. You should be using the Advanced Diagnostics; they are the diagnostics to which the remainder of this book refers.

Advanced Diagnostics Programs

For "technician level" diagnostics, IBM sells the hardware-maintenance service manuals, which include the Advanced Diagnostics disks. These disks contain the "real" diagnostics programs and, combined with the hardware-maintenance service manuals, represent the de-facto standard diagnostics information and software for IBM and compatible systems. These programs produce error messages in the form of numbers. The number codes used are the same as those used in the POST and general-diagnostics software. The meaning of the numbers is consistent across all diagnostic programs. This section explores the Advanced Diagnostics and list most of the known error-code meanings. IBM constantly adds to this error-code list as it introduces new equipment.

Using Advanced Diagnostics

If you really want to service a system in-depth, you can purchase the IBM *Hardware Maintenance Service Manual* (for about $235). This single book covers all the earlier systems, including the PC, XT, and AT. Updates cover the XT-286 and PS/2 Models 25 and 30. The "real" PS/2 systems have their own separate version of this book, called *PS/2 Hardware Maintenance and Service*. This book costs $268 and includes spare copies of the standard reference disks. The newer versions of the PS/2 book now cover also all PS/2 systems, those with ISA (Industry Standard Architecture) as well as MCA (Micro Channel Architecture) slots.

You might be surprised at the inclusion of these disks, especially when you read in the book that you have had the advanced diagnostics for the PS/2 systems all along. The book says that, to activate the hidden advanced diagnostics, you must enter the secret command. When the Reference Disk main menu is displayed, just press Ctrl-A (for Advanced), and the menu flips, placing you in the world of advanced diagnostics. Note that advanced diagnostics are found only on the Reference Disks included with PS/2 systems that have MCA (Micro Channel Architecture) bus slots. Non-MCA systems, such as the PS/2 25 through 40 systems, come with a Starter Disk, equivalent to the Setup and Diagnostics Disk that came with the original AT system. That is, the Starter Disk includes the Setup program and a limited diagnostics version that lacks many functions found in the advanced diagnostics. To get the advanced diagnostics for these systems, you must purchase the initial PS/2 *Hardware Maintenance and Service* (HMS) *Manual*, which includes the advanced diagnostics disks for Models 25, 30, and 30-286. For any other systems, such as Models 35 or 40, you must purchase the respective update package for the PS/2 HMS manual. These updates usually cost about $30.

Hiding from average users access to advanced diagnostics on the Reference Disks is probably a good idea. An inexperienced user can do great damage by low-level formatting of the hard disk, for instance. The remainder of the contents of the PS/2 book are skimpy because not many parts are found in the average PS/2 system, and they are easy to repair. The PS/2 book often seems to end a troubleshooting session with this advice: "Replace the system board." Although I recommend the hardware-maintenance and service manuals, if all you are looking for is the advanced-diagnostics software (and you have a PS/2 system with the MCA bus), you already have it, saving you $268!

Although the guide-to-operations manual is good only for identifying a problem component, the HMS manual provides information for you to more accurately isolate and repair the failure of any field-replaceable unit (FRU).

The HMS manual includes an Advanced Diagnostics disk and accompanying maintenance-analysis procedures (MAPs), which are instructions that help you to isolate and identify problem components. To run the advanced diagnostics tests, follow the procedures detailed in this section.

After booting the Advanced Diagnostics disk for your particular system (PC or AT), a menu similar to this one appears:

```
The IBM Personal Computer
ADVANCED DIAGNOSTICS
Version 2.07
Copyright IBM Corp. 1981,1986

ROS P/N: 78X7462
ROS DATE: 04/21/86

SELECT AN OPTION

0 - SYSTEM CHECKOUT
1 - FORMAT DISKETTE
2 - COPY DISKETTE
3 - PREPARE SYSTEM FOR MOVING
4 - SETUP
9 - END DIAGNOSTICS

SELECT THE ACTION DESIRED

?
```

Note   Again, only the fourth option is displayed on the AT diagnostics. If you are using the PC version, this item is not displayed because it does not apply.

The advanced diagnostics disks show the date of the ROM as well as the IBM part number for the particular chips in your system. The screen shows this information near the top as ROS (read-only software). The 04/21/86 date identifies the version of the ROM in this example. If you look up this date in the table in Chapter 7, "Primary System Components," which shows ROM identification information for IBM's systems, you see that the date indicates an IBM XT Model 286. The part number, read directly from the ROM, is academic information because IBM does not sell the ROM chips separately—only with a complete motherboard swap.

After you select Option 0, which invokes the diagnostic routines, each module on the disk loads and executes a presence test to determine whether the applicable piece of hardware is truly in the system. In this example, the result looks like this:

```
THE INSTALLED DEVICES ARE

1  - SYSTEM BOARD
2  - 2688KB MEMORY
3  - KEYBOARD
6  - 2 DISKETTE DRIVE(S) AND ADAPTER
7  - MATH COPROCESSOR
9  - SERIAL/PARALLEL ADAPTER
9  - - PARALLEL PORT
11 - SERIAL/PARALLEL ADAPTER
11 - - SERIAL PORT
17 - 1 FIXED DISK DRIVE(S) AND ADAPTER
74 - PERSONAL SYSTEM/2 DISPLAY ADAPTER

IS THE LIST CORRECT (Y/N)

?
```

You then answer Yes or No depending on the accuracy of the list. Remember that not everything appears on this list. An IBM Token Ring network adapter does not appear, for example, and never appears on this list because no software module designed for that option is present on the disk. The following list contains all the items that could appear on the list (as of Version 2.07 of these diagnostics). This list is different for other versions.

```
1 SYSTEM BOARD
2 MEMORY
3 KEYBOARD
4 MONOCHROME & PRINTER ADAPTER
5 COLOR/GRAPHICS MONITOR ADAPTER
6 DISKETTE DRIVE(S)
7 MATH COPROCESSOR
9 SERIAL/PARALLEL ADAPTER - PARALLEL PORT
```

```
10 ALTERNATE SERIAL/PARALLEL ADAPTER - PARALLEL PORT
11 SERIAL/PARALLEL ADAPTER - SERIAL PORT
12 ALTERNATE SERIAL/PARALLEL ADAPTER - SERIAL PORT
13 GAME CONTROL ADAPTER
14 MATRIX PRINTER
15 SDLC COMMUNICATIONS ADAPTER
17 FIXED DISK DRIVE(S) AND ADAPTER
20 BSC COMMUNICATIONS ADAPTER
21 ALT BSC COMMUNICATIONS ADAPTER
22 CLUSTER ADAPTER(S)
24 ENHANCED GRAPHICS ADAPTER
29 COLOR PRINTER
30 PC NETWORK ADAPTER
31 ALT. PC NETWORK ADAPTER
36 GPIB ADAPTER(S)
38 DATA ACQUISITION ADAPTER(S)
39 PROFESSIONAL GRAPHICS CONTROLLER
71 VOICE COMMUNICATIONS ADAPTER
73 3.5" EXTERNAL DISKETTE DRIVE AND ADAPTER
74 PERSONAL SYSTEM/2 DISPLAY ADAPTER
85 EXPANDED MEMORY ADAPTER - 2 MB -
89 MUSIC FEATURE CARD(S)
```

After certifying that the list is correct, or adding or deleting items as necessary to make it correct, you might begin testing each item listed.

The tests performed by the Advanced Diagnostics disk are far more detailed and precise than the tests on the general diagnostics disk in the GTO. In addition to identifying the problem component, the advanced diagnostics further attempt to identify the specific malfunctioning part of the device.

After a problem is identified, the HMS manual provides detailed instructions for performing adjustments, preventive maintenance, and removal and replacement of the affected part. To help you, comprehensive hardware and design information is available, including parts lists that specify replacement-part numbers and internal design specifications.

Examining Error Codes

Nearly all the personal computer error codes for the POST, general diagnostics, and advanced diagnostics are represented by the display of the device number followed by two digits other than 00. A display of the device number plus 00 indicates successful completion of a test.
This listing is a compilation from various sources including technical-reference manuals, hardware-maintenance service manuals, and hardware-maintenance reference manuals.

If a designation such as 2xx is indicated in the chart, error codes that begin with the first character or characters listed and with any character in place of x indicate errors in the device listed. For example, 7xx indicates math coprocessor errors, which also means that any displayed error codes from 700 to 799 (except 700, which means all is well) indicates that the math coprocessor is bad (or is having problems). Table 13.2 lists the error codes and their descriptions.

Table 13.2 Personal Computer Error Codes

Code	Description
1xx	System Board errors
2xx	Memory (RAM) errors
3xx	Keyboard errors
4xx	Monochrome Display Adapter (MDA) errors
4xx	PS/2 System Board Parallel Port errors
5xx	Color Graphics Adapter (CGA) errors
6xx	Floppy Drive/Controller errors
7xx	Math Coprocessor errors
9xx	Parallel Printer adapter errors
10xx	Alternate Parallel Printer Adapter errors
11xx	Primary Async Communications (serial port COM1:) errors
12xx	Alternate Async Communications (serial COM2:, COM3: and COM4:)
13xx	Game Control Adapter errors
14xx	Matrix Printer errors
15xx	Synchronous Data Link Control (SDLC) Communications Adapter errors
16xx	Display Station Emulation Adapter (DSEA) errors (5520, 525x)
17xx	ST-506/412 Fixed Disk and Controller errors
18xx	I/O Expansion Unit errors
19xx	3270 PC Attachment Card errors
20xx	Binary Synchronous Communications (BSC) Adapter errors
21xx	Alternate Binary Synchronous Communications (BSC) Adapter errors
22xx	Cluster Adapter errors
23xx	Plasma Monitor Adapter errors
24xx	Enhanced Graphics Adapter (EGA) errors
24xx	PS/2 System Board Video Graphics Array (VGA) errors errors
25xx	Alternate Enhanced Graphics Adapter (EGA) errors
26xx	XT or AT/370 370-M (Memory) and 370-P (Processor) Adapter
27xx	XT or AT/370 3277-EM (Emulation) Adapter errors
28xx	3278/79 Emulation Adapter or 3270 Connection Adapter errors
29xx	Color/Graphics Printer errors
30xx	Primary PC Network Adapter errors
31xx	Secondary PC Network Adapter errors
32xx	3270 PC or AT Display and Programmed Symbols Adapter errors
33xx	Compact Printer errors
35xx	Enhanced Display Station Emulation Adapter (EDSEA) errors
36xx	General Purpose Interface Bus (GPIB) Adapter errors

continues

Table 13.2 Continued

Code	Description
38xx	Data Acquisition Adapter errors
39xx	Professional Graphics Adapter (PGA) errors
44xx	5278 Display Attachment Unit and 5279 Display errors
45xx	IEEE Interface Adapter (IEEE-488) errors
46xx	A Real-Time Interface Coprocessor (ARTIC) Multiport/2 Adapter errors
48xx	Internal Modem errors
49xx	Alternate Internal Modem errors
50xx	PC Convertible LCD errors
51xx	PC Convertible Portable Printer errors
56xx	Financial Communication System errors
70xx	Phoenix BIOS/Chip Set Unique Error Codes
71xx	Voice Communications Adapter (VCA) errors
73xx	3 1/2-inch External Diskette Drive errors
74xx	IBM PS/2 Display Adapter (VGA card) errors
74xx	8514/A Display Adapter errors
76xx	4216 PagePrinter Adapter errors
84xx	PS/2 Speech Adapter errors
85xx	2Mb XMA Memory Adapter or Expanded Memory Adapter/A errors
86xx	PS/2 Pointing Device (Mouse) errors
89xx	Musical Instrument Digital Interface (MIDI) Adapter errors
91xx	IBM 3363 Write-Once Read Multiple (WORM) Optical Drive/ Adapter errors
096xxxx	SCSI Adapter with Cache (32-bit) errors
100xx	Multiprotocol Adapter/A errors
101xx	300/1200bps Internal Modem/A
104xx	ESDI Fixed Disk or Adapter errors
107xx	5 1/4-inch External Diskette Drive or Adapter errors
112xxxx	SCSI Adapter (16-bit w/o Cache) errors
113xxxx	System Board SCSI Adapter (16-bit) errors
129xx	Model 70 Processor Board errors; Type 3 (25MHz) System Board
149xx	P70/P75 Plasma Display and Adapter errors
165xx	6157 Streaming Tape Drive or Tape Attachment Adapter errors
166xx	Primary Token Ring Network Adapter errors
167xx	Alternate Token Ring Network Adapter errors
180xx	PS/2 Wizard Adapter errors
194xx	80286 Memory Expansion Option Memory Module errors
208xxxx	Unknown SCSI Device errors
209xxxx	SCSI Removable Disk errors
210xxxx	SCSI Fixed Disk errors
211xxxx	SCSI Tape Drive errors
212xxxx	SCSI Printer errors
213xxxx	SCSI Processor errors
214xxxx	SCSI Write-Once Read Multiple (WORM) Drive errors
215xxxx	SCSI CD-ROM Drive errors
216xxxx	SCSI Scanner errors
217xxxx	SCSI Optical Memory errors
218xxxx	SCSI Jukebox Changer errors
219xxxx	SCSI Communications errors

I have compiled in the Appendix in this book a detailed list of every IBM error code I have encountered. Also listed there are charts I have developed concerning SCSI errors. The SCSI interface has introduced a whole new set of error codes because of the large number and variety of devices that can be attached.

Aftermarket Diagnostics Programs

In addition to IBM's diagnostics programs, many more are available for IBM and compatible systems. Specific programs are available also to test memory, floppy drives, hard disks, video boards, and most other areas of the system. This section describes some of the best non-IBM diagnostics, some of which should be considered essential in any toolkit.

Replacements for IBM Advanced Diagnostics

An IBM-compatible system should be able to run the IBM advanced diagnostics. Some manufacturers offer their own diagnostics. AT&T, Zenith, and Tandy, for example, offer their own versions of service manuals and diagnostics programs for their systems. Other systems without this type of manufacturer support can use just the IBM diagnostics and repair manuals.

Several alternatives are available if you do not want IBM's diagnostics but still want a good, comprehensive diagnostics program for your system.

Numerous diagnostics packages are available, although many fall short of the level needed by professional-level troubleshooters. Many products, oriented more toward end users, lack the accuracy, features, and capabilities needed by technically proficient people who are serious about troubleshooting. I have tested virtually all diagnostics packages available; two stand out from all the others: Micro-Scope, by Micro 2000, and Service Diagnostics, by Landmark.

These two programs offer several advantages over the IBM diagnostics. Micro-Scope and Service Diagnostics usually are better at determining where a problem lies within a system, especially in IBM-compatible systems. The remainder of this section describes the advantages of these two programs.

All serial- and parallel-port loopback connectors, or "wrap plugs," are included in these packages. The plugs are required in order to properly diagnose and test serial and parallel ports. (IBM charges extra for these plugs.)

Both programs can be run in "batch" mode, which enables a series of tests to be run from the command line without operator intervention. You then can set up automated test suites, which can be especially useful in burning in a system or executing the same tests on many systems.

These programs test all types of memory including conventional (base) memory, extended memory, and expanded memory. Failures can be identified down to the individual chip (bank and bit) level.

Like IBM's diagnostics, neither program is copy-protected. Most software manufacturers long ago eliminated any form of copy protection from their software, but a few diagnostics packages still have this intolerable feature. (I try not to purchase any program that cannot be backed up easily, especially one as essential as a diagnostics program.)

Both of these recommended diagnostics programs have outstanding individual features, described next.

Micro-Scope

The Micro-Scope program is one of only a few programs on the market (other than manufacturer-specific programs) capable of low-level formatting IDE hard drives properly. Some people believe that IDE drives cannot or should not ever be low-level formatted; however, Micro-Scope *can* low-level format nearly all IDE drives. All IDE drives are preformatted at the factory, and a format certainly should not be done without good reason, but a drive might have problems later that require a low-level format.

Most IDE drives either lock out standard format programs and prevent formatting or allow an improper format to occur, possibly destroying factory-written defect and track-guidance information. Put simply, an improper format program can damage some IDE drives and require that a proper format be performed. Without the correct software, therefore, you must return the drive to the factory for reformatting.

Micro-Scope IDE format routines feature the capability to repair improperly formatted (damaged) IDE drives. The formats preserve factory-defect information; because they recognize vendor-specific IDE command codes unique to each manufacturer, they can format so-called unformattable drives such as the Conner Peripherals drives used in Compaq machines, as well as in many other IBM-compatible machines. This feature alone can be worth the price of the program.

Another Micro-Scope feature relative to hard disk formatting is that it works directly with the controller hardware and bypasses both DOS and the ROM BIOS. Format programs that work through DOS or the BIOS cannot format properly on many controllers, especially if the drive is magnetically damaged.

The Micro-Scope package is one of only a few diagnostics packages that is truly "PS/2 aware." Micro-Scope not only helps you troubleshoot PS/2 systems, but it also does some things that even IBM advanced diagnostics cannot do: for example, it can format industry-standard ESDI hard disk drives attached to the IBM PS/2 ESDI controller. When you attach an ESDI drive to the IBM ESDI controller, the BIOS on the controller queries the drive for its capacity and defect map information. IBM apparently chose a proprietary format for this information on its drives; if the controller cannot read the information, you cannot set up the drive nor format it using the PS/2 Reference Diskette.

Although IBM used an ESDI controller in its PS/2 system, you could not get just any ESDI drive to work on that system. Some drive manufacturers produced special "PS/2 versions" of their drives that had this information on them. Another way around the problem was to use an aftermarket ESDI controller in place of the IBM controller so that you could use the IBM ESDI drive as well as any other industry-standard ESDI drive. With this method, however, you could not use the Reference Disk format program anymore because it works only with IBM's controller. Micro-Scope can solve many of these problems because it can format an industry-standard ESDI drive attached to the IBM ESDI controller and save you from having to purchase an aftermarket controller or a "special" drive when you add drives to these systems.

Micro-Scope has also a hardware interrupt and I/O port address check feature that is more accurate than the same feature in other software. It enables you to accurately identify the interrupt or I/O port address a certain adapter or hardware device in your system is using—a valuable capability in solving conflicts between adapters. Some user-level diagnostics programs have this feature, but the information they report can be grossly inaccurate, and they often miss items installed in the system. Micro-Scope "goes around" DOS and the BIOS: because the program has its own operating system and its tests bypass the ROM BIOS when necessary, it can eliminate the "masking" that occurs with these elements in the way. For this reason, the program also is useful for technicians who support PCs that run under non-DOS environments such as UNIX or on Novell file servers. For convenience, you can install Micro-Scope on a hard disk and run it under regular DOS.

Finally, Micro 2000 offers excellent telephone technical support. Its operators do much more than explain how to operate the software: they help you with real troubleshooting problems. This information is augmented by good documentation and on-line help built-in to the software so that, in many cases, you don't have to refer to the manual. Micro-Scope normally costs $499; as a bonus, however, you can get a 25 percent discount when you mention this book.

Service Diagnostics

The Landmark Service Diagnostics program also has several features that distinguish it from other packages. These features are described in this section.

The Service Diagnostics program is an excellent, all-around, comprehensive diagnostics package. The program has been around for a while and has evolved to include nearly any test a troubleshooter could want. Service Diagnostics is known for its excellent memory tests, which are extremely thorough and accurate; it also gives you much control over the type of test to run. For example, you can optionally turn parity checking on or off during the tests, a feature not found in other programs. All memory errors are reported to the individual-bit level.

The Service Diagnostics program also has specific test routines for each different microprocessor that might be in a PC compatible system. In other words, it detects the type of processor in your system, and tests it using specific routines designed for the processor. You can override the processor detection and specify the processor you have. The program can recognize and test specific Intel-based systems using 8088, 8086, 286, 386, and 486 CPUs. Also, Service Diagnostics specifically recognizes and tests Harris 80C88 and AMD 386 chips, as well as Intel, Cyrix, and IIT math coprocessors. The program also tests for several known bugs in 386 and 486 systems that have been known to cause problems in some systems.

Another Service Diagnostics feature is its floppy disk alignment diagnostics, which enable you to check the alignment of both 3 1/2-inch and 5 1/4-inch drives through the use of an included Digital Diagnostics Diskette (DDD). These disks are accurate to a resolution of 500µ inches (micro-inches = millionths of an inch), accurate enough for checking alignment but not accurate enough for use in aligning a drive. For performing drive alignment, the program has a menu of analog-alignment aids, designed to be used in conjunction with a more-accurate Analog Alignment Disk (AAD) and an oscilloscope.

The Service Diagnostics progam has an excellent hard disk, low-level format program for ST-506/412 drives. You can specify not only the interleave, but also the skew factor. *Skew* is the offset of sectors from one track to the next to allow for head-switching time. This process is possible because the low-level format routines in the Service Diagnostics work at the controller register level: the program bypasses DOS and the BIOS and interacts directly with the controller hardware. The program formats most ESDI drives but is not designed for SCSI or IDE drives.

A printer-test feature in the Service Diagnostics program enables test patterns to be sent to different printers. You can quickly verify the functionality of the port, cable, and printer in one simple operation.

I recommend diagnostics programs that accommodate the special features of IBM's PS/2 systems; Service Diagnostics is no exception. It has a separate stand-alone PS/2 version of the software designed specifically for PS/2 systems. This version recognizes PS/2 hardware differences and works correctly with the unique PS/2 CMOS RAM for adapter setup and configuration.

A useful feature in limited situations is the inclusion of diagnostics in ROM chips. The ROM POST can be plugged into the BIOS-chip sockets on a PC, XT, AT, or IBM-compatible motherboard to test a system that otherwise does not function. These BIOS diagnostics do not function on all systems, but they can be useful on an IBM PC, XT, or AT, or a true clone system.

The Service Diagnostics package includes excellent documentation that describes not only how to operate the software, but also how the software routines work. Landmark offers good technical support for its products. The Service Diagnostics program is available in three primary kits: the PC, XT, AT Kit with ROM POST modules sells for $595; the PS/2 Complete Kit costs $495, and a Super Kit includes everything for $895. You can also buy special lower-cost software modules that cover specific types of systems. The price starts at about $195 per module, depending on the versions and how many modules you need.

Both the Micro-Scope and Service Diagnostics packages are excellent; I highly recommend both of them. They each have strengths in some areas, and having a "second opinion" in some cases is a good idea when you are troubleshooting. Although somewhat expensive for casual troubleshooters, these professional-level programs will save you money in the long run with increased accuracy and capabilities in troubleshooting and servicing your systems.

Disk Diagnostics

The advanced diagnostics from IBM and other manufacturers do a good job of covering most components in a system with a reasonable level of diagnostic capabilities. These programs sometimes fall short in testing disk drives, however. Because the disk drives are some of the most trouble-prone and complicated components in computer systems, it is no wonder that a diagnostics program designed to cover everything might be a little weak in this area. IBM's own advanced diagnostics for the PC are poor in the area of testing hard disks. The IBM PC version of this program (not the AT version) does not even allow for the entry of the manufacturer's defect list during a hard disk low-level format. This program also formats a hard disk at a fixed interleave value of 5 to 1, no matter what type of controller you have.

For the best floppy and hard disk diagnostics, you must use specialized software programs designed solely for these types of hardware. Several excellent programs are available specifically for testing floppy drives as well as hard disks. These programs, a welcome addition to anyone's toolkit, are an excellent supplement to the advanced diagnostics programs that "do it all."

The following section of this chapter discusses some of the best disk diagnostic and testing programs on the market and what they can do for you.

hTEST/hFORMAT

For specific troubleshooting and low-level formatting of ST-506/412 and ESDI hard disks, the hTEST/hFORMAT program, from Kolod Research, is one of the most powerful programs. At $130, it offers a great deal of power. The program operates directly at the controller register level, and includes drivers for a variety of controllers. It can operate through the ROM BIOS also if a driver is not available for your controller. The program, designed only for ST-506/412 or ESDI controllers, does not work with most IDE or SCSI interfaces.

hTEST/hFORMAT does nondestructive formatting and drive testing, without the surrounding "hype" of many remotely similar products on the market. This program definitely is not flashy or overfriendly, but it is one of the most powerful hard disk utilities. Its user interface is somewhat intimidating, in fact, if you are not thoroughly familiar with the operation of a hard disk and the interface.

One of the best parts of the hTEST/hFORMAT package is the KFDISK program, an FDISK clone that does not destroy data when it partitions a disk. Using this program, you can recover blown disk partitions without the subsequent damage in the volume that FDISK causes. This program alone is worth the price of the package.

Parts of this package might be difficult for a novice troubleshooter to master, but overall it is one of the most powerful programs of its type, and single features such as KFDISK are worth having.

HDtest

The HDtest program, by Jim Bracking, is an all-around excellent program for formatting and testing ST-506/412 hard disks and controllers. It also supports ESDI drives if the controller is not doing translation. SCSI and IDE support is limited to testing; formatting cannot be done on these drives.

The HDtest program works through the Int 13h (Interrupt 13 hex) inter-face built into the ROM BIOS; it tests a drive for defects by scanning the entire drive. If HDtest finds an unreadable sector, the program reports it to you precisely by cylinder, head, and individual sector; it also displays the exact BIOS error code returned. Many other programs are not as precise in this report.

An innovative feature is the program's capability to execute the indi-vidual Interrupt 13h BIOS commands to the drive. This capability has been helpful many times in troubleshooting systems with strange disk problems; also, it has been helpful in understanding how the BIOS and drive controller interact.

Because of the HDtest's easy user interface and explicit "educational" nature, I have been using it for several years in my seminars on trouble-shooting, upgrading, and repairing computers as well as in data-recovery seminars.

HDtest is user-supported directly by its creator, under the shareware concept. You can try the program, and if it meets your needs and you want to continue using it, you must send in the $35 registration fee. This fee ensures that you are notified if newer versions become available, and also helps finance this type of software. If everyone who uses the program contributes the required amount, new versions can be written. This program is excellent, with features not found in other programs at several times the price. HDtest has also one of the easiest-to-use inter-faces available on a program for testing and formatting disks. I encour-age you to obtain this program and send your registration to the author. You can download it from one of the many bulletin boards or from some public-domain software libraries; the best way, however, is from the author. Just send $35 to

Jim Bracking
967 Pinewood Dr.
San Jose, CA 95129
(408)725-0628

The current version of the software, released in 1989, is 1.28a. The program's creator has many good ideas for new features and better sup-port for ESDI, SCSI, and IDE drives, but no concrete plans for a new ver-sion unless users show sufficient interest. Registering the program if you use it is one way to show interest.

Drive Probe

Many programs on the market evaluate the condition of floppy disk drives by using a disk created or formatted on the same drive. A pro-gram that uses this technique cannot make a proper evaluation of a disk drive's alignment. A specially created disk produced by a tested and calibrated machine is required. This type of disk can be used as a reference standard by which to judge a drive. Accurite, the primary manufacturer of such reference standard floppy disks, helps specify floppy disk industry standards. Accurite produces the following three main types of reference standard disks used for testing drive function and alignment:

> Digital Diagnostic Diskette (DDD)
> High-Resolution Diagnostic Diskette (HRD)
> Analog Alignment Diskette (AAD)

The DDD diskette, introduced in 1982, enables you to test drive alignment using only software; no oscilloscope or special tools are needed. This disk is accurate to only 500μ-inches (millionths of an inch), good enough for a rough *test* of drive alignment but not nearly enough to use for *aligning* a drive.

The HRD diskette, introduced in 1989, represents a breakthrough in floppy disk drive testing and alignment. The disk is accurate to within 50μ-inches (millionths of an inch), accurate enough to use not only for precise testing of floppy drives, but also for aligning drives. With software that uses this HRD diskette, you can align a floppy drive using no special tools or oscilloscope. Other than the program and the HRD disk, you need only an IBM-compatible system to which to connect the drive. This product has lowered significantly the cost of aligning a drive and has eliminated a lot of hassling with special test equipment.

The AAD diskette has been the standard for drive alignment for many years. The disks, accurate to within 50μ inches (millionths of an inch), require that you use special test gear, such as an oscilloscope, to read the disk. These disks have no computer-readable data, only precisely placed analog tracks. Until HRD diskettes were available, using AADs was the only way to align drives properly.

The Accurite program Drive Probe is designed to work with the HRD diskettes (also from Accurite). Drive Probe is *the* most accurate and capable floppy disk testing program on the market, thanks to the use of HRD diskettes. Until other programs utilize the HRD diskettes for testing, Drive Probe is my software of choice for floppy disk testing. Because the Drive Probe software also acts as a disk exerciser, for use with AAD diskettes and an oscilloscope, you can move the heads to specific tracks for controlled testing.

Public-Domain Diagnostics

Many excellent diagnostic programs are available in the public domain. Numerous programs are available for diagnosing problems with memory, hard disks, floppy disks, displays and adapters, and virtually any other part of the system, and these programs can be excellent substitutes for the other "official" diagnostics programs. Many public-domain programs are commercial-quality programs distributed under a "try now, pay later" concept. This user-supported software is designed to use the typical public-domain software channels for distribution but is supported by honest users' payments for use. Some programs are "user supported" by contributions and donations from satisfied users nationwide.

Although you can find many sources for public-domain and user-supported software, including many distribution companies and electronic bulletin boards, one source stands out: the Public Software Library.

This organization, started as an outgrowth of a Houston computer users' group, has acquired the best single collection of public-domain and user-supported software. What makes this company extraordinary is that all the software is tested before entering the library. Bugged programs usually don't make it in the front door, which eliminates virus or Trojan-horse programs that damage a system. All the programs are the latest available versions, and earlier versions are purged from the library. Many other companies don't think twice about selling you a disk full of old programs. The programs in this library are not sold, but are just distributed. The authors are aware of how these programs are distributed, and no excessive fees are charged for the disk and copying services. This truly legitimate company has program authors' approval to distribute software in this manner. All disks are guaranteed, unlike many comparable organizations that seem bent on making as much money as they can. The Public Software Library offers a comprehensive monthly newsletter that reviews all popular public-domain, shareware, and user-supported programs; a complete catalog contains all the disk offerings. Although you do not have to subscribe to the newsletter to be able to order disks, I highly recommend that you do!

For a copy of the latest monthly newsletter and a list of the more than 3,000 disks in the library, call or write:

The Public (Software) Library   (800) 2424-PSL (orders)
P.O. Box 35705   (713) 524-6394 (information)
Houston, TX 77235-57055   (713) 524-6398 (FAX)
                                       71355,470 CompuServe ID

A disk costs $5 for 5 1/4-inch, 360K disks, or $6 for 3 1/2-inch, 720K disks. Certain disk sets are available for $6.99 on 3 1/2-inch, 1.44M disks.

Chapter Summary

This chapter has examined the diagnostic software you can use as a valuable aid in diagnosing and troubleshooting a system. The chapter has explained IBM error codes and included a reference chart showing the meanings of some of these codes. Advanced diagnostics were discussed also, as were some of the better aftermarket replacements. Some specialized diagnostics for particular areas of the system, such as disk drives, were discussed. The chapter ended with a discussion of public-domain and user-supported software, a rich source of fantastic utilities that are relatively inexpensive.

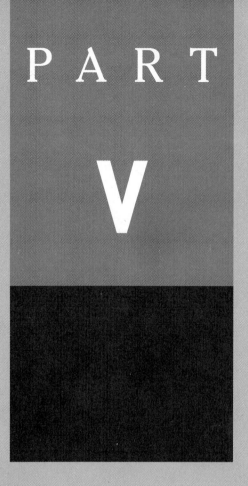

Troubleshooting Guides

PART

V

Hardware Trouble-shooting Guide

This chapter lists specific procedures for troubleshooting various system components. By now, you have a good understanding of how things work and how they should be installed. This information is the information you need for troubleshooting. To be a good trouble-shooter, you should understand a system better than average computer users.

The procedures listed here are not meant to replace the hardware-maintenance service manuals your system manufacturer provides; the procedures are designed to augment that information. These procedures are simple and concise, and they can be applied to almost any IBM or compatible system.

This chapter lists the items that fail most often in a system and recommends the items you should carry in inventory as spare parts.

Getting Started with Troubleshooting

When you troubleshoot a system, you should approach the task with a clear mind and a relaxed attitude. If you get overexcited or panic, you will make determining the problem much more difficult.

Don't start taking apart the system unit right away. First, sit back and think about the problem. Make notes and record any observations. Your notes can be valuable, especially for difficult problems. Don't throw away the notes after the problem is solved, either, because they can be valuable for a recurring problem also. You should develop a systematic approach to determining what the problem is.

Here are some basic troubleshooting rules of thumb:

1. Check the installation and configuration. Usually, if I have just assembled a system and it doesn't work properly, it's my fault. I might have set a jumper incorrectly, plugged a cable in backward (or left it unplugged), or left out some other small detail.

2. *Check the installation and configuration again.* Even when I am sure that it's correct, I still make mistakes. Double-check everything.

3. If you still have a problem, work your way through the system item by item, from those most likely to cause the problem to those least likely to cause the problem. Because power supplies often cause problems, for example, you should check the power supply before many other devices. Cables can cause many problems, and usually are easy to test. *Always check the cables before replacing any attached devices.* An improper low-level format can cause hard disk problems, so check that possibility before you assume that the disk is bad.

4. A variation of the preceding rule is to work your way through the system from the simplest, least expensive, and easiest-to-replace item to the most complex, most expensive, and hardest-to-replace item. This rule is just common sense. Check cables before adapter cards, for example, and check adapter cards before disk drives. *Check everything else before you check the motherboard.*

5. Check the environment, including incoming power, ambient temperature fluctuations, humidity, static electricity, and airborne contaminants. Environmental influences can cause many problems, and these problems can be the most difficult to track down. (How can you see temperature or humidity variations?)

6. Keep system documentation and manuals nearby. Write your own documentation for your systems and include anything you put into your system. Document the interrupt and DMA channel settings, port usage, memory usage, which slots the adapter cards are installed in, which kinds of memory chips you used in the system, and so forth. This documentation can save you from much unnecessary labor.

Keep these simple rules in mind, and your troubleshooting sessions can be enjoyable challenges.

Handling Intermittent Problems

The bane of any troubleshooter is the intermittent problem. Often you must rely on a report from a user who cannot describe the symptom in an accurate, precise manner. You must interpret the user's description and guess at what really happened. You might think that you have fixed the problem, only to discover that it occurs again.

If you can, get the system user to write down when the problem occurs and the exact symptoms. Before you begin disassembling the system, try to re-create the problem. When you have witnessed the intermittent problem, run the diagnostics software.

One of the best resources in the case of an intermittent failure is the advanced diagnostics software. This software can execute a test in endless-loop mode, which can be set to run all night or over a weekend. Another weapon commonly used to track down these types of problems is heat. You can use a hair dryer to warm up the motherboard and other electronics to help the failure along. You must be careful not to do any real damage, and I almost hesitate to mention it. Only experience and practice can give you a feel for just how hot you should make a board and when enough is enough.

Sometimes the opposite approach can work too. When a system is exhibiting a problem, you can spray on the suspected component some "component cooler" or Freon, which chills it. If the component's failure is heat-related, this chilling often restores its operation.

Static electricity and other external environmental influences often can cause what seems to be an intermittent problem. Noting the state of the surrounding environment when the problems are occurring is important. Pay attention to time too. Sometimes strange time patterns can help you discover that a problem is related to an external influence, such as turning on large motors at the same time every day.

Keep these tips in mind the next time you have an intermittent problem, and you may find it easier to handle.

Troubleshooting Flowcharts

Attempting to find a city in an unfamiliar state is made easy by the use of a road map. In the same vein, a map or flowchart can help you find a problem with a computer system. Knowing the appropriate path can get you to your destination for repairing the system with the least amount of detours. This section shows you the paths to follow to solve problems most successfully.

The Power Supply

If you suspect a power-supply problem, the simple measurements outlined in this section can help you determine whether the power supply is at fault. Because these measurements do not detect many intermittent or overload failures, you might have to use a spare power supply for long-term evaluation. If the symptoms and problems disappear with the replacement unit, you have found the source of your problem.

To test a power supply for proper output, check the voltage at the Power Good pin (P8-1 on IBM PC-XT-AT supplies) for 2.4 to 5.4 vdc. If the measurement is not within this range, the system never sees the Power Good signal and therefore never runs. In most cases, the supply is bad and must be replaced.

Continue by measuring the voltage ranges of the pins on the motherboard and drive power connectors (see table 14.1 and table 14.2). Note that the exact pin specifications and acceptable voltage ranges are for IBM PC-XT-AT power supplies as well as for most IBM-compatibles. Some systems, such as the PS/2 machines from IBM, use a different type of connector, and might accept different minimum and maximum voltages. Consult your system's technical-reference manual for this information.

Table 14.1 Motherboard Power-Connector Measurements

| | | PINS | |
Minimum voltage	Maximum voltage	-Leads	+Leads
+4.8	+5.2	P8-5	P9-4
+4.5	+5.4	P9-3	P8-6
+11.5	+12.6	P9-1	P8-3
+10.8	+12.9	P8-4	P9-2

Table 14.2 Disk Drive Power-Connector Measurements

| | | PINS | |
Minimum voltage	Maximum voltage	-Leads	+Leads
+4.8	+5.2	2	4
+11.5	+12.6	3	1

Replace the power supply if these voltages are incorrect. All these measurements must be made with the power supply installed in a system, and the system must be running. Again, these measurements are from IBM's documentation; other systems may allow different ranges to function. Most of the time on IBM-compatible systems, these ranges are acceptable:

> For output rated at +-5 volts, from 4.5 to 5.4.
> For output rated at +-12 volts, from 10.8 to 12.9.

The Appendix of this book has a detailed pin-out reference chart showing the proper voltage and signal at each power-supply connector. You can use this chart for reference when you make power-supply voltage measurements.

The types of power supplies used in these systems are called *switching* power supplies. These supplies always must have a proper load in order to function correctly. If you remove the supply from the system unit, set it on a workbench, plug it in, and power it on, the supply immediately shuts itself down. It does not run unless it's plugged into a motherboard and at least one disk drive.

The original AT systems were supplied with a huge load resistor mounted in place of the hard disk, which allowed the supply to operate properly even without a hard disk installed. If you are setting up a "diskless" system, make sure that you use a similar type of power load or you will have problems with the supply and possibly even burn it out. You can construct the same type of load resistor originally used by IBM by connecting a 6-ohm, 30-watt sandbar resistor between pins 1 and 2 on the connector. This procedure puts a 2.5-amp load on the supply's 12-volt output, which enables it to run normally. You still should connect the other power connectors to a motherboard for a load on the 5-volt outputs.

The System Board

A motherboard failure can be difficult to detect. In many cases, the system is simply nonfunctional. If the system is nonfunctional or partially functional and you suspect a motherboard failure, these troubleshooting procedures can be helpful:

> Check all connectors to ensure that they are plugged in correctly.

> Confirm that the wall outlet is a working outlet.

> Look for foreign objects such as screws you might have dropped on the motherboard, and make sure that the board is clean.

Confirm that all system-board switch settings are correct.

Run the advanced diagnostics system-board test.

Check for error codes, displayed as follows:

1xx	System board errors
101	System board error; interrupt failure
102	System board error; timer failure
103	System board error; timer-interrupt failure
104	System board error; protected mode failure
105	System board error; 8042 keyboard controller command failure
106	System board error; converting logic test
107	System board error; hot non-maskable interrupt (NMI) test
108	System board error; timer bus test
109	System board error; memory-select error
110	PS/2 system board parity-check error (PARITY CHECK 1)
111	PS/2 I/O channel (bus) parity-check error (PARITY CHECK 2)
112	PS/2 Micro Channel arbitration error; watchdog time-out
113	PS/2 Micro Channel arbitration error; DMA arbitration time-out
114	PS/2 external ROM checksum error
115	Cache parity error
121	Unexpected hardware interrupts occurred
131	PC system board cassette-port wrap test failure
131	Direct memory access (DMA) compatibility registers error
132	Direct memory access (DMA) extended registers error
133	Direct memory access (DMA) verify logic error
134	Direct memory access (DMA) arbitration logic error
151	PC Convertible; real-time clock RAM failed
151	Battery or CMOS RAM failure
152	PC Convertible; real-time clock failed
152	Real-time clock or CMOS RAM failure
160	PS/2 system board ID not recognized
161	CMOS configuration empty (dead battery)

1xx	System board errors
162	CMOS checksum error
163	CMOS error; date and time not set
164	Memory size error; CMOS setting does not match memory
165	PS/2 Micro Channel adapter ID and CMOS mismatch
166	PS/2 Micro Channel adapter time-out error
167	PS/2 CMOS clock not updating
168	CMOS configuration error; math coprocessor
170	PC Convertible LCD not in use when suspended
171	PC Convertible base 128K checksum failure
172	PC Convertible diskette active when suspended
173	PC Convertible real-time clock RAM verification error
174	PC Convertible LCD configuration changed
175	PC Convertible LCD alternate mode failed
194	System board memory error
199	User indicated INSTALLED DEVICES list is not correct

The Appendix in this book contains an extensive listing of POST (Power-On Self Test) and diagnostics error codes.

Next, check the supply voltage for 2.4 to 5.2 vdc between pins 1 and 5 (ground) at the system board. Turn off the power and remove all option adapters from the system board. Check in table 14.3 for the resistance values at the motherboard power connectors.

Table 14.3 Pin Minimums

-Lead	+Lead	Resistance
5	3	17 ohms
6	4	17 ohms
7	9	17 ohms
8	10	0.8 ohms
8	11	0.8 ohms
8	12	0.8 ohms

Improper resistance readings might indicate that the motherboard is defective, particularly if the resistance is below the minimums indicated. If the voltage measurements aren't within the parameters specified, the power supply might be defective.

Many IBM-compatible motherboards might not exhibit these same resistance characteristics. A better way to test systems that seem "dead" is to use one of the POST-code adapter cards. These cards show the manufacturer POST codes sent by the ROM BIOS to a special manufacturing-test I/O port address. These boards are described in more detail in Chapter 13. Also, the appendix lists POST codes for IBM and most other popular BIOS manufacturers. By using one of these cards plugged into a slot and reading the resulting code on the card's two-digit hex display, you often can accurately determine the cause of the system failure. Of course, if the cause is a component on the motherboard such as a DMA controller or other soldered IC chip, replacing the motherboard might be more prudent than repairing it.

Many boards use large-scale integrated chip sets that combine many functions in one chip. These chip sets, often surface mounted, are impossible to replace with conventional soldering tools; instead, special surface-mount rework solder equipment is needed. Also, obtaining a replacement part might prove very difficult, if not impossible, even if you can remove the bad one.

The Battery

A defective battery usually is indicated during the POST with a 161 error. The simplest way to determine whether a battery is defective is to replace it. Otherwise, first rerun the SETUP program; if this step doesn't correct the problem, disconnect the battery from the system board. The battery voltage between pins 1 and 4 on the battery connector should be at least 6.0 vdc. Replace the battery if it doesn't meet the correct voltage specifications.

T I P Try lithium batteries rather than the cheaper alkaline batteries when you replace the batteries in a system. If you shop prudently, you should be able to buy the standard, AT-style, 6-volt lithium battery for between $6 to $12. The alkaline batteries, although they're cheaper, do not last as long. Never use conventional batteries, because they might leak acid on the motherboard.

Many newer systems do not use a standard type of battery. Rather, they use a special module developed by Dallas Semiconductor. These "Dallas modules" are the Dallas DS-1287 or DS-1387 Real-Time Clock modules. They combine the clock and CMOS circuitry with a built-in battery. The modules look like large, square IC chips, and usually are imprinted with the Dallas name and logo, which looks like an alarm clock. The battery in these modules is supposed to be good for more than ten years in the absence of power, and even longer if the system is running. Essentially, these units should outlast the computers in which they are installed.

If the Dallas modules require replacement, you can get new modules for about $14 if you purchase directly from Dallas, or about $30 if you buy the same chip from IBM or COMPAQ. The nice thing about replacing these modules is that you are replacing the entire clock and CMOS circuit along with the battery. If the CMOS chip was damaged on a normal motherboard without the Dallas module, you would have to desolder the defective chip and solder in a replacement. The Dallas modules are installed in sockets in most systems, like those from IBM and Compaq. You should keep a few of these modules around as spares, in case of CMOS configuration problems.

The Keyboard

Keyboard errors sometimes can be difficult to detect. To troubleshoot the keyboard and cable assembly, power on and observe the POST. Write down the 3xx error if you received one.

If your 3xx error is preceded by a two-digit hexadecimal number, this number is the scan code of a failing or stuck keyswitch. A complete set of scan-code-to-key-symbol reference charts are in the Appendix of this book. These charts tell you to which key the scan code refers. By removing the keycap of the offending key and cleaning the switch, you often can solve the problem. The scan-code reference charts in the appendix cover all the keyboard types, including the original 83-key PC/XT keyboard, the 84-key AT keyboard, and the 101/102-key enhanced style keyboard.

Next, turn off the power and disconnect the keyboard. Then, turn on the power and check the voltage at the system-board keyboard connector for the specifications in table 14.4.

Table 14.4 Keyboard Connector Specifications

Pin	Voltage
1	+2.0 to +5.5
2	+4.8 to +5.5
3	+2.0 to +5.5
4	Ground
5	+2.0 to +5.5

If your measurements don't match these voltages, the motherboard might be defective. Otherwise, the keyboard cable or keyboard might be defective. Keyboard-connector pinout reference charts are included in the Appendix of this book. These charts can help you test a cable or identify the functions of the pins on the keyboard connectors on the motherboard, keyboard, and each end of the keyboard cable. If you suspect the cable as a problem, the easiest thing to do is replace the keyboard cable with a known good one and run the Advanced Diagnostics keyboard test.

A list of diagnostics keyboard error codes is displayed as follows:

3xx	Keyboard errors
301	Keyboard reset or stuck-key failure (XX 301, XX = scan code in hex)
302	System-unit keylock is locked
302	User indicated keyboard test error
303	Keyboard or system-board error; keyboard controller failure
304	Keyboard or system-board error; keyboard clock high
305	Keyboard +5v error; PS/2 keyboard fuse (on system board) error
341	Keyboard error
342	Keyboard cable error
343	Keyboard LED card or cable failure
365	Keyboard LED card or cable failure
366	Keyboard interface cable failure
367	Keyboard LED card or cable failure

The Video Adapter

If you suspect problems with the video board, make sure that the switch settings on the motherboard and video card are correct, and turn on the power. Listen for audio response during the POST (one long and two short beeps indicate a video failure).

If the adapter is supported, run the Advanced Diagnostics video adapter test for the particular adapter you want to test. Adapters that aren't supported always fail the tests even though they might be good. Error codes are displayed as follows:

4xx	**Monochrome Display Adapter (MDA)/parallel port errors**
401	Monochrome memory, horizontal sync frequency, or video-test failure
401	PS/2 system board parallel-port failure
408	User indicated display-attributes failure
416	User indicated character-set failure
424	User indicated 80x25 mode failure
432	Parallel-port test failure; Monochrome Display Adapter
5xx	**Color Graphics Adapter (CGA) errors**
501	CGA memory, horizontal sync frequency, or video-test failure
503	CGA adapter controller failure
508	User indicated display-attribute failure
516	User indicated character-set failure
524	User indicated 80x25 mode failure
532	User indicated 40x25 mode failure
540	User indicated 320x200 graphics mode failure
548	User indicated 640x200 graphics mode failure
556	User indicated light-pen test failed
564	User indicated paging-test failed
24xx	**Enhanced Graphics Adapter (EGA) errors**
24xx	**PS/2 system board Video Graphics Array (VGA) errors**
2401	Video-adapter test failure
2402	Video-display error
2408	User indicated display-attribute test failed

2409	Video-display error
2410	Video-adapter error
2416	User indicated character-set test failed
2424	User indicated 80x25 mode failure
2432	User indicated 40x25 mode failure
2440	User indicated 320x200 graphics mode failure
2448	User indicated 640x200 graphics mode failure
2456	User indicated light-pen test failure
2464	User indicated paging-test failure

25xx	**Alternate Enhanced Graphics Adapter (EGA) errors**
2501	Video-adapter test failure
2502	Video-display error
2508	User indicated display-attribute test failed
2509	Video-display error
2510	Video-adapter error
2516	User indicated character-set test failed
2524	User indicated 80x25 mode failure
2532	User indicated 40x25 mode failure
2540	User indicated 320x200 graphics mode failure
2548	User indicated 640x200 graphics mode failure
2556	User indicated light-pen test failure
2564	User indicated paging-test failure

39xx	**Professional Graphics Adapter (PGA) errors**
3901	PGA test failure
3902	ROM1 self-test failure
3903	ROM2 self-test failure
3904	RAM self-test failure
3905	Cold Start Cycle power error
3906	Data error in communications RAM
3907	Address error in communications RAM
3908	Bad data reading or writing 6845-like register

3909	Bad data in lower E0h bytes reading or writing 6845-like registers
3910	Graphics controller display-bank output-latches error
3911	Basic clock error
3912	Command-control error
3913	Vertical sync scanner error
3914	Horizontal sync scanner error
3915	Intech error
3916	Look-up table address error
3917	Look-up table red RAM chip error
3918	Look-up table green RAM chip error
3919	Look-up table blue RAM chip error
3920	Look-up table data latch error
3921	Horizontal-display error
3922	Vertical-display error
3923	Light-pen error
3924	Unexpected error
3925	Emulator-addressing error
3926	Emulator data-latch error
3927	Base for error codes 3928-3930 (emulator RAM)
3928	Emulator RAM error
3929	Emulator RAM error
3930	Emulator RAM error
3931	Emulator horizontal- or vertical-display problem
3932	Emulator cursor-position error
3933	Emulator attribute-display problem
3934	Emulator cursor-display error
3935	Fundamental emulation RAM problem
3936	Emulation character-set problem
3937	Emulation graphics-display error
3938	Emulation character-display problem
3939	Emulation bank-select error
3940	Adapter RAM U2 error

3941	Adapter RAM U4 error
3942	Adapter RAM U6 error
3943	Adapter RAM U8 error
3944	Adapter RAM U10 error
3945	Adapter RAM U1 error
3946	Adapter RAM U3 error
3947	Adapter RAM U5 error
3948	Adapter RAM U7 error
3949	Adapter RAM U9 error
3950	Adapter RAM U12 error
3951	Adapter RAM U14 error
3952	Adapter RAM U16 error
3953	Adapter RAM U18 error
3954	Adapter RAM U20 error
3955	Adapter RAM U11 error
3956	Adapter RAM U13 error
3957	Adapter RAM U15 error
3958	Adapter RAM U17 error
3959	Adapter RAM U19 error
3960	Adapter RAM U22 error
3961	Adapter RAM U24 error
3962	Adapter RAM U26 error
3963	Adapter RAM U28 error
3964	Adapter RAM U30 error
3965	Adapter RAM U21 error
3966	Adapter RAM U23 error
3967	Adapter RAM U25 error
3968	Adapter RAM U27 error
3969	Adapter RAM U29 error
3970	Adapter RAM U32 error
3971	Adapter RAM U34 error
3972	Adapter RAM U36 error

3973	Adapter RAM U38 error
3974	Adapter RAM U40 error
3975	Adapter RAM U31 error
3976	Adapter RAM U33 error
3977	Adapter RAM U35 error
3978	Adapter RAM U37 error
3979	Adapter RAM U39 error
3980	Graphics controller RAM-timing error
3981	Graphics controller read/write latch error
3982	Shift register bus output-latches error
3983	Addressing error (vertical column of memory; U2 at top)
3984	Addressing error (vertical column of memory; U4 at top)
3985	Addressing error (vertical column of memory; U6 at top)
3986	Addressing error (vertical column of memory; U8 at top)
3987	Addressing error (vertical column of memory; U10 at top)
3988	Base for error codes 3989-3991 (horizontal bank-latch errors)
3989	Horizontal bank-latch errors
3990	Horizontal bank-latch errors
3991	Horizontal bank-latch errors
3992	RAG/CAG graphics controller error
3993	Multiple write modes, nibble mask errors
3994	Row nibble (display RAM) error
3995	Graphics controller addressing error
50xx	**PC Convertible LCD errors**
5001	LCD display buffer failure
5002	LCD font buffer failure
5003	LCD controller failure
5004	User indicated PEL/drive test failed
5008	User indicated display-attribute test failed
5016	User indicated character-set test failed
5020	User indicated alternate character-set test failure
5024	User indicated 80x25 mode test failure

5032	User indicated 40x25 mode test failure
5040	User indicated 320x200 graphics test failure
5048	User indicated 640x200 graphics test failure
5064	User indicated paging-test failure
74xx	**IBM PS/2 Display Adapter (VGA card) errors**
74xx	**8514/A Display Adapter errors**
7426	8514 display error
7440	8514/A memory module 31 error
7441	8514/A memory module 30 error
7442	8514/A memory module 29 error
7443	8514/A memory module 28 error
7444	8514/A memory module 22 error
7445	8514/A memory module 21 error
7446	8514/A memory module 18 error
7447	8514/A memory module 17 error
7448	8514/A memory module 32 error
7449	8514/A memory module 14 error
7450	8514/A memory module 13 error
7451	8514/A memory module 12 error
7452	8514/A memory module 06 error
7453	8514/A memory module 05 error
7454	8514/A memory module 02 error
7455	8514/A memory module 01 error
7460	8514/A memory module 16 error
7461	8514/A memory module 27 error
7462	8514/A memory module 26 error
7463	8514/A memory module 25 error
7464	8514/A memory module 24 error
7465	8514/A memory module 23 error
7466	8514/A memory module 20 error
7467	8514/A memory module 19 error
7468	8514/A memory module 15 error

7469	8514/A memory module 11 error
7470	8514/A memory module 10 error
7471	8514/A memory module 09 error
7472	8514/A memory module 08 error
7473	8514/A memory module 07 error
7474	8514/A memory module 04 error
7475	8514/A memory module 03 error
149xx	**P70/P75 Plasma Display and Adapter errors**
14901	Plasma Display Adapter failure
14902	Plasma Display Adapter failure
14922	Plasma Display failure
14932	External Display failure

The Fixed Disk Drive

Problems with hard disks are indicated by 17xx errors. If you suspect any problems with a drive, controller, or cable, you can substitute equipment that you know works properly.

Check for proper configuration of drives (drive-select jumpers and terminating resistors). Turn off the power. Power on and boot the advanced diagnostics (or a similar program). Run the fixed disk drive and adapter tests. Error codes indicating various problems are displayed as follows:

17xx	**ST-506/412 fixed disk and controller errors**
1701	Fixed disk general POST error
1702	Drive or controller time-out error
1703	Drive-seek error
1704	Controller failed
1705	Drive sector not found error
1706	Write-fault error
1707	Drive track 0 error
1708	Head-select error
1709	Error correction code (ECC) error
1710	Sector-buffer overrun
1711	Bad address mark

1712	Internal controller diagnostics failure
1713	Data-compare error
1714	Drive not ready
1715	Track 0 indicator failure
1716	Diagnostics cylinder errors
1717	Surface-read errors
1718	Hard drive type error
1720	Bad diagnostics cylinder
1726	Data-compare error
1730	Controller error
1731	Controller error
1732	Controller error
1733	BIOS undefined error return
1735	Bad command error
1736	Data-corrected error
1737	Bad track error
1738	Bad sector error
1739	Bad initialization error
1740	Bad sense error
1750	Drive verify failure
1751	Drive read failure
1752	Drive write failure
1753	Drive random-read test failure
1754	Drive-seek test failure
1755	Controller failure
1756	Controller error-correction code (ECC) test failure
1757	Controller head-select failure
1780	Seek failure; drive 0
1781	Seek failure; drive 1
1782	Controller test failure
1790	Diagnostic cylinder read error; drive 0
1791	Diagnostic cylinder read error; drive 1

104xx	**ESDI fixed disk or adapter errors**
10450	Read/write test failed
10451	Read verify test failed
10452	Seek test failed
10453	Wrong device type indicated
10454	Controller test failed sector-buffer test
10455	Controller failure
10456	Controller diagnostic command failure
10461	Drive format error
10462	Controller head-select error
10463	Drive read/write sector error
10464	Drive primary defect map unreadable
10465	Controller; error correction code (ECC) 8-bit error
10466	Controller; error correction code (ECC) 9-bit error
10467	Drive soft-seek error
10468	Drive hard-seek error
10469	Drive soft-seek error count exceeded
10470	Controller-attachment diagnostic error
10471	Controller wrap mode interface error
10472	Controller wrap mode drive-select error
10473	Read verify test error
10480	Seek failure; drive 0
10481	Seek failure; drive 1
10482	Controller test failure
10482	Controller transfer-acknowledge error
10483	Controller reset failure
10484	Controller; head select 3 error
10485	Controller; head select 2 error
10486	Controller; head select 1 error
10487	Controller; head select 0 error
10488	Controller; read gate—command complete 2 error
10489	Controller; write gate—command complete 1 error

10490	Diagnostic area read error; drive 0
10491	Diagnostic area read error; drive 1
10499	Controller failure

SCSI device errors

096xxxx	SCSI adapter with cache (32-bit) errors
112xxxx	SCSI adapter (16-bit without cache) errors
113xxxx	System board SCSI adapter (16-bit) errors
208xxxx	Unknown SCSI device errors
209xxxx	SCSI removable disk errors
210xxxx	SCSI fixed disk errors
211xxxx	SCSI tape drive errors
212xxxx	SCSI printer errors
213xxxx	SCSI processor errors
214xxxx	SCSI Write-Once Read Mostly (WORM) drive errors
215xxxx	SCSI CD-ROM drive errors
216xxxx	SCSI scanner errors
217xxxx	SCSI optical-memory errors
218xxxx	SCSI jukebox-changer errors
219xxxx	SCSI communications errors

Check the cables to make sure that they aren't defective, and measure voltages at the drive power connector as indicated in the section "The Power Supply" earlier in this chapter.

If you are sure that the power supply is not the cause, you can attempt to replace the logic board on the drive with one from another unit. This procedure might restore the drive to operation and also enable the data to be read. If preserving the data is not important, you might attempt a low-level format without replacing the logic board. Often, intermittent hard disk read and write or boot-up problems can be caused by a drive whose low-level format has become unstable.

The Floppy Disk Drive

If you suspect that the floppy drives are defective, make sure that the problem isn't in the floppy disk being used. A number of problems can stem from improperly inserting and clamping the floppy disk in the drive. Before you continue, remove and carefully reinsert the floppy disk to be sure that it is not the problem. If the drive receives power separately from the computer, make sure that nothing is wrong with the power outlet. Be sure that all cables and connectors are plugged in correctly. Check to see that all drives are configured properly (drive-select jumpers, terminating resistors, pin 34, and media sensor) and then run the advanced diagnostics disk drive and adapter tests. Error codes are displayed as follows:

6xx	**Floppy drive and controller errors**
601	Floppy drive and controller Power-On Self Test failure
602	Diskette boot sector is not valid
603	Diskette size error
606	Diskette verify test failure
607	Write-protect error
608	Drive command error
610	Diskette initialization failure; track 0 bad
611	Drive time-out error
612	Controller chip (NEC) error
613	Direct memory access (DMA) error
614	Direct memory access (DMA) boundary-overrun error
615	Drive index timing error
616	Drive speed error
621	Drive seek error
622	Drive Cyclic Redundancy Check (CRC) error
623	Sector Not Found error
624	Address mark error
625	Controller chip (NEC) seek error
626	Diskette data-compare error
627	Diskette change error
628	Diskette removed
630	Index stuck high; drive A:
631	Index stuck low; drive A:
632	Track 0 stuck off; drive A:
633	Track 0 stuck on; drive A:

640	Index stuck high; drive B:
641	Index stuck low; drive B:
642	Track 0 stuck off; drive B:
643	Track 0 stuck on; drive B:
645	No index pulse
646	Drive track 0 detection failed
647	No transitions on read data line
648	Format test failed
649	Incorrect media type in drive
650	Drive-speed error
651	Format failure
652	Verify failure
653	Read failure
654	Write failure
655	Controller error
656	Drive failure
657	Write-protect stuck; protected
658	Changeline stuck; changed
659	Write-protect stuck; unprotected
660	Changeline stuck; unchanged
73xx	**3 1/2-inch external diskette drive errors**
7301	Diskette drive or adapter test failure
7306	Disk Changeline failure
7307	Diskette is write-protected
7308	Drive-command error
7310	Diskette initialization failure; track 0 bad
7311	Drive time-out error
7312	Controller chip (NEC) error
7313	Direct memory access (DMA) error
7314	Direct memory access (DMA) boundary overrun
7315	Drive index timing error
7316	Drive-speed error

7321	Drive-seek error
7322	Drive Cyclic Redundancy Check (CRC) error
7323	Sector not found error
7324	Address mark error
7325	Controller chip (NEC) seek error
107xx	5 1/4-inch external diskette drive or adapter errors

Check the voltages at the power connector for the floppy drives, as indicated in the section "The Power Supply" earlier in this chapter.

Test the drive for correct rotational speed using diagnostics, and adjust the speed if the drive allows a speed adjustment. Most floppy disk drives made since 1986 have no speed adjustment. Rather, these drives automatically adjust themselves to the correct speed. If a nonadjustable drive is off-speed, it must be replaced. If you use a program such as the Accurite Drive Probe, you can check the alignment of the drive.

Make sure that the cable and connectors are good, and check the cables for continuity. If the power-connector voltages don't measure as they should, the power supply might be bad.

Serial- and Parallel-Port Tests

To test serial- or parallel-port cards, run the advanced-diagnostics communications adapter tests. Most tests require that you attach a loopback connector (also called a wrap plug) to the port, to allow the port to transmit and receive signals simultaneously for test purposes. Pinout charts for all forms of serial and parallel connectors are in the Appendix of this book. Also included are wiring diagrams for serial and parallel wrap plugs if you want to make your own rather than purchase them.

The diagnostics tests display error codes as follows:

9xx	**Parallel printer adapter errors**
901	Printer adapter data-register latch error
902	Printer adapter control-register latch error
903	Printer adapter register-address decode error
904	Printer adapter address decode error
910	Status line(s) wrap connector error
911	Status line bit 8 wrap error
912	Status line bit 7 wrap error

913	Status line bit 6 wrap error
914	Status line bit 5 wrap error
915	Status line bit 4 wrap error
916	Printer adapter interrupt wrap error
917	Unexpected printer-adapter interrupt
92x	Feature-register error

10xx	**Alternate parallel printer adapter errors**
1001	Printer adapter data register latch error
1002	Printer adapter control register latch error
1003	Printer adapter register address decode error
1004	Printer adapter address decode error
1010	Status line(s) wrap connector error
1011	Status line bit 8 wrap error
1012	Status line bit 7 wrap error
1013	Status line bit 6 wrap error
1014	Status line bit 5 wrap error
1015	Status line bit 4 wrap error
1016	Printer adapter interrupt wrap error
1017	Unexpected printer-adapter interrupt
102x	Feature-register error

11xx	**Primary Async communications (serial port COM1:) errors**
1101	16450/16550 chip error
1101	PC Convertible internal modem 8250 baud generator test failed
1102	Card-selected feedback error
1102	PC Convertible internal modem test failed
1103	Port 102h register test failure
1103	PC Convertible internal modem dial-tone test 1 failed
1104	PC Convertible internal modem dial-tone test 2 failed
1106	Serial option cannot be put to sleep
1107	Cable error
1108	Interrupt request (IRQ) 3 error

1109	Interrupt request (IRQ) 4 error
1110	16450/16550 chip register failure
1111	Internal wrap test of 16450/16550 chip modem-control-line failure
1112	External wrap test of 16450/16550 chip modem-control-line failure
1113	16450/16550 chip transmit error
1114	16450/16550 chip receive error
1115	16450/16550 chip receive error; data not equal to transmit data
1116	16450/16550 chip interrupt function error
1117	16450/16550 chip baud-rate test failure
1118	16450/16550 chip receive external data wrap test failure
1119	16550 chip first-in first-out (FIFO) buffer failure
1120	Interrupt enable register error; all bits cannot be set
1121	Interrupt enable register error; all bits cannot be reset
1122	Interrupt pending; stuck on
1123	Interrupt ID register; stuck on
1124	Modem control register error; all bits cannot be set
1125	Modem control register error; all bits cannot be reset
1126	Modem status register error; all bits cannot be set
1127	Modem status register error; all bits cannot be reset
1128	Interrupt ID error
1129	Cannot force overrun error
1130	No modem-status interrupt
1131	Invalid interrupt pending
1132	No data ready
1133	No data available interrupt
1134	No transmit holding interrupt
1135	No interrupts
1136	No received line status interrupt
1137	No receive data available
1138	Transmit holding register not empty
1139	No modem-status interrupt
1140	Transmit holding register not empty

1141	No interrupts
1142	No interrupt 4
1143	No interrupt 3
1144	No data transferred
1145	Maximum baud-rate error
1146	Minimum baud-rate error
1148	Time-out error
1149	Invalid data returned
1150	Modem status register error
1151	No data set ready and Delta data set ready
1152	No data set ready
1153	No Delta data set ready
1154	Modem status register not clear
1155	No clear to send and Delta clear to send
1156	No clear to send
1157	No Delta clear to send
12xx	**Alternate Async communications (serial COM2:, COM3:, and COM4:) errors**
1201	16450/16550 chip error
1202	Card-selected feedback error
1203	Port 102h register test failure
1206	Serial option cannot be put to sleep
1207	Cable error
1208	Interrupt request (IRQ) 3 error
1209	Interrupt request (IRQ) 4 error
1210	16450/16550 chip register failure
1211	Internal wrap test of 16450/16550 chip modem control line failure
1212	External wrap test of 16450/16550 chip modem control line failure
1213	16450/16550 chip transmit error
1214	16450/16550 chip receive error
1215	16450/16550 chip receive error; data not equal to transmit data
1216	16450/16550 chip interrupt function error

1217	16450/16550 chip baud rate test failure
1218	16450/16550 chip receive external data wrap test failure
1219	16550 chip first-in first-out (FIFO) buffer failure
1220	Interrupt enable register error; all bits cannot be set
1221	Interrupt enable register error; all bits cannot be reset
1222	Interrupt pending; stuck on
1223	Interrupt ID register; stuck on
1224	Modem control register error; all bits cannot be set
1225	Modem control register error; all bits cannot be reset
1226	Modem status register error; all bits cannot be set
1227	Modem status register error; all bits cannot be reset
1228	Interrupt ID error
1229	Cannot force overrun error
1230	No modem-status interrupt
1231	Invalid interrupt pending
1232	No data ready
1233	No data available interrupt
1234	No transmit holding interrupt
1235	No interrupts
1236	No received line status interrupt
1237	No receive data available
1238	Transmit holding register not empty
1239	No modem-status interrupt
1240	Transmit holding register not empty
1241	No interrupts
1242	No interrupt 4
1243	No interrupt 3
1244	No data transferred
1245	Maximum baud rate error
1246	Minimum baud rate error
1248	Time-out error
1249	Invalid data returned

1250	Modem status register error
1251	No data set ready and Delta data set ready
1252	No data set ready
1253	No Delta data set ready
1254	Modem-status register not clear
1255	No clear to send and Delta clear to send
1256	No clear to send
1257	No Delta clear to send

For serial ports only, check for a voltage reading of -10.8 to -12.9 vdc between pins 4 and 8 (ground) and the system-board power connector. If the voltage measurement isn't within the range specified, the power supply might be defective.

The Speaker

To verify the operation of the speaker in the system unit, turn off the power. Set your meter to Ohms X1 Scale. Disconnect the speaker from the system board. Check the continuity of the speaker. If the speaker doesn't have continuity, it is defective and should be replaced.

Common Failures

Of all possible problems that can occur with a computer, some are more common than others. This section reviews some of a computer's most common failures.

Items with a High Failure Rate

The most common failures in a PC are mechanical—disk drives (floppy and hard disk) and power supplies. These items can and do fail, sometimes with no warning. Memory devices also fail periodically.

The power supply is a very failure-prone item, especially in the IBM PC in which an underrated unit was used. I usually replace the PC power supply when I upgrade a PC because most upgrades (such as hard disks) use much power—more than is available in the original supply. Having too much power supply is better than not enough.

These system components are most likely to fail:

Power supply
Hard disk low-level format
Floppy drive
Hard disk controller
Hard disk
Memory chips

Floppy Drive Failure

Only two floppy disk drive problems can be fixed quickly: the drive speed and dirty drives.

If you have other problems with a floppy disk drive, you probably have to replace the drive with a new or rebuilt unit. Because floppy disk drives are relatively inexpensive, spending a lot of time trying to fix them doesn't make sense.

Adjusting the speed of a floppy disk drive is easy if the drive is an older unit that is adjustable. You usually can do so by turning a screw on the motor-control logic board while watching the results with one of the many floppy disk testing programs available.

If you have many drives to be repaired or aligned, you should locate a service company that specializes in disk drive service and alignments. Most service companies will align a floppy drive for $25 to $50. This cost must be weighed against the replacement cost. I have purchased new, half-height 360K drives for as low as $39, so I'm not sure that I would spend $50 to align an old drive. If you want to have your drives aligned, see the vendor list in the Appendix of this book for a list of some companies that perform this service.

Cleaning disk drives is normally part of a preventive-maintenance program, but it might have been neglected. Always remember to clean a problem drive. Because some of the disk-based cleaners are abrasive to the drive heads, always use the "wet"-type cleaners—they are gentler on the heads.

Recommended Spare Components and Parts

I recommend carrying spares for these items:

Cables of all types
Power supplies

Memory chips
Floppy disk drives
Floppy drive controllers
Batteries

If the system is very important and must be up all the time, you should add a couple more items to the spares list:

Hard disk drives and controllers
Keyboards

With these items on hand, you are prepared for 90 percent of all system failures and problems.

Last-Ditch Fixes

When all else fails when you are troubleshooting a problem, a foolproof method exists for diagnosing the problem.

Locate a system identical to the failing one. The closer the match, the better. The duplicate system should be the same type, and from the same manufacturer if possible. Also, if possible, it should have the same adapter boards installed and be configured exactly the same way.

Verify that the duplicate system runs correctly and does not exhibit the symptoms of the failing unit. Begin placing items from the spare unit into the malfunctioning unit one by one, and test after replacing each item. First replace each cable, for example, using the spare system's cables. Progress to each adapter card, disk drive, power supply, motherboard, and so on.

You will know when you have found the problem part when the malfunctioning unit begins to work.

Fortunately, this "brute force" method is rarely required, but in a pinch, it works. This method requires little thought, and it's a method anyone can use. Keep it in mind when you are under pressure to fix a system.

Chapter Summary

This chapter has covered hardware troubleshooting techniques in detail. You have received some basic tips for good troubleshooting. The body of this chapter has covered specific component troubleshooting, giving you the procedures, measurements, and observations you should make to determine the location of a system fault. The last part of this chapter has focused on failure-prone items and how to handle certain troublesome situations.

Software Troubleshooting Guide

This chapter focuses on the problems that occur in PC systems because of faulty or incompatible software. First, it describes the structure of DOS and how DOS works with hardware in a functioning system. Topics of particular interest are

- DOS file structure
- DOS disk organization
- DOS programs for data and disk recovery (their capabilities and dangers)

Additionally, the chapter examines two other important software-related issues: using memory-resident software (and dealing with the problems it can cause) and distinguishing a software problem from a hardware problem.

Understanding the Disk Operating System (DOS)

Information about DOS may seem out of place in a book about hardware upgrade and repair, but if you ignore DOS and other software when you troubleshoot a system, you can miss a number of problems. The best system troubleshooters and diagnosticians know the entire system—hardware and software.

This book cannot discuss DOS in depth, but you should read more about it. Que Corporation publishes some good books on the subject (*Using PC DOS,* 3rd Edition, or *Using MS-DOS 5*, for example).

This section describes the basics of DOS: where it fits into the PC system architecture, what its components are, and what happens when a system boots (starts up). Understanding the booting process can be helpful when you're diagnosing start-up problems. This section also explains DOS configuration—an area in which many people experience problems—and the file formats DOS uses, as well as how DOS manages information on a disk.

Operating-System Basics

DOS is just one component in the total system architecture. A PC system has a distinct hierarchy of software that controls the system at all times. Even when you are operating within an application program such as 1-2-3 or another high-level application software, several other layers of programs are always executing underneath. Usually the layers can be defined distinctly, but sometimes the boundaries are vague.

Communications generally occur only between adjoining layers in the architecture, but this rule is not absolute. Many programs ignore the services provided by the layer directly beneath them and eliminate "the middleman" by skipping one or more layers. An example is a program that ignores the DOS and ROM BIOS video routines and communicates directly with the hardware in the interest of the highest possible screen performance. Although the high-performance goal is admirable, many operating environments (such as OS/2 and Windows) no longer allow direct access to the hardware. Programs that do not "play by the rules" must be rewritten to run in these new environments.

At the lowest level of the system hierarchy is the hardware. By placing various bytes of information at certain ports or locations within a system's memory structure, you can control virtually anything connected to the CPU. Maintaining control at the hardware level is difficult; doing so requires a complete and accurate knowledge of the system architecture. The level of detail required of the software operating at this level is the most intense. Commands to the system at this level are in *machine language* (binary groups of information applied directly to the microprocessor). Machine-language instructions are limited in their function: You must use many of them to perform even the smallest amount of useful work. The large number of instructions required is not really a problem because these instructions are executed extremely rapidly, with little wasted overhead.

Programmers can write programs consisting of machine-language instructions, but generally they use a tool—an *assembler*—to ease the process. They write programs using an *editor*, and then use the assembler to convert the editor's output to pure machine language. Assembler commands are still very low level, and using them effectively requires that programmers be extremely knowledgeable. No one (in his or her right mind) writes directly in machine code anymore; assembly language is the lowest level of programming environment typically used today. Even assembly language, however, is losing favor among programmers because of the amount of knowledge and work required to complete even simple tasks and because of its lack of portability between different kinds of systems.

When you start a PC system, a series of machine-code programs assume control: They are the ROM BIOS. This set of programs, always present in a system, "talks" (in machine code) to the hardware. The BIOS accepts or interprets commands supplied by programs above it in the system hierarchy and translates them to machine-code commands that then are passed on to the microprocessor. Commands at this level typically are called *interrupts* or *services*. A programmer generally can use nearly any language to supply these instructions to the BIOS. A complete list of these services is supplied in the IBM *BIOS Interface Technical Reference Manual*.

DOS itself is made up of several components. It attaches to the BIOS, and part of DOS actually becomes an extension of the BIOS, providing more interrupts and services for other programs to use. DOS provides for communication with the ROM BIOS in PCs and with higher-level software (such as applications). Because DOS gives the programmer interrupts and services to use in addition to those provided by the ROM BIOS, a lot of "reinventing the wheel" in programming routines is eliminated. For example, DOS provides an extremely rich set of functions that can open, close, find, delete, create, rename, and perform other file-handling tasks. When programmers want to include some of these functions in their programs, they can rely on DOS to do most of the work.

This standard set of functions that applications use to read from and write data to disks makes data-recovery operations possible. Imagine how tough writing programs and using computers would be if every application program had to implement its own custom disk interface, with a proprietary directory and file-retrieval system. Every application would require its own special disks. Fortunately, DOS provides a standard set of documented file-storage and -retrieval provisions that all software can use; as a result, you can make some sense out of what you find on a typical disk.

Another primary function of DOS is to load and run other programs. As it performs that function, DOS is the *shell* within which another program can be executed. DOS provides the functions and environment required by other software—including "operating environments" such as GEM and Windows—to run on PC systems in a standard way.

The System ROM BIOS

Think of the system ROM BIOS as a form of "compatibility glue" that sits between the hardware and an operating system. Why is it that IBM can sell the same DOS to run on the original IBM PC *and* on the PS/2 Model 90 XP 486—two very different hardware platforms? If DOS were written to talk directly to the hardware on all systems, it would be a very hardware-specific program. Instead, IBM developed a set of standard services and functions each system should be capable of performing and coded them as programs in the ROM BIOS. Each system then gets a completely custom ROM BIOS that talks directly to the hardware in the system and knows exactly how to perform each specific function on that hardware only.

This convention enables operating systems to be written to what amounts to a standard interface that can be made available on many different types of hardware. Any applications written to the operating-system standard interface can run on that system. Figure 15.1 shows that two very different hardware platforms can each have a custom ROM BIOS that talks directly to the hardware and still provides a standard interface to an operating system.

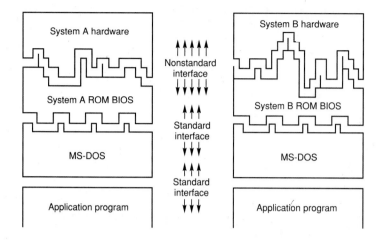

Fig 15.1

A representation of the software layers in an IBM-compatible system.

The two different hardware platforms described in figure 15.1 can run not only the exact same version of DOS, but also the same applications programs because of the standard interfaces provided by the ROM BIOS and DOS. Keep in mind, however, that the actual ROM BIOS code differs among the specific machines and that it is not usually possible therefore to run a ROM BIOS designed for one system in a different system. ROM BIOS upgrades must come from a source that has an intimate understanding of the specific motherboard on which the chip will be placed because the ROM must be custom written for that particular hardware.

The portion of DOS shown in figure 15.1 is the "system" portion, or core, of DOS. This core is found physically as the two system files on any bootable DOS disk. These hidden system files will usually have one of two sets of names, IBMBIO.COM and IBMDOS.COM (used in IBM and COMPAQ DOS), or IO.SYS and MSDOS.SYS (used in most other OEM MSDOS versions). These files must be the first and second files listed in the directory on a bootable DOS disk.

Figure 15.1 represents a simplified view of the system. In reality, some subtle but important differences exist. Ideally, applications programs are insulated from the hardware by the ROM BIOS and DOS, but in reality many programmers write portions of their programs to talk directly to the hardware, circumventing DOS and the ROM BIOS. A program therefore might work only on specific hardware, even if the proper DOS and ROM BIOS interfaces are present in other hardware.

Programs designed to go directly to the hardware are written that way mainly to increase performance. For example, many programs directly access the video hardware to improve screen-update performance. These applications often have "install" programs that require you to specify exactly what hardware is present in your system so that the program can load the correct hardware-dependent routines into the application.

Additionally, some utility programs absolutely must talk directly to the hardware to perform their function. For example, a low-level format program must talk directly to the hard disk controller hardware to perform the low-level format of the disk. Such programs are very specific to a certain controller or controller type. Another type of system-specific utility, the driver programs, enable extended memory to function as expanded memory on an 80386-based system. These drivers work by accessing the 80386 directly and utilizing specific features of the chip.

Another way that reality might differ from the simple view is that DOS itself will communicate directly with the hardware. In fact, much of the IBMBIO.COM file consists of low-level drivers designed to supplant and supersede ROM BIOS code in the system. People who own both IBM systems and compatibles might wonder why IBM never seems to have ROM BIOS upgrades to correct bugs and problems with its systems, although for vendors of most compatible systems, a ROM upgrade is at least a semiannual occurrence. The reason is simple: IBM distributes its ROM patches and upgrades in DOS. When IBM DOS loads, it determines the system type and ID information from the ROM, and loads different routines depending on which version of ROM it finds. For example, at least four different hard disk code sections are in IBM DOS, but only one is loaded for a specific system.

I have taken a single DOS boot disk with only the system files (COMMAND.COM and CHKDSK.COM) on it, and booted the disk on both an XT and an AT system, each one with an identical 640K of memory. After loading DOS, CHKDSK reported different amounts of free memory, which showed that DOS had taken up different amounts of memory in the two systems. This is due to the different code routines loaded based on the ROM ID information. In essence, DOS, the ROM BIOS, and the hardware are much more closely related than most people realize.

DOS Components

DOS consists of two primary components: the input/output (I/O) system and the shell. The I/O system consists of the underlying programs that reside in memory while the system is running; these programs are loaded first when DOS boots. The I/O system is stored in the form of two files that are hidden on a bootable DOS disk. The files are called IBMBIO.COM and IBMDOS.COM on an IBM DOS disk, but might go by other names for other manufacturers' versions of DOS. For example, IO.SYS and MSDOS.SYS are the MS-DOS file names. No matter what the exact names are, the function of these two files is basically the same for all versions of DOS.

The user-interface program, or shell, is stored in the COMMAND.COM file, which also is loaded during a normal DOS boot-up. The shell is the portion of DOS that provides the DOS prompt and that normally communicates with the user of the system.

The following sections examine the DOS I/O system and shell in more detail, to help you properly identify and solve problems that are DOS problems rather than hardware problems. Also included is a discussion on how DOS allocates disk file space.

DOS File Space Allocation

DOS allocates disk space for a file on demand (space is not preallocated). The space is allocated one *cluster* (or allocation unit) at a time. A cluster is always one or more sectors. (For more information about sectors, refer to Chapter 8.)

The clusters are arranged on a disk to minimize head movement for multisided media. DOS allocates all the space on a disk cylinder before moving to the next cylinder. It does this by using the sectors under the first head, then all the sectors under the next head, and so on until all sectors of all heads of the cylinder are used. The next sector used is sector 1 of head 0 on the next cylinder. (You will find more information on floppy disks and drives in Chapter 8 and on hard disks in Chapter 9.)

DOS version 2.X uses a simple algorithm when it allocates file space on a disk. Every time a program requests disk space, DOS scans from the beginning of the FAT until it finds a free cluster in which to deposit a portion of the file; then the search continues for the next cluster of free space, until all of the file is written. This algorithm, called the First Available Cluster algorithm, causes any erased file near the beginning of the disk to be overwritten during the next write operation, because those clusters would be the first available to the next write operation. This system prevents recovery of that file and promotes file fragmentation because the first available cluster found is used regardless of whether the entire file can be written there. DOS simply continues searching for free clusters in which to deposit the remainder of the file. The algorithm used by DOS 2.X therefore often prevents unerasing files after new data has been written to a disk, as well as promotes file fragmentation as the disk is used.

The algorithm used for file allocation in DOS 3.0 and later versions is called the Next Available Cluster algorithm. In this algorithm, the search for available clusters in which to write a file starts not at the beginning of the disk, but rather from where the last write occurred. Therefore, the disk space freed by erasing a file is not necessarily reused immediately.

Rather, DOS maintains a Last Written Cluster pointer indicating the last written cluster and begins its search from that point. This pointer is maintained in system RAM and is lost when the system is reset or rebooted, or when a disk is changed in a floppy drive.

In working with 360K drives, all versions of DOS always use the First Available Cluster algorithm because the Last Written Cluster pointer cannot be maintained for floppy disk drives that do not report a disk change (DC) signal to the controller, and because 360K drives do not supply the DC signal. With 360K floppy drives, therefore, DOS always assumes that the disk could have been changed, which flushes any buffers and resets the Last Written Cluster pointer.

The Next Available Cluster algorithm in DOS 3.0 and later versions is faster than the First Available Cluster algorithm and helps minimize fragmentation. Sometimes this type of algorithm is called "elevator seeking" because write operations occur at higher and higher clusters until the end of the disk area is reached. At that time the pointer is reset, and writes work their way from the beginning of the disk again.

Files still end up becoming fragmented using the new algorithm, because the pointer is reset after a reboot, a disk change operation, or when the end of the disk is reached. Nevertheless, a great benefit of the newer method is that it makes unerasing files more likely to succeed even if the disk has been written to since the erasure, because the file just erased is not likely to be the target of the next write operation. In fact, it might be some time before the clusters occupied by the erased file are reused.

Even when a file is "overwritten" under DOS 3.0 and later versions, the clusters occupied by the file are not actually reused in the overwrite. For example, if I accidentally save on a disk a file using the same name as an important file that already exists, the existing file clusters are marked as available, and the new file (with the same name) is written to the disk in other clusters. It is possible, therefore, that the original copy of the file can still be retrieved. I can continue this procedure by saving another copy of the file with the same name, and each file copy is saved to higher-numbered clusters, and each earlier version "overwritten" might still be recoverable on the disk. This process can continue until the system is rebooted or reset, or until the end of the available space is reached. Then the pointer is set to the first cluster, and previous file data is overwritten.

Because DOS always uses the first available directory entry when it saves or creates a file, the "overwritten" or deleted files whose data is still recoverable on the disk no longer appear in a directory listing. No commercial "quick unerase" or other unerase utilities therefore can find any record of the erased or overwritten file on the disk—true, of course, because these programs look only in the directory for a record of an erased file. Some newer undelete programs have a memory-resident delete tracking function which in essence maintains a separate directory listing from DOS. Unless an unerase program has a memory-resident delete tracking function, and that function has been activated before the deletion, no program will be able to recall the files overwritten in the directory entry.

Because unerase programs do not look at the FAT, or at the data clusters themselves (unless they use delete tracking), they see no record of the files' existence. By scanning the free clusters on the disk one by one using a disk editor tool, you can locate the data from the "overwritten" or erased file and manually rebuild the FAT and directory entries. This procedure enables you to recover erased files even though files have been written to the disk since the erasure took place. This type of powerful unerase operation and FAT and directory rebuilding are discussed in the problem-solving chapters of this book.

The I/O System

This section briefly describes the two files that make up the I/O system: IBMBIO.COM and IBMDOS.COM.

IBMBIO.COM (or IO.SYS)

IBMBIO.COM is one of the hidden files that the CHKDSK command reports on any system (bootable) disk. This file contains the low-level programs that interact directly with devices on the system and the ROM BIOS. IBMBIO.COM usually is customized by the particular original equipment manufacturer (OEM) of the system to match perfectly with that OEM's ROM BIOS. The file contains low-level drivers loaded in accord with a particular ROM BIOS, based on the ROM ID information, as well as on a system initialization routine. During boot-up, the DOS volume boot sector loads the file into low memory and gives it control of the system (see the section "DOS Volume Boot Sectors" later in this chapter). All of the file except the system initializer portion remains in memory during normal system operation.

The name used for the file that performs the functions just described varies among versions of DOS from different OEMs. Many versions of DOS, including Microsoft's MS-DOS, use IO.SYS as the name of this file. Some other manufacturers call the file MIO.SYS, and Toshiba calls it TBIOS.SYS. Using different names for this file is not normally a problem, until you try to upgrade from one OEM version of DOS to a different OEM version. If the different OEMs have used different names for this file, the

SYS command might fail with the error message No room for system on destination. Today most OEMs use the standard IBMBIO.COM name for this file to eliminate problems in upgrading and otherwise remain standard.

For a disk to be bootable, IBMBIO.COM or its equivalent must be listed as the first file in the directory of the disk and must occupy at least the first cluster on the disk (cluster number 2). The remainder of the file might be placed in clusters anywhere across the rest of the disk (versions 3 and higher). The file normally is marked with hidden, system, and read-only attributes, and placed on a disk by the FORMAT command or the SYS command.

IBMDOS.COM (or MSDOS.SYS)

IBMDOS.COM, the core of DOS, contains the DOS disk handling programs. The routines present in this file make up the DOS disk and device handling programs. IBMDOS.COM is loaded into low memory at system boot-up by the DOS volume boot sector and remains resident in memory during normal system operation.

The IBMDOS.COM program collection is less likely to be customized by an OEM but still might be present on a system by a different name than IBMDOS.COM. The most common alternative name, MSDOS.SYS, is used by Microsoft's MS-DOS and some OEM versions of DOS. Another name is TDOS.SYS (used by Toshiba). Most OEMs today stick to the IBM convention to eliminate problems in upgrading from one DOS version to another.

IBMDOS.COM or its equivalent must be listed as the second entry in the root directory of any bootable disk. This file usually is marked with hidden, system, and read-only attributes, and is normally placed on a disk by the FORMAT command or the SYS command. There are no special requirements for the physical positioning of this file on a disk.

Potential DOS Upgrade Problems

You already know that the DOS system files have special placement requirements on a hard disk. Sometimes these special requirements cause problems when you are upgrading from one version of DOS to another.

If you have attempted to upgrade a PC system from one version of DOS to another, you know that you use the DOS SYS command to replace old system files with new ones. The SYS command copies the existing system files (stored on a bootable disk with hidden, system, and read-only attributes) to the disk in the correct position and with the correct names and attributes. The COPY command does not copy hidden or system files (nor would it place the system files in the required positions on the destination disk if their other attributes had been altered so that they could be copied using COPY).

In addition to transferring the two hidden system files from one disk to another, SYS also updates the DOS volume boot sector on the destination disk so that it is correct for the new version of DOS.

The syntax of the command is

    SYS [d:][path] d:

[d:][path] specifies an optional source drive and path for the system files. If the source drive specification is omitted, the boot drive is used as the source drive. This parameter is supported in DOS 4.0 and later versions only. Versions of DOS older than 4.0 automatically look for system files on the default drive (not on the boot drive).

d: specifies the drive to which you want to transfer the system files.

When the SYS command is executed, you usually are greeted by one of two messages:

    No room for system on destination disk

or

    System transferred

If a disk has data on it before you try to write the system files to it, the SYS command from DOS versions 3.3 and earlier probably will fail because they are not capable of moving other files out of the way. The SYS command in DOS 4.0 and higher versions rarely fail because they can and do move files out of the way.

Some users think that the cause of the No room message on a system which has an older version of DOS on it is that the system files in any newer version of DOS are always larger than the previous version, and that the new version files cannot fit into the space allocated for older versions. Such users believe that the command fails because this space cannot be provided at the beginning without moving other data away. This belief is wrong. The SYS command fails in these cases because you are trying to install a version of DOS that has different file names than the names already on the disk. There is no normal reason for the SYS command to fail when you update the system files on a disk that already has them.

Although the belief that larger system files cannot replace smaller ones might be popular, it is wrong for DOS 3.0 and later versions. The system files can be placed virtually anywhere on the disk, except that the first clusters of the disk must contain the file IBMBIO.COM (or its equivalent). After that requirement has been met, the IBMDOS.COM file might be fragmented and placed just about anywhere on the disk, and the SYS command implements it with no problems whatsoever. In version 3.3 or later, even the IBMBIO.COM file can be fragmented and spread all over the disk, as long as the first cluster of the file occupies the first cluster of the disk (cluster 2). The only other requirement is that the names IBMBIO.COM and IBMDOS.COM (or their equivalents) must use the first and second directory entries.

DOS 4.0 and Later Versions

Under DOS 4.0 and later versions, the SYS command is much more powerful than under previous versions. Because the system files must use the first two entries in the root directory of the disk as well as the first cluster (cluster 2) of the disk, the DOS 4.0 and later versions' SYS command moves any files that occupy the first two entries but that do not match the new system file names to other available entries in the root directory; the SYS command also moves the portion of any foreign file occupying the first cluster to other clusters on the disk. Whereas the SYS command in older versions of DOS would fail, and require a user to make adjustments to the disk, the DOS 4.0 and later versions' SYS command automatically makes the required adjustments. For example, even if you are updating a Phoenix DOS 3.3 disk to IBM DOS 4.0, the IBM DOS SYS command relocates the Phoenix IO.SYS and MSDOS.SYS files so that the new IBMBIO.COM and IBMDOS.COM files can occupy the correct locations in the root directory as well as on the disk.

DOS 5.0

The SYS command in DOS Version 5.0 goes one step further: It replaces the old system files with the new ones. Even if the old system files had other names, DOS 5.0 ensures that they are overwritten by the new system files. If you are updating a disk on which the old system file names match the new ones, the SYS command of any version of DOS will overwrite the old system files with the new ones with no moving of files necessary. With the enhanced SYS command in DOS 4.0 and later versions, it is difficult to make a DOS upgrade fail.

DOS 3.3

The DOS 3.3 SYS command does not move other files out of the way (as SYS does in DOS 4.0 and later versions); therefore, you must ensure that the first two root directory entries are either free or contain names that match the new system file names. As in DOS 4.0 and later versions, the first cluster on the disk must contain the first portion of IBMBIO.COM; unlike DOS 4.0 and later versions, however, the SYS command under DOS 3.3 does not move any files for you. Necessary manual adjustments, such as clearing the first two directory entries or relocating a file that occupies the first cluster on the disk, must be done with whatever utility programs you have available. The DOS 3.3 system files can be fragmented and occupy various areas of the disk.

SYS under DOS 3.3 does not automatically handle updating from one version of DOS to a version that has different system file names. In that case, because the system file names are not the same, the new system files do not overwrite the old ones. If you are making this kind of system change, use a directory editing tool to change the names of the current system files to match the new names so that the system file overwrite can occur.

DOS 3.2

DOS 3.2 or earlier requires that the entire IBMBIO.COM file be contiguous starting with cluster 2 (the first cluster) on the disk. The other system file (IBMDOS.COM) can be fragmented or placed anywhere on the disk; it does not have to follow the first system file physically on the disk.

DOS 2.X

DOS 2.X requires that both system files (IBMBIO.COM and IBMDOS.COM) occupy contiguous clusters on the disk starting with the first cluster (cluster 2). The DOS 2.1 system files are slightly larger than the DOS 2.0 files in actual bytes of size, but the size change is not enough to require additional clusters on the disk. A SYS change from DOS 2.0 to DOS 2.1 therefore is successful in most cases.

Upgrading DOS from the Same OEM

Updating from one version of DOS to a later version from the same OEM by simply using the SYS command has never been a problem. I have verified this with IBM DOS. I installed IBM DOS 2.0 on a system with a hard disk through the normal FORMAT /S command. I copied all the subsequent DOS-transient programs into a \DOS subdirectory on the disk. Then I updated the hard disk, in succession, to IBM DOS 2.1, 3.0, 3.1, 3.2, 3.3, 4.0, and 5.0, using nothing more than the SYS and COPY (or XCOPY or REPLACE) commands. Between each version change, I verified that the hard disk would boot the new version of DOS with no problems. Based on this experiment, I have concluded that you never would have to use the FORMAT command to update one DOS version to a later version, as long as both versions are from the same OEM. I also verified the same operations on a floppy disk. Starting with a bootable floppy disk created by IBM DOS 2.0, I used SYS and COPY to update that disk to all subsequent versions of DOS through 5.0 without ever reformatting it. After each version change, the floppy disk was bootable with no problems.

You should be able to update a bootable hard disk or floppy disk easily from one DOS version to another without reformatting the disk. If you are having problems, you probably are attempting to upgrade to a version of DOS that uses different names for the system files than those used by the existing DOS, which means that you are moving from a DOS made by one OEM to a DOS made by a different company. If you are having trouble and this is not the case, carefully examine the list of requirements at the beginning of this section. Your problem must be that one of those requirements is not being met.

Downgrading DOS

One important and often overlooked function of the SYS command is its capability to update the DOS volume boot sector of a disk on which it is writing system files. Later versions of SYS are more complete than earlier versions in the way they perform this update; therefore, using SYS to go from a later version of DOS to an earlier version is sometimes difficult. For example, you cannot use SYS to install DOS 2.1 on a disk that currently boots DOS 3.0 and later versions. Changing from DOS 4.0 or DOS 5.0 to DOS 3.3 usually works, if the partition is less than or equal to 32 megabytes in capacity. You probably will never see a problem with a later version of SYS updating a DOS volume boot sector created by an earlier version, but earlier versions might leave something out when they attempt to change back from a later version. Fortunately, few people ever attempt to install a lower version of DOS over a higher version.

The Shell or Command Processor (COMMAND.COM)

The DOS command processor COMMAND.COM is the portion of DOS with which users normally interact. The commands can be categorized by function, but IBM DOS divides them into two types by how they are made available: *resident* or *transient*.

Resident Commands

Resident commands are built into COMMAND.COM and are available whenever the DOS prompt is present. They are generally the simpler, frequently used commands such as CLS and DIR. Resident commands execute rapidly because the instructions for them are already loaded into memory. They are *memory-resident*.

When you look up the definition of a command in the DOS manual, you will find an indication of whether the command is resident or transient. You then can determine what is required to execute that command. A simple rule is that, at a DOS prompt, all resident commands are instantly available for execution, with no loading of the program from disk required.

Transient Commands

Transient commands are often called *utilities*. These commands are not resident in the computer's memory, and the instructions to execute the command must be located on a disk. Because the instructions are loaded into memory only for execution and then are overwritten in memory after they are used, they are called *transient commands*. Most DOS commands are transient; otherwise, the memory requirements for DOS would be astronomical. Transient commands are used less frequently than resident commands and take longer to execute because they must be found and loaded before they can be run.

DOS looks only in specific places for the instructions for a transient command. The instructions that represent the command or program are in files on one or more disk drives. Files that contain execution instructions have one of three specific extensions to indicate to DOS that they are program files: .COM (command files), .EXE (executable files), or .BAT (batch files). .COM and .EXE files are machine-code programs; .BAT files contain a series of commands and instructions using the DOS batch facilities. The places in which DOS will look for these files is controlled by the current directory and the PATH command.

DOS Command File-Search Procedure

DOS performs a two- or three-level search for program instructions (the file). The first step in looking for command instructions is to see whether the command is a resident one and, if so, run it from the program code already loaded. If the command is not resident, DOS looks in the current directory for .COM, .EXE, and .BAT files, in that order, and loads and executes the first file it finds with the specified name. If the command is not resident and not in the current directory, DOS looks in all the directories specified in the DOS PATH setting (which the user can control); DOS searches for the file within each directory in the extension order just indicated. Finally, if DOS fails to locate the required instructions, it displays the error message Bad command or filename. This error message might be misleading because the command instructions usually are missing from the search areas rather than actually being bad.

Suppose that, at the DOS prompt, I type the command XYZ and press Enter. This command sends DOS on a search for the XYZ program's instructions. If DOS is successful, the program will start running within seconds. If DOS cannot find the proper instructions, an error message is displayed. Here is what happens:

1. DOS checks internally to see whether it can find the XYZ command as one of the resident commands whose instructions are already loaded. It finds no XYZ command as resident.

2. DOS looks next in the current directory on the current drive for files named XYZ.COM, then for files named XYZ.EXE, and finally for files named XYZ.BAT. I had logged on to drive C:, and the current directory was \ (the root directory); therefore, DOS did not find the files in the current directory.

3. DOS looks to see whether a PATH has been specified. If not, the search ends here. In this scenario, I do have a PATH that was specified when my system was started, so DOS checks every directory listed in that PATH for the first file it can find named XYZ.COM, XYZ.EXE, or XYZ.BAT (in that order). My PATH lists several directories, but DOS does not find an appropriate file in any of them.

4. The search ends, and DOS gives me the message Bad command or filename.

For this search-and-load procedure to be successful, I must ensure that the desired program or command file exists in the current directory on the current drive, or I must set my DOS PATH to point to the drive and directory in which the program does exist. This is why the PATH is so powerful in DOS.

A common practice is to place all simple command files or utility programs in one directory and set the PATH to point to that directory. Then each of those programs (commands) is instantly available by simply typing its name, just as though it were resident.

This practice works well only for single-load programs such as commands and other utilities. Major applications software often consists of many individual files and might have problems if they are called up from a remote directory or drive using the DOS PATH. The reason is that when the application looks for its overlay and accessory files, the DOS PATH setting has no effect.

On a hard disk system, users typically install all transient commands and utilities in subdirectories and ensure that the PATH points to those directories. The system then functions as though all the commands were resident because DOS finds the necessary files without further thought or effort on the part of the user. Major applications can be called up through batch files or aided by programs that "force-feed" a path-type setting to the programs. The software then works as though files are "here" even when they are in some other directory. The best utility for this purpose is the APPEND command in DOS 3.0 and later versions.

You can completely short-circuit the DOS command search procedure by simply entering at the command prompt the complete path to the file. For example, rather than include C:\DOS in the PATH and enter this command:

        C:>CHKDSK

you can enter the full name of the program:

        C:>C:\DOS\CHKDSK.COM

The latter command immediately locates and loads the CHKDSK program with no search through the current directory or PATH setting. This method of calling up a program speeds the location and execution of the program and works especially well to increase the speed of DOS batch-file execution.

The Boot Process

The term *boot* comes from the term "bootstrap" and describes the method by which the PC becomes operational. Just as you pull on a large boot by the small strap attached to the back, a PC can load a large operating-system program by first loading a small program that then can pull in the operating system. A chain of events begins with the application of power and finally results in an operating computer system with software loaded and running. Each event is called by the event before it and initiates the event after it.

Tracing the system-boot process might help you find the location of a problem, if you examine the error messages the system displays when the problem occurs. If you can see an error message displayed only by a particular program, you can be sure that the program in question was at least loaded and partially running. Combine this information with the knowledge of the boot sequence, and you can at least tell how far along the system's start-up procedure is. You usually want to look at whatever files or disk areas were being accessed during the failure in the boot process. Error messages displayed during the boot process as well as those displayed during normal system operation can be hard to decipher, but the first step in decoding an error message is to know where the message came from—what program actually sent or displayed the message. These programs are capable of displaying error messages during the boot process:

■ Motherboard ROM BIOS

■ Adapter card ROM BIOS extensions

■ Master-partition boot sector

■ DOS volume boot sector

■ System files (IBMBIO.COM and IBMDOS.COM)

■ Device drivers (loaded through CONFIG.SYS)

■ Shell program (COMMAND.COM)

■ Programs run by AUTOEXEC.BAT

This section examines the system start-up sequence and provides a detailed account of many of the error messages that might occur during this process.

How DOS Loads and Starts

If you have a problem with your system during start-up and you can determine where in this sequence of events your system has stalled, you know what events have occurred and you probably can eliminate each of them as a cause of the problem. The following steps occur in a typical system start-up:

1. You switch on electrical power to the system.

2. The power supply performs a self-test. When all voltages and current levels are acceptable, the supply indicates that the power is stable and sends the Power Good signal to the motherboard. The time from switch-on to Power Good is normally between .1 and .5 seconds.

3. The microprocessor timer chip receives the Power Good signal, which causes it to stop generating a reset signal to the microprocessor.

4. The microprocessor begins executing the ROM BIOS code, starting at memory address FFFF:0000. Because this location is only 16 bytes from the very end of the available ROM space, it contains a JMP (jump) instruction to the actual ROM BIOS starting address.

5. The ROM BIOS performs a test of the central hardware to verify basic system functionality. Any errors that occur are indicated by audio codes because the video system has not yet been initialized.

6. The BIOS performs a video ROM scan of memory locations C000:0000 through C780:0000, looking for video adapter ROM BIOS programs contained on a video adapter card plugged into a slot. If a video ROM BIOS is found, it is tested by a checksum procedure. If it passes the checksum test, the ROM is executed, the video ROM code initializes the video adapter, and a cursor appears on-screen. If the checksum test fails, this message appears:

   ```
   C000 ROM Error
   ```

7. If the BIOS finds no video adapter ROM, it uses the motherboard ROM video drivers to initialize the video-display hardware, and a cursor appears on-screen.

8. The motherboard ROM BIOS scans memory locations C800:0000 through DF80:0000 in 2K increments for any other ROMs located on any other adapter cards. If any ROMs are found, they are checksum-tested and executed. These adapter ROMs can alter existing BIOS routines as well as establish new ones.

9. Failure of a checksum test for any of these ROM modules causes this message to appear:

   ```
   XXXX ROM Error
   ```

10. The address XXXX indicates the segment address of the failed ROM module.

11. The ROM BIOS checks the word value at memory location 0000:0472 to see whether this start is a cold start or a warm start. A word value of 1234h in this location is a flag that indicates a warm start, which causes the memory-test portion of the POST (Power-On Self Test) to be skipped. Any other word value in this location indicates a cold start and full POST.

12. If this is a cold start, the POST executes. Any errors found during the POST are reported by a combination of audio and displayed error messages. Successful completion of the POST is indicated by a single beep.

13. The ROM BIOS searches for a DOS volume boot sector at cylinder 0, head 0, sector 1 (the very first sector) on the A: drive. This sector is loaded into memory at 0000:7C00 and tested. If a disk is in the drive but the sector cannot be read, or if no disk is present, the BIOS continues with the next step.

14. If the first byte of the DOS volume boot sector loaded from the floppy disk in A: is less than 06h, or if the first byte is greater than or equal to 06h, and the first nine words contain the same data pattern, this error message appears and the system stops:

    ```
    602-Diskette Boot Record Error
    ```

15. If the disk was prepared with FORMAT or SYS using DOS 3.3 or an earlier version and the specified system files are not the first two files in the directory, or if a problem was encountered loading them, this message appears:

    ```
    Non-System disk or disk error
    Replace and strike any key when ready
    ```

16. If the disk was prepared with FORMAT or SYS using DOS 3.3 or an earlier version and the boot sector is corrupt, you might see this message:

    ```
    Disk Boot failure
    ```

17. If the disk was prepared with FORMAT or SYS using DOS 4.0 and later versions and the specified system files are not the first two files in the directory, or if a problem was encountered loading them or the boot sector is corrupt, this message appears:

    ```
    Non-System disk or disk error
    Replace and press any key when ready
    ```

18. If no DOS volume boot sector can be read from drive A:, the BIOS looks for a master-partition boot sector at cylinder 0, head 0, sector 1 (the very first sector) of the first fixed disk. If this sector is found, it is loaded into memory address 0000:7C00 and tested for a signature.

19. If the last two (signature) bytes of the master-partition boot sector are not equal to 55AAh, software interrupt 18h (Int 18h) is invoked on most systems. On an IBM PS/2 system, a special character-graphics message is displayed that depicts inserting a floppy disk in drive A: and pressing the F1 key. For non-PS/2 systems made by IBM, an Int 18h executes the ROM BIOS-based Cassette BASIC Interpreter. On any other IBM-compatible system, a message indicating some type of boot error is displayed. For example, systems with Phoenix AT ROM BIOS display this message:

    ```
    No boot device available -
    strike F1 to retry boot, F2 for setup utility
    ```

20. The master partition boot-sector program searches its partition table for an entry with a system-indicator byte indicating an extended partition. If the program finds such an entry, it loads the extended-partition boot sector at the location indicated. The extended-partition boot sector also has a table that is searched for another extended partition. If another extended-partition entry is found, that extended-partition boot sector is loaded from the location indicated, and the search continues until either no more extended partitions are indicated or the maximum number of 24 total partitions has been reached.

21. The master-partition boot sector searches its partition table for a boot-indicator byte marking an active partition.

22. On an IBM system, if none of the partitions is marked active (bootable), ROM BIOS-based Cassette BASIC is invoked. On most IBM-compatible systems, some type of disk error message is displayed.

23. If any boot indicator in the master-partition boot record table is invalid, or if more than one indicates an active partition, this message is displayed, and the system stops:

    ```
    Invalid partition table
    ```

24. If an active partition is found in the master-partition boot sector, the volume boot sector from the active partition is loaded and tested.

25. If the DOS volume boot sector cannot be read successfully from the active partition within five retries due to read errors, this message appears and the system stops:

    ```
    Error loading operating system
    ```

26. The hard disk DOS volume boot sector is tested for a signature. If the DOS volume boot sector does not contain a valid signature of 55AAh as the last two bytes in the sector, this message appears and the system stops:

    ```
    Missing operating system
    ```

27. The volume boot sector is executed as a program. This program checks the root directory to ensure that the first two files are IBMBIO.COM and IBMDOS.COM. If these files are present, they are loaded.

28. If the disk was prepared with FORMAT or SYS using DOS V3.3 or an earlier version and the specified system files are not the first two files in the directory, or if a problem was encountered loading them, this message appears:

    ```
    Non-System disk or disk error
    Replace and strike any key when ready
    ```

29. If the disk was prepared with FORMAT or SYS using DOS V3.3 or an earlier version and the boot sector is corrupt, you might see this message:

   ```
   Disk Boot failure
   ```

30. If the disk was prepared with FORMAT or SYS using DOS V4.0 or a later version and the specified system files are not the first two files in the directory, or if a problem was encountered loading them or the boot sector is corrupt, this message appears:

   ```
   Non-System disk or disk error
   Replace and press any key when ready
   ```

31. If no problems have occurred, the DOS volume boot sector executes IBMBIO.COM.

32. The initialization code in IBMBIO.COM copies itself into the highest region of contiguous DOS memory and transfers control to the copy. The initialization code copy then relocates IBMDOS over the portion of IBMBIO in low memory that contains the initialization code, because the initialization code no longer needs to be in that location.

33. The initialization code executes IBMDOS, which initializes the base device drivers, determines equipment status, resets the disk system, resets and initializes attached devices, and sets the system default parameters.

34. The full DOS filing system is active, and the IBMBIO initialization code is given back control.

35. The IBMBIO initialization code reads CONFIG.SYS four times.

36. During the first read, all the statements except DEVICE, INSTALL, and SHELL are read and processed in a predetermined order. Thus, the order of appearance for statements other than DEVICE, INSTALL, and SHELL in CONFIG.SYS is of no significance.

37. During the second read, DEVICE statements are processed in the order in which they appear, and any device driver files named are loaded and executed.

38. During the third read, INSTALL statements are processed in the order in which they appear, and the programs named are loaded and executed.

39. During the fourth and final read, the SHELL statement is processed and loads the specified command processor with the specified parameters. If the CONFIG.SYS file contains no SHELL statement, the default \COMMAND.COM processor is loaded with default parameters. Loading the command processor overwrites the initialization code in memory (because the job of the initialization code is finished).

40. If AUTOEXEC.BAT is present, COMMAND.COM loads and runs AUTOEXEC.BAT. After the commands in AUTOEXEC.BAT have been executed, the DOS prompt appears (unless the AUTOEXEC.BAT calls an application program or shell of some kind, in which case the user might operate the system without ever seeing a DOS prompt).

41. If no AUTOEXEC.BAT is present, COMMAND.COM executes the internal DATE and TIME commands, displays a copyright message, and displays the DOS prompt.

These steps are the ones an IBM AT system performs, and most IBM-compatible systems closely emulate them. Some minor variations from this scenario are possible, such as those introduced by other ROM programs in the various adapters that might be plugged into a slot. Also, depending on the exact ROM BIOS programs involved, some of the error messages and sequences might vary. Generally, however, a computer follows this chain of events in "coming to life."

You can modify the system start-up procedures by altering the CONFIG.SYS and AUTOEXEC.BAT files. These files control the configuration of DOS and allow special start-up programs to be executed every time the system starts. The *User's Guide and Reference* that comes with DOS 5 has an excellent section on DOS configuration.

DOS Floppy Disk Formats

Since the debut of DOS version 1.0, the number of floppy disk formats supported by DOS has increased. Fortunately, newer versions of DOS from a particular OEM can always read from and write to earlier versions' disks. Table 15.1 lists all the formats supported under DOS 5.0.

Table 15.1 Floppy Disk Format Specifications

	Current formats					Obsolete formats		
Disk size (inches) Disk capacity (K)	3 1/2 2880	3 1/2 1440	3 1/2 720	5 1/4 1200	5 1/4 360	5 1/4 320	5 1/4 180	5 1/4 160
Media descriptor byte	F0h	F0h	F9h	F9h	FDh	FFh	FCh	FEh
Sides (heads)	2	2	2	2	2	2	1	1
Tracks per side	80	80	80	80	40	40	40	40
Sectors per track	36	18	9	15	9	8	9	8
Bytes per sector	512	512	512	512	512	512	512	512
Sectors per cluster	2	1	2	1	2	2	1	1
FAT length (sectors)	9	9	3	7	2	1	2	1
Number of FATs	2	2	2	2	2	2	2	2
Root directory length (Sectors)	15	14	7	14	7	7	4	4
Maximum root entries	240	224	112	224	112	112	64	64
Total sectors / disk	5760	2880	1440	2400	720	640	360	320
Total available sectors	5726	2847	1426	2371	708	630	351	313
Total available clusters	2863	2847	713	2371	354	315	351	313

DOS Disk and File Management

DOS uses several elements and structures to store and retrieve information on a disk. These elements and structures enable DOS to communicate properly with the ROM BIOS as well as application programs to process file storage and retrieval requests. Understanding these structures and how they interact will help you to troubleshoot and even repair these structures.

Interfacing to Disk Drives

DOS uses a combination of disk management components to make files accessible. These components differ slightly between floppies and hard disks and between disks of different sizes. They determine how a disk appears to DOS and to applications software. Each component used to describe the disk system fits as a layer into the complete system. Each layer communicates with the layer above and below it. When all of the components work together, an application can access the disk to find and store data.

The four primary layers of interface between an application program running on a system and any disks attached to the system consist of software routines that can perform various functions, usually to communicate with the adjacent layers. These layers are shown in this list:

- DOS Interrupt 21h (Int 21h) routines

- DOS Interrupt 25/26h (Int 25/26h) routines

- ROM BIOS disk Interrupt 13h (Int 13h) routines

- Disk controller I/O port commands

Each layer accepts various commands, performs different functions, and generates results. These interfaces are available for both floppy disk drives and hard disks, although the floppy disk and hard disk Int 13h routines differ widely. The floppy disk controllers and hard disk controllers are very different as well, but all of the layers perform the same functions for both floppy disks and hard disks.

Interrupt 21h

The DOS Int 21h routines exist at the highest level and provide the most functionality with the least amount of work. For example, if an application program needs to create a subdirectory on a disk, it can call Int 21h, Function 39h. This function performs all operations necessary to create a subdirectory on the disk, including updating the appropriate directory and FAT sectors. The only information this function needs is the name of the subdirectory to create. DOS Int 21h would do much more work by using one of the lower-level access methods to create a subdirectory on the disk. Most applications programs you run access the disk through this level of interface.

Interrupt 25h and Int 26h

The DOS Int 25h and Int 26h routines provide much lower-level access to the disk than the Int 21h routines. Int 25h reads only specified sectors from a disk, and Int 26h only writes specified sectors to a disk. If you were to write a program that used these functions to create a subdirectory on a disk, the work required would be much greater than that required by the Int 21h method. For example, your program would have to perform all these tasks:

■ Calculate exactly which directory and FAT sectors need to be updated

■ Use Int 25h to read these sectors

■ Modify the sectors appropriately to contain the new subdirectory information

■ Use Int 26h to write the sectors back out

The number of steps would be even greater considering the difficulty in determining exactly what sectors have to be modified. According to Int 25/26h, the entire DOS-addressable area of the disk consists of sectors numbered sequentially from 0. A program designed to access the disk using Int 25h and Int 26h must know the location of everything by this sector number. A program designed this way might have to be modified to handle disks with different numbers of sectors or different directory and FAT sizes and locations. Because of all the overhead required to get the job done, most programmers would not choose to access the disk in this manner, and instead would use the higher-level Int 21h—which does all of the work automatically.

Only disk- and sector-editing programs typically access a disk drive at the Int 25h and Int 26h level. Programs that work at this level of access can edit only areas of a disk that have been defined to DOS as a logical volume (drive letter). For example, DEBUG can read sectors from and write sectors to disks with this level of access.

Interrupt 13h

The next lower level of communications with drives, the ROM BIOS Int 13h routines, usually are found in ROM chips on the motherboard or on an adapter card in a slot; however, an Int 13h handler also can be implemented by using a device driver loaded at boot time. Because DOS requires Int 13h access to boot from a drive (and a device driver cannot be loaded until after boot-up), only drives with ROM BIOS-based Int 13h support can become bootable. Int 13h routines need to talk directly to the controller using the I/O ports on the controller. Therefore, the Int 13h code is very controller-specific.

If you design your own custom disk controller device, you need to write an IBM-compatible Int 13h handler package and install it on the card using a ROM BIOS that will be linked into the system at boot time. To use Int 13h routines, a program must use exact cylinder, head, and sector coordinates to specify sectors to read and write. Accordingly, any program designed to work at this level must be intimately familiar with the parameters of the specific disk on the system on which it is designed to run. Int 13h functions exist to read the disk parameters, format tracks, read and write sectors, park heads, and reset the drive.

A low-level format program needs to work with disks at the Int 13h level or lower. Most ST-506/412 controller format programs work with access at the Int 13h level, because virtually any operation a format program would need is available through the Int 13h interface. This is not true, however, for other types of controllers (such as ESDI or SCSI), for which defect mapping and other operations differ considerably from the ST-506/412 types. Controllers that must perform special operations during a low-level format, such as defining disk parameters to override the motherboard ROM BIOS drive tables, would not work with any formatter that used only the standard Int 13h interface. For these reasons, most controllers require a custom formatter designed to bypass the Int 13h interface. Most general-purpose, low-level "reformat" programs that perform a "nondestructive" format (such as Norton Calibrate and Spinrite) access the controller through the Int 13h interface (rather than going direct) and therefore cannot be used for an initial low-level format; the initial low-level format must be done by a controller-specific utility.

Few high-powered disk utility programs, other than some basic formatting software, can talk to the disk at the Int 13h level. The Kolod Research hTEST/hFORMAT utilities also can communicate at the Int 13h level, as can the DOS FDISK program. The Norton DISKEDIT and NU programs can communicate with a disk at the Int 13h level when these programs are in their "absolute sector" mode; they are two of the few utilities that can do so. These programs are important because they can be used for the worst data-recovery situations, in which the partition tables have been corrupted. Because the partition tables as well as any non-DOS partitions exist outside the area of a disk that is defined by DOS, only programs that work at the Int 13h level can access them. Most utility programs for data recovery, such as the Mace Utilities MUSE program, work only at the DOS Int 25/26h level, which makes them useless for accessing areas of a disk outside of DOS's domain.

Disk Controller I/O Port Commands

In the lowest level of interface, programs talk directly to the disk controller in the controller's own specific native language. To do this, a program must send controller commands through the I/O ports to which the controller responds. These commands are specific to the particular controller and sometimes differ even among controllers of the same type, such as different ESDI controllers. The ROM BIOS in the system must be designed specifically for the controller because the ROM BIOS talks to the controller at this I/O port level. Most manufacturer-type low-level format programs also need to talk to the controller directly, because the higher-level Int 13h interface does not provide enough specific features for many of the custom ST-506/412 or ESDI and SCSI controllers on the market.

Figure 15.2 shows the relative relationships between the various interface levels.

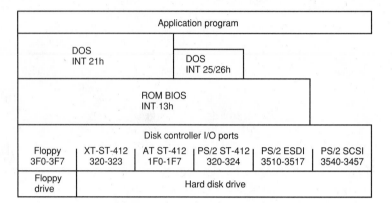

Fig. 15.2

Relative relationships
between various
interface levels.

Figure 15.2 shows that most application programs work through the Int 21h interface, which passes commands to the ROM BIOS as Int 13h commands; these commands then are converted into direct controller commands by the ROM BIOS. The controller executes the commands and returns the results through the layers until the desired information reaches the application. This process enables applications to be written without worrying about such low-level system details, leaving such details up to DOS and the ROM BIOS. It also enables applications to run on widely different types of hardware, as long as the correct ROM BIOS and DOS support is in place.

Any software can bypass any level of interface and communicate with the level below it, but doing so requires much more work. The lowest level of interface available is direct communication with the controller using I/O port commands. As figure 15.2 shows, each different type of controller has different I/O port locations as well as differences among the commands presented at the various ports, and only the controller can talk directly to the disk drive.

If not for the ROM BIOS Int 13h interface, a unique DOS would have to be written for each available type of hard and floppy disk drive and disk. Instead, DOS communicates with the ROM BIOS using standard Int 13h function calls translated by the Int 13h interface into commands for the specific hardware. Because of the standard ROM BIOS interface, DOS can be written relatively independently of specific disk hardware and can support many different types of drives and controllers.

DOS Structures

To manage files on a disk and enable all application programs to see a consistent disk interface no matter what type of disk is used, DOS uses

Hard disk volume size	Default cluster size	FAT type
0M to 16M	8 sectors or 4,096 bytes	12-bit
16M through 128M	4 sectors or 2,048 bytes	16-bit
Over 128M through 256M	8 sectors or 4,096 bytes	16-bit
Over 256M through 512M	16 sectors or 8,192 bytes	16-bit
Over 512M through 1,024M	32 sectors or 16,384 bytes	16-bit
Over 1,024M through 2,048M	64 sectors or 32,768 bytes	16-bit

In most cases, these cluster sizes, selected by the DOS FORMAT command, are the minimum possible for a given partition size. Therefore, 8K clusters are the smallest possible for a partition size of greater than 256M. Although most non-IBM OEM versions of DOS work like the IBM version, some versions might use cluster sizes different from what this table indicates. For example, COMPAQ DOS 3.31 shifts to larger cluster sizes much earlier than IBM DOS does. COMPAQ DOS shifts to 4K clusters at 64M partitions, 8K clusters at 128M partitions, and 16K clusters at 256M partitions. A 305M partition that uses 8K clusters under IBM DOS has clusters of 16K under COMPAQ DOS 3.31.

The effect of these larger cluster sizes on disk use can be substantial. A drive containing about 5,000 files, with average waste of one-half of the last cluster used for each file, wastes about 20 megabytes [5000*(.5*8)K] of file space on a disk set up with IBM DOS or MS-DOS. Using COMPAQ DOS 3.31, this wasted space doubles to 40 megabytes for the same 5,000 files. Someone using a system with COMPAQ DOS 3.31 could back up, repartition, and reformat with IBM DOS, and after restoring all 5,000 files, gain 20 megabytes of free disk space.

The reason that COMPAQ DOS 3.31 does not use the most efficient (or smallest) cluster size possible for a given partition size is that its makers were interested in improving the performance of the system at the expense of great amounts of disk space. Larger cluster sizes get you a smaller FAT, with fewer numbers to manage; DOS overhead is reduced when files are stored and retrieved, which makes the system seem faster. For example, the CHKDSK command would run much faster on a disk with a smaller FAT. Unfortunately, the trade-off for speed here is a tremendous loss of space on the disk. (COMPAQ DOS 4.0 and 5.0 use IBM DOS and MS-DOS conventions.)

The Data Area

The data area of a disk is the area that follows the boot sector, file allocation tables, and root directory on any volume. This area is managed by the FAT and the root directory. DOS divides it into allocation units that are sometimes called clusters. These clusters are where normal files are stored on a volume.

Diagnostic Read and Write Cylinder

The FDISK partitioning program always reserves the last cylinder of a hard disk for use as a special diagnostic read-and-write test cylinder. That this cylinder is reserved is one reason FDISK always reports fewer total cylinders than the drive manufacturer states are available. DOS (or any other operating system) does not use this cylinder for any normal purpose, because it lies outside the partitioned area of the disk.

On systems with ESDI or SCSI disk interfaces, the drive and controller might allocate additional area past the logical end of the drive for a bad-track table and spare sectors for replacing bad ones. This situation may account for additional discrepancies between FDISK and the drive manufacturer.

The diagnostics area enables diagnostics software such as the manufacturer-supplied Advanced Diagnostics disk to perform read and write tests on a hard disk without corrupting any user data. Low-level format programs for hard disks often use this cylinder as a scratch-pad area for running interleave tests or preserving data during "nondestructive" formats. This cylinder is also sometimes used as a head landing or parking cylinder on hard disks that do not have an automatic-parking facility.

Known Bugs in DOS

Few things are more frustrating than finding out that software you depend on every day has bugs, but DOS does. Every version of DOS ever produced has had bugs, and users must learn to expect—and watch for—them. Some problems are never resolved; you must live with them.

Sometimes the problems are severe enough, however, that IBM (and Microsoft) issues a patch disk that corrects the problems. Check with your IBM dealer periodically to find out whether these free patch disks are available. You do not have to go to the dealer where you purchased your DOS; any dealer must provide the patches for free. You just have to show that you have a legal license for DOS. The proof-of-license page from the DOS 4.0 manual satisfies as a license check. If you ask a dealer who does not know about these patches or who does not provide them for some reason, try another one. DOS is a warranted product, and the patches are part of the warranty service.

In the following section, the information is provided by IBM in the patches for DOS 3.3, 4.0, and 5.0. These versions have official IBM-produced patch disks available at no cost from your nearest IBM dealer.

DOS 3.3 Bugs and Patches

The DOS 3.3 official patches and fixes from IBM originally were issued by IBM's National Support Center on September 9, 1987. A second update was issued October 24, 1987, superseding the first update. These disks fix two general problems with DOS 3.3:

- BACKUP did not work properly in backing up a large number of subdirectories in a given directory. A new version of BACKUP was created to resolve this problem.

- Systems that had slow serial printers with small input buffers sometimes displayed a false Out of paper error message when attempting to print. A new program, I17.COM, resolves this problem.

In addition to the two general problems resolved by this patch, IBM PS/2 systems had a particular problem between their ROM BIOS and DOS 3.3; a special DASDDRVR.SYS driver was provided on the patch disk to fix these BIOS problems. The versions of DASDDRVR.SYS supplied on the DOS 3.3 patch disks have been superseded by later versions supplied elsewhere; DASDDRVR.SYS was placed on the IBM PS/2 Reference disks for more widespread distribution, and can be obtained directly from IBM on a special system-update floppy disk. This driver and the problems it can correct are discussed later in this chapter, in the section "PS/2 BIOS Update."

DOS 4.0 and 4.01 Bugs and Patches

Six different versions of IBM DOS 4.0 have been issued, counting the first version and the five patch disks subsequently released. The disks are not called patch disks anymore; rather, they are called *corrective service disks* (CSDs). Each level of CSD always contains all the previous-level CSDs. The first CSD issued for DOS 4.0 (UR22624) contained a series of problem fixes that later were incorporated into the standard released version of DOS, called 4.01. Several newer CSDs have been released since this 4.01 version appeared. Unfortunately, these more recent updates have not been integrated into the commercially packaged DOS. The only way to obtain these fixes is to obtain the CSD disks from your dealer.

If you were to purchase DOS 4.1 from an IBM dealer today, you would get the equivalent of DOS 4.0 plus CSD UR22624. You would have to ask the dealer for the current CSDs to have the corrected version of the latest release. Any truly responsible dealer automatically includes the latest CSDs with a DOS purchase, but, in my experience, a few dealers do not, and many do not even have the CSDs on hand.

The VER command in any level of DOS 4.X always shows 4.00, which causes much confusion about which level of CSD fixes are installed on a specific system. To eliminate this confusion and allow for the correct identification of installed patches, the CSD UR29015 and later levels introduce to DOS 4.X a new command: SYSLEVEL. This command is resident in COMMAND.COM and is designed to identify conclusively to the user the level of corrections installed. On a system running DOS 4.X with CSD UR35284 installed, the SYSLEVEL command reports:

DOS Version: 4.00 U.S. Date: 06/17/88

CSD Version: UR35284 U.S. Date: 09/20/91

The IBM DOS 4.0 Corrective Service Diskettes (CSDs) and when they were first available are shown in this list:

CSD	Date available
UR22624	08/15/88 (this equals 4.01)
UR24270	03/27/89
UR25066	05/10/89
UR29015	03/20/90
UR31300	06/29/90
UR35284	09/20/91

These CSDs are valid only for the IBM version of DOS 4.0. Other OEMs might provide patches or corrections in different ways; some might not even offer them. That is why I always run IBM DOS on my IBM-compatible systems: it usually is the only way to get the latest version of DOS. Because most OEMs release their versions of DOS long after IBM, they have had a chance to incorporate many (but not all) of these fixes in their standard version and therefore do not provide patch disks. For example, the regular Microsoft version of 4.01 never included all of the fixes IBM had for IBM DOS 4.0. If you have a version of DOS by a manufacturer other than IBM, contact its source to find out which patch corrections have been applied to the version of DOS you have.

Table 15.2 lists the problems fixed in IBM DOS 4.0 by the CSDs. The latest CSD contains all of the previous CSDs. The CSD indicated for each problem is the one in which the fix first appeared.

Table 15.2 IBM DOS 4.XX Corrected Problems

CSD	Item	Problem
UR22624	XMA2EMS	PS/2 Model 50Z cannot use DOS 4.00 EMS
UR22624	APPEND	APPEND /path:off not working properly
UR22624	IBMBIO	Int 2FH for Int 67H causes hang
UR22624	SHELLC	SHELL HELP index entries not alphabetic
UR22624	MODE	MODE overwrites user's application
UR22624	SELECT	Using Ctrl-Break with SHELL can hang
UR22624	MODE	MODE allows 19200 rate on PS/2 Models 25 and 30
UR22624	SHELLC	SHIFT+F9= overlays F10=
UR22624	SHELLC	Pull-down menu in files gives wrong help
UR22624	IBMDOS	BUFFERS=XX /X problem (BUFFERS to XMA)
UR22624	SHELLC	SHELL place hardware cursor with selection
UR22624	IBMDOS	Problem copying large files across NET
UR22624	PRINT	First time PRINT non-exist file message
UR22624	SHELLC	SHELL does not give error for / or \
UR22624	SELECT	Listing of printers should be reordered
UR22624	XMA2EMS	Hangs with Token Ring Net Card in slot 0
UR22624	SHELLC	SHELL will not run after run Comp. BASIC
UR22624	MODE	MODE not handling transfer correctly
UR22624	SHELLC	SHELL not handling transfer correctly
UR22624	SELECT	SELECT correct defaults for keyboards
UR22624	SELECT	SELECT/SHELL translated too big for 256K
UR22624	SHELL	PS/2 Model 30 with 8512 error color change

continues

Table 15.2 Continued

CSD	Item	Problem
UR22624	XMA2EMS	Unpredictable results using DMA to EMS
UR24270	CMOSCLK	Date does not change at midnight
UR24270	README	CSD UR22624 documentation unclear
UR24270	IBMDOS	CHKDSK shows allocation errors with 32M
UR24270	COMMAND	APPEND /x:on not working with DIR
UR24270	BACKUP	Cannot find FORMAT with LAN 1.3
UR24270	IFSFUNC	freopen() doesn't work with LAN 1.3
UR24270	MODE	Wrong number of lines on display
UR24270	RESTORE	Files backed up in 3.1 not restored
UR24270	FASTOPEN	Internal stack overflow with CHKDSK /f
UR24270	FASTOPEN	FASTOPEN /x hangs the system
UR24270	FASTOPEN	Error in EMS check
UR24270	FDISK	32M partition yields only 31M
UR24270	SELECT	Wrong partition message during SELECT
UR24270	SHELLC	Shell File System not consistent
UR24270	COMMAND	Working with LAN 1.3/DW4 reloading
UR24270	COMMAND	Batch file causes corrupted workspace
UR24270	IFSFUNC	DOS 4.0 not working with LAN 1.3
UR24270	IFSFUNC	Problems when printing to Net printer
UR24270	IFSFUNC	Certain command sequence on Net server
UR24270	ANSI	ANSI does not allow Shift-PrintScreen
UR24270	SHELLC	SHELL PSC doesn't accept null variable
UR24270	XMAEM	IBMCACHE in external memory hangs Model 70-A21
UR24270	SHELLC	SHELL Add a Program will not accept slash
UR25066	FASTOPEN	FASTOPEN second parameter causes database abort
UR25066	IBMDOS	File gets two clusters allocated

CSD	Item	Problem
UR25066	IBMBIO	DOS checks for "IBM" for valid boot sector
UR25066	XMA2EMS	Sort map table correctly
UR25066	IBMBIO	Problem using /x and page below 640K
UR25066	XMA2EMS	EMS mapping returns hex 80 from restore
UR25066	IBMDOS	Implement dynamic EMS page selection
UR25066	IBMDOS	Look-ahead buffers with file >32M
UR29015	FASTOPEN	FASTOPEN and Business Adviser REN/REST
UR29015	SHELLC	Adding programs will overlay end of disk
UR29015	SHELL	File system hangs with max program name
UR29015	SHELL	File system not handling write-protect
UR29015	SHARE	Multiple FCBs referring to same file
UR29015	BACKUP	Ctrl-Break does not terminate properly
UR29015	FORMAT	If COMMAND.COM not in boot drive with /S
UR29015	MEM	MEM.EXE and LIM EMS
UR29015	COMMAND	Invalid COMMAND.COM when APPEND changed
UR29015	IFSFUNC	File-locking errors with PCLAN and application
UR29015	FORMAT	Explicit SHARE load and FORMAT /V error
UR29015	CMOSCLK	Year-end in 00 causes error on some PS/2s
UR29015	XCOPY	Picks up wrong DBCS character for path
UR29015	NLSFUNC	Set code/page not clearing DBCS vector
UR29015	XMA2EMS	Return codes incorrect
UR29015	MODE	Should allow 19200 baud
UR29015	SYS	DOS 4.0 cannot install over OS/2 1.2
UR29015	IBMBIO	DOS 4.0 hangs with more than two hard files

continues

Table 15.2 Continued

CSD	Item	Problem
UR29015	KEYB	Multiple interrupts might cause abend
UR29015	KEYB	Keyboard error causing NL failure
UR29015	KEYB	Loss of control of SDLC interrupt
UR29015	FDISK	32M partition yields only 31M in FDISK
UR29015	KEYB	Lock keys and PS/2 mouse conflict
UR29015	IBMBIO	Device status check returns wrong status
UR29015	IBMBIO	Buffers /xs will not load properly
UR29015	SHELL	Copy to/from VDISK not working properly
UR29015	XCOPY	Hangs when downloading S/36 files
UR29015	XCOPY	Deletes source file when disk full
UR29015	IFSFUNC	Int 2F, AX=120A extended error incorrect
UR29015	IFSFUNC	Int 2F, AX=120B treated as crit error
UR29015	IBMBIO	DOS 4.01 will not accept (ECC) error
UR29015	COMMAND	No way to tell what level service
UR29015	FDISK	Does not display drives correctly if more than two hard files
UR29015	XMA2EMS	4.01 XMA2EMS fails intermittently
UR29015	SHELLB	SHEL abends if lowercase path entered
UR29015	SHARE	LOCK violation error when using LOCKs
UR29015	IBMDOS	IOCTL returns errors for off-line printer
UR29015	XMAEM	Conflict with UR25066 XMA drivers
UR29015	SHELLC	Shell hangs if mouse is not attached
UR29015	IFSFUNC	SHARE parameters ignored when using PCLP
UR29015	FORMAT	FORMAT quits on certain disk defects
UR29015	XMAEM	Stack alignment error affects performance
UR29015	FASTOPEN	FASTOPEN fails with WordPerfect 5.0
UR29015	XMA2EMS	Memory adapters not found in all slots

CSD	Item	Problem
UR29015	BACKUP	Cannot BACKUP kanji subdirectory
UR29015	IBMBIO	Hardware-related stack error
UR29015	IBMBIO	Disk drives not assigned properly
UR29015	IBMBIO	Problem trying to access more than two hard files
UR29015	KEYB	Model 70 keyboard fails when reconnected
UR31300	KEYB	Bad output from keypress in German
UR31300	SHARE	Character device driver causes abend
UR31300	SHELLC	Shell causes file system warning message
UR31300	XMA2EMS	Overlap has occurred; message with expanded memory
UR31300	IBMBIO	Cannot see non-HPFS drives when one is HPFS
UR31300	FDISK	Large message size causes failure in FDISK
UR31300	FDISK	HPFS not correctly supported in DOS FDISK
UR31300	IBMDOS	Program loader overlays program data area
UR31300	XMA2EMS	Hang on installation on Family 1 computers
UR31300	BACKUP	Abort BACKUP to hard file deletes \BACKUP files
UR31300	XMAEM	Hang on device installation on 486 machines
UR31300	MORE	First line missing with NLS MORE - Germany
UR31300	XMAEM	Int 15H, Func 87H hangs with XMAEM installed
UR35284	XMA2EMS	ADAPTER NOT FOUND message in PC 286 computer
UR35284	CHKDSK	Hangs with greater than 512 root entries message

continues

Table 15.2 Continued

CSD	Item	Problem
UR35284	IBMDOS	Intermittently wipes out hard file
UR35284	IBMBIO	DOS can overwrite HPFS partition
UR35284	FDISK	Family 1 hard file; format and track 0 bad
UR35284	XMAEM	Uses last 256 bytes ROM space

Table 15.3 shows the different versions of IBM DOS 4.0 that have been available.

Table 15.3 Versions of IBM DOS 4.0

File name	Size	Date	Ver.	SYSLEVEL	Comments
IBMBIO.COM	32810	06/17/88	4.00	—	Original release
IBMDOS.COM	35984	06/17/88			
COMMAND.COM	37637	06/17/88			
IBMBIO.COM	32816	08/03/88	4.01	CSD UR22624	EMS fixes
IBMDOS.COM	36000	08/03/88			
COMMAND.COM	37637	06/17/88			
IBMBIO.COM	32816	08/03/88	4.01	CSD UR24270	Date change fixed
IBMDOS.COM	36000	11/11/88			
COMMAND.COM	37652	11/11/88			
IBMBIO.COM	33910	04/06/89	4.01	CSD UR25066	"Death disk" fixed
IBMDOS.COM	37136	04/06/89			
COMMAND.COM	37652	11/11/88			
IBMBIO.COM	34660	03/20/90	4.01	CSD UR29015	SCSI support added
IBMDOS.COM	37248	02/20/90			
COMMAND.COM	37765	03/20/90			
IBMBIO.COM	34660	04/27/90	4.01	CSD UR31300	HPFS compatibility fixes
IBMDOS.COM	37264	05/21/90			
COMMAND.COM	37765	06/29/90			

File name	Size	Date	Ver.	SYSLEVEL	Comments
IBMBIO.COM	34692	04/08/91	4.01	CSD UR35284	HPFS and CHKDSK fixes
IBMDOS.COM	37280	11/30/90			
COMMAND.COM	37762	09/27/91			

DOS 5.0 Bugs and Patches

DOS Version 5.0 already has a CSD that fixes a couple of problems. The most significant is a defect in the XCOPY command that causes it to fail sometimes when it uses the /E or /S switches.

Listed in the following table is the IBM DOS 5.0 Corrective Service Diskette (CSD) and when it was first available:

CSD	Date available
UR35423	08/91
UR35748	10/91
UR35834	11/91

Problems fixed by this patch disk are shown in this list:

CSD	Item	Problem
UR35423	XCOPY	Wrong output when using /E and /S switches
UR35423	QBASIC	Enables QBASIC and QEDIT compatibility
UR35748	SYS	Corrupted hard file after installing UR35423
UR35834	MEUTONINI	4.0 .MEU to 5.0 .INI conversion incomplete
UR35834	DOSSHELL	DOSSHELL takes 27 seconds to load
UR35834	MEM	MEM switch hangs system with PC3270
UR35834	IBMBIO	L40SX will not SUSPEND or RESUME

continues

CSD	Item	Problem
UR35834	EMM386	Int 19H fails with EMM386 and dos=high
UR35834	FORMAT	FORMAT on unpartitioned drive; rc = 0
UR35834	REPLACE	REPLACE /a returns error
UR35834	XCOPY	XCOPY /s incorrectly sets error level
UR35834	GRAPHICS	PrtScr of graphics display produces garbage
UR35834	BACKUP	BACKUP calls wrong FORMAT.COM from OS/2
UR35834	MIRROR	MIRROR doesn't enable INTs correctly
UR35834	DOSSHELL	DOSSHELL.INI corrupted from Ctrl-Alt-Del
UR35834	BACKUP	BACKUP /a backs up too large a file
UR35834	DOSSHELL	Cannot edit dialog box if length is max

The following two charts summarize the different versions of DOS 5.0 from IBM and show what has been fixed.

File name	Size	Date	Version	SYSLEVEL	Comments
IBMBIO.COM	33430	05/09/91	5.00	—	Original release
IBMDOS.COM	37378	05/09/91			
COMMAND.COM	47987	05/09/91			
IBMBIO.COM	33430	05/09/91	5.00	CSD UR35423	XCOPY fixed
IBMDOS.COM	37378	05/09/91			QEDIT fixed
COMMAND.COM	48005	08/16/91			
IBMBIO.COM	33430	05/09/91	5.00	CSD UR35748	SYS fixed
IBMDOS.COM	37378	05/09/91			

File name	Size	Date	Version	SYSLEVEL	Comments
COMMAND.COM	48006	10/25/91			
IBMBIO.COM	33446	11/29/91	5.00	CSD UR35834	EMM386, FORMAT,
IBMDOS.COM	37378	11/29/91			DOSSHELL, BACKUP,
COMMAND.COM	48006	11/29/91			etc. fixed

PS/2 BIOS Update (DASDDRVR.SYS)

The DASDDRVR.SYS (direct-access storage device driver) file is a set of software patches that fix various ROM BIOS bugs in several models of the IBM PS/2. DASDDRVR.SYS is required for specific PS/2 systems using IBM DOS versions 3.30 or later, to correct several bugs in the IBM PS/2 ROM BIOS. When IBM DOS 4.00 was released, conflicting information indicated that DOS 4.00 would include the updates to correct the PS/2 ROM BIOS problems fixed by DASDDRVR.SYS under DOS 3.30. This information was not accurate, however. In fact, an IBM PS/2 system needs DASDDRVR.SYS with DOS 5.00 (or any higher version of DOS) even with the most current corrective service disk (CSD) update.

The PS/2 needs the DASDDRVR.SYS fixes only in the DOS environment (IBM OS/2 contains the BIOS patches). Some users assume, therefore, that the PS/2 problems with DOS are DOS bugs; they are not. The DASDDRVR.SYS program is provided on the PS/2 Reference disk (included with every PS/2 system) and is available separately on a special PS/2 system update disk. The disks contain the device driver program (DASDDRVR.SYS) and an installation program.

The PS/2 ROM BIOS bugs in the following list are fixed by DASDDRVR.SYS (the problem numbers are shown in table 15.4, and more detailed information is provided later in this section):

- Failures occur in reading some 720K program floppy disks (Models 8530, 8550, 8560, and 8580).

- Intermittent Not ready or General failure error messages appear (Models 8550, 8560, and 8580).

- 3 1/2-inch floppy disk format fails when user tries to format more than one floppy disk (Models 8550, 8560, and 8580).

- Combined 301 and 8602 error messages appear at power-on or after power interruption (Models 8550 and 8560).

- System clock loses time or combined 162 and 163 errors appear during system initialization (Models 8550 and 8560).

- User is unable to install Power-On Password program with DASDDRVR.SYS installed (Models 8550, 8560, and 8580).

- Devices attached to COM2:, COM3:, or COM4: are not detected (Model 8530).

- Devices that use Interrupt Request level 2 (IRQ2) fail (Model 8530).

- 3 1/2-inch floppy disk format fails when user tries to format more than one floppy disk (Model 8570).

- System performance degradation occurs from processor-intensive devices (Models 8550, 8555, and 8560).

- Error occurs in a microcode routine that enhances long-term reliability of 60/120M disk drives (Models 8550, 8555, 8570, and 8573).

- Time and date errors occur when user resets the time or date. Intermittent date changes occur when the system is restarted by pressing Ctrl-Alt-Del (Model 8530).

An IBM PS/2 system user running DOS 3.3 or higher and experiencing any of these problems should load the DASDDRVR.SYS file. The problems are system-specific, and DASDDRVR.SYS fixes the problems for only the systems listed.

IBM requires its dealers to distribute the System Update disk containing DASDDRVR.SYS to anyone who requests it. Neither the dealer nor the customer pays a fee for the System Update disk. You also can obtain copies directly from IBM by calling (800) IBM-PCTB (800-426-7282) and ordering the PS/2 System Update disk.

Check table 15.4 for detailed descriptions of each of these problems for the specific systems affected. Models not listed for a particular problem do not need DASDDRVR.SYS, and no benefit results from installing it.

The first three problem fixes originally were provided by the DASDDRVR.SYS version 1.10 file supplied on the first DOS 3.3 fix disk. Fixes for problems 4 and 5 were added in DASDDRVR.SYS version 1.20, included on all IBM PS/2 Reference disks (30-286, 50/60, and 70/80) version 1.02 or later as well as on an updated version of the DOS 3.3 fix disk. The fix for problem 6 was added in DASDDRVR.SYS version 1.30, included on all 50/60 and 70/80 Reference Disks version 1.03 or later. Fixes for problems 7 through 10 were added to DASDDRVR.SYS version 1.56, which is on all IBM PS/2 Reference Disks dated March 1990 or later. This version of DASDDRVR.SYS also was available separately, on the IBM PS/2 System Update disk version 1.01. The latest DASDDRVR.SYS (also called version 1.56 but dated January 1991) can be found on newer reference disks or on the IBM PS/2 System Update disk version 1.02.

Table 15.4 DASDDRVR.SYS Version Summary

Version	File size	Problems fixed	Source
1.10	648 bytes	1-3	DOS 3.3 Fix Disk (08/24/87)
1.20	698 bytes	1-5	Reference Disk, DOS 3.3 Fix Disk (09/09/87)
1.30	734 bytes	1-6	Reference Disk
1.56	1170 bytes	1-10	Reference Disk (03/90), System Update Disk 1.01 (part number 64F1500)
1.56	3068 bytes	1-12	Reference Disk (xx/xx), System Update Disk 1.02 (part number 04G3288)

By using the DASDDRVR.SYS driver file, IBM can correct specific ROM BIOS problems and bugs without having to issue a new set of ROM chips for a specific system. Using this file eliminates service time or expense in fixing simple problems, but causes the inconvenience of having to load the driver. The driver does not consume memory, nor does it remain in memory as would a typical driver or memory-resident program; it either performs functions on boot only and then terminates, or overlays existing code or tables in memory, taking no more space than what it replaced. Because DASDDRVR.SYS checks the exact ROM BIOS by model, submodel, and revision, it performs functions only on those for which it is designed. If it detects a BIOS that does not need fixing, the program terminates without doing anything. You can load DASDDRVR.SYS on any system; it functions only on systems for which it is designed.

Because a system BIOS occasionally needs revising or updating, IBM used disk-based BIOS programs for most newer PS/2 systems. The Models 57, P75, 90, and 95, in fact, load the system BIOS from the hard disk every time the system is powered up, during a procedure called *initial microcode load* (IML). You can get a ROM upgrade for these systems by simply obtaining a new Reference disk and loading the new IML file on the hard disk. This type of system makes DASDDRVR.SYS or any other such patches obsolete.

Installing DASDDRVR.SYS

To install DASDDRVR.SYS, you must update the CONFIG.SYS file with the following entry and restart the system:

DEVICE=[d:\path\]DASDDRVR.SYS

The drive and path values must match the location and name of the DASDDRVR.SYS file on your system.

Detailed Problem Descriptions

This section gives a detailed description of the problems corrected by the most current release of DASDDRVR.SYS, including an indication of the systems for which the corrections are necessary.

- Failures occur in reading some 720K program disks.

  IBM PS/2 systems affected: Model 30 286 8530-E01, -E21
  Model 50 8550-021
  Model 60 8560-041, -071
  Model 80 8580-041, -071

  Intermittent read failures on some 720K original application software disks. Example: Not ready reading drive A appears when a user attempts to install an application program. Attempting to perform DIR or COPY commands from the floppy disk also produces the error message.

- Intermittent Not ready or General failure error messages are displayed.

  IBM PS/2 systems affected: Model 50 8550-021
  Model 60 8560-041, -071
  Model 80 8580-041, -071

  A very intermittent problem with a floppy disk drive Not ready or a fixed disk General failure message. This problem might be aggravated by certain programming practices that mask off interrupts for long periods. The update ensures that interrupts are unmasked on each disk or floppy disk request.

- A 3 1/2-inch floppy disk format fails when user tries to format more than one floppy disk.

  IBM PS/2 systems affected: Model 50 8550-021
  Model 60 8560-041, -071
  Model 80 8580-041, -071

The DOS FORMAT command fails when a user tries to format multiple 3 1/2-inch floppy disks. The failure appears as an `Invalid media or Track 0 bad — disk unusable` message when the user replies Yes to the prompt `Format another (Y/N)?` after the format of the first floppy disk is complete. The error message appears when the user tries to format the second disk. If a system is booted from a floppy disk, the problem does not occur. This problem occurs only with DOS 3.3—not with later versions.

■ Combined 301 and 8602 error messages at power-on or after power interruption.

IBM PS/2 systems affected: Model 50 8550-021
Model 60 8560-041, -071

When power is interrupted momentarily or a system is otherwise switched on and off quickly, a 301 (keyboard) and 8602 (pointing device) error message might appear during the Power-On Self Test (POST). This error occurs because the system is powered on before the keyboard is ready. The problem is more likely to occur if the system was reset previously by pressing Ctrl-Alt-Del.

■ System clock loses time or combined 162 and 163 errors during system initialization.

IBM PS/2 systems affected: Model 50 8550-021
Model 60 8560-041, -071

Intermittent 162 (CMOS checksum or configuration) and 163 (Clock not updating) Power-On Self Test (POST) errors occur. Various time-of-day problems on specified IBM PS/2 Model 50 systems. For example, the user turns the machine on in the morning and finds the time set to the same time that the machine was turned off the day before.

■ User is unable to install Power-On Password program with DASDDRVR.SYS installed.

IBM PS/2 systems affected: Model 50 8550-021
Model 60 8560-041, -071
Model 80 8580-041, -071

When a user tries to install the Power-On Password feature with DASDDRVR.SYS version 1.3 or earlier installed, a message appears which says (incorrectly) that a password already exists. The user might be prompted also for a password (on warm boot) even though password security has not been implemented.

■ Devices attached to COM2:, COM3:, or COM4: are not detected.

IBM PS/2 systems affected: Model 30 286 8530-E01, -E21

■ Devices that use Interrupt Request level 2 (IRQ2) fail.

IBM PS/2 systems affected: Model 30 286 8530-E01, -E21

■ A 3 1/2-inch disk format fails when user tries to format more than one disk.

IBM PS/2 systems affected: Model 70 8570-Axx (all)
Model 80 8580-Axx (all)

The DOS FORMAT command fails when the user tries to format multiple 3 1/2-inch disks. The failure appears as an `Invalid media or Track 0 bad - disk unusable` message when the user replies Yes to the prompt `Format another (Y/N)?` after the format of the first disk is complete. The error message appears when the user tries to format the second disk. If the system is booted from a floppy disk, the problem does not occur.

■ System performance degradation occurs from processor-intensive devices.

IBM PS/2 systems affected: Model 50 8550-021, -031, -061
Model 55 SX 8555-031, -061
Model 60 8560-041, -071

■ Error occurs in a microcode routine that enhances long-term reliability of 60/120M disk drives.

IBM PS/2 systems affected: Model 50 8550-061
Model 55 SX 8555-061
Model 70 8570-061, -121, -A61, -A21, -B61, -B21
Model P70 8573-061, -121

■ Time and date errors occur when the user resets the time or date. Intermittent date changes occur when the system is restarted by pressing Ctrl-Alt-Del.

IBM PS/2 systems affected: Model 30 8530 (all)

OS/2 versions 1.2 and earlier contained these BIOS fixes in the form of a *.BIO file for each specific BIOS needing corrections. These were automatically loaded by OS/2 at boot time, depending on the specific system on which it was being loaded.

OS/2 version 1.3 and later contain the fixes directly in-line in the system files, not as separate files. When a system running OS/2 version 1.3 or later is booted, OS/2 determines the model, submodel, and revision bytes for the particular BIOS under which it is running. Based on this information, OS/2 determines the correct *.BIO file to load or the correct in-line code to run. For example, the IBM PS/2 55SX BIOS is Model F8, Submodel 0C, Revision 00, which causes IBM OS/2 version 1.2 to load the file F80C00.BIO automatically during boot-up. OS/2 version 1.3 or later uses this information to run the proper fix code contained in the system files. This procedure enables execution of the BIOS fixes necessary for only this particular system.

Any symptom described as being resolved by the DASDDRVR.SYS update might have other causes. If you install the DASDDRVR.SYS update and continue to have problems, consider the errors valid and follow normal troubleshooting procedures to find the causes.

Disk and Data Recovery

The CHKDSK, RECOVER, and DEBUG commands are the DOS damaged-disk recovery team. These commands are crude and their actions sometimes are drastic, but at times they are all that is available or needed. RECOVER is best known for its function as a data-recovery program, and CHKDSK usually is used for inspection of the file structure. Many users are unaware that CHKDSK can implement repairs to a damaged file structure. DEBUG, a crude, manually controlled program, can help in the case of a disk disaster, if you know exactly what you are doing.

The CHKDSK Command

The useful and powerful DOS CHKDSK command also is generally misunderstood. To casual users, the primary function of CHKDSK seems to be providing a disk space-allocation report for a given volume and a memory-allocation report. CHKDSK does those things, but its primary value is in discovering, defining, and repairing problems with the DOS directory and FAT system on a disk volume. In handling data-recovery problems, CHKDSK is a valuable tool, although it is crude and simplistic compared to some of the aftermarket utilities that perform similar functions.

The output of a CHKDSK command run on a typical hard disk is
as follows:

```
Volume 120M MFM created 10-07-1991 5:13a
Volume Serial Number is 1017-0CD3

117116928 bytes total disk space
    73728 bytes in 3 hidden files
   614400 bytes in 272 directories
112644096 bytes in 4516 user files
   143360 bytes in bad sectors
  3641344 bytes available on disk
     2048 bytes in each allocation unit
    57186 total allocation units on disk
     1778 available allocation units on disk

   655360 total bytes memory        565344 bytes free
```

A little-known CHKDSK function is reporting a specified file's (or files')
level of fragmentation. CHKDSK also can produce a list of all files (including hidden and system files) on a particular volume, similar to a super
DIR command. By far, the most important CHKDSK capabilities are its
detection and correction of problems with the DOS file-management
system.

The name of the CHKDSK program is misleading: It seems to be a contraction of CHECK DISK. The program does not actually check a disk, or
even the files on a disk, for integrity. CHKDSK cannot even truly show
how many bad sectors are on a disk, much less locate and mark them.
The real function of CHKDSK is to inspect the directories and FATs to
see whether they correspond with each other or contain discrepancies.
CHKDSK does not detect (and does not report on) damage in a file; it
checks only the FAT and directory areas (the "table of contents") of a
disk. Rather than CHKDSK, the command should have been called
CKDIRFAT (for CHECK DIRECTORY FAT) because its most important job
is to verify that the FATs and directories correspond with one another.
The name of the program gives no indication of the program's capability
to repair problems with the directory and FAT structures.

CHKDSK also can test files for contiguity. Files loaded into contiguous
tracks and sectors of a disk or floppy disk naturally are more efficient.
Files spread over wide areas of the disk make access operations take
longer. DOS always knows the location of all of a file's fragments by using
the pointer numbers in the file allocation table (FAT). These pointers are
data that direct DOS to the next segment of the file. Sometimes, for various reasons, these pointers might be lost or corrupted and leave DOS
incapable of locating some portion of a file. Using CHKDSK can alert you
to this condition and even let you reclaim the unused file space for use
by another file.

CHKDSK Command Syntax

The syntax of the CHKDSK command is

CHKDSK [d:][path][filename] [/F][/V]

The [d:] specifies the disk volume to analyze, and the [path] and [filename] options specify files to check for fragmentation in addition to the volume analysis. Wild cards are allowed in the file-name specification, to include as many as all of the files in a specified directory for fragmentation analysis. One flaw with the fragmentation analysis is that it does not check for fragmentation across directory boundaries, only within a specified directory.

The switch /F (Fix) enables CHKDSK to perform repairs if it finds problems with the directories and FATs. If /F is not specified, the program is prevented from writing to the disk and all repairs were not really performed.

The switch /V (Verbose) causes the program to list all the entries in all the directories on a disk and give detailed information in some cases when errors are encountered.

The drive, path, and file specifiers are optional. If no parameters are given for the command, CHKDSK processes the default volume or drive and does not check files for contiguity. If you specify [path] and [filename] parameters, CHKDSK checks all specified files to see whether they are stored contiguously on the disk. One of two messages is displayed as a result:

```
All specified file(s) are contiguous
```

or

```
[filename] Contains xxx non-contiguous blocks
```

The second message is displayed for each file that is fragmented on the disk and displays the number of fragments the file is in. A *fragmented file* is one that is scattered around the disk in pieces rather than existing in one contiguous area of the disk. Fragmented files are slower to load than contiguous files, which reduces disk performance. Fragmented files are also much more difficult to recover if a problem with the FAT or directory on the disk occurs.

Utility programs that can defragment files are discussed later in this chapter, but if you have only DOS, you have several possible ways to accomplish a full defragmentation. To defragment files on a floppy disk, you can format a new floppy disk and COPY or XCOPY all the files from the fragmented disk to the replacement. For a hard disk, you must completely BACKUP, FORMAT, and then RESTORE the disk. This procedure on a hard disk is time-consuming and dangerous, which is why so many defragmenting utilities have been developed.

CHKDSK Limitations

In several instances, CHKDSK operates only partially or not at all. CHKDSK does not process volumes or portions of volumes that have been created as follows:

- SUBST command volumes
- ASSIGN command volumes
- JOIN command subdirectories
- Network volumes

SUBST Problems

The SUBST command creates a virtual volume, which is actually an existing volume's subdirectory using another volume specifier (drive letter) as an alias. To analyze the files in a subdirectory created with SUBST, you must give the TRUENAME or actual path name to the files. TRUENAME is an undocumented command in DOS 4.0 and later versions that shows the actual path name for a SUBSTed volume.

You also can use the SUBST command to find out the TRUENAME of a particular volume. Suppose that you use SUBST to create volume E: from the C:\AUTO\SPECS directory:

    C:\>SUBST E: C:\AUTO\SPECS

After entering the following two commands to change to the E: volume and execute a CHKDSK of the volume and files there, you see the resulting error message:

    C:\>E:

    E:\>CHKDSK *.*

    Cannot CHKDSK a SUBSTed or ASSIGNed drive

To run CHKDSK on the files on this virtual volume E:, you must find the actual path the volume represents. You can do so by entering the SUBST command (with no parameters):

    E:\>SUBST

    E: => C:\AUTO\SPECS

You can also find the actual path with the undocumented TRUENAME command (in DOS 4.0 and later versions only).

    E:\>TRUENAME E:

    C:\AUTO\SPECS

After finding the path to the files, you can issue the appropriate CHKDSK command to check the volume and files:

```
E:\>CHKDSK C:\AUTO\SPECS\*.*

Volume 320M SCSI created 09-05-1991 11:22a
Volume Serial Number is 1454-12DC

314384384 bytes total disk space
    81920 bytes in 4 hidden files
  2342912 bytes in 286 directories
147865600 bytes in 4822 user files
164093952 bytes available on disk
     8192 bytes in each allocation unit
    38377 total allocation units on disk
    20031 available allocation units on disk

   655360 total bytes memory 562224 bytes free
All specified file(s) are contiguous

E:\>_
```

ASSIGN Problems

Similarly, CHKDSK does not process a disk drive that has been altered by the ASSIGN command. For example, if you have given the command ASSIGN A=B, you cannot analyze drive A: unless you first unassign the disk drive with the ASSIGN command, that is, ASSIGN A=A.

JOIN Problems

CHKDSK does not process a directory-tree section created by the JOIN command (which JOINs a physical disk volume to another disk volume as a subdirectory), nor does it process the actual JOINed physical drive, because such a drive is an `Invalid drive specification`, according to DOS. On volumes on which you have used the JOIN command, CHKDSK processes the actual portion of the volume and then displays this warning error message:

```
Directory is joined
tree past this point not processed
```

This message indicates that the command cannot process the directory on which you have used JOIN. CHKDSK then continues processing the rest of the volume and outputs the requested volume information.

Network Problems

CHKDSK does not process a networked (shared) disk on either the server or workstation side. In other words, at the file server, you cannot use CHKDSK on any volume that has any portion of itself accessible to remote network stations. At any network station, you can run CHKDSK only on volumes physically attached to that specific station and not on any volume accessed through the network software. If you attempt to run CHKDSK from a server or a workstation on a volume shared on a network, you see this error message:

```
Cannot CHKDSK a network drive
```

If you want to run CHKDSK on the volume, you must go to the specific PC on which the volume physically exists and suspend or disable any sharing of the volume during the CHKDSK.

CHKDSK Command Output

CHKDSK normally displays this information about a disk volume:

> Volume name and creation date
> Volume serial number
> Number of bytes in total disk space
> Number of files and bytes in hidden files
> Number of files and bytes in directories
> Number of files and bytes in user files
> Number of bytes in bad sectors (unallocated clusters)
> Number of bytes available on disk
> Number of bytes in total memory (RAM)
> Number of bytes in free memory
> Error messages if disk errors are encountered

By using optional parameters, CHKDSK also can show the following:

- Names and number of fragments in noncontiguous files

- Names of all directories and files on disk

If a volume name or volume serial number does not exist on a particular volume, that information is not displayed. If no clusters are marked as bad in the volume's FAT, CHKDSK returns no display of bytes in bad sectors.

As an example, suppose that a disk was formatted under DOS 4.01 with this command:

```
C:\>format a: /f:720 /s /v:floppy disk

Insert new diskette for drive A:
and press ENTER when ready...

Format complete

System transferred

730112 bytes total disk space
110592 bytes used by system
619520 bytes available on disk
  1024 bytes in each allocation unit
   605 allocation units available on disk

Volume Serial Number is 2563-16FF

Format another (Y/N)?n

C:\>_
```

The status report at the end of the format operation is similar to the output of the CHKDSK command. If you run CHKDSK on this disk now, the command and output look like this:

```
C:\>chkdsk a:

Volume FLOPPY DISK created 10-21-1991 3:57p
Volume Serial Number is 2563-16FF

730112 bytes total disk space
 72704 bytes in 3 hidden files
 37888 bytes in 1 user files
619520 bytes available on disk
  1024 bytes in each allocation unit
   713 total allocation units on disk
   605 available allocation units on disk

655360 total bytes memory    562224 bytes free
```

In this case, CHKDSK shows the volume name and serial-number information because the FORMAT command placed a volume label on the disk with the /V: parameter, and FORMAT under DOS 4.0 and later versions automatically places the volume serial number on a disk. Note that four total files are on this disk, three of which have the hidden attribute. To see the names of the hidden files, you can execute the CHKDSK command with the /V parameter:

```
C:\>chkdsk a: /v

Volume FLOPPY DISK created 10-21-1991 3:57p
Volume Serial Number is 2563-16FF

Directory A:\

A:\IBMBIO.COM
A:\IBMDOS.COM
A:\COMMAND.COM
A:\FLOPPY D.ISK

730112 bytes total disk space
 72704 bytes in 3 hidden files
 37888 bytes in 1 user files
619520 bytes available on disk
  1024 bytes in each allocation unit
   713 total allocation units on disk
   605 available allocation units on disk

655360 total bytes memory    562224 bytes free
```

With the /V parameter, CHKDSK lists the names of all directories and files across the entire disk, which in this example is only four total files. Although CHKDSK does not identify exactly which of the listed files are hidden, because COMMAND.COM is the only user (normal and unhidden) file on the disk, the other three files listed must be the hidden files. The first two are the DOS system files, and the third hidden file is the volume label, stored in the root directory as a normal directory entry just as any other file would be. The volume-label entry's starting cluster number is 0 and its size is 0 bytes, which means that it does not exist anywhere on the disk except as a sort of phony directory entry. After listing how many bytes are used by the hidden and normal files, CHKDSK lists how much total space is available on the disk.

If you are using DOS 4.0 or a later version, CHKDSK also tells you the size of each allocation unit (or cluster), the total number of allocation units present, and the number not currently being used.

Finally, CHKDSK counts the total amount of DOS-usable RAM (in this case, 640K or 655,360 bytes) and displays the number of bytes of memory currently unused or free. This information tells you the size of the largest executable program you can run.

CHKDSK under DOS versions 3.3 and earlier does not recognize the IBM PS/2 Extended BIOS Data Area (which uses the highest 1K of addresses in contiguous conventional memory) and therefore reports only 639K, or 654,336, bytes of total memory. For most IBM PS/2 systems with 640K of contiguous memory addressed before the video wall, the Extended BIOS Data Area occupies the 640th K. DOS 4.0 and later versions provide the correct 640K report.

During the FORMAT of the disk in the example, the FORMAT program did not find any unreadable sectors. Therefore, no clusters were marked in the FAT as bad or unusable, and CHKDSK did not display the xxxxxxxxx Bytes in bad sectors message. Even if the disk had developed bad sectors since the FORMAT operation, CHKDSK still would not display any bytes in bad sectors because it does not test for and count bad sectors: CHKDSK reads the FAT and reports on whether the FAT says that there are any bad sectors. CHKDSK does not really count sectors; it counts clusters (allocation units) because that is how the FAT system operates.

Although "bytes in bad sectors" sounds like a problem or error message, it is not. The report is simply stating that a certain number of clusters are marked as bad in the FAT and that DOS therefore will never use those clusters. Because nearly all hard disks are manufactured and sold with defective areas, this message is not uncommon. In fact, the higher-quality hard disks on the market tend to have more bad sectors than the lower-quality drives, based on the manufacturer defect list shipped with the drive (indicating all the known defective spots). Many of the newest controllers allow for sector and track sparing, in which the defects are mapped out of the DOS-readable area so that DOS never has to handle them. This procedure is almost standard in drives that have embedded controllers, such as IDE (Integrated Drive Electronics) or SCSI (Small Computer Systems Interface) drives.

Suppose that I use a utility program to mark two clusters (150 and 151, for example) as bad in the FAT of the 720K floppy disk I formatted earlier. CHKDSK then reports this information:

```
Volume FLOPPY DISK created 10-21-1991 3:57p
Volume Serial Number is 2563-16FF

730112 bytes total disk space
 72704 bytes in 3 hidden files
 37888 bytes in 1 user files
  2048 bytes in bad sectors
617472 bytes available on disk
  1024 bytes in each allocation unit
   713 total allocation units on disk
   603 available allocation units on disk

655360 total bytes memory    562224 bytes free
```

CHKDSK reports 2,048 bytes in bad sectors, which corresponds exactly to the two clusters I just marked as bad. These clusters, of course, are perfectly good—I simply marked them as bad in the FAT. Using disk-editor utility programs such as those supplied with the Norton or Mace Utilities, you can alter the FAT in almost any way you want.

CHKDSK Operation

Although "bytes in bad sectors" does not constitute an error or problem, CHKDSK reports problems on a disk volume with a variety of error messages. When CHKDSK discovers an error in the FAT or directory system, it reports the error with one of several descriptive messages that vary to fit the specific error. Sometimes the messages are cryptic or misleading. CHKDSK does not specify how an error should be handled; it does not tell you whether CHKDSK can repair the problem or whether you must use some other utility, and what the consequences of the error and the repair will be. Neither does CHKDSK tell you what caused the problem or how to avoid repeating the problem.

The primary function of CHKDSK is to compare the directory and FAT to determine whether they agree with one another—whether all the data in the directory for files (such as the starting cluster and size information) corresponds to what is in the FAT (such as chains of clusters with end-of-chain indicators). CHKDSK also checks subdirectory file entries, as well as the special . and . . entries that tie the subdirectory system together.

The second function of CHKDSK is to implement repairs to the disk structure. CHKDSK "patches" the disk so that the directory and FAT are in alignment and agreement. From a repair standpoint, understanding CHKDSK is relatively easy. CHKDSK almost always modifies the directories on a disk to correspond to what is found in the FAT. In only a couple of special cases does CHKDSK modify the FAT; when it does, the FAT modifications are always the same type of simple change.

Think of CHKDSK's repair capability as a directory patcher. Because CHKDSK cannot repair most types of FAT damage effectively, it simply modifies the disk directories to match whatever problems are found in the FAT.

CHKDSK is not a very "smart" repair program and often can do more damage "repairing" the disk than if it had left the disk alone. In many cases, the information in the directories is correct and can be used (by some other utility) to help repair the FAT tables. If you have run CHKDSK with the /F parameter, however, the original directory information no longer exists, and a good FAT repair is impossible. You therefore should never run CHKDSK with the /F parameter without first running it in read-only mode (without the /F parameter) to determine whether and to what extent damage exists.

Only after carefully examining the disk damage and determining how CHKDSK would "fix" the problems do you run CHKDSK with the /F parameter. If you do not specify the /F parameter when you run CHKDSK, the program is prevented from making corrections to the disk. Rather, it performs repairs in a mock fashion. This limitation is a safety feature because you do not want CHKDSK to take action until you have examined the problem. After deciding whether CHKDSK will make the correct assumptions about the damage, you might want to run it with the /F parameter.

Sometimes people place a CHKDSK /F command in their AUTOEXEC.BAT file—*a very dangerous practice*. If a system's disk directories and FAT system become damaged, attempting to load a program whose directory and FAT entries are damaged might lock the system. If, after you reboot, CHKDSK is "fixing" the problem because it is in the AUTOEXEC.BAT, it can irreparably damage the file structure of the disk. In many cases, CHKDSK ends up causing more damage than originally existed, and no easy way exists to undo the CHKDSK repair. Because CHKDSK is a simple utility that makes often-faulty assumptions in repairing a disk, you must run it with great care when you specify the /F parameter.

Problems reported by CHKDSK are usually problems with the software and not the hardware. You rarely see a case in which lost clusters, allocation errors, or cross-linked files reported by CHKDSK were caused directly by a hardware fault, although it is certainly possible. The cause is usually a defective program or a program that was stopped before it could close files or purge buffers. A hardware fault certainly can stop a program before it can close files, but many people think that these error messages signify fault with the disk hardware—almost never the case.

I recommend running CHKDSK at least once a day on a hard disk system because it is important to find out about file-structure errors as soon as possible. Accordingly, placing a CHKDSK command in your AUTOEXEC.BAT file is a good idea, but do not use the /F parameter. Also run CHKDSK whenever you suspect that directory or FAT damage might have occurred. For example, whenever a program terminates abnormally or a system crashes for some reason, I run CHKDSK to see whether any file system damage has occurred.

Common Errors

All CHKDSK can do is compare the directory and FAT structures to see whether they support or comply with one another; as a result, CHKDSK can detect only certain kinds of problems. When CHKDSK discovers discrepancies between the directory and the FAT structures, they almost always fall into one of the following categories. (These errors are the most common ones you will see with CHKDSK.)

- Lost allocation units
- Allocation errors

- Cross-linked files
- Invalid allocation units

The RECOVER Command

The DOS RECOVER command is designed to mark clusters as bad in the FAT when the clusters cannot be read properly. When a file cannot be read because of a problem with a sector on the disk going bad, the RECOVER command can mark the FAT so that those clusters are not used by another file. Used improperly, this program is highly dangerous.

Many users think that RECOVER is used to recover a file or the data within the file in question. What really happens is that only the portion of the file before the defect is recovered and remains after the RECOVER command operates on it. RECOVER marks the defective portion as bad in the FAT, and returns to available status all the data after the defect. Always make a copy of the file to be recovered before using RECOVER, because the copy command can get all the information, including that after the location of the defect.

Suppose that you are using a word processing program. You start the program and tell it to load a file called DOCUMENT.TXT. The hard disk has developed a defect in a sector used by this file, and in the middle of loading it, you see this message appear on-screen:

```
Sector not found error reading drive C
Abort, Retry, Ignore, Fail?
```

You might be able to read the file on a retry, so try several times. If you can load the file by retrying, save the loaded version as a file with a different name, to preserve the data in the file. You still have to repair the structure of the disk, to prevent the space from being used again.

After ten retries or so, if you still cannot read the file, the data will be more difficult to recover. This operation has two phases:

- Preserve as much of the data in the file as possible.
- Mark the FAT so that the bad sectors or clusters of the disk are not used again.

Preserving Data

To recover the data from a file, use the DOS COPY command to make a copy of the file with a different name; for example:

```
C>COPY document.txt document.new
```

In the middle of the copy, you see the `Sector not found` error message again. The key to this operation is to answer with the (I)gnore option. Then the bad sectors are ignored, and the copy operation can continue to the end of the file. This procedure produces a copy of the file with all of the file intact, up to the error location and after the error location. The bad sectors appear as gibberish or garbage in the new copied file, but the entire copy is readable. Use your word processor to load the new copy and remove or retype the garbled sectors. If this file were a binary file (such as a part of a program), you probably would have to consider the whole thing a total loss because you generally do not have the option of "retyping" the bytes that make up a program file. Your only hope then is to replace the file from a backup. This step completes phase one, which has recovered as much of the data as possible. Now you go to phase two, in which you mark the disk so that these areas will not be used again.

Marking Bad Sectors

You mark bad sectors on a disk with the RECOVER command. After making the attempted recovery of the data, you can use the following RECOVER command to mark the sectors as bad in the FAT:

C>RECOVER document.txt

```
Press any key to begin recovery of the
file(s) on drive C:

XXXXX of YYYYY bytes recovered
```

The DOCUMENT.TXT file still is on the disk after this operation, but it has been truncated at the location of the error. Any sectors the RECOVER command could not read are marked as bad sectors in the FAT and will show up the next time you run CHKDSK. You might want to run CHKDSK before and after running RECOVER, to see the effect of the additional bad sectors.

After using RECOVER, delete the DOCUMENT.TXT file because you have already created a copy of it that contains as much good data as possible.

This step completes phase two—and the entire operation. You now have a new file that contains as much of the original file as possible, and the disk FAT is marked so that the defective location will not be a bother.

Be very careful when you use RECOVER. Used improperly, it can do much damage to your files and the FAT. If you enter the RECOVER command without a file name for it to work on, the program assumes that you want every file on the disk recovered, and operates on every file and subdirectory on the disk; it converts all subdirectories to files, and places all file names in the root directory and gives them new names (FILE0000.REC, FILE0001.REC, and so on). This process essentially wipes out the file system on the entire disk. *Do not use RECOVER without providing a file name for it to work on.* This program is so dangerous when you misuse it that you should consider immediately deleting it from your hard disk, to prevent anyone from invoking it accidentally.

The DEBUG Program

The DOS DEBUG program is a powerful debugging tool for programmers who develop programs in assembly language. The following list shows some of the things you can do with DEBUG:

- Display data from any memory location.
- Display or alter the contents of the CPU registers.
- Display the assembly source code of programs.
- Enter data directly into any memory location.
- Input from a port.
- Move blocks of data between memory locations.
- Output to a port.
- Perform hexadecimal addition and subtraction.
- Read disk sectors into memory.
- Trace the execution of a program.
- Write disk sectors from memory.
- Write short assembly language programs.

To use the DEBUG program, make sure that DEBUG.COM is in the current directory or in the current DOS PATH. Enter this command:

DEBUG [d:][path][filename] [arglist]

[filename] specifies the file to be DEBUGged. [arglist] consists of parameters and switches that will be passed to the program; arglist might be specified if the file name is present. When the file name is loaded into memory, it is loaded as though it had been invoked with this command:

filename arglist

When the DEBUG prompt - is displayed, you can enter a DEBUG command.

Because more powerful programs are now available for debugging and assembling code, the most common use for DEBUG is patching assembly language programs to correct problems, change an existing program feature, or patch disk sectors.

DEBUG Commands and Parameters

The documentation for DEBUG no longer is provided in the standard DOS manual. If you are serious about using DEBUG, you should purchase the *DOS Technical Reference Manual*, which contains the information you need to use this program.

As a quick reference to the DEBUG program, this section gives a brief description of each command.

A address assembles macro assembler statements directly into memory.

C range address compares the contents of two blocks of memory.

D address or *D range* displays the contents of a portion of memory.

E address displays bytes sequentially and enables them to be modified.

E address list replaces the contents of one or more bytes, starting at the specified address, with values contained in the list.

F range list fills the memory locations in the range with the values specified.

G processes the program you are debugging without breakpoints.

G =address processes instructions beginning at the address specified.

G =address address processes instructions beginning at the address specified. This command stops the processing of the program when the instruction at the specified address is reached (breakpoint), and displays the registers, flags, and the next instruction to be processed. As many as ten breakpoints can be listed.

H value value adds the two hexadecimal values and then subtracts the second from the first. It displays the sum and the difference on one line.

I portaddress inputs and displays (in hexadecimal) one byte from the specified port.

L address loads a file.

L address drive sector sector loads data from the disk specified by drive and places the data in memory beginning at the specified address.

M range address moves the contents of the memory locations specified by range to the locations beginning at the address specified.

N filename defines file specifications or other parameters required by the program being debugged.

O portaddress byte sends the byte to the specified output port.

P =address value causes the processing of a subroutine call, a loop instruction, an interrupt, or a repeat-string instruction to stop at the next instruction.

Q ends the DEBUG program.

R displays the contents of all registers and flags and the next instruction to be processed.

R F displays all flags.

R registername displays the contents of a register.

S range list searches the range for the characters in the list.

T =address value processes one or more instructions starting with the instructions at CS:IP, or at =address if it is specified. This command also displays the contents of all registers and flags after each instruction is processed.

U address unassembles instructions (translates the contents of memory into assembler-like statements) and displays their addresses and hexadecimal values, together with assembler-like statements.

W address enables you to use the WRITE command without specifying parameters or by specifying only the address parameter.

W address drive sector sector writes data to disk beginning at a specified address.

XA count allocates a specified number of expanded-memory pages to a handle.

XD handle deallocates a handle.

XM lpage ppage handle maps an EMS logical page to an EMS physical page from an EMS handle.

XS displays the status of expanded memory.

Changing Disks and Files

DEBUG can be used to modify sectors on a disk. Suppose that you use this DEBUG command:

```
-L 100 1 0 1

-
```

This command loads into the current segment at an offset of 100h, sectors from drive B:\ (1), starting with sector 0 (the DOS volume boot sector), for a total of 1 or more sectors.

You then could write this sector to a file on drive C:\ by using these commands:

```
-N C:\B BOOT.SEC
-R CX
CX 0000
:200
-W
Writing 0200 bytes
-Q
```

The Name command sets up the name of the file to read or write.

The Register command enables you to inspect and change the contents of registers. The CX register contains the low-order bytes indicating the size of the file to load or save, and the BX register contains the high-order bytes. You would not need to set the BX register to anything but 0 unless the file was to be more than 65535 (64K) bytes in size. Setting the CX register to 200 indicates a file size of 200h, or 512 bytes.

The Write command saves 512 bytes of memory, starting at the default address of offset 100, to the file indicated in the Name command.

After quitting the program, your C:\ drive will have a file called B BOOT.SEC that contains an image of the DOS volume boot sector on drive B:\.

Resident-Software Conflicts

One area that gives many users trouble is memory-resident software. This software loads itself into memory and stays there, waiting for an activation key (usually a keystroke combination). Programs that can be activated by a keystroke combination are sometimes called *pop-up utilities*.

The problem with memory-resident programs is that they often conflict with each other, as well as with applications programs and even DOS. Memory-resident programs can cause many types of problems. Sometimes the problems appear consistently, and at other times they are intermittent. Some computer users do not like to use memory-resident software unless absolutely necessary because of its potential for problems.

If you are experiencing problems that you have traced to a memory-resident program conflict, a common way to correct the problem is to eliminate one of the conflicting programs. Another possibility is to change the order in which the programs load into your system. Some programs must be loaded first, and others must be loaded last. Sometimes this order preference is indicated in the documentation for the programs, but often it is discovered through trial and error.

Device drivers are a form of memory-resident software, and loading these drivers in CONFIG.SYS can cause many problems. The possible solutions are the same as for resolving other memory-resident software problems: Eliminate the programs that cause the problem and change the load order.

Unfortunately, conflicts between memory-resident programs are likely to be around as long as DOS is used. The "light at the end of the tunnel" is OS/2. The problem with DOS is that it establishes no real rules for how resident programs must interact with each other and the rest of the system. OS/2 is built on the concept of many programs being resident in memory at one time, and all multitasking. This system will put an end to the problem of resident programs conflicting with each other.

Hardware Problems versus Software Problems

One of the most aggravating situations in computer repair is opening up a system and troubleshooting all the hardware just to find that the cause of the problem is a program, not the hardware. Many people have spent large sums of money on replacement hardware such as motherboards, disk drives, adapter boards, cables, and so on, all on the premise that the hardware was causing problems, when software was actually the culprit. To eliminate these aggravating, sometimes embarrassing, and often expensive situations, you must be able to distinguish a hardware problem from a software problem.

Fortunately, making this distinction can be relatively simple. Software problems often are caused by the custom configurations many systems carry (the extensive CONFIG.SYS and AUTOEXEC.BAT files that load all kinds of memory-resident programs and specify configuration parameters). One of the first things to do when you suspect that software might be causing a problem is to boot the system from a DOS disk that has no CONFIG.SYS or AUTOEXEC.BAT configuration files on it. Then test for the problem. If it has disappeared, the cause was probably something in one or both of those files. To find the problem, begin restoring the files one command line at a time, and retest the system each time. You might be able to solve the problem by changing the order of command lines, or you might have to eliminate the offending program or configuration item.

DOS can cause other problems, such as bugs or incompatibilities with certain hardware items. For example, DOS 3.2 does not support the 1.44M floppy drive format; therefore, using DOS 3.2 on a system equipped with a 1.44M floppy drive might lead you to believe (incorrectly) that the drive is bad. Be sure that you are using the correct version of DOS and that support is provided for your hardware. Find out whether your version of DOS has any official patches available; sometimes a problem you are experiencing might be one that many others have had, and IBM or Microsoft might have released a fix disk that takes care of the problem. For example, many PS/2 users have a floppy formatting problem under DOS 3.3. They get a `track 0 bad` message after answering Yes to the `Format another diskette` message. This problem was solved by a special driver file on the DOS 3.3 patch disk.

If you are having a problem related to a piece of application software, contact the company that produces the software and explain the problem. If the software really has a bug, the company might have a patched or fixed version available, or it might be able to help you operate the software in a different way to solve the problem.

Chapter Summary

This chapter has examined the software side of your system. Often when a system has a problem, the problem is in the software and is not hardware-related. The chapter has examined DOS and showed how DOS organizes information on a disk. You have learned about the CHKDSK, RECOVER, and DEBUG commands to see how DOS can help you with data and disk recovery. Finally, the chapter has described memory-resident software and some of the problems it can cause, and has given you an idea of how to distinguish a software problem from a hardware problem.

A Final Word

The content of this book covers most of the components of an IBM or IBM-compatible personal computer system. In this book, you discovered how all the components operate and interact and how these components should be set up and installed. You saw the ways that components fail and learned the symptoms of these failures. Finally, you reviewed the steps in diagnosing and troubleshooting all the major components in a system so that you can locate and replace a failing component.

The information I have presented in this book represents years of practical experience with IBM and compatible systems. Much research and investigation have gone into each section. This information has saved companies many thousands of dollars.

Bringing microcomputer service and support in-house is one of the best ways to save money. Eliminating service contracts for most systems and reducing down-time are just two of the benefits of applying the information presented in this book. As I have indicated many times in this book, you can save a lot of money on component purchases by eliminating the middleman and purchasing the components directly from distributors or manufacturers. The vendor list in the Appendix lists the best of these sources for you to contact. Most people have not been able to take advantage of direct purchasing, however, because it requires a new level of understanding of the components involved. I hope that I have given you this deeper level of knowledge and understanding.

I have used many sources to gather the information presented in this book, starting with my own experiences. I have taught many thousands of individuals this information in a seminar series presented by my company, Mueller Technical Research. In presenting this information, I am often asked where more of this type of information can be obtained and whether I have any "secrets" for acquiring this knowledge. There are no secrets, but I can share several key sources of information that can make you a verifiable expert in PC upgrade and repair.

My four key sources for the type of information that helps me (and that can help you) solve upgrading, repairing, and general troubleshooting problems are listed as "the four Ms":

> Manuals
> Machines
> Modems
> Magazines

Manuals—let me say it again—*manuals* and documentation are the single most important source of computer information. Unfortunately, manuals are one of the most frequently overlooked sources of information. I owe much of my knowledge to poring over the various technical-reference manuals and other original equipment manufacturer's (OEM) manuals. I would not even consider purchasing a system that does not have a detailed technical-reference manual available. This statement applies also to system components, whether it's a floppy drive, hard disk, power supply, motherboard, or memory card—I have to have a detailed reference manual, to help me understand what future upgrades are possible and to provide valuable insight into proper installation, use, and support of a product.

A simple analogy explains the importance of manuals and documentation, as well as other issues concerning repair and maintenance of a system. Compare your business use of computers to a taxicab company. The company has to purchase automobiles to use as cabs. The owners purchase not one car but an entire fleet of cars. Do you think that they would purchase a fleet of automobiles based solely on reliability, performance or even gas-mileage statistics? Would they neglect to consider on-going maintenance and service of these automobiles? Would they purchase a fleet of cars that could be serviced only by the original manufacturer and for which parts could not be obtained easily? Do you think that they would buy a car that did not have available a detailed service and repair manual? Would they buy an automobile for which parts were scarce and that was supported by a sparse dealer network with few service and parts outlets, making long waits for parts and service inevitable? The answer (of course) to all these questions is No, No, No.

You can see why most taxicab companies as well as police departments use "standard" automobiles such as the Chevrolet Caprice or Ford Crown Victoria. If ever there were "generic" automobiles, these models would qualify. Dealers and parts and documentation for these cars are everywhere, and they share parts with many other automobiles as well, making them easy to service and maintain.

Doesn't your business (especially if it is large) use what amounts to a "fleet" of computers? If so, then why don't you think of this fleet as the cars of the cab company, which would go out of business quickly if these cars could not be kept running smoothly and inexpensively. Now you know why the Checker Marathon automobile used to be so popular with cab companies: its design barely changed over the span of its availability. In many ways, the standard PC and AT systems are like the venerable Checker Marathon. You can get technical information by the shelf-full for these systems. You can get parts and upgrade material from so many sources that anything you need is always immediately available and at a discounted price. I'm not saying that you should standardize on older PC or AT systems—just that there is a case for standardizing on systems that follow the "generic" physical design of the PC or AT. There is something to be said for using clone systems.

Even the PS/2 systems now are capable of being considered in this light because their installed base exceeds 10 million units. I am noticing many third parties with replacement and upgrade motherboards, power supplies, and disk drives for these systems.

It amazes me that people purchase computers that have no technical documentation and no spare-parts program, or parts available only through dealers, or that use nonstandard form-factor components, and so on. The upgrade, repair, and maintenance of a company's computer systems always seem to take a back seat to performance and style.

In addition to OEM manuals, many good reference and tutorial books are available. Que Corporation specializes in this type of computer book, and my shelf is full of books from Que and other major publishers.

The second item on the list, *machines*, refers to the systems themselves. They are one of my best sources of information. Suppose that I need to answer the question, "Will the XYZ SCSI host adapter work with the ABC tape drive?" The answer is as simple as plugging everything in and pressing the switch. (Simple to talk about, that is.) Seriously, experimenting with and observing running systems are some of the best learning tools at your disposal. I recommend trying everything; rarely does anything you try harm the equipment. Harming valuable data is definitely possible, however, if not likely, so keep regular backups as insurance. People sometimes are reluctant to experiment with systems that cost a lot of money, but much can be learned through direct tests and studies of the system.

Support personnel in larger companies have access to quantities of hardware and software I can only dream about. Some larger companies have "toy stores," where they regularly purchase equipment solely for evaluation and testing. Dealers and manufacturers also have access to an enormous variety of equipment. If you are in this position, take advantage of this access to equipment, and learn from this resource. When new systems are purchased, take notes on their construction and components.

Every time I encounter a system I have not previously worked with, I immediately open it up and start taking notes. I want to know the make and model of all the internal components, such as disk drives, power supplies, and motherboards. As far as motherboards, I record the numbers of the primary IC chips on the board, such as the processor (of course) and especially any integrated chip sets. By knowing which chip set your system uses, you can often infer other capabilities of the system, such as enhanced setup or configuration capabilities. I like to know which BIOS version is in the system, and I even make a copy of the BIOS on-disk for backup and further study purposes. I want to know the hard drive tables from the BIOS, and any other particulars involved in setting up and installing a system. Write down the type of battery a system uses so that you can obtain spares. Note any unique brackets or construction techniques such as specialized hardware (Torx screws, for example) so that you can be prepared for servicing the system later.

This discussion brings up a pet peeve of mine. Nothing burns me up as much as reading a "review" of computer systems in a major magazine, in which reviewers test systems and produce benchmark and performance results for, let's say, the hard disks or video displays in a system. Then, they do not just open up the machines and tell me (and the world) exactly which components the manufacturer of the system is using! I want to know *exactly* which disk controller, hard drive, BIOS, motherboard, video adapter, and so on are found in each system. Without this information, their review and benchmark tests are useless to me. Then they run a test of disk performance between two systems with the same disk controller and drives and say (with a straight face) that the one that came out a few milliseconds ahead of the other wins the test. With the statistical variation that normally occurs in any manufactured components, these results are meaningless. The point is perhaps to be very careful of what you trust in a normal magazine review. If it tells me exactly which components were tested, then I can draw my own conclusions and even make comparisons to other systems not included in that review. The (now defunct) *PC Tech Journal* magazine always did *excellent* reviews, and told readers what components were in the systems it tested. The review test data then was much more accurate and informative because it could be properly interpreted.

The third item, *modems*, refers to the use of public- and private-information utilities, which are a modem and a phone call away. You can tie into everything from local electronic bulletin board systems (BBSs) to vendor boards and major information networks such as CompuServe. Many hardware and software companies offer technical support and even software upgrades over their own semi-public bulletin boards. The public-access information networks such as CompuServe and other BBS systems include computer enthusiasts and technical-support people from various organizations, as well as experts in virtually all areas of computer hardware and software. Bulletin boards are a great way to have questions answered and to collect useful utility and help programs that can make your job much easier. The world of public-domain and user-supported software awaits, as well as more technical information and related experiences than you can imagine.

A favorite source of information is the public-access utility CompuServe. You can log on to this cluster of mainframe systems, based in Ohio, from virtually anywhere in the world through a local telephone call. Among CompuServe's resources are special interest groups (SIGs), sponsored by most of the major software and hardware companies, as well as enthusiasts of all types. Some interesting discussions take place in the SIGs. CompuServe, combined with a local electronic bulletin board or two, can greatly supplement the information you gather from other sources. In fact, CompuServe electronic mail is probably the most efficient method of reaching me. My CompuServe ID is 73145,1566, and if you have questions or just a comment or useful information you think I might be interested in, please send me a message. Because of the extra steps in processing, my standard mail can get backed up and it can take me awhile to answer a regular postal letter; electronic mail, however, involves fewer steps for me to send, and always seems to have a higher priority.

The last source of information, *magazines*, is one of the best sources of up-to-date reviews and technical data. Featured are "bug fixes," problem alerts, and general industry news. Keeping a printed book up-to-date with the latest events in the computer industry is extremely difficult or impossible. Things move so fast that the magazines themselves barely keep pace. I subscribe to most of the major computer magazines and am hard-pressed to pick one as the best. They all are important to me, and each one provides different information or the same information with a different angle or twist. Although the reviews sometimes leave me wanting, the magazines still are a valuable way to at least hear about products, most of which I never would have known about without the magazines' reports and advertisements. Most computer magazines now are on CD-ROM, which can ease the frantic search for a specific piece of information you remember reading about. If CD-ROM versions are too much for your needs, be aware that you can access and search most major magazines on CompuServe. This capability is valuable when you want to research everything you can about a specific subject.

Finally, the appendix lists vendors whose products are named throughout this book, as well as a list of part numbers and pricing for all of IBM's technical documentation and manuals. Additionally, you will find reference charts that contain the information I generally need most often. In fact, the appendix and the included reference charts are the most valuable part of the book to me, and the part that I use repeatedly as a reference.

I hope that *Upgrading and Repairing PCs*, 2nd Edition, is beneficial to you for your business or personal needs, and I hope that you have enjoyed reading it as much as I have enjoyed writing it.

PC Reference Information

This appendix has a great deal of useful information, primarily reference information, designed not to be read but to be looked up. This type of information can be very useful in troubleshooting or upgrading sessions, but usually is spread out among many sources. In this second edition of *Upgrading and Repairing PCs*, much information has been added to the appendix, including information I have needed during the course of normal PC troubleshooting, servicing, or upgrading.

The information in this appendix is in the form of many reference charts and tables—in particular, information about the default interrupt, DMA channel, I/O port, and memory use of the primary system and most standard options. This information is invaluable if you install new boards or upgrade a system in any way and can be important when you troubleshoot a conflict between two devices.

This appendix has information about various system connectors—from the serial and parallel ports to the power-supply connections. Diagrams for making serial and parallel wrap (test) plugs are shown also.

Tables indicate the hard disk drive tables in the two versions of the IBM XT hard disk controller, as well as all versions of the IBM AT and PS/2 system ROM BIOS to date. Many compatible BIOS drive tables also are included. This information is necessary when you add a hard disk to systems using these components.

One of the most useful tables in this appendix is a concise listing of the IBM diagnostics error codes. These codes can be generated by the POST and by the disk-based diagnostics programs. These error codes are not documented by IBM in tabular form; this compilation is the result of poring over hardware-maintenance service, technical-reference, and other manuals that IBM produces. Some of the codes come from reading the commented ROM listings in the technical-reference manuals. This information can be very useful in deciphering the codes quickly and efficiently, without having to look through a stack of books.

This appendix has also a listing of all the available IBM technical manuals and a description of all the documentation available. The included listing has part-number and pricing information as well as information useful in ordering this documentation.

Although all of this information comes from a wide range of sources, most of it comes from the technical-reference manuals and hardware-maintenance service manuals available for various systems from IBM and other manufacturers. These documents are invaluable if you want to pursue this topic more extensively.

ASCII Character Code Charts

Figures A.1 through A.3 list ASCII control, standard, and extended character values. Figure A.4 shows the IBM extended ASCII line-drawing characters in an easy-to-use format. I frequently use these extended ASCII line-drawing characters for visual enhancement in documents I create.

DOS Information

Tables A.1 through A.3 show all the resident, batch, and transient DOS commands and in which DOS version they are supported. If you are responsible for providing technical support, you should know what DOS commands are available to the users at the other end of the phone. These tables identify which commands are supported in any version of DOS released to date.

DEC	HEX	CHAR	NAME		CONTROL CODE
0	00		Ctrl-@	NUL	Null
1	01	☺	Ctrl-A	SOH	Start of Heading
2	02	●	Ctrl-B	STX	Start of Text
3	03	♥	Ctrl-C	ETX	End of Text
4	04	♦	Ctrl-D	EOT	End of Transmit
5	05	♣	Ctrl-E	ENQ	Enquiry
6	06	♠	Ctrl-F	ACK	Acknowledge
7	07	•	Ctrl-G	BEL	Bell
8	08	□	Ctrl-H	BS	Back Space
9	09	○	Ctrl-I	HT	Horizontal Tab
10	0A	■	Ctrl-J	LF	Line Feed
11	0B	♂	Ctrl-K	VT	Vertical Tab
12	0C	♀	Ctrl-L	FF	Form Feed
13	0D	♪	Ctrl-M	CR	Carriage Return
14	0E	♫	Ctrl-N	SO	Shift Out
15	0F	☼	Ctrl-O	SI	Shift In
16	10	►	Ctrl-P	DLE	Data Line Escape
17	11	◄	Ctrl-Q	DC1	Device Control 1
18	12	↕	Ctrl-R	DC2	Device Control 2
19	13	‼	Ctrl-S	DC3	Device Control 3
20	14	¶	Ctrl-T	DC4	Device Control 4
21	15	§	Ctrl-U	NAK	Negative Acknowledge
22	16	▬	Ctrl-V	SYN	Synchronous Idle
23	17	↨	Ctrl-W	ETB	End of Transmit Block
24	18	↑	Ctrl-X	CAN	Cancel
25	19	↓	Ctrl-Y	EM	End of Medium
26	1A	→	Ctrl-Z	SUB	Substitute
27	1B	←	Ctrl-[	ESC	Escape
28	1C	∟	Ctrl-\	FS	File Separator
29	1D	↔	Ctrl-]	GS	Group Separator
30	1E	▲	Ctrl-^	RS	Record Separator
31	1F	▼	Ctrl-_	US	Unit Separator

Fig. A.1

ASCII control codes.

DEC	HEX	CHAR	DEC	HEX	CHAR	DEC	HEX	CHAR	DEC	HEX	CHAR
0	0		32	20		64	40	@	96	60	`
1	1	☺	33	21	!	65	41	A	97	61	a
2	2	●	34	22	"	66	42	B	98	62	b
3	3	♥	35	23	#	67	43	C	99	63	c
4	4	♦	36	24	$	68	44	D	100	64	d
5	5	♣	37	25	%	69	45	E	101	65	e
6	6	♠	38	26	&	70	46	F	102	66	f
7	7	•	39	27	'	71	47	G	103	67	g
8	8	□	40	28	(	72	48	H	104	68	h
9	9	○	41	29	)	73	49	I	105	69	i
10	A	■	42	2A	*	74	4A	J	106	6A	j
11	B	♂	43	2B	+	75	4B	K	107	6B	k
12	C	♀	44	2C	,	76	4C	L	108	6C	l
13	D	♪	45	2D	-	77	4D	M	109	6D	m
14	E	♫	46	2E	.	78	4E	N	110	6E	n
15	F	☼	47	2F	/	79	4F	O	111	6F	o
16	10	►	48	30	0	80	50	P	112	70	p
17	11	◄	49	31	1	81	51	Q	113	71	q
18	12	↕	50	32	2	82	52	R	114	72	r
19	13	‼	51	33	3	83	53	S	115	73	s
20	14	¶	52	34	4	84	54	T	116	74	t
21	15	§	53	35	5	85	55	U	117	75	u
22	16	▬	54	36	6	86	56	V	118	76	v
23	17	↨	55	37	7	87	57	W	119	77	w
24	18	↑	56	38	8	88	58	X	120	78	x
25	19	↓	57	39	9	89	59	Y	121	79	y
26	1A	→	58	3A	:	90	5A	Z	122	7A	z
27	1B	←	59	3B	;	91	5B	[	123	7B	{
28	1C	∟	60	3C	<	92	5C	\	124	7C	|
29	1D	↔	61	3D	=	93	5D	]	125	7D	}
30	1E	▲	62	3E	>	94	5E	^	126	7E	~
31	1F	▼	63	3F	?	95	5F	_	127	7F	⌂

Fig. A.2

Standard ASCII characters (including control codes).

DEC	HEX	CHAR	DEC	HEX	CHAR	DEC	HEX	CHAR	DEC	HEX	CHAR
128	80	Ç	160	A0	á	192	C0	└	224	E0	α
129	81	ü	161	A1	í	193	C1	┴	225	E1	ß
130	82	é	162	A2	ó	194	C2	┬	226	E2	Γ
131	83	â	163	A3	ú	195	C3	├	227	E3	π
132	84	ä	164	A4	ñ	196	C4	─	228	E4	Σ
133	85	à	165	A5	Ñ	197	C5	┼	229	E5	σ
134	86	å	166	A6	ª	198	C6	╞	230	E6	µ
135	87	ç	167	A7	º	199	C7	╟	231	E7	τ
136	88	ê	168	A8	¿	200	C8	╚	232	E8	Φ
137	89	ë	169	A9	⌐	201	C9	╔	233	E9	Θ
138	8A	è	170	AA	¬	202	CA	╩	234	EA	Ω
139	8B	ï	171	AB	½	203	CB	╦	235	EB	δ
140	8C	î	172	AC	¼	204	CC	╠	236	EC	∞
141	8D	ì	173	AD	¡	205	CD	═	237	ED	φ
142	8E	Ä	174	AE	«	206	CE	╬	238	EE	ε
143	8F	Å	175	AF	»	207	CF	╧	239	EF	∩
144	90	É	176	B0	░	208	D0	╨	240	F0	≡
145	91	æ	177	B1	▒	209	D1	╤	241	F1	±
146	92	Æ	178	B2	▓	210	D2	╥	242	F2	≥
147	93	ô	179	B3	│	211	D3	╙	243	F3	≤
148	94	ö	180	B4	┤	212	D4	╘	244	F4	⌠
149	95	ò	181	B5	╡	213	D5	╒	245	F5	⌡
150	96	û	182	B6	╢	214	D6	╓	246	F6	÷
151	97	ù	183	B7	╖	215	D7	╫	247	F7	≈
152	98	ÿ	184	B8	╕	216	D8	╪	248	F8	°
153	99	Ö	185	B9	╣	217	D9	┘	249	F9	∙
154	9A	Ü	186	BA	║	218	DA	┌	250	FA	·
155	9B	¢	187	BB	╗	219	DB	█	251	FB	√
156	9C	£	188	BC	╝	220	DC	▄	252	FC	ⁿ
157	9D	¥	189	BD	╜	221	DD	▌	253	FD	²
158	9E	₧	190	BE	╛	222	DE	▐	254	FE	■
159	9F	ƒ	191	BF	┐	223	DF	▀	255	FF	

Fig. A.3

Extended ASCII characters.

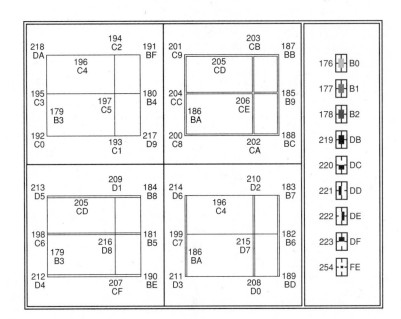

Fig. A.4

Extended ASCII line-drawing characters.

Table A.1 Resident DOS Commands

Command name	1.0	1.1	2.0	2.1	3.0	3.1	3.2	3.3	4.0	5.0
CD/CHDIR			✓	✓	✓	✓	✓	✓	✓	✓
CHCP									✓	✓
CLS			✓	✓	✓	✓	✓	✓	✓	✓
COPY	✓	✓	✓	✓	✓	✓	✓	✓	✓	✓
CTTY			✓	✓	✓	✓	✓	✓	✓	✓
DATE	✓	✓	✓	✓	✓	✓	✓	✓	✓	✓
DEL/ERASE	✓	✓	✓	✓	✓	✓	✓	✓	✓	✓
DIR	✓	✓	✓	✓	✓	✓	✓	✓	✓	✓
EXIT					✓	✓	✓	✓	✓	✓
EXPAND										✓
LOADHI/LH										✓
MD/MKDIR			✓	✓	✓	✓	✓	✓	✓	✓
PATH			✓	✓	✓	✓	✓	✓	✓	✓
PROMPT			✓	✓	✓	✓	✓	✓	✓	✓
RD/RMDIR			✓	✓	✓	✓	✓	✓	✓	✓
REN/RENAME	✓	✓	✓	✓	✓	✓	✓	✓	✓	✓
SET			✓	✓	✓	✓	✓	✓	✓	✓
TIME	✓	✓	✓	✓	✓	✓	✓	✓	✓	✓
TYPE	✓	✓	✓	✓	✓	✓	✓	✓	✓	✓
VER					✓	✓	✓	✓	✓	✓
VERIFY			✓	✓	✓	✓	✓	✓	✓	✓
VOL			✓	✓	✓	✓	✓	✓	✓	✓

Table A.2 DOS Batch File Commands

Command	1.0	1.1	2.0	2.1	3.0	3.1	3.2	3.3	4.0	5.0
CALL								✓	✓	✓
ECHO	✓	✓	✓	✓	✓	✓	✓	✓	✓	✓
FOR	✓	✓	✓	✓	✓	✓	✓	✓	✓	✓
GOTO	✓	✓	✓	✓	✓	✓	✓	✓	✓	✓
IF	✓	✓	✓	✓	✓	✓	✓	✓	✓	✓
PAUSE	✓	✓	✓	✓	✓	✓	✓	✓	✓	✓
REM	✓	✓	✓	✓	✓	✓	✓	✓	✓	✓
SHIFT	✓	✓	✓	✓	✓	✓	✓	✓	✓	✓

Table A.3 Transient DOS Commands

Command	1.0	1.1	2.0	2.1	3.0	3.1	3.2	3.3	4.0	5.0
APPEND								✓	✓	✓
ASSIGN			✓	✓	✓	✓	✓	✓	✓	✓
ATTRIB					✓	✓	✓	✓	✓	✓
BACKUP			✓	✓	✓	✓	✓	✓	✓	✓
BASIC	✓	✓	✓	✓	✓	✓	✓	✓	✓	✓
BASICA	✓	✓	✓	✓	✓	✓	✓	✓	✓	✓
CHCP								✓	✓	✓
CHKDSK	✓	✓	✓	✓	✓	✓	✓	✓	✓	✓
COMMAND			✓	✓	✓	✓	✓	✓	✓	✓
COMP	✓	✓	✓	✓	✓	✓	✓	✓	✓	✓
DEBUG	✓	✓	✓	✓	✓	✓	✓	✓	✓	✓
DISKCOMP	✓	✓	✓	✓	✓	✓	✓	✓	✓	✓
DISKCOPY	✓	✓	✓	✓	✓	✓	✓	✓	✓	✓
DOSKEY										✓
DOSSHELL									✓	✓
EDIT										✓
EDLIN	✓	✓	✓	✓	✓	✓	✓	✓	✓	✓
EMM386										✓
EXE2BIN			✓	✓	✓	✓	✓			✓
FASTOPEN								✓	✓	✓
FC										✓
FDISK			✓	✓	✓	✓	✓	✓	✓	✓
FIND			✓	✓	✓	✓	✓	✓	✓	✓
FORMAT	✓	✓	✓	✓	✓	✓	✓	✓	✓	✓
GRAFTABL			✓	✓	✓	✓	✓	✓	✓	✓
GRAPHICS			✓	✓	✓	✓	✓	✓	✓	✓
HELP										✓
JOIN					✓	✓	✓	✓	✓	✓
KEYB								✓	✓	✓
KEYBFR					✓	✓	✓			
KEYBGR					✓	✓	✓			
KEYBIT					✓	✓	✓			
KEYBSP					✓	✓	✓			
KEYBUK					✓	✓	✓			
LABEL					✓	✓	✓	✓	✓	✓
LIB	✓	✓	✓	✓	✓	✓	✓			
LINK	✓	✓	✓	✓	✓	✓	✓			
MEM									✓	✓
MIRROR										✓
MODE	✓	✓	✓	✓	✓	✓	✓	✓	✓	✓
MORE			✓	✓	✓	✓	✓	✓	✓	✓
NLSFUNC								✓	✓	✓
PRINT			✓	✓	✓	✓	✓	✓	✓	✓
QBASIC										✓
RECOVER			✓	✓	✓	✓	✓	✓	✓	✓

Command	DOS version number									
	1.0	1.1	2.0	2.1	3.0	3.1	3.2	3.3	4.0	5.0
REPLACE				✓	✓	✓	✓	✓		✓
RESTORE		✓	✓	✓	✓	✓	✓	✓		✓
SETVER										✓
SHARE					✓	✓	✓	✓		✓
SORT		✓	✓	✓	✓	✓	✓	✓		✓
SUBST				✓	✓	✓	✓	✓		✓
SYS	✓	✓	✓	✓	✓	✓	✓	✓		✓
TREE			✓	✓	✓	✓	✓	✓		✓
UNDELETE										✓
UNFORMAT										✓
XCOPY							✓	✓	✓	✓

LIB, LINK, and EXE2BIN are included with the DOS technical-reference manual for DOS versions 3.3 and higher. EXE2BIN is included with DOS V5.0.

IBM DOS 4.xx Versions

DOS 4.xx has had many revisions since being introduced in mid-1988. Since the first release, IBM has released different Corrective Service Diskettes (CSDs), which fix a variety of problems with DOS V4. Each CSD is cumulative, which means that the later ones include all previous fixes. Note that these fixes are for IBM DOS and not for any other manufacturer's version.

IBM typically provides much more support in the way of fixes and updates than any other manufacturer. Microsoft, for example, never implemented any of the fixes in the fourth through seventh releases of IBM DOS. This is the reason that I always run IBM DOS, even on clone systems.

Table A.4 shows a summary of the different IBM DOS 4.xx releases and specific information about the system files and shell so that you can identify the release you are using. To obtain the latest Corrective Service Diskettes (CSD) that update you to the latest release, contact your dealer—the fixes are free.

Table A.4 IBM DOS 4.xx Releases

File name	Size	Date	Version	SYSLEVEL	Comments
IBMBIO.COM	32810	06/17/88	4.00	—	Original release
IBMDOS.COM	35984	06/17/88			
COMMAND.COM	37637	06/17/88			
IBMBIO.COM	32816	08/03/88	4.01	CSD UR22624	EMS fixes
IBMDOS.COM	36000	08/03/88			
COMMAND.COM	37637	06/17/88			
IBMBIO.COM	32816	08/03/88	4.01	CSD UR24270	Date change fixed
IBMDOS.COM	36000	11/11/88			
COMMAND.COM	37652	11/11/88			
IBMBIO.COM	33910	04/06/89	4.01	CSD UR25066	"Death disk" fixed
IBMDOS.COM	37136	04/06/89			
COMMAND.COM	37652	11/11/88			
IBMBIO.COM	34660	03/20/90	4.01	CSD UR29015	SCSI support added
IBMDOS.COM	37248	02/20/90			
COMMAND.COM	37765	03/20/90			
IBMBIO.COM	34660	04/27/90	4.01	CSD UR31300	HPFS compatibility fixes
IBMDOS.COM	37264	05/21/90			
COMMAND.COM	37765	06/29/90			
IBMBIO.COM	34692	04/08/91	4.01	CSD UR3528	HPFS and CHKDSK fixes
IBMDOS.COM	37280	11/30/90			
COMMAND.COM	37762	09/27/91			

IBM DOS 5.xx Versions

DOS 5.xx has had several different revisions since being introduced in mid-1991. Since the first release, IBM has released various Corrective Service Diskettes (CSDs), which fix a variety of problems with DOS 5. Each CSD is cumulative, which means that the later ones include all previous fixes. You should note that these fixes are for IBM DOS and not any other manufacturer's version. IBM typically provides much more support in the way of fixes and updates than any other manufacturer. Microsoft, for example, does not have a CSD type program for DOS 5, and has not (as of this writing) released equivalent fixes to IBM's third and fourth releases. Note that IBM now supports the installation of DOS 5 on clone systems and has a special utility, the Upgrade Installation Enhancement Utility (UIEU), that facilitates the installation of IBM DOS over previous versions of MS-DOS.

Table A.5 shows a summary of the different IBM DOS 5.xx releases and specific information about the system files and shell so that you can identify the release you are using. To obtain the latest Corrective Service Diskettes (CSD) that update you to the latest release, contact your dealer—the fixes are free.

Table A.5 IBM DOS 5.xx Releases

File name	Size	Date	Version	SYSLEVEL	Comments
IBMBIO.COM	33430	05/09/91	5.00	—	Original release
IBMDOS.COM	37378	05/09/91			
COMMAND.COM	47987	05/09/91			
IBMBIO.COM	33430	05/09/91	5.00	CSD UR35423	XCOPY fixed
IBMDOS.COM	37378	05/09/91			QEDIT fixed
COMMAND.COM	48005	08/16/91			
IBMBIO.COM	33430	05/09/91	5.00	CSD UR35748	SYS fixed
IBMDOS.COM	37378	05/09/91			
COMMAND.COM	48006	10/25/91			
IBMBIO.COM	33446	11/29/91	5.00	CSD UR35834	EMM386,FORMAT, DOSHELL,
IBMDOS.COM	37378	11/29/91			BACKUP fixed
COMMAND.COM	48006	11/29/91			

DOS Formatting Information

With the DOS FORMAT command, you can perform low- and high-level formatting of floppy disks and high-level format hard disks. The following syntax is used with the FORMAT command:

```
FORMAT d: [/V[:label]] [/Q] [/U] [/F:size] [/B | /S]
FORMAT d: [/V[:label]] [/Q] [/U] [/T:tracks /N:sectors] [/B | /S]
FORMAT d: [/V[:label]] [/Q] [/U] [/1] [/4] [/B | /S]
FORMAT d: [/Q] [/U] [/1] [/4] [/8] [/B | /S]
```

Table A.6 is a concise and detailed list of all of the parameters associated with the DOS FORMAT command, including all parameters new to DOS 5. Also included are several undocumented parameters you may never have seen before.

Table A.6 FORMAT Command (Undocumented Features)

Standard parameters

/Q	Performs a Quick format
/U	Performs an Unconditional format
/S	Copies the DOS system files (IBMBIO.COM and IBMDOS.COM) and COMMAND.COM from the boot drive to the new disk
/V[:label]	Creates a volume label on the new disk. The label can be as long as 11 characters.
/F:nnnn	Specifies the format of the floppy disk. For 5 1/4-inch drives, the size can be 160K, 180K, 320K, 360K, or 1.2M. For 3 1/2-inch drives, valid sizes are 720K, 1.44M, and 2.88M.
/4	Formats a 5 1/4-inch, 360K, double-sided, double-density floppy disk in a high-density 1.2M drive
/T:nnnn	Specifies the number of tracks (1 to 1,024) per side on the disk to format
/N:nn	Specifies the number of sectors (1 to 64) per track on the disk to format

Obsolete (but still functional) parameters

/1	Formats single-sided disks (5 1/4-inch only)
/8	Formats eight sectors per track (5 1/4-inch only)
/B	Creates dummy system files and reserves room for a DOS version's SYS command to copy actual files later

Undocumented parameters (floppy disks only)

/H	Skips the message `Insert new diskette for drive d: and strike ENTER when ready`
/BACKUP	Skips the message `Insert new diskette for drive d: and press ENTER when ready`
/SELECT	Skips the message `Insert new diskette for drive d: and press ENTER when ready`. Also suppresses the disk space report, the `Format another (Y/N)?` message, and any error messages.
/AUTOTEST	Skips the `Insert new diskette for drive d: and press ENTER when ready` message. Also suppresses the disk space report, the `Format another (Y/N)?`

Notes	
/S	Looks for system files on the default drive in V3.3 or earlier versions; the boot drive is searched in V4.0 and later versions, and COMMAND.COM is copied in V5.0 and later versions
/V	Is assumed in 4.0 and later versions if /V:label is not specified; DOS 3.3 and earlier versions do not support the :label specification with /V
/F	Supported in 4.0 and later versions
/T and /N	Supported in 3.3 and later versions; /T defaults to 80, and /N defaults to 9 in DOS 3.3. No defaults are assumed in 4.0 and later versions; therefore, if one of the parameters is specified, the other must be specified as well
/H	Supported in V3.3 only
/BACKUP, /SELECT, and /AUTOTEST	Supported in V4.0 and later versions

Table A.7 shows the correct FORMAT command parameters to use when you are formatting low-density floppy disks in high-density drives. This table considers all possible permutations of floppy disk types, drive types, and DOS versions.

Table A.7 Formatting Low-Density Floppy Disks in High-Density Drives

DOS version	Drive type	Floppy disk type	Format command
DOS 3.0+	5 1/4-inch, 1.2M	DD 360K	FORMAT d: /4
DOS 3.2+	5 1/4-inch, 1.2M	DD 360K	FORMAT d: /N:9 /T:40
DOS 4.0+	5 1/4-inch, 1.2M	DD 360K	FORMAT d: /F:360
DOS 3.3+	3 1/2-inch, 1.44M	DD 720K	FORMAT d: /N:9 /T:80
DOS 4.0+	3 1/2-inch, 1.44M	DD 720K	FORMAT d: /F:720
DOS 5.0+	3 1/2-inch, 2.88M	HD 1.44M	FORMAT d: /F:1.44

+ = Includes all higher versions
d: = Specifies the drive to format
DD = Double density
HD = High density

Table A.8 shows the default cluster (allocation unit) size selected by DOS for all possible floppy disk formats and hard disk partition sizes.

Table A.8 DOS Disk Default Cluster (Allocation Unit) Sizes

Disk or volume size	Cluster/allocation unit size	FAT type
5 1/4-inch 360K	2 sectors, or 1,024 bytes	12-bit
5 1/4-inch 1.2M	1 sectors, or 512 bytes	12-bit
3 1/2-inch 720K	2 sectors, or 1,024 bytes	12-bit
3 1/2-inch 1.44M	1 sectors, or 512 bytes	12-bit
3 1/2-inch 2.88M	2 sectors, or 1,024 bytes	12-bit
$0M \leq Volume \leq 16M$	8 sectors, or 4,096 bytes	12-bit
$16M \leq Volume \leq 128M$	4 sectors, or 2,048 bytes	16-bit
$128M \leq Volume \leq 256M$	8 sectors, or 4,096 bytes	16-bit
$256M \leq Volume \leq 512M$	16 sectors, or 8,192 bytes	16-bit
$512M < Volume \leq 1,024M$	32 sectors, or 16,384 bytes	16-bit
$1,024M < Volume \leq 2,048M$	64 sectors, or 32,768 bytes	16-bit

K = 1,024 bytes
M = 1,048,576 bytes

Troubleshooting Error Codes

The following sections list a variety of system error codes. Included are manufacturer test POST codes, display POST error codes, and advanced diagnostics error codes. This section includes also a detailed list of SCSI interface error codes, which can be very helpful in troubleshooting SCSI devices.

ROM BIOS Port 80h Power-On Self Test (POST) Codes

When the ROM BIOS is performing the Power-On Self Test, in most systems the results of these tests are sent to I/O Port 80h so that they can be monitored by a special diagnostics card. These tests sometimes are called *manufacturing tests* because they were designed into the system for testing systems on the assembly line without a video display attached. The POST-code cards have a 2-digit hexadecimal display used to report the number of the currently executing test routine. Before executing each test, a hexadecimal numeric code is sent to the port, and then the test is run. If the test fails and locks up the machine, the hexadecimal code of the last test being executed remains on the card's display.

Many tests are executed in a system before the video display card is enabled, especially if the display is EGA or VGA. Therefore, many errors can occur that would lock up the system before the system could possibly display an error code through the video system. To most normal troubleshooting procedures, a system with this type of problem (such as a memory failure in Bank 0) would appear completely "dead." By using one of the commercially available POST-code cards, however, you can correctly diagnose the problem.

These codes are completely BIOS dependent because the card does nothing but display the codes sent to it. Some BIOSes have better Power-On Self Test procedures and therefore send more informative codes. Some BIOS versions also send audio codes that can be used to help diagnose such problems. The Phoenix BIOS, for example, sends the most informative set of audio codes, which eliminate the need for a Port 80h POST card. Tables A.9, A.10, and A.11 list the Port 80h codes and audio codes sent by a number of different BIOS manufacturers and versions.

Table A.9 AMI BIOS Audio POST Codes

Beep code	Fatal errors
1 short	DRAM refresh failure
2 short	Parity circuit failure
3 short	Base 64K RAM failure
4 short	System timer failure
5 short	Processor failure
6 short	Keyboard controller Gate A20 error
7 short	Virtual mode exception error
8 short	Display memory R/W test failure
9 short	ROM BIOS checksum failure

Beep code	Nonfatal errors
1 long, 3 short	Conventional/extended memory failure
1 long, 8 short	Display/retrace test failed

Table A.10 AMI 286 BIOS Plus Port 80h POST Codes

Checkpoint	Meaning
01h	NMI disabled and 286 register test about to start
02h	286 register test over
03h	ROM checksum OK
04h	8259 initialization OK
05h	CMOS pending interrupt disabled
06h	Video disabled and system timer counting OK
07h	CH-2 of 8253 test OK
08h	CH-2 of delta count test OK
09h	CH-1 delta count test OK
0Ah	CH-0 delta count test OK
0Bh	Parity status cleared
0Ch	Refresh and system timer OK
0Dh	Refresh link toggling OK
0Eh	Refresh period On/Off 50% OK
10h	Confirmed refresh On and about to start 64K memory
11h	Address line test OK
12h	64K base memory test OK
13h	Interrupt vectors initialized
14h	8042 keyboard controller test OK
15h	CMOS read/write test OK
16h	CMOS checksum/battery check OK
17h	Monochrome mode set OK
18h	Color mode set OK
19h	About to look for optional video ROM
1Ah	Optional video ROM control OK
1Bh	Display memory R/W test OK
1Ch	Display memory R/W test for alternate display OK
1Dh	Video retrace check OK
1Eh	Global equipment byte set for video OK
1Fh	Mode set call for Mono/Color OK
20h	Video test OK
21h	Video display OK
22h	Power-on message display OK
30h	Virtual mode memory test about to begin
31h	Virtual mode memory test started
32h	Processor in virtual mode
33h	Memory address line test in progress
34h	Memory address line test in progress
35h	Memory below IMB calculated
36h	Memory size computation OK
37h	Memory test in progress
38h	Memory initialization over below IMB
39h	Memory initialization over above IMB
3Ah	Display memory size
3Bh	About to start below 1M memory test
3Ch	Memory test below 1M OK

Checkpoint	Meaning
3Dh	Memory test above 1M OK
3Eh	About to go to real mode (shutdown)
3Fh	Shutdown successful and entered in real mode
40h	About to disable gate A-20 address line
41h	Gate A-20 line disabled successfully
42h	About to start DMA controller test
4Eh	Address line test OK
4Fh	Processor in real mode after shutdown
50h	DMA page register test OK
51h	DMA unit-1 base register test about to start
52h	DMA unit-1 channel OK, about to begin CH-2
53h	DMA CH-2 base register test OK
54h	About to test f/f latch for unit-1
55h	f/f latch test both unit OK
56h	DMA unit 1 and 2 programmed OK
57h	8259 initialization over
58h	8259 mask register check OK
59h	Master 8259 mask register OK, about to start slave
5Ah	About to check timer and keyboard interrupt level
5Bh	Timer interrupt OK
5Ch	About to test keyboard interrupt
5Dh	ERROR! timer/keyboard interrupt not in proper level
5Eh	8259 interrupt controller error
5Fh	8259 interrupt controller test OK
70h	Start of keyboard test
71h	Keyboard BAT test OK
72h	Keyboard test OK
73h	Keyboard global data initialization OK
74h	Floppy setup about to start
75h	Floppy setup OK
76h	Hard disk setup about to start
77h	Hard disk setup OK
79h	About to initialize timer data area
7Ah	Verify CMOS battery power
7Bh	CMOS battery verification done
7Dh	About to analyze diagnostics test result for memory
7Eh	CMOS memory size update OK
7Fh	About to check optional ROM C000:0.
80h	Keyboard sensed to enable SETUP
81h	Optional ROM control OK
82h	Printer global data initialization OK
83h	RS-232 global data initialization OK
84h	80287 check/test OK
85h	About to display soft error message
86h	About to give control to system ROM E000.0
87h	System ROM E000.0 check over
00h	Control given to Int 19, boot loader

Table A.11 AMI Color BIOS Port 80h POST Codes

Port 80h code	Test description
01h	Processor register test about to start, and NMI to be disabled
02h	NMI is disabled; power-on delay starting
03h	Power-on delay complete; any initialization before keyboard BAT is in progress
04h	Any initialization before keyboard BAT is complete; reading keyboard SYS bit to check soft reset/power-on
05h	Soft reset/power-on determined; going to enable ROM (that is, disable shadow RAM/cache if any)
06h	ROM enabled; calculating ROM BIOS checksum and waiting for KB controller input buffer to be free
07h	ROM BIOS checksum passed, KB controller I/B free; going to issue BAT command to keyboard controller
08h	BAT command to keyboard controller issued; going to verify BAT command
09h	Keyboard controller BAT result verified; keyboard command byte to be written next
0Ah	Keyboard-command byte code issued; going to write command byte data
0Bh	Keyboard controller command byte written; going to issue Pin-23,24 blocking/unblocking command
0Ch	Pin-23,24 of keyboard controller blocked/unblocked; NOP command of keyboard controller to be issued next
0Dh	NOP command processing done; CMOS shutdown register test to be done next
0Eh	CMOS shutdown register R/W test passed; going to calculate CMOS checksum and update DIAG byte
0Fh	CMOS checksum calculation done and DIAG byte written; CMOS initialization to begin (If INIT CMOS IN EVERY BOOT is set.)
10h	CMOS initialization done (if any); CMOS status register about to initialize for date and time
11h	CMOS status register initialized; going to disable DMA and interrupt controllers
12h	DMA controller #1,#2, interrupt controller #1,#2 disabled; about to disable video display and init port-B
13h	Video display is disabled and port-B initialized; chipset init/auto memory detection to begin
14h	Chipset initialization/auto memory detection over; 8254 timer test about to start
15h	CH-2 timer test halfway; 8254 CH-2 timer test to be complete
16h	Ch-2 timer test over; 8254 CH-1 timer test to be complete
17h	CH-1 timer test over; 8254 CH-0 timer test to be complete
18h	CH-0 timer test over; about to start memory refresh

Port 80h code	Test description
19h	Memory refresh started; memory refresh test to be done next
1Ah	Memory refresh line is toggling; going to check 15 micro-second On/Off time
1Bh	Memory refresh period 30 micro-second test complete; base 64K memory test about to start
20h	Base 64K memory test started; address line test to be done next
21h	Address line test passed; going to do toggle parity
22h	Toggle parity over; going for sequential data R/W test
23h	Base 64K sequential data R/W test passed; any setup before interrupt vector initialization about to start
24h	Setup required before vector initialization complete; interrupt vector initialization about to begin
25h	Interrupt vector initialization done; going to read I/O port of 8042 for turbo switch (if any)
26h	I/O port of 8042 is read; going to initialize global data for turbo switch
27h	Global data initialization is over; any initialization after interrupt vector to be done next
28h	Initialization after interrupt vector is complete; going for monochrome mode setting
29h	Monochrome mode setting is done; going for color mode setting
2Ah	Color mode setting is done; about to go for toggle parity before optional ROM test
2Bh	Toggle parity over; about to give control for any setup required before optional video ROM check
2Ch	Processing before video ROM control is done; about to look for optional video ROM and give control
2Dh	Optional video ROM control is done; about to give control to do any processing after video ROM returns control
2Eh	Return from processing after the video ROM control; if EGA/VGA not found, then do display memory R/W test
2Fh	EGA/VGA not found; display memory R/W test about to begin
30h	Display memory R/W test passed; about to look for the retrace checking
31h	Display memory R/W test or retrace checking failed; about to do alternate display memory R/W test
32h	Alternate display memory R/W test passed; about to look for the alternate display retrace checking
33h	Video display checking over; verification of display type with switch setting and actual card to begin
34h	Verification of display adapter done; display mode to be set next

continues

Table A.11 Continued

Port 80h code	Test description
35h	Display mode set complete; BIOS ROM data area about to be checked
36h	BIOS ROM data area check over; going to set cursor for power-on message
37h	Cursor setting for power-on message ID complete; going to display the power-on message
38h	Power-on message display complete; going to read new cursor position
39h	New cursor position read and saved; going to display the reference string
3Ah	Reference string display is over; going to display the Hit <Esc> message
3Bh	Hit <Esc> message displayed; virtual mode memory test about to start
40h	Preparation for virtual mode test started; going to verify from video memory
41h	Returned after verifying from display memory; going to prepare the descriptor tables
42h	Descriptor tables prepared; going to enter virtual mode for memory test
43h	Entered in virtual mode; going to enable interrupts for diagnostics mode
44h	Interrupts enabled (if diagnostics switch is on); going to initialize data to check memory wrap-around at 0:0
45h	Data initialized; going to check for memory wrap-around at 0:0 and find total system memory size
46h	Memory wrap-around test done; memory-size calculation over; about to go for writing patterns to test memory
47h	Pattern to be test-written in extended memory; going to write patterns in base 640K memory
48h	Patterns written in base memory; going to determine amount of memory below 1M memory
49h	Amount of memory below 1M found and verified; going to determine amount of memory above 1M memory
4Ah	Amount of memory above 1M found and verified; going for BIOS ROM data area check
4Bh	BIOS ROM data area check over; going to check <Esc> and clear memory below 1M for soft reset
4Ch	Memory below 1M cleared (Soft Reset); going to clear memory above 1M
4Dh	Memory above 1M cleared (Soft Reset); going to save the memory size
4Eh	Memory test started (No Soft Reset); about to display the first 64K memory test

Port 80h code	Test description
4Fh	Memory size display started; will be updated during memory test; going for sequential and random memory test
50h	Memory test below 1M complete; going to adjust memory size for relocation and shadow
51h	Memory size adjusted due to relocation/shadow; memory test above 1M to follow
52h	Memory test above 1M complete; going to prepare to go back to real mode
53h	CPU registers are saved including memory size; going to enter in real mode
54h	Shutdown successful, CPU in real mode; going to restore registers saved during preparation for shutdown
55h	Registers restored; going to disable Gate A20 address line
56h	A20 address line disable successful; BIOS ROM data area about to be checked
57h	BIOS ROM data area check halfway; BIOS ROM data area check to be complete
58h	BIOS ROM data area check over; going to clear `Hit <ESC>` message
59h	`Hit <ESC>` message cleared; `<WAIT...>` message displayed; about to start DMA and interrupt controller test
60h	DMA page-register test passed; about to verify from display memory
61h	Display memory verification over; about to go for DMA #1 base register test
62h	DMA #1 base register test passed; about to go for DMA #2 base register test
63h	DMA #2 base register test passed; about to go for BIOS ROM data area check
64h	BIOS ROM data area check halfway; BIOS ROM data area check to be complete
65h	BIOS ROM data area check over; about to program DMA unit 1 and 2
66h	DMA unit 1 and 2 programming over; about to initialize 8259 interrupt controller
67h	8259 initialization over; about to start keyboard test
80h	Keyboard test started, clearing output buffer, checking for stuck key; about to issue keyboard reset command
81h	Keyboard reset error/stuck key found; about to issue keyboard controller interface test command
82h	Keyboard controller interface test over; about to write command byte and initialize circular buffer
83h	Command byte written, global data initialization done; about to check for lock-key
84h	Lock-key checking over; about to check for memory-size mismatch with CMOS

continues

Table A.11 Continued

Port 80h code	Test description
85h	Memory size check done; about to display soft error and check for password or bypass setup
86h	Password checked; about to do programming before setup
87h	Programming before setup complete; going to CMOS setup program
88h	Returned from CMOS setup program and screen is cleared; about to do programming after setup
89h	Programming after setup complete; going to display power-on screen message
8Ah	First screen message displayed; about to display <WAIT...> message
8Bh	<WAIT...> message displayed; about to do main and video BIOS shadow
8Ch	Main and video BIOS shadow successful; Setup options programming after CMOS setup about to start
8Dh	Setup options are programmed, mouse check and initialization to be done next
8Eh	Mouse check and initialization complete; going for hard disk, floppy reset
8Fh	Floppy check returns that floppy is to be initialized; floppy setup to follow
90h	Floppy setup is over; test for hard disk presence to be done
91h	Hard disk presence test over; hard disk setup to follow
92h	Hard disk setup complete; about to go for BIOS ROM data area check
93h	BIOS ROM data area check halfway; BIOS ROM data area check to be complete
94h	BIOS ROM data area check over; going to set base and extended memory size
95h	Memory size adjusted due to mouse and hard disk type 47 support; going to verify display memory
96h	Returned after verifying display memory; going to do initialization before C800 optional ROM control
97h	Any initialization before C800 optional ROM control is over; optional ROM check and control to be done next
98h	Optional ROM control is done; about to give control to do any required processing after optional ROM returns control
99h	Any initialization required after optional ROM test over; going to set up timer data area and printer base address
9Ah	Return after setting timer and printer base address; going to set the RS-232 base address

Port 80h code	Test description
9Bh	Returned after RS-232 base address; going to do any initialization before coprocessor test
9Ch	Required initialization before coprocessor is over; going to initialize the coprocessor next
9Dh	Coprocessor initialized; going to do any initialization after coprocessor test
9Eh	Initialization after coprocessor test is complete; going to check extended keyboard, keyboard ID, and Num Lock
9Fh	Extended keyboard check is done, ID flag set, Num Lock on/off; keyboard ID command to be issued
A0h	Keyboard ID command issued; keyboard ID flag to be reset
A1h	Keyboard ID flag reset; cache memory test to follow
A2h	Cache memory test over; going to display any soft errors
A3h	Soft error display complete; going to set the keyboard typematic rate
A4h	Keyboard typematic rate set; going to program memory wait states
A5h	Memory wait states programming over; screen to be cleared next
A6h	Screen cleared; going to enable parity and NMI
A7h	NMI and parity enabled; going to do any initialization required before giving control to optional ROM at E000
A8h	Initialization before E000 ROM control over; E000 ROM to get control next
A9h	Returned from E000 ROM control; going to do any initialization required after E000 optional ROM control
AAh	Initialization after E000 optional ROM control is over; going to display the system configuration
00h	System configuration is displayed; going to give control to Int 19h boot loader

Award BIOS Port 80h POST Codes

Table A.12 provides information on the majority of Award POST codes displayed during the POST sequence. These POST codes are output to I/O port address 80h. Although this chart specifically lists all the POST codes output by the Award Modular BIOS, version 3.1, the codes are valid also for these Award Modular BIOS types:

    PC/XT Version 3.0 and greater
    AT Version 3.02 and greater

Not all these POST codes apply to all of the BIOS types. Note that the POST tests do not necessarily execute in the numeric order shown: The POST sequence may vary depending on the BIOS.

Table A.12 Award BIOS Port 80h POST Codes

Port 80h code	Code meaning
01h	Processor Test 1. Processor status verification. Tests the following processor-status flags; carry, zero, sign, and overflow. The BIOS sets each flag, verifies that they are set, and turns each flag off and verifies that it is off. Failure of a flag causes a fatal error.
02h	Determine POST Type. This test determines whether the status of the system is manufacturing or normal. The status can be set by a physical jumper on some motherboards. If the status is normal, the POST continues through and, assuming no errors, boot is attempted. If manufacturing POST is installed, POST is run in continuous loop, and boot is not attempted.
03h	8042 Keyboard Controller. Tests controller by sending TEST_KBRD command (AAh) and verifying that controller reads command.
04h	8042 Keyboard Controller. Verifies that keyboard controller returned AAh, sent in test 3.
05h	Get Manufacturing Status. The last test in the manufacturing cycle. If test 2 found the status to be manufacturing, this POST triggers a reset and POSTs 1 through 5 are repeated continuously.
06h	Initialize Chips. POST 06h performs these functions: disables color and mono video, disables parity circuits, disables DMA (8237) chips, resets math co-processor, initializes timer 1 (8255), clears DMA chip, clears all page registers, and clears CMOS shutdown byte.
07h	Processor Test 2. Reads, writes, and verifies all CPU registers except SS, SP, and BP with data pattern FF and 00.
08h	Initialize CMOS Timer. Updates timer cycle normally.
09h	EPROM Checksum. Checksums EPROM; test failed if sum not equal to 0. Also checksums sign-on message.
0Ah	Initialize Video Interface. Initializes video controller register 6845 to the following:

Port 80h code	Code meaning
	80 characters per row 25 rows per screen 8/14 scan lines per row for mono/color First scan line of cursor 6/11 Last scan line of cursor 7/12 Reset display offset to 0
0Bh	Test Timer (8254) Channel 0. These three timer tests verify that the 8254 timer chip is functioning properly.
0Ch	Test Timer (8254) Channel 1.
0Dh	Test Timer (8254) Channel 2.
0Eh	Test CMOS Shutdown Byte. Uses a walking bit algorithm to check interface to CMOS circuit.
0Fh	Test Extended CMOS. On motherboards with chipsets that support extended CMOS configurations, such as Chips & Technologies, the BIOS tables of CMOS information are used to configure the chip set. These chip sets have an extended storage mechanism that enables the user to save a desired system configuration after the power is turned off. A checksum is used to verify the validity of the extended storage and, if valid, permit the information to be loaded into extended CMOS RAM.
10h	Test DMA Channel 0. These three functions initialize the DMA (direct memory access) chip and then test the chip using an AA, 55, FF, 00 pattern. Port addresses are used to check the address circuit to DMA page registers.
11h	DMA Channel 1.
12h	DMA Page Registers.
13h	Keyboard Controller. Tests keyboard controller interface.
14h	Test Memory Refresh. RAM must be refreshed periodically to keep the memory from decaying. This function ensures that the memory-refresh function is working properly.
15h	First 64K of System Memory. An extensive parity test is performed on the first 64K of system memory. This memory is used by the BIOS.
16h	Interrupt Vector Table. Sets up and loads interrupt vector tables in memory for use by the 8259 PIC chip.

continues

Table A.12 Continued

Port 80h code	Code meaning
17h	Video I/O Operations. This function initializes the video, either CGA, MDA, EGA, or VGA. If a CGA or MDA adapter is installed, the video is initialized by the system BIOS. If the system BIOS detects an EGA or VGA adapter, the option ROM BIOS installed on the video adapter is used to initialize and set up the video.
18h	Video Memory. Tests memory for CGA and MDA video boards. This test is not performed by the system BIOS on EGA or VGA video adapters—the board's own EGA or VGA BIOS ensures that it is functioning properly.
19h	Test 8259 Mask Bits - Channel 1. These two tests verify 8259 masked interrupts by alternately turning the interrupt lines off and on. Unsuccessful completion generates a fatal error.
1Ah	8259 Mask Bits - Channel 2.
1Bh	CMOS Battery Level. Verifies that the battery status bit is set to 1. A 0 value can indicate a bad battery or some other problem, such as bad CMOS.
1Ch	CMOS Checksum. This function tests the CMOS checksum data (located at 2Eh, and 2Fh) and extended CMOS checksum, if present, to be sure that they are valid.
1Dh	Configuration from CMOS. If the CMOS checksum is good, the values are used to configure the system.
1Eh	System Memory. The system memory size is determined by writing to addresses from 0K to 640K, starting at 0 and continuing until an address does not respond. Memory size value then is compared to the CMOS value to ensure that they are the same. If they are different, a flag is set, and, at the end of POST an error message is displayed.
1Fh	Found System Memory. Tests memory from 64K to the top of the memory found by writing the pattern FFAA and 5500, and then reading the pattern back, byte by byte, and verifying that it is correct.
20h	Stuck 8259 Interrupt Bits. These three tests verify the functionality of the 8259 interrupt controller.
21h	Stuck NMI Bits (Parity or I/O Channel Check).
22h	8259 Function.

Port 80h code	Code meaning
23h	Protected Mode. Verifies protected mode: 8086 virtual mode as well as 8086 page mode. Protected mode ensures that any data about to be written to extended memory (above 1M) is checked to ensure that it is suitable for storage there.
24h	Extended Memory. This function sizes memory above 1M by writing to addresses starting at 1M and continuing to 16M on 286 and 386SX systems, and to 64M on 386 systems until there is no response. This process determines the total extended memory, which is compared with CMOS to ensure that the values are the same. If the values are different, a flag is set and at the end of POST an error message is displayed.
25h	Found Extended Memory. This function tests extended memory using virtual 8086 paging mode and writing an FFFF, AA55, 0000 pattern.
26h	Protected Mode Exceptions. This function tests other aspects of protected mode operations.
27h	Cache Control or Shadow RAM. Tests for shadow RAM and cache controller (386 and 486 only) functionality. Systems with CGA and MDA adapters indicate that video shadow RAM is enabled, even though there is no BIOS ROM to shadow (this is normal).
28h	8242. Optional Intel 8242/8248 keyboard controller detection and support.
29h	Reserved.
2Ah	Initialize Keyboard. Initialize keyboard controller.
2Bh	Floppy Drive and Controller. Initializes floppy disk drive controller and any drives present.
2Ch	Detect and Initialize Serial Ports. Initializes any serial ports present.
2Dh	Detect and Initialize Parallel Ports. Initializes any parallel ports present.
2Eh	Initialize Hard Drive and Controller. Initializes hard drive controller and any drives present.
2Fh	Detect and Initialize Math Coprocessor. Initializes math coprocessor.
30h	Reserved.
31h	Detect and Initialize Option ROMs. Initializes any option ROMs present from C800h to EFFFh.

continues

Table A.12 Continued	
Port 80h code	**Code meaning**
3Bh	Initialize Secondary Cache with OPTi chipset. Initializes secondary cache controller for systems based on the OPTi chipset (486 only).
CAh	Micronics Cache Initialization. Detects and initializes Micronics cache controller if present.
CCh	NMI Handler Shutdown. Detects untrapped Non-Maskable Interrupts during boot.
EEh	Unexpected Processor Exception.
FFh	Boot Attempt. When the POST is complete, if all the system components and peripherals are initialized, and if no error flags were set (such as memory size error), then the system attempts to boot.

Phoenix BIOS Audio and Port 80h POST Codes

Table A.13 is a list of POST fatal errors that may be reported by the Phoenix BIOS. Table A.14 is a list of nonfatal errors. Fatal errors halt the system and prevent any further processing from occurring; nonfatal errors are less severe.

Table A.13 Phoenix BIOS Fatal System-Board Errors		
Beep code	**Code at Port 80h**	**Description**
None	01h	CPU register test in progress
1-1-3	02h	CMOS write/read failure
1-1-4	03h	ROM BIOS checksum failure
1-2-1	04h	Programmable interval timer failure
1-2-2	05h	DMA initialization failure
1-2-3	06h	DMA page register write/read failure
1-3-1	08h	RAM refresh verification failure
None	09h	First 64K RAM test in progress
1-3-3	0Ah	First 64K RAM chip or data line failure, multibit

Beep code	Code at Port 80h	Description
1-3-4	0Bh	First 64K RAM odd/even logic failure
1-4-1	0Ch	Address line failure first 64K RAM
1-4-2	0Dh	Parity failure first 64K RAM
2-1-1	10h	Bit 0 first 64K RAM failure
2-1-2	11h	Bit 1 first 64K RAM failure
2-1-3	12h	Bit 2 first 64K RAM failure
2-1-4	13h	Bit 3 first 64K RAM failure
2-2-1	14h	Bit 4 first 64K RAM failure
2-2-2	15h	Bit 5 first 64K RAM failure
2-2-3	16h	Bit 6 first 64K RAM failure
2-2-4	17h	Bit 7 first 64K RAM failure
2-3-1	18h	Bit 8 first 64K RAM failure
2-3-2	19h	Bit 9 first 64K RAM failure
2-3-3	1Ah	Bit 10 first 64K RAM failure
2-3-4	1Bh	Bit 11 first 64K RAM failure
2-4-1	1Ch	Bit 12 first 64K RAM failure
2-4-2	1Dh	Bit 13 first 64K RAM failure
2-4-3	1Eh	Bit 14 first 64K RAM failure
2-4-4	1Fh	Bit 15 first 64K RAM failure
3-1-1	20h	Slave DMA register failure
3-1-2	21h	Master DMA register failure
3-1-3	22h	Master interrupt mask register failure
3-1-4	23h	Slave interrupt mask register failure
None	25h	Interrupt vector loading in progress
3-2-4	27h	Keyboard controller test failure
None	28h	CMOS power failure/checksum calculation in progress
None	29h	Screen configuration validation in progress
3-3-4	2Bh	Screen initialization failure
3-4-1	2Ch	Screen retrace failure
3-4-2	2Dh	Search for video ROM in progress
None	2Eh	Screen running with video ROM
None	30h	Screen operable
None	31h	Monochrome monitor operable
None	32h	Color monitor (40 column) operable
None	33h	Color monitor (80 column) operable

Table A.14 Nonfatal System-Board Errors

Beep code	Code at Port 80h	Description
4-2-1	34h	Timer tick interrupt test in progress or failure
4-2-2	35h	Shutdown test in progress or failure
4-2-3	36h	Gate A20 failure

continues

Table A.14 Continued		
Beep code	**Code at Port 80h**	**Description**
4-2-4	37h	Unexpected interrupt in protected mode
4-3-1	38h	RAM test in progress or address failure > FFFFh
4-3-3	3Ah	Interval timer Channel 2 test or failure
4-3-4	3Bh	Time-of-day clock test or failure
4-4-1	3Ch	Serial port test or failure
4-4-2	3Dh	Parallel port test or failure
4-4-3	3Eh	Math coprocessor test or failure
low 1-1-2	41h	System-board select failure
low 1-1-3	42h	Extended CMOS RAM failure

low *means that a lower-pitched beep precedes the other tones.*

IBM POST and Diagnostics Display Error Codes

When an IBM or compatible system is first powered on, the system runs a Power-On Self Test (POST). If errors are encountered during the POST, the errors are displayed in the form of a code number and possibly some additional text. When you are running the IBM Advanced Diagnostics, which you can purchase from IBM or which is included on many of the PS/2 Reference Diskettes, similar codes are displayed if errors are encountered during the tests. IBM has developed a system in which the first part of the error code indicates the device the error involves, and the last part indicates the exact error meaning. One of the biggest problems with these error codes is that IBM does not publish a complete list of the errors in any single publication; instead, it details specific error codes in many different publications. I have researched these codes for many years; tables A.15 and A.16 represent all the codes I have found meanings for. These codes have been selected from a number of sources, including all of IBM's technical-reference and hardware-maintenance and service manuals.

When diagnostics are run, any code ending in 00 indicates that the particular test has passed. For example, an error code of 1700 indicates that the hard disk diagnostics tests have passed.

After completing the Power-On Self Test (POST), an audio code indicates either a normal condition or that one of several errors has occurred. Table A.15 lists the audio codes for IBM systems, and table A.16 lists the IBM POST and diagnostics error codes.

Table A.15 IBM POST Audio Error Codes

Audio code	Sound graph	Fault domain
1 short beep	•	Normal POST - system OK
2 short beeps	••	POST error - error code on CRT
No beep		Power supply, system board
Continuous beep	———	Power supply, system board
Repeating short beeps	••••••	Power supply, system board
1 long, 1 short beep	-•	System board
1 long, 2 short beeps	-••	Display adapter (MDA, CGA)
1 long, 3 short beeps	-•••	Enhanced Graphics Adapter (EGA)
3 long beeps	—	3270 keyboard card

Table A.16 IBM POST and Diagnostics Error-Code List

Code	Description
1xx	System-board errors
101	System-board interrupt failure
102	System-board timer failure
102	PS/2; real-time clock (RTC)/64 byte CMOS RAM test failure
103	System-board timer interrupt failure
103	PS/2; 2K CMOS RAM extension test failure
104	System-board protected mode failure
105	System-board 8042 Keyboard Controller command failure
106	System-board converting logic test failure
107	System-board hot Non-Maskable Interrupt (NMI) test failure
108	System-board timer bus test failure
109	System-board memory select error
110	PS/2 system-board parity check error (PARITY CHECK 1)
111	PS/2 I/O channel (bus) parity check error (PARITY CHECK 2)
112	PS/2 Micro Channel Arbitration error; watchdog time-out
113	PS/2 Micro Channel Arbitration error; DMA arbitration time-out
114	PS/2 external ROM checksum error
115	Cache parity error
116	386 16/32-bit test failure
121	Unexpected hardware interrupts occurred
131	PC system-board Cassette port wrap test failure
131	Direct memory access (DMA) compatibility registers error
132	Direct memory access (DMA) extended registers error
133	Direct memory access (DMA) verify logic error
134	Direct memory access (DMA) arbitration logic error
151	PC Convertible; real-time clock RAM failed
151	Battery or CMOS RAM failure

continues

Table A.16 Continued

Code	Description
152	PC Convertible; real-time clock failed
152	Real-time clock or CMOS RAM failure
160	PS/2 system-board ID not recognized
161	CMOS configuration empty (dead battery)
162	CMOS checksum error
163	CMOS error; date and time not set
164	Memory size error; CMOS setting does not match memory
165	PS/2 Micro Channel adapter ID and CMOS mismatch
166	PS/2 Micro Channel adapter time-out error
167	PS/2 CMOS clock not updating
168	CMOS configuration error; math coprocessor
170	PC Convertible; LCD not in use when suspended
171	PC Convertible; base 128K checksum failure
172	PC Convertible; diskette active when suspended
173	PC Convertible; real-time clock RAM verification error
174	PC Convertible; LCD configuration changed
175	PC Convertible; LCD alternate mode failed
191	82385 cache controller test failure
194	System-board memory error
199	User indicated INSTALLED DEVICES list is not correct
2xx	Memory (RAM) errors
201	Memory test failure, error location may be displayed
202	Memory address error; lines 00-15
203	Memory address error; lines 16-23 (ISA) or 16-31 (MCA)
204	Memory remapped (run diagnostics again)
205	Base 128K memory error; memory remapped
207	ROM failure
211	PS/2 memory; base 64K on system-board failed
215	PS/2 memory; base 64K on daughter/SIMM 2 failed
216	PS/2 memory; base 64K on daughter/SIMM 1 failed
221	PS/2 memory; ROM to RAM copy failed (ROM shadowing)
225	PS/2 memory; wrong-speed memory on system board
231	2/4-16MB Enhanced 386 memory adapter; memory module 1 failed
241	2/4-16MB Enhanced 386 memory adapter; memory module 2 failed
251	2/4-16MB Enhanced 386 memory adapter; memory module 3 failed
3xx	Keyboard errors
301	Keyboard reset or stuck key failure (SS 301, SS = Scan Code in hex)
302	System unit keylock is locked
302	User indicated keyboard test error
303	Keyboard or system-board error; keyboard controller failure
304	Keyboard or system-board error; keyboard clock high
305	Keyboard +5v error; PS/2 keyboard fuse (on system board) error
341	Keyboard error

Code	Description
342	Keyboard cable error
343	Keyboard LED card or cable failure
365	Keyboard LED card or cable failure
366	Keyboard interface cable failure
367	Keyboard LED card or cable failure
4xx	Monochrome Display Adapter (MDA) errors
4xx	PS/2 system-board parallel port errors
401	Monochrome memory, horizontal sync frequency, or video test failure
401	PS/2 system-board parallel port failure
408	User indicated display attributes failure
416	User indicated character set failure
424	User indicated 80×25 mode failure
432	Parallel port test failure; Monochrome Display Adapter
5xx	Color Graphics Adapter (CGA) errors
501	CGA memory, horizontal sync frequency, or video test failure
503	CGA adapter controller failed
508	User indicated display attribute failure
516	User indicated character set failure
524	User indicated 80×25 mode failure
532	User indicated 40×25 mode failure
540	User indicated 320×200 graphics mode failure
548	User indicated 640×200 graphics mode failure
556	User indicated light-pen test failed
564	User indicated paging test failure
6xx	Floppy drive/controller errors
601	Floppy drive/controller Power-On Self Test failure
602	Diskette boot sector is not valid
603	Diskette size error
606	Diskette verify test failure
607	Write protect error
608	Drive command error
610	Diskette initialization failure; track 0 bad
611	Drive time-out error
612	Controller chip (NEC) error
613	Direct memory access (DMA) error
614	Direct memory access (DMA) boundary overrun error
615	Drive index timing error
616	Drive speed error
621	Drive seek error
622	Drive cyclic redundancy check (CRC) error
623	Sector not found error
624	Address mark error
625	Controller chip (NEC) seek error
626	Diskette data compare error
627	Diskette change error
628	Diskette removed
630	Index stuck high; Drive A:

continues

Table A.16 Continued

Code	Description
631	Index stuck low; Drive A:
632	Track 0 stuck off; Drive A:
633	Track 0 stuck on; Drive A:
640	Index stuck high; Drive B:
641	Index stuck low; Drive B:
642	Track 0 stuck off; Drive B:
643	Track 0 stuck on; Drive B:
645	No index pulse
646	Drive track 0 detection failed
647	No transitions on read data line
648	Format test failed
649	Incorrect media type in drive
650	Drive speed error
651	Format failure
652	Verify failure
653	Read failure
654	Write failure
655	Controller error
656	Drive failure
657	Write protect stuck protected
658	Changeline stuck changed
659	Write protect stuck unprotected
660	Changeline stuck unchanged
7xx	Math coprocessor errors
701	Math coprocessor presence/initialization error
702	Exception errors test failure
703	Rounding test failure
704	Arithmetic test 1 failure
705	Arithmetic test 2 failure
706	Arithmetic test 3 (80387 only) failure
707	Combination test failure
708	Integer load/store test failure
709	Equivalent expressions errors
710	Exception (interrupt) errors
711	Save state (FSAVE) errors
712	Protected mode test failure
713	Special test (voltage/temperature sensitivity) failure
9xx	Parallel printer adapter errors
901	Printer adapter data register latch error
902	Printer adapter control register latch error
903	Printer adapter register address decode error
904	Printer adapter address decode error
910	Status line(s) wrap connector error
911	Status line bit 8 wrap error
912	Status line bit 7 wrap error
913	Status line bit 6 wrap error
914	Status line bit 5 wrap error
915	Status line bit 4 wrap error
916	Printer adapter interrupt wrap error

Code	Description
917	Unexpected printer adapter interrupt
92x	Feature register error
10xx	Alternate parallel printer adapter errors
1001	Printer adapter data register latch error
1002	Printer adapter control register latch error
1003	Printer adapter register address decode error
1004	Printer adapter address decode error
1010	Status line(s) wrap connector error
1011	Status line bit 8 wrap error
1012	Status line bit 7 wrap error
1013	Status line bit 6 wrap error
1014	Status line bit 5 wrap error
1015	Status line bit 4 wrap error
1016	Printer adapter interrupt wrap error
1017	Unexpected printer adapter interrupt
102x	Feature register error
11xx	Primary Async communications (serial port COM1:) errors
1101	16450/16550 chip error
1101	PC Convertible internal modem 8250 baud generator test failed
1102	Card selected feedback error
1102	PC Convertible internal modem test failed
1103	Port 102h register test failure
1103	PC Convertible internal modem dial tone test 1 failed
1104	PC Convertible internal modem dial tone test 2 failed
1106	Serial option cannot be put to sleep
1107	Cable error
1108	Interrupt request (IRQ) 3 error
1109	Interrupt request (IRQ) 4 error
1110	16450/16550 chip register failure
1111	Internal wrap test of 16450/16550 chip modem control line failure
1112	External wrap test of 16450/16550 chip modem control line failure
1113	16450/16550 chip transmit error
1114	16450/16550 chip receive error
1115	16450/16550 chip receive error; data not equal to transmit data
1116	16450/16550 chip interrupt function error
1117	16450/16550 chip baud rate test failure
1118	16450/16550 chip receive external data wrap test failure
1119	16550 chip first-in first-out (FIFO) buffer failure
1120	Interrupt enable register error; all bits cannot be set
1121	Interrupt enable register error; all bits cannot be reset
1122	Interrupt pending; stuck on
1123	Interrupt ID register; stuck on
1124	Modem control register error; all bits cannot be set
1125	Modem control register error; all bits cannot be reset
1126	Modem status register error; all bits cannot be set
1127	Modem status register error; all bits cannot be reset

continues

Table A.16 Continued

Code	Description
1128	Interrupt ID error
1129	Cannot force overrun error
1130	No modem status interrupt
1131	Invalid interrupt pending
1132	No data ready
1133	No data available interrupt
1134	No transmit holding interrupt
1135	No interrupts
1136	No received sine status interrupt
1137	No receive data available
1138	Transmit holding register not empty
1139	No modem status interrupt
1140	Transmit holding register not empty
1141	No interrupts
1142	No interrupt 4
1143	No interrupt 3
1144	No data transferred
1145	Maximum baud rate error
1146	Minimum baud rate error
1148	Time-out error
1149	Invalid data returned
1150	Modem status register error
1151	No data set ready and delta data set ready
1152	No data set ready
1153	No delta data set ready
1154	Modem status register not clear
1155	No clear to send and delta clear to send
1156	No clear to send
1157	No delta clear to send
12xx	Alternate Async Communications (Serial COM2:, COM3:, and COM4:) errors
1201	16450/16550 chip error
1202	Card selected feedback error
1203	Port 102h register test failure
1206	Serial option cannot be put to sleep
1207	Cable error
1208	Interrupt request (IRQ) 3 error
1209	Interrupt request (IRQ) 4 error
1210	16450/16550 chip register failure
1211	Internal wrap test of 16450/16550 chip modem control line failure
1212	External wrap test of 16450/16550 chip modem control line failure
1213	16450/16550 chip transmit error
1214	16450/16550 chip receive error
1215	16450/16550 chip receive error; data not equal to transmit data
1216	16450/16550 chip interrupt function error

Code	Description
1217	16450/16550 chip baud rate test failure
1218	16450/16550 chip receive external data wrap test failure
1219	16550 chip first-in first-out (FIFO) buffer failure
1220	Interrupt enable register error; all bits cannot be set
1221	Interrupt enable register error; all bits cannot be reset
1222	Interrupt pending; stuck on
1223	Interrupt ID register; stuck on
1224	Modem control register error; all bits cannot be set
1225	Modem control register error; all bits cannot be reset
1226	Modem status register error; all bits cannot be set
1227	Modem Status Register error; all bits cannot be reset
1228	Interrupt ID error
1229	Cannot force overrun error
1230	No modem status interrupt
1231	Invalid interrupt pending
1232	No data ready
1233	No data available interrupt
1234	No transmit holding interrupt
1235	No interrupts
1236	No received sine status interrupt
1237	No receive data available
1238	Transmit holding register not empty
1239	No modem status interrupt
1240	Transmit holding register not empty
1241	No interrupts
1242	No interrupt 4
1243	No interrupt 3
1244	No data transferred
1245	Maximum baud rate error
1246	Minimum baud rate error
1248	Time-out error
1249	Invalid data returned
1250	Modem status register error
1251	No data set ready and delta data set ready
1252	No data set ready
1253	No delta data set ready
1254	Modem status register not clear
1255	No clear to send and delta clear to send
1256	No clear to send
1257	No delta clear to send
13xx	Game control adapter errors
1301	Game control adapter test failure
1302	Joystick test failure
14xx	Matrix printer errors
1401	Printer test failure
1402	Printer not ready error
1403	Printer no-paper error
1404	System-board time-out
1405	Parallel adapter failure
1406	Printer presence test failed

continues

Table A.16 Continued

Code	Description
15xx	Synchronous Data Link Control (SDLC) communications adapter errors
1501	SDLC adapter test failure
1510	8255 Port B failure
1511	8255 Port A failure
1512	8255 Port C failure
1513	8253 Timer #1 did not reach terminal count
1514	8253 Timer #1 stuck on
1515	8253 Timer #0 did not reach terminal count
1516	8253 Timer #0 stuck on
1517	8253 Timer #2 did not reach terminal count
1518	8253 Timer #2 stuck on
1519	8273 Port B error
1520	8273 Port A error
1521	8273 command/read time-out
1522	Interrupt Level 4 failure
1523	Ring Indicate stuck on
1524	Receive Clock stuck on
1525	Transmit Clock stuck on
1526	Test Indicate stuck on
1527	Ring Indicate not on
1528	Receive Clock not on
1529	Transmit Clock not on
1530	Test Indicate not on
1531	Data Set Ready not on
1532	Carrier Detect not on
1533	Clear to Send not on
1534	Data Set Ready stuck on
1535	Carrier Detect stuck on
1536	Clear to Send stuck on
1537	Interrupt level 3 failure
1538	Receive interrupt results error
1539	Wrap data compare error
1540	Direct memory access channel 1 error
1541	Direct memory access channel 1 error
1542	8273 error checking or status reporting error
1547	Stray Interrupt level 4
1548	Stray Interrupt level 3
1549	Interrupt presentation sequence time-out
16xx	Display Station Emulation Adapter (DSEA) errors (5520, 525x)
1604	DSEA or Twinaxial network error
1608	DSEA or Twinaxial network error
1624	DSEA error
1634	DSEA error
1644	DSEA error
1652	DSEA error
1654	DSEA error

Code	Description
1658	DSEA error
1662	DSEA interrupt level error
1664	DSEA error
1668	DSEA interrupt level error
1669	DSEA diagnostics error; use 3.0 or higher
1674	DSEA diagnostics error; use 3.0 or higher
1674	DSEA station address error
1684	DSEA device address error
1688	DSEA device address error
17xx	ST-506/412 fixed disk and controller errors
1701	Fixed disk general POST error
1702	Drive/controller time-out error
1703	Drive seek error
1704	Controller failed
1705	Drive sector not found error
1706	Write fault error
1707	Drive track 0 error
1708	Head select error
1709	Error-correction code (ECC) error
1710	Sector buffer overrun
1711	Bad address mark
1712	Internal controller diagnostics failure
1713	Data compare error
1714	Drive not ready
1715	Track 0 indicator failure
1716	Diagnostics cylinder errors
1717	Surface read errors
1718	Hard drive type error
1720	Bad diagnostics cylinder
1726	Data compare error
1730	Controller error
1731	Controller error
1732	Controller error
1733	BIOS Undefined error return
1735	Bad command error
1736	Data corrected error
1737	Bad track error
1738	Bad sector error
1739	Bad initialization error
1740	Bad sense error
1750	Drive verify failure
1751	Drive read failure
1752	Drive write failure
1753	Drive random read test failure
1754	Drive seek test failure
1755	Controller failure
1756	Controller error-correction code (ECC) test failure
1757	Controller head select failure
1780	Seek failure; drive 0
1781	Seek failure; drive 1

continues

Table A.16 Continued	

Code	Description
1782	Controller test failure
1790	Diagnostic cylinder read error; drive 0
1791	Diagnostic cylinder read error; drive 1
18xx	I/O expansion unit errors
1801	I/O expansion unit POST failure
1810	Enable/disable failure
1811	Extender card wrap test failure; disabled
1812	High-order address lines failure; disabled
1813	Wait state failure; disabled
1814	Enable/disable could not be set on
1815	Wait state failure; disabled
1816	Extender card wrap test failure; enabled
1817	High-order address lines failure; enabled
1818	Disable not functioning
1819	Wait request switch not set correctly
1820	Receiver card wrap test failure
1821	Receiver high order address lines failure
19xx	3270 PC attachment card errors
20xx	Binary synchronous communications (BSC) adapter errors
2001	BSC adapter test failure
2010	8255 Port A failure
2011	8255 Port B failure
2012	8255 Port C failure
2013	8253 Timer #1 did not reach terminal count
2014	8253 Timer #1 stuck on
2015	8253 Timer 2 did not reach terminal count
2016	8253 Timer #2 output stuck on
2017	8251 data set ready failed to come on
2018	8251 clear to send not sensed
2019	8251 data SET ready stuck on
2020	8251 clear to send stuck on
2021	8251 hardware reset failure
2022	8251 software reset failure
2023	8251 software "error reset" failure
2024	8251 transmit ready did not come on
2025	8251 receive ready did not come on
2026	8251 could not force "overrun" error status
2027	Interrupt failure; no timer interrupt
2028	Interrupt failure; transmit, replace card or planar
2029	Interrupt failure; transmit, replace card
2030	Interrupt failure; receive, replace card or planar
2031	Interrupt failure; receive, replace card
2033	Ring indicate stuck on
2034	Receive clock stuck on
2035	Transmit clock stuck on
2036	Test indicate stuck on
2037	Ring indicate stuck on
2038	Receive clock not on
2039	Transmit clock not on

Code	Description
2040	Test indicate not on
2041	Data set ready not on
2042	Carrier detect not on
2043	Clear to send not on
2044	Data set ready stuck on
2045	Carrier detect stuck on
2046	Clear to send stuck on
2047	Unexpected transmit interrupt
2048	Unexpected receive interrupt
2049	Transmit data did not equal receive data
2050	8251 detected overrun error
2051	Lost data set ready during data wrap
2052	Receive time-out during data wrap
21xx	Alternate binary synchronous communications (BSC) adapter errors
2101	BSC adapter test failure
2110	8255 Port A failure
2111	8255 Port B failure
2112	8255 Port C failure
2113	8253 Timer #1 did not reach terminal count
2114	8253 Timer #1 stuck on
2115	8253 Timer 2 did not reach terminal count
2116	8253 Timer #2 output stuck on
2117	8251 Data set ready failed to come on
2118	8251 Clear to send not sensed
2119	8251 Data set ready stuck on
2120	8251 Clear to send stuck on
2121	8251 Hardware reset failure
2122	8251 Software reset failure
2123	8251 Software "error reset" failure
2124	8251 Transmit ready did not come on
2125	8251 Receive ready did not come on
2126	8251 could not force "overrun" error status
2127	Interrupt failure; no timer interrupt
2128	Interrupt failure; transmit, replace card or planar
2129	Interrupt failure; transmit, replace card
2130	Interrupt failure; receive, replace card or planar
2131	Interrupt failure; receive, replace card
2133	Ring indicate stuck on
2134	Receive clock stuck on
2135	Transmit clock stuck on
2136	Test indicate stuck on
2137	Ring indicate stuck on
2138	Receive clock not on
2139	Transmit clock not on
2140	Test indicate not on
2141	Data set ready not on
2142	Carrier detect not on
2143	Clear to send not on
2144	Data set ready stuck on
2145	Carrier detect stuck on
2146	Clear to send stuck on

continues

Table A.16 Continued

Code	Description
2147	Unexpected transmit interrupt
2148	Unexpected receive interrupt
2149	Transmit data did not equal receive data
2150	8251 detected overrun error
2151	Lost data set ready during data wrap
2152	Receive time-out during data wrap
22xx	Cluster adapter errors
23xx	Plasma Monitor Adapter errors
24xx	Enhanced Graphics Adapter (EGA) errors
24xx	PS/2 system board Video Graphics Array (VGA) errors
2401	Video adapter test failure
2402	Video display error
2408	User indicated display attribute test failed
2409	Video display error
2410	Video adapter error; video port error
2416	User indicated character set test failed
2424	User indicated 80×25 mode failure
2432	User indicated 40×25 mode failure
2440	User indicated 320×200 graphics mode failure
2448	User indicated 640×200 graphics mode failure
2456	User indicated light-pen test failure
2464	User indicated paging test failure
25xx	Alternate Enhanced Graphics Adapter (EGA) errors
2501	Video adapter test failure
2502	Video display error
2508	User indicated display attribute test failed
2509	Video display error
2510	Video adapter error
2516	User indicated character set test failed
2524	User indicated 80×25 mode failure
2532	User indicated 40×25 mode failure
2540	User indicated 320×200 graphics mode failure
2548	User indicated 640×200 graphics mode failure
2556	User indicated light-pen test failure
2564	User indicated paging test failure
26xx	XT or AT/370 370-M (memory) and 370-P (processor) adapter errors
2601	370-M (memory) adapter error
2655	370-M (memory) adapter error
2657	370-M (memory) adapter error
2668	370-M (memory) adapter error
2672	370-M (memory) adapter error
2673	370-P (processor) adapter error

Code	Description
2674	370-P (processor) adapter error
2677	370-P (processor) adapter error
2680	370-P (processor) adapter error
2681	370-M (memory) adapter error
2682	370-P (processor) adapter error
2694	370-P (processor) adapter error
2697	370-P (processor) adapter error
2698	XT or AT/370 diagnostic diskette error
27xx	XT or AT/370 3277-EM (emulation) adapter errors
2701	3277-EM adapter error
2702	3277-EM adapter error
2703	3277-EM adapter error
28xx	3278/79 emulation adapter or 3270 connection adapter errors
29xx	Color/Graphics printer errors
30xx	Primary PC network adapter errors
3001	Processor test failure
3002	ROM checksum test failure
3003	Unit ID PROM test failure
3004	RAM test failure
3005	Host interface controller test failure
3006	±12v test failure
3007	Digital loopback test failure
3008	Host detected host interface controller failure
3009	Sync failure and no Go bit
3010	Host interface controller test OK and no Go bit
3011	Go bit and no command 41
3012	Card not present
3013	Digital failure; fall through
3015	Analog failure
3041	Hot carrier; not this card
3042	Hot carrier; this card!
31xx	Secondary PC network adapter errors
3101	Processor test failure
3102	ROM checksum test failure
3103	Unit ID PROM test failure
3104	RAM test failure
3105	Host interface controller test failure
3106	± 12v test failure
3107	Digital loopback test failure
3108	Host detected host interface controller failure
3109	Sync failure and no Go bit
3110	Host interface controller test OK and no Go bit
3111	Go bit and no command 41
3112	Card not present

continues

Table A.16 Continued

Code	Description
3113	Digital failure; fall through
3115	Analog failure
3141	Hot carrier; not this card
3142	Hot carrier; this card!
32xx	3270 PC or AT display and programmed symbols adapter errors
33xx	Compact printer errors
35xx	Enhanced display station emulation adapter (EDSEA) errors
3504	Adapter connected to Twinaxial cable during off-line test
3508	Workstation address error
3509	Diagnostic program failure
3540	Workstation address invalid
3588	Adapter address switch error
3599	Diagnostic program failure
36xx	General-purpose interface bus (GPIB) adapter errors
3601	Adapter test failure
3602	Serial poll mode register write error
3603	Adapter address error
3610	Adapter listen error
3611	Adapter talk error
3612	Adapter control error
3613	Adapter standby error
3614	Adapter Asynchronous control error
3615	Adapter Asynchronous control error
3616	Adapter error; cannot pass control
3617	Adapter error; cannot address to listen
3618	Adapter error; cannot un-address to listen
3619	Adapter error; cannot address to talk
3620	Adapter error; cannot un-address to talk
3621	Adapter error; cannot address to listen with extended addressing
3622	Adapter error; cannot un-address to listen with extended addressing
3623	Adapter error; cannot address to talk with extended addressing
3624	Adapter error; cannot un-address to talk with extended addressing
3625	Write to self error
3626	Generate handshake error
3627	Cannot detect "Device Clear" message error
3628	Cannot detect "Selected Device Clear" message error
3629	Cannot detect end with end of identify
3630	Cannot detect end of transmission with end of identify
3631	Cannot detect end with 0-bit end of string
3632	Cannot detect end with 7-bit end of string
3633	Cannot detect group execute trigger
3634	Mode 3 addressing error

Code	Description
3635	Cannot recognize undefined command
3636	Cannot detect remote, remote changed, lockout, or lockout changed
3637	Cannot clear remote or lockout
3638	Cannot detect service request
3639	Cannot conduct serial poll
3640	Cannot conduct parallel poll
3650	Adapter error; direct memory access (DMA) to 7210
3651	Data error; error on direct memory access (DMA) to 7210
3652	Adapter error; direct memory access (DMA) from 7210
3653	Data error on direct memory access (DMA) from 7210
3658	Uninvoked interrupt received
3659	Cannot interrupt on address status changed
3660	Cannot interrupt on address status changed
3661	Cannot interrupt on command output
3662	Cannot interrupt on data out
3663	Cannot interrupt on data in
3664	Cannot interrupt on error
3665	Cannot interrupt on device clear
3666	Cannot interrupt on end
3667	Cannot interrupt on device execute trigger
3668	Cannot interrupt on address pass through
3669	Cannot interrupt on command pass through
3670	Cannot interrupt on remote changed
3671	Cannot interrupt on lockout changed
3672	Cannot interrupt on service request In
3673	Cannot interrupt on terminal count on direct memory access to 7210
3674	Cannot interrupt on terminal count on direct memory access from 7210
3675	Spurious direct memory access terminal-count interrupt
3697	Illegal direct memory access configuration setting detected
3698	Illegal interrupt level setting detected
38xx	Data acquisition adapter errors
3801	Adapter test failure
3810	Timer read test failure
3811	Timer interrupt test failure
3812	Delay, binary input 13 test failure
3813	Rate, binary input 13 test failure
3814	Binary output 14, interrupt status - interrupt request test failure
3815	Binary output 0, count-in test failure
3816	Binary input strobe, count-out test failure
3817	Binary output 0, binary output clear to send test failure
3818	Binary output 1, binary input 0 test failure
3819	Binary output 2, binary input 1 test failure
3820	Binary output 3, binary input 2 test failure
3821	Binary output 4, binary input 3 test failure

continues

Table A.16 Continued

Code	Description
3822	Binary output 5, binary input 4 test failure
3823	Binary output 6, binary input 5 test failure
3824	Binary output 7, binary input 6 test failure
3825	Binary output 8, binary input 7 test failure
3826	Binary output 9, binary input 8 test failure
3827	Binary output 10, binary input 9 test failure
3828	Binary output 11, binary input 10 test failure
3829	Binary output 12, binary input 11 test failure
3830	Binary output 13, binary input 12 test failure
3831	Binary output 15, analog input CE test failure
3832	Binary output strobe, binary output GATE test failure
3833	Binary input clear to send, binary input HOLD test failure
3834	Analog input command output, binary input 15 test failure
3835	Counter interrupt test failure
3836	Counter read test failure
3837	Analog output 0 ranges test failure
3838	Analog output 1 ranges test failure
3839	Analog input 0 values test failure
3840	Analog input 1 values test failure
3841	Analog input 2 values test failure
3842	Analog input 3 values test failure
3843	Analog input interrupt test failure
3844	Analog input 23 address or value test failure
39xx	Professional Graphics Adapter (PGA) errors
3901	PGA test failure
3902	ROM1 self-test failure
3903	ROM2 self-test failure
3904	RAM self-test failure
3905	Cold start cycle power error
3906	Data error in communications RAM
3907	Address error in communications RAM
3908	Bad data reading/writing 6845-like register
3909	Bad data in lower E0h bytes reading/writing 6845-like registers
3910	Graphics controller display bank output latches error
3911	Basic clock error
3912	Command control error
3913	Vertical sync scanner error
3914	Horizontal sync scanner error
3915	Intech error
3916	Look-up table address error
3917	Look-up table red RAM chip error
3918	Look-up table green RAM chip error
3919	Look-up table blue RAM chip error
3920	Look-up table data latch error
3921	Horizontal display error

Code	Description
3922	Vertical display error
3923	Light-pen error
3924	Unexpected error
3925	Emulator addressing error
3926	Emulator data latch error
3927	Base for error codes 3928-3930 (Emulator RAM)
3928	Emulator RAM error
3929	Emulator RAM error
3930	Emulator RAM error
3931	Emulator horizontal/vertical display problem
3932	Emulator cursor position error
3933	Emulator attribute display problem
3934	Emulator cursor display error
3935	Fundamental emulation RAM problem
3936	Emulation character set problem
3937	Emulation graphics display error
3938	Emulation character display problem
3939	Emulation bank select error
3940	Adapter RAM U2 error
3941	Adapter RAM U4 error
3942	Adapter RAM U6 error
3943	Adapter RAM U8 error
3944	Adapter RAM U10 error
3945	Adapter RAM U1 error
3946	Adapter RAM U3 error
3947	Adapter RAM U5 error
3948	Adapter RAM U7 error
3949	Adapter RAM U9 error
3950	Adapter RAM U12 error
3951	Adapter RAM U14 error
3952	Adapter RAM U16 error
3953	Adapter RAM U18 error
3954	Adapter RAM U20 error
3955	Adapter RAM U11 error
3956	Adapter RAM U13 error
3957	Adapter RAM U15 error
3958	Adapter RAM U17 error
3959	Adapter RAM U19 error
3960	Adapter RAM U22 error
3961	Adapter RAM U24 error
3962	Adapter RAM U26 error
3963	Adapter RAM U28 error
3964	Adapter RAM U30 error
3965	Adapter RAM U21 error
3966	Adapter RAM U23 error
3967	Adapter RAM U25 error
3968	Adapter RAM U27 error
3969	Adapter RAM U29 error

continues

Table A.16 Continued

Code	Description
3970	Adapter RAM U32 error
3971	Adapter RAM U34 error
3972	Adapter RAM U36 error
3973	Adapter RAM U38 error
3974	Adapter RAM U40 error
3975	Adapter RAM U31 error
3976	Adapter RAM U33 error
3977	Adapter RAM U35 error
3978	Adapter RAM U37 error
3979	Adapter RAM U39 error
3980	Graphics controller RAM timing error
3981	Graphics controller read/write latch error
3982	Shift register bus output latches error
3983	Addressing error (vertical column of memory; U2 at top)
3984	Addressing error (vertical column of memory; U4 at top)
3985	Addressing error (vertical column of memory; U6 at top)
3986	Addressing error (vertical column of memory; U8 at top)
3987	Addressing error (vertical column of memory; U10 at top)
3988	Base for error codes 3989-3991 (horizontal bank latch errors)
3989	Horizontal bank latch errors
3990	Horizontal bank latch errors
3991	Horizontal bank latch errors
3992	RAG/CAG graphics controller error
3993	Multiple write modes, nibble mask errors
3994	Row nibble (display RAM) error
3995	Graphics controller addressing error
44xx	5278 display attachment unit and 5279 display errors
45xx	IEEE interface adapter (IEEE-488) errors
46xx	A real-time interface coprocessor (ARTIC) multiport/2 adapter errors
4611	ARTIC adapter error
4612	Memory module error
4613	Memory module error
4630	ARTIC adapter error
4640	Memory module error
4641	Memory module error
4650	ARTIC interface cable error
48xx	Internal modem errors
49xx	Alternate internal modem errors
50xx	PC Convertible LCD errors
5001	LCD display buffer failure
5002	LCD font buffer failure
5003	LCD controller failure
5004	User indicated PEL/drive test failed
5008	User indicated display attribute test failed

Code	Description
5016	User indicated character set test failed
5020	User indicated alternate character set test failure
5024	User indicated 80×25 mode test failure
5032	User indicated 40×25 mode test failure
5040	User indicated 320×200 graphics test failure
5048	User indicated 640×200 graphics test failure
5064	User indicated paging test failure
51xx	PC Convertible portable printer errors
5101	Portable printer interface failure
5102	Portable printer busy error
5103	Portable printer paper or ribbon error
5104	Portable printer time-out
5105	User indicated print-pattern test error
56xx	Financial communication system errors
70xx	Phoenix BIOS/chipset unique error codes
7000	Chipset CMOS failure
7001	Chipset shadow RAM failure
7002	Chipset CMOS configuration error
71xx	Voice Communications Adapter (VCA) errors
7101	Adapter test failure
7102	Instruction or external data memory error
7103	PC to VCA interrupt error
7104	Internal data memory error
7105	Direct memory access (DMA) error
7106	Internal registers error
7107	Interactive shared memory error
7108	VCA to PC interrupt error
7109	DC wrap error
7111	External analog wrap and tone-output error
7112	Microphone to speaker wrap error
7114	Telephone attachment test failure
73xx	3 1/2-inch external diskette drive errors
7301	Diskette drive/adapter test failure
7306	Disk Changeline failure
7307	Diskette is write protected
7308	Drive command error
7310	Diskette initialization failure; track 0 bad
7311	Drive time-out error
7312	Controller chip (NEC) error
7313	Direct memory access (DMA) error
7314	Direct memory access (DMA) boundary overrun
7315	Drive index timing error
7316	Drive speed error
7321	Drive seek error
7322	Drive cyclic redundancy check (CRC) error
7323	Sector not found error
7324	Address mark error
7325	Controller chip (NEC) seek error

continues

Table A.16 Continued

Code	Description
74xx	IBM PS/2 Display Adapter (VGA card) errors
74xx	8514/A display adapter errors
7426	8514 display error
7440	8514/A memory module 31 error
7441	8514/A memory module 30 error
7442	8514/A memory module 29 error
7443	8514/A memory module 28 error
7444	8514/A memory module 22 error
7445	8514/A memory module 21 error
7446	8514/A memory module 18 error
7447	8514/A memory module 17 error
7448	8514/A memory module 32 error
7449	8514/A memory module 14 error
7450	8514/A memory module 13 error
7451	8514/A memory module 12 error
7452	8514/A memory module 06 error
7453	8514/A memory module 05 error
7454	8514/A memory module 02 error
7455	8514/A memory module 01 error
7460	8514/A memory module 16 error
7461	8514/A memory module 27 error
7462	8514/A memory module 26 error
7463	8514/A memory module 25 error
7464	8514/A memory module 24 error
7465	8514/A memory module 23 error
7466	8514/A memory module 20 error
7467	8514/A memory module 19 error
7468	8514/A memory module 15 error
7469	8514/A memory module 11 error
7470	8514/A memory module 10 error
7471	8514/A memory module 09 error
7472	8514/A memory module 08 error
7473	8514/A memory module 07 error
7474	8514/A memory module 04 error
7475	8514/A memory module 03 error
76xx	4216 PagePrinter adapter errors
7601	Adapter test failure
7602	Adapter error
7603	Printer error
7604	Printer cable error
84xx	PS/2 speech adapter errors
85xx	2MB XMA memory adapter or expanded memory adapter/A errors
850x	Adapter error
851x	Adapter error
852x	Memory module error

Code	Description
8599	Unusable memory segment found
86xx	PS/2 pointing device (mouse) errors
8601	Pointing device error; mouse time-out
8602	Pointing device error; mouse interface
8603	Pointing device or system-board failure; mouse interrupt
8604	Pointing device or system-board error
89xx	Musical Instrument Digital Interface (MIDI) adapter errors
91xx	IBM 3363 Write-Once Read Multiple (WORM) optical drive/adapter errors
096xxxx	SCSI adapter with cache (32-bit) errors
100xx	Multiprotocol adapter/A errors
10001	Presence test failure
10002	Card selected feedback error
10003	Port 102h register rest failure
10004	Port 103h register rest failure
10006	Serial option cannot be put to sleep
10007	Cable error
10008	Interrupt request (IRQ) 3 error
10009	Interrupt request (IRQ) 4 error
10010	16550 chip register failure
10011	Internal wrap test of 16550 chip modem control line failure
10012	External wrap test of 16550 chip modem control line failure
10013	16550 chip transmit error
10014	16550 chip receive error
10015	16550 chip receive error; data not equal to transmit data
10016	16550 chip interrupt function error
10017	16550 chip baud rate test failure
10018	16550 chip receive external data wrap test failure
10019	16550 chip first-in first-out (FIFO) buffer failure
10026	8255 Port A error
10027	8255 Port B error
10028	8255 Port C error
10029	8254 timer 0 error
10030	8254 timer 1 error
10031	8254 timer 2 error
10032	Binary sync data set ready response to data terminal ready error
10033	Binary sync clear to send response to ready to send error
10034	8251 hardware reset test failed
10035	8251 function error
10036	8251 status error
10037	Binary sync timer interrupt error
10038	Binary sync transmit interrupt error
10039	Binary sync receive interrupt error
10040	Stray interrupt request (IRQ) 3 error
10041	Stray interrupt request (IRQ) 4 error
10042	Binary sync external wrap error
10044	Binary sync data wrap error
10045	Binary sync line status/condition error

continues

Table A.16 Continued

Code	Description
10046	Binary sync time-out error during data wrap test
10050	8273 command acceptance or results ready time-out error
10051	8273 Port A error
10052	8273 Port B error
10053	SDLC modem status change logic error
10054	SDLC timer interrupt request (IRQ) 4 error
10055	SDLC modem status change interrupt request (IRQ) 4 error
10056	SDLC external wrap error
10057	SDLC interrupt results error
10058	SDLC data wrap error
10059	SDLC transmit interrupt error
10060	SDLC receive interrupt error
10061	Direct memory access (DMA) channel 1 transmit error
10062	Direct memory access (DMA) channel 1 receive error
10063	8273 status detect failure
10064	8273 error detect failure
101xx	300/1200bps internal modem/A
10101	Presence test failure
10102	Card selected feedback error
10103	Port 102h register test failure
10106	Serial option cannot be put to sleep
10108	Interrupt request (IRQ) 3 error
10109	Interrupt request (IRQ) 4 error
10110	16450 chip register failure
10111	Internal wrap test of 16450 modem control line failure
10113	16450 transmit error
10114	16450 receive error
10115	16450 receive error data not equal transmit data
10116	16450 interrupt function error
10117	16450 baud rate test failure
10118	16450 receive external data wrap test failure
10125	Modem reset result code error
10126	Modem general result code error
10127	Modem S registers write/read error
10128	Modem turn echo on/off error
10129	Modem enable/disable result codes error
10130	Modem enable number/word result codes error
10133	Connect results for 300 baud not received
10134	Connect results for 1200 baud not received
10135	Modem fails local analog loopback test at 300 baud
10136	Modem fails local analog loopback test at 1200 baud
10137	Modem does not respond to escape/reset sequence
10138	S-Register 13 does not show correct parity or number of data bits
10139	S-Register 15 does not reflect correct bit rate
104xx	ESDI fixed disk or adapter errors

Code	Description
10450	Read/write test failed
10451	Read verify test failed
10452	Seek test failed
10453	Wrong drive type indicated
10454	Controller sector buffer test failure
10455	Controller invalid failure
10456	Controller diagnostic command failure
10461	Drive format error
10462	Controller head select error
10463	Drive read/write sector error
10464	Drive primary defect map unreadable
10465	Controller; error-correction code (ECC) 8-bit error
10466	Controller; error-correction code (ECC) 9-bit error
10467	Drive soft seek error
10468	Drive hard seek error
10469	Drive soft error count exceeded
10470	Controller attachment diagnostic error
10471	Controller wrap mode interface error
10472	Controller wrap mode drive select error
10473	Read verify test errors
10480	Seek failure; drive 0
10481	Seek failure; drive 1
10482	Controller transfer acknowledge error
10483	Controller reset failure
10484	Controller; head select 3 error
10485	Controller; head select 2 error
10486	Controller; head select 1 error
10487	Controller; head select 0 error
10488	Controller; read gate - command complete 2 error
10489	Controller; write gate - command complete 1 error
10490	Diagnostic area read error; drive 0
10491	Diagnostic area read error; drive 1
10499	Controller failure
107xx	5 1/4-inch external diskette drive or adapter errors
112xxxx	SCSI adapter (16-bit without cache) errors
113xxxx	System board SCSI adapter (16-bit) errors
129xx	Model 70 processor board errors; type 3 (25 MHz) system board
12901	Processor board; processor test failed
12902	Processor board; cache test failed
149xx	P70/P75 Plasma Display and adapter errors
14901	Plasma Display Adapter failure
14902	Plasma Display Adapter failure
14922	Plasma display failure
14932	External display failure
165xx	6157 streaming tape drive or tape attachment adapter errors
16520	Streaming tape drive failure
16540	Tape attachment adapter failure
166xx	Primary token ring network adapter errors

continues

Table A.16 Continued

Code	Description
167xx	Alternate token ring network adapter errors
180xx	PS/2 Wizard adapter errors
18001	Interrupt controller failure
18002	Incorrect timer count
18003	Timer interrupt failure
18004	Sync check interrupt failure
18005	Parity check interrupt failure
18006	Access error interrupt failure
18012	Bad checksum error
18013	Micro Channel interface error
18021	Wizard memory compare or parity error
18022	Wizard memory address line error
18023	Dynamic RAM controller failure
18029	Wizard memory byte enable error
18031	Wizard memory-expansion module memory compare or parity error
18032	Wizard memory-expansion module address line error
18039	Wizard memory-expansion module byte enable error
194xx	80286 memory-expansion option memory-module errors
208xxxx	Unknown SCSI device errors
209xxxx	SCSI removable disk errors
210xxxx	SCSI fixed disk errors
210PLSC	"PLSC" codes indicate error
	P = SCSI ID number
	L = Logical unit number (LUN)
	S = Host adapter slot number
	C = Drive capacity:
	A = 60M
	B = 80M
	C = 120M
	D = 160M
	E = 320M
	F = 400M
	U = Undetermined
211xxxx	SCSI tape drive errors
212xxxx	SCSI printer errors
213xxxx	SCSI processor errors
214xxxx	SCSI Write-Once Read Multiple (WORM) drive errors
215xxxx	SCSI CD-ROM drive errors
216xxxx	SCSI scanner errors
217xxxx	SCSI optical memory errors
218xxxx	SCSI jukebox changer errors
219xxxx	SCSI communications errors

IBM SCSI Error Codes

With the new IBM SCSI adapter and SCSI devices comes a new set of error codes. This section contains tables describing all the known IBM SCSI Power-On Self Test (POST) and advanced diagnostics error codes. These codes can be used to determine the meaning of errors that occur on the IBM SCSI adapters and any attached SCSI devices. The error codes that occur during POST and diagnostics tests have the format shown in figure A.5.

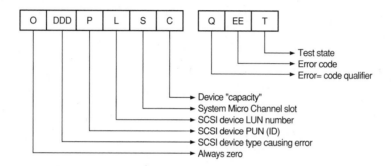

Fig. A.5

IBM SCSI POST and diagnostics error code format.

This section shows what each part of the error code indicates.

The DDD field in figure A.5 indicates the SCSI device causing the error. Table A.17 shows the device codes.

The P field indicates the SCSI device physical unit number (PUN) or SCSI ID. This value is between 0 and 7, with the host adapter normally set to 7 and the first (bootable) SCSI hard disk set to 6.

The L field indicates the SCSI device logical unit number (LUN). For most SCSI devices it is 0 because normally there is only a single LUN per physical unit or SCSI ID.

The S field indicates the system Micro Channel Architecture (MCA) slot number containing the SCSI host adapter to which the device in error is connected. If S equals 0, the error is an adapter initialization error (there is no MCA slot 0). In this case, the DDD number is 096, 112, or 113, and you must use the following adapter initialization error chart to determine the error. The specific errors in this chart are indicated by the value in the L field, which immediately precedes the S field. In this case, the L does *not* represent the logical unit number (as it normally does), but instead shows a specific initialization error for the adapter. If S is not equal to 0, no error is on the adapter (or device attached to the adapter) in slot S. You can determine these standard errors by using the rest of the tables in this section.

Table A.17 SCSI Device Error Codes

DDDxxxx xxxx	Error
096xxxx xxxx	32-bit cached SCSI host adapter
112xxxx xxxx	16-bit non-cached SCSI host adapter
113xxxx xxxx	System board SCSI host adapter
208xxxx xxxx	Unknown SCSI device type
209xxxx xxxx	Direct access (disk) device with removable media and/or other than 512 byte blocks
210xxxx xxxx	Direct access (disk) device with nonremovable media and 512 byte blocks (hard disk)
211xxxx xxxx	Sequential access device (magnetic tape)
212xxxx xxxx	Printer device
213xxxx xxxx	Processor device (host to host)
214xxxx xxxx	Write-Once, Read Multiple device (optical WORM drive)
215xxxx xxxx	Read-only device (CD-ROM drive)
216xxxx xxxx	Scanner device
217xxxx xxxx	Optical memory device (optical drive)
218xxxx xxxx	Media changer device (multiple tray CD-ROM or jukebox)
219xxxx xxxx	Communications device (LAN bridge)

DDD0LS0 0000	SCSI adapter initialization errors, where S = 0
DDD0100 0000	No extended CMOS setup data available. On systems with Non-Volatile RAM (NVRAM), this means that SCSI setup data was not located or the checksum did not verify. On systems without NVRAM (Model 50, for example), the setup data must be on the first non-SCSI fixed disk
DDD0200 0000	No hard disk at PUN 6, LUN 0. (Also expect to see 161, 162, or 165 errors)
DDD0300 0000	No space available in extended BIOS data area for SCSI data table
DDD0400 0000	ROM modules not found on SCSI adapter
DDD0500 0000	ROM checksum error in the second 16K portion of 32K SCSI adapter ROM

A value of x *indicates any number or character.*

The C field indicates the capacity of the device originating the error code. The capacity codes for each of the available IBM SCSI hard disk drives are listed in table A.18. In the case of error codes from a device with no capacity (such as a SCSI adapter or printer), this field is 0.

Table A.18 SCSI Device Capacity Codes

DDDxxxC xxxx	SCSI device capacity
DDDxxx0 xxxx	Not a storage device (that is, adapters, printers, and so on)
DDDxxxA xxxx	60M
DDDxxxB xxxx	80M
DDDxxxC xxxx	120M
DDDxxxD xxxx	160M
DDDxxxE xxxx	320M
DDDxxxF xxxx	400M
DDDxxxU xxxx	Undetermined device capacity

The Q field is the error code (EE field) qualifier. Q can have a value from 0 through 7. Depending on the value of Q, the error codes take on different meanings, because Q indicates what class of error occurred or what part of the SCSI system the error is coming from. To determine the error code meaning, use one of the following tables that correspond to the value of Q you have.

The Q value defines the origin of the EE code reported. Error codes with Q = 0 or 1 are generated by the SCSI host adapter, and all error codes with Q greater than 1 are developed using information returned by the adapter or a SCSI device. If Q = 2, the EE code indicates the value returned in the Command Error field (word 8, bits 15-8) of the SCSI Command Complete Status Block (CCSB) for values indicating hardware problems (codes of 20h or greater). If Q = 3, then EE also indicates the value returned in the Command Error field (word 8, bits 15-8) of the Command Complete Status Block (CCSB), but for values indicating software problems (codes less than 20h). If Q = 4, then EE indicates the value returned in the Sense Key field (byte 2, bits 3-0) of a Sense Data Block returned to the SCSI host adapter by a device following a SCSI Request Sense command. If Q = 5, then EE indicates the value returned in the Additional Sense Code field (byte 12) of a Sense Data Block returned by a Direct Access (Disk) device following a SCSI Request Sense command. If Q = 6, then EE indicates the value returned in the Device Error Code field (word 8, bits 7-0) of the Command Complete Status Block (CCSB). If Q = 7, a device error has occurred that normally would not be considered an error, but is now considered an error based on when the code was returned—for example, a Medium Corrupted error from a device with nonremovable media.

Although IBM has a unique format for displaying SCSI error codes, almost all except the adapter-specific errors are part of the SCSI specification. Because many of these codes come from the devices attached to the SCSI bus and not the host adapter, a new code not listed here possibly could appear because some errors can be dependent on the particular device, and some devices send manufacturer-specific errors. You then can look up the error code in the manufacturer's documentation for the device to determine the meaning. The tables in this section are standard as defined in the SCSI Common Command Set (CCS) of the ANSI SCSI-1 specification. Further information is in the IBM hardware-maintenance and service manual for the IBM SCSI adapter and the various SCSI devices.

Table A.19 SCSI Host Adapter Error Codes with Q = 0	
DDDxxxx QEEx	**Error code**
96xxxx 001x	80188 ROM test failure
96xxxx 002x	Local RAM test failure
96xxxx 003x	Power protection error (terminator or fuse)
96xxxx 004x	80188 internal peripheral test failure
96xxxx 005x	Buffer control chip test failure
96xxxx 006x	Buffer RAM test failure
96xxxx 007x	System interface control chip test failure
96xxxx 008x	SCSI interface test failure
112xxxx 001x	8032 ROM test failure
112xxxx 002x	Local RAM test failure
112xxxx 003x	Power protection device error (terminator or fuse)
112xxxx 004x	8032 internal peripheral test failure
112xxxx 005x	Buffer control chip test failure
112xxxx 006x	Undefined error condition
112xxxx 007x	System interface control chip test failure
112xxxx 008x	SCSI interface test failure
113xxxx 001x	Microprocessor ROM test failure
113xxxx 002x	Local RAM test failure
113xxxx 003x	Power protection device error (terminator or fuse)
113xxxx 004x	Microprocessor internal peripheral test failure
113xxxx 005x	Buffer control chip test failure
113xxxx 006x	Undefined error condition
113xxxx 007x	System interface control chip test failure
113xxxx 008x	SCSI interface test failure

Table A.20 SCSI Adapter Error Codes with Q = 1

DDDxxxx QEEx	Error code
DDDxxxx 107x	Adapter hardware failure
DDDxxxx 10Cx	Command completed with failure
DDDxxxx 10Ex	Command error (invalid command or parameter)
DDDxxxx 10Fx	Software sequencing error
DDDxxxx 180x	Time out
DDDxxxx 181x	Adapter busy error
DDDxxxx 182x	Unexpected interrupt presented by adapter
DDDxxxx 183x	Adapter register test failure
DDDxxxx 184x	Adapter reset (via basic control register) failure
DDDxxxx 185x	Adapter buffer test failure (cached adapter only)
DDDxxxx 186x	Adapter reset count expired
DDDxxxx 187x	Adapter registers not cleared on reset (power-on or channel reset)
DDDxxxx 188x	Card ID in adapter microcode did not match ID in POS registers
DDDxxxx 190x	Expected device did not respond (target device not powered on)
DDDxxxx 190x	DMA arbitration level conflict (if device number is 096, 112, or 113)

Table A.21 SCSI Hardware Error Codes with Q = 2

DDDxxxx QEEx	Error code
DDDxxxx 220x	Adapter hardware error
DDDxxxx 221x	Global command time-out on adapter (device did not respond)
DDDxxxx 222x	Adapter DMA error
DDDxxxx 223x	Adapter buffer defective
DDDxxxx 224x	Command aborted by adapter
DDDxxxx 280x	Adapter microprocessor detected error

Table A.22 SCSI Software Error Codes with Q = 3

DDDxxxx QEEx	Error code
DDDxxxx 301x	Invalid parameter in subsystem control block
DDDxxxx 302x	Reserved
DDDxxxx 303x	Command not supported
DDDxxxx 304x	Command aborted by system
DDDxxxx 305x	Command rejected (buffer not disabled)
DDDxxxx 306x	Command rejected (adapter diagnostic failure)
DDDxxxx 307x	Format rejected (sequence error)
DDDxxxx 308x	Assign rejected (command in progress on device)
DDDxxxx 309x	Assign rejected (device already assigned)
DDDxxxx 30Ax	Command rejected (device not assigned)
DDDxxxx 30Bx	Maximum logical block address exceeded
DDDxxxx 30Cx	16-bit card slot address range exceeded
DDDxxxx 313x	Invalid device for command
DDDxxxx 3FFx	Status not returned by adapter

Table A.23 SCSI Device Sense Key Error Codes with Q = 4

DDDxxxx QEEx	Error code
DDDxxxx 401x	Recovered error (not considered an error condition)
DDDxxxx 402x	Device not ready
DDDxxxx 403x	Device media error
DDDxxxx 404x	Device hardware error
DDDxxxx 405x	Illegal request for device
DDDxxxx 406x	Device unit attention would not clear
DDDxxxx 407x	Device data protect error
DDDxxxx 408x	Device blank check error
DDDxxxx 409x	Device vendor unique error
DDDxxxx 40Ax	Device copy aborted
DDDxxxx 40Bx	Command aborted by device
DDDxxxx 40Cx	Device search data command satisfied
DDDxxxx 40Dx	Device volume overflow (residual data still in buffer)
DDDxxxx 40Ex	Device miscompare (source and medium data don't match)
DDDxxxx 40Fx	Reserved

Table A.24 SCSI Device Extended Sense Error Codes with Q=5

DDDxxxx QEEx	Error code
DDDxxxx 501x	No index or sector signal
DDDxxxx 502x	Seek incomplete
DDDxxxx 503x	Write fault
DDDxxxx 504x	Drive not ready
DDDxxxx 505x	Drive not selected
DDDxxxx 506x	No track 0 found
DDDxxxx 507x	Multiple drives selected
DDDxxxx 508x	Logical unit communication failure
DDDxxxx 509x	Head positioning error (track following error)
DDDxxxx 50Ax	Error log overflow
DDDxxxx 50Cx	Write error
DDDxxxx 510x	CRC or ECC error on ID field
DDDxxxx 511x	Unrecoverable read error
DDDxxxx 512x	Address mark not found for ID field
DDDxxxx 513x	Address mark not found for data field
DDDxxxx 514x	Record not found
DDDxxxx 515x	Seek error
DDDxxxx 516x	Data synchronization mark error
DDDxxxx 517x	Recovered read data with retries (without ECC)
DDDxxxx 518x	Recovered read data with ECC correction
DDDxxxx 519x	Defect list error
DDDxxxx 51Ax	Parameter list length overrun
DDDxxxx 51Bx	Synchronous data transfer error
DDDxxxx 51Cx	Primary defect list not found
DDDxxxx 51Dx	Data miscompare during verify
DDDxxxx 51Ex	Recovered ID read with ECC correction
DDDxxxx 520x	Invalid command operation code
DDDxxxx 521x	Illegal logical block address (out of range)
DDDxxxx 522x	Illegal function for device type
DDDxxxx 524x	Invalid field in command descriptor block
DDDxxxx 525x	Invalid logical unit number (LUN not supported)
DDDxxxx 526x	Invalid field in parameter list
DDDxxxx 527x	Media write protected
DDDxxxx 528x	Media changed error (ready went true)
DDDxxxx 529x	Power-on or bus device reset occurred (not an error)
DDDxxxx 52Ax	Mode select parameters changed (not an error)
DDDxxxx 52Bx	Copy command can't execute because host can't disconnect
DDDxxxx 52Cx	Command sequence error
DDDxxxx 52Fx	Tagged commands cleared by another initiator
DDDxxxx 530x	Incompatible media (unknown or incompatible format)
DDDxxxx 531x	Medium format corrupted
DDDxxxx 532x	Defect spare location unavailable
DDDxxxx 537x	Rounded parameter error
DDDxxxx 539x	Saving parameters not supported

continues

Table A.24 Continued

DDDxxxx QEEx	Error code
DDDxxxx 53Ax	Media not present
DDDxxxx 53Cx	Link flag bit not supported
DDDxxxx 53Dx	Invalid bits in identify message
DDDxxxx 53Ex	Logical unit has not self-configured
DDDxxxx 53Fx	Target operating conditions have changed
DDDxxxx 540x	Device RAM failure
DDDxxxx 541x	Data path diagnostic failure
DDDxxxx 542x	Device power-on diagnostic failure
DDDxxxx 543x	Device message rejected
DDDxxxx 544x	Target device internal controller error
DDDxxxx 545x	Select/reselect failure (device unable to reconnect)
DDDxxxx 546x	Device soft reset unsuccessful
DDDxxxx 547x	SCSI interface parity error
DDDxxxx 548x	Initiator detected error
DDDxxxx 549x	Illegal command or command out of sequence error
DDDxxxx 54Ax	SCSI command phase error
DDDxxxx 54Bx	SCSI data phase error
DDDxxxx 54Cx	Logical unit failed self-configuration
DDDxxxx 54Ex	Overlapped commands attempted
DDDxxxx 560x	Status error from second-party copy command
DDDxxxx 588x	Not digital audio track
DDDxxxx 589x	Not CD-ROM data track
DDDxxxx 58Ax	Drive not in play audio state
DDDxxxx 5F0x	Format in progress (not an error)
DDDxxxx 5F1x	Spinup in progress

Table A.25 SCSI Command Complete Status Block Errors with Q=6

DDDxxxx QEEx	Error
DDDxxxx 601x	SCSI bus reset occurred
DDDxxxx 602x	SCSI interface fault
DDDxxxx 610x	SCSI selection time-out (device not available)
DDDxxxx 611x	Unexpected SCSI bus free
DDDxxxx 612x	Mandatory SCSI message rejected
DDDxxxx 613x	Invalid SCSI phase sequence
DDDxxxx 620x	Short length record error

Table A.26 SCSI Device Condition Error Codes with Q = 7

DDDxxxx QEEx	Error code
DDDxxxx 702x	Device not ready (removable media devices)
DDDxxxx 704x	Device not ready (nonremovable media devices)
DDDxxxx 728x	Media changed error would not clear
DDDxxxx 731x	Medium format corrupted (format unit interrupted—reissue format)
DDDxxxx 7F0x	Format in progress (prior format unit command being completed)
DDDxxxx 7F1x	Spinup in progress

Table A.27 shows the diagnostics test state codes used when a failure occurs. Position *T* indicates the POST *or* diagnostics test state in which the failure occurred.

Table A.27 SCSI Diagnostics Test State Codes

DDDxxxx xxxT	Test state code
DDDxxxx xxx0	Not applicable for error code
DDDxxxx xxxA	Adapter initialization
DDDxxxx xxxB	Adapter reset
DDDxxxx xxxC	Adapter register test
DDDxxxx xxxD	Adapter buffer test Phase 1 (cached adapter only)
DDDxxxx xxxE	Adapter buffer test Phase 2 (cached adapter only)
DDDxxxx xxxF	Adapter buffer test Phase 3 (cached adapter only)
DDDxxxx xxxG	Adapter buffer test Phase 4 (cached adapter only)
DDDxxxx xxxH	Adapter information test state (buffer enable and size, retry enable, etc.)
DDDxxxx xxxI	Device assignment sequence
DDDxxxx xxxJ	Device not ready (also initial unit attention clearing)
DDDxxxx xxxK	Device reset
DDDxxxx xxxL	Device starting phase (appropriate devices only)
DDDxxxx xxxM	Device in process of starting (wait for device to become ready)
DDDxxxx xxxN	Device block size determination
DDDxxxx xxxO	Device self test
DDDxxxx xxxP	Device single block (logical block address) read
DDDxxxx xxxQ	Device double block (logical block address) read
DDDxxxx xxxS	Error occurred after device testing had completed

System Memory Maps

The following maps show where memory is located logically within a system. The first map shows the processor-addressable memory in real mode. The second map shows processor-addressable memory in protected mode. The third map shows how expanded memory fits into the reserved space between 640K and 1M, and how it is not directly addressable by the processor. Expanded memory can be addressed only a small piece (*page*) at a time through a small window of memory. These maps can be useful for mapping out the logical locations of any adapter in your system. All memory locations must be uniquely supplied by a single device; the potential for conflicts does exist if two devices are mapped into the same logical locations.

1-Megabyte Conventional Memory Map Template

The following map shows the logical address locations for an Intel processor running in real mode. In this mode, the processor can see only 1 megabyte of memory, which is mapped in the following way.

. = Program-accessible memory (standard RAM)
v = Video RAM
a = Adapter board ROM and special-purpose RAM
r = Motherboard ROM BIOS
b = IBM Cassette BASIC (would be "r" in compatibles)
h = High memory area (HMA)

```
Conventional (base) memory

        : 0---1---2---3---4---5---6---7---8---9---A---B---C---D---E---F---
000000: ................................................................
010000: ................................................................
020000: ................................................................
030000: ................................................................
040000: ................................................................
050000: ................................................................
060000: ................................................................
070000: ................................................................
080000: ................................................................
090000: ................................................................
```

```
Upper memory area (UMA)

    0A0000:  vvvvvvvvvvvvvvvvvvvvvvvvvvvvvvvvvvvvvvvvvvvvvvvvvvvvvvvvvvvvvvvv
    0B0000:  vvvvvvvvvvvvvvvvvvvvvvvvvvvvvvvvvvvvvvvvvvvvvvvvvvvvvvvvvvvvvvvv
    0C0000:  aaaaaaaaaaaaaaaaaaaaaaaaaaaaaaaaaaaaaaaaaaaaaaaaaaaaaaaaaaaaaaaa
    0D0000:  aaaaaaaaaaaaaaaaaaaaaaaaaaaaaaaaaaaaaaaaaaaaaaaaaaaaaaaaaaaaaaaa
    0E0000:  rrrrrrrrrrrrrrrrrrrrrrrrrrrrrrrrrrrrrrrrrrrrrrrrrrrrrrrrrrrrrrrr
    0F0000:  rrrrrrrrrrrrrrrrrrrrrrrrbbbbbbbbbbbbbbbbbbbbbbbbbbbbbbbrrrrrrrrr

Extended memory

            : 0---1---2---3---4---5---6---7---8---9---A---B---C---D---E---F---
    100000:  hhhhhhhhhhhhhhhhhhhhhhhhhhhhhhhhhhhhhhhhhhhhhhhhhhhhhhhhhhhhhhhh
```

Note that because the first 64K of extended memory is actually in real mode, a system with a 286 or better processor can access the high memory area (HMA).

16-Megabyte Conventional and Extended Memory Map Template

The following map shows the logical address locations for an Intel processor running in protected mode. In this mode, the processor can see a full 16 megabytes of memory, which is mapped in the following way.

. = Program-accessible memory (standard RAM)
v = Video RAM
a = Adapter board ROM and special-purpose RAM
r = Motherboard ROM BIOS
b = IBM Cassette BASIC (would be "r" in compatibles)
h = High memory area (HMA)

```
Conventional (base) memory:

            : 0---1---2---3---4---5---6---7---8---9---A---B---C---D---E---F---
    000000:  ..............................................................
    010000:  ..............................................................
    020000:  ..............................................................
    030000:  ..............................................................
    040000:  ..............................................................
    050000:  ..............................................................
    060000:  ..............................................................
    070000:  ..............................................................
```

continues

```
      080000: ................................................................
      090000: ................................................................

Upper memory area (UMA)

      0A0000: vvvvvvvvvvvvvvvvvvvvvvvvvvvvvvvvvvvvvvvvvvvvvvvvvvvvvvvvvvvvvvvvvv
      0B0000: vvvvvvvvvvvvvvvvvvvvvvvvvvvvvvvvvvvvvvvvvvvvvvvvvvvvvvvvvvvvvvvvvv
      0C0000: aaaaaaaaaaaaaaaaaaaaaaaaaaaaaaaaaaaaaaaaaaaaaaaaaaaaaaaaaaaaaaaa
      0D0000: aaaaaaaaaaaaaaaaaaaaaaaaaaaaaaaaaaaaaaaaaaaaaaaaaaaaaaaaaaaaaaaa
      0E0000: rrrrrrrrrrrrrrrrrrrrrrrrrrrrrrrrrrrrrrrrrrrrrrrrrrrrrrrrrrrrrrrr
      0F0000: rrrrrrrrrrrrrrrrrrrrrrrbbbbbbbbbbbbbbbbbbbbbbbbbbbbbbrrrrrrrrr

Extended memory

           : 0---1---2---3---4---5---6---7---8---9---A---B---C---D---E---F---
      100000: hhhhhhhhhhhhhhhhhhhhhhhhhhhhhhhhhhhhhhhhhhhhhhhhhhhhhhhhhhhhhhhhhh

XMS extended memory

      110000: ................................................................
      120000: ................................................................
      130000: ................................................................
      140000: ................................................................
      150000: ................................................................
      160000: ................................................................
      170000: ................................................................
      180000: ................................................................
      190000: ................................................................
      1A0000: ................................................................
      1B0000: ................................................................
      1C0000: ................................................................
      1D0000: ................................................................
      1E0000: ................................................................
      1F0000: ................................................................
           : 0---1---2---3---4---5---6---7---8---9---A---B---C---D---E---F---
      200000: ................................................................
      210000: ................................................................
      220000: ................................................................
      230000: ................................................................
      240000: ................................................................
      250000: ................................................................
      260000: ................................................................
      270000: .........................................................
      280000: ................................................................
      290000: ................................................................
      2A0000: ................................................................
      2B0000: ................................................................
      2C0000: ................................................................
      2D0000: ................................................................
      2E0000: ................................................................
      2F0000: ................................................................
```

```
         : 0---1---2---3---4---5---6---7---8---9---A---B---C---D---E---F---
300000: ................................................................
310000: ................................................................
320000: ................................................................
330000: ................................................................
340000: ................................................................
350000: ................................................................
360000: ................................................................
370000: ................................................................
380000: ................................................................
390000: ................................................................
3A0000: ................................................................
3B0000: ................................................................
3C0000: ................................................................
3D0000: ................................................................
3E0000: ................................................................
3F0000: ................................................................
         : 0---1---2---3---4---5---6---7---8---9---A---B---C---D---E---F---
400000: ................................................................
410000: ................................................................
420000: ................................................................
430000: ................................................................
440000: ................................................................
450000: ................................................................
460000: ................................................................
470000: ................................................................
480000: ................................................................
490000: ................................................................
4A0000: ................................................................
4B0000: ................................................................
4C0000: ................................................................
4D0000: ................................................................
4E0000: ................................................................
4F0000: ................................................................
         : 0---1---2---3---4---5---6---7---8---9---A---B---C---D---E---F---
500000: ................................................................
510000: ................................................................
520000: ................................................................
530000: ................................................................
540000: ................................................................
550000: ................................................................
560000: ................................................................
570000: ................................................................
580000: ................................................................
590000: ................................................................
5A0000: ................................................................
```

continues

```
5B0000: ................................................................
5C0000: ................................................................
5D0000: ................................................................
5E0000: ................................................................
5F0000: ................................................................
       : 0---1---2---3---4---5---6---7---8---9---A---B---C---D---E---F---
600000: ................................................................
610000: ................................................................
620000: ................................................................
630000: ................................................................
640000: ................................................................
650000: ................................................................
660000: ................................................................
670000: ................................................................
680000: ................................................................
690000: ................................................................
6A0000: ................................................................
6B0000: ................................................................
6C0000: ................................................................
6D0000: ................................................................
6E0000: ................................................................
6F0000: ................................................................
       : 0---1---2---3---4---5---6---7---8---9---A---B---C---D---E---F---
700000: ................................................................
710000: ................................................................
720000: ................................................................
730000: ................................................................
740000: ................................................................
750000: ................................................................
760000: ................................................................
770000: ................................................................
780000: ................................................................
790000: ................................................................
7A0000: ................................................................
7B0000: ................................................................
7C0000: ................................................................
7D0000: ................................................................
7E0000: ................................................................
7F0000: ................................................................
       : 0---1---2---3---4---5---6---7---8---9---A---B---C---D---E---F---
800000: ................................................................
810000: ................................................................
820000: ................................................................
830000: ................................................................
840000: ................................................................
850000: ................................................................
```

```
860000: ...............................................................
870000: ...............................................................
880000: ...............................................................
890000: ...............................................................
8A0000: ...............................................................
8B0000: ...............................................................
8C0000: ...............................................................
8D0000: ...............................................................
8E0000: ...............................................................
8F0000: ...............................................................
     : 0---1---2---3---4---5---6---7---8---9---A---B---C---D---E---F---
900000: ...............................................................
910000: ...............................................................
920000: ...............................................................
930000: ...............................................................
940000: ...............................................................
950000: ...............................................................
960000: ...............................................................
970000: ...............................................................
980000: ...............................................................
990000: ...............................................................
9A0000: ...............................................................
9B0000: ...............................................................
9C0000: ...............................................................
9D0000: ...............................................................
9E0000: ...............................................................
9F0000: ...............................................................
     : 0---1---2---3---4---5---6---7---8---9---A---B---C---D---E---F---
A00000: ...............................................................
A10000: ...............................................................
A20000: ...............................................................
A30000: ...............................................................
A40000: ...............................................................
A50000: ...............................................................
A60000: ...............................................................
A70000: ...............................................................
A80000: ...............................................................
A90000: ...............................................................
AA0000: ...............................................................
AB0000: ...............................................................
AC0000: ...............................................................
AD0000: ...............................................................
AE0000: ...............................................................
AF0000: ...............................................................
     : 0---1---2---3---4---5---6---7---8---9---A---B---C---D---E---F---
B00000: ...............................................................
B10000: ...............................................................
```

continues

```
B20000:  ................................................................
B30000:  ................................................................
B40000:  ................................................................
B50000:  ................................................................
B60000:  ................................................................
B70000:  ................................................................
B80000:  ................................................................
B90000:  ................................................................
BA0000:  ................................................................
BB0000:  ................................................................
BC0000:  ................................................................
BD0000:  ................................................................
BE0000:  ................................................................
BF0000:  ................................................................
      :  0---1---2---3---4---5---6---7---8---9---A---B---C---D---E---F---
C00000:  ................................................................
C10000:  ................................................................
C20000:  ................................................................
C30000:  ................................................................
C40000:  ................................................................
C50000:  ................................................................
C60000:  ................................................................
C70000:  ................................................................
C80000:  ................................................................
C90000:  ................................................................
CA0000:  ................................................................
CB0000:  ................................................................
CC0000:  ................................................................
CD0000:  ................................................................
CE0000:  ................................................................
CF0000:  ................................................................
      :  0---1---2---3---4---5---6---7---8---9---A---B---C---D---E---F---
D00000:  ................................................................
D10000:  ................................................................
D20000:  ................................................................
D30000:  ................................................................
D40000:  ................................................................
D50000:  ................................................................
D60000:  ................................................................
D70000:  ................................................................
D80000:  ................................................................
D90000:  ................................................................
DA0000:  ................................................................
DB0000:  ................................................................
DC0000:  ................................................................
DD0000:  ................................................................
```

```
     DE0000: ...................................................................
     DF0000: ...................................................................
           : 0---1---2---3---4---5---6---7---8---9---A---B---C---D---E---F---
     E00000: ...................................................................
     E10000: ...................................................................
     E20000: ...................................................................
     E30000: ...................................................................
     E40000: ...................................................................
     E50000: ...................................................................
     E60000: ...................................................................
     E70000: ...................................................................
     E80000: ...................................................................
     E90000: ...................................................................
     EA0000: ...................................................................
     EB0000: ...................................................................
     EC0000: ...................................................................
     ED0000: ...................................................................
     EE0000: ...................................................................
     EF0000: ...................................................................
           : 0---1---2---3---4---5---6---7---8---9---A---B---C---D---E---F---
     F00000: ...................................................................
     F10000: ...................................................................
     F20000: ...................................................................
     F30000: ...................................................................
     F40000: ...................................................................
     F50000: ...................................................................
     F60000: ...................................................................
     F70000: ...................................................................
     F80000: ...................................................................
     F90000: ...................................................................
     FA0000: ...................................................................
     FB0000: ...................................................................
     FC0000: ...................................................................
     FD0000: ...................................................................
     FE0000: rrrrrrrrrrrrrrrrrrrrrrrrrrrrrrrrrrrrrrrrrrrrrrrrrrrrrrrrrrrrrrrrrrr
     FF0000: rrrrrrrrrrrrrrrrrrrrrrrrrbbbbbbbbbbbbbbbbbbbbbbbbbbbbbbrrrrrrrrrrr
```

The motherboard ROM BIOS has a duplicated address space that makes it "appear" both at the end of the 1M real mode space and at the end of the 16M protected mode space.

The addresses from 0E0000-0FFFFF are equal to FE0000-FFFFFF. This is necessary because of differences in the memory addressing during the shift between real and protected modes.

Expanded Memory

The map in figure A.6 shows how expanded memory fits with conventional and extended memory.

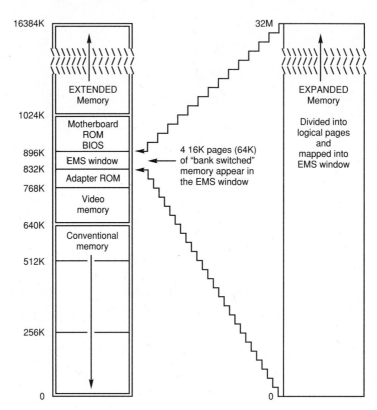

Fig. A.6

The relationship
between conventional, extended, and
expanded memory.

Hardware and ROM BIOS Data

This section has an enormous amount of detailed reference information covering a variety of hardware and ROM BIOS topics. These figures and tables cover very useful information, such as IBM PC and XT motherboard switch settings (see fig. A.7), AT CMOS RAM addresses, and diagnostic status-byte information. This section has also a variety of other hardware information, such as BIOS version data, keyboard scan codes, and a great deal of information about the expansion buses—pinouts, resources such as interrupts, DMA channels, and I/O port addresses. Finally, this section has a number of connector pinouts for serial, parallel, keyboard, video, and other connectors.

```
┌─────────────────────────────────┐        ┌──────────────────────────────┐
│ SWITCH BLOCK 1 (PC and XT)       │        │ SWITCH BLOCK 2 (PC only)     │
└─────────────────────────────────┘        └──────────────────────────────┘

Switch Block #1                             Total  │ Switch Block #2
1 2 34 56 78                                Memory (K) 1 2 3 4 5 6 7 8
│ │ ││ ││ ││                                    16  │ 1 1 1 1 0 0 0 0
│ │ ││ ││ │▼  NO. FLOPPY DRIVES:                 32  │ 1 1 1 1 1 0 0 0
│ │ ││ ││ │  11 = 1 floppy drive                 48  │ 1 1 1 1 0 0 0 0
│ │ ││ ││ │  01 = 2 floppy drives                64  │ 1 1 1 1 0 0 0 0
│ │ ││ ││ │  10 = 3 floppy drives                96  │ 0 1 1 1 1 0 0 0
│ │ ││ ││ │  00 = 4 floppy drives               128  │ 1 0 1 1 1 0 0 0
│ │ ││ ││                                       160  │ 0 0 1 1 1 0 0 0
│ │ ││ │▼  VIDEO ADAPTER:                        192  │ 1 1 0 1 1 0 0 0
│ │ ││ │  00 = Monochrome Display Adapter        224  │ 0 1 0 1 1 0 0 0
│ │ ││ │  01 = Color Graphics Adapter - 40x25    256  │ 1 0 0 1 1 0 0 0
│ │ ││ │  10 = Color Graphics Adapter - 80x25    288  │ 0 0 0 1 1 0 0 0
│ │ ││ │  11 = Video Adapter w/onboard BIOS      320  │ 1 1 1 0 1 0 0 0
│ │ ││                                          352  │ 0 1 1 0 1 0 0 0
│ │ │▼  FILLED MOTHERBOARD MEMORY BANKS:         384  │ 1 0 1 0 1 0 0 0
│ │ │  11 = Bank 0 only                          416  │ 0 0 1 0 1 0 0 0
│ │ │  01 = Banks 0 and 1                        448  │ 1 1 0 0 1 0 0 0
│ │ │  10 = Banks 0, 1 and 2                     480  │ 0 1 0 0 1 0 0 0
│ │ │  00 = All 4 Banks                          512  │ 1 0 0 0 1 0 0 0
│ │                                             544  │ 0 0 0 0 1 0 0 0
│ ▼  MATH CO-PROCESSOR:                          576  │ 1 1 1 1 0 0 0 0
│   0 = Installed                                608  │ 0 1 1 1 0 0 0 0
│   1 = Not Installed                            640  │ 1 0 1 1 0 0 0 0
▼  IBM PC:
0 = Boot From Floppy Drive                     ┌──────────────┐
1 = Do Not Boot From Floppy Drive              │ LEGEND:      │
▼  IBM XT:                                      │ 0 = Off      │
0 = Normal POST (Power-On Self Test)           │ 1 = On       │
1 = Continuous Looping POST                     └──────────────┘
```

Fig. A.7

IBM PC and XT
motherboard switch
settings.

Table A.28 shows the information maintained in the 64-byte AT CMOS
RAM module. This information controls the configuration of the system
much like the switches control the PC and XT configurations. This
memory is read and written by the system SETUP program.

Table A.28 AT CMOS RAM Addresses

Offset Hex	Dec	Field size	Function
00h	0	1 byte	Current second in binary coded decimal (BCD)
01h	1	1 byte	Alarm second in BCD
02h	2	1 byte	Current minute in BCD
03h	3	1 byte	Alarm minute in BCD
04h	4	1 byte	Current hour in BCD
05h	5	1 byte	Alarm hour in BCD
06h	6	1 byte	Current day of week in BCD
07h	7	1 byte	Current day in BCD
08h	8	1 byte	Current month in BCD
09h	9	1 byte	Current year in BCD
0Ah	10	1 byte	Status register A
			Bit 7 = Update in progress
			0 = Date and time can be read
			1 = Time update in progress
			Bits 6-4 = Time frequency divider
			010 = 32.768KHz
			Bits 3-0 = Rate selection frequency
			0110 = 1.024KHz square wave frequency

continues

Table A.28 Continued

Offset Hex	Dec	Field size	Function
0Bh	11	1 byte	Status register B
			Bit 7 = Clock update cycle
			0 = Update normally
			1 = Abort update in progress
			Bit 6 = Periodic interrupt
			0 = Disable interrupt (default)
			1 = Enable interrupt
			Bit 5 = Alarm interrupt
			0 = Disable interrupt (default)
			1 = Enable interrupt
			Bit 4 = Update-ended interrupt
			0 = Disable interrupt (default)
			1 = Enable interrupt
			Bit 3 = Status register A square wave frequency
			0 = Disable square wave (default)
			1 = Enable square wave
			Bit 2 = Date format
			0 = Calendar in BCD format (default)
			1 = Calendar in binary format
			Bit 1 = 24-hour clock
			0 = 24-hour mode (default)
			1 = 12-hour mode
			Bit 0 = Daylight Savings Time
			0 = Disable Daylight Savings (default)
			1 = Enable Daylight Savings
0Ch	12	1 byte	Status register C
			Bit 7 = IRQF flag
			Bit 6 = PF flag
			Bit 5 = AF flag
			Bit 4 = UF flag
			Bits 3-0 = Reserved
0Dh	13	1 byte	Status register D
			Bit 7 = Valid CMOS RAM bit
			0 = CMOS battery dead
			1 = CMOS battery power good
			Bits 6-0 = Reserved
0Eh	14	1 byte	Diagnostic status
			Bit 7 = Real-time clock power status
			0 = CMOS *has not* lost power
			1 = CMOS *has* lost power
			Bit 6 = CMOS checksum status
			0 = Checksum is good
			1 = Checksum is bad

Offset Hex	Dec	Field size	Function
			Bit 5 = POST configuration information status
			0 = Configuration information is valid
			1 = Configuration information is invalid
			Bit 4 = Memory size compare during POST
			0 = POST memory equals configuration
			1 = POST memory *not equal* to
			configuration
			Bit 3 = Fixed disk/adapter initialization
			0 = Initialization good
			1 = Initialization failed
			Bit 2 = CMOS time status indicator
			0 = Time is valid
			1 = Time is Invalid
			Bits 1-0 = Reserved
0Fh	15	1 byte	Shutdown code
			00h = Power on or soft reset
			01h = Memory size pass
			02h = Memory test pass
			03h = Memory test fail
			04h = POST end; boot system
			05h = JMP double word pointer with EOI
			06h = Protected mode tests pass
			07h = Protected mode tests fail
			08h = Memory size fail
			09h = Int 15h block move
			0Ah = JMP double word pointer without EOI
			0Bh = used by 80386
10h	16	1 byte	Floppy disk drive types
			Bits 7-4 = Drive 0 type
			Bits 3-0 = Drive 1 type
			0000 = None
			0001 = 360K
			0010 = 1.2M
			0011 = 720K
			0100 = 1.44M
11h	17	1 byte	Reserved
12h	18	1 byte	Hard disk types
			Bits 7-4 = Hard disk 0 type (0-15)
			Bits 3-0 = Hard disk 1 type (0-15)
13h	19	1 byte	Reserved
14h	20	1 byte	Installed equipment
			Bits 7-6 = Number of floppy disk drives
			00 = 1 floppy disk drive
			01 = 2 floppy disk drives
			Bits 5-4 = Primary display
			00 = Use display adapter BIOS
			01 = CGA 40-column

continues

Table A.28 Continued

Offset Hex	Dec	Field size	Function
			10 = CGA 80-column
			11 = Monochrome Display Adapter
			Bits 3-2 = Reserved
			Bit 1 = Math coprocessor present
			Bit 0 = Floppy disk drive present
15h	21	1 byte	Base memory low-order byte
16h	22	1 byte	Base memory high-order byte
17h	23	1 byte	Extended memory low-order byte
18h	24	1 byte	Extended memory high-order byte
19h	25	1 byte	Hard Disk 0 Extended Type (0-255)
1Ah	26	1 byte	Hard Disk 1 Extended Type (0-255)
1Bh	27	9 bytes	Reserved
2Eh	46	1 byte	CMOS checksum high-order byte
2Fh	47	1 byte	CMOS checksum low-order byte
30h	48	1 byte	Actual extended memory low-order byte
31h	49	1 byte	Actual extended memory high-order byte
32h	50	1 byte	Date century in BCD
33h	51	1 byte	POST information flag
			Bit 7 = Top 128K base memory status
			0 = Top 128K base memory not installed
			1 = Top 128K base memory installed
			Bit 6 = Setup program flag
			0 = Normal (default)
			1 = Put out first user message
			Bits 5-0 = Reserved
34h	52	2 bytes	Reserved

Table A.29 shows the values that may be stored by your system BIOS in a special CMOS byte called the *diagnostics status byte*. By examining this location with a diagnostics program, you can determine whether your system has set "trouble codes," which indicates that a problem previously has occurred.

Table A.29 CMOS RAM (AT and PS/2) Diagnostic Status Byte Codes

Bit number 7 6 5 4 3 2 1 0	Hex	Function
1	80	Real-time clock (RTC) chip lost power
. 1	40	CMOS RAM checksum is bad
. . 1	20	Invalid configuration information found at POST

Bit number 7 6 5 4 3 2 1 0	Hex	Function
. . . 1	10	Memory size compare error at POST
. . . . 1 . . .	08	Fixed disk or adapter failed initialization
. . . . . 1 . .	04	Real-time clock (RTC) time found invalid
. . . . . . 1 .	02	Adapters do not match configuration
. . . . 1	01	Time-out reading an adapter ID
. . . .	00	No errors found (Normal)

Table A.30 shows information about the different ROM BIOS versions that have appeared in various IBM systems.

Table A.30 IBM BIOS Model, Submodel, and Revision Codes

System description	CPU	Clock speed	Bus type/ width	ROM BIOS date	ID byte	Submodel byte	Revision	ST506 types drive
PC	8088	4.77 MHz	ISA/8	04/24/81	FF	—	—	—
PC	8088	4.77 MHz	ISA/8	10/19/81	FF	—	—	—
PC	8088	4.77 MHz	ISA/8	10/27/82	FF	—	—	—
PC-XT	8088	4.77 MHz	ISA/8	11/08/82	FE	—	—	—
PC-XT	8088	4.77 MHz	ISA/8	01/10/86	FB	00	01	—
PC-XT	8088	4.77 MHz	ISA/8	05/09/86	FB	00	02	—
PC*jr*	8088	4.77 MHz	ISA/8	06/01/83	FD	—	—	—
PC Convertible	80C8	4.77 MHz	ISA/8	09/13/85	F9	00	00	—
PS/2 25	8086	8 MHz	ISA/8	06/26/87	FA	01	00	26
PS/2 30	8086	8 MHz	ISA/8	09/02/86	FA	00	00	26
PS/2 30	8086	8 MHz	ISA/8	12/12/86	FA	00	01	26
PS/2 30	8086	8 MHz	ISA/8	02/05/87	FA	00	02	26
PC-AT	286	6 MHz	ISA/16	01/10/84	FC	—	—	15
PC-AT	286	6 MHz	ISA/16	06/10/85	FC	00	01	23
PC-AT	286	8 MHz	ISA/16	11/15/85	FC	01	00	23
PC-XT 286	286	6 MHz	ISA/16	04/21/86	FC	02	00	24
PS/1	286	10 MHz	ISA/16	12/01/89	FC	0B	00	44
PS/2 25 286	286	10 MHz	ISA/16	06/28/89	FC	09	02	37
PS/2 30 286	286	10 MHz	ISA/16	08/25/88	FC	09	00	37
PS/2 30 286	286	10 MHz	ISA/16	06/28/89	FC	09	02	37
PS/2 35 SX	386SX	20 MHz	ISA/16	03/15/91	F8	19	05	37
PS/2 35 SX	386SX	20 MHz	ISA/16	04/04/91	F8	19	06	37
PS/2 40 SX	386SX	20 MHz	ISA/16	03/15/91	F8	19	05	37
PS/2 40 SX	386SX	20 MHz	ISA/16	04/04/91	F8	19	06	37
PS/2 L40 SX	386SX	20 MHz	ISA/16	02/27/91	F8	23	02	37
PS/2 50	286	10 MHz	MCA/16	02/13/87	FC	04	00	32
PS/2 50	286	10 MHz	MCA/16	05/09/87	FC	04	01	32
PS/2 50Z	286	10 MHz	MCA/16	01/28/88	FC	04	02	33

continues

Table A.30 Continued

System description	CPU	Clock speed	Bus type/ width	ROM BIOS date	ID byte	Submodel byte	Revision	ST506 types drive
PS/2 50Z	286	10 MHz	MCA/16	04/18/88	FC	04	03	33
PS/2 55 SX	386SX	16 MHz	MCA/16	11/02/88	F8	0C	00	33
PS/2 55 LS	386SX	16 MHz	MCA/16	?	F8	1E	00	33
PS/2 57 SX	386SX	20 MHz	MCA/16	07/03/91	F8	26	02	None
PS/2 60	286	10 MHz	MCA/16	02/13/87	FC	05	00	32
PS/2 65 SX	386SX	16 MHz	MCA/16	02/08/90	F8	1C	00	33
PS/2 70 386	386DX	16 MHz	MCA/32	01/29/88	F8	09	00	33
PS/2 70 386	386DX	16 MHz	MCA/32	04/11/88	F8	09	02	33
PS/2 70 386	386DX	16 MHz	MCA/32	12/15/89	F8	09	04	33
PS/2 70 386	386DX	20 MHz	MCA/32	01/29/88	F8	04	00	33
PS/2 70 386	386DX	20 MHz	MCA/32	04/11/88	F8	04	02	33
PS/2 70 386	386DX	20 MHz	MCA/32	12/15/89	F8	04	04	33
PS/2 70 386	386DX	25 MHz	MCA/32	06/08/88	F8	0D	00	33
PS/2 70 386	386DX	25 MHz	MCA/32	02/20/89	F8	0D	01	33
PS/2 70 486	486DX	25 MHz	MCA/32	12/01/89	F8	0D	?	?
PS/2 70 486	486DX	25 MHz	MCA/32	09/29/89	F8	1B	00	?
PS/2 P70 386	386DX	16 MHz	MCA/32	?	F8	50	00	?
PS/2 P70 386	386DX	20 MHz	MCA/32	01/18/89	F8	0B	00	33
PS/2 P75 486	486DX	33 MHz	MCA/32	?	F8	52	00	?
PS/2 80 386	386DX	16 MHz	MCA/32	03/30/87	F8	00	00	32
PS/2 80 386	386DX	20 MHz	MCA/32	10/07/87	F8	01	00	32
PS/2 80 386	386DX	25 MHz	MCA/32	11/21/89	F8	80	01	?
PS/2 90 XP 486	486SX	20 MHz	MCA/32	?	F8	2D	00	?
PS/2 90 XP 486	487SX	20 MHz	MCA/32	?	F8	2F	00	?
PS/2 90 XP 486	486DX	25 MHz	MCA/32	?	F8	11	00	?
PS/2 90 XP 486	486DX	33 MHz	MCA/32	?	F8	13	00	?
PS/2 90 XP 486	486DX	50 MHz	MCA/32	?	F8	2B	00	?
PS/2 95 XP 486	486SX	20 MHz	MCA/32	?	F8	2C	00	?
PS/2 95 XP 486	487SX	20 MHz	MCA/32	?	F8	2E	00	?
PS/2 95 XP 486	486DX	25 MHz	MCA/32	?	F8	14	00	?
PS/2 95 XP 486	486DX	33 MHz	MCA/32	?	F8	16	00	?
PS/2 95 XP 486	486DX	50 MHz	MCA/32	?	F8	2A	00	?

The ID byte, Submodel byte, and Revision numbers are in hexadecimal.
— = This feature is not supported.
None = Only SCSI drives are supported.
? = Information unavailable.

Keyboard Key Numbers and Scan Codes

When a keyswitch on the keyboard fails, the scan code of the failed keyswitch is reported by diagnostics software, such as the POST. The tables in this section list all the scan codes for every key on the 83-, 84-, and 101-key keyboards. By looking up the reported scan code on these charts, you can determine which keyswitch is defective or needs to be cleaned.

Table A.31 83-Key (PC/XT) Keyboard Key Numbers and Scan Codes

Key number	Scan code	Key
1	01	Escape
2	02	1
3	03	2
4	04	3
5	05	4
6	06	5
7	07	6
8	08	7
9	09	8
10	0A	9
11	0B	0
12	0C	-
13	0D	=
14	0E	Backspace
15	0F	Tab
16	10	q
17	11	w
18	12	e
19	13	r
20	14	t
21	15	y
22	16	u
23	17	i
24	18	o
25	19	p
26	1A	[
27	1B	]
28	1C	Enter
29	1D	Ctrl
30	1E	a

continues

Table A.31 Continued

Key number	Scan code	Key
31	1F	s
32	20	d
33	21	f
34	22	g
35	23	h
36	24	j
37	25	k
38	26	l
39	27	;
40	28	'
41	29	`
42	2A	Left Shift
43	2B	\
44	2C	z
45	2D	x
46	2E	c
47	2F	v
48	30	b
49	31	n
50	32	m
51	33	,
52	34	.
53	35	/
54	36	Right Shift
55	37	*
56	38	Alt
57	39	Space bar
58	3A	Caps Lock
59	3B	F1
60	3C	F2
61	3D	F3
62	3E	F4
63	3F	F5
64	40	F6
65	41	F7
66	42	F8
67	43	F9
68	44	F10
69	45	Num Lock
70	46	Scroll Lock
71	47	Keypad 7 (Home)
72	48	Keypad 8 (Up arrow)
73	49	Keypad 9 (PgUp)
74	4A	Keypad -
75	4B	Keypad 4 (Left arrow)
76	4C	Keypad 5

continues

Key number	Scan code	Key
77	4D	Keypad 6 (Right arrow)
78	4E	Keypad +
79	4F	Keypad 1 (End)
80	50	Keypad 2 (Down arrow)
81	51	Keypad 3 (PgDn)
82	52	Keypad 0 (Ins)
83	53	Keypad . (Del)

Table A.32 84-Key (AT) Keyboard Key Numbers and Scan Codes

Key number	Scan code	Key
1	29	`
2	02	1
3	03	2
4	04	3
5	05	4
6	06	5
7	07	6
8	08	7
9	09	8
10	0A	9
11	0B	0
12	0C	-
13	0D	=
14	2B	\
15	0E	Backspace
16	0F	Tab
17	10	q
18	11	w
19	12	e
20	13	r
21	14	t
22	15	y
23	16	u
24	17	i
25	18	o
26	19	p
27	1A	[
28	1B	]
30	1D	Ctrl
31	1E	a
32	1F	s
33	20	d
34	21	f

continues

Table A.32 Continued

Key number	Scan code	Key
35	22	g
36	23	h
37	24	j
38	25	k
39	26	l
40	27	;
41	28	'
43	1C	Enter
44	2A	Left Shift
46	2C	z
47	2D	x
48	2E	c
49	2F	v
50	30	b
51	31	n
52	32	m
53	33	,
54	34	.
55	35	/
57	36	Right Shift
58	38	Alt
61	39	Space bar
64	3A	Caps Lock
65	3C	F2
66	3E	F4
67	40	F6
68	42	F8
69	44	F10
70	3B	F1
71	3D	F3
72	3F	F5
73	41	F7
74	43	F9
90	01	Escape
91	47	Keypad 7 (Home)
92	4B	Keypad 4 (Left arrow)
93	4F	Keypad 1 (End)
95	45	Num Lock
96	48	Keypad 8 (Up arrow)
97	4C	Keypad 5
98	50	Keypad 2 (Down arrow)
99	52	Keypad 0 (Ins)
100	46	Scroll Lock
101	49	Keypad 9 (PgUp)
102	4D	Keypad 6 (Right arrow)
103	51	Keypad 3 (PgDn)
104	53	Keypad . (Del)

Key number	Scan code	Key
105	54	SysRq
106	37	Keypad *
107	4A	Keypad –
108	4E	Keypad +

Table A.33 101/102-Key (Enhanced) Keyboard Key Numbers and Scan Codes

Key number	Scan code	Key
1	29	`
2	02	1
3	03	2
4	04	3
5	05	4
6	06	5
7	07	6
8	08	7
9	09	8
10	0A	9
11	0B	0
12	0C	-
13	0D	=
15	0E	Backspace
16	0F	Tab
17	10	q
18	11	w
19	12	e
20	13	r
21	14	t
22	15	y
23	16	u
24	17	i
25	18	o
26	19	p
27	1A	[
28	1B	]
29	2B	\ (101-key *only*)
30	3A	Caps Lock
31	1E	a
32	1F	s
33	20	d
34	21	f
35	22	g
36	23	h

continues

Table A.33 Continued

Key number	Scan code	Key
37	24	j
38	25	k
39	26	l
40	27	;
41	28	'
42	2B	# (102-key only)
43	1C	Enter
44	2A	Left Shift
45	56	\ (102-key only)
46	2C	z
47	2D	x
48	2E	c
49	2F	v
50	30	b
51	31	n
52	32	m
53	33	,
54	34	.
55	35	/
57	36	Right Shift
58	1D	Left Ctrl
60	38	Left Alt
61	39	Space bar
62	E0,38	Right Alt
64	E0,1D	Right Ctrl
75	E0,52	Insert
76	E0,53	Delete
79	E0,4B	Left arrow
80	E0,47	Home
81	E0,4F	End
83	E0,48	Up arrow
84	E0,50	Down arrow
85	E0,49	Page Up
86	E0,51	Page Down
89	E0,4D	Right arrow
90	45	Num Lock
91	47	Keypad 7 (Home)
92	4B	Keypad 4 (Left arrow)
93	4F	Keypad 1 (End)
95	E0,35	Keypad /
96	48	Keypad 8 (Up arrow)
97	4C	Keypad 5
98	50	Keypad 2 (Down arrow)
99	52	Keypad 0 (Ins)
100	37	Keypad *
101	49	Keypad 9 (PgUp)

Key number	Scan code	Key
102	4D	Keypad 6 (Left arrow)
103	51	Keypad 3 (PgDn)
104	53	Keypad . (Del)
105	4A	Keypad -
106	4E	Keypad +
108	E0,1C	Keypad Enter
110	01	Escape
112	3B	F1
113	3C	F2
114	3D	F3
115	3E	F4
116	3F	F5
117	40	F6
118	41	F7
119	42	F8
120	43	F9
121	44	F10
122	57	F11
123	58	F12
124	E0,2A,E0,37	Print Screen
125	46	Scroll Lock
126	E1,1D,45,E1,9D,C5	Pause

Hardware Interrupts

Interrupt request channels (IRQ), or hardware interrupts, are used by various hardware devices to signal the motherboard that a request must be fulfilled. These channels are represented by wires on the motherboard and in the slot connectors. When a particular interrupt is invoked, a special routine takes over the system, which first saves all the CPU register contents on a stack and then directs the system to the interrupt vector table. In this vector table is a list of program locations or addresses that correspond to each interrupt channel. Depending on which interrupt was invoked, the program corresponding to that channel is run. The pointers in this vector table point to the address of whatever software driver is used to service the card that generated the interrupt. For a network card, for example, the vector may point to the address of the network drivers that have been loaded to operate the card; for a hard disk controller, the vector may point to the ROM BIOS code that operates the controller. After the particular software routine is finished performing whatever function the card needed, the interrupt control software returns the stack contents to the CPU registers, and the system then continues whatever it was doing before the interrupt occurred.

By using interrupts, your system can respond in a timely fashion to external events. Each time a serial port presents a byte to your system, an interrupt is generated to ensure that the system responds immediately to read that byte before another comes in. Hardware interrupts are prioritized by their number, with the highest-priority interrupts having the lowest numbers. Higher-priority interrupts take precedence over lower-priority interrupts by interrupting them. In this way, several interrupts can occur concurrently in your system, each nesting within the other. If you overload the system, in this case by running out of stack resources, an `Internal stack overflow` message results. By increasing the available stack resources through the STACKS parameter in CONFIG.SYS, you can handle such situations.

The Industry Standard Architecture (ISA) bus uses *edge-triggered interrupt sensing*, in which the interrupt is sensed by the grounding of a particular wire located in the slot connector. A different wire corresponds to each hardware interrupt. Because the motherboard cannot recognize which slot contains the card that grounded the interrupt line and therefore generated the interrupt, if more than one card were set to use a particular interrupt, confusion would result. Each interrupt, therefore, usually is designated for a single hardware device, and most of the time cannot be "shared."

A device can be designed to share interrupts, and a few devices allow this; most cannot, however, because of the way interrupts are signaled in the ISA bus. Systems with the Micro Channel Architecture (MCA) bus use *level-sensitive interrupts*, which allows complete interrupt sharing to occur. In fact, all boards could be set to the same interrupt with no conflicts or problems. For maximum performance, however, interrupts should be staggered as much as possible. By eliminating interrupt conflicts as a problem, the MCA bus makes configuring boards much simpler than the ISA bus, and allows for more expansion, because you can never "run out of" interrupts.

Because interrupts usually cannot be shared in the ISA bus systems, you often will run out of interrupts when you are adding boards to a system. If two boards use the same interrupt level to signal the system, a conflict causes neither board to operate properly. The tables in the following sections show you the interrupt channels (IRQ) any standard devices use, and what may be free in your system. The AT systems have twice the number of interrupts and usually can be expanded much more easily than 8-bit ISA (PC or XT) systems.

PC and XT System Interrupts

The PC and XT have eight standard prioritized levels of interrupt, with the lower priority 6 (numbered 2-7) being bused to the system expansion slots. A special Non-Maskable Interrupt (NMI) has the highest priority. The interrupts are used as follows, in order of priority:

IRQ	Standard usage
NMI	Parity check, 8087
0	Channel 0 of the timer/counter for time-of-day clock
1	Keyboard
2	Available (most network adapters)
3	Secondary Asynchronous Communications (COM2:)
4	Primary Asynchronous Communications (COM1:)
5	Hard disk controller
6	Floppy disk controller
7	Parallel printer port 1 (LPT1:)

AT System Interrupts

The AT supports 16 standard levels of interrupts, with 11 channels bused to the expansion slots. A special Non-Maskable Interrupt (NMI) has the highest priority. Two Intel 8259A controllers are used, with 8 channels per chip. The interrupts from the second chip are cascaded through IRQ 2 on the first chip.

Because IRQ 2 now is used directly by the motherboard, the wire for IRQ 9 has been rerouted to the same position in the slot that IRQ 2 normally would occupy. Therefore, any board you install that is set to IRQ 2 is really using IRQ 9. The interrupt vector table has been adjusted accordingly to enable this deception to work. This adjustment to the system enables greater compatibility with the PC interrupt structure and enables cards set to IRQ 2 to work properly. Note that Interrupts 0, 1, 2, 8, and 13 are *not* on the bus connectors and are not accessible to adapter cards. Interrupts 8, 10, 11, 12, 13, 14, and 15 are from the second interrupt controller and are accessible only by boards that use the 16-bit extension connector, because this is where these wires are found. IRQ 9 is rewired to the 8-bit slot connector in place of IRQ 2, which means that IRQ 9 replaces IRQ 2 and therefore is available to 8-bit cards (as IRQ 2). Although the 16-bit ISA bus has twice as many interrupts as systems with the 8-bit ISA bus, you still will run out of available interrupts because only 16-bit adapters can use any of the new interrupts.

As before, although the MCA bus does follow this scheme, the interrupts can be shared without conflict. The interrupts are used as shown in this table:

IRQ	Standard usage
NMI	Parity check
0	Timer
1	Keyboard
2	Cascaded interrupts from second 8259 (IRQ 8-15)
8	Real-time clock
9	Redirected as IRQ 2 (appears as IRQ 2)
10	Available
11	Available
12	PS/2 mouse
13	Math coprocessor
14	Hard disk controller
15	Available
3	Serial port 2 (COM2:)
4	Serial port 1 (COM1:)
5	Parallel port 2 (LPT2:)
6	Floppy disk controller
7	Parallel port 1 (LPT1:)

DMA Channels

DMA channels are used by any high-speed communications devices that must send and receive information at high speed with the motherboard. For example, a hard disk controller uses DMA, but a floppy controller does not. A serial or parallel port does not use a DMA channel, but a network adapter often does. DMA channels sometimes can be shared if the devices are not of the type that would need them simultaneously. For example, you can have a network adapter and a tape backup adapter both sharing DMA channel 1, but you cannot back up while the network is running. To back up during network operation, you must ensure that each adapter used a unique DMA channel. Note that twice as many DMA channels are available in an AT-type system.

PC and XT DMA Channels

Four DMA (direct memory access) channels support high-speed data transfers between I/O devices and memory. Three of the channels are bused to the expansion slots, and are used as follows:

DMA	Standard usage
0	Used to refresh system dynamic RAM
1	Available
2	Floppy disk controller
3	Hard disk controller

AT DMA Channels

The system supports seven direct memory access (DMA) channels, with six bused to the expansion slots. DMA channel 4 is used to cascade channels 0 through 3 to the microprocessor. Channels 1-3 are available for 8-bit transfers, and DMA 0 and 5-7 are for 16-bit transfers only. The channels are used as shown in this table:

DMA	Standard usage
0	Available (16-bit only)
1	Available
2	Floppy disk controller
3	Available
4	Cascade for DMA 0-3
5	Available (16-bit only)
6	Available (16-bit only)
7	Available (16-bit only)

I/O Port Addresses

Input-output ports are addresses used by the processor to communicate directly with devices. These addresses are like memory addresses but are not for storage; 1,024 I/O ports are available in the IBM system design for both XT- and AT-type systems. Because the ports must be uniquely assigned to only a single board or device, the potential for conflicts exists. Plenty of I/O ports generally are available, but many boards do not allow their default port addresses to be changed.

Table A.34 lists all the default port addresses for any PC-type system. Note that the I/O addresses hex 000 to 0FF are reserved for the system board. Ports hex 100 to 3FF are available on the I/O channel.

Table A.34 8-Bit ISA I/O Port Addresses

Hex range	Device
000-00F	8237 DMA chip
020-021	8259 interrupt chip
040-043	8253 timer chip
060-063	8255 programmable peripheral interface chip
080	Manufacturer POST code port
080-083	DMA page registers
0A0	NMI mask register
0Cx	Reserved
0Ex	Reserved
200-20F	Game control
201	Game I/O
210-217	Expansion unit
278-27F	Parallel printer port 2
2B0-2DF	Alternate Enhanced Graphics Adapter
2E1	GPIB (Adapter 0)
2E2-2E3	Data acquisition (Adapter 0)
2F8-2FF	Serial port 2
300-31F	Prototype card
320-32F	Hard disk controller
348-357	DCA 3278
360-367	PC network (low address)
368-36F	PC network (high address)
378-37F	Parallel printer port 1
380-38F	SDLC, bisynchronous 2
390-393	Cluster
3A0-3AF	Bisynchronous 1
3B0-3BF	Monochrome Display and Printer Adapter
3C0-3CF	Enhanced Graphics Adapter
3D0-3DF	Color/Graphics Monitor Adapter
3F0-3F7	Floppy disk controller
3F8-3FF	Serial port 1
6E2-6E3	Data acquisition (Adapter 1)
790-793	Cluster (Adapter 1)
AE2-AE3	Data acquisition (Adapter 2)
B90-B93	Cluster (Adapter 2)
EE2-EE3	Data acquisition (Adapter 3)
1390-1393	Cluster (Adapter 3)
22E1	GPIB (Adapter 1)
2390-2393	Cluster (Adapter 4)
42E1	GPIB (Adapter 2)
62E1	GPIB (Adapter 3)
82E1	GPIB (Adapter 4)
A2E1	GPIB (Adapter 5)
C2E1	GPIB (Adapter 6)
E2E1	GPIB (Adapter 7)

Table A.35 lists all the default port addresses for any AT-type system. Note that the I/O addresses hex 000 to 0FF are reserved for the system board. Ports hex 100 to 3FF are available on the I/O channel.

Table A.35 16-bit ISA I/O Port Addresses

Hex range	Device
000-91F	DMA controller 1, 8237A-5
020-03F	Interrupt controller 1, 8259A, master
040-05F	Timer, 8254-2
060	8042 (keyboard)
061	System board I/O port
064	8042 (keyboard)
070-07F	Real-time clock, NMI (Non-Maskable Interrupt) mask
080	Manufacturer POST code port
080-09F	DMA page registers, 74LS612
0A0-0BF	Interrupt controller 2, 8237A-5
0F0	Clear math coprocessor busy
0F1	Reset math coprocessor
0F8-0FF	Math co-processor
1F0-1F8	Hard disk controller
21F	Voice communications adapter
278-27F	Parallel printer port 2
2B0-2DF	Alternate Enhanced Graphics Adapter
2E1	GPIB (Adapter 0)
2E2-2E3	Data acquisition (Adapter 0)
2F8-2FF	Serial Port 2
300-31F	Prototype adapter
360-363	PC network (low address)
368-36B	PC network (high address)
378-37F	Parallel printer port 1
380-38F	SDLC, bisynchronous 2
3A0-3AF	Bisynchronous 1
3B0-3BF	Monochrome Display and Printer Adapter
3C0-3CF	Enhanced Graphics Adapter
3D0-3DF	Color/Graphics Monitor Adapter
3F0-3F7	Floppy disk controller
3F8-3FF	Serial Port 1
6E2-6E3	Data acquisition (Adapter 1)
AE2-AE3	Data acquisition (Adapter 2)
EE2-EE3	Data acquisition (Adapter 3)
22E1	GPIB (Adapter 1)
42E1	GPIB (Adapter 2)
62E1	GPIB (Adapter 3)
82E1	GPIB (Adapter 4)
A2E1	GPIB (Adapter 5)
C2E1	GPIB (Adapter 6)
E2E1	GPIB (Adapter 7)

Connector Pinouts

This section lists the connector pinout specifications for a variety of connectors from the ISA and MCA bus connectors to serial and parallel ports as well as video display, keyboard, and even power-supply connectors. This information can be useful in troubleshooting cables or connections between devices.

8-Bit and 16-Bit ISA Bus Connector Pinouts

Figure A.8 shows the pinouts for the Industry Standard Architecture (ISA) PC, XT, and AT 8-bit and 16-bit expansion slot connectors.

```
8-bit PC/XT Connector:                    16-bit AT Connector:

Signal  Pin Numbers  Signal         Signal  Pin Numbers  Signal

  GROUND  —B1    A1—  -I/O CHK         GROUND  —B1    A1—  -I/O CHK
RESET DRV —B2    A2—  SD7            RESET DRV —B2    A2—  SD7
   +5 Vdc —B3    A3—  SD6               +5 Vdc —B3    A3—  SD6
    IRQ 2 —B4    A4—  SD5                IRQ 9 —B4    A4—  SD5
   -5 Vdc —B5    A5—  SD4               -5 Vdc —B5    A5—  SD4
    DRQ 2 —B6    A6—  SD3                DRQ 2 —B6    A6—  SD3
  -12 Vdc —B7    A7—  SD2              -12 Vdc —B7    A7—  SD2
-CARD SLCT —B8   A8—  SD1                 -OWS —B8    A8—  SD1
  +12 Vdc —B9    A9—  SD0              +12 Vdc —B9    A9—  SD0
   GROUND —B10   A10— -I/O RDY          GROUND —B10   A10— -I/O RDY
   -SMEMW —B11   A11— AEN               -SMEMW —B11   A11— AEN
   -SMEMR —B12   A12— SA19              -SMEMR —B12   A12— SA19
     -IOW —B13   A13— SA18                -IOW —B13   A13— SA18
     -IOR —B14   A14— SA17                -IOR —B14   A14— SA17
  -DACK 3 —B15   A15— SA16             -DACK 3 —B15   A15— SA16
    DRQ 3 —B16   A16— SA15               DRQ 3 —B16   A16— SA15
  -DACK 1 —B17   A17— SA14             -DACK 1 —B17   A17— SA14
    DRQ 1 —B18   A18— SA13               DRQ 1 —B18   A18— SA13
  -REFRESH —B19  A19— SA12             -REFRESH —B19  A19— SA12
      CLK —B20   A20— SA11                 CLK —B20   A20— SA11
    IRQ 7 —B21   A21— SA10               IRQ 7 —B21   A21— SA10
    IRQ 6 —B22   A22— SA9                IRQ 6 —B22   A22— SA9
    IRQ 5 —B23   A23— SA8                IRQ 5 —B23   A23— SA8
    IRQ 4 —B24   A24— SA7                IRQ 4 —B24   A24— SA7
    IRQ 3 —B25   A25— SA6                IRQ 3 —B25   A25— SA6
  -DACK 2 —B26   A26— SA5              -DACK 2 —B26   A26— SA5
      T/C —B27   A27— SA4                  T/C —B27   A27— SA4
     BALE —B28   A28— SA3                 BALE —B28   A28— SA3
   +5 Vdc —B29   A29— SA2               +5 Vdc —B29   A29— SA2
      OSC —B30   A30— SA1                  OSC —B30   A30— SA1
   GROUND —B31   A31— SA0               GROUND —B31   A31— SA0


                                       -MEM CS16 —D1   C1—  -SBHE
                                       -I/O CS16 —D2   C2—  LA23
                                          IRQ 10 —D3   C3—  LA22
                                          IRQ 11 —D4   C4—  LA21
                                          IRQ 12 —D5   C5—  LA20
                                          IRQ 15 —D6   C6—  LA19
                                          IRQ 14 —D7   C7—  LA18
                                          -DACK 0 —D8   C8—  LA17
                                            DRQ 0 —D9   C9—  -MEMR
                                          -DACK 5 —D10  C10— -MEMW
                                            DRQ 5 —D11  C11— SD8
                                            DACK 6 —D12  C12— SD9
                                            DRQ 6 —D13  C13— SD10
                                          -DACK 7 —D14  C14— SD11
                                            DRQ 7 —D15  C15— SD12
                                           +5 Vdc —D16  C16— SD13
                                          -MASTER —D17  C17— SD14
                                           GROUND —D18  C18— SD15
```

Fig. A.8

ISA 8- and 16-bit bus
connector pinouts.

Note: Signal names preceded by "-" are active low.

16-Bit and 32-Bit MCA Bus Connector Pinouts

Figure A.9 shows the pinouts for the Micro Channel Architecture (MCA) bus connectors in the PS/2 systems. The 16-bit connector with an optional auxiliary video-extension connector (AVEC) and the 32-bit connector with the optional matched memory extension are shown.

```
16-bit Connector with optional        32-bit Connector with optional
Auxiliary Video Extension:            Matched Memory Extension:

Signal  Pin Numbers  Signal

ESYNC   —BV10 AV10—  VSYNC
GROUND  —BV9  AV9—   HSYNC
P5      —BV8  AV8—   BLANK
P4      —BV7  AV7—   GROUND
P3      —BV6  AV6—   P6
GROUND  —BV5  AV5—   EDCLK          Signal  Pin Numbers  Signal
P2      —BV4  AV4—   DCLK
P1      —BV3  AV3—   GROUND         GROUND  —BM4  AM4—   Reserved
P0      —BV2  AV2—   P7             Reserved—BM3  AM3—   -MMC CMD
GROUND  —BV1  AV1—   EVIDEO         -MMCR   —BM2  AM2—   GROUND
Key                  Key            Reserved—BM1  AM1—   -MMC
AUDIO GND—B1   A1 —  -CD SETUP      AUDIO GND—B1   A1 —  -CD SETUP
AUDIO   —B2   A2 —   MADE 24        AUDIO   —B2   A2 —   MADE 24
GROUND  —B3   A3 —   GROUND         GROUND  —B3   A3 —   GROUND
OSC     —B4   A4 —   A11            OSC     —B4   A4 —   A11
GROUND  —B5   A5 —   A10            GROUND  —B5   A5 —   A10
A23     —B6   A6 —   A9             A23     —B6   A6 —   A9
A22     —B7   A7 —   +5 Vdc         A22     —B7   A7 —   +5 Vdc
A21     —B8   A8 —   A8             A21     —B8   A8 —   A8
GROUND  —B9   A9 —   A7             GROUND  —B9   A9 —   A7
A20     —B10  A10—   A6             A20     —B10  A10—   A6
A19     —B11  A11—   +5 Vdc         A19     —B11  A11—   +5 Vdc
A18     —B12  A12—   A5             A18     —B12  A12—   A5
GROUND  —B13  A13—   A4             GROUND  —B13  A13—   A4
A17     —B14  A14—   A3             A17     —B14  A14—   A3
A16     —B15  A15—   +5 Vdc         A16     —B15  A15—   +5 Vdc
A15     —B16  A16—   A2             A15     —B16  A16—   A2
GROUND  —B17  A17—   A1             GROUND  —B17  A17—   A1
A14     —B18  A18—   A0             A14     —B18  A18—   A0
A13     —B19  A19—   +12 Vdc        A13     —B19  A19—   +12 Vdc
A12     —B20  A20—   -ADL           A12     —B20  A20—   -ADL
GROUND  —B21  A21—   -PREEMPT       GROUND  —B21  A21—   -PREEMPT
-IRQ 9  —B22  A22—   -BURST         -IRQ 9  —B22  A22—   -BURST
-IRQ 3  —B23  A23—   -12 Vdc        -IRQ 3  —B23  A23—   -12 Vdc
-IRQ 4  —B24  A24—   ARB 0          -IRQ 4  —B24  A24—   ARB 0
GROUND  —B25  A25—   ARB 1          GROUND  —B25  A25—   ARB 1
-IRQ 5  —B26  A26—   ARB 2          -IRQ 5  —B26  A26—   ARB 2
-IRQ 6  —B27  A27—   -12 Vdc        -IRQ 6  —B27  A27—   -12 Vdc
-IRQ 7  —B28  A28—   ARB 3          -IRQ 7  —B28  A28—   ARB 3
GROUND  —B29  A29—   ARB/-GNT       GROUND  —B29  A29—   ARB/-GNT
Reserved—B30  A30—   -TC            Reserved—B30  A30—   -TC
Reserved—B31  A31—   +5 Vdc         Reserved—B31  A31—   +5 Vdc
-CHCK   —B32  A32—   -S0            -CHCK   —B32  A32—   -S0
GROUND  —B33  A33—   -S1            GROUND  —B33  A33—   -S1
-CMD    —B34  A34—   M/-IO          -CMD    —B34  A34—   M/-IO
CHRDYRTN—B35  A35—   +12 Vdc        CHRDYRTN—B35  A35—   +12 Vdc
-CD SFDBK—B36 A36—   CD CHRDY       -CD SFDBK—B36 A36—   CD CHRDY
GROUND  —B37  A37—   D0             GROUND  —B37  A37—   D0
D1      —B38  A38—   D2             D1      —B38  A38—   D2
D3      —B39  A39—   +5 Vdc         D3      —B39  A39—   +5 Vdc
D4      —B40  A40—   D5             D4      —B40  A40—   D5
GROUND  —B41  A41—   D6             GROUND  —B41  A41—   D6
CHRESET —B42  A42—   D7             CHRESET —B42  A42—   D7
Reserved—B43  A43—   GROUND         Reserved—B43  A43—   GROUND
Reserved—B44  A44—   -DS 16 RTN     Reserved—B44  A44—   -DS 16 RTN
GROUND  —B45  A45—   -REFRESH       GROUND  —B45  A45—   -REFRESH
                                    Key                  Key
                                    Key                  Key
                                    D8      —B48  A48—   +5 Vdc
```

Fig. A.9

MCA 16- and 32-bit bus connector pinouts.

Serial and Parallel Connector Pinouts

The tables in this section show the pinouts for all the different types of serial and parallel port connectors.

Table A.36 9-Pin (AT) Serial Port Connector

Pin	Description	Signal	Direction
1	Carrier detect	CD	In
✓2	Receive data	RD	In
✓3	Transmit data	TD	Out
✓4	Data terminal ready	DTR	Out
✓5	Signal ground	SG	—
6	Data set ready	DSR	In
✓7	Request to send	RTS	Out
8	Clear to send	CTS	In
9	Ring indicator	RI	In

Table A.37 25-Pin (PC, XT, and PS/2) Serial Port Connector

Pin	Description	Signal	Direction
1	Chassis Ground	—	—
2	Transmit Data	TD	Out
3	Receive Data	RD	In
4	Request to Send	RTS	Out
5	Clear to Send	CTS	In
6	Data Set Ready	DSR	In
7	Signal Ground	SG	—
8	Carrier Detect	CD	In
9	(+) Transmit Current Loop Return	—	Out
11	(−) Transmit Current Loop Data	—	Out
18	(+) Receive Current Loop Data	—	In
20	Data Terminal Ready	DTR	Out
22	Ring Indicator	RI	In
25	(−) Receive Current Loop Return	—	In

Pins 9, 11, 18, and 25 are used for a Current Loop interface only. Current Loop is not supported on the AT Serial/Parallel Adapter or PS/2 systems.

Table A.38 25-Pin (PC,XT,AT, and PS/2) Parallel Port Connector

Pin	Description	Direction
1	–Strobe	Out
2	+Data Bit 0	Out
3	+Data Bit 1	Out
4	+Data Bit 2	Out
5	+Data Bit 3	Out
6	+Data Bit 4	Out
7	+Data Bit 5	Out
8	+Data Bit 6	Out
9	+Data Bit 7	Out
10	–Acknowledge	In
11	+Busy	In
12	+Paper End	In
13	+Select	In
14	–Auto Feed	Out
15	–Error	In
16	–Initialize Printer	Out
17	–Select Input	Out
18	–Data Bit 0 Return (Ground)	In
19	–Data Bit 1 Return (Ground)	In
20	–Data Bit 2 Return (Ground)	In
21	–Data Bit 3 Return (Ground)	In
22	–Data Bit 4 Return (Ground)	In
23	–Data Bit 5 Return (Ground)	In
24	–Data Bit 6 Return (Ground)	In
25	–Data Bit 7 Return (Ground)	In

Table A.39 9-Pin to 25-Pin Serial Cable Adapter Connections

Description	Signal	9-pin	25-pin
Carrier Detect	CD	1	8
Receive Data	RD	2	3
Transmit Data	TD	3	2
Data Terminal Ready	DTR	4	20
Signal Ground	SG	5	7
Data Set Ready	DSR	6	6
Request to Send	RTS	7	4
Clear to Send	CTS	8	5
Ring Indicator	RI	9	22

Wrap Plug (Loopback) Wiring

Many third-party diagnostics packages do not have correctly wired wrap plugs. These plugs may pass their own tests, but fail tests by other diagnostics, especially IBM's Advanced Diagnostics. Figures A.10 through A.12 show the wiring of IBM's tri-connector wrap plug P/N 72X8546. These plugs pass IBM's Advanced Diagnostics as well as virtually all compatible diagnostics software tests that check serial and parallel ports.

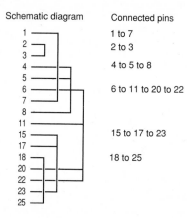

Schematic diagram	Connected pins
1	1 to 7
2	2 to 3
3	
4	4 to 5 to 8
5	
6	6 to 11 to 20 to 22
7	
8	
11	
15	15 to 17 to 23
17	
18	18 to 25
20	
22	
23	
25	

Fig. A.10

Twenty-five-pin serial loopback connector (wrap plug) wiring.

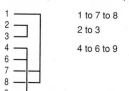

Schematic diagram	Connected pins
1	1 to 7 to 8
2	2 to 3
3	
4	4 to 6 to 9
6	
7	
8	
9	

Fig. A.11

Nine-pin serial loopback connector (wrap plug) wiring.

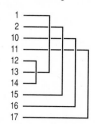

Schematic diagram	Connected pins
1	1 to 13
2	2 to 15
10	10 to 16
11	11 to 17
12	12 to 14
13	
14	
15	
16	
17	

Fig. A.12

Seventeen-pin parallel loopback connector (wrap plug) wiring.

Table A.40 shows the Monochrome Display Adapter connector pinout.

Table A.40 9-Pin Monochrome Display Adapter (MDA) Connector

Pin	Description	Direction
1	Ground	—
2	Ground	—
3	Not Used	—
4	Not Used	—
5	Not Used	—
6	+Intensity	Out
7	+Video	Out
8	+Horizontal	Out
9	—Vertical	Out

Table A.41 shows the Color Graphics Adapter connector pinout.

Table A.41 9-Pin Color Graphics Adapter (CGA) Connector

Pin	Description	Direction
		—
1	Ground	—
2	Ground	—
3	Red	Out
4	Green	Out
5	Blue	Out
6	+Intensity	Out
7	RESERVED	—
8	+Horizontal drive	Out
9	—Vertical drive	Out

Table A.42 shows the Enhanced Graphics Adapter connector pinout.

Table A.42 9-Pin Enhanced Graphics Adapter (EGA) Connector

Pin	Description	Direction
1	Ground	—
2	Secondary Red	Out
3	Red	Out
4	Green	Out
5	Blue	Out
6	Secondary Green/Intensity	Out
7	Secondary Blue/Mono video	Out
8	Horizontal Retrace	Out
9	Vertical Retrace	Out

Table A.43 shows the Video Graphics Array connector pinout.

Table A.43 15-Pin Video Graphics Array (VGA) Connector

Pin	Function	Direction
1	Red	Out
2	Green	Out
3	Blue	Out
4	Monitor ID 2	In
5	Digital Ground	—
6	Red Analog Ground	—
7	Green Analog Ground	—
8	Blue Analog Ground	—
9	Key (Plugged Hole)	—
10	Sync Ground	—
11	Monitor ID 0	In
12	Monitor ID 1	In
13	Horizontal Sync	Out
14	Vertical Sync	Out
15	Reserved	—

Figure A.13 and table A.44 show connector pinouts for each keyboard cable connectors.

Table A.44 Keyboard Connector Signals

Signal description	5-pin DIN	6-pin mini-DIN	6-pin SDL
Keyboard data	2	1	B
Ground	4	3	C
+5v	5	4	E
Keyboard clock	1	5	D
Not connected	—	2	A
Not connected	—	6	F
Not connected	3	—	—

DIN = German Industrial Norm (Deutsche Industrie Norm), a committee that sets German dimensional standards
SDL = Shielded Data Link, a type of shielded connector created by AMP and used by IBM and others for keyboard cables.

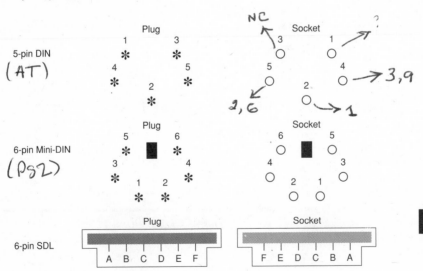

Fig. A.13

IBM keyboard connectors.

Table A.45 shows the pinouts for the PC, XT, and AT power-supply connectors.

Table A.45 PC, XT, and AT Power-Supply Connections

| | SYSTEM | |
Connector	AT, XT-286	PC, XT
P8-1	Power Good (+5)	Power Good (+5)
P8-2	+5	Key (No connect)
P8-3	+12	+12
P8-4	–12	–12
P8-5	Ground (0)	Ground (0)
P8-6	Ground (0)	Ground (0)
P9-1	Ground (0)	Ground (0)
P9-2	Ground (0)	Ground (0)
P9-3	–5	–5
P9-4	+5	+5
P9-5	+5	+5
P9-6	+5	+5
P10-1	+12	+12
P10-2	Ground (0)	Ground (0)
P10-3	Ground (0)	Ground (0)
P10-4	+5	+5
P11-1	+12	+12
P11-2	Ground (0)	Ground (0)
P11-3	Ground (0)	Ground (0)
P11-4	+5	+5
P12-1	+12	—
P12-2	Ground (0)	—
P12-3	Ground (0)	—
P12-4	+5	—

Acceptable voltage ranges are 4.5 to 5.4 for 5 volts, and 10.8 to 12.9 for 12 volts.

Disk Drives

This section has tables of information that pertain to disk drives. You can find a wealth of information here, including floppy and hard disk drive specifications and parameter data, information on the different disk interfaces from the ROM BIOS and DOS perspective, and even pinouts of the different hard disk interfaces.

Disk Software Interfaces

Figure A.14 shows a representation of the relationship between the different disk software interfaces at work in an IBM-compatible system. This figure shows the chain of command from the hardware, which is the drive controller, to the ROM BIOS, DOS, and, finally, an application program.

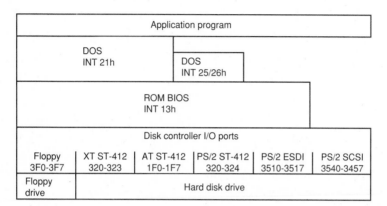

Fig. A.14

Disk software interfaces.

Table A.46 Int 13h BIOS Disk Functions

Function	Floppy disk	Hard disk	Description
00h	✓	✓	Reset disk system
01h	✓	✓	Get status of last operation
02h	✓	✓	Read sectors
03h	✓	✓	Write sectors
04h	✓	✓	Verify sectors
05h	✓	✓	Format track
06h		✓	Format bad track
07h		✓	Format drive
08h	✓	✓	Read drive parameters
09h		✓	Initialize drive characteristics
0Ah		✓	Read long
0Bh		✓	Write long
0Ch		✓	Seek
0Dh		✓	Alternate hard disk reset
0Eh		✓	Read sector buffer
0Fh		✓	Write sector buffer
10h		✓	Test for drive ready

continues

Table A.46 Continued

Function	Floppy disk	Hard disk	Description
11h		✓	Recalibrate drive
12h		✓	Controller RAM diagnostic
13h		✓	Controller drive diagnostic
14h		✓	Controller internal diagnostic
15h	✓	✓	Get disk type
16h	✓		Get floppy disk change status
17h	✓		Set floppy disk type for format
18h	✓		Set media type for format
19h		✓	Park hard disk heads
1Ah		✓	ESDI—Low-level format
1Bh		✓	ESDI—Get manufacturing header
1Ch		✓	ESDI—Get configuration

Table A.47 Int 13h BIOS Error Codes

Code	Description
00h	No error
01h	Bad command
02h	Address mark not found
03h	Write protect
04h	Request sector not found
05h	Reset failed
06h	Media change error
07h	Initialization failed
09h	Cross 64K DMA boundary
0Ah	Bad sector flag detected
0Bh	Bad track flag detected
10h	Bad ECC on disk read
11h	ECC corrected data error
20h	Controller has failed
40h	Seek operation failed
80h	Drive failed to respond
AAh	Drive not ready
BBh	Undefined error
CCh	Write fault
0Eh	Register error
FFh	Sense operation failed

Table A.48 Typical MFM Hard Disk Sector Format

Bytes	Name	Description
16	POST index gap	All 4Eh, at track beginning after index mark
		Sector data format; repeated 17 times for an MFM encoded track
13	ID VFO lock	All 00h to sync the VFO for the ID
1	Sync byte	A1h to notify controller that data follows
1	Address mark	FEh defining that ID field data follows
2	Cylinder number	A value defining actuator position
1	Head number	A value defining the head selected
1	Sector number	A value defining the sector
2	CRC	Cyclic redundancy check to verify ID data
3	Write turn-on gap	00h written by format to isolate ID from data
13	Data sync VFO lock	All 00h to sync the VFO for the DATA
1	Sync byte	A1h to notify controller that data follows
1	Address mark	F8h defining that user DATA field follows
512	Data	The area for user DATA
2	CRC	Cyclic redundancy check to verify DATA
3	Write turn-off GAP	00h written by DATA update to isolate data
15	Inter-record gap	All 00h as a buffer for speed variation
693	Pre-index gap	All 4Eh, at track end before INDEX mark

571 total bytes per sector
512 usable bytes per sector
10416 total bytes per track
8704 usable bytes per track

Characteristics of Floppy Drives and Disks

This section provides information about the physical properties of floppy disks and drives. This information shows how one type of disk or drive differs from the others in operation and use. The tables in this section explain the difference between floppy disk formats, how data is written to a disk, and how one type of media differs from the others. Knowing this information helps you prevent improper use and formatting of floppy disks, thereby preventing unnecessary future data loss.

Floppy Disk Physical Layout

Table A.49 indicates the physical geometry of each standard floppy disk format. From this information, you can see how the storage capacity of each type of disk is derived.

Table A.49 Floppy Disk Formats

5 1/4-inch	Double density	High density	
Bytes per sector	512	512	
Sectors per track	9	15	
Tracks per side	40	80	
Sides	2	2	
Capacity (K)	360	1,200	

3 1/2-inch	Double density	High density	Extra-high density
Bytes per sector	512	512	512
Sectors per track	9	18	36
Tracks per side	80	80	80
Sides	2	2	2
Capacity (K)	720	1,440	2,880

Table A.50 indicates the width of the magnetic track written by each of the standard floppy drives. Understanding this information helps you recognize when exchanging disks between two different drives is improper.

Table A.50 Floppy Disk Drive Track Width

Drive type	Number of tracks	Track width
5 1/4-inch 360K	40 per side	0.330 mm
5 1/4-inch 1.2M	80 per side	0.160 mm
3 1/2-inch 720K	80 per side	0.115 mm
3 1/2-inch 1.44M	80 per side	0.115 mm
3 1/2-inch 2.88M	80 per side	0.115 mm

For example, this table shows that because the 360K drive writes a track that is .330 millimeters wide, overwriting such a track using a 1.2M drive probably would result in a problem: when a wider track is overwritten by a narrower one, the overwrite will not be complete. Usually the 360K drive cannot further read a disk written on in this way. You also should be able to derive that full read-and-write interchangeability occurs between *all* the 3 1/2-inch drives. In other words, a 2.88M drive can write perfectly on 720K or 1.44M formatted floppy disks with no problems because the written track widths are the same between all of the standard 3 1/2-inch drives.

Floppy Disk Media Specifications

Table A.51 shows the physical differences between the various standard floppy disk media. A common misconception seems to exist among some users that double-density (DD) and high-density (HD) floppy disks are the same, especially in the 3 1/2-inch media. This is absolutely untrue! Many users who believe this myth are improperly formatting DD floppy disks as HD disks. These floppy disks are in fact very different physically and magnetically, as outlined here.

Table A.51 Floppy Disk Media Specifications

Media parameters	5 1/4-inch			3 1/2-inch		
	Double density (DD)	Quad density (QD)	High density (HD)	Double density (DD)	Extra-high density (HD)	High density (ED)
Tracks per inch (TPI)	48	96	96	135	135	135
Bits per inch (BPI)	5,876	5,876	9,646	8,717	17,434	34,868
Media formulation	Ferrite	Ferrite	Cobalt	Cobalt	Cobalt	Barium
Coercivity (oersteds)	300	300	600	600	720	750
Thickness (micro-inches)	100	100	50	70	40	100
Recording polarity	Horiz.	Horiz.	Horiz.	Horiz.	Horiz.	Vert.

This information should be used to discourage the use of "hole punchers" or other devices designed to allow someone to "fool" a drive into believing that a DD floppy disk is really a HD floppy disk. Improper formatting and use of such floppy disks causes data loss after the disk has been stored a while (usually six months to a year later) because of the inability of the lower-coercivity media to hold the magnetic patterns stable. Using devices or techniques to improperly format floppy disks in this fashion should be discouraged.

Table A.52 shows DOS parameters for each of the possible floppy drive formats through DOS V5.0. DOS uses this information when it formats a floppy disk.

Table A.52 Floppy Disk Logical (DOS) Parameters

	CURRENT FORMATS					OBSOLETE FORMATS		
Disk size (inches)	3 1/2	3 1/2	3 1/2	5 1/4	5 1/4	5 1/4	5 1/4	5 1/4
Disk capacity (K)	2880K	1440K	720K	1200K	360K	320K	180K	160K
Media descriptor byte	F0h	F0h	F9h	F9h	FDh	FFh	FCh	FEh
Sides (heads)	2	2	2	2	2	2	1	1
Tracks / side	80	80	80	80	40	40	40	40
Sectors / track	36	18	9	15	9	8	9	8
Bytes / sector	512	512	512	512	512	512	512	512
Sectors / cluster	2	1	2	1	2	2	1	1
FAT length (dectors)	9	9	3	7	2	1	2	1
Number of FATs	2	2	2	2	2	2	2	2
Root directory length (sectors)	15	14	7	14	7	7	4	4
Maximum root entries	240	224	112	224	112	112	64	64
Total sectors / disk	5760	2880	1440	2400	720	640	360	320
Total available sectors	5726	2847	1426	2371	708	630	351	313
Total available clusters	2863	2847	713	2371	354	315	351	313

Hard Disk Drives

This section has a great deal of information concerning all aspects of hard disk drives, including a table that lists a large number of different drive parameters, organized by manufacturer. Because Seagate is the largest supplier of hard disks in the world, and its product line is so extensive, a separate table references Seagate's hard disk product line, which shows the parameters of all of its drives. This section also shows BIOS hard drive parameter tables for a number of different ROM BIOS versions, including those from IBM, COMPAQ, AMI, Award, Phoenix, and Zenith. Finally, this section includes the pinouts of popular hard disk interfaces such as ST-506/412, ESDI, IDE, and SCSI.

Table A.53 shows parameters and specifications for a large number of different hard disk drives. This table can be very helpful when you are trying to install one of these drives in a system with no documentation for the drive.

Table A.53 Hard Disk Drive Specifications

Model number	Capacity (M)	Cylinders	Heads	Sectors /track	Write Pre-comp	Landing zone
Atasi						
502	46.0	755	7	17	—	—
504	46.0	755	7	17	—	—
514	117.2	1,224	11	17	—	—
519MFM	159.8	1,224	15	17	—	—
519RLL	244.4	1,224	15	26	—	—
617	149.0	1,223	7	34	—	—
628	234.2	1,223	11	34	—	—
638	319.3	1,223	15	34	—	—
3046	39.3	645	7	17	323	644
3051	42.9	704	7	17	352	703
3051+	44.7	733	7	17	368	732
3085	71.3	1,024	8	17	0	—
V130	25.8	987	3	17	128	—
V150	43.0	987	5	17	128	—
V170	60.1	987	7	17	128	—
V185	71.0	1,166	7	17	128	—
Brand Technology						
BT8085	71.3	1,024	8	17	512	—
BT8128	109.1	1,024	8	26	—	—
BT8170E	142.5	1,023	8	34	—	—
Conner Peripherals						
CP-342	42.7	981	5	17	—	—
CP-344	42.9	805	4	26	—	—
CP-3024	21.4	634	2	33	—	—
CP-3044	43.1	526	4	40	—	—
CP-3102-A	104.9	776	8	33	—	—
CP-3102-B	104.3	772	8	33	—	—
CP-3104	104.9	776	8	33	—	—
CP-3184	84.3	832	6	33	—	—
CP-3204	209.8	1,348	8	38	—	—
CP-3204F	212.9	684	16	38	—	—
CP-30104	121.6	1,522	4	39	—	—
CMI						
CM-6626	22.3	640	4	17	256	615
CM-6640	33.4	640	6	17	256	615

continues

Table A.53 Continued

Model number	Capacity (M)	Cylinders	Heads	Sectors /track	Write Pre-comp	Landing zone
Data-Tech Memories						
DTM-553	44.6	1,024	5	17	850	—
DTM-853	44.6	640	8	17	256	—
DTM-885	71.3	1,024	8	17	850	—
E.F. Industries						
3046	39.3	645	7	17	323	644
3051	42.9	704	7	17	352	703
Fujitsu						
M2225D	21.4	615	4	17	—	615
M2227D	42.8	615	8	17	—	615
M2241AS	26.3	754	4	17	128	—
M2242AS	45.9	754	7	17	128	—
M2243AS	72.2	754	11	17	128	—
M2244E	71.5	822	5	34	—	—
M2245E	100.2	822	7	34	—	—
M2246E	143.1	822	10	34	—	—
M2247E	151.3	1,242	7	34	—	—
M2248E	237.8	1,242	11	34	—	—
M2249E	324.3	1,242	15	34	—	—
M2261E	359.7	1,657	8	53	—	—
M2263E	674.5	1,657	15	53	—	—
M2611T	45.1	1,334	2	33	—	—
M2612T	90.2	1,334	4	33	—	—
M2613T	135.2	1,334	6	33	—	—
M2614T	180.3	1,334	8	33	—	—
Hewlett-Packard						
97544EF	339.9	1,456	8	57	128	—
97548EF	679.9	1,456	16	57	128	—
Hitachi						
DK511-3	30.4	699	5	17	300	699
DK511-5	42.6	699	7	17	300	699
DK511-8	71.6	823	10	17	256	—
DK512-8	71.5	822	5	34	—	—
DK512-10	85.9	822	6	34	—	—
DK512-12	100.2	822	7	34	—	—
DK512-17	143.1	822	10	34	—	—
DK514-38	329.7	902	14	51	—	—
DK522-10	85.9	822	6	34	—	—

Model number	Capacity (M)	Cylinders	Heads	Sectors /track	Write Pre-comp	Landing zone
Imprimis or CDC						
9415-519	18.2	697	3	17	128	—
9415-536	30.3	697	5	17	128	—
9415-538	31.9	733	5	17	128	—
94155-48	40.3	925	5	17	128	—
94155-56	72.5	925	9	17	128	—
94155-57	48.3	925	6	17	128	—
94155-67	56.4	925	7	17	128	—
94155-77	64.4	925	8	17	128	—
94155-85	71.3	1,024	8	17	—	—
94155-85P	71.3	1,024	8	17	128	—
94155-86	72.5	925	9	17	128	—
94155-96	80.2	1,024	9	17	—	—
94155-96P	80.2	1,024	9	17	128	—
94155-120	102.2	960	8	26	—	—
94155-120P	102.2	960	8	26	128	—
94155-135	115.0	960	9	26	—	—
94155-135P	115.0	960	9	26	128	—
94156-48	40.3	925	5	17	128	—
94156-67	56.4	925	7	17	128	—
94156-86	72.5	925	9	17	128	—
94166-101	84.3	968	5	34	—	—
94166-141	118.0	968	7	34	—	—
94166-182	151.7	968	9	34	—	—
94186-383	319.3	1,411	13	34	—	—
94186-383H	319.3	1,223	15	34	—	—
94186-442H	368.4	1,411	15	34	—	—
94196-766	663.9	1,631	15	53	—	—
94204-65	65.5	941	8	17	128	—
94204-71	71.3	1,024	8	17	128	—
94205-51	43.0	989	5	17	128	—
94205-77	65.8	989	5	26	128	—
94216-106	89.0	1,023	5	34	—	—
94244-383	338.1	1,747	7	54	—	—
94246-383	331.7	1,746	7	53	—	—
94354-135	143.3	1,072	9	29	128	—
94354-160	143.3	1,072	9	29	128	—
94354-172	177.8	1,072	9	36	—	—
94354-200	177.8	1,072	9	36	—	—
94354-230	211.0	1,272	9	36	—	—
94355-100	84.0	1,072	9	17	128	—
94355-150	128.4	1,072	9	26	128	—
94356-111	93.2	1,071	5	34	—	—
94356-155	130.5	1,071	7	34	—	—
94356-200	167.8	1,071	9	34	—	—

continues

Table A.53 Continued

Model number	Capacity (M)	Cylinders	Heads	Sectors /track	Write Pre- comp	Landing zone
Kalok						
KL320	21.4	615	4	17	—	660
KL330	32.7	615	4	26	—	660
KL343	42.5	670	4	31	—	669
Kyocera						
KC20A	21.4	616	4	17	0	—
KC20B	21.4	615	4	17	0	664
KC30A	32.8	616	4	26	0	—
KC30B	32.7	615	4	26	0	664
KC40GA	42.5	977	5	17	0	980
Lapine						
TITAN20	21.4	615	4	17	0	615
Maxtor						
LXT50S	48.0	733	4	32	—	—
LXT100S	96.1	733	8	32	—	—
LXT200A	200.5	816	15	32	—	—
LXT200S	212.9	1,320	7	45	—	—
LXT213A	212.6	683	16	38	—	—
LXT340S	352.2	1,560	7	63	—	—
LXT340AT	352.2	1,560	7	63	—	—
XT1050	39.3	902	5	17	—	—
XT1065	55.9	918	7	17	—	—
XT1085	71.3	1,024	8	17	—	—
XT1105	87.9	918	11	17	—	—
XT1120R	109.1	1,024	8	26	—	—
XT1140	119.9	918	15	17	—	—
XT1160	133.7	1,024	15	17	—	—
XT1240R	204.5	1,024	15	26	—	—
XT2085	74.6	1,224	7	17	—	—
XT2140	117.2	1,224	11	17	—	—
XT2190	159.8	1,224	15	17	—	—
XT4170E	149.2	1,224	7	34	—	—
XT4170S	149.2	1,224	7	34	—	—
XT4175	149.2	1,224	7	34	—	—
XT4230E	203.0	1,224	9	36	—	—
XT4280	234.4	1,224	11	34	—	—
XT4380E	338.4	1,224	15	36	—	—
XT4380S	338.4	1,224	15	36	—	—

Model number	Capacity (M)	Cylinders	Heads	Sectors /track	Write Pre- comp	Landing zone
XT8380E	361.0	1,632	8	54	—	—
XT8380S	361.0	1,632	8	54	—	—
XT8610E	541.5	1,632	12	54	—	—
XT8760E	676.8	1,632	15	54	—	—
XT8760S	676.8	1,632	15	54	—	—
XT8702S	617.9	1,490	15	54	—	—
XT8800E	694.7	1,274	15	71	—	—
Micropolis						
1323	35.7	1,024	4	17	—	—
1323A	44.6	1,024	5	17	—	—
1324	53.5	1,024	6	17	—	—
1324A	62.4	1,024	7	17	—	—
1325	71.3	1,024	8	17	—	—
1333	35.7	1,024	4	17	—	—
1333A	44.6	1,024	5	17	—	—
1334	53.5	1,024	6	17	—	—
1334A	62.4	1,024	7	17	—	—
1335	71.3	1,024	8	17	—	—
1353	71.2	1,023	4	34	—	—
1353A	89.0	1,023	5	34	—	—
1354	106.9	1,023	6	34	—	—
1354A	124.7	1,023	7	34	—	—
1355	142.5	1,023	8	34	—	—
1551	149.0	1,223	7	34	—	—
1554	234.2	1,223	11	34	—	—
1555	255.5	1,223	12	34	—	—
1556	276.8	1,223	13	34	—	—
1557	298.1	1,223	14	34	—	—
1558	319.3	1,223	15	34	—	—
1568-15	663.9	1,631	15	53	—	—
1653-4	86.9	1,248	4	34	—	—
1653-5	108.6	1,248	5	34	—	—
1654-6	130.4	1,248	6	34	—	—
1654-7	152.1	1,248	7	34	—	—
1664-7	337.9	1,779	7	53	—	—
1743-5	110.9	1,140	5	38	—	—
Microscience						
HH-325	21.4	615	4	17	—	615
HH-725	21.4	615	4	17	—	615
HH-1050	44.6	1,024	5	17	—	—
HH-1060	68.2	1,024	5	26	—	—
HH-1075	62.4	1,024	7	17	—	—

continues

Table A.53 Continued

Model number	Capacity (M)	Cylinders	Heads	Sectors /track	Write Pre-comp	Landing zone
HH-1090	80.1	1,314	7	17	—	—
HH-1095	95.4	1,024	7	26	—	—
HH-1120	122.4	1,314	7	26	—	—
HH-2120	124.7	1,023	7	34	—	—
HH-2160	155.4	1,275	7	34	—	—
4050	44.6	1,024	5	17	768	—
4060	68.2	1,024	5	26	768	—
4070	62.4	1,024	7	17	768	—
4090	95.4	1,024	7	26	768	—
5040-00	45.9	854	3	35	—	—
5070-00	76.5	854	5	35	—	—
5070-20	85.9	959	5	35	—	—
5100-00	107.1	854	7	35	—	—
5100-20	120.3	959	7	35	—	—
5160-00	159.3	1,270	7	35	—	—
7040-00	46.0	855	3	35	—	—
7070-00	76.6	855	5	35	—	—
7070-20	86.0	960	5	35	—	—
7100-00	107.3	855	7	35	—	—
7100-20	120.4	960	7	35	—	—

Miniscribe

Model number	Capacity (M)	Cylinders	Heads	Sectors /track	Write Pre-comp	Landing zone
1006	5.3	306	2	17	128	336
1012	10.7	306	4	17	128	336
2006	5.3	306	2	17	128	336
2012	10.7	306	4	17	128	336
3012	10.7	612	2	17	128	656
3053	44.6	1,024	5	17	512	—
3085	71.3	1,170	7	17	512	—
3130E	112.0	1,250	5	35	—	—
3180E	156.8	1,250	7	35	—	—
3180S	161.9	1,255	7	36	—	—
3212	10.7	612	2	17	128	656
3412	10.7	306	4	17	128	336
3425	21.4	615	4	17	128	656
3425P	21.4	615	4	17	128	656
3438	32.7	615	4	26	128	656
3438P	32.7	615	4	26	128	656
3650	42.2	809	6	17	128	852
3650R	64.6	809	6	26	128	852
3675	64.6	809	6	26	128	852
4010	8.4	480	2	17	128	522
4020	16.7	480	4	17	128	522
6032	26.7	1,024	3	17	512	—
6053	44.6	1,024	5	17	512	—
6079	68.2	1,024	5	26	512	—

Model number	Capacity (M)	Cylinders	Heads	Sectors /track	Write Pre-comp	Landing zone
6085	71.3	1,024	8	17	512	—
6128	109.1	1,024	8	26	512	—
7040A	42.7	981	5	17	—	—
7080A	85.4	981	10	17	—	—
8051A	42.7	745	4	28	—	—
8051S	42.7	745	4	28	—	—
8212	10.7	615	2	17	128	656
8225	20.5	771	2	26	128	810
8225A	21.4	615	4	17	—	810
8225XT	21.4	805	2	26	—	820
8412	10.7	306	4	17	128	336
8425	21.4	615	4	17	128	664
8425F	21.4	615	4	17	128	664
8425S	21.4	615	4	17	—	664
8425XT	21.4	615	4	17	—	664
8438	32.7	615	4	26	128	664
8438F	32.7	615	4	26	128	664
8450	41.1	771	4	26	128	810
8450A	42.7	745	4	28	—	810
8450XT	42.9	805	4	26	—	820
9380E	329.0	1,224	15	35	—	—
9380S	336.8	1,218	15	36	—	—
9780E	676.1	1,661	15	53	—	—
Mitsubishi						
MR522	21.3	612	4	17	300	612
MR535	42.5	977	5	17	0	—
MR535RLL	65.0	977	5	26	0	—
MR5310E	85.0	976	5	34	—	—
NEC						
D3126	21.4	615	4	17	256	664
D3142	44.7	642	8	17	128	664
D3146H	42.8	615	8	17	256	664
D3661	111.4	914	7	34	—	—
D3741	45.0	423	8	26	—	423
D5126	21.4	615	4	17	128	664
D5126H	21.4	615	4	17	128	664
D5127H	32.7	615	4	26	128	664
D5128	21.4	615	4	17	128	664
D5146H	42.8	615	8	17	128	664
D5147H	65.5	615	8	26	128	664
D5452	71.6	823	10	17	512	—
D5652	143.1	822	10	34	—	—
D5655	149.0	1,223	7	34	—	—
D5662	319.3	1,223	15	34	—	—
D5682	664.3	1,632	15	53	—	—

continues

Table A.53 Continued

Model number	Capacity (M)	Cylinders	Heads	Sectors /track	Write Pre-comp	Landing zone
Newbury						
NDR320	21.4	615	4	17	—	615
NDR340	42.8	615	8	17	—	615
NDR360	65.5	615	8	26	—	615
NDR1065	55.9	918	7	17	—	—
NDR1085	71.3	1,024	8	17	—	—
NDR1105	87.9	918	11	17	—	—
NDR1140	119.9	918	15	17	—	—
NDR2190	159.8	1,224	15	17	—	—
NDR4170	149.0	1,223	7	34	—	—
NDR4380	319.3	1,223	15	34	—	—
Pacific Magtron						
4115E	114.6	1,599	4	35	—	—
4140E	143.3	1,599	5	35	—	—
4170E	171.9	1,599	6	35	—	—
Plus Development						
IMPULSE 40AT	42.0	965	5	17	—	—
IMPULSE 80AT	84.0	965	10	17	—	—
IMPULSE 120AT	120.0	814	9	32	—	—
IMPULSE 170AT	168.5	968	10	34	—	—
IMPULSE 210AT	209.2	873	13	36	—	—
IMPULSE 52AT/LP	52.3	751	8	17	—	—
IMPULSE 80AT/LP	85.8	616	16	17	—	—
IMPULSE 105AT/LP	105.1	755	16	17	—	—
Priam						
502	46.0	755	7	17	—	—
504	46.0	755	7	17	—	—
514	117.2	1,224	11	17	—	—
519	159.8	1,224	15	17	—	—
617	143.8	751	11	34	—	—
623	196.1	751	15	34	—	—
630	319.3	1,223	15	34	—	—
V130	25.8	987	3	17	128	—
V150	43.0	987	5	17	128	—
V170	60.1	987	7	17	128	—
V185	71.0	1,166	7	17	128	—

Model number	Capacity (M)	Cylinders	Heads	Sectors /track	Write Pre-comp	Landing zone
PTI						
PT225	21.4	615	4	17	410	—
PT234	28.5	820	4	17	547	—
PT338	32.1	615	6	17	410	—
PT351	42.8	820	6	17	547	—
PT238R	32.7	615	4	26	410	—
PT251R	43.7	820	4	26	547	—
PT357R	49.1	615	6	26	410	—
PT376R	65.5	820	6	26	547	—
Quantum						
PRODRIVE 40AT	42.0	965	5	17	—	—
PRODRIVE 80AT	84.0	965	10	17	—	—
PRODRIVE 120AT	120.0	814	9	32	—	—
PRODRIVE 170AT	168.5	968	10	34	—	—
PRODRIVE 210AT	209.2	873	13	36	—	—
PRODRIVE LPS52	52.3	751	8	17	—	—
PRODRIVE LPS80	85.8	616	16	17	—	—
PRODRIVE LPS105	105.1	755	16	17	—	—
Q520	17.8	512	4	17	256	512
Q530	26.7	512	6	17	256	512
Q540	35.7	512	8	17	256	512
Rodime						
203	16.8	321	6	17	132	321
204	22.4	321	8	17	132	321
202E	22.3	640	4	17	0	640
203E	33.4	640	6	17	0	640
204E	44.6	640	8	17	0	640
3099A	80.2	373	15	28	—	—
3139A	112.5	523	15	28	—	—
3259A	212.9	990	15	28	—	—
RO3000A-NAT	43.2	625	5	27	0	—
RO3000A-XLAT	43.2	992	5	17	0	—
RO3060R	49.9	750	5	26	0	—
RO3075R	59.9	750	6	26	0	—
RO3085R	69.9	750	7	26	0	—
RO5040	32.0	1,224	3	17	0	—
RO5065	53.3	1,224	5	17	0	—
RO5090	74.6	1,224	7	17	0	—
Samsung						
SHD2020	21.8	820	2	26	—	—
SHD2021	23.5	820	2	28	—	—

continues

Table A.53 Continued

Model number	Capacity (M)	Cylinders	Heads	Sectors /track	Write Pre-comp	Landing zone
SHD2030	28.5	820	4	17	—	—
SHD2040	43.7	820	4	26	—	—
SHD2041	47.0	820	4	28	—	—
Siemens						
MEGAFILE-1200	169.2	1,215	8	34	—	—
MEGAFILE-1300	253.8	1,215	12	34	—	—
MEGAFILE-4410	321.9	1,099	11	52	—	—
Syquest						
SQ312RD	10.7	612	2	17	0	615
SQ315F	21.3	612	4	17	0	615
SQ338F	32.0	612	6	17	0	615
Tandon						
TN262	21.4	615	4	17	0	615
TN362	21.4	615	4	17	0	615
TN703	25.2	578	5	17	0	615
TN703AT	31.9	733	5	17	0	733
TN705	41.9	962	5	17	0	962
TN755	42.7	981	5	17	128	981
Toshiba						
MK-53F	36.1	830	5	17	—	—
MK-53F RLL	55.2	830	5	26	—	—
MK-54F	50.6	830	7	17	—	—
MK-54F RLL	77.3	830	7	26	—	—
MK-56F	72.2	830	10	17	—	—
MK-56F RLL	110.5	830	10	26	—	—
MK-72PC MFM	72.2	830	10	17	—	—
MK-72PC RLL	110.5	830	10	26	512	—
MK-134FA MFM	44.7	733	7	17	—	—
MK-134FA RLL	68.3	733	7	26	512	—
MK-153FA	72.2	829	5	34	—	—
MK-154FA	101.0	829	7	34	—	—
MK-156FA	144.3	829	10	34	—	—
MK-232FC	45.4	845	3	35	—	—
MK-234FC-I	106.0	845	7	35	—	—
MK-355FA	398.3	1,631	9	53	—	—
MK-358FA	663.9	1,631	15	53	—	—
Tulin						
TL226	22.3	640	4	17	—	640
TL240	33.4	640	6	17	—	640

Model number	Capacity (M)	Cylinders	Heads	Sectors /track	Write Pre- comp	Landing zone
Vertex						
V130	25.8	987	3	17	128	—
V150	43.0	987	5	17	128	—
V170	60.1	987	7	17	128	—
V185	71.0	1,166	7	17	128	—
Western Digital						
WD-93024A	21.6	782	2	27	—	—
WD-93028A	21.6	782	2	27	—	—
WD-93044A	43.2	782	4	27	—	—
WD-93048A	43.2	782	4	27	—	—
WD-95028A	21.6	782	2	27	—	—
WD-95044A	43.2	782	4	27	—	—
WD-95048A	43.2	782	4	27	—	—
WD-AC140	42.6	980	5	17	—	—
WD-AC280	85.3	980	10	17	—	—
WD-AP4200	212.2	987	12	35	—	—
WD-SP4200	209.7	1,280	8	40	—	—
WD-SC8320	326.5	949	14	48	—	—
WD-SC8400	413.2	1,201	14	48	—	—

—No write precompensation required, or no landing zone required (autopark).

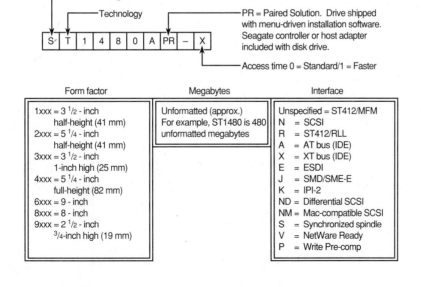

Fig. A.15

Seagate hard disk drive model code summary.

Table A.54 Seagate Hard Disk Drive Specifications

Seagate model number	Imprimis model number	Cylinders	Heads	Write Pre-comp	Landing zone	Sectors per track	Capacity (M)	Total sectors
ST124		615	4	—	670	17	21.4	41820
ST125		615	4	—	615	17	21.4	41820
ST125-1		615	4	—	615	17	21.4	41820
ST125a		404	4	—	404	26	21.5	42016
Custom/User		615	4	615	615	17	21.4	41820
ST125n		407	4	—	408	26	21.7	42328
ST137r		615	6	—	670	26	49.1	95940
ST138		615	6	—	615	17	32.1	62730
ST138a		604	4	—	604	26	32.2	62816
Custom/User		615	6	615	615	17	32.1	62730
ST138n		615	4	—	615	26	32.7	63960
ST138r		615	4	—	615	26	32.7	63960
ST151		977	5	—	977	17	42.5	83045
ST157a		560	6	—	560	26	44.7	87360
Custom/User		733	7	733	733	17	44.7	87227
ST157n		615	6	—	615	26	49.1	95940
ST157r		615	6	—	615	26	49.1	95940
ST177n		921	5	—	921	26	61.3	119730
ST212		306	4	128	319	17	10.7	20808
ST213		615	2	300	670	17	10.7	20910
ST224n		615	2	—	615	17	10.7	20910
ST225		615	4	300	670	17	21.4	41820
ST225n		615	4	—	615	17	21.4	41820
ST225r		667	2	—	670	31	21.2	41354
ST238		615	4	—	670	26	32.7	63960
ST238r		615	4	—	670	26	32.7	63960
ST250n		667	4	—	670	31	42.3	82708
ST250r		667	4	—	670	31	42.3	82708
ST251		820	6	—	820	17	42.8	83640
ST251n-0		820	4	—	820	26	43.7	85280
ST251n-1		630	4	—	630	34	43.9	85680
ST252		820	6	—	820	17	42.8	83640
ST253	94205-51	989	5	128	989	17	43.0	84065
ST274a	94204-74	948	5	—	948	27	65.5	127980
Custom/User		948	5	948	948	27	65.5	127980
ST277n-0		820	6	—	820	26	65.5	127920
ST277n-1		628	6	—	628	34	65.6	128112
ST277r		820	6	—	820	26	65.5	127920
ST278r		820	6	—	820	26	65.5	127920
ST279r	94205-77	989	5	—	989	26	65.8	128570
ST280a	94204-71	1032	5	—	1032	27	71.3	139320
Custom/User		1024	8	1024	1024	17	71.3	139264
ST280a	94204-81	1032	5	—	1032	27	71.3	139320
Custom/User		1024	8	1024	1024	17	71.3	139264

Seagate model number	Imprimis model number	Cylinders	Heads	Write Pre-comp	Landing zone	Sectors per track	Capacity (M)	Total sectors
ST296n		820	6	—	820	34	85.6	167280
ST325a		615	4	—	615	17	21.4	41820
Custom/User		615	4	615	615	17	21.4	41820
ST325a/x		615	4	—	615	17	21.4	41820
Custom/User		615	4	615	615	17	21.4	41820
ST325n		654	2	—	654	32	21.4	41856
ST325x		615	4	—	615	17	21.4	41820
ST351a		820	6	—	820	17	42.8	83640
Custom/User		820	6	820	820	17	42.8	83640
ST351a/x		820	6	—	820	17	42.8	83640
Custom/User		820	6	820	820	17	42.8	83640
ST351x		820	6	—	820	17	42.8	83640
ST406		306	2	128	319	17	5.3	10404
ST412		306	4	128	319	17	10.7	20808
ST419		306	6	128	319	17	16.0	31212
ST425		306	8	128	319	17	21.3	41616
ST506		153	4	128	157	17	5.3	10404
ST1057a		1024	6	—	1024	17*	53.5	104448
Custom/User		1024	6	1024	1024	17*	53.5	104448
ST1090a	94354-90	1072	5	—	1072	29	79.6	155440
Custom/User		335	16	335	335	29	79.6	155440
ST1090n	94351-90	1068	5	—	1068	29	79.3	154860
ST1096n		906	7	—	906	26	84.4	164892
ST1100	94355-100	1072	9	—	1072	17	84.0	164016
ST1102a		1024	10	—	1024	17*	89.1	174080
Custom/User		1024	10	1024	1024	17*	89.1	174080
ST1106r		977	7	—	977	26	91.0	177814
ST1111a	94354-111	1072	5	—	1072	36	98.8	192960
Custom/User		402	10	402	402	48	98.8	192960
ST1111e	94356-111	1072	5	—	1072	36	98.8	192960
ST1111n	94351-111	1068	5	—	1068	36	98.4	192240
ST1126a	94354-126	1072	7	—	1072	29	111.4	217616
Custom/User		469	16	469	469	29	111.4	217616
ST1126n	94351-125	1068	7	—	1068	29	111.0	216804
ST1133a	94354-133	1272	5	—	1272	36	117.2	228960
Custom/User		477	8	477	477	60	117.2	228960
ST1133n	94351-133s	1268	5	—	1268	36	116.9	228240
ST1144a		1001	15	—	1001	17*	130.7	255255
Custom/User		1001	15	1001	1001	17*	130.7	255255
ST1150r	94355-150	1072	9	300	1072	26	128.4	250848
ST1156a	94354-156	1072	7	—	1072	36	138.3	270144
Custom/User		536	9	536	536	56	138.3	270144
ST1156e	94356-156	1072	7	—	1072	36	138.3	270144
ST1156n	94351-155	1068	7	—	1068	36	137.8	269136
ST1156r	94355-156	1072	7	300	1072	36	138.3	270144
ST1162a	94354-162	1072	9	—	1072	29	143.3	279792
Custom/User		603	16	603	603	29	143.3	279792
ST1162n	94351-160	1068	9	—	1068	29	142.7	278748

3½" half height AT ohs (IDE) (handwritten annotation)

continues

Table A.54 Continued

Seagate model number	Imprimis model number	Cylinders	Heads	Write Pre-comp	Landing zone	Sectors per track	Capacity (M)	Total sectors
ST1182e		972	9	—	972	36	161.2	314928
ST1186a	94354-186	1272	7	—	1272	36	164.1	320544
Custom/User		636	9	636	636	56	164.1	320544
ST1186n	94351-186	1268	7	—	1268	36	163.6	319536
ST1201a	94354-201	1072	9	—	1072	36	177.8	347328
Custom/User		804	9	804	804	48	177.8	347328
ST1201e	94356-201	1072	9	—	1072	36	177.8	347328
ST1201n	94351-200	1068	9	—	1068	36	177.2	346032
ST1239a	94354-239	1272	9	—	1272	36	211.0	412128
Custom/User		954	12	954	954	36	211.0	412128
ST1239n	94351-230	1268	9	—	1268	36	210.3	410832
ST1400a		1475	7	—	1018	62*	327.8	640150
Custom/User		1018	12	1018	1018	53*	331.5	647448
ST1400n		1476	7	—	1476	62*	328.0	640584
ST1400ns		1476	7	—	1476	62*	328.0	640584
ST1401a		1132	9	—	1132	65*	339.1	662220
Custom/User		726	15	726	726	61*	340.1	664290
ST1401n		1100	9	—	1100	66*	334.5	653400
ST1401ns		1100	9	—	1100	66*	334.5	653400
ST1480a		1474	9	—	1474	62*	421.1	822492
Custom/User		895	15	895	895	62*	426.2	832350
ST1480n		1476	9	—	1476	62*	421.7	823608
ST1480ns		1476	9	—	1476	62*	421.7	823608
ST1480nv		1476	9	—	1476	62*	421.7	823608
ST1481n		1476	9	—	1476	62*	421.7	823608
ST1481nd		1476	9	—	1476	62*	421.7	823608
ST1581n		1476	9	—	1476	77*	523.7	1022868
ST1581nd		1476	9	—	1476	77*	523.7	1022868
ST1980n		1732	13	—	1732	74*	853.1	1666184
ST1980nd		1732	13	—	1732	74*	853.1	1666184
ST11200n		1875	15	—	1875	72*	1036.8	2025000
ST11200nd		1875	15	—	1875	72*	1036.8	2025000
ST2106e	94216-106	1024	5	—	1024	36	94.4	184320
ST2106n	94211-106	1024	5	—	1024	36	94.4	184320
ST2106n	94211-091	1024	5	—	1024	36	94.4	184320
ST2106nm	94211-106	1024	5	—	1024	36	94.4	184320
ST2125n	94221-125	1544	3	—	1544	45*	106.7	208440
ST2125nm	94221-125	1544	3	—	1544	45*	106.7	208440
ST2125nv	94221-125	1544	3	—	1544	45*	106.7	208440
ST2182e	94246-182	1453	4	—	1453	54	160.7	313848
ST2209n	94221-209	1544	5	—	1544	45*	177.9	347400
ST2209nm	94221-209m	1544	5	—	1544	45*	177.9	347400
ST2209nv	94221-209	1544	5	—	1544	45*	177.9	347400
ST2274a	94244-274	1747	5	—	1747	54	241.5	471690

Seagate model number	Imprimis model number	Cylinders	Heads	Write Pre-comp	Landing zone	Sectors per track	Capacity (M)	Total sectors
Custom/User		536	16	536	536	55	241.5	471680
ST2383a	94244-383	1747	7	—	1747	54	338.1	660366
Custom/User		737	16	737	737	56	338.1	660352
ST2383e	94246-383	1747	7	—	1747	54	338.1	660366
ST2383n	94241-383	1260	7	—	1260	74*	334.2	652680
ST2383nm	94241-383	1260	7	—	1260	74*	334.2	652680
ST2502n	94241-502	1756	7	—	1755	69*	434.3	848148
ST2502nm	94241-502	1756	7	—	1755	69*	434.3	848148
ST2502nv	94241-502	1756	7	—	1755	69*	434.3	848148
ST3051a		820	6	—	820	17	42.8	83640
Custom/User		820	6	820	820	17	42.8	83640
ST3096a		1024	10	—	1024	17	89.1	174080
Custom/User		1024	10	1024	1024	17	89.1	174080
ST3120a		1024	12	—	1024	17*	107.0	208896
Custom/User		1024	12	1024	1024	17*	107.0	208896
ST3144a		1001	15	—	1001	17*	130.7	255255
Custom/User		1001	15	1001	1001	17*	130.7	255255
ST3283a		978	14	—	978	35*	245.4	479220
Custom/User		978	14	978	978	35*	245.4	479220
ST3283n		1691	5	—	1691	57*	246.8	481935
ST4026		615	4	—	670	17	21.4	41820
ST4038		733	5	—	733	17	31.9	62305
ST4038m		733	5	—	733	17	31.9	62305
ST4051		977	5	—	977	17	42.5	83045
ST4053		1024	5	—	1024	17	44.6	87040
ST4085		1024	8	—	1024	17	71.3	139264
ST4086	94155-86	925	9	—	925	17	72.5	141525
ST4086p	94155-86p	925	9	128	925	17	72.5	141525
ST4096		1024	9	—	1024	17	80.2	156672
ST4097	94155-96	1024	9	—	1024	17	80.2	156672
ST4097p	94155-96p	1024	9	128	1024	17	80.2	156672
ST4135r	94155-135	960	9	—	960	26	115.0	224640
ST4144r		1024	9	—	1024	26	122.7	239616
ST4182e	94166-182	969	9	—	969	36	160.7	313956
ST4182e	94166-155	969	9	—	969	36	160.7	313956
ST4182n	94161-182	967	9	—	967	36	160.4	313308
ST4182nm	94161-182	967	9	—	967	36	160.4	313308
ST4350n	94171-300	1412	9	—	1412	46*	299.3	584568
ST4350n	94171-307	1412	9	—	1412	46*	299.3	584568
ST4350n	94171-327	1412	9	—	1412	46*	299.3	584568
ST4350n	94171-350	1412	9	—	1412	46*	299.3	584568
ST4350nm	94171-327	1412	9	—	1412	46*	299.3	584568
ST4376n	94171-344	1549	9	—	1549	45*	321.2	627345
ST4376n	94171-376	1549	9	—	1549	45*	321.2	627345
ST4376nm	94171-344	1549	9	—	1549	45*	321.2	627345
ST4376nv	94171-344	1549	9	—	1549	45*	321.2	627345
ST4383e	94186-383	1412	13	—	1412	36	338.3	660816

continues

Table A.54 Continued

Seagate model number	Imprimis model number	Cylinders	Heads	Write Pre-comp	Landing zone	Sectors per track	Capacity (M)	Total sectors
ST4384e	94186-383h	1224	15	—	1224	36	338.4	660960
ST4385n	94181-385h	791	15	—	791	55*	334.1	652575
ST4385nm	94181-385h	791	15	—	791	55*	334.1	652575
ST4385nv	94181-385h	791	15	—	791	55*	334.1	652575
ST4442e	94186-442	1412	15	—	1412	36	390.4	762480
ST4702n	94181-702	1546	15	—	1546	50*	593.7	1159500
ST4702nm	94181-702	1546	15	—	1546	50*	593.7	1159500
ST4766e	94196-766	1632	15	—	1632	54	676.8	1321920
ST4766n	94191-766	1632	15	—	1632	54	676.8	1321920
ST4766nm	94191-766	1632	15	—	1632	54	676.8	1321920
ST4766nv	94191-766	1632	15	—	1632	54	676.8	1321920
ST4767e		1399	15	—	1399	63	676.9	1322055
ST4767n	94601-767h	1356	15	—	1356	64*	666.5	1301760
ST4767nm	94601-767h	1356	15	—	1356	64*	666.5	1301760
ST4767nv	94601-767h	1356	15	—	1356	64*	666.5	1301760
ST4769e		1552	15	—	1552	53	631.7	1233840
ST41200n	94601-12g	1931	15	—	1931	70*	1038.1	2027550
ST41200nm	94601-12g	1931	15	—	1931	70*	1038.1	2027550
ST41200nv	94601-12g	1931	15	—	1931	70*	1038.1	2027550
ST41520n		2101	17	—	2101	77*	1408.1	2750209
ST41600n		2098	17	—	2098	74*	1351.3	2639284
ST41601n		2098	17	—	2098	74*	1351.3	2639284
ST41650n		2107	15	—	2110	87*	1407.8	2749635
ST41650nd		2107	15	—	2110	87*	1407.8	2749635
ST41651n		2107	15	—	2110	87*	1407.8	2749635
ST41651nd		2107	15	—	2110	87*	1407.8	2749635
ST42100n		2573	15	—	2573	96*	1897.0	3705120
ST42100nd		2573	15	—	2573	96*	1897.0	3705120
ST42101n		2573	15	—	2573	96*	1897.0	3705120
ST42101nd		2573	15	—	2573	96*	1897.0	3705120
ST42400n		2627	19	—	2627	83*	2121.1	4142779
ST42400nd		2627	19	—	2627	83*	2121.1	4142779
ST43400n		2627	21	—	2627	100*	2824.6	5516700
ST43401n		2627	21	—	2627	100*	2824.6	5516700
ST43401nd		2627	21	—	2627	100*	2824.6	5516700
ST9051a		654	4	—	654	32	42.9	83712
Custom/User		820	6	820	820	17	42.8	83640
ST9052a		980	5	—	980	17*	42.6	83300
Custom/User		980	5	980	980	17*	42.6	83300
ST9077a		802	4	—	802	39	64.1	125112
Custom/User		669	11	669	669	17	64.1	125103
ST9096a		980	10	—	980	17*	85.3	166600
Custom/User		980	10	980	980	17*	85.3	166600
ST9144a		980	15	—	980	17*	127.9	249900
Custom/User		980	15	980	980	17*	127.9	249900

Seagate model number	Imprimis model number	Cylinders	Heads	Write Pre-comp	Landing zone	Sectors per track	Capacity (M)	Total sectors
ST——	9415-521	697	3	0	697	17	18.2	35547
ST——	9415-525	697	4	0	697	17	24.3	47396
ST——	9415-536	697	5	0	697	17	30.3	59245
ST——	9415-538	733	5	0	733	17	31.9	62305
ST——	94151-42	921	5	—	921	17	40.1	78285
ST——	94151-62	921	7	—	921	17	56.1	109599
ST——	94151-80	921	9	—	921	17	72.1	140913
ST——	94155-48	925	5	—	925	17	40.3	78625
ST——	94155-48p	925	5	128	925	17	40.3	78625
ST——	94155-57	925	6	—	925	17	48.3	94350
ST——	94155-57p	925	6	128	925	17	48.3	94350
ST——	94155-67	925	7	—	925	17	56.4	110075
ST——	94155-67p	925	7	128	925	17	56.4	110075
ST——	94155-92	989	9	—	989	17	77.5	151317
ST——	94155-92p	989	9	128	989	17	77.5	151317
ST——	94155-130	1024	9	128	1024	26	122.7	239616
ST——	94156-48	925	9	—	925	17	72.5	141525
ST——	94156-67	925	7	—	925	17	56.4	110075
ST——	94156-86	925	7	—	925	17	56.4	110075
ST——	94161-86	969	5	—	969	35	86.8	169575
ST——	94161-103	969	6	—	969	35	104.2	203490
ST——	94161-121	969	7	—	969	35	121.6	237405
ST——	94161-138	969	8	—	969	35	138.9	271320
ST——	94166-86	969	5	—	969	35	86.8	169575
ST——	94166-103	969	6	—	969	35	104.2	203490
ST——	94166-121	969	7	—	969	35	121.6	237405
ST——	94166-138	969	8	—	969	35	138.9	271320
ST——	94244-219	1747	4	—	1747	54	193.2	377352
Custom/User		536	16	536	536	44	193.2	377344

Because these intelligent drives use zone-bit recording, the sectors-per-track value is an average, rounded down to the next-lower integer.

Model-number extension	Meaning
None	ST412 MFM interface
r	ST412 RLL interface
e	ESDI interface
x	XT-BUS embedded interface
a	AT-BUS embedded interface
a/x	Switchable XT or AT embedded interface
n	SCSI interface
nm	SCSI interface, Macintosh-compatible drive
nv	SCSI interface, NetWare-ready drive
ns	SCSI interface, synchronized spindle
nd	SCSI differential interface

Hard Disk Interface Pinouts

This section details the pinouts of each of the popular hard disk drive interfaces, including ST-506/412, ESDI, IDE, and SCSI (see figs. A.16, A.17, A.18, and A.19).

```
34-pin Control Connector:              20-pin Data Connector:

Signal Pin Numbers Signal              Signal Pin Numbers Signal

GROUND  ─1    2─  -HD SLCT 2(3)  -DRV SLCTD  ─1    2─  GROUND
GROUND  ─3    4─  -HD SLCT 2(2)    Reserved  ─3    4─  GROUND
GROUND  ─5    6─  -WRITE GATE      Reserved  ─5    6─  GROUND
GROUND  ─7    8─  -SEEK CMPLT      Reserved  ─7    8─  Key
GROUND  ─9   10─  -TRACK 0            Spare  ─9   10─  Spare
GROUND  ─11  12─  -WRITE FAULT      GROUND  ─11   12─  GROUND
GROUND  ─13  14─  -HD SLCT 2(0)  +MFM WRITE  ─13   14─  -MFM WRITE
Key     ─15  16─  Reserved          GROUND  ─15   16─  GROUND
GROUND  ─17  18─  -HD SLCT 2(1)   +MFM READ  ─17   18─  -MFM READ
GROUND  ─19  20─  -INDEX            GROUND  ─19   20─  GROUND
GROUND  ─21  22─  -READY
GROUND  ─23  24─  -STEP
GROUND  ─25  26─  -DRV SLCT 1
GROUND  ─27  28─  Reserved
GROUND  ─29  30─  Reserved
GROUND  ─31  32─  Reserved
GROUND  ─33  34─  -DIRECTION IN

Note: Signal names preceded by "-" are active low.
```

Fig. A.16

ST-506/412 hard
disk interface pinout.

```
34-pin Control Connector:              20-pin Data Connector:

Signal Pin Numbers Signal              Signal Pin Numbers Signal

GROUND  ─1    2─  -HD SLCT 2(3)  -DRV SLCTD  ─1    2─  -SECTOR
GROUND  ─3    4─  -HD SLCT 2(2)  -CMD COMPL  ─3    4─  -ADDR MK EN
GROUND  ─5    6─  -WRITE GATE       GROUND  ─5    6─  GROUND
GROUND  ─7    8─  -CNFG/STATUS  +WRITE CLK  ─7    8─  -WRITE CLK
GROUND  ─9   10─  -XFER ACK         GROUND  ─9   10─  +RD/REF CLK
GROUND  ─11  12─  -ATTENTION   -RD/REF CLK  ─11   12─  GROUND
GROUND  ─13  14─  -HD SLCT 2(0)  +NRZ WRITE  ─13   14─  -NRZ WRITE
Key     ─15  16─  -SECTOR          GROUND  ─15   16─  GROUND
GROUND  ─17  18─  -HD SLCT 2(1)   +NRZ READ  ─17   18─  -NRZ READ
GROUND  ─19  20─  -INDEX            GROUND  ─19   20─  -INDEX
GROUND  ─21  22─  -READY
GROUND  ─23  24─  -XFER REQ
GROUND  ─25  26─  -DRV SLCT 1
GROUND  ─27  28─  -DRV SLCT 2
GROUND  ─29  30─  Reserved
GROUND  ─31  32─  -READ GATE
GROUND  ─33  34─  -CMD DATA

Note: Signal names preceded by "-" are active low.
```

Fig. A.17

Enhanced Small
Device Interface (ESDI)
pinout.

Hard Disk Parameter Tables

When a hard disk drive is installed in a system, the system BIOS must be informed about the physical geometry of the drive in order for the Int 13h BIOS functions to work. Usually, the BIOS is informed through a table contained in the motherboard or controller BIOS that has entries defining various drive geometries. The disk installer then selects the entry that matches the drive being installed and normally informs the

BIOS through the system's SETUP utility. After entering the drive type through SETUP, the type information usually is maintained in CMOS RAM by virtue of a long-life lithium battery. With XT-class systems, the Int 13h BIOS support usually is found directly on the hard disk controller in a built-in BIOS. In this case, selection of a specific drive type usually is done by moving jumpers on the controller card.

```
ATA 40-pin Connector:

    Signal  Pin Numbers  Signal

        -RESET  —1      2—  GROUND
            D7  —3      4—  D8
            D6  —5      6—  D9
            D5  —7      8—  D10
            D4  —9     10—  D11
            D3  —11    12—  D12
            D2  —13    14—  D13
            D1  —15    16—  D14
            D0  —17    18—  D15
        GROUND  —19    20—  Key
      Reserved  —21    22—  GROUND
          -IOW  —23    24—  GROUND
          -IOR  —25    26—  GROUND
      Reserved  —27    28—  ALE
      Reserved  —29    30—  GROUND
        IRQ 14  —31    32—  -I/O CS16
            A1  —33    34—  -PDIAG
            A0  —35    36—  A2
        -CS1FX  —37    38—  -CS3FX
 -SLAVE PRESENT —39    40—  GROUND

Note: Signal names preceded by "-" are active low.
```

AT Attachment (ATA)
Integrated Drive
Electronics (IDE)
pinout.

```
Unshielded Internal              Shielded "D" Style
Header Connector:                External Connector:

Signal  Pin Numbers Signal       Signal  Pin Numbers  Signal

GROUND  —1    2—  DB 0           GROUND  —1    26—  DB 0
GROUND  —3    4—  DB 1           GROUND  —2    27—  DB 1
GROUND  —5    6—  DB 2           GROUND  —3    28—  DB 2
GROUND  —7    8—  DB 3           GROUND  —4    29—  DB 3
GROUND  —9   10—  DB 4           GROUND  —5    30—  DB 4
GROUND  —11  12—  DB 5           GROUND  —6    31—  DB 5
GROUND  —13  14—  DB 6           GROUND  —7    32—  DB 6
GROUND  —15  16—  DB 7           GROUND  —8    33—  DB 7
GROUND  —17  18—  DB P           GROUND  —9    34—  DB P
GROUND  —19  20—  GROUND         GROUND  —10   35—  GROUND
GROUND  —21  22—  GROUND         GROUND  —11   36—  GROUND
Reserved —23  24— Reserved       Reserved —12  37—  Reserved
Open    —25  26—  TERMPWR        Open    —13   38—  TERMPWR
Reserved —27  28— Reserved       Reserved —14  39—  Reserved
GROUND  —29  30—  GROUND         GROUND  —15   40—  GROUND
GROUND  —31  32—  -ATN           GROUND  —16   41—  -ATN
GROUND  —33  34—  GROUND         GROUND  —17   42—  GROUND
GROUND  —35  36—  -BSY           GROUND  —18   43—  -BSY
GROUND  —37  38—  -ACK           GROUND  —19   44—  -ACK
GROUND  —39  40—  -RST           GROUND  —20   45—  -RST
GROUND  —41  42—  -MSG           GROUND  —21   46—  -MSG
GROUND  —43  44—  -SEL           GROUND  —22   47—  -SEL
GROUND  —45  46—  -C/D           GROUND  —23   48—  -C/D
GROUND  —47  48—  -REQ           GROUND  —24   49—  -REQ
GROUND  —49  50—  -I/O           GROUND  —25   50—  -I/O

Note: Signal names preceded by "-" are active low.
```

SCSI-1 and SCSI-2
(single-ended)
interface pinouts.

In the case of the battery-maintained CMOS memory, this Setup procedure usually is performed only during these conditions:

■ The system is new and has not yet been set up.

■ A new peripheral is installed. CMOS normally stores information about these items only:

> Floppy drive types
> Hard drive types
> Base and extended memory amount
> Video Display Adapter and mode
> Math coprocessor—installed or not
> Date and time

■ The battery is dead or dying.

The Setup program comes on a disk for systems made by IBM or COMPAQ; most compatibles made after 1987, however, have the Setup program built directly into the BIOS. As a feature of some of the newer PS/2 systems (Models 57, 90, and 95), the Setup program, as well as the entire ROM BIOS, is stored on the hard disk in a special hidden, 3-megabyte partition—the system partition. Having the Setup built into the motherboard BIOS or loaded from a system partition as in the newer PS/2 systems is very convenient, and eliminates the need for a separate floppy disk containing the Setup program. Most of the time these BIOS-based Setup programs are activated by a particular keystroke sequence either at any time or only during the Power-On Self Test. The four popular compatible BIOS manufacturers use these keystrokes to activate Setup:

> Phoenix BIOS   Ctrl-Alt-Esc or Ctrl-Alt-S
> AMI BIOS   Del key during the POST
> Award BIOS   Ctrl-Alt-Esc
> IBM PS/2 BIOS   Ctrl-Alt-Ins after Ctrl-Alt-Del

With the Phoenix, Award, or IBM BIOS, you must hold the three keys down simultaneously to invoke Setup. With AMI, you just press the Del key during the POST. Note that only certain PS/2 models support Initial Microcode Load (IML) from the hard disk, which means that the BIOS and Reference disk (Setup) can be invoked with the indicated keystrokes.

To select the correct hard disk type for most ST-506/412, IDE, or ESDI type drives, you first must know your drive's physical characteristics. With most IDE drives, you need to know just the total number of sectors on the drive. SCSI drives almost always automatically configure to the system by entering a disk type of "0."

This step enables the SCSI BIOS to execute a SCSI Read Capacity command and supply the parameters to the system "on the fly."

Drive-parameter information can be found in the technical-reference documentation that came with your drive or system. If you did not get this documentation, call your vendor and demand it. After knowing the parameters for your drive, you need to find a table entry in your specific BIOS that matches the drive parameters. If none is an exact match, in some cases you can use an entry that is close as long as the entries for cylinders, heads, or sectors per track are not more than the drive is capable of. You also should match as close as possible the Write Precompensation starting cylinder value for reliable operation on the drive's inner cylinders. See Chapter 9, "Hard Disk Drives," for more information on selecting a correct type.

Because a variety of BIOS manufacturers are available in the marketplace, your systems may contain different tables. Each BIOS manufacturer has defined its own drive tables, usually starting with entries that are the same as IBM's. Most BIOS drive tables are similar to IBM for the first 15 or 23 entries, but from there they vary from manufacturer to manufacturer. For this reason, a drive manufacturer cannot simply stamp the drive type on the drive itself. For example, the correct drive type used for a Seagate ST-251 drive varies according to the BIOS manufacturer:

IBM BIOS	Type 8
COMPAQ BIOS	Type 5
AMI BIOS	Type 40
Award BIOS	Type 40
Phoenix BIOS	Type 44

Note that because of the lack of a user-definable type in the IBM and COMPAQ BIOS, this drive is not used to full capacity in those systems (especially in the IBM). So, if Seagate were to put the drive type on the drive, which number should it use? Obviously, it cannot do so, and the installer or data-recovery specialist must make the correct selection.

The tables in this section show the contents of the disk tables for a variety of BIOS manufacturers including IBM, COMPAQ, Phoenix, AMI, and Award. This information is helpful in determining the correct drive type for a particular drive and system combination. Note that some BIOS vendors now provide user-definable entries in their tables, which means that the values in the table can be typed directly from the keyboard, thereby allowing for virtually infinite customization without having to modify the BIOS itself.

Also included are tables for IBM's XT controllers, whose table format differs slightly from the tables in AT-class systems.

Table A.55 IBM 10M XT Hard Disk Controller (Xebec 1210) Drive

Entry	Type	Cylinders	Heads	WPC	Ctrl	LZ	S/T	Meg	MB
10M									
0	—	306	2	0	00h	00h	00h	5.08	5.33
1	—	375	8	0	05h	00h	00h	24.90	26.11
2	—	306	6	256	05h	00h	00h	15.24	15.98
3	—	306	4	0	05h	00h	00h	10.16	10.65
20M									
0	1	306	4	0	05h	305	17	10.16	10.65
1	16	612	4	0	05h	663	17	20.32	21.31
2	2	615	4	300	05h	615	17	20.42	21.41
3	13	306	8	128	05h	319	17	20.32	21.31

Entry = Controller table position
Jumper pins 1 and 2 define Drive 0 (C:); 3 and 4 define Drive 1 (D:).
Type = Drive type number
Heads = Total number of heads
WPC = write precompensation starting cylinder
Ctrl = Control byte; values according to following table:

Bit number	Hex	Meaning
Bit 0	01h	Drive step rate (see table)
Bit 1	02h	Drive step rate
Bit 2	04h	Drive step rate
Bit 3	08h	More than eight heads
Bit 4	10h	Imbedded servo drive
Bit 5	20h	OEM defect map at (cylinders + 1)
Bit 6	40h	Disable ECC retries
Bit 7	80h	Disable disk access retries

Table A.56 Xebec 1210 Drive Step Rate Coding (Control Byte)

Hex value	Definition
00h	3-millisecond step rate
04h	200-microsecond buffered step
05h	70-microsecond buffered step
06h	30-microsecond buffered step
07h	15-microsecond buffered step

```
           Controller Table Entry
Jumper pins #0    #1    #2    #3

          1   o=o   o=o   o o   o o
          2   o=o   o o   o=o   o o
          3   o=o   o=o   o o   o o
          4   o=o   o o   o=o   o o
```

Fig. A.20

Xebec 1210 drive table selection (jumper W5).

AT Motherboard BIOS Hard Drive Tables

Table A.57 shows the IBM motherboard ROM BIOS hard disk parameters for AT or PS/2 systems using ST-506/412 (standard or IDE) controllers.

Table A.57 IBM AT and PS/2 BIOS Hard Disk

Type	Cylinders	Heads	WPC	Ctrl	LZ	S/T -	Meg	MB
1	306	4	128	00h	305	17	10.16	10.65
2	615	4	300	00h	615	17	20.42	21.41
3	615	6	300	00h	615	17	30.63	32.12
4	940	8	512	00h	940	17	62.42	65.45
5	940	6	512	00h	940	17	46.82	49.09
6	615	4	65535	00h	615	17	20.42	21.41
7	462	8	256	00h	511	17	30.68	32.17
8	733	5	65535	00h	733	17	30.42	31.90
9	900	15	65535	08h	901	17	112.06	117.50
10	820	3	65535	00h	820	17	20.42	21.41
11	855	5	65535	00h	855	17	35.49	37.21
12	855	7	65535	00h	855	17	49.68	52.09
13	306	8	128	00h	319	17	20.32	21.31
14	733	7	65535	00h	733	17	42.59	44.66
15	0	0	0	00h	0	0	0	0
16	612	4	0	00h	663	17	20.32	21.31
17	977	5	300	00h	977	17	40.55	42.52
18	977	7	65535	00h	977	17	56.77	59.53
19	1024	7	512	00h	1023	17	59.50	62.39
20	733	5	300	00h	732	17	30.42	31.90
21	733	7	300	00h	732	17	42.59	44.66
22	733	5	300	00h	733	17	30.42	31.90
23	306	4	0	00h	336	17	10.16	10.65
24	612	4	305	00h	663	17	20.32	21.31
25	306	4	65535	00h	340	17	10.16	10.65
26	612	4	65535	00h	670	17	20.32	21.31

continues

Table A.57 Continued

Type	Cylinders	Heads	WPC	Ctrl	LZ	S/T	Meg	MB
27	698	7	300	20h	732	17	40.56	42.53
28	976	5	488	20h	977	17	40.51	42.48
29	306	4	0	00h	340	17	10.16	10.65
30	611	4	306	20h	663	17	20.29	21.27
31	732	7	300	20h	732	17	42.53	44.60
32	1023	5	65535	20h	1023	17	42.46	44.52
33	614	4	65535	20h	663	25	29.98	31.44
34	775	2	65535	20h	900	27	20.43	21.43
35	921	2	65535	20h	1000	33	29.68	31.12
36	402	4	65535	20h	460	26	20.41	21.41
37	580	6	65535	20h	640	26	44.18	46.33
38	845	2	65535	20h	1023	36	29.71	31.15
39	769	3	65535	20h	1023	36	40.55	42.52
40	531	4	65535	20h	532	39	40.45	42.41
41	577	2	65535	20h	1023	36	20.29	21.27
42	654	2	65535	20h	674	32	20.44	21.43
43	923	5	65535	20h	1023	36	81.12	85.06
44	531	8	65535	20h	532	39	80.89	84.82
45	0	0	0	00h	0	0	0.00	0.00
46	0	0	0	00h	0	0	0.00	0.00
47	0	0	0	00h	0	0	0.00	0.00

LZ = Landing zone cylinder for head parking
S/T = Number of sectors per track
Meg = Drive capacity in megabytes
MB = Drive capacity in millions of bytes
The Landing zone and Sectors per Track fields are not used in the 10MB (original) controller and contain 00h values for each entry.

Table entry 15 is reserved to act as a pointer to indicate that the type is greater than 15. Most IBM systems do not have every entry in this table. The maximum usable type number varies for each particular ROM version. The maximum usable type for each IBM ROM is indicated in the table on IBM ROM versions, earlier in this appendix. If you have a compatible, this table may be inaccurate for many of the entries past type 15. Instead, you should see whether one of the other tables listed here applies to your specific compatible ROM. Most compatibles follow the IBM table for at least the first 15 entries.

Most IBM PS/2 systems now are supplied with hard disk drives that have the defect map written as data on the cylinder one cylinder beyond the highest reported cylinder. This special data is read by the IBM PS/2 Advanced Diagnostics low-level format program. This process automates the entry of the defect list and eliminates the chance of human error, as long as you use only the IBM PS/2 Advanced Diagnostics for hard disk low-level formatting.

This type of table does not apply to IBM ESDI or SCSI hard disk controllers, host adapters, and drives. Because the ESDI and SCSI controllers or host adapters query the drive directly for the required parameters, no table-entry selection is necessary. Note, however, that the table for the ST-506/412 drives can still be found currently in the ROM BIOS of most of the PS/2 systems, even if the model came standard with an ESDI or SCSI disk subsystem.

Table A.58 shows the COMPAQ motherboard ROM BIOS hard disk parameters for the COMPAQ Deskpro 386.

Table A.58 COMPAQ Deskpro 386 Hard Disk								
Type	**Cylinders**	**Heads**	**WPC**	**Ctrl**	**LZ**	**S/T**	**Meg**	**MB**
1	306	4	128	00h	305	17	10.16	10.65
2	615	4	128	00h	638	17	20.42	21.41
3	615	6	128	00h	615	17	30.63	32.12
4	1024	8	512	00h	1023	17	68.00	71.30
5	940	6	512	00h	939	17	46.82	49.09
6	697	5	128	00h	696	17	28.93	30.33
7	462	8	256	00h	511	17	30.68	32.17
8	925	5	128	00h	924	17	38.39	40.26
9	900	15	65535	08h	899	17	112.06	117.50
10	980	5	65535	00h	980	17	40.67	42.65
11	925	7	128	00h	924	17	53.75	56.36
12	925	9	128	08h	924	17	69.10	72.46
13	612	8	256	00h	611	17	40.64	42.61
14	980	4	128	00h	980	17	32.54	34.12
15	0	0	0	00h	0	0	0	0
16	612	4	0	00h	612	17	20.32	21.31
17	980	5	128	00h	980	17	40.67	42.65
18	966	6	128	00h	966	17	48.11	50.45
19	1023	8	65535	00h	1023	17	67.93	71.23
20	733	5	256	00h	732	17	30.42	31.90
21	733	7	256	00h	732	17	42.59	44.66
22	805	6	65535	00h	805	17	40.09	42.04
23	924	8	65535	00h	924	17	61.36	64.34
24	966	14	65535	08h	966	17	112.26	117.71
25	966	16	65535	08h	966	17	128.30	134.53
26	1023	14	65535	08h	1023	17	118.88	124.66
27	966	10	65535	08h	966	17	80.19	84.08
28	748	16	65535	08h	748	17	99.34	104.17
29	805	6	65535	00h	805	26	61.32	64.30
30	615	4	128	00h	615	25	30.03	31.49

continues

Table A.58 Continued

Type	Cylinders	Heads	WPC	Ctrl	LZ	S/T	Meg	MB
31	615	8	128	00h	615	25	60.06	62.98
32	905	9	128	08h	905	25	99.43	104.26
33	748	8	65535	00h	748	34	99.34	104.17
34	966	7	65535	00h	966	34	112.26	117.71
35	966	8	65535	00h	966	34	128.30	134.53
36	966	9	65535	08h	966	34	144.33	151.35
37	966	5	65535	00h	966	34	80.19	84.08
38	611	16	65535	08h	611	63	300.73	315.33
39	1023	11	65535	08h	1023	33	181.32	190.13
40	1023	15	65535	08h	1023	34	254.75	267.13
41	1023	15	65535	08h	1023	33	247.26	259.27
42	1023	16	65535	08h	1023	63	503.51	527.97
43	805	4	65535	00h	805	26	40.88	42.86
44	805	2	65535	00h	805	26	20.44	21.43
45	748	8	65535	00h	748	33	96.42	101.11
46	748	6	65535	00h	748	33	72.32	75.83
47	966	5	128	00h	966	25	58.96	61.82

Table entry 15 is reserved to act as a pointer to indicate that the type is greater than 15.

Table A.59 shows the COMPAQ motherboard ROM BIOS hard disk parameters for the COMPAQ Deskpro 286 Revision F.

Table A.59 COMPAQ Deskpro 286 Revision F Hard Disk

Type	Cylinders	Heads	WPC	Ctrl	LZ	S/T	Meg	MB
1	306	4	128	00h	305	17	10.16	10.65
2	615	4	128	00h	638	17	20.42	21.41
3	615	6	128	00h	615	17	30.63	32.12
4	1024	8	512	00h	1023	17	68.00	71.30
5	940	6	512	00h	939	17	46.82	49.09
6	697	5	128	00h	696	17	28.93	30.33
7	462	8	256	00h	511	17	30.68	32.17
8	925	5	128	00h	924	17	38.39	40.26
9	900	15	65535	08h	899	17	112.06	117.50
10	980	5	65535	00h	980	17	40.67	42.65
11	925	7	128	00h	924	17	53.75	56.36
12	925	9	128	08h	924	17	69.10	72.46
13	612	8	256	00h	611	17	40.64	42.61
14	980	4	128	00h	980	17	32.54	34.12
15	0	0	0	00h	0	0	0	0
16	612	4	0	00h	612	17	20.32	21.31

Type	Cylinders	Heads	WPC	Ctrl	LZ	S/T	Meg	MB
17	980	5	128	00h	980	17	40.67	42.65
18	966	6	128	00h	966	17	48.11	50.45
19	1023	8	65535	00h	1023	17	67.93	71.23
20	733	5	256	00h	732	17	30.42	31.90
21	733	7	256	00h	732	17	42.59	44.66
22	768	6	65535	00h	768	17	38.25	40.11
23	771	6	65535	00h	771	17	38.40	40.26
24	966	14	65535	08h	966	17	112.26	117.71
25	966	16	65535	08h	966	17	128.30	134.53
26	1023	14	65535	08h	1023	17	118.88	124.66
27	966	10	65535	08h	966	17	80.19	84.08
28	771	3	65535	00h	771	17	19.20	20.13
29	578	4	65535	00h	578	17	19.19	20.12
30	615	4	128	00h	615	25	30.03	31.49
31	615	8	128	00h	615	25	60.06	62.98
32	966	3	65535	00h	966	34	48.11	50.45
33	966	5	65535	00h	966	34	80.19	84.08
34	966	7	65535	00h	966	34	112.26	117.71
35	966	8	65535	00h	966	34	128.30	134.53
36	966	9	65535	08h	966	34	144.33	151.35
37	966	5	65535	00h	966	34	80.19	84.08
38	1023	9	65535	08h	1023	33	148.35	155.56
39	1023	11	65535	08h	1023	33	181.32	190.13
40	1023	13	65535	08h	1023	33	214.29	224.70
41	1023	15	65535	08h	1023	33	247.26	259.27
42	1023	16	65535	08h	1023	34	271.73	284.93
43	756	4	65535	00h	756	26	38.39	40.26
44	756	2	65535	00h	756	26	19.20	20.13
45	768	4	65535	00h	768	26	39.00	40.89
46	768	2	65535	00h	768	26	19.50	20.45
47	966	5	128	00h	966	25	58.96	61.82

Table entry 15 is reserved to act as a pointer to indicate that the type is greater than 15.

Table A.60 shows the COMPAQ motherboard ROM BIOS hard disk parameters for the COMPAQ Deskpro 286e Revision B (03/22/89).

Table A.60 COMPAQ Deskpro 286e Revision B Hard Disk								
Type	Cylinders	Heads	WPC	Ctrl	LZ	S/T	Meg	MB
1	306	4	128	00h	305	17	10.16	10.65
2	615	4	128	00h	638	17	20.42	21.41
3	615	6	128	00h	615	17	30.63	32.12

continues

Table A.60 Continued

Type	Cylinders	Heads	WPC	Ctrl	LZ	S/T	Meg	MB
4	1024	8	512	00h	1023	17	68.00	71.30
5	805	6	65535	00h	805	17	40.09	42.04
6	697	5	128	00h	696	17	28.93	30.33
7	462	8	256	00h	511	17	30.68	32.17
8	925	5	128	00h	924	17	38.39	40.26
9	900	15	65535	08h	899	17	112.06	117.50
10	980	5	65535	00h	980	17	40.67	42.65
11	925	7	128	00h	924	17	53.75	56.36
12	925	9	128	08h	924	17	69.10	72.46
13	612	8	256	00h	611	17	40.64	42.61
14	980	4	128	00h	980	17	32.54	34.12
15	0	0	0	00h	0	0	0	0
16	612	4	0	00h	612	17	20.32	21.31
17	980	5	128	00h	980	17	40.67	42.65
18	966	5	128	00h	966	17	40.09	42.04
19	754	11	65535	08h	753	17	68.85	72.19
20	733	5	256	00h	732	17	30.42	31.90
21	733	7	256	00h	732	17	42.59	44.66
22	524	4	65535	00h	524	40	40.94	42.93
23	924	8	65535	00h	924	17	61.36	64.34
24	966	14	65535	08h	966	17	112.26	117.71
25	966	16	65535	08h	966	17	128.30	134.53
26	1023	14	65535	08h	1023	17	118.88	124.66
27	832	6	65535	00h	832	33	80.44	84.34
28	1222	15	65535	08h	1222	34	304.31	319.09
29	1240	7	65535	00h	1240	34	144.10	151.10
30	615	4	128	00h	615	25	30.03	31.49
31	615	8	128	00h	615	25	60.06	62.98
32	905	9	128	08h	905	25	99.43	104.26
33	832	8	65535	00h	832	33	107.25	112.46
34	966	7	65535	00h	966	34	112.26	117.71
35	966	8	65535	00h	966	34	128.30	134.53
36	966	9	65535	08h	966	34	144.33	151.35
37	966	5	65535	00h	966	34	80.19	84.08
38	611	16	65535	08h	611	63	300.73	315.33
39	1023	11	65535	08h	1023	33	181.32	190.13
40	1023	15	65535	08h	1023	34	254.75	267.13
41	1630	15	65535	08h	1630	52	620.80	650.96
42	1023	16	65535	08h	1023	63	503.51	527.97
43	805	4	65535	00h	805	26	40.88	42.86
44	805	2	65535	00h	805	26	20.44	21.43
45	748	8	65535	00h	748	33	96.42	101.11
46	748	6	65535	00h	748	33	72.32	75.83
47	966	5	128	00h	966	25	58.96	61.82

Table entry 15 is reserved to act as a pointer to indicate that the type is greater than 15.

Table A.61 shows the AMI ROM BIOS (286 BIOS Version 04/30/89) hard disk parameters.

Table A.61 AMI ROM BIOS (286 BIOS Version 04/30/89) Hard Disk

Type	Cylinders	Heads	WPC	Ctrl	LZ	S/T	Meg	MB
1	306	4	128	00h	305	17	10.16	10.65
2	615	4	300	00h	615	17	20.42	21.41
3	615	6	300	00h	615	17	30.63	32.12
4	940	8	512	00h	940	17	62.42	65.45
5	940	6	512	00h	940	17	46.82	49.09
6	615	4	65535	00h	615	17	20.42	21.41
7	462	8	256	00h	511	17	30.68	32.17
8	733	5	65535	00h	733	17	30.42	31.90
9	900	15	65535	08h	901	17	112.06	117.50
10	820	3	65535	00h	820	17	20.42	21.41
11	855	5	65535	00h	855	17	35.49	37.21
12	855	7	65535	00h	855	17	49.68	52.09
13	306	8	128	00h	319	17	20.32	21.31
14	733	7	65535	00h	733	17	42.59	44.66
15	0	0	0	00h	0	0	0	0
16	612	4	0	00h	663	17	20.32	21.31
17	977	5	300	00h	977	17	40.55	42.52
18	977	7	65535	00h	977	17	56.77	59.53
19	1024	7	512	00h	1023	17	59.50	62.39
20	733	5	300	00h	732	17	30.42	31.90
21	733	7	300	00h	732	17	42.59	44.66
22	733	5	300	00h	733	17	30.42	31.90
23	306	4	0	00h	336	17	10.16	10.65
24	925	7	0	00h	925	17	53.75	56.36
25	925	9	65535	08h	925	17	69.10	72.46
26	754	7	526	00h	754	17	43.81	45.94
27	754	11	65535	08h	754	17	68.85	72.19
28	699	7	256	00h	699	17	40.62	42.59
29	823	10	65535	08h	823	17	68.32	71.63
30	918	7	874	00h	918	17	53.34	55.93
31	1024	11	65535	08h	1024	17	93.50	98.04
32	1024	15	65535	08h	1024	17	127.50	133.69
33	1024	5	1024	00h	1024	17	42.50	44.56
34	612	2	128	00h	612	17	10.16	10.65
35	1024	9	65535	08h	1024	17	76.50	80.22
36	1024	8	512	00h	1024	17	68.00	71.30
37	615	8	128	00h	615	17	40.84	42.82
38	987	3	805	00h	987	17	24.58	25.77
39	987	7	805	00h	987	17	57.35	60.14
40	820	6	820	00h	820	17	40.84	42.82
41	977	5	815	00h	977	17	40.55	42.52
42	981	5	811	00h	981	17	40.72	42.69

continues

Table A.61 Continued

Type	Cylinders	Heads	WPC	Ctrl	LZ	S/T	Meg	MB
43	830	7	512	00h	830	17	48.23	50.57
44	830	10	65535	08h	830	17	68.90	72.24
45	917	15	65535	08h	918	17	114.18	119.72
46	1224	15	65535	08h	1223	17	152.40	159.81
47	0	0	0	00h	0	0	0.00	0.00

Table entry 15 is reserved to act as a pointer to indicate that the type is greater than 15. This BIOS uses type 47 as a user-definable entry.

Table A.62 shows the Award ROM BIOS (286 BIOS Version 04/30/89) (Modular 286, 386SX, and 386 BIOS Version 3.05) hard disk parameters.

Table A.62 Award ROM BIOS Version 3.05 Hard Disk

Type	Cylinders	Heads	WPC	Ctrl	LZ	S/T	Meg	MB
1	306	4	128	00h	305	17	10.16	10.65
2	615	4	300	00h	615	17	20.42	21.41
3	615	6	300	00h	615	17	30.63	32.12
4	940	8	512	00h	940	17	62.42	65.45
5	940	6	512	00h	940	17	46.82	49.09
6	615	4	65535	00h	615	17	20.42	21.41
7	462	8	256	00h	511	17	30.68	32.17
8	733	5	65535	00h	733	17	30.42	31.90
9	900	15	65535	08h	901	17	112.06	117.50
10	820	3	65535	00h	820	17	20.42	21.41
11	855	5	65535	00h	855	17	35.49	37.21
12	855	7	65535	00h	855	17	49.68	52.09
13	306	8	128	00h	319	17	20.32	21.31
14	733	7	65535	00h	733	17	42.59	44.66
15	0	0	0	00h	0	0	0	0
16	612	4	0	00h	663	17	20.32	21.31
17	977	5	300	00h	977	17	40.55	42.52
18	977	7	65535	00h	977	17	56.77	59.53
19	1024	7	512	00h	1023	17	59.50	62.39
20	733	5	300	00h	732	17	30.42	31.90
21	733	7	300	00h	732	17	42.59	44.66
22	733	5	300	00h	733	17	30.42	31.90
23	306	4	0	00h	336	17	10.16	10.65
24	977	5	65535	00h	976	17	40.55	42.52
25	1024	9	65535	08h	1023	17	76.50	80.22
26	1224	7	65535	00h	1223	17	71.12	74.58
27	1224	11	65535	08h	1223	17	111.76	117.19

Type	Cylinders	Heads	WPC	Ctrl	LZ	S/T	Meg	MB
28	1224	15	65535	08h	1223	17	152.40	159.81
29	1024	8	65535	00h	1023	17	68.00	71.30
30	1024	11	65535	08h	1023	17	93.50	98.04
31	918	11	65535	08h	1023	17	83.82	87.89
32	925	9	65535	08h	926	17	69.10	72.46
33	1024	10	65535	08h	1023	17	85.00	89.13
34	1024	12	65535	08h	1023	17	102.00	106.95
35	1024	13	65535	08h	1023	17	110.50	115.87
36	1024	14	65535	08h	1023	17	119.00	124.78
37	1024	2	65535	00h	1023	17	17.00	17.83
38	1024	16	65535	08h	1023	17	136.00	142.61
39	918	15	65535	08h	1023	17	114.30	119.85
40	820	6	65535	00h	820	17	40.84	42.82
41	1024	5	65535	00h	1023	17	42.50	44.56
42	1024	5	65535	00h	1023	26	65.00	68.16
43	809	6	65535	00h	808	17	40.29	42.25
44	820	6	65535	00h	819	26	62.46	65.50
45	776	8	65535	00h	775	33	100.03	104.89
46	0	0	0	00h	0	0	0.00	0.00
47	0	0	0	00h	0	0	0.00	0.00

Table entry 15 is reserved to act as a pointer to indicate that the type is greater than 15. This BIOS uses types 46 and 47 as user-definable entries.

Table A.63 shows the Award ROM BIOS hard disk parameters (modular 286, 386SX, and 386 BIOS Version 3.1).

Table A.63 Award ROM BIOS Version 3.1 Hard Disk

Type	Cylinders	Heads	WPC	Ctrl	LZ	S/T	Meg	MB
1	306	4	128	00h	305	17	10.16	10.65
2	615	4	300	00h	615	17	20.42	21.41
3	615	6	300	00h	615	17	30.63	32.12
4	940	8	512	00h	940	17	62.42	65.45
5	940	6	512	00h	940	17	46.82	49.09
6	615	4	65535	00h	615	17	20.42	21.41
7	462	8	256	00h	511	17	30.68	32.17
8	733	5	65535	00h	733	17	30.42	31.90
9	900	15	65535	08h	901	17	112.06	117.50
10	820	3	65535	00h	820	17	20.42	21.41
11	855	5	65535	00h	855	17	35.49	37.21
12	855	7	65535	00h	855	17	49.68	52.09
13	306	8	128	00h	319	17	20.32	21.31
14	733	7	65535	00h	733	17	42.59	44.66
15	0	0	0	00h	0	0	0	0

continues

Type	Cylinders	Heads	WPC	Ctrl	LZ	S/T	Meg	MB
Table A.63 Continued								
16	612	4	0	00h	663	17	20.32	21.31
17	977	5	300	00h	977	17	40.55	42.52
18	977	7	65535	00h	977	17	56.77	59.53
19	1024	7	512	00h	1023	17	59.50	62.39
20	733	5	300	00h	732	17	30.42	31.90
21	733	7	300	00h	732	17	42.59	44.66
22	733	5	300	00h	733	17	30.42	31.90
23	306	4	0	00h	336	17	10.16	10.65
24	977	5	65535	00h	976	17	40.55	42.52
25	1024	9	65535	08h	1023	17	76.50	80.22
26	1224	7	65535	00h	1223	17	71.12	74.58
27	1224	11	65535	08h	1223	17	111.76	117.19
28	1224	15	65535	08h	1223	17	152.40	159.81
29	1024	8	65535	00h	1023	17	68.00	71.30
30	1024	11	65535	08h	1023	17	93.50	98.04
31	918	11	65535	08h	1023	17	83.82	87.89
32	925	9	65535	08h	926	17	69.10	72.46
33	1024	10	65535	08h	1023	17	85.00	89.13
34	1024	12	65535	08h	1023	17	102.00	106.95
35	1024	13	65535	08h	1023	17	110.50	115.87
36	1024	14	65535	08h	1023	17	119.00	124.78
37	1024	2	65535	00h	1023	17	17.00	17.83
38	1024	16	65535	08h	1023	17	136.00	142.61
39	918	15	65535	08h	1023	17	114.30	119.85
40	820	6	65535	00h	820	17	40.84	42.82
41	1024	5	65535	00h	1023	17	42.50	44.56
42	1024	5	65535	00h	1023	26	65.00	68.16
43	809	6	65535	00h	852	17	40.29	42.25
44	809	6	65535	00h	852	26	61.62	64.62
45	776	8	65535	00h	775	33	100.03	104.89
46	684	16	65535	08h	685	38	203.06	212.93
47	615	6	65535	00h	615	17	30.63	32.12

Table entry 15 is reserved to act as a pointer to indicate that the type is greater than 15. This BIOS uses types 48 and 49 as user-definable entries.

Table A.64 shows the Phoenix 286 ROM BIOS (80286 ROM BIOS version 3.01, dated 11/01/86) hard disk parameters.

Table A.64 Phoenix 286 (80286 ROM BIOS Version 3.01) Hard Disk

Type	Cylinders	Heads	WPC	Ctrl	LZ	S/T	Meg	MB
1	306	4	128	00h	305	17	10.16	10.65
2	615	4	300	00h	638	17	20.42	21.41
3	615	6	300	00h	615	17	30.63	32.12
4	940	8	512	00h	940	17	62.42	65.45
5	940	6	512	00h	940	17	46.82	49.09
6	615	4	65535	00h	615	17	20.42	21.41
7	462	8	256	00h	511	17	30.68	32.17
8	733	5	65535	00h	733	17	30.42	31.90
9	900	15	65535	08h	901	17	112.06	117.50
10	820	3	65535	00h	820	17	20.42	21.41
11	855	5	65535	00h	855	17	35.49	37.21
12	855	7	65535	00h	855	17	49.68	52.09
13	306	8	128	00h	319	17	20.32	21.31
14	733	7	65535	00h	733	17	42.59	44.66
15	0	0	0	00h	0	0	0.00	0.00
16	612	4	0	00h	633	17	20.32	21.31
17	977	5	300	00h	977	17	40.55	42.52
18	977	7	65535	00h	977	17	56.77	59.53
19	1024	7	512	00h	1023	17	59.50	62.39
20	733	5	300	00h	732	17	30.42	31.90
21	733	7	300	00h	733	17	42.59	44.66
22	733	5	300	00h	733	17	30.42	31.90
23	0	0	0	00h	0	0	0.00	0.00
24	0	0	0	00h	0	0	0.00	0.00
25	0	0	0	00h	0	0	0.00	0.00
26	0	0	0	00h	0	0	0.00	0.00
27	0	0	0	00h	0	0	0.00	0.00
28	0	0	0	00h	0	0	0.00	0.00
29	0	0	0	00h	0	0	0.00	0.00
30	0	0	0	00h	0	0	0.00	0.00
31	0	0	0	00h	0	0	0.00	0.00
32	0	0	0	00h	0	0	0.00	0.00
33	0	0	0	00h	0	0	0.00	0.00
34	0	0	0	00h	0	0	0.00	0.00
35	0	0	0	00h	0	0	0.00	0.00
36	1024	5	512	00h	1024	17	42.50	44.56
37	830	10	65535	08h	830	17	68.90	72.24
38	823	10	256	08h	824	17	68.32	71.63
39	615	4	128	00h	664	17	20.42	21.41
40	615	8	128	00h	664	17	40.84	42.82
41	917	15	65535	08h	918	17	114.18	119.72
42	1023	15	65535	08h	1024	17	127.38	133.56
43	823	10	512	08h	823	17	68.32	71.63
44	820	6	65535	00h	820	17	40.84	42.82
45	1024	8	65535	00h	1024	17	68.00	71.30
46	925	9	65535	08h	925	17	69.10	72.46
47	1024	5	65535	00h	1024	17	42.50	44.56

Table entry 15 is reserved to act as a pointer to indicate that the type is greater than 15.

Table A.65 shows the Phoenix 286 ROM BIOS (286 BIOS Plus, version 3.10) hard disk parameters.

Table A.65 Phoenix 286 ROM BIOS (286 BIOS Plus Version 3.10) Hard Disk								
Type	**Cylinders**	**Heads**	**WPC**	**Ctrl**	**LZ**	**S/T**	**Meg**	**MB**
1	306	4	128	00h	305	17	10.16	10.65
2	615	4	300	00h	615	17	20.42	21.41
3	615	6	300	00h	615	17	30.63	32.12
4	940	8	512	00h	940	17	62.42	65.45
5	940	6	512	00h	940	17	46.82	49.09
6	615	4	65535	00h	615	17	20.42	21.41
7	462	8	256	00h	511	17	30.68	32.17
8	733	5	65535	00h	733	17	30.42	31.90
9	900	15	65535	08h	901	17	112.06	117.50
10	820	3	65535	00h	820	17	20.42	21.41
11	855	5	65535	00h	855	17	35.49	37.21
12	855	7	65535	00h	855	17	49.68	52.09
13	306	8	128	00h	319	17	20.32	21.31
14	733	7	65535	00h	733	17	42.59	44.66
15	0	0	0	00h	0	0	0	0
16	612	4	0	00h	663	17	20.32	21.31
17	977	5	300	00h	977	17	40.55	42.52
18	977	7	65535	00h	977	17	56.77	59.53
19	1024	7	512	00h	1023	17	59.50	62.39
20	733	5	300	00h	732	17	30.42	31.90
21	733	7	300	00h	732	17	42.59	44.66
22	733	5	300	00h	733	17	30.42	31.90
23	306	4	0	00h	336	17	10.16	10.65
24	0	0	0	00h	0	0	0.00	0.00
25	615	4	0	00h	615	17	20.42	21.41
26	1024	4	65535	00h	1023	17	34.00	35.65
27	1024	5	65535	00h	1023	17	42.50	44.56
28	1024	8	65535	00h	1023	17	68.00	71.30
29	512	8	256	00h	512	17	34.00	35.65
30	615	2	615	00h	615	17	10.21	10.71
31	989	5	0	00h	989	17	41.05	43.04
32	1020	15	65535	08h	1024	17	127.00	133.17
33	0	0	0	00h	0	0	0.00	0.00
34	0	0	0	00h	0	0	0.00	0.00
35	1024	9	1024	08h	1024	17	76.50	80.22
36	1024	5	512	00h	1024	17	42.50	44.56
37	830	10	65535	08h	830	17	68.90	72.24
38	823	10	256	08h	824	17	68.32	71.63
39	615	4	128	00h	664	17	20.42	21.41
40	615	8	128	00h	664	17	40.84	42.82
41	917	15	65535	08h	918	17	114.18	119.72

Type	Cylinders	Heads	WPC	Ctrl	LZ	S/T	Meg	MB
42	1023	15	65535	08h	1024	17	127.38	133.56
43	823	10	512	08h	823	17	68.32	71.63
44	820	6	65535	00h	820	17	40.84	42.82
45	1024	8	65535	00h	1024	17	68.00	71.30
46	925	9	65535	08h	925	17	69.10	72.46
47	699	7	256	00h	700	17	40.62	42.59

Table entry 15 is reserved to act as a pointer to indicate that the type is greater than 15. This BIOS uses types 48 and 49 as user-definable entries.

Table A.66 shows the Pheonix 386 ROM BIOS (A386 BIOS 1.01 Reference ID 08, dated 04/19/90) hard disk parameters.

Table A.66 Phoenix 386 ROM BIOS (A386 BIOS 1.01) Hard Disk

Type	Cylinders	Heads	WPC	Ctrl	LZ	S/T	Meg	MB
1	306	4	128	00h	305	17	10.16	10.65
2	615	4	300	00h	615	17	20.42	21.41
3	615	6	300	00h	615	17	30.63	32.12
4	940	8	512	00h	940	17	62.42	65.45
5	940	6	512	00h	940	17	46.82	49.09
6	615	4	65535	00h	615	17	20.42	21.41
7	462	8	256	00h	511	17	30.68	32.17
8	733	5	65535	00h	733	17	30.42	31.90
9	900	15	65535	08h	901	17	112.06	117.50
10	820	3	65535	00h	820	17	20.42	21.41
11	855	5	65535	00h	855	17	35.49	37.21
12	855	7	65535	00h	855	17	49.68	52.09
13	306	8	128	00h	319	17	20.32	21.31
14	733	7	65535	00h	733	17	42.59	44.66
15	0	0	0	00h	0	0	0	0
16	987	12	65535	08h	988	35	202.41	212.24
17	977	5	300	00h	977	17	40.55	42.52
18	977	7	65535	00h	977	17	56.77	59.53
19	1024	7	512	00h	1023	17	59.50	62.39
20	733	5	300	00h	732	17	30.42	31.90
21	733	7	300	00h	732	17	42.59	44.66
22	1024	16	0	08h	0	17	136.00	142.61
23	914	14	0	08h	0	17	106.22	111.38
24	1001	15	0	08h	0	17	124.64	130.69
25	977	7	815	00h	977	26	86.82	91.04
26	1024	4	65535	00h	1023	17	34.00	35.65
27	1024	5	65535	00h	1023	17	42.50	44.56
28	1024	8	65535	00h	1023	17	68.00	71.30
29	980	10	812	08h	990	17	81.35	85.30

continues

Table A.66 Continued								
Type	Cylinders	Heads	WPC	Ctrl	LZ	S/T	Meg	MB
30	1024	10	0	08h	0	17	85.00	89.13
31	832	6	832	00h	832	33	80.44	84.34
32	1020	15	65535	08h	1024	17	127.00	133.17
33	776	8	0	00h	0	33	100.03	104.89
34	782	4	0	00h	862	27	41.24	43.24
35	1024	9	1024	08h	1024	17	76.50	80.22
36	1024	5	512	00h	1024	17	42.50	44.56
37	830	10	65535	08h	830	17	68.90	72.24
38	823	10	256	08h	824	17	68.32	71.63
39	980	14	65535	08h	990	30	200.98	210.74
40	615	8	128	00h	664	17	40.84	42.82
41	917	15	65535	08h	918	17	114.18	119.72
42	1023	15	65535	08h	1024	17	127.38	133.56
43	823	10	512	08h	823	17	68.32	71.63
44	820	6	65535	00h	820	17	40.84	42.82
45	1024	8	65535	00h	1024	17	68.00	71.30
46	0	0	0	00h	0	0	0.00	0.00
47	0	0	0	00h	0	0	0.00	0.00

Table entry 15 is reserved to act as a pointer to indicate that the type is greater than 15. This BIOS uses types 46 and 47 as user-definable entries.

Table A.67 shows the Zenith motherboard BIOS (80286 Technical Reference 1988) hard disk parameters.

Table A.67 Zenith Motherboard BIOS Hard Disk								
Type	Cylinders	Heads	WPC	Ctrl	LZ	S/T	Meg	MB
1	306	4	128	00h	305	17	10.16	10.65
2	615	4	300	00h	615	17	20.42	21.41
3	699	5	256	00h	710	17	29.01	30.42
4	940	8	512	00h	940	17	62.42	65.45
5	940	6	512	00h	940	17	46.82	49.09
6	615	4	65535	00h	615	17	20.42	21.41
7	699	7	256	00h	710	17	40.62	42.59
8	733	5	65535	00h	733	17	30.42	31.90
9	900	15	65535	08h	901	17	112.06	117.50
10	925	5	0	00h	926	17	38.39	40.26
11	855	5	65535	00h	855	17	35.49	37.21
12	855	7	65535	00h	855	17	49.68	52.09
13	306	8	128	00h	319	17	20.32	21.31
14	733	7	65535	00h	733	17	42.59	44.66
15	0	0	0	00h	0	0	0	0
16	612	4	0	00h	663	17	20.32	21.31
17	977	5	300	00h	977	17	40.55	42.52
18	977	7	65535	00h	977	17	56.77	59.53

Type	Cylinders	Heads	WPC	Ctrl	LZ	S/T	Meg	MB
19	1024	7	512	00h	1023	17	59.50	62.39
20	733	5	300	00h	732	17	30.42	31.90
21	733	7	300	00h	732	17	42.59	44.66
22	733	5	300	00h	733	17	30.42	31.90
23	306	4	0	00h	336	17	10.16	10.65
24	612	2	65535	00h	611	17	10.16	10.65
25	615	6	300	00h	615	17	30.63	32.12
26	462	8	256	00h	511	17	30.68	32.17
27	820	3	65535	00h	820	17	20.42	21.41
28	981	7	65535	00h	986	17	57.00	59.77
29	754	11	65535	08h	754	17	68.85	72.19
30	918	15	65535	08h	918	17	114.30	119.85
31	987	5	65535	00h	987	17	40.96	42.95
32	830	6	400	00h	830	17	41.34	43.35
33	697	4	0	00h	696	17	23.14	24.27
34	615	4	65535	00h	615	17	20.42	21.41
35	615	4	128	00h	663	17	20.42	21.41
36	1024	9	65535	08h	1024	17	76.50	80.22
37	1024	5	512	00h	1024	17	42.50	44.56
38	820	6	65535	00h	910	17	40.84	42.82
39	615	4	306	00h	684	17	20.42	21.41
40	925	9	0	08h	924	17	69.10	72.46
41	1024	8	512	00h	1023	17	68.00	71.30
42	1024	5	1024	00h	1023	17	42.50	44.56
43	615	8	300	00h	615	17	40.84	42.82
44	989	5	0	00h	988	17	41.05	43.04
45	0	0	0	00h	0	0	0.00	0.00
46	0	0	0	00h	0	0	0.00	0.00
47	0	0	0	00h	0	0	0.00	0.00

Table entry 15 is reserved to act as a pointer to indicate that the type is greater than 15.

Type = Drive type number

Cyls = Total number of cylinders

Heads = Total number of heads

WPC = Write precompensation starting cylinder

      65535 = No Write precompensation

         0 = Write precompensation on all cylinders

Ctrl = Control byte, with values according to the following table:

Bit number	Hex	Meaning
Bit 0	01h	Not used (XT = drive step rate)
Bit 1	02h	Not used (XT = drive step rate)
Bit 2	04h	Not used (XT = drive step rate)
Bit 3	08h	More than eight heads
Bit 4	10h	Not used (XT = imbedded servo drive)
Bit 5	20h	OEM defect map at (cyls + 1)
Bit 6	40h	Disable ECC retries
Bit 7	80h	Disable disk access retries

LZ = Landing-zone cylinder for head parking

S/T = Number of sectors per track

Meg = Drive capacity in megabytes

MB = Drive capacity in millions of bytes

Printer and Modem Codes

This section lists the command and control codes for popular printers and modems. If you ever have had to work with these devices without the original documentation, you will appreciate these tables.

Table A.68 IBM Printer-Control Codes

Function	Codes in ASCII	Codes in Hex	Pro-Printer	Graphics printer	Color printer
Job-control commands					
Escape (command start)	<ESC>	1B	✓	✓	✓
Null (command end)	<NUL>	00	✓	✓	✓
Ring bell	<BELL>	07	✓	✓	✓
Cancel (clear printer buffer)	<CAN>	18	✓	✓	✓
Select printer	<DC1>	11	✓		✓
Deselect printer n	<ESC>Q#	1B 51#	✓		✓
Deselect printer	<DC3>	13	✓		✓
Automatic ribbon band shift	<ESC>a	1B 61			✓
Select ribbon band 1	<ESC>y	1B 79			✓
Select ribbon band 2	<ESC>m	1B 6D			✓
Select ribbon band 3	<ESC>c	1B 63			✓
Select ribbon band 4 (black)	<ESC>b	1B 62			✓
Home print head	<ESC><	1B 3C		✓	✓
Form feed	<FF>	0C	✓	✓	✓
Horizontal tab	<HT>	09	✓	✓	✓
Backspace	<BS>	08	✓		✓
Initialize function On	<ESC>?<SOH>	1B 3F 01			✓
Initialize function Off	<ESC>?<NUL>	1B 3F 00			✓
Unidirectional printing On	<ESC>U<SOH>	1B 55 01	✓	✓	✓
Unidirectional printing Off	<ESC>U<NUL>	1B 55 00	✓	✓	✓
Space #/120 forward to next character	<ESC>d##	1B 64##			✓
Space #/120 backward to next character	<ESC>e##	1B 65##			✓
Set aspect ratio to 1:1	<ESC>n<SOH>	1B 6E 01			✓
Set aspect ratio to 5:6	<ESC>n<NUL>	1B 6E 00			✓
Select control values = binary	<ESC>@#<NUL>	1B 40# 00			✓
Select control values = ASCII	<ESC>@<SOH>	1B 40 01			✓
Printer-control commands					
Ignore paper end On	<ESC>8	1B 38		✓	
Ignore paper end Off	<ESC>9	1B 39		✓	
Set length of page in lines (1-127)	<ESC>C#	1B 43#	✓	✓	✓
Set length of page in inches (1-22)	<ESC>C<SOH>#	1B 43 00#	✓	✓	✓

Function	Codes in ASCII	Codes in Hex	Pro-Printer	Graphics printer	Color printer
Automatic line justification On	<ESC>M<SOH>	1B 4D 01			✓
Automatic line justification Off	<ESC>M<NUL>	1B 4D 00			✓
Perforation skip On (1-127)	<ESC>N#	1B 4E#	✓	✓	✓
Perforation skip Off	<ESC>O	1B 4F	✓	✓	✓
Set top of page (form)	<ESC>4	1B 34	✓		✓
Set left and right margins	<ESC>X##	1B 58##			✓
Clear tabs (set to power-on defaults)	<ESC>R	1B 52	✓		✓
Set horizontal tab stops	<ESC>D#...#<NUL>	1B 44#...#00	✓	✓	✓
Set vertical tab stops	<ESC>B#...#<NUL>	1B 42#...#00	✓	✓	✓
Carriage return	<CR>	0D	✓	✓	✓
Line feed	<LF>	0A		✓	✓
Set $n/72$ lines per inch	<ESC>A#	1B 41#	✓	✓	✓
Set $n/216$ lines per inch	<ESC>3#	1B 33#	✓	✓	#/144"
Set 8 lines per inch	<ESC>0	1B 30	✓	✓	✓
Set 7/72nd line per inch	<ESC>1	1B 31	✓	✓	6/72"
Start new line spacing	<ESC>2	1B 32	✓	✓	✓
Vertical tab	<VT>	0B	✓	✓	✓
Reverse line feed	<ESC>]	1B 5D			✓
Automatic line feed On	<ESC>5<SOH>	1B 35 01	✓		✓
Automatic line feed Off	<ESC>5<NUL>	1B 35 00	✓		✓

Font selection

Function	Codes in ASCII	Codes in Hex	Pro-Printer	Graphics printer	Color printer
Select char set 1	<ESC>7	1B 37	✓	✓	✓
Select char set 2	<ESC>6	1B 36	✓	✓	✓
10 characters per inch (compressed Off)	<DC2>	12	✓	✓	✓
17.1 characters per inch (compressed On)	<SI>	0F	✓	✓	✓
Doublestrike On	<ESC>G	1B 47	✓	✓	✓
Doublestrike Off	<ESC>H	1B 48	✓	✓	✓
Doublewidth On (lines)	<ESC>W<SOH>	1B 57 01	✓	✓	✓
Doublewidth Off (lines)	<ESC>W<NUL>	1B 57 00	✓	✓	✓
Doublewidth by line On	<SO>	0E	✓	✓	✓
Doublewidth by line Off	<DC4>	14	✓	✓	✓
Emphasized printing On	<ESC>E	1B 45	✓	✓	✓
Emphasized printing Off	<ESC>F	1B 46	✓	✓	✓
Subscript On	<ESC>S<SOH>	1B 53 01	✓	✓	✓
Superscript On	<ESC>S<NUL>	1B 53 00	✓	✓	✓
Subscript/superscript Off	<ESC>T	1B 54	✓	✓	✓
Set draft quality	<ESC>I<SOH>	1B 49 01			✓
Set text quality (near-letter quality)	<ESC>I<STX>	1B 49 02	✓		✓
Set letter quality	<ESC>I<ETX>	1B 49 03			✓
Proportional spacing On	<ESC>P<SOH>	1B 50 01			✓
Proportional spacing Off	<ESC>P<NUL>	1B 50 00			✓
12-characters-per-inch spacing	<ESC>:	1B 3A	✓		✓
Print all characters	<ESC>\##	1B 5C##	✓		✓
Print next character	<ESC>^	1B 5E	✓		✓

continues

Table A.68 Continued

Function	Codes in ASCII	Codes in Hex	Pro-Printer	Graphics printer	Color printer
Underline On	<ESC>-<SOH>	1B 2D 01	✓	✓	✓
Underline Off	<ESC>-<NUL>	1B 2D 00	✓	✓	✓
Graphics					
Graphics, 60 dots per inch (DPI)	<ESC>K#	1B 4B#	✓	✓	
Graphics, 70/84 DPI	<ESC>K#	1B 4B#			✓
Graphics, 120 DPI half speed	<ESC>L#	1B 4C#	✓	✓	
Graphics, 140/168 DPI half speed	<ESC>L#	1B 4C#			✓
Graphics, 120 DPI normal speed	<ESC>Y#	1B 59#	✓	✓	
Graphics, 140/168 DPI normal speed	<ESC>Y#	1B 59#			✓
Graphics, 240 DPI half speed	<ESC>Z#	1B 5A#	✓	✓	
Graphics, 280/336 DPI half speed	<ESC>Z#	1B 5A#			✓

 # indicates a variable number in the code.

Table A.69 Epson Printer-Control Codes

Function	Codes in ASCII	Codes in Hex
Job-control commands		
Ring bell	<BELL>	07
Clear line	<CAN>	18
Select printer	<DC1>	11
Deselect printer	<DC3>	13
Set justification	<ESC>a	1B 61
Cut sheet-feeder control	<ESC>	EM1B 19
Select character space	<ESC>	SP1B 20
Select mode combinations	<ESC>!	1B 21
Select active character set	<ESC>%	1B 25
Copies ROM to user RAM	<ESC>:	1B 3A
Defines user characters	<ESC>&	1B 26
Set MSB = 0	<ESC>>	1B 3E
Set MSB = 1	<ESC>=	1B 3D
Select international character set	<ESC>R#	1B 72#
Select 15 width	<ESC>g	1B 67
Select immediate print (typewriter mode)	<ESC>i	1B 69
Half-speed printing Off	<ESC>s<NUL>	1B 73 00
Half-speed printing On	<ESC>s<SOH>	1B 73 01
Set horizontal tab unit	<ESC>e<NUL>	1B 65 00
Set vertical tab unit	<ESC>e<SOH>	1B 6D 01
Special character-generator selection (control codes accepted)	<ESC>m<NUL>	1B 6D 00
Special character-generator selection (graphic characters accepted)	<ESC>m<SOH>	1B 6D 01
Unidirectional printing On	<ESC>U<SOH>	1B 55 01
Unidirectional printing Off	<ESC>U<NUL>	1B 55 00
Turn unidirectional (left to right) On	<ESC><	1B 3C
Form feed	<FF>	0C
Horizontal tab	<HT>	09
Initialize printer	<ESC>@	1B 40
Backspace	<BS>	08
Printer-control commands		
Ignore paper end On	<ESC>8	1B 38
Ignore paper end Off	<ESC>9	1B 39
Set length of page in lines (1-127)	<ESC>C#	1B 43#
Set length of page in inches (1-22)	<ESC>C<NUL>#	1B 43 00#
Set absolute tab	<ESC>$	1B 24
Set vertical tab	<ESC>/	1B 2F
Set vertical tab	<ESC>b	1B 62
Set horizontal tab unit	<ESC>e<NUL>	1B 65 00
Set vertical tab unit	<ESC>e<SOH>	1B 65 01
Set horizontal skip position	<ESC>f<NUL>	1B 66 00

continues

Table A.69 Continued

Function	Codes in ASCII	Codes in Hex
Set vertical skip position	<ESC>f<SOH>	1B 66 01
Perforation skip On (1-127)	<ESC>N#	1B 4E#
Perforation skip Off	<ESC>O	1B 4F
Set horizontal tab stop	<ESC>D	1B 44
Set vertical tab stop	<ESC>B	1B 42
Carriage return	<CR>	0D
Line feed	<LF>	0A
Set variable line feed to #/72 inch (1-85)	<ESC>A#	1B 41#
Set variable line feed to #/216 inch	<ESC>J#	1B 4A#
Set spacing at 1/8 inch	<ESC>0	1B 30
Set spacing at 7/72 inch	<ESC>1	1B 31
Set line spacing at 1/6 inch	<ESC>2	1B 32
Set #/216 inch line feed (0-225)	<ESC>3#	1B 33#
Vertical tab	<VT>	0B

Font selection

Function	Codes in ASCII	Codes in Hex
Deactivate high-order control codes	<ESC>6	1B 36
Turn alternate character (italics) On	<ESC>4	1B 34
10 CPI (compressed Off) spacing	<DC2>	12
17.1 CPI (compressed On) spacing	<SI>	0F
Doublestrike On	<ESC>G	1B 47
Doublestrike Off	<ESC>H	1B 48
Doublewidth On (lines)	<ESC>W<SOH>	1B 57 01
Doublewidth Off (lines)	<ESC>W<NUL>	1B 57 00
Enlarged print mode On	<SO>	0E
Enlarged print mode Off	<DC4>	14
Emphasized printing On	<ESC>E	1B 45
Emphasized printing Off	<ESC>F	1B 46
Turn alternate character (italics) On	<ESC>4	1B 34
Turn alternate character (italics) Off	<ESC>5	1B 35
Elite mode On (Pica mode off)	<ESC>M	1B 4D
Select family of type styles	<ESC>k	1B 6B
Proportional printing Off	<ESC>p<NUL>	1B 70 00
Proportional printing On	<ESC>p<SOH>	1B 70 01
Select letter- or draft-quality printing	<ESC>z	1B 7A
Subscript On	<ESC>S<SOH>	1B 53 01
Superscript On	<ESC>S<NUL>	1B 53 00
Subscript/superscript Off	<ESC>T	1B 54
Control code select	<ESC>I	1B 49
Elite mode Off (Pica mode On)	<ESC>P	1B 50
Nine-pin graphics mode	<ESC>^	1B 5E
Underline On	<ESC>-<SOH>	1B 2D 01
Underline Off	<ESC>-<NUL>	1B 2D 00

Function	Codes in ASCII	Codes in Hex
Graphics		
Normal-density bit image	<ESC>K	1B 4B##
Dual-density bit image	<ESC>L	1B 4C##
Double-speed, dual-density bit image	<ESC>Y	1B 59##
Quadruple-density bit image	<ESC>Z	1B 5A##

International character sets:

0 = U.S.
1 = France
2 = Germany
3 = England
4 = Denmark
5 = Sweden
6 = Italy
7 = Spain
8 = Japan
9 = Norway
10 = Denmark II

Characters in brackets are ASCII code names.

 # indicates a variable numeric value.

Table A.70 HP LaserJet Printer-Control Codes

Function type	Function	Codes in ASCII	Codes in Hex
Job-control commands			
Printer control	Reset printer	<ESC>	E1B 45
	Self test mode	<ESC>z	1B 7A
	Number of copies	<ESC>&l#X	1B 26 6C # 58
	Long-edge offset registration	<ESC>&l#U	1B 26 6C # 55
	Short-edge offset registration	<ESC>&l#Z	1B 26 6C # 5A
Printer-control commands			
Paper source	Eject page	<ESC>&l0H	1B 26 6C 30 48
	Paper-tray auto feed	<ESC>&l1H	1B 26 6C 31 48
	Manual feed	<ESC>&l2H	1B 26 6C 32 48
	Manual envelope feed	<ESC>&l3H	1B 26 6C 33 48

continues

Table A.70 Continued

Function type	Function	Codes in ASCII	Codes in Hex
	Feed from lower cassette	<ESC> &l4H	1B 26 6C 34 48
Page size	Executive	<ESC>&l1A	1B 26 6C 31 41
	Letter	<ESC>&l2A	1B 26 6C 32 41
	Legal	<ESC>&l3A	1B 26 6C 33 41
	A4	<ESC>&l26A	1B 26 6C 32 36 41
	Monarch (envelope)	<ESC>&l80A	1B 26 6C 38 30 41
	COM 10 (envelope)	<ESC>&l81A	1B 26 6C 38 31 41
	DL (envelope)	<ESC>&l90A	1B 26 6C 39 30 41
	C5 (envelope)	<ESC>&l91A	1B 26 6C 39 31 41
Orientation	Portrait mode	<ESC>&l0O	1B 26 6C 30 4F
	Landscape mode	<ESC>&l1O	1B 26 6C 31 4F
	Reverse portrait	<ESC>&l2O	1B 26 6C 32 4F
	Reverse landscape	<ESC>&l3O	1B 26 6C 33 4F
	Print direction	<ESC>&a#P	1B 26 61 # 50
Page settings	Page length	<ESC>&l#P	1B 26 6C # 50
	Top margin	<ESC>&l#E	1B 26 6C # 45
	Text length	<ESC>&l#F	1B 26 6C # 46
	Clear horizontal margins	<ESC>9	1B 39
	Set left margin	<ESC>&a#L	1B 26 61 # 4C
	Set right margin	<ESC>&a#M	1B 26 61 # 4D
	Perforation skip enable	<ESC>&l1L	1B 26 6C 31 4C
	Perforation skip disable	<ESC>&l0L	1B 26 6C 30 4C
Line spacing	Vertical motion index	<ESC>&l#C	1B 26 6C # 43
	Horizontal motion index	<ESC>&k#H	1B 26 6B # 4B
	1 line/inch	<ESC>&l1D	1B 26 6C 31 44
	2 lines/inch	<ESC>&l2D	1B 26 6C 32 44
	3 lines/inch	<ESC>&l3D	1B 26 6C 33 44
	4 lines/inch	<ESC>&l4D	1B 26 6C 34 44
	6 lines/inch	<ESC>&l6D	1B 26 6C 36 44
	8 lines/inch	<ESC>&l8D	1B 26 6C 38 44
	12 lines/inch	<ESC>&l12D	1B 26 6C 31 32 44
	16 lines/inch	<ESC>&l16D	1B 26 6C 31 36 44
	24 lines/inch	<ESC>&l24D	1B 26 6C 32 34 44
	48 lines/inch	<ESC>&l48D	1B 26 6C 34 38 44
	Half line feed	<ESC>=	1B 3D
Stacking position	Default	<ESC>&l0T	1B 26 6C 30 54
	Toggle	<ESC>&l1T	1B 26 6C 31 54

Cursor positioning

Function type	Function	Codes in ASCII	Codes in Hex
Vertical position	Number of rows	<ESC>&a#R	1B 26 61 # 52
	Number of dots	<ESC>*p#Y	1B 2A 70 # 59
	Number of decipoints	<ESC>&a#V	1B 26 61 # 56

Function type	Function	Codes in ASCII	Codes in Hex
Horizontal position	Number of rows	<ESC>&a#C	1B 26 61 # 43
	Number of dots	<ESC>*p#X	1B 2A 70 # 58
	Number of decipoints	<ESC>&a#H	1B 26 61 # 48
End-of-line	CR=CR; LF=LF; FF=FF	<ESC>&k0G	1B 26 6B 30 47
	CR=CR+LF; LF=LF; FF=FF	<ESC>&k1G	1B 26 6B 31 47
	CR=CR; LF=CR+LF; FF=CR+FF	<ESC>&k2G	1B 26 6B 32 47
	CR=CR+LF; LF=CR+LF; FF=CR+FF	<ESC>&k3G	1B 26 6B 33 47
Push/Pop position	Push position	<ESC>&f0S	1B 26 66 30 53
	Pop position	<ESC>&f1S	1B 26 66 31 53

Font selection

Function type	Function	Codes in ASCII	Codes in Hex
Font symbol set	Roman-8	<ESC>(8U	1B 28 38 55
	USASCII	<ESC>(0U	1B 28 30 55
	Danish/Norwegian	<ESC>(0D	1B 28 30 44
	British (U.K.)	<ESC>(1E	1B 28 31 45
	French	<ESC>(1F	1B 28 31 46
	German	<ESC>(1G	1B 28 31 47
	Italian	<ESC>(0I	1B 28 30 49
	Swedish/Finnish	<ESC>(0S	1B 28 30 53
	Spanish	<ESC>(2S	1B 28 32 53
	Legal	<ESC>(1U	1B 28 31 55
	Linedraw	<ESC>(0B	1B 28 30 42
	Math8	<ESC>(8M	1B 28 38 4D
	Math7	<ESC>(0A	1B 28 30 41
	PiFont	<ESC>(15U	1B 28 31 35 55
	ECMA-94 Latin	<ESC>(0N	1B 28 30 4E
	PC-8	<ESC>(10U	1B 28 31 30 55
	PC-8 D/N	<ESC>(11U	1B 28 31 31 55
	PC 850	<ESC>(12U	1B 28 31 32 55
Primary spacing	Proportional	<ESC>(s1P	1B 28 73 31 50
	Fixed	<ESC>(s0P	1B 28 73 30 50
Character pitch	10 characters per inch	<ESC>(s10H	1B 28 73 31 30 48
	12 characters per inch	<ESC>(s12H	1B 28 73 31 32 48
	16.6 characters per inch	<ESC>(s16.6H	1B 28 73 31 36 2E 36 48
	Standard pitch (10 cpi)	<ESC>&k0S	1B 26 6B 30 53
	Compressed pitch (16.6 cpi)	<ESC>&k2S	1B 26 6B 32 53
	Elite (12.0)	<ESC>&k4s	1B 26 6B 34 53
Character point size	7 point	<ESC>(s7V	1B 28 73 37 56
	8 point	<ESC>(s8V	1B 28 73 38 56
	8.5 point	<ESC>(s8.5V	1B 28 73 38 2E 35 56
	10 point	<ESC>(s10V	1B 28 73 31 30 56
	12 point	<ESC>(s12V	1B 28 73 31 32 56
	14.4 point	<ESC>(s14.4V	1B 28 73 31 34 2E 34 56
Character style	Upright	<ESC>(s0S	1B 28 73 30 53
	Italic	<ESC>(s1S	1B 28 73 31 53
Character weight	Ultra thin	<ESC>(s-7B	1B 28 73 -37 42
	Extra thin	<ESC>(s-6B	1B 28 73 -36 42

continues

Table A.70 Continued

Function type	Function	Codes in ASCII	Codes in Hex
	Thin	<ESC>(s-5B	1B 28 73 -35 42
	Extra light	<ESC>(s-4B	1B 28 73 -34 42
	Light	<ESC>(s-3B	1B 28 73 -33 42
	Demi light	<ESC>(s-2B	1B 28 73 -32 42
	Semi light	<ESC>(s-1B	1B 28 73 -31 42
	Medium (normal)	<ESC>(s0B	1B 28 73 30 42
	Semi bold	<ESC>(s1B	1B 28 73 31 42
	Demi bold	<ESC>(s2B	1B 28 73 32 42
	Bold	<ESC>(s3B	1B 28 73 33 42
	Extra bold	<ESC>(s4B	1B 28 73 34 42
	Black	<ESC>(s5B	1B 28 73 35 42
	Extra black	<ESC>(s6B	1B 28 73 36 42
	Ultra black	<ESC>(s7B	1B 28 73 37 42
Character typeface	Courier	<ESC>(s3T	1B 28 73 33 54
	Univers	<ESC>(s52T	1B 28 73 35 32 54
	Line printer	<ESC>(s0T	1B 28 73 30 54
	CG Times	<ESC>(s4101T	1B 28 73 34 31 30 31 54
	Helvetica	<ESC>(s4T	1B 28 73 34 54
	TMS RMN	<ESC>(s5T	1B 28 73 33 54
Font default	Primary font	<ESC>(3@	1B 28 33 40
	Secondary font	<ESC>)3@	1B 29 33 40
Underlining	Underline On	<ESC>&d#D	1B 26 64 30 44
	Underline floating	<ESC>&d3D	1B 26 64 33 44
	Underline Off	<ESC>&d@	1B 26 64 40
Transparent print	Number of bytes	<ESC>&p#X[Data]	1B 26 70 # 58

Font management

Assign font ID	Font ID number	<ESC>*c#D	1B 2A 63 # 44
Font and character control	Delete all fonts	<ESC>*c0F	1B 2A 63 30 46
	Delete all temp fonts	<ESC>*c1F	1B 2A 63 31 46
	Delete last font ID specified	<ESC>*c2F	1B 2A 63 32 46
	Delete last font ID and char code	<ESC>*c3F	1B 2A 63 33 46
	Make temporary font	<ESC>*c4F	1B 2A 63 34 46
	Make permanent font	<ESC>*c5F	1B 2A 63 35 46
	Copy/assign font	<ESC>*c6F	1B 2A 63 36 46
Select font (ID)	Primary font ID number	<ESC>(#X	1B 28 # 58
	Secondary font ID number	<ESC>)#X	1B 29 # 58

Soft font creation

Font descriptor	Create font	<ESC>)s#W[Data]	1B 29 73 # 57
	Download character	<ESC>(s#W[Data]	1B 28 73 # 57
	ASCII char code number	<ESC>*c#E	1B 2A 63 # 45

Function type	Function	Codes in ASCII	Codes in Hex
Graphics			
Vector graphics	Enter HP-GL/2 mode	<ESC>%0B	1B 25 30 42
	HP-GL/2 plot horz size	<ESC>%1B	1B 25 31 42
	HP-GL/2 plot vert size	<ESC>*c#K	1B 2A 63 # 4B
	Set picture frame	<ESC>*0T	1B 2A 63 30 54
	Picture frame horz size	<ESC>*c#X	1B 2A 63 # 58
	Picture frame vert size	<ESC>*c#Y	1B 2A 63 # 59
Raster resolution	75 dpi resolution	<ESC>*t75R	1B 2A 74 37 35 52
	100 dpi resolution	<ESC>*t100R	1B 2A 74 31 30 30 52
	150 dpi resolution	<ESC>*t150R	1B 2A 74 31 35 30 52
	300 dpi resolution	<ESC>*t300R	1B 2A 74 33 30 30 52
	Start at leftmost position	<ESC>*r0A	1B 2A 72 30 41
	Start at current cursor	<ESC>*r1A	1B 2A 72 31 41
Raster graphics presentation	Rotate image	<ESC>*r0F	1B 2A 72 30 46
	LaserJet landscape compatible	<ESC>*r3F	1B 2A 72 33 46
	Left raster graphics margin	<ESC>*r0A	1B 2A 72 30 41
	Current cursor	<ESC>*r1A	1B 2A 72 31 41
	Raster Y offset	<ESC>*b0M	1B 2A 62 # 59
Set raster compression	Uncoded	<ESC>*b0M	1B 2A 62 30 41
	Mode run-length encoded	<ESC>*b1M	1B 2A 62 31 41
	Tagged image file format	<ESC>*b2M	1B 2A 62 32 41
	Delta row	<ESC>*b3M	1B 2A 62 33 41
	Transfer graphic rows	<ESC>*b#W[Data]	1B 2A 62 # 57
	End graphics	<ESC>*rB	1B 2A 72 42
	Raster height	<ESC>*r#T	1B 2A 72 # 54
	Raster width	<ESC>*r#S	1B 2A 72 # 53
The print model			
Select pattern	Solid black (default)	<ESC>*v0T	1B 2A 76 30 54
	Solid white	<ESC>*v1T	1B 2A 76 31 54
	HP-defined shading pattern	<ESC>*v2T	1B 2A 76 32 54
	HP-defined cross-hatched pattern	<ESC>*v3T	1B 2A 76 33 54
Select source	Transparent	<ESC>*v0N	1B 2A 76 30 42
Transparency	Opaque	<ESC>*v1N	1B 2A 76 31 42
Select pattern	Transparent	<ESC>*v0O	1B 2A 76 30 43
Transparency	Opaque	<ESC>*v1O	1B 2A 76 31 43
Rectangle width	Horz # dots in pattern	<ESC>*c#A	1B 2A 63 # 41
	Horz # decipoints in pattern	<ESC>*c#H	1B 2A 63 # 48

continues

Table A.70 Continued

Function type	Function	Codes in ASCII	Codes in Hex
Rectangle height	Vert # dots in pattern	<ESC>*c#B	1B 2A 63 # 42
	Vert # decipoints in pattern	<ESC>*c#V	1B 2A 63 # 56
Fill rectangular Area	Solid black	<ESC>*c0P	1B 2A 63 30 50
	Erase (solid white area fill)	<ESC>*c1P	1B 2A 63 31 50
	Shade fill	<ESC>*c2P	1B 2A 63 32 50
	Cross-hatched fill	<ESC>*c3P	1B 2A 63 33 50
	User defined	<ESC>*c4P	1B 2A 63 34 50
	Current pattern	<ESC>*c5P	1B 2A 63 35 50
Pattern ID	Percent of shading or type of pattern	<ESC>*c#G	1B 2A 63 # 47
Shading	Print 2% gray scale	<ESC>*c2G	1B 2A 63 32 47
	Print 10% gray scale	<ESC>*c10G	1B 2A 63 31 30 47
	Print 15% gray scale	<ESC>*c15G	1B 2A 63 31 35 47
	Print 30% gray scale	<ESC>*c30G	1B 2A 63 33 30 47
	Print 45% gray scale	<ESC>*c45G	1B 2A 63 34 35 47
	Print 70% gray scale	<ESC>*c70G	1B 2A 63 37 30 47
	Print 90% gray scale	<ESC>*c90G	1B 2A 63 39 30 47
	Print 100% gray scale	<ESC>*c100G	1B 2A 63 31 30 30 47
Pattern	1 horizontal line	<ESC>*c1G	1B 2A 63 31 47
	2 vertical lines	<ESC>*c2G	1B 2A 63 32 47
	3 diagonal lines	<ESC>*c3G	1B 2A 63 33 47
	4 diagonal lines	<ESC>*c4G	1B 2A 63 34 47
	5 square grid	<ESC>*c5G	1B 2A 63 35 47
	6 diagonal grid	<ESC>*c6G	1B 2A 63 36 47

Macros

Function type	Function	Codes in ASCII	Codes in Hex
Macro ID	Macro ID number	<ESC>&f#Y	1B 26 66 # 59
Macro control	Start macro	<ESC>&f0X	1B 26 66 30 58
	Stop macro definition	<ESC>&f1X	1B 26 66 31 58
	Execute macro	<ESC>&f2X	1B 26 66 32 58
	Call macro	<ESC>&f3X	1B 26 66 33 58
	Enable overlay	<ESC>&f4X	1B 26 66 34 58
	Disable overlay	<ESC>&f5X	1B 26 66 35 58
	Delete macros	<ESC>&f6X	1B 26 66 36 58
	Delete all temporary macros	<ESC>&f7X	1B 26 66 37 58
	Delete macro ID	<ESC>&f8X	1B 26 66 38 58
	Make temporary	<ESC>&f9X	1B 26 66 39 58
	Make permanent	<ESC>&f10X	1B 26 66 31 30 58

Function type	Function	Codes in ASCII	Codes in Hex
Programming hints			
Display functions	Display functions On	<ESC>Y	1B 59
	Display functions Off	<ESC>Z	1B 5A
End-of-line wrap	Enable	<ESC>&s0C	1B 26 73 30 43
	Disable	<ESC>&s1C	1B 26 73 31 43

 # indicates a variable numeric value.
[Data] indicates a bitstream of appropriate data.

Table A.71 shows the commands recognized by the popular Hayes and USRobotics modems. These modems have a standard command set that can get quite complicated in the higher-end models. This table comes in handy when you need to reconfigure a modem without the original manual. Even if your modem is not Hayes or USRobotics, it probably follows most of these commands because this command set has become somewhat of a standard.

Table A.71 USRobotics and Hayes Modem Commands and Supported Features

		USR		Hayes	
Command	Function/options	Dual	2400	2400	1200
&	See Extended Command Set	X			
%	See Extended Command Set	X			
A	Force Answer mode when modem has not received an incoming call	X	X	X	X
A/	Reexecute last command once	X	X	X	X
A>	Repeat last command continuously	X			
Any key	Terminate current connection attempt; exit Repeat mode	X	X		
AT	Attention: must precede all other commands, except A/, A>, and +++	X	X	X	X
Bn	Handshake options	X		X	
	B0 CCITT answer sequence	o		o	
	B1 Bell answer tone	o		o	
Cn	Transmitter On/Off	X	X	X	X
	C0 Transmitter Off	o	o	o	o
	C1 Transmitter On-Default	o	o	o	o
Dn	Dial the number that follows and go into originate mode				
	Use any of these options:	X	X	X	X
	P Pulse dial-Default	o	o	o	o
	T Touch-Tone dial	o	o	o	o

continues

Table A.71 Continued

Command	Function/options		USR Dual	2400	Hayes 2400	1200
	,	(Comma) Pause for 2 seconds	o	o	o	o
	;	Return to command state after dialing	o	o	o	o
	"...	Dial the letters that follow	o	o		
	!	Flash switch-hook to transfer call	o	o	o	
	W	Wait for second dial tone (if X3 or higher is set)	o	o	o	
	@	Wait for an answer (if X3 or higher is set)	o	o	o	
	R	Reverse frequencies	o	o	o	o
	S	Dial stored number			o	
DL	Dial the last-dialed number		X			
DSn	Dial number stored in NVRAM at position n		X			
En	Command mode local echo; not applicable after a connection has been made		X	X	X	X
	E0	Echo Off	o	o	o	o
	E1	Echo On	o	o	o	o
Fn	Local echo On/Off when a connection has been made		X	X	X	X
	F0	Echo On (Half duplex)	o	o	o	o
	F1	Echo Off (Full duplex)-Default	o	o	o	o
Hn	On/Off hook control		X	X	X	X
	H0	Hang up (go on hook)-Default	o	o	o	o
	H1	Go off hook	o	o	o	o
In	Inquiry		X	X	X	X
	I0	Return product code	o	o	o	o
	I1	Return memory (ROM) checksum	o	o	o	o
	I2	Run memory (RAM) test	o	o	o	
	I3	Return call duration/real time	o	o		
	I4	Return current modem settings	o	o		
	I5	Return NVRAM settings	o			
	I6	Return link diagnostics	o			
	I7	Return product configuration	o			
Kn	Modem clock operation		X			
	K0	ATI3 displays call duration-Default	o			
	K1	ATI3 displays real time; set with ATI3=HH:MM:SSK1	o			
Ln	Loudness of speaker volume;				X	
	L0	Low			o	
	L1	Low			o	
	L2	Medium			o	
	L3	High			o	
Mn	Monitor (speaker) control		X	X	X	X
	M0	Speaker always Off	o	o	o	o
	M1	Speaker On until carrier is established-Default	o	o	o	o
	M2	Speaker always On	o	o	o	o
	M3	Speaker On after last digit dialed, Off at carrier detect	o	o	o	o

Command	Function/options		USR Dual	2400	Hayes 2400	1200
O	Return on-line after command execution		X	X	X	X
	O0	Return on-line, normal	o	o	o	o
	O1	Return on-line, retrain	o	o	o	o
P	Pulse dial		X	X	X	X
Qn	Result codes display		X	X	X	X
	Q0	Result codes displayed	o	o	o	o
	Q1	Result codes suppressed (quiet mode)	o	o	o	o
	Q2	Quiet in answer mode only	o			
Sr=n	Set Register commands: r is any S-register; n must be a decimal number between 0 and 255.		X	X	X	X
Sr.b=n	Set bit .b of register r to n (0/Off or 1/On)		X			
Sr?	Query register r		X	X	X	X
T	Tone dial		X	X	X	X
Vn	Verbal/Numeric result codes		X	X	X	X
	V0	Numeric mode	o	o	o	o
	V1	Verbal mode	o	o	o	o
Xn	Result code options		X	X	X	X
Yn	Long space disconnect				X	
	Y0	Disabled			o	
	Y1	Enabled; disconnects after 1.5-second break			o	
Z	Software reset		X	X	X	X
+++	Escape code sequence, preceded and followed by at least one second of no data transmission		X	X		
/	(Slash) Pause for 125 msec		X			
>	Repeat command continuously or up to 10 dial attempts		X	X		
	Cancel by pressing any key					
$	Online Help - Basic command summary		X	X		
&$	Online Help - Ampersand command summary		X			
%$	Online Help - Percent command summary		X			
D$	Online Help - Dial command summary		X	X		
S$	Online Help - S-register summary		X	X		
<Ctrl>-S	Stop/restart display of HELP screens			X		
<Ctrl>-C	Cancel display HELP screens			X		
<Ctrl>-K	Cancel display HELP screens			X		

Extended command set

Command	Function/options		USR Dual	2400	Hayes 2400	1200
&An	ARQ result codes 14-17, 19		X			
	&A0	Suppress ARQ result codes	o			
	&A1	Display ARQ result codes-Default	o			
	&A2	Display HST and V.32 result codes	o			
	&A3	Display protocol result codes	o			
&Bn	Data Rate, terminal-to-modem (DTE/DCE)		X			
	&B0	DTE rate follows connection rate-Default	o			
	&B1	Fixed DTE rate	o			
	&B2	Fixed DTE rate in ARQ mode; variable DTE rate in non-ARQ mode	o			

continues

Table A.71 Continued

Command	Function/options		USR Dual	2400	Hayes 2400	1200
&Cn	Carrier Detect (CD) operations		X		X	
	&C0	CD override	o		o	
	&C1	Normal CD operations	o		o	
&Dn	Data Terminal Ready (DTR) operations		X		X	
	&D0	DTR override	o		o	
	&D1	DTR Off; goes to command state			o	
	&D2	DTR Off; goes to command state and on hook	o		o	
	&D3	DTR Off; resets modem			o	
&F	Load factory settings into RAM		X		X	
&Gn	Guard tone		X		X	
	&G0	No guard tone; U.S., Canada-Default	o		o	
	&G1	Guard tone; some European countries	o		o	
	&G2	Guard tone; U.K., requires B0	o		o	
&Hn	Transmit Data flow control		X			
	&H0	Flow control disabled-Default	o			
	&H1	Hardware (CTS) flow control	o			
	&H2	Software (XON/XOFF) flow control	o			
	&H3	Hardware and software control	o			
&In	Received Data software flow control		X			
	&I0	Flow control disabled-Default	o			
	&I1	XON/XOFF to local modem and remote computer	o			
	&I2	XON/XOFF to local modem only	o			
	&I3	Host mode, Hewlett-Packard protocol	o			
	&I4	Terminal mode, Hewlett-Packard protocol	o			
	&I5	ARQ mode-same as &I2; non-ARQ mode; look for incoming XON/XOFF	o			
&Jn	Telephone jack selection				X	
	&J0	RJ-11/ RJ-41S/ RJ-45S			o	
	&J1	RJ-12/ RJ-13			o	
&Kn	Data compression		X			
	&K0	Disabled	o			
	&K1	Auto enable/disable-Default	o			
	&K2	Enabled	o			
	&K3	V.42bis only	o			
&Ln	Normal/Leased line operation		X		X	
	&L0	Normal phone line-Default	o		o	
	&L1	Leased line	o		o	
&Mn	Error Control/Synchronous Options		X		X	
	&M0	Normal mode, no error control	o		o	
	&M1	Synch mode	o		o	
	&M2	Synch mode 2 - stored number dialing			o	
	&M3	Synch mode 3 - manual dialing			o	
	&M4	Normal/ARQ mode-Normal if ARQ connection cannot be made-Default	o			
	&M5	ARQ mode-hang up if ARQ connection cannot be made	o			

Command	Function/options	USR Dual	2400	Hayes 2400	1200
&Nn	Data Rate, data link (DCE/DCE)	X			
&N0	Normal link operations-Default	o			
&N1	300 bps	o			
&N2	1200 bps	o			
&N3	2400 bps	o			
&N4	4800 bps	o			
&N5	7200 bps	o			
&N6	9600 bps	o			
&N7	12K bps	o			
&N8	14.4K bps	o			
&Pn	Pulse dial make/break ratio	X		X	
&P0	North America-Default	o		o	
&P1	British Commonwealth	o		o	
&Rn	Received Data hardware (RTS) flow control	X		X	
&R0	CTS tracks RTS	o		o	
&R1	Ignore RTS-Default	o		o	
&R2	Pass received data on RTS high; used only if terminal equipment supports RTS	o			
&Sn	Data Set Ready (DSR) override	X		X	
&S0	DSR override (always On-Default)	o		o	
&S1	Modem controls DSR	o		o	
&S2	Pulsed DSR; CTS follows CD	o			
&S3	Pulsed DSR	o			
&Tn	Modem Testing	X		X	
&T0	End testing	o		o	
&T1	Analog loopback	o		o	
&T2	Reserved	o			
&T3	Digital loopback	o		o	
&T4	Grant remote digital loopback	o		o	
&T5	Deny remote digital loopback	o		o	
&T6	Initiate remote digital loopback	o		o	
&T7	Remote digital loopback with self test	o		o	
&T8	Analog loopback with self test	o		o	
&W	Write current settings to NVRAM	X		X	
&Xn	Synchronous timing source	X		X	
&X0	Modem's transmit clock-Default	o		o	
&X1	Terminal equipment	o		o	
&X2	Modem's receiver clock	o		o	
&Yn	Break handling. Destructive breaks clear the buffer; expedited Breaks are sent immediately to remote system.	X			
&Y0	Destructive, but don't send break	o			
&Y1	Destructive, expedited-Default	o			
&Y2	Nondestructive, expedited	o			
&Y3	Nondestructive, unexpedited	o			
&Zn=L	Store last-dialed phone number in NVRAM at position n	X			
&Zn=s	Write phone number(s) to NVRAM at position n (0-3); 36 characters maximum	X			

continues

Table A.71 Continued

Command	Function/options		USR Dual	2400	Hayes 2400	1200
&Zn?	Display phone number in NVRAM at position n (n=0-3)		X		X	
%Rn	Remote access to Rack Controller Unit (RCU)		X			
	%R0	Disabled	o			
	%R1	Enabled	o			
%T	Enable Touch-Tone recognition		X			

Register	Function		USR Dual	2400	Hayes 2400	1200
S-Register functions and defaults						
S0	Set number of rings before automatic answering when DIP switch 5 is UP. Default = 1. S0 = 0 disables Auto Answer, equivalent to DIP switch 5 Down		SW-5	SW-5	0	SW-5
S1	Counts and stores number of rings from incoming call		0	0	0	0
S2	Define escape code character. Default = +		43	43	43	43
S3	Define ASCII carriage return		13	13	13	13
S4	Define ASCII line feed		10	10	10	10
S5	Define ASCII Backspace		8	8	8	8
S6	Set number of seconds modem waits before dialing		2	2	2	2
S7	Set number of seconds modem waits for a carrier		60	30	30	30
S8	Set Duration, in seconds, for pause (,) option in Dial command and pause between command reexecutions for Repeat (>) command		2	2	2	2
S9	Set duration, in tenths of a second, of remote carrier signal before recognition		6	6	6	6
S10	Set duration, in tenths of a second, modem waits after loss of carrier before hanging up		7	7	7	7
S11	Set duration and spacing, in milliseconds, of dialed Touch-Tones		70	70	70	70
S12	Define guard time, in 50ths of a second, for escape code sequence		50	50	50	50
S13	Bit-mapped register:		0			
	1	Reset when DTR drops				
	2	Auto answer in originate mode				
	4	Disable result code pause				
	8	DS0 on DTR low-to-high				
	16	DS0 on power up, ATZ				
	32	Disable HST modulation				
	64	Disable MNP Level 3				
	128	Watchdog hardware reset				
S15	Bit-mapped register:		0			
	1	Disable high-frequency equalization				
	2	Disable on-line fallback				
	4	Force 300-bps back channel				

Register	Function	USR Dual	2400	Hayes 2400	1200
	8 Set non-ARQ transmit buffer to 128 bytes				
	16 Disable MNP Level 4				
	32 Set Del as Backspace key				
	64 Unusual MNP incompatibility				
	128 Custom applications only				
S16	Bit-mapped register:	0	0	0	
	1 Analog loopback				
	2 Dial test				
	4 Test pattern				
	8 Initiate remote digital loopback				
	16 Reserved				
	32 Reserved				
	64 Reserved				
	128 Reserved				
S18	&Tn Test timer, disabled when S18 is set to 0 seconds	0		0	
S19	Set inactivity timer in minutes	0			
S21	Length of Break, DCE to DTE, in 10-millisecond units	10		0	
S22	Define ASCII XON	17		17	
S23	Define ASCII XOFF	19		19	
S24	Sets duration, in 20-millisecond units, of pulsed DSR when modem is set to &S2 or &S3	150			
S25	Delay to DTR 5				
S26	Sets duration, in 10-millisecond units, of delay between RTS and CTS, synchronous mode	1		1	
S27	Bit-mapped register:	0			
	1 Enable V.21 modulation, 300 bps				
	2 Enable unencoded V.32 modulation				
	4 Disable V.32 modulation				
	8 Disable 2100 Hz answer tone				
	16 Disable MNP handshake				
	32 Disable V.42 Detect phase				
	64 Reserved				
	128 Unusual software incompatibility				
S28	Sets duration, in tenths of a second, of V.21/V.23 handshake delay	8			
S32	Voice/Data switch options:	1			
	0 Disabled				
	1 Go off hook in originate mode				
	2 Go off hook in answer mode				
	3 Redial last-dialed number				
	4 Dial number stored at position 0				
	5 Auto answer toggle On/Off				
	6 Reset modem				
	7 Initiate remote digital loopback				
S34	Bit-mapped register:	0			
	1 Disable V.32bis				
	2 Disable enhanced V.32 mode				
	4 Disable quick V.32 retrain				

continues

Table A.71 Continued

Register	Function	USR Dual	2400	Hayes 2400	1200
	8 Enable V.23 modulation				
	16 Change MR LED to DSR				
	32 Enable MI/MIC				
	64 Reserved				
	128 Reserved				
S38	Sets duration, in seconds, before disconnect when DTR drops during an ARQ call	0			

ARQ = Automatic repeat request

ASCII = American Standard Code for Information Interchange

BPS = Bits per second

CCITT = Consultative Committee for International Telephone and Telegraph

CD = Carrier cetect

CRC = Cyclic redundancy check

DCE = Data communications equipment

DTE = Data terminal equipment

EIA = Electronic Industries Association

HDLC = High-level data link control

HST = High-speed technology

Hz = Hertz

LAPM = Link access procedure for modems

MI/MIC = Mode indicate/Mode indicate common

MNP = Microcom networking protocol

NVRAM = Non-volatile memory

RAM = Random-access memory

ROM = Read-only memory

SDLC = Synchronous Data Link Control

MR = Modem ready

LED = Light-emitting diode

DTR = Data terminal ready

CTS = Clear to send

RTS = Ready to send

DSR = Data set ready

IBM Technical Manuals and Updates

IBM has an extensive array of documentation available to help a system troubleshooter responsible for upgrading and repairing any system. These manuals are primarily in two categories: technical-reference manuals and hardware-maintenance service manuals. You purchase these manuals in basic form and then buy updates that reflect changes in newer systems as they are introduced. All of the manuals together with the updates present a bewildering—and expensive—array of documentation. If you are interested in obtaining any of this documentation, this section is very useful.

This section explains each manual type and gives information needed for ordering this documentation, and tables describe all the available manuals and updates, including part numbers and prices.

Guide to Operations and Quick-Reference Manuals

These publications contain instructions for system operation, testing, relocation, and option installation. A diagnostics floppy disk is included.

Table A.72 Guide to Operations and Quick Reference Manual Part Numbers and Prices

Description	Part number	Price
PS/2		
Model 25	75X1051	$28.75
Model 25 286	15F2179	42.50
Model 30	68X2230	54.25
Model 30 286	15F2143	42.50
Model 50-031 and 50-061	68X2321	54.25
Model 55 SX	01F0238	39.75
Model 60	68X2213	54.25
Model 65 SX	15F2171	47.50
Model 70	68X2308	54.25
Model 70 486	15F2183	48.50
Model P70 386	68X2380	16.50
Model 80	15F2186	63.75

continues

Table A.72 Continued		
Description	**Part number**	**Price**
PC		
AT	6280066	$ 49.50
AT Model 339	6280102	80.00
PC	6322510	50.00
PC Convertible	6280629	71.50
PC*jr*	1502292	23.25
Portable PC	6936571	66.75
XT	6322511	50.00
XT Models 089 268 278	6280085	88.00
XT Model 286	6280147	65.00

Hardware-Maintenance Manuals

The single-volume hardware-maintenance manuals provide the information needed to isolate and replace a field-replaceable unit (FRU). The color printer and the graphics- and compact-printer manuals are designed to be used with the system-maintenance manuals.

Table A.73 Hardware-Maintenance Manual Part Numbers and Prices		
Description	**Part number**	**Price**
Color Printer Model 5182	68X2237	$61.50
Graphics and Compact Printer	6280079	41.50
PC*jr*	1502294	96.75
PC Convertible	6280641	97.25
Supplement to 6280641		
Speech adapter	59X9964	23.00

PS/2 Hardware-Maintenance Library

The PS/2 Hardware-Maintenance Library consists of a two-part set of manuals, intended for trained service representatives.

The PS/2 Hardware-Maintenance Service manual contains all the information necessary to diagnose a failure. Maintenance-analysis procedures (MAPs), the parts catalog, and Reference Disks containing the advanced diagnostics tests are in this manual.

The PS/2 Hardware-Maintenance Reference contains product descriptions, field-replaceable unit (FRU) locations and removal procedures, and information about the diagnostics programs.

To maintain an accurate library, you should add all available supplements. (The PS/2 Model 25 and Model 30 supplements update the PC maintenance library.)

Table A.74 PS/2 Hardware-Maintenance Manual Part Numbers and Prices

Description	Part number	Price
PS/2 Hardware-Maintenance Service (includes the following service pamphlets)	15F2200	$268.00
General Information	15F2189	3.60
Model 25/30	15F2191	3.60
Model 30 286	15F2192	1.55
Model 50	15F2193	1.55
Model 55 SX	15F2195	1.55
Model 60	15F2194	1.55
Model 65 SX	15F2196	1.45
Model 70 (includes Model 70 486)	15F2197	1.55
Model P70 386	15F2198	1.55
Model 80	15F2199	1.55
Supplements to 15F2200		
Model 25 286	15F2181	2.60
External SCSI Devices	64F1426	3.05
300/1200/2400 Internal Modem/A	68X2384	10.50
PS/2 Hardware Maintenance Reference Manual	15F2190	63.75
PS/2 Hardware Maintenance Library Supplement Model 25 286	15F2180	26.75

PC (Including PS/2 Models 25 and 30) Hardware-Maintenance Library

The PC Hardware Maintenance library consists of a two-part set of manuals and is intended for trained service representatives. The PC Hardware Maintenance Service manual contains all of the information necessary to diagnose a failing system. Maintenance analysis procedures (MAPs), jumper-position switch settings, parts catalog, and floppy disks containing the advanced diagnostics are included in this manual.

The PC Hardware Maintenance Reference contains general information about the systems. It describes the diagnostics procedures and field-replaceable unit (FRU) location, adjustment, and removal.

All available supplements should be added to maintain an accurate library.

Table A.75 PC (Including PS/2 Model 25 and 30) Hardware-Maintenance Manual Part Numbers and Prices

Description	Part number	Price
PC Hardware Maintenance Service PC, XT, AT, and Portable	6280087	$ 235.00
Supplements to 6280087		
Personal System/2 Model 25	75X1054	39.50
Personal System/2 Model 30	68X2202	36.25
Personal System/2 Model 30-001	15F2105	29.50
Personal System/2 Model 30 286	01F0235	26.75
AT Model 339	6280139	11.75
XT Model 286	68X2211	11.75
XT Models 089, 268, 278	6280109	11.75
Display Adapter	68X2216	36.25
PC Music Feature	75X1049	50.00
2MB Expanded Memory Adapter	74X9923	64.75
3 1/2-inch internal floppy disk drive	6280159	6.80
3 1/2-inch external floppy disk drive	6280111	12.00
5 1/4-inch external floppy disk drive	68X2273	12.00
20MB hard disk drive Model 25	01F0246	8.90
Service Summary Card Models 25/30	15F2216	1.75
Service Summary Card Models 30 286	01F0236	1.55
Empty supplement binder	1502561	9.10
PC Hardware Maintenance Reference PC, XT, AT, and Portable	6280088	180.00
Supplements to 6280088		
Personal System/2 Model 25	75X1059	10.75
Personal System/2 Model 30	68X2203	12.00
Personal System/2 Model 30 286	01F0234	6.65
AT Model 339	6280138	7.15
XT Model 286	68X2212	11.75
XT Models 089, 268, and 278	6280108	7.15
Display Adapter	68X2238	7.25

Description	Part number	Price
Color Display 8514	68X2218	$ 7.25
3 1/2-inch internal floppy disk drive	6280160	7.15
3 1/2-inch external floppy disk drive	(Included in 68X22)	
20MB hard disk drive Model 25	01F0244	4.15
Empty supplement binder	01F0200	20.25

Use these empty binders to store hardware-maintenance supplements:

Description	Part number	Price
Empty HMS (Service) Binder	1502561	$ 7.25
Empty HMR (Reference) Binder	01F0200	17.00

System Hardware Technical-Reference Library

The publications listed in table A.76 provide system-specific hardware and software interface information for the IBM PC and PS/2 products. They are intended for developers who provide hardware and software products to operate with these systems. The library is divided into system, options and adapters, and BIOS interface publications.

Table A.76 System Hardware Technical-Reference Manual Part Numbers and Prices

Description	Part number	Price
Personal System/2 Model 25	75X1055	$ 34.50
Supplement to 75X1055		
20MB hard disk drive	01F0245	4.05
Personal System/2 Model 30	68X2201	90.75
Personal System/2 Model 30 286	01F0237	29.25
Supplement to 01F0237		
Model 25 286	15F2182	26.75
Personal Computer	6322507	36.25
Personal Computer AT	6280070	126.00

continues

Table A.76 Continued

Description	Part number	Price
Supplement to 6280070		
Personal Computer AT Model 339	6280099	$ 59.75
Personal Computer XT Model 286	68X2210	60.50
Personal Computer XT and Portable	6280089	59.75
PC Convertible	6280648	90.75
Supplements to 6280648		
Speech Adapter	59X9965	23.00
256KB Memory and Enhanced Modem	75X1035	5.20
PC*jr*	1502293	49.50

Hardware Interface Technical Reference

These publications provide interface and design information for the system units. Information is included for the system board, math coprocessor, power supply, video subsystem, keyboard, instruction sets, and other features of the system.

Table A.77 Hardware Interface Technical Reference Manual Part Numbers and Prices

Description	Part number	Price
IBM Personal System/2 Hardware Interface Technical Reference	68X2330	$ 150.00
Supplements to 68X2330		
Model 55 SX	01F0242	11.50
Model 65 SX	15F2174	14.50
Model 70-A21 (includes updates to Setup sections)	68X2344	57.75
Model 70 486	15F2136	37.75
Model P70 386	15F2150	18.25
Model 80	15F2147	23.00
Micro Channel Architecture	15F2160	15.50

BIOS Interface Technical Reference

This publication provides basic input-output system (BIOS) interface information. It is intended for developers of hardware or software products that operate with the IBM PC and PS/2 products.

Table A.78 BIOS Interface Technical Reference Manual Part Numbers and Prices		
Description	**Part number**	**Price**
IBM Personal System/2 and Personal Computer BIOS Interface Technical Reference (second edition)	68X2341	$ 150.00
Supplements to 68X2341		
BIOS and ABIOS updates (includes SCSI support)	15F2161	18.25

Options and Adapters Technical Reference

These publications provide interface and design information for the options and adapters available for various systems. This information includes a hardware description, programming considerations, interface specifications, and BIOS information (where applicable).

Table A.79 Options and Adapters Technical Reference Manual Part Numbers and Prices		
Description	**Part number**	**Price**
Options and Adapters Technical Reference includes: Asynchronous Communications Adapter Bisynchronous Communications Adapter Cluster adapter Color display Color/Graphics Monitor adapter Color printer Expansion unit Hard disk drive adapter Game control adapter Graphics printer	6322509	$ 150.00

continues

Table A.79 Continued

Description	Part number	Price
Monochrome display		
Monochrome/printer adapter		
Printer adapter		
SDLC adapter		
Slimline floppy disk drive		
10M hard disk drive		
5.25-inch floppy disk drive		
5.25-inch floppy disk drive adapter		
64/256K memory option		
Engineering/scientific, includes:	6280133	$ 40.75
Data acquisition and control adapter (DAC)		
DAC distribution panel		
General purpose interface bus adapter		
Professional graphics controller		
Professional graphics display		
Personal Computer AT, includes:	6280134	15.50
Double-sided floppy disk drive		
Hard disk and floppy disk drive adapter		
High-capacity floppy disk drive		
Serial/parallel adapter		
128K memory expansion option		
20MB hard disk drive		
512K memory expansion option		
Communications		
Dual Async Adapter/A (Second Edition)	68X2315	7.25
Multiprotocol Adapter/A (Second Edition)	68X2316	14.25
300/1200 Internal Modem/A	68X2275	7.25
300/1200/2400 Internal Modem/A	68X2378	6.20
Displays		
PS/2 Color Display 8514	68X2214	7.25
PS/2 Display Adapter	68X2251	12.00
PS/2 Display Adapter 8514/A	68X2248	12.00
PS/2 Displays 8503,8512,and 8513	68X2206	7.25
Enhanced Graphics Adapter	6280131	11.75
Enhanced Color Display		
Graphics Memory Expansion Card		
Floppy disk drive and adapters		
3 1/2-Inch External Drive	59X9945	6.50
3 1/2-Inch External Drive Adapter	59X9946	6.50
3 1/2-Inch 720B/1.44MB Drive	68X2225	7.25
5 1/4-Inch External Drive (360K)	68X2272	12.00
5 1/4-Inch External Drive (1.2MB)	68X2348	11.50
5 1/4-Inch Internal Drive (1.2MB)	68X2350	11.50

Description	Part number	Price
5 1/4-Inch Drive Adapter (1.2MB)	68X2349	11.50
Floppy Disk Drive Half High (XT,AT)	6280093	$ 7.15
Hard disk drive and adapters		
Hard Disk Drive Adapter/A	68X2226	14.25
Hard Disk Drive Adapter/A, ESDI	68X2234	14.25
Hard Disk and Diskette Drive Adapter (for XT Model 286)	68X2215	7.25
20MB Drive (XT-089,-278,-286)	68X2208	8.45
20MB Adapter (XT-089,-268,-278)	6280092	7.15
20MB Drive and Adapter (Model 25)	01F0247	3.35
3 1/2-Inch 20MB Drive (Model 30)	68X2205	7.25
3 1/2-Inch 20MB Drive (Model 50)	68X2219	12.00
30MB Drive (AT)	68X2310	22.25
30MB Drive (Model 50-031)	68X2324	12.00
44MB Drive (Second Edition)	68X2317	7.25
60MB Adapter (50-021 and 50-031)	68X2343	4.80
60/120MB Drives (Models 50 and 70)	68X2314	10.75
70/115/314MB Drives	68X2236	7.25
Other storage devices and adapters		
CD-ROM drive	15F2134	12.50
Micro Channel SCSI adapter	68X2397	15.75
Micro Channel SCSI adapter w/cache	68X2365	16.75
Memory		
128/640K memory adapter	1502544	7.15
256K memory expansion	6280132	11.75
512KB/2MB memory adapter	6183075	7.15
2MB expanded memory adapter	75X1086	10.50
Expanded memory adapter/A (0-8MB)	01F0228	7.50
80286 memory expansion option	68X2227	7.25
80286 memory expansion option 2-8MB	68X2356	7.35
80386 memory expansion option 2-6MB	68X2257	12.00
80386 memory expansion option 2-8MB	68X2339	14.25
Other		
PS/2 speech adapter	68X2207	15.25
Voice communications adapter	55X8864	7.15
Mouse	68X2229	7.25
PC music feature	75X1048	21.00
Empty options and adapters binder	6280115	8.95
Developer's Guide		
8514/A Adapter Application Developer's Guide	68X2279	25.00

continues

Table A.79 Continued

Description	Part number	Price
Software reference manuals		
Basic Reference Version 3.30	6280189	$ 45.00
DOS Technical Reference Version 3.30	6280059	85.00
IBM OS/2 Technical Reference Version 1.0	6280201	200.00

Ordering Information

IBM technical and service publications can be ordered by calling toll-free 1-800-IBM-PCTB (1-800-426-7282), Monday through Friday, 8 a.m. to 8 p.m. Eastern time. In Canada, call toll-free 1-800-465-1234, Monday through Friday, from 8:30 a.m. to 4:30 p.m. Eastern time. In British Columbia, call toll-free 112-800-465-1234. In Alaska, call 1-414-633-8108.

When you order by telephone, you can use a credit card. You also may call to request additional copies of the Technical Directory (catalog) or to inquire about the availability of IBM PC or IBM PS/2 technical information on newly announced products that may not be listed here.

Commonly Used IBM Phone Numbers

IBM authorized dealer locator	800-447-4700
IBM CAD assistance	303-924-7262
IBM customer relations	201-930-3443
IBM direct (supplies: order/retail pricing)	800-426-2468
IBM employee sales	800-426-3675
IBM general information	800-426-3333
IBM multimedia help line	800-627-0920
IBM NSD hardware service (PC repair)	800-IBM-SERV
IBM part number ID and lookup	303-924-4015
IBM parts order center	303-924-4100
IBM technical manuals	800-IBM-PCTB
IBM National Support Center for Persons with Disabilities	800-426-2133
Independent developer information/registration	407-982-6178
Scientific Research Associates (SRA Products)	800-SRA-1277

Note: These are voice numbers—not modem lines.

Industry and Worldwide Standards Information

The following list shows official sources for documentation on industry and worldwide standards that relate to the computer industry.

FIPS or CCITT Recommendations
National Technical Information Service
Springfield, VA 22161
(703) 487-4650

Standard Reference Materials (SRMs)
Office of Standards Reference Materials
National Bureau of Standards
Room B311, Chemistry Building
Gaithersburg, MD 20899
(301) 975-6776, Telex: 197674 NBS UT

ANSI or ISO Standards
National Standards Institute
1430 Broadway, New York, NY 10018
Document sales: (212) 642-4900

X3 Standards
X3 Secretariat
CBEMA
311 First Street, N.W., Suite 500
Washington, DC 20001
(202) 737-8888

or

Global Engineering Documents
2805 McGaw, Irvine, CA 92714
(800) 854-7179, (714) 261-1455

EIA Standards
Electronic Industries Association
Engineering Department
2001 Eye Street, N.W., Washington, DC 20006
(202) 457-4500

MIL Standards
Navy Publication Center
Philadelphia, PA
(215) 697-2667 orders
(215) 697-2191 publications
(215) 697-4834 customer services

IEEE Standards
IEEE Service Center,
445 Hoes Lane,
Piscataway, NJ 08854
(201) 981-0060

or

IEEE Computer Society Press
Worldway Postal Center
Los Angeles, CA 90080
(714) 821-8380

Federal Telecommunications Standards (FED-STD)
General Services Administration
Specifications Sales (WFRI)
7th and D Streets, S.W.
Washington, DC 20407
(202) 472-2205

ECMA standards
European Computer Manufacturers Association
114 Rue de Rhone
CH-1204 Geneva, Switzerland

Vendor List

One of the most frustrating things about supporting PCs is finding a specific adapter board, part, driver program, or whatever you need to make a system work. Over the years I have compiled a list of companies whose products are popular or that I have found to work exceptionally well. I use these contacts regularly to provide information and components to enable me to support PC systems effectively.

Many companies have been mentioned in this book, but others not specifically mentioned have been added here. These companies carry many computer products that you often will have contact with, or that I simply recommend. I have tried to list as many vendors as possible that are important in day-to-day work with PC systems. These vendors can supply documentation for components you have, provide parts and service, and be used as a source for new equipment and even software. This list is as up-to-date as possible, but companies move or go out of business all the time. If you find in this list information that no longer is accurate, please call me or leave me a message on CompuServe. My number and address are under the listing for Mueller Technical Research.

Standard phone numbers rather than 800 numbers are given for all companies listed so that international readers can easily contact these companies. Also included are 800 numbers where available. Following each address is a short description of the products or services the company provides. I hope that this list is as useful to you as it is to me!

3M Data Storage Products Division
3M Center Building #223-5N-01
St. Paul, MN 55144
(612)736-1866

Manufactures magnetic disk and tape media. DC-600 and DC-2000 media are standards for tape-backup data cartridges.

Accurite Technologies, Inc.
231 Charcot Ave.
San Jose, CA 95131
(408)433-1980

Manufactures Accurite Drive Probe floppy disk diagnostics program, as well as HRD, DDD, and ADD industry-standard test disks.

Acer Technologies Corporation
401 Charcot Avenue
San Jose, CA 95131
(408)922-0333
(800)538-1542

Manufactures PC-compatible systems, monitors, and printers.

Acme Electric/Safe Power
20 Water Street
Cuba, NY 14727
(716)968-2400
(800)325-5848

Manufactures uninterruptible power supplies (UPS) systems and power conditioners.

Adaptec
691 S. Milpitas Boulevard
Milpitas, CA 95035
(408)945-8600

Manufactures hard disk controllers and SCSI host adapters.

Addison-Wesley Publishing Co, Inc.
Route 128
Reading, MA 01867
(617)944-3700

Publishes technical publications and books.

Adobe Systems, Inc.
1585 Charleston Road
Box 7900
Mountain View, CA 94039
(415)961-0911
(800)447-3577

Manufactures and created the PostScript language and a variety of graphics software.

Advanced Digital Information Corporation
14737 NE 87th Street
Box 2996
Redmond, WA 98073
(206)881-8004
(800)336-1233

Manufactures high-capacity tape-backup subsystems.

Advanced Logic Research (ALR)
9401 Jeronimo Street
Irvine, CA 92718
(714)581-6770
(800)444-4257

Manufactures PC compatibles featuring ISA, EISA, and MCA buses.

Advanced Micro Devices (AMD)
901 Thompson Place
Box 3453
Sunnyvale, CA 94088
(408)732-2400

Manufactures 386-compatible chips and math coprocessors.

Aldus Corporation
411 1st Avenue South
Seattle, WA 98104
(206)622-5500
(800)333-2538

Manufactures PageMaker desktop publishing software and a variety of other graphical programs.

ALL Computers, Inc.
1220 Yonge Street
Second Floor
Toronto, ONT, M4T1W1
(416)960-0111
(800)387-2744

Manufactures the ALL Chargecard memory coprocessor.

Allied Computer Services, Inc.
3417 Center Point Road N.E.
Cedar Rapids, IA 52402
(319)378-1383

Specializes in PC troubleshooting and data-recovery products.

Alloy Computer Products
165 Forest Street
Marlborough, MA 01752
(508)481-8500
(800)544-7551

Manufactures tape-backup subsystems.

ALPS America
3553 N. First Street
San Jose, CA 95134
(408)432-6000

Supplies 5 1/4-inch and 3 1/2-inch floppy drives to IBM for use in the
original XT, AT, and now the PS/2 systems. Also manufactures a line of
printers and scanners.

Altex Electronics, Inc.
300 Breesport
San Antonio, TX 78216
(512)349-8795
(800)531-5369

Supplies mail-order electronics parts.

Amdek Corporation
3471 N. First Street
San Jose, CA 95134
(408)473-1200
(800)722-6335

Division of Wyse Technology that manufactures monitors.

American Megatrends, Inc. (AMI)
1346 Oakbrook Drive
#120
Norcross, GA 30093
(404)263-8181
(800)828-9264

Manufactures an IBM-compatible BIOS, and ISA and EISA bus
motherboards.

American National Standards Institute
11 West 42nd Street
13th Floor
New York, NY 10036
(212)642-4900

ANSI committees set standards throughout the computer industry.
Copies of any ANSI-approved standard can be ordered here.

AMP, Inc.
AMP Building
Harrisburg, PA 17105
(717)564-0100
(800)522-6752

Manufactures a variety of computer connectors, sockets, and cables
used by many OEMs, including IBM.

AndraTech
P.O. Box 222
Milford, OH 45150
(513)831-9708

Manufactures an excellent EPROM programmer that runs from a parallel
port. The device can program up to 4Meg EPROMS and includes software for operation on IBM-compatible systems.

Anvil Cases
15650 Salt Lake Avenue
Industry, CA 91745
(818)968-4100
(800)359-2684

Manufactures heavy-duty equipment cases.

AOX, Inc.
486 Totten Pond Road
Waltham, MA 02154
(617)890-4402
(800)726-0269

Manufactures PS/2 MCA bus master 386 and 486 processor upgrade
boards.

Apple Computer, Inc.
20525 Mariani Avenue
Cupertino, CA 95014
(408)996-1010
(800)538-9696

Manufactures a line of Apple-compatible systems, peripherals, and
software.

Archive Technology/Ardat, Inc.
1650 Sunflower Avenue
Costa Mesa, CA 92626
(714)641-1230
(800)537-2724

Manufactures high-capacity tape drives.

Areal Technology, Inc.
2075 Zanker Road
San Jose, CA 95131
(408)436-6800

Manufactures high-capacity 3 1/2-inch hard disk drives.

Arrow Electronics, Inc.
25 Hub Drive
Melville, NY 11747
(516)391-1300
(800)521-3430

System and peripheral distributor.

AST Research, Inc.
16215 Alton Parkway
Irvine, CA 92718
(714)727-7902
(800)876-4278

Manufactures an extensive line of adapter boards and peripherals for
IBM and compatible computers, as well as a line of IBM-compatible
systems.

ATI Technologies, Inc.
3761 Victoria Park Avenue
Scarborough, ONT M1W3S2
(416)756-0718

Manufactures video cards and chipsets.

AT&T
55 Corporate Drive
Bridgewater, NJ 08807
(404)446-4734
(800)247-1212

Manufactures a line of IBM-compatible computer systems.

AT&T National Parts Sales Center
2551 E. 40th Avenue
Denver, CO 80205
(800)222-7278

Supplies parts and components for AT&T computer systems. Call and ask for the free AT&T parts catalog.

Autodesk, Inc.
2320 Marinship Way
Sausalito, CA 94965
(415)332-2344
(800)445-5415

Manufactures AutoCAD software.

Award Software, Inc.
130 Knowles Drive
Los Gatos, CA 95030
(408)370-7979

Manufactures a line of IBM-compatible ROM BIOS software.

Beckman Industrial
3883 Ruffin Road
San Diego, CA 92123
(619)495-3200
(800)854-2708

Manufactures diagnostics and test equipment.

Belden Wire and Cable
P.O. Box 1980
Richmond, IN 47375
(317)983-5200
(800)235-3361

Manufactures cable and wire products.

Bitstream, Inc.
215 1st Street
Cambridge, MA 02142
(617)497-6222
(800)522-3668

Manufactures fonts and font software.

Black Box Corporation
P.O. Box 12800
Pittsburgh, PA 15241
(412)746-5530

Manufactures and distributes a variety of communications products
including network adapters, cables, and connectors for a variety of
applications.

Boca Research, Inc.
6413 Congress Avenue
Boca Raton, FL 33487
(407)997-6227

Manufactures a low-cost line of adapter card products for
IBM-compatibles.

Bondwell Industrial Company, Inc.
47485 Seabridge Drive
Fremont, CA 94538
(415)490-4300

Manufactures a line of laptop systems.

Borland International
1800 Green Hills Road
Scotts Valley, CA 95066
(408)439-1411
(800)331-0877

Software manufacturer that features Turbo language products, Paradox,
as well as dBASE IV and Framework, acquired from Ashton-Tate.

Boston Computer Exchange
55 Temple Place
Boston, MA 02111
(617)542-4414

A broker for used IBM and compatible computers.

Bracking, Jim
967 Pinewood Drive
San Jose, CA 95129
(408)725-0628

Manufactures the HDtest hard disk test and format program. This program, distributed as shareware, is excellent for testing and educational
use.

Brightbill-Roberts
120 E. Washington Street
#421
Syracuse, NY 13202
(315)474-3400
(800)444-3490

Manufactures the ShowPartner FX presentation graphics program.

Bureau of Electronic Publishing
141 New Road
Parsippany, NJ 07054
(201)808-2700
(800)828-4766

Distributes and publishes software on CD-ROM disks.

Byte Information Exchange (BIX)
One Phoenix Mill Lane
Peterborough, NH 03458
(603)924-7681

An on-line computer information and messaging system.

***Byte* Magazine**
One Phoenix Mill Lane
Peterborough, NH 03458
(603)924-9281

A monthly magazine covering all lines of microcomputers.

C. Itoh Electronics, Inc.
19300 S Hamilton Avenue
Box 9116
Torrance, CA 90508
(213)327-9100

Cable Connection
557 Salmar Avenue
#B
Campbell, CA 95008
(408)379-9224

Manufactures a variety of cable, connector, and switch products.

Cables To Go
26 W. Nottingham
#200
Dayton, OH 45405
(513)275-0886
(800)826-7904

Manufactures a variety of cable, connector, and switch products.

Cache Computers, Inc.
46600 Landing Parkway
Fremont, CA 94538
(510)266-9922

Manufactures a line of 386 and 486 motherboards.

Cal-Abco
6041 Variel Avenue
Woodland Hills, CA 91367
(818)704-7733
(800)669-2226

Distributes computer systems and peripherals.

Canon USA, Inc.
One Canon Plaza
Lake Success, NY 11042
(516)488-6700

Manufactures a line of printer and video equipment as well as floppy drives. Supplies floppy drives to COMPAQ and IBM.

Casio, Inc.
15 Gardner Road
Fairfield, NJ 07006
(201)575-7400

Manufactures personal data systems and digital watches.

Central Point Software, Inc.
15220 NW Greenbrier Parkway
Beaverton, OR 97006
(503)690-8088
(800)888-8199

Manufactures the PC Tools and Copy II PC software.

Cherry Electrical Products
3600 Sunset Avenue
Waukegan, IL 60087
(708)662-9200

Manufactures a line of keyboards for IBM-compatible systems.

Chicago Case Company
4446 S. Ashland Avenue
Chicago, IL 60609
(312)927-1600

Manufactures equipment-shipping and travel cases.

Chinon America, Inc.
660 Maple Avenue
Torrance, CA 90503
(213)533-0274
(800)441-0222

Manufactures a line of floppy disk and CD-ROM drives.

Chips & Technologies, Inc.
3050 Zanker Road
San Jose, CA 95134
(408)434-0600
(800)944-6284

Manufactures specialized chipsets for compatible motherboard manufacturers.

Ci Design Company
1711 Langley Avenue
Irvine, CA 92714
(714)261-5524

Manufactures custom-made 3 1/2-inch drive mounting kits used by Toshiba, Panasonic, and NEC for their drive products. Also makes drive faceplates, enclosures, and custom cable assemblies.

Cipher Data Products, Inc.
10101 Old Grove Road
San Diego, CA 92131
(619)578-9100
(800)424-7437

Manufactures a line of tape-backup products. Also supplies tape-backup systems to IBM.

Ciprico, Inc.
2955 Xenium Lane
Minneapolis, MN 55441
(612)559-2034
(800)727-4669

Manufactures high-performance SCSI host adapters.

Citizen America Corporation
2050 Broadway
#600
Santa Monica, CA 90411
(213)453-0614

Manufactures a line of printers and floppy disk drives.

CMS Enhancements, Inc.
2722 Michelson Drive
Irvine, CA 92715
(714)222-6000

Distributes a variety of system and peripheral products, and specializes
in hard disk drives.

Colorado Memory Systems, Inc.
800 S. Taft Avenue
Loveland, CO 80537
(303)669-8000
(800)346-9881

Manufactures tape-backup subsystems.

Columbia Data Products
1070B Rainer Drive
Altamonte Springs, FL 32714
(407)869-6700

Manufactures SCSI drivers for Western Digital FASST host adapters.

Comb
720 Anderson Avenue
Street Cloud, MN 56372
(612)654-4800
(800)328-0609

Liquidates and distributes a variety of discontinued products, including
PC compatible systems and peripherals.

COMPAQ Computer Corporation
20555 State Hwy.
#249
Houston, TX 77070
(713)370-0670
(800)231-0900

Manufactures IBM-compatible computer systems.

CompUSA, Inc.
15151 Surveyor
#A
Addison, TX 75244
(214)702-0055
(800)932-2667

Computer retail superstore and mail-order outlet.

CompuServe Information Service (CIS)
5000 Arlington Centre Boulevard
Columbus, OH 43220
(614)457-8600
(800)848-8199

Largest on-line information and messaging service; offers manufacturer- and vendor-sponsored forums for technical support.

Computer Component Source, Inc.
135 Eileen Way
Syosset, NY 11791
(516)496-8727
(800)356-1227

Distributes a large number of computer components for repair. Specializes in display parts such as flyback transformers and other components.

***Computer Hotline* Magazine**
15400 Knoll Trail
#500
Dallas, TX 75248
(214)233-5131
(800)866-3241

Publication featuring advertisers offering excellent sources of replacement and repair parts as well as new and used equipment at wholesale prices.

***Computer Shopper* Magazine**
5211 S. Washington Avenue
Titusville, FL 32780
(305)269-3211

Monthly magazine for experimenters and bargain hunters that features a large number of advertisements.

Comtech Publishing Ltd.
P.O. Box 12340
Reno, NV 89510
(702)825-9000
(800)456-7005

Manufactures Salvage Professional, the best dBASE data-recovery software.

Connector Resources Unlimited (CRU)
1005 Ames Avenue
Milpitas, CA 95035
(408)942-9077

Manufactures a large variety of disk enclosures, mounting kits, cables, and connectors for IBM and Mac systems.

Conner Peripherals, Inc.
3081 Zanker Road
San Jose, CA 95134
(408)456-4500

Manufactures 3 1/2-inch hard disk drives. Partly owned by COMPAQ, and supplies most of COMPAQ's hard drives.

Core International, Inc.
7171 North Federal Hwy.
Boca Raton, FL 33487
(407)997-6055

Distributes a variety of different manufacturers' hard disk drives including Seagate and Western Digital.

Corel Systems, Inc.
1600 Carling Avenue
Ottawa, ONT, K1Z8R7
(613)728-8200

Manufactures a variety of optical disk products and CorelDraw software.

Cumulus Corporation
23500 Mercantile Road
Cleveland, OH 44120
(216)464-2211

Manufactures processor-upgrade products and clone systems.

Curtis Manufacturing Co, Inc.
30 Fitzgerald Drive
Jaffrey, NH 03452
(603)532-4123
(800)548-4900

Manufactures a line of computer accessories, cables, and toolkits.

Cyrix Corporation
2703 N. Central Expressway
Richardson, TX 75080
(214)234-8387
(800)327-6284

Manufactures fast Intel-compatible math coprocessors for 286-, 386SX-, and 386DX-based systems.

Manufactures a line of printers and disk drives.

Dak Industries, Inc.
8200 Remmet Avenue
Canoga Park, CA 91304
(818)888-8220
(800)325-0800

Liquidates and distributes a variety of discontinued products, including PC compatible systems and peripherals.

Dallas Semiconductor
4401 S. Beltwood Parkway
Dallas, TX 75244
(214)450-0400

Manufactures real-time clock and non-volatile RAM modules used by a number of OEMs including IBM, COMPAQ, and others.

Damark International, Inc.
7101 Winnetka Avenue North
Minneapolis, MN 55429
(800)729-9000

Liquidates and distributes a variety of discontinued products, including PC compatible systems and peripherals.

Data Depot
1525 Sandy Lane
Clearwater, FL 34615
(813)446-3402
(800)275-1913

Manufactures the PocketPOST diagnostics card for ISA and EISA systems.

Data Spec
20120 Plummer Street
Chatsworth, CA 91311
(818)993-1202
(800)431-8124

Manufactures a complete line of switch boxes for parallel, serial, video, and many other connections.

Data Technology Corporation (DTC)
500 Yosemite Drive
Milpitas, CA 95035
(408)262-7700

Manufactures excellent hard disk controllers for ISA and EISA bus systems.

Datastorm Technologies, Inc.
3212 Lemone Boulevard
Columbia, MO 65201
(314)443-3282

Manufactures ProCOMM and ProCOMM Plus communications software.

Dell Computer Corporation
9505 Arboretum Boulevard
Austin, TX 78759
(512)338-4400
(800)426-5150

Manufactures a line of low-cost, high-performance IBM-compatible computer systems.

DiagSoft, Inc.
5615 Scotts Valley Drive
Scotts Valley, CA 95066
(408)438-8247

Manufactures QAPlus PC diagnostics software.

Digital Research, Inc.
70 Garden Court
Monterey, CA 93942
(408)649-2893
(800)848-1498

Manufactures the DR DOS operating system.

Direct Drives
1107 Euclid Lane
Richton Park, IL 60417
(708)481-1111

Distributes hard disk drives and controllers. Carries an enormous selection of drives and controllers. Also publishes the *Hard Disk Buyers Reference*, a comprehensive and accurate listing of drive and controller specs.

Distributed Processing Tech. (DPT)
140 Candace Drive
Maitland, FL 32751
(407)830-5522

Manufactures high-performance caching SCSI host adapters.

Diversified Technology
112 E. State Street
Ridgeland, MS 39158
(201)891-8718
(800)443-2667

Manufactures industrial and rack-mount PC compatible systems as well as a variety of backplane-design CPU boards and multifunction adapters.

DTK Computer, Inc.
17700 Castleton Street
Industry, CA 91748
(818)810-8880

Manufactures PC-compatible systems and BIOS software.

Dynatech Computer Power Inc.
5800 Butler Lane
Scotts Valley, CA 95066
(408)438-5760
(800)638-9098

Manufactures a line of computer power-protection devices.

Edmund Scientific
101 E. Gloucester Pike
Barrington, NJ 08007
(609)573-6250

Supplies scientific supplies including optical equipment and components, test equipment, and a variety of electronic components and gadgets. Its catalog is a hacker's dream!

Elek-Tek, Inc.
7350 North Linder Avenue
Skokie, IL 60077
(708)677-7660
(800)395-1000

Computer retail superstore offering a large selection of brand-name
equipment at discount pricing.

Emerson Computer Power
15041 Bake Parkway
#L
Irvine, CA 92718
(714)380-1005
(800)222-5877

Manufactures a line of computer power-protection devices.

Endl Publications
14426 Black Walnut Court
Saratoga, CA 95070
(408)867-6642

Publishes SCSI technical documentation such as *The SCSI Bench
Reference* and *The SCSI Encyclopedia*.

Epson America, Inc.
20770 Madrona Avenue
Torrance, CA 90509
(213)782-0770
(800)289-3776

Manufactures printers, floppy disk drives, and complete PC-compatible
systems.

Everex Systems, Inc.
48431 Milmont Drive
Fremont, CA 94538
(415)498-1111
(800)922-8911

Manufactures PC-compatible systems and peripherals.

Exabyte Corporation
1685 38th Street
Boulder, CO 80301
(303)447-7359

Manufactures high-performance 8mm tape-backup systems.

Excel, Inc.
2200 Brighton-Henrietta Townline Road
Rochester, NY 14623
(716)272-8770
(800)624-2001

Distributes refurbished IBM PC, XT, AT, and PS/2 systems as well as printers, modems, displays, and so on.

Fedco Electronics, Inc.
184 W. 2nd Street
Fond du Lac, WI 54936
(414)922-6490
(800)542-9761

Manufactures and supplies a large variety of computer batteries.

Fessenden Technologies
116 N. 3rd Street
Ozark, MO 65721
(417)485-2501

Service company that offers hard disk drive and monitor repair and reconditioning. Also offers floppy disk and hard disk test equipment.

Fifth Generation Systems, Inc.
10049 N. Reiger Road
Baton Rouge, LA 70809
(504)291-7221
(800)873-4384

Manufactures a variety of software utility products including FASTBACK, the Mace Utilities, and the Brooklyn Bridge.

Forbin Project
P.O. Box 702
Cedar Falls, IA 50613
(319)266-0543

Manufactures the Qmodem communications software.

Fox Software, Inc.
134 W. South Boundary
Perrysburg, OH 43551
(419)874-0162

Manufactures FoxPro and FoxBase dBASE-compatible software.

Fujitsu America, Inc.
3055 Orchard Drive
San Jose, CA 95134
(408)432-1300
(800)626-4686

Manufactures a line of high-capacity hard disk drives.

Future Domain Corporation
2801 McGaw Avenue
Irvine, CA 92714
(714)253-0400

Manufactures a line of high-performance SCSI host adapters and
software.

GammaTech
P.O. Box 70
Edmond, OK 73083
(405)359-1219

Manufactures the GammaTech HPFS Utilities, which can undelete and
recover files on an OS/2 HPFS partition.

Gateway 2000
610 Gateway Drive
North Sioux City, SD 57049
(605)232-2000
(800)523-2000

Manufactures a line of PC-compatible systems sold by mail order.

GigaTrend, Inc.
2234 Rutherford Road
Carlsbad, CA 92008
(619)931-9122

Manufactures high-capacity tape drives.

Global Engineering Documents
2805 McGaw
Irvine, CA 92714
(714)261-1455
(800)854-7179

A source of ANSI-standard documents. Unlike ANSI, you can get draft
documents of standards that are not yet ANSI-approved.

Globe Manufacturing, Inc.
1159 Route 22
Mountainside, NJ 07092
(908)232-7301
(800)227-3258

Manufactures assorted PC adapter card brackets.

Golden Bow Systems
842 E. Washington Street
#B
San Diego, CA 92103
(619)298-9349
(800)284-3269

Manufactures Vopt, the best and fastest disk optimizer software available.

GoldStar Technology, Inc.
3003 N. First Street
San Jose, CA 95134
(408)432-1331

Manufactures a line of PC systems, monitors, and fax machines.

Great Software Ideas, Inc. (GSI)
17951 H Sky Park Circle
Irvine, CA 92714
(714)261-7949
(800)468-7800

Manufactures a line of floppy controllers, including units with IDE hard disk interfaces, security locks, and support for 2.88M drives. Also offers complete 2.88M drive upgrade kits.

Hauppauge Computer Works, Inc.
91 Cabot Court
Hauppauge, NY 11788
(516)434-1600
(800)443-6284

Manufactures upgrade motherboards for PC-compatible systems.

Hayes Microcomputer Products
5835 Peachtree Corners East
Norcross, GA 30092
(404)449-8791
(800)874-2937

Manufactures a complete line of modems.

Heathkit
Heath Company
Benton Harbor, MI 49022
(616)982-3411
(800)253-0570

Manufactures various electronic device kits assembled by the purchaser. Has incredible kits for learning electronics and computer design.
Also sells Zenith computers and technical documentation.

Hewlett-Packard
19310 Pruneridge Avenue
Cupertino, CA 95014
(800)752-0900

Manufactures printers and PC-compatible systems.

Hewlett-Packard, Disk Memory Division
11413 Chinden Boulevard
Boise, ID 83714
(208)323-6000

Manufactures high-capacity 3 1/2-inch hard disk drives.

Hitatchi America, Ltd.
50 Prospect Avenue
Tarrytown, NY 94005
(914)332-5800

Manufactures computer peripherals, including hard disks and LCD
devices.

Honeywell Inc.
4171 N. Mesa Street
Building D
El Paso, TX 79902
(915)543-5566
(800)445-6939

Manufactures a variety of high-quality keyboards for PC-compatible
systems.

Hyundai Electronics America
166 Baypointe Parkway
San Jose, CA 95134
(408)473-9200
(800)544-7808

Manufactures PC-compatible systems.

IBM Desktop Software
472 Wheelers Farm Road
Milford, CT 06460
(800)426-7699

Supports IBM PC applications software such as DisplayWrite and
PC Storyboard.

IBM National Distribution Division (NDD)
101 Paragon Drive
Montvale, NJ 07645
(800)426-9397

Manufactures and supports IBM DOS and OS/2.

IBM OEM Division
1133 Westchester Avenue
White Plains, NY 10604
(914)642-6049

Manufactures and distributes IBM products such as high-capacity
3 1/2-inch hard disk drives, and networking and chipset products.

IBM Parts Order Center
P.O. Box 9022
Boulder, CO 80301
(303)924-4100

IBM's nationwide service parts ordering center.

IBM Personal Systems Division
11400 Burnet Road
Austin, TX 78758
(512)823-2851

Manufactures and supports IBM's PS/2 products.

IBM Technical Directory
P.O. Box 2009
Racine, WI 53404
(414)633-8108
(800)426-7282

The source for books, reference manuals, documentation, software
toolkits, and language products for IBM systems.

InfoChip Systems, Inc.
2840 San Tomas Expressway
Santa Clara, CA 95051
(408)727-0514
(800)447-0200

Manufactures the Expanz data-compression coprocessor products.

***InfoWorld* Magazine**
375 Cochituate Road
Framingham, MA 01701
(508)879-0446

Publishes *InfoWorld* magazine, featuring excellent product reviews.

Inline, Inc.
625 S. Palm Street
La Habra, CA 90631
(213)690-6767
(800)882-7117

Manufactures a complete line of video-connection accessories including distribution amplifiers, scan converters, line drivers, projector interfaces, and cables.

Inmac
2951 Zanker Road
San Jose, CA 95134
(408)435-1700

Distributes a large variety of computer supplies, floppy disks, cables, and so on.

Integrated Information Technology (IIT)
2445 Mission College Boulevard
Santa Clara, CA 95054
(408)727-1885
(800)832-0770

Manufactures fast Intel-compatible math coprocessors for 286-, 386SX-, and 386DX-based systems.

Intel Corporation
3065 Bowers Avenue
Santa Clara, CA 95051
(408)765-8080
(800)548-4725

Manufactures microprocessors used in IBM and compatible systems. Also makes a line of memory and accelerator boards.

Intel PC Enhancement Operations
5200 NE Elam Young Parkway
Hillsboro, OR 97124
(503)629-7354
(800)538-3373

Manufactures a variety of PC expansion boards including AboveBoard memory adapters and modems.

Interface Group
300 First Avenue
Needham, MA 02194
(617)449-6600

Produces the annual COMDEX/Fall and COMDEX/Spring computer shows.

Intex Solutions, Inc.
161 Highland Avenue
Needham, MA 02194
(617)449-6222

Manufactures and distributes software, especially Lotus enhancement products such as the Rescue Plus Lotus Data Recovery program.

Iomega Corporation
1821 West 4000 South
Roy, UT 84067
(801)778-1000
(800)456-5522

Manufactures the Bernoulli box removable-cartridge drive.

IQ Technologies, Inc.
22032 23rd Drive SE
Bothell, WA 98021
(206)483-3555
(800)752-6526

Manufactures PC interconnect cables and devices, including the SmartCable RS232 devices.

Irwin Magnetic Systems, Inc.
2101 Commonwealth Boulevard
Ann Arbor, MI 48105
(313)930-9000
(800)421-1879

Manufactures a line of tape-backup products from DC-2000 to DAT and
8mm units. Also supplies IBM tape-backup systems.

Jameco Computer Products
1355 Shoreway Road
Belmont, CA 94002
(415)592-8097

Supplies computer components, parts, and peripherals by way of mail
order.

JDR Microdevices
2233 Branham Lane
San Jose, CA 95124
(408)559-1200
(800)538-5000

A vendor for chips, disk drives, and various computer and electronic
parts and components.

Jensen Tools
7815 S. 46th Street
Phoenix, AZ 85044
(602)968-6231
(800)426-1194

Supplies and manufactures high-quality tools and test equipment.

Kalok Corporation
1289 Anvilwood Avenue
Sunnyvale, CA 94089
(408)747-1315

Manufactures a line of low-cost 3 1/2-inch hard disk drives.

Kenfil Distribution
16745 Saticoy Street
Van Nuys, CA 91406
(818)785-1181

A major software distributor.

Kensington Microware, Ltd.
251 Park Avenue South
New York, NY 10010
(212)475-5200
(800)535-4242

Manufactures and supplies computer accessories.

Key Tronic Corporation
North 4424 Sullivan Road
Spokane, WA 99216
(509)928-8000
(800)262-6006

Manufactures and supplies low-cost PC-compatible keyboards. Supplies COMPAQ with keyboards.

Kimpsion International
1335 Rothland Court
San Jose, CA 95131
(408)729-6654

Manufactures low-cost hard disk controllers and other adapter boards.

Kingston Technology Corporation
17600 Newhope Street
Fountain Valley, CA 92708
(714)435-2600

Manufactures the SX/Now! processor upgrade module, windows enhancement video boards, and a variety of high-quality memory modules.

Kolod Research, Inc.
1898 Techny Court
Northbrook, IL 60062
(708)291-1586

Manufactures hTEST/hFORMAT, a very powerful hard disk formatting and diagnostics software package.

Landmark Research International
703 Grand Central Street
Clearwater, FL 34616
(813)443-1331
(800)683-6696

Manufactures the Service Diagnostics PC diagnostics program, as well as the Kickstart diagnostic adapter cards. Known also for the Landmark System Speed Test program.

Laser Magnetic Storage
4425 Arrowswest Drive
Colorado Springs, CO 80907
(719)593-7900
(800)777-5764

Manufactures a variety of optical disk products.

Lexmark
740 New Circle Road
Lexington, KY 40511
(606)232-6814

Manufactures IBM keyboards and printers for retail distribution. Spun off from IBM in 1991, sells to other OEMs and distributors.

Liuski International, Inc.
10 Hub Drive
Melville, NY 11747
(516)454-8220
(800)347-5454

Hardware distributor that carries a variety of peripherals and systems.

Longshine Computer, Inc.
2013 N. Capitol Avenue
San Jose, CA 95132
(408)942-1746

Manufactures various PC adapters including floppy, hard disk, SCSI, Token Ring, Ethernet, and so on.

Lotus Development Corporation
55 Cambridge Parkway
Cambridge, MA 02142
(617)577-8500
(800)343-5414

Manufactures Lotus 1-2-3, Symphony, and Magellan software.

LSI Logic, Inc.
1551 McCarthy Boulevard
Milpitas, CA 95035
(408)433-8000

Manufactures motherboard logic and chipsets.

Manzana Microsystems, Inc.
P.O. Box 2117
Goleta, CA 93118
(805)968-1387

Manufactures floppy disk upgrade subsystems and controllers.

Mastersoft, Inc.
6991 E. Camelback Road
Scottsdale, AZ 85251
(602)277-0900
(800)624-6107

Manufactures Word for Word, a word processing file-conversion program.

Maxell Corporation of America
22-08 Route 208
Fair Lawn, NJ 07410
(201)795-5900
(800)533-2836

Manufactures magnetic media products including disks and tape cartridges.

Maxi Switch, Inc.
2901 E. Elvira Road
Tuscon, AZ 85706
(602)294-5450

Manufactures a line of good-quality PC keyboards, including some designed for harsh or industrial environments.

Maxoptix
2520 Junction Avenue
San Jose, CA 95134
(408)954-9700
(800)848-3092

Manufactures a line of optical WORM and magneto-optical drives. Joint venture with Maxtor Corporation and Kubota Corporation.

Maxtor Corporation
211 River Oaks Parkway
San Jose, CA 95134
(408)432-1700
(800)262-9867

Manufactures a line of large-capacity, high-quality hard disk drives.

Maynard Electronics, Inc.
36 Skyline Drive
Lake Mary, FL 32746
(407)263-3500
(800)821-8782

Manufactures a line of tape-backup products.

McAfee Associates
4423 Cheeney Street
Santa Clara, CA 95054
(408)988-3832

Manufactures the SCAN virus-scanning software, which is nonresident
and updated frequently to handle new viruses as they are discovered.

McGraw-Hill, Inc.
Princeton Road N-1
Highstown, NJ 08520
(619)426-5000
(800)822-8158

Publishes technical information and books.

Megahertz Corporation
4505 S. Wasatch Boulevard
Salt Lake City, UT 84124
(801)272-6000
(800)527-8677

Manufactures laptop modems and external network adapters. Also
makes AT-speedup products.

Memorex Computer Supplies
1200 Memorex Drive
Santa Clara, CA 95050
(408)957-1000

Manufactures a line of computer diskette media, tape cartridges, and
various other supplies.

Mentor Electronics, Inc.
7560 Tylor Boulevard
#E
Mentor, OH 44060
(216)951-1884

Supplies surplus IBM PC (10/27/82) ROM BIOS update chips.

Merisel
200 Continental Boulevard
El Segundo, CA 90245
(213)615-3080
(800)645-7778

A large distributor of PC hardware and software products from many
manufacturers.

Merrill & Bryan Enterprises, Inc.
9770 Carroll Center Road
#C
San Diego, CA 92126
(619)689-8611

Manufactures the InfoSpotter system inspection and diagnostics
program.

Merritt Computer Products, Inc.
5565 Red Bird Center Drive
#150
Dallas, TX 75237
(214)339-0753

Manufactures the SafeSkin keyboard protector.

Micro 2000, Inc.
1100 E. Broadway
Third Floor
Glendale, CA 91205
(818)547-0125

Manufactures the MicroScope PC diagnostics program, as well as the
POSTProbe ISA, EISA, and MCA POST diagnostics card. Is extending 25
percent discount to anyone who mentions this book when purchasing.

Micro Accessories, Inc.
2012 Hartog Drive
San Jose, CA 95131
(408)441-1242
(800)777-6687

Manufactures a variety of cables and disk drive mounting brackets and
accessories, including PS/2 adapter kits.

Micro Channel Developers Association
2 Greenwich Plaza
#100
Greenwich, CT 06830
(203)622-7614

An independent organization that facilitates evolution of the Micro
Channel Architecture. Resolves technical issues related to the MCA bus.

Micro Design International
6985 University Boulevard
Winter Park, FL 32792
(407)677-8333
(800)241-1853

Manufactures the SCSI Express driver software for integration of SCSI
peripherals in a variety of environments.

Micro House
P.O. Box 10492
Clearwater, FL 34617
(813)443-6194
(800)741-3282

Publishes the *Encyclopedia of Hard Disks*, an excellent reference book
that shows hard disk drive and controller jumper settings.

Micro Solutions, Inc.
132 W. Lincoln Hwy.
DeKalb, IL 60115
(815)756-3411

Manufactures a complete line of floppy controllers and subsystems including 2.88M versions. Also offers floppy drive and tape-backup systems that run from a standard parallel port, using no expansion slots.

Microcom, Inc.
500 River Ridge Drive
Norwood, MA 02062
(617)551-1000
(800)822-8224

Manufactures error-correcting modems, and develops the MNP
communications protocols.

MicroComputer Accessories, Inc.
5405 Jandy Place
Los Angeles, CA 90066
(213)301-9400
(800)821-8270

Manufactures a variety of computer and office accessories.

Micrografx, Inc.
1303 E. Arapaho
Richardson, TX 75081
(214)497-6431
(800)733-3729

Manufactures the Micrografx Designer, Draw Plus, and Charisma software. Specializes in Windows and OS/2 development.

Microlink/Micro Firmware, Inc.
1430 W. Lindsey Street
Norman, OK 83069
(405)321-8333
(800)767-5465

The largest distributor of Phoenix ROM BIOS upgrades. Develops custom versions for specific motherboards and supplies many other BIOS vendors with products.

Micron Technologies
2805 E. Columbia Road
Boise, ID 83706
(208)368-3900
(800)642-7661

Manufactures various memory chips, SIMMs, and memory boards.

Micronics Computers, Inc.
232 Warren Avenue
Fremont, CA 94539
(415)651-2300

Manufactures PC-compatible motherboards and complete laptop and portable systems.

Micropolis Corporation
21211 Nordhoff Street
Chatsworth, CA 91311
(818)709-3300

Manufactures a line of high-capacity 5 1/4- and 3 1/2-inch hard disk drives.

Pacific Magtron, Inc.
568-8 Weddell Drive
Sunnyvale, CA 94089
(408)774-1188

Manufactures hard disk drives.

Packard Bell
9425 Canoga Avenue
Chatsworth, CA 91311
(800)733-4411

Manufactures an excellent line of low-cost PC-compatible computer
systems.

Panasonic Communications & Systems
2 Panasonic Way
Secaucus, NJ 07094
(201)348-7000
(800)233-8182

Manufactures monitors, optical drive products, floppy drives, printers,
and PC-compatible laptop systems.

Parts Now, Inc.
810 Stewart Street
Madison, WI 53713
(608)276-8688
(800)233-8182

Sells a large variety of laser printer parts for HP, Canon, Apple, and other
laser printers using Canon engines.

PC Connection
6 Mill Street
Marlow, NH 03456
(603)446-7721
(800)800-5555

Distributes many different hardware and software packages by way of
mail order.

PC **Magazine**
One Park Avenue
New York, NY 10016
(212)503-5446

Magazine featuring product reviews and comparisons.

PC Power & Cooling, Inc.
5995 Avenida Encinas
Carlsbad, CA 92008
(619)931-5700
(800)722-6555

Manufactures a line of high-quality, high-output power supplies for IBM and compatible systems, including COMPAQ. Known for high-power output and quiet fan operation.

PC Repair Corporation
2010 State Street
Harrisburg, PA 17103
(717)232-7272
(800)727-3724

Service company and parts distributor that performs board repair of IBM PCs and PS/2s, printers, and typewriters as well as COMPAQ systems repair. Also offers an extensive parts line for these systems.

***PC Week* Magazine**
10 Presidents Landing
Medford, MA 02155
(617)693-3753

Weekly magazine featuring industry news and information.

***PC World* Magazine**
375 Chochituate Road
Framingham, MA 01701
(508)879-0700
(800)435-7766

A monthly magazine featuring product reviews and comparisons.

PC-SIG/Spectra Publishing
1030 E. Duane Avenue
#D
Sunnyvale, CA 94086
(408)730-9291
(800)245-6717

Publishes public-domain software and shareware available on CD-ROM.

Philips Consumer Electronics
One Philips Drive
Knoxville, TN 37914
(615)521-4366

Manufactures Magnavox PCs, monitors, and CD-ROM drives.

Phoenix Technologies, Ltd.
846 University Avenue
Norwood, MA 02062
(617)551-4000
(800)677-3000

Manufactures IBM-compatible BIOS software for a number of ISA, EISA, and MCA systems.

Pivar Computing Services, Inc.
165 Arlington Heights Road
Buffalo Grove, IL 60089
(708)459-6010
(800)266-8378

Service company that specializes in data and media conversion.

PKWare, Inc.
9025 N. Deerwood Drive
Brown Deer, WI 53223
(414)354-8699

Manufactures the PKZIP, PKUNZIP, PKLite, and PKZMENU data compression software. Widely used on BBS systems and by manufacturers for software distribution.

Plus Development Corporation
1778 McCarthy Boulevard
Milpitas, CA 95035
(408)434-6900
(800)624-5545

Manufactures the Plus Hardcard product line. A division of Quantum Corporation.

Priam Systems Corporation
1140 Ringwood Court
San Jose, CA 95131
(408)441-4180

Provides service and repair for Priam drives; original Priam has gone out of business.

***Processor* Magazine**
P.O. Box 85518
Lincoln, NE 68501
(800)247-4880

Publication that offers excellent sources of replacement and repair parts as well as new equipment at wholesale prices.

Programmer's Shop
90 Industrial Park Road
Hingham, MA 02043
(617)740-2510
(800)421-8006

Distributes programming tools and utility software.

PTI Industries
269 Mount Hermon Road
Scott Valley, CA 95066
(408)438-3900

Manufactures a line of computer power-protection devices.

Public Brand Software
P.O. Box 51315
Indianapolis, IN 46251
(317)856-7571
(800)426-3475

Publishes a public domain and shareware library.

Public Software Library
P.O. Box 35705-F
Houston, TX 77235
(713)524-6394
(800)242-4775

Top-notch distributor of high-quality public domain and shareware software. Its library is the most well-researched and -tested available. Also offers an excellent newsletter that reviews the software.

Quadram
One Quad Way
Norcross, GA 30093
(404)923-6666

Manufactures a line of adapter boards and upgrades for IBM and compatible systems.

Quaid Software Limited
45 Charles Street East
Third Floor
Toronto, ON, M4Y1S2,
(416)961-8243

Manufactures the Quaid Copywrite disk copy program and other disk utilities.

Qualitas, Inc.
7101 Wisconsin Avenue
#1386
Bethesda, MD 20814
(301)907-6700

Manufactures the 386Max memory-manager utility programs.

Quantum Corporation
500 McCarthy Boulevard
Milpitas, CA 95035
(408)894-4000

Manufactures a line of 3 1/2-inch hard disk drives. Supplies drives to Apple Computer.

Quarterdeck Office Systems
150 Pico Boulevard
Santa Monica, CA 90405
(213)392-9851

Manufactures the popular DESQview, QEMM, and QRAM memory-manager products.

Que Corporation
11711 N. College Avenue
Carmel, IN 46032
(317)573-2500
(800)992-0244

Publishes the highest-quality computer applications software and hardware books in the industry.

Qume Corporation
500 Yosemite Drive
Milpitas, CA 95035
(408)942-4000
(800)223-2479

Manufactures a variety of peripherals including displays, printers, and printer supplies such as toner cartridges. Qume owns DTC, a disk controller manufacturer.

Rancho Technology, Inc.
8632 Archibald Avenue
#109
Rancho Cucamonga, CA 91730
(714)987-3966

Manufactures an extensive line of SCSI products including host adapters for ISA, EISA, and MCA bus systems, SCSI extenders and interface software.

Reply Corporation
4435 Fortran Drive
San Jose, CA 95134
(408)942-4804
(800)955-5295

Manufactures PS/2-compatible systems with MCA bus slots. These systems are available in a variety of expandable configurations and are truly MCA compatible.

Rodime, Inc.
901 Broken Sound Parkway
Boca Raton, FL 33487
(407)994-6200

Manufactures a line of hard disk drives.

Rotating Memory Repair, Inc.
23382-J Madero Road
Mission Viejo, CA 92691
(714)472-0159

Repair company that specializes in hard drive and floppy drive repair. Also repairs power supplies and displays.

Rotating Memory Services
4919 Windplay
El Dorado Hills, CA 95630
(916)939-7500

Repair company that specializes in hard disk drives.

Rupp Corporation
7285 Franklin Avenue
Los Angeles, CA 90046
(213)850-5394

Manufactures the FastLynx program, which performs system-to-system transfers over serial or parallel ports.

Safeware Insurance Agency, Inc.
2929 N. High Street
Columbus, OH 43202
(614)262-0559
(800)848-3469

Insurance company that specializes in insurance for computer equipment.

SAMS
11711 N. College Avenue
Carmel, IN 46032
(317)573-2500

Publishes technical books on computers and electronic equipment.

Seagate Technology
920 Disc Drive
Scotts Valley, CA 95066
(408)438-6550
(800)468-3472

Largest hard disk manufacturer in the world. Offers the most extensive product line of any disk manufacturer, ranging from low-cost units to the highest-performance, -capacity, and -quality drives available.

SGS-Thomson Microelectronics/Inmos
1000 E. Bell Road
Phoenix, AZ 85022
(602)867-6100

Manufactures custom chipsets, and has been licensed by IBM to produce IBM-designed XGA chipsets for ISA, EISA, and MCA bus systems.

Sharp Electronics Corporation
Sharp Plaza
Mahwah, NJ 07430
(201)529-8200
(800)237-4277

Manufactures a wide variety of electronic and computer equipment including LCD displays and panels, scanners, printers, and complete laptop and notebook systems.

Shugart Corporation
9292 Jeronimo Road
Irvine, CA 92714
(714)770-1100

Manufactures hard disk, floppy disk, and tape drives.

Sigma Data
P.O. Box 1790
New London, NH 03257
(603)526-6909
(800)446-4525

Distributes a complete line of memory chips and SIMM memory modules, hard drives, and processor upgrades.

Silicon Valley Computer
441 N Whisman Road
Building 13
Mountain View, CA 94043
(415)967-1100

Manufactures a complete line of IDE interface adapters, including a unique model that supports 16-bit IDE (ATA) drives on PC and XT systems (8-bit ISA bus) and models including floppy drive support as well as serial and parallel ports.

SMS Technology, Inc.
550 E. Brokaw Road
Box 49048
San Jose, CA 95161
(408)954-1633

Manufactures the OMTi disk controllers, formerly known as Scientific Micro Systems.

Sola Electric
1717 Busse Road
Elk Grove, IL 60007
(708)439-2800
(800)289-7652

Manufactures a line of computer power-protection devices.

Sony Corporation of America
Sony Drive
Park Ridge, NJ 07656
(201)930-1000

Manufactures all types of high-quality electronic and computer equipment including displays and magnetic- and optical-storage devices.

Sota Technology
559 Weddell Drive
Sunnyvale, CA 94089
(408)745-1111
(800)933-7682

Manufactures processor upgrade products including the SOTA Express/386 upgrade module for AT systems and 386/si turbo board for PC/XT systems.

Specialized Products Company
3131 Premier Drive
Irving, TX 75063
(214)550-1923
(800)527-5018

Distributes a variety of tools and test equipment.

Sprague Magnetics, Inc.
15720 Stagg Street
Van Nuys, CA 91406
(818)994-6602
(800)553-8712

Manufactures a unique and interesting magnetic developer fluid that can be used to view sectors and tracks on a magnetic disk or tape. Also repairs tape drives.

Stac Electronics
5993 Avenida Encinas
Carlsbad, CA 92008
(619)431-7474
(800)522-7822

Manufactures the Stacker real-time data-compression adapter and software.

Standard Microsystems Corporation
35 Marcus Boulevard
Hauppauge, NY 11788
(516)273-3100
(800)992-4762

Manufactures ARCnet and EtherNet network adapters.

Star Micronics America, Inc.
200 Park Avenue
Pan Am Building
#3510
New York, NY 10166
(212)986-6770
(800)447-4700

Manufactures a line of low-cost printers.

STB Systems, Inc.
1651 N. Glenville
Richardson, TX 75085
(214)234-8750

Manufactures various adapter boards, and specializes in a line of high-resolution VGA video adapters.

Storage Dimensions, Inc.
2145 Hamilton Avenue
San Jose, CA 95125
(408)879-0300
(800)765-7895

Distributes Maxtor hard disk and optical drives as complete subsystems. Also manufactures the Speedstor hard disk utility software.

Symantec Corporation
10201 Torre Avenue
Cupertino, CA 95014
(408)253-9600
(800)441-7234

Manufactures a line of utility and applications software featuring the Norton Utilities for IBM and Apple systems.

SyQuest Technology
47071 Bayside Parkway
Fremont, CA 94538
(415)226-4000
(800)245-2278

Manufactures removable-cartridge hard disk drives.

Sysgen, Inc.
556 Gibraltar Drive
Milpitas, CA 95035
(408)263-4411
(800)821-2151

Manufactures a line of tape-backup storage devices.

Sytron
117 Flanders Road
Box 5025
Westboro, MA 01581
(508)898-0100

Manufactures the SyTOS tape-backup software for DOS and OS/2, the most widely used tape software in the industry.

Tadiran
2975 Bowers Avenue
Santa Clara, CA 95051
(408)727-0300

Manufactures a variety of batteries for computer applications.

Tandon Corporation
405 Science Drive
Moorpark, CA 93021
(805)523-0340

Manufactures IBM-compatible computer systems and disk drives. Supplied to IBM most of the full-height floppy drives used in the original PC and XT systems.

Tandy Corporation/Radio Shack
1800 One Tandy Center
Fort Worth, TX 76102
(817)390-3700

Manufactures a line of IBM-compatible systems, peripherals, and accessories. Also distributes electronic parts and supplies.

Tatung Company of America, Inc.
2850 El Presidio Street
Long Beach, CA 90810
(213)979-7055
(800)827-2850

Manufactures monitors and complete compatible systems.

TDK Electronics Corporation
12 Harbor Park Drive
Port Washington, NY 11050
(516)625-0100

Manufactures a line of magnetic and optical media including disk and tape cartridges.

Teac America, Inc.
7733 Telegraph Road
Montebello, CA 90640
(213)726-0303

Manufactures a line of floppy and tape drives, including a unit that combines both 3 1/2-inch and 5 1/4-inch drives in one half-height package.

Tech Data Corporation
5350 Tech Data Drive
Clearwater, FL 34620
(813)539-7429
(800)237-8931

Distributes computer equipment and supplies.

Tecmar, Inc.
6225 Cochran Road
Solon, OH 44139
(216)349-0600
(800)344-4463

Manufactures a variety of adapter boards for IBM and compatible systems.

Toshiba America, Inc.
9740 Irvine Boulevard
Irvine, CA 92718
(714)583-3000
(800)999-4823

Manufactures a complete line of 5 1/4- and 3 1/2-inch floppy and hard disk drives, CD-ROM drives, display products, printers, and a popular line of laptop and notebook IBM-compatible systems.

TouchStone Software Corporation
2130 Main Street
#250
Huntington Beach, CA 92648
(714)969-7746
(800)531-0450

Manufactures the CheckIt user-level diagnostics program.

Trantor Systems, Ltd.
5415 Randall Place
Fremont, CA 94538
(510)770-1400

Manufactures the MiniSCSI Parallel Port SCSI adapter, including hard disk and CD-ROM drivers.

Traveling Software, Inc.
18702 N. Creek Parkway
Bothell, WA 98011
(206)483-8088
(800)662-2652

Manufactures the LapLink file-transfer program for PC and Mac systems
as well as several other utility programs.

Tripp Lite Manufacturing
500 N. Orleans
Chicago, IL 60610
(312)329-1777

Manufactures a line of computer power-protection devices.

Tseng Labs, Inc.
10 Pheasant Run
Newtown Commons
Newtown, PA 18940
(215)968-0502

Manufactures video controller chipsets, BIOS, and board design for
OEMs.

Tulin Corporation
2156 O'Toole Avenue
San Jose, CA 95131
(408)432-9025

Manufactures a line of hard disk drives.

Ultrastor Corporation
15 Hammond Street
#310
Irvine, CA 92718
(714)581-4100

Manufactures a complete line of high-performance ESDI, SCSI, and IDE
disk controllers for ISA and EISA bus systems.

Ultra-X, Inc.
2005 De La Cruz Boulevard
#115
Santa Clara, CA 95050
(408)988-4721
(800)722-3789

Manufactures the QuickPost PC, QuickPost PS/2, and Racer II diagnostic
cards.

UNISYS
Township Line and Union Meeting roads
Blue Bell, PA 19424
(215)542-2691
(800)448-1424

Manufactures PC-compatible systems that are part of the government
Desktop IV contract.

Universal Memory Products
1378 Logan Avenue
#F
Costa Mesa, CA 92626
(714)751-9445
(800)678-8648

Distributes memory components including chip and SIMM modules.

Upgrades Etc.
15251 NE 90th Street
Redmond, WA 98052
(818)884-6417
(800)541-1943

Distributes AMI, Award, and Phoenix BIOS upgrades.

U.S. Robotics, Inc.
8100 N. McCormick Boulevard
Skokie, IL 60076
(708)982-5010
(800)982-5151

Manufactures a complete line of modems and communications products.
Its modems support more protocols than most others, including V.32bis,
HST, and MNP protocols.

V Communications, Inc.
4320 Stevens Creek Boulevard
#275
San Jose, CA 95129
(408)296-4224

Manufactures the Sourcer disassembler and other programming tools.

Varta Batteries, Inc.
300 Executive Boulevard
Elmsford, NY 10523
(914)592-2500

Manufactures a complete line of computer batteries.

Verbatim Corporation
1200 WT Harris Boulevard
Charlotte, NC 28262
(704)547-6500

Manufactures a line of storage media including optical and magnetic disks and tapes.

VESA - Video Electronic Standards Organization
1330 S. Bascom Avenue
San Jose, CA 95128
(408)971-7525

Organization of manufacturers dedicated to setting and maintaining video display and adapter standards.

Video Seven
46221 Landing Parkway
Fremont, CA 94538
(415)623-7857

Manufactures an extensive line of high-resolution VGA graphics adapters.

Visiflex Seels
16 E. Lafayette Street
Hackensack, NJ 07601
(201)487-8080

Manufactures form-fitting clear keyboard covers and other computer accessories.

VLSI Technology, Inc.
8375 S. River Parkway
Tempe, AZ 85284
(602)752-8574

Manufactures chipsets and circuits for PC-compatible motherboards and adapters. IBM uses these chipsets in some of the PS/2 system designs.

Walling Company
4401 S. Juniper
Tempe, AZ 85282
(602)838-1277

Manufactures the DataRase EPROM eraser, which can erase as many as four EPROM chips simultaneously using ultraviolet light.

Wang Laboratories, Inc.
One Industrial Avenue
Lowell, MA 01851
(508)656-1550
(800)225-0654

Manufactures a variety of PC-compatible systems including some with MCA bus slots.

Wangtek, Inc.
41 Moreland Road
Simi Valley, CA 93065
(805)583-5525
(800)992-9916

Manufactures a complete line of tape-backup drives including QIC, DAT, and 8mm drives for ISA, EISA, and MCA bus systems.

Warshawski/Whitney & Co.
1916 S. State Street
Chicago, IL 60680
(312)431-6100

Distributes an enormous collection of bargain-priced tools and equipment. Its products are primarily for automotive applications, but many of the tools have universal uses.

Washburn & Co.
3800 Monroe Avenue
Pittsford, NY 14534
(716)248-3627
(800)836-8026

Distributes AMI BIOS and motherboard products, as well as the Second Nature hard disk drive table expansion ROMs. Definitive source of AMI products and technical support.

Wave Mate Inc.
2341 205th Street
#110
Torrance, CA 90501
(213)533-8190

Manufactures a line of high-speed replacement motherboards for IBM
and compatible systems.

Weitek Corporation
1060 E. Arques
Sunnyvale, CA 94086
(408)738-8400

Manufactures high-performance math coprocessor chips.

Western Digital Corporation
8105 Irvine Center Drive
Irvine, CA 92718
(714)932-5000
(800)832-4778

Manufactures many products including IDE and SCSI hard drives; SCSI
and ESDI adapters for ISA, EISA, and MCA bus systems; and EtherNet,
Token Ring, and Paradise video adapters. Supplies IBM with IDE and SCSI
drives for PS/2 systems.

Westlake Data Corporation
P.O. Box 1711
Austin, TX 78767
(512)328-1041

Manufactures the Diskminder disk editor utilities.

WordPerfect Corporation
1555 N. Technology Way
Orem, UT 84057
(801)225-5000
(800)451-5151

Manufactures the popular WordPerfect word processing program.

WordStar International, Inc.
201 Alameda del Prado
Novato, CA 94949
(415)382-8000
(800)227-5609

Manufactures the WordStar and WordStar 2000 programs.

Wyse Technology
3471 N. 1st Street
San Jose, CA 95134
(408)473-1200
(800)438-9973

Manufactures PC-compatible systems and terminals.

Xebec
3579 Gordon
Carson City, NV 89701
(702)883-4000

Manufactures ISA disk controllers originally used by IBM in the XT.

Xerox Corporation
Xerox Square
Rochester, NY 14644
(716)423-5078

Manufactures the Ventura desktop publishing software as well as an extensive line of computer equipment, copiers, and printers.

Xidex Corporation
5100 Patrick Henry Drive
Santa Clara, CA 95050
(408)970-6574

Manufactures disk and tape media.

Xircom
26025 Mureau Road
Calbasas, CA 91302
(818)878-7600
(800)874-7875

Manufactures external Token Ring and EtherNet adapters that attach to a parallel port.

Y-E Data America, Inc.
3030 Business Park Drive
#1
Norcross, GA 30071
(404)446-8655

Manufactures a line of floppy disk drives, tape drives, and printers. Supplied 5 1/4-inch floppy drives to IBM for use in XT, AT, and PS/2 systems.

Zenith Data Systems
2150 E. Lake Cook Road
Buffalo Grove, IL 60089
(708)699-4800
(800)553-0331

Manufactures a line of IBM-compatible systems.

Zeos International, Ltd.
530 5th Avenue NW
St. Paul, MN 55112
(612)633-4591
(800)423-5891

Manufactures a line of good, low-cost PC-compatible ISA and EISA bus systems sold by way of mail order.

Glossary

The glossary contains computer and electronics terms that are applicable to the subject matter in this book. The glossary is meant to be as comprehensive as possible on the subject of upgrading or repairing PCs. Many terms correspond to the latest technology in disk interfaces, modems, video and display equipment, and many standards that govern the PC industry. Although a glossary is a resource not designed to be read from beginning to end, you should find that scanning through this one is interesting, if not enlightening, with respect to some of the newer PC technology.

The computer industry is filled with acronyms used as shorthand for a number of terms. This glossary defines many acronyms, as well as the term on which the acronym is based. The definition of an acronym usually is included under the acronym. For example, Video Graphics Array is defined under the acronym VGA rather than under *Video Graphics Array*. This organization makes it easier to look up a term—IDE, for example—even if you do not know in advance what it stands for (integrated drive electronics).

For additional reference, *Que's Computer User's Dictionary*, 2nd Edition, is a comprehensive, general-purpose computer dictionary of computer terminology.

80286 An Intel microprocessor with 16-bit registers, a 16-bit data bus, and a 24-bit address bus. Can operate in real and protected virtual modes.

80287 An Intel math coprocessor designed to perform floating-point math with much greater speed and precision than the main CPU. The 80287 can be installed in most 286- and some 386DX-based systems, and adds more than 50 new instructions to what is available in the primary CPU alone.

80386 *See* 80386DX.

80386DX An Intel microprocessor with 32-bit registers, a 32-bit data bus, and a 32-bit address bus. This processor can operate in real, protected virtual, and virtual real modes.

80386SX An Intel microprocessor with 32-bit registers, a 16-bit data bus, and a 24-bit address bus. This processor, designed as a low-cost version of the 386DX, can operate in real, protected virtual, and virtual real modes.

80387DX An Intel math coprocessor designed to perform floating-point math with much greater speed and precision than the main CPU. The 80387DX can be installed in most 386DX-based systems, and adds more than 50 new instructions to what is available in the primary CPU alone.

80387SX An Intel math coprocessor designed to perform floating-point math with much greater speed and precision than the main CPU. The 80387SX can be installed in most 386SX-based systems, and adds more than 50 new instructions to what is available in the primary CPU alone.

80486 *See* 80486DX.

80486DX An Intel microprocessor with 32-bit registers, a 32-bit data bus, and a 32-bit address bus. The 486DX has a built-in cache controller with 8K of cache memory as well as a built-in math co-processor equivalent to a 387DX. The 486DX can operate in real, protected virtual, and virtual real modes.

80486SX An Intel microprocessor with 32-bit registers, a 32-bit data bus, and a 32-bit address bus. The 486SX is the same as the 486DX except that it lacks the built-in math coprocessor function, and was designed as a low-cost version of the 486DX. The 486SX can operate in real, protected virtual, and virtual real modes.

80487SX An Intel microprocessor with 32-bit registers, a 32-bit data bus, and a 32-bit address bus. The 487SX has a built-in cache controller with 8K of cache memory as well as a built-in math coprocessor equivalent to a 387DX. The 486DX can operate in real, protected virtual, and virtual real modes. This processor is a complete processor and math coprocessor unit, not just a math coprocessor. The 487SX is designed to upgrade systems with the 486SX processor, which lacks the math coprocessor function. When a 487SX is installed in a system, it shuts down the 486SX and takes over the system. In effect, the 487SX is a full-blown 486DX modified to be installed as an upgrade for 486SX systems.

8086 An Intel microprocessor with 16-bit registers, a 16-bit data bus, and a 20-bit address bus. This processor can operate only in real mode.

8087 An Intel math coprocessor designed to perform floating-point math with much greater speed and precision than the main CPU. The 8087 can be installed in most 8086- and 8088-based systems, and adds more than 50 new instructions to what is available in the primary CPU alone.

8088 An Intel microprocessor with 16-bit registers, an 8-bit data bus, and a 20-bit address bus. This processor can operate only in real mode, and was designed as a low-cost version of the 8086.

8514/A An analog video display adapter from IBM for the PS/2 line of personal computers. Compared to previous display adapters such as EGA and VGA, it provides a high resolution of 1024×768 pixels with as many as 256 colors or 64 shades of gray. It provides a video coprocessor that performs two-dimensional graphics functions internally, thus relieving the CPU of graphics tasks. It is an inter-laced monitor: It scans every other line every time the screen is refreshed.

abend Short for *ab*normal *end*. Used when the execution of a program or task is terminated unexpectedly because of a bug or crash.

AC Alternating current. The frequency is measured in cycles per sec-onds (cps), or hertz. The standard value running through the wall outlet is 120 volts at 60 Hertz, through a fuse or circuit breaker that usually can handle about 20 amps.

accelerator board An add-in board replacing the computer's CPU with circuitry that enables the system to run faster.

access time The time that elapses from the instant information is re-quested to the point that delivery is completed. Usually described in nanoseconds for memory chips. The IBM PC requires memory chips with an access time of 200 nanoseconds, and the AT requires 150-nanosecond chips. For hard disk drives, access time is de-scribed in milliseconds. Most manufacturers rate average access time on a hard disk as the time required for a seek across one-third of the total number of cylinders plus one-half of the time for a single revolution of the disk platters (latency).

accumulator A register (temporary storage) in which the result of an operation is formed.

active high Designates a digital signal that has to go to a high value to produce an effect. Synonymous with positive true.

active low Designates a digital signal that has to go to a low value to produce an effect. Synonymous with negative true.

actuator The device that moves a disk drive's read/write heads across the platter surfaces. Also known as an access mechanism.

adapter The device that serves as an interface between the system unit and the devices attached to it. Used by IBM to be synonymous with circuit board, circuit card, or card.

address Refers to where a particular piece of data or other information is found in the computer. Also can refer to the location of a set of instructions.

address bus One or more electrical conductors used to carry the binary-coded address from the microprocessor throughout the rest of the system.

alphanumeric characters A character set that contains only letters (A-Z) and digits (0-9). Other characters, such as punctuation marks, also may be allowed.

ampere The basic unit for measuring electrical current. Also called amp.

analog loopback A modem self-test in which data from the keyboard is sent to the modem's transmitter, modulated into analog form, looped back to the receiver, demodulated into digital form, and returned to the screen for verification.

analog signals Continuously variable signals in which the slightest change may be significant. Analog circuits are more subject to distortion and noise but are capable of handling complex signals with relatively simple circuitry. An alternative to analog is digital, in which signals are in only one of two states.

AND A logic operator having the property that if P is a statement, Q is a statement, R is a statement,..., then the AND of P,Q,R,... is true if all statements are true and is false if any statement is false.

AND gate A logic gate in which the output is 1 only if all inputs are 1.

ANSI Acronym for American National Standards Institute, a non-governmental organization founded in 1918 to propose, modify, approve, and publish data processing standards for voluntary use in the United States. Also the U.S. representative to the

International Standards Organization (ISO) in Paris and the International Electrotechnical Commission (IEC). For more information, contact ANSI, 1430 Broadway, New York, NY 10018.

answer mode A state in which the modem transmits at the predefined high frequency of the communications channel and receives at the low frequency. The transmit/receive frequencies are the reverse of the calling modem, which is in originate mode.

APA All points addressable. A mode in which all points of a displayable image can be controlled by the user or a program.

API An acronym for application program interface. A system call (routine) that gives programmers access to the services provided by the operating system. In IBM-compatible systems, the ROM BIOS and DOS together present an API that a programmer can use to control the system hardware.

arbitration A method by which multiple devices attached to a single bus can bid or arbitrate to get control of that bus.

archive bit The bit in a file's attribute byte that sets the archive attribute. Tells whether the file has been changed since it last was backed up.

archive medium A storage medium (floppy disk, tape cartridge, or removable cartridge) to hold files that need not be accessible instantly.

ARCnet An acronym for *A*ttached *R*esource *C*omputer *Net*work, a baseband, token-passing local area network technology offering a flexible bus/star topology for connecting personal computers. Operates at 2.5 megabits per second, is one of the oldest LAN systems, and has become popular in low-cost networks. Originally developed by John Murphy, of Datapoint Corporation, although ARCnet interface cards are available from a variety of vendors.

ARQ *A*utomatic *r*epeat *r*equest. A general term for error-control protocols that feature error detection and automatic retransmission of defective blocks of data.

ASCII An acronym for American Standard Code for Information Interchange, a standard seven-bit code created in 1965 by Robert W. Bemer to achieve compatibility among various types of data processing equipment. The standard ASCII character set consists of 128 decimal numbers, ranging from 0 through 127, assigned to letters, numbers, punctuation marks, and the most common special characters. In 1981 IBM introduced the extended ASCII character set with the IBM PC, extending the code to eight bits and adding characters from 128 through 255 to represent additional special mathematical, graphics, and foreign characters.

ASCII character A 1-byte character from the ASCII character set, including alphabetic and numeric characters, punctuation symbols, and various graphics characters.

assemble To translate a program expressed in an assembler language into a computer machine language.

assembler language A computer-oriented language whose instructions are usually in one-to-one correspondence with machine language instructions.

asymmetrical modulation A duplex transmission technique that splits the communications channel into one high-speed channel and one slower channel. During a call under asymmetrical modulation, the modem with the greatest amount of data to transmit is allocated the high-speed channel. The modem with less data is allocated the slow, or back, channel (450 bps). The modems dynamically reverse the channels during a call if the volume of data transfer changes.

asynchronous communication Data transmission in which the length of time between transmitted characters may vary. Timing is dependent on the actual time for the transfer to take place, as opposed to synchronous communication, which is timed rigidly by an external clock signal. Because the receiving modem must be signaled about when the data bits of a character begin and end, start and stop bits are added to each character.

ATA An acronym for AT Attachment interface, an IDE disk interface standard introduced in March 1989 that defines a compatible register set and a 40-pin connector and its associated signals. *See also* IDE.

attribute byte A byte of information, held in the directory entry of any file, that describes various attributes of the file, such as whether it is read-only or has been backed up since it last was changed. Attributes can be set by the DOS ATTRIB command.

audio A signal that can be heard, such as through the speaker of the PC. Many PC diagnostics tests use both visual (on-screen) codes and audio signals.

audio frequencies Frequencies that can be heard by the human ear (approximately 20 to 20,000 hertz).

auto answer A feature in modems enabling them to answer incoming calls over the phone lines without the use of a telephone receiver.

auto dial A feature in modems enabling them to dial phone numbers without the use of a telephone transmitter.

AUTOEXEC.BAT A special batch file that DOS executes at start-up. Contains any number of DOS commands that are executed automatically.

automatic head parking Disk drive head parking performed whenever the drive is powered off. Found in all hard disk drives with a voice-coil actuator.

average latency The average time required for any byte of data stored on a disk to rotate under the disk drive's read/write head. Equal to one-half the time required for a single rotation of a platter.

average seek time The average time required for a disk drive's read/write heads to move from one track to another. Usually expressed as the time required for a seek across one-third of the total number of tracks.

backup The process of duplicating a file or library onto a separate piece of media. Good insurance against loss of an original.

backup disk Contains information copied from another disk. Used to make sure that original information is not destroyed or altered.

bad sector A disk sector that cannot hold data reliably because of a media flaw or damaged format markings.

bad track table A label affixed to the casing of a hard disk drive that tells which tracks are flawed and cannot hold data. The listing is entered into the low-level formatting program.

balun Short for *bal*anced/*un*balanced. A type of transformer that enables balanced cables to be joined with unbalanced cables. Twisted pair (balanced) cables, for example, can be joined with coaxial (unbalanced) cables if the proper balun transformer is used.

bandwidth Generally the measure of the range of frequencies within a radiation band required to transmit a particular signal. Measures in millions of cycles per second the difference between the lowest and highest signal frequencies. The bandwidth of a computer monitor is a measure of the rate that a monitor can handle information from the display adapter. The wider the bandwidth, the more information the monitor can carry, and the greater the resolution.

bank The collection of memory chips that make up a block of memory readable by the processor in a single bus cycle. This block therefore must be as large as the data bus of the particular microprocessor. In IBM systems, the processor data bus is usually 8, 16, or 32 bits, plus a parity bit for each 8 bits, resulting in a total of 9, 18, or 36 bits for each bank.

bar code The code used on consumer products and inventory parts for identification purposes. Consists of bars of varying thicknesses to represent characters and numerals that are read with an optical reader. The most common version is called the Universal Product Code (UPC).

baseband The transmission of digital signals over a limited distance. ARCnet and EtherNet local area networks utilize baseband signaling. Contrasts with broadband transmission, which refers to the transmission of analog signals over a greater distance.

BASIC An acronym for Beginner's All-purpose Symbolic Instruction Code, a popular computer programming language. Originally developed by John Kemeny and Thomas Kurtz, in the mid-1960s at Dartmouth College. Normally an interpretive language, meaning that each statement is translated and executed as it is encountered; but can be a compiled language, in which all the program statements are compiled before execution.

batch file A set of commands stored in a disk file for execution by the operating system. A special batch file called AUTOEXEC.BAT is executed by IBM DOS each time the system is started. All DOS batch files have a BAT file extension.

baud A unit of signaling speed denoting the number of discrete signal elements that can be transmitted per second. The word *baud* is derived from the name of J.M.E. Baudot (1845-1903), a French pioneer in the field of printing telegraphy and the inventor of Baudot code. Although technically inaccurate, baud rate commonly is used to mean *bit rate*. Because each signal element or baud may translate into many individual bits, bits per second (bps) normally differs from baud rate. A rate of 2400 baud means that 2400 frequency or signal changes per second are being sent, but each frequency change may signal several bits of information. Most people are surprised to learn that 2400 and 1200 bps modems transmit at 600 baud, and that 9600 and 14400 bps modems transmit at 2400 baud.

Baudot code A 5-bit code used in many types of data communications including teletype (TTY), radio teletype (RTTY), and telecommunications devices for the deaf (TDD). Baudot code has been revised and extended several times.

baud rate *See* baud.

bay An opening in a computer cabinet that holds disk drives.

BBS An acronym for bulletin board system, a computer that operates with a program and a modem to enable other computers with modems to communicate with it, often on a round-the-clock basis. Thousands of IBM- and Apple-related bulletin board systems offer a wealth of information and public-domain software that can be downloaded.

bezel A cosmetic panel that covers the face of a drive or some other device.

bidirectional Refers to lines over which data can move in two directions, like a data bus or a telephone line. Also refers to the capability of a printer to print from right to left and from left to right alternately.

binary Refers to the computer numbering system that consists of two numerals, 0 and 1. Also called base-2.

BIOS Basic input-output system. The part of an operating system that handles the communications between the computer and its peripherals. Often burned into read-only memory (ROM) chips.

bisynchronous *Bi*nary *synchronous* control. An earlier protocol developed by IBM for software applications and communicating devices operation in synchronous environments. The protocol defines operations at the link level of communications—for example, the format of data frames exchanged between modems over a phone line.

bit *Bi*nary digi*t*. Represented logically by 0 or 1 and electrically by 0 volts and (typically) 5 volts. Other methods are used to represent binary digits physically (tones, different voltages, lights, and so on), but the logic is always the same.

bit map A method of storing graphics information in memory in which a bit devoted to each pixel (picture element) on-screen indicates whether that pixel is on or off. A bit map contains a bit for each point or dot on a video display screen and allows for fine resolution because any point or pixel on-screen can be addressed. A greater number of bits can be used to describe each pixel's color, intensity, and other display characteristics.

block A string of records, words, or characters formed for technical or logic reasons and to be treated as an entity.

block diagram The logical structure or layout of a system in graphics form. Does not necessarily match the physical layout and does not specify all the components and their interconnections.

BNC An acronym for British National Connector, a type of connector plug and jack system. Originally designed in England for television set antennas, the BNC is a type of connector designed for use with coaxial cabling. Male and female BNCs are available. Although the term is redundant, BNCs usually are referred to as *BNC connectors*. Often used in local area network cabling systems that use coaxial cable, such as EtherNet and ARCnet, and also used frequently for video cabling systems.

Boolean operation Any operation in which each of the operands and the result take one of two values.

boot Load a program into the computer. The term comes from the phrase "pulling a boot on by the bootstrap."

boot record A one-sector record that tells the computer's built-in operating system (BIOS) the most fundamental facts about a disk and DOS. Instructs the computer how to load the operating system files into memory, thus booting the machine.

bootstrap A technique or device designed to bring itself into a desired state by means of its own action.

bps Bits per second. The number of binary digits, or bits, transmitted per second. Sometimes confused with baud.

bridge In local area networks, an interconnection between two networks. Also the hardware equipment used to establish such an interconnection.

broadband A term used to describe analog transmission. Requires modems for connecting terminals and computers to the network. Using frequency division multiplexing, many different signals or sets of data can be transmitted simultaneously. The alternate transmission scheme is baseband, or digital, transmission.

bubble memory A special type of nonvolatile read/write memory introduced by Intel in which magnetic regions are suspended in crystal film and data is maintained when the power is off. A typical bubble memory chip contains about 512K, or more than 4 million bubbles. Failed to catch on because of slow access times measured in several milliseconds. Has found a niche use as solid-state "disk" emulators in environments in which conventional drives are unacceptable, such as military or factory use.

buffer A block of memory used as a holding tank to store data temporarily. Often positioned between a slower peripheral device and the faster computer. All data moving between the peripheral and the computer passes through the buffer. A buffer enables the data to be read from or written to the peripheral in larger chunks, which improves performance. A buffer that is x bytes in size usually holds the last x bytes of data that moved between the peripheral and CPU. This method contrasts with that of a cache, which adds intelligence to the buffer so that the most often accessed data rather than the last accessed data remains in the buffer (cache). A cache can improve performance greatly over a plain buffer.

bug An error or defect in a program.

burn-in The operation of a circuit or equipment to stabilize components and to screen for failures.

bus An electrical pathway over which power, data, and other signals travel.

bus master An intelligent device that when attached to the Micro Channel bus can bid for and gain control of the bus to perform its specific task.

byte A collection of bits that makes up a character or other designation. Generally, a byte is eight data bits plus one parity (error-checking) bit.

cache An intelligent buffer. By using an intelligent algorithm, a cache contains the data that is accessed most often between a slower peripheral device and the faster CPU.

CAM An acronym for Common Access Method, a committee formed in 1988 consisting of a number of computer peripheral suppliers and dedicated to developing standards for a common software interface between SCSI peripherals and host adapters. The CAM committee also has set a standard for IDE drives called the ATA interface.

capacitor A device consisting of two plates separated by insulating material and designed to store an electrical charge.

card A printed circuit board containing electronic components that form an entire circuit, usually designed to plug into a connector or slot. Sometimes also called an adapter.

carpal tunnel syndrome A painful hand injury that gets its name from the narrow tunnel in the wrist which connects ligament and bone. When undue pressure is put on the tendons, they can swell and compress the median nerve, which carries impulses from the brain to the hand, causing numbness, weakness, tingling, and burning in the fingers and hands. Computer users get carpal tunnel syndrome primarily from improper keyboard ergonomics that result in undue strain on the wrist and hand.

carrier A continuous frequency signal capable of being either modulated or impressed with another information-carrying signal. The reference signal used for the transmission or reception of data. The most common use of this signal with computers involves modem communications over phone lines. The carrier is used as a signal on which the information is superimposed.

carrier detect signal A modem interface signal which indicates to the attached data terminal equipment (DTE) that it is receiving a signal from the distant modem. Defined in the RS-232 specification. Same as the received line-signal detector.

cathode ray tube A device that contains electrodes surrounded by a glass sphere or cylinder and displays information by creating a beam of electrons that strike a phosphor coating inside the display unit.

CCITT An acronym for the Comité Consultatif Internationale de Télégraphique et Téléphonique (in English, the International Telegraph and Telephone Consultative Committee or the Consultative Committee for International Telegraph and Telephone). An international committee organized by the United Nations to set international communications recommendations, which frequently are adopted as standards, and to develop interface, modem, and data network recommendations. The Bell 212A standard for 1200 bps communication in North America, for example, is observed internationally as CCITT V.22. For 2400 bps communication, most U.S. manufacturers observe V.22bis, and V.32 and V.32bis are standards for 9600 and 14400 bps, respectively. Work is now under way to define a new standard for 19200 bps called V.32fast.

CCS An acronym for the Common Command Set, a set of SCSI commands specified in the ANSI SCSI-1 Standard X3.131-1986 Addendum 4.B. All SCSI devices must be capable of using the CCS in order to be fully compatible with the ANSI SCSI-1 standard.

CD-ROM An acronym for compact disc read-only memory. A computer peripheral device that employs compact disc (CD) technology to store large amounts of data for later retrieval. Phillips and Sony developed CD-ROM in 1983. Current CD-ROM discs hold approximately 600M of information. CD-ROM drives are much slower than conventional hard disks, with normal average-access times of 380 milliseconds or greater and data transfer rates of about 1.2 megabits per second. Most CD-ROM drives use the SCSI (Small Computer Systems Interface) bus for connection to a system.

ceramic substrate A thin, flat, fired ceramic part used to hold an IC chip (usually made of beryllium oxide or aluminum oxide).

CGA An acronym for Color Graphics Adapter, a type of PC video display adapter introduced by IBM on August 12, 1981, that supports text and graphics. Text is supported at a maximum resolution of 80×25 characters in 16 colors with a character box of 8×8 pixels. Graphics is supported at a maximum resolution of 320×200 pixels in 16 colors or 640×200 pixels in 2 colors. The CGA outputs a TTL (digital) signal with a horizontal scanning frequency of 15.75 KHz, and supports TTL color or NTSC composite displays.

channel A path along which signals can be sent.

character A representation, coded in binary digits, of a letter, number, or other symbol.

checksum Short for *sum*mation *check*, a technique for determining whether a package of data is valid. The package, a string of binary digits, is added up and compared with the expected number.

chip Another name for an IC, or integrated circuit. Housed in a plastic or ceramic carrier device with pins for making electrical connections.

chip carrier A ceramic or plastic package that carries an integrated circuit.

circuit A complete electronic path.

circuit board The collection of circuits gathered on a sheet of plastic, usually with all contacts made through a strip of pins. The circuit board usually is made by chemically etching metal-coated plastic.

CISC An acronym for complex instruction-set computer. Refers to traditional computers that operate with large sets of processor instructions. Most modern computers, including the Intel 80xxx processors, are in this category. CISC processors have expanded instruction sets that are complex in nature and require several to many execution cycles to complete. This structure contrasts with RISC (reduced instruction-set computer) processors, which have far fewer instructions that execute quickly.

clean room A dust-free room in which certain electronic components (such as hard disk drives) must be manufactured and serviced to prevent contamination. Rooms are rated by Class numbers. A Class 100 clean room must have fewer than 100 particles larger than .5 microns per cubic foot of space.

clock The source of a computer's timing signals. Synchronizes every operation of the CPU.

clock speed A measurement of the rate at which the clock signal for a device oscillates, usually expressed in millions of cycles per second (MHz).

clone An IBM-compatible computer system that physically as well as electrically emulates the design of one of IBM's personal computer systems, usually the AT or XT. For example, an AT clone has parts (motherboard, power supply, and so on) that are physically interchangeable with the same parts in the IBM AT system.

cluster Also called allocation unit. A group of sectors on a disk that forms a fundamental unit of storage to the operating system. Cluster or allocation unit size is determined by DOS when the disk is formatted.

CMOS Complementary Metal-Oxide Semiconductor. A type of chip design that requires little power to operate. In an AT-type system, a battery-powered CMOS memory and clock chip is used to store and maintain the clock setting and system configuration information.

coated media Hard disk platters coated with a reddish iron-oxide medium on which data is recorded.

coaxial cable Also called coax cable. A data-transmission medium noted for its wide bandwidth, immunity to interference, and high cost compared to twisted-pair wire. Signals are transmitted inside a fully shielded environment, in which an inner conductor is surrounded by a solid insulating material and then an outer conductor or shield. Used in many local area network systems such as EtherNet and ARCnet.

COBOL An acronym for *Common business-oriented language*, a high-level computer programming language. The business world's preferred programming language on mainframe computer systems, it has never achieved popularity on smaller computers.

code page switching A DOS feature in versions 3.3 and later that changes the characters displayed on-screen or printed on an output device. Primarily used to support foreign-language characters. Requires an EGA or better video system and an IBM-compatible graphics printer.

coercivity A measurement in units of oersteads of the amount of magnetic energy to switch or "coerce" the flux change in the magnetic recording media. High-coercivity disk media requires a stronger write current.

Color Graphics Adapter *See* CGA.

COM port A serial port on a PC that conforms to the RS-232 standard. *See also* RS-232.

COMDEX The largest international computer trade show and conference in the world. COMDEX/Fall is held in Las Vegas during October, and COMDEX/Spring usually is held in Chicago or Atlanta during April. The 14th annual COMDEX/Fall is in 1992.

command An instruction that tells the computer to start, stop, or continue an operation.

COMMAND.COM An operating system file that is loaded last when the computer is booted. The command interpreter or user interface and program-loader portion of DOS.

common The ground or return path for an electrical signal. If a wire, usually is colored black.

common mode noise Noise or electrical disturbances that can be measured between a current- or signal-carrying line and its associated ground.

compiler A program that translates a program written in a high-level language into its equivalent machine language. The output from a compiler is called an object program.

composite video Television picture information and sync pulses combined. The IBM Color Graphics Adapter (CGA) outputs a composite video signal.

computer Device capable of accepting data, applying prescribed processes to this data, and displaying the results or information produced.

CONFIG.SYS A file that can be created to tell DOS how to configure itself when the machine starts up. Can load device drivers, set the number of DOS buffers, and so on.

configuration file A file kept by application software to record various aspects of the software's configuration, such as the printer it uses.

console The unit, such as a terminal or a keyboard, in your system with which you communicate with the computer.

contiguous Touching or joined at the edge or boundary, in one piece.

continuity In electronics, an unbroken pathway. Testing for continuity normally means testing to determine whether a wire or other conductor is complete and unbroken (by measuring 0 ohms). A broken wire shows infinite resistance (or infinite ohms).

control cable The wider of the two cables that connect an ST-506/412 or ESDI hard disk drive to a controller card. A 34-pin cable that carries commands and acknowledgments between the drive and controller.

controller The electronics that control a device such as a hard disk drive and intermediate the passage of data between the device and the computer.

controller card An adapter holding the control electronics for one or more devices such as hard disks. Ordinarily occupies one of the computer's slots.

convergence Describes the capability of a color monitor to focus the three colored electron beams on a single point. Poor convergence causes the characters on-screen to appear fuzzy and can cause headaches and eyestrain.

coprocessor An additional computer processing unit designed to handle specific tasks in conjunction with the main or central processing unit.

core An "old-fashioned" term for computer memory.

CP/M An acronym for Control Program/Microcomputer, an operating system created by Gary Kildall, the founder of Digital Research. Created for the old 8-bit microcomputers that used the 8080, 8085, and Z-80 microprocessors. Was the dominant operating system in the late 1970s and early 1980s for small computers used in a business environment.

cps Characters per second. A data transfer rate generally estimated from the bit rate and the character length. At 2400 bps, for example, 8-bit characters with start and stop bits (for a total of 10 bits per character) are transmitted at a rate of approximately 240 characters per second (cps). Some protocols, such as V.42 and MNP, employ advanced techniques such as longer transmission frames and data compression to increase cps.

CPU Central processing unit. The computer's microprocessor chip, the brains of the outfit. Typically, an IC using VLSI (very-large-scale integration) technology to pack several different functions into a tiny area. The most common electronic device in the CPU is the transistor, of which several thousand to several million or more are found.

crash A malfunction that brings work to a halt. A system crash usually is caused by a software malfunction, and ordinarily you can restart the system by rebooting the machine. A head crash, however, entails physical damage to a disk and probable data loss.

CRC An acronym for cyclic redundancy checking, an error-detection technique consisting of a cyclic algorithm performed on each block or frame of data by both sending and receiving modems. The sending modem inserts the results of its computation in each data block in the form of a CRC code. The receiving modem compares its results with the received CRC code and responds with either a positive or negative acknowledgment. In the ARQ protocol implemented in high-speed modems, the receiving modem accepts no more data until a defective block is received correctly.

CRT Cathode-ray tube. A term used to describe a television or monitor screen tube.

current The flow of electrons, measured in amperes.

cursor The small flashing hyphen that appears on-screen to indicate the point at which any input from the keyboard will be placed.

cyclic redundancy checking *See* CRC.

cylinder The set of tracks on a disk that are on each side of all the disk platters in a stack and are the same distance from the center of the disk. The total number of tracks that can be read without moving the heads. A floppy drive with two heads usually has 160 tracks, which are accessible as 80 cylinders. A typical 20M hard disk has 2 platters with 4 heads and 615 cylinders, in which each cylinder is 4 tracks.

daisy chain Stringing up components in such a manner that the signals move serially from one to the other. Most microcomputer multiple disk drive systems are daisy-chained. The SCSI bus system is a daisy-chain arrangement, in which the signals move from computer to disk drives to tape units, and so on.

daisywheel printer An impact printer that prints fully formed characters one at a time by rotating a circular print element composed of a series of individual spokes, each containing two characters that radiate from a center hub. Produces letter-quality output.

DAT An acronym for *d*igital *a*udio*t*ape, a small cassette tape for storing large amounts of digital information. Also sometimes called 4mm tape. DAT technology emerged in Europe and Japan in 1986 as a way to produce high-quality, digital audio recordings. One DAT cassette can hold approximately 1.3 gigabytes of data.

data Groups of facts processed into information. A graphic or textural representation of facts, concepts, numbers, letters, symbols, or instructions used for communication or processing.

Also, an android from the 24th century with a processing speed of 60 trillion operations per second and 80 quadrillion bits of storage who serves on the USS Enterprise NCC-1701-D with the rank of lieutenant commander.

data cable The narrower of two cables that connects a hard disk drive to a controller card.

data communications A type of communication in which computers and terminals can exchange data over an electronic medium.

data transfer rate The maximum rate at which data can be transferred from one device to another.

DC Direct current, such as that provided by a power supply or batteries.

DC-600 Data Cartridge 600, a data-storage medium invented by 3M in 1971 that uses a quarter-inch-wide tape 600 feet in length.

DCE Data communications equipment. The hardware that does the communication—usually a dial-up modem that establishes and controls the data link through the telephone network. *See also* DTE.

DEBUG The name of a utility program included with DOS and used for specialized purposes such as altering memory locations, tracing program execution, patching programs and disk sectors, and performing other low-level tasks.

dedicated line A user-installed telephone line used to connect a specified number of computers or terminals within a limited area, such as a single building. The line is a cable rather than a public-access telephone line. The communications channel also may be referred to as nonswitched because calls do not go through telephone company switching equipment.

dedicated servo surface In voice-coil-actuated hard disk drives, one side of one platter given over to servo data that is used to guide and position the read/write heads.

default Any setting assumed at start-up or reset by the computer's software and attached devices and operational until changed by the user. An assumption the computer makes when no other parameters are specified. When you type *dir* without specifying the drive to search, for example, the computer assumes that you want it to search the default drive. The term is used in software to describe any action the computer or program takes on its own with imbedded values.

density The amount of data that can be packed into a certain area on a specific storage media.

device driver A memory-resident program, loaded by CONFIG.SYS, that controls an unusual device, such as an expanded memory board.

Dhrystone A benchmark program used as a standard figure of merit indicating aspects of a computer system's performance in areas other than floating-point math performance. Because the program does not use any floating-point operations, performs no I/O, and makes no operating system calls, it is most applicable to measuring the processor performance of a system. The original Dhrystone program was developed in 1984 and was written in Ada, although the C and Pascal versions became more popular by 1989.

diagnostics Programs used to check the operation of a computer system. These programs enable the operator to check the entire system for any problems and to indicate in what area the problems lie.

digital loopback A test that checks the modem's RS-232 interface and the cable that connects the terminal or computer and the modem. The modem receives data (in the form of digital signals) from the computer or terminal and immediately returns the data to the screen for verification.

digital signals Discrete, uniform signals. In this book, the term refers to the binary digits 0 and 1.

DIP Dual In-line Package. A family of rectangular, integrated-circuit flat packages that have leads on the two longer sides. Package material is plastic or ceramic.

DIP switch A tiny switch (or group of switches) on a circuit board. Named for the form factor of the carrier device in which the switch is housed.

direct memory access A process by which data moves between a disk drive (or other device) and system memory without direct control of the central processing unit, thus freeing it up for other tasks.

directory An area of a disk that stores the titles given to the files saved on the disk and serves as a table of contents for those files. Contains data that identifies the name of a file, the size, the attributes (system, hidden, read-only, and so on), the date and time of creation, and a pointer to the location of the file. Each entry in a directory is 32 bytes long.

disk operating system DOS. A collection of programs stored on the DOS disk that contain routines enabling the system and user to manage information and the hardware resources of the computer. DOS must be loaded into the computer before other programs can be started.

diskette A floppy disk. Made of a flexible material coated with a magnetic substance, the disk spins inside its protective jacket, and the read/write head comes in contact with the recording surface to read or write data.

DMA Direct memory access. A circuit by which a high-speed transfer of information may be facilitated between a device and system memory. This transfer is managed by a specialized processor that relieves the burden of managing the transfer from the main CPU.

dot-matrix printer An impact printer that prints characters composed of dots. Prints characters one at a time by pressing the ends of selected wires against an inked ribbon and paper.

dot pitch A measurement of the width of the dots that make up a pixel. The smaller the dot pitch, the sharper the image.

double density (DD) An indication of the storage capacity of a floppy drive or disk in which eight or nine sectors per track are recorded using MFM encoding.

down-time Operating time lost because of a computer malfunction.

drive A mechanical device that manipulates data storage media.

DTE Data terminal (or terminating) equipment. The device, usually a computer or terminal, that generates or is the final destination of data. *See also* DCE.

duplex Indicates a communications channel capable of carrying signals in both directions.

Dvorak keyboard A keyboard design by August Dvorak that was patented in 1936 and approved by ANSI in 1982. Provides increased speed and comfort and reduces the rate of errors by placing the most frequently used letters in the center for use by the strongest fingers. Finger motions and awkward strokes are reduced by more than 90 percent in comparison with the familiar QWERTY keyboard. The Dvorak keyboard has the five vowel keys, AOEUI, together under the left hand in the center row, and the five most frequently used consonants, DHTNS, under the fingers of the right hand.

edit The process of rearranging data or information.

EGA An acronym for Enhanced Graphics Adapter, a type of PC video display adapter first introduced by IBM on September 10, 1984, that supports text and graphics. Text is supported at a maximum resolution of 80×25 characters in 16 colors with a character box of 8×14 pixels. Graphics is supported at a maximum resolution of 640×350 pixels in 16 (from a palette of 64) colors. The EGA outputs a TTL (digital) signal with a horizontal scanning frequency of 15.75, 18.432, or 21.85 KHz, and supports TTL color or TTL monochrome displays.

EIA Electronic Industries Association, which defines electronic standards in the United States.

EISA An acronym for Extended Industry Standard Architecture, an extension of the Industry Standard Architecture (ISA) bus developed by IBM for the AT. The EISA design was led by COMPAQ Corporation. Later, eight other manufacturers (AST, Epson, Hewlett-Packard, NEC, Olivetti, Tandy, Wyse, and Zenith) joined COMPAQ in a consortium founded September 13, 1988. This group became known as the "gang of nine." The EISA design was patterned largely after IBM's Micro Channel Architecture (MCA) in the PS/2 systems, but unlike MCA, EISA allows for backward compatibility with older plug-in adapters.

electronic mail A method of transferring messages form one computer to another.

electrostatic discharge (ESD) Static electricity, a sudden flow of electricity between two objects at different electrical potentials. ESD is a primary cause of integrated circuit damage or failure.

embedded servo data Magnetic markings embedded between or inside tracks on disk drives that use voice-coil actuators. These markings enable the actuator to fine-tune the position of the read/write heads.

EMS An acronym for Expanded Memory Specification. Sometimes also called the LIM spec because it was developed by Lotus, Intel, and Microsoft. Provides a way for microcomputers running under DOS to access additional memory. EMS memory management provides access to a maximum of 32M of expanded memory through a small (usually 64K) window in conventional memory. EMS is a cumbersome access scheme designed primarily for pre-286 systems that could not access extended memory.

emulator A piece of test apparatus that emulates or imitates the function of a particular chip.

encoding The protocol by which data is carried or stored by a medium.

encryption The translation of data into unreadable codes to maintain security.

Enhanced Graphics Adapter *See* EGA.

Enhanced Small Device Interface *See* ESDI.

EPROM Erasable programmable read-only memory. A type of read-only memory (ROM) in which the data pattern can be erased to allow a new pattern. Usually is erased by ultraviolet light and recorded by a higher than normal voltage programming signal.

equalization A compensation circuit designed into modems to counteract certain distortions introduced by the telephone channel. Two types are used: fixed (compromise) equalizers and those that adapt to channel conditions (adaptive). Good-quality modems use adaptive equalization.

error control Various techniques that check the reliability of characters (parity) or blocks of data. V.42, MNP, and HST error-control protocols use error detection (CRC) and retransmission of errored frames (ARQ).

error message A word or combination of words to indicate to the user that an error has occurred somewhere in the program.

ESDI An acronym for Enhanced Small Device Interface, a hardware standard developed by Maxtor and standardized by a consortium of 22 disk drive manufacturers on January 26, 1983. A group of 27 manufacturers formed the ESDI steering committee on September 15, 1986, to enhance and improve the specification.

A high-performance interface used primarily with hard disks, ESDI provides for a maximum data transfer rate to and from a hard disk of between 10 and 24 megabits per second.

EtherNet A type of network protocol developed in the late 1970s by Bob Metcalf, at Xerox Corporation, and endorsed by the IEEE. One of the oldest LAN communications protocols in the personal computing industry. EtherNet networks use a collision-detection protocol to manage contention.

expanded memory Otherwise known as EMS memory, memory that conforms to the EMS specification. Requires a special device driver and conforms to a standard developed by Lotus, Intel, and Microsoft.

eXtended graphics array *See* XGA.

extended memory Direct processor-addressable memory that is addressed by an Intel (or compatible) 286, 386, or 486 processor in the region beyond the first megabyte. Addressable only in the processor's protected mode of operation.

extended partition A nonbootable DOS partition containing DOS volumes. Starting with DOS V3.3, the DOS FDISK program can create two partitions that serve DOS: an ordinary, bootable partition (called the primary partition) and an extended partition, which may contain as many as 23 volumes from D: through Z:.

extra-high density (ED) An indication of the storage capacity of a floppy drive or disk in which 36 sectors per track are recorded using a vertical recording technique with MFM encoding.

FIFO An acronym for *first-in first-out*, a method of storing and retrieving items from a list, table, or stack such that the first element stored is the first one retrieved.

file A collection of information kept somewhere other than in random-access memory.

file allocation table A table held near the outer edge of a disk that tells which sectors are allocated to each file and in what order.

file attribute Information held in the attribute byte of a file's directory entry.

file defragmentation The process of rearranging disk sectors so that files are compacted on consecutive sectors in adjacent tracks.

file name The name given to the disk file. Must be one to eight characters long and may be followed by a file-name extension, which can be one to three characters long. Can be made up of any combination of letters and numbers but should be descriptive of the information contained in the file.

firmware Software contained in a read-only memory (ROM) device. A cross between hardware and software.

fixed disk Also called a hard disk, a disk that cannot be removed from its controlling hardware or housing. Made of rigid material with a magnetic coating and used for the mass storage and retrieval of data.

floppy tape A tape standard that uses drives connecting to an ordinary floppy disk controller.

flow control A mechanism that compensates for differences in the flow of data input to and output from a modem or other device.

FM encoding Frequency modulation encoding. An outdated method of encoding data on the disk surface that uses up half the disk space with timing signals.

form factor The physical dimensions of a device. Two devices with the same form factor are physically interchangeable. The IBM PC, XT, and XT Model 286, for example, all use power supplies that are internally different but have exactly the same form factor.

FORMAT.COM The DOS format program that performs both low- and high-level formatting on floppy disks but only high-level formatting on hard disks.

formatted capacity The total number of bytes of data that can fit on a formatted disk. The unformatted capacity is higher because space is lost defining the boundaries between sectors.

formatting Preparing a disk so that the computer can read or write to it. Checks the disk for defects and constructs an organizational system to manage information on the disk.

FORTRAN An acronym for *for*mula *tran*slator, a high-level programming language for programs dealing primarily with mathematical formulas and expressions, similar to algebra and used primarily in scientific and technical applications. One of the oldest languages but still widely used because of its compact notation, the many mathematical subroutines available, and the ease with which arrays, matrices, and loops can be handled. FORTRAN was written in 1954 by John Backus at IBM, and the first successful FORTRAN program was executed by Harlan Herrick.

frame A data communications term for a block of data with header and trailer information attached. The added information usually includes a frame number, block size data, error-check codes, and start/end indicators.

full duplex Signal flow in both directions at the same time. In microcomputer communications, also may refer to the suppression of the on-line local echo.

full-height drive A drive unit that is 3.25 inches high, 5.75 inches wide, and 8.00 inches deep.

function keys Special-purpose keys that can be programmed to perform various operations. Serve many different functions depending on the program being used.

gas-plasma display Commonly used in portable systems, a type of display that operates by exciting a gas, usually neon or an argon-neon mixture, through the application of a voltage. When sufficient voltage is applied at the intersection of two electrodes, the gas glows an orange-red. Because gas-plasma displays generate light, they require no backlighting.

giga A multiplier indicating 1 billion (1,000,000,000) of some unit. Abbreviated as g or G. When used to indicate a number of bytes of memory storage, the multiplier definition changes to 1,073,741,824. One gigabit, for example, equals 1,000,000,000 bits, and one gigabyte equals 1,073,741,824 bytes.

gigabyte A unit of information storage equal to 1,073,741,824 bytes.

global backup A backup of all information on a hard disk, including the directory tree structure.

half duplex Signal flow in both directions but only one way at a time. In microcomputer communications, may refer to activation of the on-line local echo, which causes the modem to send a copy of the transmitted data to the screen of the sending computer.

half-height drive A drive unit that is 1.625 inches high, and either 5.75 or 4.00 inches wide and 4.00 or 8.00 inches deep.

hard disk A high-capacity disk storage unit characterized by a normally nonremovable rigid substrate media. The platters in a hard disk normally are constructed of aluminum or glass.

hard error An error in reading or writing data that is caused by damaged hardware.

hardware Physical components that make up a microcomputer, monitor, printer, and so on.

HDLC High-Level Data Link Control. A standard protocol developed by the International Standards Organization for software applications and communicating devices operating in synchronous environments. Defines operations at the link level of communications—for example, the format of data frames exchanged between modems over a phone line.

head A small electromagnetic device inside a drive that reads, records, and erases data on the media.

head actuator The device that moves read/write heads across a disk drive's platters. Most drives use a stepper-motor or a voice-coil actuator.

head crash A (usually) rare occurrence in which a read/write head strikes a platter surface with sufficient force to damage the magnetic medium.

head parking A procedure in which a disk drive's read/write heads are moved to an unused track so that they will not damage data in the event of a head crash or other failure.

head seek The movement of a drive's read/write heads to a particular track.

heat sink A mass of metal attached to a chip carrier or socket for the purpose of dissipating heat.

helical scan A type of recording technology that has vastly increased the capacity of tape drives. Invented for use in broadcast systems and now used in VCRs. Conventional longitudinal recording records a track of data straight across the width of a single-track tape. Helical scan recording packs more data on the tape by positioning the tape at an angle to the recording heads. The heads spin to record diagonal stripes of information on the tape.

hexadecimal number A number encoded in base-16, such that digits include the letters A through F as well as the numerals 0 through 9 (for example, 8BF3, which equals 35,827 in base-10).

hidden file A file that is not displayed in DOS directory listings because the file's attribute byte holds a special setting.

high density (HD) An indication of the storage capacity of a floppy drive or disk in which 15 or 18 sectors per track are recorded using MFM encoding.

high-level formatting Formatting performed by the DOS FORMAT program. Among other things, it creates the root directory and file allocation tables.

history file A file created by utility software to keep track of earlier use of the software. Many backup programs, for example, keep history files describing earlier backup sessions.

HPT High-pressure tin. A PLCC socket that promotes high forces between socket contacts and PLCC contacts for a good connection.

HST High-speed technology. The USRobotics proprietary high-speed modem-signaling scheme, developed as an interim protocol until the V.32 protocol could be implemented in a cost-effective manner. Incorporates trellis-coded modulation for greater immunity from variable phone-line conditions, and asymmetrical modulation for more efficient use of the phone channel at speeds of 4800 bps and above. The forward channel transmits at either 9600 bps (older designs) or 14400 bps, and the reverse channel transmits at 450 bps. This technique eliminated the need for the V.32 echo-cancellation hardware that was more costly at the time HST was developed. HST also incorporates MNP-compatible error-control procedures adapted to the asymmetrical modulation.

Hz A mnemonic for *hertz*, a frequency measurement unit used internationally to indicate one cycle per second.

I/O Input/output. A circuit path that enables independent communications between the processor and external devices.

IBMBIO.COM One of the DOS system files required to boot the machine. The first file loaded from disk during the boot. Contains extensions to the ROM BIOS.

IBMDOS.COM One of the DOS system files required to boot the machine. Contains the primary DOS routines. Loaded by IBMBIO.COM, it in turns loads COMMAND.COM.

IC An acronym for integrated circuit, a complete electronic circuit contained on a single chip. May consist of only a few transistors, capacitors, diodes, or resistors, or thousands of them, and generally is classified according to the complexity of the circuitry and the approximate number of circuits on the chip. SSI (small-scale integration) equals 2 to 10 circuits. MSI (medium-scale integration) equals 10 to 100 circuits. LSI (large-scale integration) equals 100 to 1,000 circuits. VLSI (very-large-scale integration) equals 1,000 to 10,000 circuits. ULSI (ultra-large-scale integration) equals more than 10,000 circuits.

IDE An acronym for integrated drive electronics. Describes a hard disk with the disk controller circuitry integrated within it. The first IDE drives commonly were called hard cards. Also refers to the ATA interface standard, the standard for attaching hard disk drives to ISA bus IBM-compatible computers. IDE drives typically operate as though they were standard ST-506/412 drives. *See also* ATA.

incremental backup A backup of all files that have changed since the last backup.

initiator A device attached to the SCSI bus that sends a command to another device (the target) on the SCSI bus. The SCSI host adapter plugged into the system bus is an example of an SCSI initiator.

inkjet printer A type of printer that sprays one or more colors of ink on the paper. Can produce output with quality approaching that of a laser printer at a lower cost.

input Data sent to the computer from the keyboard, the telephone, the video camera, another computer, paddles, joysticks, and so on.

instruction Program step that tells the computer what to do for a single operation.

integrated circuit *See* IC.

interface A communications device or protocol that enables one device to communicate with another. Matches the output of one device to the input of the other device.

interleave ratio The number of sectors that pass beneath the read/write heads before the "next" numbered sector arrives. When the interleave ratio is 3:1, for example, a sector is read, two pass by, and then the next is read. A proper interleave ratio, laid down during low-level formatting, enables the disk to transfer information without excessive revolutions due to missed sectors.

internal command In DOS, a command contained in COMMAND.COM so that no other file must be loaded in order to perform the command. DIR and COPY are two examples of internal commands.

internal drive A disk or tape drive mounted inside one of a computer's disk drive bays (or a hard disk card, which is installed in one of the computer's slots).

interpreter A translator program for a high-level language that translates and executes the program at the same time. The program statements that are interpreted remain in their original source language, the way the programmer wrote them—that is, the program does not need to be compiled before execution. Interpreted programs run slower than compiled programs and always must be run with the interpreter loaded in memory.

interrupt A suspension of a process, such as the execution of a computer program, caused by an event external to that process and performed in such a way that the process can be resumed. An interrupt can be caused by internal or external conditions such as a signal indicating that a device or program has completed a transfer of data.

interrupt vector A pointer in a table that gives the location of a set of instructions that the computer should execute when a particular interrupt occurs.

IRQ lines An acronym for *i*nterrupt *req*uest lines. Physical connections between external hardware devices and the interrupt controllers. When a device such as a floppy controller or a printer needs the attention of the CPU, an IRQ line is used to get the attention of the system to perform a task. On PC and XT IBM-compatible systems, 8 IRQ lines are included, numbered IRQ0 through IRQ7.

On the AT and PS/2 systems, 16 IRQ lines are numbered IRQ0 through IRQ15. IRQ lines must be used by only a single adapter in the ISA bus systems, but Micro Channel Architecture (MCA) adapters can share interrupts.

ISDN An acronym for Integrated Services Digital Network, an international telecommunications standard that enables a communications channel to carry digital data simultaneously with voice and video information.

ISO An acronym for International Standards Organization. The ISO, based in Paris, develops standards for international and national data communications. The U.S. representative to the ISO is the American National Standards Institute (ANSI).

J-lead J-shaped leads on chip carriers. Can be surface-mounted on a PC board or plugged into a socket that then is mounted on a PC board, usually on .050-inch centers.

JEDEC Joint Electron Devices Engineering Council. A group that establishes standards for the electronics industry.

jumper A small, plastic-covered, metal clip that slips over two pins protruding from a circuit board. Sometimes also called a *shunt*. When in place, the jumper connects the pins electrically and closes the circuit. By doing so, it connects the two terminals of a switch, turning it "on."

Kermit A protocol designed for transferring files between microcomputers and mainframes. Developed by Frank DaCruz and Bill Catchings, at Columbia University (and named after the talking frog on *The Muppet Show*). Widely accepted in the academic world. The complete Kermit protocol manual and the source for various versions is available from Kermit Distribution, Columbia University Center for Computing Activities, 612 West 115 Street, New York, NY 10025, (212) 854-3703.

key disk In software copy protection, a distribution floppy disk that must be present in a floppy disk drive for an application program to run.

keyboard macro A series of keystrokes automatically input when a single key is pressed.

kilo A multiplier indicating one thousand (1,000) of some unit. Abbreviated as *k* or *K*. When used to indicate a number of bytes of memory storage, the multiplier definition changes to 1,024. One kilobit, for example, equals 1,000 bits, and one kilobyte equals 1,024 bytes.

kilobyte A unit of information storage equal to 1,024 bytes.

landing zone An unused track on a disk surface on which the read/write heads can land when power is shut off. The place that a parking program or a drive with an autopark mechanism parks the heads.

LAPM *Link-access procedure for modems*, an error-control protocol incorporated in CCITT Recommendation V.42. Like the MNP and HST protocols, uses cyclic redundancy checking (CRC) and retransmission of corrupted data (ARQ) to ensure data reliability.

laptop computer A computer system smaller than a briefcase but larger than a notebook, and that usually has a clamshell design in which the keyboard and display are on separate halves of the system, which are hinged together. These systems normally run on battery power.

laser printer A type of printer that is a combination of an electrostatic copying machine and a computer printer. The output data from the computer is converted by an interface into a raster feed, similar to the impulses that a TV picture tube receives. The impulses cause the laser beam to scan a small drum that carries a positive electrical charge. Where the laser hits, the drum is discharged. A toner, which also carries a positive charge, then is applied to the drum. This toner, a fine black powder, sticks only to the areas of the drum that have been discharged electrically. As it rotates, the drum deposits the toner on a negatively charged sheet of paper. Another roller then heats and bonds the toner to the page.

latency The amount of time required for a disk drive to rotate half of a revolution. Represents the average amount of time to locate a specific sector after the heads have arrived at a specific track. Latency is part of the average access time for a drive.

LCC Leadless chip carrier. A type of integrated circuit package that has input and output pads rather than leads on its perimeter.

LCD An acronym for liquid crystal display, a display that uses liquid crystal sealed between two pieces of polarized glass. The polarity of the liquid crystal is changed by an electric current to vary the amount of light that can pass through. Because LCD displays do not generate light, they depend on either the reflection of ambient light or backlighting the screen. The best type of LCD, the active-matrix or thin-film transistor (TFT) LCD, offers fast screen updates and true color capability.

LED An acronym for light-emitting diode, a semiconductor diode that emits light when a current is passed through it.

LIF Low insertion force. A type of socket that requires only a minimum of force to insert a chip carrier.

light pen A hand-held input device with a light-sensitive probe or stylus, connected to the computer's graphics adapter board by a cable. Used for writing or sketching on-screen or as a pointing device tool for making selections. Unlike mice, not widely supported by software applications.

local echo A modem feature that enables the modem to send copies of keyboard commands and transmitted data to the screen. When the modem is in command mode (not on-line to another system), the local echo normally is invoked through an ATE1 command, which causes the modem to display your typed commands. When the modem is on-line to another system, the local echo is invoked by an ATF0 command, which causes the modem to display the data it transmits to the remote system.

logical drive A drive as named by a DOS drive specifier, such as C: or D:. Under DOS 3.3 or later, a single physical drive can act as several logical drives, each with its own specifier.

logical unit number *See* LUN.

lost clusters Clusters that have been marked accidentally as "unavailable" in the file allocation table even though they belong to no file listed in a directory.

low-level formatting Formatting that divides tracks into sectors on the platter surfaces. Places sector-identifying information before and after each sector and fills each sector with null data (usually hex F6). Specifies the sector interleave and marks defective tracks by placing invalid checksum figures in each sector on a defective track.

LUN An acronym for logical unit number, a number given to a device (a logical unit) attached to a SCSI physical unit and not directly to the SCSI bus. Although as many as eight logical units can be attached to a single physical unit, normally a single logical unit is a built-in part of a single physical unit. A SCSI hard disk, for example, has a built-in SCSI bus adapter that is assigned a physical unit number or SCSI ID, and the controller and drive portions of the hard disk are assigned a logical unit number (usually 0).

magnetic domain A tiny segment of a track just large enough to hold one of the magnetic flux reversals that encode data on a disk surface.

magneto-optical recording An erasable optical disk recording technique that uses a laser beam to heat pits on the disk surface to the point at which a magnet can make flux changes.

master partition boot sector On hard disks, a one-sector record that gives essential information about the disk and tells the starting locations of the various partitions. Always the first physical sector of the disk.

MCA An acronym for Micro Channel Architecture. Developed by IBM for the PS/2 line of computers and introduced on April 2, 1987. Features include a 16- or 32-bit bus width and multiple master control. By allowing several processors to arbitrate for resources on a single bus, the MCA is optimized for multitasking, multiprocessor systems. Offers switchless configuration of adapters, which eliminates one of the biggest headaches of installing older adapters.

MCGA An acronym for MultiColor Graphics Array, a type of PC video display circuit introduced by IBM on April 2, 1987, that supports text and graphics. Text is supported at a maximum resolution of 80×25 characters in 16 colors with a character box of 8×16 pixels. Graphics is supported at a maximum resolution of 320×200 pixels in 256 (from a palette of 262,144) colors or 640×480 pixels in 2 colors. The MCGA outputs an analog signal with a horizontal scanning frequency of 31.5 KHz, and supports analog color or analog monochrome displays.

MDA An acronym for Monochrome Display Adapter, a type of PC video display adapter introduced by IBM on August 12, 1981, that supports text only. Text is supported at a maximum resolution of 80×25 characters in four colors with a character box of 9×14 pixels. *Colors*, in this case, indicates black, white, bright white, and underlined. Graphics modes are not supported. The MDA outputs a digital signal with a horizontal scanning frequency of 18.432 KHz, and supports TTL monochrome displays. The IBM MDA also included a parallel printer port.

mean time between failure *See* MTBF.

mean time to repair *See* MTTR.

medium The magnetic coating or plating that covers a disk or tape.

mega A multiplier indicating 1 million (1,000,000) of some unit. Abbreviated as *m* or *M*. When used to indicate a number of bytes of memory storage, the multiplier definition changes to 1,048,576. One megabit, for example, equals 1,000,000 bits, and one megabyte equals 1,048,576 bytes.

megabyte A unit of information storage equal to 1,048,576 bytes.

memory Any component in a computer system that stores information for future use.

memory caching A service provided by extremely fast memory chips that keeps copies of the most recent memory accesses. When the CPU makes a subsequent access, the value is supplied by the fast memory rather than by relatively slow system memory.

memory-resident program A program that remains in memory after it has been loaded, consuming memory that otherwise might be used by application software.

menu software Utility software that makes a computer easier to use by replacing DOS commands with a series of menu selections.

MFM Modified Frequency Modulation encoding. A method of encoding data on the surface of a disk. The coding of a bit of data varies by the coding of the preceding bit to preserve clocking information.

MHz An abbreviation for *megahertz*, a unit of measurement for indicating the frequency of one million cycles per second. One hertz (Hz) is equal to one cycle per second. Named after Heinrich R. Hertz, a German physicist who first detected electromagnetic waves in 1883.

MI/MIC Mode Indicate/Mode Indicate Common, also called forced or manual originate. Provided for installations in which equipment other than the modem does the dialing. In such installations, the modem operates in dumb mode (no auto-dial capability) yet must go off-hook in originate mode to connect with answering modems.

micro A prefix indicating one millionth (1/1,000,000 or .000001) of some unit. Abbreviated as *u*.

microprocessor A solid-state central processing unit much like a computer on a chip. An integrated circuit that accepts coded instructions for execution.

microsecond A unit of time equal to one millionth (1/1,000,000 or .000001) of a second. Abbreviated as *us*.

MIDI An acronym for Musical Instrument Digital Interface, an interface standard for connecting a musical instrument to a microcomputer. Multiple musical instruments can be daisy-chained and played simultaneously with the help of the computer and related software. The various operations of the instruments can be captured, saved, edited, and played back.

milli A prefix indicating one thousandth (1/1,000 or .001) of some unit. Abbreviated as *m*.

millisecond A unit of time equal to one thousandth (1/1,000 or .001) of a second. Abbreviated as *ms*.

MIPS An acronym for million instructions per second. Refers to the average number of machine-language instructions a computer can perform or execute in one second. Because different processors can perform different functions in a single instruction, MIPS should be used only as a general measure of performance among different types of computers.

MNP Microcom Networking Protocol. Asynchronous error-control and data-compression protocols developed by Microcom, Inc. and now in the public domain. Ensure error-free transmission through error detection (CRC) and retransmission of errored frames. MNP Levels 1 through 4 cover error control and have been incorporated into CCITT Recommendation V.42. MNP Level 5 includes data compression but is eclipsed in superiority by V.42bis, an international standard that is more efficient. Most high-speed modems will connect with MNP Level 5 if V.42bis is unavailable.

modem *Mo*dulator-*dem*odulator. A device that converts electrical signals from a computer into an audio form transmittable over telephone lines, or vice versa. Modulates, or transforms, digital signals from a computer into the analog form that can be carried successfully on a phone line; also demodulates signals received from the phone line back to digital signals before passing them to the receiving computer.

module An assembly that contains a complete circuit or subcircuit.

Monochrome Display Adapter *See* MDA.

MOS An acronym for Metal-Oxide Semiconductor. Refers to the three layers used in forming the gate structure of a field-effect transistor (FET). MOS circuits offer low power dissipation and enable transistors to be jammed close together before a critical heat problem arises. PMOS, the oldest type of MOS circuit, is a silicon-gate P-channel MOS process that uses currents made up of positive charges. NMOS is a silicon-gate N-channel MOS process that uses currents made up of negative charges and is at least twice as fast as PMOS. CMOS, Complementary MOS, is nearly immune to noise, runs off almost any power supply, and is an extremely low-power circuit technique.

MTBF An acronym for *m*ean *t*ime *b*etween *f*ailure, a statistically derived measure of the probable time a device will continue to operate before a hardware failure occurs, usually given in hours. Because no standard technique exists for measuring MTBF, a device from one manufacturer can be significantly more or significantly less reliable than a device with the same MTBF rating from another manufacturer.

MTTR An acronym for *mean time to repair*, a measure of the probable time it will take a technician to service or repair a specific device, usually given in hours.

motherboard The main circuit board in the computer. Also called planar, system board, or backplane.

MultiColor Graphics Array *See* MCGA.

multitask Run several programs simultaneously.

multiuser system A system in which several computer terminals share the same central processing unit (CPU).

nano A prefix indicating one billionth (1/1,000,000,000 or .000000001) of some unit. Abbreviated as *n*.

nanosecond A unit of time equal to one billionth (1/1,000,000,000 or .000000001) of a second. Abbreviated as *ns*.

network A system in which a number of independent computers are linked in order to share data and peripherals, such as hard disks and printers.

nonvolatile memory (NVRAM) Random-access memory whose data is retained when power is turned off. Sometimes nonvolatile RAM is retained without any power whatsoever, as in EEPROM or flash memory devices. In other cases the memory is maintained by a small battery. Nonvolatile RAM that is battery maintained is sometimes also called CMOS memory. CMOS NVRAM is used in IBM-compatible systems to store configuration information. True NVRAM often is used in intelligent modems to store a user-defined default configuration loaded into normal modem RAM at power-up.

nonvolatile RAM disk A RAM disk powered by a battery supply so that it continues to hold its data during a power outage.

NTSC An acronym for the National Television Standards Committee, which governs the standard for television and video playback and recording in the United States. Organized in 1941 when TV broadcasting first began on a wide scale. The NTSC standard provides for 525 scan lines of resolution and is transmitted at 60 half-frames per second. It is an interlaced signal, which means that it scans every other line each time the screen is refreshed. The signal is generated as a composite of red, green, and blue signals for color and includes an FM frequency for audio and a signal for stereo. Twenty years later, higher standards were adopted in Europe with the PAL and SECAM systems, both incompatible with the NTSC standard of North America.

null modem A serial cable wired so that two data terminal equipment (DTE) devices, such as personal computers, or two data communication equipment (DCE) devices, such as modems or mice, can be connected. Also sometimes called a modem-eliminator. To make a null-modem cable with DB-25 connectors, you wire these pins together: 1-1, 2-3, 3-2, 4-5, 5-4, 6-20, 20-6, and 7-7.

OCR An acronym for optical character recognition, an information-processing technology that converts human-readable text into computer data. Usually a scanner is used to read the text on a page, and OCR software converts the images to characters.

OEM An acronym for original equipment manufacturer, any manufacturer that sells its product to a reseller. Usually refers to the original manufacturer of a particular device or component. Most COMPAQ hard disks, for example, are made by Conner Peripherals, who is considered the OEM.

on-line fallback A feature that enables high-speed error-control modems to monitor line quality and fall back to the next lower speed if line quality degrades. The modems fall forward as line quality improves.

operating system A collection of programs for operating the computer. Operating systems perform housekeeping tasks such as input and output between the computer and peripherals and accepting and interpreting information from the keyboard. DOS and OS/2 are examples of popular operating systems.

optical disk A disk that encodes data as a series of reflective pits that are read (and sometimes written) by a laser beam.

originate mode A state in which the modem transmits at the pre-defined low frequency of the communications channel and receives at the high frequency. The transmit/receive frequencies are the reverse of the called modem, which is in answer mode.

OS/2 A universal operating system developed through a joint effort by IBM and Microsoft Corporation. The latest operating system for microcomputers using the Intel 80286 or better microprocessors, OS/2 is the successor to DOS (developed also by Microsoft and IBM) and Windows. OS/2 uses the protected mode operation of the processor to expand memory from 1M to 16M and to support fast, efficient multitasking. The OS/2 Presentation Manager, an integral part of the system, is a graphical interface similar to Microsoft Windows and the Apple Macintosh system. The latest version runs DOS, Windows, and OS/2-specific software.

output Information processed by the computer; or the act of sending that information to a mass storage device such as a video display, a printer, or a modem.

overlay Part of a program that is loaded into memory only when it is required.

overrun A situation in which data moves from one device faster than a second device can accept it.

overwrite To write data on top of existing data, thus erasing the existing data.

package A device that includes a chip mounted on a carrier and sealed.

PAL An acronym for phase alternating line system. Invented in 1961 and refers to a system of TV broadcasting used in England and other European countries. With its 625-line picture delivered at 25 frames/second, PAL provides a better image and an improved color transmission over the NTSC system used in North America. PAL also can stand for Programmable Array Logic, a type of chip that has logic gates specified by a device programmer.

palmtop computer A computer system smaller than a notebook that is designed so that it can be held in one hand while being operated by the other.

parallel A method of transferring data characters in which the bits travel down parallel electrical paths simultaneously—for example, eight paths for eight-bit characters. Data is stored in computers in parallel form but may be converted to serial form for certain operations.

parity A method of error checking in which an extra bit is sent to the receiving device to indicate whether an even or odd number of binary 1 bits were transmitted. The receiving unit compares the received information with this bit and can obtain a reasonable judgment about the validity of the character. The same type of parity (even or odd) must be used by two communicating computers, or both may omit parity. When parity is used, a parity bit is added to each transmitted character. The bit's value is 0 or 1, to make the total number of 1s in the character even or odd, depending on which type of parity is used.

park program A program that executes a seek to the highest cylinder or just past the highest cylinder of a drive so that the potential of data loss is minimized if the drive is moved.

partition A section of a hard disk devoted to a particular operating system. Most hard disks have only one partition, devoted to DOS. A hard disk can have as many as four partitions, each occupied by a different operating system. DOS V3.3 or higher can occupy two of these four partitions.

Pascal A high-level programming language named for the French mathematician Blaise Pascal (1623-1662). Developed in the early 1970s by Niklaus Wirth for teaching programming and designed to support the concepts of structured programming. Easy to learn and often the first language taught in schools.

peripheral Any piece of equipment used in computer systems that is an attachment to the computer. Disk drives, terminals, and printers are all examples of peripherals.

PGA Pin-grid array. A chip package that has a large number of pins on the bottom designed for socket mounting. Also can mean Professional Graphics Adapter, a limited-production, high-resolution graphics card for XT and AT systems from IBM.

physical drive A single disk drive. DOS defines logical drives, which are given a specifier, such as C: or D:. A single physical drive may be divided into multiple logical drives. Conversely, special software can span a single logical drive across two physical drives.

physical unit number *See* PUN.

pixel A mnemonic term meaning picture element. Any of the tiny elements that form a picture on a video display screen. Also called a pel.

planar board A term equivalent to motherboard, used by IBM in some of its literature.

plated media Hard disk platters plated with a form of thin metal film media on which data is recorded.

platter A disk contained in a hard disk drive. Most drives have two or more platters, each with data recorded on both sides.

PLCC Plastic leaded-chip carrier. A popular chip-carrier package with J-leads around the perimeter of the package.

port Plug or socket that enables an external device such as a printer to be attached to the adapter card in the computer. Also a logical address used by a microprocessor for communications between itself and various devices.

port address One of a system of addresses used by the computer to access devices such as disk drives or printer ports. You may need to specify an unused port address when installing any adapter boards in a system unit.

portable computer A computer system smaller than a transportable system, but larger than a laptop system. Most portable systems conform to the lunchbox style popularized by COMPAQ, or the briefcase style popularized by IBM, each with a fold-down (removable) keyboard and built-in display. These systems characteristically run on AC power and not on batteries, include several expansion slots, and can be as powerful as full-blown desktop systems.

POS An acronym for Programmable Option Select. The Micro Channel Architecture's POS eliminates switches and jumpers from the system board and adapters by replacing them with programmable registers. Automatic configuration routines store the POS data in a battery-powered CMOS memory for system configuration and operations. The configuration utilities rely on adapter description (ADF) files that contain the setup data for each card.

POST Power-On Self Test. A series of tests run by the computer at power-on. Most computers scan and test many of their circuits and sound a beep from the internal speaker if this initial test indicates proper system performance.

PostScript A page-description language developed primarily by John Warnock, of Adobe Systems, for converting and moving data to the laser-printed page. Instead of using the standard method of transmitting graphics or character information to a printer, telling it where to place dots one-by-one on a page, PostScript provides a way for the laser printer to interpret mathematically a full page of shapes and curves.

power supply An electrical/electronic circuit that supplies all operating voltage and current to the computer system.

Presentation Manager The graphical, icon- and window-based software interface offered with OS/2.

primary partition An ordinary, single-volume bootable partition. *See also* extended partition.

processor speed The clock rate at which a microprocessor processes data. A standard IBM PC, for example, operates at 4.77 MHz (4.77 million cycles per second).

program A set of instructions or steps telling the computer how to handle a problem or task.

PROM Programmable read-only memory. A type of memory chip that can be programmed to store information permanently—information that cannot be erased.

proprietary Anything invented by a company and not used by any other company. Especially applies to cases in which the inventing company goes to lengths to hide the specifications of the new invention. The opposite of standard.

protected mode A mode available in all Intel 80286- or 80386-compatible processors. In this mode, memory addressing is extended to 16 or 4096 megabytes, and restricted protection levels can be set to trap software crashes and control the system.

protocol A system of rules and procedures governing communications between two or more devices. Protocols vary, but communicating devices must follow the same protocol in order to exchange data. The data format, readiness to receive or send, error detection, and error correction are some of the operations that may be defined in protocols.

PUN An acronym for *p*hysical *u*nit *n*umber, a term used to describe a device attached directly to the SCSI bus. Also known as a SCSI ID. As many as eight SCSI devices can be attached to a single SCSI bus, and each must have a unique PUN or ID assigned from 7 to 0. Normally the SCSI host adapter is assigned the highest-priority ID, which is 7. A bootable hard disk is assigned an ID of 6, and other nonbootable drives are assigned lower priorities.

QAM An acronym for quadrature amplitude modulation, a modulation technique used by high-speed modems that combines both phase and amplitude modulation. This technique enables multiple bits to be encoded in a single time interval. The V.32bis standard-codes six data bits plus an additional trellis coding bit for each signal change. An individual signal is evaluated with respect to phase and amplitude compared to the carrier wave. A plot of all possible QAM signal points is referred to as the signal constellation pattern. The V.32bis constellation pattern has 128 discrete signal points.

QIC Quarter-Inch Committee. An industry association that sets hardware and software standards for tape-backup units that use quarter-inch-wide tapes.

QWERTY keyboard The standard typewriter or computer keyboard, with the characters Q, W, E, R, T, and Y on the top row of alpha keys. Because of the haphazard placement of characters, this keyboard can hinder fast typing.

rails Plastic strips attached to the sides of disk drives mounted in IBM ATs and compatibles so that the drives can slide into place. These rails fit into channels in the side of each disk drive bay position.

RAM An acronym for random-access memory, all memory accessible at any instant (randomly) by a microprocessor.

RAM disk A "phantom disk drive" in which a section of system memory (RAM) is set aside to hold data, just as though it were a number of disk sectors. To DOS, a RAM disk looks like and functions like any other drive.

random-access file A file in which all data elements (or records) are of equal length and written in the file end to end, without delimiting characters between. Any element (or record) in the file can be found directly by calculating the record's offset in the file.

random-access memory *See* RAM.

read-only file A file whose attribute setting in the file's directory entry tells DOS not to allow software to write into or over the file.

read-only memory *See* ROM.

read/write head A tiny magnet that reads and writes data on a disk track.

real mode A mode available in all Intel 8086-compatible processors that enables compatibility with the original 8086. In this mode, memory addressing is limited to one megabyte.

real time When something is recorded or processed as it is happening in the outside world.

refresh cycle A cycle in which the computer accesses all memory locations stored by dynamic RAM chips so that the information remains intact. Dynamic RAM chips must be accessed several times a second, or else the information fades.

register Storage area in memory having a specified storage capacity, such as a bit, a byte, or a computer word, and intended for a special purpose.

remote digital loopback A test that checks the phone link and a remote modem's transmitter and receiver. Data entered from the keyboard is transmitted from the initiating modem, received by the remote modem's receiver, looped through its transmitter, and returned to the local screen for verification.

remote echo A copy of the data received by the remote system, returned to the sending system, and displayed on-screen. A function of the remote system.

resolution A reference to the size of the pixels used in graphics. In medium-resolution graphics, pixels are large. In high-resolution graphics, pixels are small.

RISC An acronym for Reduced Instruction Set Computer, as differentiated from CISC, Complex Instruction Set Computer. RISC processors have simple instruction sets requiring only one or a few execution cycles. These simple instructions can be utilized more effectively than CISC systems with appropriately designed software, resulting in faster operations.

RLL An acronym for Run-Length Limited, a type of encoding that derives its name from the fact that the techniques used limit the distance (run length) between magnetic flux reversals on the disk platter. Several types of RLL encoding techniques exist. (1,7)RLL encoding increases storage capacity 25 percent over MFM encoding, (2,7)RLL encoding increases storage capacity by 50 percent over MFM encoding, and (3,9)RLL encoding roughly doubles that of MFM. Most IDE, ESDI, and SCSI hard disks use one of these forms of RLL encoding.

RMA number Return-merchandise authorization number. A number given to you by a vendor when you arrange to return an item for repairs. Used to track the item and the repair.

ROM An acronym for read-only memory, a type of memory that has values permanently or semi-permanently burned in. These locations are used to hold important programs or data that must be available to the computer when the power initially is turned on.

ROM BIOS Read-only memory basic input-output system. A BIOS encoded in a form of read-only memory for protection. Often applied to important start-up programs that must be present in a system for it to operate.

root directory The main directory of any hard or floppy disk. Has a fixed size and location for a particular disk volume and cannot be resized dynamically the way subdirectories can.

routine Set of frequently used instructions. May be considered as a subdivision of a program with two or more instructions that are related functionally.

RS-232 An interface introduced in August 1969 by the Electronic Industries Association. The RS-232 interface standard provides an electrical description for connecting peripheral devices to computers.

scratch disk A disk that contains no useful information and can be used as a test disk. IBM has a routine on the Advanced Diagnostics disks that creates a specially formatted scratch disk to be used for testing floppy drives.

SCSI An acronym for Small Computer System Interface, a standard originally developed by Shugart Associates (then called SASI for Shugart Associates System Interface) and later approved by ANSI in 1986. Uses a 50-pin connector and permits multiple devices (up to eight including the host) to be connected in daisy-chain fashion.

SDLC Synchronous Data Link Control. A protocol developed by IBM for software applications and communicating devices operation in IBM's Systems Network Architecture (SNA). Defines operations at the link level of communications—for example, the format of data frames exchanged between modems over a phone line.

SECAM A mnemonic term for sequential and memory. Refers to a system of TV broadcasting used in France and in a modified form in the USSR. Uses an 819-line picture that provides a better resolution than the (British) PAL 625-line and (U.S.) NTSC 525-line formats.

sector A section of one track, defined with identification markings and an identification number. Most sectors hold 512 bytes of data.

security software Utility software that uses a system of passwords and other devices to restrict an individual's access to subdirectories and files.

seek time The amount of time required for a disk drive to move the heads across one-third of the total number of cylinders. Represents the average time it takes to move the heads from one cylinder to another randomly selected cylinder. Seek time is a part of the average access time for a drive.

semiconductor A substance, such as germanium or silicon, whose conductivity is poor at low temperatures but is improved by minute additions of certain substances or by the application of heat, light, or voltage. Depending on the temperature and pressure, a semiconductor can control a flow of electricity. Semiconductors are the basis of modern electronic-circuit technology.

sequential file A file in which varying-length data elements are recorded end to end, with delimiting characters placed between each element. To find a particular element, you must read the whole file up to that element.

serial The transfer of data characters one bit at a time, sequentially, using a single electrical path.

servo data Magnetic markings written on disk platters to guide the read/write heads in drives that use voice-coil actuators.

settling time The time required for read/write heads to stop vibrating after they have been moved to a new track.

shadow ROM A copy of a system's slower access ROM BIOS placed in faster access RAM, usually during the start-up or boot procedure. This setup enables the system to access BIOS code without the penalty of additional wait states required by the slower ROM chips.

shell The generic name of any user interface software. COMMAND.COM is the standard shell for DOS. OS/2 comes with three shells: a DOS command shell, an OS/2 command shell, and the OS/2 Presentation Manager, a graphical shell.

shock rating A rating (usually expressed in G force units) of how much shock a disk drive can sustain without damage. Usually two different specifications exist for a drive powered on or off.

SIMM Single in-line memory module. An array of memory chips on a small PC board with a single row of I/O contacts.

SIP Single In-line Package. A DIP-like package with only one row of leads.

skinny dip Twenty-four- and 28-position DIP devices with .300-inch row-to-row centerlines.

SO-J Small Outline J-lead. A small DIP package with J-shaped leads for surface mounting or socketing.

soft error An error in reading or writing data that occurs sporadically, usually because of a transient problem such as a power fluctuation.

software A series of instructions loaded in the computer's memory that instructs the computer in how to accomplish a problem or task.

spindle The central post on which a disk drive's platters are mounted.

SQL An acronym for structured query language. A standard relational database language used especially on midrange and mainframe computers.

ST-506/412 A hard disk interface invented by Seagate Technology and introduced in 1980 with the ST-506 5M hard drive. The ST-506 interface requires that the read/write head be stepped or moved across the disk one track at a time by carefully timed pulses. Because these pulses cause the read/write head's stepper motor to advance a notch, they cannot be sent faster than the disk drive can move the heads. The ST-412 interface introduced with the ST-412 10M drive adds buffered seeking, which eliminates this problem. Instead of requiring the controller to slow the pulse rate to whatever the mechanism can handle, ST-412 simply counts the pulses as they come in and then decides how far to step the head to move the required number of tracks. ST-506/412 was formerly the interface of choice for IBM-compatible systems but has since been superceded by the IDE, ESDI, and SCSI interfaces.

standby power supply A backup power supply that quickly switches into operation during a power outage.

start/stop bits The signaling bits attached to a character before the character is transmitted during asynchronous transmission.

starting cluster The number of the first cluster occupied by a file. Listed in the directory entry of every file.

stepper motor actuator An assembly that moves disk drive read/write heads across platters by a sequence of small partial turns of a stepper motor.

storage Device or medium on or in which data can be entered or held, and retrieved at a later time. Synonymous with memory.

streaming In tape backup, a condition in which data is transferred from the hard disk as quickly as the tape drive can record the data so that the drive does not start and stop or waste tape.

string A sequence of characters.

subdirectory A directory listed in another directory. Subdirectories themselves exist as files.

subroutine A segment of a program that can be executed by a single call. Also called program module.

surface mount Chip carriers and sockets designed to mount to the surface of a PC board.

surge protector A device in the power line that feeds the computer, that provides minimal protection against voltage spikes and other transients.

synchronous communication A form of communication in which blocks of data are sent at strictly timed intervals. Because the timing is uniform, no start or stop bits are required. Compare with asynchronous communication. Some mainframes support only synchronous communications unless a synchronous adapter and appropriate software have been installed.

system crash A situation in which the computer freezes up and refuses to proceed without rebooting. Usually caused by faulty software. Unlike a hard disk crash, no permanent physical damage occurs.

system files The two hidden DOS files IBMBIO.COM and IBMDOS.COM; they represent the interface between the BIOS and DOS (IBMBIO) and the interface between DOS and other applications (IBMDOS).

system integrator A computer consultant or vendor who tests available products and combines them into highly optimized systems.

target A device attached to a SCSI bus that receives and processes commands sent from another device (the initiator) on the SCSI bus. A SCSI hard disk is an example of a target.

TCM An acronym for trellis-coded modulation, an error-detection and correction technique employed by high-speed modems to enable higher-speed transmissions that are more resistant to line impairments. In TCM encoding, the first two data bits of an encoded group are used to generate a third TCM bit that is added to the group. For example, in V.32bis, the first two bits of a 6-bit group are used to generate the TCM bit, which then is placed as the first bit of a new 7-bit group. By reversing the encoding at the other end, the receiving modem can determine whether the received group is valid.

temporary backup A second copy of a work file, usually having the extension BAK. Created by application software so that you easily can return to a previous version of your work.

temporary file A file temporarily (and usually invisibly) created by a program for its own use.

tera A multiplier indicating 1 trillion (1,000,000,000,000) of some unit. Abbreviated as *t* or *T*. When used to indicate a number of bytes of memory storage, the multiplier definition changes to 1,099,511,627,776. One terabit, for example, equals 1,000,000,000,000 bits, and one terabyte equals 1,099,511,627,776 bytes.

terabyte A unit of information storage equal to 1,099,511,627,776 bytes.

terminal A device whose keyboard and display are used for sending and receiving data over a communications link. Differs from a microcomputer in that it has no internal processing capabilities. Used to enter data into or retrieve processed data from a system or network.

terminal mode An operational mode required for microcomputers to transmit data. In terminal mode, the computer acts as though it were a standard terminal such as a teletypewriter rather than a data processor. Keyboard entries go directly to the modem, whether the entry is a modem command or data to be transmitted over the phone lines. Received data is output directly to the screen. The more popular communications software products control terminal mode and enable more complex operations, including file transmission and saving received files.

terminator A piece of hardware that must be attached to both ends of an electrical bus. Functions to prevent the reflection or echoing of signals that reach the ends of the bus and to ensure that the correct impedance load is placed on the driver circuits on the bus.

thin-film media Hard disk platters that have a thin film (usually 3 millionths of an inch) of medium deposited on the aluminum substrate through a sputtering or plating process.

through-hole Chip carriers and sockets equipped with leads that extend through holes in a PC board.

throughput The amount of user data transmitted per second without the overhead of protocol information such as start and stop bits or frame headers and trailers.

TIFF An acronym for Tagged Image File Format, a way of storing and exchanging digital image data. Developed by Aldus Corporation, Microsoft Corporation, and major scanner vendors to help link scanned images with the popular desktop publishing applications. Supports three main types of image data: black-and-white data, halftones or dithered data, and gray-scale data.

Token ring A type of local area network in which the workstations relay a packet of data called a token in a logical ring configuration. When a station wants to transmit, it takes possession of the token, attaches its data, then frees the token after the data has made a complete circuit of the electrical ring. IBM's token ring system is a standard network hardware implementation supported by many manufacturers. It is currently the highest-performance-standard LAN system and transmits at speeds of 16 million bits per second. Because of the token-passing scheme, access to the network is controlled, unlike the slower EtherNet system, in which collisions of data can occur, wasting time. The token ring network also uses twisted-pair wiring, which is cheaper than the coaxial cable used by EtherNet and ARCnet.

TPI Tracks per inch. Used as a measurement of magnetic track density. Standard $5\frac{1}{4}$-inch 360K floppy disks have a density of 48 TPI, and the 1.2M disks have a 96-TPI density. All $3\frac{1}{2}$-inch disks have a 135.4667-TPI density, and hard disks can have densities greater than 2,000 TPI.

track One of the many concentric circles that hold data on a disk surface. Consists of a single line of magnetic flux changes and is divided into some number of 512-byte sectors.

track density The number of tracks that can be fit on a platter side, as measured by the total number of tracks on a side or in tracks per inch (TPI).

track-to-track seek time The time required for read/write heads to move between adjacent tracks.

transportable computer A computer system larger than a portable system, and similar in size and shape to a portable sewing machine. Most transportables conform to a design similar to the original COMPAQ portable, with a built-in CRT display. These systems are characteristically very heavy, and run only on AC power. Because of advances primarily in LCD and plasma-display technology, these systems are largely obsolete and have been replaced by portable systems.

troubleshooting The task of determining the cause of a problem.

TSR An acronym for terminate-and-stay-resident, a program that remains in memory after being loaded. Because they remain in memory, TSR programs can be reactivated by a predefined keystroke sequence or other operation while another program is active. Usually called resident programs.

TTL An acronym for transistor-to-transistor logic. Digital signals often are called TTL signals. A TTL display is a monitor that accepts digital input at standardized signal voltage levels.

twisted pair A type of wire in which two small insulated copper wires are wrapped or twisted around each other to minimize interference from other wires in the cable. Two types of twisted-pair cables are available: unshielded and shielded. Unshielded twisted-pair wiring commonly is used in telephone cables and provides little protection against interference. Shielded twisted-pair wiring is used in some networks or any application in which immunity from electrical interference is more important. Twisted-pair wire is much easier to work with than coaxial cable and is cheaper as well.

UART An acronym for Universal Asynchronous Receiver Transmitter, a chip device that controls the RS-232 serial port in a PC-compatible system. Originally developed by National Semiconductor, several UART versions are in PC-compatible systems: the 8250B is used in PC- or XT-class systems, and the 16450 and 16550A are used in AT-class systems.

unformatted capacity The total number of bytes of data that can be fit on a disk. The formatted capacity is lower because space is lost defining the boundaries between sectors.

uninterruptible power supply Also known as UPS. A device that supplies power to the computer from batteries so that power will not stop, even momentarily, during a power outage. The batteries are recharged constantly from a wall socket.

Universal Asynchronous Receiver Transmitter *See* UART.

UPC An acronym for Universal Product Code, a ten-digit computer-readable bar code used in labeling retail products. The code in the form of vertical bars includes a five-digit manufacturer identification number and a five-digit product code number.

update To modify information already contained in a file or program with current information.

utility Programs that carry out routine procedures to make computer use easier.

UTP An acronym for unshielded twisted pair, a type of wire often used indoors to connect telephones or computer devices. Comes with two or four wires twisted inside a flexible plastic sheath or conduit and utilizes modular plugs and phone jacks.

V.21 A CCITT standard for modem communications at 300 bps. Modems made in the U.S. or Canada follow the Bell 103 standard but can be set to answer V.21 calls from overseas. The actual transmission rate is 300 baud and employs FSK (*f*requency *s*hift *k*eying) modulation, which encodes a single bit per baud.

V.22 A CCITT standard for modem communications at 1200 bps, with an optional fallback to 600 bps. V.22 is partially compatible with the Bell 212A standard observed in the United States and Canada. The actual transmission rate is 600 baud, using DPSK (*d*ifferential-*p*hase *s*hift *k*eying) to encode as much as 2 bits per baud.

V.22bis A CCITT standard for modem communications at 2400 bps. Includes an automatic link-negotiation fallback to 1200 bps and compatibility with Bell 212A/V.22 modems. The actual transmission rate is 600 baud, using QAM (quadrature amplitude modulation) to encode as much as 4 bits per baud.

V.23 A CCITT standard for modem communications at 1200 or 600 bps with a 75-bps back channel. Used in the United Kingdom for some videotext systems.

V.25 A CCITT standard for modem communications that specifies an answer tone different from the Bell answer tone used in the U.S. and Canada. Most intelligent modems can be set with an ATB0 command so that they use the V.25 2100 Hz tone when answering overseas calls.

V.32 A CCITT standard for modem communications at 9600 bps and 4800 bps. V.32 modems fall back to 4800 bps when line quality is impaired and fall forward again to 9600 bps when line quality improves. The actual transmission rate is 2400 baud, using QAM (quadrature amplitude modulation) and optional TCM (trellis-coded modulation) to encode as much as 4 data bits per baud.

V.32bis A CCITT standard that extends the standard V.32 connection range and supports 4800-, 7200-, 9600-, 12000-, and 14400-bps transmission rates. V.32bis modems fall back to the next lower speed when line quality is impaired, fall back further as necessary, and fall forward to the next higher speed when line quality improves. The actual transmission rate is 2400 baud, using QAM (quadrature amplitude modulation) and TCM (trellis-coded modulation) to encode as much as 6 data bits per baud.

V.32 fast A proposed CCITT standard that will extend the standard V.32bis connection range, supporting 19200-bps transmission rates as well as all the functions and rates of V.32bis. Products following this proposed standard should become available in 1993.

V.42 A CCITT standard for modem communications that defines a two-stage process of detection and negotiation for LAPM error control. Also supports MNP error-control protocol, Levels 1 through 4.

V.42bis An extension of CCITT V.42 that defines a specific data-compression scheme for use with V.42 and MNP error control.

vaccine A type of program used to locate and eradicate virus code from infected programs or systems.

VESA An acronym for the Video Electronics Standards Association. Founded in the late 1980s by NEC Home Electronics and eight other leading video board manufacturers, with the main goal to standardize the electrical, timing, and programming issues surrounding 800-by-600 resolution video displays, commonly known as Super VGA. Super VGA has been superseded by the XGA standard subsequently introduced by IBM.

VGA An acronym for Video Graphics Array, a type of PC video display circuit (and adapter) first introduced by IBM on April 2, 1987, that supports text and graphics. Text is supported at a maximum resolution of 80×25 characters in 16 colors with a character box of 9×16 pixels. Graphics is supported at a maximum resolution of 320×200 pixels in 256 (from a palette of 262,144) colors or 640×480 pixels in 16 colors. The VGA outputs an analog signal with a horizontal scanning frequency of 31.5 KHz, and supports analog color or analog monochrome displays.

video graphics array *See* VGA.

virtual disk A RAM disk or "phantom disk drive" in which a section of system memory (usually RAM) is set aside to hold data, just as though it were a number of disk sectors. To DOS, a virtual disk looks like and functions like any other "real" drive.

virtual memory A technique by which operating systems (including OS/2) load more programs and data into memory than they can hold. Parts of the programs and data are kept on disk and constantly swapped back and forth into system memory. The applications software programs are unaware of this setup and act as though a large amount of memory is available.

virtual real mode A mode available in all Intel 80386-compatible processors. In this mode, memory addressing is limited to 4,096 megabytes, restricted protection levels can be set to trap software crashes and control the system, and individual real mode compatible sessions can be set up and maintained separately from one another.

virus A type of resident program designed to attach itself to other programs. Usually at some later time, when the virus is running, it causes an undesirable action to take place.

voice-coil actuator A device that moves read/write heads across hard disk platters by magnetic interaction between coils of wire and a magnet. Functions somewhat like an audio speaker, from which the name originated.

voltage regulator A device that smooths out voltage irregularities in the power fed to the computer.

volume A portion of a disk signified by a single drive specifier. Under DOS V3.3 and later, a single hard disk can be partitioned into several volumes, each with its own logical drive specifier (C:,D:,E:, and so on).

volume label An identifier or name of up to 11 characters that names a disk.

VRAM An acronym for video random-access memory. VRAM chips are modified DRAMs on video boards that enable simultaneous access by the host system's processor and the processor on the video board. A large amount of information thus can be transferred quickly between the video board and the system processor. Sometimes also called dual-ported RAM.

wait states Pause cycles during system operation that require the processor to wait one or more clock cycles until memory can respond to the processor's request. Enables the microprocessor to synchronize with lower-cost, slower memory. A system that runs with "zero wait states" requires none of these cycles because of the use of faster memory or a memory cache system.

Whetstone A benchmark program developed in 1976 and designed to simulate arithmetic-intensive programs used in scientific computing. Remains completely CPU-bound and performs no I/O or system calls. Originally written in ALGOL, although the C and Pascal versions became more popular by the late 1980s. The speed at which a system performs floating-point operations often is measured in units of Whetstones.

Winchester drive Any ordinary, nonremovable (or fixed) hard disk drive. The name originates from a particular IBM drive in the 1960s that had 30M of fixed and 30M of removable storage. This 30-30 drive matched the caliber figure for a popular series of rifles made by Winchester, so the slang term Winchester was applied to any fixed platter hard disk.

word length The number of bits in a data character without parity, start, or stop bits.

WORM An acronym for write once, read many (or multiple). An optical mass-storage device capable of storing many megabytes of information but that can be written to only once on any given area of the disk. A WORM disk typically holds more than 200M of data. Because a WORM drive cannot write over an old version of a file, new copies of files are made and stored on other parts of the disk whenever a file is revised. WORM disks are used to store information when a history of older versions must be maintained.

write precompensation A modification applied to write data by a controller in order to alleviate partially the problem of bit shift, which causes adjacent 1s written on magnetic media to read as though they were further apart. When adjacent 1s are sensed by the controller, precompensation is used to write them closer together on the disk, thus enabling them to be read in the proper bit cell window. Drives with built-in controllers normally handle precompensation automatically. Precompensation normally is required for the inner cylinders of oxide media drives.

XGA An acronym for eXtended Graphics Array, a type of PC video display circuit (and adapter) first introduced by IBM on October 30, 1990, that supports text and graphics. Text is supported at a maximum resolution of 132×60 characters in 16 colors with a character box of 8×6 pixels. Graphics is supported at a maximum resolution of 1024×768 pixels in 256 (from a palette of 262,144) colors or 640×480 pixels in 65536 colors. The XGA outputs an analog signal with a horizontal scanning frequency of 31.5 or 35.52 KHz, and supports analog color or analog monochrome displays.

Xmodem A file-transfer protocol—with error checking—developed by Ward Christensen in the mid-1970s and placed in the public domain. Designed to transfer files between machines running the CP/M operating system and using 300- or 1200-bps modems. Until the late 1980s, because of its simplicity and public-domain status, Xmodem remained the most widely used microcomputer file-transfer protocol. In standard Xmodem, the transmitted blocks are 128 bytes. 1K-Xmodem is an extension to Xmodem that increases the block size to 1,024 bytes. Many newer file-transfer protocols that are much faster and more accurate than Xmodem have been developed, such as Ymodem and Zmodem.

XON/XOFF Standard ASCII control characters used to tell an intelligent device to stop or resume transmitting data. In most systems, typing Ctrl-S sends the XOFF character. Most devices understand Ctrl-Q as XON; others interpret the pressing of any key after Ctrl-S as XON.

Y-connector A Y-shaped splitter cable that divides a source input into two output signals.

Ymodem A file-transfer protocol first released as part of Chuck Forsberg's YAM (*yet another modem*) program. An extension to Xmodem, designed to overcome some of the limitations of the original. Enables information about the transmitted file, such as the file name and length, to be sent along with the file data and increases the size of a block from 128 to 1,024 bytes. Ymodem-batch adds the capability to transmit "batches" or groups of files without operator interruption. YmodemG is a variation that sends the entire file before waiting for an acknowledgment. If the receiving side detects an error in midstream, the transfer is aborted. YmodemG is designed for use with modems that have built-in error-correcting capabilities.

ZIF Zero insertion force. Sockets that require no force for the insertion of a chip carrier. Usually accomplished through movable contacts and used primarily in test devices in which chips will be inserted and removed many times.

ZIP Zigzag in-line package. A DIP package that has all leads on one edge in a zigzag pattern and mounts in a vertical plane.

Zmodem A file-transfer protocol commissioned by Telenet and placed in the public domain. Like Ymodem, designed by Chuck Forsberg, and developed as an extension to Xmodem to overcome some of that original protocol's limitations. Among the key features are a 32-bit CRC offering a degree of error detection many times greater than Xmodem CRC, a server facility, batch transfers, and fast error recovery. One feature of Zmodem is the capability to continue transmitting a file from where it left off if the connection has been broken. Zmodem also was engineered specifically to avoid sending certain sequences, such as ESCape-carriage return-ESCape, that the Telenet network uses to control the connection. Its speed, accuracy, and file-recovery capabilities make Zmodem the leading protocol for high-speed modem file transfers.

Symbols

C

Y-Z

Computer Books from Que Mean PC Performance!

Spreadsheets

1-2-3 Beyond the Basics	$24.95
1-2-3 Database Techniques	$29.95
1-2-3 for DOS Release 2.3 Quick Reference	$ 9.95
1-2-3 for DOS Release 2.3 QuickStart	$19.95
1-2-3 for Windows Quick Reference	$ 9.95
1-2-3 for Windows QuickStart	$19.95
1-2-3 Graphics Techniques	$24.95
1-2-3 Macro Library, 3rd Edition	$39.95
1-2-3 Release 2.2 PC Tutor	$39.95
1-2-3 Release 2.2 QueCards	$19.95
1-2-3 Release 2.2 Workbook and Disk	$29.95
1-2-3 Release 3 Workbook and Disk	$29.95
1-2-3 Release 3.1 Quick Reference	$ 8.95
1-2-3 Release 3.1 + QuickStart, 2nd Edition	$19.95
Excel for Windows Quick Reference	$ 8.95
Quattro Pro Quick Reference	$ 8.95
Quattro Pro 3 QuickStart	$19.95
Using 1-2-3/G	$29.95
Using 1-2-3 for DOS Release 2.3, Special Edition	$29.95
Using 1-2-3 for Windows	$29.95
Using 1-2-3 Release 3.1+, 2nd Edition	$29.95
Using Excel 3 for Windows, Special Edition	$29.95
Using Quattro Pro 3, Special Edition	$24.95
Using SuperCalc5, 2nd Edition	$29.95

Databases

dBASE III Plus Handbook, 2nd Edition	$24.95
dBASE IV PC Tutor	$29.95
dBASE IV Programming Techniques	$29.95
dBASE IV Quick Reference	$ 8.95
dBASE IV 1.1 QuickStart	$19.95
dBASE IV Workbook and Disk	$29.95
Que's Using FoxPro	$29.95
Using Clipper, 2nd Edition	$29.95
Using DataEase	$24.95
Using dBASE IV	$29.95
Using ORACLE	$29.95
Using Paradox 3	$24.95
Using PC-File	$24.95
Using R:BASE	$29.95

Business Applications

Allways Quick Reference	$ 8.95
Introduction to Business Software	$14.95
Introduction to Personal Computers	$19.95
Norton Utilities Quick Reference	$ 8.95
PC Tools Quick Reference, 2nd Edition	$ 8.95
Q&A Quick Reference	$ 8.95
Que's Computer User's Dictionary, 2nd Edition	$10.95
Que's Using Enable	$29.95
Que's Wizard Book	$12.95
Quicken Quick Reference	$ 8.95
SmartWare Tips, Tricks, and Traps, 2nd Edition	$26.95
Using DacEasy, 2nd Edition	$24.95
Using Managing Your Money, 2nd Edition	$19.95
Using Microsoft Works: IBM Version	$22.95
Using Norton Utilities	$24.95
Using PC Tools Deluxe	$24.95
Using Peachtree	$27.95
Using PROCOMM PLUS, 2nd Edition	$24.95
Using Q&A 4	$27.95
Using Quicken: IBM Version, 2nd Edition	$19.95
Using SmartWare II	$29.95
Using Symphony, Special Edition	$29.95
Using TimeLine	$24.95
Using TimeSlips	$24.95

CAD

AutoCAD Quick Reference	$ 8.95
Que's Using Generic CADD	$29.95
Using AutoCAD, 3rd Edition	$29.95
Using Generic CADD	$24.95

Word Processing

Microsoft Word Quick Reference	$ 9.95
Using LetterPerfect	$22.95
Using Microsoft Word 5.5: IBM Version, 2nd Edition	$24.95
Using MultiMate	$24.95
Using PC-Write	$22.95
Using Professional Write	$22.95
Using Word for Windows	$24.95
Using WordPerfect 5	$27.95
Using WordPerfect 5.1, Special Edition	$27.95
Using WordStar, 3rd Edition	$27.95
WordPerfect PC Tutor	$39.95
WordPerfect Power Pack	$39.95
WordPerfect 5 Workbook and Disk	$29.95
WordPerfect 5.1 QueCards	$19.95
WordPerfect 5.1 Quick Reference	$ 8.95
WordPerfect 5.1 QuickStart	$19.95
WordPerfect 5.1 Tips, Tricks, and Traps	$24.95
WordPerfect 5.1 Workbook and Disk	$29.95

Hardware/Systems

DOS Tips, Tricks, and Traps	$24.95
DOS Workbook and Disk, 2nd Edition	$29.95
Fastback Quick Reference	$ 8.95
Hard Disk Quick Reference	$ 8.95
MS-DOS PC Tutor	$39.95
MS-DOS 5 Quick Reference	$ 9.95
MS-DOS 5 QuickStart, 2nd Edition	$19.95
MS-DOS 5 User's Guide, Special Edition	$29.95
Networking Personal Computers, 3rd Edition	$24.95
Understanding UNIX: A Conceptual Guide, 2nd Edition	$21.95
Upgrading and Repairing PCs	$29.95
Using Microsoft Windows 3, 2nd Edition	$24.95
Using MS-DOS 5	$24.95
Using Novell NetWare	$29.95
Using OS/2	$29.95
Using PC DOS, 3rd Edition	$27.95
Using Prodigy	$19.95
Using UNIX	$29.95
Using Your Hard Disk	$29.95
Windows 3 Quick Reference	$ 8.95

Desktop Publishing/Graphics

CorelDRAW! Quick Reference	$ 8.95
Harvard Graphics Quick Reference	$ 8.95
Que's Using Ventura Publisher	$29.95
Using Animator	$24.95
Using DrawPerfect	$24.95
Using Harvard Graphics, 2nd Edition	$24.95
Using Freelance Plus	$24.95
Using PageMaker 4 for Windows	$29.95
Using PFS: First Publisher, 2nd Edition	$24.95
Using PowerPoint	$24.95
Using Publish It!	$24.95

Macintosh/Apple II

The Big Mac Book, 2nd Edition	$29.95
The Little Mac Book	$12.95
Que's Macintosh Multimedia Handbook	$24.95
Using AppleWorks, 3rd Edition	$24.95
Using Excel 3 for the Macintosh	$24.95
Using FileMaker	$24.95
Using MacDraw	$24.95
Using MacroMind Director	$29.95
Using MacWrite	$24.95
Using Microsoft Word 4: Macintosh Version	$24.95
Using Microsoft Works: Macintosh Version, 2nd Edition	$24.95
Using PageMaker: Macintosh Version, 2nd Edition	$24.95

Programming/Technical

C Programmer's Toolkit	$39.95
DOS Programmer's Reference, 2nd Edition	$29.95
Network Programming in C	$49.95
Oracle Programmer's Guide	$29.95
QuickC Programmer's Guide	$29.95
UNIX Programmer's Quick Reference	$ 8.95
UNIX Programmer's Reference	$29.95
UNIX Shell Commands Quick Reference	$ 8.95
Using Assembly Language, 2nd Edition	$29.95
Using BASIC	$24.95
Using Borland C++	$29.95
Using C	$29.95
Using QuickBASIC 4	$24.95
Using Turbo Pascal	$29.95

For More Information, Call Toll Free!

1-800-428-5331

All prices and titles subject to change without notice.
Non-U.S. prices may be higher. Printed in the U.S.A.

Enhance Your Personal Computer System With Hardware And Networking Titles From Que!

Upgrading and Repairing PCs
Scott Mueller

This book is the ultimate resource for personal computer upgrade, maintenance, and troubleshooting information! It provides solutions to common PC problems and purchasing decisions and includes a glossary of terms, ASCII code charts, and expert recommendations.

IBM Computers & Compatibles
$29.95 USA
0-88022-395-2, 724 pp., 7 3/8 x 9 1/4

Hard Disk Quick Reference

Que Development Group

Through DOS 4.01

$8.95 USA

0-88022-443-6, 160 pp., 4 3/4 x 8

Introduction To Personal Computers, 2nd Edition

Katherine Murray

IBM, Macintosh, & Apple

$19.95 USA

0-88022-758-3, 400 pp., 7 3/8 Xx9 1/4

Networking Personal Computers, 3rd Edition

Michael Durr & Mark Gibbs

IBM & Macintosh

$24.95 USA

0-88022-417-7, 400 pp., 7 3/8 x 9 1/4

Que's Computer Buyer's Guide, 1992 Edition

Que Development Group

IBM & Macintosh

$14.95 USA

0-88022-759-1, 250 pp., 8 x 10

Que's Guide to Data Recovery

Scott Mueller

IBM & Compatibles

$29.95 USA

0-88022-541-6, 500 pp., 7 3/8 x 9 1/4

Que's PS/1 Book

Katherine Murray

Covers Microsoft Works & Prodigy

$22.95 USA

0-88022-690-0, 450 pp., 7 3/8 x 9 1/4

Using Novell NetWare

Bill Lawrence

Version 3.1

$29.95 USA

0-88022-466-5, 728 pp., 7 3/8 x 9 1/4

Using Your Hard Disk

Robert Ainsbury

DOS 3.X & DOS 4

$29.95 USA

0-88022-583-1, 656 pp., 7 3/8 x 9 1/4

To Order, Call:
(800) 428-5331 OR (317) 573-2500

Find It Fast With Que's Quick References!

Que's Quick References are the compact, easy-to-use guides to essential application information. Written for all users, Quick References include vital command information under easy-to-find alphabetical listings. Quick References are a must for anyone who needs command information fast!

To Order, Call:
(800) 428-5331 OR (317) 573-2500

Teach Yourself
With QuickStarts From Que!

The ideal tutorials for beginners, Que's QuickStart books use graphic illustrations and step-by-step instructions to get you up and running fast. Packed with examples, QuickStarts are the perfect beginner's guides to your favorite software applications.

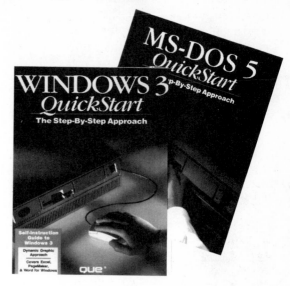

Learning is Easy with Easy Books from Que!

Easy WordPerfect

Shelley O'Hara

The ideal coverage of WordPerfect for beginners! 4-color illustrations and text as well as before-and-after screen shots illustrate each task. The book also includes a command summary and a glossary.

Version 5.1

$19.95 USA
0-88022-797-4, 200 pp., 8 x 10

Que's Easy Series offers a revolutionary concept in computer training. The friendly, 4-color interior, easy format, and simple explaniations guarantee success for even the most intimidated computer user!

Easy Quattro Pro

Shelley O'Hara

Versions 3.X, 4.X, & 5

$19.95 USA
0-88022-798-2, 200 pp., 8 x 10

Easy Lotus 1-2-3

Shelley O'Hara

Releases 2.01 & 2.2

$19.95 USA
0-88022-799-0, 200 pp., 8 x 10

Easy Windows

Shelley O'Hara

Versions 3 & 4

$19.95 USA
0-88022-800-8, 200 pp., 8 x 10

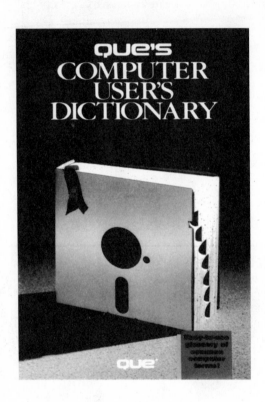

Free Catalog!

Mail us this registration form today, and we'll send you a free catalog featuring Que's complete line of best-selling books.

Name of Book _____

Name _____

Title _____

Phone ( ) _____

Company _____

Address _____

City _____

State _____ ZIP _____

Please check the appropriate answers:

1. Where did you buy your Que book?
   - ☐ Bookstore (name: _____)
   - ☐ Computer store (name: _____)
   - ☐ Catalog (name: _____)
   - ☐ Direct from Que
   - ☐ Other: _____

2. How many computer books do you buy a year?
   - ☐ 1 or less
   - ☐ 2-5
   - ☐ 6-10
   - ☐ More than 10

3. How many Que books do you own?
   - ☐ 1
   - ☐ 2-5
   - ☐ 6-10
   - ☐ More than 10

4. How long have you been using this software?
   - ☐ Less than 6 months
   - ☐ 6 months to 1 year
   - ☐ 1-3 years
   - ☐ More than 3 years

5. What influenced your purchase of this Que book?
   - ☐ Personal recommendation
   - ☐ Advertisement
   - ☐ In-store display
   - ☐ Price
   - ☐ Que catalog
   - ☐ Que mailing
   - ☐ Que's reputation
   - ☐ Other: _____

6. How would you rate the overall content of the book?
   - ☐ Very good
   - ☐ Good
   - ☐ Satisfactory
   - ☐ Poor

7. What do you like *best* about this Que book?
   _____
   _____

8. What do you like *least* about this Que book?
   _____
   _____

9. Did you buy this book with your personal funds?
   - ☐ Yes   ☐ No

10. Please feel free to list any other comments you may have about this Que book.
    _____
    _____

QUe

Order Your Que Books Today!

Name _____

Title _____

Company _____

City _____

State _____ ZIP _____

Phone No. ( ) _____

Method of Payment:

Check ☐   (Please enclose in envelope.)

Charge My: VISA ☐   MasterCard ☐

American Express ☐

Charge # _____

Expiration Date _____

Order No.	Title	Qty.	Price	Total

You can **FAX** your order to **1-317-573-2583**. Or call **1-800-428-5331, ext. ORDR** to order direct.
Please add $2.50 per title for shipping and handling.

Subtotal _____

Shipping & Handling _____

Total _____

QUe